PENGUIN REFERENCE

Roget's Thesaurus

Betty Kirkpatrick was editor of the *Chambers Twentieth Century Dictionary* and Reference Director at Chambers Books for six years before embarking on a freelance career which has included editing the last edition of Roget's Thesaurus, writing a weekly column for the *Glasgow Herald* on language, and editing and writing a wide variety of major reference works.

Roget's Thesaurus
of English words and phrases

New edition prepared by
BETTY KIRKPATRICK MA

PENGUIN BOOKS

PENGUIN BOOKS

Published by the Penguin Group
Penguin Books Ltd, 80 Strand, London WC2R 0RL, England
Penguin Putnam Inc., 375 Hudson Street, New York, New York 10014, USA
Penguin Books Australia Ltd, Ringwood, Victoria, Australia
Penguin Books Canada Ltd, 10 Alcorn Avenue, Toronto, Ontario, Canada M4V 3B2
Penguin Books India (P) Ltd, 11 Community Centre, Panchsheel Park, New Delhi – 110 017, India
Penguin Books (NZ) Ltd, Cnr Rosedale and Airborne Roads, Albany, Auckland, New Zealand
Penguin Books (South Africa) (Pty) Ltd, 24 Sturdee Avenue, Rosebank 2196 South Africa

Penguin Books Ltd, Registered Offices: 80 Strand, London WC2R 0RL, England

www.penguin.com

First published 1852
Abridged edition first published in Great Britain by Penguin Books 1988. Based on
Roget's Thesaurus revised and edited by Betty Kirkpatrick, first published by
Longman Group UK Limited 1987
Revised edition published 2000

3

This edition copyright © Longman Group UK Limited, 1962, 1982, 1987
New material in 2000 edition © Penguin Books Ltd, 2000
All rights reserved

Printed in England by Clays Ltd, St Ives plc
Filmset in PostScript ITC Stone Serif and Stone Sans
Typesetting by Rowland Phototypesetting Limited, Bury St Edmunds, Suffolk.

Preface to the first edition, 1852

It is now nearly fifty years since I first projected a system of verbal classification similar to that on which the present Work is founded. Conceiving that such a compilation might help to supply my own deficiencies, I had, in the year 1805, completed a classed catalogue of words on a small scale, but on the same principle, and nearly in the same form, as the Thesaurus now published. I had often during that long interval found this little collection, scanty and imperfect as it was, of much use to me in literary composition, and often contemplated its extension and improvement; but a sense of the magnitude of the task, amidst a multitude of other avocations, deterred me from the attempt. Since my retirement from the duties of Secretary of the Royal Society, however, finding myself possessed of more leisure, and believing that a repertory of which I had myself experienced the advantage might, when amplified, prove useful to others, I resolved to embark in an undertaking which, for the last three or four years, has given me incessant occupation, and has, indeed, imposed upon me an amount of labour very much greater than I had anticipated. Notwithstanding all the pains I have bestowed on its execution, I am fully aware of its numerous deficiencies and imperfections, and of its falling far short of the degree of excellence that might be attained. But, in a work of this nature, where perfection is placed at so great a distance, I have thought it best to limit my ambition to that moderate share of merit which it may claim in its present form; trusting to the indulgence of those for whose benefit it is intended, and to the candour of critics who, while they find it easy to detect faults, can at the same time duly appreciate difficulties.

P. M. Roget
29 April, 1852

Preface to the 2000 edition

First published in 1852, *Roget's Thesaurus* has long been recognized as one of the greatest English language reference books in the world. Generations of writers and speakers of English have come to regard it as an invaluable companion and they swear by it. Nowadays more and more emphasis is being placed on the importance of communication skills in all manner of contexts and the need for a reliable vocabulary guide is greater than ever. An ever-increasing number of people require a book which will help them to use the right word in the right place and *Roget's Thesaurus* is there to provide just this kind of help. This paperback edition has all the merits of the parent edition, while being slightly reduced in extent for ease of handling.

Despite its age, the Thesaurus still has remarkable relevance to this modern age. It is a tribute to the methodology of Peter Mark Roget that his unique classification system has not only stood the test of time remarkably well, but also has demonstrated an in-built capacity for absorbing new vocabulary as the years have gone on. Language holds a mirror up to life and is a reflection of what is happening in society. In recent decades changes in various aspects of society have been fast and furious and English has witnessed a corresponding boom in vocabulary additions. With the help of successive editors who have expanded or adapted the system where necessary, the *Thesaurus* has shown itself to be more than capable of allowing for such additions.

Recent vocabulary additions reflect the broad spectrum of interests that are common in the modern age, including such areas as science, medicine, computing, sport and leisure, music and entertainment, food and drink, marketing and shopping terminology, social issues, environmental concerns and traffic control. The sheer range and diversity of these interests have brought in their wake such a mass of vocabulary changes that it is becoming more and more impossible for language reference books to be truly comprehensive. The problem has been exacerbated by the advent of the Internet which is spawning new words at an alarming rate – as well as taking over our lives. Some degree of selectivity is required and the present edition of the *Thesaurus* has plucked from the current superabundance of vocabulary items a representative selection which reflects what is happening in our lives and marries well with the linguistic information given in previous editions.

Users of the *Thesaurus* may access information either by means of the classification system, outlined on p. ix and clarified on p. xiii, or by means of the index, explained on p. xi. Either way they will find valuable assistance in shaping their thoughts and translating these into competent, and hopefully polished, English. Those who are in need of inspiration will find that as well as the right words, the Thesaurus, because of the thematic way it is structured, has the capacity to suggest ideas as well as words. It thus has a decidedly creative dimension to it, unlike some reference books on the market, which are entitled thesauruses but which are, in fact, synonym dictionaries. This creative dimension also makes the *Thesaurus* an ideal medium for browsing, a pursuit much enjoyed by the many people who have an interest in language.

This new edition of the Thesaurus will keep its users up to date with the linguistic changes going on around them. The publishers are sure that it will be a welcome source of information and interest both to its established loyal readership and to those who have just become aware of its unique value. We are all indebted to the genius of Peter Mark Roget.

The Text

The *Thesaurus* is divided into six *Classes*. The first three Classes cover the external world: Class One, *Abstract Relations*, deals with such ideas as number, order and time; Class Two, *Space*, is concerned with movement, shapes and sizes, while Class Three, *Matter*, covers the physical world and humankind's perception of it by means of the five senses. The last three Classes deal with the internal world of human beings: the human mind (Class Four, *Intellect*), the human will (Class Five, *Volition*), and the human heart and soul (Class Six, *Emotion, Religion and Morality*). There is a logical progression from abstract concepts, through the material universe, to mankind itself, culminating in what Roget saw as mankind's highest achievements: morality and religion.

Roget borrowed his scheme from natural history, with its hierarchy of Phyla, Classes, Orders and Families. His system has also been compared to a tree, with ever smaller ramifications diverging from the main branches. This is a workable way of dividing up human experience, as can be seen from the way Roget's system has survived intact through numerous revisions. But life, as Roget himself points out, is not easily compartmentalized. 'Choice', for example, involves both the will (Class Five) and the intellect (Class Four). The language which reflects our experience is equally complex, more like a web than a tree, for it interconnects at all points. Also one word may have many meanings depending on its context. Roget was aware of this problem. His solution was to use copious cross-references to link related groups of words, a method which succeeded in both reflecting the complexity of language and coming to terms with it.

To see at a glance how Roget's system works, look up the *Plan of Classification* on pp. xiii–xiv. This shows the Six Classes, further subdivided into *Sections*. Each Section deals with a particular aspect of the Class within which it is found. So under Class One, *Abstract Relations*, we find Sections for *Quantity*, *Order*, *Time* and so on. The Sections themselves are further subdivided into *Heads*. Within Class One Section Six, *Time*, for instance, there are 35 Heads dealing with, among others, the ideas of *Present Time*, *Past Time*, *Transience*, and *Age*. Each Head is numbered. There are 990 in the present edition, a slight reduction from Roget's original 1,000. It is the Heads which form the basic units of the book, and they follow each other in a logical progression. It is a sign of Roget's skill in compiling the *Thesaurus* that this basic framework has remained virtually intact through edition after edition of the copyright version, of which this is the most recent.

The Heads themselves are divided into paragraphs, grouped together according to their part of speech. Head **852**, *Hope*, for example, has three paragraphs of nouns (marked **N.**), two of adjectives (**Adj.**), two of verbs (**Vb.**) one of adverbs (**Adv.**) and one of interjections (**Int.**). Not all Heads have a full complement of parts of speech, nor are the labels themselves applied too strictly, words and phrases being allocated to the part of speech which most closely describes their function. Each paragraph begins with a word in italics known as the *keyword*. This is both a clue to the kind of words found in that paragraph, and also itself part of the vocabulary. It is not a synonym of the words which follow: it was Roget's intention to offer words which express every aspect of an idea, rather than to list the synonyms. It is called the *keyword* because it is both the 'key' to the rest of the paragraph, and the 'open sesame' to the whole book, being used to identify the position of other words in the index and cross-references.

Within the paragraphs, words are grouped between semicolons according to their meaning, context or level of usage (i.e. colloquial, formal, etc.). These groups follow one another in a logical sequence, exploring every aspect of the idea under considera-tion. By comparing, whether consciously or not, the words and phrases offered, you can now select the most appropriate. It was Roget's expectation that his readers would "recognize" the word they wanted, guided by "an instinctive tact". On this assumption, words having more than one meaning or context are not usually repeated within paragraphs, nor are transitive and intransitive verbs listed separately. Where the right word is not immediately apparent, but an unfamiliar one seems from the context as if it might answer, it is advisable, especially for non-English speakers, to check with a dictionary. Yet more ideas can be obtained by looking up the cross-references. These are found at the end of some groups of words and consist of a Head number and a word in italics. The latter, besides being an item of vocabulary in its own right, is also the *keyword* of a paragraph in the given Head. It is also worth consulting the Heads before and after the one originally looked up. Most Heads are in pairs, representing the positive and negative aspects of an idea, e.g. **852** *Hope*, **853** *Hopelessness*. Sometimes several heads between them cover an idea—'education' is dealt with in **534** *Teaching*, **535** *Misteaching*, **536** *Learning*, **537** *Teacher*, **538** *Learner* and **539** *School*.

A few conventions should be explained. These have mainly been designed to avoid repetition and save space. Conjugate forms are often indicated by the use of 'etc.' For instance, 'be content,—satisfied etc. adj.' suggests that readers can form further verbs for themselves on the same pattern. In the same way, 'darkness etc. adj.' suggests how more nouns may be formed from the adjectives already given. Where consecutive expressions use the same word, two means are used to avoid repeating it. The phrases may be linked by '*or*', as in 'drop a brick *or* a clanger', 'countryman *or* -woman'. Alternatively, the repeated word is simply indicated by its first letter, followed by a full stop: 'weasel word, loan w., nonce w.,' and so on. Brackets within the text are occasionally used to clarify the context of a word, as in 'dissolve (a marriage)'. 'Tdmk' in brackets following a noun indicates a registered trade mark. An 'e' in brackets added to the end of a word means that it is of French origin and requires a final 'e' if applied to a woman. '**See** . . .' is used to refer the reader to another paragraph within the same Head, where the idea under consideration is dealt with more thoroughly. This often happens where a general paragraph, such as '*killing*' in Head **362**, is followed by more specific paragraphs, in this case '*homicide*' and '*slaughter*'.

The Index

Once familiar with Roget's *Plan of Classification*, readers will be able to find their own way round the book, and this is certainly the most rewarding method of using the *Thesaurus*. However, new readers, and those in a hurry, will probably prefer to use the Index at the back of this book.

The Index is based on a complete computer-listing of all the items in the book. It is intended as a guide to the text rather than as a catalogue of its contents, and the reader should not assume that a word is missing from the book simply because it is not in the Index. Nor is the list of references at each entry intended to be exhaustive. The reader should bear in mind that the Heads offer words to express a given idea or ideas; it really does not matter whether you look up a noun, a verb or an adjective, as once you have found the right Head, all the parts of speech conveying that idea will be available to you.

The Index consists of a list of items, each of which is followed by one or more references to the text. These references consist of: a Head number; a *keyword* in italics, and a part of speech label (n. for nouns, adj. for adjectives, vb. for verbs, adv. for adverbs, and int. for interjections). The *keyword* is given to identify the paragraph which contains the word you have looked up; it also gives an indication of the ideas contained in that paragraph, so it can be used as a clue where a word has several meanings and therefore several references. To use the Index, look up your word, turn to the Head number given in your chosen reference, and under the relevant part of speech you will find a paragraph beginning with the *keyword* given in the Index.

Where several references are given choose the most appropriate *keyword*. For instance, suppose you need another expression for 'feeling happy'. Look up 'happy' in the Index, and you will find a list of references. The *keywords* given include 'apt', 'willing' and 'drunk', which refer to other uses of the word 'happy'. But the *keywords* 'cheerful' and 'happy' are obviously relevant, and looking up **833** *cheerful* and **824** *happy* will offer you an abundance of suitable terms.

Some points to note

1) *Items are listed in alphabetical order*, whether they are words or phrases. For example: "hall, halleluja, halliard, hallmark, hall of residence, halloo, hallow, hallowed, hallowed by custom, Hallowe'en". 'The', 'a', and 'be' are disregarded for this purpose.

2) *References to the same Head* are not usually repeated under different grammatical forms of the same word. For example: "abundance" has references to Heads **32, 171, 632, 625** and **637**, while "abundant" has reference to none of these, but lists **104, 800** and **813**. This means that the adjective is found in three Heads which do not list the noun form: the idea of "abundance", however, is present in all the Heads listed. It is a good idea to check other forms of the word you are looking up, to obtain the fullest list of references to suitable Heads. Forms that do not follow each other immediately are linked by the direction '*See . . .*'.

Obvious derivatives of words, such as nouns ending in '-ness', adjectives in '-ing' or '-ed' and adverbs in '-ly', are not usually given an entry of their own unless they have a different meaning from the parent word.

3) *Objects* should be looked up in their simplest form, e.g. "ship" rather than "clipper",

"dog" rather than "wolfhound" and "flag" rather than 'banneret". An object with a compound name, such as "money box" may be dealt with under either or both of its constituent parts.

4) *Phrases* are listed in alphabetical order as noted above. In idioms where the first word is variable, such as "have (*or* know) by heart", the phrase will be indexed under both, or under the next word in the phrase.

5) *General expressions* such as "good example", "bad health", "no meaning" and "not mind" have been retained in the Index as useful guides for the reader.

6) *(s) after a word* indicates that references may apply to either the singular or the plural form.

7) *Alternative spellings* are given after the main form.

Plan of classification

Abstract relations

Existence

1 Existence

N. *existence*, being, entity; aseity, self-existence; monad, a being, an entity, ens, quiddity; Platonic idea; subsistence 360 *life*; eternity 115 *perpetuity*; preexistence 119 *priority*; this life 121 *present time*; prevalence 189 *presence*; realization, evolution 147 *conversion*; creation 164 *production*; potentiality 469 *possibility*; metaphysics; realism, materialism, idealism, existentialism 449 *philosophy*.

reality, realness, actuality; material e. 319 *materiality*; historicity, factuality, factualness 494 *truth*; fact, fact of life, undeniable f., positive f., stubborn f., matter of f., fait accompli 154 *event*; real thing, not a dream, no joke; nitty-gritty, basics, fundamentals, bedrock, nuts and bolts, brass tacks 638 *important matter*.

essence, nature, very n., quiddity, inner being, sum and substance 5 *essential part*; soul, heart, heart of the matter, core, centre 224 *interiority*.

Adj. *existing*, existent; existential; essential 5 *intrinsic*; absolute, given; in existence, under the sun, living 360 *alive*; preexistent 119 *prior*; coexistent 121 *present*; undying, immortal, eternal, enduring 115 *perpetual*; extant, surviving, indestructible 113 *lasting*; rife, prevalent 189 *ubiquitous*; metaphysical.

real, essential, not imagined, actual, positive, factual, well-documented, historical, well-g. 494 *true*; natural, physical, flesh and blood 319 *material*; concrete, solid, tangible 324 *dense*.

Vb. *be*, exist, have being; be the case 494 *be true*; consist in, reside in 5 *be intrinsic*; preexist; coexist, coincide, subsist 121 *be now*; continue 146 *go on*; endure 113 *last*; pass the time, live out one's life, drag out one's l.; be alive, breathe, live, have one's being, draw breath 360 *live*; be found, be met with, lie 186 *be situated*; be here 189 *be present*; prevail, be rife 189 *per-*vade; take place, come about, occur 154 *happen*; hold good 494 *be true*;

become, come to be, come into existence, first see the light of day 360 *be born*; spring up 68 *begin*; develop, grow, take shape 316 *evolve*; turn out, change into, metamorphose 147 *be turned to*.

Adv. *actually*, really, essentially, substantially; ipso facto; in essence, to all intents and purposes; in fact, in point of f. 494 *truly*.

2 Nonexistence

N. *nonexistence*, nothingness, nullity; blank, vacuum 190 *emptiness*; nothing, sweet n., nil, cipher, zilch 103 *zero*; a nothing, nonentity 4 *insubstantial thing*; no such thing, no one, nonperson 190 *nobody*; nihilism, negativeness.

extinction, oblivion, nirvana; dying out, obsolescence 51 *decay*; annihilation, nihilism 165 *destruction*; cancellation, erasure, clean slate 550 *obliteration*.

Adj. *nonexistent*, without being; missing, omitted 190 *absent*; negatived, nullified, null and void; cancelled, wiped out.

unreal, without reality, baseless, groundless, unfounded, without foundation; fictitious, fabulous, visionary 513 *imaginary*; intangible 4 *insubstantial*; only supposed.

unborn, uncreated, unmade; unbegotten, unconceived; undiscovered, uninvented, unimagined; as yet unborn, yet to come.

extinct, died out, vanished, lost and gone forever; no more, dead and gone, defunct 361 *dead*; obsolete, dead as the dodo; finished, over and done with 125 *past*.

Vb. *not be*, have no existence *or* life, be null and void; fail to materialize, not come off, abort; be yet unborn.

pass away, cease to exist, become extinct *or* obsolete, die out; be no more 361 *die*; come to nothing, abort 728 *miscarry*; sink into oblivion 506 *be forgotten*; go, vanish, be lost to sight; dematerialize, melt into thin air, go up in a puff of smoke 446 *disappear*; evaporate 338 *vaporize*; dissolve 337 *liquefy*.

nullify, reduce to nothing, annul, annihilate, extinguish; render null and void, suspend 752 *abrogate*; neutralize, negative 533 *negate*; cancel 550 *obliterate*; abolish, wipe out 165 *destroy*.

3 Substantiality

N. *substantiality*, essentiality 1 *reality*; substantivity, objectivity; corporeality, visibility, tangibility, palpability, solidity 319 *materiality*; weight 322 *gravity*; pithiness, meatiness; material 319 *matter*.

substance, core, nub, nitty-gritty 5 *essential part*; entity, thing, something, somebody 319 *object*; living matter 360 *life*; concretion 324 *solid body*; pith, marrow, meat 224 *interiority*.

Adj. *substantial*, real, actual, objective, natural, corporeal, phenomenal, physical 319 *material*; concrete, solid, tangible, palpable 324 *dense*; considerable 638 *important*; bulky 195 *large*; heavy 322 *weighty*; pithy, meaty, meaningful, full of substance.

Adv. *substantially*, really 1 *actually*; essentially 5 *intrinsically*; largely, in the main 32 *greatly*.

4 Insubstantiality

N. *insubstantiality*, nothingness 2 *nonexistence*; naught, nothing, nothing at all, zilch, not a whit *or* jot, not a scrap 103 *zero*; no one, not a soul 190 *nobody*; incorporeality 320 *immateriality*; lack of substance; meagreness, sparseness 325 *rarity*; superficiality 212 *shallowness*; intangibility, impalpability, invisibility; vacuity, vacancy, void, hollowness 190 *emptiness*; fatuity 497 *absurdity*; hallucination, self-delusion 542 *deception*; dream world, fantasy 513 *ideality*; unreality.

insubstantial thing, token, symbol 547 *indication*; soul 447 *spirit*; abstraction, shadow, ghost, phantom, spectre, vision, dream, mirage, optical illusion 440 *visual fallacy*; air, thin a., mist; bubble, gossamer, snowflake; bauble; vanity, inanity, fatuity, fool's paradise 499 *folly*; flight of fancy, figment of the imagination, pipe dream, castle in the air 513 *fantasy*; all talk, moonshine, cock and bull story; hot air, idle talk, gossip, speculation, rumour 515 *empty talk*; cry of 'wolf' 665 *false alarm*; mockery, pretence 875 *ostentation*; chimera, figment, courtesy title; nine days' wonder, flash in the pan; cipher, figurehead, man of straw 639 *nonentity*; stuffed shirt 873 *vain person*; fictitious person; pseudonym, stage name 562 *no name*.

Adj. *insubstantial*, inessential; non-physical, nonmaterial 320 *immaterial*; bodiless, incorporeal; aetherial 323 *light*; thin, gossamer 422

transparent; pale 426 *colourless*; misty 336 *gaseous*; fragile, delicate, ghostly, spectral 970 *spooky*; vague 419 *dim*, vacuous, vacant, void 190 *empty*; inane; honorary, nominal, fictitious; emblematic, symbolic, token; without substance, groundless, without foundation, unfounded; visionary, chimerical 513 *imaginary*; senseless 515 *meaningless*; blank, characterless, null; superficial 212 *shallow*.

Vb. *not be*, pass away, nullify.

5 Intrinsicality

N. *intrinsicality*, inherence, immanence; essentialness; inwardness, introversion, autism; subjectiveness, subjectivity; ego 80 *self*; subjectivism.

essential part, sine qua non; prime constituent 1 *essence*; principle, property, attribute 89 *concomitant*; virtue; quintessence, flower, distillation; stuff, quiddity 3 *substance*; incarnation, embodiment; life, lifeblood, heart's blood, sap; jugular vein, artery; heart, heart of the matter, soul, inner man 447 *spirit*; gumption, backbone, marrow, pith, fibre; core, kernel 225 *centre*; nub, nitty-gritty, nuts and bolts, business end, nucleus 638 *chief thing*.

character, nature, quality; make-up, personality, type, breed 77 *sort*; constitution, characteristics, traits, ethos; cast, colour, complexion; features; diagnosis.

temperament, temper, frame of mind, humour, disposition, mood, spirit 817 *affections*; strain, trait 179 *tendency*; idiosyncrasy, peculiarity 80 *speciality*.

heredity, DNA, chromosome, gene, inherited characteristic, genome, genetic map; original sin; ancestry 169 *genealogy*; Mendel's law; genetics, genetic counselling, genetic engineering, transgenics 358 *biology*.

Adj. *intrinsic*, immanent, deep down, deep-seated, deep-set, deep-rooted, ingrained; inherent, integral 58 *component*; inward, internal 224 *interior*; implicit, part and parcel of, built-in 78 *included*; indispensable, unalienable, inseparable 13 *identical*; autistic, subjective, introversive, reflexive, inward-looking, introspective, introverted; characteristic; indigenous, native; natural, instinctive, automatic; organic 156 *fundamental*; a priori, original, elemental, cardinal; essential, constitutional.

genetic, inherited, hereditary, familial, atavistic; native, inborn, innate, congenital, inbred; transgenic, genetically-modified.

characteristic, typical, representative, 80 *special*; characterizing, qualitative, indicative, unchanging 153 *established*.

Vb. *be intrinsic*, – immanent etc. adj.; inherit,

take after, run in the family; bear the mark of, involve, boil down to 523 *imply*.

6 Extrinsicality

N. *extrinsicality*, objectiveness, objectivity; transcendence 34 *superiority*; otherness, the other, externality, outwardness, outer space 223 *exteriority*; externalization; projection, extrovert; accidence 7 *modality*; accident, contingency 159 *chance*; accessory.

Adj. *extrinsic*, foreign 59 *extraneous*; transcendent 34 *superior*; outward, external, extramural 223 *exterior*; outward-looking, extroverted; environmental, acquired, implanted, inbred, instilled, inculcated; accessory, annexed, appended 38 *additional*; incidental, accidental, contingent, fortuitous 159 *casual*; nonessential, inessential; subsidiary, subordinate 35 *inferior*.

Vb. *be extrinsic*, lie without, be out-with; transcend 34 *be superior*; come from without.
make extrinsic, objectify, realize, project.

7 State: absolute condition

N. *state*, condition; lot, walk of life, station in l., lifestyle; plight 8 *circumstance*; position, place, echelon, category, status, footing, standing, rank; habit, disposition, attitude, frame of mind, vein, temper, disposition, humour, mood 817 *affections*; state of mind, spirits, morale; state of health; kilter, fettle.

modality, mode, manner, way, fashion, trend, style; mould 243 *form*; shape, fabric 331 *structure*; aspect, character, guise 445 *appearance*.

8 Circumstance: relative condition

N. *circumstance*, situation, circumstances, conditions, factors, the times; environment, milieu 230 *surroundings*; context 9 *relation*; status quo, state of affairs, how things stand; régime, set-up 7 *state*; aspect, appearances 445 *appearance*; lie of the land 186 *situation*; footing, standing, status, relative position 73 *serial place*, awkward situation, catch-22 s., plight, pickle, pretty pass, corner, fix, hole, jam, quandary, dilemma 700 *predicament*.

juncture, conjuncture, stage, point 154 *event*; contingency, eventuality; crossroads, turning point, point of no return; moment, hour, right time, opportunity 137 *occasion*; critical moment, crucial m., when the chips are down.

Adj. *circumstantial*, situated; surrounding, environmental, contextual; limiting; modifying 468 *qualifying*; temporary 114 *transient*; variable 152 *changeful*; relative, contingent, incidental; critical, crucial; suitable, seemly 24 *agreeing*; appropriate, convenient 642 *advisable*.

Adv. *thus*, so; like this, in this way. *if*, should it be that; in the event of, in the case of, in case;

provided that; given that, supposing, assuming, granting, allowing; if not, unless, except, without.

SECTION TWO

Relation

9 Relation

N. *relation*, relatedness, connectedness, rapport, reference, respect, regard; bearing, direction; concern, interest, import 638 *importance*; involvement, implication 5 *intrinsicality*; relationship, homogeneity, affinity; filiation, kinship 11 *consanguinity*; classification; affiliation, alliance 706 *association*; relations, friendly terms, intimacy 880 *friendship*; liaison, connection, merger, take-over, link, tie-up 47 *bond*; something in common, common interest, common denominator; context, milieu, environment 8 *circumstance*.

relativeness, relativity, interconnection, mutual relation 12 *correlation*; correspondence 13 *identity*, 28 *equality*; analogy 18 *similarity*; comparability 462 *comparison*; apposition, approximation 289 *approach*, 200 *nearness*, 202 *contiguity*, 89 *accompaniment*; collaterality 219 *parallelism*, 245 *symmetry*; perspective, proportion, ratio; cause and effect 156 *cause*; dependence 157 *effect*; relative position, status, rank, echelon 27 *degree*; serial order 65 *sequence*.

relevance, logicality, logical argument 475 *reasoning*; thread; due proportion 24 *conformance*; suitability, application, appositeness, pertinence, propriety, comparability 24 *fitness*; case in point, good example, classic e.

referral, reference, cross-r.; application, allusion, mention; citation, quotation; frame of reference, referent.

Adj. *relative*, not absolute 8 *circumstantial*; relational, respective; referable; related, connected, associated, en rapport, linked, bearing upon, concerning; of import 638 *important*; belonging, appertaining, in common; mutual, reciprocal, corresponding, answering to 12 *correlative*; in the same category 62 *arranged*; consecutive 65 *sequential*; affiliated, filiated, cognate, kindred 11 *akin*; analogous, like 18 *similar*; comparative, comparable 462 *compared*; approximating, approaching 200 *near*; collateral; proportional, proportionate, varying as, in ratio, to scale; in due proportion, commensurate 245 *symmetrical*; in perspective; contextual.

relevant, apposite, pertinent, applicable; to the point, well-directed 475 *rational*; proper, appropriate, suitable, fitting 24 *apt*; alluding, allusive; quotable, worth mentioning.

Vb. be related, have a relationship; have reference to, refer to, have to do with; bear upon, have a bearing on, be a factor 178 *influence*; touch, concern, deal with, interest, affect; be a relation 11 *be akin*; belong, pertain, appertain; approximate to 289 *approach*; answer to, correspond, reciprocate 12 *correlate*; have a connection, tie in with; be proportionate, vary as; be relevant, serve as an example; come to the point, get down to brass tacks, get down to the nitty-gritty.

relate, put in perspective; connect with, gear to, apply, bring to bear upon; link, connect, bracket together, treat as one, tie up with 45 *tie*; put in its context, provide a background, sketch in the b.; compare 18 *liken*; balance 28 *equalize*; establish a connection, draw a parallel; make a reference to, refer to, touch on, allude to, mention, mention in passing, refer to en passant.

Adv. *relatively*, not absolutely, in relation to; to some extent, comparatively; proportionally, in ratio, to scale, in perspective; depending on circumstance.

concerning, touching, regarding; as to, as regards, with regard *or* respect to; relative to, relating to, vis-à-vis, with reference to, about, re, on; in connection with; in relation to; speaking of, apropos, by the way, by the bye, on the subject of; on the point of; in the matter of; whereas; forasmuch, inasmuch; concerning which, whereto; thereto; hereto; whereof, thereof; hereof.

10 Unrelatedness: absence of relation
N. *unrelatedness*, absoluteness; independence 744 *freedom*; arbitrariness; unilateralism; separateness, isolation 46 *separation*; individuality 80 *speciality*; homelessness, no fixed abode; lack of connection; unclassifiability; randomness 61 *disorder*; inconsequence (**see** *irrelevance*); dissociation 46 *disunion*, 72 *discontinuity*; wrong association 495 *error*; disproportion, asymmetry 246 *distortion*; incommensurability, disparity 29 *inequality*; diversity, multifariousness 15 *difference*, 17 *nonuniformity*, 82 *multiformity*; incongruence 84 *nonconformity*; irreconcilability 14 *contrariety*; intrusiveness 138 *untimeliness*; no business of, nobody's b.; square peg in a round hole, fish out of water 25 *misfit*; exotic, intruder, cuckoo in the nest 59 *extraneousness*.

irrelevance, irrelevancy; illogicality 477 *sophism*; inapplicability; inconsequence, non sequitur; parenthesis; diversion, red herring, dust in the eyes 282 *deviation*; incidental 154 *event*; nonessential 639 *unimportance*.

Adj. *unrelated*, absolute; independent; owing nothing to 21 *original*; irrespective, regardless, unilateral, arbitrary; unclassified, unidentified;

homeless, of no fixed abode; wandering, astray; insular 88 *alone*; uninvolved 860 *indifferent*; floating, detached, unconnected, without context, unallied; parenthetic; episodic, incidental 72 *discontinuous*; separate, individual 80 *special*; without interest, nothing to do with; inessential 6 *extrinsic*; exotic, foreign, alien, strange, extraterrestrial 59 *extraneous*; intrusive; inappropriate, incompatible 25 *disagreeing*; not comparable, incommensurable, disparate 29 *unequal*; disproportionate, out of proportion, asymmetrical 246 *distorted*; discordant 84 *unconformable*; irreconcilable 14 *contrary*; multifarious 82 *multiform*.

irrelevant, illogical; inapposite, inapplicable; impertinent, inept 25 *unapt*; misapplied; misdirected 495 *erroneous*; off-target, off the beam, off-centre, peripheral; wandering 570 *diffuse*; beside the point, beside the mark, neither here nor there; trivial, inessential 639 *unimportant*; inconsequential; incidental 159 *casual*; remote, far-fetched, forced, strained, laboured; academic, immaterial.

Vb. *be unrelated*, have nothing to do w., have no bearing on; owe nothing to; have no right to be there; not be one's business, be nobody's b.; not concern, not touch; be irrelevant, be beside the p., cloud the issue, draw a red herring, throw dust in one's eyes; force, strain, labour; drag in by the heels, drag in screaming; ramble, wander, lose the thread, stray from the point 570 *be diffuse*.

11 Consanguinity: relations of kindred
N. *consanguinity*, kinship, kindred, blood 169 *parentage*; affiliation, relationship, affinity, propinquity; blood relationship; ancestry, lineage, descent 169 *genealogy*; connection, alliance, family; ties of family, clanship, tribalism, nationality 371 *nation*; nepotism; atavism 5 *heredity*.

kinsman, kinswoman; kin, kindred, kith and kin, kinsfolk, relations; near relative, next of kin; distant relation, blood r., kissing cousin; one of the family, relation by marriage, in-law, grandparents, father, mother 169 *parentage*; children, offspring, issue, one's flesh and blood 170 *posterity*; twin, identical t., sibling, sister, brother *or* s., blood b. *or* s., half-b. *or* -s., stepbrother *or* -s.; cousin, first c., second c., cousin once removed; uncle, aunt, auntie, great-uncle, great-great-u., great-aunt, great-great-a.; nephew, niece, grand-nephew, grand-niece; clansman, tribesman, compatriot.

family, matriarchy, patriarchy; motherhood, fatherhood, brotherhood, sisterhood; fraternity, sorority; adopted son *or* daughter, foster child, godchild, stepchild, adopted c.; adoptive mother or father, biological mother or father, natural mother, birth m., surrogate m., in-laws; one's people, one's folks; family circle, home c. 882 *fellowship*; the old folks at home, household, hearth and home 192 *home*; nuclear family, extended f.; tribe, clan.

race, stock, breed, strain, line, house, tribe, clan, sept; ethnic group; nation, people.

Adj. *akin*, kindred, twin-born; matrilineal, out of; patrilineal, by; maternal, paternal 169 *parental*; sibling, fraternal, brotherly, sisterly, cousinly; avuncular; related, family, allied; german; near, related 9 *relative*; once removed, twice r.; next-of-kin.

ethnic, racial, tribal, clannish 371 *national*; interbred, inbred 43 *mixed*; Caucasoid, Negroid.

Vb. *be akin*, share the blood of; claim relationship etc. n.; own a connection 9 *be related*; marry into 894 *wed*; father, sire 167 *generate*; be brother or sister to; affiliate, adopt, foster.

12 Correlation: double or reciprocal relation

N. *correlation*, correlativity 9 *relation*; proportion 245 *symmetry*; design, pattern 62 *arrangement*; grid 222 *network*; correspondence 18 *similarity*; opposite number 13 *identity*; mutuality, interrelation, interconnection; interdependence, mutual dependence; interaction, interplay; alternation, turn and turn about, swings and roundabouts, seesaw 317 *oscillation*; reciprocity, reciprocation 151 *interchange*; each, each other, one another; give and take 770 *compromise*; exchange, change, payment in kind 791 *barter*; trade-off, tit for tat 714 *retaliation*.

Adj. *correlative*, reciprocal 9 *relative*; corresponding, opposite, answering to, analogous, parallel 18 *similar*; proportional, proportionate 245 *symmetrical*; complementary, interdependent; interconnecting; mutual, requited; reciprocating; alternating, alternate, seesaw; balancing 28 *equivalent*; interlocking, geared, interacting; patterned, woven; interchangeable, exchangeable; inter-, international; two-way.

Vb. *correlate*, interrelate, interconnect, interlock, interplay, interact; interdepend; vary as, be a function of; correspond, be analogous to, answer to, reflect 18 *resemble*; react 280 *recoil*; alternate 317 *oscillate*; reciprocate 714 *retaliate*; exchange, swap, barter, trade off 791 *trade*; balance 28 *equalize*; set off, act as a foil to 31 *compensate*.

Adv. *correlatively*, proportionately, as . . . so . . . ; mutually, reciprocally, each to each, each other, one another; interchangeably, in mutual exchange; in kind; alternately, by turns, turn and turn about; vice versa 14 *contrarily*; between, shuttlewise 317 *to and fro*.

13 Identity

N. *identity*, identicalness, sameness; the same, the very same, the very one; genuineness 494 *authenticity*; the real thing, it 21 *no imitation*; the very words, ditto, tautology, redundancy 106 *repetition*; alter ego, genius, double; identification, coincidence, congruence 24 *agreement*; coalescence, absorption 299 *reception*; convertibility, interchangeability, equivalence 28 *equality*; no difference, indistinguishability; synonymity, synonymy 514 *meaning*; same kind, homogeneity 16 *uniformity*; no change, invariability, constant 153 *fixture*; duplicate 22 *copy*; look-alike, dead ringer, spitting image; fellow, pair, match, twin 18 *analogue*; homonym, homophone, synonym 559 *word*.

Adj. *identical*, same, self, selfsame, of that ilk; one and the same, one and only 88 *one*; coalescent, merging, absorbed; identified with, indistinguishable, look-alike, interchangeable, confusable, unisex, convertible, equivalent 28 *equal*; synonymous, congruent 24 *agreeing*; always the same, invariable, constant, unchanging, unaltered 153 *unchangeable*; monotonous 838 *tedious*; homogeneous, monolithic 16 *uniform*; tautologous, redundant, repetitive, repetitional 106 *repeated*.

Vb. *be identical*, look the same, be as like as two peas in a pod, be look-alikes, be a dead ringer for, be the spitting image of, ditto 106 *repeat*; coincide, coalesce, merge, be one with; be congruent, agree in all respects, be unanimous 24 *accord*; phase 123 *synchronize*.

identify, make as one, unify; treat as the same, not distinguish; equate, tar with the same brush 28 *equalize*; assimilate, match, pair 18 *liken*.

Adv. *identically*, ibidem; ditto; same here.

14 Contrariety

N. *contrariety*, world of d. 15 *difference*; exclusiveness, irreconcilability 10 *unrelatedness*; antipathy, repugnance, hostility 888 *hatred*; adverseness, contrariness, antagonism 704 *opposition*; antidote 182 *counteraction*; conflict, confrontation, clash 279 *collision*; discord 25 *disagreement*; contradistinction, contrast, relief, light r., variation, undertone, counterpoint 15 *differentiation*; contradiction 533 *negation*; contraindication 467 *counterevidence*; antonym 514 *meaning*; inconsistency 17 *nonuniformity*; paradox, ambivalence 518 *equivocalness*; oppositeness, antithesis, direct opposite, antipodes, poles apart; other extreme, quite the contrary, quite the reverse; other side, opposite s. 240 *contraposition*; reverse, wrong side 238 *rear*; inverse 221 *inversion*; converse, reverse image, mirror i., mirror 417 *reflection*; opposite direction, contraflow; headwind, undertow, counter-current 182 *counteraction*.

polarity, contraries 704 *opposites*; positive and negative; north and south; east and west; day and night; light and darkness; hot and cold; fire and water; chalk and cheese; black and white; good and evil; yin and yang, male and female.

Adj. *contrary*, nonidentical, as different as chalk from cheese, anything but 15 *different*; contrasting, contrasted, incompatible, clashing, conflicting, discordant 25 *disagreeing*; inconsistent, not uniform 17 *nonuniform*; ambivalent, bittersweet, love-hate, sweet and sour; contradictory, antithetic 533 *negative*; antithetical, antonymous; diametrically opposite, poles apart, antipodean 240 *opposite*; reverse, converse, inverse; antipathetic, hostile; adverse, antagonistic 704 *opposing*; antidotal; counter-, contra-, anti-.

Vb. *be contrary*, have nothing in common, be poles apart 10 *be unrelated*, 15 *differ*; contrast 25 *disagree*; conflict with; run counter to 240 *be opposite*; speak with two voices 518 *be equivocal*; contravene 704 *oppose*, 738 *disobey*; contradict, contraindicate 533 *negate*; cancel out 182 *counteract*; turn the tables 221 *invert*.

Adv. *contrarily*, on the other hand, conversely, contrariwise; vice versa, topsy-turvy, upside down; inversely; on the contrary; otherwise, the other way round; in contrast, in opposition to.

15 Difference

N. *difference*, unlikeness 19 *dissimilarity*; disparity, odds 29 *inequality*; margin, differential, minus, plus 41 *remainder*; wide margin, clear blue water 199 *distance*; narrow margin 200 *nearness*; heterogeneity, variety, diverseness, diversity 17 *nonuniformity*; divergence, departure from 282 *deviation*; otherness, differentia, distinctness 10 *unrelatedness*, 21 *originality*; discrepancy, incongruity 25 *disagreement*; incompatibility, antipathy 861 *dislike*; disharmony, discord, variance 709 *dissension*; contrast 14 *contrariety*; opposite, antithesis 240 *contraposition*; variation, modification, alteration 143 *change*, 147 *conversion*.

differentiation 463 *discrimination*; contradistinction, distinction, nice d., subtle d.; nuance, nicety 514 *meaning*; conjugation, declension 564 *grammar*.

variant, different thing, another t., something else, something else again; quite another matter, different kettle of fish, a different ball game; another story, horse of another colour, another light on, the other side of the coin; freak,

mutation; sport 84 *nonconformist*; new edition 589 *edition*.

Adj. *different*, differing, unlike 19 *dissimilar*; original 126 *new*; various, diverse, diversified, heterogeneous 17 *nonuniform*; multifarious 82 *multiform*; assorted, all manner of 43 *mixed*; distinct, distinguished, differentiated, discriminated 46 *separate*; departing from; odd 84 *unusual*; discordant, clashing, incongruent, incongruous 25 *disagreeing*; disparate 29 *unequal*; contrasting, contrasted, far from it, wide apart, poles apart 14 *contrary*; other, not the same; in a different class 34 *superior*, 35 *inferior*; the same yet not the same, altered 147 *converted*.

distinctive, diagnostic, indicative 5 *characteristic*; differentiating, distinguishing; comparative, superlative.

Vb. *differ*, be different etc. adj.; vary from, diverge f. 282 *deviate*; contrast, conflict 25 *disagree*; be at variance 709 *quarrel*; change one's tune, modify, vary, make alterations; suffer a sea change 143 *change*.

differentiate, distinguish, single out 463 *discriminate*; refine, make a distinction; widen the gap 46 *set apart*.

16 Uniformity

N. *uniformity*, uniformness, consistency, constancy, steadiness 153 *stability*; persistence 71 *continuity*, 146 *continuance*; unfailing regularity, conveyor belt 141 *periodicity*; order, regularity, method, centralization 60 *order*; homogeneity 18 *similarity*; monolithic quality; unity, unison, correspondence, accordance 24 *agreement*; evenness, levelness, flushness 258 *smoothness*; roundness 245 *symmetry*; sameness 13 *identity*; monotony; mixture as before, same old story; even pace, rhythm; daily round, routine, treadmill 610 *habit*; monotone; droning, sing-song, monologue; monolith; pattern, mould; type, stereotype 22 *copy*; stamp, set, assortment; suit; standard dress 228 *uniform*; standardization, mass production, automation, computerization 83 *conformity*; cliché 106 *repetition*; regimentation, totalitarianism, closed shop 740 *compulsion*.

uniformist, regimenter, leveller, egalitarian.

Adj. *uniform*, all of a piece, one-piece; same all through, monolithic; of one kind; homogeneous 18 *similar*; same, consistent, constant, steady 153 *fixed*; undeviating, unchanging, invariable 144 *permanent*; equable 823 *inexcitable*; rhythmic 258 *smooth*; undifferentiated, unrelieved 573 *plain*; without contrast, lacking variety, uniformed, characterless, featureless, blank; monotonous, droning, sing-song, monotone; monochrome; repetitive 106 *repeated*; normal 83 *typical*; patterned, standardized, stereotyped, mass-produced, conveyor belt, unisex; sorted, assorted, sized; drilled, aligned, in line; orderly, regular 245 *symmetrical*; straight, even, flush, level, dead 1. 216 flat.

Vb. *be uniform*, – homogeneous etc. adj.; follow routine 610 *be wont*; sing in unison, chorus 24 *accord*; typify 83 *conform*; toe the line, follow the crowd, fall in, wear uniform.

make uniform, homogenize; characterize, run through 547 *mark*; level, abolish differentials 28 *equalize*; assimilate 18 *liken*; size, grade; drill, align; regiment, institutionalize; standardize, stereotype; mass-produce; put into uniform; regularize 83 *make conform*.

17 Nonuniformity

N. *nonuniformity*, variability, patchiness 72 *discontinuity*; unpredictability 152 *changeableness*; inconstancy, inconsistency, capriciousness, whimsy 604 *caprice*; irregularity, haphazardness 61 *disorder*; asymmetry 244 *amorphism*; unevenness 259 *roughness*; heterogeneity 15 *difference*; contrast 14 *contrariety*, 19 *dissimilarity*; divergence 282 *deviation*; diversity, variety 82 *multiformity*; all shapes and sizes, mixed bag, ragbag, lucky dip, hotchpotch, odds and ends 43 *medley*; patchwork, motley, crazy paving, mosaic 437 *variegation*; abnormality, exception, special case, sport, mutation, freak 84 *nonconformity*; odd man out, rogue elephant 59 *extraneousness*; uniqueness.

Adj. *nonuniform*, variable, unpredictable 152 *changeful*; sporadic 142 *fitful*; inconstant, inconsistent 604 *capricious*; temperamental 822 *excitable*; patchy 29 *unequal*; random, haphazard, unsystematic; asymmetrical 244 *amorphous*; untidy, out of order; uneven, bumpy 259 *rough*; erratic, out of step, out of time; contrasted 14 *contrary*; heterogeneous, diverse 15 *different*, 19 *dissimilar*; multifarious, miscellaneous, of all sorts 82 *multiform*; multicoloured, decorated 844 *ornamental*; divergent, diversified; dissenting 25 *disagreeing*; atypical 84 *unconformable*; unusual, unconventional 84 *abnormal*; unique, lone 80 *special*; individual, hand-made; out of uniform, in mufti.

18 Similarity

N. *similarity*, resemblance, likeness, similitude; seeming, look 445 *appearance*; fashion, trend, style 243 *form*; point of resemblance 9 *relation*; congruity 24 *agreement*; affinity, kinship 11 *consanguinity*; homogeneity, comparability, analogy, correspondence, parallelism 12 *correlation*; equivalence, parity 28 *equality*; no difference 13 *identity*; family likeness; close resemblance, perfect likeness; faithful 1., photographic 1. 551

representation; life-likeness 494 *accuracy*; approximation 200 *nearness*; faint resemblance; suggestion, hint.

assimilation, likening 462 *comparison*; identification 13 *identity*; simulation, camouflage 20 *imitation*; parable, allegory, metaphor; portrayal 590 *description*; portraiture 553 *picture*; alliteration, assonance, rhyme 593 *prosody*; pun, play on words 518 *equivocalness*.

analogue, the like, suchlike, the likes of; type, perfect example, classic e. 83 *example*; correlative 12 *correlation*; simile, parallel, metaphor, allegory, parable; equivalent 150 *substitute*; twin; match, pair, fellow, mate, companion; complement, counterpart, other half, better half 89 *concomitant*; alter ego, genius, doppelgänger; double, dead ringer, look-alike; likeness, reflection, shadow, the picture of 551 *image*; dead spit of, spitting image, living image, chip off the old block; two peas, couple, pair 90 *duality*; two of a kind, birds of a feather; clone 22 *duplicate*.

Adj. *similar*, resembling, like, alike, twin, matching, like as two peas (in a pod), out of the same mould; much of a muchness, 13 *identical*; of a piece 16 *uniform*; analogous; parallel 28 *equivalent*; corresponding, bracketed with; homogeneous, close, approximate 200 *near*; representative; reproducing, reflecting; after, après, in the style of, à la; much the same, something like, such as, quasi.

lifelike, realistic, exact, faithful, typical; just one, true to life, true to type; graphic, vivid.

simulating 20 *imitative*; seeming, deceptive; mock, quasi, pseudo 542 *spurious*; synthetic, artificial, simulated, ersatz 150 *substituted*.

Vb. *resemble*, be similar to, pass for, bear a resemblance; mirror, reflect 20 *imitate*; seem like, sound 1., look as if; look like, take after, favour, put one in mind of, have the look of; savour of, smack of; come near to 289 *approach*; match, answer to 24 *accord*; typify 551 *represent*.

liken, approximate 462 *compare*; reduce to 13 *identify*; pair, twin, bracket with 28 *equalize*; allegorize, portray 20 *imitate*.

Adv. *similarly*, as, like, as if, quasi, so to speak, as it were; likewise, so, in the same category, by the same token.

19 Dissimilarity

N. *dissimilarity*, incomparability 10 *unrelatedness*; disparity 29 *inequality*; divergence 15 *difference*; variation, variety 17 *nonuniformity*, 82 *multiformity*; contrast 14 *contrariety*; little in common, nothing in c., no common ground, not a pair 25 *disagreement*; novelty, uniqueness 21 *originality*; dissemblance; 527 *disguise*; poor

1. 552 *misrepresentation*; foreign body, 59 *extraneousness*; odd man out 25 *misfit*.

Adj. *dissimilar*, unlike, diverse 15 *different*; various 82 *multiform*; disparate 29 *unequal*; unalike, not comparable 10 *unrelated*; unpaired 17 *nonuniform*; unique, peerless, matchless, nonpareil, one and only, original 21 *inimitable*; incongruent 25 *disagreeing*; untypical, atypical, exotic 84 *unconformable*; novel 126 *new*; a far cry from 199 *distant*; not true to life, unrealistic.

Vb. *be unlike*, – dissimilar etc. adj.; bear no resemblance, have nothing in common 15 *differ*.

make unlike, discriminate, distinguish 15 *differentiate*; modify 143 *change*, 147 *convert*; 246 *distort*; dissemble 542 *deceive*; disguise 525 *conceal*; 541 *fake*.

20 Imitation

N. *imitation*, copying etc. vb; sincerest form of flattery; rivalry, emulation 716 *contention*; doing as Rome does 83 *conformity*; want of originality, slavish imitation; imitativeness, parrotry (**see** *mimicry*); affectedness 850 *affectation*; mimesis 551 *representation*; reflection, mirror, echo, shadow 18 *assimilation*; translation 520 *interpretation*; borrowing, cribbing, plagiarism, piracy 788 *stealing*; forgery, falsification, counterfeit, fake 541 *falsehood*; copying, transcribing, tracing 22 *copy*; duplication 166 *reproduction*, 551 *photography*.

mimicry, mimesis 551 *representation*; onomatopoeia; mime, pantomime, sign language, gesticulation 547 *gesture*; ventriloquism 579 *speech*; portraiture 553 *painting*, 590 *description*; realism 494; *accuracy*; mockery, caricature, parody, spoof, burlesque 851 *satire*; travesty 552 *misrepresentation*, 246 *distortion*; mimicking, apishness, parrotry 106 *repetition*, 850 *affectation*; conjuring, illusionism; simulation, semblance, disguise, cosmetics, make-up, camouflage, mockery.

imitator, copycat, ape, sedulous a.; mockingbird, parrot, myna bird, echo; sheep 83 *conformist*; poseur; mocker, parodist, caricaturist 839 *humorist*; mime, ventriloquist, mimic, impersonator, female i., drag artiste, illusionist 594 *entertainer*; actor, portraitist 556 *artist*; copyist, tracer; translator, paraphraser 520 *interpreter*; simulator, hypocrite 545 *impostor*; borrower, plagiarist, pirate; counterfeiter, forger; duplicator, spirit d., copier, photocopier, Xerox (tdmk), stencil.

Adj. *imitative*, mimetic; emulating; onomatopoeic, echoic; aping, parrot-like; following; echoing; posing 850 *affected*; disguised, camouflaged; mock, mimic; simulating, shamming

541 *hypocritical*; pseudo, quasi, sham, imitation, phony, counterfeit 541 *false*; artificial, ersatz, synthetic, man-made 150 *substituted*; run-of-the-mill, hackneyed 610 *usual*; unimaginative, derivative, second-hand, handed down 106 *repeated*; paraphrastic, modelled; copied, slavish; caricatured, parodied, travestied, burlesque.

Vb. *imitate*, emulate, ape, parrot, echo, mirror, reflect 18 *resemble*; pretend, masquerade, make-believe, make as if, make like; act, mimic, mime, portray 551 *represent*; parody, take off, spoof, lampoon, caricature, burlesque, travesty 851 *ridicule*; sham, simulate, put on, feign 541 *dissemble*; camouflage 525 *conceal*.

copy, trace; catch; set up 587 *print*; reprint, duplicate, mimeograph, cyclostyle, photocopy, xerox, photostat; copy out, transcribe, type, paraphrase, translate 520 *interpret*; crib, plagiarize, pirate, lift, borrow 788 *steal*; counterfeit, forge 541 *fake*.

do likewise, do as the Romans do, mould oneself on; take a leaf out of another's book; follow suit, tread in the steps of, follow my leader 284 *follow*; echo, ditto, chorus 106 *repeat*; follow precedent, follow another's example, jump on the bandwagon 83 *conform*; emulate.

21 Originality

N. *originality*, creativeness, inventiveness 513 *imagination*; all my own work, a poor thing but mine own, 164 *production*; original thought, originality 119 *priority*, 10 *unrelatedness*; uniqueness, the one and only 88 *unity*; new departure 68 *beginning*; something new, novelty, innovation, freshness 126 *newness*; eccentricity, idiosyncrasy, individuality 84 *nonconformity*.

no imitation, genuineness, sincerity 494 *authenticity*; real thing, the real McCoy, the genuine article 80 *self*; autograph, holograph, manuscript, one's own hand.

Adj. *original*, creative, inventive 513 *imaginative*; underived; archetypal; primordial, primary; first, first-hand, first in the field, pioneering 119 *prior*; unprecedented, fresh, novel 126 *new*; individual; idiosyncratic 84 *unconformable*.

inimitable, incomparable, out of reach 34 *superior*; not imitated, not emulated, uncopied, atypical 15 *different*; unique, one and only 88 *one*; true 494 *genuine*.

22 Copy

N. *copy*, exact c.; clone 166 *reproduction*; replica, facsimile, tracing; fair copy, transcript, transcription; cast, death mask; ectype, stamp, seal, impression, imprint; stereotype, lithograph, print, offprint; 555 *engraving*; photocopy, Xerox (tdmk), photograph 551 *photography*; Photostat (tdmk). microfilm, microfiche 548 *record*; an

imitation, dummy, pastiche; fake 542 *sham*;
plagiarism, piracy, crib 20 *imitation*; a likeness,
semblance 18 *similarity*; portrait, drawing 553
picture; icon, image 551 *representation*; model,
effigy, statue 554 *sculpture*; reflex, echo, mirror
106 *repetition*, 417 *reflection*; poor likeness, apology for, mockery of 552 *misrepresentation*; caricature, cartoon, travesty, take-off, spoof,
lampoon, parody 851 *ridicule*; shadow; outline,
sketch, draft; metaphrase, paraphrase 520 *translation*.

duplicate, carbon copy; stencil, master copy;
transfer, rubbing; photograph 551 *photography*;
reprint, reissue 589 *edition*.

23 Prototype

N. *prototype*, archetype; type, norm, everyman
30 *average*; protoplasm 358 *organism*; original,
protoplast 68 *origin*; precedent 119 *priority*;
guide, rule, maxim 693 *precept*; standard, criterion, touchstone, standard of comparison,
yardstick, bench mark, barometer, frame of reference 9 *referral*; ideal 646 *perfection*; keynote,
tuning fork, metronome 465 *gauge*; module;
specimen, sample 83 *example*; model; exemplar,
pattern, template, paradigm; dummy, mock-up;
copybook, copy, text, manuscript; blueprint,
design, master plan, scheme 623 *plan*; rough
plan, outline, draft, sketch.

living model, model, artist's m., poser, sitter,
subject; fashion model, mannequin; stroke,
pacer, pacemaker; trendsetter, bandleader, conductor.

mould, matrix, mint; stencil, negative; frame
243 *form*; wax figure, lay f., tailor's dummy;
last; die, stamp, punch, seal, intaglio 555
printing.

Vb. *be an example*, set an e., serve as e., act as
a pattern; serve as a model, model, sit for, pose.

24 Agreement

N. *agreement*, consent 488 *assent*; accord, accordance, chorus, unison 16 *uniformity*; harmony
410 *melody*; consonance, concordance; concert,
understanding, mutual understanding, rapport,
entente; concordat, convention, pact 765 *compact*; unity, solidarity, unanimity 488 *consensus*;
consortium 706 *cooperation*; union 50 *combination*; peace 710 *concord*.

conformance 83 *conformity*; congruence, coincidence 13 *identity*; consistency, congruity 16 *uniformity*; coherence, consequence, logic, logical
conclusion 475 *reasoning*; correspondence, parallelism 18 *similarity*.

fitness, aptness, qualification, capability 694
aptitude; suitability, propriety 642 *good policy*;
the right man or woman in the right place, the
very thing 13 *identity*; relevancy, pertinence,

admissibility, appositeness, case in point, good
example 9 *relevance*; commensurability, proportion 9 *relation*; timeliness, right moment
137 *occasion*; mot juste.

adaptation, harmonization, synchronization,
matching 18 *assimilation*; reconciliation 719
pacification; accommodation, negotiation 770
compromise; attunement, adjustment 62 *arrangement*; compatibility, fitting, suiting, good fit,
perfect f.

Adj. *agreeing*, right, in accord, in accordance
with, in keeping with; corresponding, answering; proportional, proportionate, commensurate, according to 12 *correlative*; coinciding,
congruent, congruous 28 *equal*; consistent
with, conforming 83 *conformable*; in conformity, in step, in phase, in tune, synchronized 123
synchronous; of a piece with, consistent;
harmonized 410 *harmonious*; combining, mixing; suiting, matching 18 *similar*; becoming 846
tasteful; sympathetic; reconcilable, compatible,
coexisting, symbiotic; consentient, agreeable,
acquiescent, cool 488 *assenting*; concurrent,
agreed, at one, in unison, unanimous; united,
concerted; in rapport with, like-minded; in
treaty, negotiating 765 *contractual*.

apt, applicable, admissible, germane, appropriate, pertinent, to the point, well-aimed 9 *relevant*; to the purpose, bearing upon; pat, in
place, apropos; right, happy, felicitous 575
elegant; at home, in one's element; opportune
137 *timely*.

fit, fitting, befitting, seemly, decorous; suited,
well-adapted, capable, qualified, groomed for,
cut out for 694 *skilful*; suitable, up one's street
642 *advisable*; proper 913 *right*.

adjusted, well-a. 60 *orderly*, 494 *accurate*;
synchronized; focused, tuned, fine-t.; strung,
pitched, attuned 412 *musical*; trimmed, balanced 28 *equal*; well-cut, fitting, well-fitting;
bespoke, made to measure, tailored, tailor-
made.

Vb. *accord*, agree, concur 488 *assent*, 758 *consent*; respond, echo, chorus, chime in, ditto 106
repeat; coincide, mesh with, dovetail 45 *join*; fit,
fit like a glove, fit like a second skin, fit to a T;
tally, correspond, match 18 *resemble*; go with,
tone in w., harmonize; come naturally to; take
to like a duck to water; fit in, belong, feel at
home, be in one's element; answer, do, meet,
suit, suit down to the ground 642 *be expedient*;
prove timely, fit the occasion; pull together 706
cooperate; be consistent, hang together 475 *be
reasonable*; negotiate 766 *make terms*; get on
with, be of one mind, be on the same wavelength, hit it off, fraternize 880 *befriend*.

adjust, make adjustments 654 *rectify*; readjust,
repair 656 *restore*; fit, suit, adapt, accommodate,

conform; attune, tune, pitch, string 410 *harmonize*; modulate; regulate 60 *order*; graduate, proportion 12 *correlate*; align 62 *arrange*; balance 28 *equalize*; cut, trim 31 *compensate*; tailor, make to measure; focus, synchronize.

25 Disagreement

N. *disagreement*, disaccord; nonagreement, agreement to disagree 489 *dissent*; conflict of opinion, controversy 475 *argument*; confrontation, wrangling, bickering 709 *quarrel*; disunity, faction 709 *dissension*; dissidence 978 *schism*; clash 279 *collision*; challenge, defiance, rupture, breach 718 *war*; variance, divergence, discrepancy 15 *difference*; ambiguity, ambivalence 518 *equivocalness*; inconsistency, credibility gap; variety, inconsistency 17 *nonuniformity*; contradiction, conflict 14 *contrariety*; dissonance, inharmoniousness 411 *discord*; incongruence, incongruity 10 *unrelatedness*; disparity 29 *inequality*; disproportion, asymmetry 246 *distortion*; incompatibility, irreconcilability, hostility 881 *enmity*.

inaptitude, unfitness, incompetence 695 *unskilfulness*; unfittingness, unsuitability, impropriety 643 *inexpedience*, inapplicability, inadmissibility, irrelevancy 10 *irrelevance*; interruption 138 *untimeliness*; maladjustment, incompatibility 84 *nonconformity*.

misfit, maladjustment, bad fit; bad match, mésalliance 894 *marriage*; incongruity, false note, jar 411 *discord*; fish out of water, square peg in a round hole; outsider, alien, foreigner, foreign body 59 *intruder*; dissident 84 *nonconformist*; joker, odd man out, freak, mutation 84 *abnormality*; eccentric, oddity 851 *laughingstock*.

Adj. *disagreeing*, dissenting, not unanimous 489 *dissenting*; in opposition, at odds, at cross purposes, at variance; at one another's throats, at loggerheads, at war 718 *warring*; bickering 709 *quarrelling*; hostile, antagonistic 881 *inimical*; antipathetic; conflicting, contradictory 14 *contrary*; unnatural, against the grain, out of character; incompatible. odd, alien, foreign 59 *extraneous*; out of proportion, unsymmetrical 246 *distorted*; grating 411 *discordant*; mismatched; ill-matching, badly matched, ill-assorted, incongruous 497 *absurd*.

unapt, unsuited, incompetent 695 *unskilful*; inept, maladjusted 695 *clumsy*; wrong, unfitting, unsuitable, unbecoming, not for one, improper, undue, inappropriate 643 *inexpedient*; impracticable 470 *impossible*; unfit for, ineligible; ill-timed 138 *inopportune*; inapplicable, inadmissible 10 *irrelevant*; out of character, out of keeping; out of one's element, like a fish out of water, like a square peg in a round hole; out

of place, out of joint, out of tune, out of time, out of step, out of phase.

Vb. *disagree* 489 *dissent*; differ, dispute 475 *argue*; fall out 709 *quarrel*, clash, confront, collide, contradict 14 *be contrary*; be unapt etc. adj.; diverge 15 *differ*; not play, not play ball 702 *be obstructive*; have nothing to do with 10 *be unrelated*; be incongruous, stick out like a sore thumb, jar.

SECTION THREE

Quantity

26 Quantity

N. *quantity*, amount, sum 38 *addition*; total 52 *whole*; extent 465 *measurement*; mass, substance, body, bulk 195 *size*; dimension, dimensions, longitude 203 *length*; width, thickness 205 *breadth*; altitude 209 *height*; deepness 211 *depth*; area, volume, extension 183 *space*; weight 322 *gravity*, 323 *lightness*; force, flow, potential, pressure, tension, stress, strain, torque 160 *energy*; numbers 104 *multitude*; quotient, fraction, multiple.

finite quantity, limited amount; lower limit, upper 1., ceiling 236 *limit*; quantum, quota, quorum; measure, dose 465 *measurement*; avoirdupois 322 *weighing*; ration, whack 783 *portion*; spoonful, thimbleful, teaspoonful, dessertspoonful, tablespoonful, cupful; capful, bagful; lot, batch; load, lorryload, containerful 193 *contents*; lock stock and barrel 52 *whole*; large amount, masses, heaps, mountains 32 *great quantity*; small amount, bit 33 *small quantity*; greater amount, more, most, majority 36 *increase*; smaller amount, less, not so much 37 *decrease*.

Adj. *quantitative*, some, certain, any.

27 Degree: relative quantity

N. *degree*, relative quantity, proportion, ratio, scale 9 *relativeness*, 462 *comparison*; ration, stint 783 *portion*, 53 *part*; amplitude, extent, intensity, frequency, magnitude, size 26 *quantity*; level, pitch, altitude 209 *height*, 211 *depth*; key, register 410 *musical note*; reach, compass, scope 183 *range*; rate, tenor, way, speed 265 *motion*; gradation, graduation, calibration 15 *differentiation*; differential, shade, nuance; grade, remove, stepping-stone; step, rung, tread, stair 308 *ascent*; point, stage, milestone, turning point, crisis 8 *juncture*; mark, peg, notch, score 547 *indicator*; bar, line, interval 410 *notation*; valuation, value 465 *measurement*; ranking, grading, league table 77 *classification*; class, kind 77 *sort*; standard, rank, grade 73 *serial place*; military rank, lieutenancy, captaincy, majority, colonelcy; ecclesiastical rank 985 *church office*; hierarchy 733 *authority*; sphere, station, status, social class, caste, standing, footing 8 *circumstance*; gradualism, gradualness 278 *slowness*.

comparative, relative, proportional, in scale 9 *relative*; within the bounds of; measured by.

Vb. *graduate*, rate, class, rank 73 *grade*; scale, calibrate; compare, measure.

Adv. *by degrees*, gradually, little by little, step by step, drop by drop, bit by bit, inch by inch; by inches, slowly but surely, by slow degrees; to some extent, just a bit; however little, however much.

28 Equality: sameness of quantity or degree

N. *equality*, parity, equal opportunity, sexual equality, gender e., level playing field, coincidence 24 *agreement*; symmetry, balance; evenness. 216 *horizontality*; equability.

equivalence, likeness 18 *similarity*; sameness 13 *identity*, 219 *parallelism*; equation; interchangeability 151 *interchange*; isotropy; synonym; reciprocation, exchange, fair e., trade-off 791 *barter*; par, quits; equivalent, value 809 *price*; six of one and half a dozen of the other, nothing to choose between, nothing in it, level-pegging; even money.

equilibrium, equipoise, equiponderance, balance; even keel, steadiness; balance of nature, balance of power, balance of trade, balance of payments; deadlock, stalemate, logjam 145 *stop*; stable state, homoeostasis; sea legs, seat; fin, aileron, spoiler 153 *stabilizer*; balance.

equalization, equation; balancing 322 *weighing*; coordination, adjustment, levelling up or down 656 *restoration*, 31 *compensation*; positive discrimination, affirmative action, equal opportunities legislation, equal division, going halves 92 *bisection*; reciprocity 12 *correlation*; tit for tat 714 *retaliation*, 151 *interchange*; equalizer, counterpoise.

draw, drawn game, no result, drawn battle; level-pegging; tie, dead heat; stalemate, deadlock; neck and neck race, photo finish; love all, deuce.

compeer, peer, equal, match, mate, twin; fellow, brother 18 *analogue*; equivalent, parallel, opposite number, pair, counterpart, shadow.

Adj. *equal*, same 13 *identical*; like 18 *similar*; coordinate, coincident, congruent, homologous 24 *agreeing*; equidistant; isotropic; balanced, in equilibrium; homoeostatic, steady, stable 153 *fixed*; even, level, round, square, flush 258 *smooth*; equilateral, regular 16 *uniform*, 245 *symmetrical*; equable, unvarying; well-matched, drawn, tied; parallel, level-pegging; running level, abreast, neck-and-neck, nip and

tuck; bracketed; sharing; equally divided, half-and-half, fifty-fifty; impartial, equitable 913 *just*; on equal terms, on the same footing, on a par, on a level; par, quits, upsides with.

equivalent, comparable, parallel, interchangeable, synonymous, corresponding, reciprocal 12 *correlative*; tantamount, virtually the same, more or less identical, indistinguishable; much the same, all one, as broad as it is long, pot calling the kettle black (**see** *equivalence*) 18 *similar*; worth.

Vb. *be equal*, equal, counterbalance, compensate; come to the same thing, coincide with, agree w. 24 *accord*; be equal to, measure up to; cope with 160 *be able*; make the grade, come up to scratch, pass muster 635 *suffice*; hold one's own, keep up with, keep pace w., be level; parallel; match, twin 18 *resemble*; tie, draw; break even; go halves.

equalize, equate; bracket, match; parallel 462 *compare*; balance, strike a b., poise; trim, dress, square, round off, make flush, level 258 *smooth*, 16 *make uniform*; fit, accommodate, readjust 24 *adjust*; counterpoise, even up; redress the balance, handicap 31 *compensate*; set on an even keel, equilibrate, restore to equilibrium 153 *stabilize*; right oneself, keep one's balance.

29 Inequality: difference of quantity or degree

N. *inequality*, difference of degree 34 *superiority*, 35 *inferiority*; irregularity, patchiness 17 *nonuniformity*; unevenness 259 *roughness*; disproportion, asymmetry 246 *distortion*, 25 *disagreement*; oddness, lopsidedness 220 *obliquity*; disparity 15 *difference*; unlikeness 19 *dissimilarity*; imbalance; dizziness, the staggers; tilting of the scales, preponderance, top-hamper 322 *gravity*; short weight 323 *lightness*; inadequacy 636 *insufficiency*; odds 15 *difference*; counterpoise; partiality, discrimination 481 *bias*.

Adj. *unequal*, disparate, incongruent 15 *different*, 19 *dissimilar*; unique, unequalled; 644 *excellent*; below par 35 *inferior*; disproportionate, asymmetrical 246 *distorted*; irregular, scalene, lopsided 17 *nonuniform*; awry; odd, uneven; variable, patchy 437 *variegated*; deficient, defective, falling short, inadequate 636 *insufficient*; underweight 323 *light*; overweight 322 *weighty*; unbalanced, swaying; untrimmed, unballasted, uncompensated; overloaded, top-heavy, unwieldy 695 *clumsy*; listing, leaning, canting, heeling; off balance, dizzy, giddy, falling; unequitable, partial, 481 *biased*.

Vb. *be unequal*, be mismatched 25 *disagree*; not balance, not equate 15 *differ*; fall short 35 *be inferior*; preponderate, have the advantage, give points to, outclass, outrank 34 *be superior*; outstrip 306 *outdo*; be deficient 636 *not suffice*; overcompensate, overweight, tip the scales 322 *weigh*; be underweight 323 *be light*; unbalance, throw off balance; overbalance, capsize; list, tilt, lean 220 *be oblique*; rock, sway 317 *fluctuate*; vary 143 *change*.

30 Mean

N. *average*, medium, mean, median; middle term 73 *serial place*; balance; happy medium, golden mean 177 *moderation*; standard product 79 *generality*; ruck, ordinary run 732 *averageness*; norm, par; the normal 610 *habit*.

middle point, midpoint, middle distance, half way 70 *middle*; middle years 131 *middle age*; middle class 869 *middle classes*; middle of the road, midway, middle course, middle ground 625 *middle way*; splitting the difference 770 *compromise*; neutrality 606 *no choice*; central position 225 *centre*.

common man 869 *commoner*, everywoman, man *or* woman in the street; joe soap 79 *everyman*; average specimen 732 *averageness*.

Adj. *median*, mean, average 70 *middle*, 225 *central*; lukewarm; intermediate, grey; standard, par, ordinary, commonplace, run-of-the-mill, mediocre 732 *middling*; moderate, middle-of-the-road 625 *neutral*; middle class, middle brow.

Vb. *average out*, average, take the mean; split the difference, go halfway 770 *compromise*; strike a balance 28 *equalize*.

31 Compensation

N. *compensation*, weighting 28 *equalization*; rectification 654 *amendment*; reaction, neutralization, antidote, nullification 182 *counteraction*; commutation 151 *interchange*, 150 *substitution*; redemption, recoupment, recovery; retrieval 771 *acquisition*; indemnification, reparation, damages, redress 787 *restitution*, 656 *restoration*; amends, expiation 941 *atonement*; reimbursement, refund, one's money back; recompense, repayment 962 *reward*, 910 *revenge*, 714 *retaliation*; reciprocity, measure for measure 12 *correlation*.

Adj. *compensatory*, compensating, redeeming, countervailing, balancing 28 *equivalent*; self-correcting, self-cancelling; reimbursing, restitutory; amendatory, expiatory 941 *atoning*; weighed against 462 *compared*.

Vb. *compensate*, offer compensation, make amends, make compensation etc. n.; do penance 941 *atone*; indemnify, restore, pay back 787 *restitute*; make good, make up, make up for; add a make-weight, ballast; pay, repay 714 *retaliate*; bribe, square 962 *reward*; reimburse, pay

overtime 804 *pay*; redeem, out-weigh; overcompensate, lean over backwards.

recoup, recover 656 *retrieve*; make up leeway, take up the slack; indemnify oneself, take back, get back 786 *take*; make a comeback 656 *be restored*.

32 Greatness

N. *greatness*, largeness, bigness, girth 195 *size*; large scale, generous proportions, ample p., vastness, enormousness, gigantism; muchness, abundance 635 *plenty*; amplitude, ampleness, fullness, maximum 54 *completeness, plenitude*; superabundance, superfluity, embarras de richesses, arm and a leg, more than enough 637 *redundance*; immoderation 815 *prodigality*; exorbitance, excessiveness, excess 546 *exaggeration*; enormity, immensity, boundlessness 107 *infinity*; numerousness, countlessness 104 *multitude*; dimensions, magnitude 26 *quantity*, 27 *degree*; extension, extent 203 *length*, 205 *breadth*, 209 *height*, 211 *depth*; expanse, area, volume, capacity 183 *space*; spaciousness 183 *room*; might, strength, intensity 160 *power*, 178 *influence*; intensification, magnification, multiplication 197 *expansion*; aggrandizement 36 *increase*; seriousness, significance 638 *importance*; eminence 34 *superiority*; grandeur, grandness 868 *nobility*, 871 *pride*; majesty 733 *authority*; fame, renown 866 *repute, prestige*; noise, din 400 *loudness*.

great quantity, galore 635 *plenty*; crop, profusion, abundance 171 *productiveness*; superfluity, superabundance, torrent 637 *redundance*, 350 *stream*; expanse, lake, sea, ocean, world, universe, sight of, world of; much, lot, whole l., fat l., deal, good d., great d.; not a little, not peanuts, not chickenfeed, not to be sneezed at; too much, more than one bargained for; stock, mint, mine 632 *store*; quantity, peck, bushel, pints, gallons; lump, heap, mass, stack, mountain 74 *accumulation*; load (of), shipload, lorryload, sackload, containerful 193 *contents*; quantities, lots, lashings, oodles, scads, gobs, wads, pots, bags; heaps, loads, masses, stacks; pots of money, bomb, packet, telephone numbers; oceans, seas, floods, streams; volumes, reams, sheets, pages and pages, screeds; numbers, quite a flood, crowds, masses, millions, hosts, swarms, multitudes 104 *multitude*; all, entirety, corpus, caboodle 52 *whole*.

Adj. *great*, greater, main, most, major 34 *superior*; maximum, greatest 34 *supreme*; grand, big, muckle, mickle 195 *large*; fair-sized, largish, biggish; substantial, considerable, respectable; sizable, king-size, full-s., man-s., life-s.; bulky, massive, heavy 322 *weighty*; prolonged, lengthy 203 *long*; wide, thick 205 *broad*; swollen; ample, generous, voluminous, capacious 183 *spacious*; profound 211 *deep*; tall, lofty 209 *high*; 162 *strong*; mighty 160 *powerful*, 178 *influential*; intense, violent 174 *vigorous*; noisy 400 *loud*; soaring, climbing; culminating, at the peak, at its height, through the ceiling, at the limit *or* zenith, at the summit 213 *topmost*; plentiful, abundant, overflowing 635 *plentiful*; superabundant 637 *redundant*; many, swarming, teeming, hotching, alive with 104 *multitudinous*; antique, ancient, venerable, immemorial 127 *olden*, 131 *ageing*; imperial, august, of value 644 *valuable*, 868 *noble*; exalted 821 *impressive*; glorious, famed, famous 866 *renowned, worshipful*; grave, solemn, serious 638 *important*; excelling, excellent, cool, wicked, awesome 644 *best*.

extensive, wide-ranging, far-flung, far-reaching, widespread, prevalent, epidemic; worldwide, global, universal, cosmic; mass, wholesale, full-scale, all-embracing, across-the-board, comprehensive 78 *inclusive*.

enormous, immense, vast, colossal, giant, gigantic, monumental 195 *huge*; towering, sky-high 209 *high*.

prodigious, marvellous, astounding, amazing, astonishing 864 *wonderful*; fantastic, fabulous, incredible, unbelievable, passing belief; 472 *improbable*, 470 *impossible*; stupendous, tremendous, terrific; dreadful, frightful 854 *frightening*; breathtaking, overwhelming, out of this world 821 *impressive*.

remarkable, signal, noticeable 866 *noteworthy*; outstanding, extraordinary, exceptional, singular, uncommon 84 *unusual*; eminent, distinguished, marked 638 *notable*.

flagrant, blatant, flaring, glaring, stark, staring, staring one in the face; shocking 867 *discreditable*.

unspeakable, unutterable, indescribable, beyond description, indefinable, ineffable; past speaking 517 *inexpressible*.

exorbitant, extortionate, harsh, stringent, severe, Draconian 735 *oppressive*; excessive, extreme, monstrous, outrageous, swingeing, unconscionable; unbearable 827 *intolerable*; inordinate, unwarranted, preposterous, extravagant, astronomical; beyond the pale, going too far.

consummate 54 *complete*; flawless 646 *perfect*; entire 52 *whole*; thorough, thoroughgoing, utter, total, out and out, dyed in the wool, arch, crass, gross, arrant, rank, regular, downright, desperate, unmitigated.

absolute, essential, positive, unequivocal; stark, pure, sheer, mere 44 *unmixed*; unlimited, unrestricted 107 *infinite*.

Vb. *be great* – large, etc. adj.; loom, loom up; stretch 183 *extend*; rear, tower, soar, mount 308

ascend; scale, transcend 34 *be superior*; clear, overtop; exceed, know no bounds, run to extremes, go off the deep end 306 *overstep*; enlarge 36 *augment*; 197 *expand*.

Adv. *greatly*, much, well; very, right, so; very much, mighty, ever so; fully, quite, entirely, utterly, without reservation, 54 *completely*; thoroughly, wholesale; widely, extensively, universally 79 *generally*; largely, mainly, mostly, to a large extent; something, considerably, fairly, pretty, pretty well; a sight, a deal, a great d., ever so much; materially, substantially; increasingly, more than ever, doubly, trebly; specially, particularly; dearly, deeply; vitally; exceptionally; on a large scale, in a big way; vastly, hugely, enormously, gigantically, colossally; heavily, strongly, powerfully, mightily; actively, strenuously, vigorously, heartily, intensely; closely, narrowly, intensively, zealously, fanatically, hotly, bitterly, fiercely; acutely, sharply, shrewdly, exquisitely; enough, more than e., abundantly, profusely, prodigiously; generously, richly, worthily, magnificently, splendidly, nobly; supremely, preeminently, superlatively; rarely, unusually, wonderfully, incomparably, strangely; indefinitely, immeasurably, incalculably, infinitely, unspeakably, ineffably.

extremely, ultra, to extremes, to the highest degree, to the maximum, to the limit, to the nth degree; no end of, no limit to; beyond measure, beyond all bounds; beyond comparison, beyond compare, incomparably, drop dead; overly, unduly, improperly, to a fault; out of all proportion; bitterly, harshly, drastically, rigorously, unconscionably, with a vengeance; immoderately, uncontrollably, desperately, madly, frantically, frenziedly, furiously, fanatically, bitterly; exceedingly, excessively, exorbitantly, inordinately, outrageously, prohibitively, preposterously; foully, abominably, grossly, monstrously, horribly; confoundedly, deucedly, devilishly, damnably, hellishly; tremendously, terribly, fearfully, dreadfully, awfully, frightfully, horribly.

remarkably, noticeably, markedly, pointedly; notably, strikingly, conspicuously, signally, emphatically, prominently, glaringly, flagrantly, blatantly, unashamedly; publicly 400 *loudly*; preeminently 34 *eminently*; outstandingly, unco; singularly, peculiarly, curiously, oddly, queerly, strangely, strangely enough, uncommonly, unusually; surprisingly, astonishingly, amazingly, astoundingly, incredibly, magically.

33 Smallness

N. *smallness*, small size, diminutiveness, minuteness 196 *littleness*; brevity 204 *shortness*; leanness, meagreness 206 *thinness*; briefness, momentariness 114 *transience*; paucity 105 *fewness*; rareness, sparseness, sparsity 140 *infrequency*; scarceness, scarcity, inadequacy 636 *insufficiency*, 307 *shortfall*; exiguousness, scantiness; moderateness, moderation; pettiness, insignificance, meanness 639 *unimportance*, 35 *inferiority*; mediocrity 30 *average*, 732 *averageness*; tenuity 4 *insubstantiality*; compression, abbreviation, abridgment 198 *contraction*; diminution 37 *decrease*; miniaturization.

small quantity, fraction, modicum, minimum 26 *finite quantity*; minutiae, trivia; peanuts, chickenfeed 639 *trifle*; detail, petty detail 80 *particulars*; nut-shell 592 *compendium*; drop in the bucket, drop in the ocean; homoeopathic dose, trifling amount, infinitesimal a.; thimbleful, spoonful, mouthful, cupful, trickle, dribble, sprinkling, sprinkle, dash, splash, squirt, squeeze; tinge, tincture, trace, smidgen, lick, smell, breath, whisper, suspicion, vestige, soupçon, thought, suggestion, hint, nuance, shade, touch; vein, strain, streak; spark, gleam, flash, flicker, ray; pinch, snatch, handful; snack, sip, bite, scrap, morsel, sop; dole, pittance, iron ration; fragment 53 *piece*; whit, bit, mite; iota, jot, tittle, fig, toss; ounce, gram, pennyweight, scruple, minim 322 *weighing*; inch, micron, millimetre 200 *short distance*; second, moment, nanosecond 116 *instant*.

small thing 196 *miniature*; microcosm; particle, atom; dot, point, pinpoint; dab, spot, fleck, speck, mote; grain, granule, seed, crumb 332 *powder*; drop, droplet; thread, wisp, shred, rag, tatter, fragment 53 *piece*; smithereens, little pieces; flake, snip, snippet, gobbet, small slice, finger; confetti; splinter, chip, clipping, paring, shaving; shiver, sliver, slip; pinprick, prick, nick; hair 208 *filament*; groat, mite, widow's m.; dime, sou; gnat, flea; shrimp, minnow, sprat; manikin, midget 196 *dwarf*.

Adj. *small*, exiguous, not much, moderate, modest, homoeopathic, minimal, infinitesimal; microscopic, tiny, teeny, teeny-weeny, teensy, weeny, wee, minute, diminutive, miniature 196 *little*; smaller 35 *lesser*; least, minimum; small-sized, small-framed, small-built, small-boned, undersized 196 *dwarfish*; slim, slender, lean, meagre, thin, anorexic 206 *narrow*; slight, feeble, puny, frail 163 *weak*; delicate, dainty, fragile 330 *brittle*; flimsy 323 *light*; fine, subtle, quiet, soft, low, faint, hushed 401 *muted*; squat 210 *low*; brief, minute, skimpy, abbreviated 204 *short*; shortened, abridged, cut, concise, compact, thumbnail; scanty, scant, scarce 307

deficient; dribbling, trickling 636 *insufficient*; reduced, limited, restricted 747 *restrained*; declining, ebbing, at low ebb, less 37 *decreasing*.

inconsiderable, minor, lightweight, trifling, trivial, petty, paltry, not to be taken seriously, insignificant 639 *unimportant*; not many 105 *few*; imperceptible; marginal, negligible, laughable, remote, slight; superficial, cursory 4 *insubstantial*; so-so 30 *median*; modest, humble, tolerable 732 *middling*; not much of a, no great shakes, second-rate 35 *inferior*.

Vb. *be small*, fit into a nutshell, be put onto a thumbnail; be less 307 *fall short*; get less 37 *decrease*; shrink 198 *become small*.

Adv. *slightly*, exiguously, little; lightly, softly, faintly, feebly; superficially, cursorily, gradually, little by little, imperceptibly, insensibly, invisibly; on a small scale, in a small way, modestly; fairly, moderately, tolerably, quite; comparatively, relatively, rather; indifferently, poorly, badly; hardly, scarcely, barely, only just, just and no more; narrowly, by the skin of one's teeth, by one's fingernails; hardly at all, no more than, at least, at the very least.

partially, to some degree, in some measure, to a certain extent, to some e.; somehow, after a fashion, sort of, in a kind of way, in a manner of speaking; some, somewhat, a little, a bit, just a bit, ever so little; not fully; in part, partly; not perfectly.

almost, all but, within an ace of, within an inch of, on the brink of, on the verge of, within sight of, in a fair way to 200 *near*; close upon, approximately 200 *nearly*; pretty near, just short of, not quite, virtually.

about, somewhere, somewhere about, thereabouts; more or less; near enough; at a guess, say.

in no way, no ways, no wise, by no means, not by any manner of means, in no respect, not at all, not in the least, not a bit, not the least bit, not in the slightest; not a whit, not a jot, not by a long chalk.

34 Superiority

N. *superiority*, higher position; loftiness 209 *height*; transcendance 32 *greatness*, 306 *overstepping*; top 213 *summit*; excellence 644 *goodness*; ne plus ultra 646 *perfection*; seniority 64 *precedence*, 119 *priority*; eminence 866 *prestige*; higher rank, higher degree 27 *degree*, 868 *nobility*, *aristocracy*; paramountcy, supremacy, sovereignty, majesty 733 *authority*; ascendancy, domination, predominance 178 *influence*; leadership 689 *management*; prevalence 29 *inequality*; win, championship 727 *victory*; prominence 638 *importance*; one-upmanship 698 *cunning*, 727 *success*; excess 637 *superfluity*;

climax, zenith, culmination 725 *completion*; maximum, top, ceiling, peak, pinnacle, crest, crest of the wave; record, high, new h. 213 *summit*.

advantage, handicap, favour 615 *benefit*; head start, flying s., lead, commanding 1., winning position, pole p.; odds, points, vantage, pull, edge; seeded position; command, upper hand, whip h.; one up, something in hand, reserves; trump card, card up one's sleeve; ace up one's sleeve; leverage, clout; vantage ground.

superior, superman *or* woman, wonderwoman 864 *prodigy*; select few 644 *elite*; high-ups, one's betters, top people, best p. 638 *bigwig*; aristocracy 868 *upper class*; overlord, sovereign 741 *master*; commander, chief, guide 690 *leader*; boss, foreman 690 *manager*; primate, president, prime minister, premier, primus inter pares 690 *director*; star, virtuoso 696 *proficient person*; mastermind 500 *sage*; world-beater, record-breaker; chart-topper; prizewinner, champion, record-holder 727 *victor*; prima donna, first lady, head boy *or* girl; big fish in a small pond.

Adj. *superior*, greater 32 *great*; upper, higher, senior, supernormal, above average, in a different class, in a class by himself *or* herself 15 *different*; better, a cut above, head and shoulders above 644 *excellent*; more than a match for; one up, ahead, always one step a., streets a. 64 *preceding*; record, exceeding, overtopping, vaulting, outclassing; in the lead, on top, winning, victorious 727 *successful*; distinguished 866 *noteworthy*; rare, 84 *unusual*; top-level, high-l., high-powered; 638 *important*; commanding, in authority 733 *ruling*.

supreme, arch-, greatest 32 *great*; highest, above all others, uppermost 213 *topmost*; first, chief, foremost 64 *preceding*; main, principal, leading, overruling, overriding, cardinal, capital 638 *important*; excellent, superlative, super, champion, tip-top, top-notch, first-rate, first-class, A1, 5-star, front-rank, world-beating 644 *best*; facile princeps, top of the class, second to none, none such, nonpareil; dominant, paramount, preeminent, sovereign; incomparable, unrivalled, matchless, peerless, unparalleled, unequalled 21 *inimitable*; unsurpassed, ultimate, the last word in; beyond compare 646 *perfect*; transcendental, out of this world.

Vb. *be superior*, transcend, rise above, surmount, overtop, tower over, overlook, command 209 *be high*; go beyond 306 *overstep*; exceed, out-Herod Herod, take the cake, take the biscuit; carry off the laurels, bear the palm, wear the crown; pass, surpass, beat the record, reach a new high; improve on, better, go one b., cap, trump; excel 644 *be good*; assert one's

superiority, be too much for; steal the show, outshine, eclipse, overshadow, throw into the shade; put another's nose out of joint, have the laugh on 851 *ridicule*; best, outrival, outclass, outrank 306 *outdo*; outplay, outpoint, outmanoeuvre, outwit; overtake, leave behind, lap 277 *outstrip*; get the better of, worst, trounce, beat, beat hollow, knock into a cocked hat, beat all comers 727 *defeat*.

predominate, preponderate, tip the scale, turn the s.; change the balance 29 *be unequal*; override, sit on 178 *prevail*; have the advantage, have the whip hand, have the upper h., have the edge on; hold all the cards, hold all the aces; lead, hold the l., be up on, be one up.

culminate, come to a head; cap, cap it all, crown all 213 *crown*; rise to a peak; set a new record, reach new heights, reach a new high 725 *climax*.

Adv. *beyond*, more, over; over the mark, above the m., above par, over the average; above the limit, upwards of, in advance of; over and above; at the top of the scale, on the crest, at its height, at the peak, at the zenith.

eminently, preeminently, outstandingly, surpassingly, prominently, superlatively, supremely; above all, of all things; to crown it all, to cap it all; par excellence; principally, especially, particularly, peculiarly, singularly; a fortiori; far and away, by far 32 *extremely*.

35 Inferiority

N. *inferiority*, minority, littleness 33 *smallness*; subordinacy, subordination, dependence 745 *subjection*; supporting role, second fiddle 639 *unimportance*; lowliness 872 *humility*; second rank, third class, back seat, obscurity; handicap 702 *hindrance*; defect 647 *imperfection*; inadequateness 307 *shortfall*, 636 *insufficiency*; failure 728 *defeat*; second best 645 *badness*, 812 *cheapness*; kitsch 847 *bad taste*; shabbiness 801 *poverty*; decline 655 *deterioration*; low, all-time l., minimum, lowest point, nadir, the bottom, rock b. 214 *base*; depression, trough 210 *lowness*.

inferior, subordinate, subaltern, sub, underling, assistant, sidekick, subsidiary 707 *auxiliary*; agent 755 *deputy*, 150 *substitute*; tool, pawn 628 *instrument*; retainer 742 *dependant*; menial, hireling 742 *servant*; poor relation, small fry 639 *nonentity*; subject, underdog 742 *slave*; backbencher, private, other ranks, lower classes 869 *commonalty*; second, second best, second string, second fiddle, second-rater; also-ran; reject 607 *rejection*; lesser creation, younger, junior, minor.

Adj. *lesser*, less, minor, small-time, one-horse, hick, small-beer 639 *unimportant*; small

33 *inconsiderable*; smaller, diminished 37 *decreasing*; reduced.

inferior, lower, junior; subordinate, subaltern 742 *serving*; dependent, parasitical 745 *subjected, subject*; secondary, tributary, ancillary, subsidiary, auxiliary 703 *aiding*, 639 *unimportant*; second, second-best, second-class, second-rate; third-rate 922 *contemptible*; lowly, below the salt; low-ranking; subnormal, substandard, not up to the mark, not up to scratch; underweight 307 *deficient*; spoilt; defective 647 *imperfect*; failing 636 *insufficient*; shoddy, jerry-built, crummy 645 *bad*, 812 *cheap*, 847 *vulgar*; low 869 *plebeian*; makeshift 670 *unprepared*; temporary, provisional 114 *ephemeral*; feeble 163 *weak*; in a lower class, outclassed, outshone, trounced, beaten 728 *defeated*; unworthy, not fit, not fit to hold a candle to, not in the same league, not a patch on.

Vb. *be inferior*, fall short, come short of, fall below 307 *fall short*; lag, fall behind; want, lack 636 *not suffice*; not make the grade, not come up to scratch, not pass 728 *fail*; bow to 739 *obey*; concede the victory; yield, give in, cede, yield the palm, hand it to, knuckle under 721 *submit*; play second fiddle, play a supporting role 742 *serve*; take a back seat, retire into the shade; sink into obscurity; lose face 867 *lose repute*; get worse 655 *deteriorate*; sink, sink without trace, touch rock bottom, reach one's nadir 309 *descend*.

Adv. *less*, minus, short of; beneath 210 *under*; below average.

36 Increase

N. *increase*, increment, augmentation, waxing, crescendo; progress 285 *progression*; growth, growth area, development a., boom town; buildup, development 164 *production*; extension, protraction; widening; spread, escalation, amplification, inflation, dilation 197 *expansion*; proliferation, swarming 171 *productiveness, abundance*; multiplication; adding 38 *addition*; enlargement, aggrandizement 32 *greatness*; heightening, raising 310 *elevation*; concentration 324 *condensation*; intensification, stepping up, redoubling 91 *duplication*, acceleration, speeding 277 *spurt*; hotting up 381 *heating*; excitation 174 *stimulation*; exacerbation 832 *aggravation*; advancement, boost 654 *improvement*; rise, spiral, upward curve, upward trend, upswing, upturn 308 *ascent*; uprush, upsurge, flood, tide, surge 350 *wave*; progressiveness, cumulativeness, snowball 74 *accumulation*.

increment, augmentation, bulge; accretion, accrual, accession, contribution 38 *addition*; supplement, salary increase, pay rise 40 *extra*; padding, stuffing 303 *insertion*; percentage, commission, expenses, rake-off 771 *earnings*.

Adj. *increasing*, spreading, progressive, escalating; growing, waxing, filling, crescent, on the increase, on the up and up; supplementary 38 *additional*; ever-increasing, snowballing, cumulative 71 *continuous*; intensive; fruitful 171 *prolific*; increased, stretched, enlarged.

Vb. *grow*, increase, gain, develop, escalate; dilate, swell, bulge, wax, fill 197 *expand*; fill out, fatten, thicken; broad; become larger, put on weight 322 *weigh*; sprout, bud, burgeon, flower, blossom 167 *reproduce itself*; breed, spread, swarm, proliferate, mushroom, multiply 104 *be many*, 171 *be fruitful*; grow up 669 *mature*; spring up, shoot up, grow taller, grow by leaps and bounds 209 *be high*; spiral, climb, mount, rise, go through the ceiling, rocket, skyrocket, take off 308 *ascend*; 417 *shine*; gain strength 656 *be restored*, 162 *be strong*; improve 654 *get better*; flourish, thrive, prosper; gain ground, advance, snowball, accumulate 285 *progress*; earn interest 771 *be profitable*; gain in value, appreciate, rise in price 811 *be dear*; boom, break all records, surge, exceed, overflow 637 *superabound*, 32 *be great*; rise to a maximum 34 *culminate*.

augment, increase, bump up, double; redouble; duplicate 106 *repeat*; multiply 166 *reproduce*; propagate, grow, raise, rear 369 *breed stock*; enlarge, magnify, distend, inflate, blow up 197 *expand*; amplify, develop, build up, fill out, fill in, pad out 54 *make complete*; supplement, enrich; contribute to; accrue 38 *add*; extend, prolong, stretch 203 *lengthen*; broaden, widen, thicken, deepen; heighten, enhance, send up 209 *make higher*; raise, exalt 310 *elevate*; advance, aggrandize 285 *promote*; speed up 277 *accelerate*; intensify, redouble, step up, stimulate, energize 174 *invigorate*; give a boost to, boost 685 *refresh*, 656 *restore*, 162 *strengthen*; glorify 546 *exaggerate*, 482 *overrate*; stoke, add fuel to the flame, exacerbate 832 *aggravate*; maximize.

37 Decrease: no increase

N. *decrease*, lessening, dwindling, falling off, de-escalation; waning, fading; dimming 419 *dimness*; wane 198 *contraction*; shrinking, ebb, reflux, retreat 286 *regression*; ebb tide, neap 210 *lowness*; descending order 71 *series*; subsidence, sinking, decline, declension, downward curve, downward spiral, downward trend, downturn, fall, drop, plunge 309 *descent*, 165 *ruin*; deflation, recession, slump 655 *deterioration*; retrenchment, cutback, cut, cutting back 814 *economy*; loss of value, depreciation 812 *cheapness*; weakening; shortage 636 *scarcity*; diminishing returns, exhaustion 190 *emptiness*;

shrinkage, erosion, decay, crumbling 655 *dilapidation*.

diminution, making less; deduction 39 *subtraction*; abatement, reduction, de-escalation, restriction 747 *restraint*; deceleration 278 *slowness*; retrenchment, cut, economization 814 *economy*; cutting back, pruning, paring, shaving, clipping, docking, curtailment, abridgment, abbreviation 204 *shortening*; compression, squeeze 198 *contraction*; abrasion, erosion 333 *friction*; weeding out, elimination 62 *sorting*, 300 *ejection*; mitigation, minimization 177 *moderation*; belittlement, undervaluation 483 *underestimation*, 926 *detraction*; demotion, degradation 872 *humiliation*.

Adj. *decreasing*, dwindling; waning, fading; evaporating; de-escalating; declining, going down, sinking, ebbing; decaying.

Vb. *abate*, diminish, decrease, de-escalate, lessen, take away, detract from, deduct 39 *subtract*; except 57 *exclude*; reduce, scale down, whittle, pare, scrape 206 *make thin*; clip, trim 46 *cut*; shrink, abridge, abbreviate, boil down 204 *shorten*; squeeze, compress, contract 198 *make smaller*; limit, curtail 747 *restrain*; cut down, cut back, retrench 814 *economize*; decelerate 278 *retard*; depress 311 *lower*; minimize, mitigate, extenuate 177 *moderate*; allay, alleviate 831 *relieve*; deflate, puncture; disparage, decry, belittle, depreciate, undervalue 483 *underestimate*; dwarf, overshadow 34 *be superior*; steal one's thunder, put in the shade; degrade, demote 872 *humiliate*; exhaust 300 *empty*; let evaporate, boil away 338 *vaporize*; crumble 332 *pulverize*; rub away, abrade, file 333 *rub*; gnaw, nibble at, eat away 301 *eat*; erode, rust 655 *impair*; strip, peel, denude 229 *uncover*; unman 161 *disable*; dilute 163 *weaken*; thin out, weed o., depopulate 105 *render few*; decimate 165 *destroy*; damp down, crack down on.

decrease, grow less, lessen, de-escalate; abate, slacken, ease, moderate, subside, die down; dwindle, shrink, contract 198 *become small*; wane, waste, decay, wear away, wither away, degenerate 655 *deteriorate*; fade, die away, grow dim 419 *be dim*; retreat, withdraw, ebb 286 *regress*, 290 *recede*; run low, run down, ebb away, drain away, fail 636 *not suffice*; tail off, taper off, peter out; 293 *converge*; subside, sink 313 *plunge*; come down, decline, fall, drop, slump, collapse 309 *descend*; level off, bottom out, lag 278 *decelerate*; melt away 446 *disappear*; evaporate 338 *vaporize*; thin out 105 *be few*; become endangered, become extinct 2 *pass away*; reduce, lose weight, become anorexic 323 *be light*, 946 *starve*; lose one's voice, shut up 578 *be mute*; lose, shed; cast off.

38 Addition

N. *addition*, adding to, annexation, agglutination 45 *union*; superimposing 187 *location*; affixture 65 *sequence*; supplementation, contribution 703 *aid*; superaddition, imposition, load 702 *encumbrance*; accession, accretion, accrual, supervention; interposition, interjection 303 *insertion*, 78 *inclusion*; reinforcement 36 *increase*; increment, supplement, additive, E numbers; add-on; addendum, appendage, tailpiece, appendix 40 *adjunct*; extra time, overtime 113 *protraction*; appurtenance 89 *accompaniment*; summation, adding up, counting up, totalling, total.

Adj. *additional*, additive; added, included etc. vb.; adventitious; supplementary, conjunctive; subsidiary, auxiliary, contributory 703 *aiding*; supernumerary; another, further, more; extra, spare 637 *superfluous*; interjected, interposed 303 *inserted*, prefixed 64 *preceding*.

Vb. *add*, add up, sum, total; carry over 272 *transfer*; add to, annex, append; attach, pin to, clip to, tag on, tack on; hitch to, yoke to, unite to 45 *join*, tie; stick on, glue on; add on, preface, prefix, affix, suffix, infix; introduce; interpose, interject; engraft, let in 303 *insert*; contribute to 36 *augment*; swell, extend, expand 197 *enlarge*; supplement: superadd, superimpose; ornament, embellish 844 *decorate*; mix with 43 *mix*; annex 786 *take*.

accrue, be added 78 *be included*; supervene 295 *arrive*; join 708 *join a party*; combine with 50 *combine*; make one more; reinforce, swell the ranks.

Adv. *in addition*, additionally, more, plus, extra; with interest, with a vengeance, with knobs on; and, too, also, item, furthermore, further; likewise, and also, to boot; else, besides; et cetera; and so on, and so forth, moreover, into the bargain, over and above, including, inclusive of, with, as well as, apart from, not to mention, let alone, not forgetting; together with, along w., coupled w., in conjunction w..

39 Subtraction

N. *subtraction*, deduction, taking away; diminution 37 *decrease*; abstraction, removal, withdrawal; elimination 62 *sorting*; clearance 300 *ejection*; unpacking 188 *displacement*, 304 *extraction*; precipitation, sedimentation, ablation; abrasion, erosion, detrition 333 *friction*; retrenchment, cutting back, curtailment 204 *shortening*; severance, detruncation, amputation, excision 46 *scission*; mutilation 655 *impairment*; expurgation; deletion 550 *obliteration*; minuend 85 *numerical element*; subtrahend.

Vb. *subtract*, take away, deduct, do subtraction; detract from, diminish, decrease 37 *abate*;

cut 810 *discount*; take off, knock o., allow;
except, take out, leave o. 57 *exclude*; expel 300
eject; abstract 786 *take*, 788 *steal*; withdraw,
remove; unload 188 *displace*; shift 272 *transfer*;
draw off 300 *empty*; abrade, scrape away, file
down, erode 333 *rub*; eradicate, uproot, pull up,
pull out 304 *extract*; pick, pick out, put on one
side 605 *select*; cross out, blot o., delete, censor
550 *obliterate*; expurgate, mutilate 655 *impair*;
sever, separate, amputate, excise; shear, shave
off, clip 46 *cut*; retrench, cut back, cut down,
whittle, lop, prune, pare, decapitate, behead,
dock, curtail, abridge, abbreviate 204 *shorten*;
geld, castrate, caponize, spay, emasculate 161
unman; peel, skin, fleece, strip, divest, denude
229 *uncover*.

40 Adjunct: thing added
N. *adjunct*, addition, additive, something
added, add-on, contribution 38 *addition*; addendum, carry-over; supplement, annex; attachment, fixture; inflection, affix, suffix, prefix,
adjective, adverb 564 *part of speech*; ticket, tag
547 *label*; appendage, tailpiece, train, following
67 *sequel*; wake 65 *sequence*; appendix, postscript, P.S., P.P.S., envoi, coda, ending 69
extremity; codicil, rider 468 *qualification*; marginalia, annotation, footnotes; corollary, complement 725 *completion*; appurtenance, accessory
89 *concomitant*; companion piece, fellow, pair
18 *analogue*; extension, continuation, second
part; annexe, wing (of a house), outhouse 164
edifice; offshoot 53 *branch*; arm, extremity 53
limb; accretion 59 *extraneousness*; increment 36
increase; patch, reinforcement 656 *repair*; padding, stuffing 227 *lining*; interpolation 303 *insertion*; interlude, intermezzo 231 *interjacency*;
insertion, gusset 228 *garment*; flap, lappet, lapel;
ingredient 58 *component*; fringe, 234 *edge*;
embroidery 844 *ornamentation*; garnish, seasoning; frills, trimmings; trappings, accoutrements
228 *dressing*.

extra, additive, addendum, increment, something over and above, by-product; percentage,
interest 771 *gain*; bonus, tip, perk, perquisite,
graft 962 *reward*; free gift, freebie, giveaway, gratuity, golden handshake, golden hello 781 *gift*;
windfall; allowance; oddment, odds and ends;
supernumerary; spare parts, spares 633 *provision*; reinforcement 707 *auxiliary*; surplus 637
superfluity; extra time, injury time, overtime.

41 Remainder: thing remaining
N. *remainder*, residue; result; balance; surplus;
relic, rest, remains, remnant 105 *fewness*; rump,
stump, stub, scrag end, fag e., butt e. 69 *extremity*; torso, trunk 53 *piece*; fossil, skeleton, bones
363 *corpse*; husk, shell; wreck, wreckage, debris

165 *ruin*; ashes 332 *powder*; track, spoor, fingerprint 548 *record, trace*; afterglow 67 *sequel*; memorabilia 505 *remembrance*; survival 113
durability; vestige.

leavings, leftovers; precipitate, deposit, sediment; alluvium, silt 344 *soil*; drift, loess,
moraine, detritus 272 *thing transferred*: grounds,
lees, dregs; scum, dross, slag, sludge; bilge, scrap-
ings, shavings, filings, sawdust, crumbs 332
powder; husks, chaff, stubble; peel, peelings;
skin, slough, scurf; combings, trimmings, clippings, remnants, off-cuts; scraps, candle-ends,
odds and ends, bin-ends, lumber 641 *rubbish*;
rejects 779 *derelict*; sweepings, scourings, off-
scourings; waste, sewage 302 *excrement*; refuse,
litter, 649 *dirt*.

Adj. *remaining*, surviving, left, vestigial,
resultant; residual; deposited, sedimentary, precipitated; discarded 779 *not retained*; on the
shelf 860 *unwanted*; left over, odd; net, surplus;
unused; outstanding; spare; superfluous 637
redundant; orphaned, widowed.

Vb. *be left*, remain, result, survive.
leave over, leave out 57 *exclude*; leave, discard,
abandon 607 *reject*.

42 Decrement: thing deducted
N. *decrement*, deduction, depreciation, cut 37
diminution; allowance; remission; clawback,
rebate 810 *discount*; refund, shortage, slippage,
defect 307 *shortfall*, 636 *insufficiency*; loss, sacrifice, forfeit 963 *penalty*; leak, leakage, escape
298 *out-flow*; consumption 634 *waste*; subtrahend, rake-off 786 *taking*; toll 809 *tax*.

43 Mixture
N. *mixture*, mingling, mixing, stirring; blending, harmonization; admixture 38 *addition*;
commixture 45 *union*; intermixture, interpolation 231 *interjacency*; interweaving, interlac-
ing 222 *crossing*; amalgamation, integration 50
combination; merger 706 *association*; eclecticism; fusion, interfusion, infusion, suffusion,
transfusion, instillation, impregnation; adulteration 655 *impairment*; contamination, infection 653 *insalubrity*; infiltration, penetration
297 *ingress*; crossbreeding; interbreeding, miscegenation, intermarriage 894 *marriage*; syngamy,
allogamy 167 *propagation*; cross-fertilization,
hybridism, hybridization, mongrelism; misci-
bility, solubility 337 *liquefaction*.

tincture, ingredient 58 *component*; strain,
streak, element, vein; sprinkling, infusion;
tinge, touch, drop, dash, soupçon 33 *small quantity*; smack, hint, suspicion, flavour 386 *taste*;
seasoning; colour, dye 425 *hue*; stain 845
blemish.

a mixture, mélange; blend, harmony 710 *con-*

cord; composition 331 *structure*; amalgam, fusion, compound, confection, potpourri, concoction 50 *combination*; pastiche; alloy, bronze, brass, pewter, steel; paste; soup, stew, goulash, ragout, olla podrida, salmagundi 301 *dish*; cocktail, punch, brew; solution, infusion.

medley, variety 17 *nonuniformity*, 82 *multiformity*; motley, mosaic 437 *variegation*; miscellany, miscellanea, mixed bag, job lot, ragbag, lucky dip; gallimaufry, hotchpotch, hodgepodge, mishmash, potpourri; jumble; conglomeration 74 *accumulation*; entanglement, imbroglio 61 *confusion*; phantasmagoria, kaleidoscope; clatter 411 *discord*; motley crew 74 *crowd*; circus 369 *zoo*; variety show 594 *stage show*; all sorts, odds and ends, paraphernalia.

hybrid, cross, cross-breed, mongrel; mule; half-breed, half-caste; mulatto.

Adj. *mixed*, mixed up, stirred; mixed up in, involved in; blended, harmonized; syncretic, eclectic; fused, alloyed 50 *combined*; tempered, qualified, adulterated, sophisticated, watered down 163 *weakened*; merged, amalgamated; composite, half-and-half, fifty-fifty; confused, jumbled; unclassified, out of order; heterogeneous 17 *nonuniform*; kaleidoscopic, phantasmagoric 82 *multiform*; patchy, dappled, motley 437 *variegated*; shot; miscellaneous, random 464 *indiscriminate*; miscible, soluble; pervasive 653 *infectious*; hybrid, mongrel; cross-bred, crossed; half-caste; of mixed blood, multiracial.

Vb. *mix*, mix up, stir, shake; shuffle, scramble 63 *jumble*; knead, mash 332 *pulverize*; brew 56 *compose*; fuse, alloy, merge, amalgamate 45 *join*; blend, harmonize 50 *combine*; mingle, intermingle, intersperse 437 *variegate*; interleave 303 *insert*; intertwine, interweave 222 *weave*; tinge, dye 425 *colour*; imbue, instil, impregnate; sprinkle 341 *moisten*; water down, adulterate 163 *weaken*; temper, doctor, tamper with 143 *modify*; season, spice, fortify, lace, spike; hybridize, mongrelize, cross, cross-fertilize, cross-breed 167 *generate*.

Adv. *among*, amongst, amid, amidst, with; in the midst of; inter alia.

44 Simpleness: freedom from mixture

N. *simpleness*, homogeneity 16 *uniformity*; purity 648 *cleanness*; oneness 88 *unity*; absoluteness, sheerness; fundamentality 1 *essence*; indivisibility, insolubility; simplicity 516 *intelligibility*, 573 *plainness*, 699 *artlessness*.

Adj. *simple*, homogeneous, monolithic 16 *uniform*; sheer, mere, utter, nothing but; single, unified 88 *one*; elemental, indivisible, entire 52 *whole*; primary, fundamental, nuts and bolts, basic, bog standard, no-frills, without bells and whistles 5 *intrinsic*; elementary, uncomplicated,

simplified 516 *intelligible*; direct, unadulterated, unalloyed; unsophisticated; 699 *artless*; sincere; naked.

unmixed, pure and simple, without alloy; clear, pure, undefiled, unpolluted, clarified, purified 648 *clean*; thoroughbred 868 *noble*; free from, excluding; unblemished, untarnished 646 *perfect*; unblended, unalloyed, uncompounded, uncombined; undiluted, unadulterated, neat 162 *strong*; unqualified, unmodified; unfortified; unseasoned.

Vb. *simplify*, render simple 16 *make uniform*; break down, factorize 51 *decompose*; disentangle, unscramble; unite.

45 Union

N. *union*, junction, joining etc. vb.; coming together, meeting, concurrence, conjunction 293 *convergence*; clash 279 *collision*; contact 202 *contiguity*, 378 *touch*; congress, concourse, reunion 74 *assembly*; confluence, rendezvous, meeting-place 76 *focus*; coalescence, fusion, merger 43 *mixture*; unification, synthesis 50 *combination*; cohesion, agglutination 48 *coherence*; concretion, consolidation, solidification, coagulation 324 *condensation*; coalition, alliance, symbiosis 706 *association*; connection, linkage, tieup, hookup, linkup 47 *bond*; syngamy, wedlock 894 *marriage*; interconnection, interlocking 222 *crossing*; communication 305 *passage*; network, intercommunication, intercourse 882 *sociability*; trade, traffic, exchange 151 *interchange*, 791 *trade*; involvement 9 *relation*.

sexual intercourse, coition, coitus, copulation, sexual intercourse, sex, fucking (vulg.), bonking, intimacy, carnal knowledge; generation 167 *propagation*; pairing, mating, coupling; union 894 *marriage*; consummation; sexual assault 951 *rape*; unprotected sex, casual s., safe s. 172 *contraception*; foreplay, fellatio, blowjob, cunnilingus; cybersex.

joint, joining, juncture; crease 261 *fold*; suture, seam, stitching 47 *bond*; bonding, English bond, Flemish b.; weld; splice; mitre, mitre joint; dovetail, dovetail and mortise joint; ball and socket j.; hasp, latch, sneck, catch 218 *pivot*; hinge-joint; finger, thumb, wrist, ankle, knuckle, knee, hip, elbow; node; junction, meeting-point, intersection, crossroads 222 *crossing*; decussation, figure X 222 *cross*.

Adj. *conjunctive*, adjunctive, connective, copulative, adhesive 48 *cohesive*; coagulating, astringent; coincident; copulatory, coital, venereal, intimate.

firm, close, fast, secure, sound 153 *fixed*; solid, set, solidified 324 *dense*; glued, cemented, stuck 48 *cohesive*; put, pat; planted, rooted, deep-set;

ingrown, impacted; close-set, crowded, tight, tight-fitting, wedged, jammed, stuck; inextricable, inseparable, immovable, unshakable; packed, jam-p. 54 *full*.

tied, bound, knotted, roped, lashed, secured, belayed, spliced; stitched, sewn, gathered; attached, fastened, adhering 48 *cohesive*; well-tied, tight, taut, tense, fast, secure; intricate, involved, tangled, inextricable, indissoluble.

Vb. *join*, conjoin, couple, yoke, hyphenate, harness together; pair, match 18 *liken*, 462 *compare*, 894 *marry*; bracket, bracket together 28 *equalize*; put together, throw t., piece t., unite 50 *combine*; gather 74 *bring together*; add to, amass, accumulate 38 *add*, 632 *store*; associate, ally, twin (town); merge 43 *mix*; incorporate, unify; 16 *make uniform*; lump together, roll into one; include, embrace 78 *comprise*; grip, grapple 778 *retain*; hinge, articulate, dovetail, mortise, mitre, rabbet; fit, set, interlock, jam 303 *insert*; weld, solder, fuse, cement, glue; lace, knit, sew, seam, stitch; pin, buckle; do up, fasten, button up, zip up 264 *close*; lock, latch; darn, patch, mend, heal over 656 *repair*.

connect, attach, annex (**see** *affix*); staple, clip, pin together; string t., rope t., link t., contact 378 *touch*; make contact, plug in, earth; network, interconnect; link, bridge, span; communicate, intercommunicate; put through to, put in touch; hook up with, link up w.; tie up w. 9 *relate*.

affix, attach, fix, fasten; yoke, leash, harness, saddle, bridle; tie up, moor, anchor, tie to, tether, pin on, hang on, hook on, screw on, nail on; stick on, cement on, sellotape on, gum on; suffix, prefix 38 *add*; splice, engraft, implant 303 *insert*; impact, set, frame 235 *enclose*; drive in, knock in, hammer in 279 *strike*; wedge, jam; screw, nail, rivet, bolt, clamp, clinch.

tie, knot, hitch, lash, belay; knit, sew, seam, stitch, suture; tack, baste; braid, plait, crochet, twine, twist, intertwine, lace, interlace, interweave 222 *weave*; truss, string, rope, strap; do up, lace up, lash up; tether, picket, moor; pinion, manacle, handcuff; hobble, shackle 747 *fetter*; bind, splice, gird, girdle; bandage.

tighten, constrict, compress; fasten, screw up, make firm, make fast, secure; tauten, draw tight, pull t..

unite with, join, meet 293 *converge*; hold t., fit closely, adhere, hang together, stick t. 48 *cohere*; mesh, interlock, engage, grip, grapple, clinch; embrace, entwine; link up with, hold hands; associate with, partner, mix w. 882 *be sociable*; marry, get hitched 894 *wed*; live with, cohabit; go to bed with, lie with, sleep w., make love, have intercourse, have sex w., fuck (vulg.), bonk, have carnal knowledge; consummate a

marriage *or* a union; know, enjoy, possess, have, do; lay, make, bed, tumble; knock off, have it off *or* away with; deflower, rape, ravish, violate, take by force 951 *debauch*; copulate, couple, mate, pair 167 *generate*; mount, tup, cover, serve; cross with, breed w.

46 Disunion

N. *disunion*, disjunction, disconnection, disconnectedness, incoherence, break 72 *discontinuity*; diffusion, dispersal 75 *dispersion*; breakup, disintegration, dissolution, decay 51 *decomposition*, 655 *dilapidation*; absent-mindedness 456 *abstractedness*; dissociation, withdrawal, retirement 621 *relinquishment*, 753 *resignation*; moving apart, growing a., widening 294 *divergence*, 282 *deviation*; split, schism (**see** *separation*); detachment, neutrality 860 *indifference*; isolation, quarantine, segregation 883 *seclusion*; insularity 620 *avoidance*; lack of unity 709 *dissension*; separateness, isolationism, separatism; no connection, no common ground 10 *unrelatedness*; distance apart; dichotomy 15 *difference*; interval, breathing space, space, opening, hole, breach, break, rent, rift, tear, split; fissure, crack, cleft, chasm; cleavage, slit, cut, gash, incision 201 *gap*.

separation, disjoining, severance, parting; uncoupling, breaking up, splitting up 896 *divorce*; untying, undoing, unfastening, unravelling; loosening, freeing 746 *liberation*; setting apart, discrimination, segregation, ghettoization, apartheid 883 *seclusion*; exemption 57 *exclusion*; boycott 620 *avoidance*; expulsion 300 *ejection*; selection 605 *choice*; putting aside 632 *storage*; taking away 39 *subtraction*; expropriation; detaching, withdrawal 188 *displacement*, 272 *transference*; stripping, peeling, plucking 229 *uncovering*; disjointing, dislocation; scattering 75 *dispersion*; dissolution, resolution, disintegration 51 *decomposition*; dissection, analysis, breakdown; disruption, fragmentation 165 *destruction*; splitting, fission, nuclear f. 160 *nucleonics*; breaking, cracking, rupture, fracture 330 *brittleness*; dividing line, caesura; wall, fence, hedge, ha-ha 231 *partition*; curtain 421 *screen*; boundary 236 *limit*; Styx.

scission, section, cleavage, cutting, tearing; division, dichotomy 92 *bisection*; subdivision, segmentation; partition 783 *apportionment*; abscission, cutting off, decapitation, curtailment, retrenchment 204 *shortening*, 37 *diminution*; cutting away, resection, circumcision; cutting open, incision, opening 658 *surgery*; dissection; rending; clawing, laceration, tearing off, nipping, pinching, biting etc. vb.

Adj. *separate*, apart, asunder; adrift, lost; unjoined, unfixed, unfastened, unattached, unannexed, unassociated; distinct, discrete, differentiated, separable, distinguishable 15 *different*; exempt, excepted; hived off, abstracted; unassimilated 44 *unmixed*; alien, foreign 59 *extraneous*; external 6 *extrinsic*, 223 *exterior*; insular, lonely, isolated 88 *alone*; shunned, dropped, avoided, boycotted, sent to Coventry; cast-off; set apart 605 *chosen*; abandoned, left 41 *remaining*; hostile, antipathetic 881 *hostile*, 14 *contrary*, 240 *opposite*; divorced; disjunctive, separative; dichotomous, dividing; selective, diagnostic 15 *distinctive*.

Vb. *separate*, stand apart 620 *avoid*; go away 296 *depart*; part, go different ways, radiate 294 *diverge*; go another way 282 *deviate*; part, part company, cut adrift, cut loose, divorce, split up; hive off; get free, get loose 667 *escape*; disengage, cast off, unmoor, leave, quit, fall away 621 *relinquish*; scatter, break up 75 *disperse*; spring apart 280 *recoil*; come apart, fall a., break, come to bits, disintegrate 51 *decompose*; come undone, unravel; fall off 49 *come unstuck*; split, crack 263 *open*.

disunite, dissociate, divorce; split up, break up, part, separate, sunder, sever; uncouple, unhitch, disconnect, unplug; disengage; disjoint, displace, dislocate, wrench; detach, unseat; remove, detract, deduct 39 *subtract*, 272 *transfer*; skin, strip, flay, peel, pluck 229 *uncover*; unfasten, undo, unbutton, unhook, unlace, unzip, unclasp, unlock, unlatch 263 *open*; untie, cut the knot, sever the tie, disentangle; unstitch, unpick; loosen, relax, slacken, unstring 177 *moderate*; unbind, unchain, unfetter, unloose, loose, free, set f., release 746 *liberate*; expel 300 *eject*; dispel, scatter, break up, disband, demobilize 75 *disperse*; disintegrate, break down 51 *decompose*, 332 *pulverize*, 165 *destroy*.

set apart, put aside set a. 632 *store*; mark out, tick off, distinguish 15 *differentiate*, 463 *discriminate*; single out 605 *select*; exempt, leave out 57 *exclude*; boycott, send to Coventry 620 *avoid*; taboo, black, blacklist 757 *prohibit*; insulate, isolate, cut off 235 *enclose*; zone, compartmentalize, screen off, declare a no-go area 232 *circumscribe*; segregate, ghettoize, sequester, quarantine, maroon 883 *seclude*; keep apart, hold a., drive a.; drive a wedge between, estrange, alienate, set against.

sunder (**see** *disunite*); divide, fragment, fractionate, segment, sectionalize, fractionalize; reduce, factorize, analyse; dissect 51 *decompose*; dichotomize, halve 92 *bisect*; divide up, split, partition, parcel out 783 *apportion*; dismember, quarter, carve (**see** *cut*); behead, decapitate, curtail, dock, amputate 204 *shorten*; take apart, take to pieces, cannibalize, dismantle, break up,

dismount; force open 263 *open*; slit, split; cleave 263 *pierce*. **See** *break*.

cut, hew, hack, slash, gash 655 *wound*; prick, stab, knife 263 *pierce*; cut through, cleave, saw, chop; cut open, slit 263 *open*; cut into, make an incision, incise 555 *engrave*; cut deep, cut to the bone, carve, slice; cut round, pare, whittle, chisel, chip, trim, bevel; clip; snip; cut short, shave 204 *shorten*; cut down, fell, scythe, mow; cut off, lop, prune, dock, curtail (**see** *sunder*); cut up, chop up, quarter, dismember; dice, shred, mince, make mincemeat of, pound 332 *pulverize*; bite 301 *chew*; scratch, score, plough 262 *groove*; nick 260 *notch*.

rend, tear (**see** *sunder*); scratch, claw; gnaw, fret, fray, make ragged; rip, slash, slit (**see** *cut*); lacerate, dismember; tear limb from limb, tear to pieces, tear to shreds, 165 *destroy*; mince, grind, crunch, scrunch, pound 301 *chew*, 332 *pulverize*; blow to pieces, burst.

break, fracture, rupture, bust; split, burst; break in pieces, smash, smash to smithereens, shatter, splinter, shiver 165 *demolish*; fragment, crumble, grind 332 *pulverize*; disintegrate, cave in 51 *decompose*; break up, dismantle (**see** *sunder*); chip, crack, damage 655 *impair*; bend, buckle, warp 246 *distort*; break in two, snap; cleave, force apart 263 *open*.

Adv. *separately*, severally, singly, one by one, bit by bit, piecemeal, in bits, in pieces, in halves, in twain, discontinuously, unconnectedly, disjointedly.

apart, open, asunder, adrift; to pieces, to bits, to smithereens, to shreds; limb from limb.

47 Bond: connecting medium

N. *bond*, connecting medium, vinculum, chain, shackle, fetter, handcuff, tie, band, hoop, yoke; sympathy, empathy, fellow feeling 905 *pity*; nexus, connection, link, liaison 9 *relation*; junction, hinge 45 *joint*; ramification, network 53 *branch*; hyphen, dash, bracket 547 *punctuation*; cement (**see** *adhesive*); bondstone, binder; tie-beam, stretcher, girder 218 *beam*; strut, stay 218 *prop*; channel, passage, corridor 624 *access*; stepping-stone, causeway 624 *bridge*; span, arch; isthmus, neck; col, ridge; stair, steps, stepladder, ladder 308 *ascent*; lifeline; umbilical cord.

cable, line, guy, hawser, painter, moorings; guest-rope, towline, towrope, ripcord, lanyard, communication cord; rope, cord, whipcord, string, tape, twine 208 *fibre*; chain, wire, earth.

ligature, ligament, tendon, muscle; tendril, osier, raffia 208 *fibre*; lashing, binding; string, cord, thread, tape, sticky tape, Sellotape (tdmk), Scotch tape (tdmk), Velcro (tdmk), band, fillet, ribbon, ribband; bandage, tourniquet; drawstring, thong, lace, tag; braid, plait 222 *network*;

tie, stock, cravat 228 *neckwear;* knot, hitch, clinch, bend; running k., slip k., granny k., reef k.; half hitch, clove h.; sheepshank; Gordian k.

fastening, fastener, snap f., press-stud, pop-fastener, popper, zip fastener, zip; drawstring; stitch, basting; button, buttonhole, eyelet, loop, frog; hook and eye; Velcro (tdmk); stud, cufflink; garter, suspender, braces; tiepin, brooch 844 *jewellery;* clip, grip, slide, clasp, curlers; hairpin, hatpin; skewer, spit, pin, drawing p., safety p., toggle p., cotter p., linch p., king p.; peg, dowel, treenail, trenail, nail, brad, tack, tintack 256 *sharp point;* Blutack (tdmk), Sellotape (tdmk), Scotch tape (tdmk); holdfast, staple, clamp, brace, batten, cramp 778 *pincers;* nut, bolt, screw, rivet; buckle, clasp, morse; hasp, hinge 45 *joint;* catch, safety c., spring c.; latch, bolt; lock, lock and key 264 *closure;* combination lock, yale l., mortise l.; padlock, handcuffs, bracelets 748 *fetter;* ring, cleat; hold, bar, post, pile, pale, stake, bollard.

adhesive, glue, fish glue, lime, birdlime, gum, epoxy resin; fixative, hair lacquer, hair spray, brilliantine, grease; solder; paste, size, clay, cement, putty, mortar, stucco, plaster, grout 226 *facing;* wafer, sealing wax; sticker, stamp, adhesive tape, sticky t., Sellotape (tdmk), Scotch tape (tdmk), Blu-tack (tdmk); flypaper 542 *trap;* sticking plaster, Elastoplast (tdmk), Band-Aid (tdmk) 48 *coherence.*

48 Coherence

N. *coherence,* connection, connectedness 71 *continuity;* chain 71 *series;* cohesion, cohesiveness; tenacity 778 *retention;* adherence, adhesion, adhesiveness; stickiness 354 *viscidity;* cementation, cementing, sticking, soldering, agglutination 45 *union;* compaction, conglomeration, consolidation, set 324 *condensation;* inseparability, indivisibility, union 88 *unity;* phalanx, serried ranks, unbroken front, united f.; birds of a feather; monolith, agglomerate, concrete 324 *solid body.*

Adj. *cohesive,* adhesive, adherent; clinging, tenacious; sticky, tacky, gummy, gluey, viscous 354 *viscid;* well-knit, coagulated, concrete, frozen 324 *dense;* shoulder to shoulder, side by side, serried; monolithic 16 *uniform;* united, indivisible, inseparable, inextricable; close, tight, close-fitting, skintight, figure-hugging, clinging, moulding.

Vb. *cohere,* hang together, grow together 50 *combine;* stick close, hold fast; bunch, close the ranks, rally 74 *congregate;* take hold of 778 *retain;* hug, clasp, embrace, twine round; close with; fit, fit tight, mould the figure; adhere, cling, stick; stick to, cleave to, stick on to, freeze on to; stick like a limpet, cling like a shadow,

cling like ivy; cake, coagulate, conglomerate, solidify.

49 Noncoherence

N. *noncoherence,* incoherence 72 *discontinuity;* uncombined state, noncombination, chaos 51 *decomposition;* scattering 75 *dispersion;* separability; looseness, bagginess; loosening, relaxation, freedom 46 *separation;* wateriness 335 *fluidity;* slipperiness 258 *smoothness;* frangibility, friability 330 *brittleness;* nonadhesion, aloofness.

Vb. *come unstuck,* peel off, melt, thaw, run 337 *liquefy;* totter, slip 309 *tumble;* dangle, flap 217 *hang;* rattle, shake, flap.

50 Combination

N. *combination,* composition; coalescence, symphysis 45 *union;* fusion, blending, conflation, synthesis, syncretism 43 *mixture;* amalgamation, merger, assimilation, digestion, absorption 299 *reception;* uniting, unification, integration, centralization 88 *unity;* incorporation, embodiment; synchronization 706 *cooperation;* marriage, union, league, alliance 706 *association;* cabal 623 *plot;* counterpoint 412 *music;* chorus 24 *agreement;* harmony, orchestration 710 *concord;* assembly 74 *assemblage;* synopsis, conspectus, bird's-eye view 592 *compendium.*

compound, alloy, amalgam, blend, composite 43 *a mixture.*

Adj. *combined,* united, unified 88 *one;* integrated, centralized; embodied; inbred, ingrained, absorbed 5 *intrinsic;* fused 43 *mixed;* blended, adapted 24 *adjusted;* connected, linked, networked, conjoint; aggregated; synchronized 123 *synchronous;* in harmony, on the same wavelength, in partnership, in league; associated 706 *cooperative;* conspiratorial.

Vb. *combine,* put together; make up 56 *compose;* interweave 222 *weave;* harmonize, synchronize 24 *accord;* bind, tie 45 *join;* unite, unify, centralize; incorporate, embody, integrate, absorb, assimilate; merge, amalgamate, pool; blend, fuse 43 *mix;* impregnate, imbue, instil, inoculate; bracket together; lump together 38 *add;* group, rally 74 *bring together;* band together, associate; ally; go into partnership with, join hands, join forces with, team up with 706 *cooperate;* fraternize, make friends 880 *be friendly;* marry 894 *wed;* mate 90 *pair;* conspire 623 *plot;* coalesce, grow together.

51 Decomposition

N. *decomposition* 46 *disunion;* division, partition, 46 *separation;* dissection, dismemberment; anatomization, analysis, breakdown; factorization;

syllabification, parsing 564 *grammar*; resolution, electrolysis, hydrolysis, photolysis, cataly-
sis; atomization; dissolving, dissolution 337
liquefaction; fission 160 *nucleonics*; hiving off,
decentralization, devolution, delegation;
regionalism; collapse, breakup, disintegration,
entropy 165 *destruction*; chaos 17 *nonuniformity*.

decay 655 *dilapidation*; erosion, wear and tear
37 *diminution*; disintegration 361 *death*; corruption, mouldering, rotting, putridness, putrefaction, adipocere, mortification, necrosis,
gangrene, caries 649 *uncleanness*; rot, rust,
mould 659 *blight*; carrion 363 *corpse*.

Vb. *decompose*, resolve, reduce, factorize 44
simplify; separate, parse, dissect; break down,
analyse, take to pieces 46 *sunder*; electrolyse,
catalyse; split, fission 46 *disunite*; atomize 165
demolish; disband, break up, hive off 75 *disperse*;
decentralize 783 *apportion*; unsettle, disturb 63
derange; melt 337 *liquefy*; erode 37 *abate*; rot,
rust, moulder, decay, consume, waste away,
crumble, wear, perish 655 *deteriorate*; corrupt,
putrefy, mortify, gangrene 649 *be unclean*; disintegrate, go to pieces 165 *be destroyed*.

52 Whole. Principal part

N. *whole*, wholeness, fullness 54 *completeness*;
integration, indivisibility, integrity, oneness 88
unity; whole number, integer, entity 88 *unit*;
entirety, ensemble, corpus, complex, totality,
summation, sum 38 *addition*; holism, univer-
salization, generalization 79 *generality*; comprehensiveness, inclusiveness 78 *inclusion*;
collectivity, system, world, globe, cosmos 321
universe; microcosm; Lebensraum; bird's-eye v.,
panorama, overview, conspectus.

all, no exceptions, one and all, everybody,
everyone 79 *everyman*; all the world 74 *crowd*;
total, aggregate, sum; ensemble, be-all and end-
all, lock, stock and barrel; hook, line and sinker,
inventory 87 *list*; lot, whole l., the whole
caboodle, the whole bang shoot, the works, the
full monty.

chief part, best part, major p., nitty-gritty,
nuts and bolts 638 *chief thing*; ninety-nine per
cent, bulk, mass; heap 32 *great quantity*; tissue,
staple, stuff; body, torso, trunk, bole, stem,
stalk; hull, hulk, skeleton; lion's share, biggest
slice of the cake; gist, sum and substance, the
long and the short of it; almost all, nearly all,
everything but the kitchen sink; all but a few,
majority.

Adj. *whole*, total, universal; integral, pure 44
unmixed; sound 646 *perfect*; gross, full 54 *complete*; integrated 88 *one*; in one piece; fully
restored.

intact, untouched, unaffected; unspoiled, virgin 126 *new*; undivided, undiminished,

unclipped, uncut; undissolved; unbroken,
unimpaired 646 *undamaged*; uncut, unabridged,
unedited, uncensored, unexpurgated.

indivisible, 324 *indissoluble*; inseparable,
monolithic 16 *uniform*.

comprehensive, omnibus, all-embracing, all-
encompassing, across-the-board, full-length 78
inclusive; wholesale, all singing all dancing,
sweeping 32 *extensive*; widespread, epidemic 79
general; international, world, world-wide, global, cosmic 79 *universal*, 189 *ubiquitous*.

Adv. *on the whole*, by and large, all in all, all
things considered, in the long run; substantially, in essence; virtually, to all intents and
purposes, in effect; as good as; mainly, in the
main 32 *greatly*; almost, all but 200 *nearly*.

collectively, one and all, all together; compre-
hensively; in bulk; in the aggregate; en masse,
en bloc.

53 Part

N. *part*, portion; proportion, fraction, half, quarter, tithe, percentage; factor, aliquot 85 *number*;
surplus 41 *remainder*; quota, contingent; dividend, share 783 *portion*; item, particular, detail
80 *particulars*; clause, sentence, paragraph 563
phrase; ingredient, member, constituent,
element 58 *component*; schism, faction 708
party; heat, leg, lap, round 110 *period*; side 239
laterality; group, species (**see** *subdivision*);
detachment; attachment 40 *adjunct*; page, leaf,
folio, sheet 589 *book*; excerpt, extract, passage,
quotation, quote 605 *choice*; text; segment, sector, section 46 *scission*; arc 248 *curve*; hemisphere 252 *sphere*; instalment, advance, down
payment, deposit, earnest 804 *payment*; fragment (**see** *piece*).

limb, member, organ, appendage; hind limb
267 *leg*; forelimb 271 *wing*; flipper, fin 269 *propeller*; arm, hand 378 *feeler*.

subdivision, segment, sector, section 46 *scission*; division, compartment; group, subgroup,
species, subspecies, family 74 *group*; classification 62 *arrangement*; ward, community,
parish, department, region 184 *district*; chapter,
paragraph, clause, subordinate clause, phrase,
verse; part, number, issue, instalment, volume
589 *edition*; canto 593 *poem*.

branch, ramification, offshoot 40 *adjunct*;
bough, limb, spur, twig, tendril, leaf, switch,
shoot, scion, sucker, slip, sprig, spray 366
foliage.

piece, torso, trunk, stump 41 *remainder*; limb,
segment, section (**see** *part*); patch, insertion 40
adjunct; length, roll 222 *textile*; strip, swatch;
fragment 55 *incompleteness*; bit, scrap, offcut,
shred, wisp, rag 33 *small thing*; morsel, bite,
crust, crumb 33 *small quantity*; splinter, skelf,

sliver, chip, snippet; cut, wedge, finger, slice, rasher; collop, cutlet, chop, gigot c., steak; hunk, chunk, wad, wodge, portion, slab, lump, mass 195 *bulk*; clod, turf, divot, sod 344 *soil*; shard, flake, scale; dose 783 *portion*; bits and pieces, odds and ends, oddments 43 *medley*; bin ends; clippings, parings, brash, rubble, scree, detritus, moraine, debris 41 *leavings*; parcel, plot, allotment.

Adj. *fragmentary*, broken, crumbly 330 *brittle*; in bits, in pieces, in smithereens; not whole 647 *imperfect*; partial, bitty, scrappy 636 *insufficient*; fractional, aliquot; segmental, sectional, divided; shredded, sliced, minced, ground 33 *small*.

Vb. *part*, divide, partition, segment; compartmentalize 46 *sunder*; share out 783 *apportion*; fragment 46 *disunite*.

54 Completeness

N. *completeness*, entireness, wholeness 52 *whole*; integration 88 *unity*; solidarity 706 *cooperation*; harmony 710 *concord*; self-sufficiency 635 *sufficiency*; entirety, totality 52 *all*; comprehensiveness 79 *generality*; the ideal 646 *perfection*; ne plus ultra, the limit 236 *limit*; peak, culmination, zenith, crown 213 *summit*; finish 69 *end*; last touch, finishing t. 725 *completion*; fulfilment, consummation 69 *finality*; the whole hog, the full monty.

plenitude, fullness, amplitude, capacity, maximum, one's fill, saturation 635 *sufficiency*; saturation point 863 *satiety*; completion, filling; filling up, brimming, overrunning, swamping, drowning; full house, complement, full c.; requisite number, quorum; full measure, bumper; bellyful, skinful, repletion; full size, full length, full volume.

Adj. *complete*, plenary, full; total; integral 52 *whole*; entire 52 *intact*; full-blown, full-grown, fully-fledged, 669 *matured*; unbroken, undivided 324 *dense*; self-contained, self-sufficient 635 *sufficient*; fully furnished; all-in, comprehensive 78 *inclusive*; exhaustive, detailed 570 *diffuse*; absolute, extreme; thorough, thoroughgoing, sweeping, wholesale, regular 32 *consummate*; unmitigated, downright, plumb, plain 44 *unmixed*; crowning, culminating, consummating, complementary.

full, replete 635 *filled*; topped up; well-filled, bulging; brimful, brimming; overwhelmed; overflowing, running over, slopping, swamped, drowned; saturated, oozing; bursting at the seams; gorged, fit to burst, full to bursting 863 *sated*; chock-full, chock-a-block, crammed, stuffed, packed, jam-p., packed like sardines; laden, heavy-1., fully charged, all seats taken, standing room only; infested, overrun, crawl-

ing with, hotching w., alive w., seething w., jumping w., lousy w., stiff w.; full of, rolling in; soaked in, dripping with.

Vb. *be complete*, be integrated; culminate, come to a head 725 *climax*; come to a close, be all over 69 *end*; be self-sufficient 635 *have enough*; want nothing, lack n. 828 *be content*; become complete, fill out, reach maturity 669 *mature*; be filled.

make complete, complete, complement, integrate 45 *join*; make whole 656 *restore*; build up, construct, make up, piece together 56 *compose*; eke out, supplement; do thoroughly, leave nothing undone, carry out 725 *carry through*; put the finishing touch, put the icing on the cake, round off 69 *terminate*.

fill, fill up, brim, top; saturate 341 *drench*; overfill, swamp, drown, overwhelm; top up, replenish 633 *provide*; satisfy 635 *suffice*, 828 *content*, 863 *sate*; fill to capacity, cram, pack, stuff, line, bulge out, pack in, pile in, squeeze in, ram in, jam in 303 *insert*; load, charge, ram down; freight; fill space, occupy 226 *cover*; reach to, extend to 183 *extend*; spread over, overrun 189 *pervade*; fit tight, be full to overflowing, be chock-a-block 45 *tighten*; fill in, enter 38 *add*.

Adv. *completely*, fully, wholly, totally, entirely, utterly, extremely 32 *greatly*; all told, in all, in toto; on all counts, in all respects, in every way; quite, altogether; outright, downright; thoroughly; to one's fill, to the top of one's bent, to the utmost, to the end, to the full; out and out, all out, heart and soul; head and shoulders, head over heels, neck and crop; to the brim, up to the hilt, up to the neck, up to the ears, up to the eyes; hook, line and sinker; root and branch; down to the ground; with a vengeance, with knobs on, with all the trimmings, and then some; to the last man, to the last breath; every whit, every inch; at full length, full out, in full; as far as possible; to capacity, not an inch to spare.

throughout, all the way, from first to last, from beginning to end, from end to end, from one end to the other, the length and breadth of, from coast to coast, from sea to sea, from Land's End to John o' Groats 183 *widely*; from north and south and east and west; fore and aft; high and low; from top to bottom; from top to toe, from head to foot, cap-à-pie; to the bitter end, to the end of the road, to the end of the chapter.

55 Incompleteness

N. *incompleteness*, defectiveness; unfinished state 647 *imperfection*; immaturity 670 *undevelopment*; sketch, outline, 623 *plan*; skeleton, torso, trunk 53 *piece*; half measures, a lick and a promise 726 *noncompletion*; perfunctoriness, superficiality, 458 *negligence*; nonfulfilment, deficiency, slippage 307 *shortfall*, 636 *insufficiency*; dissatisfaction 829 *discontent*; impairment 655 *deterioration*; omission, break, gap, lacuna, missing link 72 *discontinuity*, 201 *interval*; part payment 53 *part*.

deficit, screw loose, missing link, omission 647 *defect*; shortfall, slippage; 772 *loss*; default 930 *improbity*; want, lack, need 627 *requirement*.

Adj. *incomplete*, inadequate, defective 307 *deficient*; short, scant, unsatisfactory 636 *insufficient*; like Hamlet without the Prince 641 *useless*; omitting, wanting, lacking, needing, requiring; short of, shy of; halting, mutilated; without, -less, -free; garbled, impaired; cropped, abbreviated, shortened 204 *short*; flawed 647 *imperfect*; partial 53 *fragmentary*; half-finished, neglected 726 *uncompleted*; not ready 670 *unprepared*; undeveloped, underdeveloped, unripe 670 *immature*; raw, crude, rough-hewn 244 *amorphous*; sketchy, scrappy, bitty; thin, poor 4 *insubstantial*; perfunctory, half-hearted, half-done, undone 458 *neglected*; left in the air, left hanging; omitted, missing, lost 190 *absent*; interrupted 72 *discontinuous*.

unfinished, in progress, in hand; in embryo, begun 68 *beginning*; in preparation, on the stocks; on the back-burner.

Vb. *be incomplete*, miss, lack, need 627 *require*, 307 *fall short*; be wanting 190 *be absent*; default, leave undone 458 *neglect*; omit, miss out 57 *exclude*; break off, interrupt 72 *discontinue*; leave in the air, leave dangling, leave hanging 726 *not complete*.

56 Composition

N. *composition*, constitution, setup, make-up; formation, construction, build-up, build 331 *structure*; organization 62 *arrangement*; nature, humour, character, condition 5 *temperament*; embodiment 78 *inclusion*; compound 43 *mixture*, 50 *combination*, 358 *organism*; syntax, sentence 563 *phrase*; artistic composition 412 *music*, 551 *art*, 553 *painting*, 554 *sculpture*; architecture 164 *edifice*; authorship 586 *writing*, 593 *poetry*; dramatic art 594 *drama*; composing, printing, typography 587 *print*; compilation 74 *assemblage*; construction 164 *production*; choreography 594 *ballet*; orchestration, instrumentation, score 412 *musical piece*; work of art, picture, portrait, sculpture, piece of s., model; literary work 589 *book*, 593 *poem*, 591 *dissertation*, 592 *anthology*; play 594 *stage play*; 837 *dance*; pattern, design 12 *correlation*.

Vb. *constitute*, compose, form, make; make up; inhere, belong to, enter into.

contain, subsume, include, consist of 78 *comprise*; hold, have, take in, absorb 299 *admit*; comprehend, embrace, embody 235 *enclose*.

compose, compound 43 *mix*, 50 *combine*; organize, set in order, put in o. 62 *arrange*; synthesize, put together, make up 45 *join*; compile, assemble 74 *bring together*; compose, set up, computer-set 587 *print*; draft, draw up 586 *write*; orchestrate, score 413 *compose music*; draw 553 *paint*; sculpt, construct, build, make, fabricate 164 *produce*; knit 222 *weave*.

57 Exclusion

N. *exclusion*, preemption; forestalling 702 *hindrance*; exclusiveness, monopoly, closed shop, dog-in-the-manger policy; possessiveness 932 *selfishness*; exception; special case; exemption, dispensation 746 *liberation*; leaving out, including o., omission 607 *rejection*; blackball; no entry, no admission, no-go area, no-man's-land, exclusion order; closed door, lockout; picket line; embargo, ban, bar, taboo 757 *prohibition*; ostracism, boycott 620 *avoidance*; segregation, quarantine, caste system, colour bar, apartheid, 883 *seclusion*; intolerance, repression, suppression, discrimination 481 *prejudice*; expulsion, eviction; disbarment, dismissal, suspension, excommunication; deportation, exile, expatriation; removal, elimination, eradication 188 *displacement*; dam, wall, barricade, screen, partition, pale, curtain, Iron C., Bamboo C. 235 *barrier*; great wall of China 713 *defence*; customs' barrier, economic zone, tariff wall 809 *tax*; ghetto.

Adj. *excluding*, exclusive, exemptive; restrictive, clannish, cliquish; preventive, prohibitive; preemptive.

Vb. *be excluded* not belong, stay outside, not gain admission; suffer exile, go into e., go into voluntary e. 296 *depart*, 190 *be absent*.

exclude, preclude 470 *make impossible*; preempt, forestall 64 *come before*; keep out, warn off 747 *restrain*; blackball, vote against, deny entry, shut out, debar, shut the door on, spurn 607 *reject*; bar, ban, put an embargo on, taboo, black, disallow 757 *prohibit*; ostracize, cold-shoulder, boycott, send to Coventry 620 *avoid*, not include, leave out, include o.; count o.; exempt, dispense, excuse 746 *liberate*; except, make an exception, treat as a special case 19 *make unlike*; omit, miss out, pass over, disregard 458 *neglect*; lay aside, put a., relegate 46 *set apart*; take out, strike o., cross o., cancel 550 *obliterate*; disbar, strike off, remove, disqualify 188 *displace*, 963 *punish*; rule out, draw the line; wall off, fence off, screen off, curtain off, quarantine 232 *circumscribe*, 235 *enclose*; excommunicate, segregate, sequester 883 *seclude*; thrust out, dismiss, sack, declare redundant, deport, extradite, exile, banish, outlaw, expatriate; weed, sift, sieve, sort out; eradicate, uproot 300 *eject*; expurgate, bowdlerize, censor 648 *purify*; deny 760 *refuse*; abandon 779 *not retain.*

Adv. *exclusive of*, excepting, barring, bar, not counting, including out, except, with the exception of, save; short of; let alone, apart from.

58 Component

N *component*, component part, integral p., element, item; piece, bit, segment; link, stitch; word, letter; constituent, part and parcel 53 *part*; factor, leaven 178 *influence*; additive, appurtenance, feature 40 *adjunct*; one of, member, one of us; staff, workforce, crew, men, company, complement 686 *personnel*; ingredient 193 *contents*, 43 *tincture*; works, inner workings, insides, interior 224 *interiority*; nuts and bolts, machinery 630 *machine*; spare part 40 *extra*; components, set, outfit 88 *unit.*

Adj. *component*, constituent, ingredient; belonging, proper, native, inherent 5 *intrinsic*; built-in; admitted, one of, on the staff.

59 Extraneousness

N. *extraneousness*, foreignness 6 *extrinsicality*, 223 *exteriority*; foreign parts; foreign body, foreign substance, accretion 38 *addition*; alien element, 84 *nonconformity*; exotica.

foreigner, alien, stranger, emmet, outlander; Southerner, Northerner, Easterner, Westerner; Martian, extraterrestrial being, little green men; Celtic fringe; Sassenach, pommie (derog), limey (derog), rooineck (derog); Yank, Yankee, Aussie, Kiwi; wog (derog), wop (derog), dago (derog); gringo (derog), whitey (derog), honkie (derog), paleface; colonial, Creole 191 *settler*; resident alien, expatriate; migrant, migrant worker, guest w., Gastarbeiter, emigrant, émigré, exile; immigrant, refugee, diaspora, ten lost tribes.

intruder, interloper, alien, trespasser, cuckoo in the nest, squatter; uninvited guest, gatecrasher, stowaway; outsider; not one of us, stranger in our midst; arrival, new a., nouveau arrivé, newcomer, new boy, tenderfoot 297 *incomer*; invader 712 *attacker.*

Adj. *extraneous*, ulterior, outside 223 *exterior*, 6 *extrinsic*; ultramundane, extragalactic 199 *distant*; not indigenous, imported; foreign, alien, unearthly; strange, outlandish, barbarian; overseas, transatlantic; continental, extraterrestrial; exotic, unacclimatized; gypsy, nomad, wandering; unassimilated, unintegrated 46 *separate*; immigrant, intrusive, interloping, trespassing, gate-crashing; infringing, invading; exceptional 84 *unusual*; not of this world, unnatural, paranormal, supernatural 983 *magical*; inadmissible.

Order

60 Order

N. *order*, state of order, orderliness, tidiness, neatness 648 *cleanness*, 258 *smoothness*; quiet 266 *quietude*; harmony 710 *concord*; system, method, methodology, prioritization; fixed order, pattern, rule 81 *regularity*, 16 *uniformity*; custom, routine 610 *habit*; rite 988 *ritual*; discipline 739 *obedience*; due order, hierarchy, gradation, subordination, rank, position 73 *serial place*; unbroken order, even tenor, progression, series 71 *continuity*; logical order, alphabetical o. 65 *sequence*, 12 *correlation*; organization, array 62 *arrangement*, 56 *composition*; a place for everything and e. in its place.

Adj. *orderly*, harmonious, 245 *symmetrical*; well-behaved, decorous 848 *well-bred*; disciplined 739 *obedient*; well-regulated, according to rule 81 *regular*; ordered, classified 62 *arranged*; methodical, systematic; strict 16 *uniform*; steady 610 *habitual*; correct, shipshape, Bristol fashion, trim, neat, tidy, neat and tidy, neat as a pin, out of a bandbox; spick and span, spruce, dapper, well-groomed 648 *clean*; in good trim, well-kept, in apple-pie order, in perfect o., in its proper place 62 *arranged*; direct 249 *straight*; lucid 516 *intelligible.*

Vb. *order*, dispose, prioritize 62 *arrange*; schematize, systematize, organize 62 *regularize*; regulate 24 *adjust*; normalize, standardize 16 *make uniform*; keep order, call to order, police, govern 733 *rule*, 737 *command.*

be in order, be shipshape, harmonize 24 *accord*; range oneself, draw up, line up; fall into place, find one's level; take one's place, station oneself, take up one's position 187 *place oneself*; keep one's place; rally round 74 *congregate*; follow routine 610 *be wont.*

61 Disorder

N. *disorder*, random order, nonclassification; incoordination, muddle, no system; bedlam, chaotic state, chaos, mayhem 734 *anarchy*; irregularity, anomalousness, anomaly 17 *nonuniformity*; disunion, disaccord 25 *disagreement*; disharmony 411 *discord*; disorderliness, unruliness, lack of discipline 738 *disobedience*; outbreak (**see** turmoil); nihilism 738 *sedition*; untidiness, clutter, littering, slovenliness 649 *uncleanness*; neglect 458 *negligence*; discomposure, disarray, dishevelment 63 *derangement*; scattering 75 *dispersion*, 51 *decomposition*; upheaval 149 *revolution*; subversion 221 *overturning*; destruction; welter, jumble, shambles, hugger-mugger, mix-up, medley, embroilment, imbroglio 43 *mixture*; chaos, scramble 74 *crowd*; muddle, litter, clutter, lumber 641 *rubbish*; farrago, mess, mishmash, hash, hotchpotch, ragbag, Babel, bedlam, madhouse (**see** *turmoil*).

complexity, complication, snarl-up 700 *difficulty*, 702 *hindrance*; implication, involvement, imbroglio, embroilment; intricacy, kink 251 *convolution*; maze, labyrinth, warren; web 222 *network*; coil, tangle, twist, snarl, ravel; knot, Gordian k. 47 *ligature*; puzzle 517 *unintelligibility*; awkward situation, how d'ye do, how-do-you-do, pretty kettle of fish, pickle 700 *predicament*.

turmoil, turbulence, tumult, frenzy, ferment, storm, convulsion 176 *violence*; pandemonium, inferno; hullabaloo, hubbub, racket, row, riot, uproar 400 *loudness*; affray, fracas, dustup, stramash, brawl, mêlée 716 *fight*; hurly-burly, todo, rumpus, ruction, shemozzle, spot of bother, pother, trouble, disturbance 318 *commotion*; whirlwind, tornado, hurricane 352 *gale*; beargarden, shambles, madhouse, Bedlam; shindig, breach of the peace; roughhouse, rough and tumble, free for all, fisticuffs, all hell broken loose, bull in a china shop; street fighting, gang warfare 709 *quarrel*; fat in the fire, devil to pay, hell to p.

slut, sloven, slag, slattern, draggletail, litterer, litterlout 649 *dirty person*; ragamuffin, tatterdemalion 801 *poor person*.

anarchist, nihilist; lord of misrule, sons of Belial 738 *rioter*.

Adj. *complex*, intricate, involved, elaborate, sophisticated, complicated, over-c., overinvolved 251 *coiled*, problematic 517 *puzzling*; winding, inextricable; entangled, enmeshed, balled up, snarled 702 *hindered*; knotted 45 *tied*.

disorderly, undisciplined, unruly; out of control, out of step, out of line, tumultuous, rumbustious; frantic 503 *frenzied*; orgiastic, Saturnalian, Bacchic, Dionysiac 949 *drunken*; rough, tempestuous, turbulent 176 *violent*, anarchical, nihilistic, lawless 954 *lawbreaking*; wild, harum-scarum, rantipole, tomboyish, boisterous, scatterbrained 456 *light-minded*.

Vb. *be disordered*, fall into disarray, scatter, break up 75 *disperse*; get in a mess, fall into confusion 49 *come unstuck*; get out of hand, riot, 738 *disobey*; jump the queue 64 *come before*; disorder 63 *derange*.

rampage, go on the r., storm; rush, mob; riot 738 *revolt*; romp 837 *amuse oneself*; play the fool 497 *be absurd*; give a riotous welcome 876 *celebrate*.

62 Arrangement: reduction to order

N. *arrangement*, reduction to order; ordering, disposal, disposition, marshalling, arraying, placing 187 *location*; grouping, 74 *assemblage*; division, distribution, allocation, allotment 783 *apportionment*; method, systematization, organization, prioritization, reorganization; restructuring, perestroika; rationalization; streamlining 654 *improvement*; centralization 48 *coherence*; decentralization, hiving off 49 *noncoherence*; administration 689 *management*; planning 623 *contrivance*, 669 *preparation*; taxonomy, categorization, classification 561 *nomenclature*; analysis 51 *decomposition*; codification, consolidation; syntax, conjugation 564 *grammar*; grading, gradation, subordination, graduation, calibration 465 *measurement*, 71 *series*; synchronization 123 *synchronism*; construction 56 *composition*; array, system, form 60 *order*; cosmos 321 *universe*; orchestration, score 412 *music*; layout, pattern; choreography 837 *dance*; collection, assortment 74 *accumulation*; schematism; computer program; register, file 548 *record*; inventory, catalogue, table 87 *list*; code, digest; class, group, sub-g. 77 *classification*.

sorting, grading, seeding, league table; cross-reference 12 *correlation*; file, computer f., folder, filing system, Filofax (tdmk), personal organizer, card index, pigeonhole, slot; sieve, strainer 263 *porosity*.

Adj. *arranged*, disposed, marshalled, arrayed etc. vb.; ordered, schematic, tabulated, tabular; methodical, systematic, organizational; precise, definite, cut and dried; classified; straightened out; regulated 81 *regular*; sorted, seeded, graded, streamed, banded.

Vb. *arrange*, set, dispose, set up, set out, lay out; formulate, form, knock into shape, orchestrate, score 56 *compose*; range, rank, align, line up, form up; position 187 *place*; marshal, array; rally 74 *bring together*; put in order; grade, size, group, space; collocate, thread together 45 *connect*; settle, fix, determine, define; allot, allocate, assign, distribute, deal, parcel out 783 *apportion*; rearrange, trim, neaten, tidy, tidy up, arrange for, make arrangements 669 *prepare*, 623 *plan*, 689 *manage*.

regularize, reduce to order, straighten out, put to rights 654 *rectify*, 24 *adjust*; regulate; organize, systematize, prioritize, methodize, schematize; standardize, normalize, centralize 16 *make uniform*.

class, classify, subsume, group; specify 561 *name*; process; analyse, divide; dissect 51 *decompose*; rate, rank, grade, evaluate 480 *estimate*; sort, sift, sieve, seed; tag, label 547 *mark*; file, pigeonhole; index, cross-r.; tabulate, alphabetize; catalogue; register 548 *record*; program.

63 Derangement

N. *derangement*, shuffling 151 *interchange*; translocation, displacement 272 *transference*; obstruction 702 *hindrance*; disarrangement, disorganization, discomposure, dishevelment; dislocation 46 *separation*; disturbance, interruption 138 *untimeliness*; creasing, corrugation 261 *fold*; madness 503 *mental disorder*; upsetting 221 *inversion*; convulsion 176 *violence*, 318 *agitation*; state of disorder 61 *disorder*.

Vb. *derange*, disarrange, disorder, put out of gear, get out of order; disturb, touch 265 *move*; interfere 702 *hinder*; lose 188 *misplace*; disorganize, muddle, confuse, convulse, throw into confusion, make havoc; tamper, spoil, mar, damage, sabotage 655 *impair*; strain, bend, twist 176 *force*; unhinge, dislocate, sprain, rick 188 *displace*; unseat, dislodge, derail, throw off the rails; throw off balance, upset, overturn, capsize 221 *invert*, 149 *revolutionize*; declassify; shake, jiggle, toss 318 *agitate*; trouble, perturb, unsettle, discompose, disconcert, ruffle, rattle, flurry, fluster 456 *distract*; interrupt 138 *mistime*; misdirect, disorientate, throw one off his bearings 495 *mislead*, 655 *pervert*; unhinge, dement, drive mad 503 *make mad*, 891 *enrage*.

jumble, shuffle, get out of order 151 *interchange*, 272 *transpose*; mix up 43 *mix*; toss, tumble 318 *agitate*; ruffle, dishevel, tousle; rumple, crumple, crease, wrinkle, crush 261 *fold*; untidy, mess, muck up; muddle, mess up, scatter, fling about 75 *disperse*.

bedevil, throw into confusion, make a mess *or* hash of; confound, complicate, perplex, involve, ravel, ball up, foul up, entangle, tangle, embroil; turn topsy-turvy, turn upside down 221 *invert*; send haywire.

64 Precedence

N. *precedence*, antecedence, going before, coming b., queue-jumping 283 *preceding*; front position, prosthesis 237 *front*; higher position, pride of place 34 *superiority*; preference 605 *choice*; preeminence, excellence 638 *importance*; captaincy, leadership, hegemony 733 *authority*; the lead, the pas; leading, guiding, pioneering; precedent 66 *precursor*; past history 125 *past time*.

Adj. *preceding*, foregoing, outgoing; former, ex-, previous 119 *prior*; before-mentioned, above-m.; aforesaid, said; forewarning, premonitory, prodromal; preliminary, prefatory, preparatory.

Vb. *come before*, be first to arrive 283 *precede*; go first, jump the queue; lead, guide, conduct,

show the way, point the way 547 *indicate*; be the forerunner of, pioneer, clear the way, blaze the trail 484 *discover*; head, take the lead 237 *be in front*; have precedence, take p. 34 *be superior*; lead the dance, set the fashion, be a trend-setter 178 *influence*; open, lead off, kick off, bully off 68 *begin*; preface; introduce, usher in, herald, ring in 68 *auspicate*; get ahead; antedate 125 *be past*.

put in front, send a reconnaisance party, send ahead, station before 187 *place*; prefix 38 *add*; front, top 237 *be in front*; presuppose 512 *suppose*; preface.

Adv. *before*, in advance; preparatory to, as a prelude to, as a preliminary; earlier 119 *before* (in time); ante, supra, above 237 *in front*.

65 Sequence

N. *sequence*, coming after, descent, line, lineage 120 *posteriority*; going after; inference 475 *reasoning*; suffixion 38 *addition*; succession, successorship, mantle, Elijah's m. 780 *transfer*; rota, Buggin's turn; series 71 *continuity*; successiveness, alternation, serialization; continuation, prolongation 113 *protraction*, 146 *continuance*; pursuance 619 *pursuit*; overtaking 306 *overstepping*, 727 *success*; subordination, second place, proxime accessit 35 *inferiority*; last place 238 *rear*; consequence 67 *sequel*.

Adj. *sequential*, following, succeeding; ensuing; next 200 *near*; posterior, latter, later 120 *subsequent*; another, second 38 *additional*; successive, consecutive 71 *continuous*; alternating 12 *correlative*; alternate, consequent, resulting 157 *caused*.

Vb. *come after*, ensue 284 *follow*; follow close, sit on one's tail, drive bumper to bumper, breathe down one's neck, tread on the heels; succeed, inherit, step into the shoes of, supplant 150 *substitute*; alternate, relieve, take over.

place after, suffix, append.

Adv. *after*, following; afterwards 120 *subsequently*, 238 *rearward*; at the end, as follows, consequentially; in the end 69 *finally*; next, later; infra, below.

66 Precursor

N. *precursor*, predecessor, ancestor, forbear 169 *parentage*; Adam and Eve, early man 371 *humankind*; the ancients 125 *antiquity*; eldest, firstborn; discoverer, inventor 461 *experimenter*; pioneer, pathfinder, explorer 268 *traveller*; guide, pilot 690 *leader*; scout, reconnaissance party; vanguard, avant-garde, innovator, trailblazer; trend-setter; forerunner; herald, harbinger, announcer 529 *messenger*; anticipation, foretaste, preview, premonition, 511 *omen*; trailer; prequel; precedent 83 *example*; antecedent, prefix, preposition 40 *adjunct*; eve, vigil, day before 119 *priority*.

prelude, preliminary, preamble, preface, front matter, prologue, foreword; opening, introduction 68 *beginning*; lead, heading, frontispiece 237 *front*; 669 *preparation*; aperitif, appetizer, hors d'oeuvre, starter; overture 412 *musical piece*; presupposition 512 *supposition*, 475 *premise*.

Adj. *precursory*, preliminary, exploratory 669 *preparatory*; introductory, prefatory 68 *beginning*; inaugural; precedent 64 *preceding*.

67 Sequel

N. *sequel*, consequence, result, aftermath, by-product, spin-off 157 *effect*; conclusion 69 *end*; aftereffect; hangover, morning after 949 *crapulence*; aftertaste; afterglow, fallout; afterbirth, placenta 167 *obstetrics*; inheritance, legacy 777 *dower*; surprise 508 *lack of expectation*; afterthought, second thoughts; second try, second bite at the cherry; end matter, epilogue, postscript; envoi, last words; follow-up 725 *completion*; continuation, sequel 589 *book*; tailpiece, colophon, coda 238 *rear*; appendage, appendix, codicil, supplement 40 *adjunct*; suffix, affix, inflection 564 *grammar*; afters, pudding, dessert 301 *dish*; afterlife, 124 *future state*; hereafter.

retinue, following, followers, camp f., groupies 284 *follower*; queue 71 *series*; train, cortege 71 *procession*; tailback, wake 89 *concomitant*; trailer 274 *vehicle*.

successor, descendant, future generations 170 *posterity*; heir 776 *beneficiary*; next man in; replacement, supplanter 150 *substitute*; newcomer, nouveau arrivé 297 *incomer*; satellite, hanger-on 742 *dependant*.

68 Beginning

N. *beginning*, birth, rise (**see** *origin*); infancy, babyhood 130 *youth*, 126 *newness*; primitiveness 127 *oldness*; commencement; onset 295 *arrival*; emergence 445 *appearance*; inception, institution, constitution, foundation 156 *causation*; origination, invention 484 *discovery*; creation 164 *production*; innovation 21 *originality*; initiative, introduction 66 *prelude*; alpha, first letter, initial; heading, headline; title page, front matter; van, front, forefront 237 *front*; dawn 128 *morning*; running in, teething troubles, growing pains; first sight, first impression, first lap, first round, first stage; early stages, early days; rudiments, elements, first principles, alphabet, ABC; leading up to 289 *approach*; onset 712 *attack*; starter 538 *beginner*; preliminaries 669 *preparation*.

debut, coming out, presentation, initiation, launching; inauguration, opening, unveiling;

first night, premiere, first appearance, first offence; first step, first move; gambit; maiden voyage, maiden speech; baptism of fire.

start, outset; zero hour, D-day; send-off, embarkation, countdown 296 *departure*; rising of the curtain; kick-off; house-warming, honeymoon; flying start.

origin, derivation, conception, genesis, birth, nativity; provenance, ancestry 169 *parentage*; fount, fons et origo; rise 156 *source*; nest, womb; bud, germ, seed; egg, embryo, pre-embryo, protoplasm 358 *organism*; first beginnings, cradle 192 *home*.

entrance 297 *way in*; inlet 345 *gulf*; mouth, opening 263 *orifice*; threshold 624 *access*; porch 194 *lobby*; gateway 263 *doorway*; border 236 *limit*; suburbs 230 *surroundings*; foothills, outlier; pass, corridor 289 *approach*, 305 *passage*.

Adj. *beginning*, introductory, prefatory 66 *precursory*; inaugural; rudimental 156 *fundamental*; primeval, primordial 127 *primal*; rudimentary, elementary; embryonic, nascent, budding, incipient, in preparation 726 *uncompleted*; early, infant 126 *new*.

first, initial, primary, maiden, starting, natal; pioneering 21 *original*; unprecedented 126 *new*; foremost, front 237 *frontal*; leading, principal, major, head, chief 34 *supreme*.

Vb. *begin*, commence; open, dawn, spring up; arise, emerge, appear; rise; spring from; sprout, germinate; come into existence, come into the world, see the light of day 360 *be born*; make one's debut, come out; start, enter upon, embark on 296 *start out*; fire away, kick off, strike up; start work, clock in; roll up one's sleeves, limber up 669 *prepare*; run in; begin at the beginning, start from scratch; put one's hand to the plough, put one's shoulder to the wheel, set to, set to work, get cracking, get moving, get weaving; attack, tackle, address oneself; go to it 672 *undertake*.

initiate, found, launch; originate, invent 484 *discover*; usher in, herald, ring in, open the door to, introduce; start, start up, kick-start, switch on, ring up the curtain; set in motion, get under way; put to work 622 *employ*; handsel, run in; take the initiative, lead, lead off, lead the way, take the lead, pioneer, break new ground 64 *come before*; broach, open, raise the subject; break the ice, kick off, set the ball rolling; throw the first stone, open fire; take the first step, take the plunge; trigger off, spark off, set off.

auspicate, inaugurate, open; establish 156 *cause*; be a founder member, be in on the ground floor, be in with the bricks; baptize, christen, launch 561 *name*; initiate, blood; lay the foundations, cut the first turf 669 *prepare*.

Adv. *initially*, originally, in the beginning; at the very start, from its inception; from the beginning, from the word go; first, firstly, in the first place, primarily, first of all, first and foremost; as a start, for starters, for a kick-off, for a beginning; from scratch; back to basics.

69 End

N. *end*, close, conclusion, consummation 725 *completion*; payoff, result, end r. 157 *effect*; expiration, lapse; termination, closure, guillotine; finishing stroke, death blow, quietus, coup de grace; knockout, clincher 279 *knock*; denouement; ending, finish, finale, curtain; term, period, stop, halt 145 *cessation*; final stage, latter end 129 *evening*; beginning of the end, last words, swan-song, envoi, coda 67 *sequel*; last stage, last round, last lap, home stretch; last over; last breath, last gasp 361 *decease*; terminal illness; final examination, finals 459 *exam*. See *finality*.

extremity, omega; extreme, pole, antipodes; extreme case, ne plus ultra; farthest point, world's end, ultima Thule, where the rainbow ends; fringe, verge, brink 234 *edge*; frontier, boundary 236 *limit*; end of the road, end of the line, terminus, terminal 295 *goal*, 617 *objective*; dregs; foot, toe, bottom, nadir 214 *base*; bottom dollar, last cent, last penny 801 *poverty*; tip, cusp, point 256 *sharp point*; vertex, peak, head, top, zenith 213 *summit*; tail, tail end 67 *sequel*; arm, stump 53 *limb*; shirt-tail, coat-t. 217 *hanging object*; end, butt end, gable e., fag e. 238 *rear*; tag, epilogue, postscript, end matter, appendix 40 *adjunct*; inflection, suffix 564 *grammar*.

finality, bitter end; time, time up, deadline; conclusion 54 *completeness*; breakup, wind-up 145 *cessation*; dissolution 165 *destruction*; doom, destiny 596 *fate*; last trump, crack of doom, Götterdämmerung; Day of Judgment, end of the world 124 *future state*.

Adj. *ending*, final, terminal, last, ultimate, supreme, closing; extreme, polar; definitive, conclusive, crowning, hindmost, rear 238 *back*; caudal.

Vb. *end*, come to an end, expire, run out, become invalid 111 *elapse*; close, finish, conclude, be all over; die out 361 *die*, 2 *pass away*; come to a close, draw to a c., have run its course; stop, clock out, go home 145 *cease*.

terminate, conclude, close, settle; apply the closure, bring to an end, put an end to, put a stop to, put paid to, pull the plug on; discontinue, drop; finish, consummate, see it out 725 *carry through*; ring down the curtain, put up the shutters, shut up shop, wind up, close down, call it a day; switch off, ring off, hang up, cut off, stop 145 *halt*.

Adv. *finally*, in conclusion; at last, at long last; once for all, for good and all; never again, nevermore; in the end, in the long run, in the final analysis, when all's said and done.

70 Middle

N. *middle*, midst, midpoint; mean 30 *average*; medium; thick, thick of things; heart, heart of the matter, kernel; nave, hub, navel 225 *centre*; nucleus 224 *interiority*; midweek, midwinter, half tide; midstream 625 *middle way*; bisection, midline, equator, the Line 28 *equalization*; midriff, diaphragm 231 *partition*; equidistance, halfway house; mezzo floor.

Adj. *middle*, medial, mean, mezzo, mid 30 *median*; middlemost 225 *central*; intermediate, betwixt and between 231 *interjacent*; equidistant; mediterranean, equatorial.

71 Continuity: uninterrupted sequence

N. *continuity*, continuousness, uninterruptedness, monotony 16 *uniformity*; continuation; successiveness, succession; line, lineage, descent, dynasty; one thing after another, serialization 65 *sequence*; continuum 115 *perpetuity*; assembly line, conveyor belt 146 *continuance*; endless band 315 *rotation*; recurrence, cycle 106 *repetition*, 141 *periodicity*, 139 *frequency*; cumulativeness, snowball 36 *increase*; course, career, flow, steady f., trend 179 *tendency*; progressiveness 285 *progression*; circuit, round 314 *circuition*; daily round, routine, rut, practice, custom 610 *habit*; track, trail, wake 67 *sequel*; chain, food c.; chain reaction; round robin, chain letter; circle 250 *circularity*.

series, gradation 27 *degree*; succession, run; progression; ascending order 36 *increase*; descending order 37 *decrease*; family tree, lineage 169 *genealogy*; chain, line, string, thread; train, parade; unbroken line, line of battle; array 62 *arrangement*; row; range, ridge; colonnade, peristyle, portico; ladder, steps, stairs, staircase 308 *ascent*; range, tier, storey 207 *layer*; set, group, raft; suite, suit (of cards); assortment 77 *classification*; spectrum; gamut, scale 410 *musical note*; stepping stones 624 *bridge*; hierarchy, pyramid.

Adj. *continuous*, continued, run-on; consecutive, running, successive 65 *sequential*; serial, serialized; seriate, catenary; progressive; overlapping, unbroken, solid, smooth, uninterrupted, circular; continuing, ongoing, continual, incessant, ceaseless, unremitting, nonstop, constant 115 *perpetual*; cyclical, rhythmic 110 *periodic*; repetitive, recurrent, monotonous 106 *repeated*, 16 *uniform*; linear, lineal, rectilinear 249 *straight*.

continue, run on, prolong, 203 *lengthen*;

serialize, arrange in succession, catenate, string 45 *connect*; maintain continuity, keep the kettle boiling 600 *persevere*; keep the succession, provide an heir.

Adv. *continuously*, consecutively etc. adj.; successively, in succession, in turn; one after another; at a stretch, together, running; at one go, without stopping, on the trot; around the clock, night and day 115 *for ever*; progressively; in procession, in file, in single f., in Indian f., in a crocodile, nose to tail.

72 Discontinuity: interrupted sequence
N. *discontinuity*, intermittence; discontinuation 145 *cessation*; interval, hiatus, pause, time lag 145 *lull*; disconnectedness, randomness 61 *disorder*; unevenness 17 *nonuniformity*, 259 *roughness*; dotted line; broken ranks; ladder, run 46 *disunion*; disruption, interruption, intervention; parenthesis 231 *interjection*; caesura, division 46 *separation*, 547 *punctuation*; break, fracture, flaw, fault, split, crack, cut 201 *gap*; lacuna; missing link; broken thread, anacoluthon, non sequitur; alternation 141 *periodicity*; irregularity 142 *fitfulness*.

Adj. *discontinuous*, nonrecurrent; discontinued; interrupted, broken; disconnected; discrete 46 *separate*; few and far between 140 *infrequent*; irregular, intermittent 142 *fitful*; alternate, alternating, stop-go, on-off 141 *periodical*; spasmodic 17 *nonuniform*; jerky, bumpy, uneven 259 *rough*; incoherent; parenthetic, episodic.

Vb. *be discontinuous*, halt, rest 145 *pause*; alternate.

discontinue, suspend, break off, refrain from, desist; interrupt, intervene, chip in, butt in, break, break in upon 231 *interfere*; interpose, interject, punctuate; disconnect, break the connection, break *or* interrupt one's train of thought, snap the thread 46 *disunite*.

73 Term: serial position
N. *serial place*, term, order, remove 27 *degree*; echelon, rank, ranking, grade, gradation; station, place, position, slot; status, standing, footing, social class, caste; point, mark, pitch, level, storey; step, tread, round, rung; stage, milestone, watershed.

Vb. *grade*, rank, rate, place, classify, class; stagger, space out 201 *space*, 27 *graduate*.

74 Assemblage
N. *assemblage*, collection 50 *combination*, 62 *arrangement*; collocation; compilation, corpus, anthology 56 *composition*; gathering, harvest 370 *agriculture*, 771 *acquisition*; consolidation, concentration; centering, focusing, zeroing in on; levy, call-up 718 *war measures*; parade 875

pageant; march, demonstration, rally; roundup, lineup; herding, shepherding 369 *animal husbandry*; collectivization, collective, 370 *farm*; conspiracy, caucus 708 *party*; collective noun 564 *grammar*.

assembly, getting together, ganging up; forgathering, congregation, concourse, conflux, concurrence 293 *convergence*; gathering, meeting, mass m., protest m., sit-in, meet; coven; conventicle; convention, convocation 985 *synod*; legislature, conclave 692 *council*; eisteddfod, mod, festival 876 *celebration*; reunion, get-together, gathering of the clans, ceilidh 882 *social gathering*; company, at home, party 882 *fellowship*; circle, sewing-bee; encounter group 658 *therapy*; discussion group, symposium, focus group, quality circle 584 *conference*.

group, constellation, galaxy, cluster 321 *star*; pride (lions), leap (leopards), troop, bevy, swarm, flock, herd; drove, team; pack, kennel; stable, string; nest, eyrie; brood, hatch, litter, kindle (kittens); gaggle, flight, skein, covey, wing (plovers), charm (finches), exaltation (larks); shoal, school; unit, brigade 722 *formation*; batch, lot, clutch; brace, pair, span 90 *duality*; leash, four-in-hand 96 *quaternity*; set, class, genus, species, sub-s. 77 *sort*; breed, tribe, clan, household 11 *family*; brotherhood, sisterhood, fellowship, guild, union 706 *association*; club 708 *society*; sphere, quarter, circle 524 *informant*; charmed circle, coterie 644 *elite*; social group, the caste system, the classes 868 *nobility*, 869 *commonalty*; in-group, us and them, they 80 *self*; age group, peer g., year g., stream 538 *class*; hand (at cards), set 71 *series*.

band, company, troupe; cast 594 *actor*; brass band, dance b., pop group, rock g. 413 *orchestra*; team, string, fifteen, eleven, eight; knot, bunch; set, coterie, clique, ring; gang, squad, party, work p.; crew, complement, manpower, workforce, staff 686 *personnel*; following 67 *retinue*; squadron, troop, platoon; unit, regiment, corps 722 *formation*; squad, posse; force, body, host 722 *armed force*, 104 *multitude*; (Boy) Scouts, Girl Guides 708 *society*; band of brothers, sisters, merry men 880 *friendship*; committee, commission 754 *consignee*; panel 87 *list*.

crowd, throng 104 *multitude*; huddle, cluster, swarm, colony; knot, bunch; the masses, the hoi polloi, mass, mob, ruck 869 *rabble*; sea of faces, full house 54 *completeness*; congestion, press, squash, squeeze, jam, scrum, rush, crush; rush hour 680 *haste*; flood, spate, deluge, stream, streams of 32 *great quantity*; volley, shower, hail, storm; infestation, invasion 297 *ingress*.

bunch, assortment, lot, mixed l. 43 *medley*; clump, tuft, wisp, handful; pencil (of rays), fan;

bag 194 *receptacle*; hand (tobacco), bundle, packet, wad; batch, pack, package, parcel; portfolio, file, dossier 548 *record*; bale, roll, bolt; load, pack 193 *contents*; fascine, faggot; fascicle; tussock, shock, sheaf, stook, truss, heap; swathe, rick, stack 632 *storage*; thicket, copse 366 *wood*; bouquet, nosegay, posy, spray; skein, hank.

accumulation, agglomeration, conglomeration; massing, amassment; concentration, centralization; pileup 279 *collision*; pile, heap; snowdrift; snowball 36 *increment*; debris, detritus 41 *leavings*; dustheap, midden, dump 641 *rubbish*; cumulus, storm cloud 355 *cloud*; store, storage 633 *provision*, 799 *treasury*; magazine, battery, armoury, quiver 723 *arsenal*; bus garage, car park, parking lot; set, lot 71 *series*; mixed lot, mixed bag 43 *medley*; kit, gear, stock; range, selection, assortment 795 *merchandise*; display 522 *exhibit*; museum 632 *collection*; menagerie, aquarium 369 *zoo*; literary collection 589 *library*; miscellanea, miscellany, compilation 56 *composition*; symposium, festschrift 591 *dissertation*.

Vb. *congregate*, meet, forgather, rendezvous; assemble; associate, come together, get t., join t., flock t., gather, gather round, collect, troop, rally, roll up, swell the ranks; resort to, centre on, focus on, zero in on, make for 293 *converge*; band together, gang up; mass, concentrate; conglomerate, huddle, cluster, bunch, crowd; throng, swarm, seethe, mill around; surge, stream, flood 36 *grow*; swarm in, infest, invade.

bring together, assemble, put together, draw t. 45 *join*; draw 291 *attract*; gather, collect, rally, muster, call up, mobilize; concentrate, consolidate; collocate, lump together, group, brigade, unite; compile 56 *compose*; bring into focus, focus, zero in on, centre; convene, convoke, convocate, summon, hold a meeting; herd, shepherd, get in, whip in, call in, round up, corral 235 *enclose*; mass, aggregate, rake up, dredge up; accumulate, conglomerate, heap, pile, amass; catch, take, rake in, net 771 *acquire*; scrape together, garner 632 *store*; truss, bundle, parcel, package; bunch, bind 45 *tie*; pack, cram, stuff 54 *fill*; build up, pile up, stack 310 *elevate*.

Adv. *together*, as one, in a oner; collectively, all together, en masse.

75 Nonassembly. Dispersion

N. *dispersion*, scattering, diffraction, breakup 46 *separation*; branching out, fanning o., spread, scatter, radiation 294 *divergence*; sprawl, suburbia; distribution 783 *apportionment*; delegation, decentralization, regionalization; disintegration 51 *decomposition*; evaporation 338 *vaporization*, 337 *liquefaction*; dissipation 634

waste; circulation, diffusion; dissemination, broadcasting; spraying, sprinkling; dispersal; disbandment, demobilization.

Vb. *be dispersed*, disperse, scatter, spread, fan out, thin o. 325 *rarefy*; spread like wildfire, be rampant, flood; radiate, branch, branch out 294 *diverge*; break up, break ranks, fall out 46 *separate*; break away 49 *come unstuck*; hive off, go each his *or* her own way 267 *wander*; drift away, drift apart; straggle, trail, fall behind 282 *stray*; spread over, sprawl over, cover, litter 226 *overlie*; explode, blow up, burst, fly apart; evaporate, melt 338 *vaporize*, 337 *liquefy*; disintegrate, dissolve, decay 51 *decompose*.

disperse, scatter, diffract; spread out, splay 294 *diverge*; separate 46 *sunder*; thin out, string o.; disseminate, diffuse, broadcast, sow, strew, spread; dissipate, dispel, disintegrate 51 *decompose*; scatter to the winds 634 *waste*; dispense, deal, deal out, dole out, allot 783 *apportion*; decentralize, regionalize; break up, disband, disembody, demobilize, dismiss, send home 46 *disunite*; draft, draft off, hive off, detach 272 *send*; sprinkle, splash, spray, spatter 341 *moisten*; circulate; rout 727 *defeat*.

76 Focus: place of meeting

N. *focus*, focal point, junction, town centre, city c. 293 *convergence*, 225 *centre*; crossroads; switchboard, exchange, nerve centre; hub, nub, core, heart, kernel 70 *middle*; civic centre, community c.; village hall, village green, town square; campus, quad; market place 796 *market*; stamping ground; club, pub, local 192 *tavern*; headquarters, HQ, depot; rallying point; venue, rendezvous, trysting place 192 *meeting place*; fireside, campfire; cynosure, centre of attraction, honeypot 291 *attraction*; place of pilgrimage, Mecca, Lourdes, Rome, Zion, promised land 295 *goal*, 617 *objective*.

Vb. *focus*, centre on 293 *converge*; centralize, concentrate, focus upon, zero in on; point to.

77 Class

N. *classification*, categorization 62 *arrangement*; taxonomy; diagnosis, specification, designation; category, class, bracket; set, subset; head, heading, subhead, section, subsection 53 *subdivision*; division, branch, department, faculty; pocket, pigeonhole, slot 194 *compartment*; tier, rank, caste, status, social class, standing 27 *degree*; province, domain, field, sphere, range; sex, gender; blood group, age g., stream 74 *group*; coterie, clique 74 *band*; persuasion, school of thought, denomination 978 *sect*.

sort, order, type, version, variety, kind, species; manner, genre, style; nature, quality, grade, calibre 5 *character*; mark, brand 547 *label*;

ilk, stripe, kidney, feather, colour; stamp, mould, shape, frame, make 243 *form*; assortment, kit, gear, set, suit, lot 71 *series*.

breed, strain, blood, family, kin, tribe, clan, sept, caste, line 11 *race*, 169 *genealogy*; kingdom, phylum, class, order, genus, species, subspecies; genotype, monotype.

78 Inclusion

N. *inclusion*, comprising; incorporation, embodiment, assimilation, encapsulation; comprehension, admission, integration 299 *reception*; admissibility, eligibility; membership 775 *participation*; inclusiveness, coverage, full c., blanket c. 79 *generality*; all-roundness, versatility 694 *skill*; comprehensiveness; set, complete s., complement, package 52 *whole*; package deal 765 *compact*; constitution 56 *composition*; accommodation 183 *room*.

Adj. *inclusive*, including, comprising, counting, containing, having; holding, consisting of; incorporating; fully-furnished, all-inclusive, all-in; overall, all-embracing 52 *comprehensive*; wholesale, blanket, sweeping 32 *extensive*; total, across-the-board, global.

included, admitted, counted; admissible, eligible; integrated; constituent, making up; inherent 58 *component*, 5 *intrinsic*; belonging, pertinent 9 *relative*; classified with, in the same league 18 *similar*, 11 *akin*; entered, noted, recorded, on the list; merged 38 *additional*.

Vb. *be included*, be contained, be comprised, make one of; enlist, enrol oneself, swell the ranks, join 708 *join a party*; come under, go u., fall u.; merge in; appertain to, pertain, refer to 9 *be related*; come in, go in, enter into 297 *enter*; constitute 56 *compose*; overlap, inhere, belong 5 *be intrinsic*.

comprise, include, involve, mean, imply, consist of, hold, have, count, boast 56 *contain*; take, measure 28 *be equal*; receive, take in 299 *admit*; accommodate, find room for; comprehend, encapsulate, cover; embody, incorporate; encompass, embrace, encircle, envelop 235 *enclose*.

Adv. *including*, inclusively; from A to Z; et cetera.

79 Generality

N. *generality*, universality; catholicity, catholicism; ecumenicity, ecumenicalism 976 *orthodoxy*; universalism; generalization, universal; macrocosm 321 *universe*; globalization, global view, world-view; panorama, synopsis, conspectus, bird's-eye view 52 *whole*; inclusiveness, dragnet 78 *inclusion*; prevalence, custom 610 *habit*, 848 *fashion*; pervasiveness, ubiquity 189 *presence*; pandemic, epidemic 651 *disease*; impre-

cision 495 *inexactness*, 464 *indiscrimination*; commonness, ruck, run of the mill 30 *average*; ordinariness 732 *averageness*.

everyman, everywoman; man *or* woman in the street, Mr *or* Mrs average, man on the Clapham omnibus, joe soap, common type 30 *common man*; everybody, every one, each one, one and all, the long and the short and the tall, all and sundry, every mother's son, every man Jack, all hands 52 *all*; all the world and his wife, Tom, Dick and Harry, Uncle Tom Cobley and all, the masses, the hoi polloi, the rabble, 869 *commonalty*; all sorts, anyone, whosoever, N or M; anything, whatsoever, what have you, what you will 562 *no name*.

Adj. *general*, generic, typical, representative, standard; encyclopaedic, broad-based; collective, all-embracing, blanket, across-the-board 52 *comprehensive*; broad, sweeping, panoramic; prevalent 189 *ubiquitous*; usual, normal, run-of-the-mill, customary 610 *habitual*; vague, loose, indefinite 495 *inexact*; unspecified, impersonal 10 *unrelated*; common, ordinary, average 30 *median*; commonplace 83 *typical*; popular, mass, vulgar 869 *plebeian*; multipurpose.

universal, catholic, ecumenical; national, international, cosmopolitan, global, worldwide, nationwide, widespread 32 *extensive*; pervasive, prevalent, epidemic, pandemic 189 *ubiquitous*; every, each, any, all, all without exception 52 *whole*.

Vb. *generalize*, render general etc. adj.; broaden, widen, universalize, globalize; spread, broadcast, diffuse 75 *disperse*.

Adv. *generally*, without exception, universally etc. adj.; mainly; generally speaking, by and large; loosely, vaguely.

80 Speciality

N. *speciality*, personality, uniqueness; singularity 88 *unity*; originality, individuality, particularity; make-up 5 *character*; characteristic, one's middle name; idiosyncrasy, eccentricity, peculiarity, distinctive feature, trademark, mannerism, quirk, foible; trait, mark, feature, attribute; sine qua non 89 *accompaniment*; distinction, differentiae 15 *difference*; idiom; slang, jargon, brogue, patois 560 *dialect*; idiolect 557 *language*; version, lection 15 *variant*; exception, nonce word, special case 84 *nonconformity*; specialty, gift, special study, specialization 694 *skill*.

particulars, details, the nitty gritty, minutiae, items, special points, specification; circumstances; the ins and outs of.

self, ego, id, identity, selfhood, personality 320 *subjectivity*; psyche, soul 447 *spirit*; I, myself, number one, me generation; we, ourselves; yourself, himself, herself, itself, themselves; us, in-group 74 *group*; being 371 *person*.

Adj. *special*, specific, particular; peculiar, singular, unique 88 *one*; individual, idiosyncratic, characteristic, idiomatic, original 21 *inimitable*; personal, private; appropriate 24 *apt*; diagnostic 5 *characteristic*; distinctive, marked, out of the ordinary 84 *unusual*.

definite, definitive, defining; determinate, quantified, specified; distinct, concrete, explicit, clear-cut, cut and dried; certain, exact, precise 494 *accurate*; itemized, detailed.

private, intimate, esoteric, personal, personalized, exclusive; off the record, for one's private ear, confidential, secret 523 *latent*.

Vb. *specify*, enumerate, quantify 86 *number*; particularize, itemize, detail, 87 *list*; cite, reel off, mention, name names 561 *name*; enter into detail, spell out 570 *be diffuse*; define, determine 236 *limit*, 463 *discriminate*; pinpoint, locate 187 *place*; come to the point, explain 520 *interpret*; point out 547 *indicate*; realize, translate into fact, substantiate 156 *cause*; individualize, personalize 15 *differentiate*; specialize.

Adv. *specially*, especially, in particular; personally, for one's own part; specifically, ad hoc, to order.

severally, each, apiece, one by one; respectively, in turn; in detail, bit by bit.

namely, that is to say, videlicet, viz., to wit, i.e..

81 Rule

N. *rule*, norm, formula, canon, code; maxim, principle 693 *precept*; law, law of nature, universal principle; firm principle, hard and fast rule; strict law, law of the Medes and Persians; law of the jungle, sod's law, Murphy's law, Parkinson's law; unwritten rule *or* law, rule of thumb; statute, by-law 953 *law*; regulation, order, party line; guide, precedent, model, pattern 23 *prototype*; form, standard, keynote 83 *example*.

regularity, constancy 16 *uniformity*; order; 60 *order*; normality, normal state; form, routine, drill, practice, custom 610 *habit*; fixed ways, rut, groove; treadmill; methodicalness, method, system 62 *arrangement*; convention 83 *conformity*.

Adj. *regular*, constant, steady 141 *periodical*; even 258 *smooth*; standardized 16 *uniform*; regulated, according to rule, according to the rulebook, methodical, systematic 60 *orderly*; normal, unexceptional 83 *typical*; customary 610 *usual*; conventional 83 *conformable*.

82 Multiformity

N. *multiformity*, multiplicity; heterogeneity, variety, diversity 17 *nonuniformity*; multifariousness, many-sidedness 101 *plurality*;

schizophrenia, split personality 503 *personality disorder*; changeability 152 *changeableness*, 437 *variegation*; Proteus, Jekyll and Hyde; kaleidoscope.

Adj. *multiform*, multifarious, polymorphous, polymorphic; multifid; multiple, multiplex, multiplicate, manifold, many-headed, many-sided, many-faceted, hydra-headed, protean, versatile, all-round; variform, heterogeneous, diverse 17 *nonuniform*; motley, mosaic, kaleidoscopic 43 *mixed*; many-coloured 437 *variegated*; divers, sundry; of all sorts and kinds 15 *different*; changeable 152 *changeful*; schizophrenic.

83 Conformity

N. *conformity*, conformation 24 *conformance*; faithfulness 768 *observance*; accommodation, adjustment, reconciliation, conciliation 24 *agreement*, *adaptation*; malleability 327 *softness*; acquiescence 721 *submission*; assimilation, acclimatization, naturalization 147 *conversion*, 18 *similarity*; conventionality 848 *etiquette*; political correctness, PC; traditionalism; orthodoxness 976 *orthodoxy*; formalism, strictness 735 *severity*; convention, form 848 *fashion*, 610 *practice*; emulation 106 *repetition*, 925 *flattery*, 20 *imitation*; ordinariness 79 *generality*.

example, exemplar, type, pattern, model 23 *prototype*; exemplification, stock example, classic e.; case, case in point, instance; illustration, practical demonstration, object lesson; sample, random s., cross-section; representative, specimen, representative selection; trailer, teaser, foretaste 66 *precursor*; precedent.

conformist, conventionalist, traditionalist; company man; formalist, copycat, yes-man 20 *imitator*, 925 *flatterer*; follower, loyalist.

Adj. *conformable*, adaptable, adjustable; malleable, pliant 327 *flexible*; accommodating 24 *agreeing*; conforming, following, faithful, loyal, true-blue 768 *observant*; conventional; politically correct, PC; on-message; traditional 976 *orthodox*; slavish, servile 20 *imitative*.

typical, normal, natural, of daily occurrence, everyday, ordinary, common, common or garden 79 *general*; average 30 *median*, 732 *middling*; true to type; commonplace, prosaic; conventional; habitual 610 *usual*; representative, standard; exemplary.

Vb. *conform*, correspond, conform to 24 *accord*; adapt oneself, accommodate o., adjust o., mould o.; fit in; bend, yield, take the shape of 327 *soften*; fall into line, toe the l., fall in with 721 *submit*; comply with 768 *observe*; fit in with 24 *accord*; stick to the rules, obey regulations, follow precedent 739 *obey*; keep in step, follow the fashion, follow the trend, follow the crowd, do as others do, do as the Romans do;

join in the cry, jump on the bandwagon, keep up with the Joneses 848 *be in fashion*; follow suit 20 *imitate, copy*; drift with the tide, swim with the stream 601 *be irresolute*; keep to the beaten track, run on tramlines, run in a groove, stick in a rut 610 *be wont*.

make conform, conform, assimilate, naturalize 18 *liken*; acclimatize 610 *habituate*; systematize 62 *regularize*; normalize, conventionalize, standardize; drill 16 *make uniform*; train, lead 689 *direct*; bend, twist, force 740 *compel*; accommodate, fit, fit in, trim, cut down to size, knock *or* lick into shape 24 *adjust*.

exemplify, illustrate, cite, quote, reel off, instance.

84 Nonconformity

N. *nonconformity*, nonconformance, unconformity, inconsistency 25 *disagreement*, 17 *nonuniformity*; contrast 14 *contrariety*; exceptionality, strangeness 59 *extraneousness*; nonconformism, unorthodoxy 977 *heterodoxy*; disconformity, dissidence 489 *dissent*, 769 *nonobservance*; deviationism 744 *independence*; anomalousness, eccentricity, irregularity 282 *deviation*; unconventionality; freakishness, oddity; rarity 140 *infrequency*; infringement, infraction 954 *illegality*; breach of practice; wonder, miracle 864 *prodigy*; anomaly, exception 57 *exclusion*; exemption, escape clause 919 *nonliability*; special case 80 *speciality*; individuality, trait, idiosyncrasy, quirk, kink, peculiarity, singularity, mannerism; uniqueness 21 *originality*.

abnormality, aberration 282 *deviation*; mutation 15 *variant*; abortion, teratogenesis, monstrosity, monster; sexual abnormality, bisexuality; homosexuality, lesbianism, Sapphism; fetishism, necrophilia, sadism, masochism, sadomasochism; transvestism, gender bending; hermaphroditism 161 *impotence*.

nonconformist, dissident, deviationist, dissenter, maverick 489 *dissentient*, 977 *heretic*, 978 *sectarian*; blackleg, scab 938 *cad*; unconventionalist, Bohemian, hippie, beatnik, dropout, rebel, angry young man, punk, recalcitrant 738 *revolter*; contra; fanatic 504 *crank*; outlaw, criminal 904 *offender*; pariah 883 *outcast*; hermit, loner 883 *solitary*; gypsy, nomad, New Age traveller, tramp, bag lady 268 *wanderer*; odd man out, joker; square peg in a round hole, fish out of water 25 *misfit*; deviant, mutant, albino, freak, monster, oddity, original, character, card, caution, odd customer, queer c., oddball, weirdo 504 *crank*; queer fish 851 *laughingstock*; curiosity, rarity; neither fish, flesh, fowl nor good red herring; transsexual, hermaphrodite; homosexual, lesbian, lez *or* les, gay; pansy, fairy nancy, poof, poofter, homo, fruit, queen queer;

dyke *or* dike; transvestite, drag artist, crossdresser, transsexual, gender-bender 143 *transformation*; pervert, perv; sadist, masochist sadomasochist; mongrel, cur 43 *hybrid*.

rara avis, unicorn, phoenix, griffin, roc; sphinx, hippogriff, chimera, centaur, Minotaur; dragon, wyvern, fire-drake, cockatrice, basilisk, salamander, hydra; sea serpent, leviathan, kraken, Loch Ness monster; merman, mermaid, siren, Lorelei; gorgon, cyclops 970 *mythical being*; Snark, Jabberwocky, hobbit 513 *fantasy*.

Adj. *unconformable*, unmalleable 326 *rigid*, 602 *obstinate*; recalcitrant 711 *defiant*; eccentric; a law to oneself 744 *independent*; freakish, outlandish; unique 80 *special*; solitary 883 *unsociable*; blacklegging; nonconformist, dissident 489 *dissenting*, 978 *sectarian*; unorthodox, heretical; nonpractising 769 *nonobservant*; unconventional, weird, offbeat, Bohemian, hippie, beatnik, irregular, not done; infringing, lawless, criminal 954 *illegal*; aberrant, off the rails; misplaced, out of one's element, out of place, ectopic, out of order; incongruous, out of step, out of line, off-message, out of tune, out of keeping 25 *disagreeing*; alien, exotic, 59 *extraneous*; wandering; ambiguous 518 *equivocal*.

unusual, uncustomary, unwonted 611 *unhabituated*; unfamiliar 491 *unknown*; newfangled 126 *new*; exotic 59 *extraneous*; out of the ordinary, extraordinary, way-out; phenomenal; unparalleled; singular, unique 80 *special*, 140 *infrequent*; rare, choice, recherché 644 *excellent*; strange, bizarre, curious, odd, queer, rum, unco; funny, peculiar, fantastic, grotesque 849 *ridiculous*; noteworthy, remarkable, surprising, astonishing, miraculous 864 *wonderful*; mysterious, inexplicable, unaccountable 523 *occult*; unimaginable, incredible 470 *impossible*, 472 *improbable*; monstrous, teratoid, teratological; unnatural, preternatural, supernatural; outsize 32 *enormous*; outré.

abnormal, unnatural, supernatural, preternatural (**see** *unusual*); aberrant, teratological, teratoid, freakish; uncharacteristic, untypical, atypical, unrepresentative, exceptional; anomalous 17 *nonuniform*; kinky, deviant; homosexual, lesbian, lez *or* les, gay, bent, queer; bisexual, AC/DC; epicene, androgynous, gynandrous; mongrel, hybrid 43 *mixed*; irregular, solecistic; nonstandard, substandard, below par, subnormal; supernormal 32 *great*; asymmetrical, deformed, amorphous, shapeless 246 *distorted*.

Vb. *be unconformable*, unconventional etc. adj.; not fit in, be a fish out of water, be a square peg, be out of one's element; be the exception that proves the rule; infringe custom; break a law, commit a breach of etiquette, break a habit, break with custom; violate a law; drop

out, freak o., do one's own thing 744 *be free*;
make an exception; leave the beaten track.

SECTION FIVE

Number

85 Number
N. *number*, real number, imaginary n.; natural
n., cardinal n., ordinal n.; round n., complex
n.; prime n., odd n., even n., whole n., integer;
irrational n., transcendental n.; numeral,
cipher, digit, figure, character; numerals, Arabic
n., Roman n., algorithm; decimal system,
binary s.; quantity, unknown q., unknown, X,
symbol, constant; mapping; operator, sign;
function, variable, argument; vector, matrix,
tensor, quaternion; surd; expression, equation,
quadratics; formula, series; set.
numerical element, minuend, subtrahend;
multiplicand, multiplier; coefficient, multiple,
dividend, divisor, aliquant, aliquot; quotient,
factor, submultiple, fraction, proper f.,
improper f., vulgar f.; mixed number; numerator, denominator; decimal, recurring d., repetend; common factor, common denominator;
reciprocal, complement; parameter; power,
root, square r., cube r.; exponent, index, loga-
rithm, natural l., mantissa, antilogarithm;
modulus, differential, derivative, integral, inte-
grand, determinant, fluxion.
ratio, proportion; progression, arithmetical
progression, geometrical p., harmonic p.; trigonometrical ratio, sine, tangent, secant; cosine,
cotangent, cosecant; percentage, per cent, percentile.
numerical result, answer, product, equation;
sum, total, aggregate 52 *whole*; difference,
residual 41 *remainder*; bill, score, tally 38
addition.
Adj. *numerical*, numerary, numeral, digital;
arithmetical; cardinal, ordinal; round, whole;
even, odd; prime; figurate; positive, negative,
surd, radical; divisible, aliquot; multiple;
reciprocal, complementary; fractional, decimal;
incommensurable; commensurable, proportional; exponential, logarithmic, differential, fluxional, integral; algebraic, transcendental; rational, irrational.

86 Numeration
N. *numeration*, numbering, enumeration, census, counting, ciphering, figuring, reckoning,
calculating, computing; sum, tally, score;
count, countdown; summation, calculation,
computation 465 *measurement*; pagination;
algorithm, decimal system; accountancy 808
accounts; poll, capitation; head-count.

mathematics, pure m., applied m., arithmetic,
algebra; quadratic equations; set theory,
modern maths; differential calculus, integral c.,
infinitesimal c., vector c.; fluxions; calculus of
variations; topology; geometry, trigonometry;
graphs, logarithms; algorithm, systems analysis
(**see** data *processing*); operational research, critical path analysis, linear programming 623
policy; axiomatics 475 *reasoning*.
statistics, figures, tables, averages; mode,
mean 30 *average*; significance, deviation, normal d., standard d., standard error; distribution
curve, skew; regression; correlation, rank c. test,
chi-squared t.; statistical enquiry, market
research, poll, Gallup p. (tdmk) 605 *vote*; census, capitation; roll call, muster, muster roll,
account 87 *list*; demography, birth rate, death
r.; vital statistics; price index, retail p. i., cost of
living, cost-of-living index 809 *price*; bar graph,
histogram, scatter diagram, pie chart, flow
c. 623 *plan*; cartogram 551 *map*.
computing data processing, electronic d. p.,
EDP, desk-top publishing, computation, computer literacy; computer technology, cybernetics; software, program, computer p.; input,
output, throughput, feedback; storage,
retrieval; batch processing, time-sharing, multi-
programming, downtime; machine code, computer language, hardware (**see** *counting
instrument*); keyboard, keypad, mouse; data, bit,
byte; magnetic tape, floppy disk, disk drive; processor, word processor; central processing unit;
database, data bank, memory, menu, visual display unit, VDU, visual display terminal, VDT
445 *appearance*; hard copy, printout; spell-
check, spelling check; viewdata, Prestel (tdmk),
Ceefax (tdmk), Oracle (tdmk), teletext 524 *information*; information superhighway, Internet,
the Internet, the Net, World Wide Web, the
Web, website, web page, home page, search
engine, browser, net surfing, surfing; service provider; cyberspace, virtual reality; e-mail; spam;
e-commerce, e-business, dot com company;
cyberpreneur, cybersex; computer virus; e-mail
v., microvirus, computer bug, millennium b.;
computer programmer, computernik, hacker;
mouse potato; computer crime, computer
fraud; e-health; cyberlaw; computer game,
video g. 837 *indoor game*.
counting instrument, abacus; ready reckoner,
multiplication table; tape measure, yardstick
465 *gauge*; sliding rule, slide r.; Cuisenaire rods,
Napier's bones *or* rods; comptometer, adding
machine, calculating m., calculator, electronic
c., pocket c.; cash register, till, totalizator, tote;
computer.
computer digital c., analogue c; mainframe;
minicomputer, microcomputer, micropro-

cessor, personal computer, PC, home c., desktop c., lap-top c.; workstation.

Adj. *statistical*, expressed in numbers, digital, ciphered, numbered; mathematical, arithmetical, algebraical; geometrical, trigonometrical; in ratio, in proportion, percentile, quartile.

computerized, automatic, robotic, electronic, on-line, off-line; programmable; real-time, random-access, on-screen, user friendly; analogue, digital, binary, alphanumeric.

Vb. *number*, cast, count, reckon, calculate, compute, tell; score, keep the s., notch up; tick off, count down; paginate; enumerate, poll, count heads, count hands; take a poll, take a census; muster, take roll call; take stock, inventory 87 *list*; go over 106 *repeat*; check, audit, balance, keep accounts 808 *account*; aggregate, amount to, add up to, total, tot up to, come to.

computerize, automate; digitize, digitalize; program, process; debug; compute, log on, boot, reboot, key in, keyboard, dump, log off, download; scroll, browse 173 *operate*; hack; benchmark; surf the Net, surf.

87 List

N. *list*, enumeration; inventory, stock list; chart, table, catalogue, listing; portfolio 767 *security*; statement, schedule, manifest, bill of lading; checklist; invoice; score; price list, tariff, bill, account 809 *price*; registry, Domesday Book; file, register 548 *record*; ticket, docket, tag, tally 547 *label*; ledger, books; table of contents, index, card i. 547 *indication*; menu, 86 *data processing*; bill of fare, menu 301 *eating*; playbill, programme, prospectus, synopsis, syllabus 592 *compendium*; roll, electoral r., voting list 605 *electorate*; constituency list, top-up l.; payroll; Army List, Navy L., active l. 686 *personnel*; census 86 *numeration*; book list, bibliography 589 *reading matter*; rota, roster, panel; waiting list, short l., short leet; dramatis personae; family tree, pedigree 169 *genealogy*; scroll, roll of honour, martyrology, beadroll, diptych; blacklist 928 *accused person*, 924 *censure*; sick list 651 *sick person*; book of days, calendar, engagement book, diary 505 *reminder*; questionnaire; alphabetical list, A–Z, alphabet 60 *order*.

word list, vocabulary, glossary, lexicon, thesaurus 559 *dictionary*.

directory, gazetteer, atlas; almanac, calendar, timetable 117 *chronology*; Bradshaw, ABC 524 *guidebook*; Army List, Navy L., Crockford, Debrett, Burke's Peerage, Who's Who 589 *reference book*; telephone directory, phone book, Yellow Pages.

Vb. *list*, enumerate; itemize, reel off, inventory, catalogue, index, tabulate; file, docket, schedule, enter, book 548 *register*; enlist, matriculate, enrol, empanel, inscribe.

88 Unity

N. *unity*, oneness, absoluteness 44 *simpleness*; integration, wholeness 52 *whole*; uniqueness, individuality 80 *speciality*; monotheism; monism; singleness 895 *celibacy*; isolation, solitude, loneliness 883 *seclusion*; union, undividedness, indivisibility, solidarity 48 *coherence*, 706 *association*; unification 50 *combination*.

unit, integer, one, ace, item, article, piece; individual, atom, monad, entity 371 *person*; single piece, monolith; nonce word; isolated case, only exception; solo, monologue; single person, single, bachelor, bachelor girl 895 *celibate*; single parent 896 *divorce*; hermit, lone wolf, loner 883 *solitary*; set, kit, outfit, package 78 *inclusion*.

Adj. *one*, singular, sole, single, solitary; unique, only, lone, one and only; unrepeated, only-begotten; one-off, custom-built; a, an, a certain 562 *anonymous*; individual 80 *special*; absolute, universal 79 *general*; unitary, unific, univocal, unicameral, unilateral, unicellular; unisex; mono-; monolithic 16 *uniform*.

alone, lonely, homeless, orphaned, deserted, abandoned, forsaken; lonesome, solitary, lone 883 *unsociable*; isolated; insular 199 *distant*; single-handed, on one's own; by oneself, on one's tod; unaccompanied, unescorted, unchaperoned; celibate.

Adv. *singly*, one by one, one at a time; once, once only, once and for all, for the nonce, just this once, never again, only, solely, simply; alone, on one's own, by oneself, per se.

89 Accompaniment

N. *accompaniment*, concomitance 71 *continuity*, 45 *union*, 5 *intrinsicality*; inseparability; society 882 *sociability*; companionship, togetherness 880 *friendship*; partnership, marriage 706 *association*; coexistence 181 *concurrence*; coincidence, contemporaneity, simultaneity 123 *synchronism*; attendance, company; parallel course 219 *parallelism*.

concomitant, attribute, sine qua non 5 *essential part*; complement 54 *completeness*; accessory, appendage, appurtenance, fixture 40 *adjunct*; by-product, corollary; symptom, syndrome 547 *indication*; coincidence 159 *chance*; context, circumstance 7 *state*; background; accompaniment, obbligato; accompanist 413 *musician*; entourage, court 742 *retainer*; attendant, following, suite 67 *retinue*; groupie, camp follower; convoy, escort, guide 690 *leader*; chaperon, bodyguard 660 *protector*, 749 *keeper*; suitor, wooer 887 *lover*; tracker 619 *hunter*; inseparable, shadow, tail 284 *follower*; consort, cohabitee, lover 894 *spouse*; comrade, companion, boon c., best friend 880 *friend*; stable companion, mate, co-worker, partner, associate 707 *colleague*; accomplice 707 *collaborator*; twin, pair, fellow 18 *analogue*; satellite, parasite, hanger-on 742 *dependant*.

Vb. *accompany*, coexist; cohabit, live with, keep company w., consort w., walk out w.; string along with; bear one company, squire, chaperon, protect 660 *safeguard*; convoy, escort, guide, conduct, lead, usher 64 *come before*; track, dog, tail, shadow 619 *pursue*; associate with, partner 706 *cooperate*; gang up with, chum up w. 880 *befriend*; carry with, bring in its train, bring in its wake 156 *cause*; be inseparable, go hand in hand with, follow as night follows day 157 *depend*; belong, go with, go together 9 *be related*.

Adv. *with*, together with, along w., in company w.; in the same boat; hand in hand, arm in arm, side by side; cheek by jowl.

90 Duality

N. *duality*, dualism; double-sidedness; double life, dual personality, split p., Jekyll and Hyde; positive and negative, yin and yang 14 *polarity*; dyad, two, deuce, duo, twain, partnership, couple, item, Darby and Joan, Jack and Jill, Romeo and Juliet; brace, pair, couple; doublets, twins, Castor and Pollux, Gemini, Siamese twins, identical t., Tweedledum and Tweedledee 18 *analogue*; yoke; couplet; twosome, duel; duet; Janus; double whammy.

Adj. *dual*, binary, binomial; bilateral, bicameral; twin, biparous; bisexual, double-barrelled, duplex 91 *double*; paired, coupled etc. vb.; two abreast, two by two; in twos, both; in pairs, tête-à-tête, à deux; double-sided, double-edged, bipartisan; amphibious; ambidextrous 91 *double*; bifocal; biform, two-dimensional, two-faced.

Vb. *pair*, couple, match, bracket, yoke; mate, pair off.

91 Duplication

N. *duplication*, doubleness; doubling 261 *fold*; reduplication, encore, repeat, iteration, echo, parrotry 106 *repetition*; renewal 656 *restoration*; copy, carbon c., photocopy, Xerox (tdmk) 22 *duplicate*; living image, look-alike 18 *analogue*.

Adj. *double*, doubled, twice; duplex; biform; twofold, two-sided, two-headed, two-edged; double-faced, two-faced; amphibious, ambidextrous; dual-purpose, two-way; ambiguous 518 *equivocal*; ambivalent; bisexual, AC/DC, hermaphrodite; twin, duplicate; dualistic 90 *dual*.

Vb. *double*, redouble, square; encore, echo, second 106 *repeat*; renew 656 *restore*; duplicate, twin; reduplicate, stencil, xerox, photocopy 20 *copy*.

92 Bisection

N. *bisection*, bipartition, dichotomy; dividing by two, halving etc. vb.; hendiadys; half, moiety, fifty per cent 53 *part*; hemistich; hemisphere 252 *sphere*.

bifurcation, forking, branching, furcation 294 *divergence*; swallowtail, fork, prong 222 *cross*.

dividing line, diameter, diagonal, equator, parting, seam; date line; party wall, garden fence 231 *partition*.

Adj. *bisected*, halved etc. vb.; bifid; bipartite; bicuspid; bifurcated, forked; dichotomous; split, cloven.

Vb. *bisect*, transect; divide, split, cleave 46 *sunder*; cut in two, share, go halves, go fifty-fifty 783 *apportion*; halve, divide by two.

bifurcate, separate, fork; branch off, ramify 294 *diverge*.

93 Triality

N. *triality*, trinity; triplicity 94 *triplication*.

three, triad; Faith, Hope and Charity; threesome, triumvirate, troika; triplet, trio; trimester, triennium; trefoil, shamrock, triangle, trident, tripod, trivet; three-wheeler, tricycle; three-headed monster, Cerberus; triphthong, triptych, trilogy; third power, cube; third person; Third World.

Adj. *three*, triform, trinomial; three in one, tripartite; tricolour; three-dimensional, three-sided, triangular, deltoid, trigonal, trilateral; three-pointed; trifoliate, three-leaved *or* leafed; three-pronged, three-cornered; tricorn, tricuspid; three-monthly, trimestrial, quarterly.

94 Triplication

N. *triplication*, triplicity; trebleness; hat trick; tercentenary.

Adj. *treble*, triple; trine, trinal, ternary; triplex, triplicate, threefold, three-ply; third, tertiary; trihedral; trilateral.

Vb. *treble*, triple, triplicate, cube.

95 Trisection

N. *trisection*, tripartition, trichotomy; third, third part; tierce.

Vb. *trisect*, divide into three parts, divide by three; trifurcate.

96 Quaternity

N. *quaternity*, four, tetrad, tetrarchy; square, tetragon, quadrilateral, quadrangle, quad; tetrahedron; quadrature, quarter; fylfot, swastika 222 *cross*; tetrapod, tetrameter, quatrain; tetragram; quartet, foursome; four winds, four evangelists; four-in-hand, quadriga; quatrefoil; quadruplet, quad; quadruped, tetrapod; quadrennium; four corners of 52 *whole*.

Adj. *four*, quaternary, quadratic; quadrate, square, quadrilateral, tetrahedral, foursquare; four-footed, quadrupedal; quadrennial.

97 Quadruplication
N. *quadruplication*, quadruplicity; squaring; quatercentenary.

Adj. *fourfold*, quadruple, quadruplicate, quadruplex; squared.

Vb. *quadruple*, quadruplicate, multiply by four; square, quadrate.

98 Quadrisection
N. *quadrisection*, quartering, fourth, fourth part; quarterly; quart, quarter; farthing, quarto.

Vb. *quadrisect*, quarter, divide into four parts, divide by four.

99 Five and over
N. *five*, cinque, quintuplet, quin; quintet; pentagon, pentagram; pentameter; Pentateuch; pentathlon; cinquefoil; quinquereme; five senses, Five Towns, Cinque Ports; five-a-side; a bunch of fives.

over five, six, half-a-dozen, sextet, hexad, sixer; hexagon, hexagram; Hexateuch; hexameter; seven, heptad, week, sabbatical year; septennium; septenary, septet; pleiad; Heptateuch; Seven Deadly Sins, Seven Wonders of the World, Seven Seas; eight, octave, octet, octad; octagon; one over the eight, piece of eight, figure of eight; nine, three times three; nonary; novena; nine Muses, nine days' wonder; ten, tenner, decade; decagon, decahedron, Decalogue; Ten Commandments; eleven, hendecasyllable; twelve, dozen; dodecahedron; twelve apostles, the Twelve, twelve tribes; thirteen, baker's dozen, double figures, teens.

twenty and over, twenty, a score; icosahedron; four and twenty, two dozen; twenty-five, pony; forty, two score; fifty, half a hundred, jubilee; sixty, three score; sexagenarian; seventy, three score and ten, septuagenarian; eighty, four score, octogenarian; ninety, nonagenarian.

hundred, century, ton, centenary, centennial; hundredweight; centurion; centenarian; centipede; the hundred days; Old Hundredth; hundred per cent; treble figures.

over one hundred, a gross; hundreds and hundreds; thousand, grand; millennium; ten thousand, myriad; hundred thousand, lakh; million; ten million; thousand million, milliard; billion; million million; trillion, quadrillion, centillion; multimillion; zillion.

100 Multisection
N. *multisection*, decimation.

Adj. *multifid*, multipartite; decimal, tenth, tithe; duodecimal, twelfth; sexagesimal, sexagenary; hundredth, centesimal; millesimal.

Vb. *multisect*, decimate, decimalize.

101 Plurality
N. *plurality*, the plural; multiplicity 104 *multitude*; many-sidedness 82 *multiformity*; polygon, polyhedron; polytheism; a number; a few; majority.

Adj. *plural*, composite, multiple; polydactyl, polypod; multiparous; polymorphic, multiform; many-sided; multilateral, multipurpose; in the majority 104 *many*.

102 Fraction: less than one
N. *fraction*, decimal f. 85 *numerical element*; fragment 53 *part*, 783 *portion*; shred 33 *small quantity*.

Adj. *fractional*, partial 53 *fragmentary*, 33 *small*.

103 Zero
N. *zero*, nil, zilch, nothing, simply n., next to nothing, naught, nought, nix; no score, love, duck, blank; cipher; nothingness 2 *nonexistence*, 4 *insubstantiality*; none, nobody, not a soul 190 *absence*; nadir, rock bottom.

Adj. *not one*, not any, zero; infinitely little, null 4 *insubstantial*, 2 *nonexistent*.

104 Multitude
N. *multitude*, numerousness, multiplicity; large number, million 99 *over one hundred*; lots, loads, heaps, masses 32 *great quantity*; numbers, scores, myriads, millions, trillions, zillions; a sea of, a mass of, a world of, a sight of; forest, thicket; host, array, fleet, battalions 722 *army*; throng, mob, all the world and his wife 74 *crowd*; tribe, horde.

Adj. *many*, myriad, several, sundry, divers, various, a thousand and one; quite a few, a good f.; considerable, numerous, very many, a good many, ever so m., many more, no end of, umpteen, n, in telephone numbers; untold, unnumbered, innumerable, uncounted 107 *infinite*; multifarious, manifold 82 *multiform*; ever-recurring 139 *frequent*, 106 *repeated*; much, ample, multiple; profuse, in profusion, abundant, superabundant, generous, lavish, overflowing, galore 635 *plentiful*, 32 *great*.

multitudinous, massed, crowded, thronged 54 *full*; populous, peopled, populated, high-density 324 *dense*; teeming, crawling, humming, lousy with, hotching w., alive w., bristling w. 171 *prolific*; thick, thick on the ground, thick as flies; coming thick and fast 139 *frequent*; incalculable, innumerable, inexhaustible, countless, endless 107 *infinite*.

Vb. *be many*, – various etc. adj.; swarm with, crawl w., hum w., bristle w., teem w., be hotching w., be lousy w., be alive w. 54 *fill*; clutter, crowd, throng, swarm, mass, flock, troop 74 *congregate*; swarm like ants, swarm like locusts, swarm like bees round a honey-pot; flood, overflow, snow under, swamp, overwhelm 637 *superabound*; infest, overrun; swell the ranks 36 *augment*; outnumber, make a majority 32 *be great*.

105 Fewness

N. *fewness*, paucity; exiguity, thinness, sparsity, sparseness, rarity 140 *infrequency*; scantiness 636 *scarcity*; a few, a handful; wisps, tuft; poor turnout; small number, trickle, soupçon, smidgen 33 *small quantity*; limited number, no quorum; minority, one or two, not enough to matter, a derisory amount.

Adj. *few*, precious few, scant, scanty, little 636 *scarce*; thin on the ground, sparse, rare, low-density, few and far between 140 *infrequent*; not many, hardly any; to be counted on the fingers of one hand; too few, in a minority, without a quorum.

Vb. *be few*, be few in number, be underpopulated; seldom occur.

render few, reduce, diminish, pare 198 *make smaller*; scale down, slim down, cut back, decimate; eliminate, weed, thin, sort out 300 *eject*; understaff.

Adv. *here and there*, in dribs and drabs, in twos and threes, in a trickle; sparsely, rarely, infrequently.

106 Repetition

N. *repetition*, iteration, reiteration; doubling, ditto, reduplication 20 *imitation*, 91 *duplication*; recapitulation; renewal, resumption, reprise 68 *beginning*; saying again, repeating, anaphora 574 *ornament*; tautology, redundancy 570 *diffuseness*; stammering, stuttering 580 *speech defect*; repeat, repeat performance, encore; second helping, seconds; playback, replay, return match, revenge; chorus, refrain 412 *vocal music*; echo, repercussion, reverberation 404 *resonance*; quotation, plagiarism; hardy annual (**see** *recurrence*); old story, chestnut 838 *tedium*; reprint, reissue 589 *edition*; remake, rehash, recast, revival 656 *restoration*.

recurrence, repetitiveness, repetitive strain injury, RSI 139 *frequency*; cycle, round, return, rebirth, renaissance, reincarnation 141 *regular return*; succession, run, series, serial; serial killing, serial monogamy 71 *continuity*; recurring

decimal, repetend, throwback, atavism 5 *heredity*; reappearance, comeback, curtain call; rhythm, drumming, hammering 141 *periodicity*; alliteration, assonance, rhyme 18 *assimilation*, 593 *prosody*; 838 *tedium*; same old round, mixture as before, rehash, routine 610 *habit*.

Adj. *repeated*, repetitional; recurrent, recurring, ever-r. 141 *periodical*; haunting 505 *remembered*; tautological, redundant, repetitive, repetitious, harping, iterative; stale, clichéridden 572 *feeble*; echoing, rhyming, alliterative, assonant 18 *similar*; monotonous, singsong 16 *uniform*, 838 *tedious*; rhythmical, drumming, hammering; incessant, habitual 139 *frequent*; retold, said before, quoted, cited; above-mentioned, aforesaid 66 *precursory*; plagiarized 20 *imitative*; reheated, rehashed, recycled.

Vb. *repeat*, do again, iterate, cut and come again; duplicate, reduplicate, redouble 91 *double*; multiply 166 *reproduce*; reiterate, say again, recapitulate, go over, ring the changes on; retell, restate, reword, rephrase; trot out; recite, reel off, say over, say after; echo, ditto, parrot, plagiarize 20 *copy*, 925 *flatter*; quote, cite 505 *remember*; go over the same ground, retrace one's footsteps, practise, rehearse; play back, rerun, rewind; recycle, reprocess; begin again, restart, resume 68 *begin*; replay, give an encore; reprint, reissue, republish; rehash, remake, renew, revive 656 *restore*; reheat.

again, afresh, anew, over again, for the second time, once more; ditto; encore; de novo.

107 Infinity

N. *infinity*, infiniteness, boundlessness, limitlessness, illimitability; infinite space, outer s. 183 *space*; eternity 115 *perpetuity*.

Adj. *infinite*, indefinite; immense, measureless; eternal 115 *perpetual*; countless, innumerable, immeasurable, illimitable, interminable; incalculable, unfathomable, incomprehensible, unapproachable, beyond comprehension; inexhaustible, without number, without limit, without end, no end of; without measure, limitless, endless, boundless; untold, unnumbered 104 *many*; unlimited.

Adv. *infinitely*, ad infinitum; indefinitely; immeasurably 32 *greatly*.

SECTION SIX

Time

108 Time

N. *time*, tide; tense 564 *grammar*; duration, extent 113 *long duration*; season, term, semester, tenancy, tenure; tour, shift, shot, spell, stint; span, space 110 *period*; a bit, a while; quality time; the whole time, the entire period, life, life-time; eternity 115 *perpetuity*; passage of time, lapse of time, lapse, course 111 *course of time*; years, days; Time, Father Time, Time's scythe, Time's hourglass, sands of time, ravages of t., t. the enemy, t. the healer; fourth dimension; time zone; indefinite time; past time, past tense 125 *past time*, 119 *priority*; prospective time 124 *futurity*; contemporaneity 121 *present time*; recent time 126 *newness*; antiquity, distant time 127 *oldness*.

date, day, age, reign 110 *era*; vintage, year, time of life 117 *chronology*; birthday, Saint's day 141 *anniversary*; day of the week, calends, ides, nones; time of day 117 *clock time*; moment 116 *instant*; target date, zero hour, D-day; term, fixed day, quarter day, payday.

Adj. *continuing*, permanent 115 *perpetual*, in process of, pending; repetitive, recurrent 106 *repeated*; temporal 141 *periodical*.

Vb. *continue*, endure, drag on 113 *last*; roll on, pass 111 *elapse*; live through, sustain; stay, remain, abide, survive 113 *outlast*; wait 136 *be pending*.

pass time, vegetate, breathe, subsist, exist 360 *live*; age; spend time, consume t., use t., employ t. 678 *be busy*; while away time, kill t., summer, winter, weekend; waste time, fritter away t. 679 *be inactive*; mark time.

fix the time, date, put a date to, settle on a date for 117 *time*.

Adv. *while*, whilst, during, pending; day by day 113 *all along*; in the course of, so long as; for the time being, for now, meantime, meanwhile; between whiles, in the meantime, in the interim; from day to day, from hour to hour; hourly 139 *often*, for a time, for a season; till, until, up to, yet; always, the whole time, all the time 139 *perpetually*; all along 54 *throughout*.

when, what time; one day, once upon a time, one fine morning; in the days of, in the time of, in the year of.

109 Neverness

N. *neverness*, Greek Calends; month of Sundays, blue moon, when pigs fly; jam tomorrow, mañana; dies non; eternity 115 *perpetuity*.

Adv. *never*, not ever, at no time, at no period, on no occasion; not in donkey's years; nevermore, never again; over one's dead body; never before, never in one's born days; without date, sine die.

110 Period

N. *period*, matter of time; season; time of day, morning, evening; time of year, spring, summer, autumn, fall, winter 128 *morning*, 129 *evening*; term; time up, full time 69 *finality*;

spell, go, tour, stint, shot, shift, span, stretch, sentence; innings, turn; round, bout, lap; watch; length of time, second, minute, hour; particular time, rush hour; pause, interval; day, weekday, working day; week, working w., five-day w.; fortnight, month, calendar m., lunar m., quarter, trimester; half year, semester; twelve month, year, solar y., sidereal y., light y., leap y.; fiscal y.; quinquennium; decade, Gay Nineties, Hungry Thirties, Swinging Sixties; golden wedding, jubilee 141 *anniversary*; century, millennium.

era, time, period, generation, age, days; epoch; aeon; cycle, Ice Age; Stone A., Iron A., Dark Ages, Middle A. 125 *antiquity*; Renaissance, Age of Enlightenment, A. of Reason, belle époque, fin de siècle; modern times, Computer A., Space A.; Golden A., A. of Aquarius.

Adj. *periodic* 141 *seasonal*; hourly, annual, biennial, quinquennial, centennial; period 127 *olden*.

111 Course: indefinite duration

N. *course of time*, matter of t., process of t., lapse of t., march of t., flight of t.; duration 108 *time*, 146 *continuance*.

Vb. *elapse*, pass, lapse, flow, run, roll, proceed, advance, press on 285 *progress*; wear on, drag on, crawl 278 *move slowly*; flit, fly, fleet, slip, slide, glide 277 *move fast*; run its course; go by, pass by, slip by, fly past.

Adv. *in time*, in due time, in due season; in the course of time, in the process of t., in the fullness of t., with the years.

112 Contingent duration

Adv. *provisionally*, precariously, by favour; at the pleasure of; for the present; so long as it lasts; as or so long as.

113 Long duration

N. *long duration*, a long t., unconscionable t.; a month of Sundays, years, donkey's years, years on end, yonks; a lifetime; generations, a century, an age, ages, aeons 115 *perpetuity*; longevity 131 *old age*; corridor of t., antiquity 125 *past time*.

durability, lasting quality, endurance; stamina, staying power 162 *strength*; survival 146 *continuance*; permanence 153 *stability*; long standing, good age, ripe old a. 127 *oldness*; long run, long innings.

protraction, prolongation, extension; dragging out, spinning o., padding o., filibustering, stonewalling 702 *hindrance*, 715 *resistance*; interminability, long haul 136 *delay*, 278 *slowness*; extra time, injury t., overtime.

Adj. *lasting*, abiding; secular, agelong,

lifelong, livelong; longtime, longstanding, inveterate, deep-seated, deep-rooted; of long duration, long-term, long-service, marathon 203 *long*; unconscionable; durable, enduring 162 *strong*; long-lived 127 *immemorial*; evergreen, unfading, fresh 126 *new*; eternal, perennial 115 *perpetual*; persistent, chronic 602 *obstinate*; indestructible 162 *unyielding*; constant, stable, permanent 153 *unchangeable*.

Vb. *last*, endure, stand, stay, remain, abide, continue 146 *go on*; defy time, stand the test of time, never end 115 *be eternal*; wear well 162 *be strong*.

outlast, outlive, outwear, outstay, survive; remain 41 *be left*; live to fight another day; have nine lives.

Adv. *for a long time*, long, for long, for ages, for years, since time immemorial, many a long day; for good, for ever, for all time, for better for worse; all one's life, from the cradle to the grave; till blue in the face; till the cows come home.

all along, all day, all day long, the livelong day, as the day is long; all the year round, round the clock; day in day out, year in year out; ever since.

long ago, long since, in the distant past, long long ago, when the world was young; in the past, in ancient days, in bygone times 125 *formerly*.

at last, at long last, in the end, in the long run, after many days, not before time.

114 Transience

N. *transience*, transientness, transitoriness 4 *insubstantiality*; impermanence; evanescence 446 *disappearance*; volatility 338 *vaporization*; fugacity 277 *velocity*; fragility 330 *brittleness*; mortality, perishability 361 *death*; frailty, fragility 163 *weakness*; mutability 152 *changeableness*; capriciousness, fickleness 604 *caprice*; suddenness 116 *instantaneity*; temporariness, interregnum.

brief span, short space of time, a minute or two, short while; briefness, momentariness, brevity 204 *shortness*; mortal span, short life and a merry one; summer lightning, shooting star, meteor, flash in the pan, nine days' wonder; ephemera, bubble, mayfly, snow on a dyke, snows of yesteryear, smoke in the wind; April shower, summer cloud 4 *insubstantial thing*; bird of passage, ship that passes in the night; brief encounter; short run 110 *period*, 277 *spurt*; spasm, moment 116 *instant*.

Adj. *transient*, temporal, impermanent, transitory, fading, passing 4 *insubstantial*; cursory, flying, fleeting, flitting, fugitive 277 *speedy*; volatile, written in water; evanescent;

unsettled, restless; flickering, changeable 152 *changeful*.

ephemeral, of a day, short-lived, fleeting, disposable; mortal 361 *dying*; frail, fragile 163 *weak*, 330 *brittle*; impermanent, temporary.

brief, short-term, short-service 204 *short*; summary, short and sweet, to the point 569 *concise*; quick, fleet, brisk 277 *speedy*; sudden, momentary, meteoric, like a flash 116 *instantaneous*; hurried 680 *hasty*.

Vb. *be transient*, – transitory etc. adj.; not stay, not last; flit, fleet, fly, gallop 277 *move fast*; fade, flicker, vanish, evanesce, melt, evaporate 446 *disappear*; fade like a dream, flit like a shadow, pass like a summer cloud, burst like a bubble.

115 Perpetuity: endless duration

N. *perpetuity*, endless time 107 *infinity*; everlastingness, eternity, timelessness; never-endingness, interminability 113 *long duration*; endurance 144 *permanence*, 71 *continuity*; immortality 146 *continuance*; perpetuation, immortalization.

Adj. *perpetual*, perennial, longlasting, enduring, durable 113 *lasting*; agelong 127 *immemorial*; nonstop, constant, continual, ceaseless, incessant; flowing, ever-flowing, uninterrupted 71 *continuous*; dateless, ageless, unageing, unchanging, immutable 144 *permanent*; evergreen, unfading, everlasting; imperishable, undying, deathless, immortal; unending, never-ending, interminable; endless, without end, timeless, eternal.

Vb. *perpetuate*, make permanent, continue, establish; immortalize, eternalize.

be eternal, – perpetual etc. adj.; last for ever, endure for e., live for e.; go on for e., have no end, never cease.

Adv. *for ever*, in perpetuity, on and on; ever and always, for always and always, for aye, evermore, for ever and ever, for ever and a day; time without end, world without e.; for keeps, for good and all, for better for worse; to the end of time, till doomsday, to the crack of doom; to infinity 107 *infinitely*.

116 Instantaneity: point of time

N. *instantaneity*, instantaneousness, immediateness, immediacy; simultaneity 121 *present time*; suddenness, abruptness 508 *lack of expectation*; precise time 135 *punctuality*; momentariness 114 *transience*.

instant, moment, precise m., point, point of time; second, split s., half a s., tick, trice, jiffy, half a j., mo, half a mo; breath; burst; crack; stroke, coup; flash, lightning f.; twinkle, twinkling, the twinkling of an eye; two shakes, two shakes of a lamb's tail; the very moment, the very hour, the stroke of.

Adj. *instantaneous*, immediate, instant, sudden, abrupt, snap; quick as lightning, with the speed of light, quick as a flash, like a flash 277 *speedy*.

117 Chronometry

N. *chronometry*, chronoscopy, horology; watchmaking; calendar-making, timetabling; timing, dating; timekeeping 108 *time*.

clock time, right time, BBC t., astronomer's t., solar t., sidereal t., Greenwich Mean T., G.M.T., British Standard T., British Summer T., B.S.T., local t., Central European T., continental t.; time of day, time of night; bedtime; summer time, double summer t., daylight saving t.

timekeeper, chronometer, timepiece; clock, dial, face; hand, pendulum 317 *oscillation*; electric clock, digital c., quartz c., long-case c., grandfather c., grandmother c., calendar c., carriage c., cuckoo c., alarm c., travelling alarm, travel clock, clock radio, alarum; Big Ben; water-clock; watch, ticker; fob-watch, hunter, repeater; wristwatch, digital watch, analogue w.; sundial; hour-glass, sand-glass, egg timer; chronograph, chronoscope; time signal, pip, siren, hooter; gong, bell, five-minute b., time-clock, timer, stopwatch; Tim, speaking clock; parking meter, traffic light 305 *traffic control*; time fuse, time switch, time bomb; metronome.

chronology, dendrochronology; radio-carbon dating; dating; date, age, epoch, style 110 *era*; old style, O.S., new style, N.S.; almanac, calendar, perpetual c., fixed c., Gregorian c., Julian c.; ephemeris, astronomical almanac; chronicle, annals, book of days, diary, journal, log-book 548 *record*; date list, time-chart 87 *list*; tide-table, timetable, schedule 87 *directory*.

chronologist, chronographer, chronologer, calendar-maker, calendarist; chronicler, annalist, diarist 549 *recorder*.

Vb. *time*, clock; timetable, schedule; match times 123 *synchronize*; phase 24 *adjust*; set the alarm 669 *make ready*; calendar, chronologize, chronicle 548 *record*; date, be dated; measure time, mark t., beat t., keep t.; count the minutes, watch the clock; clock in 68 *begin*; clock out 145 *cease*.

Adv. *o'clock*, a.m., p.m.

118 Anachronism

N. *anachronism*, parachronism, wrong date, wrong day, chronological error; mistiming, previousness, prolepsis 135 *anticipation*; disregard of time, unpunctuality 136 *lateness*; neglect of time 506 *oblivion*; wrong moment 138 *untimeliness*.

Adj. *anachronistic*, misdated; antedated, foredated, previous, before time, too early 135 *early*; parachronistic, postdated 136 *late*; too late, overdue, unpunctual, behind time; out of due time, out of season, out of date, old-fashioned 127 *antiquated*.

119 Priority

N. *priority*, antecedence, previousness, preexistence; primogeniture, birthright; eldest, firstborn, son and heir; flying start 64 *precedence*; leading 283 *preceding*; the past, yesteryear, yesterday 125 *past time*; eve, day before; precedent, antecedent; foretaste, trailer, teaser, preview, prerelease; herald 66 *precursor*; prequel.

Adj. *prior*, earliest, first, first in the field, precedent 64 *preceding*; previous, earlier, anterior, antecedent; antediluvian, prehistoric; pre-Christian, BC; pre-war, preexisting, prenatal, antenatal; elder, eldest, firstborn; former, ci-devant, onetime, erstwhile, sometime, ex-, retired, emeritus; foregoing, aforementioned, above-mentioned; aforesaid, said; introductory, prefatory, preliminary 66 *precursory*; given, presupposed 512 *supposed*.

Vb. *do before*, presuppose 512 *suppose*; predecease, prefabricate, prearrange, preempt, prejudge, preview; be previous, anticipate, forestall, be beforehand with, jump the gun, jump the queue; steal a march on, have a start on 277 *outstrip*; lead 283 *precede*, 64 *come before*.

Adv. *before*, prior to, beforehand, by; just before, on the eve of; earlier, previously, formerly; ultimo, ult.; afore, ere; aforetime, ere now, before n.; ere then, before t., already, yet; in anticipation; until now, up to now, hitherto, heretofore.

120 Posteriority

N. *posteriority*, subsequence; succession 65 *sequence*, days to come, time to come 124 *futurity*; line, lineage, descent, successor, descendant 170 *posterity*; cadet; aftermath 67 *sequel*.

Adj. *subsequent*, posterior, following, ensuing, next, to come, after, later; last in date, junior, cadet, younger, youngest 130 *young*; successive, consecutive, consequent; succeeding, designate, to be 124 *future*; postnatal; posthumous; postwar; after Christ, AD; postprandial 65 *sequential*.

Vb. *ensue*, supervene, follow after 65 *come after*; go after 284 *follow*, 157 *result*; succeed, follow in the footsteps of, step into the shoes of 771 *inherit*.

Adv. *subsequently*, later, in the process of time; after, afterwards; at a later date; next, next time; thereafter, thereupon; since, from that time, from that moment; from the start, from the word 'go'; after a while, after a time; soon after, close upon; next month, proximo.

121 Present time

N. *present time*, contemporaneity, contemporaneousness, topicality 126 *modernism*; time being, the present, present time, present day, present moment; this hour, this moment, this moment in time, this instant 116 *instantaneity*; juncture, opportunity, crisis 137 *occasion*; the nonce; the times, modern t., these days, this day and age; today, twenty-first century, nowadays; one's age, present generation, one's contemporaries 123 *contemporary*.

Adj. *present*, actual, instant, current, extant 1 *existing*; of this date, of today's d.; topical, contemporary, contemporaneous; present-day, latter-day, latest, up-to-the-minute, up-to-date, bang up-to-date 126 *modern*.

Adv. *at present*, now, right now, at this time, at this moment, at this moment in time; live; at the present time, contemporaneously, contemporarily; today, nowadays; at this time of day, at this stage, even now; already, but now, just now; this time, on the present occasion; for the time being, for now, for the nonce; on the spot; now or never; now as always.

until now, to this day, to the present day, up to now, to date; through; from the start, from the word 'go' 113 *all along*.

122 Different time

N. *different time*, other times 124 *futurity*, 125 *past time*; another time, some other t., not now, not today, any time but this 109 *neverness*; parachronism 118 *anachronism*.

123 Synchronism

N. *synchronism*, synchrony; coexistence, coincidence, concurrence, concomitance 89 *accompaniment*; simultaneity, simultaneousness, same time 116 *instantaneity*; contemporaneity, contemporaneousness, same date, same day 121 *present time*; coevality, same age, twin birth 28 *equality*; level-pegging, neck-and-neck, nip and tuck, dead heat 28 *draw*; synchronization, sync, phasing, isochronism.

contemporary, coeval, twin 28 *compeer*; one's contemporaries, one's own generation; age group, peer g., class, year 74 *group*.

Adj. *synchronous*, synchronal, synchronic; contemporary, contemporaneous 121 *present*, 126 *modern*; simultaneous, coinstantaneous, coincident, coexistent, coeternal, conterminous, concomitant 24 *agreeing*; level, neck and neck 28 *equal*; matched in age, coeval, twin; of the same age, of the same year, of the same gen-

eration, of the same vintage; synchronized, timed, phased, isochronous, on the beat.

Vb. *synchronize*, sync, concur, coexist 89 *accompany*; encounter, coincide 295 *meet*; keep time 410 *harmonize*; say together, say in unison, chorus; tune, phase 24 *adjust*; be level-pegging, run neck and neck 28 *be equal*; pace, keep in step with; isochronize.

124 Futurity: prospective time

N. *futurity*, future tense; womb of time, time to come, days and years to come; morrow 120 *posteriority*; future, time ahead, prospect, outlook 507 *expectation*; coming events, fate 154 *event*, 155 *destiny*; near future, tomorrow, mañana, the day after tomorrow, next week, next year 121 *present time*, 200 *nearness*; advent 289 *approach*; long run, distant future 199 *distance*; future generations, descendants, heirs, heritage 170 *posterity*; successorship.

future state, what fate holds in store 155 *destiny*, 596 *fate*; latter days; doomsday, crack of doom 69 *finality*; afterlife, life after death, life to come, hereafter, kingdom come 971 *heaven*; damnation 972 *hell*; good time coming, mañana, jam tomorrow, millennium 730 *prosperity*; reincarnation 106 *repetition*.

Adj. *future*, to be, to come; coming 289 *approaching*; nigh, just round the corner, close at hand 200 *near*; on the horizon, in the wind; due, destined, fated, threatening, imminent, overhanging 155 *impending*; in the future, ahead, yet to come, waiting; in embryo, on the stocks 669 *preparatory*; prospective, designate, earmarked 605 *chosen*; promised, looked for, anticipated 507 *expected*, 471 *probable*; predicted, foreseeable; later, ulterior, posterior 120 *subsequent*.

Vb. *be to come*, lie ahead, lie in the future; have in store, be destined, threaten, overhang 155 *impend*; near, draw nigh 289 *approach*; be imminent, be just round the corner, cast its shadow before, stare one in the face.

henceforth, in future, from this time forth, from now on.

125 Past Time: retrospective time

N. *past time* 119 *priority*; retrospection, looking back 505 *remembrance*; past tense, historic t., preterite, perfect, pluperfect 564 *grammar*; the past, recent p., only yesterday 126 *newness*; distant past, history, antiquity; old story, matter of history 127 *oldness*; past times, days of yore, days of old, olden days, good old d., bygone d.; auld lang syne, yesterday, yesteryear, former times.

antiquity, rust of a., eld; creation, when time began, when the world was young, time immemorial; prehistory, protohistory, ancient world, mediaeval times; Stone Age, prehistoric a.; Dark Ages, Middle A. 110 *era*; the ancients, cavemen, Neanderthal man 371 *humankind*; relics, neolith, microlith, 41 *remainder*; 127 *archaism*; ruin, ancient monument, megalith, Stonehenge 548 *monument*, 253 *earthwork*; excavation, dig, archaeology 484 *discovery*; museum 632 *collection*; ancient lineage 169 *genealogy*.

fossil, fossilized remains *or* relics, petrified forest, trilobite, ammonite; trace fossil 548 *record*; coal forest 385 *fuel*; sponge, coral 358 *organism*; Neanderthal man 371 *humankind*; mammoth, dinosaur 365 *animal*.

palaeology, palaeontology, palaeozoology, palaeography; palaeoanthropology 371 *humankind*; archaeology; antiquarianism.

antiquarian, palaeontologist, archaeologist; palaeologist, palaeographer; antiquary 492 *scholar*; historian, prehistorian; medievalist 549 *chronicler*; Egyptologist, classicist 557 *linguist*.

Adj. *past*, in the p., historical; ancient, prehistoric 127 *olden*; early, primitive 127 *primal*; gone, gone for good, bygone, lost, dead and buried 506 *forgotten*; passed away, no more, died out, dead as the Dodo 2 *extinct*, 361 *dead*; passé, has-been, obsolete 674 *disused*, 127 *antiquated*; fossilized 326 *hard*; over, blown o., done, over and done with, behind one; elapsed, lapsed, expired, run out, ended, finished 69 *ending*.

former, late, quondam, sometime, ex-119 *prior*; retired, emeritus, outgoing.

foregoing, last, latter 64 *preceding*; recent.

retrospective, looking back, backward-looking; reminiscing 505 *remembering*; historical; retroactive, going back; with hindsight, from experience.

Vb. *be past*, have elapsed, have expired; have run its course, have had its day, be burnt out; pass, die, elapse, blow over, be o., be at an end 69 *end*; be a dead letter.

Adv. *formerly*, aforetime, of old, of yore; time was, ago, in olden times; long ago, long since; a long while, a long time ago; once upon a time; years ago, ages a.; lately, some time ago, some time back; yesterday, the day before yesterday; yestreen, yesteryear; last year, last season, last month, last week.

126 Newness

N. *newness*, recentness; recent date, recent occurrence, recent past 125 *past time*, 121 *present time*; innovation 560 *neology*, 21 *originality*; novelty, freshness, dewiness 648 *cleanness*; greenness, immaturity, callowness, rawness 130

youth; renovation, restoration, renewal, resurrection 656 *revival*; clean slate, new leaf, new broom.

modernism, modernity, modernness, modernization; up-to-dateness, topicality, contemporaneity 121 *present time*; the latest, the latest thing, the in-thing, latest fashion; the last word, dernier cri; new look, contemporary style, trendiness 848 *fashion*.

modernist, neologist, neoteric, futurist; advanced thinker, avant-garde; bright young thing, trendy, yuppy, baby-boomer; modern generation, younger g.

Adj. *new*, newish, recent, of recent date, of recent occurrence; upstart, parvenu, nouveau arrivé, nouveau riche, mushroom; novel, inventive, innovative, unprecedented, unheard of 21 *original*; brand-new, spick and span, like new, in mint condition 648 *clean*; green, evergreen, dewy, juicy; fresh, fresh as a daisy, fresh as paint; maiden, virgin, virginal; newborn 130 *young*; raw, unfledged, callow 670 *immature*; just out, just published, hot from the press; new-made, new-laid; straight from the oven, factory-fresh; untouched by human hand; unused, first-hand; untried, untrodden, unbeaten, unexplored 491 *unknown*; untested 461 *experimental*; aspiring, budding, wannabe 68 *beginning*.

modern, late, latter-day; contemporary, topical 121 *present*; up-to-the-minute, up-to-date, bang up-to-date, with it; à la mode, in the latest fashion, trendy 848 *fashionable*; leading-edge, state-of-the-art, ultramodern, modernistic, advanced, avant-garde, futuristic, revolutionary; innovating, innovative, neoteric, newfangled, new-fashioned.

Vb. *modernize*, do up, renovate, refurbish; update, bring up to date, give a new lease of life; have the new look, go modern, go contemporary, get with it; move with the times 285 *progress*.

127 Oldness

N. *oldness*, primitiveness 68 *beginning*; olden times 110 *era*; age, eld; dust of ages, ruins 125 *antiquity*; maturity, mellowness 129 *autumn*; decline, rust 51 *decay*; senility 131 *old age*.

archaism, antiquities 125 *antiquity*; ancien régime; thing of the past, relic of the p.; listed building, ancient monument; museum piece, antique, heirloom, bygone, Victoriana; dodo, dinosaur 125 *fossil*; golden oldie; old fogy, old fossil, fuddy-duddy, archaist, square, old-timer, has-been, back number.

tradition, lore, folklore, mythology; inveteracy, custom 610 *habit*; common law; word of mouth 579 *speech*.

Adj. *olden,* old, ancient, antique, anti-quarian; veteran, vintage; venerable; archaic, ancient; time-worn; prehistoric, mythological; feudal, medieval; historical 125 *past,* 866 *renowned.*

primal, prime, primitive, primeval, primor-dial, aboriginal 68 *beginning;* fossil, palaeozoic; eolithic, palaeolithic, mesolithic, neolithic; early, antediluvian, before the Flood.

antiquated, of other times, of another age, archaic; old as the hills, old as Methuselah, old as time, age-old 113 *lasting;* old-world, old-time; olde worlde, ye olde; prewar 119 *prior;* anachronistic 125 *retrospective;* fossilized, ossi-fied; behind the times, out of date, out of fashion, dated, antediluvian, before the Flood, out of the ark, horse-and-buggy, silent-screen, black-and-white; conservative, Victorian, old-fashioned, old-school, square, not with it; out-worn, outdated, outmoded; passé, démodé, vieux jeu, old hat; gone by 125 *past;* perished 655 *dilapidated;* mouldering; obsolete, obsoles-cent; superannuated 674 *disused;* old 131 *ageing.*

Vb. *be old,* – antiquated etc. adj.; belong to the past, have had its day, be burnt out 69 *end;* age; decline, fade, wither 655 *deteriorate.*

128 Morning. Spring. Summer

N. *morning,* morn, forenoon, a.m.; small hours, wee sma' hours 135 *earliness;* matins; dawn, dawning, cockcrow, dawn chorus 66 *precursor;* sunrise, sun-up, daybreak 417 *light;* peep of day, break of d.; first blush of day; daylight, daytime; full day, full light of day; Aurora, rosy-fingered Dawn; daystar, orb of day 321 *sun.*

noon, high noon, meridian, midday, noon-day, noontide; eight bells, twelve o'clock, twelve noon.

spring, springtime, springtide, Eastertide, ver-nal season, spring s., seed-time, blossom-time, maying; first cuckoo; vernal equinox, first point of Aries.

summer 379 *heat;* summertime, summertide, Whitsuntide; midsummer, summer solstice, Midsummer's Day, high summer, dog days; hay-making; aestivation; Indian summer.

129 Evening. Autumn. Winter

N. *evening,* eventide, even, eve, dewy e.; even-song, vespers, afternoon, p.m.; matinée; after-noon tea, five o'clock; sundowner, soirée; dog-watches; sunset, sundown, setting sun, going down of the sun; evening star, Hesperus, Ves-per; dusk, crepuscule, twilight, gloaming 419 *half-light;* candlelight, cockshut, dewfall; moon-rise, moonset 321 *moon;* close of day, nightfall, dark, night-time, night-owl 418 *darkness;* bed-

time 679 *sleep;* curfew, last post 136 *lateness,* 69 *finality.*

midnight, dead of night, witching time; night-watch, small hours.

autumn, back-end, fall, harvest, harvest-time; harvest moon; Michaelmas; Indian summer.

winter 380 *wintriness;* wintertime, wintertide; yuletide, Christmas; midwinter, winter solstice; hibernation; nuclear winter.

Adj. *wintry,* winter, brumal, brumous, snow-bound 380 *cold;* stark, bleak.

130 Youth

N. *youth,* freshness 126 *newness,* 174 *vigor-ousness;* young blood, youthfulness, youngness, juvenility; babyhood, infancy, childhood, child-ish years, tender age 68 *beginning;* puppyhood; boyhood, girlhood; one's teens, adolescence, pubescence, age of puberty, boyishness, girl-ishness, awkward age, growing pains; younger generation, rising g., yoof, middle youth 132 *youngster;* growing boy *or* girl, minor, ward; Peter Pan.

nonage, tender age, immaturity, minority, infancy, pupillage, wardship; cradle, nursery, kindergarten.

salad days, school d., student d., college d., happiest days of one's life; heyday, heyday of the blood, springtime of youth; prime of life, bloom of youth, florescence.

Adj. *young,* youthful, childlike, boyish, girl-ish; virginal, maidenly, sweet-sixteen; adoles-cent, pubescent; teenage, preteen, juvenile; maturing, developing, growing; budding, bur-geoning, blooming, flowering; unripe, green, callow, awkward, raw, unfledged 670 *immature;* school-age, under-age, minor, infant, pre-school; younger, minor, junior, cadet; young-est; childish; juvenescent; young at heart, ageless.

131 Age

N. *age,* time of life, years, lifespan 113 *long duration.*

middle age, middle years, middle life, middle youth, adultescent, sandwich generation, years of discretion 134 *adultness;* maturity, prime of life; a certain age, climacteric, change of life, the change, menopause, male m., mid-life crisis; middle-aged spread.

old age, anno domini; pensionable age, retire-ment age; advanced years, three-score years and ten, allotted span, grey hairs, white hairs 133 *old person;* senescence, declining years, vale of years, evening of one's days, autumn *or* winter of life; infirmity, debility 163 *weakness;* second childhood, dotage, senility, Alzheimer's disease 655 *deterioration;* longevity, ripe old age.

seniority, old man's privilege 64 *precedence*; primogeniture 119 *priority*; higher rank 34 *superiority*; doyen; gerontocracy, elders, presbytery, senate 692 *council*.

gerontology, nostology, geriatrics, care of the aged 658 *therapy*, old people's home, sheltered housing, eventide home.

Adj. *ageing*, aged, old, elderly, matronly; middle-aged, adultescent, ripe, mature, mellow 669 *matured*; overblown, overripe, run *or* gone to seed; of a certain age, not so young as one was, no chicken; past one's prime, getting on, getting old, going grey, greying; white-haired, grey-h., hoary, hoary-headed, long in the tooth; senescent, waning, declining, moribund 361 *dying*; wrinkled, lined, marked with crow's feet, rheumy-eyed, toothless, shrivelled, wizened, decrepit, rickety; drivelling, doddering, gaga 499 *foolish*; senile, failing; advanced in years, stricken in y., living on borrowed time, with one foot in the grave; longeval, old as the hills, old as Methuselah; well-preserved 650 *healthy*; venerable, patriarchal; too old, past it; retired 681 *leisurely*; superannuated, passé(e) 127 *antiquated*; gerontologic, geriatric.

older, major; elder, senior 34 *superior*; first-born, eldest, primogenital 119 *prior*; eldest, maximus.

132 Young person. Young animal. Young plant

N. *child*, children, small fry; babe, baby, bundle of joy; infant, nursling, suckling, weanling, fosterling; bairn, little one, tiny tot, little chap, mite, moppet, toddler; brat, kid, kiddie; papoose, bambino; little darling, little angel, little monkey, little imp; cherub, young innocent; changeling. **See** *young creature*.

youngster, juvenile, young person, young adult, young hopeful, young 'un; young people 130 *youth*; boy, schoolboy, stripling, adolescent; youth, young man, lad, laddie, sonny; urchin, nipper, cub, young shaver, whippersnapper; yob; Ted, mod, rocker, punk, skinhead; girl, young woman; schoolgirl, lass, lassie, missie, wench, maid, maiden, virgin; chit, slip, chick, miss; teenager, teenybopper, weenybopper, groupie; tomboy, hoyden; little minx, baggage; colleen, mademoiselle, damsel, nymph, nymphet. **See** *young creature*.

young creature, young animal, yearling, lamb, kid, calf, heifer; piglet; fawn, colt, foal, filly; kitten; puppy, pup, whelp, cub; chick, chicken, pullet; duckling, gosling, cygnet 365 *animal*, *bird*; fledgling, nestling, fry, litter, farrow, clutch, spawn, brood; larva, pupa, nymph; caterpillar, grub; chrysalis, cocoon; tadpole; embryo, pre-embryo, foetus 156 *source*.

young plant, seedling, set; sucker, runner, spur, shoot, offshoot, sprout, slip; twig, sprig, scion, sapling 366 *plant*.

133 Old person

N. *old person*, elderly p., retired p., pensioner, old-age p., O.A.P., senior citizen; old dear, old body.

old man, elderly gentleman, patriarch, elder statesman; grandfather, grandad 169 *paternity*; veteran, old soldier, old hand, old stager, old trouper, old-timer 696 *expert*; old 'un, old boy, gaffer; old geezer, o. codger, o. buffer, dotard; old fogy.

old woman, elderly lady, dowager; grandmother, grandma, gran, granny; old girl, old trout, old duck, old bag; old dutch 894 *spouse*; no spring chicken, mutton dressed as lamb; gammer, crone, hag.

old couple, Darby and Joan.

134 Adultness

N. *adultness*, adulthood, grown-upness, development; years of discretion, matureness; age of consent, legal age, majority, man's *or* woman's estate; manhood, womanhood, virility, nubility 372 *male*, 373 *female*; key of the door; maturity, prime of life 131 *middle age*.

adult, grown-up, big boy *or* girl; man, gentleman 372 *male*; woman, lady, matron 373 *female*.

Adj. *grown-up*, adult, of age, at the age of consent, old enough to know better; mature, fully-developed, full-grown 669 *matured*; nubile; virile, manly 372 *male*; womanly, matronly 373 *female*; full-blown, full-fledged; in one's prime, adult, X-rated, 18.

135 Earliness

N. *earliness*, early hour, unearthly h.; early stage, primitiveness 68 *beginning*; early riser, early bird; first arrival 66 *precursor*; original settler, earliest inhabitant 191 *native*.

punctuality, timeliness 137 *occasion*; promptitude 678 *activity*; immediacy 116 *instantaneity*.

anticipation, a stitch in time 510 *foresight*, 669 *preparation*; prematurity, precocity; forestalling 64 *precedence*.

Adj. *early*, bright and e., good and e., in the small hours, in the wee sma' hours; timely, in time, on t., in good t., punctual, prompt; forward, in advance; precocious, ahead of its time 126 *new*; immediate 116 *instantaneous*, 508 *unexpected*; coming shortly, forthcoming, ready 669 *prepared*; imminent, at hand 200 *near*; premature 670 *immature*.

Vb. *be early*, – premature etc. adj.; be betimes, be beforehand etc. adv.; nip in the bud;

forestall, preempt 64 *come before*; take the opportunity, take time by the forelock; steal a march
on, catch napping 306 *outdo*; engage, book,
reserve; secure, order; lose no time 680 *hasten*;
jump the gun.

Adv. *betimes*, early, soon; before long; first
thing, at the first opportunity; with time to
spare; punctually, to the minute, in time, in
good time.

beforehand, in advance; precipitately; pre-
cociously, prematurely, untimely, too soon.

suddenly, without notice 508 *unexpectedly*;
forthwith, right away; at the drop of a hat.

136 Lateness

N. *lateness*, late hour, small hours, wee sma'
hours 129 *midnight*; eleventh hour, last minute;
backwardness, slow development 670 *nonpreparation*, 499 *unintelligence*; tardiness, lagging, dragging one's feet 278 *slowness*; afterthought, delayed reaction; latecomer; late
developer 538 *learner*; late riser 278 *slowcoach*;
laggard 679 *idler*; Fabius Cunctator.

delay, cunctation, Fabian policy 858 *caution*;
delaying tactics, gaining time, stonewalling,
filibustering 113 *protraction*, 702 *hindrance*;
deceleration 278 *slowness*; holdup 747 *restraint*;
postponement, adjournment, cooling-off
period; pause, time lag, jet lag 145 *lull*; defer-
ment, moratorium, respite, days of grace; suspension, stay of execution; reprieve 752
abrogation; putting off, procrastination,
mañana 679 *sluggishness*; dilatoriness, bureaucracy, red tape 678 *overactivity*; shelving, putting
on ice, putting on hold, putting on the back-
burner, cold storage 679 *inactivity*.

Adj. *late*, late in the day, eleventh-hour, last-
minute, deathbed; too late, time up; overdue,
delayed, belated, benighted; held up, bogged
down 702 *hindered*; behindhand, lagging,
behind time, behind schedule; sluggish, tardy;
backward 278 *slow*; Fabian 858 *cautious*;
unpunctual; procrastinating, dilatory 679
inactive; delayed-action; deferred etc. vb.; on
ice, on hold, in cold storage, on the back-
burner, posthumous 120 *subsequent*.

Vb. *be late*, sit up late, rise late, keep late
hours, burn the midnight oil, burn the candle
at both ends; lag behind 284 *follow*; drag
one's feet, linger, loiter 278 *move slowly*; hang
back 679 *be inactive*; miss a chance, miss the
boat, oversleep 138 *lose a chance*; be behindhand, have leeway to make up, have a backlog;
not move with the times; lose, stop (clock).

wait 507 *await*; bide one's time, hold one's
horses, take one's time, wait and see 145 *pause*;
sleep on it 677 *not act*; hang fire; hang on, hold
on, hold the line; stand about, sit a., hang a.; be

kept waiting, wait impatiently, cool one's heels,
play the waiting game; count to ten.

put off, defer, postpone, adjourn; hold over;
file, pigeonhole; table; shelve, put in cold storage, keep on ice, put on the back-burner; hold
in abeyance; procrastinate, protract, delay,
retard, set back, hold up, gain time, stonewall,
filibuster; temporize, tide over; stall, keep one
waiting.

Adv. *late*, after time, behind t.; late in the
day, at sunset, at the eleventh hour, at the last
minute, last thing; at length, at last, at long l.,
ultimately; till all hours; too late.

137 Occasion: timeliness

N. *occasion*, happy chance 154 *event*; juncture
181 *concurrence*; timeliness, opportuneness, ripe-
ness; fittingness 24 *fitness*, right time; auspicious hour, right moment, nick of time.

opportunity, favourable opportunity, golden
o. 469 *possibility*; one's chance, break, lucky
moment, piece of luck 159 *chance*; opening,
look-in, field 744 *scope*; freedom of choice 744
freedom; convenience, clear field 159 *fair chance*;
stepping-stone 624 *bridge*.

crisis, critical time, key moment; turning
point, psychological moment, crucial m., crux,
emergency, extremity; eleventh hour, last
minute 136 *lateness*; the chips are down.

Adj. *timely*, in time, within the time limit; on
time, to the minute, on the dot, punctual 135
early; well-timed; just in time, not before time,
in the nick of t., at the eleventh hour.

opportune, favourable, providential, heaven-
sent, auspicious, propitious; fortunate, lucky,
happy 730 *prosperous*; fitting 24 *apt*.

crucial, critical, key, momentous, climactic,
pivotal, decisive 638 *important*.

Vb. *profit by*, seize or grab the chance, take
the opportunity, create an opening; take time
by the forelock, carpe diem, strike while the
iron is hot, make hay while the sun shines; cash
in on, capitalize, exploit, turn to good account
673 *use*.

incidentally, by the way, by the by; en passant, apropos; parenthetically, by way of parenthesis; while speaking of, while on this
subject, talking of, that reminds me.

138 Untimeliness

N. *untimeliness*, wrong time, inopportuneness
643 *inexpedience*; mishap, contretemps; evil
hour 731 *misfortune*; off day, time of the
month; disturbance 72 *discontinuity*; mistiming
118 *anachronism*.

Adj. *ill-timed*, mistimed, ill-judged, ill-
advised; out-of-turn, untimely, untoward; mala-
propos, inconvenient 25 *unapt*, 643 *inexpedient*;

unseasonable, unpunctual, not in time 136 *late*; premature, too soon for 135 *early*.

inopportune, untoward, inauspicious, unpropitious, unfavourable, ill-omened, ill-starred, unlucky, unhappy, unfortunate 731 *adverse*.

Vb. *mistime*, time it *or* things badly 481 *misjudge*; disturb, find engaged.

be engaged, be busy, be occupied, be not at home; be otherwise engaged, have a previous engagement, have other fish to fry 678 *be busy*.

lose a chance, miss the bus, miss the boat 728 *fail*; bungle 695 *be unskilful*; lose one's chance, let the opportunity slip 136 *be late*; let slip through one's fingers 458 *neglect*; stand in one's own light, shut the stable door after the horse has bolted 695 *act foolishly*.

139 Frequency

N. *frequency*, rapid succession 71 *continuity*; oftenness, unfailing regularity 141 *periodicity*; redoubling 106 *repetition*; frequenting, haunting, regular visits.

Adj. *frequent*, recurrent 106 *repeated*; common, of common occurrence 104 *many*; thick on the ground 104 *multitudinous*; continual, constant, steady; regular 141 *periodical*; haunting, frequenting, assiduous 610 *habitual*.

Vb. *recur* 106 *reoccur*; do nothing but; keep, keep on 146 *go on*, frequent, haunt 882 *visit*; pester 827 *trouble*.

Adv. *often*, oft, many a time, time after t., time and time again, times without number; a thousand t.; frequently, commonly, generally; more often than not; not infrequently, again and again; in quick succession, in rapid succession; thick and fast; regularly, daily, hourly; ad libitum.

perpetually, continually, constantly, incessantly, steadily, without respite 71 *continuously*; at all times, night and day, day and night, day after day, day in, day out, morning, noon and night.

sometimes, occasionally, every so often, once in a while; at times, now and then, now and again, every now and again; from time to time.

140 Infrequency

N. *infrequency*, rarity 105 *fewness*; seldomness, uncommonness; intermittence 72 *discontinuity*.

Adj. *infrequent*, uncommon, sporadic, occasional; intermittent, few and far between 72 *discontinuous*; scarce, rare, scarce *or* rare as hen's teeth 105 *few*; like gold dust 811 *of price*; almost unheard of, unprecedented 84 *unusual*.

Adv. *seldom*, little, once in a while; rarely, scarcely, hardly, only occasionally; not often, infrequently; scarcely ever, hardly e., once in a

blue moon, once in a month of Sundays; few and far between.

141 Periodicity: regularity of recurrence

N. *periodicity*, regularity, rhythm, steadiness, evenness 16 *uniformity*; timing, phasing, serialization 71 *continuity*; alternation, turn and turn about, shot about; reciprocity 12 *correlation*; ebb and flow, alternating current, AC, wave movement 317 *fluctuation*; to-and-fro movement, pendulum m., piston m., shuttle m.; shuttle service; shuttle diplomacy; pulsation, pulse, tick, beat, throb, rhythm, swing 317 *oscillation*; chorus, refrain 106 *recurrence*; drumbeat, tattoo 403 *roll*; tide 350 *wave*; frequency, wave f.; turn, go, round, circuit, lap; shift, relay 110 *period*, cycle.

regular return, rota, cycle, circuit, revolution, life cycle, wheel of life 314 *circuition*, 315 *rotation*; biorhythm; menstrual cycle, menses; yearly cycle, seasons 128 *morning*, 129 *evening*; fixed interval 110 *period*; routine, daily round 60 *order*, 610 *habit*.

anniversary, birthday, saint's day, jubilee, silver j., diamond j., wedding anniversary, silver wedding, ruby w., golden w.; diamond w., centenary, bicentenary; St George's Day, St Andrew's D., St Patrick's D., St David's D., St Valentine's Day 988 *holy day*; Fourth of July, Independence Day, 14 Juillet, Bastille Day 876 *special day*.

Adj. *periodical*, periodic, cyclic, revolving; fluctuating; rhythmical, steady, even, regular, constant, punctual, clock-like, like clockwork 81 *regular*; breathing, pulsating, throbbing, beating; recurrent, intermittent, sporadic, spasmodic, on-again-off-again 106 *repeated*; reciprocal, alternate, alternating 12 *correlative*; serial, successive, serialized 65 *sequential*, 71 *continuous*.

seasonal, anniversary; hourly, daily, nightly, diurnal, quotidian, tertian, biweekly, weekly, hebdomadal, hebdomadary, fortnightly, monthly; menstrual; yearly, annual, biennial, triennial, quadrennial, quinquennial, sextennial, septennial, octennial, decennial; bissextile; centennial, sesquicentennial, bicentennial, tercentennial, quadricentennial, quincentennial, millennial; secular.

Adv. *periodically*, rhythmically etc. adj.; at regular intervals; at fixed periods; punctually etc. adj.; seasonally, hourly, daily, weekly, monthly, yearly; per diem, per annum; at intervals, intermittently, sporadically, spasmodically, fitfully, every now and then, every so often, every once in a while.

142 Fitfulness: irregularity of recurrence

N. *fitfulness*, irregularity 61 *disorder*; fits and starts 17 *nonuniformity*, 318 *spasm*; remission 114 *transience*, 72 *discontinuity*; unsteadiness, variability 152 *changeableness*, 143 *change*; capriciousness, unpredictability 604 *caprice*; eccentricity; lurching 317 *oscillation*.

Adj. *fitful*, periodic, intermittent, on-off, on-again-off-again, stop-go 72 *discontinuous*; irregular 84 *unconformable*; uneven 29 *unequal*; occasional 140 *infrequent*; unsteady, unstable, fluttering 17 *nonuniform*; inconstant, variable 152 *changeful*; spasmodic, jerky, restless; halting, wavering, flickering, unsystematic; erratic 604 *capricious*; moody.

SECTION SEVEN

Change

143 Change: difference at different times

N. *change*, alteration, variation 15 *difference*; mutation, permutation, modulation, inflexion, declension; mutability, variability 152 *changeableness*; modification, adjustment, process, treatment 468 *qualification*; sea change 147 *conversion*; sudden change 149 *revolution*; break, break with the past, innovation, new look 126 *newness*; winds of change; change for the better, reformation 654 *improvement*; change for the worse 655 *deterioration*; change of direction, U-turn, diversion, shift, turn 282 *deviation*, 286 *regression*; relocation, change of position, transition 305 *passage*; translation, transposition 272 *transference*, 151 *interchange*; alternation 141 *periodicity*; overthrow 221 *inversion*; change of mind, c. of heart 603 *change of mind*.

transformation, transfiguration; transmogrification; make-over, sea change, metamorphosis, metasomatism; metabolism, anabolism, catabolism; transmutation, transubstantiation 147 *conversion*; transmigration of souls; reincarnation, avatar; version, adaptation, transcription, translation 520 *interpretation*, 521 *misinterpretation*.

Adj. *changeable*, variable, mutable; fickle 604 *capricious*; affected, changed etc. vb.; newfangled 126 *new*; transitional, provisional, alternative, transmutative; chequered, kaleidoscopic 437 *variegated*.

Vb. *change*, be changed, alter 152 *vary*; wax and wane 36 *grow*, 37 *decrease*; change one's clothes; change colour, change countenance 426 *lose colour*; change one's tune 603 *tergiversate*; vacillate, blow hot and cold, chop and change, channel-hop, channel-graze 604 *be*

capricious; turn, shift, veer, change course, do a U-turn 282 *deviate*; relocate, seek pastures new, make a transition, pass to 305 *pass*; turn the corner 656 *be restored*; turn over a new leaf, be converted 654 *get better*; submit to change 83 *conform*; move with the times 126 *modernize*.

modify, alter, vary, modulate, diversify 437 *variegate*; superimpose 38 *add*; introduce changes, innovate 126 *modernize*; computerize, automate; turn upside down, subvert 149 *revolutionize*, 221 *invert*; reverse, turn back 148 *revert*; make changes, rearrange, reorder, change the rules, move the goalposts; reset 62 *arrange*; adapt 24 *adjust*; conform 83 *make conform*; recast, remould, reshape 243 *form*; process, treat; revise, edit, correct 654 *rectify*; reform 654 *make better*; revamp, patch, darn 656 *restore*; change for the worse 655 *pervert*; tamper with, meddle w., spoil 655 *impair*; warp, bend, deform 246 *distort*; dye, discolour 425 *colour*, adulterate, doctor, qualify 43 *mix*, 163 *weaken*; cover, mask, disguise 525 *conceal*; change round, ring the changes 151 *interchange*, 272 *transpose*; effect a change, leaven 156 *cause*; turn the scale 178 *influence*; transform, transfigure, metamorphose, transmute, transubstantiate, 147 *convert*; metabolize, digest.

144 Permanence: absence of change

N. *permanence*, permanency, status quo; invariability, immutability 153 *stability*; persistence 600 *perseverance*; endurance, duration 113 *durability*, 115 *perpetuity*; fixity of purpose, immobility, intransigence 602 *obstinacy*; firmness, bedrock, foundation, solidity 324 *density*; conservation 666 *preservation*, 146 *continuance*; rule 81 *regularity*; fixed law, entrenched clause 153 *fixture*; standing, long s., inveteracy 127 *oldness*; tradition, custom, practice 610 *habit*; fixed attitude, conservatism; routine, rut 60 *order*.

Adj. *permanent*, enduring, durable 113 *lasting*; persisting, continuing, maintained; 115 *perpetual*; inveterate, rocklike, long-standing 127 *immemorial*; perpetuated, standing, well-established, entrenched, in with the bricks, fixed, unchangeable, immutable 153 *established*; well-preserved 666 *preserved*; unchanging, conservative, reactionary, dyed in the wool, true blue, diehard 602 *obstinate*; stationary, static, immobile 266 *quiescent*; always the s. 13 *identical*.

Vb. *stay*, come to stay, be here for good, set in, take root; abide, endure, subsist, outlast 113 *last*; persist, hold, hold good; hold on, hold it, maintain, sustain, keep up, keep on 146 *go on*; rest, remain, tarry, live 192 *dwell*; stand fast, refuse to budge, dig one's toes in, dig one's heels in 600 *persevere*; stand one's ground, keep one's footing 599 *stand firm*; stand still, resist change 266 *be quiescent*; grow moss 127 *be old*; remain the same, not change one's spots.

145 Cessation: change from action to rest

N. *cessation*, ceasing; desistance, discontinuance, discontinuation 72 *discontinuity*; arrest 747 *restraint*; withdrawal 753 *resignation*, 621 *relinquishment*.

stop, halt, dead stop; logjam, impasse, standstill, deadlock, gridlock, stalemate 28 *draw*; checkmate 728 *defeat*; breakdown 728 *failure*; stoppage; shutdown, closing down, nonresumption 69 *end*; hitch, check 702 *hindrance*; blockage 264 *closure*; interruption 72 *discontinuity*; breaking-off, walkout 709 *dissension*; closure of debate, guillotine 399 *silence*.

strike, stopping work 679 *inactivity*, 715 *resistance*; industrial action, general strike, 'national holiday'; work to rule; stoppage, walkout, sit-in, work-in, sit-down strike, lightning s.; unofficial strike, wildcat s., mutiny 738 *disobedience*; lockout 57 *exclusion*.

lull, interval, pause, remission, letup; break, breather, rest 685 *refreshment*; holiday, day off, time o., gap year, leisure time 681 *leisure*; interlude, cooling-off period, breathing space; abeyance, suspension; close season, respite, moratorium, truce, armistice, cease-fire, standstill 136 *delay*.

stopping place, port of call, port, harbour; stop, halt, pull-up, whistle-stop, station; bus stop, request s.; terminus, terminal, air t. 271 *air travel*; dead end, blind alley, cul-de-sac; billet, destination, the grave; 295 *goal*.

Vb. *cease*, stay, desist, refrain, hold, hold one's hand, stay one's h.; stop, halt, pull up, draw up; stand, rest, rest on one's oars, repose on one's laurels 683 *repose*; have done with, see the last of, end, finish 69 *terminate*; interrupt, leave off, knock o.; break o., let up 72 *discontinue*; ring off, hang up 578 *be mute*; withhold one's labour, stop work, down tools, strike, come out, walk out, vote with one's feet 715 *resist*; lock out 57 *exclude*; pipe down 399 *be silent*; come to an end, dry up, peter out, run o., run down 636 *not suffice*; slacken off, fade out, fade away 446 *disappear*; come off, end its run, be taken off; fold up, collapse 728 *fail*; die away, blow over, clear up 125 *be past*; stand down, withdraw, retire 753 *resign*; leave, leave off; give up, give over 621 *relinquish*; shut up, shut down, close; shut up shop, put up the shutters, go out of business, wind up; shut off steam, switch off; cease fire 719 *make peace*; sound the last post, ring down the curtain, call it a day 266 *be quiescent*, 679 *sleep*.

halt, stop, put a stop to; arrest, check, stem

702 *obstruct*; hold up, call off; pull up, cut short, call a halt, interrupt 747 *restrain*; call out, stage a strike; bring to a standstill, cause a logjam, freeze; checkmate, stalemate, thwart 702 *hinder*; check oneself, stop short, stop in one's tracks, stop dead; grind to a halt, seize, seize up, stall, jam, stick, catch; brake, put on the b. 278 *retard*.

pause, halt for a moment, take a breather; hold back, hang fire 278 *move slowly*; stay one's hand, hold one's horses, hesitate 679 *be inactive*; wait awhile, suspend, adjourn, shelve, put on ice, mothball, put on the back-burner 136 *wait*; rest 683 *repose*.

146 Continuance in action

N. *continuance*, continuation 71 *continuity*, 144 *permanence*; flow 179 *tendency*; extension, prolongation 113 *protraction*; maintenance, perpetuation 115 *perpetuity*; sustained action, persistence 600 *perseverance*; progress 285 *progression*; uninterrupted course, break, run, rally 71 *series*; recurrence 106 *repetition*.

Vb. *go on*, keep going, march on, drive on, proceed, advance 285 *progress*; run on, never end 115 *be eternal*; – and – (e.g. rain and rain, pour and pour); roll on, pursue its course, take its c.; endure, stick, hold, abide, rest, remain, linger 144 *stay*; haunt, frequent 139 *recur*; keep at it, persist, carry on, peg away 600 *persevere*; stick it out to the bitter end, sit it out, wait, wait till the end, see the end of, hang on 725 *carry through*; be not out; survive; live out one's time 69 *end*.

sustain, maintain, uphold 218 *support*; follow through 71 *continue*; keep up 666 *preserve*; keep on, harp on 106 *repeat*; keep it up, prolong, protract; 115 *perpetuate*; keep things moving, keep the pot boiling, keep the ball rolling.

147 Conversion: change to something different

N. *conversion*, converting, turning into, making i.; processing 164 *production*; reduction, crystallization; fermentation, leaven; chemistry, alchemy; mutation, transfiguration 143 *transformation*; enchantment 983 *sorcery*; course, lapse, flux 111 *course of time*; development 36 *increase*; evolution 358 *biology*; degeneration 655 *deterioration*; regeneration, reformation 654 *improvement*; rebirth 656 *restoration*; naturalization 78 *inclusion*; denaturalization 916 *loss of right*; brainwashing 178 *influence*; evangelization 534 *teaching*, 612 *inducement*; convertibility 469 *possibility*.

transition, transit 305 *passage*; movement, shift, relocation, translation, transfer 272 *transference*; alteration 143 *change*; life cycle.

Adj. *converted*, turned into, made i. etc. vb.;

assimilated, naturalized; reborn, born again; brainwashed; becoming, transitional; evolving, embryonic, developing, growing into; transformed, metamorphosed, transfigured, bewitched, unrecognizable 15 *different*.

Vb. *be turned to*, be converted into, become, get; come to, turn to, ferment, develop into, evolve i., ripen i. 316 *evolve*; fall into, pass i., slide i., shift i. 305 *pass*; melt into, merge i.; settle into, sink i.; mellow 669 *mature*; wax 36 *grow*; degenerate 655 *deteriorate*; take the shape of, assume the character of; be transformed; undergo a personality change, suffer a sea change, turn over a new leaf 143 *change*; metamorphose.

convert, reduce, process, ferment, leaven; make into, reduce to, resolve into, turn i., conjure i., enchant 983 *bewitch*; metamorphose; transmute, alchemize; render, make, mould, shape, hew into shape, knock or lick into s. 243 *form*; brainwash 178 *influence*; proselytize, evangelize 534 *teach*; win over 485 *convince*; regenerate 656 *revive*; paganize 655 *pervert*.

transform, transfigure; landscape 844 *decorate*; camouflage, disguise, paper over the cracks 525 *conceal*; render 520 *translate*; traduce 521 *misinterpret*; reshape, deform 246 *distort*; change the face of, change out of recognition 149 *revolutionize*; metamorphose 143 *modify*; reform, make something of 654 *make better*; remodel, reorganize, restructure, rationalize.

148 Reversion

N. *reversion*, reverting, going back, return, regress, retrogression, retreat, withdrawal, ebb 286 *regression*; tracing back, derivation 156 *source*; return to the past, turning the clock back, harking back 127 *archaism*; atavism, throwback 5 *heredity*; looking back, retrospection 505 *remembrance*; retroaction; reaction 182 *counteraction*, 31 *compensation*; repercussion, boomerang effect, backlash, backfire, ricochet 280 *recoil*; revulsion, disenchantment 830 *regret*; counter-revolution, reversal 149 *revolution*; retraction, backdown 603 *change of mind*; volte face, about-turn, U-t., right-about t. 240 *contraposition*; backsliding, recidivism 657 *relapse*; retroversion; 246 *distortion*; giving back, cession, replacement, reinstatement 787 *restitution*; getting back, recovery, retrieval 771 *acquisition*; taking back; reply, feedback 460 *answer*; retort 479 *confutation*; turn, turning point, watershed, crucial point, turn of the tide, calm before the storm 137 *crisis*; alternation, swing, swings and roundabouts, give-and-take, swing of the pendulum 141 *periodicity*, 106 *recurrence*, 317 *oscillation*; recycling; to-and-fro movement, coming and going, shuttling,

commuting; round trip, there and back; return journey, return ticket, day return; back where one started, status quo.

Vb. *revert*, go back, turn b., turn, return, retrace 286 *regress*; reverse, face about, turn a., do a U-turn 221 *invert*; ebb, retreat, withdraw 290 *recede*; kick back, rebound, backfire, ricochet, boomerang 280 *recoil*; slip back, slide b., backslide 657 *relapse*; back down, retract 603 *recant*; hark back, start again, turn the clock back, go back to the beginning, restore the status quo, revive 656 *restore*; disenchant, open one's eyes, remove the spell 613 *dissuade*.

149 Revolution: sudden or violent change

N. *revolution*, full circle, circuit 315 *rotation*; radical change, organic c.; tabula rasa, clean slate, clean sweep 550 *obliteration*; sudden change, catastrophe, coup d'état 508 *lack of expectation*; landslide; violent change, bouleversement, upset, overthrow 221 *overturning*; convulsion, shake-up, upheaval, reorganization, restructuring, perestroika; eruption, explosion, cataclysm 176 *outbreak*; avalanche, crash, debacle 309 *descent*, rebellion, counter-revolution 148 *reversion*, 738 *revolt*; total change, sea c., metamorphosis, nullification 752 *abrogation*, deposal.

revolutionist, abolitionist, radical, revolutionary, Marxist, Red 738 *revolter*; seditionist 738 *agitator*; anarchist 168 *destroyer*; idealist 654 *reformer*.

Adj. *revolutionary* 126 *new*; innovating, radical, thoroughgoing, out-and-out, root and branch 54 *complete*; cataclysmic, catastrophic, seismic, earth-shaking, world-shaking 176 *violent*; seditious, subversive, Marxist, red 738 *disobedient*; anarchistic 165 *destructive*.

Vb. *revolutionize*, overturn 221 *invert*; switch over 603 *tergiversate*; uproot, eradicate, make a clean sweep 550 *obliterate*, 165 *demolish*; break with the past, remodel, restructure, reorganize, refashion 126 *modernize*; change the face of, metamorphose 147 *transform*.

150 Substitution: change of one thing for another

N. *substitution*, subrogation, surrogation; commutation, exchange, switch, shuffle 151 *interchange*; supplanting, replacement, transfer 272 *transference*.

substitute, sub, proxy, alternate, agent, representative 755 *deputy*; surrogate; twofer; understudy, stand-in, body double 594 *actor*; ghost, ghost-writer 589 *author*; locum tenens, locum 658 *doctor*; reserve, twelfth man 707 *auxiliary*; supply, replacement; relief 67 *successor*; double, ringer, look-alike, changeling 545 *impostor*; mother figure, father f., foster parent; synonym, doublet 559 *word*; metaphor, symbol 551 *representation*; prosthesis, artificial limb, pacemaker; transplant; alternative, second best, ersatz 35 *inferiority*; whipping boy, scapegoat, sacrifice 981 *oblation*; makeshift, temporary measure, stopgap; sticking plaster, Band-Aid (tdmk) 177 *moderator*; expedient, modus vivendi 770 *compromise*.

Adj. *substituted*, vicarious 931 *disinterested*; interchangeable 28 *equivalent*; dummy, imitation, plastic, mock, ersatz, counterfeit, false 542 *spurious*; makeshift, stopgap, provisional, acting, temporary 114 *ephemeral*.

Vb. *substitute*, change for; exchange, switch 151 *interchange*; take *or* offer in exchange, swap, compound 770 *compromise*; palm off with, fob off w. 542 *deceive*; make do with, put up w., make shift w.; put in the place of, replace with; count as, treat as, regard as; replace, step into the shoes of, succeed 65 *come after*; supersede, supplant, displace, oust 300 *eject*; replace, take the place of, be substitute for, do duty f., count f., stand in f., act f., understudy f. 755 *deputize*; act the part of, ghost for; hold the fort; shoulder the blame for, accept responsibility for, take the rap f., cover up f.; rob Peter to pay Paul.

Adv. *instead*, in place, in lieu; in favour of; in loco parentis; by proxy; alternatively, as an alternative; in default of, for want of better, faute de mieux.

151 Interchange: double or mutual change

N. *interchange*, interchangeability, reciprocality; swap, exchange, trade-off 791 *barter*; commutation, permutation; transposition, metathesis, mutual transfer; all change; castling (chess), shuffle, shuffling 272 *transference*; reciprocity, mutuality; cross-fire, interplay, two-way traffic, reciprocation 12 *correlation*; quid pro quo; rally (tennis), give and take; retort, repartee 460 *rejoinder*; measure for measure, tit for tat, eye for an eye, tooth for a tooth 714 *retaliation*.

Vb. *interchange*, exchange, counter-change; change money, convert; swap, barter, trade off 791 *trade*; permute, commute, shuttle; change places; switch, shuffle, castle (chess) 272 *transpose*; give and take 770 *compromise*; reciprocate 12 *correlate*; requite, give as good as one gets 714 *retaliate*; bandy words, answer back, return the compliment, rejoin, retort 460 *answer*; take in each other's washing, scratch each other's back 706 *cooperate*.

152 Changeableness

N. *changeableness*, changeability, mutability 143 *change*; changefulness, variability, variety 17 *nonuniformity*, 437 *variegation*; inconsistency, inconstancy, irregularity; instability, imbalance 29 *inequality*; unsteadiness, rockiness; pliancy 327 *softness*; fluidness 335 *fluidity*; lubricity, slipperiness 258 *smoothness*; mobility, restlessness, fidgeting, disquiet 318 *agitation*; fluctuation, alternation 317 *oscillation*; turning, veering, chopping and changing 142 *fitfulness*; impermanence, flash 114 *transience*; vacillation, hesitation, wavering 601 *irresolution*; yea and nay 603 *change of mind*; fickleness, capriciousness 604 *caprice*; flightiness, light-mindedness 456 *inattention*; versatility 694 *aptitude*.

changeable thing, moon, Proteus, chameleon; kaleidoscope; shifting sands; man of straw; wax, clay; mercury, quick-silver 335 *fluid*; wind, weathercock, weathervane; eddy; April showers; wheel, whirligig; mobile 265 *motion*; fortune, wheel of Fortune; vicissitude, luck 159 *chance*; variable quantity 85 *numerical element*; mobile features 445 *appearance*; grasshopper mind 456 *inattention*; floating voter, don't know 603 *tergiversator*.

Adj. *changeful*, changing, mutable, alterable, phased 143 *changeable*; shifting, vicissitudinous; varying, variant, variable 17 *nonuniform*; kaleidoscopic; protean 82 *multiform*; quickchange, versatile 694 *skilful*; uncertain, unreliable, vacillating, wavering 601 *irresolute*; moody, unpredictable, unaccountable 508 *unexpected*; never the same, ever-changing, volatile, mercurial 15 *different*; rootless, of no fixed abode, vagrant, wandering; wayward, fickle, whimsical 604 *capricious*; vibratory, tidal 141 *periodical*; malleable, plastic 327 *soft*; giddy, dizzy, flighty, wanton, irresponsible, frivolous 456 *light-minded*; shifty, inconstant, unfaithful, disloyal, traitorous.

Vb. *vary*, be off with the old and on with the new, show variety 437 *variegate*; ring the changes, go through phases 143 *change*; chop and change, change and change about; dodge, double 620 *avoid*; shuffle, be shifty 518 *be equivocal*; writhe 251 *wriggle*; dart, flit, flitter 265 *be in motion*; leap, dance, flicker, gutter 417 *shine*; twinkle, flash; wave, flutter, flap 217 *hang*; shake, tremble 318 *be agitated*; wobble, stagger, teeter, totter, rock, reel, sway, swing, vibrate 317 *oscillate*; shuttle, alternate, ebb and flow, wax and wane 317 *fluctuate*; veer, tack, yaw 282 *deviate*, 269 *navigate*; puff 352 *blow*; vacillate, waver, shilly-shally, hesitate, float, drift, change one's mind 601 *be irresolute*; hover, blow hot and cold, play fast and loose 603 *tergiversate*; be inconstant 604 *be capricious*.

153 Stability

N. *stability*, immutability; irreversibility, constancy 16 *uniformity*; firmness 144 *permanence*; rest, immobility, immovability 266 *quiescence*; stableness, steadiness, steady state, homoeostasis, balance 28 *equality*; nerve, iron n., aplomb 599 *resolution*; stiffness, inflexibility 326 *hardness*, 602 *obstinacy*.

fixture, establishment, firm foundation; foundations, cornerstone, rock, bedrock, pillar, tower, pyramid; invariant, constant; fast colour, indelible ink; leopard's spots; law, law of the Medes and Persians, the Twelve Tables, the Ten Commandments, written constitution, droit du seigneur 953 *legality*.

stabilizer, fin, spoiler, keel; counterweight, ballast; buttress 218 *prop*.

Adj. *unchangeable*, inflexible 602 *obstinate*; unwavering, rocklike 599 *resolute*; predictable, reliable 473 *certain*; immutable, unalterable, inconvertible; changeless, unchanging, inalterable, irreversible; unshrinkable, shrinkproof; stereotyped, unvarying, invariable, constant 16 *uniform*; steady, undeviating 81 *regular*; durable, as the hills 113 *lasting*, 144 *permanent*; undying, perennial, evergreen 115 *perpetual*; imperishable, indestructible, inextinguishable 660 *invulnerable*. **See** *fixed*.

fixed, steadfast, firm, secure, immovable, irremovable; unassailable, unshakable, rocklike, steady as a rock; steady, stable, balanced, homoeostatic; fast, ingrained, indelible; engraved; ineradicable, rooted, deep-r.; deepseated, entrenched, in with the bricks, foursquare, well-founded, built on a rock; standing, pat; tethered, moored, anchored 45 *tied*; at rest, at anchor; run aground, stuck fast, stranded, grounded, high and dry; pinned down, transfixed; immobile, frozen, rooted to the ground *or* spot, like a statue, still as a stone 266 *still*.

Vb. *stabilize*, root, entrench, found, establish, build on a rock 115 *perpetuate*; erect, set up, set on its feet 218 *support*; float, set afloat; fix, set, stereotype; make valid, validate, confirm, ratify 488 *endorse*; retain, stet; bind, make sure, make fast 45 *tie*; keep steady, hold the road, retain equilibrium, balance 28 *equalize*.

154 Present events

N. *event*, phenomenon; fact, matter of f., actual f. 1 *reality*; case, circumstance, situation, state of affairs 7 *state*; occurrence, eventuality, incidence, realization, happening, turn of events; incident, episode, adventure 137 *occasion*; milestone, watershed 8 *juncture*; fortune, accident, casualty, contingency 159 *chance*; misadventure, mishap 731 *misfortune*; emergency, pass 137 *crisis*; coincidence 181 *concurrence*; advent

289 *approach*; encounter, meeting; transaction, proceeding, affairs 676 *action*; result, product, consequence, issue, outcome, upshot, bottom line 157 *effect*; denouement, solution 316 *evolution*; catastrophe 69 *end*.

affairs, matters, doings, transactions 676 *deed*; agenda; involvement, concern, concerns, interests, business i., irons in the fire, axes to grind 622 *business*; world, life, situation 8 *circumstance*; current affairs, affairs in general, state of affairs; course of events 111 *course of time*; chapter of accidents, ups and downs of life, vicissitudes 730 *prosperity*, 731 *adversity*.

Vb. *happen*, become, come into existence 360 *be born*; materialize, appear, be realized, come off 727 *succeed*; take place, occur, come about, come to pass, fulfil expectations; befall, betide 159 *chance*; turn up, pop up, crop up, start up, spring up, arise 295 *arrive*; present itself 189 *be present*; supervene 284 *follow*; issue, transpire, emanate 157 *result*; turn out, fall o., work o., pan o.; be afoot, take its course, advance 285 *progress*; continue 146 *go on*; go off, pass o. 125 *be past*; fall to one's lot, be one's good fortune *or* misfortune; be the case, be so, prove, prove to be; bring about, occasion 156 *cause*.

meet with, incur, encounter 295 *meet*; realize, happen on, chance upon, stumble u.; find 484 *discover*; experience, pass through, go t.; have been through 490 *know*, 818 *feel*; have adventures, endure, undergo 825 *suffer*.

Adv. *eventually*, ultimately; in due course, in the course of things, in the natural course of t., in the ordinary course of t.; as times go; as the world goes.

155 Destiny: future events

N. *destiny*, what's to come, one's stars 596 *fate*; horoscope, forecast 511 *prediction*; prospect, outlook 507 *expectation*; coming events, future plans 124 *futurity*, 617 *intention*; trouble in store, danger 900 *threat*; proximity 200 *nearness*, 289 *approach*; future existence, hereafter 124 *future state*; next world, Hades, afterworld, world to come, life after death 971 *heaven*; predestination 596 *necessity*, 473 *certainty*.

Adj. *impending*, overhanging, louring, hovering, imminent; preparing, brewing, cooking 669 *preparatory*; destined, predestined, in the stars, in the lap of the gods 596 *fated*; predicted, forthcoming, forecast 511 *predicting*; inescapable, inevitable, going to be, bound to happen 473 *certain*; due, owing 596 *necessary*; in the wind, on the cards 471 *probable*; on the agenda, intended, decided on 608 *predetermined*; in prospect, in view, in the offing, on the horizon, looming on the h., in the distance 443 *visible*; in the future, to come, in the womb of time 124 *future*; at hand, close 200 *near*, 289 *approaching*; instant, immediate, about to be, on the point of 116 *instantaneous*; pregnant with, heavy w. 511 *presageful*; in store, in reserve, ready, kept r., on the stocks 669 *prepared*; in embryo, embryonic 68 *beginning*.

Vb. *impend* 124 *be to come*; hang over, lie o., hover, lour, loom, be on the horizon 900 *threaten*; come on, draw nigh 289 *approach*; front, face, stare one in the f. 237 *be in front*; breathe down one's neck; ripen 669 *mature*.

SECTION EIGHT

Causation

156 Cause: constant antecedent

N. *causation*, causality, cause and effect, aetiology 158 *attribution*; authorship; origination, creation 21 *originality*; invention 484 *discovery*; inspiration 178 *influence*; evocation, provocation 164 *production*; stimulation, fomentation, encouragement, motivation 612 *motive*; planting, cultivation 370 *agriculture*; abetment 706 *cooperation*.

cause, material c., prime mover, God 965 *the Deity*; creator, maker 164 *producer*; begetter, father 169 *parentage*; author, inventor, originator, founder; agent, leaven; stimulus 174 *stimulant*; contributor, factor, contributory f., moment, determinant; inspirer, mainspring 612 *motivator*; fomenter, aider, abettor; power behind the throne, undercurrents 178 *influence*; planetary influence, astrological i., stars 155 *destiny*; fate 596 *necessity*; force 740 *compulsion*.

source, fountain, fount 68 *origin*; spring, fountainhead, wellspring; mine, quarry 632 *store*; birthplace 192 *home*; genesis, ancestry, lineage, descent 169 *parentage*; parent, ancestor, progenitor; loins 167 *genitalia*; rudiment, element, principle, first p.; nucleus, germ, seed, sperm, spore; egg, foetus, embryo, pre-embryo; chrysalis, cocoon 132 *young creature*; bud, stem, stock, rootstock; root, bulb 366 *plant*; radix, radical, etymon, derivation, etymology; foundation, fundamentals, the nitty gritty, bedrock 214 *base*; groundwork, spadework, beginnings 68 *beginning*; nuts and bolts, raw material, ore 631 *materials*.

reason why, reason, cause, the why and wherefore; explanation, key 460 *answer*, 520 *interpretation*; excuse 614 *pretext*; ground, basis, rationale, motive, idea, occasion, raison d'être.

Adj. *fundamental*, primary, elemental, ultimate; foundational, radical, basic 5 *intrinsic*; crucial, central 638 *important*; original, aboriginal 68 *first*; primitive, primordial 127 *primal*.

Vb. *cause*, originate, bring into being, create, make 164 *produce*; beget, be the author of 167 *generate*; invent 484 *discover*; be the reason 158 *account for*; underlie, be or lie at the bottom of, be at the root of; sow the seeds of, be answerable, be responsible, have a hand in, be to blame; institute, found, lay the foundations, inaugurate 68 *auspicate*; set up, erect 310 *elevate*; launch, set afloat, set afoot, set going, trigger off, spark off, touch o. 68 *begin*; open, open up, broach 68 *initiate*; seed, sow, plant, water 370 *cultivate*; contrive, effect, effectuate, bring about, bring off, bring to pass 727 *succeed*; procure, provide the means, put up the wherewithal; stage-manage, engineer 623 *plan*; bring on, induce, precipitate 680 *hasten*; bring out, draw o., evoke, elicit 291 *attract*; provoke, arouse, awaken 821 *excite*; stimulate 174 *invigorate*; kindle, inspire, incite, tempt 612 *induce*; occasion 612 *motivate*; have an effect, be a factor, show its result, make or mar 178 *influence*; be the agent, do the deed 676 *do*; determine, decide, give the decision 480 *judge*; decide the result, turn the scale, come down on one side or the other, give the casting vote 178 *prevail*, 34 *predominate*.

157 Effect: constant sequel

N. *effect*, consequence, corollary 65 *sequence*; result; derivation, derivative, precipitate 41 *remainder*; upshot, outcome, issue, denouement 154 *event*; final result, end r., termination 725 *completion*; visible effect, mark, print, impress 548 *trace*; by-product, side-effect, spin-off; aftermath, legacy, backwash, wake, repercussion 67 *sequel*; resultant action, response 460 *answer*; performance 676 *deed*; reaction, backlash, boomerang effect 182 *counteraction*; offspring 170 *posterity*; handiwork 164 *product*; karma 596 *fate*; moral effect 178 *influence*.

growth, development, expansion 36 *increase*; carcinoma 651 *cancer*; bud, blossom, florescence, fruit; ear, spike; produce, crop, harvest; profit 771 *gain*; growth industry.

Adj. *caused*, owing to, due to, attributed to; consequential, resulting from, consequent upon 65 *sequential*; contingent, depending, dependent on 745 *subject*; resultant, derivative, descended; secondary 20 *imitative*; arising, emergent, emanating, developed from, evolved f.; born of, out of, by; ending in, issuing in; effected, done.

Vb. *result*, be the r., come of; follow on, ensue, wait on, accrue 284 *follow*; be owing to, be due to; owe everything to, borrow from 785 *borrow*; have a common origin 9 *be related*; take its source, have its roots in, derive from, descend f., originate f. or in, come from or out of; issue, proceed, emanate 298 *emerge*; grow from, spring f., arise f., flow f.; develop, unfold 316 *evolve*; bud, sprout, germinate 36 grow; show a trace, show an effect, receive an impression, bear the stamp 522 *be plain*; bear the consequences 154 *meet with*, 963 *be punished*; turn out, fall o., pan o., work o., eventuate 154 *happen*; result in 164 *produce*.

depend, hang upon, hinge on, pivot on, turn on, centre on 12 *correlate*, 745 *be subject*.

158 Attribution: assignment of cause

N. *attribution*, reference to, imputation, ascription; theory, hypothesis, assumption, conjecture 512 *supposition*; explanation 520 *interpretation*; aetiology 459 *enquiry*; rationale 156 *reason why*; affiliation 169 *parentage*; derivation, etymology 156 *source*; attribute 89 *concomitant*; credit, credit title, acknowledgment 915 *dueness*.

Vb. *attribute*, ascribe, impute; say of 532 *affirm*; accord, grant, allow 781 *give*; put down to, set down to; assign to, refer to, point to, trace to, connect with, derive from 9 *relate*; lay at the door of, affiliate, father upon; charge with, saddle with *or* on; found upon; make responsible, make a scapegoat, blame for 928 *accuse*; bring home to 478 *demonstrate*; credit, credit with, acknowledge.

account for, explain 520 *interpret*; theorize, hypothesize, assume 512 *suppose*.

Adv. *hence*, thence, therefore; whence, wherefore; for, since, on account of, because, owing to, thanks to, on that account, from this cause, from that cause, ergo, thus, so; that's why.

159 Chance: no assignable cause

N. *chance*, blind c., fortuity, randomness; fortuitousness; unpredictability 474 *uncertainty*; inexplicability 517 *unintelligibility*; lot, fortune, wheel of f., lady luck 596 *fate*; potluck, luck of the draw; good fortune, luck, good 1., run of good 1. 730 *prosperity*; bad luck, run of bad 1. 731 *misfortune*; hazard, accident, misadventure, casualty, coincidence, chapter of accidents 154 *event*; lucky shot, lucky strike, fluke 618 *nondesign*; chance in a million 140 *infrequency*; chance meeting, chance encounter 508 *lack of expectation*; serendipity 484 *discovery*.

equal chance, even c., fifty-fifty 28 *equality*; toss-up, spin of the coin, heads or tails, throw of the dice, turn of the card, spin of the wheel; lucky dip, random sample; lottery, National Lottery, scratch card, raffle, tombola, sweepstake, premium bond 618 *gambling*.

fair chance, sporting c., fighting c., 469 *possibility*; half a chance, small c. 472 *improbability*; good chance 137 *opportunity*; long odds, odds

on, odds 34 *advantage*; safe bet, sure thing, the probabilities 471 *probability*.

Adj. *casual*, fortuitous, serendipitous, chance, haphazard, hit-or-miss, random, stray, out of a hat; adventitious, accidental, unexpected, incidental; coincidental; 10 *unrelated*; chancy, fluky, dicey, incalculable.

Vb. *chance*, turn up, crop up, fall to one's lot, so happen 154 *happen*; chance upon, come u., light u., hit u., stumble u., bump into, run across 154 *meet with*, 484 *discover*; go out on a limb, risk it, try one's luck, chance it, leave it to chance 618 *gamble*.

Adv. *by chance*, by accident; accidentally, fortuitously, serendipitously; perchance, perhaps; according to chance, as it may be.

160 Power

N. *power*, potency, mightiness 32 *greatness*; prevalence, predominance 34 *superiority*; omnipotence, almightiness 733 *authority*; control, sway 733 *governance*; moral power, ascendancy 178 *influence*; spiritual power, charisma, mana; witchcraft 983 *sorcery*; staying power, endurance 153 *stability*; driving force 612 *motive*; physical power, might, muscle, brute force *or* strength 162 *strength*; might and main, effort, endeavour 682 *exertion*; force 740 *compulsion*; stress, strain, shear; weight 322 *gravity*; weight of numbers; manpower 686 *personnel*; position of power, position of strength, vantage ground 34 *advantage*.

ability, ableness, capability, potentiality 469 *possibility*; competence, efficiency, efficacy, effectuality 694 *skill*; capacity, faculty, virtue, property 5 *intrinsicality*; qualification 24 *fitness*; attribute 89 *concomitant*; native wit, gift, flair, what it takes 694 *aptitude*; grasp 183 *range*; enablement.

energy, liveliness, vigour, drive, pep, zip, dynamism 174 *vigorousness*; work, kinetic energy, electrical energy, atomic e., nuclear e.; mechanical energy, engine power, horsepower; inertia; resistance 333 *friction*; force, field of f.; force of gravity 322 *gravity*; pressure, head, charge, steam; steam up; tension, high t.; electromotive force; pulling power 288 *traction*; thrust, jet propulsion 287 *propulsion*; momentum, impetus 279 *impulse*; magnetic field 291 *attraction*; 292 *repulsion*; suction 299 *reception*; expulsion 300 *ejection*; unit of work, erg, joule; calorie.

sources of energy, coal, gas, oil 385 *fuel*; nuclear power; wind p., solar energy, alternative e; hydroelectricity; power house, power station, hydroelectrics 350 *waterfall*; windmill, wind farm; solar panel 383 *heater*; generator 630 *machine*.

electricity, static e.; lightning; electrodynamics, electrostatics, electromagnetism; induction, inductance, capacitance; resistance, conduction; oscillation, pulsation, frequency; electric charge, pulse, shock; electric current, direct c., alternating c.; circuit, short c., closed c.; electrode, anode, cathode; positive, negative; conductor, semiconductor, non-conductor, insulator; lightning conductor, earth 662 *safeguard*; electrification, live wire 661 *danger*.

electronics, optics; lasers 417 *radiation*; integrated circuit, microprocessor; computer electronics 86 *data processing*; automation 630 *machine*; television, radio 531 *telecommunication*; electrical engineering, electricity supply; power line, lead, flex 47 *cable*; distributor; pylon, grid, national g.; generator, magneto, dynamo; oscillator, alternator; transformer, commutator, power pack; battery, accumulator; cell, photo c., photoelectric c.; valve, tube, transistor; voltage, volt, watt, kilowatt, megawatt; ohm; amperage, ampere, amp.

nucleonics, nuclear physics; fission, fusion, thermonuclear reaction; cyclotron, synchrotron; atomic pile, nuclear reactor, fast breeder r.; fuel rods, coolant; radioactivity, fallout 417 *radiation*; radioactive waste 659 *poison*; nuclear warhead, nuclear missile, atomic bomb 723 *bomb*; nuclear winter.

Adj. *powerful*, potent 162 *strong*; mighty 32 *great*; prevalent, prevailing, predominant 178 *influential*; almighty, omnipotent, irresistible 34 *supreme*; empowered 733 *authoritative*; competent, capable, able, adequate, equal to, up to 635 *sufficient*; with resources 800 *rich*; more than a match for, efficacious, effectual, effective 727 *successful*; operative, workable, having teeth; in force, valid 153 *established*; cogent, compulsive 740 *compelling*.

dynamic, energetic, peppy 174 *vigorous*; supercharged, souped-up; magnetic; propelling; locomotive, kinetic 265 *moving*; powered, engined; mechanized, automated 630 *mechanical*; electric, electrical, electromagnetic, electronic; computerized, atomic, nuclear, thermonuclear; hydroelectric, wave-powered, solar-p., wind-driven, water-d., steam-operated.

Vb. *be able*, – powerful etc. adj.; can, have it in one's power, have it in one; be capable of, have the talent for, have the virtue, have the property; manage 676 *do*; measure up to 635 *suffice*; have power, exercise p., control 733 *dominate*; force 740 *compel*.

161 Impotence

N. *impotence*, lack of power; invalidity, 163 *weakness*; inability, incapacity; incapability, incompetence, inefficiency 728 *failure*; 695 *unskilfulness*; ineptitude, unfitness 25 *inaptitude*;

decrepitude 131 *age*; frailness 114 *transience*; invalidation, disqualification 752 *abrogation*; sterility, barrenness 172 *unproductiveness*, *contraception*; disarmament, demilitarization 719 *pacification*; demobilization 75 *dispersion*.

helplessness, defencelessness 661 *vulnerability*; harmlessness 935 *innocence*; powerlessness 745 *subjection*, 747 *restraint*; stamping of feet, gnashing of teeth 891 *anger*; prostration, exhaustion 684 *fatigue*; collapse, breakdown 728 *failure*; unconsciousness, faint, swoon, coma, catatonia; numbness, narcosis 375 *insensibility*; stroke, cerebrovascular accident, CVA, apoplexy, paralysis, hemiplegia, paraplegia 651 *disease*; atrophy 655 *deterioration*; senility, old age 131 *age*; incontinence; dementia, Alzheimer's disease 503 *mental disorder*; imbecility 499 *unintelligence*; pupillage, minority 130 *nonage*; babyhood, infancy 130 *youth*; invalid 651 *sick person*, 163 *weakling*.

Adj. *powerless*, impotent, unable; unauthorized; nominal, figurehead 4 *insubstantial*; invalid, null and void; without a leg to stand on 163 *weak*; inoperative, not working, unemployed, disemployed 677 *nonactive*; suspended, in abeyance, cancelled, withdrawn; abolished, gone by the board; obsolete; mothballed, laid up, out of circulation, kaput; disqualified, deposed; inept 25 *unapt*; unworkable, dud, good for nothing 641 *useless*; inadequate 636 *insufficient*; ineffective, inefficacious, ineffectual, feeble 728 *unsuccessful*; incapable, incompetent, inefficient 695 *unskilful*; unpowered, unengined.

impotent, powerless, feeble 163 *weak*; emasculated, castrated, gelded, unsexed, unmanned, spayed, sterilized; sexless; sterile, barren, infertile 172 *unproductive*; worn out, exhausted, used up, effete; senile, gaga 131 *ageing*; paralytic, arthritic, stiff 326 *rigid*; unconscious, comatose, drugged, hypnotized, catatonic 375 *insensible*; incapacitated, disabled, paralysed 163 *crippled*; incontinent; all in, dead-beat, clapped out 684 *fatigued*; prostrated 216 *supine*; shell-shocked 854 *nervous*; helpless, rudderless; laid on one's back; thwarted, gnashing one's teeth, stamping one's feet 702 *hindered*.

Vb. *disable*, incapacitate 641 *make useless*; disqualify 916 *disentitle*; deprive of power, invalidate 752 *abrogate*; disarm, demilitarize 163 *weaken*; neutralize 182 *counteract*; undermine, sap 255 *make concave*; exhaust, use up, consume 634 *waste*; wind, prostrate, bowl over, knock out 279 *strike*; paralyse 679 *make inactive*; sprain, rick, wrench, twist, dislocate, break, fracture; cripple, lame, maim, hobble, nobble, hamstring 702 *hinder*, 655 *impair*; stifle, smother, throttle, suffocate, strangle 362 *kill*; muzzle, deaden 399 *silence*; spike the guns, draw the teeth, clip the wings, tie one's hands, cramp one's style; sabotage, put a spoke into one's wheel, throw a spanner in the works; deflate, take the wind out of one's sails; put out of action, put out of commission 674 *stop using*.

unman, unnerve, devitalize 163 *weaken*; emasculate, castrate, neuter, spay, geld, unsex.

162 Strength

N. *strength*, might, potency, horsepower, HP 160 *power*; energy 174 *vigorousness*; force 735 *brute force*; resilience; load-bearing capacity, tensile strength; steel 326 *hardness*; heart of oak 329 *toughness*; staying power, survivability, endurance, grit 600 *stamina*.

vitality, healthiness, fitness 650 *health*; vim, vigour, liveliness 360 *life*; virility 855 *manliness*; guts, nerve, spunk, pluck, backbone 599 *resolution*; aggressiveness 718 *bellicosity*; physique, muscularity, muscle, biceps, sinews, thews and sinews; beefiness, burliness, brawn 195 *size*; grip, iron g., vicelike g. 778 *retention*; Titanic strength, strength of Hercules.

athletics 837 *sport*, 716 *contest*; athleticism, gymnastics, acrobatics, body-building, pumping iron, feats of strength, callisthenics, aerobics 682 *exercise*; stadium, gymnasium, astrodome 724 *arena*.

athlete, gymnast, tumbler, acrobat, contortionist, trapeze artist, circus rider, bareback r., stunt man, escapologist 594 *entertainer*; marathon runner; Blue, all-rounder 716 *contender*; wrestler 716 *wrestling*; heavyweight 722 *pugilist*; weight-lifter, body-builder, strong man; champion 644 *exceller*; he-man, muscle man 372 *male*; Mr Universe, Tarzan, Hercules; Samson, Goliath, Atlas, Titan 195 *giant*; tower of strength 707 *auxiliary*.

Adj. *strong*, lusty, vigorous, youthful 130 *young*; mighty, potent, armed 160 *powerful*; high-powered, high-tension; all-powerful, omnipotent, overpowering, overwhelming 34 *superior*; incontestable, irresistible, more than a match for, victorious; sovereign, supreme 733 *ruling*; valid, in full force; like a giant refreshed; in high feather, in fine fettle, in tip-top condition, at one's peak, in top form, in good nick, fit as a fiddle, sound as a bell 650 *healthy*; heavy 322 *weighty*; forceful; urgent, compulsive 740 *compelling*; emphatic 532 *assertive*; hard as iron, steely, adamantine 326 *hard*; case-hardened, toughened 329 *tough*; solid, substantial, stable 153 *fixed*; well-built, stout; strong as a horse, strong as a lion, strong as an ox; heady, alcoholic 949 *intoxicating*; undiluted, neat; strengthened, fortified, double-strength; entrenched, unassailable 660 *invulnerable*; unyielding,

staunch 599 *resolute*; stubborn, intransigent 602 *obstinate*; persistent; shatterproof, unbreakable, solid 324 *dense*; impregnable 660 *invulnerable*; indomitable, unconquerable, invincible, unbeatable; unquenchable, unallayed; unflagging, tireless, unexhausted 678 *industrious*; unwithered, indestructible; waterproof, showerproof, weatherproof, rustproof, dampproof, impermeable, gasproof, leakproof, hermetic; fireproof, bulletproof, bombproof.

stalwart, stout, sturdy, hardy, rugged, robust, doughty 174 *vigorous*; of good physique, able-bodied, abled, muscular, brawny; sinewy, wiry 678 *active*; strapping, well-knit, well set-up, broadshouldered, barrel-chested, thickset, stocky, mesomorphic, burly, beefy, husky, hulking, hefty 195 *large*; gigantic, colossal, titanic, Herculean, Atlantean 195 *huge*.

manly, masculine, macho 372 *male*; amazonian; virile, red-blooded, manful 855 *courageous*; in the prime of manhood 134 *grown-up*.

Vb. *be strong*, – mighty etc. adj.; pack a punch; come in force; overpower, be more than a match for 727 *overmaster*; recover, convalesce, revive 656 *be restored*; blow hard, blow great guns 352 *blow*.

strengthen, confirm, give strength to, lend force to 36 *augment*; underline, stress 532 *emphasize*; reinforce, fortify; prop, sustain 218 *support*; brace, steel, screw up one's courage 855 *give courage*; stiffen, stiffen one's resolve, stiffen one's upper lip, toughen, temper, case-harden 326 *harden*; energize, act like a tonic, put body into, put beef into 174 *invigorate*; beef up, tone up, reinvigorate 685 *refresh*; set one on his legs 656 *cure*; set up, build up 310 *elevate*; power, engine.

163 Weakness

N. *weakness*, lack of strength, feebleness, puniness; vulnerability, helplessness 161 *impotence*; slightness 323 *lightness*; flimsiness, fragility, frailness 330 *brittleness*; delicacy, tenderness 374 *sensibility*; unsteadiness, shakiness, giddiness, vertigo, disequilibrium 29 *inequality*; feet of clay, instability 152 *changeableness*; ineffectiveness; moral weakness, frailty, infirmity of purpose 601 *irresolution*; debility, infirmity, decrepitude, senility 131 *old age*; delicate health 651 *ill health*; flaccidity, flabbiness 327 *softness*; fleshiness, corpulence 195 *bulk*; loss of strength, enervation, inactivity 679 *sluggishness*; exhaustion, prostration, collapse 684 *fatigue*; decline 655 *deterioration*; weakening, softening, mitigation 177 *moderation*; relaxation 734 *laxity*; loosening 46 *disunion*; adulteration, watering, watering down, dilution 43 *mixture*; debili-

tation 655 *impairment*; emasculation, eviscera-
tion; invalidation 752 *abrogation*; crack, fault
201 *gap*; flaw 845 *blemish*; inadequacy 636 *insufficiency*; weak point, fatal flaw, Achilles' heel
647 *defect*.

weakling, pansy, patsy; lightweight, small fry
639 *nonentity*; softy, sissy, milksop, namby-
pamby; old woman, invalid, hypochondriac
651 *sick person*; lame dog, lame duck 731
unlucky person; infant, babe-in-arms, kitten 132
young creature; baby, big baby, crybaby, chicken
856 *coward*; mummy's boy, mother's darling,
teacher's pet 890 *favourite*; doormat, pushover,
jellyfish, drip, weed, wimp, nerd, wet.

weak thing, broken reed, thread, rope of sand;
sandcastle, house built on sand, house of cards,
house of straw, cobweb 4 *insubstantial thing*;
matchstick, eggshell, paper, tissue p.; glass,
china 330 *brittleness*; water, dishwater, milk and
water.

Adj. weak, powerless, 161 *impotent*; unconfirmed 161 *powerless*; unfortified, unstrength-
ened, vulnerable; harmless 935 *innocent*;
namby-pamby, cissy or sissy, babyish; effeminate, limp-wristed, womanish 373 *female*; poor,
feeble, frail, delicate, slight, puny 33 *small*; lightweight 323 *light*; slightly built, anorexic, skeletal, of poor physique 196 *little*; thin 206 *lean*;
feeble-minded, weak or soft in the head, dim-
witted, imbecile 499 *foolish*; weak-willed, half-
hearted 601 *irresolute*; spineless, weak-kneed,
lily-livered, chicken-hearted, yielding 721 *submitting*; pale 426 *colourless*; limp, flaccid, flabby,
floppy 327 *soft*; drooping, sagging, giving 217
hanging; slack, loose, relaxed 734 *lax*; watery,
wishy-washy, milk-and-water, insipid, wersh
387 *tasteless*; low, quiet, faint 401 *muted*;
decrepit, old 131 *ageing*; past it, weak as a baby,
weak as a kitten; wavering, unreliable 604
capricious.

weakened, debilitated, enervated, diminished,
deflated 37 *decreasing*; depleted, impoverished,
drained, dissipated; effete; sapped, under-
mined, disarmed, disabled, laid low; exhausted,
wearied 684 *fatigued*; strained, overstrained 246
distorted; the worse for wear, not what it was,
on its last legs, tottering; deactivated, neu-
tralized 175 *inert*; diluted, adulterated, watered,
watered down 43 *mixed*. **See** *crippled*.

weakly, infirm, delicate, sickly 651 *unhealthy*;
groggy, rocky; run down, seedy, under the
weather, coming apart at the seams, below par,
one degree under, poorly; underweight, anorexic, skinny 206 *lean*; listless; faint; sallow, wan,
pallid, lacklustre 426 *colourless*.

crippled, disabled, impaired, incapacitated,
handicapped 161 *impotent*; halt, lame, game,
gammy, limping, hobbling; hamstrung,

hobbled; knock-kneed 246 *deformed*; arthritic,
rheumatic, gouty; limbless, legless, armless,
handless, eyeless 647 *imperfect*.

flimsy, gossamer, wispy, tenuous 4 *insubstantial*; delicate, dainty 331 *textural*; frail, fragile
330 *brittle*; gimcrack, jerry-built, makeshift,
shoddy 641 *useless*; rickety, ramshackle, tumbledown, on its last legs, shaky, tottery, teetering,
wobbly, wonky, creaky, tumbledown 655 *dilapidated*.

Vb. be weak, grow w., grow feeble, weaken;
sicken, be in poor health 651 *be ill*; faint, fail,
languish, flag 684 *be fatigued*; drop, fall 309
tumble; dwindle 37 *decrease*; decline 655 *deteriorate*; droop, wilt, fade; wear thin, crumble;
yield, give way, sag 327 *soften*; split 263 *open*;
dodder, totter, teeter, sway, stagger, reel 317
oscillate; tremble, shake 318 *be agitated*; halt,
limp, go lame 278 *move slowly*; have one foot in
the grave, not have long to go, be on the way
out 127 *be old*.

weaken, debilitate, enervate; loosen 46 *disunite*; soften up 327 *soften*; strain, sprain 161 *disable*; hurt, injure 655 *wound*; cramp 702
obstruct; disarm, take the edge off, cushion 257
blunt; impoverish, starve; deprive, rob 786 *take
away*; reduce, degrade, extenuate, thin, lessen
37 *abate*; dilute, adulterate 43 *mix*; devitalize,
eviscerate; deactivate, neutralize 182 *counteract*;
decimate 105 *render few*; muffle 401 *mute*; invalidate 752 *abrogate*; sap, deplete, undermine.

164 Production

N. *production*, producing, creation; origination,
invention, innovation, original work 21 *originality*, 484 *discovery*; productivity 171 *productiveness*; endeavour 671 *attempt*, 672 *undertaking*;
composition, authorship 551 *art*, 553 *painting*,
554 *sculpture*, 586 *writing*; musicianship; performance, output, turnout 676 *action*;
execution, accomplishment, achievement; concoction, brewing 669 *preparation*; craftsmanship
243 *formation*; planning, design 623 *plan*;
organization 331 *structure*, 62 *arrangement*;
engineering, construction; building design, geomancy, feng shui; establishment, erection 310
elevation; making, fabrication, manufacture,
industry, sunrise i. 622 *business*; processing, process 147 *conversion*; production line 71 *continuity*, 630 *machine*; technology,
computerization, new technology, high-tech,
robotics, third wave, increased output, Kaizen,
mass production; productivity deal 706
cooperation; development, growth 36 *increase*,
171 *abundance*; factory farming 370 *agriculture*;
breeding 369 *animal husbandry*; procreation 167
propagation.

product, creature, creation, result 157 *effect*;

output; printout; end-product, by-p.; extract,
essence; handiwork, artifact, manufacture,
article, thing 319 *object*; goods, wares 795 *merchandise*; goods and services, gross national
product, GNP; earthenware 381 *pottery*; stoneware, hardware, ironware; fabric, cloth 222 *textile*; production, work, opus, oeuvre, piece 56
composition; chef d'oeuvre, magnum opus,
crowning achievement 694 *masterpiece*; fruit,
flower, blossom, berry; produce, yield, harvest,
crop, vintage 157 *growth*; interest, increase,
return 771 *gain*; brainwave, brainchild, conception 451 *idea*; fiction 513 *ideality*; offspring,
young, egg, spawn, seed 132 *young creature*.

edifice, building, structure, erection, pile,
dome, tower, high-rise building, skyscraper 209
high structure; sick building; pyramid, ancient
monument 548 *monument*; church 990 *temple*;
mausoleum 364 *tomb*; habitation, mansion,
hall 192 *house*; college 539 *school*; fortress 713
fort.

producer, creator, maker. Nature; the Creator
965 *the Deity*; originator, inventor, discoverer,
mover, prime m., instigator 612 *motivator*;
founding father, founder, founder member,
establisher 156 *cause*; begetter 169 *parentage*; creative worker, poet, writer 589 *author*; composer
413 *musician*; painter, sculptor 556 *artist*;
deviser, designer 623 *planner*; developer, con-
structor, builder, architect, engineer; manufacturer, industrialist 686 *agent*; executive 676
doer; labourer 686 *worker*; artificer, craftsman *or*
-woman 686 *artisan*; grower, planter, cultivator,
agriculturalist, gardener 370 *farmer*; stock
farmer, stock breeder, sheep farmer, rancher
369 *breeder*; miner, extractor; play-producer 594
stage manager; film producer, film director, 445
cinema.

Vb. *produce*, create, originate, make; invent
484 *discover*; think up, conceive 513 *imagine*;
write, design 56 *compose*; operate 676 *do*; frame,
fashion, shape, mould 243 *form*; knit, spin 222
weave; sew, run up 45 *tie*; forge, chisel, carve,
sculpture, cast; coin 797 *mint*; manufacture,
fabricate, prefabricate, process, turn out, mill,
machine; mass-produce, churn out, multiply
166 *reproduce*; construct, build, raise, rear, erect,
set up, run up 310 *elevate*; put together, make
up, assemble, compose, cobble together 45 *join*;
synthesize, blend 50 *combine*; mine, quarry 304
extract; establish, found, constitute, institute 68
initiate; organize, get up 62 *arrange*; develop,
exploit; industrialize, mechanize, automate,
computerize; engineer, contrive 623 *plan*; perform, implement, execute, achieve, accomplish
725 *carry out*; bring about, yield results, effect
156 *cause*; unfold, develop 316 *evolve*; breed,
hatch, rear 369 *breed stock*; sow, grow, farm 370

cultivate; bear young 167 *reproduce itself*; bring
up, educate 534 *train*.

165 Destruction

N. *destruction*, undoing 148 *reversion*; blotting
out 550 *obliteration*; blowing out, annihilation,
nullification 2 *extinction*; abolition, suppression
752 *abrogation*; suffocation, smothering, stifling, silencing 399 *silence*; subversion 221 *overturning*, 149 *revolution*; overthrow 311 *lowering*;
felling, levelling, razing, flattening 216 *horizontality*; dissolution 51 *decomposition*; breaking up,
tearing down, knocking d., demolition, demol-
ishment 655 *dilapidation*, 46 *disunion*; disruption 46 *separation*; crushing, grinding,
pulverization 332 *powderiness*; incineration 381
burning; liquidation, elimination, extermination; extirpation, eradication, rooting out,
uprooting 300 *ejection*; wiping out, mopping up
725 *completion*; decimation, mass murder, massacre, genocide 362 *slaughter*; hatchet job;
destructiveness, vandalism, iconoclasm 176 *violence*; sabotage 702 *hindrance*; fire-raising, arson
381 *incendiarism*.

ruin, downfall, ruination, perdition, one's
undoing; crushing blow 731 *adversity*; catastrophe, disaster, act of God 731 *misfortune*; collapse, débâcle, landslide 149 *revolution*;
breakdown, meltdown, break-up, crack-up 728
failure; crash, smash, smash-up 279 *collision*;
wreck, shipwreck, wreckage, wrack, rack and
ruin; sinking, loss; Waterloo 728 *defeat*; knockout blow, KO 279 *knock*; beginning of the end,
slippery slope, road to ruin 655 *deterioration*;
coup de grace 725 *completion*; apocalypse,
doom, crack of doom, knell, end 69 *finality*, 961
condemnation; ruins 127 *oldness*.

Adj. *destructive*, destroying, internecine,
annihilating etc. vb.; root and branch 54 *complete*; consuming, ruinous 634 *wasteful*; sacrificial, costly 811 *dear*; exhausting, crushing,
apocalyptic, cataclysmic, overwhelming 176
violent; raging 176 *furious*; merciless 906 *pitiless*;
mortal, suicidal, cut-throat, life-threatening
362 *deadly*; subversive, subversionary 149 *revolutionary*; incendiary, mischievous, pernicious
645 *harmful*; poisonous 653 *toxic*.

Vb. *destroy*, undo, unmake, dismantle, take
apart 148 *revert*; destruct, self-d.; abolish,
annihilate, liquidate, nuke, exterminate, axe,
invalidate 2 *nullify*; devour, consume 634 *waste*;
swallow up, engulf 299 *absorb*; swamp, overwhelm, drown 341 *drench*; incinerate, burn up,
gut 381 *burn*; wreck, shipwreck, sink (**see** *suppress*); end, exterminate, put an end to 69 *terminate*; do for, do in, put down, put away, do
away with, make away w., get rid of 362 *kill*;
poison 362 *murder*; decimate 105 *render few*;

exterminate, leave no survivor 362 *slaughter*, 906 *be pitiless*; remove, extirpate, eradicate, deracinate, uproot, root up 300 *eject*; wipe out, expunge, efface, erase, delete, rub out, blot out, strike out, cancel 550 *obliterate*; annul, revoke, tear up 752 *abrogate*; dispel, scatter, dissipate 75 *disperse*; dissolve 337 *liquefy*; evaporate 338 *vaporize*; mutilate, deface 244 *deform*; knock out, flatten out; put the kibosh on, nip in the bud, put the skids under, make short work of, seal the doom of, make mincement of, mop up; spifflicate, trounce 726 *defeat*; dish, cook one's goose, sabotage 702 *obstruct*; play hell with, play the deuce with 63 *bedevil*, 634 *waste*; ruin, bring to ruin, be the ruin of, be one's undoing.

demolish, unbuild, dismantle, break down, knock d., pull d., tear d. 46 *disunite*; level, raze, raze to the ground, lay in the dust 216 *flatten*; throw down, steamroller, bulldoze 311 *fell*; blow down, blow away, carry a.; cut down, mow d. 362 *slaughter*; knock over, kick o.; subvert, overthrow, overturn, topple, cause the downfall of, overset, upset 221 *invert*; explode, blast, blow up, blow sky-high; bombard, bomb, blitz, blow to bits 712 *fire at*; wreck, break up, smash up; smash, shatter, shiver, smash to smithereens 46 *break*; pulp, crush, grind 332 *pulverize*; crush to pieces, atomize, grind to bits, make mincemeat of; rend, tear up, rend to pieces, tear to bits, tear to shreds, tear to rags, pull to pieces 46 *sunder*; shake to pieces 318 *agitate*; beat down, batter, ram 279 *strike*; gut, strip bare 229 *uncover*.

suppress, quench, blow out, put o., snuff o. 382 *extinguish*; put the kibosh on, nip in the bud, cut short, cut off, abort 72 *discontinue*; quell, put down, stamp out, trample out, trample under foot, stamp on, sit on, clamp down on 735 *oppress*; squelch, squash 216 *flatten*; quash, revoke 752 *abrogate*; blanket, stifle, smother, suffocate, strangle 161 *disable*; keep down, repress 745 *subjugate*; cover 525 *conceal*; drown, submerge, sink, scuttle, scupper, torpedo, sink without trace 313 *plunge*; 311 *lower*.

consume, devour, eat up, lick up, gobble up; swallow up, engulf, envelop 299 *absorb*; squander 634 *waste*.

be destroyed, go west, go under, be lost 361 *perish*; sink, go down 313 *plunge*; have had it, be all over with, be all up with 69 *end*; cop it, fall, bite the dust 309 *tumble*; founder, go on the rocks, break up, split, go to pieces, crumple up; fall into ruin, go to rack and ruin, crumble 655 *deteriorate*; go to the wall, succumb; go downhill, go to pot, go to the dogs, go to hell, go to blazes.

166 Reproduction

N. *reproduction*, procreation 167 *propagation*; remaking, re-fashioning, reshaping, remoulding, reconstruction 164 *production*; redoing 106 *repetition*; reduplication, mass production 171 *productiveness*; multiplication, duplication, printing 587 *print*; renovation, renewal 656 *restoration*; regeneration, resuscitation 656 *revival*; resurrection, resurgence; reappearance 106 *recurrence*; atavism 5 *heredity*; reincarnation 124 *future state*; copy 22 *duplicate*; Phoenix.

Vb. *reproduce*, remake, refashion, remould, reconstruct; rebuild; duplicate, clone 20 *copy*, 106 *repeat*; inherit 18 *resemble*, 148 *revert*; renovate, renew 656 *restore*; regenerate, revivify, resuscitate, reanimate 656 *revive*; reappear 106 *reoccur*; resurrect, mass-produce, multiply; breed 167 *reproduce itself*, 104 *be many*.

167 Propagation

N. *propagation* 166 *reproduction*; fertility, fecundity 171 *productiveness*; proliferation, multiplication 36 *increase*; breeding, hatching, incubation 369 *animal husbandry*; eugenics 358 *biology*; sex, facts of life, birds and the bees; copulation 45 *coition*; procreation 156 *source*; parthenogenesis, virgin birth; spontaneous generation; fertilization, pollination, fecundation, impregnation, insemination, artificial i., AID, test-tube baby; fertility treatment, assisted reproduction, reproductive medicine, fertility drug, Gift, gamete intra-fallopian transfer, intra-cytoplasmic sperm injection, in-vitro fertilization, IVF, egg donation; 171 *fertilizer*; conception, pregnancy, germination, gestation (**see** *obstetrics*); birth, nativity, happy event 68 *origin*; stillbirth, abortion 728 *failure*; birth rate; development 157 *growth*; fruition, flowering 669 *maturation*; puberty 134 *adultness*; parenthood, maternity, paternity 169 *parentage*; procreator, begettor; inseminator, donor; fertilizer, pollinator; propagator, cultivator 370 *gardener*.

obstetrics, midwifery; parturition, birth, childbirth, natural c., active birth, water b., childbed, confinement, lying in; epidural 375 *anaesthetic*; labour, labour pains, contractions; delivery, breech d., forceps d., Caesarian section, Caesarian; amniotic fluid, waters, bag of w., caul, umbilical cord; placenta, afterbirth; amniocentesis, alpha-fetoprotein test 658 *diagnostic*; birthing pool; gynaecologist, obstetrician, midwife 658 *nurse*; stork, gooseberry bush.

genitalia, loins, womb 156 *source*; genitals, reproductive organs, sex organs; pudenda, private parts, privates; male member, penis, phallus, cock (vulg), prick (vulg); testicles, scrotum, balls (vulg), goolies (vulg); lunch box; prostate, p. gland; vas deferens; vulva, clitoris, vagina, cunt (vulg), fanny (vulg), pussy (vulg), uterus, cervix, ovary, Fallopian tubes; ovum, egg; semen, seminal fluid, sperm, spermatozoa; seed, pollen.

Adj. *fertilized*, impregnated; pregnant, enceinte, gravid; in an interesting *or* delicate condition; heavy with, big with; expecting, expecting a happy event, expectant, carrying, with child, in the family way; up the spout, up the pole, in the club, having a bun in the oven, fallen, preggers; parturient; obstetric.

Vb. *reproduce itself*, yield, give increase 171 *be fruitful*; hatch, breed, spawn, multiply, teem, 104 *be many*; germinate, sprout, burgeon 36 *grow*; bloom, flower, fruit, bear fruit, fructify 669 *mature*; seed; conceive, get pregnant, fall; carry, bear; be brought to bed of, bring forth, give birth, have a baby; have children, have young; lay (eggs), drop, farrow, lamb, foal, calve, cub, pup, whelp, kitten, litter; have one's birth 360 *be born*.

generate, evolve 164 *produce*; bring into being, bring into the world, give life to, bring into existence, beget, get, engender, spawn, father, sire; copulate 45 *unite with*; impregnate, inseminate, pollinate; procreate, propagate; breed, hatch, incubate, raise, bring up, rear 369 *breed stock*; raise from seed, take cuttings, bud, graft, layer 370 *cultivate*.

168 Destroyer

N. *destroyer*, demolisher, leveller; Luddite, iconoclast, annihilationist, nihilist, anarchist 149 *revolutionist*; wrecker, vandal, arsonist, pyromaniac 381 *incendiarism*; despoiler, ravager, pillager, raider 712 *attacker*, 789 *robber*; saboteur; defacer, eraser, extinguisher 550 *obliteration*; hatchet man, hitman, killer, assassin 362 *murderer*; executioner, hangman; barbarian, Vandal, Hun; time, hand of t., time's scythe 111 *course of time*; angel of death 361 *death*; destructive agency, locust 947 *glutton*; moth, woodworm, dry rot, rust, erosion 51 *decay*; corrosive, acid, mildew, blight, poison 659 *bane*; earthquake, fire, flood; grim-visaged war 718 *war*; instrument of destruction, sword 723 *weapon*; gunpowder, dynamite, blasting powder 723 *explosive*; block-buster 723 *bomb*; nuclear warhead; juggernaut, bulldozer 216 *flattener*; Four Horsemen of the Apocalypse, Exterminating Angel.

169 Parentage

N. *parentage*, paternity, maternity; parenthood, fatherhood, motherhood; loins, womb 156 *source*; kinship 11 *family*; adoption, fostering, guardianship, surrogateship, surrogacy 660 *protection*; parent, first parents, Adam and Eve 371

humankind; single parent 896 *divorce*, godparent, guardian, appropriate person 660 *protection*.

genealogy, family tree, lineage, kin 11 *consanguinity*; pedigree, heredity; line, blood, strain; blue blood 868 *nobility*; stock, stem, tribe, house, clan 11 *race*; descent, extraction, birth, ancestry 68 *origin*.

paternity, fatherhood; father, dad, daddy, pop, papa, pater, governor, the old man; head of the family, paterfamilias; procreator, begetter, author of one's existence; grandfather, grandsire, grandad, grandpa, great-grandfather 133 *old man*; ancestor, progenitor, forefather, forbear, patriarch, predecessor 66 *precursor*; father figure; adoptive father, foster-f., natural f., biological f., stepfather, father-in-law; fatherland.

maternity, motherhood; maternal instinct 887 *love*; expectant mother, mother-to-be 167 *propagation*; mother, unmarried m., dam; mamma, mummy, mum, mater; grandmother, grandma, granny, gran, nan; materfamilias, matron, matriarch; ancestress, progenitrix; grandam 133 *old woman*; mother substitute; foster-mother, stepmother, adoptive mother, natural m., biological m., surrogate m.; mother-in-law; Mother Church, mother country, motherland.

Adj. *parental*, paternal; maternal, matronly; fatherly, fatherlike; motherly, stepmotherly; family, lineal, patrilineal, matrilineal; ancestral, hereditary 5 *genetic*; patriarchal 127 *immemorial*; racial 11 *ethnic*.

170 Posterity

N. *posterity*, progeny, issue, offspring, young, little ones 132 *child*; breed 11 *race*; brood, seed, litter, farrow, spawn 132 *young creature*; children, grandchildren 11 *family*; succession, heirs, inheritance, heritage 120 *posteriority*; rising generation 130 *youth*.

descendant, son, daughter; chip off the old block, infant 132 *child*; scion, shoot, sprout 132 *young plant*; heir, heiress 776 *beneficiary*; love child 954 *bastardy*; branch, ramification, colony; graft, offshoot, offset.

171 Productiveness

N. *productiveness*, productivity, mass production 164 *production*; boom, booming economy 730 *prosperity*; overproductivity, superabundance, glut, butter mountain, wine lake 637 *redundance*; menarche, fecundity, fertility, luxuriance, lushness, exuberance, richness, embarras de richesses 635 *plenty*; baby boom, population explosion; procreation, multiplication 167 *propagation*; fructification 669 *ripening*; fertilization, pollination.

fertilizer, organic f., manure, farmyard m., dung, guano, compost, bonemeal; artificial fertilizer, chemical f.; phosphates, nitrates, potash, lime; top-dressing, mulch 370 *agriculture*; semen, sperm, seed; fertility drug, gonadotrophin 167 *propagation*.

abundance, wealth, riot, profusion, harvest 32 *great quantity*; mother earth; hotbed, nursery, propagator; cornucopia, horn of plenty, land flowing with milk and honey; milch cow; aftermath 67 *sequel*; rabbit warren, ant heap 104 *multitude*.

Adj. *prolific*, fertile, productive, fecund; teeming, spawning; fruitful, fruitbearing, fructiferous; pregnant, heavy with, parturient; exuberant, rife, lush, leafy, verdant, luxuriant, rich, fat 635 *plentiful*; copious, streaming, pouring; paying 640 *profitable*; creative, scribacious.

Vb. *make fruitful*, make productive etc. adj.; fertilize, irrigate, impregnate, inseminate; procreate, propagate 167 *generate*.

be fruitful, – prolific etc. adj.; flourish; burgeon, bloom, blossom; germinate; conceive, bear, give birth, have children 167 *reproduce itself*; teem, proliferate, swarm, multiply, mushroom 104 *be many*; boom; 36 *augment*; populate.

172 Unproductiveness

N. *unproductiveness*, unproductivity, dearth, famine 636 *scarcity*; sterility, barrenness, infertility, infecundity 161 *impotence*; deforestation, erosion; defoliation; scorched earth policy, desertification, desertization; falling birthrate, zero population growth 37 *decrease*; virginity 895 *celibacy*; change of life, the change, menopause; abortion; unprofitableness 772 *loss*; unprofitability, fruitlessness 641 *uselessness*; aridity, aridness, fallowness, stagnation; slump, idleness 679 *inactivity*.

contraception, birth control, planned parenthood, family planning; contraceptive, barrier c.; pill, minipill, morning after pill, abortion p.; coil, loop, diaphragm, Dutch cap, French letter, condom, sheath; spermicide, C-film; rhythm method, Billing's m.; chastity 747 *restraint*; sterilization, vasectomy, hysterectomy.

desert, dryness, aridity, aridness 342 *dryness*; desolation, waste, barren w., wastelands, lunar landscape; heath, moor, bush, wild, wilderness; desert sands, sand dunes, Sahara; dustbowl 634 *waste*; desert island; salt flat 347 *marsh*; Arctic wastes 380 *ice*.

Adj. *unproductive*, dried up, exhausted, spent; sparse, scarce 636 *insufficient*; waste, desert, desolate; treeless, bleak, gaunt, bare 190 *empty*; poor, stony, shallow, eroded; barren, infertile, sour, sterile; withered, shrivelled, blasted;

unprolific, unfruitful, arid, unirrigated 342 *dry*; fallow, stagnating 674 *disused*; unsown, untilled, uncultivated; impotent, sterilized, sterile, on the pill; childless, without issue; celibate; fruitless, unprofitable 641 *profitless*; inoperative, out of action, null and void, of no effect 161 *impotent*; ineffective 728 *unsuccessful*; addled, abortive 670 *unprepared*.

173 Agency

N. *agency*, operation, work, doing 676 *action*; job, position, office 622 *function*; exercise 673 *use*; force, strain, swing 160 *power*; interworking 178 *influence*; procurement 689 *management*; service 628 *instrumentality*; effectiveness, efficiency 156 *causation*; quickening power 174 *stimulation*; support 703 *aid*; co-agency 706 *cooperation*; execution; process.

Adj. *operative*, effectual, efficient, efficacious 727 *successful*; operational, functional, up and running; in force, in play, at work; 673 *used*; afoot, up and doing 678 *active*.

Vb. *operate*, be in action, be operative, be in play, play; act, work, go, run 676 *do*; serve, execute, perform 622 *function*; do its job, do its stuff, do one's thing 727 *be successful*; take effect 156 *cause*; have effect 178 *influence*; take action, take industrial a., strike 678 *be active*; crew, man; make operate, bring into play, bring into action, wind up, turn on, plug in, switch on, flick or flip the switch, press the button; actuate, power, drive 265 *move*.

174 Vigour: physical energy

N. *vigorousness*, lustiness, energy, vigour, life 678 *activity*; dynamism, pressure, force, impetus 160 *energy*; intensity 162 *strength*; dash, élan, pizzazz, impetuosity 680 *haste*; exertion, effort 682 *labour*; fervour, enthusiasm 571 *vigour*; gusto, relish, zest, zestfulness 824 *joy*; liveliness, spirit, vim, zing, zip, éclat; fire, mettle, pluck, smeddum, blood 855 *courage*; fizz, verve, snap, pep, drive, go, get up and go; enterprise, initiative 672 *undertaking*; vehemence 176 *violence*; aggressiveness, oomph, thrust, push, kick, punch 712 *attack*; grip, bite, teeth, backbone, spunk 599 *resolution*; guts, grit 600 *stamina*; virility 162 *vitality*.

stimulation, activation, turning on, galvanizing, whipping up; intensification, boost stepping up 36 *increase*; excitement 821, *excitation*; stir; bustle 678 *activity*; perturbation 318 *agitation*; ferment, fermentation.

stimulant, energizer, activator, booster; yeast, leaven, catalyst; stimulus, fillip, shot, shot in the arm; Viagra (tdmk), crack of the whip, spur, prick, prod, jolt, goad, lash 612 *incentive*; restorative, tonic, pep pill 658 *tonic*; pick-me-up, aperitif, appetizer 390 *savouriness*; seasoning, spice 389 *sauce*; liquor, alcohol 301 *alcoholic drink*; aphrodisiac, philtre; love potion; pep talk, rousing cheer, egging on 821 *excitant*.

Adj. *vigorous*, energetic 678 *active*; forceful, vehement 176 *violent*; vivid, vibrant 160 *dynamic*, intense, strenuous 678 *industrious*; enterprising, go-getting, go-ahead 285 *progressive*; aggressive, keen, 597 *willing*; potent 160 *powerful*; hearty, virile, full-blooded 162 *strong*; full of beans, peppy, zippy, zingy, zestful, lusty, mettlesome 819 *lively*; blooming, bouncing 650 *healthy*; spry, brisk, nippy, snappy; fizzy, effervescent, heady, racy; tonic, bracing, rousing, invigorating, stimulating 821 *exciting*; thriving, lush 171 *prolific*.

keen, acute, sharp, trenchant 571 *forceful*; mordant, biting, pointed, sarcastic; virulent, corrosive, caustic 388 *pungent*; acrimonious, acrid, acid 393 *sour*.

Vb. *be vigorous*, thrive, be full of zip *or* zing, enjoy life 650 *be healthy*; burst with energy 162 *be strong*; show energy 678 *be active*; be always on the go, be up and doing 682 *exert oneself*; drive; cut right through 176 *force*; get up steam, put on a spurt, get psyched up, pull out all the stops 277 *accelerate*; be thorough, strike home 725 *carry through*; show one's power, make an impression 178 *influence*, 821 *impress*; throw one's weight about 678 *meddle*.

invigorate, energize, activate, push one's buttons; galvanize, electrify, intensify, double, redouble; wind up, step up, bump up, hike up, pep up, ginger up, boost, soup up 162 *strengthen*; rouse, kindle, inflame, stimulate, psych up, enliven, quicken 821 *excite*; act like a tonic, hearten, animate, egg on 833 *cheer*; go to one's head, intoxicate 949 *inebriate*; freshen, revive 685 *refresh*; give an edge to 256 *sharpen*.

175 Inertness

N. *inertness*, inertia 677 *inaction*; lifelessness, languor, paralysis, torpor, torpidity 375 *insensibility*; rest, vegetation, stagnation, passivity 266 *quiescence*; dormancy 523 *latency*; apathy, sloth 679 *sluggishness*; immobility, passive resistance 602 *obstinacy*; impassiveness, stolidity 823 *inexcitability*.

Adj. *inert*, passive, dead 677 *nonactive*; lifeless, languid, torpid, numb 375 *insensible*; heavy, lumpish, sluggish 278 *slow*, 679 *inactive*; hibernating 679 *sleepy*; quiet, vegetating, stagnant 266 *quiescent*; fallow 172 *unproductive*; slack; limp, flaccid 163 *weak*; apathetic, neutral 860 *indifferent*, 820 *impassive*; deactivated, suspended, in abeyance; dormant 523 *latent*.

176 Violence

N. *violence*, vehemence, frenzy, fury, ferment, impetuosity 174 *vigorousness*; destructiveness, vandalism 165 *destruction*; boisterousness, turbulence, storminess 318 *commotion*; uproar, riot, row, roughhouse, rumpus, ruckus, brouhaha, stramash, furore 61 *turmoil*; roughness, rough handling 735 *severity*; force, fisticuffs, hammer blows, strong-arm tactics, terrorism 735 *brute force*; torture 898 *cruel act*; brutality, savagery, domestic violence 898 *inhumanity*; fierceness, ferocity 906 *pitilessness*; rage, road r., trolley r., hysterics 822 *excitable state*; fit, throes, paroxysm 318 *spasm*; shock, clash 279 *collision*.

outbreak, outburst 318 *agitation*; flood, tidal wave 350 *wave*; cataclysm, convulsion, earthquake, quake, tremor 149 *revolution*; eruption, volcano 383 *furnace*; explosion, blow-up, flare-up, burst, blast 165 *destruction*; bursting open 46 *disunion*; detonation 400 *loudness*; sortie 712 *attack*; gush, torrent 350 *stream*.

storm, turmoil, turbulence, war of the elements; weather, dirty w., rough w., inclement w., inclemency; squall, tempest, typhoon, hurricane, tornado, cyclone 352 *gale*; thunder, thunder and lightning; rainstorm, downpour, cloudburst 350 *rain*; hailstorm, snowstorm, blizzard 380 *wintriness*; sandstorm, duststorm, sirocco 352 *gale*; magnetic storm.

violent creature, brute, beast, wild b., savage b.; dragon, tiger, wolf, she w., mad dog; demon, devil, hellhound, Hound of the Baskervilles, hellcat 938 *monster*; savage, barbarian, vandal, iconoclast 168 *destroyer*; he-man, cave m., Neanderthal m. 372 *male*; man of blood, assassin, executioner, Herod 362 *murderer*; homicidal maniac, psychopath 504 *madman*; rough, tough, rowdy, thug, mugger 904 *ruffian*; hooligan, football h., lager lout; bully, bully boy, bovver b., boot b., terror, holy t. 735 *tyrant*; firebrand, incendiary, pyromaniac 738 *agitator*; revolutionary, militant, nihilist, terrorist 149 *revolutionist*; termagant, Amazon; spitfire, scold 892 *shrew*.

Adj. *violent*, vehement, forcible 162 *strong*; acute 256 *sharp*; unmitigated; excessive, outrageous, extravagant 32 *exorbitant*; rude; extreme, severe, tyrannical, heavy-handed 735 *oppressive*; barbarous, savage, brutal, bloody 898 *cruel*; hot-blooded 892 *irascible*; aggressive, bellicose 718 *warlike*; rampant, charging; struggling, kicking, thrashing about 61 *disorderly*; rough, wild, furious, raging, blustery, tempestuous, stormy 352 *windy*; drenching, torrential 350 *rainy*; uproarious, obstreperous 400 *loud*; rowdy, turbulent, tumultuous, boisterous; incendiary, nihilistic 149 *revolutionary*; intemperate, immoderate, unbridled, unrestrained;

ungovernable, unruly, uncontrollable 738 *disobedient*; irrepressible, inextinguishable 174 *vigorous*; ebullient, hot, red-hot, inflamed 381 *heated*; inflammatory, scorching, flaming 379 *fiery*; eruptive, cataclysmic, overwhelming, volcanic, seismic 165 *destructive*; detonating, explosive, bursting; convulsive, spasmodic; full of violence, disturbed, troublous.

furious, fuming, boiling, towering; infuriated, mad, like a mad bull, mad with rage, maddened 891 *angry*; impetuous, rampant, gnashing; roaring, howling; headstrong 680 *hasty*; desperate 857 *rash*; savage, tameless, wild; blustering, threatening 899 *cursing*; vicious, fierce, ferocious 898 *cruel*; blood-thirsty, ravening, rabid, berserk, out of control 362 *murderous*; tigerish; frantic, frenetic, hysterical 503 *frenzied*.

Vb. *force*, use f., smash 46 *break*; tear, rend 46 *sunder*, bruise, crush 332 *pulverize*; blow up 165 *demolish*; strain, wrench, pull, dislocate, fracture, sprain; twist, warp, deform 246 *distort*; force open, prise o., pry o., lever o.; jimmy 263 *open*; blow open, burst o.; shock, shake 318 *agitate*; do violence to, mug, beat up, abuse 675 *misuse*; violate, ravish, rape 951 *debauch*; torture 645 *ill-treat*.

177 Moderation

N. *moderation*, nonviolence; mildness, gentleness 736 *leniency*; harmlessness, innocuousness 935 *innocence*; moderateness, reasonableness 502 *sanity*; golden mean 732 *averageness*; temperateness, restraint, self-control 942 *temperance*; soberness 948 *sobriety*, 874 *modesty*; impassivity 823 *inexcitability*; neutrality 625 *middle way*; correction, adjustment, modulation; mitigation 831 *relief*; relaxation, remission, letup 734 *laxity*; easing, alleviation; détente 719 *pacification*; tranquillization, sedation; quiet, calm, dead c. 266 *quietude*; control, check 747 *restraint*.

moderator, palliative 658 *remedy*; alleviative 658 *balm*; soothing syrup, milk, oil on troubled waters; calmative, sedative, tranquillizer, Valium (tdmk); lullaby; nightcap, bromide, barbiturate, sleeping pill, Mogadon (tdmk); anodyne, opiate, opium, laudanum 375 *anaesthetic*; dummy, pacifier 264 *stopper*; wet blanket, damper, killjoy 613 *dissuasion*; cooler, cold water, cold shower 382 *extinguisher*; clamp, brake 747 *restraint*; neutralizer; anaphrodisiac 658 *antidote*; cushion, shock absorber 327 *softness*; mollifier, peacemaker 720 *mediator*; rein.

Adj. *moderate*, unextreme, nonviolent, reasonable, within reason 913 *just*; innocuous 935 *innocent*, 163 *weak*; measured, restricted, low-key 747 *restrained*; self-controlled, tempered 942 *temperate*, 948 *sober*; cool, calm,

composed 823 *inexcitable*; still, quiet, untroubled 266 *tranquil*; peaceable, pacific 717 *peaceful*; leftish, pink, nonextreme, nonreactionary, middle-American, middle-of-the-road 625 *neutral*, 860 *indifferent*.

Vb. *moderate*, mitigate, temper; correct 24 *adjust*; tame, check, curb, control, chasten, govern, limit, keep within limits 747 *restrain*; lessen, diminish, slacken 37 *abate*; palliate, extenuate, qualify 163 *weaken*; take the edge off 257 *blunt*; break the fall, cushion 218 *support*; play down, soft-pedal, tone down, blue-pencil, euphemize 648 *purify*; sober, sober down, dampen, damp, cool, chill, throw cold water on 382 *refrigerate*, 613 *dissuade*; put a damper on, bank down the fires; blanket, muffle, smother, subdue, quell 382 *extinguish*.

assuage, ease, pour balm, mollify 327 *soften*; alleviate, lighten 831 *relieve*; deactivate, neutralize, act as an antidote, take the sting out 182 *counteract*; allay, dull, deaden 375 *render insensible*; soothe, calm, tranquillize, comfort, still, quiet, hush, lull, rock, cradle, rock to sleep 266 *bring to rest*; disarm, appease, smooth over, bring round, pour oil on troubled waters 719 *pacify*; assuage one's thirst, quench one's t., slake 301 *drink*.

178 Influence

N. *influence*, capability, power, potency 160 *ability*; prevalence, predominance 34 *superiority*; mightiness 32 *greatness*, 638 *importance*; upper hand, whip h., casting vote, final say; vantage ground, footing, hold, grip; leverage, play 744 *scope*; purchase 218 *pivot*; clout, weight, pressure; pull, drag, magnetism 291 *attraction*; counterattraction 292 *repulsion*, 182 *counteraction*; impact 279 *impulse*; climate 8 *circumstance*; occult influence, mana, magic, spell 983 *sorcery*; stars, astrology, horoscope, heavens, destiny 596 *fate*; hypnotism, mesmerism; curse, ruin 659 *bane*; persuasion, insinuation, inspiration 612 *motive*; personality, je ne sais quoi, charisma 866 *prestige*; ascendancy, domination, tyranny 733 *authority*; sway, control, dominance, control freakery, reign 733 *governance*; sphere of influence, orbit; factor, contributing f., vital role, leading part 156 *cause*; power dressing; indirect influence, patronage, favour, pull, friend at court, wire-pulling 703 *aid*; strings, lever 630 *tool*; secret influence, hidden hand, hand that rocks the cradle, woman behind the great man, power behind the throne, kingmaker, power broker, Grey Eminence 523 *latency*; lobby, pressure group, vested interest 612 *inducement*; manipulator, mover, manoeuvrer 612 *motivator*; big noise, big shot 638 *bigwig*; superpower; Big Brother, the Establishment 733 *government*.

Adj. *influential*, dominant, predominant, prevalent, prevailing 34 *supreme*; ruling, reigning, commanding, in the driving seat, obeyed; recognized, with authority 733 *authoritative*; rising, ascendant 36 *increasing*; strong, potent, mighty, multinational 32 *great*, 160 *powerful*; leading, guiding; inspiring; active in, busy, meddling 678 *active*; contributing, effective; weighty, key, momentous, decisive, world-shattering, earth-shaking 638 *important*; telling, moving, attractive; fascinating, charismatic; irresistible, hypnotic, mesmeric 740 *compelling*; persuasive, suggestive, insinuating; addictive; instructive 534 *educational*; pervasive 189 *ubiquitous*.

Vb. *influence*, have i., carry weight, cut ice; be well-connected, know the right people, have friends at court, have friends in high places; have a hold on, have in one's power; have the ear of, be obeyed 737 *command*; dominate, tower over, bestride; lead by the nose, have under one's thumb, wind round one's little finger, wear the trousers 34 *be superior*; exert influence, make one's presence felt, assert oneself; put pressure on, lobby, pull strings 612 *motivate*; make one's voice heard 455 *attract notice*; have a voice, have a say in; affect, be a factor in, turn the scale; bear upon, tell u. 821 *impress*; work on 925 *flatter*; inspire, persuade, carry with one 612 *induce*; force 740 *compel*; brainwash, prejudice 481 *bias*; hypnotize, mesmerize 291 *attract*; put off 292 *repel*; militate against, counterbalance 182 *counteract*; actuate, work 173 *operate*; have a rôle, play a part, play a leading p., guide 689 *direct*; lead the dance, set the fashion, establish a trend, be the model for 23 *be an example*.

prevail, outweigh, override, turn the scale 34 *predominate*; overawe, overcome, subdue, subjugate; hold the whip hand, gain the upper hand, hold all the cards, master 727 *overmaster*; control, rule, monopolize 733 *dominate*; hold 778 *retain*; take root, take hold, settle 144 *stay*; permeate, catch on, spread, rage, be rife, spread like wildfire.

179 Tendency

N. *tendency*, trend, tenor; tempo, rhythm, set, drift 281 *direction*; course, stream, main current, main stream, Zeitgeist, spirit of the times, spirit of the age; climate 178 *influence*; gravitation, affinity 291 *attraction*; polarity 240 *contraposition*; aptness 24 *fitness*; gift, talent, instinct for 694 *aptitude*; proneness, proclivity, propensity, predisposition, readiness, inclination, penchant, predilection, liking, leaning, bias, prejudice; weakness 180 *liability*; cast, cast of mind, bent, turn, grain; a strain of 43 *tincture*; vein,

humour, mood; tone, quality, nature, characteristic 5 *temperament*; special gift, genius, idiosyncrasy 80 *speciality*.

Vb. *tend*, verge, lean, incline; set towards, gravitate t. 289 *approach*; turn 178 *influence*; lead to 156 *conduce*; be calculated to 471 *be likely*.

180 Liability

N. *liability*, liableness, weakness 179 *tendency*; exposure 661 *vulnerability*; susceptibility 374 *sensibility*; potentiality 469 *possibility*; likelihood 471 *probability*; obligation, responsibility, accountability, amenability 917 *duty*.

Adj. *liable*, apt to; subject to, given to 745 *subject*; open to, exposed to, in danger of 661 *vulnerable*; dependent on, contingent 157 *caused*; incident to, incidental; possible, within the realms of possibility, on the cards, within the range of 469 *possible*; susceptible 819 *impressible*; answerable, reportable, responsible, accountable 917 *obliged*.

Vb. *be liable*, – subject to etc. adj.; be responsible, the buck stops here, answer for 917 *incur a duty*; incur, lay oneself open to, stand the chance of; run the risk of 661 *be in danger*.

181 Concurrence: combination of causes

N. *concurrence*, combined operation, joint effort, collaboration, synergy, synergism 706 *cooperation*; coincidence 24 *conformance*, 83 *conformity*; concord, harmony 24 *agreement*; compliance 758 *consent*; consensus 488 *assent*; acquiescence, nonresistance 721 *submission*; concert, pooling of resources, two heads are better than one, two minds with but a single thought, joint planning, collusion, conspiracy 623 *plot*; league, alliance, partnership 706 *association*; conjunction, liaison 45 *union*; think tank.

Vb. *concur*, acquiesce 488 *assent*; collude, connive, conspire 623 *plot*; agree, harmonize 24 *accord*; hang together, stick t., pull t. 706 *cooperate*; contribute, help, aid, abet, aid and abet, serve 703 *minister to*; promote, subserve 156 *conduce*; go with, go along w., go hand in hand w., keep pace w., keep abreast of, run parallel to 89 *accompany*; unite, stand together 48 *cohere*.

182 Counteraction

N. *counteraction*, polarity 240 *contraposition*; antagonism, antipathy, clash, aggro, conflict, mutual c. 14 *contrariety*, 279 *collision*; reaction, retroaction, repercussion, backfire, backlash, boomerang effect 280 *recoil*; recalcitrance, kicking back 715 *resistance*, 704 *opposition*; inertia, friction, drag, check 702 *hindrance*; interference, counterpressure, repression, suppression 747 *restraint*; intolerance, persecution 735 *severity*; neutralization, deactivation 177 *moderation*; nullification, cancellation 165 *destruction*; crosscurrent, headwind 702 *obstacle*; counterspell, counterirritant, neutralizer 658 *antidote*; counterbalance, counterweight; counterblast, countermove 688 *tactics*; defensive measures, deterrent 713 *defence*; prevention, preventive, preventative; contraception; inhibitor 757 *prohibition*.

Vb. *counteract*, counter, run c., cross, traverse, work against, go a., militate a.; not conduce to

702 *hinder*; react 280 *recoil*; persecute 881 *be inimical*; fight against, resist, withstand, defend oneself 704 *oppose*; antagonize, conflict with 14 *be contrary*; clash 279 *collide*; interfere 678 *meddle*; cancel out, counterpoise, counterbalance; repress 165 *suppress*; undo, cancel 752 *abrogate*; neutralize, act as an antidote, deactivate, demagnetize; cure 658 *remedy*; recover 656 *retrieve*; obviate, be a way round, prevent, inhibit 757 *prohibit*.

Adv. *although*, in spite of, despite, notwithstanding; against, contrary to 704 *in opposition*.

Space

Space in general

183 Space: indefinite space

N. *space*, expanse, expansion; extension, extent, surface, area; volume, cubic content; continuum, stretch 71 *continuity*; space-time 108 *time*; empty space 190 *emptiness*; abyss 211 *depth*; roominess; infinite s. 107 *infinity*; sky, aerospace, air-space, outer space 321 *heavens*; world, length and breadth of the land; vastness, immensity; terrain, open space, open country; green belt, wide open spaces 348 *plain*; upland, moorland, veld, prairie, steppe 348 *grassland*; outback, hinterland 184 *region*; wild, wilderness, waste 172 *desert*.

measure, proportions, dimension 203 *length*, 205 *breadth*, 209 *height*, 211 *depth*; area, surface a.; square measure, acreage, acres, rods, poles and perches; square inch, square yard, square metre, hectare, hide; volume, cubic content 195 *size*.

range, reach, carry, compass; stretch, grasp, span; radius, latitude, amplitude; sweep, spread, ramification; play, swing, margin 744 *scope*; sphere, field, arena 184 *region*; prospect 438 *view*; perspective, focal distance 199 *distance*; aim; magnifying power.

room, space, accommodation; capacity, stowage, storage space 632 *storage*; seating capacity, seating; standing room; margin, clearance, windage; elbowroom, legroom, room to swing a cat; headroom, headway; leeway, latitude; opening, way 263 *open space*; Lebensraum.

Adj. *spacious* 32 *extensive*; expansive, roomy, commodious; ample, vast, capacious, broad, deep, wide; voluminous, baggy, loose-fitting 195 *large*; broad-based 79 *general*; far-reaching, far-flung, widespread, wide-ranging, comprehensive, worldwide, global, world 52 *whole*; uncircumscribed, boundless 107 *infinite*; extending, branching.

Vb. *extend*, spread, outspread, spread out, range, cover, encompass; span, straddle, bestride; extend to, reach to 202 *be contiguous*; branch.

Adv. *widely*, extensively, everywhere, with no stone unturned; far and near, far and wide, all over, globally, universally, the whole world over; under the sun, on the face of the earth, in all quarters, from end to end, from pole to pole, from coast to coast, from Land's End to John o' Groats 54 *throughout*; from all the points of the compass, from the furthest corners of the earth; to the four winds, to the uttermost parts of the earth; here, there and everywhere, right and left, high and low.

184 Region: definite space

N. *region*, locality, locale, parts 185 *place*; sphere, orb, hemisphere; zone, section, belt; latitude, parallel, meridian; clime, climate; tract, terrain, country, ground, soil 344 *land*; geographical unit, island, peninsula, continent, landmass; sea 343 *ocean*; Third World 733 *political organization*; compass, circumference, circle, circuit 233 *outline*; boundaries, bounds, shore, confines, marches 236 *limit*; pale, precincts, close, enclave, salient 235 *enclosure*; corridor 624 *access*; area, field, theatre 724 *arena*; economic zone, exclusive area, charmed circle. **See** *territory*.

territory, sphere, zone; catchment area; beat, pitch, ground; plot, lot, holding, claim 235 *enclosure*; grounds, park 777 *estate*; national boundaries, domain, territorial waters, economic zone; continental shelf, airspace; possession, dependency, protectorate, dominion; colony, settlement; motherland, fatherland, homeland 192 *home*; commonwealth, republic, kingdom, realm, state, empire 733 *political organization*; no-man's-land, Tom Tiddler's ground 774 *nonownership*; no-go area; turf war.

district, purlieus, neighbourhood, haunt 187 *locality*; subregion, quarter, division 53 *subdivision*; state, province, county, shire, bailiwick, riding, lathe, wapentake, hundred, soke, rape, tithing; diocese, bishopric, archbishopric; parish, ward, constituency; borough, community, township, municipality; county, district, metropolitan area; canton, department, arrondissement, commune; hamlet, village, town, market t., county t. 192 *abode*; built-up area 192 *housing*; garden city, new town; suburb, suburbia, dormitory suburb, stockbroker belt; green belt 183 *space*; Home Counties, provinces, back of beyond, the sticks; outback, backwoods, bush, brush, bundu; hinterland, heartland.

city, metropolis, conurbation; Greater London, the Big City, the Big Smoke, the Big Apple; City, Wall Street.

185 Place: limited space

N. *place*, emplacement, site, location, position 186 *situation*; station, substation; quarter, locality 184 *district*; pitch, beat, billet, socket, groove; centre, meeting place, rendez-vous 76 *focus*; birthplace, dwelling place, fireside 192 *home*; address, habitat 187 *locality*, 192 *quarters*; premises, building, mansion 192 *house*; spot, plot; point, dot, pinpoint; niche, nook, corner, cranny, hole, pigeonhole, pocket, slot 194 *compartment*; confines, bounds, baseline, crease (cricket) 236 *limit*; confined place, prison, coffin, grave; precinct, paddock, compound, pen 235 *enclosure*; close, quadrangle, quad, square, town s.; yard, area, backyard, courtyard, court 263 *open space*; farmyard, field 370 *farm*; every nook and cranny.

186 Situation

N. *situation*, position, setting; scene, locale; time and place, when and where; location, address, whereabouts; point, stage, milestone 27 *degree*; site, seat, emplacement, base 185 *place*; habitat, ecosphere, ecosystem, biotype, range 184 *region*; post, station; standpoint, standing, ground, footing 7 *state*; side, aspect, feng shui; attitude, posture; frontage, orientation 239 *laterality*, 240 *contraposition*; geography, topography, chorography, cosmography, ecology 321 *earth sciences*; chart 551 *map*.

Vb. *be situated*, be located, be sited, be situate, centre on; be found at, have one's address at, be, lie, stand; be stationed, be posted; live, live at 192 *dwell*; touch.

187 Location

N. *location*, placing, siting, placement, emplacement, collocation, disposition; posting, stationing, relocation; locating, pinpointing; radiolocation, radar; centering, localization 200 *nearness*; settlement, resettlement, lodgment,

establishment, fixation, installation; deposition; putting in 303 *insertion*.

locality, quarters, purlieus, environs, environment, surroundings, milieu, neighbourhood, parts, neck of the woods 184 *district*; vicinity; address, postal district, street, place of residence, habitat 192 *abode*; seat, site 185 *place*; meeting place, venue, haunt 76 *focus*.

station, seat, site, emplacement, position 186 *situation*; depot, base, military b.; barracks, naval base, air b.; colony, settlement; anchorage, roadstead, mooring 662 *shelter*; cantonment, lines, police l.; camp, encampment, laager, bivouac, campsite, caravan site, temporary abode; hostel 192 *abode*; halting place, lay-by, car park, parking bay, parking lot, parking place, park-and-ride 145 *stopping place*.

Vb. *place*, collocate, assign a place 62 *arrange*; situate, position, site, locate, relocate; base, centre, localize; narrow down, pinpoint, pin down; find the place, put one's finger on; place right, aim well, hit, hit the nail on the head, hit the mark 281 *aim*; put, lay, set, seat; station, post, park; install, ensconce, set up, establish, fix 153 *stabilize*; fix in, root, plant, implant, embed, graft, slot in 303 *insert*; bed, bed down, put to bed, tuck in, tuck up, cradle; accommodate, find a place for, find room for, put one up, lodge, house, quarter, billet; quarter upon, billet on; impose; moor, tether, picket, anchor 45 *tie*; dock, berth 266 *bring to rest*; deposit, lay down, put d., set d.; stand, put up, erect 310 *elevate*; place with, transfer, bestow, invest 780 *assign*; array, deploy.

place oneself, stand, take one's place, take one's stand, anchor, drop a. 266 *come to rest*; settle, strike root, take r., gain a footing, get a foothold, entrench oneself, dig in 144 *stay*; perch, alight, sit on, sit, squat, park; pitch on, pitch one's tent, encamp, camp, bivouac; stop at, lodge, put up; burrow; ensconce oneself, locate oneself, establish o., find a home, move in, put down roots; settle, colonize, populate, people 192 *dwell*.

188 Displacement

N. *displacement*, dislocation, derailment 63 *derangement*; misplacement, wrong place, ectopia 84 *abnormality*; shift, move 265 *motion*; red shift, Doppler effect; parallax; aberration, perturbation (astronomy) 282 *deviation*; translocation, transposition, transhipment, transfer 272 *transference*; mutual transfer 151 *interchange*; relief, replacement 150 *substitution*; uprooting, removal, taking away 304 *extraction*; unloading, unpacking; expulsion 300 *ejection*; weeding, eradication 300 *voidance*; exile, banishment 883 *seclusion*; refugee 268 *wanderer*; fish out of water, square peg in a round hole 25 *misfit*; docker, stevedore, removal man.

displaced person, homeless person, the homeless, bag lady, bag people, rough sleeper, skell; fish out of water; square peg in a round hole.

Vb. *displace*, disturb, disarrange, disorientate, derail, dislocate; dislodge, disestablish, unseat, unfix, unstick 46 *disunite*; dispel, scatter, send flying 75 *disperse*; shift, remove 265 *move*; cart away, transport 272 *transfer*; change round; transpose 151 *interchange*; dispatch, post 272 *send*; relegate, banish, exile, kick upstairs 300 *dismiss*; set aside, supersede 150 *substitute*, 752 *depose*; turn out, evict, unhouse 300 *eject*; wipe out, eradicate, uproot 165 *destroy*; discharge, unload, off-load, unship, tranship; clear away, rake, sweep, sweep up 648 *clean*; take away, take off, cart off; lift, raise, uplift 310 *elevate*; draw, draw out, pull o. 304 *extract*.

misplace, mislay, lose, lose touch with, lose track of.

189 Presence

N. *presence*, being there, existence; whereabouts 186 *situation*; being somewhere, ubiety; being everywhere, ubiquity, ubiquitousness, omnipresence; permeation, pervasion, diffusion; availability, bird in the hand; attendance, presenteeism; residence, occupancy, occupation, sit-in 773 *possession*; visit, descent, stay; nowness, present moment 121 *present time*; man on the spot; spectator, attendee, bystander 441 *onlookers*.

Adj. *ubiquitous*, omnipresent, permeating, pervading, pervasive 79 *universal*.

Vb. *be present*, exist, be; take up space, occupy; colonize, inhabit 192 *dwell*; hold 773 *possess*; stand, lie 186 *be situated*; look on, stand by, observe, witness 441 *watch*; frequent, haunt; occur 154 *happen*; stay, sojourn, summer, winter, revisit 882 *visit*; attend, assist at, grace the occasion, honour with one's presence; take part; show up, turn up, present oneself; announce o. 295 *arrive*; be in evidence, show one's face, put in an appearance, look in on; face, confront 711 *defy*.

pervade, permeate, fill 54 *make complete*; be diffused through, be disseminated, imbue, impregnate, soak, saturate, run through; overrun, swarm over, spread, filter through, meet one at every turn 297 *infiltrate*; make one's presence felt 178 *influence*.

190 Absence

N. *absence*, nonpresence, disappearing trick 446 *disappearance*; lack 636 *scarcity*; deprivation 772 *loss*; being nowhere; inexistence 2 *nonexistence*;

being elsewhere, alibi; nonresidence, living out; leave of absence, sick leave, compassionate leave, maternity l., paternity l., parental l., vacation, holiday, sabbatical, furlough 681 *leisure*; nonattendance, nonappearance, truancy, skiving, bunking off, absenteeism 620 *avoidance*; absentee, truant 620 *avoider*; absentee landlord; backwoodsman, nonvoter.

emptiness, bareness, empty space, void, vacuity, inanity, vacancy; blank 201 *gap*; nothing inside, hollowness, shell; vacuum, air pocket, empties, dead men (empty bottles); blank cartridge, blank paper, clean sheet, tabula rasa; virgin territory, no-man's-land; waste, desolation, wilderness 172 *desert*; vacant lot, bomb site 183 *room*.

nobody, no one, nobody present, nobody on earth; not a soul, not a single person, not a living thing; empty seats.

Adj. *absent*, not present, not found, unrepresented; away, not resident; gone from home, on tour, on location; out, not at home; gone, flown, disappeared; lacking, wanting, missing, wanted; absent without leave, AWOL; truant, absentee; unavailable, unobtainable, off the menu, off 636 *unprovided*; lost, mislaid, missing, nowhere to be found; inexistent 2 *nonexistent*; exempt from, spared, exempted; on leave, on holiday, on vacation, on sabbatical, on furlough; omitted, left out.

empty, vacant, vacuous, inane; void, devoid, bare; blank, clean; characterless, featureless; hollow; vacant, unoccupied, unlived-in, uninhabited, untenanted; unstaffed, crewless; depopulated; desert, deserted; unpeopled, unsettled, uncolonized; godforsaken, lonely; bleak, desolate 172 *unproductive*; uninhabitable.

Vb. *be absent*, have no place in, take no part in; absent oneself, not show up, stay away, keep away, keep out of the way, cut, skip, skive, play truant *or* hookey, bunk off, take French leave 620 *avoid*; be missed, leave a gap, be conspicuous by one's absence.

go away, withdraw, leave 296 *depart*; make oneself scarce, slip out, slip away, be off, naff off, retreat 296 *decamp*, 667 *escape*; vanish 446 *disappear*; vacate.

191 Inhabitant

N. *dweller*, inhabitant, habitant, denizen; sojourner, migrant, expatriate 59 *foreigner*; mainlander, Continental; islander; boat-dweller, water gipsy; landsman *or* -woman, hill-dweller, dalesman, daleswoman, high-lander, lowlander, plains-dweller, fenman, fenwoman, forest-dweller, bush-d.; frontiersman *or* -woman, borderer; city-dweller, town-d., urbanite, suburbanite, commuter; metropolitan, provincial; country-dweller, countryman *or* -woman, ruralist, villager, parishioner; peasant 370 *farmer*; desert-dweller, tent-d., bedouin; cave-dweller, troglodyte; slum-dweller 801 *poor person*. See *native*.

resident, householder, ratepayer, housewife, hausfrau, chatelaine, housekeeper; cottager, crofter; addressee, owner-occupier, occupier, occupant, incumbent, residentiary 776 *possessor*; locum tenens 150 *substitute*; tenant, sitting t., protected t., renter, lessee, leaseholder; inmate, in-patient; house surgeon, house physician, house officer 658 *doctor*; garrison, crew 686 *personnel*; lodger, boarder, au pair, paying guest, p.g.; guest, visitor, commensal; cuckoo, squatter 59 *intruder*; parasite 659 *bane*.

native, aboriginal, abo (derog), aborigines, autochthones, indigenes, first-comers 66 *precursor*; people, tribe, clan 371 *nation*; local, local inhabitant; parishioner, villager, townsperson, townee, city person, urbanite, city slicker, cockney, suburbanite, weekender, holiday-homer; yokel, rustic 869 *country-dweller*; fellow countryman *or* -woman, fellow citizen; national, patrial, citizen, burgher, burgess, voter; John Bull, Uncle Sam; Briton, Britisher, Brit; Celt, Gael, Scot, North Briton, Caledonian; Welshman *or* -woman. Irishman *or* -woman, Hibernian; Jock, Jimmy, Taffy, Paddy; Englishman *or* -woman, Northerner, Southerner, Midlander, East Anglian, Westcountryman *or* -woman; Londoner, Brummie, Bristolian, Mancunian, Liverpudlian, Scouse, Geordie, Glaswegian, Aberdonian; New Yorker, Parisian, Muscovite 59 *foreigner*; earth-dweller, terrestrial, tellurian; extraterrestrial, ET, space-dweller, Martian, Venusian, little green men.

settler, pioneer, Pilgrim Fathers 66 *precursor*; immigrant, colonist, colonial; planter 370 *farmer*; resident alien 59 *foreigner*.

Adj. *native*, vernacular, popular, national, ethnic; indigenous, autochthonous, aboriginal; earthbound, terrestrial, tellurian; home, home-made; domestic, domiciliary, domesticated; settled, domiciled, naturalized; resident.

occupied, occupied by, inhabited, lived in, tenanted, populated; garrisoned by, taken over by, manned, staffed.

192 Abode: place of habitation or resort
N. *abode*, habitat, haunt, station 186 *situation*; place of residence 187 *locality*; habitation, street, house, home, second h.; address, house number, number; domicile, residence, residency; town, city, postal district 184 *district*; headquarters, base, seat 76 *focus*; temporary abode, hangout, camp, pad, pied-à-terre;

weekend cottage, country seat, holiday home, timeshare flat *or* apartment, watering place, hill station 837 *pleasure ground*; cantonment, lines 187 *station*; bivouac, encampment; camp, refugee c.; campsite, caravan park; home from home.

quarters, living q., married q., accommodation, lodging, billet, berth, squat; barrack, lodgings, rooms, chambers, digs; residential hotel, guest house, boarding h., lodging h., pension; boarding school, hostel, youth hostel, hostel for the homeless, foyer; dormitory, dorm; hall of residence; convent 986 *monastery*; cardboard city.

dwelling, roof over one's head 226 *roof*; prehistoric dwelling, lake d., pile d., crannog; tower, keep; cave, hut, kraal, igloo; wigwam, tepee, wickiup, tent, 226 *canopy*; lair, den, hole, form, burrow, warren, earth, sett 662 *shelter*.

nest, nidus, drey; branch 366 *tree*; aerie, eyrie, perch, roost; covert, heronry, rookery, swannery, hatchery, aviary, apiary, beehive, skep; bike, wasp's nest, antheap, anthill.

home, home-sweet-home, hearth and home, place where one hangs one's hat, hearth, fireside, fireplace, chimney corner, inglenook, rooftree, roof, paternal r., ancestral halls; homestead, household; bosom of one's family, family circle, cradle, birthplace, 'house where I was born' 68 *origin*; native land, la patrie, motherland, fatherland, homeland, one's country, God's own country, the Old Country, Blighty, Albion; native soil, native sod, native ground, native heath, home ground, home town, own backyard.

house, building 164 *edifice*; abode, home, residence, dwelling, dwelling house; country house, town h.; villa, detached house, semi-detached h., semi, terraced house; Queen Anne house, Georgian h., Regency h.; council h., council flat, high-rise f., prefab; ranch house, chalet, bungalow, chalet-b.; seat, place, mansion, hall, stately home; palace, dome, alcazar; chateau, castle, keep, tower, manor house, dower h.; manor, grange, lodge, priory, abbey; vicarage 986 *parsonage*; farmhouse, farmstead, croft, hacienda 370 *farm*; official residence, Buckingham Palace, Holyrood P., Chequers, Mansion House, White House, embassy, consulate.

small house, bijou residence; two-up two-down, back-to-back; chalet, lodge, cottage, thatched c., cot, but and ben; cabin, log c., hut, Nissen h., shanty, bothy; hovel, dump, hole, slum dwelling; box, hunting-box *or* -lodge; shed, shack, lean-to, outhouse, outbuilding; shelter, tent 226 *canopy*; kiosk, booth, stall, shieling; houseboat 275 *boat*; mobile home,

Dormobile (tdmk), caravan, trailer 274 *vehicle.* See *flat.*

housing, high-density h.; bricks and mortar 631 *building material*; built-up area, urban sprawl; asphalt jungle, concrete j.; urban blight; urbanization, conurbation; town, satellite t., new t., commuter t., dormitory t., burgh, suburb, garden city 184 *city*; housing estate, residential area 184 *district*; villadom, suburbia; crescent, close, terrace, circus, square, avenue, street 624 *road*; block, court, row, mansions, villas, buildings; houses, tenements, high-rise flats; inner city, ghetto, slum; shanty town; hamlet, village, community.

flat, flatlet, granny flat, tenement f., high-rise f., council f., furnished f., service f., mews f., penthouse; apartment, suite, chambers; bedsitting room, bed-sitter, bed-sit 194 *chamber*; maisonette, duplex; block of flats, apartment block, tower b.; mews, tenements.

stable, byre, cowshed; kennel, dog-house; sty, pigpen, fold, sheepfold 235 *enclosure*; dovecote, pigeon loft; stall, cage, coop, hencoop, hutch, battery; stabling, mews, coach-house, garage, carport, hangar; boathouse; marina, dock, dry d., graving d.; basin, wharf, roads, roadstead, port 662 *shelter*; berth, quay, jetty, pier.

inn, hotel, boarding house, guest-house, hostelry, roadhouse, motel, bed and breakfast (**see** *quarters*); doss-house, bunk-h., kip, flophouse; youth hostel; auberge, trattoria.

tavern, alehouse, pothouse, boozer; public house, pub, local; free house, tied h.; gin palace, saloon; speakeasy, dive, joint, honky-tonk; shebeen; wine cellar, wine bar, bodega; beer cellar, beer hall, beer garden; bar, public b., spit-and-sawdust b., lounge b., saloon b., snug; tap-room; theme pub, theme bar.

café, restaurant, self-service r., cafeteria; eating-house, eatery, steakhouse, diner, brasserie, bistro, pizzeria, kebab house, creperie, spaghetti house, trattoria, grill room, rotisserie; coffee bar, milk b., juice b., soup b., sushi b.; ice-cream parlour, soda fountain; lunch counter, fast-food c., snack bar, sandwich bar; teahouse, teashop, tearoom; buffet, canteen, Naafi; fish and chip shop, fish and chicken bar, chippie, baked potato shop, pancake house, take-away; coffee stall, pull-in, transport café; motorway services; cybercafé.

meeting place, conventicle, meeting house 990 *church*; day centre, community c., village hall; assembly rooms, pump r.; club, clubhouse, night club, working men's c., holiday camp 837 *place of amusement*; football ground, racecourse, dog track 724 *arena*; theatre, concert hall, opera house, stadium, stand 441 *onlookers*; astro-

dome, sports centre, gymnasium, drill hall, parade ground; piazza, quadrangle, quad, campus, village green, town square 76 *focus*; shopping centre, shopping mall 796 *market*.

park, park, grounds, pleasure g., pleasance, gardens, green; walk, mall, avenue, parade, promenade, boulevard; national park, theme p., adventure p., safari p.; parkland, chase 837 *pleasure ground.*

pavilion, kiosk, stand, bandstand, rotunda, folly, bower, grotto 194 *arbour*; stoa, colonnade, arcade, peristyle; tent, marquee 226 *canopy*.

retreat, sanctuary, sanctum sanctorum, refuge, asylum, haven, ark 662 *shelter*; priesthole, hidey-hole 527 *hiding-place*; cubbyhole, den, snuggery, snug, sanctum, study 194 *chamber*; cell, hermitage 883 *seclusion*; cloister 986 *monastery*; almshouse, grace and favour house; workhouse, poorhouse; orphanage, home, old people's h., rest h., hostel, foyer, hospice, halfway house, sheltered housing; 188 *displaced person.*

Adj. *provincial*, parochial, parish-pump, local, domestic, vernacular; up-country, countrified, rural, rustic.

architectural, designer, architect-d. 243 *formed*; Gothic 990 *churchlike*; classical, Byzantine, Romanesque, Norman, Tudor, Renaissance, Elizabethan, Jacobean, baroque, neo-classical, Palladian, Queen Anne, rococo, Georgian, Victorian, neo-gothic, Bauhaus 127 *olden.*

Vb. *dwell*, dwell in, inhabit, populate, people 189 *be present*; settle, colonize 786 *appropriate*; frequent, haunt 882 *visit*; take up one's abode, take up residence, hang up one's hat, move in; reside, remain, abide, sojourn, live 186 *be situated*; take rooms, put up at, stay, keep, lodge, lie, sleep at; live in, board out, be in digs; have an address, hang out at; tenant, occupy, squat 773 *possess*; nestle, perch, roost, nest, hive, burrow, stable; camp, encamp, bivouac, squat, doss down, pitch one's tent, make one's quarters 187 *place oneself*; tent, shelter 662 *seek refuge*; berth, dock, anchor 266 *come to rest.*

193 Contents: things contained

N. *contents*, ingredients, items, components, constituents, parts 58 *component*; inventory 87 *list*; furnishings, equipment 633 *provision*; load, payload, cargo, lading, freight, shipment, cartload, shipload, containerful 272 *thing transferred*; enclosure, inside 224 *insides*; stuffing, filling, stopping, wadding 227 *lining*; fistful, handful, cupful, quiverful 33 *small quantity*, 32 *great quantity.*

Vb. *load*, lade, freight, charge, burden; palletize, containerize; take in, take on board, ship;

overload, overburden 322 *weigh*; pack, package, pack in, fit in, tuck in 303 *insert*; pack tight, squeeze in, cram, stuff 54 *fill*.

194 Receptacle

N. *receptacle*, container, holder; frame 218 *prop*; hutch, cage 748 *prison*; folder, wrapper, envelope, cover, file 235 *enclosure*; net, safety n., fishing n. 222 *network*; sheath, chrysalis, cocoon; packaging 226 *wrapping*; capsule, ampoule; pod, calyx, boll; mould 243 *form*; socket, mortise 255 *cavity*; groove, slot 262 *furrow*; pigeon-hole, hole, cave, cavity 263 *opening*; bosom, lap 261 *fold*; pincushion; catch-all, trap; well, reservoir, hold, repository 632 *store*; drain, cesspit, sump 649 *sink*; crockery, chinaware, glassware 381 *pottery*.

stomach, maw, tummy, tum, abdomen, belly, corporation, pot belly, paunch 253 *swelling*; gizzard, gullet, crop, craw, jaws, mouth, oesophagus 263 *orifice*.

compartment, cell, cellule, loculus, follicle, ventricle; tray, cage; cubicle, carrel, booth, stall; sentry box; box 594 *theatre*; pew, choirstall 990 *church interior*; niche, nook, cranny, recess, bay, oriel; pigeonhole, cubbyhole; drawer, locker; shelving, rack 218 *shelf*; storey, floor, deck 207 *layer*.

cabinet, closet, commode, wardrobe, press, chest of drawers, chiffonier, tallboy; cupboard, corner c., built-in c., unit; whatnot, dresser, Welsh d., china cabinet; buffet, sideboard 218 *stand*; freezer, fridge-freezer 384 *refrigerator*; cocktail cabinet, dumbwaiter, lazy Susan, tea trolley; secretaire, escritoire, davenport, bureau, desk, writing d.; console; book-case.

basket, creel; hamper, picnic basket; pannier, trug, punnet, skep, rush basket; crib, cradle, bassinet; clothesbasket, laundry basket; workbasket, workbox; wastepaper basket.

box, chest, ark; coffer, locker; case, canteen; safe, till, moneybox 799 *treasury*; coffin, sarcophagus 364 *tomb*; packing case, tea chest; tuckbox; attaché case, briefcase, dispatch box; suitcase, expanding s., overnight case, vanity c.; trunk, valise, portmanteau; sea chest, ditty-box; bandbox, hat box; ammunition chest, canister, caisson 723 *ammunition*; boxes, luggage, baggage, impedimenta, paraphernalia, bits and pieces, gear; boot, trunk, luggage van.

small box, pill b., snuff b., cigar b., pencil b., matchbox; cardboard box, carton, packet; plastic box, lunch box, metal box, can, tin, caddy, tea caddy, canister; casket, pyx 988 *ritual object*; salt cellar, pepper mill; castor; nest of boxes.

bag, sack, poke; handbag, vanity case, reticule, clutch bag, dorothy b., shoulder b., tote b.; shopping bag, carrier b., polythene b., poly

b., plastic b., paper b.; cornet, twist, sachet; Gladstone bag, carpet b., travelling b., overnight b., flight b., sponge b.; sleeping bag; bedding-roll; holdall, grip; haversack, knapsack, rucksack, backpack; kitbag, ditty bag, duffle b.; pouch, sling; pannier, saddlebag, nosebag; school bag, satchel, sports bag.

case, étui, housewife; wallet, pocket book, notecase, billfold; spectacle case, cigarette c., compact; attaché case, briefcase, portfolio; file, box f.; scabbard, sheath; pistol case, holster; arrow case, quiver 632 *store*.

vat, butt, water b., cask, barrel, tun, tub, keg; drum 252 *cylinder*; wine cask, pipe, hogshead, firkin, kilderkin 465 *metrology*; hopper, cistern, tank 632 *store*.

vessel, vase, urn, jar, amphora, ampulla, cruse, crock, pot, water p.; pipkin, pitcher, ewer, jug, toby jug; gourd, calabash 366 *plant*; carafe, decanter, bottle; leather bottle, chagal *or* chagul, blackjack, wineskin; wine bottle, demijohn, magnum, jeroboam, rehoboam, methuselah, balthazar; flask, hip f., flagon, vial, phial; honeypot, jamjar; gallipot, carboy, crucible, retort, pipette, test tube, cupel 461 *testing agent*; chamber pot, bedpan, toilet bowl 649 *latrine*; pail, bucket, wooden b.; churn, can, watering c.; flowerpot, planter, jardinière; bin, litter b., rubbish b., dustbin 649 *sink*; scuttle, coal s., hod; skip, kibble; bath, tin b., tub.

pot 383 *heater*; boiler, copper, kettle, cauldron, cooking pot, skillet, pan, saucepan, stewpan, steamer, double-boiler; frying pan, wok, omelette pan, grill p., girdle; casserole, Dutch oven, tandoor, bain-marie; mess tin, dixie, billy-can; tea urn, teapot, samovar, coffeepot, cafetière, percolator; vacuum flask, Thermos (tdmk) f.; warming pan.

cup, eggcup, coffee cup, teacup, breakfast cup; tea service, tea set; chalice, goblet, beaker; drinking cup, loving c.; quaich; horn, drinking h.; tankard, stoup, can, cannikin, pannikin, mug, stein, toby, noggin, rummer, schooner, tassie; tumbler, glass, liqueur g., wine-glass, brandy balloon, pony.

bowl, basin, hand b., wash b., finger b.; toilet b.; pudding basin, mixing bowl, punch b., drinking b., jorum; porringer, ramekin; manger, trough; colander, strainer, vegetable dish, tureen, terrine, gravy boat; rose bowl, vase 844 *ornamentation*.

plate, salver, silver s.; tray, platter, ashet, trencher, charger, dish; palette; saucer; pan, scale 322 *scales*; pallet; mortarboard, hod.

ladle, skimmer, dipper, baler, scoop, cupped hands; spoon, tablespoon, dessertspoon, teaspoon, eggspoon, soupspoon; spade, trowel, spatula, slice, shovel.

chamber, room, apartment 192 *flat*; cockpit, cubicle, cab; cabin, stateroom; audience chamber, throne room; cabinet, closet, study, den, snug, snuggery, sanctum 192 *retreat*; library, studio, atelier, workroom, office 687 *workshop*; playroom, rumpus room, nursery; reception room, drawing room, front r., sitting r., living r., lounge, parlour, salon, boudoir; bedroom, dormitory; dressing room; bathroom, washroom, toilet, shower room, sauna; dining room, breakfast r., dinette; messroom, mess, hall, refectory, canteen 192 *café*; gunroom, wardroom; smoking room, billiard r.; bar, snug 192 *tavern*; cookhouse, galley, kitchen, kitchenette; scullery, pantry, larder, stillroom; dairy, laundry, utility room, offices, outhouse; coachhouse, garage 192 *stable*; storeroom, box room, lumber r., glory hole 632 *storage*; cloakroom, smallest room, lavatory 649 *latrine*. See *compartment*.

lobby, vestibule, foyer, anteroom, antechamber, waiting room; corridor, passage, hall, entrance h.; gallery, verandah, stoop, patio, piazza, loggia, balcony, portico, porch 263 *doorway*; extension, lean-to.

cellar, cellarage, vault, crypt, basement, garden flat 214 *base*; coalhole, bunker 632 *storage*; hold, dungeon 748 *prison*.

attic, loft, hayloft; penthouse, garret 213 *summit*.

arbour, alcove, bower, grotto, grot, summerhouse, gazebo, folly, pergola 192 *pavilion*; sun lounge, solarium, conservatory, orangery, greenhouse, glasshouse, hothouse 370 *garden*.

SECTION TWO

Dimensions

195 Size

N. *size*, magnitude, order of m.; proportions, dimensions, measurements 183 *measure*; extent, expanse, area 183 *space*; extension 203 *length*, 209 *height*, 211 *depth*; width, amplitude 205 *breadth*; volume; girth, circumference 233 *outline*; bulk, mass, weight 322 *gravity*; capacity, intake, tonnage; measured size, calibre 465 *measurement*; real size, true dimensions 494 *accuracy*; greatest size, maximum 32 *greatness*; full size, life size 54 *plenitude*; large size, king s., queen s., magnum; largest portion 52 *chief part*; excessive size, hypertrophy, giantism, gigantism.

bulk, mass, weight, heaviness, avoirdupois 322 *gravity*; lump, dod, block, clod, boulder 324 *solid body*; hunk, chunk 53 *piece*; mound, heap 32 *great quantity*; mountain, pyramid 209 *high structure*; massiveness, bulkiness; turgidity 197

dilation; obesity, corpulence, fatness, stoutness, chubbiness, plumpness, embonpoint, chunkiness, fleshiness, meatiness, beefiness; flesh and blood, double chin, rotund figure, spare tyre, corporation 253 *swelling*; muscle man 162 *athlete*; fat person, fatty, tub, dumpling, mound of flesh, tub of lard, hulk; Billy Bunter, Bessie B., Falstaff.

giant, giantess, colossus 209 *tall creature*; mountain of a man *or* woman, young giant; ogre, monster, King Kong; leviathan, behemoth, Triton among the minnows; whale, hippopotamus, elephant, jumbo; mammoth, dinosaur; giantry, Titan, Titaness, Gargantua, Pantagruel, Brobdingnagian, Gog and Magog, Typhon, Atlas, Cyclops, Polyphemus, Goliath.

Adj. *large*, big 32 *great*; large size, economy s., king s., queen s., jumbo; fair-sized, considerable, sizable, good-sized; bulky, massive, massy 322 *weighty*; ample, capacious, voluminous, baggy; comprehensive 205 *broad*; vast, extensive 183 *spacious*; monumental, towering, mountainous 209 *tall*; fine, magnificent, spanking, thumping, thundering, whacking; man-size, life-s., large as life; well-grown, well-built, large-limbed, elephantine; macroscopic, large-scale, megalithic.

huge, immense, enormous, vast, mighty, stonking, mega, grandiose, stupendous, monstrous 32 *prodigious*; record size; colossal, mammoth, dinosaurian, gigantic, giant, giant-like, mountainous; Brobdingnagian, titanic, Herculean, gargantuan; Cyclopean, megalithic; outsize, oversize, overlarge, overweight 32 *exorbitant*; limitless 107 *infinite*.

fleshy, fat, stout, obese, overweight; well-covered, well-upholstered, Falstaffian; plump, ample, plumpish, sonsie, chubby, cuddly, fubsy, podgy, pudgy 205 *thick*; squat, squab, square, dumpy, chunky, stocky 205 *broad*; tubby, portly, corpulent, paunchy, pot-bellied 253 *convex*; puffy, bloated, bosomy, busty; round, rotund, roly-poly, full, full-faced, chubby-f.; double-chinned, dimpled, dimply, buxom, jolly, on the plump side; in condition, in good c., well-fed, well-grown, strapping, hunky, lusty, burly, beefy, brawny 162 *stalwart*; plump as a partridge, fat as butter, fat as a pig.

unwieldy, cumbersome, hulking, lumbering, gangling, lolloping; hulky, lumpy, lumpish, lubberly; too big, elephantine, whale-like, overweight; awkward, muscle-bound 695 *clumsy*.

196 Littleness

N. *littleness*, daintiness etc. adj.; small size 33 *smallness*; lack of height 204 *shortness*; diminutiveness, dwarfishness, stuntedness; scantiness, paucity, exiguity 105 *fewness*; meagreness 206 *thinness*.

minuteness, point; pinpoint, pinhead; crystal; atom, molecule, particle, electron, neutron, proton, quark; nucleus, cell; corpuscle; drop, droplet, dust, grain, g. of sand; seed, mustard s. 33 *small thing*; bubble, button, molehill 639 *trifle*.

miniature 553 *picture*; microphotograph, microdot, microfilm, microfiche 551 *photography*; pocket edition, duodecimo 589 *edition*; thumbnail sketch, epitome 592 *compendium*; model, microcosm; mini version.

dwarf, midget, minikin, pigmy, Lilliputian, halfling, hobbit; little people 970 *elf*; chit, slip, titch; teeny, mite, tot, tiddler 132 *child*; cocksparrow, bantam 33 *small quantity*; pipsqueak, squirt 639 *nonentity*; manikin, doll, puppet, Pinocchio; Tom Thumb, Thumbelina, Hop-o'-my-thumb, homunculus; shrimp, runt, weakling.

Adj. *little 33 small*; petite, dainty, dinky, dolly, elfin; diminutive, mini, pigmy, Lilliputian; no bigger than; wee, titchy, tiny, teeny, teeny-weeny, itsy-witsy; toy, baby, pocket, pocket-size, pocket-handkerchief, pint-size, duodecimo, mini-; miniature, model; portable, handy, compact, bijou; snug, cosy, poky, cramped, no room to swing a cat 206 *narrow*; puny 163 *weak*; petty 33 *inconsiderable*; one-horse 639 *unimportant*.

dwarfish, dwarf, dwarfed, Lilliputian, pigmy, undersized, stunted, wizened, shrunk; squat, dumpy 204 *short*; knee-high, knee-high to a grasshopper.

Vb. *be little*, take up no room, lie in a nutshell, roll up into a ball, fit on the head of a pin.

197 Expansion

N. *expansion*, enlargement, augmentation, aggrandizement 36 *increase*; amplification, supplementation, reinforcement 38 *addition*; hypertrophy, giantism, gigantism; hyperbole 546 *exaggeration*; stretching, extension, spread, deployment, fanning out 75 *dispersion*; ribbon development, urban sprawl 192 *housing*; increment, accretion 40 *adjunct*; upgrowth, overgrowth, development 157 *growth*, 171 *productiveness*; overstaffing, Parkinson's law 637 *superfluity*.

dilation, dilatation, distension, diastole; inflation, reflation, puffing, puff 352 *blowing*; swelling up, turgescence, turgidity, tumescence, intumescence, tumefaction; puffiness, dropsy, tumour 253 *swelling*.

Vb. *expand*, wax, grow larger, increase, snowball 36 *grow*; widen, broaden, flare, splay; spread, extend, sprawl; fan out, deploy, 75 *be dispersed*; spread over, spread like wildfire, overrun, straddle 226 *cover*; rise, prove (e.g. dough);

gather, swell, distend, dilate, fill out; mushroom, balloon, belly; get fat, gain flesh, put on weight, put on the flab; burst at the seams; grow up, spring up, bud, burgeon, shoot, sprout, open, put forth, burst f., blossom, flower, blow, bloom, be out 171 *be fruitful*.

enlarge, aggrandize; make larger, expand; rarefy (by expansion); leaven 310 *elevate*; bore, ream; widen, broaden, let out; open, pull out; stretch, extend 203 *lengthen*; intensify, heighten, deepen, draw out; amplify, supplement, reinforce 38 *add*; double, redouble; develop, build up 36 *augment*; distend, inflate, reflate, pump up, blow up, puff, puff up, puff out 352 *blow*; bulk, thicken; stuff, pad 227 *line*; cram, fill to bursting 54 *fill*; feed up, fatten, plump up, bloat 301 *feed*; enlarge, blow up 551 *photograph*; magnify, overenlarge, overdevelop 546 *exaggerate*.

198 Contraction

N. *contraction*, reduction, abatement, lessening, deflation 37 *diminution*; decrease, shrinkage, diminuendo; curtailment, abbreviation, elision 204 *shortening*; consolidation 324 *condensation*; freezing 382 *refrigeration*; contracting, systole; contractions, labour pains 167 *obstetrics*; attenuation, emaciation, consumption, withering, atrophy; decline, retreat, recession, slump 655 *deterioration*; neck, isthmus, bottleneck, hourglass, wasp-waist 206 *narrowness*; epitome 592 *compendium*.

compression, pressure, compressure, compaction, squeeze, squeezing, stenosis, strangulation; constriction, constringency, astriction, astringency; contractility, contractibility, compressibility.

Vb. *become small*, grow less, lessen, dwindle; take a pay cut, downshift; wane, ebb, fall away 37 *decrease*; shrivel, wither, waste away 51 *decompose*; lose weight, lose flesh 323 *be light*; level off, bottom out; contract, shrink, narrow, taper, taper off, draw in; condense 324 *be dense*; evaporate 338 *vaporize*; pucker, purse.

make smaller, lessen, reduce, scale down, downsize 37 *abate*; contract, shrink, abridge, take in, cut down to life size, dwarf, stunt 204 *shorten*; diet, slim, take off weight 323 *lighten*; taper, narrow, attenuate, thin, emaciate 206 *make thin*; puncture, deflate, rarefy; boil down, evaporate 338 *vaporize*; dehydrate 342 *dry*; cramp, constrict, pinch, nip, squeeze, bind, bandage, corset; draw in, draw tight, strain, tauten 45 *tighten*; draw together, clench 264 *close*, 45 *join*; hug, crush, strangle, strangulate; compress, compact, constipate, condense, nucleate 324 *be dense*; huddle, crowd together; squeeze in, pack tight, pack like sardines, cram, jam 54 *fill*;

squash 216 *flatten*; cramp, restrict 747 *restrain*; limit 232 *circumscribe*; chip away, whittle away, shave, shear, clip, trim, prune, pollard 46 *cut*; scrape, file, grind 332 *pulverize*; fold up, crumple 261 *fold*; roll, press, flatten 258 *smooth*.

199 Distance

N. *distance*, astronomical d., light years 183 *space*; measured distance, mileage, footage 203 *length*; focal distance; elongation, aphelion, apogee; far distance, horizon, skyline; background 238 *rear*; periphery, circumference 233 *outline*; drift, dispersion 282 *deviation*; reach, grasp, compass, span, stride, giant's s. 183 *range*; far cry, long way, fair w., tidy step, day's march, long long trail, marathon.

Adj. distant, distal, peripheral, terminal; far, farther; ulterior; ultimate, farthest, furthest, furthermost; long-distance, long-range; yon, yonder; not local, away, far away; outlying, peripheral; offshore, on the horizon; remote, aloof, farflung, godforsaken; hyperborean, antipodean; out of range, telescopic; lost to sight, lost to view, out of sight 444 *invisible*; off-centre, wide, wide of the mark.

Vb. *be distant*, stretch to, reach to, extend to, spread to, go to, get to, stretch away to, carry to, carry on to 183 *extend*; carry, range; outdistance, outrange, outreach 306 *outdo*; keep one's distance, remain at a d., stay at arm's length, keep off, hold off, stand off, lie off; keep clear of, stand aloof, stand clear of, keep a safe distance, give a wide berth 620 *avoid*.

Adv. *beyond*, further, farther; further on, ahead, in front; clear of, wide of, wide of the mark; below the horizon; up over, down under, over the border, over the hills and far away.

too far, at the back of beyond, out of reach, out of range, out of sight, out of hearing, out of earshot, out of the sphere of, out of bounds.

200 Nearness

N. *nearness*, proximity, propinquity, closeness, near distance, foreground 237 *front*; vicinage, vicinity, neighbourhood 230 *surroundings*; brink, verge 234 *edge*; adjacency 202 *contiguity*; collision course 293 *convergence*; approximation 289 *approach*.

short distance, no d., shortest d., bee-line, short cut; step, short s., no distance, walking d.; striking distance, close quarters, close grips; close range, earshot, stone's throw, spitting distance; short span, inch, millimetre, finger's breadth, hair's breadth 201 *gap*; close-up, close finish, photo f., needle race, near thing 716 *contest*.

Adj. *near*, proximate, proximal; very near, approximate; approximating, close, getting

warm, warm 289 *approaching*; about to meet 293 *convergent*; nearby, wayside, roadside 289 *accessible*; not far, hard by, inshore; near at hand, close at hand, at hand, handy, at one's fingertips, present; near the surface 212 *shallow*; home, local, vicinal, in the neighbourhood; close to, next to, next-door to, neighbouring, bordering on, verging on, adjacent, adjoining, jostling, rubbing shoulders; fronting, facing 237 *frontal*; close, intimate, inseparable; bumper-to-bumper; on one's tail, breathing down one's neck; at close quarters, at close grips; close-run, neck-and-neck, nip and tuck, with nothing between, level, level-pegging; near in blood, related 11 *akin*.

Adv. *near*, not far, locally, in the neighbourhood, in the vicinity; nigh, hard by, fast by, close to, close up to, close upon, in the way, at close range, at close quarters; close behind, right b.; within call, within hearing, within earshot, within a stone's throw, only a step, at no great distance, not far from; on one's doorstep, in one's own backyard; at one's door, at one's feet, at one's elbow, at one's side, under one's nose, at one's fingertips, within reach, close at hand; in the presence of, face to face, eyeball to eyeball; in juxtaposition, next door, side by side, cheek by jowl, tête-à-tête, arm in arm, beside, alongside; on the circumference, on the periphery, on *or* in the confines of, on the skirts of, on the outskirts, at the threshold; brinking on, verging on, on the brink of, on the verge of, on the tip of one's tongue.

nearly, practically, almost, all but; more or less, near enough, roughly, around, somewhere around; in the region of; about, much a., hereabouts, thereabouts, nearabouts, there or thereabouts, circa; closely, approximately, hard on, close on; well-nigh, as good as, on the way to; within an ace of, just about to.

201 Interval

N. *interval*, distance between, space; narrow interval, half-space, hairspace 200 *short distance*; interspace, daylight, head, length; clearance, margin, freeboard 183 *room*; interval of time, timelag; pause, break, intermission, breather, time out, gap year, truce 145 *lull*; hiatus 72 *discontinuity*; interruption, incompleteness, jump, leap; musical interval, tone, semitone, third, fourth, fifth 410 *musical note*.

gap, interstice, mesh 222 *network*; lacuna, cavity, hole, opening, aperture 263 *orifice*; pass, defile, ghat, wind-gap 305 *passage*; firebreak 662 *safeguard*; ditch, dike, trench 351 *drain*; water jump, ha-ha, sunk fence 231 *partition*; ravine, gorge, gully, couloir, chimney, crevasse, canyon 255 *valley*; cleft, crevice, chink, crack, rift, cut, gash, tear, rent, slit 46 *scission*; flaw, fault, breach, break, split, fracture, rupture, fissure, chap 46 *separation*; slot, groove 262 *furrow*; indentation 260 *notch*; seam, join 45 *joint*; leak 298 *outlet*; abyss, chasm 211 *depth*; yawning gulf, void 190 *emptiness*; inlet, creek, gulch 345 *gulf*.

Vb. *space*, interval, space out, place at intervals 46 *set apart*; crack, split, start, gape, dehisce 263 *open*; win by a head, win by a length; clear, show daylight between; lattice, mesh, reticulate.

202 Contiguity

N. *contiguity*, juxtaposition, apposition, proximity, close p. 200 *nearness*; touching 378 *touch*; no interval 71 *continuity*; contact, tangency; abuttal, abutment; intercommunication, osculation; meeting, encounter, confrontation, interface 293 *convergence*; conjunction, syzygy (astronomy) 45 *union*; close contact, adhesion, cohesion 48 *coherence*; coexistence, coincidence, concomitance 89 *accompaniment*; grazing contact, tangent; border, fringe 234 *edge*; borderland, frontier 236 *limit*; buffer state 231 *interjacency*.

Vb. *be contiguous*, overlap 378 *touch*; make contact, come in c., brush, rub, skim, scrape, graze, kiss; join, meet 293 *converge*; stick, adhere 48 *cohere*; lie end to end, abut; abut on, adjoin, reach to, extend to 183 *extend*; sit next to, rub shoulders with, crowd, jostle, elbow; be bumper to bumper, be elbow to elbow, border with, march w., skirt 234 *hem*; coexist, coincide 89 *accompany*; osculate, intercommunicate 45 *connect*; get in touch, contact.

203 Length

N. *length*, longitude; extent, extension; reach, long arm; full length, overall l.; stretch, span, mileage, footage 199 *distance*; perspective 211 *depth*.

line, bar, rule, tape, measuring tape, strip, stripe, streak; spoke, radius; single file, line ahead, crocodile, queue 65 *sequence*; straight line, right l. 249 *straightness*; bent line, fractal 248 *curvature*.

long measure, linear m., measurement of length, micrometry 465 *measurement*; unit of length, finger, hand, hand's breadth, palm, span, cubit; arm's length, fathom; head, length; pace, step; inch, foot, yard; rod, pole, perch; chain, furlong; mile, statute m., geographical m., nautical m., knot, league; millimetre, centimetre, metre, kilometre; degree of latitude, degree of longitude; micro-inch, micron, wavelength; astronomical unit, light year, parsec.

Adj. *long*, lengthy, extensive, a mile long; long-drawn out; lengthened, elongated, outstretched, extended, strung out; shoulderlength, ankle-length, down to . . . ; wire-drawn, lank 206 *lean*; lanky, leggy, long-legged 209 *tall*; as long as my arm, long as a wet week; interminable, no end to 838 *tedious*; polysyllabic, sesquipedalian 570 *diffuse*; uncut, full-length 54 *complete*.

longitudinal, oblong, linear; one-dimensional.

Vb. *lengthen*, stretch, elongate, draw out, wiredraw 206 *make thin*; pull out, stretch o., spreadeagle 197 *expand*; spread oneself out, sprawl 216 *be horizontal*; spread out, string o., deploy 75 *disperse*; extend, pay out, uncoil, unfurl, unroll, unfold 316 *evolve*; let down, drop the hem; produce, continue; prolong, protract; drawl 580 *stammer*.

Adv. *longwise*, longways, lengthwise; along, longitudinally, radially, in line ahead, in single file, in Indian f.; one in front and one behind, in tandem; in a crocodile; in a line, in perspective; at full length, end to end, overall; fore and aft; head to foot, head to tail, stem to stern, top to toe, head to heels, from the crown of the head to the sole of the foot.

204 Shortness

N. *shortness*, squatness etc. adj.; brevity, briefness; transience 114 *brief span*; inch, centimetre 200 *short distance*; low stature, dwarfishness, short legs, duck's disease 196 *littleness*; lack of inches, no height 210 *lowness*; shrinkage; scantiness, exiguity; scarceness 636 *insufficiency*; slippage; concision 569 *conciseness*; short hair, short back and sides, bob, crew cut; shorts, miniskirt.

shortening, abridgment, abbreviation; précis, summary 592 *compendium*; curtailment, cutback, cut, reduction 37 *diminution*; contraction 198 *compression*.

Adj. *short*, brief 114 *transient*; not big, dwarfish, stunted 196 *little*; knee-high to a grasshopper, not tall, squab, squabby, squat, dumpy, fubsy, stumpy, stocky, thickset, stubby 195 *fleshy*, 205 *thick*; not high 210 *low*; pug-nosed, snub-n.; snub, retroussé, blunt; not long, inch-long; skimpy, scanty 636 *insufficient*; foreshortened 246 *distorted*; abbreviated, abridged; shortened, sawn-off; cut, curtailed, docked, beheaded, decapitated, truncated, topless, headless; shaven, shorn, mown; sparing of words, terse 569 *concise*; elliptical (of style); halffinished 55 *unfinished*; epitomized, potted, compact; compacted, compressed.

Vb. *shorten*, abridge, abbreviate, cut; pot, epitomize, boil down, summarize 592 *abstract*; sum up, recapitulate 569 *be concise*; compress, contract, telescope 198 *make smaller*; reduce, diminish 37 *abate*; foreshorten 246 *distort*; take up, put a tuck in, raise the hem, turn up, tuck up, kilt; behead, decapitate, guillotine, axe, chop up 46 *sunder*; cut short, dock, curtail, truncate; cut back, cut down, slash, lop, prune; shear, shave, trim, crop, clip, bob, shingle 46 *cut*; mow, scythe; nip in the bud, stunt, check the growth of 278 *retard*; scrimp, skimp.

205 Breadth. Thickness

N. *breadth*, width, latitude; width across, span, fingerspan, wingspan, wingspread; diameter, radius, gauge, broad g., bore, calibre; broadness, expanse, superficial extent, amplitude 183 *range*; wideness, fullness, bagginess.

Adj. *broad*, wide, expansive, unspanned 183 *spacious*; wide-cut, full, flared, ample, baggy; fan-like, umbelliferous; outspread, outstretched, splayed out; bell-bottomed, broad-b., broad-based; callipygian, steatopygous, wide-hipped; broad in the beam, beamy, widebodied; wide as a church door; broad-brimmed, wide-angle (lens); wide-mouthed 263 *open*; broad-shouldered, broad-chested 162 *stalwart*; wide-ranging, global 79 *general*.

thick, stout, dumpy, squat 204 *short*; thickset, tubby, beefy, stubby 195 *fleshy*; thick-lipped, full-l.; thick-necked, bull-n.; thick-skinned, pachydermatous; thick-ribbed, barrel-chested, broad-shouldered 162 *strong*; thick as a rope; pyknic, endomorphic; solidly built 324 *dense*; semiliquid, ropy, lumpy, to be cut with a knife 354 *viscid*.

Adv. *broadways*, broadwise, breadthways, breadthwise; widthways, widthwise; broadways on 239 *sideways*.

206 Narrowness. Thinness

N. *narrowness*, tightness etc. adj.; narrow interval, closeness, tight squeeze, crack, chink, hair's breadth, finger's b. 200 *short distance*; lack of breadth, length without b., line, strip, stripe, streak; vein, capillary 208 *filament*; knife-edge, razor's edge, tightrope, wire; narrow gauge; bottleneck, narrows, strait 345 *gulf*; ridge, col, saddle 209 *high land*; ravine, gully 255 *valley*; pass, defile 305 *passage*; neck, isthmus, landbridge 624 *bridge*.

thinness, tenuity, fineness 325 *rarity*; slenderness, gracility; skinniness, emaciation, anorexia (nervosa), consumption; scrag, skin and bone, skeleton; miserable specimen, scarecrow, rake, beanpole, broomstick, shadow, spindle-shanks, barebones; haggardness, lantern jaws, hatchet face, sunken cheeks; thread, paper, tissue 422 *transparency*; shaving, splinter 33 *small thing*; slip, wisp 208 *filament*.

Adj. *narrow*, not wide, single track; strait,

tight, close; compressed, pinched, unexpanded; not thick, fine, thin, wafer-thin 422 *transparent*; attenuated, spun, fine-s., wire-drawn 203 *long*; thread-like, capillary; tapering 293 *convergent*; slight, slightly-built, wispy, delicate 163 *weak*; gracile, attenuate, slender, slim, svelte, slinky, sylph-like; willowy, rangy, skinny; long-legged, leggy, lanky, gangling; narrow-waisted, wasp-w.; isthmian; bottlenecked.

lean, thin, ectomorphic, spare, rangy, wiry; meagre, skinny, bony; cadaverous, fleshless, skin-and-bone, skeletal, raw-boned, haggard, gaunt, drawn, lantern-jawed, sunken-eyed, hatchet-faced; twiggy, spindly, spindle-shanked, spidery; undersized, weedy, scrawny, scrubby, scraggy; consumptive, emaciated, anorexic, wasted, withered, wizened, pinched, peaky 651 *sick*; sere, shrivelled 131 *ageing*; starved, starveling 636 *underfed*; wraith-like, scarecrow-like, worn to a shadow, thin as a rake, thin as a lath, without an ounce of flesh to spare.

Vb. *make thin*, contract, compress, pinch, nip 198 *make smaller*; starve, diet, reduce, lose weight; slim; draw, wiredraw, spin, spin fine 203 *lengthen*; attenuate 325 *rarefy*.

207 Layer

N. *layer*, stratum, substratum, underlay, floor 214 *base*; outcrop 254 *projection*; bed, course, range, row; zone, vein, seam, lode; thickness, ply; storey, tier, floor, mezzanine f.; entresol, landing; stage, planking, platform 218 *frame*; deck, top d., lower d., upper d., orlop d., quarterdeck, bridge 275 *ship*; film 423 *opacity*; bloom, dross, scum; patina, coating, coat, undercoat, veneer, top layer, top-dressing, topcoat 226 *covering*; scale, scab, membrane, peel, pellicle, sheathe, bark, integument 226 *skin*; level, water l., water table 216 *horizontality*; atmospheric layer 340 *atmosphere*.

208 Filament

N. *filament*, flagellum, cilium, lash, eyelash, beard, down 259 *hair*; barb, feather, harl 259 *plumage*; flock, lock, shred of wool, thread, lock of hair, strand, wisp, curl; fringe 234 *edging*; fibre, fibril, fibrilla, rootlet, stalk, tendril 366 *plant*; whisker, antenna, antennule 378 *feeler*; gossamer, cobweb, web 222 *network*; capillary, vein, venule, veinlet 351 *conduit*; ramification, branch; wire, element, wick 420 *torch*.

fibre, natural f., animal f., hair, camel h., rabbit h.; Angora, goat's hair, mohair, cashmere; llama hair, alpaca, vicuna; wool, Shetland w., botany w., merino; silk, real s., wild silk, tussore, floss; vegetable fibre, cotton, cotton wool, silk cotton, kapok; linen, flax; manila, hemp; jute, sisal, coir; hards; tow, oakum; bast, raffia;

worsted, yarn; spun yarn, continuous filament y.; thread, twine, twist, strand, cord, string, line, rope 47 *cable*; artificial fibre, man-made f., acrylic f., rayon, nylon 222 *textile*; staple, denier 331 *texture*.

strip, fascia, band, bandage; belt, cord, thong, braid, tape, strap, ribbon, ribband; fillet; lath, slat, batten, stave; shaving, wafer; splinter, shiver, shred 53 *piece*; streak, stripe, strake 203 *line*.

209 Height

N. *height*, perpendicular length; altitude, elevation, ceiling, pitch 213 *summit*; loftiness, steepness, dizzy height; tallness, stature; eminence, sublimity; sky, stratosphere 340 *atmosphere*; zenith.

high land, height, highlands, heights, steeps, uplands, moor, moorland, downs, rolling country; rising ground, rise, bank, ben, brae, slope, climb 220 *incline*; hill, eminence, mount, mountain; fell, scar, tor, alp, Mont Blanc, Everest, mountain range, chain, sierra, cordillera, massif, Alps, Himalayas, Andes, Rockies; ridge, col, saddle, spur, headland, foothill 254 *projection*; crest, peak, pike, hilltop 213 *summit*; steepness, precipice, cliff, white cliffs of Dover; crag, scar, bluff, steep, escarpment; gorge, canyon, ravine 255 *valley*; summit level, mesa; plateau, tableland 216 *horizontality*.

high structure, column, pillar, turret, tower, pile, noble p., skyscraper, high-rise flats, tower block 164 *edifice*; chimney stack, steeple, spire, flèche, belfry, campanile 990 *church exterior*; minaret; obelisk, Cleopatra's Needle; dome, cupola 226 *roof*; colossus 554 *sculpture*; mausoleum, pyramid 364 *tomb*; pagoda 990 *temple*; ziggurat, Tower of Babel; Eiffel Tower; mast, topmast; flagstaff, pikestaff; pole, maypole; lamppost, standard; pylon, radio mast; masthead 213 *summit*; watchtower, lookout, crow's nest, eyrie 438 *view*; column of smoke, mushroom cloud.

tall creature, giraffe, elephant, mammoth, ostrich, longlegs, beanpole, six-footer, grenadier, colossus 195 *giant*.

Adj. *high*, high-up, sky-high; eminent, uplifted, exalted, lofty, sublime, supernal; highest 213 *topmost*; perching, hanging (gardens); aerial, airborne, flying; soaring, aspiring; towering, skyscraping; steep, dizzy, giddy; knee-high, thigh-h., breast-h., shoulder-h..

tall, lanky, leggy, rangy 206 *narrow*; long-legged, ostrich-necked, giraffelike, beanpole-like; colossal.

Vb. *be high*, – tall etc. adj.; tower, rear, soar; surmount, clear, overtop, overlook, dominate, command 34 *be superior*; overhang, overshadow

226 *cover*; beetle, impend 254 *jut*; hover, hang over 217 *hang*; culminate, peak, be at the zenith 725 *climax*; mount, bestride, bestraddle; grow taller, shoot up, add to one's inches; rise 308 *ascend*; stand on tiptoe, stand on another's shoulders 310 *lift oneself*.

make higher, heighten, build up, raise, hold aloft 310 *elevate*.

210 Lowness

N. *lowness*, debasement 311 *lowering*; prostration; sea level, flatness 216 *horizontality*; flats, levels 347 *marsh*; levelness, steppe 348 *plain*; low elevation, lowlands, pimple 196 *littleness*; gentle slope, nursery s., slight gradient 220 *incline*; lower level, foothill 35 *inferiority*; bottom, hollow, depression 255 *valley*; sea-floor 343 *ocean*; depths, cellar, nether regions, basement, well, mine 211 *depth*; floor, foot 214 *base*; underside 240 *contraposition*; nadir, lowest point, the pits; low water, low ebb, low tide 350 *current*.

Adj. *low*, not high, squat 204 *short*; crouched, crouching, stooping, slouching, bending; recumbent, laid low, prostrate 216 *supine*; low-lying, flat, at sea level 216 *flat*; low-level, single-storey; lower, under, nether, 35 *inferior*; sunken, lowered 255 *concave*; flattened, rounded, blunt; subterranean, subterraneous, underground, below the surface, submarine 523 *latent*, 211 *deep*; underfoot 745 *subjected*.

Adv. *under*, beneath, underneath, neath; below, at the foot of; underfoot, underground, downstairs, below stairs; at a low ebb; below par.

211 Depth

N. *depth*, drop, fall; deepness etc. adj.; perspective 203 *length*; vertical range, profundity, lowest point, nadir; deeps, deep water 343 *ocean*; unknown depths, unfathomable d. 663 *pitfall*; depression, bottom 255 *valley*; hollow, pit, shaft, mine, well 255 *cavity*; abyss, abysm, chasm 201 *gap*; vault, crypt, dungeon 194 *cellar*; cave, pothole, catacomb, bowels of the earth 210 *lowness*; pot-holing, deep-sea diving 309 *descent*; caisson disease, the bends, underworld, bottomless pit 972 *hell*; diving bell, submarine.

Adj. *deep*, steep, plunging, profound; abysmal, yawning, cavernous; abyssal, deep-sea; deep-seated, deep-rooted 153 *fixed*; unplumbed, bottomless, fathomless; unsounded, unfathomed, subterranean, underground, underwater, undersea, submarine; buried, deep in, immersed, submerged; drowned; knee-deep, ankle-d.; infernal; benthic; depth-measuring, bathymetric.

Vb. *be deep*. – profound etc. adj.; deepen,

hollow, fathom, sound, take soundings, plumb, heave the lead; drop, lower 311 *let fall*; go deep, plumb the depths, touch bottom, reach rock bottom, be on one's knees, reach one's nadir; sink to the bottom, plunge 313 *founder*.

212 Shallowness

N. *shallowness*, no depth, superficiality 4 *insubstantiality*; film 223 *exteriority*; veneer, thin coat 226 *skin*; superficial wound, scratch, pinprick, graze 639 *trifle*; shoals, shallows; pond, puddle 346 *lake*; light soil, stony ground 344 *soil*.

Adj. *shallow*, slight, superficial 4 *insubstantial*; surface, skin-deep; shoaly, light, thin 206 *narrow*.

213 Summit

N. *summit*, sky, heaven, seventh h., cloud nine; pole, north p., south p.; top, peak, crest, apex, pinnacle, crown; maximum height, pitch; zenith, meridian, high noon, culmination, apogee; culminating point, crowning p.; acme, ne plus ultra, peak of perfection 646 *perfection*; crest of the wave, top of the tree 730 *prosperity*; high-water mark 236 *limit*; climax, turning point 137 *crisis*; dividing line, watershed, Great Divide 231 *partition*; copingstone, keystone; lintel, pediment, entablature, architrave, epistyle; capital, cornice.

vertex, apex, crown, top, cap, brow, head; tip, cusp, spike, point, nib, end 69 *extremity*; spire, finial 990 *church exterior*; stairhead, landing 308 *ascent*; acropolis 713 *fort*; summit level, hilltop, mountaintop, plateau, tableland 209 *high land*; treetop, housetop, rooftop; gable, gable-end; leads, ceiling 226 *roof*; upper chamber, garret, loft 194 *attic*; top storey; topside, upper deck, bridge 275 *ship*; topmast, masthead, crow's nest 209 *high structure*.

head, headpiece, pate, poll, sconce; noddle, nob, nut, noggin, coco, conk, bonce, crumpet, bean, block, chump; upper storey, belfry; brow, dome, temple, forehead; loaf, brain, grey matter 498 *intelligence*; epicranium, pericranium; scalp, crown, double c.; skull, cranium, brainpan 255 *cavity*; fontanelle; craniology, craniometry, cranioscopy, craniotomy; phrenology; brain scanning, brain scan, neuroradiology, brain surgery, neurosurgery.

Adj. *topmost*, top, highest 209 *high*; uppermost, upmost 34 *supreme*; polar, apical, crowning; capital, head; culminating, meridian; tiptop, super 644 *best*.

Vb. *crown*, cap, head, top, pinnacle, tip, surmount, crest, overtop 209 *be high*; culminate, consummate 725 *climax*; go up top, take top place, go into the lead 34 *be superior*; top out, put the finishing touches to 54 *make complete*.

214 Base

N. *base*, foot, toe, skirt 210 *lowness*; bottom, fundus, root; lowest point, the depths, rock bottom, nadir, low water; footing, foundation 218 *basis*; the nitty gritty; fundamental 68 *origin*; groundwork, substructure, infrastructure, chassis 218 *frame*; baseboard, plinth, pedestal 218 *stand*; substratum, floor, underlayer, bed, bedrock; subsoil, pan, hardpan; ground, earth, foundations; footing, sill; damp course, dampproof course; basement, ground floor 194 *cellar*; flooring, pavement, paving-stone, flagstone; carpet 226 *floor-cover*; skirting board, wainscot, plinth, dado; keel, keelson; hold, bilge; sump, drain 649 *sink*.

foot, feet, tootsies, dogs, plates; beetle-crusher; forefoot, hindfoot; sole, heel, Achilles' tendon, instep, arch; toe, toe-nail, big toe, hallux; trotter, hoof, cloven h.; paw, pad; claw, talon 778 *pincers*; ankle, ankle-bone, tarsus, metatarsus, fetlock, pastern.

215 Verticality

N. *verticality*, the vertical, erectness, uprightness, upright carriage; steepness, sheerness, precipitousness 209 *height*; perpendicularity, right angle, square; elevation, azimuth circle; vertical line, plumbline, plummet; vertical structure, upright, pole, stalagmite 218 *pillar*; precipice, cliff, bluff, scarp, steep 209 *high land*; perpendicular drop, vertical height, rise.

Adj. *vertical*, upright, erect, standing; perpendicular, rectangular, sheer, abrupt, steep, precipitous 209 *high*; straight, plumb; straight up, straight down; upstanding, standing up, on one's feet, on one's legs, on one's hindlegs; bolt upright, stiff as a ramrod, unbowed; rampant, rearing; on end.

Vb. *be vertical*, stick up, cock up, bristle, stand on end; stand erect, stand upright, hold oneself straight; sit up, stand up, straighten up; rise, stand, be upstanding, rise to one's feet, get to one's feet, ramp, rear; keep standing, have no seat, sit on one's thumb.

216 Horizontality

N. *horizontality*, horizontalness; horizontal angle, azimuth; horizontal line, rule; horizontal course, strike; flatness 258 *smoothness*; level, plane, level plane; sea level, water l., water table; stratum; slab, tablet, table 207 *layer*; level stretch, steppe 348 *plain*; flats 347 *marsh*; platform, ledge 254 *projection*; terrace, esplanade; plateau, tableland 209 *high land*; billiard table, bowling green, cricket ground, croquet lawn 724 *arena*; gridiron, platter 194 *plate*; spirit level, T square 465 *gauge*; skyline, horizon, false h., horizon line 236 *limit*.

flattener, iron, flatiron, steam iron, mangle, press, trouser p.; rolling pin, roller, garden r., steamroller 258 *smoother*; bulldozer, juggernaut 168 *destroyer*.

Adj. *flat*, horizontal, two-dimensional, level, plane, even, flush 258 *smooth*; trodden, flat as a pancake; unwrinkled, smooth, smooth as a baby's bottom, smooth as glass, calm, calm as a millpond.

supine, flat on one's back, flat out; prone, face down, prostrate; recumbent; lying down, couchant; abed, laid up, laid out; stretched out, sprawling, spreadeagled, lolling.

Vb. *be horizontal*, lie, lie down, lie flat, lie prostrate, lie on one's back; measure one's length, recline, couch, sprawl, spread-eagle, loll 311 *sit down*; straighten out, level out, bottom o.

flatten, lay out, roll o., lay down, spread; lay flat, beat f., tread f., stamp down, trample d., squash; make flush, align, level, even, grade, plane 28 *equalize*; iron, iron out, roll out 258 *smooth*; pat down, smooth d, prostrate, knock down, floor, ground 311 *fell*.

217 Pendency

N. *pendency*, suspension, hanging, dangle; set, hang, drape; droop.

hanging object, hanging ornament, mobile, pendant, dangler, drop, eardrop, earring, dangling e. 844 *jewellery*; tassel, bobble, tag 844 *trimming*; hangings, draperies, drapes, curtains, arras, tapestry 226 *covering*; train, skirt, coat-tails; flap, lappet, tippet 228 *headgear*; pigtail, tail 67 *sequel*, 259 *hair*; dewlap, lobe, appendix 40 *adjunct*; pendulum, bob, swing, hammock 317 *oscillation*; chandelier 420 *lamp*; icicle, stalactite.

hanger, coat h., curtain rod, curtain ring, runner, rack; hook, coathook, peg, knob, nail, hatstand 218 *prop*; suspender, braces, suspender belt 228 *underwear*; clothesline 47 *cable*; clothes-horse, airer 218 *frame*; crane; spar, mast 218 *pillar*; gallows, gibbet 964 *pillory*.

Adj. *hanging*, pendent, pendulous, pensile; hanging from, dependent, suspended, dangling etc. vb.; hanging the head, nodding, drooping, lowering, overhanging; beetling 254 *projecting*.

Vb. *hang*, be pendent, drape, set; hang down, draggle, trail, flow; hang on to, swing from; swing, sway, dangle, bob; hang the head, nod, loll, droop, sag, swag; hang in the wind, hang over, hover, lour; suspend, hang up, append 45 *join*.

218 Support

N. *support*, support, mounting, bearing; carriage, undercarriage, carrier, underframe, chassis; buttress, flying b., abutment, bulwark, embankment, wall, retaining w.; underpinning, shore, jack; flagstaff, jackstaff, stanchion, rod, bar, transom, brace, strut; stay, mainstay, guy, shrouds, rigging; sprit, boom, spar, mast, yard, yard-arm, crosstree 254 *projection*; trunk, stem, stalk, caudex, pedicle, pedicel, peduncle 366 *plant*; arch, ogive 248 *curve*; keystone, headstone, cornerstone, springer; cantilever; pier (**see** *pillar*); strapping, bandage, elastic b., jockstrap, truss, splint; stiffener, whalebone; corset 228 *underwear*; yoke 217 *hanger*; rest, headrest, backrest, footrest, stirrup; banisters, handrail (**see** *handle*); foothold 778 *retention*; wedge 702 *obstacle*; staff, baton, stick, cane, alpenstock, crutch, crook, shepherd's c.; leg support, splint, calliper, irons; bracket (**see** *shelf*); trivet, hob (**see** *stand*); life-support machine, collarbone, worldbearer, patron.

handle, holder, pen h., cigarette h. 194 *receptacle*; hilt, pommel, haft; knob, doorhandle; lug, ear, loop; railing, handrail, rail, poop r., taffrail, banisters, balustrade; shaft; handlebar, tiller; winder, crank, crankhandle; lever, trigger 630 *tool*.

basis, foundation, footings, deck; pallet, sleeper; substratum 207 *layer*; ground, groundwork, floor, bed, bedrock, rock bottom 214 *base*; sill *or* cill; flooring, pavement 226 *paving*; terra firma 344 *land*.

stand, tripod, trivet, hob; table mat, coaster; anvil, block, bench; trolley, tea trolley; table, console t., coffee t., card t., gateleg t., drop-leaf t., refectory t., board; sideboard, dresser, Welsh d. 194 *cabinet*; work table, desk, counter; pedestal, plinth, podium; platform, launching pad, launchpad, gantry; emplacement; footplate; landing; landing stage, pier; dais, pulpit, stage; doorstep, threshold; step, stair, tread, rung.

seat, throne, woolsack; bank, bench, form, settle; bucket seat, box s., rumble s., dicky; pew, choirstall, misericord 990 *church interior*; stall, fauteuil 594 *theatre*; chair, armchair, easy chair, wing c., club c., rocking c., revolving c., basket c., Windsor c., high c., deck c., lounger; chaise longue; sofa, settee, futon, divan, couch, studio c., ottoman, chesterfield, loveseat, windowseat; pouffe, stool, footstool, kitchen stool, campstool; prie-dieu, hassock; saddle, pillion, pad, howdah; ducking-stool 964 *pillory*; electric chair; lap; mat 226 *floor-cover*.

bed, cot, crib, cradle, bassinet; marriage bed, bridal b., double b., single b., king-size b., bunk b., bunk; bed settee, daybed, couch; tester, four-poster; charpoy, truckle bed, trundle b., camp b., pallet, airbed, futon, bedroll, shakedown; hammock 217 *hanging object*; sick bed, litter, hurdle, stretcher 658 *hospital*; bier 364 *funeral*;

bedding, duvet 226 *coverlet*; bedstead, divan; headboard.

cushion, pillow; bolster; mattress, palliasse; squab, hassock, kneeler.

beam, balk, joist, girder, box g., rafter, purlin, tie beam, truss 47 *bond*; summer, bressummer; wall-plate 226 *roof*; crossbeam, transom, crossbar, traverse; architrave, lintel.

pillar, shaft, pier, pile, pole, stake, stud 331 *structure*; post, king post, queen p., crown p.; jamb, door j., doorpost; stanchion, puncheon; newelpost, banister, baluster; mullion; pilaster, column, Doric c., Ionic c., Corinthian c., Tuscan c.; caryatid, telamon, atlantes; spinal column, spine, backbone, vertebral column, vertebrae; neck, cervix.

pivot, fulcrum, lever, purchase; hinge 45 *joint*; pole, axis; gimbals; axle, swivel, spindle, arbor, pintle 315 *rotator*; bearing, gudgeon, trunnion; rowlock, tholepin; centreboard, keel.

shelf, bookshelf, ledge 254 *projection*; corbel, bracket, console; retable, niche 194 *compartment*; sill, windowsill, mantelpiece, mantelshelf, rack, dresser 194 *cabinet*; desktop, counter, worktop, plank, board, table, leaf, slab.

frame, skeleton, ribs; framework, infrastructure, staging, scaffolding 331 *structure*; trellis, espalier; chassis, fuselage, body (of a car), undercarriage; trestle; easel, clotheshorse; housing 235 *enclosure*; picture frame, window f., sash 233 *outline*.

Vb. *support*, sustain, bear, carry, hold, shoulder; uphold, hold up, bear up, buoy up; prop, shore up, underprop, underpin, jack up 310 *elevate*; buttress, bolster, bolster up, cushion; reinforce, underset 162 *strengthen*; bandage, brace, truss 45 *tighten*; steady, stay; cradle, pillow, cup, cup one's chin; maintain, give aliment, give alimony 633 *provide*; give one a hand, back up, give support, lend s., furnish s., afford s., supply s. 703 *aid*; frame, set, mount 235 *enclose*; be the infrastructure, bottom, ground, found, base 153 *stabilize*; stand, endure, survive, stand up to, stand the strain, take the s. 635 *suffice*.

219 Parallelism

N. *parallelism*, non-convergence, nondivergence, equidistance, coextension, collimation, concentricity; parallel, correspondence 28 *equality*; parallel lines, lines of latitude; tramlines, rails, railway lines; parallel bars; parallelogram, parallelepiped.

220 Obliquity

N. *obliquity*, obliqueness, skewness; diagonal; rhomboid 247 *angular figure*; oblique angle,

inclination 247 *angularity*; indirection, indirectness, squint; curvature, camber, bend, z-bend, chicane, humpback 248 *curve*; crookedness, zigzag, chevron; switchback 251 *meandering*; oblique motion, circumlocution, digression, swerve, lurch, stagger 282 *deviation*; splay, bias, twist, warp 246 *distortion*; leaning, list, tip, cant; slope, slant, tilt, pitch, rakish angle; sloping face; sloping edge, bevel, bezel; inclined plane, ramp, chute, slide; Tower of Pisa, leaning tower; measurement of inclination 247 *angular measure*.

incline, rise, ascent; ramp, acclivity, gradient; hill, rising ground, hillock; hillside 239 *laterality*; declivity, fall, dip, downhill 309 *descent*; gentle slope, nursery s.; escarpment, steepness, cliff, precipice 215 *verticality*; scarp 713 *fortification*; talus, bank, scree, landslip, landslide.

Adj. *sloping*, uphill, rising; downhill, falling, declining, dipping; anticlinal, synclinal; declivitous, steep, abrupt, sheer, precipitous, vertiginous, breakneck 215 *vertical*.

Vb. *be oblique*, be askew, be awry, be agley; incline, lean, tilt; pitch, slope, slant, shelve, dip, decline 309 *descend*; rise, climb 308 *ascend*; cut, cut across, transect 222 *cross*; lean, list, tip, lean over, bank, heel, careen, cant; bend, sag, give; bend over 311 *stoop*; walk sideways, edge, sidle, sidestep; look sideways, squint; zigzag; jink, dodge, duck, swerve; diverge, converge.

221 Inversion

N. *inversion*, turning back to front, palindrome; turning inside out, eversion; turning backwards, retroversion, reversal 148 *reversion*; turning inward, introversion; turning over, capsizal (**see** *overturning*); turn of the tide, return 286 *regression*; oppositeness 14 *contrariety*, 240 *contraposition*; transposition, metathesis 151 *interchange*; inverted order, chiasmus 519 *trope*; spoonerism.

overturning, capsizal, upset, purler, spill; somersault, summerset, cartwheel, handspring; subversion, undermining, overthrowing 149 *revolution*.

Vb. *be inverted*, turn round, go r., wheel r., swing r., turn about, face a., right about turn 286 *turn back*; turn over, heel o., keel o., capsize, turn head over heels, turn turtle, turn topsyturvy, be arsy-versy; tilt over 220 *be oblique*; go over, topple o. 309 *tumble*; do a handstand, stand on one's head; loop the loop; reverse, back, back away, go backwards 286 *regress*; be back to front, be inside out.

invert, transpose, put the cart before the horse 151 *interchange*; reverse, turn the tables; turn back; turn down 261 *fold*; introvert, turn inside out, upend, upturn, overturn, tip over, spill, upset, overset, capsize; turn topsy-turvy.

Adv. *inversely*, vice versa; contrariwise, quite the reverse, just the opposite, on the contrary, other way round; back to front, upside down; arsy-versy, topsy-turvy, head over heels; face down, face downwards, bottom side up.

222 Crossing: intertexture

N. *crossing*, crisscross, transection, intersection; decussation, X-shape; intertexture, interlacement, intertwinement, interweaving 844 *pattern*; braid, wreath, plait, pigtail 251 *convolution*; entanglement, intricacy, skein, cat's cradle 61 *complexity*; crossroads, intersection, roundabout, interchange, road junction 624 *road*; level crossing 624 *railway*; viaduct, flyover, overpass, underpass, subway 624 *bridge*, 305 *traffic control*.

cross, crux, rood, crucifix 988 *ritual object*; pectoral 989 *vestments*; ankh, ansate cross, tau c., Latin c., c. of Lorraine, Greek c., Maltese c., Celtic c., St Anthony's C., St Andrew's C.; saltire, crosslet 547 *heraldry*; gammadion, swastika, fylfot; crossbones, skull and c. 547 *flag*; crossbar, transom 218 *beam*.

network, reticulation, meshwork, netting, wire n., chicken wire; webbing, matting, wickerwork, basketwork, trellis, wattle; honeycomb, lattice, grating, grid, grille, gridiron; craquelure; tracery, fretwork, filigree 844 *ornamental art*; lace, crochet, knitting, darning, tatting, macramé 844 *needlework*; web, cobweb; net, fishnet, seine, purse-s., drag-net, trawl, beam t. 235 *enclosure*; plexus, mesh, reticle; chain, group, interconnection.

textile, weave, web, loom; woven stuff; bolt, roll, length, piece, cloth, stuff, material; broadcloth, fabric, tissue, suiting; batik 844 *ornamental art*; jute, hessian, gunny, sacking, hopsack, canvas, sailcloth, duck; ticking, crash, huckaback, towelling, terry t., candlewick; chintz, cretonne, damask, brocade, brocatelle, grosgrain, rep, chenille, tapestry 226 *covering*; mohair, cashmere; alpaca, vicuna, angora 208 *fibre*; wool, worsted, grogram; frieze, felt, baize; homespun, khadar, duffel, kersey, tweed, serge, shalloon, bombazine, gabardine, doeskin; flannel, swanskin, swansdown; paisley, jacquard 844 *pattern*; stockinette, jersey, tricot, nainsook, flannelette, winceyette; velvet, velveteen, velour; corduroy, needlecord; cotton, denim, drill, nankeen, cavalry twill, khaki; fustian, moleskin, sharkskin; poplin, calico, dimity, gingham, madras, seersucker, piqué; batiste, organdie, organza; silesia, cheesecloth, muslin, mull, voile, percale; cambric, lawn, toile, holland, linen; silk, surah, foulard, georgette, crêpe

de chine, chiffon, mousseline; satin, sateen, taffeta, moire; tussore *or* tussah, shantung, pongee; ninon; tulle, net, gauze; lace, guipure; rayon, nylon, Terylene (tdmk), Crimplene (tdmk), polyester, Courtelle (tdmk), Acrilan (tdmk), fibreglass 208 *fibre*.

weaving, texture; web, warp, weft, woof, selvedge; nap, pile 259 *hair*; frame, loom, shuttle; weaver, knitter; knitting machine, sewing m.; spinning wheel, distaff, whorl; spinner, spider, weaverbird; Arachne, Penelope.

Adj. *crossed*, crossing, cross, crisscross; quadrivial; diagonal, transverse, cross-eyed, squinting; decussate, X-shaped, quincunxial; cross-legged, cruciform, crucial, cruciate, forked, furcate 247 *angular*; plexiform; knotted, matted, tangled, balled-up, ravelled 61 *complex*; pleached, plashed, plaited, braided, interlaced, interwoven; textile, loomed, woven, hand-woven, tweedy; twill, herringbone; trellised, latticed, honeycombed, mullioned, barred; corded, ribbed, streaked, striped 437 *variegated*.

Vb. *cross*, crisscross, cross over, cross under 305 *pass*; intersect, cut 220 *be oblique*; decussate, inosculate, interdigitate; splice, dovetail, link 45 *join*; reticulate, mesh, net, knot; fork, bifurcate.

weave, loom; pleach, plash, plait, braid; felt, twill, knit, crochet, darn; spin, slub.

223 Exteriority

N. *exteriority*, the external; outwardness, externality 230 *surroundings*; periphery, circumference, sidelines 233 *outline*; exterior, outward appearance 445 *appearance*; superficiality, surface, superstratum, crust, cortex, shell, integument 226 *skin*; outer side, face, facet, façade 237 *front*; other side 240 *contraposition*; externalism; externalization, extroversion, extrovert 6 *extrinsicality*; outside, out of doors, open air; outer space 199 *distance*; extraterritoriality 57 *exclusion*; foreignness 59 *extraneousness*; eccentricity 84 *nonconformity*; outsider 84 *nonconformist*.

Adj. *exterior*, exoteric, outward; external 10 *unrelated*; peripheral; outer, outermost, outlying, extraterrestrial 199 *distant*; outside, outboard; outdoor, extramural; foreign 59 *extraneous*; extraterrestrial, extraterritorial 57 *excluding*; extrovert, outward-looking 6 *extrinsic*; centrifugal; exogenous, eccentric; surface, superficial, epidermal, cortical; skin-deep 212 *shallow*; facial 237 *frontal*.

Adv. *externally*, outwardly, outwards, superficially, on the surface; on the face of it, to the outsider; outside, out, out of doors, in the cold, in the sun, in the open, in the open air, al fresco.

224 Interiority

N. *interiority*, interior, inside, indoors; inner surface, undersurface; endoderm 226 *skin*; sapwood, heartwood 366 *wood*; inmost being, heart's blood, soul; heart, centre, breast, bosom 225 *centrality*; inland, Midlands, heartland, hinterland, up-country; the nitty gritty, pith, marrow 3 *substance*; substratum 214 *base*; pervasion 189 *presence*, 231 *interjacency*; deepness, cave, pit, pothole, recesses 211 *depth*; introversion 5 *intrinsicality*; self-absorption, egocentrism 932 *selfishness*.

insides 193 *contents*; inner man or woman, viscera, vitals; heart; lungs, lights; liver, kidneys, spleen; offal 301 *meat*; bowels, entrails, innards, guts, tripe; intestines, colon, rectum; abdomen, belly, paunch, underbelly; womb, uterus; stomach, tummy 194 *stomach*; chest, breast, bosom, solar plexus.

Adj. *interior*, internal, inward 5 *intrinsic*; inside, inner, innermost 225 *central*; inland; domestic, home; intimate, familiar 490 *known*; indoor, intramural, shut in, enclosed; built-in, inwrought; endemic; deep-seated, deep-rooted, in-grown 153 *fixed*; intestinal, visceral; intravenous, subcutaneous; interstitial 231 *interjacent*; inward-looking, introvert 5 *intrinsic*; endogamous; endogenous.

Adv. *inside*, within, in, deep down; inwardly, intimately; deeply, profoundly, at heart; within doors, indoors, at home, en famille, chez, at the sign of.

225 Centrality

N. *centrality*, centralness; concentricity; centralization, focalization, concentration 324 *condensation*; central position 231 *interjacency*; midriff, waistline, centreline.

centre, dead c.; centroid, centre of gravity, centre of pressure, metacentre; nerve centre, ganglion; centre of activity, focal point 76 *focus*; epicentre; storm centre; heart, core, kernel 5 *essential part*; nub, hub; nucleus, nucleolus; navel, umbilicus; spine, backbone, vertebrae, midrib; marrow, pith 224 *interiority*; pole, axis, fulcrum, centreboard 218 *pivot*; centre point, mid p. 70 *middle*; fess-point 547 *heraldry*; eye, pupil; bull's-eye, target 617 *objective*.

Adj. *central*, centric, centrical; nuclear, nucleolar; centremost, midmost 70 *middle*; axial, focal, pivotal; umbilical; concentric; geocentric; spinal, vertebral; centripetal; metropolitan, chief, head 34 *supreme*.

Vb. *centralize*, centre, focus; zero in on, centre upon; concentrate, nucleate, consolidate 324 *be dense*.

226 Covering

N. *covering*, capping etc. vb.; superimposition, overlaying; overlap, overlapping; coating, stratification 207 *layer*; veneer, top layer, top dressing, mulch, topsoil 344 *soil*; topping, icing, frosting 844 *ornamentation*; cover, lid; ledger 364 *tomb*; hatch, trapdoor; flap, shutter; film 423 *opacity*; glass, watch glass, crystal 422 *transparency*; cap, top, plug, bung, cork 264 *stopper*; plaster, Elastoplast (tdmk), Band-Aid (tdmk) 658 *surgical dressing*; carapace, shell, tortoiseshell 326 *hardness*; mail, plate 713 *armour*; shield, cowl, bonnet, hood (of a car); scab; crust, fur 649 *dirt*; capsule, ferrule, sheath, involucre, envelope 194 *receptacle*; pillowcase, pillowslip, cushion cover; table cloth, tray c.; chair cover, antimacassar; soft furnishings, loose covers; hangings, curtains, drapes 217 *hanging object*; wallpaper 227 *lining*.

roof, cupola 253 *dome*; mansard roof, hipped r., pitched r., gable r., flat r., housetop, rooftop 213 *vertex*; leads, slates, slating, tiles, tiling, pantile, shingle, thatch, thatching, corrugated iron 631 *building material*; eaves 234 *edge*; ceiling, deck; vaulting, vault; rafters 218 *beam*.

canopy, tilt, awning, sunblind 421 *screen*; marquee, pavilion, big top; tent, bell tent, ridge t., frame t.; tepee 192 *dwelling*; tentcloth, canvas, tarpaulin, fly sheet; mosquito net 222 *network*.

shade, hood, eyelid, eyelash; blind, venetian b., jalousie, shutters, slats; curtain, veil; umbrella, gamp, brolly; parasol, sunshade; sun hat, sun helmet, topee 228 *headgear*; visor, eye shade 421 *screen*; peak (of a cap); dark glasses, sunglasses, shades 442 *eyeglass*.

wrapping, wrapper, paper, tissue p., cellophane, polythene; polystyrene 227 *lining*; packaging, blister pack, bubble pack, gift box, shrinkpack 194 *receptacle*; bandage, roller; plaster cast 658 *surgical dressing*; book cover, binding, boards, dust jacket or cover 589 *bookbinding*; tunic, coat 228 *jacket*; mantle 228 *cloak*; comforter, scarf 228 *neckwear*; life belt, life jacket 662 *safeguard*; cocoon, chrysalis; shroud, winding sheet 364 *grave clothes*.

skin, epithelium; outer skin, scarf s., epidermis, cuticle; true skin, cutis, dermis, derma, corium; tegument 223 *exteriority*; integument, peel, bark, crust, rind, coat, cortex; pericarp, husk, hull, shell, pod, jacket; pellicle, membrane, film; scalp 213 *head*; scale; pelt, fleece, fell, fur; leather, hide, rawhide, imitation leather, leatheroid; shagreen, patent leather; crocodile, alligator; pigskin, morocco, calf, kid, chamois, suede, buff, buckskin, doeskin; rabbitskin, moleskin, sealskin; sheepskin, lamb, Persian l., astrakhan; mink, sable, ermine, miniver, cony; chinchilla 208 *fibre*; feathers, coverts 259 *plumage*.

paving, flooring, floor, parquet, quarry tiles; deck, floorboards, duckboards; pavement, sidewalk, pavé; flags, paving stone, crazy paving; sett, cobble, cobblestone; gravel, chippings, asphalt, tarmac 624 *road*.

coverlet, bedspread, counterpane, bedding, bedclothes, bed linen; sheet, quilt, eiderdown, duvet, continental quilt, Downie (tdmk); blanket, rug; caparison, housings, trappings; saddlecloth, horsecloth; pall.

floor-cover, carpeting, carpet, fitted c., wall-to-wall; broadloom, pile carpet, Persian c.; mat, doormat, bath mat, prayer m.; rug, hearth r.; linoleum, lino, vinyl, tiles; matting, coconut m.; red carpet 875 *formality*.

facing, cladding; veneer, coating, varnish, japan, lacquer, enamel, glaze; roughcast, pebbledash; ashlar, weather-boarding 631 *building material*; stucco, compo, plaster, pargeting, rendering, screed; wash, whitewash, distemper, emulsion, paint; stain, polish, smearing, anointment; coat of paint 425 *pigment*.

Vb. *cover*, superimpose; roof, cork, cap, tip; ice, frost, decorate (a cake); spread, lay (a table); overlay, smother; insulate, lag 227 *line*; lap, wrap up, enfold, envelope 235 *enclose*; blanket, shroud, mantle, muffle; hood, veil 525 *conceal*; case, bind, cover (books); box, pack, vacuum-pack; wrap, shrink-w.; bandage, swathe, wrap round, dress 658 *doctor*; sheathe, encapsulate, encase 303 *insert*; wall in, wall up; cover up, keep under cover.

coat, revet, face, front; grout, roughcast, encrust, shingle; stucco, plaster, pebbledash; render, parget 844 *decorate*; thatch, tile; veneer, varnish, lacquer, japan, enamel, glaze, size; paint, whitewash, colourwash, distemper, emulsion, stain 425 *colour*; creosote; tar, pitch, pay; daub, bedaub, scumble, overpaint, grease, lard, lay it on thick; smear, butter, anoit, powder, sprinkle, gild, plate, silver; electroplate, silverplate; waterproof, fireproof, damp-proof 660 *safeguard*.

227 Lining

N. *lining*, liner, coating, inner c.; stuffing, wadding, padding, quilting; kapok, foam, polystyrene 631 *materials*; lagging, insulation, double-glazing, damp-proofing, soundproofing; backing, facing; doublure 589 *bookbinding*; upholstery; papering, wallpaper; wainscotting, panelling, wainscot, skirting board, dado, brattice; metal lining; brake lining; packing, dunnage; packaging 226 *wrapping*; filling, stopping (dentistry); washer.

Vb. *line*, encrust 226 *coat*; insulate 226 *cover*; interlard, inlay; back, face, paper, wallpaper, upholster, cushion; stuff, pad, wad; fill, pack.

228 Dressing

N. *dressing*, investment, investiture; clothing, covering, dressing up, toilet, toilette; overdressing, foppishness; underdressing, casualness 848 *fashion*; vesture, dress, garb, attire, rig, gear, clobber; panoply, array; garniture, trim, accoutrements, caparison, harness, housing, trappings; traps, paraphernalia, accessories; rigout, turn-out; tailoring, dressmaking, millinery; haute couture; the rag trade, the fashion world; power dressing.

clothing, wear, apparel, raiment, linen; clothes, garments, vestments, habiliments; togs, gear, kit, clobber; outfit, wardrobe, trousseau; maternity wear; layette, baby clothes, swaddling c., Babygro (tdmk); old clothes, duds, reach-me-downs, cast-offs, rags, tatters; working clothes, hand-me-downs, second-hand clothes, uniform; leisure wear, sportswear, tracksuit, casual clothes; best c.; Sunday best, best bib and tucker; party dress, glad rags; ostrich feathers, frippery 844 *finery*; fancy dress, masquerade; motley; national costume.

garment, article of clothing; neck, collar (**see** *neckwear*, *neckline*); top, bodice, bosom; corsage, bib, stomacher; shirt-front, dickey; waistline (**see** *belt*); peplum, bustle, train; crutch, codpiece; arms (**see** *sleeve*); flaps, coat tails 217 *hanging object*; placket, fly 263 *opening*; patch pocket; flap, gusset, gore, pleat, kick pleat; lapel, turn-up 261 *fold*; cuff, hemline 234 *edging*.

formal dress, correct d., court d., full d. 875 *formality*; grande toilette, evening dress, tails, white tie and tails; dinner jacket, black tie, tuxedo; morning dress; academic dress, academicals, cap and gown, subfusc; mourning, black, widow's weeds.

uniform, regimentals; dress uniform, undress, mess kit; battledress, fatigues, khaki; school uniform, academic dress; robes, vestments, clerical dress 989 *canonicals*.

informal dress, undress, mufti, civvies; casual clothes, leisure wear, slacks, jeans; dress-down Friday; déshabillé, dishabille; dressing gown, loungewear, peignoir, bathrobe, robe, wrapper, housecoat; smoking jacket, slippers.

robe, gown, robes, sari; kimono, caftan; jubbah, djellaba, toga, cassock 989 *canonicals*.

dress, frock, gown; creation, number, ballgown, cocktail dress, little black d.; sheath d., tube d., cheongsam, chemise, shift, sack;

shirtwaister, coatdress, overdress, pinafore dress, jumper, gymslip; sundress.

suit, outfit, ensemble; coordinates, separates; lounge suit, zoot s., drape s., pinstripe s.; costume, tweeds, trouser suit, pantsuit; jumpsuit, catsuit, leotard, body-suit, body stocking; overalls, dungarees, boiler suit, siren s., tracksuit, leisure suit, skinsuit, wetsuit; G-suit, spacesuit.

jacket, coat, tail c., dinner jacket, tuxedo; monkey jacket, mess j., Eton j.; blazer, reefer, sports jacket, Norfolk j., hacking j., riding habit, hunting pink; donkey jacket, lumber j. (**see** *overcoat*); parka, windcheater, anorak, kagoule; bomber jacket, blouson; jerkin, tunic, tabard, surcoat, waistcoat, vest, gilet, spencer; bolero, coatee, matinee jacket.

jersey, pullover, woolly, knit, homeknit, handknit, jumper, sweater, V-neck, polo neck, turtle neck, crew neck, sloppy joe, sweatshirt, guernsey, Fair Isle, cardigan, cardi, shrug, tank top, twin set.

trousers, pants, trews, breeks; cords, flannels, pinstripes; hipsters, drainpipes, bell-bottoms, flares; slacks, bags, Oxford b., plus fours; breeches, britches, jodhpurs, knickerbockers, pedal-pushers, leggings, tights; chaps, dungarees, denims jeans, blue j., Levi's (tdmk); shorts, Bermuda s., hot pants; lederhosen; bloomers, pantaloons, rompers.

skirt, maxi s., midi s., miniskirt; pleated s., flared s., A-line s., gored s., full s., dirndl, bubble skirt, kilt, kirtle, filibeg; sarong; straight skirt, slit s., hobble s.; sports s., divided s., culottes; ballet skirt, tutu; crinoline, farthingale, hoop.

shirt, smock, angel top; polo neck, tee shirt, sweatshirt; blouse, camisole, top.

underwear, underclothes, undies, linen; lingerie, smalls, unmentionables; underpants, shorts, pants, Y-fronts, boxer shorts; briefs, panties, scanties, French knickers, camiknickers, teddy knickers, bloomers, drawers; combinations, long johns, thermal underwear; singlet, vest, string v., undershirt, semmit; camisole, chemise, slip, half-slip, underskirt, petticoat; foundation garment, body stocking, corset, stays, girdle, pantie-g., roll-on; brassiere, bra; suspender belt, braces.

nightwear, nightclothes, sleeping suit; nightgown, nightdress, nightie, negligee; nightshirt, pyjamas; bedsocks, bed jacket, nightcap.

beachwear, sunsuit, sundress; bikini, bankini, monokini; swimming costume, swimsuit, onepiece s., bathing suit, trunks, bathers; beach robe.

overcoat, coat (**see** *jacket*); fur coat 226 *skin*; topcoat, greatcoat, frock coat; ulster, car coat, duffel c.; waterproof, oilskins; mac, mackin-tosh, raincoat, gabardine; Burberry (tdmk), trench coat; light coat, duster; fitted coat.

cloak, cape, cycling c.; poncho.

neckwear, scarf, fichu; stole, boa, tippet; comforter, muffler; neckerchief, jabot, cravat, necktie, tie, bow t.; necklace 844 *jewellery*; ruff, collar, dog c. 989 *canonicals*; Eton collar, mandarin c., Peter Pan c., Vandyke c., Bertha, sailor c., shawl c.; button-down c., stand-up c. **See** *neckline*.

headgear, millinery; hat, cap, lid, titfer, tile; headdress, mantilla; plumes, ribbons 844 *finery*; crown, coronet, tiara 743 *regalia*; fillet, snood; juliet cap, skull c., coif; headscarf, kerchief, bandanna, headband, sweatband, Alice band; turban; hood, cowl, wimple; veil, yashmak 421 *screen*; fez, tarboosh; kepi, busby, bearskin, helmet 713 *armour*; tin hat, crash helmet, safety h. 662 *safeguard*; woolly hat, bobble h., ski h.; rainhat, sou'wester; cap, cloth c., beret, tam-o'-shanter, tammy; Balmoral, glengarry, deerstalker; Homburg, trilby, pork-pie hat, billycock, fedora, beaver, bowler, derby; slouch hat, stetson, ten-gallon hat, sombrero, shovel hat, picture h., straw h., boater, panama, coolie hat, bush h., sunhat, pith helmet 226 *shade*; bonnet, Easter b., poke b., mob cap, toque, cloche, pillbox; top hat, topper, silk hat, stovepipe h.; cocked h., mortarboard; biretta 989 *canonicals*; witch's hat, wizard's h., dunce's cap.

neckline, boat neck, crew n., cowl n., turtle n., roll n., polo n., halter n., V-n., round n.; low n. 229 *bareness*.

belt, waistband; cummerbund, sash, obi; money belt, belt-bag, bum-bag; shoulder-belt, bandolier, baldric.

sleeve, arm, armhole; leg-of-mutton sleeve, raglan s., dolman s., batwing s., magyar s., puff s., cap s., short s., long s.; wristband, cuff.

glove, gauntlet, driving gloves, long g., evening g.; mitten, mitt, muff.

legwear, hosiery; stockings, nylons, tights, fleshings; trunks, hose; socks, knee-length s., over-the-knee s., ankle s., bootees; leggings, gaiters, spats, puttees; garter, suspender 47 *fastening*.

footwear, footgear; slipper, carpet s., mule; patten, clog, sabot; flipflops, jelly sandals, jellies, sandals, Jesus boots, chappals; rope-soled shoes, espadrilles, rubber-soled shoes, crepe-soled s., creepers, brothel creepers, sneakers, plimsolls, gym shoes, trainers, high-tops, tennis shoes; pumps, ballet shoes, moccasins, slip-ons, casuals; winklepickers, beetlecrushers, clodhoppers; shoe, court s., high heels, stiletto h., platform h., Cuban h., wedge h.; peep-toed shoes, slingbacks, flat shoes, driving s., lace-ups, buckled shoes; Oxfords, brogues; boots, fashion b., high b., cowboy b.; thigh b., waders, wellingtons, wellies, gumboots; Doc Martens (tdmk), Dr Martens (tdmk), DMs; skiboots 274 *sled*; running shoes, spikes.

clothier, outfitter, costumier; tailor, couturier; couturière; fashion designer 848 *fashion*; dressmaker, seamstress, modiste; shoemaker, bootmaker; cobbler 686 *artisan*; hosier, hatter, milliner, draper, haberdasher; Savile Row, Carnaby Street; boutique; valet, batman 742 *domestic*; dresser, mistress of the wardrobe.

Adj. *tailored*, tailor-made, bespoke, made-to-measure, custom-made; designer, ready-to-wear, off-the-peg; fully fashioned.

Vb. *dress*, clothe, array, garb, attire; robe, drape, sheet, mantle; invest, put in uniform, equip, rig out, fit o., harness 669 *make ready*; dress up, deck, prink 843 *primp*; envelop, wrap, lap, enfold, wrap up, fold up, muffle up, roll up in, swaddle, swathe, shroud, sheathe 226 *cover*.

wear, put on, don, slip on, slip into; clothe oneself, attire o., get dressed, get one's clothes on; have on, dress in, dress up 875 *be ostentatious*.

229 Uncovering

N. *uncovering*, divestment, undressing etc. vb.; opening, openness, glasnost; exposure, indecent e. 526 *disclosure*; nudism, naturism; stripping, dance of the seven veils, striptease 594 *stage show*; undress, dishabille, déshabillé 228 *informal dress*; moulting, ecdysis, shedding; decortication, exfoliation, abscission, excoriation, peeling, desquamation; depilation, shaving; denudation, devastation.

bareness, décolleté, décolletage, bare neck, plunging neckline; nudity, nakedness, birthday suit, the altogether, the buff, the raw, starkers, not a stitch on, streaking.

stripper, ecdysiast, striptease artiste, flasher, dirty old man in a raincoat, streaker; nudist, naturist; nude model, hair-remover, depilatory, wax, electrolysis.

uncovered person, nude, nudist, naturist; baldheaded person, baldie, slaphead.

Adj. *uncovered*, bared; exposed, unveiled 522 *manifest*; divested; debagged; stripped; unclad, unclothed, undressed, unattired; décolleté(e), bare-necked, off-the-shoulder, topless; bare-backed, bare-armed, barelegged; barefoot, unshod, hatless, bareheaded; en déshabillé, in one's shirt-sleeves; miniskirted, bikini-clad, swimsuited; indecently dressed; bare, naked, nude, raw; mother naked, in a state of undress, in the buff, in one's birthday suit, with nothing on, without a stitch on; stark, stark naked, starkers; unsheathed.

hairless, bald, baldheaded, beardless, shaved, shaven, clean-s., tonsured; bald as a coot, bald as an egg, bald as a billiard ball; threadbare; thin on top.

Vb. *uncover*, unveil, undress, unclothe; divest, debag; strip, skin, scalp, flay, tear off; pluck, peel, pare, bark, excoriate; hull, pod, shell, stone; bone, fillet 300 *empty*; denude, expose, bare, lay open 526 *disclose*; unsheathe, draw (a sword) 304 *extract*; unwrap, unpack; uncap, uncork 263 *open*; abrade 333 *rub*.

230 Surroundings

N. *surroundings* 223 *exteriority*; ambience, atmosphere, aura; ambient music; medium, matrix; encompassment, containment, surrounding 235 *enclosure*; compass, circuit, circumference, periphery, perimeter 233 *outline*; milieu, environment, entourage; background, setting, scene, scenario 186 *situation*; neighbourhood, vicinity; outskirts, environs, suburbs, precincts 192 *housing*; sticks, outpost, cordon.

Vb. *surround*, lie around, encompass, lap; encircle 314 *circle*; begird 235 *enclose*; twine around; embrace, cuddle, hug 889 *caress*; contain, keep in, cloister, shut in, close round, hem in 232 *circumscribe*; blockade 712 *besiege*.

Adv. *around*, about, on every side, round about, all round; on all sides; outside, in the outskirts.

231 Interjacency

N. *interjacency*, intermediacy, intervention, penetration, permeation, infiltration 189 *presence*; dovetailing 45 *union*.

partition, curtain, Iron C., bamboo c. 421 *screen*; Great Wall of China 713 *defences*; Berlin Wall 57 *exclusion*; wall, party w., garden fence 235 *fence*; divide, watershed, parting 46 *separation*; division, panel 53 *subdivision*; hedge, ditch 201 *gap*.

intermediary, medium, link 47 *bond*; negotiator, go-between, pander, broker 720 *mediator*; agent 755 *deputy*; middle-man, retailer 794 *merchant*; advocate 707 *patron*; buffer, bumper, fender, crumple zone, cushion, air bag 662 *safeguard*; air lock, buffer state, no-man's-land, no-go area, halfway house 70 *middle*.

interjection, sandwiching; interpolation 303 *insertion*; embolism 264 *closure*; interruption, intrusion, chipping in, butting in 72 *discontinuity*; interference, meddling 702 *hindrance*; episode, parenthesis 40 *adjunct*; insert.

interjector, interpolator; intruder, interloper.

Adj. *interjacent*, sandwiched; episodic, parenthetical, in brackets, in parentheses; intermediary, intervening etc. vb.; mediating; intrusive 59 *extraneous*; interplanetary; intermediate 303 *inserted*; median, medium, mean 70 *middle*; partitioning, dividing.

Vb. *lie between*, come b., stand b.; mediate, intervene.

introduce, let in 299 *admit*; throw in, work in, edge in, force in, thrust in 303 *insert*; ingrain; splice, dovetail, mortise 45 *join*; smuggle in, worm in, insinuate 297 *infiltrate*.

interfere, come between, intercept 702 *hinder*; step in, intervene, intercede 720 *mediate*; interrupt, put in, chip in, get a word in; obtrude, thrust in, poke one's nose in, horn in, butt in 297 *intrude*; invade, trespass 306 *encroach*; put one's oar in; have a finger in the pie 678 *meddle*.

Adv. *between*, betwixt, 'twixt, betwixt and between; among, amongst, amid, amidst, mid, midst; in the middle of; in the thick of; parenthetically.

232 Circumscription

N. *circumscription*, enclosing 235 *enclosure*; encircling, encompassing, circle, balloon; ringing round, hedging r., fencing r.; surrounding, framing, girdling; siege, blockade 712 *attack*; envelopment, encirclement, containment, confinement, limitation 747 *restriction*; ring 235 *fence*.

Vb. *circumscribe*, describe a circle, ring round, circle, encircle, encompass; envelop, close in, cut off, cordon off, rope off, mark off, invest, beleaguer, blockade, picket 712 *besiege*; beset, hem in, pen in; enclose, rail in, hedge in, fence in; box, cage, wall in, immure, cloister 747 *imprison*; frame 230 *surround*; encase, enfold, enshrine, edge, border 236 *limit*; clasp 889 *caress*, embrace.

233 Outline

N. *outline*, circumference, perimeter, periphery; surround, frame, rim 234 *edge*; compass, circuit 250 *circle*; delineation, configuration, features 445 *feature*; profile, relief 239 *laterality*; silhouette, skyline, horizon 553 *picture*; sketch, rough s., draft 623 *plan*; figure, diagram, layout; trace, tracing; skeleton, framework 331 *structure*; contour, contour line, shape 243 *form*; coastline, bounds 236 *limit*.

Vb. *outline*, describe a circle 232 *circumscribe*; frame 230 *surround*; delineate, draw, silhouette, profile, trace 551 *represent*; etch 555 *engrave*; map, block out, rough o., sketch o., sketch; diagrammatize.

234 Edge

N. *edge*, verge, brim; tip, brink, skirt, fringe, margin 69 *extremity*; confines, bounds, boundary, frontier, border 236 *limit*; coast, beach, strand, seaside, seashore, water's edge,

waterfront 344 *shore*; wharf, quay, dock 192 *stable*; sideline, side, brim, kerb or curb, wayside, roadside, bank 239 *laterality*; hedge 235 *fence*; lip, ledge, eave, cornice, rim, welt, flange 254 *projection*; horizon, skyline; knife edge, razor e.; sharpness, acrimony; advantage, upper hand.

threshold, sill, doorstep, door, portal, porch 263 *doorway*; mouth.

edging, frame 233 *outline*; selvedge; hem, border; binding, piping; fringe, frill, ruffle, flounce, furbelow, valance 844 *trimming*; scallop.

Adj. *marginal*, border, coastal; riverside, roadside, wayside; labial, edged, trimmed, bordered; borderline, peripheral.

Vb. *hem*, edge, lower e., border, trim, piping, fringe; crenellate 260 *notch*; bound, confine 236 *limit*.

235 Enclosure

N. *enclosure*, envelope, case 194 *receptacle*; wrapper, packaging 226 *wrapping*; ring, perimeter, circumference, periphery 233 *outline*; surround, frame; cloister, courtyard 185 *place*; reserve 883 *seclusion*; lot, holding, claim 184 *territory*; fold, pen, sheepfold, sty 369 *cattle pen*; park 370 *garden*; compound, yard, pound, paddock, field; car park, parking lot 192 *stable*; corral, stockade, lines 713 *defences*; net, trawl 222 *network*; cell, cage 748 *prison*.

fence, ring f., barbed-wire f., razor-wire fence, electric f. 222 *network*; hurdle, wooden fence, picket f., sunk f., ha-ha, hedge, privet h., quickset h., hedgerow, espalier; rails, balustrade, banisters, paling, railing; pale, wall, boundary w.; moat, dike, ditch, fosse, trench 713 *defences*.

barrier, wall, cavity w., brick w., dry-stone w. 231 *partition*; soundproofing, double-glazing, damp-proofing 660 *protection*; barricade, cordon, pale; balustrade, parapet; turnstile 702 *obstacle*; palisade, stockade 713 *fort*; portcullis, gate, door, bolt, bar, padlock 264 *closure*.

Vb. *enclose*, fence in, cordon off, rope off, surround, wall; pen, hem, ring, corral 232 *circumscribe*; cloister, immure, wall up, confine, cage 747 *imprison*; wrap, enfold 261 *fold*; hug, embrace, cuddle 889 *caress*; frame.

236 Limit

N. *limit*, limitation, constraint 747 *restriction*, 468 *qualification*; delimitation, demarcation 783 *apportionment*; parameter, upper limit, ceiling, high-water mark 213 *summit*; lower limit, threshold 214 *base*; legal limit, Plimsoll line; saturation point 54 *completeness*; utmost, uttermost, extreme, ne plus ultra, pole 69 *extremity*; ends of the earth; terminus, terminal 69 *end*;

goal, target, winning post, touch, touch-line, home, base 617 *objective*; turning point, watershed 137 *crisis*; point of no return 599 *resolution*; Rubicon, threshold of pain, tolerance, capacity, end of one's tether; outside edge, perimeter, periphery, circumference 233 *outline*; tidemark, sea line 344 *shore*; landmark, boundary stone; milestone 27 *degree*; kerb *or* curb, kerbstone 624 *road*; boundary, verge; frontier, border, marches 234 *edge*; demarcation 1., international date 1., divide, parting 231 *partition*; skyline, horizon, equator, deadline, time limit, term 110 *period*; ultimatum 900 *threat*; speed limit 278 *slowness*; sound barrier.

Vb. *limit*, bound, border, edge 234 *hem*; top 213 *crown*; confine; restrict 747 *restrain*; encompass 232 *circumscribe*; delimit, demarcate; rope off, mark out 547 *mark*.

237 Front

N. *front*, fore, forefront 64 *precedence*; prefix, frontispiece, preface, foreword, front matter; forelock 259 *hair*; forecourt, anteroom, entrance, hall 263 *doorway*; foreground 200 *nearness*; front rank, front line; leading edge; forward line, centre forward; avant-garde, vanguard, advance guard; spearhead; outpost, scout, reconnaissance party; forerunner, pioneer 66 *precursor*; prequel.

face, frontage, façade, fascia; face of a coin, obverse, head; right side, outer s., recto; front view, front elevation; physiognomy; features, visage, countenance; phiz, phizog, mug, mush, dial, clock 445 *feature*.

Adj. *frontal*, fore, forward, front, obverse; full frontal, head-on, oncoming, facing 240 *opposite*; anterior, prefixed 64 *preceding*.

Vb. *be in front*, stand in front etc. adv. front, confront, face, eyeball, face up to 240 *be opposite*; breast; come to the fore, forge ahead, take the lead, head 283 *precede*.

Adv. *in front*, before, in advance, in the lead, in the van; ahead, ahead of one's time, further on 199 *beyond*; far ahead, before one's eyes; face to face, eyeball to eyeball, in the foreground, in the forefront, in the limelight.

238 Rear

N. *rear*, back end, rear end, tail end, stern 69 *extremity*; tailpiece, heel, colophon; coda 412 *musical piece*; tail, brush, scut 67 *sequel*; wake, train 67 *retinue*; booby prize, wooden spoon, back seat 35 *inferiority*; rearguard 67 *successor*; background, backdrop 594 *stage set*; hinterland, far corner 199 *distance*; behind, backstage, back side; reverse side, wrong s., verso 240 *contraposition*; reverse, other side, flip side, B-side; back door, back entrance, tradesmen's e., postern

263 *doorway*; back (of the body), dorsum; spine 218 *prop*; back of the neck, scruff of the n., nape; back of the head.

buttocks, backside, behind, rear end, derrière, posterior; bottom, btm, seat, sit-upon; bum, arse (vulg), ass, butt, fanny; rear, stern, tail; hindquarters; hips, haunches, hams, hunkers; rump; lower back, coccyx; anus.

Adj. *back*, rear; posterior, after, hind, hinder, hindermost, rearmost, tail-end; backswept 253 *convex*; reverse 240 *opposite*; placed last 35 *inferior*; spinal, vertebral, dorsal, lumbar; anal; caudal, caudate.

Vb. *be behind*, back on, back; back up 703 *aid*; follow, bring up the rear 65 *come after*; lag, trail, drop behind 278 *move slowly*; trail, tail, shadow, dog 619 *pursue*; follow at heel 284 *follow*; bend backwards 220 *be oblique*.

Adv. *rearward*, behind; in the rear, at the end; at the back, in the background; behind one's back; behind the scenes, offstage; after; aft, abaft, astern, aback; to the rear, hindward, backward, above; overleaf; hard on the heels of, at the back of, close behind; one behind the other, back to back.

239 Laterality

N. *laterality*, side movement 317 *oscillation*; sidestep 282 *deviation*; sideline, side, bank 234 *edge*; coast 344 *shore*; siding, side entrance, side door; broadside; beam; quarter; flank, ribs; wing, fin, arm, hand; cheek, jowl; gills; side whiskers 259 *hair*; temples; profile, side elevation; lee side, leeward; windward 281 *direction*; off side, on s., near s. 241 *dextrality*, 242 *sinistrality*.

Adj. *lateral*, side 234 *marginal*; sidelong; winglike; flanking, skirting; flanked, sided; manysided, multilateral, unilateral, bilateral, trilateral, quadrilateral; collateral; edging, sidling.

Vb. *flank*, side, edge, skirt, border 234 *hem*; coast, move sideways, skirt; side-step 282 *deviate*.

Adv. *sideways*, crabwise, laterally; askance, asquint; in profile, sideways on; sidelong, broadside on; aside; side by side, cheek by jowl 200 *near*.

240 Contraposition

N. *contraposition*, antithesis, opposition, antipodes 14 *contrariety*; opposite side, other s., other s. of the fence; reverse, back 238 *rear*; polarity, polarization; opposite poles, poles apart, North and South; crosscurrent, headwind 704 *opposition*; reversal, inverse 221 *inversion*.

Adj. *opposite*, contrapositive, reverse, inverse; contrary 14 *contrary*; facing, face to face, vis-à-vis, eyeball to eyeball, confronting 237 *frontal*; diametrically opposed, antipodean, antithetical; polarized, polar.

Vb. *be opposite*, – facing, etc. adj.; stand opposite, lie o.; subtend; face, confront 237 *be in front*; run counter 182 *counteract*; oppose, contrapose.

Adv. *against*, poles apart; facing, face to face, eyeball to eyeball, vis-à-vis; back to back; on the other side, on the other side of the fence, overleaf; contrariwise, vice versa.

241 Dextrality

N. *dextrality*, right hand, right-handedness; ambidextrousness 694 *skill*; right, offside, starboard; right-hand page, recto; right wing, rightwinger; dextral, ambidexter.

242 Sinistrality

N. *sinistrality*, left hand, left-handedness, cackhandedness; left, near side, on s.; larboard, port; left-hand page, verso; left wing, leftwinger; sinistral, southpaw.

SECTION THREE

Form

243 Form

N. *form*, idea; essence 3 *substance*; art form 551 *art*, 593 *verse form*; word form; shape, turn, lines, architecture; formation, conformation, configuration, fashion, style, trend, design 331 *structure*; contour, silhouette, relief, profile, frame, outline; figure, cut, set, trim, build, cut of one's jib, lineament 445 *feature*; physiognomy 237 *face*; look, expression, appearance 445 *mien*; posture, attitude, stance; get-up, turnout, rig, gear; type, kind, pattern, stamp, cast, mould, blank 23 *prototype*; format; morphology.

formation, forming, shaping, creation 164 *production*; formulation 62 *arrangement*; designing 844 *ornamental art*; weaving, knitting 222 *network*; tailoring 844 *needlework*; throwing 381 *pottery*; moulding 554 *sculpture*; joinery 694 *skill*; word-formation.

Adj. *formed*, created etc. vb.; sculptured, carved, moulded, thrown, turned; shaped, fashioned, fully f., styled; designer, tailor-made, custom-built; ready-made, off the peg; matured, ready 669 *prepared*; solid, concrete 324 *dense*.

Vb. *form*, create, make 164 *produce*; formalize, shape, fashion; throw (pots), blow (glass); turn; cut, tailor; cut out, silhouette 233 *outline*; sketch, draft, draw 551 *represent*; model, carve, whittle, chisel 554 *sculpt*; hew, rough-h. 46 *cut*; mould, cast; stamp, coin, mint; hammer out, block o., punch o.; forge; knead, work, work up into; construct, build, frame 310 *elevate*; express, put into words, verbalize, formulate, put into shape, lick into s., knock into s.

244 Amorphism: absence of form

N. *amorphism*, formlessness; chaos 61 *disorder*; amorphousness, shapelessness; vagueness, fuzziness; uncouthness 670 undevelopment; raw material 631 *materials*; rough diamond; disfigurement, defacement, deformity 246 *distortion*.

Adj. *amorphous*, formless, unformed, unstructured, structureless; liquid 335 *fluid*; shapeless, characterless; chaotic; undefined, ill-defined, indistinct, nondescript, nebulous, vague, fuzzy, blurred 419 *shadowy*; unformed; embryonic 68 *beginning*; raw, callow 670 *immature*; unhewn 55 *incomplete*; rude, uncouth, barbaric 699 *artless*; rugged 259 *rough*; unshapely 842 *unsightly*; malformed, misshapen 246 *deformed*.

Vb. *deform*, deprive of form 165 *destroy*; melt 337 *liquefy*; knock out of shape, batter 46 *break*; grind, pulp 332 *pulverize*; warp, twist 246 *distort*; deface, disfigure 842 *make ugly*; mutilate 655 *impair*; jumble 63 derange.

245 Symmetry: regularity of form

N. *symmetry*, proportion 12 *correlation*; balance 28 *equilibrium*; regularity, evenness 16 *uniformity*; branching, ramification 219 *parallelism*; shapeliness, regular features, classic f. 841 *beauty*; harmony, congruity 24 *agreement*; rhythm 141 *periodicity*; finish 646 *perfection*.

Adj. *symmetrical*, balanced, well-balanced 28 *equal*; proportioned, well-p. 12 *correlative*; rhythmical, harmonious, congruous 24 *agreeing*; congruent; corresponding; analogous 18 *similar*; smooth, even 16 *uniform*; squared, rounded; evensided, isosceles, equilateral 81 *regular*; arborescent.

246 Distortion: irregularity of form

N. *distortion*, asymmetry, disproportion, disproportionateness 10 *unrelatedness*; fractal; imbalance, disequilibrium 29 *in equality*; lop-sidedness, crookedness, skewness 220 *obliquity*; projection 551 *map*; contortion, twisting; thrust, stress, strain, shear; bias, warp; buckle, bend, screw, twist 251 *convolution*; grimace, moue, snarl 547 *gesture*.

deformity, malformation, disfigurement, monstrosity, mutation, abortion 84 *abnormality*; curvature of the spine 248 *curvature*; clubfoot, knock knees, bow legs, rickets, hunchback 845 *blemish*; ugliness 842 *eyesore*; teratology.

Adj. *distorted*, contorted etc. vb.; irregular, asymmetric, scalene, unsymmetrical, disproportionate 17 *nonuniform*; weighted, biased; not true, not straight; out of shape, warped, mutative 244 *amorphous*; mangled, buckled, twisted, gnarled 251 *convoluted*; wry, awry, askew, crazy, crooked, cock-eyed, on one side; grimacing.

deformed, ugly 842 *unsightly*; ill-proportioned; defective 647 *imperfect*; mutative, ill-made, malformed, misshapen; hunchbacked, bandy-legged, bowlegged, knock-kneed; pigeon-toed, splay-footed, club-footed, web-footed; round-shouldered, pigeon-chested; hare-lipped; stunted 204 *short*.

Vb. *distort*, weight, bias; contort, screw, twist, knot 251 *twine*; bend, warp 251 *crinkle*; buckle, crumple; strain, sprain, skew, wrest, rack 63 *derange*; misshape, botch 244 *deform*; mangle, batter, knock out of shape 655 *impair*; pervert 552 *misrepresent*; misconstrue 521 *misinterpret*; grimace 547 *gesticulate*; frown.

247 Angularity

N. *angularity*, crotchet, bracket, crook, hook; bend, scythe, sickle, scimitar 248 *curvature*; chevron, zigzag 220 *obliquity*; V-shape, elbow, knee; withers 253 *camber*; knuckle, ankle, groin 45 *joint*; crotch 222 *cross*; fork, branching 222 *crossing*; corner, cranny, nook, niche, recess 194 *compartment*; nose, Roman n., hook n. 254 *protuberance*; flexure 261 *fold*; indentation 260 *notch*.

angle, right a., acute a., obtuse a., salient a., solid a.

angular measure, trigonometry, altimetry; angular elevation, angular distance; zenith distance; second, degree, minute; radian; altimeter; clinometer, level, theodolite; transit circle; sextant, quadrant; protractor, set square.

angular figure, triangle, isosceles t., equilateral t., scalene t.; parallelogram, rectangle, square, quadrangle; quadrilateral, diamond; rhomb; trapezium, tetragon, polygon, pentagon, hexagon, heptagon, octagon, nonagon, decagon, dodecahedron, icosahedron; cube, pyramid, wedge; prism.

Adj. *angular*, hooked, Roman-nosed, aquiline; angled, sharp-a., cornered; staggered, crooked, zigzag; jagged, serrated, crinkled; bony, jointed; akimbo; knock-kneed; forked, bifurcate, V-shaped.

248 Curvature

N. *curvature*, curvation; inward curve 255 *concavity*; outward curve 253 *convexity*; flexure, inflexion, bending 261 *fold*; stooping 311 *obeisance*; bending down; turning away, swerve, detour 282 *deviation*; downward bend 309 *descent*; curliness, sinuosity 251 *convolution*; curvature of the spine 246 *deformity*.

curve, elbow 247 *angularity*; turn, bend, Z-bend, hairpin b., U-turn; horse-shoe; bay, bight 345 *gulf*; figure of eight 250 *loop*; S-shape; curl 251 *convolution*; bow, Cupid's b., rainbow 250 *arc*; arch, ogee a., arcade, vault 253 *dome*;

sickle, scimitar, crescent, half-moon, lens; trajectory, parabola, hyperbola, conic section; cone biopsy; arch (of the foot), instep; swan neck.

Adj. *curved*, cambered etc. vb.; bent; bowed, stooping; bowlike, curvilinear; rounded, curvaceous, curvy, bosomy, busty, wavy, billowy 251 *undulatory*; aquiline, hook-nosed 247 *angular*; beaked, beaklike; bent back, retroussé, turned-up; circumflex; ogival, vaulted 253 *arched*; bow-legged, bandy-legged 246 *deformed*; hooked, semicircular 250 *round*; crescent, lunate, lunar; heart-shaped, bell-s., pear-s., hour-glass.

Vb. *be curved*, -bent etc. adj.; curve, swerve, bend, loop, wind, arch, sweep, sag, give 217 *hang*; bend, crook; turn, round; bend in, bend back, bend over, bend down, bow, incline 311 *stoop*; turn over 261 *fold*; turn away 282 *deflect*; arch; coil 251 *twine*; loop, curl, kink, wave, perm 251 *crinkle*; loop the loop.

249 Straightness

N. *straightness*, directness; perpendicularity 215 *verticality*; inflexibility, intransigence, rigidity 326 *hardness*; chord, radius, tangent 203 *line*; straight line, beeline; Roman road; straight stretch; short cut 200 *short distance*.

Adj. *straight*, direct, even, right, true; in a line, linear; straight-lined, rectilinear, rectilineal; perpendicular 215 *vertical*; stiff, inflexible 326 *rigid*; straightened, dead straight, undeviating, unswerving, undeflected, on the beam, straight as an arrow; straight as a die 929 *honourable*; not bent, heterosexual 83 *typical*.

Vb. *straighten*, align; iron out 216 *flatten*; unbend (a bow); uncross (legs), unfold (arms); uncurl 258 *smooth*; uncoil, unroll, unfurl, unfold 316 *evolve*.

250 Circularity: simple circularity

N. *circularity*, roundness 252 *rotundity*.

circle, full c., circumference 233 *outline*; equator; orb; areola; plate, saucer; round, disc, disk, discus; coin, button, sequin; washer, hoop, ring, bracelet, quoit; eye, iris; eyelet, loophole, keyhole 263 *orifice*; circuit, circus, roundabout; zodiac; fairy ring; smoke ring; crop circle.

loop, figure of eight 251 *convolution*; bow; ringlet, curl, kink 259 *hair*; bracelet, armlet, torque 844 *finery*; crown, coronet 743 *regalia*; halo; wreath, garland 228 *headgear*; collar, neckband, necklace, choker 228 *neckwear*; band, cordon, sash, girdle, cummerbund 228 *belt*; lasso.

wheel, pulley, castor 315 *rotator*; hub, tyre; spare t., radial t., roller 252 *rotundity*.

arc, semicircle; half-moon, crescent, rainbow

248 *curve*; sector, quadrant, sextant; ellipse, oval.

orbit, cycle; circuit; circulation 314 *circuition*.

Adj. *round*, rounded, circular, cyclic, discoid; orbicular, ringlike, annular; semicircular, hemicyclic; oval; elliptic, ovoid, egg-shaped, crescent-s., pear-s. 248 *curved*; cycloidal, spherical 252 *rotund*.

251 Convolution: complex circularity

N. *convolution*, involution, circumvolution; intricacy; sinuosity, sinuousness; tortuosity, tortuousness, reticulation 222 *network*; twist 208 *fibre*; ripple 350 *wave*; kink, wrinkle, corrugation 261 *fold*; indentation, scallop 260 *notch*; waviness, undulation, ogee 248 *curve*.

coil, roll, twist; turban 228 *headgear*; spiral, helix; screw, worm, corkscrew; spring, coiled s.; intrauterine device 172 *contraception*; whorl, snailshell, whirlpool 350 *eddy*, 315 *vortex*; tendril 366 *plant*; scalloped edge 234 *edging*; kink, curl; ringlet, lovelock 259 *hair*; scroll, flourish, twirl, curlicue, squiggle 844 *ornamentation*.

meandering, winding, twists and turns 282 *deviation*; labyrinth, maze 61 *complexity*; switchback, zigzag 220 *obliquity*.

serpent, snake, eel, worm 365 *reptile*; wriggler.

Adj. *convoluted*, twisted, contorted 246 *distorted*; cranky; winding, looping, twining, sinuous, tortuous, indented, ragged; crumpled, buckled.

snaky, serpentine, eel-like, wormlike, vermiform, undulating, curvy, sinuous, squirming, wriggling, S-shaped.

undulatory, undulating, rolling, heaving; up-and-down, switchback; wavy, curly, frizzy, kinky, crinkly; crimped, curled, permed; scolloped, wrinkled, corrugated, indented.

coiled, spiral, helical, cochlear; convolute, involute, turbinate, whorled, coiling, spiralling.

intricate, involved, complicated, knotted 61 *complex*.

Vb. *twine*, twist, twirl, roll, coil, spiral 315 *rotate*; entwine; be convoluted, twisted etc. adj.; turn and twist, bend 248 *be curved*.

crinkle, crimp, frizz, perm, curl; wave, undulate, ripple, wrinkle, corrugate 261 *fold*; indent 260 *notch*; crumple 246 *distort*.

meander, loop, snake, twist and turn, zigzag, corkscrew. **See** *twine*.

wriggle, writhe, squirm, shimmy, shake; worm.

252 Rotundity

N. *rotundity*, roundness 250 *circularity*; sphericality, globularity, cylindricality.

sphere, globe, spheroid, ellipsoid, globoid,

bladder; balloon 276 *airship*; soap bubble 355 *bubble*; ball, football, pelota, billiard ball, marble; crystal ball; cannonball, bullet, shot, pellet; bead, pearl, pill, pea, boll, globule; drop, droplet, dewdrop, blot; vesicle, bulb, onion, knob, pommel 253 *swelling*; boulder; round head.

cylinder, roll; roller, rolling pin; round, rung; round tower, martello t., column; trunk, stalk, stem; pipe, drainpipe 263 *tube*; funnel, chimneypot; hat b., pillbox; drum, barrel, cask.

cone, conoid; penumbra; cornet, horn 194 *cup*; top, spinning t.; pear shape.

Adj. *rotund*, 250 *round*; spherical, globular, global; round-headed, bullet-headed, beadlike, hemispherical; spheroidal, ovoid, egg-shaped; pot-bellied 195 *fleshy*.

253 Convexity

N. *convexity*, convexness; arching 248 *curvature*; sphericality 252 *rotundity*; bulginess, lumpiness, humpiness, bulge, bump, lump; projection, protrusion, protuberance 254 *prominence*; tumescence, swelling 197 *dilation*; pot-belliedness 195 *bulk*; pimpliness, wartiness.

swelling, bump, lump, bulge, growth, excrescence, gall, knot, node, nodule; knuckle; oedema, emphysema; sarcoma, tumour, neoplasm, carcinoma 651 *cancer*; goitre; Adam's apple; bunion, corn, wart, verruca; cyst, boil, carbuncle, stye, pimple, blister, vesicle; polyp, adenoids, haemorrhoids, piles; proud flesh, weal, welt; cauliflower ear; drop 252 *sphere*; air bubble 355 *bubble*; knob; bulb, button, bud; belly, potbelly, paunch 195 *bulk*; billow, swell 350 *wave*.

bosom, bust, breasts; boobs, bristols, knockers, tits; mamma, mamilla, papilla, nipple, pap, dug, teat, udder; thorax, chest; silicone implant, breast reduction, breast enlargement; breast-feeding; breastcancer, mammogram; mastectomy, lumpectomy, breastplate.

dome, cupola, vault 226 *roof*; beehive; brow, forehead 237 *face*; skull 213 *head*; hemisphere, mound; hillock, molehill, anthill, mushroom, umbrella.

earthwork, tumulus; barrow, hill fort 713 *defences*; embankment.

camber, 248 *curve*; arch, bow, rainbow; hump, humpback 246 *deformity*.

Adj. *convex*, protruding 254 *projecting*; hemispheric, domelike 252 *rotund*; lentiform, lenticular; humpy, lumpy, bumpy; curvaceous, bosomy, busty, billowy 248 *curved*; bulging, bouffant; swelling, swollen; bloated, potbellied, barrel-chested 195 *fleshy*; turgid, tumid, tumescent, tumorous, tuberous; nubbly 259 *rough*; warty, pimply, spotty, acned; blistery, vesicular.

arched, cambered, bowed 248 *curved*; rounded.

254 Prominence

N. *prominence*, eminence 209 *high land*; conspicuousness 443 *visibility*.

projection, salient; outstretched arm, forefinger, index f.; bowsprit; tongue of land, point, mull, promontory, foreland, headland, ness 344 *land*; peninsula 349 *island*; spur, foothill; jetty, breakwater, pier 662 *shelter*; outwork 713 *fortification*; buttress 218 *prop*; shelf, sill, ledge, balcony; eaves 226 *roof*; overhang 220 *obliquity*; lip 234 *edge*; nozzle, spout; tongue; tenon 45 *joint*; stump, outcrop; landmark 209 *high structure*.

protuberance, bump 253 *swelling*; nose, snout, schnozz, schnozzle, conk, hooter; neb, pecker, bill, beak, rostrum; muzzle, proboscis, trunk; antenna 378 *feeler*; chin, jaw, forehead, brow, beetle brow 237 *face*; figurehead; horn, antler 256 *sharp point*.

Adj. *projecting*, jutting, prominent, salient, bold; protuberant, protruding, bulging, popping etc. vb.; bug-eyed, goggle-e., pop-e., with eyes out on stalks; toothy; beetle-browed; raised, embossed, in relief, ridged, nobbly 259 *rough*.

Vb. *jut*, project, protrude, pout, pop, pop out; stand out, stick o., stick out like a sore thumb, hang o. 443 *be visible*; prick up, cock up 259 *roughen*; shoot up, swell up 197 *expand*; overhang 217 *hang*.

255 Concavity

N. *concavity*, concaveness 248 *curvature*; hollowness 190 *emptiness*; depression, dint, dimple, dent; impression, stamp, imprint, footprint 548 *trace*; intaglio 555 *engraving*; furrowing 262 *furrow*; indentation 260 *notch*; gap, lacuna 201 *interval*.

cavity, hollow, niche, nook, cranny 194 *compartment*; hole, den, burrow, warren; chasm, abyss 211 *depth*; cave, cavern; grotto, alcove 194 *arbour*; bowl, cup, saucer, basin, trough 194 *vessel*; sump 649 *sink*; cell, follicle, pore 263 *orifice*; dimple, pockmark; saltcellar, armpit; honeycomb, sponge 263 *porosity*; funnel, tunnel 263 *tube*; groove, socket 262 *furrow*; sinus; bay, bight, cove, creek, inlet 345 *gulf*; channel, ditch, moat, canal 351 *conduit*; shaft, dip, depression, pothole, crater, pit.

valley, vale, dell, dingle, corrie, strath; glen, dip, depression, ravine, gorge, canyon, gully 201 *gap*.

excavation, dugout, grave, gravepit 364 *tomb*; opencast mining; shaft, bore-hole, well, mine, coal m., shale m., diamond m., pit, coal p., colliery, quarry 632 *store*; trench, burrow, warren; underground railway, tube 263 *tunnel*; archaeological excavation, dig; cutting.

Adj. *concave*, hollow, cavernous; vaulted, arched 248 *curved*; hollowed out, dug o.; caved in; depressed, sunk, sunken; spoonlike, cup-shaped; funnel-shaped; bell-shaped; cellular, dented, dimpled, pockmarked; full of holes, pincushion-like, honeycombed; spongy, porous.

Vb. *make concave*, depress, press in, stamp, impress; buckle, dent, dint, stave in; crush, push in, beat in; excavate, hollow, dig, canalize 262 *groove*; mine, undermine, burrow, tunnel, bore; perforate 263 *pierce*; scoop out, hollow o., dig o. 300 *eject*; pockmark; indent 260 *notch*.

256 Sharpness

N. *sharpness*, acuity, acuteness, pointedness, sting; serration 260 *notch*; thorniness, prickliness; acridity 388 *pungency*.

sharp point, sting, thorn, prick, point, cusp 213 *vertex*; nail, tack, drawing pin, staple 47 *fastening*; nib, tag, pin, needle, knitting-needle, stylus, bodkin, skewer, spit; awl, gimlet, drill, auger 263 *perforator*; arrow, shaft, bolt, arrowhead; barb, swordpoint, rapier, lance, pike 723 *spear*; gaff, harpoon; dagger, dirk, stiletto 723 *side arms*; spike, barbed wire 713 *defences*; spur; goad 612 *incentive*; fork, prong, tine, pick, horn, antler; claw, talon, nails 778 *pincers*; spire, steeple; peak 213 *summit*.

prickle, thorn, brier, bramble, thistle, nettle, cactus; bristle 259 *hair*; beard; spine, needle, quill.

tooth, tusk, fang; milktooth; canine-tooth, eyetooth, incisor, grinder, molar, wisdom tooth; dentition, front tooth, back t., set of teeth, denture, false teeth, gold t., plate, bridge; comb, saw; cog, ratchet, sprocket.

sharp edge, cutting e.; jagged edge, broken glass; cutlery, steel, razor; blade, razor blade; ploughshare 370 *farm tool*; spade, mattock, trowel, shovel; scythe, sickle, hook, billhook; cutter, lawn mower; scissors, shears, clippers, secateurs, pruners; scalpel; chisel, plane, scraper 258 *smoother*; knife, bread-k., kitchen-k., cook's k., carving k., fish k., penknife, pocketknife, flick-knife, sheath knife, jack k., hunting k., bowie k.; machete; chopper, cleaver, wedge; hatchet, axe, adze; battleaxe 723 *axe*; sword, broadsword, cutlass, scimitar 723 *side arms*.

Adj. *sharp*, stinging, keen, acute; edged, cutting; swordlike; pointed; sharp-pointed, barbed; spiky, spiny, spinose, thorny, thistly; needle-like, needle-sharp, acicular; prickly, bristly; spear-like, bayonet-like; craggy, jagged 259 *rough*; comblike, serrated; sharp-edged, knife-e., razor-e.; sharp as a razor, sharp as a needle; sharpened, whetted etc. vb.; razor-sharp.

toothed, toothy; tusky, fanged, dental, denticulate, dentiform; cogged, serrated, sawedged.

Vb. *be sharp*, – stinging etc. adj.; have a point, prick, sting; bristle with; have an edge, bite, pierce 46 *cut*; taper, come to a point, end in a point 293 *converge*.

sharpen, edge, put an edge on, whet, hone, grind, file, strop; barb, point.

257 Bluntness

N. *bluntness*, obtuseness, flatness, bluffness; curves 258 *smoothness*; rustiness, dullness; toothlessness, toothless tiger, lack of bite; blunt instrument, foil; blunt edge, blade, flat.

Vb. *blunt*, make blunt; take off the point, bate (a foil); obtund, dull, rust; draw the teeth 161 *disable*; be blunt.

258 Smoothness

N. *smoothness*, evenness etc. adj.; silkiness; silk, satin, velvet, velour; fleeciness, down, swansdown 327 *softness*; sleekness; baby's bottom; millpond; marble, glass, ice; dance floor, ice rink; flatness, levelness, lawn, bowling green, billiard table 216 *horizontality*; tarmac 226 *paving*; polish, wax, varnish, gloss, glaze, shine, finish; slipperiness, slipway, slide, chute; lubricity, oiliness, greasiness 334 *lubrication*; calm, dead c. 266 *quiescence*.

smoother, roller, garden r., road r., steamroller; bulldozer; rolling pin 216 *flattener*; iron, electric i., smoothing-i., flatiron; mangle, wringer; press, trouser p.; plane 256 *sharp edge*; rake, harrow; card, comb, brush; sandpaper, glass-paper, emery paper, emery board; file, nail f.; polish, French p., varnish, enamel 226 *facing*; lubricator, grease, oil, grease gun, oilcan 334 *lubricant*.

Adj. *smooth*, streamlined; slippery; lubricious, oily, greasy, buttery, soapy; greased, oiled 334 *lubricated*; polished, shiny, gleaming, varnished, waxed, enamelled, lacquered, glazed; soft, suave, bland, soothing; silky, satiny, velvety; peachlike, downy, woolly; marble, glassy; bald 229 *hairless*; sleek, slick, brushed; combed, carded; rolled, even, level, flush 216 *flat*; glassy, calm, c. as a millpond 266 *still*; blunt; smooth-skinned; smooth-haired; smooth as glass, smooth as a baby's bottom, smooth as velvet, satin-smooth; slippery as an eel.

Vb. *smooth*, streamline; oil, grease 334 *lubricate*; smoothen, plane, even, level; rake, comb; file, rub down 333 *rub*; roll, calender, press, iron 216 *flatten*; mow, shave, cut 204 *shorten*; smooth over, slick down, plaster d.; iron out;

shine, burnish 417 *make bright*; buff, polish, glaze, wax, varnish 226 *coat*.

259 Roughness

N. *roughness*, asperity, harshness; broken ground; rough water, choppiness 350 *wave*; turbulence 352 *wind*; brokenness, jaggedness, broken glass, barbed wire 256 *sharp edge*; serration, saw edge, scalloped e. 260 *notch*; ruggedness, cragginess; sierra 209 *high land*; rough going, dirt road, dirt track; unevenness 17 *nonuniformity*; kink, corrugation, ripple, corrugated iron 261 *fold*; rut 262 *furrow*; coarseness, coarse grain 253 *convexity*; washboard, grater, file, sandpaper, glasspaper, emery paper, emery board; sackcloth, tweed, homespun 222 *textile*; gooseflesh, goose pimples; chap, hack, crack; shagginess; hairiness; stubble, five o'clock shadow, burr, bristle, scrubbing brush, nailbrush.

hair 208 *filament*; head of h., shock of h., matted h., thatch, fuzz, wool; crop, mop, mane, fleece, shag; bristle, stubble, five o'clock shadow; locks, flowing l.; crowning glory, tresses, curls, ringlet; kiss curl; strand, plait, braid; pigtail, ponytail, bunches, rat's tails; topknot, forelock, lovelock, dread locks; fringe, bangs, cowlick, quiff, widow's peak; roll, French pleat, bun, chignon 843 *hair-dressing*; false hair, hairpiece, hair extension, switch, wig, toupee 228 *head-gear*; wisp; beard, full b., beaver, goatee, imperial, Van Dyke, Abe Lincoln; whiskers, sideboards, sideburns, mutton-chops; moustache, moustachio, toothbrush, handlebars; facial hair; eyebrows, eyelashes; woolliness, fleeciness, downiness, fluffiness; down, pubic hair, wool, fur 226 *skin*; tuft, flock; mohair, cashmere, Angora 208 *fibre*; fluff, fuzz; horsehair 227 *lining*.

plumage, feathering, quill, feathers; neck feathers, hackle; ruff, frill, plume, crest; peacock's feathers, ostrich f. 844 *finery*.

Adj. *rough*, irregular, uneven; rippling, choppy, storm-tossed; stony, rocky, rutted, pitted, potholed, bumpy; roughcast; lumpy, stony, nodular, studded, roughened, frosted; nubbly, slubbed, bouclé; crinkled 251 *undulatory*; knotted, gnarled, coarse-grained, coarse; cracked, hacked, chapped; lined, wrinkled, corrugated, ridged; rough-edged; craggy, jagged; scabby, pockmarked, acned, warty, scaly, blistered; ruffled, unkempt, unpolished; unsifted.

hairy, woolly, fleecy, furry; hirsute, shaggy, matted; bristly 256 *sharp*; wispy, straggly, fringed, bearded, moustached; unshaven, unshorn; curly, frizzy, fuzzy, permed, woolly.

Vb. *be rough*, – hairy etc. adj.; bristle 254 *jut*;

creep (of flesh); scratch; jolt, bump, jerk 278 *move slowly*.

roughen, roughcast, rough-hew; serrate, indent 260 *notch*; stud, boss; corrugate, wrinkle, ripple, kink 251 *crinkle*; disorder, ruffle, tousle, tangle 63 *derange*; rumple, crumple, crease 261 *fold*; rub up the wrong way, set on edge; chap, crack, hack.

260 Notch

N. *notch*, serration, ragged edge 256 *sharpness*; indentation, deckle edge; crenellation 713 *fortification*; nick, snip, cut, gash, crenation 201 *gap*; indent, dent, dint, dimple 255 *concavity*; scallop, dogtooth 844 *pattern*; sprocket, cog, ratchet, cogwheel; saw, hacksaw, chain saw, circular saw 256 *tooth*; battlement.

Vb. *notch*, serrate, tooth, cog; nick, score, scratch, scarify, bite, slice 46 *cut*; crenellate, indent, scallop, jag, pink, slash; dent, knurl 259 *roughen*; pinch, snip, crimp 261 *fold*.

261 Fold

N. *fold*, flexure, doubling; facing, revers, hem; lapel, cuff, turnup; plait, braid, ply, pleat, box p., accordion p., knife-edge p.; tuck, gather, pucker, ruche, ruffle; flounce, frill; wrinkle, ruck; frown, lines, wrinkles, age zones, crow's feet 131 *age*; joint.

Vb. *fold*, double, turn over, bend over, roll; corrugate, furrow, wrinkle 262 *groove*; pucker; ruffle, gather, frill, ruck, shirr, smock; hem, cuff; turn up; enfold, wrap, swathe 235 *enclose*; fold up, furl.

262 Furrow

N. *furrow*, groove, slot, slit, rabbet, mortise; crack, split, chink, cranny 201 *gap*; trough, hollow 255 *cavity*; flute, fluting, goffering; chamfer, bezel, incision, gash, slash, scratch, score 46 *scission*; streak, striation 437 *stripe*; rut 548 *trace*; gutter, ditch, dike, trench, dugout, moat, channel 351 *conduit*; ravine 255 *valley*; wrinkle, corrugation; corduroy, corrugated iron, washboard, ploughed field; ripple.

Vb. *groove*, slot, flute, chamfer; gash, scratch, score, incise 46 *cut*; claw, tear 655 *wound*; striate, streak 437 *variegate*; carve, bite in, etch 555 *engrave*; furrow, plough, channel, rut, wrinkle, line; corrugate, goffer 261 *fold*.

263 Opening

N. *opening*, throwing open, openness, glasnost; uncorking, uncapping 229 *uncovering*; yawn, yawning, splitting; gaping; hiatus, lacuna, space, interval 201 *gap*; aperture, split, crack, leak 46 *disunion*; hole, potato; hollow 255 *cavity*; placket.

perforation, piercing, body-piercing, tattooing; puncture, acupuncture; pinhole, eyelet.

porosity, porousness, sponge; sieve, sifter, riddle, screen 62 *sorting*; strainer, tea s., colander; grater; honeycomb, pincushion.

orifice, aperture, slot; oral cavity, mouth, gob, trap, kisser, mush, moosh, jaws, muzzle; throat, gullet 194 *stomach*; sucker; vagina, anus; flue pipe 353 *air pipe*; nozzle, spout, vent, vent-hole 298 *outlet*; blowhole, air-hole; nostril; rivermouth, pore; hole, crater, pothole 255 *cavity*; manhole, armhole, keyhole, buttonhole, punch hole, pin h.; pigeonhole 194 *compartment*; eye, eye of a needle, eyelet; ring 250 *loop*.

window, fenestration; shop window, plateglass w., glass front; embrasure 713 *fortification*; lattice, grille; casement window, leaded w., sash w., bay w., oriel w., dormer w., French w., picture w.; rose window, lancet w. 990 *church interior*; light, fanlight, skylight, sunshine roof; companion, cabin window, port, porthole; peephole, keyhole; car window, windscreen, windshield; window frame, casement, sash, mullion, transom; window pane 422 *transparency*.

doorway, archway; doorstep, threshold 68 *entrance*; approach, drive, driveway, entry 297 *way in*; exit, way out; passage, corridor, gangway, drawbridge 624 *access*; gate, gateway; portal, porch; door, front d., Dutch d.; swing doors, revolving d., double d.; church d., lychgate; back door, tradesmen's d., postern 238 *rear*; small door, wicket; cat-flap; hatch, hatchway; trapdoor, companionway; stairwell; door jamb, gatepost, lintel; concierge 264 *doorkeeper*; entryphone.

open space 183 *space*; yard, court 185 *place*; opening, clearing, glade, panorama, vista 438 *view*; landscape, open country 348 *plain*.

tunnel, boring; subway, underpass, underground railway, underground, tube, metro; Channel Tunnel, chunnel; mine, shaft, pit, gallery, adit 255 *excavation*; cave 255 *cavity*; bolthole, rabbit hole, fox h., mouse h. 192 *dwelling*; funnel 252 *cone*; sewer 351 *drain*; qanat.

tube, pipe, duct 351 *conduit*; tubule, pipette, cannula; catheter, tubing, piping, pipeline, hose; artery, vein, capillary; colon, gut 224 *insides*; funnel, fistula.

opener, key, master k., skeleton k.; doorknob, handle; corkscrew, tin opener, can o., bottle o.; aperient, purgative; password, open sesame; passport.

perforator, piercer, borer, corer; gimlet, corkscrew; auger, drill, pneumatic d.; bit, brace and b.; trepan; probe, lancet, lance, bodkin, needle, hypodermic n.; awl, bradawl 256 *sharp point*;

pin, nail 47 *fastening*; skewer, spit, broach, stiletto 723 *weapon*; punch, card p., stapler; dibble; pickaxe, pick, ice p.

Adj. *open*, exposed to view, on view 522 *manifest*; uncapped, uncorked, ajar; unbolted, unlocked, unbarred, unobstructed 289 *accessible*; wide-open, gaping, yawning, openmouthed, gaping; opening, aperient; in bloom, out.

porous, permeable, spongy, percolating, leachy, leaky, leaking.

Vb. *open*, declare open, give the open sesame, give a passport to, unfold, unwrap, unpack, unpackage, undo, unlock, unlatch, unbolt, open the door, fling wide the gates 299 *admit*; uncover, bare; unplug, unstop, uncap, uncork; lay open, throw o. 522 *show*; force open 176 *force*; cut open, tear o., crack o.; fly open, split, gape, yawn; burst, explode; open out, fan o., deploy 75 *be dispersed*; unclench, bloom, be out.

pierce, transfix, impale; gore, run through, stick, pink, lance, bayonet, spear 655 *wound*; spike, skewer, spit; prick, puncture, tattoo, body-pierce; probe, stab, poke; inject; perforate, hole, riddle, pepper, honeycomb; knock holes in, punch, punch full of holes; bore, drill, trepan; burrow, tunnel, mine 255 *make concave*; cut through, penetrate 297 *enter*.

Adv. *openly*, frankly, unguardedly, out in the open.

264 Closure

N. *closure*, closing, closing down, shutting etc. vb.; occlusion, stoppage; contraction, strangulation 198 *compression*; sealing off, blockade 232 *circumscription*; 235 *enclosure*; embolism, obstruction, infarction, constipation, strangury; dead end, cul-de-sac, impasse, blank wall, road block 702 *obstacle*; caecum.

stopper, cork, plug, bung, peg; ramrod, piston; valve; wedge, tampon; wadding, padding, stuffing, stopping 227 *lining*; gag, muzzle 748 *fetter*; shutter 421 *screen*; tourniquet; damper, choke; tap, faucet, stopcock, top, lid, cap, cover, seal 226 *covering*; lock, Yale (tdmk) lock, mortise l., key, bolt, latch, bar 47 *fastening*.

doorkeeper, doorman, gatekeeper, porter, janitor, commissionaire, concierge; sentry, sentinel, night watchman 660 *protector*; warden, guard, guard dog, vigilante, 749 *keeper*; jailer, prison warder, turnkey, Cerberus 749 *gaoler*.

Adj. *closed*, unopened, shut etc. vb.; shuttered, bolted, barred, locked; stoppered, corked, unpierced, nonporous, impervious, impermeable 324 *dense*; impenetrable, impassable 470 *impracticable*; dead-end; clogged up, stuffed up, bunged up; strangulated.

Vb. *close*, shut, occlude, seal; clinch, fix,

bind, make tight 45 *tighten*; put the lid on, cap 226 *cover*; batten down the hatches; slam, bang (a door); lock, fasten, plug, bung up, cork, stopper, button, zip up, do up 45 *join*; knit, furrow, clench (fist); block, dam, staunch, choke, throttle, strangle, smother, asphyxiate 702 *obstruct*; blockade 712 *besiege*; enclose, surround, shut in, seal off 232 *circumscribe*; trap, bolt, latch, bar, lock in 747 *imprison*; shut down, clamp d., batten d., ram d., tamp d., put up the shutters; close down, go out of business, flop, go bust, fail.

SECTION FOUR

Motion

265 Motion: successful change of place

N. *motion*, movement, move, march; speed, acceleration, pace, tempo; locomotion, motility, mobility, movableness; kinetic energy, motive power; forward motion, advance, progress, headway 285 *progression*; backward motion 286 *regression*, 290 *recession*; motion towards 289 *approach*, 293 *convergence*; motion away, shift 294 *divergence*, 282 *deviation*; motion into 297 *ingress*; motion out of 298 *egress*; upward motion, rising 308 *ascent*; downward motion, sinking, plummeting 309 *descent*, 313 *plunge*; motion round, circumnavigation 314 *circuition*; axial motion 315 *rotation*, 316 *evolution*; to and fro movement, fluctuation 317 *oscillation*; irregular motion 318 *agitation*; stir, bustle, unrest, restlessness 678 *activity*; rapid motion 277 *velocity*; slow motion 278 *slowness*; regular motion 16 *uniformity*, 71 *continuity*; recurring movement, cycle, rhythm 141 *periodicity*; motion in front 283 *preceding*; motion after 284 *following*, 619 *pursuit*; conduction, conductivity 272 *transference*; current, flow, flux, drift 350 *stream*; course, career, run; traffic, flow of traffic; transit 305 *passage*; transportation 272 *transport*; running, jogging, walking, footslogging, marathoning 267 *pedestrianism*; riding 267 *equitation*; travel 267 *land travel*, 269 *water travel*, 271 *air travel*; dancing, tangoing, gliding, sliding, skating, rolling, skipping; manoeuvre, manoeuvring, footwork; exercise, aerobics, gymnastics 162 *athletics*; gesticulation 547 *gesture*; motion picture, film 445 *cinema*; laws of motion, kinetics, dynamics.

gait, walk, carriage 688 *conduct*; pace, step, stride; run, lope, jog; hop, skip, jump 312 *leap*; skid, slide, slip; waddle, shuffle; undulate, swagger, stalk, strut, goosestep 875 *formality*; march; trot, amble, canter, gallop 267 *equitation*.

Adj. *moving*, rolling etc. vb.; in motion, under way; motive, motor; motile, movable, mobile; progressive, regressive; locomotive, automotive; transitional, shifting; mercurial 152 *changeful*; restless 678 *active*; nomadic; drifting, erratic, meandering, runaway; kinetic; cinematographic.

Vb. *be in motion*, move, go, hie, gang, wend, trail; budge, stir; flutter, wave, flap 217 *hang*; march, tramp 267 *walk*; tread; trip, dance 312 *leap*; shuffle, waddle 278 *move slowly*; toddle, patter; run, jog 277 *move fast*; run on wheels, roll, taxi; stream, roll on, drift 350 *flow*; paddle 269 *row*; skitter, slide, slither, skate, ski, sledge, toboggan, glide; fly, frisk, flit, dart, hover; climb 308 *ascend*; sink, plunge, plummet 309 *descend*; coast, cruise, steam, chug, proceed 146 *go on*; make one's way, push one's w., elbow one's w., shoulder one's w. 285 *progress*; pass through, wade t., pass by 305 *pass*; make a move, shift, dodge, duck, shift about, jink, jouk, tack, manoeuvre 282 *deviate*; twist 251 *wriggle*; creep, crawl, worm one's way, go on all fours; hover about, hang a. 136 *wait*; move house, flit, relocate; change places 151 *interchange*; move over, make room 190 *go away*; travel, stray 267 *wander*.

move, put in m.; set going; put skates under; put a bomb under, galvanize, actuate, switch on, put into operation 173 *operate*; stir up, jerk 318 *agitate*; budge, shift, trundle, roll, wheel 188 *displace*; push, shove 279 *impel*; move on, drive, hustle 680 *hasten*; tug, pull 288 *draw*; fling, throw 287 *propel*; convey, transport 272 *transfer*, dispatch 272 *send*; mobilize 74 *bring together*; scatter 75 *disperse*; raise, uplift 310 *elevate*; throw down, drop 311 *let fall*; motion, gesture 547 *gesticulate*; transpose 151 *interchange*.

266 Quiescence

N. *quiescence*, motionlesness; subsidence 145 *cessation*; rest, stillness; deadness; stagnation, 679 *inactivity*; pause, truce, standstill 145 *lull*; stoppage, halt; deadlock, gridlock, full stop, dead s. 145 *stop*; embargo, freeze 757 *prohibition*; immobility, rigidity, stiffness 326 *hardness*; equilibrium 153 *stability*; trance.

quietude, quiet, quietness, stillness, hush 399 *silence*; tranquillity, peacefulness 717 *peace*; rest 683 *repose*; eternal rest 361 *death*; sleepiness, slumber 679 *sleep*; calm, millpond 258 *smoothness*; not a breath of air; dead quiet, not a mouse stirring; composure, cool 823 *inexcitability*; passivity, quietism; tranquillizer, sedation 177 *moderator*.

Adj. *quiescent*, quiet, still; asleep 679 *sleepy*; resting, at rest, becalmed; at anchor, anchored, moored, docked; at a standstill, stopped, idle 679 *inactive*; unemployed, disemployed, out of commission, inoperative; dormant, stagnant,

vegetating, static, stationary 175 *inert*; sedentary; on one's back 216 *supine*; disabled, housebound, confined to bed 747 *restrained*; settled; unmoved 860 *indifferent*.

tranquil, undisturbed, sequestered 883 *secluded*; peaceful, restful; unhurried, easygoing 681 *leisurely*; uneventful 16 *uniform*; calm, like a millpond, airless; glassy 258 *smooth*; sunny, halcyon 730 *palmy*; at ease, comfortable, relaxed 683 *reposeful*; tranquillized, sedated, under sedation; cool, unruffled, serene 823 *inexcitable*.

still, unmoving, unstirring, not fizzy, flat 387 *tasteless*; immobile, motionless, expressionless, deadpan, poker-faced 820 *impassive*; steady, unblinking 153 *unchangeable*; rooted to the ground *or* spot 153 *fixed*; transfixed, spellbound; immovable, becalmed, stuck; stiff, frozen 326 *rigid*; paralysed 375 *insensible*; quiet, so quiet you could hear a pin drop, hushed, soundless 399 *silent*; stock-still, still as a statue, still as death; quiet as a mouse.

Vb. *be quiescent*, – still etc. adj.; subside, die down 37 *decrease*; pipe down 399 *be silent*; stand still, lie s., keep quiet; stagnate, vegetate; stand, mark time 136 *wait*; stay put, sit tight, remain in situ, remain 144 *stay*; ride at anchor; tarry 145 *pause*; rest, sit down, take a breather, rest on one's laurels, rest on one's oars 683 *repose*; retire, go to bed, doss down, turn in 679 *sleep*; settle down 187 *place oneself*; stick fast; jam; stand firm; not move a muscle, not stir a step; be at a standstill 145 *cease*.

come to rest, stop, stop short, stop in one's tracks, stop dead in one's tracks, freeze 145 *halt*; pull up, draw up; anchor, alight 295 *land*; relax, cool it, rest, pause 683 *repose*.

bring to rest, quiet, quieten, quell, hush 399 *silence*; lull, soothe, calm down, tranquillize, sedate 177 *assuage*; lull to sleep, cradle, rock; let alone, let well alone, let sleeping dogs lie 620 *avoid*; bring to a standstill, bring to, heave to; brake, put the brake on 278 *retard*; stay, immobilize 679 *make inactive*.

Int. stop! stay! halt! whoa! hold hard! hold on! hold it! don't move! freeze!

267 Land travel

N. *land travel*, travel, travelling; globe-trotting; tourism; walking, hiking, riding, driving, motoring, cycling, biking; journey, voyage, odyssey; course, passage; pilgrimage, quest, expedition, safari, trek, field trip; reconnaissance, exploration, orienteering, youth hostelling, backpacking; visit, trip, business t., tour, grand t., coach t.; package t.; circuit, turn, round, patrol, commuting; round trip, day t. 314 *circuition*; jaunt, hop, spin; ride, bike r., joy r., drive, lift;

excursion, outing, airing; ramble, constitutional, promenade. See *pedestrianism*.

pedestrianism, walking, going on foot, footing it, Shanks's pony; foot-slogging, striding, tramping, marching, backpacking; perambulation; walkabout 314 *circuition*; walk, promenade, constitutional; stroll, saunter, amble, ramble; hike, tramp, march, walking tour; run, cross-country run, jog, trot, jog t., lope 265 *gait*; foot race, racewalking, marathon 716 *racing*; sleepwalking, somnambulism.

marching, marching and countermarching; march, forced m., route m., quick march, slow m.; march past, parade, cavalcade, procession 875 *formality*.

equitation, equestrianism, horsemanship *or* horsewomanship, manège, dressage 694 *skill*; show jumping, eventing, gymkhana, steeplechasing, point-to-point racing 716 *contest*; horse racing; riding, bareback r. 162 *athletics*.

conveyance, lift, elevator, escalator, travelator 274 *conveyor*; feet, own two f. 214 *foot*; legs, Shanks's pony; horseback, mount 273 *horse*; bicycle, moped, scooter, motor cycle, car, bus, train, coach, taxi, ambulance 274 *vehicle*; traffic.

leg, limb, foreleg, hindleg; shank, shin, calf; thigh, ham, hamstrings; knee, kneecap 247 *angularity*; tibia, fibula, legs, pegs, pins 218 *prop*; stumps, stilts; stump, wooden leg, artificial l., prosthesis 150 *substitute*; bow legs, bandy l., knock-knees 845 *blemish*; thick legs, piano l., legs like tree stumps; long legs, spindle shanks.

itinerary, route 624 *way*; course 281 *direction*; route map, road m., plan, chart 551 *map*; guide, Baedeker, timetable, Bradshaw, A-Z 524 *guidebook*; milestone, fingerpost 547 *signpost*.

Vb. *travel*, journey, tour, see the world, go globetrotting, go on a world cruise, visit, explore 484 *discover*; get around, knock about, go places, sightsee, rubberneck; go on a pilgrimage; go on a trip, go on a journey; go on safari, trek, hump bluey; hike, backpack; be always on the move, live out of a suitcase; set out, take wing 296 *depart*; migrate, emigrate, immigrate, settle 187 *place oneself*; shuttle, commute; take oneself off, swan off, slope o.; go to, hie to, repair to, resort to, betake oneself to 295 *arrive*, 882 *visit*; go 265 *be in motion*; wend one's way, stir one's stumps, bend one's steps, shape one's course, tread a path, follow the road; make one's way, pick one's way, thread one's w., elbow one's w., force a w., plough through; jog on, trudge on, shuffle on, pad on, plod on, tramp on, march on, chug on 146 *sustain*; course, race, post 277 *move fast*; proceed, advance 285 *progress*; coast, free-wheel, glide, slide, skate, ski, skim, roll along, bowl a., fly a.

traverse, cross, range, pass through, range t.

305 *pass*; go round, beat the bounds 314 *circle*; go the rounds, make one's rounds, patrol; scout, reconnoitre 438 *scan*; scour, sweep, sweep through.

wander, migrate; rove, roam, bum around; ramble, amble, stroll, saunter, mosey along, potter, dawdle, walk about, trail around; gad, traipse, gallivant, gad about, hover, flit about, dart a. 265 *be in motion*; prowl, skulk 523 *lurk*; straggle, trail 75 *be dispersed*; lose the way, get lost, wander away 282 *stray*.

walk, step, tread, pace, stride; stride out 277 *move fast*; strut, stalk, prance, mince 871 *be proud*; tread lightly, tiptoe, trip, skip, dance, curvet 312 *leap*; tread heavily, lumber, clump, stamp, tramp, goosestep; toddle, patter, pad; totter, stagger, lurch, reel, stumble 317 *oscillate*; limp, hobble, waddle, shuffle, shamble, dawdle 278 *move slowly*; paddle, wade; go on foot, go by Shanks's pony, foot it, hoof it, hike, footslog, wear out shoe leather; plod, stump, trudge, jog; go, go for a walk, perambulate, pace up and down; go for a run *or* a jog, take the air, take one's constitutional; march, troop; file, file past, defile, march in procession 65 *come after*; walk behind 284 *follow*; walk in front 283 *precede*.

ride, mount, hack; trot, amble, canter, gallop; prance, caper; cycle, bicycle, bike, motorcycle; freewheel, coast; drive, motor; go by bike, go by car, go by bus, bus it, go by coach, go by taxi, go by cab; go by road, go by tube, go by train; go by air 271 *fly*; take a lift, take a ride, cadge a lift, thumb a l., hitchhike.

Int. come along! move along there! move it! get along! get going! get out! git! go away! be off! buzz off! piss off (vulg)! hop it! skedaddle! scram!

268 Traveller

N. *traveller*, itinerant, wayfarer; explorer, adventurer, voyager 270 *mariner*; air traveller, spaceman *or* -woman, astronaut 271 *aeronaut*; pioneer, pathfinder, explorer 66 *precursor*; alpinist, mountaineer, cragsman 308 *climber*; pilgrim; walker, hiker, rambler, trekker; backpacker, camper, caravanner, youth hosteller; globe-trotter, tourist, rubberneck, sightseer 441 *spectator*; tripper, day-t., excursionist; sunseeker, holidaymaker, visitor; roundsman, hawker 794 *pedlar*; doorstepper, canvasser; travelling salesman, commercial traveller, rep 793 *seller*; messenger, errandboy 529 *courier*; daily traveller, commuter.

wanderer, migrant, bird of passage, visitant 365 *bird*; floating population, nomad, bedouin; gypsy; didicoi, Romany; New Age traveller, rover, ranger, rambler, promenader, stroller;

strolling player, wandering minstrel, touring company 594 *entertainer*; rolling stone, drifter, vagrant, vagabond, tramp, knight of the road, bag lady; swagman, sundowner, hobo, bum; loafer, beachcomber 679 *idler*; emigrant, émigré, refugee, deportee, exile 59 *foreigner*; runaway, fugitive, escapee 620 *avoider*; waif, stray, the homeless, rough sleeper, skell 801 *poor person*.

pedestrian, foot passenger, walker, tramper; jogger, sprinter, runner 716 *contender*; toddler; wader, paddler; skater, skier; skateboarder, roller-skater; hiker, hitch-h., foot-slogger; marcher 722 *infantry*; somnambulist, sleepwalker; prowler, loiterer; footpad 789 *robber*.

rider, horse-rider, camel-r., cameleer; elephant-rider, mahout; horseman, horsewoman, equestrian; postilion, postboy 529 *courier*; mounted police, Mounties; cavalier, knight, knight errant 722 *cavalry*; hunt, huntsman 619 *hunter*; jockey, steeplechaser, show jumper, eventer 716 *contender*; trainer, breaker 369 *breeder*; roughrider, bareback r., broncobuster, cowboy, cowgirl, cowpuncher, gaucho, rodeo rider; cyclist, bicyclist, biker; circus rider, trick rider 162 *athlete*; motorcyclist, moped rider, scooterist;

driver, coachman; carter, waggoner, drayman; car driver, chauffeur, motorist, white-van man, roadhog; joy rider; L-driver 538 *beginner*; taxi driver, cab d., cabby; bus driver, coach d.; lorry d., truck d., van d., trucker, routier, teamster; tractor d.; motorman, train driver, engine d.; pilot 271 *aeronaut*.

269 Water travel

N. *water travel*, seafaring, life on the ocean wave; navigation, voyaging, sailing, cruising; coasting, longshore sailing; boating, yachting, rowing (**see** *aquatics*); voyage, navigation, cruise, sail; course, run, passage, crossing, ferry c.; circumnavigation 314 *circuition*; sea trip, river t., canal t., breath of sea air 685 *refreshment*; way, headway, steerage way, sternway, seaway 265 *motion*; leeway, driftway 282 *deviation*; wake, track, wash, backwash 350 *eddy*; sea-path, sea lane, approaches 624 *route*; boat, sailing ship 275 *ship*; sailor 270 *mariner*.

navigation, piloting, steering, pilotage 689 *directorship*; astronavigation; plane sailing, plain s., spherical s., great-circle s., parallel s.; compass reading, dead reckoning 465 *measurement*; pilotship, seamanship 694 *skill*.

aquatics, boating, sailing, yachting, cruising; rowing, sculling, canoeing; yacht racing, speedboat r., ocean r. 716 *racing*; water skiing, surf riding, surfing, wind s., skiboarding, boardsailing; jet-skiing; rafting, white-water r., hydrospeeding; watersports 837 *sport*; natation, swimming, floating; stroke, breast s., side s., crawl, back c., front c., butterfly, dogpaddle; diving, plunging 313 *plunge*; wading, paddling; swimsuit 228 *beachwear*.

sailing aid, navigational instrument, sextant, quadrant 247 *angular measure*; chronometer, ship's c. 117 *timekeeper*; log, line; lead, plummet 211 *depth*; anchor 662 *safeguard*; compass, astrocompass, magnetic c., ship's c.; needle, magnetic n.; card, compass c. *or* rose; binnacle; gyrocompass 689 *directorship*; radar 484 *detector*; helm, wheel, tiller, rudder, steering oar, sea mark, buoy, lighthouse, pharos, lightship 547 *signpost*; chart, Admiralty c., portolano 551 *map*; nautical almanac, ephemeris 524 *guidebook*.

propeller, screw, twin screw, blade, rotor 287 *propellant*; paddle wheel, stern w., floatboard; oar, sweep, paddle, scull; pole, punt p., barge p.; fin, flipper, fish's tail 53 *limb*; sails 275 *sail*.

Vb. *go to sea*, join the navy; become a sailor, get one's sea legs; sail before the mast; go sailing, boat, yacht, cruise.

voyage, sail, go by sea, go by ship, go by boat, take the ferry, take the sea route; work one's passage; embark, go on board, put to sea, set sail, up anchor 296 *start out*; disembark, land 295 *arrive*; cruise; steam, ply, run, tramp, ferry; coast, hug the shore; roll, pitch, toss.

navigate, man a ship, work a s., crew; put to sea, set sail; launch, push off, boom off; unmoor, cast off, weigh anchor; get up steam; hoist sail, spread canvas; get under way, gather w., make w., carry sail 265 *be in motion*; drop the pilot; set a course, make for, head for 281 *steer for*; read the chart, go by the card 281 *orientate*; pilot, steer, hold the helm, captain 689 *direct*; stroke, cox, cox-swain; trim the sails, square, square away; change course, veer, gybe, yaw 282 *deviate*; put about, wear ship 282 *turn round*; run before the wind, scud 277 *move fast*; put the helm up, fall to leeward, pay off; put the helm down, luff, bring into the wind; beat to windward, luff, tack, weather; back and fill; round, double a point, circumnavigate 314 *circle*; be caught amidships 700 *be in difficulty*; careen, list, heel over 220 *be oblique*; turn turtle, capsize, overturn 221 *invert*; ride out the storm, weather the s., keep afloat 667 *escape*; run for port 662 *seek refuge*; lie to, lay to, heave to 266 *bring to rest*; take soundings, heave the lead 465 *measure*; tide over 507 *await*; tow, haul, warp, kedge, clubhaul 288 *draw*; ground, run aground, wreck, be cast away 165 *destroy*; sight land, make a landfall, take on a pilot 289 *approach*; make port; cast anchor, drop a.; moor, tie up, dock, disembark 295 *land*; cross one's bows, take the wind out of one's sails, outmanoeuvre, gain the weather gauge 702 *obstruct*; foul 279 *collide*; back, go astern 286 *regress*; surface, break water 298 *emerge*; flood the tank dive 313 *plunge*; shoot, shoot a bridge, shoot the rapids 305 *pass*.

row, ply the oar, get the sweeps out; pull, stroke, scull; feather; catch a crab; ship oars; punt; paddle, canoe; boat; shoot the rapids.

swim, go swimming, do the breast stroke, do the crawl (**see** aquatics); aquaplane; strike out, breast the current, stem the stream; tread water; dive 313 *plunge*; bathe, dip, duck; wade, paddle.

270 Mariner
N. *mariner*, sailor, sea-man, seafaring man; salt, old s., seadog, shellback; tar, Jack Tar, limey, matelot; bad sailor, fairweather s., landlubber 697 *bungler*; skipper, master mariner, master, ship m.; mate, boatswain, bosun; coxswain; able seaman, A.B. 696 *expert*; deckhand, swabbie; ship's steward, cabin boy 742 *servant*; shipmates, hearties; crew, complement, ship's c., men, watch 686 *personnel*; trawler, whaler, deep-sea fisherman; sea rover, privateer, buccaneer, sea king, Viking, pirate 789 *robber*; sea scout, sea cadet.

navigator, pilot, sailing master, helmsman, steersman, wheelman, man at the wheel, quartermaster; coxswain, cox 690 *leader*; leadsman, lookout man; foretop-man, reefer; boatswain, bosun's mate; circumnavigator; compass 269 *sailing aid*.

nautical personnel, marine, submariner, naval cadet, bluejacket, rating 722 *naval man*; petty officer, midshipman, middy, lieutenant, sub-l., commander, captain, commodore, admiral 741 *naval officer*; Admiralty, Sea Lord; Trinity House, lighthouse keeper, coastguard 660 *protector*; lifeboatman 703 *aider*; river police, naval patrol, harbour p., harbourmaster.

boatman, waterman, rowing man, wet bob; gigsman; galley slave; oar, oarsman, sculler, rower, punter; paddler, canoeist; yachtsman *or* -woman; gondolier, ferryman; wherryman, bargeman, bargee, lighterman; stevedore, docker, longshoreman; lock keeper.

271 Aeronautics
N. *aeronautics*, aeromechanics, aerodynamics, aerostatics; aerostation, ballooning; aerospace, astronautics; aeroballistics, rocketry 276 *rocket*; volitation, flight, vertical f., horizontal f.; subsonic f., supersonic f. 277 *velocity*; stratospheric flight, hypersonic f., space f.; aviation, flying, night f., blind f., instrument f.; shoran, teleran; gliding, powered g., hang-g.; parachuting, skydiving, free fall; flypast, formation flying, stunt f., aerobatics 875 *ostentation*; skywriting, vapour trail; planing, volplaning, looping the loop; spin, roll, side-slip; volplane, nose dive, pull-out; crash dive, crash, prang 309 *descent*; pancake, landing, belly l., crash l., forced l.; talkdown, touchdown 295 *arrival*; takeoff, vertical t. 296 *departure*.

air travel, air transport, airlift 272 *transport*; air service, airline; shuttle service, scheduled flight, charter f.; air miles; airlane, airway, air route 624 *route*; flight path, glide p., line of flight 281 *direction*; airspace 184 *territory*; takeoff, touchdown, landing; airbase; airstrip, runway, tarmac, airfield, aerodrome, airport; heliport, helipad; terminal, air t., check-in desk, luggage carousel, baggage reclaim, airside, landside 295 *goal*; hangar 192 *stable*; fear of flying, aerophobia; jetlag.

space travel, space flight, manned s.f., spacefaring 276 *spaceship*; lift-off, blast-off; orbit, flyby; docking, space walk; reentry, splashdown, soft landing; cosmodrome, spaceport, space station, space platform, space shuttle; launching pad, silo; spacesuit.

aeronaut, balloonist; glider, hang g., sky diver, parachutist; paratrooper 722 *soldier*; aviator, aviatrix, airwoman, airman, birdman; astronaut, cosmonaut, spaceman, spacewoman, space traveller; air traveller, air passenger, jet set 268 *traveller*; air hostess, steward, stewardess, cabin personnel 742 *servant*; flier, pilot, test p., jet p., copilot; automatic pilot, autopilot; navigator, air crew; pilot officer, flying o. 741 *air officer*; aircraftman 722 *air force*; air personnel, ground crew 686 *personnel*.

wing, pinion, feathers, flight f., wing feather, wing spread 259 *plumage*; sweptback wing, deltawing, swingwing, variable w.; aerofoil, aileron, flaps.

Vb. *fly*, wing, be on the w.; wing one's way, be wafted; soar, rise 308 *ascend*; hover, hang over 217 *hang*; flutter, flit 265 *be in motion*; taxi, take off, leave the ground, climb, circle 296 *depart*; be airborne, have lift-off; aviate, glide, plane; float, drift 323 *be light*; hit an air pocket, experience turbulence, stunt, spin, roll, side-slip, loop the loop, volplane; hedgehop, skim the rooftops, buzz; stall, dive, power-dive, nose-d., spiral 313 *plunge*; crash, prang, forceland, crash-land, pancake, ditch 309 *tumble*; pull out, flatten o.; touch down 295 *land*; bale out, jump, parachute, eject; blast off, lift o., take o.; orbit, go into o. 314 *circle*.

272 Transference
N. *transference*, relocation, transplantation, transhipment, transfer, bussing, commuting, shuttling; shifting, shift, drift, longshore d.,

continental d. 282 *deviation*; posting 751 *mandate*; transposition, metathesis 151 *interchange*; removal, moving house, flitting, relegation, deportation, expulsion 300 *ejection*; unpacking, unloading, airdrop 188 *displacement*; exportation, export 791 *trade*; trade-off, mutual transfer 791 *barter*; importation, import 299 *reception*; distribution, logistics 633 *provision*; transmittal, forwarding, sending, remittance, dispatch; recalling, recall, extradition 304 *extraction*; recovery, retrieval 771 *acquisition*; handing over, delivery; takeover 792 *purchase*; conveyance, transfer of property, donation 780 *transfer*; committal, trust 751 *commission*; gaol delivery, habeas corpus, release 746 *liberation*; transition, metastasis; passing over, ferry, ferriage 305 *passage*; transmigration 143 *transformation*; transmission, throughput; conduction, convection; transfusion; decantation; diffusion, dispersal 75 *dispersion*; communication, contact 378 *touch*; contagion, infection, contamination 178 *influence*; transcription, transumption, copying, transliteration 520 *translation*.

transport, transportation; conveyance, carriage, shipping, shipment; carrying, humping, portage, porterage, haulage, draught 288 *traction*; carting; freightage, air freight, airlift; rail, road 274 *vehicle*; sea, canal 275 *ship*; pipeline, conveyor belt 274 *conveyor*; flotsam, jetsam, trust 767 *security*; legacy, bequest 781 *gift*; lease 777 *property*; cargo, load, payload, freight; consignment, shipment 193 *contents*; goods, mails; luggage, baggage, impedimenta; container, container-load, lorryload, trainload, coachload, busload; person transferred, passenger, rider, commuter 268 *traveller*.

Vb. *transfer*, hand over, deliver 780 *assign*; leave 780 *bequeath*; commit, entrust 751 *commission*; transmit, hand down, hand on, pass on; make over, turn over, hand to, pass to; transfer responsibility to, delegate, pass the buck; export, transport, convey, ship, airlift, fly, ferry 273 *carry*; infect, contaminate 178 *influence*; conduct, convect; carry over 38 *add*; transfer itself to, come off on, adhere, stick 48 *cohere*.

transpose, shift, move 188 *displace*; transfer, relocate, switch, shunt, shuffle, castle (chess) 151 *interchange*; detach, detail, draft; relegate, deport, expel, sack 300 *eject*; drag, pull 288 *draw*; push, shove 279 *impel*; containerize 193 *load*; channel, funnel, pour in *or* out, transfuse, decant, strain off, siphon off 300 *empty*; unload, remove 188 *displace*; download, upload; shovel, ladle, spoon out, bail out 255 *make concave*; transliterate 520 *translate*.

send, remit, transmit, dispatch; direct, consign, address; post, mail; redirect, readdress, post on, forward; send by hand, deliver in person, send by post; send for, order, mailorder, tele-order 627 *require*; send away, detach, detail 287 *propel*.

Adv. *in transit*, en route, on the way; in the post; in the pipeline.

273 Carrier

N. *carrier*, haulier, carter, waggoner; shipper, transporter, exporter, importer; ferryman 270 *boatman*; lorry driver, truck d., van d., bus d. 268 *driver*; delivery boy; delivery van, lorry, truck, juggernaut, cart, goods train 274 *vehicle*; barge, cargo vessel, freighter, tramp 275 *ship*; chassis, undercarriage 218 *prop*; pallet, container; carrier bag, plastic b., poly b. 194 *bag*; conveyor belt, escalator 274 *conveyor*.

beast of burden, packhorse, packmule; ass, she-a., donkey, moke, Neddy, cuddy, burro; ox, oxen, bullock, draught animals 365 *cattle*; sledge dog, husky; camel, dromedary, ship of the desert; elephant 365 *mammal*.

horse, equine species, quadruped, horseflesh; dobbin, gee-gee; nag; Rosinante; mount, steed, trusty s.; stallion, gelding, mare, colt, filly, foal; stud horse, brood mare, stud, stable; carthorse; circus horse, liberty h.; roan, strawberry r., grey, dapple g., bay, chestnut, sorrel, black, piebald, skewbald, pinto, dun, palomino; purebred, blood-horse, bloodstock; Arab, Barbary horse; pacer, stepper, high-s., trotter; courser, race-horse, racer, goer, stayer; sprinter; steeplechaser, hurdler, fencer, jumper, hunter, foxhunter; warhorse, charger, courser, steed 722 *cavalry*; winged horse, Pegasus; Houyhnhnm.

draught horse, carthorse, dray h.; shaft-horse, trace-h.; carriage-horse, coach-h., post-h.; plough-h., shire-h , Clydesdale, punch, Suffolk P., Percheron, pit pony.

saddle horse, mount, hack, roadster; jade; screw, nag; pad, pad-nag, ambler; mustang, bronco; palfrey, jennet.

pony, cob, galloway, garron, sheltie; Shetland pony, fell p., Welsh p., Dartmoor p., Exmoor p., New Forest p.

Adj. *equine*, horsy, horse-faced; neighing; roan, grey etc. n.; asinine; mulish.

Vb. *carry*, bear 218 *support*; hump, humf, lug, heave, tote; caddy; shoulder, bear on one's back, carry on one's shoulders; fetch, bring, reach; fetch and carry; transport, cart, truck, railroad; ship, waft, raft; lift, fly 272 *transfer*; carry over, carry across, traject, ferry; convey, conduct, convoy, escort 89 *accompany*; be saddled with, be lumbered with, be burdened w.; be loaded with, be fraught 54 *be complete*.

274 Vehicle

N. *vehicle*, conveyance, public c.; public service vehicle, transport, public t.; vehicular traffic, motorized t., road t., wheeled t.; pedal power, horse p.; sedan chair, palanquin; litter, horse l.; brancard, stretcher, hurdle, crate; ambulance, bloodwagon, fire engine; Black Maria, paddy wagon; tumbril, hearse; snowplough, snowmobile, weasel; breakdown van, recovery vehicle; tractor, caterpillar t., tracked vehicle, bulldozer, JCB (tdmk); amphibian, moon buggy, space vehicle; rollercoaster, switchback, dodgem car; time machine.

sled, sledge, sleigh, dogsleigh; bobsleigh, bobsled, toboggan, sand yacht, surfboard, sailboard; skate, ice s., roller s., skateboard; snowshoes, skis.

bicycle, cycle, pedal c., bike, push b.; wheel, gridiron, crate; velocipede, hobbyhorse, boneshaker, penny-farthing, sit-up-and-beg; folding bicycle, sports model, racer, tourist, roadster, mountain bicycle *or* bike; ladies' bicycle, man's b.; five-speed, ten-s.; BMX (tdmk), Chopper (tdmk); stabilized bicycle; small-wheeler; tandem, randem; monocycle, unicycle, tricycle, fairy cycle, trike, quadricycle; motorized bicycle, moped; scooter, motor s., motorcycle, motorbike, trail bike, scrambler, quad bike; motorcycle combination, sidecar; invalid carriage; cycle-rickshaw, trishaw.

pushcart, perambulator, pram, baby buggy, buggy, pushchair, stroller; bath chair, wheelchair, invalid c.; rickshaw; barrow, wheelbarrow, handcart, cart, gocart; trolley, truck, float.

cart, ox-c., bullock-c., horse-and-cart; dray, milk float; farm cart, haywain, hay waggon; wain, waggon, covered w., prairie schooner; caravan, mobile home, trailer, horse-box, loose-b.; dustcart, watercart. See *lorry*.

carriage, horse-drawn c., equipage, turnout, rig; chariot, coach, state c. coach and four; barouche, landau, landaulet, berlin, victoria, brougham, phaeton, clarence; surrey, buckboard, buggy, wagonette; travelling carriage, chaise, shay, calèche, calash, britzka, droshky, troika; racing chariot, quadriga; four-in-hand, drag, brake, charabanc; two-wheeler, cabriolet, curricle, tilbury, whisky, jaunting car; trap, gig, ponycart, dogcart, governess cart; carriole, sulky; shandrydan, rattletrap.

war chariot, scythed c.; gun carriage, caisson, limber, ammunition waggon; tank, armoured car 722 *cavalry*; jeep, staff car.

cab, hackney carriage, horsecab, fourwheeler, hansom, fly; fiacre, droshky; gharry, tonga; taxicab, taxi, minicab; rickshaw, jinrickisha, pedicab, cycle-rickshaw.

bus, horsebus, motorbus; omnibus, doubledecker, single-d.; autobus, trolleybus, motor coach, coach, postbus, minibus; airbus.

tram, horse t., tramcar, trolley, streetcar, cablecar.

automobile, horseless carriage, car, motor car; motor, auto; limousine, limo, gas guzzler; saloon, two-door s., four-d. s.; tourer, roadster, runabout, buggy; hard-top, soft-t., convertible; coupé, sports car; racing car, stock c., dragster, hot-rod; go-kart, go-cart, kart; fastback, hatchback, estate car, people carrier; station waggon, shooting brake; Land Rover (tdmk), jeep, four-by-four, off-roader; police car, patrol c., panda c.; veteran car, vintage car, model T; tin Lizzie, banger, bus, jalopy, old crock, rattletrap; beetle, bubble car, minicar; invalid car, three-wheeler; minibus, camper, Dormobile (tdmk); cannibalized car, Frankencar; automatic car, gear-shift c.; zero-emission vehicle; car theft, auto-theft, twoc, joy-riding, hotting; drive-by crime.

lorry, truck, pickup t., dump t.; refuse lorry, dustcart; container lorry, articulated l., roadliner, juggernaut; tanker, bowser; car transporter, low-loader; van, delivery v., removal v., pantechnicon; breakdown van; electric van, float.

train, railway t., passenger t., excursion t., boat t.; motorail; express train, through t., intercity t., high-speed t., HST, slow train, stopping t.; goods train, freight t., freightliner; milk train, mail t., night mail; rolling stock; coach, carriage, compartment, first-class c., second-class c., smoker, nonsmoker; Pullman, wagonlit, sleeping car, sleeper; restaurant car, dining c., buffet c., observation c.; guard's van, luggage v., brake v., caboose; truck, waggon, tank w., hopper w., trolley; bogie; steam train, diesel t., electric t., tube t., model t.; live rail, third r., overhead wires, pantograph; cable railway, electric r., underground r. 624 *railway*; Orient Express, Eurostar, Le Shuttle.

locomotive, diesel engine, steam engine, tender; choo-choo, puff-puff, traction engine, steam roller.

conveyor; conveyor belt, escalator, moving staircase, moving pavement, moving walkway, travelator; shovel, hod 194 *ladle*; fork, trowel 370 *farm tool*; crane.

275 Ship

N. *ship*, vessel, boat, craft; bark, barque; great ship, tall s.; little ship, cockleshell; bottom, keel, sail; hooker, tub, hull; hulk, prisonship; Argo, Golden Hind, Noah's Ark; steamer, screw s., steamship, steamboat, motor vessel; paddle steamer, paddleboat, stern-wheeler, riverboat, showboat; passenger ship, liner, luxury l., cruise ship; channel steamer, ferry; hovercraft, hydrofoil; rotor ship; mail-boat, packet, steam p.; dredger, hopper, icebreaker; transport, hospital ship; storeship, tender, escort vessel; pilot vessel; tug, launch; lightship; weather ship; underwater craft, submarine, U-boat 722 *warship*; aircraft carrier.

merchant ship, galleon, argosy, Indiaman; banana boat, tea clipper; slave ship; cargo boat, freighter, tramp; coaster; lugger, collier, tanker, oil t., supertanker; containership.

fishing boat, inshore f. boat.; fishing smack, drifter, trawler, purse-seiner; factory ship; whaler, whale-catcher.

sailing ship, sailing boat, sailboat, sailer; windjammer, clipper, tall ship; square-rigged ship; four-masted ship, three-masted s., threemaster; barque, barquentine; two-masted ship, brig, hermaphrodite b., brigantine, schooner, pinnace; frigate, corvette 722 *warship*; cutter, sloop, ketch, yawl; wherry; yacht, racing y.; sailing dinghy, catamaran, smack; xebec, felucca, caïque, dhow, junk, sampan.

sail, sailcloth, canvas; square sail, lug-sail, lug, lateen sail, fore-and-aft s., leg-of-mutton s., spanker; course, mainsail, foresail, topsail, topgallant sail, royal, skysail; jib, staysail, spinnaker, balloon sail, studding s.; rigging; mast, foremast, mainmast, mizzenmast 218 *prop*.

boat, skiff, foldboat, cockboat; lifeboat; ship's boat, tender, dinghy, pram; longboat, jolly boat; whaleboat, dory; pinnace, cutter, gig; bumboat, surf boat; barge, lighter, pontoon; ferry, ferryboat, canalboat, narrowboat; houseboat; towboat, tugboat, tug; sailing boat, sailboat, sailing dinghy, yacht, catamaran; powerboat, motorboat, motor launch; pleasureboat, cabin cruiser; speedboat.

rowing boat, galley; eight, racing e.; sculler, shell, randan; skiff, dinghy, rubber dinghy; coracle, currach; punt, gondola; canoe, outrigger, dugout; pirogue, proa, kayak, umiak.

shipping, craft, argosy, fleet, armada, flotilla, squadron 722 *navy*; marine, mercantile marine, merchant navy, shipping line; flag of convenience 547 *flag*.

Adj. marine, maritime, naval, nautical, seagoing, ocean-g.; sea-worthy, snug, shipshape, shipshape and Bristol fashion.

276 Aircraft

N. *aircraft* 271 *aeronautics*; flying machine; aeroplane, airplane, crate; plane, monoplane, biplane, triplane; amphibian; hydroplane, seaplane, flying boat; airliner, airbus, transport, freighter; warplane, fighter, bomber 722 *air force*; stratocruiser, jet plane, jet, jumbo j., jump

j., supersonic j., turbojet, turboprop, turbofan, propfan; VTOL, STOL, HOTOL; microlight; helicopter, autogyro, whirlybird, chopper, copter; ornithopter; hovercraft 275 *ship*; glider, sailplane; flying instruments, controls, flight recorder, black box, autopilot, automatic pilot, joystick, rudder; aerofoil, fin, tail; flaps, aileron 271 *wing*; prop 269 *propeller*; cockpit, flight deck; undercarriage, landing gear; safety belt, life jacket, parachute, ejection seat; test bed, wind tunnel; flight simulator; aerodrome, airport 271 *air travel*.

airship, aerostat, balloon, Montgolfier b., hot-air b.; captive balloon, barrage b., observation b., weather b., blimp; dirigible, Zeppelin; kite, box-k.; parachute, chute; hang glider; magic carpet; balloon-basket, nacelle, car, gondola.

rocket, rocketry; step rocket, multistage r.: booster: nose cone, warhead; guided missile, intercontinental ballistic m., ICBM, Exocet (tdmk), nuclear missile. Cruise m. 723 *missile weapon*; V2; Star Wars, Strategic Defence Initiative, SDI.

spaceship, spacecraft, space probe, space shot, space capsule, space shuttle, spaceplane, aerospaceplane; space lab; lunar module; space tug, orbital manoeuvring vehicle; space platform, space station, sputnik 321 *satellite*; flying saucer, UFO, unidentified flying object.

277 Velocity

N. *velocity*, celerity, rapidity, speed, swiftness, fleetness, quickness, liveliness, alacrity, agility; speed of thought 116 *instantaneity*; promptness, expedition, dispatch; speed, tempo, rate, pace, bat 265 *motion*; speed-rate, miles per hour, mph, knots; mach number; speed of light, speed of sound, supersonic speed; lightning speed; maximum speed, full s., full steam; utmost speed, press of sail, full s.; precipitation, hurry, flurry 680 *haste*; breakneck speed 857 *rashness*; streak of lightning, flash, lightning f.; flight, jet f., supersonic f.; gale, hurricane, tempest, torrent; electricity, telegraph, lightning, greased l.; speed measurement, tachometer, speedometer 465 *gauge*; wind gauge; log, logline; speed trap, radar t. 542 *trap*.

spurt, acceleration, speed-up, overtaking; burst of speed; thrust, drive, impetus 279 *impulse*; jump. spring, bound, pounce 312 *leap*; whizz, swoop, swoosh, vroom, zip, zing, zap, uprush, zoom; down rush, dive, power d.; flying start, rush, dash, scamper, run, sprint, gallop.

Adj. *speedy*, swift, fast, quick, rapid, nimble, volant, darting, dashing, lively, brisk, smart, snappy, nifty, zippy 174 *vigorous*; expeditious, hustling 680 *hasty*; double-quick, rapid-fire; prompt 135 *early*; immediate 116 *instantaneous*;

fast-track, high-speed, streamlined, souped-up.
go-go; speeding, racing, ton-up; running, charging, runaway; flying, whizzing, hurtling, pelting; whirling, tempestuous; breakneck, headlong, precipitate 857 *rash*; fleet, fleet of foot, light-footed, nimble-f.; darting, starting, flashing; swift-moving, agile, nimble, mercurial, like quicksilver 152 *changeful*; like a bird; arrowy, like an arrow; like a shot; like a flash, like greased lightning, like the wind, quick as lightning, quick as thought, quick as a flash, quick as the wind, like a bat out of hell; meteoric, jet-propelled.

Vb. *move fast*, move, shift, travel, speed: drive, pelt, streak, flash, shoot; scorch, burn up the miles, tear up the road; scud, careen; skim, nip, cut; bowl along; sweep along, tear a., rattle a., thunder a.; storm a.; tear, rip, vroom, zip, zing, zap, rush, dash; fly, wing, whizz, skirr; hurtle, zoom, dive; dash off, tear o., dart o., dash on, dash forward; plunge, lunge, swoop; run, trot, double, lope, spank, gallop; bolt, cut and run, hotfoot it, leg it, scoot, skedaddle, scamper, scurry, skelter, scuttle; show a clean pair of heels, be unable to be seen for dust 620 *run away*; hare, run like a h., run like the wind, run like mad, run like the clappers; start, dart, dartle, flit; frisk, whisk; spring, bound, leap, jump, pounce; ride hard, put one's best foot forward, stir one's stumps, get cracking, get a move on, get one's finger out; hie, hurry, post, haste 680 *hasten*; chase, charge, stampede, career, go full tilt, go full pelt, go full lick, go full steam, go all out; break the speed limit, break the sound barrier.

accelerate, speed up, raise the tempo; gather momentum, gather speed, spurt, sprint, put on speed, pick up s., step on it, step on the gas, put one's foot down, open the throttle, open up, let it rip; crowd on sail; quicken one's speed, get a move on; put on one's running shoes, set off at a run, get off to a flying start; make up time, make up for lost time, make forced marches; quicken, step up, drive, spur, urge forward, urge on; lend wings to, put a bomb under, hustle, expedite 680 *hasten*.

outstrip, overtake, overhaul, catch up, catch up with; lap, outpace, outrun 306 *outdo*; gain on, outdistance, leave behind, leave standing, leave at the starting post; lose, shake off; make the running, romp home, win the race, outclass 34 *be superior*.

Adv. *swiftly*, rapidly etc. adj.; trippingly, apace; posthaste, at full speed, at full tilt; in full gallop, all out, flat out; helter-skelter, headlong, lickety-split, hell for leather; pronto, smartish, p.d.q.; like greased lightning, like a shot, like the clappers, in a flash, before you could say

Jack Robinson; in full sail, under press of sail *or* canvas, full speed ahead; on eagle's wings, with giant strides; nineteen to the dozen, hand over fist; at a rate of knots, at the double, in double-quick time, as fast as one's legs would carry one; at full speed, for all one is worth; by leaps and bounds, like wildfire.

278 Slowness

N. *slowness*, slackness, languor 679 *sluggishness*; inertia 175 *inertness*; deliberation 823 *inexcitability*; tentativeness, Fabian tactics; hesitation 858 *caution*; reluctance 598 *unwillingness*; go-slow, working to rule 145 *strike*; slowing down, slow-down, deceleration, retardation 113 *protraction*; drag 333 *friction*; brake, curb 747 *restraint*; leisureliness, no hurry, time to spare, time on one's hands, all the time in the world, easy stages 681 *leisure*; slow motion, low gear; slow march, dead m.; slow time, andante; slow pace, foot p., snail's p., crawl, creep, dawdle; dragging one's feet; amble 265 *gait*; limping, hobbling; standing start, slow s.; lag, time lag 136 *delay*.

slowcoach, snail, tortoise, tardigrade; stopping train, slow t.; funeral procession, dawdler, loiterer, lingerer; slow learner, late developer; laggard, sluggard, sleepyhead, slouch; drone 679 *idler*.

Adj. *slow*, painfully s.; low-geared, slow-motion, time-lapse; snail-like, tortoise-1., creeping, crawling, dragging; tardigrade, slow-moving 695 *clumsy*; limping, halting; taking one's time, dragging one's feet, hanging fire, tardy, dilatory, lagging 136 *late*; unhurried 681 *leisurely*; sedate 875 *formal*; deliberate 823 *patient*; painstaking 457 *careful*; Fabian 858 *cautious*; groping, tentative 461 *experimental*; languid, slack, sluggish 679 *lazy*; apathetic, phlegmatic 375 *insensible*; gradual, imperceptible.

Vb. *move slowly*, go slow, amble, crawl, creep, inch; trickle, dribble 350 *flow*; drift 282 *deviate*; hover; slouch, shuffle; toddle, waddle, mince; plod, trudge, lumber, wobble, totter, teeter, stagger, lurch; struggle, toil, labour, chug, limp, hobble; drag one's steps, flag, falter 684 *be fatigued*; trail, lag, fall behind 284 *follow*; hang fire, drag one's feet, drag oneself 598 *be unwilling*; tarry, be long about it, take one's time 136 *be late*; laze, idle 679 *be inactive*; take it easy, linger, stroll, saunter, dawdle 267 *walk*; march in slow time, tick over; grope, feel one's way 461 *be tentative*; soft-pedal, hesitate 858 *be cautious*; speak slowly, drawl, spin something out 580 *stammer*.

decelerate, slow down, slow up, ease up, let up, lose momentum; reduce speed, slacken s., slacken one's pace, slacken off; relax, slacken, ease off 145 *pause*; lose ground, flag, falter, waver 684 *be fatigued*.

retard, check, curb, rein in, throttle down 177 *moderate*; reef, shorten sail, take in s., strike s 269 *navigate*; brake, put on the b., put on the drag 747 *restrain*; backpedal, backwater, backpaddle, put the engines astern, reverse 286 *regress*; handicap, impair, clip the wings 702 *hinder*.

Adv. *slowly*, deliberately etc. adj.; lazily, sluggishly; at low speed, in low gear, in bottom g.; at a snail's p., at a funeral p.; with leaden step; in one's own good time; in slow time, adagio, largo; by easy stages, by degrees, little by little, step by step.

279 Impulse

N. *impulse*, impulsion, pressure; impetus, momentum; boost 174 *stimulant*; encouragement 612 *incentive*; thrust, push, shove, heave; stroke; throw, fling 287 *propulsion*; lunge, kick 712 *attack*; beating, tapping, drumming; beat, drumbeat 403 *roll*; thud; ramming, bulldozing, hammering; butting, butt (**see** *collision*); shaking, rattling; shock, impact; slam, bang; flick, clip, tap 378 *touch*; shake, jerk, wrench 318 *agitation*; pulsation, pulse 318 *spasm*; mechanics, dynamics.

knock, dint, dent 255 *concavity*; rap, tap, clap; dab, pat, fillip, flip, flick; nudge, dig 547 *gesture*; smack, slap; cuff, clip on *or* round the ear, clout, buffet, box on the ears; blow, fourpenny one; bunch of fives, knuckle sandwich; lash, stroke, hit, crack; cut, drive (cricket); thwack, thump, biff, bang, slug; punch, rabbit p., left, right, straight left, upper-cut, jab, hook; body blow, swipe; knockout blow; stamp, kick; swat; spanking, trouncing, dusting, pasting, licking, leathering, whipping, flogging, thrashing, beating, bashing, hammering, pummelling, rain of blows; hiding 963 *corporal punishment*; assault, assault and battery 712 *attack*; exchange of blows, fisticuffs, cut and thrust, hammer and tongs 61 *turmoil*.

collision, encounter, meeting, confrontation; head-on collision; bird strike; graze, scrape 333 *friction*; clash 14 *contrariety*; cannon; impact, bump, shock, crash, smash, smashup, accident; brunt, charge, force 712 *attack*; collision course 293 *convergence*; multiple collision, pileup 74 *accumulation*; motorway madness.

hammer, sledge h., steam h., trip h.; hammerhead, peen; punch, puncher; beetle, maul, mallet; flail; cosh, black-jack, knuckle-duster, cudgel, club, sandbag 723 *weapon*; pestle, anvil.

ram, battering r., bulldozer; JCB (tdmk); piledriver, monkey; ramrod; rammer, tamper; cue, billiard c., pusher 287 *propellant*.

Vb. *impel*, fling, heave, throw 287 *propel*; give an impetus, impart momentum; slam, bang 264 *close*; press, press in, press up, press down; push, thrust, shove; ram down, tamp; shove off, push off, pole, punt; hustle, prod, urge, spur, railroad, pressurize 277 *accelerate*; fillip, flip, flick; jerk, shake, rattle, shock, jog, jolt, jostle 318 *agitate*; shoulder, elbow, push out of the way, push around 282 *deflect*; throw out, run out, expel 300 *eject*; frogmarch; drive forward, flog on, whip on; goad 612 *incite*; drive, start, run, set going, set moving 173 *operate*; raise 310 *elevate*; plunge, dip, douse 311 *lower*.

collide, impinge 306 *encroach*; come into collision 293 *converge*; meet, encounter, confront, clash; cross swords, fence 712 *strike at*; ram, butt, batter, bash, dint, dent; bulldoze 165 *demolish*; cannon into, bump into, bump against; graze 333 *rub*; butt against; drive into, crash i., smash i., run i., run down, run over; clash with, collide w., fall foul of; run one's head against, run into a brick wall, run against, dash a.; bark one's shins, stub one's toe; trip over 309 *tumble*; knock together, knock heads t., clash the cymbals, clap one's hands.

strike, smite, hit, land a blow, fetch one a b.; aim a blow, hit out at; lunge at; lash out at, lace into, let fly; hit wildly, swing, flail; strike hard, slam, bang, knock; knock for six, knock into the middle of next week, send flying; knock down, floor 311 *fell*; tap, rap; slap, smack; bop, clock, clout, bash, clobber, box the ears of, clip one's ear; box, spar, fisticuff 716 *fight*; buffet, punch, paste, thump, thwack, whack, wham, rain blows, pummel, trounce, beat up, sock it to, let one have it; give one a black eye *or* a bloody nose, make one see stars; pound, batter, bludgeon 332 *pulverize*; biff, bash, dash, slosh, sock, slog, slug, cosh, cudgel, club, mug, spifflicate; blackjack, sandbag, hit over the head, crown; concuss, stun, knock out, leave senseless; spank, wallop, thrash, lash, lam, lambast, beat, whip, cane 963 *flog*; leather, strap, belt, tan one's hide, give a hiding 963 *punish*; thresh, flail; hammer, drum; swat 216 *flatten*; maul 655 *wound*; throw stones at, stone, pelt; head (a football); bat, swipe, lob, smash, volley 287 *propel*.

280 Recoil

N. *recoil*, revulsion, reaction, retroaction, reflux 148 *reversion*; repercussion, reverberation, echo 404 *resonance*; reflex 417 *reflection*; kick, kickback, backlash; ricochet, cannon; rebound, bounce, spring, springboard, trampoline 328 *elasticity*; ducks and drakes; swing-back, swing of the pendulum 317 *oscillation*; volley, return (at tennis), boomerang; rebuff, repulse 292 *repulsion*; riposte, return fire.

Vb. *recoil*, react 182 *counteract*; shrink, wince, blench, quail, start, flinch, jib, shy, jump back 620 *avoid*; kick back, hit b.; ricochet, cannon, cannon off; uncoil, spring back, fly b., rebound; return, swing back 148 *revert*; have repercussions; reverberate, echo 404 *resound*; be reflected, reflect 417 *shine*; boomerang 714 *retaliate*.

281 Direction
N. *direction*, bearing, compass reading; lie of the land 186 *situation*; orientation, collimation, alignment; set, drift 350 *current*; tenor, trend, bending 179 *tendency*; aim, course, beam; beeline, straight shot, line of sight, optical axis 249 *straightness*; course, tack; line, line of march, track, way, path, road 624 *route*; steering, steerage; aim, target 295 *goal*; compass, pelorus 269 *sailing aid*; collimator, sights; fingerpost 547 *signpost*; direction finder, range f. 465 *gauge*; orienteering.

Adj. *directed*, orientated, directed towards, signposted; aimed, well-directed, well-placed 187 *located*; bound for; aligned with; axial, diagonal; sideways 239 *lateral*; facing 240 *opposite*; direct, undeviating 249 *straight*; unswerving, straightforward, one-way, directive, guiding.

Vb. *orientate*, orientate oneself, box the compass, take one's bearings, shoot the sun, plot one's course 269 *navigate*; find which way the wind blows, see how the land lies; ask the way, ask for directions; signpost, direct, show the way, put on the right track 547 *indicate*; pinpoint, locate 187 *place*.

steer for, shape a course for, be bound f., head f., make f., aim f.; make towards, bend one's steps to, go to, go towards, go straight for, direct oneself towards, make a beeline for; go straight to the point, hold the line, keep on the beam, keep the nose down.

point to, point out, point, show, point towards, signpost 547 *indicate*; incline towards.

aim, level, point; take aim, aim at; train one's sights, draw a bead on, level at; have one covered; collimate, set one's sights; hit the mark, get a bull's-eye.

Adv. *towards*, versus, facing; on the way, on the road to, through, via, en route for, by way of; straight, direct, straight forwards; point blank, straight as an arrow; in a direct line, in a straight line, in a line with, in a line for; directly, full tilt at, as the crow flies; upstream, downstream; upwind, downwind; before the wind, close to the w., near the w.; against the w., in the wind's eye, seaward, landward, homeward; downtown; cross-country; up-country; in

all directions 183 *widely*; from or to the four winds; hither, thither; clockwise, anticlockwise, counterclockwise, widdershins.

282 Deviation
N. *deviation*, disorientation, misdirection, wrong course, wrong turning; aberration, deflection, refraction; diversion, digression; shift, veer, slew, swing; departure, declension 220 *obliquity*; flection, flexion, swerve, bend 248 *curvature*; branching off 294 *divergence*; deviousness, detour, long way round, scenic route, tourist r. 626 *circuit*; vagrancy; fall, lapse 495 *error*; wandering mind 456 *abstractedness*; drift, leeway; sidestep, sideslip; break, leg b., off b., googly (cricket); knight's move (chess); yaw, tack; zigzag, slalom course.

Vb. *deviate*, digress, make a detour, go a roundabout way, go the long way round; branch out 294 *diverge*; turn, filter, turn a corner, turn aside, swerve, slew; go out of one's way, depart from one's course; step aside, make way for; alter course, change direction, yaw, tack; veer, back (wind); bend, curve 248 *be curved*; zigzag, twist 251 *meander*; swing 317 *oscillate*; steer clear of, give a wide berth, sheer off; sidle, skid, sideslip; break (cricket); fly off at a tangent 220 *be oblique*; sidestep 620 *avoid*.

turn round, turn about, about turn, wheel, wheel about, face a., face the other way, do a U-turn, change one's mind; reverse, reverse direction, return 148 *revert*; go back 286 *turn back*.

stray, err, ramble, maunder, straggle 267 *wander*; go astray, go adrift, lose one's way, get lost; miss one's footing, lose one's bearings, lose one's sense of direction, take the wrong turning 495 *blunder*; lose track of, lose the place, lose the thread 456 *be inattentive*.

deflect, bend, crook; warp, skew; put off the scent, lead astray, draw a red herring, throw dust in one's eyes, set off on a wild-goose chase, misdirect, misaddress 495 *mislead*; avert; divert, change the course of; sidetrack, draw aside, push a., pull a.; elbow a., bias, slice, pull, hook, glance, bowl a break, bowl wide (cricket); shift, switch, shunt 151 *interchange*.

283 Preceding: going before
N. *preceding* 119 *priority*, 64 *precedence*; going before, going ahead of, leading, heading, flying start; preemption, queue-jumping; pride of place, head of the table, head of the river (bumping races); lead, leading role, star role 34 *superiority*; pioneer 66 *precursor*; van, vanguard, avant-garde 237 *front*; prequel, foreword, prelude.

Vb. *precede*, go before, go ahead of, be the

forerunner of, herald, be the precursor of, be
the prelude to; usher in, introduce; head, spearhead, lead, be in the vanguard, head the queue;
go in front, go in advance, clear the way, light
the w., lead the w.; lead the dance, guide, conduct 689 *direct*; take the lead, have a head start;
steal a march on, preempt, steal one's thunder;
get in front, jump the queue; get ahead of, lap
277 *outstrip*; be beforehand 135 *be early*; take
precedence over, take priority over, have right
of way 64 *come before*.

284 Following: going after

N. *following* 65 *sequence*; run, suit 71 *series*; subsequence 120 *posteriority*; pursuit, pursuance
619 *chase*; succession, reversion 780 *transfer*;
last place 238 *rear*.

follower, pursuer, tail, stalker, attendant, suitor, hanger-on, camp follower, groupie 742
dependant; train, tail, wake, cortege, suite, followers 67 *retinue*; following, party, adherent,
supporter, fan 703 *aider*; satellite, moon, artificial satellite, space station 276 *spaceship*;
trailer, caravan 274 *cart*; tender 275 *ship*.

Vb. *follow*, come behind, succeed, follow on,
follow after, follow close upon, sit on one's tail,
breathe down one's neck, be bumper to
bumper, follow in the wake of, tread on the
heels of, tread in the steps of, follow the footprints of, come to heel 65 *come after*; stick like a
shadow, tag after, hang on the skirts of, beset;
attend, wait on, dance attendance on 742 *serve*;
tag along 89 *accompany*; dog, shadow, trail, tail,
track, chase 619 *pursue*; trail, dawdle 278 *move
slowly*; bring up the rear 238 *be behind*.

285 Progression: motion forwards

N. *progression*, going forward; procession,
march, way, course, career; march of time 111
course of time; progress, steady p., forward
march 265 *motion*; giant strides, leap, quantum
l., jump, leaps and bounds 277 *spurt*; irresistible progress, relentless p., majestic p., flood,
tide 350 *current*; gain, ground gained, advance,
headway 654 *improvement*; getting ahead, overtaking 283 *preceding*; encroachment 306 *overstepping*; next step, development, evolution 308
ascent, 71 *continuity*; furtherance, promotion,
step up the ladder, advancement, preferment;
rise, raise, lift, leg-up 310 *elevation*; progressiveness; enterprise, go-getting, go-go 672 *undertaking*; achievement 727 *success*; economic
progress 730 *prosperity*.

Adj. *progressive*, enterprising, resourceful, go-
ahead, go-go, go-getting, forward-looking,
reformist; advancing etc. vb.; flowing on 265
moving; advanced, state-of-the-art, leading-edge
126 *modern*.

Vb. *progress*, proceed 265 *be in motion*;
advance, go forward, take a step forward, come
on, develop 316 *evolve*; show promise, promise
well 654 *get better*; get on, get ahead, do well
730 *prosper*; march on, run on, flow on, pass on,
jog on, wag on, rub on, hold on, keep on, slog
on 146 *go on*; move with the times 126
modernize; never look back, hold one's lead;
press on, push on, drive on, push forward, press
f., press onwards 680 *hasten*; make a good start,
make good progress; gain, gain ground, make
headway, make strides 277 *move fast*; get a
move on, get ahead, forge a., advance by leaps
and bounds; gain on, distance, outdistance,
overtake, leave behind 277 *outstrip*; rise, climb
the ladder 308 *climb*; reach out to, make up leeway, recover lost ground 31 *recoup*; gain time,
make up t.

promote, further, contribute to, advance 703
aid; upgrade, move up, raise, lift 310 *elevate*;
bring forward, develop 174 *invigorate*; speed up
277 *accelerate*; put ahead 64 *put in front*; favour,
make for 156 *cause*.

Adv. *forward*, forwards, onward, forth, on,
ahead, forrard; progressively, by leaps and
bounds, with giant strides.

286 Regression: motion backwards

N. *regression*, regress; reverse direction,
retroflexion, retrocession, retrogression, retro-
gradation, retroaction, backward step 148 *reversion*; retreat, withdrawal, retirement,
disengagement 290 *recession*; regurgitation 300
voidance; reversing, backing; falling away,
decline, drop, fall, downward trend, slump 655
deterioration.

return, remigration, homeward journey;
homecoming 295 *arrival*; reentrance, reentry
297 *ingress*; going back, turn of the tide, reflux,
ebb, regurgitation 350 *current*; veering, backing,
relapse, backsliding 603 *change of mind*; U-turn,
volte-face, about turn 148 *reversion*; countermarch, countermovement, countermotion 182
counteraction; turn, turning point 137 *crisis*;
resilience 328 *elasticity*; reflex 280 *recoil*.

Vb. *regress*, recede, retrogress, retreat, sound a
r., beat a r.; retire, withdraw, fall back, draw b.;
turn away, turn tail 620 *run away*; back out,
back down 753 *resign*; backtrack, backpedal;
give way, give ground; recede into the distance
446 *disappear*; fall behind 278 *move slowly*;
reverse, back, go backwards; run back, regurgitate; slip back; ebb, slump, fall, drop, decline
309 *descend*; bounce back 280 *recoil*.

turn back, retrace one's steps; remigrate, go
back, go home, return 148 *revert*; look back,
look over one's shoulder, hark back 505 *retrospect*; turn one's back, turn on one's heel; veer

round, wheel r., about face, execute a volte-face, do a U-turn 603 *tergiversate*; double back, countermarch.

287 Propulsion

N. *propulsion*, jet p., drive; impulsion, push, forward thrust 279 *impulse*; projection, throwing, tossing, hurling, pelting, slinging, stone-throwing; precipitation; cast, throw, chuck, toss, fling, sling, shy, cock-shy; pot shot, pot, shot, long s.; shooting, firing, discharge, volley 712 *bombardment*; bowling, pitching, throw-in, full toss, yorker, lob (cricket); kick, punt, dribble (football); stroke, drive, swipe 279 *knock*; pull, slice (golf); rally, volley, smash (tennis); ballistics, gunnery, musketry, sniping, pea-shooting; archery, toxophily; marksmanship 694 *skill*; gunshot, bowshot, stone's throw 199 *distance*.

missile, projectile, shell, rocket, cannonball, grapeshot, ball, bullet, shot, small s.; pellet, brickbat, stone, snowball; arrow, dart 723 *missile weapon*; ball, tennis b., golf b., cricket b., hockey b.; football, rugby ball; bowl, boule, wood, jack, puck, curling stone; quoit, discus; javelin; hammer, caber.

propellant, thrust, driving force, jet, steam 160 *energy*; spray, aerosol, CFC, chlorofluorocarbons; thruster, pusher, shover 279 *ram*; tail wind, following w. 352 *wind*; lever, treadle, pedal, bicycle p.; oar, sweep, paddle; screw, blade, paddlewheel 269 *propeller*; coal, petrol, diesel oil 385 *fuel*; gunpowder, dynamite 723 *explosive*; shotgun, rifle 723 *firearm*; revolver 723 *pistol*; airgun, pop gun, water pistol; blow-pipe, pea-shooter; catapult, sling, bow 723 *missile weapon*.

Vb. *propel*, launch, project, set on its way; throw, cast, deliver, heave, pitch, toss, cant, chuck, shy, bung; bowl, lob, york; hurl, fling, sling, catapult; dart, flick, pelt, stone, shower, snowball; precipitate, get moving, send flying, send headlong; expel, pitchfork 300 *eject*; blow up, explode, put dynamite under, put a bomb under; serve, return, volley, smash, kill (tennis); bat, slam, slog, wham; sky, loft; drive, cut, pull, hook, glance (cricket); slice 279 *strike*; kick, dribble, punt (football); putt, push, shove, shoulder, ease along 279 *impel*; wheel, pedal, roll, bowl, trundle 315 *rotate*; move on, drive, hustle 265 *move*; sweep, sweep before one, carry before one; put to flight 727 *defeat*.

shoot, fire, open fire; fire a volley; discharge, explode, let off, set off; let fly, draw a bead on, pull the trigger; bombard 712 *fire at*; snipe, pot, take a potshot at, pepper 263 *pierce*.

288 Traction

N. *traction*, drawing etc. vb.; retraction; retractability; magnetism 291 *attraction*; haulage; pull, haul; tug, tow; towrope; rake, harrow; trawl, dragnet; hauler, haulier; retractor; lugsail, square sail 275 *sail*; windlass; tug 275 *ship*; tractor, traction engine 274 *locomotive*; loadstone; rowing; tug of war 716 *contest*; trailer, caravan 274 *cart*.

Vb. *draw*, pull, haul, kedge 269 *navigate*; tug, tow, take in tow; lug, drag, trail, trawl; rake, harrow; winch, reel in, wind in, lift, heave, hitch 310 *elevate*; drag down 311 *lower*; suck in 299 *absorb*; pluck; pull out 304 *extract*; wrench, twist 246 *distort*; yank, jerk, twitch, tweak, pluck at 318 *agitate*, pull towards 291 *attract*; pull back, draw in, retract.

289 Approach: motion towards

N. *approach*, advance 285 *progression*; approximation 200 *nearness*; meeting, confluence 293 *convergence*; access, accession, advent, coming 295 *arrival*, 189 *presence*; overtaking, overlapping 619 *pursuit*; onset 712 *attack*; advances, pass, overture 759 *offer*; way in 624 *access*.

Adj. *approaching*, nearing, getting warm etc. vb.; close 200 *near*; meeting 293 *convergent*; closing in, imminent 155 *impending*; advancing, oncoming.

accessible, approachable, get-at-able; within easy reach; attainable 469 *possible*; available, obtainable, on tap; nearby 200 *near*; welcoming, inviting, 882 *sociable*; well-paved, made-up, metalled.

Vb. *approach*, draw near; approximate; come within range 295 *arrive*; come into view 443 *be visible*; come closer, meet 293 *converge*; near, draw n., go n., walk up to, run up to; roll up 74 *congregate*; come in 297 *enter*; accost 884 *greet*; make overtures, make passes 889 *court*; lean towards, incline 179 *tend*; move towards 265 *be in motion*; advance 285 *progress*; advance upon, bear down on 712 *attack*; close in, close in on 232 *circumscribe*; hover 155 *impend*; overtake 277 *outstrip*; narrow the gap, breathe down one's neck, tread on one's heels, sit on one's tail, drive bumper to bumper, run one close; be in sight of, be within shouting distance of.

290 Recession: motion from

N. *recession*, retirement, withdrawal, retreat, stepping back 286 *regression*; emigration, evacuation 296 *departure*; resignation 621 *relinquishment*; flight 667 *escape*; shrinking, shying, flinching 620 *avoidance*; revulsion 280 *recoil*.

Vb. *recede*, retire, withdraw, fall back, draw b., retreat 286 *regress*; ebb, subside, shrink, decline 37 *decrease*; fade from view 446 *dis-*

appear; go, go away, leave, clear out, evacuate, emigrate 296 *depart*; move from, move away, put space between, widen the gap 199 *be distant*; stand aside, make way, sheer off 282 *deviate*; drift away 282 *stray*; back away, flinch 620 *avoid*; flee 620 *run away*; get away 667 *escape*; go back 286 *turn back*; jump back 280 *recoil*; come unstuck 46 *separate*.

291 Attraction

N. *attraction*, pull, drag, draw, tug; suction; magnetism, magnetic field; force of gravity; itch for 859 *desire*; affinity, sympathy, empathy; attractiveness, seductiveness, allure, appeal, sex a., it; allurement, seduction, temptation, lure, bait, decoy, charm, siren song 612 *inducement*; charmer, temptress, siren, Circe 612 *motivator*; centre of attraction, cynosure, honeypot 890 *favourite*.

Vb. *attract*, magnetize, pull, drag, tug 288 *draw*; adduct, exercise a pull, draw towards, pull t., drag t.; appeal, charm, move, pluck at one's heartstrings 821 *impress*; lure, allure, bait, seduce 612 *tempt*; decoy 542 *ensnare*.

292 Repulsion

N. *repulsion*, repulsiveness 842 *ugliness*; reflection 280 *recoil*; driving off, beating o. 713 *defence*; repulse, rebuff, snub, refusal, the cold shoulder, the bird 607 *rejection*; brush-off, dismissal 300 *ejection*.

Adj. *repellent*, repelling etc. vb.; repulsive, off-putting, antipathetic.

Vb. *repel*, put off, make sick 861 *cause dislike*; push away, butt a. 279 *impel*; drive away, repulse, beat off, stonewall, talk out; dispel 75 *disperse*; head off, turn away, reflect 282 *deflect*; be deaf to 760 *refuse*; rebuff, snub, brush off, reject one's advances 607 *reject*; give one the bird, cold-shoulder, keep at arm's length, make one keep his distance; show the door to, shut the door in one's face, send one off with a flea in his ear, send packing, send one about his business, give one his marching orders; boot out, give the boot, kick out, sack 300 *dismiss*.

293 Convergence

N. *convergence*, narrowing gap; confrontation, collision course 279 *collision*; concourse, confluence, conflux, meeting 45 *union*; congress, concurrence, concentration, resort, assembly 74 *assemblage*; closing in 232 *circumscription*; centering, focalization, zeroing in 76 *focus*; narrowing, tapering, taper 206 *narrowness*; tangent; perspective, vanishing point 438 *view*.

Adj. *convergent*, converging etc. vb.; focusing, zeroing in on, focused; centering; confluent,

concurrent 45 *conjunctive*; tangential; pointed, conical, pyramidal; knock-kneed.

Vb. *converge*, come closer, close in; narrow the gap; come together 295 *meet*; unite, gather together, get t. 74 *congregate*; enter in 297 *enter*; close with, intercept, close in upon 232 *circumscribe*; concentrate, focus, bring into f.; centre on, zero in on 225 *centralize*; taper, come to a point, narrow down.

294 Divergence

N. *divergence*, divergency, clear blue water 15 *difference*; contradiction 14 *contrariety*; moving apart, drifting a., parting 46 *separation*; aberration, declination 282 *deviation*; spread, fanning out, deployment 75 *dispersion*; parting of the ways, fork, bifurcation, crossroads, watershed, points 222 *crossing*; radiation, ramification, branching out; Y-shape 247 *angularity*.

Adj. *divergent*, diverging etc. vb.; separated; radiating, radiant, palmate, stellate; centrifugal, centrifuge; aberrant.

Vb. *diverge* 15 *differ*; radiate; ramify, branch off, branch out; split off, fork, bifurcate; part, part company, come to the parting of the ways 46 *separate*; file off, go one's own way; change direction, switch; glance off, fly off, fly off at a tangent 282 *deviate*; deploy, fan out, spread, scatter 75 *be dispersed*; straddle, spread-eagle; splay, splay apart.

295 Arrival

N. *arrival*, advent, accession, appearance, entrance 289 *approach*, 189 *presence*; onset 68 *beginning*; coming, reaching, making; landfall, landing, touchdown, docking, mooring 266 *quiescence*; debarkation, disembarkation 298 *egress*; rejoining, meeting, encounter 154 *event*; greeting, handshake, golden hello, formalities 884 *courteous act*; homecoming 286 *return*; prodigal's return, reception, welcome 876 *celebration*; guest, visitor, visitant, new arrival, nouveau arrivé, recent a., homing pigeon 297 *incomer*; finish, close f., neck-and-neck f., needle f., photo f. 716 *contest*; last lap, home stretch.

goal 617 *objective*; journey's end, point of no return, terminus 69 *extremity*; stop, halt 145 *stopping place*; pier; harbour, haven, anchorage, roadstead 662 *shelter*; aerodrome, airport, airfield, heliport, terminal, air t. 271 *air travel*; terminus, railway t., railway station, bus s., depot, rendezvous 192 *meeting place*.

Vb. *arrive*, come, reach, fetch up at, end up at, get there 189 *be present*; reach one's destination, make port; dock, moor, drop anchor 266 *come to rest* (**see** *land*); draw up, pull up, park; come home, return h. 286 *regress*; hit, make, win to, gain, attain; finish the race, breast the tape; achieve one's aim, reach one's goal 725 *carry through*; be on the doorstep 297 *enter*; make an entrance; appear, show up, pop up, turn up, roll up, drop in, blow in 882 *visit*; put in, pull in, stop 145 *pause*; clock in 135 *be early*; arrive at, find 484 *discover*; arrive at the top 727 *be successful*, 730 *prosper*; be brought, come to hand.

land, beach, run aground; touch down, make a landing; step ashore, disembark, get off, get out, get down, alight, light on, perch 309 *descend*; dismount.

meet, join, see again; receive, greet, welcome, shake hands 882 *be sociable*; go to meet, come to m.; rendezvous; come upon, encounter, come in contact, run into, meet by chance; hit, bump into, knock i., collide with 279 *collide*; upon, light upon, gather, assemble 74 *congregate*.

Int. welcome! greetings! hullo! hi! pleased to meet you! aloha! shalom! salaam!

296 Departure

N. *departure*, leaving, parting, removal, going away; walk-out, exit 298 *egress*; pulling out, emigration 290 *recession*; migration, exodus, general e., Hegira; flight, moonlight flit, decampment, elopement, getaway 667 *escape*; embarkation 297 *ingress*; saddling 267 *equitation*; setting out, outset 68 *start*; takeoff, blast-off 308 *ascent*; zero hour, time of departure, moment of leave-taking; point of departure.

valediction, farewell, valedictory, funeral oration, epitaph, obituary 364 *obsequies*; leave-taking, congé, dismissal; goodbyes, goodnights, farewells, adieus; last handshake, waving goodbye, wave of the handkerchief 884 *courteous act*; send-off, farewell address; last post, last words, final goodbye, parting shot; stirrup cup, doch-an-dorris, one for the road, nightcap.

Vb. *depart*, quit, leave, abandon 621 *relinquish*; retire, withdraw, retreat 286 *turn back*; remove, move house, flit, leave the neighbourhood, leave the country, leave home, emigrate, absent o. 190 *go away*; fly the nest, take one's leave, take one's departure, be going, be getting along; bid farewell, say goodbye, say good night, make one's adieus, tear oneself away, part, part company; receive one's congé, get one's marching orders; leave work, cease w. 145 *cease*; clock out, go home 298 *emerge*; quit the scene, leave the stage, bow out, give one's swan song, exit, make one's e. 753 *resign*; depart this life 361 *die*.

decamp, up sticks, strike tents, break camp, break up; walk out, march out, pack up, clear off; clear out, pull out, evacuate; make tracks;

be off, beetle o., buzz o., slope o., swan o., push o., shove o., make oneself scarce; take wing 271 *fly*; vamoose, skedaddle, beat it, hop it, scram, bolt, scuttle, skip, slip away, cut and run 277 *move fast*; flee, take flight, make a break for it 620 *run away*; flit, make a moonlight f., make one's getaway 446 *disappear*; elope, abscond, give one the slip 667 *escape*.

start out, be off, get going, get on one's way, set out 68 *begin*; set forth, sally f., take up one's bed and walk, issue f., strike out, light out, march out 298 *emerge*; gird oneself, be ready to start, warm up 669 *make ready*; take ship, embark, go on board 297 *enter*; hoist the Blue Peter, unmoor, cast off, weigh anchor, push off, get under way, set sail, put out to sea 269 *navigate*; mount, bridle, harness, saddle 267 *ride*; hitch up, pile in, hop on; catch a train, catch a plane, catch a bus; pull out, drive off, take off, be on one's way, see off.

Int. goodbye! farewell! adieu! au revoir! auf Wiedersehen! arrivederci! adios! be seeing you! see you later! cheerio! ciao! bye-bye! ta-ta! so long! pleasant journey! have a good trip! bon voyage! God be with you!

297 Ingress: motion into

N. *ingress*, incoming, entry, entrance; reentry 286 *return*; inflow, influx, flood 350 *stream*; inpouring, inrush; intrusion, trespass 306 *overstepping*; invasion, forced entry, inroad, raid, irruption, incursion 712 *attack*; immersion, diffusion, osmosis; penetration, infiltration, insinuation 231 *interjacency*, 303 *insertion*; immigration; intake 299 *reception*; import, importation 272 *transference*; right of entry, admission, admittance, access, entrée 756 *permission*; free trade 791 *trade*.

way in, way, path 624 *access*; entrance, entrance hall, entry, door 263 *doorway*; mouth, opening 263 *orifice*; inlet 345 *gulf*; channel 351 *conduit*; open door, free port 796 *market*.

incomer, newcomer, Johnny-come-lately; new arrival, nouveau arrivé, new member, new face; new boy, new girl 538 *beginner*; visitant, visitor, caller 882 *sociable person*; immigrant, migrant, colonist, settler 59 *foreigner*; stowaway, unwelcome guest 59 *intruder*; invader, raider 712 *attacker*; house-breaker, burglar 789 *thief*; entrant, competitor 716 *contender*.

Vb. *enter*, turn into, go in, come in, move in, drive in, run in, breeze in, venture in, sidle in, step in, walk in, file in; follow in 65 *come after*; set foot in, cross the threshold, darken the doors; let oneself in; unlock the door, turn the key 263 *open*; gain admittance, have entrée to, be invited; look in, drop in, pop in, blow in, call 882 *visit*; mount, board, get aboard; get in, hop in, jump in, pile in; squeeze into, creep in, slip in, edge in, slink in, sneak in, steal in; work one's way into, buy one's way into, insinuate oneself; worm into, bore i. 263 *pierce*; bite into, eat i., cut i. 260 *notch*; put one's foot in, tread in, fall into, drop i. 309 *tumble*; sink into, plunge i., dive i. 313 *plunge*; join, enlist in, enroll oneself; immigrate, settle in 187 *place oneself*; let in 299 *admit*; put in 303 *insert*; enter oneself, enter for 716 *contend*.

infiltrate, percolate, seep, soak through; leak into, sink in, penetrate, permeate, mix in, taint, infect 655 *impair*; filter in, worm one's way in.

intrude, trespass, gatecrash, outstay one's welcome, be de trop; horn in, barge in, push in, muscle in, break in upon, burst in u., interrupt 63 *derange*; break in, burgle 788 *steal*.

298 Egress: motion out of

N. *egress*, egression, going out; exit; walkout, exodus, general e., evacuation 296 *departure*; emigration, expatriation, exile 883 *seclusion*; emergence, emerging, debouchment; emersion, surfacing; emanation, efflux, issue; evaporation 388 *evaporation*; eruption, outburst 176 *outbreak*; sortie, breakout 667 *escape*; export, exportation 272 *transference*.

outflow, effluence, efflux, effusion; emission 300 *ejection*; issue, outpouring, gushing, streaming; exudation, oozing, dribbling, weeping; bleeding 302 *haemorrhage*; perspiration, sweating, sweat; percolation, filtration; leak, escape, leakage, seepage 634 *waste*; drain, running sore 772 *loss*; discharge, drainage, draining 300 *voidance*; overflow, spill, flood 350 *waterfall*; jet, fountain, spring 156 *source*; gush, squirt 350 *stream*; geyser; streaming eyes, runny nose, postnasal drip.

outlet, vent, chute; spout, nozzle, tap, faucet; pore, blowhole 263 *orifice*, 352 *respiration*; sluice, floodgate 351 *conduit*; exhaust pipe; drainpipe, overflow, gargoyle; exit, way out, path 624 *access*; escape, loophole 667 *means of escape*.

Vb. *emerge*, pop out, stick out, project 254 *jut*; peep out, peer out 443 *be visible*; surface 308 *ascend*; emanate, transpire 526 *be disclosed*; egress, issue, debouch, make a sortie; issue forth, sally f., come f., go f.; issue out of, go out, come o., creep o., sneak o., march o, flounce o., fling o. 267 *walk*; jump out, bale o. 312 *leap*; clear out, evacuate 296 *decamp*; emigrate 267 *travel*; exit, walk off 296 *depart*; erupt, break out 667 *escape*.

exude, perspire, sweat, steam 379 *be hot*; ooze, seep through, soak t., leak t.; percolate, strain, strain out, filter, filtrate, distil; run, dribble, drip, drop, drivel, drool, slaver, slobber, sali-

vate, water at the mouth 341 *be wet*; exhale 352 *breathe*.

299 Reception

N. *reception*, admission, admittance, entrance, entrée, access 297 *ingress*; invitation 759 *offer*; receptivity, acceptance; open arms, welcome, liberty hall 876 *celebration*; enlistment, enrolment 78 *inclusion*; initiation, baptism, baptismal fire 68 *debut*; asylum, sanctuary, shelter, refuge 660 *protection*; introduction; importation, import 272 *transference*; radio receiver, telephone r. 531 *telecommunication*; inhalation 352 *respiration*; sucking, suction; assimilation, digestion, absorption, resorption; engulfing, engulfment, swallowing, ingurgitation; ingestion (of food) 301 *eating*; imbibition, fluid intake 301 *drinking*; intake, consumption 634 *waste*; infusion 303 *insertion*; interjection 231 *interjacency*; admissibility.

Vb. *admit*, receive, accept, take in; grant asylum, afford sanctuary, shelter, give refuge 660 *safeguard*; welcome; invite, call in 759 *offer*; enlist, enrol, take on 622 *employ*; give entrance or admittance to, allow in, allow access, give a ticket to, grant a visa to; throw open, open the door 263 *open*; bring in, import, land 272 *transfer*; let in, show in, usher in, introduce 64 *come before*; send in 272 *send*; initiate, baptize 534 *teach*.

absorb, incorporate, engross, assimilate, digest; suck in; soak up, sponge, mop up, blot 342 *dry*; take in, ingest, imbibe; lap up, swallow, engulf, gulp, gobble, devour 301 *eat*, *drink*; breathe in, inhale 352 *breathe*; sniff 394 *smell*; get the taste of 386 *taste*.

300 Ejection

N. *ejection*, ejaculation, expulsion; precipitation 287 *propulsion*; disbarment, striking off, disqualification, excommunication 57 *exclusion*; throwing out, chucking o., bum's rush; drumming out, marching orders; the heave ho; dismissal, discharge, redundancy, golden handshake, sack, boot, push, kick upstairs 607 *rejection*; deportation, extradition; relegation, downgrading, exile, banishment 883 *seclusion*; eviction, dislodgment 188 *displacement*; dispossession, deprivation 786 *expropriation*; jettison, throwing overboard 779 *nonretention*; clean sweep, elimination 165 *destruction*; emission, effusion, shedding, spilling 298 *outflow*; libation 981 *oblation*; secretion, salivation 302 *excretion*; radioactivity 417 *radiation*.

voidance, clearance, cleavage, drainage, curettage, aspiration; eruption, eruptiveness 176 *outbreak*; egestion, regurgitation, disgorgement; vomiting, throwing up, nausea, vomit, puke;

gas, wind, burp, belch, fart; breaking wind, belching; elimination, evacuation 302 *excretion*.

vomiting, sick, sickened, nauseated, sick to one's stomach, throwing up, green, g. around the gills; seasick, airsick, carsick; sick as a dog.

Vb. *eject*, expel, send down 963 *punish*; strike off, strike off the register, disbar, excommunicate 57 *exclude*; export, send away 272 *transfer*; deport, expatriate; exile, banish, transport 883 *seclude*; throw up, cast up, wash up; spit out, cough up, spew out; put out, push o., turf o., throw o., chuck o., fling o., bounce 287 *propel*; kick out, boot o., give the bum's rush, throw out on one's ear, give the heave-ho, bundle out, hustle o.; drum out; precipitate 287 *propel*; pull out 304 *extract*; unearth, root out, weed o., uproot, eradicate 165 *destroy*; rub out, scratch o., eliminate 550 *obliterate*; exorcise, rid, get rid of, rid oneself, get shot of; shake off, brush o.; dispossess, expropriate 786 *deprive*; out, oust, evict, dislodge, turn out, turn adrift, turn out of house and home 188 *displace*; smoke out 619 *hunt*; jettison, discard, throw away, throw overboard 779 *not retain*; blackball 607 *reject*.

dismiss, discharge, lay off, make redundant, drop 674 *stop using*; axe, sack, fire, give the sack, give the boot, give the push, give the heave-ho, give marching orders to 779 *not retain*; turn away, send one about his business, send one away with a flea in his ear, send packing 292 *repel*; see off, shoo away 854 *frighten*; show the door, show out; bowl out, run o., catch o.; exorcize, order off, order away 757 *prohibit*.

empty, drain, void; evacuate, eliminate 302 *excrete*; discharge; pour out, decant 272 *transpose*; drink up, drain to the dregs 301 *drink*; drain off, strain off, ladle out, bail o., pump o., suck o., run off, siphon o., open the sluices, open the floodgates, turn on the tap 263 *open*; draw off, tap, broach 263 *pierce*; milk, bleed, let blood, catheterize 304 *extract*; clear, sweep away, clear a., clean up, mop up, make a clean sweep of, clear the decks 648 *clean*; clean out, clear out; unload, unpack 188 *displace*; disembowel, eviscerate, gut, clean, bone, fillet 229 *uncover*; disinfest 648 *purify*; depopulate, desertize, 105 *render few*.

emit, let out, give vent to; send out 272 *send*; emit rays 417 *radiate*; emit a smell, give off, exhale, breathe out, perfume, scent 394 *smell*; vapour, fume, smoke, steam, puff 338 *vaporize*; spit, splutter; pour, spill, shed, sprinkle, spray; spurt, squirt, jet, gush 341 *moisten*; bleed, weep; drip, drop, ooze; dribble, drool, slobber 298 *exude*; sweat, perspire 379 *be hot*; secrete 632 *store*; egest, pass 302 *excrete*; drop (a foal), lay (an egg) 167 *generate*.

vomit, be sick, be sick to one's stomach, bring up, throw up, regurgitate, disgorge, retch, gag; spew, puke, cat, honk, poop, chunder, be seasick, feel nausea, heave, have a bilious attack.

eruct, belch, burp; break wind, blow off, fart; hiccup, cough, hawk, clear the throat, expectorate, spit, gob.

301 Food: eating and drinking

N. *eating*, munching etc. vb.; ingestion; alimentation, nutrition; feeding, drip-f., force-f., gavage; consumption, devouring; swallowing, downing, getting down, bolting; biting, chewing, mastication; rumination, digestion; chewing the cud; cropping; table, diet, dining, lunching, breakfasting, supping, having tea, snacking, grazing; dining out 882 *sociability*; partaking; tasting, nibbling, pecking, licking, playing with one's food, toying with one's f.; eating disorder; anorexia, anorexia nervosa; guzzling, gobbling; overeating, overindulgence, bingeing, bulimia nervosa, seesaw eating 944 *sensualism*, 947 *gluttony*; obesity 195 *bulk*; appetite, voracity, wolfishness 859 *hunger*; omnivorousness 464 *indiscrimination*; eating habits, table manners 610 *practice*; carnivorousness, man-eating, cannibalism; herbivorousness, vegetarianism, veganism; edibility, digestibility, food chain.

feasting, eating and drinking, gormandizing, guzzling, swilling; banqueting, eating out, dining out, having a meal out; regalement; orgy, bacchanalia, feast; reception, wedding breakfast, annual dinner, do 876 *celebration*; harvest supper, beanfeast, bunfight, thrash; Christmas dinner, blowout, spread (**see** *meal*); loaded table, festive cheer, festive board, groaning b.; fleshpots 635 *plenty*.

dieting, dietetics 658 *therapy*; weightwatching, slimming 206 *thinness*; reducing, losing weight 946 *fasting*; diet, balanced d., crash d., macrobiotic d.; nouvelle cuisine, cuisine minceur, lean cuisine; regimen, regime, course, diet sheet, calorie counter; malnutrition 651 *disease*; calories, vitamins (**see** *food content*); vitamin pill; additive, E number.

gastronomy, epicureanism, epicurism 944 *sensualism*; gourmandism, foodism, good living, high 1. 947 *gluttony*; refined palate 463 *discrimination*.

cookery, cooking, baking, cuisine, haute c., nouvelle c., lean c., fusion c.; food preparation, dressing; domestic science, home economics, catering 633 *provision*; food processing (**see** *provisions*); baker, cook, chef, sous c., commis c., cuisinier, cordon bleu 633 *caterer*; bakery, rotisserie, delicatessen, restaurant 192 *café*; kitchen, cookhouse, galley; microwave, oven 383 *furnace*; cooking medium, butter, margarine, ghee,

Olestra (tdmk), corn oil, vegetable o., sunflower o., olive o. 357 *oil*; dripping, lard 357 *fat*; yeast 323 *leaven*; flour, cornflour 332 *powder*; vinegar, balsamic v., malt v. 393 *sourness*; recipe, cookery book, cookbook.

eater, feeder, consumer, partaker, taster etc. vb.; nibbler, picker, pecker; messmate; diner, banqueter, feaster, picnicker; diner-out, dining club 882 *sociability*; connoisseur, gourmet, epicure; gourmand, trencherman, trencherwoman, bon vivant, foodie 947 *glutton*; flesheater, meat-e., carnivore; man-eater, cannibal; vegetarian, vegan, veggie, herbivore; omnivore, hearty eater; wolf, gannet, vulture, hyena, locust.

provisions, stores, commissariat; provender, foodstuff, groceries; tinned *or* canned food, frozen f., convenience f., junk f., fast f.; keep, board, maintenance, aliment, sustenance 633 *provision*; self-sufficiency; commons, rations, iron r.; helping 783 *portion*.

provender, animal food, fodder, feed, pasture, pasturage, forage; corn, oats, barley, grain, hay, grass, clover, lucerne, silage; beechmast, acorns; foodstuffs, winter feed; chicken feed, pigswill, cattle cake; saltlick.

food, meat, bread, staff of life; aliment, nutriment, liquid n.; alimentation, nutrition; nurture, sustenance, nourishment, food and drink, pabulum; manna; nectar and ambrosia, amrita; daily bread, staple food, wheat, maize, rice, pulses, beans, potatoes; foodstuffs, comestibles, eats, victuals, viands, provender, grub, tucker, nosh, scoff, chow, chuck, scran; biscuit, salt pork, pemmican; stodge 391 *unsavouriness*; processed food, carrion, offal; wholefood, health food, functional f., organic foodstuff, high-fibre food, low-fat f.; genetically-modified f., genetically-altered f., Frankenstein f., Frankenfood, irradiated f.; good food, cakes and ale; tibits, snacks, delicacies, Gucci food, garnish, flavouring, herbs, sauce 389 *condiment*.

food content, vitamins; calories, roughage, bulk, fibre; minerals, salts; calcium, iron; protein, amino acid; fat, oil, cholesterol, saturated fats, polyunsaturates, essential fatty acid, transfatty a. 357 *fat*; carbohydrates, starch; sugar, glucose, sucrose, lactose, fructose 392 *sweet thing*; additive, preservative, artificial flavouring; E numbers.

mouthful, bite, nibble, morsel 33 *small quantity*; sop, sip, swallow; titbit; sandwich, open s., club s., snack, savoury, tortilla, wrap, nacho; petit four, biscuit, chocolate, sweet, toffee, chewing gum (**see** *sweetmeat*); popcorn, crisps, nuts.

meal, refreshment, fare; snack, bite to eat; piece, butty, sandwich, open s., club s., toasted s., toastie, hamburger, hot dog, fish and chips;

packed lunch, ploughman's l.; square meal, three-course m., sit-down meal, repast, collation, spread, feed, blowout, beanfeast (**see** *feasting*); beano, thrash, junket 837 *festivity*; picnic, barbecue; bread and cheese 1., potluck; take away, food to go; breakfast, elevenses, luncheon, lunch, brunch, tiffin; tea, afternoon t., high tea; dinner, supper, fork s., buffet s.; table d'hôte, à la carte, cover, helping 783 *portion*; seconds.

dish, course; main dish; salad, side dish, entre-mets; dessert, pudding, savoury; speciality, pièce de résistance, plat du jour, dish of the day; meat and two veg (**see** *meat*); casserole, stew, Irish s., hotpot, Lancashire h., ragout 43 *a mixture*; meat loaf, hamburger; goulash, curry; moussaka; pilau, pilaff, paella, risotto, biryani; chop suey, chow mein, stir-fry; dhal, bhaji; pasta, ravioli, lasagne, macaroni, spaghetti, tagliatelle, fettuccine, vermicelli, tortellini, penne, cannelloni, noodles; pancake, pizza, taco, tortilla, burrito, chimichanga, fajita; pasty, pie, flan, quiche; fricassee, fritters, croquettes, spring roll; fry-up, mixed grill, fritto misto, kebabs; tandoori; fondue, soufflé, omelette, fu yung; Welsh rabbit *or* rarebit, buck r., scrambled eggs, poached e., boiled e., fried e.; bread and cheese, bread and dripping; cauliflower cheese, ratatouille, bubble and squeak; pease pudding, baked beans, nut cutlet; leftovers.

hors-d'oeuvres, antipasto, smorgasbord; starter, appetiser, canapé; angels on horseback, devils on h.; taramasalata, hummus, raita, mezze; vol-au-vent: blini, samosa, pakora; soup, cream s., clear s.; broth, brew, potage, consommé; stock, bouillon, julienne, bisque, chowder, purée; cock-a-leekie, mulligatawny, minestrone, borscht, gazpacho, bouillabaisse; cold meats, cooked m., cold cuts, salami, pâté, terrine, galantine; salad, side s., green s., mixed s., potato s., Russian s., Waldorf s., coleslaw, macedoine; mayonnaise, dressing, French d. 389 *sauce*.

fish food, fish 365 *marine life*; fish and chips, fish pie, fish cakes, gefilte fish, fish fingers, quenelles, kedgeree; white fish, oily f., fresh f., smoked f; freshwater fish, trout, salmon, lox, gravlax, eel; seafish, cod, coley, rock salmon, dogfish, whiting, plaice, sole, skate, hake, halibut, haddock, smoked h., finnan haddie, turbot, mullet, mackerel, herring, rollmops, brisling, whitebait, sprats; sardine, pilchard, anchovies, tuna, tunny; kippers, bloaters, Arbroath smoky; Bombay duck; seafood, shellfish, oyster, lobster, crayfish, crab, shrimp, prawn, scampi; scallop, cockle, winkle, mussel, whelk, jellied eel; roe, soft r., hard r., caviar; sushi.

meat, flesh; red meat, white m.; beef, mutton, lamb, veal, pork, venison, game; pheasant, grouse, partridge, chicken 365 *table bird, poultry*; soya flour, textured vegetable protein, TVP 150 *substitute*; roast meat, Sunday roast, S. joint, roast beef and Yorkshire pudding; boiled beef and carrots; haggis, black pudding; shepherd's pie, cottage p.; minced meat, mince; meatballs, rissoles, hamburgers; sausage, banger, chipolata, frankfurter, smoked sausage; toad in the hole, Cornish pasty, steak and kidney pudding; cut, joint, leg; baron of beef, sirloin; shoulder, hand of pork, skirt, scrag end, breast, brisket; shin, loin, flank, ribs, topside, silverside; cutlet, chop, loin c., chump c., gigot c., escalope; steak, fillet s., rump s., porterhouse s., entrecôte s., sirloin s.; pork pie, ham, bacon, bacon rasher, streaky b., back b., boiled b., gammon; tongue, knuckle, brawn, oxtail, cowheel, pig's trotters, sweetbreads, tripe, chitterlings; offal, kidney, liver 224 *insides*.

dessert, pudding, sweet; milk pudding, rice p., semolina, tapioca, bread-and-butter pudding; steamed p., suet p., Christmas p., plum p., summer p., roly-poly, spotted dick; jam tart, mince pies, (**see** *pastries*); crumble, charlotte, strudel; sticky toffee pudding, baklava; stewed fruit, compôte, fool; fresh fruit, fruit salad; ice cream, sorbet, mousse, tiramisu, soufflé, sundae, trifle, blancmange, jelly, custard 392 *sweet thing*; cheese board; yoghourt.

sweets, boiled s., confectionery; candy, chocolate, caramel, toffee, fudge, Turkish delight, marshmallows, mints, liquorice; acid drops, pear d., barley sugar, humbugs, butterscotch, nougat; gob-stopper, aniseed ball, chewing gum, bubble g.; lolly, lollipop 392 *sweet thing*; sweetmeat, comfit, bonbon; crystallized fruit; toffee apple, candy floss.

fruit and vegetables, soft fruit, berry, gooseberry, strawberry, raspberry, loganberry, blackberry, tayberry, bilberry, mulberry; currant, redcurrant, blackcurrant, whitecurrant; apricot, peach, nectarine, plum, greengage, damson, cherry; apple, crab a., pippin, russet, pear; citrus fruit, orange, grapefruit, pomelo, lemon, lime, tangerine, clementine, mandarin; banana, pineapple, grape; rhubarb; date, fig; dried fruit, currant, raisin, sultana, prune; pomegranate, persimmon, Sharon fruit, passion fruit, guava, lichee, star fruit; mango, avocado; melon, water m., cantaloupe, honeydew; pawpaw, papaya; breadfruit; nut, coconut, Brazil nut, cashew n., pecan, peanut, groundnut, monkey nut; almond, walnut, chestnut, pine nut, hazel n., cob n., filbert; bottled fruit, tinned f., preserves 392 *sweet thing; vegetable, greens 366 plant*; turnip, swede, parsnip, carrot, Jerusalem artichoke;

potato, sweet p., yam; spud, baked potato, roast p., boiled p., mashed p., duchesse p., fried p., sauté p., French fries, chips; green vegetable, cabbage, Chinese c., red c., green c., white c., savoy, cauliflower, broccoli, calabrese, kohlrabi, kale, curly k., seakale; sprouts, Brussel s., spring greens; peas, petits pois, mangetout, beans, French b., broad b., runner b.; okra, lady's fingers, sorrel, spinach, chard, spinach beet, seakale b., asparagus, globe artichoice; leek, onion, shallots, garlic (**see** *herb*); marrow, courgette, zucchini, cucumber, pumpkin squash; aubergine, eggplant, capsicum, pepper, green p., red p., yellow p., chilli; sweetcorn; salads, lettuce, cos l., chicory, endive; spring onion, scallion, radish, celery, beetroot; tomato, beef t., cherry t., tomatoes on the vine, sun-dried tomatoes, love-apple; beansprouts, bamboo shoots; cress, watercress, mustard and cress; pulses, lentils, split peas, chick p.; haricot beans, butter b., kidney b., soya b., adzuki b.; mushroom, boletus, truffle; laver, laverbread, samphire; tofu, bean curd, Quorn (tdmk).

herb, bouquet garni, fines herbes; marjoram, sweet m., oregano, rosemary, sage, mint, parsley, chervil, chives, thyme, basil, balm, bergamot, savory, tarragon, bayleaf, dill, fennel, borage, hops, seasoning 389 *condiment*.

spice, spicery; coriander, cumin, cardamom, pepper, cayenne, paprika, chilli, curry powder, turmeric, allspice, mace, cinnamon, ginger, nutmeg, clove, caraway, juniper berries, capers, vanilla pod 389 *condiment*.

cereals, grains, wheat, buckwheat, oats, rye, maize, mealies, corn; rice, brown r., unpolished r., wild r., long grain r., patna r., basmatti r., short grain r., pudding r., millet, sorghum; breakfast cereal, cornflakes, muesli, oatmeal, porridge, gruel, skilly, brose; flour, meal, wholemeal, wheat germ, bran; bread, dough, flour, yeast; crust, crumb; white bread, sliced b., soda b., brown b., wholemeal b., malt b., granary b., black b., rye b., pumpernickel, corn b., pitta b., ciabatta; toast, rusk, croûtons; loaf, pan l., cottage l., cob, tin, farmhouse, bloomer, baguette, French stick, bread s.; roll, breakfast r., bridge r., bap, bagel, croissant, brioche, bun, currant b.; crumpet, muffin, scone, drop s., pancake, crêpe; tea-cake, oatcake, bannock; pappadum, chapatti, nan, paratha, polenta, tortilla, taco, waffle, wafer, crispbread, cracker, cream c.

pastries and cakes, confectionery; patty, pasty, turnover, dumpling; tart, flan, quiche, pie, piecrust; pastry, shortcrust p., flaky p., puff p., rough p. p., choux p.; patisserie, gateau, cake, lardy c., fruit c., Dundee c., seed c., sponge c., Madeira c., angel c., battenburg c., layer c., galette, cheesecake; brownies, fairy cakes, cup cakes, meringue, eclair, macaroon; Chelsea bun, Bath b., doughnut, flapjack, brandysnap, gingerbread, shortbread, cookies, biscuits, crackers, digestive biscuits, Nice b., tea b., garibaldi b., custard creams, gingernuts.

dairy product (**see** *milk*); cream, clotted c., curds, whey, junket, yoghourt, fruit y.; fromage frais; cheese, goat's c., cream c., cottage c., fullfat c., crowdie, mascarpone, ricotta; Cheddar, Cheshire, Leicestershire, Double Gloucester, Caerphilly, Lancashire, Wensleydale, sage Derby, red Windsor; Emmental, Gruyère, Gouda, Edam, Hayarti; Camembert, Brie; Bel Paese, Parmesan; ripe cheese, blue c., blue vinny, Roquefort, Gorgonzola, Stilton, Danish blue, Dolcellate, Lymeswold (tdmk); vegetarian cheese.

drinking, imbibing, sipping, wine-tasting 463 *discrimination*; gulping; swilling, alcoholism 949 *drunkenness*; libation 981 *oblation*.

draught, drink, beverage, dram, bevvy; gulp, swallow, sip, sup; bottle, bowl, glass 194 *cup*; cuppa, pinta; glassful, bumper; swig, nip, noggin, jigger, tot, slug; peg, double peg, snorter, snifter, chaser; long drink; short; quick one, quickie, snort; sundowner, nightcap; loving cup, stirrup c., doch-an-dorris, one for the road; health, toast; mixed drink, concoction, cocktail, punch, spritzer 43 *mixture*; potion, decoction, infusion 658 *medicine*; nectar.

soft drink, nonalcoholic beverage; water, drinking w., spring water, fountain; soda water, soda, cream s., soda fountain, siphon; table water, carbonated w., mineral w., Perrier (tdmk), tonic w., barley w., squash, low calorie drink, mixer; energy drink; iced drink, frappé; milk, milk shake; ginger beer, ginger ale, Coca Cola *or* Coke (tdmk), Pepsi (tdmk); fizz, pop, lemonade, orangeade; cordial, fruit juice, apple j., tomato j., vegetable j., juice box; coconut milk; tea, iced t., lemon t., herbal t., char, pekoe, orange p., Indian t., China t., green t., black t., Russian t., herb t., tisane 658 *tonic*; coffee, decaffeinated coffee, decaf, café au lait, café noir, black coffee, Irish c., Turkish c., espresso, cappuccino, latte; cocoa (**see** *milk*); sherbet, syrup, julep, hydromel.

alcoholic drink, strong d., booze, bevvy, tipple, poison; brew, intoxicating l. (**see** *wine*); alcohol; malt liquor, John Barleycorn, beer, small b.; draught beer, keg b., bottled b.; strong beer; heavy, export; ale, real ale; barley wine; stout, lager, bitter, porter, mild, home brew; lowalcohol beer, no-alcohol b., nab; shandy; cider, scrumpy; perry, mead, Athole brose; palm wine, rice beer, toddy, sake, mescal, tequila; distilled liquor, spirituous l., spirits, ardent s., raw s., aqua vitae, firewater, hooch, moonshine, moun-

tain dew, rotgut, hard stuff; brandy, cognac, eau-de-vie, armagnac, marc, applejack, Calvados, kirsch, slivovitz, jambava; gin, mother's ruin, geneva, sloe gin, schnapps; whisky, usquebaugh, Scotch whisky, scotch; rye, bourbon; Irish whiskey, poteen; vodka, aquavit, ouzo, raki, arrack; rum, white r., Bacardi (tdmk), margarita; aperitif, Pernod (tdmk), absinthe; liqueur, cassis, Cointreau (tdmk), Drambuie (tdmk), curaçao, crème de menthe, grog, hot toddy, punch, rum p.; spiced wine, mulled w., negus, posset, claret cup; Pimms (tdmk), gin and tonic, pink gin, highball, brandy and soda, whisky and s.; mint julep; cocktail, Manhattan, Bloody Mary.

wine, the grape, ampelology, ampelography; red wine, white w., vin rosé, blush wine, vermouth; spumante, sparkling wine; sweet w., dry w., full-bodied w., vintage w.; vin ordinaire, vin de table, vin du pays; vino, plonk; table wine, dessert w.; fortified w., sack, sherry, port, vintage p., ruby p., white p., tawny p., madeira, marsala; champagne, champers, fizz, bubbly; claret, Bordeaux; burgundy, Beaujolais; Muscadet, hock, Sauternes, Moselle, Riesling; Spätlese, Auslese, Beerenauslese, Trockenbeerenauslese; Tokay, retsina, chianti; alcohol-free wine, lowalcohol w.; vintage wine, first great growth, premier cru.

milk, top of the m., cream; cow's milk, beestings; goat's milk, mare's m., koumiss; mother's milk, breast m.; buttermilk, dried m., skimmed m., semi-skimmed m., condensed m., evaporated m., pasteurized m.; milk drink, m. shake, malted m., cocoa, chocolate, hot c., Horlicks (tdmk); curdled milk, curds, junket. **See** *dairy product*.

Adj. *feeding*, eating, grazing etc. vb.; flesheating, meat-e.; carnivorous, creophagous, cannibalistic; omophagic, omophagous; insectivorous; herbivorous, graminivorous, frugivorous; vegetarian, vegan; omnivorous 464 *indiscriminating*.

edible, eatable; kosher; digestible; potable, drinkable; palatable, succulent, moreish, delicious 386 *tasty*.

nourishing, sustaining, nutritious, nutritive, nutritional; protein-rich, body-building; wholesome 652 *salubrious*.

culinary, dressed, oven-ready, ready-to-cook, made-up, ready-to-serve; cooked, done to a turn, well-done; al dente; underdone, red, rare, raw; over-cooked, burnt, b. to a cinder; roasted etc. vb. (**see** *cook*); à la meunière, au gratin, au naturel, mornay, au fromage, à la campagne, à la mode, à la maison, à la meunière; gastronomic, epicurean; prandial, post-p., afterdinner; meal-time.

Vb. *eat*, feed, mess; partake 386 *taste*; take a meal, have a feed, break one's fast, break bread; breakfast, have brunch, snack, graze, eat between meals, lunch, have tea, take tea, dine, sup; dine out, feast, banquet, carouse 837 *revel*; do justice to, be a good trencherman *or* woman, ask for more; water at the mouth, drool, raven 859 *be hungry*; fall to, set to, tuck in, lay into; stuff oneself, binge 863 *sate*; guzzle, gormandize 947 *gluttonize*; eat up, leave a clean plate; lick the platter clean 165 *consume*; swallow, gulp down, devour, dispatch, bolt, wolf, make short work of; feed on, live on, fatten on, batten on, prey on; nibble, peck, lick, play with one's food, toy with one's f., be anorexic; nibble at, peck at, sniff at; be a seesaw eater; ingest, digest 299 *absorb*.

chew, masticate, champ, chomp, munch, crunch, scrunch; gnaw, grind 332 *pulverize*; chew up 46 *cut*.

graze, browse, crop, feed; ruminate, chew the cud; nibble.

drink, imbibe, suck 299 *absorb*; quaff, drink up, drink one's fill, drain, drink like a fish, slake one's thirst, lap, sip, gulp; wet one's lips, wet one's whistle; crack a bottle; lap up, soak up, wash down; booze, swill, swig, tipple, tope 949 *get drunk*; drain one's glass, knock it back; raise one's glass, pledge 876 *toast*; take one for the road, have one over the eight; refill one's glass 633 *replenish*.

feed, nourish, nurture, sustain, cater 633 *provide*; nurse, breast-feed, give suck; pasture, graze, put out to grass; fatten, fatten up 197 *enlarge*; dine, wine and dine, feast, fête, banquet 882 *be hospitable*.

cook, pressure-cook; microwave, bake, brown; roast, spit-roast, pot-r., braise; broil, grill, charcoal-grill, barbecue, spatchcock, griddle, devil, curry; sauté, fry, deep-f., shallow-f., stir-f.; fry sunny side up, scramble, poach; boil, parboil; coddle, simmer, steam; casserole, stew; baste, lard, bard; whip, whisk, beat, blend, liquidize, stir; draw, gut, bone, fillet; stuff, dress, garnish; dice, shred, mince, grate; sauce, flavour, herb, spice 388 *season*.

Int. bon appétit! here's health! here's to you! here's mud in your eye! bottoms up! down the hatch! slàinte! prosit! skol! cheers!

302 Excretion

N. *excretion*, discharge, secretion 300 *ejection*; emanation 298 *egress*; exhalation, breathing out 352 *respiration*; exudation, perspiration, sweating 298 *outflow*; suppuration 651 *infection*; cold, common c., coryza, catarrh, hay fever, allergic rhinitis, allergy; salivation, expectoration, spitting; coughing, hawking, cough; urination, micturition, peeing, pissing (vulg), slashing; waterworks, plumbing; incontinence.

haemorrhage, bleeding, haemophilia 335 *blood*; menses, menarche, period, time of the month, curse; dysmenorrhoea, menorrhagia.

defecation, evacuation, elimination, clearance 300 *voidance*; bowel movement, shit (vulg), crap (vulg), motion; bodily functions; diarrhoea, the trots 651 *digestive disorders*; constipation.

excrement, waste matter; faeces, stool, shit (vulg), crap (vulg), excreta, ordure; dung, cowpat, manure, muck; droppings, guano; urine, piss (vulg), water; sweat; spittle, spit, gob, sputum; saliva, slaver, slobber; rheum, phlegm; catarrh, mucus, snot; matter, pus; afterbirth, lochia.

Vb. *excrete*, secrete; pass, move; move one's bowels, defecate, shit (vulg), crap (vulg); be taken short, have the trots; relieve oneself, answer the call of nature, go, go to the lavatory; urinate, micturate, piddle, pee; have a pee, piss (vulg), have a p. (vulg), have a slash, take a leak; make water, spend a penny; wet oneself; sweat, perspire 379 *be hot*; salivate, slobber, snivel; cough, hawk, spit, gob 300 *eruct*; weep 298 *exude*.

303 Insertion: forcible ingress

N. *insertion*, interpolation, parenthesis 231 *interjection*; adding 38 *addition*; introduction, insinuation 297 *ingress*; impaction; planting 370 *agriculture*; inoculation, injection, jab, shot; infusion, enema, catheter; insert, inset; implant, silicone i.; stuffing 227 *lining*.

Vb. *insert*, introduce; weave into; put into, thrust i., intrude; poke into, jab i., stick i.; transfix, run through 263 *pierce*; ram into, jam i., stuff i., pack i., push i., shove i., tuck i., press i., pop i. 193 *load*; pocket; ease into place, slide in, fit in; knock into, hammer i., drive i. 279 *impel*; put in, inlay, inset 227 *line*; subjoin 38 *add*; interpose 231 *put between*; drop in, put in the slot 311 *let fall*; pot, hole; bury 364 *inter*.

implant, plant, transplant, plant out, prick o., bed o., dibble; graft, engraft, bud; inoculate, vaccinate; embed, bury.

immerse, bathe, steep, souse, marinate, soak 341 *drench*; baptize, duck, dip 311 *lower*; submerge; immerse oneself 313 *plunge*.

304 Extraction: forcible egress

N. *extraction*, withdrawal, removal 188 *displacement*; elimination, eradication 300 *ejection*; abortion 172 *unproductiveness*; extermination 165 *destruction*; extrication, unravelment, disengagement, liberation 668 *deliverance*; tearing out, ripping o.; cutting out, excision; Caesarian birth, forceps delivery; expression, squeezing out; suction, sucking out, aspiration; vacuuming, pumping; drawing out, pull, tug, wrench 288 *traction;* digging out 255 *excavation;* mining, quarrying; fishery; distillation 338 *vaporization;* drawing off, tapping, milking; thing extracted, essence, extract.

Vb. *extract,* remove, pull 288 *draw;* draw out, elicit; unfold 316 *evolve;* pull out, take o., get o., pluck; withdraw, excise, cut out, rip o., tear o., whip o.; excavate, mine, quarry, dig out, unearth; dredge, dredge up; expel, lever out, winkle o., smoke o. 300 *eject;* extort, wring from; express, press out, squeeze o., gouge o.; force out, wring o., wrench o., drag o.; draw off, milk, tap; syphon off, aspirate, suck, void, pump; wring from, squeeze f., drag f.; pull up, dig up, grub up, rake up; eliminate, weed out, root up, uproot, eradicate, extirpate 165 *destroy;* prune, thin out 105 *render few;* distil 338 *vaporize;* extricate, unravel, free 746 *liberate;* unpack, unload 188 *displace;* eviscerate, gut 300 *empty;* unwrap 229 *uncover;* pick out 605 *select.*

305 Passage: motion through

N. *passage,* transmission 272 *transference;* transportation 272 *transport;* passing, passing through, traversing; traverse, crossing, journey, patrol 267 *land travel;* penetration, permeation, infiltration; osmosis, 297 *ingress;* intervention 231 *interjacency;* right of way 624 *access;* stepping-stone, flyover, underpass, subway 624 *bridge;* track, route, orbit 624 *path;* intersection, junction 222 *crossing;* waterway, channel 351 *conduit.*

traffic control, traffic engineering; traffic calming, traffic c. measures, speed bump, sleeping policeman, road hump, chicane; road pricing, road tolling; flow of traffic; traffic jam, tailback; rush hour; highway code, Green Cross C., green man 693 *precept;* traffic lane, motorway l., bus l., cycle l., one-way street, carriageway, dual c., clearway 624 *road;* diversion, alternative route 282 *deviation;* contraflow, lane closure; white lines, yellow l., double yellow l., red l., red route; cat's-eyes (tdmk), sleeping policemen; street furniture, traffic lights, lampposts, roundabout; pedestrian crossing, zebra c., pelican c., subway (**see** *passage*); Belisha beacon, bollard, refuge, island; parking, zone p., off-street p.; car park, parking lot, parking place, parking zone, park-and-ride; parking meter, parking ticket, waiting, loading, unloading; lay-by; point duty, road patrol, speed trap, radar t., speed camera; traffic police, traffic cop; traffic warden, meter maid; lollipop man *or* lady; road user 268 *pedestrian.*

Vb. *pass,* pass by, leave on one side, skirt, coast; flash by 277 *move fast,* 114 *be transient;* go past, not stop 146 *go on,* 265 *be in motion;* pass along, circulate, weave; pass through, transit, traverse; shoot through, shoot the rapids 269 *navigate;* pass out, come out the other side 298 *emerge;* go through, soak t., seep t., percolate, permeate 189 *pervade;* pass and repass, patrol, walk up and down, work over, beat, scour, go over the ground; pass into, penetrate, infiltrate 297 *enter;* bore, perforate 263 *pierce;* thread, thread through, string 45 *connect;* rake; force a passage; worm one's way, squeeze through, elbow t., clear the way 285 *progress;* cross, go across, cross over, make a crossing, reach the other side 295 *arrive;* wade across, ford; get through, get past, negotiate; pass beyond 306 *overstep;* pass in front, cut across 702 *obstruct;* step over, straddle; bridge 226 *cover;* carry over, carry across, transmit 272 *send;* pass to, hand, reach, pass from hand to hand, hand over 272 *transfer.*

306 Overstepping: motion beyond

N. *overstepping,* going beyond, overstepping the mark, stretching a point 305 *passage;* transcendence 34 *superiority,* digression 282 *deviation;* transgression 936 *guilty act;* encroachment 916 *arrogation;* infringement, intrusion 916 *undueness;* expansionism, greediness 859 *desire;* excessiveness 637 *redundance;* overdoing it, going overboard 546 *exaggeration;* overindulgence 943 *intemperance.*

Vb. *overstep,* overstep the mark; go too far, throw out the baby with the bathwater; exceed, exceed the limit; overrun, overshoot the mark, aim too high; overlap; cross the Rubicon, pass the point of no return, burn one's boats; overfill, spill o. 54 *fill;* overgrow 637 *superabound;* overdo 546 *exaggerate;* strain, stretch a point; overbid, have one's bluff called, overestimate 482 *overrate;* overindulge 943 *be intemperate;* outstay one's welcome, oversleep 136 *be late.*

encroach, invade, make inroads on 712 *attack;* infringe, transgress, trespass 954 *be illegal;* poach 788 *steal;* squat, usurp 786 *appropriate;* barge in, horn in, butt in 297 *intrude;* impinge; eat away, erode 655 *impair;* infest, overrun; overflow, flood 341 *drench.*

outdo, exceed, surpass, outclass; transcend, rise above, soar a., outrival 34 *be superior;* go one better, outbid; outwit; outmanoeuvre, outflank, steal a march on, steal one's thunder; outpace, outrun, outride, outdistance; overtake; leave standing, leave at the starting post 277 *outstrip;* leave behind, beat hollow 727 *defeat.*

307 Shortfall

N. *shortfall,* falling short etc. vb.; negative equity, inadequacy 636 *insufficiency;* a minus, deficit, short measure, shortage, slippage, loss; leeway, drift 282 *deviation;* unfinished state 55 *incompleteness;* nonfulfilment, 726 *noncompletion;* half measures 641 *lost labour;* shortcoming 647 *imperfection;* something missing, want, lack, need 627 *requirement.*

Adj. *deficient,* short, short of, minus, wanting, lacking, missing; underpowered, substandard; undermanned, short-staffed, half-done 55 *incomplete;* inadequate 636 *insufficient;* failing, running short 636 *scarce;* below par 647 *imperfect.*

Vb. *fall short,* run s. 636 *not suffice;* not reach to; lack, want, be without 627 *require;* underachieve, not make the grade, not come up to scratch; miss the mark; lag 136 *be late;* stop short, fall by the way, fall out, not stay the course; break down, get bogged down; fall behind, lose ground, slip back; slump, collapse 286 *regress;* fall through, come to nothing, fizzle out, fail 728 *miscarry;* labour in vain 641 *waste effort;* not come up to expectations 509 *disappoint.*

308 Ascent: motion upwards

N. *ascent,* ascension, lift, upward motion; levitation; taking off, takeoff, lift-off, blast-off 296 *departure;* soaring, spiral; zoom 271 *aeronautics;* culmination 213 *summit;* surfacing; going up, rising; rise, upturn, upward trend; uprush, upsurge, crescendo 36 *increase;* updraught, thermal; sunrise, sun-up, dawn 128 *morning;* mounting, climbing; hill-climbing, rock-c., mountaineering, alpinism; ladder-scaling, escalade 712 *attack;* jump, vault, pole v., pole jump 312 *leap;* bounce 280 *recoil;* rising ground, hill 209 *high land;* gradient, slope, ramp 220 *incline;* rising pitch 410 *musical note;* stairs, steps, stile, flight of stairs, stair-case, spiral s., stairway, landing; ladder, step 1., accommodation 1., Jacob's 1., companionway; rope ladder, ratlines; stair, step, tread, rung; lift, ski 1., chair 1., elevator, escalator; fire escape 667 *means of escape.*

climber, mountaineer, rock-climber, alpinist, cragsman *or* -woman, fell walker; steeplejack.

Vb. *ascend,* rise, rise up, go up, leave the ground; defy gravity, levitate; take off, become airborne, have lift-off, fly up 271 *fly;* gain height, mount, soar, spiral, zoom, climb; reach the top, get to the top of the ladder, reach the zenith, culminate; float up, bob up, surface, break water; jump up, spring, vault 312 *leap;* bounce 280 *recoil;* push up, grow up, shoot up 36 *grow;* curl upwards; tower, aspire, spire 209 *be high;* gush, spirt, spout, jet, play; get up, start

up, stand up, rear, rear up, ramp 215 *be vertical;* rise to one's feet, get up 310 *lift oneself;* slope upwards 220 *be oblique.*

climb, walk up, struggle up; mount, make one's way up, work one's way up; go climbing, go mountaineering, mountaineer; clamber, scramble, swarm up, shin up, go up hand over fist; surmount, top, breast, conquer, scale, scale the heights 209 *be high;* go over the top, escalade 712 *attack;* go upstairs, climb a ladder; mount (a horse).

Adv. *up,* uphill, upstairs; upwards 209 *aloft.*

309 Descent

N. *descent,* declension 282 *deviation;* falling, dropping; cadence; downward trend, decline, drop, slump 37 *decrease;* sunset, moonset; comedown, demotion 286 *regression;* downfall, collapse, setback 165 *ruin;* trip, stumble; lurch, capsize 221 *overturning;* tumble, crash, spill, fall; cropper, purler; downrush, swoop, stoop, pounce; dive, header, bellyflop 313 *plunge;* nosedive, power-dive 271 *aeronautics;* landing, crash 1., splashdown 295 *arrival;* sliding down, glissade; subsidence, landslide, avalanche; downdraught 352 *wind;* downpour, shower 350 *rain;* cascade 350 *waterfall;* downthrow (geology); declivity, slope, tilt, dip 220 *incline;* chute, slide, helter-skelter; precipice, sheer drop 215 *verticality;* submergence, sinkage, slippage 311 *lowering;* burrowing, mining, undermining 255 *excavation;* speleology, pot-holing, caving.

Vb. *descend,* come down, go d., dip d.; decline, abate, ebb 37 *decrease;* slump, plummet, fall, drop, sink; sink like a lead balloon, sink without trace 322 *weigh;* soak in, seep down 297 *infiltrate;* reach the depths, touch bottom; bottom out, reach one's nadir 35 *be inferior;* sink to the bottom, gravitate, precipitate, settle, set; fall down, fall in, cave in, fall to the ground, collapse; sink in, subside, slip, give way; hang down, prolapse, droop, sag, swag 217 *hang;* go under water, draw; submerge, dive 313 *plunge;* drown 313 *founder;* go underground, dig down, burrow, mine, undermine 255 *make concave;* parachute; swoop, stoop, pounce; fly down, flutter d., float d.; lose height, drop down, swing low; touch down, alight, light, perch 295 *land;* lower oneself, abseil; get down, climb d., step d., get off, fall o., dismount; coast down, slide down, glissade, toboggan; fall like rain, shower, cascade, drip 350 *rain;* bow down, dip, duck 311 *stoop;* flop, plop, splash down.

tumble, fall; topple, keel over, overbalance, capsize, tumble head over heels 221 *be inverted;* miss one's footing, trip, stumble; lose one's balance; take a header, dive 313 *plunge;* fall off, take a fall, be thrown, come a cropper, fall heavily, crash to the ground, fall flat on one's face, fall prostrate, bite the dust, measure one's length; plummet, plump down 311 *sit down*; slump, nosedive.

Adv. *down*, downwards; downhill, downstairs, downstream.

310 Elevation

N. *elevation*, raising etc. vb.; erection, uplift, upheaval; picking up, lift; hoist, boost; leg-up 703 *aid*; levitation; exaltation, Assumption; uprising, uptrend, growth, upswing 308 *ascent*; eminence 209 *high land*, 254 *prominence*; height above sea level 209 *height*.

Vb. *elevate*, heighten 209 *make higher*; puff up, blow up, swell, leaven 197 *enlarge*; raise, erect, set up, put up, run up, rear up, build up, build; lift, lift up, raise up, heave up; uplift; jack up, lever up, hike up, prop 218 *support*; stand on end; hold up, bear up; buoy up; raise aloft, hold a., hold up, wave; hoist, haul up; pick up, take up; pull up, wind up; weigh; fish up, drag up, dredge up, pump up 304 *extract*; chair, shoulder, carry shoulder-high; exalt, put on a pedestal 866 *honour*; mount 213 *crown*; jump up, bounce up 285 *promote*; give a lift, give a leg-up 703 *aid*; throw in the air, throw up, cast up, toss up; loft; send up, shoot up, lob 287 *propel*; perk up (one's head), prick up (one's ears); bristle, bristle up 215 *be vertical*.

lift oneself, arise, rise 308 *ascend*; stand up, get up, get to one's feet, pick oneself up, jump up, leap up, spring up, spring to one's feet; pull oneself up; hold oneself up, hold one's head up, draw oneself up to one's full height, stand on tiptoe 215 *be vertical*.

311 Lowering

N. *lowering*, depression, hauling down etc. vb.; pushing down 279 *impulse*; ducking, sousing 313 *plunge*; debasement, demotion, reduction 872 *humiliation*; subversion 149 *revolution*; overthrow, prostration; overturn, upset 221 *overturning*; precipitation, defenestration 287 *propulsion*; suppression; depression, dent, dip, dimple, hollow 255 *cavity*; low pressure 340 *weather*.

obeisance, reverence, bow, salaam, kowtow 884 *courtesy*; curtsy, bob, duck, nod, salute 884 *courteous act*; kneeling, genuflexion 920 *respect*.

Vb. *lower*, depress, push down, thrust d. 279 *impel*; shut down (a lid) 264 *close*; hold down, keep d., hold under 165 *suppress*; lower, let down, take d.; lower a flag, dip; haul down, strike; deflate, puncture, flatten, squash, crush 198 *make smaller*; let drop (**see** *let fall*); sink, scuttle, drown 309 *descend*; duck, souse, douse,

dip 313 *plunge*; weigh on, press on 322 *weigh*; tip, hollow 255 *make concave*.

let fall, drop, shed; let go 779 *not retain*; let slip *or* slide through one's fingers; pour, pour out, decant 300 *empty*; spill, slop 341 *moisten*; sprinkle, shower, scatter, dust, dredge; sow, broadcast 75 *disperse*; lay down, put d., set d., throw d., fling d. (**see** *fell*); pitch *or* chuck overboard, jettison, drop over the side; precipitate, send headlong 287 *propel*.

fell, overthrow; prostrate; lay low, lay one on his back 216 *flatten*; knock down, bowl over; floor, raze to the ground, trample in the dust 165 *demolish*; hew down, cut d., axe 46 *cut*; bring down; shoot down 287 *shoot*.

abase, debase, lower one's sights; demote, reduce to the ranks, cashier 752 *depose*; humble, deflate, puncture, debunk, take down a peg, cut down to size, take the wind out of one's sails 872 *humiliate*; crush, squash, grind down 165 *suppress*.

sit down, sit, sit oneself down, be seated, squat, hunker; sink, lower oneself; take a seat, seat oneself, take a pew, park oneself; perch, alight 309 *descend*.

stoop, bend, bend down; bend over, bend forward, bend backward; lean forward, lean over backwards; cringe, crouch, cower 721 *knuckle under*; slouch, hunch one's back 248 *make curved*; bow, scrape, duck, bob, curtsy, bob a c. 884 *pay one's respects*; nod, incline one's head, bow down, make obeisance, kiss hands, salaam, prostrate oneself, kowtow 920 *show respect*; kneel, kneel to, genuflect, kiss the ground.

312 Leap

N. *leap*, leapfrogging; jump, hop, skip; spring, bound, vault, pole v.; high jump, long j., running j.; triple j., hop, skip and jump; bungee jump; caper, gambol, frolic; kick, cancan; jeté, entrechat; prance; dance step; dance, breakdance, reel, jig, Highland fling 837 *dancing*.

Vb. *leap*, jump, take a running j.; spring, bound, vault, pole-v., hurdle, steeplechase, take one's fences; skip, hop, leapfrog, bob, bounce, rebound, buck, bob up and down 317 *oscillate*; stamp 837 *dance*; caper, cut capers, gambol, frisk, romp; prance; start, give a jump; jump on, pounce; jump up, leap up, spring up 308 *ascend*; jump over, clear.

313 Plunge

N. *plunge*, swoop, pounce, stoop, plummet 309 *descent*; nosedive, power dive 271 *aeronautics*; dive, header, bellyflop; swallow dive, duck d.; dip, ducking; immersion, submergence; crash dive.

diver, skin d., scuba d., deepsea d., frogman; underwater swimmer, aquanaut; the bends, caisson disease.

Vb. *plunge*, dip, duck 341 *be wet*; fall in, jump in, plump, plop, plummet; dive, take a header, go headfirst; souse, douse, immerse, submerse, drown; submerge, crash-dive 309 *descend*; sink, scuttle, send to Davy Jones's locker 311 *lower*.

founder, go down 309 *descend*; get out of one's depth; drown, go to the bottom, go down like a stone 211 *be deep*; plummet, sink, sink without trace, sink like lead 322 *weigh*.

314 Circuition: curvilinear motion

N. *circuition*, circulation, circumnavigation, circling, wheeling, spiral 315 *rotation*; turning, cornering, turn, U-turn 286 *return*; orbit; lap; circuit, milk round, tour, round trip, full circle; figure of eight 250 *loop*; helix 251 *coil*; circuitousness, roundabout way, scenic route, tourist r. 626 *circuit*.

Adj. *circuitous*, turning etc. vb.; peripatetic; devious 626 *roundabout*.

Vb. *circle*, circulate, go the rounds, make the round of; circuit, make a c., lap; do the round trip; go round, skirt; circumnavigate, go round the world, go globetrotting; turn, round, weather a point; round a corner, turn a c.; revolve, orbit; wheel, spiral, come full circle, chase one's tail 315 *rotate*; do a U-turn, turn round, bend r.; put about, wheel a., face a., turn on one's heel 286 *turn back*; draw a circle, describe a circle 232 *circumscribe*; curve, wind, twist, wind one's way 251 *meander*; make a detour 626 *circuit*.

315 Rotation: motion in a continued circle

N. *rotation*, revolving, orbiting; revolution, full circle; gyration, circling, wheeling, spiralling; circulation; circumrotation; rolling 285 *progression*; spiral, roll, spin, flat s.; turn, twirl, pirouette, waltz 837 *dance*; whirl; dizzy round, rat race, milk round 678 *overactivity*.

vortex, whirl; whirlwind, tornado, cyclone 352 *gale*; waterspout, whirlpool, swirl 350 *eddy*; whirlpool bath, Jacuzzi (tdmk); maelstrom, Charybdis; smoke ring 250 *loop*.

rotator, rotor, spinner; whirligig, top, spinning t., humming t.; merry-go-round; churn, whisk; potter's wheel, lathe, circular saw; spinning wheel, spinning jenny; catherine wheel; flywheel, roulette w., wheel of Fortune 250 *wheel*; Hula-Hoop (tdmk); gyroscope, turntable; gramophone record, disc, magnetic tape, cassette, compact disc; wind pump, windmill, fan, sail; propeller, prop, screw; turbine; winder, capstan; swivel, hinge; spit, jack; spindle, axle,

axis, shaft 218 *pivot*; spool, reel, roller 252 *cylinder*; rolling stone, planet, satellite 268 *wanderer*.

Vb. *rotate*, revolve, orbit, go into orbit 314 *circle*; turn right round, chase one's own tail; spin, twirl, pirouette; corkscrew 251 *twine*; gyrate, waltz, wheel; whirl, hum 404 *resound*; mill around, swirl, eddy 350 *flow*; bowl, trundle; roll, roll along; twirl, twiddle, twizzle; churn, whisk 43 *mix*; turn, crank, wind, reel, spool, spin; slew, slew round, swing round, swivel r.; roll up, furl 261 *fold*; roll itself up, curl up.

316 Evolution: motion in a reverse circle

N. *evolution*, unrolling, unfolding, unfurling; development 157 *growth*; evolutionism, Darwinism 358 *biology*.

Vb. *evolve*, unfold, unfurl, unroll, unwind, uncoil, uncurl, untwist, untwine, disentangle; develop, grow into 147 *be turned to*, 1 *become*; roll back 263 *open*.

317 Oscillation: reciprocating motion

N. *oscillation*, harmonic motion, pendular m., swing of the pendulum; vibration, tremor; vibrancy, resonance 141 *periodicity*; pulsation, rhythm; throbbing, drumming, pulse, beat, throb; pitter-patter, flutter, palpitation 318 *agitation*; breathing 352 *respiration*; undulation, wave motion, frequency, frequency band, wavelength 417 *radiation*; sound wave, radio w.; tidal w. 350 *wave*; seismic disturbance, earthquake, tremor 176 *violence*; seismology, seismograph; oscillator, vibrator; metronome; pendulum, bob, yoyo 217 *hanging object*. **See** *fluctuation*.

fluctuation, wave motion (**see** *oscillation*); alternation, reciprocation 12 *correlation*; to and fro movement, coming and going, shuttling; ups and downs, boom and bust, ebb and flow, flux and reflux; night and day 14 *contrariety*; rolling, pitching; roll, pitch, lurch, shake, nod, wag; swing, seesaw; shuttle; wavering, vacillation 601 *irresolution*.

Vb. *oscillate*, emit waves 417 *radiate*; wave, undulate; vibrate, pulsate, pulse, beat, drum; tick, throb, palpitate; pant, heave 352 *breathe*; play, sway, nod; swing, dangle 217 *hang*; seesaw, rock; lurch, stagger, totter, teeter, waddle, wobble, wiggle, waggle, wag; bob, bounce, bob up and down, dance 312 *leap*; toss, roll, pitch; rattle, chatter, shake; flutter, quiver, shiver 318 *be agitated*; flicker 417 *shine*; echo 404 *resound*. **See** *fluctuate*.

fluctuate, alternate, reciprocate 12 *correlate*; ebb and flow, come and go, pass and repass, shuttle.

brandish, wave, wag, waggle, shake, flourish;

wave to and fro, shake up and down; flutter 318 *agitate*.

Adv. *to and fro*, backwards and forwards, back and forth; in and out, up and down, side to side; zigzag, seesaw, like a yoyo; shuttlewise.

318 Agitation: irregular motion

N. *agitation*, jerkiness, fits and starts, unsteadiness, shakiness 152 *changeableness*; joltiness, bumpiness, choppiness, pitching, rolling 259 *roughness*; flicker, twinkle 417 *flash*; start, jump 508 *lack of expectation*; hop 312 *leap*; shake, toss 287 *propulsion*; shock, jar, jolt, jerk, judder, bounce, bump 279 *impulse*; nudge, dig, jog 547 *gesture*; vibration, thrill, throb, pulse, pit-a-pat, palpitation, flutter 317 *oscillation*; shuddering, shudder, shiver, frisson; quiver, quaver, tremor; tremulousness, trembling (**see** *spasm*); restlessness, feverishness, fever; tossing, turning; jiving, rock 'n roll, breakdancing 678 *activity*, 837 *dancing*; itchiness, itch 378 *formication*; twitchiness, twitch, grimacing, grimace; perturbation, disquiet 825 *worry*; trepidation, jumpiness, twitter, flap, butterflies, collywobbles 854 *nervousness*; delirium tremens, dt's, the shakes; Parkinson's disease, Parkinsonism; shivers, jumps, jitters, fidgets.

spasm, ague, shivering, chattering; twitch, tic, nervous t.; chorea, St Vitus' dance; lockjaw, tetanus; cramp, the cramps; throe 377 *pang*; convulsion, paroxysm, orgasm 503 *frenzy*; fit, epilepsy 651 *nervous disorders*; pulse, throb 317 *oscillation*; attack, seizure, stroke.

commotion, turbulence, tumult 61 *turmoil*; hurly-burly, hubbub, brouhaha, hassle; fever, flurry, rush, bustle 680 *haste*; furore 503 *frenzy*; fuss, to-do, bother, kerfuffle, shemozzle 678 *restlessness*; racket, din 400 *loudness*; stir, ferment

821 *excitation*; boiling, fermentation, ebullition, effervescence 355 *bubble*; ground swell, heavy sea 350 *wave*; squall, tempest, thunderstorm, magnetic storm 176 *storm*; whirlpool 315 *vortex*; whirlwind 352 *gale*; disturbance, atmospherics.

agitated, shaken; shaking, etc. vb; troubled; restless; jittery, jumpy, twitchy, wound up, wired up, flustered, in a flap 854 *nervous*.

Vb. *be agitated*, ripple, boil 355 *bubble*; stir, move, dash; shake, tremble, quiver, quaver, shiver; have a fever, throw a fit, be all of a doodah, be all of a dither; be in a flap; be like a cat on hot bricks; writhe, squirm, twitch 251 *wriggle*; toss, turn, toss about, thresh a.; kick, plunge, rear; flounder, flop, wallow, roll, reel, pitch 317 *fluctuate*; sway 220 *be oblique*; pulse, beat, thrill, vibrate, judder, shudder; wag, waggle, wobble, stagger, lurch, dodder, totter, teeter, dither 317 *oscillate*; whirr, whirl 315 *rotate*; jig around, jig up and down, jump about, hop, bob, bounce, dance 312 *leap*; flicker, twinkle, gutter, sputter 417 *shine*; flap, flutter, twitter, start, jump; throb, pant, palpitate, miss a beat, go pit-a-pat 821 *be excited*; bustle, rush, mill around 61 *rampage*; ramp, roar 891 *be angry*.

agitate, disturb, rumple, ruffle, untidy 63 *derange*; discompose, perturb, worry, hassle, throw into a panic 827 *trouble*; ripple, muddy; stir, stir up 43 *mix*; whisk, whip, beat, churn 315 *rotate*; shake up, shake; wag, waggle, wave, flourish 317 *brandish*; flutter, fly (a flag); jog, joggle, jolt, jounce, nudge, dig; jerk, pluck, twitch.

effervesce, froth, spume, foam, foam at the mouth, bubble up 355 *bubble*; boil, boil over, seethe, simmer, sizzle, spit 379 *be hot*; ferment, work.

Matter

Matter in general

319 Materiality

N. *materiality*, materialness; corporeality, bodiliness; world of nature 3 *substantiality*; physical condition 1 *existence*; plenum 321 *world*; concreteness, tangibility, palpability, solidity 324 *density*; weight 322 *gravity*; personality, individuality 80 *speciality*; embodiment, incarnation, reincarnation, realization, materialization; materialism; worldliness, sensuality 944 *sensualism*.

matter, stuff; prime matter; mass, material, fabric, body, frame 331 *structure*; substance, corpus; flesh, flesh and blood, plasma, protoplasm 358 *organism*.

object, bird in the hand; inanimate object; body, flesh and blood, real person 371 *person*; thing, gadget, gizmo, something, commodity, article, item.

element, principle, nitty-gritty 68 *origin*; the four elements, earth, air, fire, water; factor, ingredient, nuts and bolts 58 *component*; isotope; atom, molecule; elementary particle, electron, neutron, meson, proton, quark 196 *minuteness*; nucleus, nucleon; photon; quantum; ion.

physics, physical science, natural s.; natural history 358 *biology*; chemistry, organic c., inorganic c., physical c.; mechanics, theory of relativity; thermodynamics; electromagnetism; atomic physics, nuclear physics 160 *nucleonics*; applied physics, technology 694 *skill*; natural philosophy 490 *science*.

Adj. *material*, real, natural; solid, concrete, palpable, tangible, weighty; physical, objective, impersonal, clinical, neuter; substantial; incarnate, embodied; corporeal, bodily, fleshly, of flesh and blood, in the flesh, carnal; reincarnated, realized, materialized; materialistic, worldly, unspiritual 944 *sensual*.

Vb. *materialize*, substantiate, objectify 223

externalize; realize, body forth; embody, incarnate, personify.

320 Immateriality

N. *immateriality*, unreality 4 *insubstantiality*; incorporeality, disembodiment, intangibility, impalpability, ghostliness, shadowiness; immaterialism, idealism, Platonism; spirituality, otherworldliness; animism; spiritualism 984 *occultism*.

subjectivity, personality, myself, me, yours truly 80 *self*; me generation; ego, id, superego; Conscious, Unconscious; psyche 447 *spirit*.

Adj. *immaterial*, incorporeal; abstract 447 *mental*; aery, ethereal, ghostly, shadowy 4 *insubstantial*; intangible; bodiless, disembodied; unearthly; psychic, astral 984 *psychical*; spiritual, otherworldly 973 *religious*.

321 Universe

N. *universe*, whole; matter; world, globe, creation; cosmos, macrocosm, microcosm; outer space, intergalactic s.; void; big bang theory, steady state t. 68 *start*.

world, wide w., four corners of the earth; earth, mother e.; planet earth, space, globe, sphere; geosphere, biosphere, ecosphere; continental drift 344 *land*; waters of the earth 343 *ocean*; atlas 551 *map*; Old World, New World 184 *region*; Ptolemaic system; personal world 8 *circumstance*.

heavens, sky, ether, celestial sphere, hemisphere; firmament; music of the spheres; aurora borealis, northern lights, aurora australis.

star, heavenly body, celestial b. 420 *luminary*; constellation, Great Bear, Little B., Plough, Big Dipper, Charles' Wain, Cassiopeia's Chair, Pleiades, Orion, Orion's belt, Southern Cross; starlight; blue star, white s., yellow s., red s; double star, binary; multiple star; variable star, cepheid; giant, supergiant, red giant; subgiant, dwarf, red d., white d.; X-ray star, radio s. 417 *radiation*; quasi-stellar object, quasar, pulsar, neutron star, black hole, white h.; nova, supernova; Pole Star, North Star, Polaris; Pointers; Dog star, Sirius; Star of David, Star of Bethlehem; Milky Way, Galaxy; star cluster, globular c., galaxy, radio g.; island universe; nebula.

zodiac, signs of the z., Aries (the Ram), Taurus (the Bull), Gemini (the Twins), Cancer (the Crab), Leo (the Lion), Virgo (the Virgin), Libra (the Balance), Scorpio (the Scorpion), Sagittarius (the Archer), Capricornus (the Goat), Aquarius (the Watercarrier), Pisces (the Fishes); cusp.

planet, asteroid, planetoid; Mercury; Venus, morning star, evening s., Lucifer, Vesper, Hesperus; Mars, red planet; Earth, Jupiter, Saturn, Uranus, Neptune, Pluto; comet, wandering star, Halley's comet.

meteor, falling star, shooting s., fireball, bolide; meteorite, aerolite, siderite, chondrite; chondrule; meteoroid; micro-meteorite.

sun, day-star, eye of heaven; midnight sun; sunlight, sunshine, sun spot, solar flare, corona; solar wind; Phoebus, Apollo; solar system, Copernican s.

moon, satellite; new moon, waxing moon, waning m., half-m., crescent m., horned m., full m., harvest m., hunter's m.; mock moon; moonscape, crater, mare, rill; Queen of the night, Diana, Phoebe, man in the moon; moonlight, moonshine.

satellite, moon; earth satellite, artificial s., sputnik, weather satellite, communications s., comsat; space station, skylab, space lab; space shuttle 276 *spaceship.*

astronomy, stargazing; satellite tracking; radioastronomy; astrophysics; uranography; astrology, horoscope 511 *divination*, observatory, planetarium; tracking station; telescope, refracting t., reflecting t., Newtonian t., Cassegrainian t., Gregorian t. 442 *telescope*; astronomical telescope, altazimuth, equatorial; transit instrument; radio telescope, parabolic reflector, dish; spectroscope 551 *photography.*

earth sciences, geography, orography, oceanography, physiography, geomorphology, speleology; geology, geodesy, geodetics; hydrology, hydrography.

Adj. *cosmic*, universal, cosmological; interplanetary; galactic, intragalactic; extragalactic.

celestial, heavenly, ethereal, empyreal; starry; sidereal, astral, stellar; solar, zodiacal; lunar, lunate; nebular, nebulous; heliocentric, geocentric; meteoric; equinoctial.

astronomic, astronomical, astrophysical, stargazing, star-watching; astrological, telescopic, spectroscopic.

geographic, geographical, oceanographic, orographical; geological, geomorphic, speleologi-

cal; geodesic, geodetic; hydrographic, hydrological.

322 Gravity

N. *gravity*, gravitation, force of gravity, gravitational pull; gravity feed; weight, weightiness, heaviness, ponderousness 195 *bulk*; specific gravity; pressure, displacement, sinkage, draught; encumbrance, load, lading, freight; burden; ballast, makeweight, counterpoise; mass, lump 324 *solid body*; plummet 313 *diver.*

weighing, balancing, equipoise 28 *equalization*; weights, avoirdupois weight, troy w., apothecaries' w.; grain, carat, scruple, pennyweight, drachm; ounce, pound, stone, quarter, quintal, hundredweight, ton; milligram, gram, kilogram, kilo; megaton, kiloton; axle load, laden weight.

scales, weighing machine; steelyard, weighbeam; balance, spring b.; bathroom scales, kitchen s., pan, scale, weight; calibrator; platform scale, weighbridge.

Adj. *weighty*, heavy, heavyweight, ponderous; leaden; weighing etc. vb.; cumbersome, cumbrous 195 *unwieldy*; massive 324 *dense*; heavy-handed, heavy-footed, pressing, incumbent, oppressive; weighing, with a weight of; weighted, loaded, laden, charged, burdened; overburdened, overloaded, top-heavy 29 *unequal.*

Vb. *weigh*, balance 28 *be equal*; counterpoise, counterweigh 31 *compensate*; outweigh 34 *predominate*; tip the scales, turn the s., tip the balance; settle 313 *founder*, 309 *descend*; lie heavy; press, weigh on, weigh one down, oppress, hang like a millstone 311 *lower*; load, cumber 702 *hinder*; find the weight of, put on the scales, lay in the scale 465 *measure*; weigh oneself, stand on the scales.

make heavy, weight, hang weights on; charge, burden, overweight, overburden, overload 193 *load.*

323 Lightness

N. *lightness*, portability; thinness, air, ether 325 *rarity*; buoyancy; volatility 338 *vaporization*; weightlessness; levitation 308 *ascent*; feather, thistledown, cobweb, gossamer; fluff, oose, dust, straw 4 *insubstantial thing*; cork, buoy, lifebelt, life jacket; balloon, bubble; hot air, helium.

leaven, raising agent; ferment, enzyme, barm, yeast, baking-powder, self-raising flour.

Adj. *light*, underweight 307 *deficient*; lightweight, featherweight; portable, handy 196 *little*; light-footed; light on one's feet; having a light touch; weightless, lighter than air; ethereal, airy, gaseous, volatile 325 *rare*; doughy, barmy, yeasty, fermenting, zymotic, enzymic; aerated, frothy, bubbly, sparkling, pétillant, foamy, whipped; floating, buoyed up, buoyant, feathery, cobwebby, fluffy; light as a feather.

Vb. *be light*, buoyant, etc. adj.; levitate, surface, float, swim; drift, waft, glide, be airborne 271 *fly*; soar, hover 308 *ascend*.

lighten, make light, make lighter, lose weight; ease 701 *disencumber*; jettison 300 *empty*; vaporize 340 *aerate*; leaven; raise, levitate 310 *elevate*.

SECTION TWO

Inorganic matter

324 Density

N. *density*, solidity, consistency; compactness, solidness, concreteness, thickness, concentration; incompressibility 326 *hardness*; impenetrability, impermeability; indissolubility, indivisibility; coalescence, cohesion, inseparability 48 *coherence*; relative density, specific gravity.

condensation, consolidation, concentration; constipation; thickening etc. vb.; concretion; solidification, consolidation; coagulation; thrombosis; congealment, gelatinization; glaciation; ossification, petrifaction, fossilization; crystallization; sedimentation, precipitation.

solid body, solid; block, mass 319 *matter*; knot, nugget, lump, chunk, dod, burl; condensation, nucleus, hard core; aggregate, conglomerate, concretion; concrete, cement; stone, crystal, hard-pan 344 *rock*; precipitate, deposit, sediment, silt, clay, cake, clod, clump; bone, ossicle; gristle, cartilage 329 *toughness*; coagulum, curd, clot, blood-c.; solid mass.

Adj. *dense*, thick; close, heavy, stuffy (air); foggy, murky, smoky, to be cut with a knife; lumpy, clotted, coagulated, curdled; caked, matted, knotted, tangled 48 *cohesive*; consistent, monolithic; firm, close-textured, knotty, gnarled; substantial, massy, massive 322 *weighty*; concrete, solid, set, gelled or jelled, frozen, solidified etc. vb.; crystalline, crystallized; condensed, nucleated; costive, constipated; compact, close-packed, firm-p. 54 *full*; thick, bushy, luxuriant 635 *plentiful*; serried, massed; impenetrable, impermeable, impervious; indivisible.

indissoluble, insoluble, infusible; precipitated, sedimentary.

Vb. *be dense*, – solid etc. adj.; become solid, solidify, consolidate; conglomerate, cement 48 *cohere*; condense, nucleate, thicken; precipitate, deposit; freeze, glaciate 380 *be cold*; set, gell *or* jell; congeal, coagulate, clot, curdle; cake, crust;

crystallize; fossilize, petrify, ossify 326 *harden*; compact, compress, firm down, contract, squeeze 198 *make smaller*; crowd 74 *bring together*.

325 Rarity

N. *rarity*, low pressure, vacuum, near v. 190 *emptiness*; compressibility, sponginess 327 *softness*; tenuity, fineness 206 *thinness*; lack of substance 4 *insubstantiality*, 323 *lightness*; incorporeality, ethereality 320 *immateriality*; airiness, ether, gas 336 *gaseousness*, 340 *air*; rarefaction, expansion, dilatation, attenuation.

Adj. *rare*, tenuous, thin, fine, subtle, flimsy, airy, airy-fairy, slight 4 *insubstantial*; low-pressure, uncompressed; spongy 328 *elastic*; rarefied, aerated 336 *gaseous*; void, hollow 190 *empty*; ethereal, aery 323 *light*; incorporeal 320 *immaterial*; wispy, straggly 75 *unassembled*.

Vb. *rarefy*, reduce the pressure, expand, dilate; make a vacuum, hermetically seal, pump out, exhaust 300 *empty*; attenuate, refine, thin; dilute, adulterate 163 *weaken*; gasify 338 *vaporize*.

326 Hardness

N. *hardness*, intractability, intransigence, resistance 329 *toughness*; starchiness, stiffness, rigour, rigidity, inflexibility; inelasticity; firmness, callosity, callousness, lumpiness, nodosity, nodularity; grittiness, stoniness, rockiness, cragginess; grit, stone, pebble, boulder; flint, silica, quartz, granite, marble, diamond 344 *rock*; adamant, metal, duralumin; steel, iron, wrought i., cast i.; nails, hardware, stoneware; cement, concrete, reinforced c., brick; block, board, heartwood, duramen; hardwood, teak, oak, heart of o. 366 *wood*; bone, gristle, cartilage; spine, backbone; lump, nodule, callosity, callus, corn, wart; horn, ivory; crust, shell, hard s.; hard core, hard centre, jawbreaker; brick wall; stiffener, starch, wax; whalebone, corset, splint 218 *prop*; ossification, sclerosis, hardening of the arteries.

Adj. *hard*, adamantine; indestructible, unbreakable 162 *strong*; shatterproof, fortified, armoured, armour-plated; steeled, proof; iron, cast-i.; steel, steely, hard as iron, hard as steel, hard as stone, rock-hard; sun-baked; stony, rocky, flinty; gritty, gravelly, pebbly; granitic, crystalline, vitreous, glassy; horny; calloused; bony; gristly 329 *tough*; hardened, tempered, case-hardened; vitrified, petrified, fossilized, ossified; icy, frozen.

rigid, stubborn, resistant, intractable, unmalleable, intransigent; firm, inflexible, unbending 162 *unyielding*; starchy, starched; boned, reinforced; muscle-bound 695 *clumsy*; braced,

tense, taut, tight, set, solid; crisp 330 *brittle*; stiff, stiff as a poker, stiff as a board.
Vb. *harden*, render hard etc. adj.; steel 162 *strengthen*; temper, vulcanize, toughen; crisp, bake 381 *heat*; petrify, fossilize, ossify; calcify, vitrify, crystallize 324 *be dense*; set, gell or jell, glaciate, freeze 382 *refrigerate*; stiffen, back, bone, starch, wax (a moustache), tauten 45 *tighten*.

327 Softness
N. *softness*, tenderness; pliableness etc. adj.; compliance 739 *obedience*; pliancy, pliability, flexibility, plasticity, ductility, tractability; malleability, adaptability; suppleness, litheness; springiness, suspension 328 *elasticity*; impressibility, doughiness 356 *pulpiness*; sponginess, flaccidity, flabbiness, floppiness; laxity, looseness 354 *semiliquidity*; sogginess, squelchiness, marshiness, bogginess 347 *marsh*; downiness; velvetiness; butter, grease, oil, wax, putty, paste, Plasticine (tdmk), clay, dough, soap, plastic; padding, foam-filling, wadding, pad 227 *lining*; cushion, pillow, armchair, feather bed 376 *euphoria*; velvet, plush, down, thistledown, fluff, fleece 259 *hair*; feathers 259 *plumage*; snow, snowflake 323 *lightness*.

Adj. *soft*, tender 301 *edible*; melting 335 *fluid*; giving, yielding, compressible; springy, sprung 328 *elastic*; pneumatic, foam-filled, cushiony, padded, podgy; impressible, waxy, doughy, spongy, soggy, mushy, squelchy, boggy 347 *marshy*; juicy, overripe; fleecy; turfy, mossy, grassy; velvety, silky 258 *smooth*; unstiffened, unstarched, limp; flaccid, flabby, floppy; unstrung, relaxed, slack, loose; soft as butter, soft as wax, soft as soap, soft as down, soft as velvet, soft as silk; tender as a chicken; softening, emollient.

flexible, bendable; pliant, pliable, putty-like; ductile, tractile, malleable, tractable, mouldable, plastic; stretchable 328 *elastic*; lithe, willowy, supple, lissom, limber, loose-limbed, double-jointed; acrobatic.

Vb. *soften*, tenderize; mellow 669 *mature*; oil, grease 334 *lubricate*; knead, massage, mash, pulp, squash 332 *pulverize*; macerate, marinade, steep 341 *drench*; melt, thaw 337 *liquefy*; cushion, featherbed; relax, unstring 46 *disunite*; yield, give, give way, relax, loosen up, hang loose 328 *be elastic*.

328 Elasticity
N. *elasticity*, give, stretch; spring, springiness; suspension; stretchability, tensibility; resilience, bounce 280 *recoil*; buoyancy, rubber, india r., foam r.; caoutchouc, guttapercha; elastic band, rubber band, rubber ball;

bouncy castle; stretch jeans; gum, chewing g., bubble g.

Adj. *elastic*, stretchy, stretchable, tensile; rubbery, springy, bouncy, resilient; buoyant; flexible; sprung, well-s.; ductile 327 *soft*.

329 Toughness
N. *toughness*, durability, survivability, infrangibility 162 *strength*; tenacity, cohesion 48 *coherence*; viscidity 354 *semiliquidity*; leatheriness, inedibility, indigestibility; leather, gristle, cartilage 326 *hardness*.

Adj. *tough*, durable; strong-fibred 162 *strong*; tenacious, retentive, clinging, sticky 48 *cohesive*; viscid 354 *semiliquid*; infrangible, unbreakable, indestructible, shockproof, shatter-proof; vulcanized, toughened, strengthened; weather-beaten; hardboiled, overdone; stringy, sinewy, woody, fibrous; gristly, cartilaginous; rubbery, leathery, tough as old boots or shoe leather; chewy, indigestible, inedible; stubborn 326 *rigid*.

330 Brittleness
N. *brittleness*, crispness etc. adj.; frangibility; friableness, crumbliness 332 *powderiness*; fissility 46 *scission*; laminability, flakiness; fragility, frailty, flimsiness 163 *weakness*; eggshell, matchwood, shale, slate; glass, porcelain 381 *pottery*, greenhouse,

Adj. *brittle*, breakable, frangible; inelastic 326 *rigid*; fragile, papery, parchment like; splintery; friable, crumbly 332 *powdery*; crisp, flaky, laminable; fissile, splitting; frail, flimsy, eggshell 163 *weak*.

331 Structure. Texture
N. *structure*, organization, pattern, plan; complex, syndrome 52 *whole*; build 243 *form*; constitution, make-up, set-up, content, substance 56 *composition*; construction, make, works, workings, nuts and bolts; architecture; fabric, brickwork, stonework, woodwork, timberwork 631 *materials*; infrastructure, superstructure 164 *edifice*; scaffold, framework, chassis, shell 218 *frame*; infilling 303 *insertion*; lamination, cleavage; body, carcass, physique, anatomy 358 *organism*; skeleton, anatomy, physiology, histology 358 biology.

texture, tissue, fabric, stuff 222 *textile*; staple, denier 208 *fibre*; web, weave, warp and woof, warp and weft 222 *weaving*; nap, pile 259 *hair*; grain, grit; fineness of grain 258 *smoothness*; coarseness of grain 259 *roughness*; surface 223 *exteriority*; feel 378 *touch*.

Adj. *textural*, textile, woven 222 *crossed*; fine-woven, close-w.; ribbed, twilled; grained, granular; fine-grained, silky, satiny 258 *smooth*;

coarse-grained, gritty 259 *rough*; fine, cob-webby, filmy; coarse, rough, homespun, tweedy 259 *hairy*.

332 Powderiness

N. *powderiness*, friability, crumbliness 330 *brittleness*; dustiness 649 *dirt*; sandiness, grittiness; granulation; friability, crumbliness 330 *brittleness*; pulverization, attrition, attenuation, disintegration, erosion 51 *decomposition*; grinding, milling; abrasion, filing 333 *friction*; fragmentation 46 *disunion*; sprinkling, dusting, powdering, frosting.

powder, face p., foot p., talcum p.; talc, chalk; pollen, spore; dust, coaldust; soot, ash 649 *dirt*; icing sugar, flour, cornflour, farina, arrowroot, starch; grist, meal, bran; sawdust, filings; efflorescence, flowers; scurf, dandruff; debris, detritus 41 *leavings*; sand, grit, gravel, shingle; grain, seed, crumb 53 *piece*; granule, speck 33 *small thing*; flake, snowflake; smut, smoke; dust cloud; fog, smog 355 *cloud*; sandstorm, dust storm 176 *storm*.

pulverizer, miller, grinder; roller, crusher, masher, atomizer; mill, millstone, muller, quern, quernstone; pestle, pestle and mortar; hand mill, coffee m., pepper m.; grater, grindstone, file; abrasive, sandpaper, emery paper, emery board; molar 256 *tooth*; chopper 256 *sharp edge*; sledgehammer 279 *hammer*; bulldozer 279 *ram*.

Adj. *powdery*, chalky, dusty, sooty, smoky 649 *dirty*; sandy 342 *dry*; farinaceous, floury; granulated, granular; gritty, gravelly; flaky, efflorescent; ground, sifted, sieved; crumbly, friable 330 *brittle*.

Vb. *pulverize*, powder, reduce to p.; granulate; crush, mash, smash, shatter, fragment, disintegrate 46 *break*; grind, mill, mince, beat, bruise, pound; crumble; crunch, scrunch 301 *chew*; abrade 333 *rub*; erode 51 *decompose*.

333 Friction

N. *friction*, frictional force, drag 278 *slowness*; rubbing etc. vb.; attrition, rubbing against, rubbing together 279 *collision*; rubbing out, erasure 550 *obliteration*; abrasion, excoriation, scraping; filing 332 *powderiness*; wearing away, erosion 165 *destruction*; scrape, graze, scratch; brushing, rub; polish, elbow grease; massage, facial m., cosmetic scrub, exfoliator, exfoliant, facial 843 *beautification*; pumice stone; eraser, rubber, rosin; whetstone.

Vb. *rub*, rub against, strike (a match); gnash, grind; fret, fray, chafe; graze, scratch, bark, take the skin off 655 *wound*; rub off, abrade, excoriate; skin, flay; scuff, scrape, scrub, scour, burnish; brush, rub down, towel, curry,

curry-comb 648 *clean*; polish, buff 258 *smooth*; rub out, erase 550 *obliterate*; erode, wear away 165 *consume*; rasp, file, grind 332 *pulverize*; shampoo, massage; rub in; anoint 334 *lubricate*; wax, rosin, chalk (one's cue); catch, stick; rub gently, stroke 889 *caress*; iron 258 *smooth*.

334 Lubrication

N. *lubrication*, greasing; anointment, unction, oiling etc. vb.; lubricity 357 *unctuousness*; nonfriction 258 *smoothness*.

lubricant, graphite, plumbago, black lead; glycerine, wax, grease, axle g. 357 *oil*; soap, lather 648 *cleanser*; saliva, spit, spittle; ointment, salve 658 *balm*; emollient, lenitive 357 *unguent*; lubricator, oil-can, grease-gun.

Vb. *lubricate*, oil, grease, wax, soap, lather; butter 357 *grease*; anoint.

335 Fluidity

N. *fluidity*, fluidness, liquidity, liquidness; wateriness, rheuminess 339 *water*; juiciness, sappiness 356 *pulpiness*; haemophilia; solubility, solubleness, liquescence 337 *liquefaction*; gaseous character 336 *gaseousness*; viscosity 354 *semiliquidity*; fluid mechanics.

fluid, liquid; water, running w. 339 *water*; drink 301 *draught*; milk, whey; juice, sap, latex; humour, chyle, rheum, mucus, saliva 302 *excrement*; serum, lymph, plasma; pus, matter; gore (see *blood*); hydrocele, dropsy 651 *disease*.

blood, lifeblood 360 *life*; bloodstream, circulation; red blood 162 *vitality*; blue blood 868 *nobility*; blood of the gods; gore; clot, blood c., coagulation 324 *solid body*; corpuscle, red c., white c., platelet; lymph, plasma, serum, blood s.; haemoglobin; factor VIII; haematosis; blood group, Rhesus factor; blood count; haematology; blood transfusion; haemophilia, anaemia, leukaemia, AIDS.

Adj. *liquid*, in suspension; uncoagulated, unclotted, clarified; soluble, liquescent, melting; viscous 354 *viscid*; fluent, running 350 *flowing*; runny, rheumy 339 *watery*; serous; suppurating 653 *toxic*. *haematic*, sanguineous, haemic, haemal; serous, lymphatic, plasmatic; bloody, sanguinary; gory, bleeding; haemophilic, haemolytic.

336 Gaseousness

N. *gaseousness*, vaporousness etc adj.; windiness, flatulence 352 *wind*; aeration, gasification; volatility 338 *vaporization*; *aerostatics, aerodynamics*.

gas, vapour, ether 340 *air*; effluvium, exhalation, miasma 298 *egress*; flatus 352 *wind*; fumes, reek, smoke; steam, water vapour 355 *cloud*; laughing gas, coal g., natural g., North

Sea g., methane 385 *fuel*; marsh gas, poison g. 659 *poison*; damp, after-d., black d., choke d., fire d.; gasbag; balloon 276 *airship*; gasworks, gas plant, gasification p. 687 *workshop*; gasometer 632 *storage*; gas-light, neon light 420 *lamp*; gas stove, gas cooker 383 *furnace*; gas meter 465 *meter*.

Adj. *gaseous*, gasiform; vaporous, steamy, volatile 338 *vaporific*; aerial, airy, aeriform, ethereal 340 *airy*; carbonated, effervescent, pétillant 355 *bubbly*; gassy, windy, flatulent; effluvial, miasmic; pneumatic, aerostatic, aerodynamic.

Vb. *gasify*, steam, emit vapour 338 *vaporize*; let off steam, blow off s. 300 *emit*; oxygenate 340 *aerate*; carbonate; hydrogenate, hydrogenize.

337 Liquefaction

N. *liquefaction*, liquidization; fluidization; solubility, deliquescence 335 *fluidity*; fusion 43 *mixture*; dissolution; thaw, melting 381 *heating*; solvent, dissolvent, flux; liquefier, liquefacient; liquidizer; anticoagulant 658 *antidote*.

solution, decoction, infusion; aqua; suspension; flux, lye.

Vb. *liquefy*, liquidize, unclot, clarify, liquate, dissolve, deliquesce, run 350 *flow*; unfreeze, thaw, melt, smelt 381 *heat*; render, clarify; leach; fluidize.

338 Vaporization

N. *vaporization*, gasification; exhalation 355 *cloud*; evaporation, volatilization, distillation, sublimation; steaming, fumigation, vapourability, volatility; atomization.

vaporizer, evaporater; atomizer, spray, aerosol; retort, still, distillery, vaporimeter.

Adj. vaporific, volatilized etc. vb.; reeking; vapouring, steaming etc. vb.; vaporous, vapoury, vapourish; steamy, gassy, smoky; evaporable, volatile.

Vb. *vaporize*, evaporate; 336 *gasify*; volatilize, distil, sublimate, exhale, transpire, emit vapour, blow off steam 300 *emit*; smoke, fume, reek, steam; fumigate, spray; atomize.

339 Water

N. *water*, H_2O; heavy water, D_2O; hard water, soft w.; drinking water, tap w., Adam's ale; mineral w., soda w. 301 *soft drink*; water vapour, steam 355 *cloud*; rain water 350 *rain*; spring water, running w., fresh w. 350 *stream*; holy water 988 *ritual object*; weeping, tears 836 *lamentation*; sweat, saliva 335 *fluid*; high water, high tide, spring t., neap t., low water 350 *wave*; standing water, still w., stagnant w. 346 *lake*; sea water, salt w., brine, briny 343 *ocean*; water cure, taking the waters, hydrotherapy, hydropa-

thy 658 *therapy*; bath water, bath, tub, Jacuzzi (tdmk), shower, douche, splash 648 *ablutions*; lotion, lavender water 843 *cosmetic*; diluent, adulteration, dilution 655 *impairment*; wateriness, damp, humidity, wet; watering; jug, ewer 194 *vessel*; tap, faucet, stand-pipe, hydrant 351 *conduit*; waterer, hose 341 *irrigator*; water supply, waterworks; hot spring, geyser; well, artesian w., borehole 632 *store*; hydrometry.

Adj. *watery*, aqueous, aquatic, lymphatic 335 *fluid*; hydrated, hydrous; hydrological, hydrographic 321 *geographic*; adulterated, diluted, 163 *weak*; wet, moist, drenching 341 *humid*; hydrotherapeutic; sudorific 658 *medical*.

340 Air

N. *air* 336 *gas*; thin air, ether 325 *rarity*; air pocket 190 *emptiness*; blast 352 *wind*; oxygen, nitrogen, argon; welkin, blue, blue sky 355 *cloud*; open air, open, out of doors, exposure 183 *space*; sea air, ozone; fresh air, country a., smokeless zone 648 *cleanness*; airing 342 *desiccation*; aeration 338 *vaporization*; fanning 352 *ventilation*; air-conditioning, air-cooling 382 *refrigeration*; ventilator, blower, fan, air-conditioner 384 *refrigerator*; air-filter 648 *cleanser*; humidifier, vaporizer, atomizer, ionizer 341 *moisture*.

atmosphere, troposphere, tropopause, stratosphere, ionosphere; mesosphere, exosphere; aerosphere; aerospace; ozone layer, hole in the ozone layer, CFC, chlorofluorocarbons, greenhouse effect 381 *heating*.

weather, the elements; fine weather; balmy days, halcyon days; dry spell, heat wave, Indian summer 379 *heat*; doldrums; atmospheric pressure, anticyclone, high pressure; cyclone, depression, low pressure; rough weather 176 *storm*, 352 *gale*; bad weather, foul w., wet w. 350 *rain*; cold weather 380 *wintriness*; changeable weather; meteorology; weather forecast 511 *prediction*; isobar; glass, mercury, barometer; vane, weathervane, weathercock; hygrometer; weather ship, weather station, rain gauge; weatherman *or* -woman, meteorologist; climate, microclimate; climatology, climatography; climatologist.

Adj. *airy*, ethereal 4 *insubstantial*; aerial; pneumatic, aerated, oxygenated; inflated, blown up; flatulent 336 *gaseous*; breezy 352 *windy*; well-ventilated, fresh, air-conditioned 382 *cooled*; meteorological, weather-wise; atmospheric, barometric; cyclonic, anticyclonic; high-pressure 324 *dense*; low-pressure 325 *rare*; climatic, climatological.

Vb. *aerate*, oxygenate; air, expose 342 *dry*; ventilate, freshen 648 *clean*; fan, winnow, make a draught 352 *blow*; take the air 352 *breathe*.

Adv. *alfresco,* out of doors, in the open air, en plein air, in the open.

341 Moisture

N. *moisture,* humidity, sap, juice 335 *fluid;* dampness, wetness, moistness, dewiness; dew point; dankness, condensation, rising damp; sogginess, swampiness, marshiness, bogginess; saturation, saturation point 54 *plenitude;* leakiness 298 *outflow;* raininess, showeriness; rainfall, high r., wet weather 350 *rain;* damp, wet; spray, spindrift, froth, foam 355 *bubble;* mist, haar, fog, fog bank 355 *cloud;* Scotch mist, drizzle, smirr, drip, dew, morning d.; drop, droplet, raindrop, dewdrop, teardrop; tears 836 *lamentation;* saliva, salivation, slabber, slobber, spit, spittle 302 *excrement;* ooze, slime, mud, squelch, fen, bog 347 *marsh;* sop.

irrigator, sprinkler, waterer, water-cart; watering can; spray, rose; hose, garden h., syringe, squirt; pump, fire engine; shadoof, Archimedes' screw; water butt, dam, reservoir 632 *store;* catheter; sluice, water pipe, qanat 351 *conduit.*

Adj. *humid,* moistened, wet 339 *watery;* pluvial; drizzling, drizzly; damp, moist, dripping; dank, muggy, foggy, misty 355 *cloudy;* steaming, reeking; undrained, oozy, muddy, slimy, sloppy, slushy, squashy, squelchy, splashy, plashy, fenny, boggy 347 *marshy;* dewy, fresh, bedewed; juicy, sappy 335 *fluid;* dribbling, seeping, percolating; wetted, steeped, soaked, sprinkled.

Vb. *be wet,* – moist etc. adj.; be soaking wet, be wringing wet; be soaking, be sopping; squelch; slobber, salivate, sweat, perspire 298 *exude;* steam, reek 300 *emit;* percolate, seep 297 *infiltrate;* weep, bleed, stream; ooze, drip, leak; trickle, smirr, drizzle, smurr, rain, pour, rain cats and dogs 350 *rain;* get wet, get wet through, get drenched, dip, duck; bathe, wash, shower, douche; paddle.

moisten, humidify, wet, dampen; dilute, hydrate; lick, lap, wash; splash, splatter; spill, slop; flood, shower, spatter, bespatter; sprinkle, besprinkle, syringe; bedew.

drench, saturate, imbue; soak, deluge, wet through; leach; wash, bathe, shower, douche; hose down, sluice, slosh, rinse 648 *clean;* baptise 988 *perform ritual;* plunge, dip, duck, submerge, drown 303 *immerse;* swamp, flood, inundate, flood out, waterlog; dunk, douse, souse, steep; macerate, marinate.

irrigate, water, hose, pump; flood, submerge; percolate 297 *infiltrate;* squirt, inject, douche.

342 Dryness

N. *dryness,* aridity; thirst 859 *hunger;* drought, drouth, low rainfall, sandiness, desertification,

desertization 172 *desert;* dry climate, dry season; sun, sunniness 379 *heat.*

desiccation, drying, drying up; airing, evaporation 338 *vaporization;* draining, drainage, catheterization; dehydration, sunning 381 *heating;* withering, searing 426 *achromatism.*

dryer, dehydrator, desiccator, evaporator; dehydrant, siccative, silica gel, sand, blotting paper; absorbent; mop, swab, sponge, towel, towelling; paper towel, kitchen t., tissue, toilet roll; hair drier, hand d., spin d., tumble d.; wringer, mangle; airer, clotheshorse 217 *hanger;* airing cupboard.

Adj. *dry,* thirsty 859 *hungry;* arid; sandy, dusty, desertized 332 *powdery;* bare, brown; desert, Saharan; dehydrated, desiccated; shrivelled, withered, seared, sere; dried up, parchment-like; sunned; aired; sun-dried, wind-d.; burnt, scorched, baked, parched 379 *hot;* sunny, fine, cloudless, fair; dried out, drained, evaporated; squeezed dry, wrung out, mangled; waterproofed, waterproof, rainproof, showerproof, dampproof; watertight; high and dry; dry as a bone.

Vb. *dry,* dehumidify, desiccate, freeze-dry; dehydrate; drain, catheterize, pump out, suck dry 300 *empty;* wring out, mangle; spin-dry, tumble-d., drip-d.; hang out, peg o., air, evaporate 338 *vaporize;* sun, expose to sunlight, solarize, sun-dry; smoke, kipper, cure; parch, scorch, bake, burn 381 *heat;* sere, sear, shrivel, wither; mummify 666 *preserve;* dry up, stop the flow, apply a tourniquet 350 *staunch;* blot, blot up, mop, mop up, soak up, sponge 299 *absorb;* swab, wipe, wipe up, wipe dry.

343 Ocean

N. *ocean,* sea, blue, salt water, brine, briny; waters, billows, waves, tide 350 *wave;* Davy Jones's locker; main, deep, deep sea; high seas, great waters; trackless deep, watery waste; herring pond, drink; sea lane, shipping lane; ocean floor, sea bed, sea bottom, ooze, benthos; the seven seas; Atlantic Ocean, Pacific O., Indian O., Arctic O., Antarctic O., Red Sea, Mediterranean, Baltic, North Sea, Irish S., Caspian S., Black S., Caribbean S., Tasman S., Bering S., Dead S., Barents S., Beaufort S., Tethys.

sea god, Oceanus, Neptune, Poseidon, Triton; Nereus, merman 970 *mythical being.*

sea nymph, Oceanid, Nereid, siren; Amphitrite, Thetis; Calypso, Undine; mermaid; bathing beauty; water sprite 970 *fairy.*

344 Land

N. *land,* dry l., terra firma; earth, ground, earth's crust 321 *world;* continent, mainland; heartland, hinterland; midland, inland, interior

224 *interiority*; peninsula, delta, promontory
254 *projection*; isthmus; terrain, heights, highlands 209 *high land*; lowlands 210 *lowness*;
reclaimed land, polder; steppe, fields 348 *plain*;
wilderness 172 *desert*; oasis; isle 349 *island*;
zone, clime; country, district, tract 184 *region*;
territory, possessions, acres, estate, real e. 777
lands; landscape.

shore, coastline 233 *outline*; coast 234 *edge*;
strand, beach, sands, shingle; seaboard, seashore, seaside; sea cliff, sea wall; plage, lido, riviera; marina; bank, river bank, riverside;
continental shelf.

soil, farmland, arable land 370 *farm*; pasture
348 *grassland*; deposit, moraine, loess, silt, alluvium; topsoil, sand, dust, subsoil; mould, leaf
m., humus; loam, clay, bole, marl; Fuller's
earth; argil, potter's clay, china clay, kaolin 381
pottery; gravel; stone, pebble, flint; turf, sod,
clod 53 *piece*.

rock, cliff, scar, crag; stone, boulder; reef;
stack, skerry; dyke, sill; igneous rock, plutonic
r., granite, basalt; volcanic rock; lava; sedimentary rock, sandstone, shale, limestone, chalk;
schist, marble; ore 359 *mineralogy*; precious
stone, semi-p. s. 844 *gem*.

345 Gulf: inlet
N. *gulf*, bay, bight, cove, creek, lagoon; slough;
natural harbour, road, roadstead; inlet, outlet,
fleet, bayou; fjord, sea loch; ria; mouth, estuary;
firth, frith, kyle; sound, strait, channel.

346 Lake
N. *lake*, lagoon; loch, lough, linn; fresh-water
lake, salt l.; Dead Sea; oxbow lake, bayou l.;
broads; sheet of water, standing w., stagnant
w., backwater; mud flat, wash 347 *marsh*; pool,
tarn, mere, pond, dewpond; fishpond, stew;
millpond; swimming pool; swimming baths,
Jacuzzi (tdmk) 648 *ablutions*; birthing pool; artificial lake, dam, reservoir 632 *storage*; well 339
water; water feature, waterhole, puddle.

347 Marsh
N. *marsh*, morass; marshland; flat, mud f., salt
marsh; fen, fenland, bog, peat b., quagmire,
quicksand; saltpan; mudhole, slough, mire,
mud; swamp, swampland, mangrove swamp;
Slough of Despond.

Adj. *marshy*, paludal; swampy, boggy, fenny;
quaggy; squelchy, spongy 327 *soft*; slushy;
muddy, miry 649 *dirty*; waterlogged.

348 Plain
N. *plain*, peneplain; dale, levels 216 *horizontality*; lowlands 255 *valley*; flats 347 *marsh*;
delta, alluvial plain; sands, desert s., waste 172

desert; tundra; ice field, ice floe 380 *ice*; grass-
lands, steppe, prairie, pampas, savanna, llanos,
campos; heath, common, wold, downland,
downs, moor, moorland, fell; upland, plateau,
tableland 209 *high land*; bush, veld, range 183
space; fields, green belt, parkland, national park,
safari p. 263 *open space*; lowlands, low countries
210 *lowness*.

grassland, pasture, pasturage, grazing 369 *animal husbandry*; sheeprun, sheep track, sheep
walk; field, meadow, mead, lea; chase, park,
grounds; green, greensward, lawn, turf.

349 Island
N. *island*, isle, islet, skerry; eyot, inch, holm;
atoll, reef, coral r.; cay, key; sandbank; iceberg,
ice floe; peninsula; archipelago; insularity.

350 Stream: water in motion
N. *stream*, running water, watercourse, river,
subterranean r.; waterway; tributary, branch,
streamlet, rivulet, brook, bourne, burn, rill,
beck, gill, runnel, runlet; freshet, torrent; wadi;
spring, fountain, fountainhead, headwaters 156
source; jet, spout, gush; geyser, hot spring, well
632 *store*; water feature.

current, flow, flux 285 *progression*; effluence
298 *egress*; confluence 293 *convergence*; inflow
297 *ingress*; outflow, reflux 286 *regression*; undercurrent, undertow, crosscurrent 182 *counteraction*; tide, spring t., neap t.; tidal flow, tidal
current, ebb and flow 317 *fluctuation*; bore,
eagre; tidal race; millrace, millstream; bloodstream.

eddy, whirlpool, swirl, maelstrom 315 *vortex*;
whirlpool bath, Jacuzzi (tdmk); wake 67 *sequel*.

waterfall, falls, cataract, Niagara, Victoria;
linn, cascade, rapids, weir; water power 160
sources of energy.

wave, bow w.; wash, backwash; ripple,
cat's-paw 262 *furrow*; swell, ground s.; billow,
roller, comber; breaker, surf, spume; white
horses; tidal wave; bore, eagre; choppiness 259
roughness; sea, choppy s., waviness, undulation.

rain, rainfall 341 *moisture*; precipitation;
drizzle, mizzle, Scotch mist, smirr; sleet, hail
380 *wintriness*; shower, downpour, deluge,
cloudburst, thunderstorm 176 *storm*; flurry 352
gale; pouring rain, teeming r., driving r., torrential r., sheets of rain; raininess, wet spell, foul
weather; rainy season, the rains, monsoon;
lovely weather for ducks; patter; dripping etc.
vb.; rain-making, cloud-seeding; rain gauge.

Adj. *flowing*, falling etc. vb.; runny 335 *fluid*;
fluent, riverine, fluvial, tidal; running, coursing, racing; streaming; in flood, overflowing, in
spate; flooding, inundatory, cataclysmic; pouring, lashing, driving, dripping, gushing.

VB. *flow*, run, course, pour; ebb 286 *regress*; surge, gush, rush, spirt, spout, spew, play, squirt; well, well up, bubble up, issue 298 *emerge*; pour, stream; trickle, dribble 298 *exude*; drip, drop 309 *descend*; wash, slosh, splash 341 *moisten*; trill, murmur, babble, bubble, burble, gurgle; flow over, cascade, fall, flood, inundate, deluge 341 *drench*; flow into, drain i. 297 *enter*; run off; leak, percolate, pass through 305 *pass*; ooze.

rain, shower, stream, pour, pelt; snow, sleet, hail; fall, come down, bucket, piss down, rain hard, pour with rain, rain cats and dogs; come down in torrents, come down in sheets, come down in stair-rods, rain pitchforks; patter, drizzle, mizzle, smirr, drip, spit, sprinkle; be wet, rain and rain.

staunch, apply a tourniquet; plug 264 *close*; stem, dam, dam up 702 *obstruct*.

351 Conduit

N. *conduit*, water channel, tideway, riverbed; arroyo, wadi; trough, basin, river b.; canyon, ravine, gorge, gully 255 *valley*; inland waterways, canal system; canal, channel, watercourse, qanat; ditch, dike; trench, moat; gutter, mill race; duct, aqueduct; water pipe, water main; pipe, hose, garden h.; stand-pipe, hydrant, siphon, tap, spout, funnel 263 *tube*; valve, flume, sluice, weir, lock, floodgate, watergate, spillway; chute 350 *waterfall*; oilpipe, pipeline; vein, artery.

drain, gully, gutter, gargoyle, water-spout; overflow, wastepipe, drainpipe 298 *outlet*; culvert; ditch, sewer 649 *sink*; alimentary canal; catheter 300 *voidance*.

352 Wind: air in motion

N. *wind* 340 *air*; draught, downdraught, updraught; blast, blow (**see** *breeze, gale*); air stream, jet s.; current, air c., crosswind, headwind 182 *counteraction*; tailwind, following wind 287 *propellant*; air flow, slip stream; air pocket; cold draught, icy blast; hot wind, sirocco, monsoon, etesian winds; prevailing w., trade w., Roaring Forties; north wind, Boreas, mistral, tramontano; south wind, föhn, chinook; east wind, levanter; west wind, Zephyr, wind god, Aeolus.

breeze, zephyr; breath of air, waft, whiff, puff, gust, sough, light breeze, gentle b., fresh b., sea breeze, cooling b.

gale, high wind; blow, blast, gust, flurry; squall; nor'wester, sou'wester, hurricane, whirlwind, cyclone, tornado, twister, typhoon, simoom 315 *vortex*; thunderstorm, dust storm, sandstorm, dust devil, blizzard 176 *storm*; microburst; gale force.

blowing, insufflation, inflation 197 *dilation*;

blowing up, pumping up; pumping out 300 *voidance*; pump, air p., stirrup p., bicycle p.; bellows, windbag, bag-pipe; woodwind, brass 414 *musical instrument*; blowpipe; exhaust pipe, exhaust 298 *outlet*.

ventilation, airing 340 *air*; draught; fanning, cooling; ventilator 353 *air pipe*; blower, fan, extractor f., electric f., punkah, air-conditioner, air-conditioning 384 *refrigerator*.

respiration, breathing, inhalation, exhalation, expiration, inspiration; gills, lungs, bellows; respirator, iron lung, oxygen tent; windpipe 353 *air pipe*; sigh, sob, gulp, hiccup, catching of the breath, yawn; panting, gasping, huffing and puffing.

Adj. *windy*, airy, exposed, draughty, breezy, blowy; ventilated, fresh; blowing, gusty, gusting, squally; blustery, stormy, tempestuous, boisterous 176 *violent*; windswept, windblown; storm-tossed, storm-bound; flatulent; fizzy, gassy 336 *gaseous*; aeolian, boreal, zephyrous; cyclonic; gale-force, hurricane f.

Vb. *blow*, puff, blast; insufflate, blow up, get up, blow hard, blow great guns, blow a hurricane, rage, storm; howl, roar 409 *ululate*; screech, scream, whistle, pipe, sing in the shrouds 407 *shrill*; hum, moan, mutter, sough, sigh 401 *sound faint*; wave, flap, shake, flutter, flourish 318 *agitate*; draw, ventilate, fan 382 *refrigerate*; waft 287 *propel*; veer, back 282 *deviate*; die down, subside, drop, abate.

breathe, respire, breathe in, inhale; draw or take a deep breath, fill one's lungs; breathe out, exhale; aspirate, puff, huff, huff and puff, whiff; sniff, sniffle, snuffle, snort; breathe hard; gasp, pant, heave; wheeze, sneeze, cough 407 *rasp*; sigh, catch one's breath.

blow up, pump up, inflate, dilate 197 *enlarge*; pump out, exhaust 300 *empty*.

353 Air pipe

N. *air pipe*, airway, air shaft, air well; wind tunnel; blowpipe, peashooter 287 *propellant*; windpipe, trachea, larynx; bronchia, bronchus; throat, gullet, oesophagus; nose, nostril, spiracle, blowhole, nozzle, vent, mouthpiece 263 *orifice*; flue pipe, mouth organ 414 *organ*; gas main, gas pipe; tobacco pipe, pipe, briar, hookah 388 *tobacco*; funnel, flue, exhaust pipe.

354 Semiliquidity

N. *semiliquidity*, mucosity, viscidity; thickness, stodginess; semiliquid, colloid, emulsion, gore, albumen, mucus, phlegm, clot 324 *solid body*; pus, matter; juice, sap 335 *fluidity*; soup, slop, gruel, cream, curds 356 *pulpiness*; molten lava; oil slick; mud, glaur, slush, sludge, thaw, ooze, slime; silt 347 *marsh*.

thickening, coagulation, clotting 324 *condensation*; gelatinization; emulsification; thickener, starch, arrowroot, flour, cornflour, gelatine, isinglass, pectin.

viscidity, viscosity, glutinousness, stickiness, adhesiveness 48 *coherence*; glue, gluten, gum 47 *adhesive*; emulsion, colloid; glair, size, paste, glaze; gel, jelly; treacle, jam, syrup, honey, goo; wax, mastic 357 *resin*; flypaper.

Adj. *viscid*, viscous, gummy, gooey 48 *cohesive*; slimy, sticky, tacky; jammy, treacly, syrupy, gluey; glairy, glaireous; mucous.

Vb. *thicken*, inspissate, congeal 324 *be dense*; coagulate 48 *cohere*; emulsify; gelatinize, gel, jelly, jell; starch 326 *harden*; curdle, clot; churn, whip up, beat up, mash, pulp 332 *pulverize*.

355 Bubble. Cloud: air and water mixed

N. *bubble*, suds, soapsuds, lather, foam, froth; head; sea foam, spume, surf, spray, spindrift 341 *moisture*; mousse, soufflé, meringue, candyfloss, yeast, barm 323 *leaven*; scum 649 *dirt*.

cloud, scud; cloudbank; rain cloud, storm c.; woolpack, cumulus, altocumulus, cirrus, cirrocumulus, stratus, cirrostratus, nimbostratus; mackerel sky, mare's tail; vapour, steam 338 *vaporization*; brume, haze, mist, haar, fog, smog, pea-souper; cloudiness, film 419 *dimness*; nebulosity; nephology, nephoscope.

Adj. *bubbly*, bubbling etc. vb.; effervescent, fizzy, sparkling, pétillant 336 *gaseous*; mousseux, foamy; spumy, spumous; frothy, soapy, lathery; yeasty, aerated 323 *light*; scummy 649 *dirty*.

cloudy, clouded, overcast, nebulous; cirrose, foggy, hazy, misty, filmy, brumous 419 *dim*; steamy 338 *vaporific*.

Vb. *bubble*, spume, foam, froth, cream, form a head; boil, simmer, seethe, fizzle, gurgle 318 *effervesce*; work, ferment, fizz, sparkle; aerate, carbonate; steam 338 *vaporize*.

cloud, cloud over, be cloudy etc. adj.; befog, mist up 419 *be dim*.

356 Pulpiness

N. *pulpiness*, doughiness, sponginess; fleshiness, juiciness, 327 *softness*; poultice, pulp, pith, paste, putty, porridge, pap, puree; mush, mash, squash; dough, batter, sponge; jam 354 *viscidity*; puree, mousse 355 *bubble*; slush, papier mâché, wood pulp.

357 Unctuousness

N. *unctuousness*. unctuosity, oiliness, greasiness, lubricity, soapiness 334 *lubrication*; fattiness; saponification; anointment, unction.

oil, volatile o., essential o.; animal oil, whale

o., sperm o., train o., cod-liver o.; vegetable oil, corn o., sunflower o., olive o., virgin olive o., coconut o., almond o., linseed o., cotton-seed o., castor o., rape o., groundnut o., palm o., jojoba o.; mineral oil, shale o., rock o., crude o., petroleum; refined oil, coal o.; fuel oil, paraffin, kerosene, petrol, gasoline, gas 385 *fuel*; lubricating oil 334 *lubricant*; bath oil, suntan o.

fat, animal f., grease, adipocere, body fat, excess f., liposuction; saturated fat, unsaturated f., polyunsaturated f., monounsaturated f., essential fatty acid, trans-fatty a., triglyceride; blubber, tallow, spermaceti; sebum, wax, beeswax; suet, lard, dripping, bacon fat 301 *cookery*; glycerine, stearin, olein; margarine, butter, ghee, spread; cream, Devonshire c., Cornish c.; top of the milk; buttermilk; soap, carbolic s., soft s., toilet s., liquid s., soap flakes, washcream 648 *cleanser*.

unguent, salve, unction, ointment, liniment, embrocation, lanolin; pomade, brilliantine; cream, cold cream 843 *cosmetic*.

resin, rosin, gum, gum arabic, tragacanth, myrrh, frankincense, camphor; lac, amber, ambergris; pitch, tar, bitumen, asphalt; varnish, mastic, shellac, lacquer, japan; epoxy resin; polyurethane, plastics.

Adj. *fatty*, fat, adipose, blubbery, flabby 195 *fleshy*; sebaceous, waxy, waxen; lardaceous; saponaceous, soapy; buttery, creamy, milky, rich 390 *savoury*.

Vb. *grease*, oil, anoint 334 *lubricate*; baste, lard; butter; saponify; resin, rosin.

SECTION THREE

Organic matter

358 Organisms: living matter

N. *organism*, organic matter; living beings; animal and vegetable kingdom, flora and fauna, biota; ecosystem; ecotype, bio-type 77 *breed*; living matter 360 *life*; microscopic life; cell, protoplasm, cytoplasm, nucleus, nucleolus; nucleic acid, RNA, DNA; chromatin, chromosome, chromatid, gene 5 *heredity*; albumen, protein; rogue protein, prion; enzyme, globulin; antioxidants; organic remains 125 *fossil*.

biology, microbiology; natural history, nature study, biochemistry, biophysics, molecular biology, cell b., cytology; histology; morphology, embryology; anatomy, physiology 331 *structure*; zoography 367 *zoology*; phytography 368 *botany*; ecology, biodiversity; biogeography; marine biology; genetics, eugenics, genetic engineering; biotechnology, biotech, biomedicine; evolution, natural selection, survival of the fittest; Darwinism; biogenesis.

Adj. *biological*, physiological, zoological, palaeontological; biogenetic; evolutionary, Darwinian.

359 Mineral: inorganic matter

N. *mineral*, inorganic matter, earth's crust 344 *rock*; ore, metal, precious m., base m.; alloy 43 *a mixture*; mineralogical deposit, coal measures 632 *store*.

mineralogy, geology, lithology, petrography, petrology; metallurgy, metallography; speleology, glaciology 321 *earth sciences*.

360 Life

N. *life*, living, being 1 *existence*; the living, living being, being, soul, spirit; plant life 366 *vegetable life*; animal life 365 *animality*; human life 371 *humankind*; gift of life, birth, nativity 68 *origin*; renaissance 656 *revival*; life to come, the hereafter 124 *future state*; immortal life 971 *heaven*; animation; vitality, vital force, élan vital, life force; soul 447 *spirit*; will to live, survival, cat's nine lives, longevity 113 *long duration*; liveliness, animation 819 *moral sensibility*; breathing 352 *respiration*; lifeblood, heart's blood 5 *essential part*; vital spark; heart, artery; staff of life 301 *food*; biological function, parenthood 167 *propagation*; sex, sexual activity 45 *coition*; living matter, protoplasm, living tissue; cell, unicellular organism 358 *organism*; symbiosis 706 *association*; life-support system; lifetime, one's born days; life expectancy, allotted span, life cycle; survivability, viability, viableness 469 *possibility*.

Adj. *alive*, living, quick, live, animate; breathing, alive and kicking; animated 819 *lively*; incarnate, in the flesh; surviving, in the land of the living, above ground, with us, on this side of the grave; long-lived 113 *lasting*; survivable, viable; vital, enlivened.

born, begotten, fathered, sired; mothered, dammed; foaled, dropped; out of, by 11 *akin*; spawned, littered; laid, new-l., hatched.

Vb. *live*, be alive, have life, have being; draw breath 352 *breathe*; exist 1 *be*; come to life, come to, liven up, quicken, revive 656 *be restored*; be spared, survive 41 *be left*; cheat death, have nine lives; live in 192 *dwell*.

be born, come into the world, come into existence, first see the light 68 *begin*; have one's nativity; draw breath; be begotten, be conceived.

vitalize, give birth to, beget, conceive, support life 167 *generate*; vivify, enliven, breathe life into, bring to life 174 *invigorate*; revitalize, give a new lease of life, put new life into, ginger, put zest into, reanimate 656 *revive*; maintain, provide for, keep body and soul together, make

ends meet, keep the wolf from the door 301 *feed*.

361 Death

N. *death*, no life 2 *extinction*; dying (**see** *decease*); mortality, ephemerality 114 *transience*; sentence of death, doom, death knell; execution, martyrdom; curtains, deathblow, quietus 362 *killing*; necrosis, mortification 51 *decay*; the beyond, the great divide, crossing the Styx or Lethe; eternal rest, long sleep 266 *quietude*; Abraham's bosom 971 *heaven*; the grave 364 *tomb*; jaws of death, shadow of d.; nether regions, Stygian darkness, Hades 972 *hell*; Death, the Grim Reaper, the Great Leveller; Angel of Death; post mortem, autopsy, necroscopy 364 *inquest*; mortuary, charnel house, morgue 364 *cemetery*.

decease, clinical death, brain d., cerebral d.; extinction, exit, demise, curtains 69 *end*; departure, passing, passing away, passing over; natural death, quiet end, euthanasia 376 *euphoria*; welcome end, loss of life, fatality; sudden death, violent d., untimely end; death by drowning, watery grave; death on the roads; accidental death, death by misadventure; karoshi 362 *suicide*; fatal disease, terminal illness or disease 651 *disease*; dying day, last hour; valley of the shadow of death; deathbed, deathbed repentance, death scene; last gasp, dying breath; swan song, death rattle, rigor mortis 69 *finality*; extreme unction; passing bell 364 *obsequies*.

the dead, forefathers 66 *precursor*; dear departed, souls 968 *saint*; the shades, ghosts, phantoms 970 *ghost*; dead body 363 *corpse*; next world 124 *future state*; world of spirits, netherworld, Styx; Hades, Stygian shore 972 *mythic hell*; Elysian fields, happy hunting grounds, Davy Jones's locker 971 *mythic heaven*.

death roll, mortality, fatality, collateral damage, death toll, death rate; casualty list; death register 87 *list*; death certificate 548 *record*; martyrology; obituary, obit, deaths column, death notice; the dead, the fallen, the lost; casualties, the dead and dying.

Adj. *dying*, expiring etc. vb.: mortal, ephemeral, perishable 114 *transient*; moribund, with one foot in the grave, deathly; all over with, all up with, not long for this world, not long to go; done for, had it; going, slipping away, sinking fast; sick unto death 651 *sick*; on the danger list, in a critical condition, terminally ill, on one's deathbed, at death's door; life hanging by a thread; at the last gasp; on one's last legs, at the point of death; under sentence of death, doomed.

dead, deceased; passed over, passed away,

departed, gone, gone before; dead and gone, dead and buried, in the grave, six feet under; stillborn; lifeless; extinct, bereft of life; cold, stiff; dead as a doornail, dead as a dodo; kaput, done for, gone for a burton; out of one's misery; departed this life, called to one's eternal rest, gathered to one's fathers, in Abraham's bosom, on the other side, beyond the grave; gone to join one's forefathers, gone to the happy hunting-grounds; defunct, late, late-lamented, gone but not forgotten, of sainted memory; martyred, slaughtered, massacred, killed.

Vb. *die* (**see** *perish*); be dead, lie in the grave, be gone, be no more, cease to be, lose one's life 2 *pass away*; die young, not make old bones; die a natural death, die in one's sleep, die in bed; end one's life, decease; expire, give up the ghost, breathe one's last; close one's eyes, sleep one's last sleep; pass over, be taken; depart this life 296 *depart*; ring down the curtain, shuffle off this mortal coil, go the way of all flesh, go to one's last home; cross the Styx, join the angels, meet one's Maker, reach a better world; croak, peg out, snuff it; cop it, have bought it; cash in one's chips, conk out, pop off, go west, go for a burton, hop the twig, kick the bucket, bite the dust, turn up one's toes, push up the daisies, flatline.

perish, die out, become extinct 2 *pass away*; go to the wall 165 *be destroyed*; wither, come to dust 51 *decompose*; meet one's end, meet one's fate; die in harness, die with one's boots on; get killed, be killed, fall in action, lose one's life, be lost; lay down one's life; become a martyr, make the supreme sacrifice; die young, drop down dead; meet a sticky end, die a violent death, break one's neck; bleed to death; drown, go to Davy Jones's locker 313 *founder*; be put to death, walk the plank; commit suicide 362 *kill oneself*.

362 Killing: destruction of life
N. *killing*, slaying 165 *destruction*; taking life; blood sports, hunting, poaching, lamping, shooting 619 *chase*; blood-shedding, blood-letting; vivisection; cull; mercy killing, euthanasia; murder, serial killing, assassination, bumping off (**see** *homicide*); poisoning, drowning, suffocation, strangulation, hanging; immolation, sacrifice; martyrdom; crucifixion, execution 963 *capital punishment*; judicial murder, auto da fé, burning alive, the stake; death-blow, coup de grâce, quietus; death by misadventure, violent death, fatal accident, death on the roads, car crash, train c., plane crash.

homicide, manslaughter; murder, premedi-

tated m., capital m.; assassination; thuggery; crime passionel 911 *jealousy*; regicide, tyrannicide, parricide, patricide, matricide, uxoricide, fratricide; infanticide, genocide (**see** *slaughter*).

suicide, self-destruction, felo de se; suttee, hara-kiri; assisted suicide, doctor-assisted s., physician-assisted s.; parasuicide, attempted suicide; mass suicide, Gadarene swine, lemmings.

slaughter, bloodshed, butchery, carnage; bloodbath, massacre, fusillade, holocaust; pogrom, purge, liquidation, decimation, extermination, annihilation 165 *destruction*; genocide, ethnic cleansing; war, battle 718 *warfare*; Roman holiday, gladiatorial combat 716 *duel*; slaughter-house, abattoir, knacker's yard, shambles; bull-ring 724 *arena*; battlefield 724 *battleground*; killing-fields; gas chamber, Auschwitz, Belsen.

killer, slayer; mercy killer 905 *pity*; soldier, guerrilla, urban g. 722 *combatant*; slaughterer, butcher; huntsman 619 *hunter*; trapper, mole-catcher, ratcatcher, pest exterminator; toreador, picador, matador 162 *athlete*; executioner, hangman; homicide (**see** *murderer*); lynch mob; homicidal maniac, psychopath; head-hunter, cannibal; predator, bird of prey, beast of prey, man-eater, insecticide.

murderer, homicide, killer, Cain; assassin, terrorist; poisoner, strangler, garrotter, thug; hatchet man, hitman, gangster, contract killer, gunman; cut-throat 904 *ruffian*.

Adj. *deadly*, killing, lethal; fell, mortal, fatal, deathly; life-threatening, capital; death-bringing, malignant, poisonous 653 *toxic*; asphyxiant, suffocating, stifling; miasmic 653 *insalubrious*; inoperable, incurable, terminal.

murderous, homicidal, genocidal; suicidal, self-destructive; internecine, death-dealing, trigger-happy; sanguinary, bloody, gory, blood-stained, red-handed; bloodthirsty 898 *cruel*; head-hunting, man-eating, cannibalistic.

Vb. *kill*, slay, take life, deprive of l.; do in, do for 165 *destroy*; nip in the bud, shorten one's life; put down, put to sleep; hasten one's end, drive to one's death, work to d., put to d., send to the scaffold, hang, behead, guillotine, electrocute, send to the electric chair 963 *execute*; stone to death; string up, lynch; make away with, do away w., dispatch, get rid of; deal a deathblow, give the coup de grâce, put one out of his misery, give one his quietus; shed blood, knife, put to the sword, lance, bayonet, stab, run through 263 *pierce*; shoot down, pick off, blow the brains out 287 *shoot*; strangle, garrotte, choke, suffocate, smother, stifle, drown; wall up, bury alive; brain, poleaxe, sandbag 279 *strike*; send to the stake 381 *burn*; immolate, sacrifice, offer up; martyr, condemn to death, sign the death warrant, ring the knell 961 *condemn*.

slaughter, butcher, poleaxe, cut the throat of; massacre, put to the sword; decimate, scupper, wipe out; cut to pieces, cut to ribbons, cut down, shoot d., mow d.; give no quarter, spare none 906 *be pitiless*; annihilate, exterminate, liquidate, purge, send to the gas chamber, commit genocide 165 *destroy*.

murder, commit m., commit homicide, commit manslaughter, assassinate, finish off, make away with, do in, do to death, do for, fix, settle, bump off, wipe out, liquidate, rub out; make to walk the plank; smother, suffocate, strangle, poison, gas.

kill oneself, do oneself in, do away with oneself, make away with oneself, commit suicide, suicide; commit hara-kiri, commit suttee; hang oneself, shoot o., blow out one's brains, cut one's throat, slash one's wrists; fall on one's sword, die Roman fashion; put one's head in the oven, gas oneself; take poison, take an overdose; jump overboard, drown oneself.

363 Corpse
N. *corpse*, dead body, body; dead man *or* woman, victim; stiff; cadaver, carcass, skeleton, dry bones; death's-head, skull; mummy; mortal remains, relics, ashes; carrion, food for worms, food for fishes.

364 Interment
N. *interment*, burial, entombment; inhumation, cremation, incineration; scattering of the ashes; embalming, mummification; embalmment, myrrh, spices, coffin, cist, shell, casket, urn; sarcophagus; pyre, funeral pile, crematorium; mortuary, morgue, charnel house; undertaker's, funeral parlour; sexton, gravedigger; undertaker, funeral director; mortician; embalmer.

obsequies, mourning, weeping and wailing, wake 836 *lamentation*; lying-in-state; last rites, burial service; funeral rites, cortege; knell; dead march, muffled drum, last post; memorial service, requiem, funeral hymn, funeral oration; elegy, dirge 836 *lament*; inscription, epitaph, obituary; tombstone, gravestone, headstone; cross, war memorial; cenotaph 548 *monument*; necrologist, obituary-writer.

funeral, hearse, bier, pall, coffin; mourner, weeper, keener; pallbearer; lychgate (**see** *obsequies*).

grave clothes, shroud, winding sheet.

cemetery, burial place, golgotha; churchyard, graveyard, God's Acre; catacombs, cinerarium; necropolis, city of the dead; garden of remembrance, garden of rest.

tomb, vault, crypt; burial chamber; pyramid;

mausoleum, sepulchre; pantheon; grave, long home; cist; barrow 253 *earthwork*; cromlech, dolmen, menhir 548 *monument*; shrine, memorial, cenotaph.

inquest 459 *enquiry*; necropsy, autopsy, postmortem; exhumation, disinterment, disentombment.

Adj. *funereal*, funebrial; sombre, sad 428 *black*; mourning, elegiac, mortuary, cinerary, crematory, sepulchral; obsequial, obituary; epitaphic; necrological, dirgelike 836 *lamenting*.

Vb. *inter*, inhume, bury; lay out; embalm, coffin; urn, entomb; lay in the grave, consign to earth, lay to rest; cremate, incinerate 381 *burn*; pay one's last respects, go to a funeral, toll the knell, sound the last post; mourn, keen, hold a wake 836 *lament*.

exhume, disinter; disentomb; unearth, dig up.

365 Animality. Animal
N. *animality*, animal life, wild life; animal kingdom, fauna; physique, flesh, flesh and blood; anthropomorphism; zoomorphism, Pan; animalism 944 *sensualism*; animal liberation movement, animal rights m.; antivivisectionist, animalist, animal liberationist.

animal, living thing; birds, beasts and fishes; creature, brute, beast, dumb animal, creeping thing; protozoon, metazoon; zoophyte; mammal, amphibian, fish, bird, reptile; worm, mollusc, arthropod; crustacean, insect, arachnid; invertebrate, vertebrate; biped, quadruped; carnivore, herbivore, insectivore, ruminant, maneater; wild animal, game, big game; prey, beast of prey; pack, flock, herd 74 *group*; stock, livestock 369 *stock farm*; tame animal, domestic a.; pet a., household pet, animal companion; cyberpet, virtual pet, Tamagotchi (tdmk); goldfish, cagebird, hamster, gerbil, guinea pig, tortoise; young animal 132 *young creature*; draught animal 273 *horse, beast of burden*; endangered species, blue whale, oryx; extinct animal, dodo, auk, aurochs, prehistoric animal, pterodactyl, ichthyosaur, plesiosaur, dinosaur, brontosaurus, tyrannosaurus rex, megathere, mammoth, mastodon, sabre-toothed tiger; fabulous beast, heraldic b., unicorn, griffin 84 *rara avis*.

mammal, viviparous animal; man 371 *humankind*; primate, ape, anthropoid ape, gorilla, orang-outang, chimpanzee, gibbon, baboon, mandrill, monkey; marmoset, lemur; marsupial, kangaroo, wallaby, wombat, koala bear, opossum; rodent, rat, mouse, field m., dormouse, shrew, vole, porcupine, mongoose, chipmunk, skunk, polecat, squirrel; aardvark, ant-eater, mole; bat, bush baby, raccoon, badger, hedgehog; stoat, weasel, ferret; fox, dog f., vixen, Reynard; jackal, hyena, lion (**see** *cat*); herbivorous mammal (**see** *sheep* etc.); hare, mountain h., rabbit, bunny; otter, beaver, water rat, water vole; walrus, seal, sea lion; cetacean, dolphin, porpoise, whale, sperm w., right w.; pachyderm, elephant, rhinoceros, hippopotamus; bear, polar b., black b., brown b., grizzly b; giant panda; ungulate, giraffe, zebra (**see** *cattle*); deer, stag, hart, buck, doe, fawn, pricket; red deer, fallow d., roe d., muntjac; reindeer, caribou; elk, moose; gazelle, antelope, chamois, springbok, eland, hartebeest, wildebeest, gnu; horse, donkey, camel 273 *beast of burden*; pet passport, animal p.

bird, winged thing, fowls of the air; fledgling, squab 132 *young creature*; avifauna, birdlife; cagebird, canary, budgerigar; parrot, polly, macaw, mynah bird; songbird, songster, warbler, nightingale, philomel, bulbul, lark, thrush, throstle, mavis, blackbird, linnet; curlew, plover, lapwing, peewit; dove, turtle d., ring d., pigeon, wood p.; woodpecker, jay, magpie, pie; jackdaw, rook, raven, crow; finch, goldfinch, greenfinch, chaffinch; tit, blue t., great t., wren, robin, sparrow, hedge s., house s.; yellowhammer, wagtail; humming b., sunbird, weaver b., b. of paradise, lyrebird; hoopoe, golden oriole; migrant, cuckoo, swallow, swift, martin; redwing, fieldfare, snow bunting; emu, ostrich, rhea, cassowary, kiwi, penguin; nightbird, owl, tawny o., barn o., screech o., nightjar; vulture, marabou, carrion crow; bird of prey, eagle, golden e; kite, kestrel, harrier, osprey, buzzard; hawk, sparrowhawk, falcon, peregrine f., merlin, shrike; fishing bird, pelican, kingfisher, gannet, cormorant, shag, skua, Arctic s.; gull, herring g., kittiwake, tern, oyster-catcher, puffin, guillemot; ocean bird, albatross, petrel, stormy p., Mother Carey's chickens; marsh bird, wader, stork, crane, heron, bittern; spoonbill, ibis, flamingo; water bird, waterfowl, swan, cob, pen, cygnet; duck, drake, duckling; goose, gander, gosling; merganser, pintail, teal, mallard, widgeon; moorhen, coot, lily-trotter, diver, dipper, grebe, dabchick.

table bird, game b., woodcock, wood pigeon, squab; peafowl, peacock, peahen; grouse, ptarmigan, capercaillie, pheasant, partridge, quail; goose, duck, snipe; turkey, guinea fowl, guinea hen.

poultry, fowl, hen; cock, cockerel, rooster; chicken, pullet; boiler, broiler, roaster, capon; Rhode Island Red, Leghorn, bantam.

cattle, kine, livestock 369 *stock farm*; bull, cow, calf, heifer, yearling; bullock, steer; beef cattle, highland c., Aberdeen Angus, Luing cattle, Hereford, Charolais; dairy cattle, milch cow, Guernsey, Jersey, Friesian; Simmental,

dual-purpose cattle, Redpoll, shorthorn; zebu, brahmin, zho; ox, oxen; buffalo, beefalo, bison; yak, musk ox.

goat. billy g., nanny g., mountain g., ibex.

sheep, ram, tup, wether, bell w., ewe, lamb; teg; Southdown, Lincoln, Cheviot, Herdwick, Merino; mountain sheep, mouflon.

pig, swine, boar, warthog; hog, sow, piglet, pigling, sucking pig, porker; Large White, Wessex Saddleback, Berkshire, Tamworth.

dog, canine, bow-wow, man's best friend; bitch, whelp, pup, puppy; cur, hound, tyke, pooch, mutt; mongrel, pariah dog, pye-d.; guide dog, hearing d., house d., watch d., police dog, bloodhound, mastiff; sheepdog, Old English S., collie, Border c.; Doberman pinscher, bull terrier; bulldog, boxer; wolfhound, borzoi, Afghan hound, Alsatian, Dalmatian; Great Dane; St Bernard; greyhound, courser, whippet; foxhound, staghound, beagle; basset, dachshund; gun dog, retriever, golden r., Labrador r., Labrador, golden l., pointer, setter, Irish s.; terrier, smooth-haired t., wire-h. t., fox t., sealyham, Scottish t., Scottie, West Highland terrier, Yorkshire t.; spaniel, cocker s., springer s., King Charles s.; show dog, fancy d., toy d., chihuahua, Pomeranian, chow; lap dog, Pekinese, peke, pug; Welsh corgi; poodle, French p., miniature p., toy p.; husky, sledge dog; wild dog, dingo; wolf, coyote; dangerous dog, fighting d., bandog.

cat, feline; grimalkin, moggie, puss, pussy, kitten, pussycat; tom, tom cat, tabby; mouser; Cheshire Cat; Persian c., Siamese c., Manx c., calico c., tortoiseshell c., marmalade c., tabby c.

big cat, lion, lioness, King of Beasts; tiger, tigress, tigon, leopard, leopardess, cheetah, panther, puma, jaguar, cougar, ocelot; wildcat, bobcat, lynx.

amphibian, frog, bullfrog, tree frog, platanna f.; frogspawn, tadpole; paddock, puddock, toad, natterjack; newt, eft; salamander, axolotl.

reptile, ophidian, serpent, sea s.; snake, water s., grass s., venomous s., viper, adder, asp; cobra, king c., hamadryad; puff adder, mamba, horned viper, rattlesnake; anaconda, boa constrictor, python; crocodile, alligator, cayman; lizard, slowworm, blindworm; chameleon, iguana, monitor, gecko; turtle, tortoise, terrapin.

marine life, denizens of the deep; marine organisms, nekton, benthos; cetacean (**see** *mammal*); sea urchin, sea horse, sea anemone, coral, coral reef, jellyfish, Portuguese man of war, starfish, brittle-star; shellfish, mollusc, bivalve, clam, oyster, mussel, cockle; whelk, winkle, limpet; cephalopod, cuttlefish, squid, octopus; crustacean, crab, lobster, crayfish, shrimp; barnacle.

fish, flying f., swordfish, angelfish, dogfish, shark; piranha, barracuda; stingray, electric ray; tunny fish, turbot, bass, conger eel 301 *fish food*; coelacanth; blenny; pike, roach, perch, bream, carp; trout, grayling; salmon, grilse; eel, elver, lamprey; minnow, gudgeon, stickleback.

insect, larva, pupa, imago; fly, house f., horse f., gadfly, cleg, bluebottle; mayfly, caddis fly; gnat, midge, tsetse fly, mosquito; greenfly, blackfly, aphid; thunder fly; ladybird, lacewing, hoverfly; firefly, glow-worm; dragonfly, crane fly, daddy longlegs; butterfly, cabbage white, red admiral, moth, hawk m., clothes m.; bee, bumble bee, humble b., honey b., queen b., worker b., drone; wasp, hornet; beetle, stag b., dung b., cockroach; vermin, parasites, bug, bed bug, flea, louse, nit, mite, tick; jigger; woodworm, weevil, borer, cockchafer, deathwatch beetle 659 *blight*; emmet, ant, soldier a., worker a., white a., termite; stick insect, praying mantis; locust, grasshopper, cicada, cricket.

creepy-crawly, grub, maggot, caterpillar, looper, inchworm; worm, earthworm, lugworm, wireworm, roundworm, flatworm, tapeworm, fluke; myriapod, centipede, millipede; slug, snail; earwig, woodlouse; spider, money s.; black widow s., tarantula; scorpion.

Adj. *animal*, brutish, beastly, bestial; feral, domestic; human, manly, subhuman; therianthropic, theriomorphic, anthropomorphic, zoomorphic; zoological; vertebrate, invertebrate; mammalian; anthropoid, simian; equine, asinine, mulish; deerlike, cervine; bovine, taurine, ruminant; ovine, sheepish; goat-like, goatish; porcine, piggy; bearish, ursine; elephantine; canine, doggy; lupine, wolfish; feline, catlike, cattish, tigerish, leonine; vulpine, foxy; avian, birdlike; aquiline, vulturine; passerine; owlish; dovelike; gallinaceous, anserine; coldblooded, fishy, piscine, molluscan, molluscoid; amphibian, amphibious, saliential; reptilian, saurian, ophidian, snaky, serpentine, viperish; vermicular, wormy, weevilly; verminous; lepidopterous, entomological.

366 Vegetable life

N. *vegetable life*, vegetable kingdom; flora, vegetation; biomass; flowering, blooming, florescence; lushness, rankness, luxuriance 635 *plenty*, 171 *abundance*; wood nymph 967 *nymph*.

wood, timber, lumber, softwood, hardwood, heartwood, sapwood; forest, virgin f., primeval f.; rain f., jungle; coniferous forest, taiga; bush, heath, scrub, maquis, chaparral; woods, timberland, greenwood, woodland, bocage, copse, coppice, spinney; thicket, bosk, brake, covert; park, chase, game preserve; hurst, holt;

plantation, arboretum, pinetum, pinery; orchard, orangery 370 *garden*; grove, clump; clearing, glade; brushwood, underwood, undergrowth; bushiness, bushes, shrubbery, windbreak, hedge, hedgerow.

forestry, dendrology, silviculture, treeplanting, afforestation; forester, woodcutter, dendrologist 370 *gardener*.

tree, shrub, bush, sapling, scion, stock; pollard; bonsai; shoot, sucker, trunk, bole; limb, branch, bough, twig; conifer, greenwood t., evergreen t., deciduous t., softwood t., hardwood t.; fruit tree, timber t.; mahogany, ebony, teak, walnut, oak, elm, ash, beech, sycamore, maple, plane, lime, linden; horse chestnut, copper beech; cedar of Lebanon, redwood, larch, fir, Douglas fir, spruce, pine, Scots p., lodgepole p.; poplar, Lombardy p., aspen, alder, sallow, willow, weeping w., pussy w.; birch, silver b., rowan, mountain ash; crab apple, sweet chestnut; hazel, elder, spindle, hawthorn, may, blackthorn, sloe; privet, yew, holly, ivy, box, bay, laurel; rhododendron, camellia, azalea; magnolia, laburnum, lilac; wisteria, Virginia creeper; acacia, jacaranda; palm, date p., coconut p., oil p.; baobab, banyan, mangrove; gum tree, eucalyptus, rubber tree 370 *agriculture*.

foliage, foliation, frondescence; greenery, verdure; leafiness, leafage; herbage; umbrage; limb, branch, bough, twig, shoot; spray, sprig; treetop; leaf, simple l., compound l.; frond, flag, blade; leaflet, foliole; pine needle; seed-leaf, cotyledon; leaf-stalk, petiole, stipule, node, stalk, stem; tendril, prickle, thorn.

plant, herb, wort, weed; root, tuber, rhizome, bulb, corm 156 *source*; stolon, rootstock, cutting 132 *young plant*; culinary herb 301 *herb*; medicinal herb 658 *remedy*; fodder 301 *vegetable*, *fruit*, *provender*; national plant, rose, leek, daffodil, thistle, shamrock, fleur-de-lis; garden plant, pansy, primula, marigold, lupin, iris, dahlia, gladiolus, hyacinth, chrysanthemum, snapdragon, sweet william, pink, carnation, lily; lavender, honeysuckle 396 *fragrance*; wild plant, daisy, dandelion, buttercup, poppy, primrose, snowdrop, bluebell, harebell, foxglove, cowslip, forget-me-not, clover, heather; water lily, marsh marigold, flag; cactus, succulent; prickly plant, bramble, gorse, whin; insectivorous plant, Venus's flytrap, sundew; deadly nightshade 659 *poisonous plant*; creeper, climber, twiner, vine, bine, convolvulus, bindweed, liane; parasite, mistletoe; horsetail, fern, bracken; moss, clubmoss, bog m., sphagnum; liverwort; lichen, fungus, mushroom, toadstool, agaric, puffball; mould, penicillin; seaweed, wrack, bladderwrack, kelp, gulfweed; algae.

flower, floweret, floret, blossom, bloom, bud, burgeon; inflorescence, head, corymb, panicle, cyme, umbel, spike, catkin; petal, sepal; corolla, calyx; ovary, ovule, receptacle; pistil, style, stigma, stamen, anther, pollen; nectary; fruit, berry, nut, drupe; seed vessel, pod, capsule, cone; pip, spore, seed 156 *source*; annual, biennial, perennial; house plant, pot p.; hothouse p., exotic; garden flower, wild flower; flowerbed, seedbed, propagator, growbag; gardening, horticulture, floriculture 370 *garden*.

grass, hay; pasture, pasturage, herbage 348 *grassland*; verdure, turf, sod, lawn; meadow grass, rye g., couch g., bent g., fescue; sedge, rush, bulrush, reed, papyrus; marram grass, esparto g.; Pampas grass, elephant g., bamboo, sugar cane; grain plant, wheat, oats, barley, rye, millet, sorghum, rice 301 *cereals*; grain, husk, bran, chaff, stubble, straw.

Adj. *wooden*, wood, treen, woody, ligneous, ligniform.

Vb. *vegetate*, germinate, sprout, shoot 36 *grow*; plant, garden 370 *cultivate*; afforest.

367 Zoology: the science of animals

N. *zoology*, morphology 331 *structure*; embryology 358 *biology*; animal behaviour; anthropography 371 *anthropology*; ornithology, bird watching, twitching; ichthyology, herpetology, ophiology, mammalogy, primatology, cetology, malacology, helminthology, nematology, entomology, lepidopterology, arachnology, conchology; palaeontology.

zoologist, ornithologist, ichthyologist, entomologist, lepidopterist, anthropologist etc. n.

368 Botany: the science of plants

N. *botany*, taxonomy; plant ecology; dendrology 366 *forestry*; mycology, fungology, bryology, algology; palaeobotany; botanical garden 370 *garden*; herbarium; botanist, herbalist, taxonomist etc. n.

369 Animal husbandry

N. *animal husbandry*, manège; breeding, stock-b.; veterinary science; horse-breeding, cattle-raising; dairy farming, beef f. 365 *cattle*; sheep farming, hill f., pig-f., bee-keeping, poultry farming; stirpiculture, pisciculture, aviculture, apiculture, sericulture; veterinary surgeon, vet, veterinarian, animal doctor, horse d. 658 *doctor*; groom 742 *servant*.

stock farm, stud f., dairy farm, cattle f., rancho, hacienda, ranch; fish farm, trout f., hatchery; fish pond, fish tank; duck pond; pig farm, piggery; beehive, hive, apiary; pasture, grazing, sheep farm, hill f., sheeprun, sheepwalk 348 *grassland*; poultry farm, chicken run,

hen r., broiler house, battery, deep litter; factory farm; game preserve.

cattle pen, byre, cowshed 192 *stable*; sheepfold 235 *enclosure*; hutch, coop, hencoop, hen run, henhouse; cowshed, pigsty; swannery; bird cage, aviary.

zoo, zoological gardens, menagerie, circus; Noah's Ark; aviary, vivarium, terrarium, aquarium, dolphinarium; reptile house, monkey temple; bear pit; wildlife park, safari p.; game park, game reserve.

breeder, apiarist; fancier, pigeon-f.

herdsman, herd; cowherd, stockman, cattleman, byreman, cowman, rancher; cowboy, cowgirl, cowpuncher; broncobuster, gaucho; shepherd, shepherdess; swineherd; goatherd; goosegirl; milkmaid, dairymaid; kennel maid.

Vb. *break in*, tame, domesticate, acclimatize 610 *habituate*; train 534 *teach*; yoke, harness, hitch, bridle, spur 267 *ride*; mount, whip, saddle; round up, herd, corral, cage 235 *enclose*.

breed stock, breed, rear, raise, grow, hatch, culture, incubate, nurture, fatten; farm 370 *cultivate*.

groom, currycomb, rub down.

370 Agriculture

N. *agriculture*, agronomy, agronomics; Common Agricultural Policy, decerealization; butter mountain, grain m., wine lake; agribusiness, agro-industry, agrochemical i. 622 *business*; cultivation, ploughing, sowing, reaping; growth, harvest, produce, crop, vintage 632 *store*; cash crop, fodder c.; husbandry, farming, mixed f., factory f.; cattle farming, dairy f., horsiculture 369 *animal husbandry*; cereal farming, arable f.; hydroponics, tank farming; irrigation; tillage, tilth; green fingers; floriculture, flower-growing; horticulture, gardening, market g.; bonsai; vegetable growing, fruit g., soft-fruit g., mushroom g.; viticulture, viniculture, wine-growing; arboriculture, silviculture, afforestation 366 *forestry*; landscape gardening, landscape architecture.

farm, home f., grange; arable farm, dairy f., sheep f., hill f., cattle f. 369 *stock farm*; ranch, rancho, hacienda; model farm; farmstead, steading, farmhouse; farmyard, barnyard 235 *enclosure*; state farm, collective f., kolkhoz, kibbutz; farmland, arable land, ploughed land, fallow 344 *soil*; rice paddy, paddyfield; pasturage, pasture, corn field, crop circle, fields, meadows 348 *grassland*; demesne, manor farm, estate, holding, smallholding, croft 777 *lands*; allotment, kitchen garden; market garden, herb g.; nursery; vineyard, vinery; fruit farm, orchard; tea garden, tea estate, coffee e., sugar plantation, rubber p.

garden, botanical g., flower g., rose g., Dutch g., herb g., rock g., alpine g., indoor g., container g., winter g.; vegetable garden, cabbage patch, kitchen garden, allotment; fruit garden, orchard; arboretum, pinetum, pinery 366 *wood*; patch, plot, lawn, park 235 *enclosure*; shrubbery, border, herbaceous b., bed, flowerbed, parterre 844 *ornamental art*; seedbed, frame, cold f., propagator 167 *propagation*; cloche, conservatory, hothouse, greenhouse, glasshouse, orangery; grow bag, growing-bag; jardinière, planter, flower-pot; water feature, patio.

farmer, husbandman, farm manager, grieve, factor, farm agent, bailiff; cultivator, planter, tea p., coffee p.; agronomist, agriculturalist; peasant, paysan; serf; villein; tenant farmer; gentleman farmer, yeoman; hill farmer; smallholder, crofter, allotment-holder; fruit grower; wine-grower, vigneron; farm hand, farm labourer, orraman, agricultural worker; land girl; ploughman, tractor driver, sower, reaper, harvester, gleaner; thresher; potato picker, hop p., fruit p.

gardener, horticulturist, flower grower; topiarist, landscape gardener; seedsman, nurseryman or -woman; market gardener; fruit-grower, vinegrower, vigneron; arborist, arboriculturalist, silviculturist 366 *forestry*.

farm tool, tractor plough, ploughshare; harrow; cultivator, rotary c., spade, fork, farm f., graip, hoe, Dutch h., rake, trowel; dibble, drill; hayfork, pitchfork; scythe, sickle, shears, pruners, secateurs 256 *sharp edge*; flail; winepress, ciderpress; mowing machine, mower, Flymo (tdmk), rotary m., cylinder m., trimmer, binder, baler, combine harvester, pea viner.

Vb. *cultivate*, bring under cultivation 171 *make fruitful*; farm, ranch, garden, grow; till, till the soil, dig, trench, dibble; sow, scatter the seed, set, plant, prick out, dibble in, transplant, plant out, bed o.; plough, harrow, rake, hoe; weed, prune, thin out, deadhead 204 *shorten*; graft 303 *implant*; layer, take cuttings; force; fertilize, topdress, mulch, manure 174 *invigorate*; grass over, rotate the crop; leave fallow 674 *not use*; harvest 632 *store*; glean, reap, mow, cut, scythe, cut a swathe; bind, bale, stook, sheaf; flail, thresh, winnow, sift, bolt 46 *separate*; crop, pluck, pick, gather; tread out the grapes; ensile; ditch, drain, reclaim; water 341 *irrigate*.

371 Humankind

N. *humankind*, mankind, homo sapiens, womankind; humanity, human nature; flesh, mortality, human frailty; human race, human species, man; earthling; human being, Adam, Eve, civilized world 654 *civilization*; barbarians,

savages; bushmen, aborigines; Stone-Age man, Cro-Magnon man, Neanderthal man, cavemen and -women, troglodytes; apemen and -women, Pithecanthropus, Australopithecus, Peking man, Java man, ethnic type 11 *race*.

anthropology, anthropography; somatology; ethnology, ethnography, folklore; social anthropology, demography; social science, humanitarianism 901 *sociology*; humanism; anthroposophy; anthropomorphism, pathetic fallacy; anthropologist, craniologist, ethnographer, demographer, folklorist, humanist.

person, individual, human being, everyman, everywoman; creature, mortal, body, bod; a being, soul, living s.; one, somebody, someone, so and so, such a one; party, customer, character, type, element; chap, fellow 372 *male*; girl, female, bird 373 *woman*; personage, figure, person of note, VIP 638 *bigwig*; celebrity, star 890 *favourite*; dramatis personae, all those concerned 686 *personnel*; unit, head, hand, nose.

social group, society, community, ethnic group, ghetto 74 *group*; kinship group 11 *family*; primitive society, tribalism; organized society; people, persons, folk; public, general p., man or woman in the street, joe soap, the average punter, everyman, you and me, the 'me' generation 79 *generality*; population, populace, citizenry 191 *inhabitants*; the masses 869 *commonalty*; social classes 869 *lower classes*, middle c., 868 *upper class*, aristocracy.

nation, nationality, statehood, nationalism; chauvinism, jingoism, gung-ho nationalism, expansionism, imperialism, colonialism; Lebensraum; body politic, people, demos; state; realm, commonwealth 733 *political organization*; democracy, republic 733 *government*.

Adj. *national*, state, civic, general, communal, tribal, social, societal; cosmopolitan, international.

372 Male

N. *male*, male sex, man, he, him; Adam; manliness, masculinity, manhood; virility, machismo; male chauvinism, male-dominated society, patriarchy, men's movement, mannishness, virilism; gentleman, sir, esquire, master; lord, my l., his lordship; Mr, mister, monsieur, Herr, señor, don, dom, senhor, signor, sahib; tovarich, comrade, citoyen; squire, guvnor, guv; buster, Mac, Jock, Jimmy; mate, buddy, butty, pal 880 *chum*; goodman, wight, swain; gaffer, buffer 133 *old man*; fellow, guy, scout, bloke, chap, chappie, johnny, gent; codger, card, cove, joker; blade, rake, gay dog 952 *libertine*; he-man, caveman, macho, Alpha Man; male chauvinist pig, MCP, New Lad, lad, laddism; New Man; sissy, mummy's boy 163 *weakling*; homosexual, homo, queer 84 *nonconformist*; eunuch, castrato; escort, beau, boy friend; bachelor, widower; bridegroom 894 *bridal party*; married man, husband, house h., man, live-in 894 *spouse*; family man, paterfamilias, patriarch; father 169 *paternity*; uncle, brother, nephew; lad, stripling, boy 132 *youngster*; blue-eyed boy, son; spear side; stag party, menfolk.

male animal, jack, cock, cockerel, rooster; drake, gander, cob; buck, stag, hart; horse, stallion, stud horse, colt; bull, bull-calf, bullock, ox, steer; boar, hog; ram, tup; he-goat, billy g.; dog, dog fox, tom cat; gelding, capon.

Adj. *male*, he, masculine, manly, gentlemanly, chivalrous; virile, macho; mannish, manlike, butch, unfeminine, unwomanly.

373 Female

N. *female*, feminine sex, woman, she, her, -ess; Eve, femininity, feminineness; womanhood 134 *adultness*; womanliness, girlishness; feminism, gynography, women's rights, Women's Lib *or* Liberation, Women's Movement; matriarchy, gynocracy, regiment of women; girl, little g. 132 *youngster*; virgin, maiden; nun, unmarried woman, old maid 895 *spinster*; bachelor girl, career woman; feminist, sister, women's libber, bra burner; suffragette; bride, married woman, wife, 'trouble and strife', woman, live-in, squaw, widow, matron 894 *spouse*; dowager 133 *old woman*; mother, grandmother 169 *maternity*; unmarried mother, working wife *or* mother, superwoman, housewife; aunt, auntie, niece, sister, daughter; wench, lass, lassie, nymph, colleen, damsel; petticoat, skirt, doll, chick, bird, totty; honey, hinny, baby; brunette, blonde, platinum b., redhead; girl friend, sweetheart 887 *loved one*; moll, bint, crumpet, bit of fluff; broad, courtesan 952 *loose woman*; lesbian, dyke *or* dike 84 *nonconformist*; minx, hussy, baggage, jade; shrew, virago, stramullion, Amazon, lady, gentlewoman; dame; milady, her ladyship, donna; madam, ma'am, marm, mistress, Mrs, missus, Ms, miss, madame, mademoiselle, Frau, Fräulein; signora, signorina, señora, señorita, memsahib; goodwife; gynaecology; obstetrics 167 *propagation*.

womankind, second sex, female s., fair s., gentle s., weaker s.; the distaff side, womenfolk, women; hen party; women's quarters, purdah, seraglio, harem.

female animal, hen, bitch; mare, filly; cow, heifer; sow; ewe, ewelamb; nanny goat; hind, doe; vixen, tigress, lioness, leopardess.

Adj. *female*, she, feminine, petticoat, girlish, womanly, ladylike, maidenly, matronly; child-bearing; feminist, feministic; Amazonian; lesbian, lez *or* les, dykey *or* dikey; womanish, effeminate, unmanly, pansy.

374 Physical sensibility

N. *sensibility*, sensitivity; sensitiveness, soreness, tenderness, delicateness, threshold of pain; exposed nerve; perceptivity, awareness, consciousness 819 *moral sensibility*; susceptibility; allergy; funny bone; sensuousness, aestheticism, aesthetics; aesthete 846 *people of taste*; touchy person, sensitive plant, thin skin.

sense, sense organ, nervous system, sensorium; five senses; touch, hearing, taste, smell, sight; sensation, impression 818 *feeling*; effect, response, reaction, reflex, autosuggestion; sixth sense, feyness, second sight, extrasensory perception, ESP; telepathy, thought-transference 984 *psychics*.

Adj. *sentient*, perceptive, sensitive, sensitized; sensible, susceptible; sensory, perceptual; sensuous, aesthetic 818 *feeling*; percipient, aware, conscious 490 *knowing*; acute, sharp, keen 377 *painful*; ticklish, itchy; tender, raw, sore, exposed; impressionable, alive, alive to, warm, responsive; allergic, oversensitive, hypersensitive 819 *impressible*.

Vb. *have feeling*, sense, become aware; come to one's senses, awaken, wake up; perceive, realize 490 *know*; be sensible of 818 *feel*; react, tingle 819 *be sensitive*; have all one's senses, hear, see, touch, taste, smell; be alert, have one's wits about one, be on the ball, be on the qui vive.

cause feeling, stir the senses, stir the blood; arouse, awaken, excite, make *or* produce an impression 821 *impress*; cause a sensation 508 *surprise*; sensitize.

375 Physical insensibility

N. *insensibility*, insensitiveness; imperceptiveness, obtuseness 499 *unintelligence*; impassivity 820 *moral insensibility*; anaesthesia; analgesia; hypnosis, hypnotism, autosuggestion; suspended animation; apoplexy, paralysis, palsy; numbness; catalepsy, stupor, coma, trance, freak-out; faint, swoon, blackout, unconsciousness, senselessness; narcolepsy, narcotism, sleeping sickness 651 *disease*; narcosis 679 *sleep*.

anaesthetic, dope 658 *drug*; local anaesthetic, general a.; ether, chloroform, morphine, cocaine; gas, nitrous oxide, laughing gas; gas and air, epidural, pethidene; narcotic, sleeping tablets, Mogadon (tdmk), draught; opium, laudanum; painkiller, analgesic 177 *moderator*.

Adj. *insensible*, insensitive, insentient; obtuse, imperceptive 499 *unintelligent*; unaware, oblivious; unhearing 416 *deaf*; unseeing 439 *blind*; senseless, unconscious; inert 679 *inactive*; out cold, out for the count, dead 266 *quiescent*; numb, frozen; paralysed, paralytic, palsied; doped, dopy, drugged; freaked out, spaced o.; stoned 949 *dead drunk*; anaesthetized, hypnotized; dazed, stupefied; semiconscious, in a trance; catatonic, cataleptic, comatose.

unfeeling, cold, callous, insensitive, inured, toughened, hardened; pachydermatous, thick-skinned; stony, shock-proof 820 *impassive*.

Vb. *render insensible*, blunt, deaden; paralyse, benumb; freeze 382 *refrigerate*; put to sleep, send to sleep, hypnotize, mesmerize 679 *make inactive*; anaesthetize, put under, gas, chloroform; drug, dope; dull, stupefy; stun, concuss, brain, knock out, render unconscious 279 *strike*.

376 Physical pleasure

N. *pleasure*, thrill 821 *excitation*; enjoyment, gratification, sensuousness, sensuality; self-indulgence, luxuriousness, hedonism 944 *sensualism*; dissipation 943 *intemperance*; treat, diversion, entertainment, divertissement 837 *amusement*; feast, thrash 301 *feasting*; epicurism, epicureanism, relish 386 *taste*; gusto, zest, delight, happiness, ecstasy 824 *joy*.

euphoria, well-being, contentment 828 *content*, 824 *happiness*; quiet.

Adj. *pleasant*, pleasure-giving 826 *pleasurable*; pleasing, titillating, arousing; delightful; welcome, gratifying, satisfying 685 *refreshing*; genial, congenial, friendly, matey, cordial, heart-warming; nice, agreeable, enjoyable 837 *amusing*; palatable, delicious 386 *tasty*; tuneful 410 *melodious*; lovely 841 *beautiful*.

comfortable, affording comfort, comfy, homely, snug, cosy, warm, comforting, restful 683 *reposeful*; convenient; cushy; downy 327 *soft*; luxurious; in comfort, at one's ease; pampered, featherbedded, in clover, on a bed of roses, on velvet; happy, gratified 828 *content*; relieved.

sensuous, appealing to the s.; bodily, physical 319 *material*; voluptuous, pleasure-loving, luxuriating, enjoying, epicurean, hedonistic 944 *sensual*.

Vb. *enjoy*, relish, like, love, adore; feel pleasure, experience p., take p. in 824 *be pleased*; thrill to 821 *be excited*; luxuriate in, revel in, bask in, roll in, wallow in; gloat over, get a kick out of; lick one's lips, smack one's l. 386 *taste*; live on the fat of the land, live comfortably, live in clover, rest on a bed of roses 730 *prosper*; give pleasure 826 *please*.

Adv. *in comfort*, at one's ease; in clover, on velvet, on a bed of roses.

377 Physical pain

N. *pain*, threshold of pain; discomfort, malaise; distress, hell 731 *adversity*; strain, stress 684 *fatigue*; hurt, bruise, sprain, break, fracture; cut, gash 655 *wound*; aching, smarting, throbbing; heartache, anguish, agony 825 *suffering*; torment, torture; crucifixion, martyrdom, vivisection; rack, wheel, thumbscrew 964 *instrument of torture*; painfulness, soreness, tenderness.

pang, throes; stab, labour pangs, hunger p., twinge, nip, pinch; pins and needles 378 *formication*; stitch, crick, cramp, convulsion 318 *spasm*; smart, sting, sharp pain, shooting p.; ache, headache, splitting head, migraine; toothache, earache; stomachache, bellyache, colic, collywobbles; neuritis, neuralgia, angina; arthritis, rheumatoid a., rheumatism, fibrositis, repetitive strain injury, sciatica, lumbago, backache 651 *ill health*.

Adj. *painful*, aching, agonizing, excruciating, harrowing, racking, tormenting; burning, biting, searing, stabbing, shooting, tingling, smarting, throbbing; sore, raw, tender, exposed, grazed; bittersweet 393 *sour*; disagreeable.

Vb. *give pain*, hurt, pain, sting, graze; excruciate, lacerate, torment, twist the arm of 963 *torture*; flog, whip, crucify, martyr 963 *punish*; vivisect, tear, lacerate 46 *cut*; prick, stab 263 *pierce*; gripe, nip, pinch, tweak, twinge, shoot, throb; bite, gnaw; grate, jar, set on edge; fret, chafe, gall 333 *rub*; irritate 832 *aggravate*; put on the rack, break on the wheel; grate on the ear 411 *discord*; annoy, distress 827 *trouble*.

feel pain, feel the pangs 825 *suffer*; agonize, ache, smart, chafe; twitch, wince, flinch, writhe, squirm, creep, shiver, quiver 318 *be agitated*; tingle, get pins and needles; be a martyr, go through it 731 *have trouble*, groan 408 *cry*.

378 Touch: sensation of touch

N. *touch*, tactility, palpability; handling, feeling, palpation, manipulation; massage, kneading, squeeze, pressure 333 *friction*; graze, contact 202 *contiguity*; stroke, pat, caress; flick, flip, tap 279 *knock*; precision 494 *accuracy*; artistry 694 *skill*.

tingling, tingle, pins-and-needles, formication; creeps, gooseflesh *or* -bumps *or* -pimples, someone walking over one's grave; scratchiness, itchiness, itch; urticaria, nettlerash, hives, allergic reaction; rash, prickly heat 651 *skin disease*.

feeler, antenna, whisker, tentacle; proboscis, tongue; digit, forefinger, thumb (**see** *finger*); hand, paw, flipper.

finger, forefinger, index, middle finger, ring f., little f., pinkie; thumb, pollex; big toe 214 *foot*;

five fingers, bunch of fives, knuckle sandwich, dukes, fingernail, talon, claw.

Adj. *tactual*, tactile; prehensile; touching, licking, grazing etc. vb.; touchable, tangible, palpable 319 *material*.

handed, right-handed; left-handed; manual.

Vb. *touch*, make contact, come into c.; graze, scrape, shave, brush, glance; kiss 202 *be contiguous*; impinge; hit, meet 279 *collide*; feel, palpate; finger, thumb, pinch, nip, massage 333 *rub*; palm, run the hand over; stroke 258 *smooth*; tap, tip, pat, dab, flick, flip, tickle, scratch; lick; nuzzle, rub noses; paw, fondle 889 *caress*; handle, twiddle, fiddle with, play with; manipulate, wield, ply, manhandle 173 *operate*; jab, poke, goose, bruise, crush 377 *give pain*; grope; put out a feeler 461 *be tentative*.

379 Heat

N. *heat*, radiant heat; convected heat; emission of heat, incandescence, flame, glow, flush, hot flush, blush; warmth, fervour, ardour; tepidity, lukewarmness; specific heat, blood h., body h.; sweat, perspiration, swelter; pyrexia, fever, inflammation 651 *disease*; high temperature, white heat, ebullition, boiling point, flash p., melting p.; tropical heat, sweltering h.; high summer, flaming June, Indian summer; dog days, heat haze 128 *summer*; heat wave, scorcher, sizzler; hot wind, simoom, sirocco; hot springs, thermal s., geyser, hot water, steam; tropics, torrid zone; sun, midday s., sunshine, solar heat 381 *heating*.

fire, flames; bonfire, beacon fire; St Elmo's f. 417 *glow*; hellfire; pyre 364 *obsequies*; coal fire, gas f., electric f., wood-burning stove 383 *furnace*; Greek fire, wild f. 723 *bomb*; conflagration, holocaust; forest fire, bush f.; fireball, blaze, flame, tongue of f., wall of f.; spark, scintillation, flicker, arc 417 *flash*; flare 420 *torch*; eruption, volcano; pyrotechnics; arson 381 *incendiarism*; fire worship 981 *worship*.

thermometry, thermometer, clinical t., Fahrenheit t., centigrade *or* Celsius t., Réaumur t.; feverscan; thermostat; calorimeter; British Thermal Unit, BTU, therm, calorie; thermodynamics; thermography.

Adj. *hot*, heated, superheated; inflamed, fervent, fervid; flaming, glowing, fiery, red-hot, white-h.; hot as hell; piping hot; feverish, febrile, fevered; sweltering, sweating, perspiring; steaming, smoking; dripping with sweat; on the boil, boiling, seething, ebullient, scalding; tropical, torrid, scorching, grilling, broiling, searing, blistering, baking, toasting, roasting etc. vb.; scorched, scalded 381 *heated*; thirsty, burning, parched 342 *dry*.

fiery, burning, blazing, flaming; smoking, smouldering; ablaze, afire, on fire, aflame; candescent, incandescent, glowing, aglow 431 *red*; pyrogenic, igneous; ignited, lit, alight, kindled, volcanic, erupting.

warm, tepid, lukewarm; temperate, mild, genial, balmy; fair, set f., sunny, sunshiny 417 *undimmed*; summery; tropical, equatorial; torrid, sultry; stuffy, close, muggy; overheated, unventilated; oppressive, suffocating, stifling, like a hothouse 653 *insalubrious*; warm as toast; snug 376 *comfortable*; at room temperature, at blood heat.

Vb. *be hot*, be warm, get warm etc. adj.; incandesce; burn, kindle, catch fire, draw; blaze, flare, flame, burst into flame, go up in flames; glow, flush; smoke, smoulder, reek, fume, steam 300 *emit*; boil, seethe 318 *effervesce*; toast, grill, broil, roast, sizzle, crackle, fry, bake 381 *burn*; get burnt, scorch, boil dry; bask, sun oneself, sunbathe; get sunburnt, tan; swelter, sweat, perspire, glow; thaw 337 *liquefy*; parch; suffocate, stifle, pant, gasp for breath, fight for air; be in a fever, be feverish, have a fever, run a temperature; keep warm, wrap up, insulate, keep out the cold.

380 Cold

N. *coldness*, low temperature, drop in t.; cool, coolness, freshness; cold, freezing c., absolute zero; freezing point, frigidity; iciness, frostiness, chilliness, windchill factor, hypothermia, shivering, shivers, chattering of the teeth, chittering, gooseflesh, goose pimples, frostbite, chilblains, chap, hack; chill, common cold, coryza, a cold in the head; cold climate, Siberia, North Pole, South P.; Arctic, Antarctica; snowline, permafrost; Ice Age.

wintriness, winter, hard winter; nip in the air, cold snap; cold front; arctic conditions, degrees of frost; snowstorm, hailstorm, blizzard; frost, touch of f., Jack Frost, rime, hoarfrost, hard frost; sleet, hail, hailstone, black ice, freeze.

snow, snowfall, snowflake; avalanche, snowdrift, snowfield; snowstorm; snow line, snowcap, snowball, snowman; snowplough, snowshoe, snowmobile, snow tyre; winter sports 837 *sport*; snow blindness; snowbound.

ice, ice cube; icicle; ice cap, ice field, ice sheet, ice shelf, floe, ice f., iceberg, tip of the iceberg, glacier, icefall; pack ice; icebreaker, ice yacht; ice house, icebox 384 *refrigerator*; glaciation 382 *refrigeration*.

Adj. *cold*, cool; shady, chilly, parky, nippy, perishing; unheated; fresh, raw, keen, bitter, biting, piercing; freezing, ice-cold; frigid 129 *wintry*; winterbound, frosty, snowy, snow-covered; sleety, icy; glacial, ice-capped, glaciated; boreal, polar, arctic, Siberian.

chilly, shivering, chattering, chittering, shivery, blue with cold; perishing, starved with cold, chilled to the bone, hypothermic, frozen, frostbitten, like ice, cold as charity, cold as marble, stone-cold, cold as death.

Vb. *be cold*, – chilly etc. adj.; grow cold, lose heat, drop in temperature; feel cold, chatter, chitter, shiver, tremble, shake, quake, quiver, shudder; freeze, starve, perish with cold, suffer from hypothermia; catch cold, get a chill; chill 382 *refrigerate*.

381 Heating
N. *heating*, superheating, warming, keeping warm; space heating, central heating 383 *heater*; solar heating, sunning 342 *desiccation*; greenhouse effect; melting, thawing 337 *liquefaction*; smelting, boiling, seething, simmering, ebullition; baking, cooking 301 *cookery*.

burning, combustion; inflammation, kindling, ignition; afterburning; conflagration 379 *fire*; incineration, roasting; cremation 364 *interment*; suttee, self-burning 362 *suicide*; holocaust 981 *oblation*; cauterization, branding; scorching, singeing, charring, inflammability, flammability, combustibility; burner 383 *furnace*; vitriol; branding iron; match, touchpaper 385 *lighter*; burn, scorch mark, brand, sunburn, tan, sunstroke.

arson, fire-raising, pyromania, incendiarism; incendiary, arsonist, fire-raiser, fire-bug.

pottery, ceramics; earthenware, stoneware, lustre ware, glazed w.; majolica, faience, chinaware, porcelain; crockery, china, bone c., Wedgwood (tdmk) c., Spode c., Worcester c., Doulton c., Chelsea c., Staffordshire c., Derby c., Sèvres c., Dresden c.; delft, willow pattern, terracotta; tile, brick, adobe; pot, urn 194 *vessel*; potter's wheel.

Adj. *heated*, superheated 379 *hot*; centrally-heated, winterized, insulated; fired; cooked; warmed up; overheated; steamy, smoky.

heating, warming etc. vb.; calefactory, calorific, solid-fuel, coal-burning, oil-fired, gas-fired; incendiary, inflammatory; inflammable, flammable; anti-freeze.

Vb. *heat*, raise the temperature, warm; winterize, insulate; keep the cold out, take the chill off; hot up, warm up, stoke up; rub one's hands, stamp one's feet; thaw, thaw out; inflame, foment; overheat, stifle, suffocate; parch, shrivel, sear 342 *dry*; roast 301 *cook*; defrost 337 *liquefy*.

kindle, ignite, light, strike a l.; set fire to, light the touchpaper, light the fuse, touch off; add

fuel to the fire, poke the f.; lay the fire, rub two sticks together.

burn, burn up, burn out; consign to the flames; make a bonfire of, send to the stake; fire, set fire to, set on fire, set alight; cremate, incinerate; boil dry 342 *dry*; char, singe, sear, scorch; cauterize, brand; scald.

382 Refrigeration
N. *refrigeration*, cooling, reduction of temperature; icing etc. vb.; freezing, freezing up, glaciation 380 *ice*; solidification 324 *condensation*; exposure; cold storage 384 *refrigerator*; cryonic suspension 364 *interment*; cryogenics, cryosurgery.

extinguisher, fire e.; foam, water, hose, sprinkler, hydrant, standpipe; fire engine, fire truck, fire brigade, fire tender, fire station; fireman, firefighter.

Adj. *cooled*, chilled etc. vb.; ventilated, air-conditioned; iced up; frozen, deep-frozen, freeze-dried; frosted, iced, glacé, frappé; with ice, on the rocks 380 *cold*; cooling etc. vb.; refrigeratory.

Vb. *refrigerate*, cool, air-cool, water-c.; reduce the temperature, turn off the heat; freeze, deep-freeze, freeze-dry; ice up, ice over; chill, benumb, starve, nip, pinch, bite, pierce, chill to the marrow, make one's teeth chatter; expose to the cold, frost-bite.

extinguish, quench, put out, blow o., snuff out; choke, suffocate, stifle, smother 165 *suppress*; damp, douse, damp down, bank d.; stamp out; stub o.; go out, burn o., die down.

383 Furnace
N. *furnace*, fiery f.; the stake 964 *means of execution*; volcano, touchhole, gun barrel; forge, blast furnace; kiln; oasthouse; incinerator, crematorium; brazier, stove, kitchen s., wood-burning s., gas s., electric s., primus s., oil s.; oven, gas o., electric o., microwave o.; range, kitchen r.; cooker, gas c., electric c., split-level c., turbo-fan c., ceramic hob; gas ring, burner, bunsen b.; blowlamp, oxyacetylene lamp; fire, open f., coal f., log f. 379 *fire*; brand 385 *lighter*; fireplace, grate, hearth, ingle; fire-irons, andirons, firedog; poker, tongs, shovel; hob, trivet; fireguard, fender; flue.

heater, space h., paraffin h., radiator, solar panel; hot-air duct, hot-water pipe, immersion heater, geyser, boiler, back b., central-heating b., combi-boiler, copper, kettle, electric k. 194 *pot*; hotplate; warming pan, hot-water bottle; electric blanket; still, retort, crucible 461 *testing agent*; blowpipe, bellows, damper; hot baths, Turkish bath, sauna, Jacuzzi (tdmk) 648 *ablutions*; hotbed, hothouse, greenhouse, conservatory 370 *garden*; sun trap, solarium; kitchen, galley, cookhouse; grill, frying pan, saucepan; toaster, electric t.; iron, flat i., electric i., steam i., soldering i., curling tongs; flame, sunlight 381 *heating*; gas, electricity, solar energy, greenhouse effect 160 *sources of energy*; steam, hot air; wood, coal, peat 385 *fuel*.

384 Refrigerator

N. *refrigerator*, cooler; frigidarium; refrigerating plant, fridge, chiller, wine cooler, ice bucket; coolant, snow, ice; icehouse, icebox, ice pack, ice cubes, rocks; cold storage, freezer, fridge-freezer, cooler cupboard, deep-freeze 382 *refrigeration*.

385 Fuel

N. *fuel*, inflammable material, flammable m., combustible; kindling; wood, brushwood, firewood, faggot, log, Yule l.; turf, peat; lignite, brown coal, charcoal; coal, natural gas, petroleum 357 *oil*, 336 *gas*; nuclear fuel 160 *nucleonics*; petrol, high octane p., two-star, three-s, four-s.; juice, gasoline, gas; diesel oil, derv; biodiesel, alternative fuel; paraffin, kerosene; methylated spirit, North Sea gas, coal g., acetylene, propane, butane, methane.

coal, black diamond, anthracite, briquette; coal dust, slack; coal seam, coal deposit, coalfield 632 *store*; embers; coke; smokeless fuel.

lighter, fire-1., cigarette l., igniter, light, pilot l., illuminant, taper, spill, candle 420 *torch*; fire ship, incendiary bomb 723 *bomb*; touchpaper, match, percussion cap, detonator; safety match, lucifer, vesta, fusee; flint, steel, tinder, touchwood.

386 Taste

N. *taste*, savour; flavour, flavouring; smack, tang, aftertaste; relish, gusto, zest, appetite 859 *liking*; palate, tastebuds.

Adj. *tasty*, palatable, mouth-watering, tempting, appetizing 390 *savoury*; well-seasoned, tangy 388 *pungent*; flavoured, spiced, spicy, herbed, herby, rich, strong, full-bodied, fruity, well-matured, mellow, vintage.

Vb. *taste*, lick one's lips, lick one's fingers 376 *enjoy*; savour, sample, sip, lick, sup, nibble 301 *eat*; have a taste, taste of, savour of, smack of 18 *resemble*; taste good, tickle the palate, tempt the appetite, stimulate the tastebuds 390 *make appetizing*.

387 Insipidity

N. *insipidity*, vapidity, vapidness, tastelessness, wateriness, wershness etc. adj., pap.

Adj. *tasteless*, wersh; vapid, insipid, watery; adulterated 163 *weakened*; wishy-washy; unap-

petizing 391 *unsavoury*; flavourless, unspiced, unseasoned.

388 Pungency

N. *pungency*, piquancy, poignancy, sting, kick, bite, edge; causticity; spiciness, acridity, sharpness, acerbity, acidity 393 *sourness*; roughness, harshness; strength, tang; bad taste 391 *unsavouriness*; salt, brine, pepper, pickle, spice 389 *condiment*; sal volatile, smelling salts 656 *revival*.

tobacco, baccy, snout, nicotine; the weed; tobacco leaf, Virginia tobacco, Turkish t., smoking mixture; snuff; plug, quid, twist; chewing tobacco, nicotine chew, tobacco sachet, tobacco teabag; pipe tobacco, shag; cigar, cigarillo, cheroot, panatella, Havana, corona; smoke, cigarette, cig, ciggie, fag, gasper, coffin-nail; reefer, joint 949 *drug-taking*; filter tip, cork tip, low-tar cigarette, menthol c., roll-up; butt, stub, fag-end, dog-end; tobacco pipe, clay p., churchwarden; briar, corncob; meerschaum; water pipe, hubble-bubble, hookah, narghile; pipe of peace, calumet; bowl, stem; smoker's cough; snuff taker, smoker, pipe s., cigarette s., cigar s., chain s.; smoking, passive s.; tobacconist, cigarette machine; snuff box, cigarette case, cigar c., cigarette box, cigar b.; pipe rack; pipe cleaner, tobacco pouch, tobacco jar, smokeroom; smoker, non-smoker, smoking compartment, smoking zone; smoke-free zone or area.

Adj. *pungent*, strong; stinging, biting 256 *sharp*; caustic, smoky; harsh 259 *rough*; bitter, acrid, tart, astringent 393 *sour*; strong-flavoured, high, gamy, off; highly-seasoned, hot, gingery, peppery, fiery; zesty, tangy, piquant, aromatic 390 *savoury*.

salty, salt, brackish, briny, saline, pickled.

Vb. *season*, salt, marinade, souse, pickle; flavour, spice, herb, season, pepper, devil, curry; smoke, kipper 666 *preserve*.

smoke, smoke a pipe, pull, draw, suck, inhale; puff, blow smoke rings; chain-smoke, smoke like a chimney; chew a quid, suck tobacco sachets; take a pinch.

389 Condiment

N. *condiment*, seasoning, flavouring, dressing, relish, garnish; aspic; salt, garlic s., celery s.; mustard, French m., Dijon m., German m., English m.; pepper, black p., white p., peppercorn; vinegar, malt v., balsamic v. 393 *sourness*; onion, garlic 301 *herb*; curry powder 301 *spice*; vanilla.

sauce, roux; gravy, stock; brown sauce, white s., béchamel; parsley sauce, bread s., tartar s., mint s., horseradish s., sauce piquante; béarnaise sauce; apple sauce, cranberry s. 392 *sweet*

thing; tomato sauce, ketchup; chilli sauce, salsa, Tabasco s. (tdmk), soy s., Worcester s.; chutney, sweet c., mango c., pickles, piccalilli, pickled onions, gherkins; salad dressing, French d., Thousand Island d., mayonnaise, vinaigrette.
Vb. *spice* 388 *season.*

390 Savouriness
N. *savouriness*, tastiness, palatability; gaminess; body, bouquet; savoury, relish, appetizer; delicacy, dainty, titbit 301 *mouthful*; hors d'oeuvre.
Adj. *savoury*, seasoned, flavoured, spicy, herby 386 *tasty*; tempting, appetizing, aromatic, piquant 388 *pungent*; palatable, toothsome; delectable, delicious, choice, epicurean; ambrosial, fit for the gods, fit for a king; scrumptious, yummy, moreish; succulent; gamy, high; full-flavoured.
Vb. *make appetizing*, garnish, spice, pep up 388 *season*; tempt the appetite, tickle the palate, stimulate the tastebuds; smell good, taste good.

391 Unsavouriness
N. *unsavouriness*, unpalatability, sourness, rankness, rottenness, over-ripeness, unwholesomeness 653 *insalubrity*; acerbity, acridity 393 *sourness*; austerity, prison fare, bread and water, nursery fare, iron rations; aloes, rue; bitter pill, gall and wormwood.
Adj. *unsavoury*, tasteless; unpalatable, unappetizing, wersh; underdone, undressed 670 *uncooked*; overdone, burnt, burnt to a cinder, uneatable, inedible; stale, leathery 329 *tough*; soggy 327 *soft*; bitter, acrid, acid 393 *sour*; undrinkable, corked; overripe, rank, rancid, putrid, rotten, gone off, high, stinking 397 *fetid*; revolting, disgusting, loathsome 827 *unpleasant*; nauseating; poisonous 653 *toxic*.
Vb. *be unpalatable*, – unappetizing etc. adj.; disgust, repel, sicken, nauseate, turn the stomach 861 *cause dislike*; poison; pall.

392 Sweetness
N. *sweetness*, sweetening, sugariness, sweet tooth.
sweet thing, sweetening, honey, honeycomb, honeypot; saccharin, sucrose, glucose, dextrose, fructose, lactose, galactose; sugar, cane s., beet s., invert s.; granulated s., caster s., icing s., demerara; molasses, syrup, maple s.; treacle; artificial sweetener; custard, condensed milk; julep, nectar, hydromel, mead; conserve, preserve; candied peel, glacé cherries; jam, marmalade, jelly; marzipan, icing, fondant, sugar coating; fudge, candy, sugar c. 301 *sweets*; jujube, cachou, lozenge, pastille; lollipop, ice cream, candyfloss, rock; confectionery, confection, cake 301 *pastries, dessert*.

Adj. *sweet*, sweetened, honeyed, candied, crystallized; iced, glacé; sugared, sugary, saccharine, melliferous; ambrosial, luscious, delicious 376 *pleasant*; sweet as a nut; cloying; 390 *savoury*.
Vb. *sweeten*, sugar, add sugar, candy, crystallize, ice, glaze; sugar the pill; mull.

393 Sourness
N. *sourness*, acerbity; astringency; tartness, bitterness, vinegariness; sharpness 388 *pungency*; acidity, acidosis; acid, tartar; lemon, lime, vinegar, malt v., white wine v., red wine v., cider v., raspberry v., sherry v., tarragon v., balsamic v.; sloe, crab apple; alum, bitter aloes, bitters; gall, wormwood, absinth.
Adj. *sour*, sourish, acid, acidy, acidulous, acidulated, acetic, tartaric; acerbic, crabbed, tart, bitter; sharp, astringent 388 *pungent*; vinegary 391 *unsavoury*; unripe, green 670 *immature*; sugarless; unsweetened, dry.
Vb. *be sour*, – acid etc. adj.; sour, turn, turn sour; acetify, acidify, acidulate; ferment; set one's teeth on edge.

394 Odour
N. *odour*, smell, aroma, bouquet, nose; perfume, scent, essence 396 *fragrance*; pong, niff, stink 397 *stench*; smoke, fume, reek; whiff; odorousness, redolence; tang, scent 548 *trace*; olfaction, sense of smell; olfactories.
Adj. *odorous*, odoriferous, smelling; scented, perfumed 396 *fragrant*; smelly, redolent, reeking; malodorous, whiffy, niffy, ponging 397 *fetid*.
Vb. *smell*, have an odour, smell of, reek of, reek, pong of, pong; exhale; smell a mile off; smell out, scent, get wind of 484 *detect*; get a whiff of, get a niff of; sniff, inhale 352 *breathe*.

395 Inodorousness
N. *inodorousness*, odourlessness, scentlessness; absence of smell, loss of s.; deodorant, deodorizer, incense, mouthwash; deodorization, fumigation, purification.
Adj. *odourless*, inodorous, scentless; unscented, unperfumed; deodorized; deodorizing.

396 Fragrance
N. *fragrance*, sweet smell, perfume; redolence, aroma, bouquet 394 *odour*; flower garden, rose g. 370 *garden*; buttonhole, nosegay; fumigation; perfumery, perfumer.
scent, perfume, aromatic gum; balm, myrrh, incense, frankincense, spikenard; spicery 389 *condiment*; cloves, cachou; musk, civet, ambergris, camphor; sandalwood, patchouli; essential

oil, otto, attar; lavender, thyme, spearmint, chypre, vanilla, citronella oil; frangipani, bergamot, orris root, tonka bean; honeysuckle, toilet water, eau-de-toilette, lavender water, rose w., attar of roses, eau-de-cologne; scented soap 843 *cosmetic*; lavender bag, pomander, potpourri, scent bottle, joss stick, censer, thurible.

Adj. *fragrant*, redolent, odorous, odoriferous, aromatic, scented, perfumed 376 *pleasant*; balmy; sweet-scented; musky, spicy, fruity.

397 Stench

N. *stench*, fetidity, fetidness; bad smell, bad odour; body odour, BO, armpits; bad breath, halitosis; stink, pong, niff, reek; mephitis; fumes, miasma 336 *gas*; rancidity, putrefaction 51 *decay*; foulness 649 *dirt*; mustiness, fustiness, staleness, fug; fungus, stinkhorn, garlic, asafoetida; hydrogen sulphide, ammonia; skunk, polecat; stink bomb, bad egg; dung 302 *excrement*; latrine, sewer, septic tank 649 *sink*.

Adj. *fetid*, reeking, ill-smelling, malodorous, smelly, whiffy, niffy, pongy, humming; stinking, rank; high; bad, gone b., rancid; putrid; stale, musty, fusty, fuggy, smoky, stuffy, suffocating; foul, noisome, noxious, sulphurous, ammoniacal, miasmic 653 *toxic*; acrid 388 *pungent*.

Vb. *stink*, smell, reek, pong, niff, hum; fart, blow off; have bad breath, have halitosis; have a bad smell, smell bad 51 *decompose*; stink to high heaven; smell like a bad egg, stink out.

398 Sound

N. *sound*, audibility, reception 415 *hearing*; sounding, sonancy; audio, mono, monophonic sound, binaural s., stereophonic s., stereo, quadraphonic sound, surround-sound system; sound waves, vibrations 417 *radiation*; sound effect; sound track, voice-over; sonority, sonorousness 404 *resonance*; noise, loud sound 400 *loudness*; softness 401 *faintness*; tone, pitch, level, cadence; accent, intonation, twang, timbre 577 *voice*; tune, strain 410 *melody*, 412 *music*; types of sound 402 *bang*, 403 *roll*, 404 *resonance*, 405 *nonresonance*, 406 *sibilation*, 407 *stridor*, 408 *cry*, 409 *ululation*, 411 *discord*; transmission, telephone, cellular t., radio 531 *telecommunication*; recorded sound, high fidelity, hi-fi; record-player 414 *gramophone*; ghetto blaster, personal stereo; loudspeaker 415 *hearing aid*; decibel, phon, sone; sonic barrier, sound b.

speech sound, phone, syllable, polysyllable; consonant, fricative, plosive, sibilant; dental, alveolar, labial, nasal, palatal, guttural, glottal stop; click; aspirate, surd; semivowel; glide; vowel, diphthong 577 *voice*; ablaut; umlaut; voc-

able 559 *word*; International Phonetic Alphabet, IPA 586 *script*.

Adj. *sounding*, sonic; supersonic; audible, distinct; resounding, sonorous 404 *resonant*; stentorian 400 *loud*; auditory, acoustic; monaural, monophonic, mono; binaural, stereophonic, stereo, high fidelity, hi-fi; audio, audiovisual; phonic, phonetic; voiced; unvoiced, voiceless.

399 Silence

N. *silence*, soundlessness, inaudibility, total silence, not a sound, not a squeak; stillness, hush, lull, rest, peace, quiet 266 *quiescence*; taciturnity, muteness, speechlessness 578 *voicelessness*; solemn silence, dead s., perfect s., uncanny s., deathly hush; enforced silence, gagging order.

Adj. *silent*, still, hushed; calm, peaceful, quiet 266 *quiescent*; soft, faint 401 *muted*; noiseless, soundless, inaudible; soundproof; speechless, taciturn, mute 578 *voiceless*; unspoken; silent as the grave.

Vb. *be silent*, not open one's mouth, not say a word, hold one's tongue 582 *be taciturn*; not speak 578 *be mute*; make not a sound, not utter a squeak; become silent, relapse into silence, pipe down, be quiet, lose one's voice, fall silent.

silence, still, lull, hush, quiet, quieten, make silent; soft-pedal; stifle, muffle, gag, stop, stop someone's mouth, muzzle; drown the noise.

Int. hush! sh! silence! quiet! peace! soft! whist! hold your tongue! keep your mouth shut! shut up! keep your trap shut! dry up! pipe down! cut the cackle! stow it! mum's the word!

400 Loudness

N. *loudness*, audibility; noise; high volume; broken silence, shattered s., knock, knocking; burst of sound, report; sonic boom, slam, clap, thunderclap, burst, shell b., explosion 402 *bang*; siren, alarm, honk, toot 665 *danger signal*; reverberation, boom, rattle 403 *roll*; thunder 176 *storm*; war in heaven, hissing 406 *sibilation*; gunfire, artillery, blitz 712 *bombardment*; shrillness, blast, blare, bray, fanfare, flourish 407 *stridor*; trumpet blast, clarion call, view halloo 547 *call*; sonority, clang 404 *resonance*; bells, peal, chimes; crescendo, fortissimo, full blast; clamour, outcry, roaring, shouting, bawling, yelling, screaming, whoop, shout, howl, shriek, scream, roar 408 *cry*, 409 *ululation*; cachinnation 835 *laughter*; stertorousness 352 *respiration*; noisiness, din, row; racket, crash, clash, clatter, hubbub, hullabaloo, ballyhoo, song and dance, slamming, banging, stamping, chanting, hooting, uproar, stramash, shemozzle, tumult, bedlam, pandemonium, all hell let loose 61 *turmoil*.

megaphone, amplifier, loud pedal; public address system, loudhailer, loudspeaker, speaker, microphone, mike; ear trumpet 415 *hearing aid*; loud instrument, whistle, siren, ghetto blaster; town crier.

Adj. *loud*, audible; at full volume, at full pitch, at the top of one's voice; noisy, uproarious, rowdy, rumbustious 61 *disorderly*; clamorous, shouting, yelling, whooping, screaming, bellowing; sonorous, booming, full-throated, stentorian, ringing, carrying; deafening; dinning; piercing, ear-splitting, thunderous, rattling, crashing; pealing, shrill 407 *strident*; blaring; crescendo; fortissimo, enough to waken the dead.

Vb. *be loud*, – noisy etc. adj.; break the silence; raise the voice, caterwaul; skirl, scream, whistle 407 *shrill*; shout 408 *cry*; cachinnate 835 *laugh*; clap, stamp, raise the roof, raise the rafters; roar, bellow, howl 409 *ululate*; din, sound, boom; rattle, thunder, fulminate, storm, clash; ring, peal, clang, crash; bray, blare; slam 402 *bang*; explode, detonate; knock, hammer, drill; deafen, stun; shatter the eardrums, ring in the ear; waken the dead; raise Cain, kick up a shindy 61 *rampage*.

Adv. *loudly*, distinctly etc. adj.; noisily, aloud, at the top of one's voice; in full cry, full blast; fortissimo, crescendo.

401 Faintness

N. *faintness*, softness, indistinctness, inaudibility; low volume, sound-proofing, noise abatement; thud, thump, bump 405 *nonresonance*; whisper, bated breath; muffled tones 578 *voicelessness*; undertone; murmur, hum, drone 403 *roll*; sigh, sough, moan; scratch, squeak, creak, tick, click; tinkle, clink, chink; buzz, whirr; purr, swish; burble, gurgle; rustle, frou-frou; patter, pitter-p., pit-a-pat; soft footfall, pad; quiet tone, hushed tones, conversation level.

Adj. *muted*, distant, faint, inaudible, barely audible, sotto voce; half-heard; weak, feeble, unemphatic, unstressed, unaccented; soft, low, gentle, piano, subdued, hushed, stealthy, whispered; dull; muffled, suppressed, stifled, bated 407 *hoarse*.

Vb. *sound faint*, lower one's voice; whisper, breathe, murmur, mutter; hum; croon, purr; buzz, drone; babble, ripple, lap, gurgle 350 *flow*; tinkle, chime; moan, sigh, sough 352 *blow*; rustle, swish; tremble, melt; float on the air; fade away; squeak, creak; tick, click; clink, chink; thud, thump.

mute, soften, dull, deaden, dampen, soft-pedal; turn down the volume; hush, muffle, stifle 399 *silence*.

402 Bang: sudden and violent noise

N. *bang*, report, explosion, detonation, blast, blowout, backfire, sonic boom; peal, thunderclap, crash 400 *loudness*; crackle; smack, crack, snap; slap, clap, tap, rap, rat-tat-tat; thump, knock, slam; pop; burst, burst of fire, firing, volley, round, salvo; shot, pistol-s.; cracker, banger, squib.

Vb. *crackle*, sizzle, spit 318 *effervesce*; crack, split; click, rattle; snap, clap, rap, tap, slap, smack.

bang, slam, wham, clash, crash, boom; explode, blast, detonate; pop, go p.; backfire; burst.

403 Roll: repeated and protracted sounds

N. *roll*, rumbling, grumbling; mutter, witter, murmur, background m., rhubarb rhubarb, blahblah; din, rattle, racket, clack, clatter, chatter; booming, clang, ping, reverberation 404 *resonance*; chugging; knocking, drumming, tattoo; rub-a-dub, rat-a-tat, pit-a-pat; peal, carillon; dingdong, tick-tock, cuckoo 106 *repetition*; trill, tremolo, vibrato 410 *musical note*; quaver; hum, whirr, buzz, drone; ringing, singing; drumfire, barrage, cannonade.

Vb. *roll*, drum, tattoo, beat a t.; tap, thrum; chug, rev up, vroom; drum in the ear; boom, roar, din in the ear; grumble, rumble, drone, hum, whirr; trill, chime, peal, toll; tick, beat 317 *oscillate*; rattle, chatter, clatter, clack; reverberate, clang, ping, ring, sing, sing in the ear; quaver, shake, tremble, vibrate; patter 401 *sound faint*.

404 Resonance

N. *resonance*, sonorousness; vibration 317 *oscillation*; reverberation; echo 106 *recurrence*; twanging; ringing, ringing in the ear, tinnitus; singing, bell ringing, tintinnabulation; peal, carillon; sonority, boom; clang, peal, blare, bray; sounding brass, tinkling cymbal; tinkle, jingle; chink, clink; ping, ring, ting-a-ling, chime; low note 410 *musical note*; bass, baritone, basso profondo, bass contralto.

Adj. *resonant*, vibrant, reverberant, reverberative; carrying 400 *loud*; resounding etc. vb.; booming, echoing, lingering, sonorous; ringing, tintinnabulary; deep-toned; booming, hollow, sepulchral.

Vb. *resound*, vibrate, reverberate, echo 403 *roll*; whirr, buzz; hum, ring in the ear, sing; ping, ring, ding; jingle, jangle, chink, clink, clank, clunk; ting, tinkle; twang, thrum; gong, chime, tintinnabulate; tootle, toot, trumpet, blare, bray 400 *be loud*.

405 Nonresonance
N. *nonresonance*, nonvibration, thud, thump, bump; plump, plop, plonk, plunk; cracked bell 411 *discord*; muffled sound, muffled drums 401 *faintness*; mute, damper.

406 Sibilation: hissing sound
N. *sibilation*, sibilance, hissing, hiss; sibilant; sputter, splutter; splash, rustle, frou-frou 407 *stridor*; squelch, squish; swish, swoosh.

Vb. *hiss*, sibilate; snort, wheeze, snuffle, whistle; buzz, fizz, fizzle, sizzle, sputter, splutter; spit; splash 318 *effervesce*; swish, swoosh, whizz; squelch, squish, suck; rustle 407 *rasp*.

407 Stridor: harsh sound
N. *stridor*, stridency, discordance, cacophony 411 *discord*; roughness, raucousness, hoarseness, huskiness, gruffness; guttural; squeakiness, rustiness 333 *friction*; scrape, scratch, jarring, creak, squeak; stridulation; shriek, screech, squawk, yawp, yelp, braying 409 *ululation*; high pitch, shrillness, piping, whistling, wolf whistle; bleep; piercing note, sharp n. 410 *musical note*; soprano, treble, falsetto, tenor, countertenor; nasality, twang, drone; skirl, brass, blare.

Adj. *strident*, grating, rusty, creaky, creaking, jarring (**see** *hoarse*); harsh, metallic; high-pitched, acute, shrill, bleeping; piercing, tinny, ear-splitting 400 *loud*; blaring, braying; reedy, squeaky, squawky, screechy, scratchy; cracked; cacophonous 411 *discordant*.

hoarse, husky, throaty, guttural, raucous, rough, gruff; rasping, jarring, scraping, creaking; grunting, growling; hollow, deep, sepulchral; snoring, stertorous.

Vb. *rasp*, grate, crunch, scrunch, grind, saw, scrape, scratch, squeak; snore, snort; cough, hawk, clear the throat, hem, choke, gasp, sob; bray, croak, caw, screech 409 *ululate*; grunt, burr, break (of the voice); jar, grate on the ear, set the teeth on edge, clash, jangle, twang, clank, clink 411 *discord*.

shrill, bleep; drone, skirl; trumpet, blare 400 *be loud*; whistle, catcall, caterwaul 408 *cry*; scream, squeal, yelp, yawl, screech, squawk; buzz, hum, whine 409 *ululate*; go right through one; strain one's vocal chords.

408 Human cry
N. *cry*, animal cry 409 *ululation*; exclamation, ejaculation 577 *voice*; utterances 579 *speech*; talk, chat, chitchat, conversation 584 *interlocution*; raised voice, vociferousness, shouting, clamour, hullabaloo 400 *loudness*; yodel, song, chant, chorus 412 *vocal music*; shout, yell, whoop, bawl; howl, scream, shriek, screech 407 *stridor*, 377 *pain*; halloo, hail 547 *call*; view halloo, tallyho, hue and cry 619 *chase*; cheer, hurrah, hip-hip-hurrah, hooray 835 *rejoicing*; laugh, giggle, titter 835 *laughter*; hoot, boo, guffaw 924 *disapprobation*; sob, sigh 836 *lamentation*; caterwaul, yawl, squeal, wail, whine, boohoo; grunt, gasp 352 *respiration*; cheerleader; barker; town crier.

Vb. *cry*, cry out, exclaim, ejaculate, pipe up 579 *speak*; call, call out, hail 884 *greet*; whoop; hoot, boo, whistle 924 *disapprove*; cheer, hurrah (**see** *vociferate*); scream, screech, yawl, yowl, howl, groan 377 *feel pain*; snigger, titter, giggle 835 *laugh*; caterwaul, squall, boohoo, whine, whimper, wail, fret, mewl, pule 836 *weep*; yammer, moan, sob, sigh 836 *lament*; mutter, grumble 401 *sound faint*, 829 *be discontented*; gasp, grunt, snort, snore 352 *breathe*; squeak, squawk, yap, bark 409 *ululate*.

vociferate, clamour, shout, bawl, yell, yawl, yowl, holler; chant, chorus 413 *sing*; cheer, give three cheers, hurrah, hooray, huzza, exult 835 *rejoice*; hiss, hoot, boo, shout down 924 *disapprove*; roar, bellow 409 *ululate*; yell, cry out, sing o., thunder o.; raise the voice, give v., strain one's voice, make oneself hoarse, shout at the top of one's voice.

409 Ululation: animal sounds
N. *ululation*, howling, wailing, yowling, yawling; barking, baying; buzzing, humming, drone; chattering, twittering, chirping, chirruping; warble, call, cry, note, woodnote, birdsong; squeak, cheep, twitter, tweet-tweet; buzz, hum; croak, caw, coo, hiss, quack, cluck, squawk, screech, yawp; baa, moo, neigh, whinny, heehaw; cock-a-doodle-doo, cuckoo, tu-whit tu-whoo; miaow, mew, bark, yelp, yap, snap, snarl, growl. **See** *ululate*.

Vb. *ululate*, cry, call, give tongue; squawk, screech, yawp; caterwaul, yowl, yawl, howl, wail; roar, bellow, bell; hum, drone, buzz, spit 406 *hiss*; woof, bark, bay; yelp, yap; snap, snarl, growl, whine; trumpet, bell, troat; bray, neigh, whinny, whicker; bleat, baa; low, moo; miaow, mew, mewl, purr; quack, cackle, gaggle; gobble, gabble, cluck, clack; grunt, gruntle, snort, squeal; pipe, pule; chatter, sing, chirp, chirrup, cheep, peep, tweet, twitter, chuckle, churr, whirr, coo; caw, croak; hoot, honk, boom; grate, squeak 407 *rasp*; warble, carol, whistle 413 *sing*.

410 Melody: concord
N. *melody*, musicalness, melodiousness, tonality, euphony, euphoniousness;

harmoniousness, chime, harmony, concord, concert 24 *agreement*; assonance; unison; resolution (of a discord), cadence, perfect c.; harmonics, harmonization, counterpoint; part, second, chorus; orchestration, instrumentation; tone; phrasing; passage, theme, leitmotiv, coda; movement 412 *musical piece*.

musical note, note, keys, keyboard, manual; black notes, white n., sharp, flat, double f., double sharp, accidental, natural, tone, semitone; keynote, fundamental note; tonic, supertonic, mediant, subdominant, dominant, submediant, subtonic, leading note; interval, second, third, fourth, fifth, sixth, seventh, octave, ninth; diatesseron, diapason; gamut, scale (**see** *key*); chord, common c., triad, tetrachord, arpeggio; grace note, grace, ornament, crush note, appoggiatura, acciaccatura, mordent, turn, shake, trill, tremolo, vibrato, cadenza; tone, tonality, register, pitch, concert p., high p., low p.; high note 407 *stridor*; low note 404 *resonance*; undertone, overtone, harmonic, upper partial; sustained note, monotone, drone.

notation, musical n., tonic solfa; score; signature, key s., clef, treble c., bass c., tenor c., alto c.; bar, stave, staff; line, ledger l., space, brace; rest, pause, interval; breve, semibreve, minim, crotchet, quaver, semiquaver, demisemiquaver, hemidemisemiquaver.

tempo, time, beat; rhythm 593 *prosody*; measure, timing; syncopation; upbeat, downbeat; suspension, long note, short n., suspended n.; prolonged n.; tempo rubato; rallentando, andante, adagio; metronome.

key, signature, clef, modulation, transposition, major key, minor k.; scale, gamut, major scale, minor s., diatonic s., chromatic s., harmonic s., melodic s., enharmonic s., twelvetone s.; series, tone row; mode, Lydian m., Phrygian m., Dorian m., mixolydian; Indian mode, raga.

Adj. *melodious*, melodic, musical, lyrical, lilting, tuneful, catchy, tripping; dulcet, mellifluous, sweet-sounding; chiming; silver-toned; golden-toned; euphonious, euphonic.

harmonious, harmonizing, consonant 24 *agreeing*; in pitch; in chorus; assonant, rhyming, matching 18 *similar*; symphonic, symphonious.

Vb. *harmonize*, blend 24 *accord*; chorus 413 *sing*; attune, tune, tune up, pitch, string 24 *adjust*; be in key, be in unison, be on the beat; compose, put to music, set to music, score, symphonize, orchestrate 413 *compose music*; modulate, transpose.

411 Discord

N. *discord*, discordance, dissonance, disharmony, jangle 25 *disagreement*; atonality, twelvetone scale; imperfect cadence; preparation (of a discord); harshness, hoarseness, jarring, cacophony; Babel, cat's concert, caterwauling, yowling 400 *loudness*; row, din, noise, pandemonium, bedlam, tumult, racket 61 *turmoil*; atmospherics, wow.

Adj. *discordant*, dissonant, jangling, discording 25 *disagreeing*; conflicting 14 *contrary*; jarring, grating, scraping, rasping, harsh, raucous, cacophonous 407 *strident*; inharmonious; unmelodious, unmusical; untuned, cracked; off pitch, off key, out of tune, sharp, flat; atonal, toneless, tuneless, droning, singsong.

Vb. *discord*, lack harmony 25 *disagree*; jangle, jar, grate, clash, crash; saw, scrape 407 *rasp*; be harsh, be out of tune, be off key; play sharp, play flat; thrum, drone, whine; prepare a discord.

412 Music

N. *music*, harmony; 410 *melody*; musicianship 413 *musical skill*; minstrelsy, music-making, playing; strumming, thrumming, vamping; improvisation; orchestration, instrumentation, composing, composition; instrumental music, pipe m., military m.; counterpoint, contrapuntal music; classical music, chamber m., organ m., choral m., operatic m., ballet m., sacred m., soul m.; light music, popular m., pop m., pop, indie p., Britpop, bhangra; descriptive music, programme m.; house, acid h., gabba, garage, electronic music, techno, trance, musique concrète; live music, recorded music, canned m., piped m., musical wallpaper, wall-to-wall m., Muzak (tdmk), ambient music; disco music, dance m., waltztime; hot music, syncopation, jazz, progressive j., modern j., cool j., acid j., blue note, blues, mainstream jazz, traditional j., trad, Dixieland, ragtime, swing, swingbeat, doowop, bebop, bop, boogie-woogie; salsa, skiffle, jive, rock 'n roll, rock music, hard r., soft r., heavy metal, black m., grunge, goth, jungle, jazz-funk, electro, hip-hop, new wave, mod, punk; ska, reggae; soul; rhythm 'n blues, country and western, blue grass, folk; sheet music, the music, score, full s.; concert, orchestral c., choral c., promenade c., prom; singsong; music festival, eisteddfod, mod; conservatoire; Tin Pan Alley, Nashville.

tune, melody, strain; theme song, signature tune; descant; reprise, refrain; melodic line; air, popular a., aria, solo; peal, chime, carillon; phrase, passage, measure.

musical piece, piece, composition, opus, work; tape, cassette, recording 414 *gramophone*; orchestration, instrumentation; arrangement, adaptation, setting, transcription; accompaniment, obbligato; voluntary, prelude, overture, intermezzo, finale; incidental music, background m., wallpaper m., wall-to-wall m.; romance, rhapsody, extravaganza, impromptu, fantasia, caprice, divertissement, variations, raga; medley, potpourri; étude, study; suite, fugue, canon, toccata; sonata, sonatina, concerto, symphony, sinfonietta; symphonic poem, tone p.; pastorale, scherzo, rondo, gigue, jig, reel, strathspey; gavotte, minuet, tarantella, mazurka, polonaise, polka, waltz 837 *dance*; march, grand m., bridal m., wedding m., dead m., funeral m., dirge, pibroch; nocturne, serenade, berceuse, lullaby; introductory phrase, anacrusis; statement, exposition, development, recapitulation, variation; theme, motive, leitmotiv; movement; passage, phrase; chord 410 *musical note*; cadenza, coda.

vocal music, singing, vocalism, lyricism; vocalization; part; opera, operetta, light opera, comic o., musical comedy, musical 594 *stage play*; choir-singing, oratorio, cantata, chorale; hymn-singing, psalmody, hymnology; descant, chant, plain c., Gregorian c., Ambrosian c., plainsong; cantus, c. firmus, recitative; bel canto, coloratura, bravura; solfège, solfa; introit, anthem, canticle, psalm 981 *hymn*; song, lay, roundelay, carol, lyric, lilt; canzonet, cavatina, lieder, lied, ballad; folk song, popular *or* pop s., rap, gangsta; top twenty, hit parade, the charts; karaoke, ditty, shanty, calypso; spiritual, blues; part song, glee, madrigal, round, catch, canon; chorus, refrain, burden; choral hymn, antiphony, dithyramb; boat song, barcarole; lullaby, cradle song, berceuse; serenade, aubade; bridal hymn, wedding h., epithalamium, prothalamium; love song, amorous ditty; song, birdsong, bird call, dawn chorus; requiem, dirge, threnody, coronach 836 *lament*; musical declamation, recitative; lyrics, libretto; songbook, hymnbook, psalter.

Adj. *musical* 410 *melodious*; philharmonic, symphonic; melodic; vocal, hummable; operatic, recitative; lyric; choral; hymnal, psalmodic; harmonized 410 *harmonious*; contrapuntal; orchestrated, scored; set to music, arranged; instrumental, orchestral, for strings; syncopated; doo-wop.

Adv. *adagio*, lento, largo, larghetto, andante, andantino, maestoso, moderato; allegro, allegretto; spiritoso, vivace, accelerando, presto, prestissimo; piano, mezzo-p., pianissimo, forte, mezzo-f., fortissimo, sforzando, con brio, capriccioso, scherzando; glissando, legato, sostenuto; staccato; crescendo, diminuendo, rallentando; affettuoso, cantabile, parlante; tremolo, pizzicato, vibrato; rubato; da capo.

413 Musician

N. *musician*, artiste, virtuoso, soloist; bravura player 696 *proficient person*; player, performer, concert artist; bard, minstrel, troubadour, trovatore, minnesinger; street musician, busker; composer, symphonist, contrapuntist; scorer, arranger, harmonist; syncopator, jazzman; librettist, lyricist, liederwriter, hymnwriter, hymnographer, psalmist; musical director, music teacher, music master, kapellmeister, master of the music, bandmaster, conductor (**see** *orchestra*); musicologist, musicotherapist, music critic, concertgoer, operagoer 504 *enthusiast*.

instrumentalist, pianist, accompanist; organist, cembalist, harpsichordist, accordionist, concertina player, harmonica p.; violinist, fiddler; violist, cellist; harpist, lyre player, lute p., lutanist, sitarist, guitarist, bassist, mandolinist, banjoist; strummer, thrummer; piper, fifer, piccolo player, flautist, flutist, clarinettist, oboist, bassoonist; saxophonist, horn player, trumpeter, bugler; cornetist; bell ringer, carilloneur, campanologist; drummer, drummer boy, drum major; percussionist, timpanist; organgrinder, hurdy-gurdy man.

orchestra, symphony o., chamber o., sinfonietta, quartet, quintet; ensemble, wind e.; strings, brass, woodwind, percussion, drums; band, string b., jazz b., ragtime b.; brass b., military b., pipe b.; skiffle group, steel band; rock b. *or* group, punk b. *or* g., pop g.; conductor, maestro, bandmaster; bandleader, leader, first violin; orchestra player, bandsman.

vocalist, singer, songster, caroller; chanteuse, songstress; troubadour, madrigal singer, minstrel, busker; ballad singer, folk s., pop s.; crooner, jazz singer, blues s.; opera singer, prima donna, diva; castrato; treble, soprano, mezzo-s., contralto, alto, tenor, counter-tenor, baritone, bass b., bass, basso, basso profondo.

choir, chorus, waits, wassailers, carol singers, glee club, barbershop quartet; massed choirs, eisteddfod; chorister, choirboy *or* -girl; precentor, cantor, choirmaster, choirleader.

Vb. *compose music*, compose; set to music, score, arrange, transpose, orchestrate, harmonize, improvise, extemporize.

play music, play, perform, execute, render, interpret; pick out a tune; conduct, wield the baton, beat time, syncopate; play the piano, accompany; pedal, vamp, strum; tickle the ivories; harp, pluck, pick, strike the lyre, pluck the guitar, bottleneck; thrum, twang; fiddle, bow, scrape, saw; play the concertina, squeeze the box, grind the organ; play the harmonica; wind, wind the horn, blow, bugle, blow the b., sound the horn, sound, trumpet, sound the t., toot, tootle; pipe, flute, whistle; clash the cymbals; drum, tattoo, beat, tap, ruffle, beat the drum 403 *roll*; ring, peal the bells, ring a change; toll, knell; tune, string, set to concert pitch; practise, do scales, improvise, jam, extemporize, play a voluntary, prelude; strike up.

sing, chant; intone, descant; warble, carol, lilt, trill, croon, hum, whistle, yodel; belt out; harmonize; chorus; serenade; chirp, chirrup, twitter, pipe 409 *ululate*; purr 401 *sound faint*.

414 Musical instruments

N. *musical instrument*, band, concert 413 *orchestra*; strings, brass, wind, woodwind, percussion; sounding board, diaphragm, sound box; synthesizer.

stringed instrument, harp, Aeolian harp; lyre, lute, sitar; theorbo; cithara, cithern, zither, gittern, guitar, acoustic g., semi-acoustic g., electric g., mandolin, ukulele, banjo, balalaika, zither; psaltery, vina; plectrum, fret.

viol, violin, Cremona, Stradivarius, fiddle, kit, crowd, rebec; viola *or* tenor violin, viola d'amore, viola da gamba *or* bass viol, cello *or* violoncello, double bass *or* contrabasso; musical saw; bow, fiddlestick; string, catgut; bridge; resin.

piano, pianoforte, grand piano, concert grand, baby g.; upright piano, cottage p.; virginals, dulcimer, harpsichord, cembalo, spinet, clavichord, celesta; piano-organ, player piano, Pianola (tdmk); clavier, keyboard, manual, keys, ivories; loud pedal, soft p., damper.

organ, pipe o., church o., Hammond o., electric *or* electronic o., steam o., calliope; reed organ, harmonium, American organ, melodeon; mouth organ, harmonica; kazoo, comb; accordion, piano a., concertina; barrel organ, hurdy-gurdy; great organ, swell o., choir o.; organ pipe, flue p., organ stop, flue s.; manual, keyboard.

flute, fife, piccolo, flageolet, cornetto, recorder; woodwind, reed instrument, clarinet, bass c., basset horn; saxophone, sax, tenor s.; shawm, hautboy, oboe, tenor o., cor Anglais; bassoon, double b.; ocarina; pipe, oaten p., reed, straw; chanter, bagpipes, musette; pan pipes, Pandean p., syrinx; nose flute; whistle, penny w., tin w.; pitch-pipe; bazooka; mouthpiece, embouchure.

horn, brass; bugle horn, post h., hunting h.; bugle, trumpet, clarion; alpenhorn, French horn, flugelhorn, saxhorn, althorn, helicon horn, bass h.; sousaphone; euphonium, ophicleide, serpent, bombardon; cornet, trombone, sackbut, tuba, saxtuba, bass tuba; conch, shell.

gong, bell, tintinnabulum; treble bell, tenor b.; church bell, alarm bell, tocsin 665 *danger signal*; tintinnabulation, peal, carillon, chimes, bells; bones, rattle, clappers, castanets, maracas; cymbals; xylophone, marimba; vibraphone, vibes; musical glasses, harmonica; tubular bell, glockenspiel; triangle; tuning fork; Jew's harp; sounding board; percussion instrument.

drum, big d., bass d., tenor d., side d., snare d., kettle d., timpani, steel drum; war drum, tomtom, bongo; tabor, tambourine; tabla.

gramophone, record player, phonograph, radiogram; tape recorder, cassette r., high-fidelity system, hi-fi, stereo set, stereo system, music centre, stack system, stereo tower, hi-fi t.; personal stereo, personal hi-fi, personal headset, Walkman (tdmk), ghetto blaster, compact disc player, CD player, playback; recording, tape r., tape, cassette; gramophone record, disc, compact d., CD laser d., platter, long-playing record, LP; EP, 33, 45, 78; album, single, track; jukebox; head, needle, stylus, pickup, cartridge; deck, turntable; amplifier, speaker, tweeter, woofer.

415 Hearing

N. *hearing*, audition; sense of hearing, acute hearing; good ear, sharp e., ear for music; audibility, good reception; earshot, range, reach.

listening, hearkening 455 *attention*; aural examination 459 *enquiry*; listening-in; lip-reading 520 *interpretation*; eavesdropping, wiretapping, bugging 523 *latency*; sound recording 548 *record*; audition, voice testing 461 *experiment*; interview, audience, hearing 584 *conference*; legal hearing 959 *legal trial*.

listener, hearer, audience, auditorium; stalls. pit, gallery, the gods, bums or seats 441 *spectator*; radio listener, radio ham, CB user; hi-fi enthusiast, audiophile; disciple, lecture-goer 538 *learner*; monitor, auditor, examiner 459 *questioner*; eavesdropper, listener-in, little pitcher.

ear, lug, lobe, earhole, lughole; external ear, middle e., internal e.; aural cavity, cochlea, eardrum, tympanum; auditory canal, labyrinth; otology; aurist, otologist, otolaryngologist, otorhinolaryngologist, ENT specialist, ear, nose and throat s.; Ménière's disease.

hearing aid, deaf-aid, ear trumpet; stethoscope, otoscope, auriscope; loudspeaker, loudhailer, Tannoy (tdmk), public address system 528 *publication*; microphone, mike, amplifier 400 *megaphone*; speaking tube; telephone, phone, cellular telephone, car t., mobile t., blower; receiver, handset, earpiece, extension, headphones, headset, earphones; walkie-talkie 531 *telecommunication*; sound recorder, asdic, sonar, Dictaphone (tdmk), Dictograph (tdmk) 549 *recording instrument*; radiogram 414 *gramophone*, 531 *broadcasting*.

Adj. *auditory*, hearing, auricular, aural; audio-visual 398 *sounding*; otic, otological, stethoscopic; auditive, acoustic, audile, within earshot, within hearing distance, audible.

Vb. *hear*, catch; list, listen, lip-read 520 *interpret*; listen in, switch on, tune in, tune to; lift the receiver, answer the phone; overhear, eavesdrop, listen at keyholes, keep one's ears open; intercept, bug, tap; hearken, lend an ear, give audience, interview, grant an interview 459 *interrogate*; hear confession 526 *confess*; be all ears, hang on the lips of, lap up 455 *be attentive*; strain one's ears, prick up one's e.; hear it said, hear it on *or* through the grapevine, come to one's ears 524 *be informed*.

416 Deafness

N. *deafness*, defective hearing, imperfect h., hardness of hearing; deaf-mutism; deaf-and-dumb speech, sign language, dactylogy; deaf-and-dumb person, deaf-mute; inaudibility 399 *silence*.

Adj. *deaf*, hard of hearing, dull of h., hearing-impaired, profoundly deaf, stone-deaf, deaf as a post, deaf and dumb, deaf-mute; deafened, unable to hear, with ears bunged up; deaf to, not listening 456 *inattentive*; tone-deaf; inaudible, out of earshot, out of hearing 399 *silent*.

Vb. *be deaf*, hear nothing, fail to catch; not listen, shut one's ears, close one's e., plug one's e. 458 *disregard*; turn a deaf ear to 760 *refuse*; have hearing difficulties, have impaired hearing, be hard of hearing, use a hearing aid; lip-read, use lip-reading 520 *translate*; talk with one's fingers, use sign language.

deafen, make deaf, split the eardrum, drown one's voice 400 *be loud*.

417 Light

N. *light*, daylight, light of day, noon, high n., broad daylight 128 *morning*; sunbeam, sunlight, sun 420 *luminary*; starlight, moonlight, moonshine, half-light, twilight, gloaming 419 *dimness*; artificial light, electric light, gaslight, candlelight, firelight 420 *lighting*; floodlight, son et lumière; illumination, irradiation, splendour, resplendence, effulgence, refulgence, intensity, brightness, vividness, brilliance; luminousness, luminosity, luminance, candle power, magnitude; incandescence, radiance; sheen, shine, gloss, polish, lustre (**see** *reflection*); blaze, blaze of light; glare, dazzle; flare, flame 379 *fire*; halo, nimbus, aureole; spectrum, iridescence, rainbow 437 *variegation*.

flash, lightning; beam, stream, shaft, ray; streak, meteor flash; scintillation, sparkle, spark; glint, glitter, glisten, play of light; blink,

twinkle, twinkling, flicker, flickering, glimmer, gleam, shimmer, shimmering; spangle, tinsel; strobe light, searchlight, torchlight 420 *lamp*; firefly.

glow, flush, afterglow, dawn, rosy-fingered d., sunset; lambent light; aurora, aurora borealis, aurora australis; northern lights; zodiacal light 321 *heavens*; radiance, incandescence 379 *heat*; luminescence, fluorescence, phosphorescence, thermoluminescence; will-o'-the-wisp.

radiation, emission, absorption; radioactivity, irradiation 160 *nucleonics*; radioisotope; Geiger counter; fallout, nuclear f., mushroom cloud 659 *poison*; radiation belt, Van Allen layer 340 *atmosphere*; radio wave, frequency w.; long w., short w., medium w. 317 *oscillation*; wavelength, waveband; high frequency, VHF, UHF; interference, static 160 *electricity*; electromagnetic radiation, microwave; infrared radiation, radiant heat *or* energy; ultraviolet radiation; X-ray, gamma r., cosmic radiation; magnetic storm; photon; photoelectric cell; curie, millicurie, roentgen, rem, rad; half-life, radiology, industrial r., medical r., diagnostic r., radiotherapy; food irradiation.

reflection, refraction; diffraction, dispersion, scattering, interference, polarization; polish, gloss, sheen, shine, glisten, gleam, lustre; glare, dazzle, blink.

Adj. *luminous*, lucid; light, lit, well-lit, floodlit, bright, gay, shining, fulgent, resplendent, splendid, brilliant, flamboyant, vivid; colourful; radiant, effulgent, refulgent; dazzling, blinding, glaring, lurid, garish; incandescent, flaring, flaming, aflame, aglow, afire, ablaze 379 *fiery*; glowing, blushing, auroral 431 *red*; luminescent, fluorescent, phosphorescent; soft, lambent, beaming; glittery, flashing, glinting etc. vb.; scintillating, sparkling; lustrous, chatoyant, shimmering, shiny, sheeny, glossy, polished; reflecting; refractive; optical, photosensitive.

undimmed, clear, bright, fair; cloudless, unclouded, sunny, sunshiny; moonlit, starlit, starry; burnished, polished, glassy, gleaming; lucid, pellucid.

Vb. *shine*, burn, blaze, flame, flare 379 *be hot*; glow, incandesce, luminesce, phosphoresce; glare, dazzle, bedazzle, blind; dance; flash, glisten, glister, blink; glimmer, flicker, twinkle; glitter, shimmer, glance; scintillate, sparkle, spark; come up, gleam, glint.

radiate, beam, shoot, shoot out rays, send out r. 300 *emit*; reflect, refract; be radioactive, bombard; X-ray.

make bright, lighten, dawn, rise, wax (moon); clear, clear up, lift, brighten; light, ignite 381 *kindle*; light up, shed lustre, throw light on;

shine upon, flood with light, irradiate, illuminate, illume; transilluminate; burnish, rub up 648 *clean*.

418 Darkness

N. *darkness*, dark; black 428 *blackness*; night, dark n., night-time, nightfall; dead of night, witching time 129 *midnight*; pitch darkness; Stygian gloom; murk, murkiness, gloom, dusk, gloaming, twilight, half-dark, semi-darkness; shadiness, shadows 419 *dimness*; shade, shadow; penumbra; silhouette, negative, radiograph; darkroom.

darkening, obfuscation 419 *dimness*; blackout; fadeout, eclipse, total e. 446 *disappearance*; lights out; sunset, sundown 129 *evening*; blackening, shading; chiaroscuro; dark lantern; dimmer, dip switch.

Adj. *dark*, sombre, dark-coloured, swarthy, dusky 428 *black*; poorly lit, obscure, pitch-dark, sooty, inky, jet-black, black as night; black as ink, black as hell, black as pitch, black as the ace of spades, murky; funereal, gloomy, sombre; louring; shady 419 *shadowy*; darkened; nocturnal; hidden, secret 523 *occult*.

unlit, unlighted, unilluminated; sunless, moonless, starless; eclipsed, overcast; hazy, cloudy 423 *opaque*; extinguished; dimmed, blacked out; obscured.

Vb. *be dark*, grow d., get d., lour; cloud over, look black.

darken, black out; lower the light, dim the l., put out the l., switch off the l., eclipse 226 *cover*; curtain, shutter, veil 421 *screen*; obscure, obfuscate; cloud, dim, tone down 419 *bedim*; overcast, overshadow, spread gloom; cast a shadow; silhouette 551 *represent*; shade, underexpose 428 *blacken*.

419 Dimness

N. *dimness*, indistinctness, vagueness, fuzziness, blur, lack of definition, soft focus; loom; faintness, paleness 426 *achromatism*; grey 429 *greyness*; dullness, lacklustre; matt finish; leaden skies; cloudiness, smokiness, poor visibility, impaired v., white-out 423 *opacity*; mistiness, fogginess; murk, gloom 418 *darkness*; fog, mist, haar 355 *cloud*; shadowiness, shadow, shade.

half-light, semidarkness, half-dark, bad light; waning light, gloaming 129 *evening*; twilight, dusk; daybreak, break of day, penumbra, half-shadow, partial eclipse.

Adj. *dim*, darkish, sombre, dusky, dusk, twilight, wan, dun, grey, pale 426 *colourless*; faint, faded, waning; imperceptible, indistinct, blurred, bleary; dull, lustreless, lacklustre, leaden; flat, matt; filmy, hazy, fuzzy, foggy, fogbound, misty, nebulous 355 *cloudy*; thick,

smoky, sooty, muddy 423 *opaque*; dingy, grimy, rusty, rusted, mildewed, unpolished, unburnished 649 *dirty*.

shadowy, shady, shaded, overshadowed, overcast; vague, indistinct, undefined, ill-defined, obscure, confused, fuzzy, blurry; deceptive; half-glimpsed, half-hidden 444 *invisible*; half-lit 418 *unlit*; dreamlike, ghostly 4 *insubstantial*; coming and going.

Vb. *be dim*, – faint etc. adj.; be indistinct; lose definition, fade, wane, grow pale 426 *lose colour*; lour; glimmer, flicker, gutter.

dim, dip; bedim; lower or turn down the lights, fade out; obscure, blur; smear, besmirch, sully; rust, mildew, muddy, dirty 649 *make unclean*; fog, mist; becloud; overcast; shade, shadow, veil 226 *cover*.

420 Luminary: source of light

N. *luminary*, naked light, flame 379 *fire*; flare; sun; moon; starlight 321 *star*; bright star, first magnitude s., Sirius, Aldebaran, Betelgeuse, Canopus, Alpha Centauri; evening star, Hesperus, Vesper, Venus; morning star, Lucifer; shooting star, fireball 321 *meteor*; galaxy, Milky Way, northern lights 321 *heavens*; lightning, bolt of l., sheet l., forked l., ball l., summer l., lightning flash, levin; scintilla, spark, sparkle 417 *flash*.

torch, brand; torchlight, flambeau, match 385 *lighter*; candle, bougie, tallow candle, wax c.; flower c., cake c., Christmas c; taper, wax t.; spill, wick, dip, rushlight, nightlight, naked light, flare, gas jet, burner, Bunsen b.

lamp, lamplight; lantern; safety lamp, Davy l., acetylene l.; oil lamp, hurricane l., paraffin l., spirit l.; gas lamp, Calor gas (tdmk) lamp, gas mantle; electric lamp, flash gun, torch, pocket t., penlight, flashlight, searchlight, arc light, floodlight; headlamp; headlight, side light; foglamp; tail light, brake l., reflector, bulb, flashbulb, photoflood, electric bulb, light b.; strobe light, stroboscope, strobe; vapour light, neon l., strip l., fluorescent l.; street l., mercury vapour lamp, sodium l.; Chinese lantern, fairy lights, Christmas tree l.; magic lantern, projector; light fitting, chandelier, candelabra; standard lamp, table l., desk l., reading l., Anglepoise (tdmk) l.; sun l., sunray l.; lamppost; candle holder, candlestick.

lighting, illumination, irradiation 417 *light*; artificial lighting, street l.; indirect lighting; gas lighting, electric l., neon l., fluorescent l.; floodlighting, son et lumière; limelight, spotlight, footlights, houselights.

signal light, warning l. 665 *danger signal*; traffic light, red l., green l., amber l., trafficator, indicator; Very light, Bengal l., rocket, star shell, parachute flare, flare; flare path, beacon, beacon fire, balefire 547 *signal*; lighthouse, lightship.

421 Screen

N. *screen*, shield 660 *protection*; shelter; bower 194 *arbour*; shady nook 418 *darkness*; sunshade, parasol; sun hat, solar topee 226 *shade*; awning 226 *canopy*; sunscreen, visor; lampshade; eyeshade, blinkers; eyelid, eyelashes 438 *eye*; dark glasses, tinted g., sun g., shades 442 *eyeglass*; smoked glass, frosted g., opaque g., polarized g. 424 *semitransparency*; stained glass 437 *variegation*; double glazing, soundproofing, partition, wall, hedge 235 *fence*; filter 57 *exclusion*; mask 527 *disguise*; hood, veil, mantle 228 *cloak*; cloud; mist; smokescreen.

curtain 226 *shade*; window curtain, net c., bead c.; drapes, shade, blind, sunblind; persienne, jalousie, venetian blind, roller b.; shutter.

Vb. *screen*, shield, shelter 660 *safeguard*; protect 713 *defend*; ward off, fend off, keep at bay; keep off, keep out, filter out 57 *exclude*; cover up, veil, hood 226 *cover*; mask, hide, shroud 525 *conceal*; intercept 702 *obstruct*; blinker, blindfold 439 *blind*; shade, shadow, darken; curtain, curtain off, canopy, draw the curtains, pull down the blind; put up the shutters, close the s. 264 *close*; cloud, fog.

422 Transparency

N. *transparency*, transmission of light; transparence, translucence; thinness; lucidity, pellucidity, limpidity; clearness, clarity; glassiness; water, ice, crystal, Perspex (tdmk), cellophane, shrink-wrapping, bubble pack, blister p., glass, plate g., magnifying g., lens, eyepiece 442 *eyeglass*; pane, window p.; sheer silk, gossamer, gauze, lace, chiffon 4 *insubstantial thing*.

Adj. *transparent*, diaphanous, revealing, sheer, see-through; thin, fine, filmy, gauzy, pellucid, translucent; lucent 424 *semitransparent*; liquid, limpid; crystal, crystalline, glassy; clear, lucid; crystal-clear.

423 Opacity

N. *opacity*, opaqueness; thickness, solidity 324 *density*; filminess, frost; turbidity, muddiness, dirtiness 649 *dirt*; fog, mist, haar, dense fog, smog, pea-souper 355 *cloud*; film, scale 421 *screen*; smoke-screen.

Adj. *opaque*, nontransparent, thick, impervious to light, blank, windowless; not clean, unclarified, cloudy, milky, filmy, turbid, muddy, muddied; foggy, hazy, misty, murky, smoky, sooty 419 *dim*; frosted, misted, clouded.

424 Semitransparency

N. *semitransparency*, milkiness; pearliness, opalescence; smoked glass, ground g., frosted g., tinted spectacles, dark glasses; gauze, muslin, net; pearl, opal 437 *variegation*.

Adj. *semitransparent*, gauzy, filmy; translucent, opalescent; milky, pearly; frosted; smoked 419 *dim*, 355 *cloudy*.

425 Colour

N. *colour*, primary c.; three primaries; chromatism, chromatic aberration; chromatic scale; prism, spectrum, rainbow 437 *variegation*; colour scheme, palette; coloration 553 *painting*; colour photography, Technicolor (tdmk); heraldic colour, tincture, chromatics; spectroscope, prism.

hue, chromaticity, tone; brilliance, intensity, warmth, loudness; softness, deadness, dullness; coloration, livery; pigmentation, colouring, complexion; flush, blush, glow; rosy cheek, ruddiness 431 *redness*; sickly hue, pallor 426 *achromatism*; discoloration; tint, shade, nuance, cast, dye; tinge, patina; half-tone, half-light, mezzotint.

pigment, colouring matter, rouge, blusher, warpaint 843 *cosmetic*; dyestuff, dye, fast d.; natural d., vegetable d., madder, cochineal 431 *red pigment*; indigo 436 *purpleness*; woad 435 *blueness*; artificial dye, synthetic d., aniline d.; stain, fixative, mordant; wash, colourwash, whitewash, distemper; paint, emulsion p., gloss p., undercoat; oil paints, acrylic p., watercolours.

Adj. *florid*, colourful, high-coloured; overstated; ruddy 431 *red*; intense, deep, strong, emphatic; unfaded, vivid, brilliant 417 *luminous*; warm, glowing, rich, painted, gay, bright; gaudy, garish, showy, flashy; glaring, flaring, flaunting, spectacular; harsh, stark, raw, crude; lurid, loud, screaming, shrieking; clashing, discordant 25 *disagreeing*.

soft-hued, soft, quiet, under-stated, tender, delicate, refined, discreet; pearly, creamy 427 *whitish*; light, pale, pastel, muted; simple; faded; weathered, mellow; harmonious 24 *agreeing*.

Vb. *colour*, colorize, colour in, block in, crayon, daub 553 *paint*; rouge 431 *redden*, 843 *primp*; pigment, tattoo; dye, tie-dye, dip, imbue; tint, touch up; shade; tincture, tinge; wash, colourwash, distemper, lacquer 226 *coat*; stain, run, discolour; come off (e.g. on one's fingers); tan, weather, mellow; illuminate, emblazon; whitewash; enamel 437 *variegate*.

426 Achromatism: absence of colour

N. *achromatism*, achromaticity, colourlessness; discoloration, etiolation, weathering, fading, bleaching 427 *whiteness*; overexposure 551 *photography*; pallor, pallidity, paleness; lightness, faintness etc. adj.; absence of colour, anaemia, bloodlessness; pigment deficiency, albinism, albinoism; neutral tint; monochrome; black and white; albino, blond(e), platinum b., peroxide b., artificial b.

bleacher, decolorant, peroxide, bleaching powder, bleach, lime.

Adj. *colourless*, neutral; uncoloured, achromatic; bleached, etiolated, overexposed, weathered; faint, faded, fading; unpigmented, albino, light-skinned, fair-s., fair, blond(e) 433 *yellow*, 427 *whitish*; lustreless, mousy; bloodless, anaemic; without colour, drained of colour, washed out, wishy-washy, peaky; pale, pallid 427 *white*; ashen, livid, whey-faced; pasty, doughy, sallow, sickly 651 *unhealthy*; dingy, dull 429 *grey*; lacklustre; wan 419 *dim*; deathly, deathly pale, white as a sheet, ghostlike.

Vb. *lose colour* 419 *be dim*; pale, fade, bleach, blanch, turn pale, change countenance, go as white as a sheet 427 *whiten*; run.

427 Whiteness

N. *whiteness*, etiolation; albinism, albinoism 426 *achromatism*; whitishness, creaminess, off-whiteness, pearliness; hoariness; white light 417 *light*; white heat 379 *heat*; white, Caucasian, paleface; albino.

white thing, alabaster, marble; hoar frost, snow, new-fallen s.; chalk, paper, milk, flour, salt, ivory, lily, swan; albino; silver, pewter, platinum; pearl, teeth.

Adj. *white*, pure; light, bright 417 *luminous*; silvery, silver, alabaster, marble; chalky, snowy, snow-covered; hoary, frosty, frosted; foaming, spumy, foam-flecked; soapy, lathery; white hot 379 *hot*; white as a sheet, white as the driven snow; pure white, lily-white, milk-w., snow-w., white-skinned, Caucasian; whitened, whitewashed, bleached 648 *clean*.

whitish, pearly, milky, creamy 424 *semitransparent*; ivory, waxen, sallow, pale 426 *colourless*; off-white, oyster-w., mushroom, magnolia; ecru, beige 430 *brown*; hoary, grizzled 429 *grey*; pepper-and-salt 437 *mottled*; blond(e), fair, Nordic; ash-blond(e), platinum b., fair-haired, golden-h., flaxen-h., tow-headed.

Vb. *whiten*, white, blanco, pipeclay, white-wash, wash 648 *clean*; blanch, bleach; pale, fade; frost, silver, grizzle.

428 Blackness

N. *blackness*, 418 *darkness*; inkiness, lividity, black, sable; melanism, swarthiness, duskiness, pigmentation, dark colouring, colour; depth, deep tone; black and white; blackening, darkening 418 *obscuration*; black, Negro, Negress; coloured.

black thing, coal, charcoal, soot, pitch, tar; ebony, jet, ink, smut; blacklead; burnt cork; melanin; sable; bruise, black eye; blackberry, sloe; crow, raven, blackbird; black clothes, mourning.

Adj. *black*, sable; inky, black as thunder 418 *dark*; sooty, smoky, smudgy, smutty 649 *dirty*; blackened, singed, charred; black-haired, raven-haired, dark-headed; black-eyed, sloe-e.; dark, brunette; black-skinned, Negroid; pigmented, coloured; sombre, gloomy, mourning 364 *funereal*; coal-black, jet-b., pitch-b.; blue-b.; black as ink, black as pitch, black as the ace of spades, black as hell; black as night.

blackish, swarthy, dusky, dark, dark-skinned, tanned, sun-t.; coloured, pigmented; livid, black and blue.

Vb. *blacken*, black, blacklead, japan, ink, ink in; dirty, blot; char 381 *burn*.

429 Greyness

N. *greyness*, neutral, greige, grisaille; pepper and salt, grey hairs, hoary head; pewter, silver; gunmetal, ashes, slate; grey, dove g. etc. adj.; oyster, taupe.

Adj. *grey*, neutral, dull, sombre, leaden, livid; greying, grizzled, grizzly, hoary; silvery, pearly, frosted 427 *whitish*; greige; light-grey, pale-g., ash-g., dove-g., pearl-g.; mouse-coloured, mousy, dun, drab, donkey-grey, steely, charcoal-g.; slate-coloured; greyish, ashen, smoky; dapple-grey.

430 Brownness

N. *brownness*, brown, bronze, copper, amber; tobacco leaf, autumn colours; cinnamon, coffee, chocolate; butterscotch, caramel, toffee, burnt almond; walnut, mahogany; dark skin or complexion, suntan; brunette.

brown pigment, bistre, ochre, sepia, burnt sienna, burnt umber, Vandyke brown.

Adj. *brown*, bronze, mahogany etc. n.; browned, toasted; bronzed, tanned, sunburnt; dark, brunette; nut-brown, hazel; light brown, ecru, oatmeal, beige, buff, fawn, biscuit, mushroom, café-au-lait; brownish, greyish-brown, dun, mud-coloured; yellowish-brown, snuff-coloured, khaki; tawny, tan; reddish-brown, bay, roan, sorrel, chestnut, auburn, copper-coloured; russet, rust-coloured; maroon; puce; dark brown, peat-b., mocha, chocolate, coffee-

coloured etc. n.; brown as a berry, brown as a nut.
Vb. *brown*, bronze, tan, sunburn; singe, char, toast 381 *burn*.

431 Redness

N. *redness*, blush, flush, hectic f.; sunset, dawn, rosy-fingered d. 417 *glow*; reddening, warmth; rosiness, ruddiness, bloom, red cheeks, rosy c., cherry lips; high colour, floridness; red colour, crimson, scarlet, red etc. adj.; carnation, rose, geranium, poppy; cherry, tomato; burgundy, port, claret; gore 335 *blood*; ruby, garnet, cornelian; flame 379 *fire*; red ink, rubric; red planet, Mars; redbreast, robin r.; redskin, Red Indian; redhead, carrot-top, gingernob.

red pigment, red dye, cochineal, carmine, kermes; cinnabar, vermilion; madder; crimson lake, Venetian red, red ochre, red lead, rouge, blusher, lipstick 843 *cosmetic*.

Adj. *red*, reddish; ruddy, sanguine, florid, blowzy; warm, hot, fiery, glowing, red-hot 379 *hot*; flushed, fevered; flushing, blushing; red-cheeked, rosy-c.; bright red, red as a lobster, red as a beetroot; red-haired, ginger-h.; carroty, sandy, auburn, titian-red, flame-coloured; russet, rusty, rust-coloured; pink, roseate, rosy, rose-coloured, peach-c., flesh-c., salmon-pink, shocking-p.; coral, carnation, damask, crushed strawberry; crimson, cherry-red, cerise, carmine, cramoisy; fuchsia, magenta, maroon 436 *purple*; wine-coloured; oxblood, sanguine; scarlet, cardinal-red, vermilion, pillarbox red; reddened, rouged, painted.

Vb. *redden*, rouge, apply blusher, raddle 843 *primp*; dye red, flush, blush, glow; colour, colour up, crimson, go red, go pink.

432 Orange

N. *orange*, red and yellow, gold, old gold; amber; sunflower, marigold; apricot, tangerine; marmalade; ochre, cadmium orange, henna.

Adj. *orange*, apricot etc. n.; coppery; ginger; orangeish, orangey, orange-coloured, flame-c., copper-c., brass-c., brassy.

433 Yellowness

N. *yellowness*, yellow, sunshine y. etc. adj.; brass, gold, old gold, topaz, amber, old ivory; sulphur, brimstone; buttercup, daffodil, primrose, dandelion; lemon, honey; saffron, mustard; jaundice, yellow fever; sallow skin, fair hair, golden hair; blond(e), ash b., platinum b., strawberry b.; yellow rain, cadmium yellow, chrome y., lemon y., yellow ochre, xanthin.

Adj. *yellow*, gold, amber etc. n.; tawny, sandy; fair-haired, golden-h., yellow-h. 427 *whitish*; honey-coloured, straw-c.; pale yellow,

acid y., lemon y.; primrose y., jasmine, chartreuse, champagne; canary yellow, sunshine y., bright y.; sulphur y., mustard y.; golden, gilded; deep yellow, yellowy, yellowish, flavescent, xanthic; sallow, jaundiced, bilious; yellow with age.

434 Greenness

N. *greenness*, green etc. adj.; verdancy, greenery, greenwood; verdure; grass, moss, turf, green leaf 366 *foliage*; lime, greengage; jade, emerald, beryl, aquamarine, olivine; verdigris; Lincoln green.

Adj. *green*, verdant; grassy, leafy; bright green, deep g., dark g., pale g.; grass-green, leaf-g., moss-g.; emerald, sea-green 435 *blue*; jade-green, bottle-g.; sage-g., willow-g.; pea-g., acid-g., apple-g., lime-g., chartreuse; eau-de-Nil, avocado, olive, olive-green; greenish.

435 Blueness

N. *blueness*, blue, azure; blue sky, blue sea; sapphire, aquamarine, turquoise, lapis lazuli; bluebell, cornflower, forget-me-not; gentian blue etc. adj.; bluishness, cyanosis; lividness.

blue pigment, blue dye, indigo, woad; cobalt blue; bluebag.

Adj. *blue*, cyanic, azure; sky-blue; duck-egg blue, eggshell b., turquoise; light blue, pale blue, ice-b., powder-b., Cambridge-b.; air-force b., Saxe-b., slate-b., steel-b., electric-b.; sapphire, aquamarine, peacock-b., kingfisher-b.; bright b., royal-b., ultramarine, deep blue, dark b., Oxford-b., midnight-b., navy-b., navy, French n.; indigo; blue-black, black and blue, livid; cold, steely, bluish.

436 Purpleness

N. *purpleness*, purple, blue and red; imperial purple; amethyst; lavender, violet, heliotrope, heather, foxglove; plum, damson, aubergine; gentian violet; amaranth, lilac, mauve.

Adj. *purple*, plum etc. n.; purplish, violet, mauve, pale purple, lavender, lilac; bright purple, fuchsia, magenta, plum-coloured, damson-coloured, puce; heliotrope; deep purple, dark purple, mulberry; purple with rage.

437 Variegation

N. *variegation*, variety, diversification, diversity 15 *difference*; dancing light; play of colour, shot colours, iridescence, chatoyance; tiger's eye, opal, nacre, mother-of-pearl; shot silk, moire; peacock's tail, tortoiseshell, chameleon; Joseph's coat, motley, harlequin, patchwork, patchwork quilt; enamelwork; stained glass, kaleidoscope; rainbow, spectrum, prism; collage.

chequer, check, Prince of Wales c., hound's tooth, pepper-and-salt; plaid, tartan;

chessboard, draughtboard; marquetry, inlay, inlaid work 844 *ornamental art*; mosaic, crazy paving 43 *medley*.

stripe, striation; line, streak, band, bar, bar code; agate; zebra, tiger; streakiness, mackerel sky; crack, craze; reticulation 222 *network*.

mottle, maculation; dappling, stippling, marbling; spottiness, patchiness 17 *nonuniformity*; patch, speck, speckle, macula, spots, pimples, pockmarks 845 *blemish*; freckle, fleck, dot, polka d.; blotch, splotch, splodge, splash; leopard, Dalmatian.

Adj *variegated*, fretted etc. vb.; diversified; patterned, embroidered, worked 844 *ornamental*; colourful 425 *florid*; multi-coloured, parti-c., motley, patched; tortoiseshell, chameleon, harlequin, kaleidoscopic 82 *multiform*; plaid, tartan; rainbow-coloured, prismatic; mosaic, tessellated, parquet.

pied, parti-coloured, black-and-white, pepper-and-salt, grizzled, piebald, skewbald, roan, pinto, chequered, check, dappled, patchy.

mottled, marbled, veined, reticulated; studded, maculose, spotted, patchy; speckled, freckled; streaked, striated, lined, barred, banded, striped 222 *crossed*; brindled, tabby; pocked, pockmarked.

Vb *variegate*, diversify, pattern; chequer; patch 656 *repair*; embroider, work 844 *decorate*; braid, quilt; inlay, tessellate; stud, pepper, dot with, mottle, speckle, freckle, spangle; spot; tattoo, stipple, dapple; streak, stripe, striate; craze, crack; marble, vein; discolour 649 *make unclean*; make iridescent.

438 Vision

N. *vision*, sight, power of s; eyesight; seeing, visualization, mind's eye 513 *imagination*; perception, recognition; acuity (of vision), good eyesight; long sight, far s.; defective vision, short sight 440 *dim sight*; second sight 984 *occultism*; double vision, binocular v.; magnification; winking, blinking, tic, squint; eyetesting; oculist, optician, ophthalmologist, optometrist; optometer, ophthalmoscope.

eye, eyeball, iris, pupil, white, cornea, retina, optic nerve; optics, orbs, sparklers, peepers; saucer eyes, goggle e.; eyelashes, eyelid 421 *screen*; lashes; naked eye; sharp e., gimlet e., X-ray e.; weak eyes 440 *dim sight*; glass e. 439 *blindness*; evil eye 983 *sorcery*; hawk, eagle, cat, lynx; basilisk, cockatrice.

look, glance, sideways look, squint; tail *or* corner of the eye; glint, blink, flash; gaze, steady g.; observation, close o., contemplation, watch; stare, fixed s.; come-hither look, glad eye, sheep's eyes, ogle, leer 889 *wooing*; wink

524 *hint*; grimace, dirty look, scowl, evil eye; peep, peek, glimpse, rapid g., brief g.

inspection, examination, autopsy 459 *enquiry*; view, preview, sneak p. 522 *manifestation*; supervision 689 *management*; survey, overview, bird's-eye view; reconnaissance, reconnoitre, recce, surveillance; sight-seeing, rubbernecking, gawping; look, butcher's, lookaround, look-see, dekko, once-over, shufti, second glance, double take; review, revision; viewing, home v. 445 *cinema*, 531 *broadcasting*; discernment, espial, view, first sight; looking round, observation, prying, spying; espionage; peeping, voyeurism, peeping Tom.

view, eyeful; vista, prospect, outlook, perspective; aspect 445 *appearance*; panorama, bird's-eye view; horizon, false h.; line of vision; range of view; field of view; scene, setting, stage 594 *theatre*; angle of vision, point of view, viewpoint, standpoint; vantage point, lookout, crow's nest, watchtower 209 *high structure*; camera obscura; astrodome, conning tower; observatory; grandstand, ringside seat 441 *onlookers*; peephole 263 *window*.

Adj. *seeing*, glimpsing etc. vb.; visual, perceptible 443 *visible*; panoramic, ocular, ophthalmic; optical, optometric; stereoscopic, binocular; orthoptic, perspicacious, sharp-eyed, gimlet-e., eagle-e., vigilant, with eyes in the back of one's head.

Vb. *see*, behold, visualize; perceive, discern, distinguish, make out, pick o., recognize; take in, see at a glance 498 *be wise*; descry, discover 484 *detect*; sight, espy, spy, spot, observe 455 *notice*; lay *or* set eyes on, catch sight of, sight; catch a glimpse of, glimpse; view, command a view of, have in sight; look on 441 *watch*.

gaze, quiz, gaze at, look, look at; look straight at, look in the eyes; look intently, eye, stare, peer; stare at, stare hard, goggle, gape, gawk, gawp; focus, rivet one's eyes, fix one's gaze; glare, glower, look daggers, give a black look, look black 891 *be angry*; glance, glance at; squint, look askance, look down one's nose; wink, blink 524 *hint*; make eyes at, give the glad eye, give a come-hither look, ogle, leer 889 *court*; feast one's eyes on, gloat over 824 *be pleased*; steal a glance, peep, peek, take a peep; direct one's gaze, turn one's eyes on; notice, take n., look upon 455 *be attentive*; lift up one's eyes, look up; look down, look round, look behind, look in front; look ahead 858 *be cautious*; look away, avert one's gaze 439 *be blind*; exchange glances.

scan, scrutinize, inspect, examine, take stock of, look one up and down; contemplate, pore over 536 *study*; look over, look through, read t., riffle t., leaf t., skim t.; have *or* take a look at, have a dekko, have a butcher's, take a shufti at, take a gander *or* a squint at, run one's eye over, give the once-over; see, go and see, take in, sight-see, rubberneck, gawp; go to see 882 *visit*; view, survey, sweep, reconnoitre; scout, spy out the land, take a recce; peep, peek 453 *be curious*; spy, pry, snoop; observe, keep under observation, keep under surveillance, watch 457 *invigilate*; hold in view, keep in sight; watch out for, look out f. 507 *await*; keep watch, look out, keep a lookout for, keep an eye out for, keep a weather eye open for, keep cave, keep looking, keep one's eyes skinned *or* peeled; strain one's eyes, peer; squint at, squinny; crane, crane one's neck, stand on tiptoe.

439 Blindness
N. *blindness*, unawareness 491 *ignorance*; sightlessness; glaucoma, river blindness, cataract; night blindness, snow b., colour b.; dim-sightedness 440 *dim sight*; blind spot 444 *invisibility*; tunnel vision; blind eye 456 *inattention*; word blindness, dyslexia; glass eye, artificial e.; blind man *or* woman, the blind; Braille, talking book; white stick, guide dog.

Adj. *blind*, sightless, unsighted, visually challenged, dark; unseeing, undiscerning, unperceiving, unobserving 456 *inattentive*; blinded, blindfold, blinkered; in the dark, benighted; 440 *dim-sighted*; stone-blind; blind as a bat.

Vb. *be blind*, not use one's eyes; go blind, lose one's sight, not see; grope in the dark, feel one's way 461 *be tentative*; be blindfolded, wear blinkers; be blind to 491 *not know*; ignore, have a blind spot, not see for looking, not see what is under one's nose; not see the wood for the trees, shut the eyes to, turn a blind eye, avert one's gaze, look the other way 458 *disregard*; blink, squint 440 *be dim-sighted*.

blind, gouge one's eyes out; dazzle; obscure 419 *bedim*; screen from sight; blinker, blindfold, bandage 421 *screen*; throw dust in one's eyes 495 *mislead*.

440 Dim-sightedness: imperfect vision
N. *dim sight*, failing sight, defective eyesight, dim-sightedness, purblindness 439 *blindness*; defective v., impaired v.; eyestrain; short s., near s., near-sightedness, myopia; hypermetropia, presbyopia, long sight, far s.; double vision; astigmatism; cataract; glaucoma; colour-blindness; snow-blindness, night-blindness; ophthalmitis; conjunctivitis, pink eye; cast; strabismus, squint, cross-eye; wall-eye; wink, blink, nictitation, nervous tic; eyeshade, blinker 421 *screen*; tunnel vision, blind spot 444 *invisibility*.

visual fallacy, refraction 417 *reflection*; aberration of light 282 *deviation*; false light 552 *misrep-*

resentation; optical illusion, trick of light, mirage 542 *deception*; spectre, apparition 970 *ghost*; vision, dream 513 *fantasy*; distorting mirror, hall of mirrors, magic lantern.

Adj. *dim-sighted*, purblind, half-blind, semi-b.; visually impaired, bespectacled; myopic, short-sighted, near-s.; hypermetropic, presbyopic, long-sighted, far-sighted, astigmatic; colour-blind; wall-eyed, squinting; strabismal, strabismic, cross-eyed; boss-eyed, bug-e.; nystagmic, blinking, dazzled; blinded, temporarily b. 439 *blind*; cataractous, glaucomatous.

Vb. *be dim-sighted*, – myopic etc. adj.; not see well, need spectacles; have a mist before the eyes; get something in one's e.; peer, screw up the eyes, squint; blink, wink, nictitate, have a nervous tic; see double, be blinded by, dazzle; grow blurred, dim, fail; see through a glass darkly.

blur, confuse; dim, mist, fog, smudge; be indistinct, be hazy.

441 Spectator
N. *spectator*, beholder; viewer, observer, watcher, invigilator; inspector, examiner, scrutinizer, overseer 690 *manager*; witness, eyewitness; bystander, onlooker; gazer, starer, gaper, gawper, goggler; ogler, voyeur, Peeping Tom; window shopper; sightseer, rubberneck, tourist, globetrotter 268 *traveller*; stargazer, astronomer; bird watcher, twitcher, train spotter, lookout 484 *detector*; watchman, night-w., security officer, security man, sentinel, sentry, 664 *warner*; patrolman, patrol; scout, spy, mole, spook, snoop 459 *detective*; filmgoer, cinemagoer 445 *cinema*; theatregoer 594 *playgoer*; televiewer, viewer, TV addict, square-eyes; captive audience.

onlookers, audience, auditorium, sea of faces; box office, gate; house, gallery, gods, circle, dress c., pit, stalls; stadium, grandstand, terraces; crowd, supporters, followers, aficionados, fans 707 *patron*, 504 *enthusiast*; bums on seats.

Vb. *watch*, spectate, look on, look at, view 438 *see*; witness 189 *be present*; follow with the eyes, observe 455 *be attentive*; attend, eye, ogle, give the glad eye, quiz; gape, gawk, stare; spy, spy out, scout, scout out, reconnoitre 438 *scan*.

442 Optical instrument
N. *eyeglass*, spectacles, specs, goggles, glasses, reading g., pince-nez, sunglasses, shades, dark glasses, Polaroid (tdmk) g., bifocals; pebble glasses; contact lens, hard c. 1., soft c. 1.; lorgnette, monocle; magnifying glass.

telescope, terrestrial telescope, astronomical t. 321 *astronomy*; collimator; sight, finder, viewfinder, rangefinder; periscope; spyglass, night glass; binoculars, prism b., field glasses, opera g.

microscope, electron m., photomicroscope, ultramicroscope.

mirror, reflector; concave mirror, speculum; rear-view mirror, wing m.; glass, looking g., cheval g., full-length mirror, dressing-table m., hand m.

camera, camera lucida, camera obscura, spectrograph 321 *astronomy*; box camera, disc c.; instant c., Polaroid (tdmk) c.; cinecamera; television camera, videopack, camcorder; electric eye, closed-circuit television 484 *detector*; shutter, aperture, stop; flashgun 420 *lamp*; film 551 *photography*; telephoto lens, zoom l., wide-angle l.; light meter; slide projector, overhead p., magic lantern 455 *cinema*.

443 Visibility

N. *visibility*, perceptibility; 445 *appearance*; sight, exposure; distinctness, clearness, clarity, definition, conspicuousness, prominence; eye-witness, visible evidence, object lesson 522 *manifestation*; visual aid 534 *teaching*; scene, field of view, field of vision 438 *view*; seeing, impaired visibility, reduced v.; horizon, skyline, visible distance 183 *range*; landmark 547 *signpost*; symptom.

Adj. *visible*, perceptible, perceivable, discernible, observable, detectable; noticeable, remarkable; recognizable, unmistakable, palpable, tangible; symptomatic; apparent 445 *appearing*; showing 522 *manifest*; exposed, open, naked; exposed to view, in full view; before one's eyes, under one's nose, for all to see; visible to the naked eye; telescopic, panoramic.

obvious, showing, for all to see 522 *shown*; plain, clear, clear-cut, crystal-clear, as clear as day; definite, well-defined, well-marked; distinct, unblurred; undisguised; conspicuous, pointed, prominent; eye-catching, striking, shining 417 *luminous*; glaring, staring; pronounced, highlighted, spotlit; vivid, eidetic; under one's nose, before one's very eyes, staring one in the face, plain to see, plain as plain, plain as a pikestaff, plain as the nose on your face.

Vb. *be visible*, be seen, – obvious etc. adj.; show, shine through; attract attention, ask to be noticed 455 *attract notice*; strike, catch the eye, stand out, act as a landmark; come to light, dawn upon; heave in sight, come into view, show its face 445 *appear*; pop up, crop up, turn up, show up 295 *arrive*; spring up, start up, arise 68 *begin*; surface, break s. 308 *ascend*; come out, creep out 298 *emerge*; stick out, project 254 *jut*; show, materialize, develop; manifest itself, expose i., betray i. 522 *be plain*; symptomize

547 *indicate*; make one's entry, make an entrance 297 *enter*; step forward, advance; dazzle; break through the clouds 417 *shine*; stay in sight; make visible, expose 522 *manifest*.

444 Invisibility

N. *invisibility*, imperceptibility, indistinctness, poor definition; poor visibility, reduced v., obscurity 419 *dimness*; distance 199 *farness*; smallness 196 *minuteness*; privacy 883 *seclusion*; submergence 523 *latency*; hiding 525 *concealment*; mystery 525 *secrecy*; smoke screen, mist, fog, haar, veil, curtain; blind spot, blind eye 439 *blindness*; blind corner, 663 *pitfall*; hidden menace 661 *danger*.

Adj. *invisible*, imperceptible, indiscernible; indistinguishable, unrecognizable; unseen; sightless; unnoticed 458 *neglected*; out of sight; not in sight, remote 199 *distant*; sequestered 883 *secluded*; lurking 523 *latent*; camouflaged 525 *concealed*; shadowy, mysterious; obscured, eclipsed.

indistinct, unclear, poorly-defined, indefinite, indistinct 419 *dim*; faint, microscopic; confused, vague, blurred, out of focus; fuzzy, misty, hazy 424 *semi-transparent*.

Vb. *be unseen*, hide, lie low, go to earth, go to ground, lie in ambush 523 *lurk*; escape notice, blush unseen 872 *be humble*; pale, fade, die 419 *be dim*; be lost to view, vanish 446 *disappear*; hide away, submerge 525 *conceal*; veil 421 *screen*; darken, eclipse 419 *bedim*.

445 Appearance

N. *appearance*, first appearance 68 *beginning*; materialization, bodying forth, presence 1 *existence*; exhibition, display, view, demonstration 522 *manifestation*; 471 *probability*; revelation 484 *discovery*; outside 223 *exteriority*; appearances, look of things; visual impact, face value; first impressions, effect; image, front, public persona, façade 541 *duplicity*; veneer, show, seeming, semblance; side, aspect, facet; guise 228 *dressing*; shape, dimension 243 *form*; look; emanation; vision 513 *fantasy*; mirage, hallucination, illusion 440 *visual fallacy*; spectre 970 *ghost*; reflection, image; likeness 551 *representation*.

spectacle, impression, effect, something to write home about; decoration 844 *ornamentation*; eyeful, vision, sight, sight for sore eyes, scene; scenery, landscape, seascape, townscape, estatescape; panorama, bird's-eye view 438 *view*; display, pageantry, pageant, parade, review 875 *ostentation*; revue, extravaganza, pantomime, floor show 594 *stage show*; television, video 531 *broadcasting*; illuminations, son et lumière; pyrotechnics; presentation, show, demonstration, exhibition, exposition 522 *exhibit*; art exhibition 553 *picture*; visual entertainment, in-flight e., peep show, slide s., film s., picture s., home movies; kaleidoscope 437 *variegation*; panorama, staging, tableau; set, decor, scenario 594 *stage set*.

cinema, cinematography; big screen, silver s., Hollywood, film industry; film studio, film production, film-making, shooting 551 *photography*; direction, continuity, editing, cutting, montage, projection; photoplay, screenplay, scenario, script, shooting s.; credits, titles; special effects, animation; voiceover, sound effects, soundtrack; cinematograph, projector; multiplex cinema; picture house, drive-in cinema, flea pit 594 *theatre*; film director, film star 594 *actor*; filmgoer 504 *enthusiast*.

film, films, pictures, motion p., movies, flicks; Technicolor (tdmk), 3-D, Cinerama (tdmk), Cinemascope (tdmk); silent film, talkie; 15, 18, PG, U; big picture, B p., B movie, supporting film, newsreel, trailer; cartoon, animated c., travelogue, documentary, docu-drama, feature film; art film, nouvelle vague; epic, blockbuster, musical; low-budget movie; weepie, bodice-ripper, thriller, cliffhanger, war film, horror film; blue movie, skinflick; Western, spaghetti w.; space odyssey; oldie, remake; rush, preview; general release.

look, mien, face; expression; countenance, looks; complexion, colour, cast; air, demeanour, carriage, bearing, deportment, poise, presence; gesture, posture, behaviour 688 *conduct*.

feature, trait, mark, lineament; lines, cut, shape, fashion, figure 243 *form*; outline, contour, relief, elevation, profile, silhouette; visage, physiognomy, cut of one's jib 237 *face*.

Adj. *appearing*, apparent; seeming, ostensible; deceptive; outward, external, superficial 223 *exterior*; on view 443 *visible*; visual, showing, exhibited, hung 522 *shown*; impressive, effective, spectacular 875 *showy*; revealed 522 *manifest*; dreamlike 513 *imaginary*.

Vb. *appear*, show 443 *be visible*; seem 18 *resemble*; have the look of, have an air of, take the shape of; figure in, cut a figure 875 *be ostentatious*; be on show; be showing; appear on television, star in; exhibit 522 *manifest*; arise; dawn, break 68 *begin*; materialize, pop up 295 *arrive*.

446 Disappearance

N. *disappearance*, loss, vanishing; disappearing trick, escapology 542 *sleight*; flight 667 *escape*; exit 296 *departure*; evaporation 338 *vaporization*; dissipation, dissolution 51 *decomposition*; extinction 2 *nonexistence*; occupation, eclipse 418 *obscuration*; fadeout; thin air 444 *invisibility*.

Vb. *disappear*, vanish, do the vanishing trick; dematerialize, melt into thin air; evaporate 338 *vaporize*; dissolve, melt away 337 *liquefy*; dwindle to vanishing point 37 *decrease*; fade away 114 *be transient*; suffer an eclipse 419 *be dim*; disperse, dissipate, diffuse, scatter 75 *be dispersed*; fail to appear, play truant, bunk off, take French leave, go AWOL 190 *be absent*; go, be gone, depart 296 *decamp*; run away, get a. 667 *escape*; hide, lie low, be in hiding 523 *lurk*; leave no trace 525 *conceal*; be lost to sight 444 *be unseen*; become extinct 2 *pass away*; erase, dispel 550 *obliterate*.

Intellect: the exercise of the mind

4.1
Formation of Ideas

SECTION ONE

General

447 Intellect
N. *intellect*, mind, psyche, mentality; understanding, conception; powers of thought; rationality, reasoning power; reason, association of ideas 475 *reasoning*; philosophy 449 *thought*; awareness, sense, consciousness, self-c., stream of c. 455 *attention*; cognition, perception, percipience, insight; extra-sensory perception, ESP, instinct, sixth sense 476 *intuition*; flair, judgment 463 *discrimination*; intellectualism; mental capacity, brains, wits, senses, sense, grey matter, IQ, intelligence quotient 498 *intelligence*; genius; brain.

spirit, soul, inner mind; inner sense, inner being; heart, breast, bosom, inner man 5 *essential part*; double, genius 80 *self*; psyche, id, ego, superego, animus, self, the unconscious, the subconscious; personality, dual p., multiple p., split p. 503 *personality disorder*; spiritualism, psychical research 984 *occultism*; spiritualist, occultist.

psychology, parapsychology 984 *psychics*; Freudian psychology, Jungian p., Adlerian p.; Gestalt psychology, behaviourism; psychopathology, psychiatry, psychotherapy, psychodrama, psychoanalysis 658 *therapy*; psychological profiling; profiling; psycholinguistics.

psychologist, psychoanalyst, psychiatrist, psychotherapist 658 *doctor*; analyst, head shrinker, shrink, trick cyclist.

Adj. *mental*, thinking, reasoning 475 *rational*; cerebral, intellectual, conceptual; theoretical; perceptual, perceptive; cognizant 490 *knowing*.

perceive, perceive 490 *know*; realize, sense, become aware of, become conscious of; note 438 *see*; mark 455 *notice*; reason; use one's head, understand 498 *be wise*; conceptualize, intellectualize 449 *think*; conceive, invent 484 *discover*; imagine.

448 Absence of intellect
N. *absence of intellect*, stocks and stones; brainlessness, mindlessness 450 *absence of thought*; brain damage, unsound mind, insanity 503 *mental disorder*.

Adj. *mindless*, unintelligent; inanimate; unreasoning; brainless, empty-headed, vacuous 499 *foolish*; moronic, wanting 503 *mentally disordered*.

449 Thought
N. *thought*, mental process, thinking, thought processes; intellectual exercise, mental e., cogitation, cerebration, thinking cap; brainwork; hard thought, concentration 455 *attention*; deep thought, profundity 498 *wisdom*; thoughts, ideas 451 *idea*; conception, inmost thoughts 513 *ideality*; train of thought; association of ideas, reason 475 *reasoning*; brown study, deep thought, reverie 456 *abstractedness*; thinking out; second thoughts, after-thought 67 *sequel*; retrospection, hindsight, wisdom after the event 505 *memory*; forethought, forward planning, telepathy 984 *psychics*.

meditation, thoughtfulness, speculation 459 *enquiry*; lateral thinking; reflection, deep thought, brooding, rumination, consideration, pondering; contemplation 438 *inspection*; absorption, pensiveness; introspection, self-communing; transcendental meditation; retreat, mysticism 979 *piety*; deliberation, thinking out 480 *judgment*; application 536 *study*.

philosophy, metaphysics, ethics; speculation, abstract thought, scientific thought, natural philosophy; philosophical system, philosophical theory 512 *supposition*; school of philosophy 485 *opinion*; idealism, conceptualism, transcendentalism; phenomenalism, phenomenology, realism, nominalism, positivism, analytic philosophy 475 *reasoning*; existentialism, voluntarism; determinism, mechanism; vitalism; holism, organicism, structuralism, functionalism, reductionism, reductivism; rationalism, humanism, hedonism; utilitarianism, materialism; empiricism, pragmatism; relativism, relativity; agnosticism, scepticism, irrationalism 486 *doubt*; eclecticism; atheism 974 *irreligion*; nihilism, fatalism 596 *fate*; Pythagoreanism, Platonism, Aristotelianism; Scepticism, Stoicism, Epicureanism, Cynicism; Neo-Platonism, gnosticism; scholasticism, Thomism; Cartesianism, Kantianism, Hegelianism, Neo-H., dialectical materialism, Marxism; anthroposophy, theosophy; Hinduism, Buddhism, Sufism, Yoga, Zen 973 *religion*.

Adj. *thoughtful*, speculative; cogitative, deliberative; pensive, meditative, ruminative, contemplative, reflective; introspective; wrapt in thought; absorbed 455 *obsessed*; musing, daydreaming, dreamy 456 *abstracted*; concentrated 455 *attentive*; studying 536 *studious*; considerate 901 *philanthropic*; prudent 510 *foreseeing*.

Vb. *think*, ween 512 *suppose*; form ideas, fancy 513 *imagine*; ponder, cogitate (see *meditate*); put on one's thinking cap, use one's grey matter; concentrate, collect one's thoughts 455 *be attentive*; apply the mind, trouble one's head about, cerebrate, mull over, puzzle over 536 *study*; think hard, rack one's brains; think through, reason out 475 *reason*; think up, invent 484 *discover*; devise 623 *plan*; take into one's head, harbour a notion, have a sudden fancy, have an idea, toy with an i., kick an i. around; cherish an i. 485 *believe*; become obsessed, get a bee in one's bonnet, have a hang-up about 481 *be biased*; bear in mind, take account of, think on 505 *remember*.

meditate, ruminate; wonder about, enquire into 459 *enquire*; reflect, contemplate, study; speculate, philosophize, theorize; think about, consider, take into account, take into consideration; take stock of, ponder, weigh 480 *estimate*; think over, run over in the mind 505 *memorize*; reconsider, have second thoughts; think better of; take counsel, sleep on it 691 *consult*; brood, brood upon, muse, fall into a brown study.

dawn upon, occur to, cross the mind; come into one's head, come to one in a blinding flash, strike one.

cause thought, provoke thought, make one think, make one stop and think 821 *impress*; sink in, become a hang-up, obsess 481 *bias*.

absorb, engross, absorb, preoccupy, monopolize; be never out of one's thoughts, go round and round in one's head, occupy the mind, be uppermost in one's mind; prey on one's mind, obsess 481 *bias*; fascinate 983 *bewitch*.

450 Absence of thought

N. *absence of thought*, blank mind, abstraction 456 *abstractedness*; inanity, vacuity, blankness, fatuity, empty head 499 *unintelligence*; thoughtlessness 456 *inattention*; conditioned reflex; knee-jerk response, gut reaction; instinct 476 *intuition*.

451 Idea

N. *idea*, notion, a thought; abstract idea, concept; theory 512 *supposition*; mental image; Platonic idea; conception, perception, apprehension 447 *intellect*; observation 449 *thought*; impression, fancy 513 *imagination*; figment of imagination; associated ideas, complex; stream of consciousness, free association of ideas; invention, brainchild; brain wave, happy thought 484 *discovery*; wheeze, device 623 *contrivance*; point of view, slant, way of thinking, attitude 485 *opinion*; principle, main idea; obsession, hang-up 481 *prejudgment*.

452 Topic

N. *topic*, food for thought; gossip, rumour 529 *news*; subject matter, subject; contents, chapter, section 53 *subdivision*; what it is about, argument, plot, theme, message; text, commonplace, burden, motif; musical topic, statement, leitmotiv 412 *musical piece*; concern, interest, human i.; matter, affair; shop 622 *business*; topic for discussion, business on hand, agenda, any other business, AOB, order paper 623 *policy*; item on the agenda, motion 761 *request*; resolution 480 *judgment*; problem, problematics, gist, drift; theorem, proposition 512 *supposition*; thesis, case, point 475 *argument*; issue, moot point, debatable p., point at issue; field of enquiry, field of study 536 *study*.

Adj. *topical*, thematic; thought about, uppermost in the mind, fit for consideration, worthy of discussion.

Adv. *in question*, in one's thoughts; afoot, on the agenda, on the table; before the house, before the committee, under consideration, under discussion.

SECTION TWO

Precursory conditions and operations

453 Curiosity: desire for knowledge

N. *curiosity*, intellectual c., speculativeness, enquiring mind, thirst or itch for knowledge 536 *study*; interest, inquisitiveness, curiousness; zeal, meddlesomeness, officiousness, nosiness 678 *overactivity*; quizzing 459 *question*; sightseeing, rubbernecking 267 *land travel*; morbid curiosity, ghoulishness; voyeurism 951 *impurity*.

Adj. *inquisitive*, curious, interested; speculating, searching, seeking, avid for knowledge, hungry for information 536 *studious*; morbidly curious, ghoulish, prurient; newsmongering, agog, all ears 455 *attentive*; burning with curiosity, consumed with c., eaten up with c.; itching, hungry for; overcurious, nosy, snoopy, prying, spying, peeping, peeking; questioning, inquisitorial 459 *enquiring*; meddlesome, interfering, officious.

Vb. *be curious*, want to know; look for 459 *search*; research 461 *experiment*; be interested, take an interest; show interest, show curiosity, prick up one's ears, be all agog 455 *be attentive*; mosey around, dip into; dig up, nose out; peep, peek, spy 438 *scan*; snoop, pry, nose into 459 *enquire*; eavesdrop, tap the line, intercept, bug, listen, listen in, eavesdrop 415 *hear*; poke *or* stick one's nose in, be nosy, interfere, act the busybody 678 *meddle*; quiz, question, bombard with questions 459 *interrogate*; stand and stare, gape, gawk 438 *gaze*.

454 Incuriosity

N. *incuriosity*, lack of curiosity; mental inertia; uninterest, unconcern 860 *indifference*; apathy, phlegmatism 820 *moral insensibility*.

Adj. *incurious*, uninquisitive; uninterested; aloof, distant, blasé; unconcerned, uninvolved 860 *indifferent*; inert, apathetic 820 *impassive*.

Vb. *be incurious*, – indifferent etc. adj.; have no curiosity, take no interest 456 *be inattentive*; feel no concern, couldn't care less, not trouble oneself, not bother with 860 *be indifferent*; mind one's own business, go one's own way 820 *be insensitive*; look the other way 458 *disregard*.

455 Attention

N. *attention*, notice, regard 438 *look*; consideration 449 *thought*; heed, alertness, readiness, attentiveness, solicitude, observance 457 *carefulness*; observation, watchfulness, vigilance, watch, guard, invigilation 457 *surveillance*; wariness, circumspection 858 *caution*; contemplation, introspection 449 *meditation*; intentness, earnestness, seriousness 599 *resolution*; undivided attention; concentration, application, studiousness, close study 536 *study*; examination, scrutiny, checkup, review 438 *inspection*; close attention; meticulousness, attention to detail, minuteness, pernicketiness; diligence, trouble 678 *assiduity*; rapt attention; single-mindedness; absorption, preoccupation 456 *inattention*; interest 453 *curiosity*; one-track mind, fixation, obsession, hang-up.

Adj. *attentive*, intent, diligent, assiduous 678 *industrious*; considerate, caring, thoughtful 884

courteous; heedful, mindful; alert, ready, on one's toes, on the qui vive, on the ball, with it; wakeful, awake, wide-a.; awake to, alive to, sensing 819 *sensitive*; aware, conscious, thinking 449 *thoughtful*; observant, sharp-eyed, watching, watchful 457 *vigilant*; attending, rapt, missing nothing; all eyes, all agog 438 *seeing*; all ears; concentrating; serious, earnest; eager to learn 536 *studious*; meticulous, punctilious 494 *accurate*; on the lookout 507 *expectant*.

obsessed, single-minded, engrossed, preoccupied, wrapped up in, taken up with, into, hooked on, addicted to, hung up; haunted by 854 *fearing*; monomaniacal 503 *crazy*.

Vb. *be attentive*, attend, pay attention; heed, pay h., take notice of, mind 457 *be careful*; care, take trouble, take pains, put oneself out for, bother 682 *exert oneself*; listen, prick up one's ears, sit up and take notice; take seriously; devote *or* give one's attention to, bend the mind to, direct one's thoughts to 449 *think*; think of nothing else, be obsessed with, be preoccupied with 481 *be biased*; keep one's eye on the ball, concentrate, miss nothing; watch, be all eyes, be all agog 438 *gaze*; be all ears, drink in, hang on the lips of 415 *hear*; focus one's mind on, rivet one's attention to, concentrate on, fix on; scrutinize; study closely.

be mindful, keep in mind, bear in m., have in m., be thinking of 505 *remember*; not forget, think of, spare a thought for, regard, look on 438 *see*; lend an ear to 415 *hear*; take care of, see to 457 *look after*; have regard to, have an eye to.

notice, note, take n., register; mark, recognize, spot; take cognizance of, take into consideration, take into account, review, reconsider 449 *meditate*; take account of, consider, weigh 480 *judge*; comment upon, remark on, talk about 584 *converse*; mention, just m., mention in passing, refer to en passant, touch on 524 *hint*; think worthy of attention, have time for, spare time f.; acknowledge.

attract notice, draw the attention, hold the a., engage the a., focus the a., rivet the a., be the cynosure of all eyes, draw the crowds, cut a figure 875 *be ostentatious*; stick out like a sore thumb, arouse notice, interest 821 *impress*; excite attention, demand a.; catch the eye 443 *be visible*; bring to one's notice *or* attention 522 *show*; call attention to, advertise, publicize 528 *publish*; point out, point to, show 547 *indicate*; stress, underline 532 *emphasize*; fascinate; warn 665 *raise the alarm*; call to attention 737 *command*.

456 Inattention

N. *inattention*, inadvertence, forgetfulness 506 *oblivion*; oversight; lapse 495 *error*; lack of interest 454 *incuriosity*; unconcern, apathy 860 *indifference*; disregard 458 *negligence*; thoughtlessness, heedlessness 857 *rashness*; carelessness, inconsiderateness 481 *misjudgment*, 932 *selfishness*; deaf ears 416 *deafness*; unseeing eyes, blind spot, tunnel vision 439 *blindness*; diversion, distraction, dust in the eyes, wild-goose chase, red herring 612 *inducement*; attention deficit disorder; absent-mindedness 450 *absence of thought*; stargazer, daydreamer, woolgatherer, head in the clouds, Johnny-head-in-air, Walter Mitty; scatterbrain, grasshopper mind, butterfly.

abstractedness, abstraction, absent-mindedness, wandering attention; woolgathering, daydreaming, stargazing, doodling; reverie; distraction, divided attention.

Adj. *inattentive*, careless 458 *negligent*; off one's guard, with one's trousers *or* pants down 508 *inexpectant*; unobservant, unnoticing 454 *incurious*; unseeing 439 *blind*; unhearing 416 *deaf*; undiscerning 464 *indiscriminating*; unmindful, unheeding, inadvertent, not thinking, unreflecting; half asleep; uninterested 860 *indifferent*; apathetic, unaware 820 *impassive*; oblivious 506 *forgetful*; inconsiderate, thoughtless, tactless, heedless; regardless 857 *rash*; cavalier, offhand, cursory, superficial 212 *shallow*.

abstracted, distrait(e), absent-minded, not with it, miles away; lost in thought; rapt, with one's head in the clouds, stargazing; bemused, sunk in a brown study, deep in reverie, pensive, dreamy, daydreaming, mooning, woolgathering; half-awake 679 *sleepy*.

distracted, preoccupied, engrossed; diverted; put off, put off one's stroke; unnerved 854 *nervous*.

light-minded, desultory, trifling; frivolous, flippant, light-headed; mercurial, bird-witted, flighty, giddy; grasshopper-minded, scatty, scatterbrained, harebrained, featherbrained; harum-scarum, inconstant 604 *capricious*.

Vb. *be inattentive*, pay no attention, pay no heed; turn a blind eye 439 *be blind*; stop one's ears 416 *be deaf*; not register, not use one's eyes; not get the message, not click; overlook 495 *blunder*; be off one's guard, be caught with one's trousers *or* pants down, let the cat out of the bag, let slip, be caught out; lose track of, lose sight of; not remember 506 *forget*; dream, nod 679 *sleep*; trifle, play at, toy with; be abstracted, let one's thoughts wander; go woolgathering, build castles in Spain, build castles in the air 513 *imagine*; fall into a brown study, muse, be lost in thought, moon, stargaze, have one's head in the clouds; idle, doodle 679 *be inactive*; be distracted, digress, lose the thread, lose the train of thought, fluff one's lines 282 *stray*; be

disconcerted, be rattled 854 *be nervous*; be put off, be put off one's stroke 702 *hinder* (**see** *distract*); disregard, ignore 458 *neglect*.

distract, divert, divert one's attention; put out of one's head, drive out of one's mind; entice, throw a sop to Cerberus 612 *tempt*; muddle 63 *derange*; disturb, interrupt 72 *discontinue*; disconcert, upset, perplex, hassle, fluster, bother, flurry, rattle 318 *agitate*; put one off his stroke 702 *obstruct*; bewilder, flummox, throw off the scent, draw a red herring 474 *puzzle*; fuddle.

457 Carefulness

N. *carefulness*, attentiveness, diligence, pains 678 *assiduity*; heed, care, utmost c. 455 *attention*; anxiety, solicitude 825 *worry*; loving care 897 *benevolence*; orderliness, neatness 60 *order*; attention to detail, thoroughness, meticulousness; exactitude 494 *accuracy*; perfectionism 862 *fastidiousness*; scruples 929 *probity*; vigilance, watchfulness, alertness, readiness; wariness 858 *caution*; forethought 510 *foresight*.

surveillance, watching, guarding, neighbourhood watch, home w. 660 *protection*; houseminding, homesitting, caretaking, vigilance, invigilation, inspection; baby-sitting, childminding, chaperonage; lookout, weather eye, Hoolivan, electronic surveillance; vigil, watch, deathwatch; doomwatch

carer, nurse, care assistant, home help, buddy; baby-sitter, child-minder, minder; house-sitter, home-s.

guard, sentinel, sentry 660 *protector*, 749 *keeper*.

Adj. *careful*, thoughtful, considerate, heedful 455 *attentive*; painstaking; solicitous, anxious; cautious; conscientious, scrupulous; diligent, assiduous 678 *industrious*; meticulous; nice, exact 494 *accurate*; pedantic, perfectionist 862 *fastidious*; neat 60 *orderly*; miserly 816 *parsimonious*.

vigilant, alert, ready 669 *prepared*; on the alert, on guard, on the qui vive, on one's toes; keeping cave, watchful, wide-awake; observant, sharp-eyed, eagle-eyed 438 *seeing*; prudent, farsighted 510 *foreseeing*; circumspect, guarded, wary 858 *cautious*.

Vb. *be careful*, heed, beware 455 *be attentive*; take precautions, think twice; be on the qui vive, be on the alert, have one's eyes open, have one's wits about one, keep a lookout, keep cave, watch one's step, mind how one goes; look before one leaps; feel one's way 461 *be tentative*; be on one's guard, mind one's Ps and Qs; dot one's i's and cross one's t's.

look after, look to, see to, take care of, caretake, homesit 689 *manage*; take charge of; care for, mind, tend, keep 660 *safeguard*; baby-sit, childmind; nurse, foster, take into care, cherish 889 *pet*; keep a sharp eye on, keep tabs on, monitor; escort, chaperon.

invigilate, keep vigil, watch; stand sentinel; keep watch, keep a sharp lookout, watch out for; keep one's wits about one, keep one's eyes peeled, keep one's weather-eye open, sleep with one eye o., keep one's ear to the ground; mount guard, post sentries.

458 Negligence
N. *negligence*, carelessness 456 *inattention*; forgetfulness 506 *oblivion*; neglect, oversight, omission; default 918 *undutifulness*; unwariness, unguarded hour *or* minute, unpreparedness 670 *nonpreparation*; disregard; unconcern, don't-care attitude, couldn't-care-less a. 860 *indifference*; recklessness 857 *rashness*; procrastination 136 *delay*; laziness 679 *inactivity*; slovenliness, sluttishness, untidiness 61 *disorder*; sloppiness, inexactitude 495 *inexactness*; offhandedness, casualness, laxness 734 *laxity*; perfunctoriness, superficiality 212 *shallowness*; trifling, scamping, skipping, dodging, botching 695 *bungling*; scamped work, skimped w., botched job, loose ends 728 *failure*.

Adj. *negligent*, neglectful, careless 456 *inattentive*; remiss 918 *undutiful*; thoughtless; oblivious 506 *forgetful*; uncaring; reckless 857 *rash*; heedless 769 *nonobservant*; casual, offhand 734 *lax*; sloppy, slipshod, slapdash, couldn't care less, perfunctory, superficial, with a lick and a promise; hit-and-miss, hurried 680 *hasty*; inaccurate 495 *inexact*; slack 679 *lazy*; procrastinating 136 *late*; sluttish, untidy, slovenly 649 *dirty*; unwary, unguarded, off guard 508 *inexpectant*; improvident 670 *unprepared*; disregarding, ignoring; lapsed 974 *irreligious*.

neglected, uncared for, untended; unkempt 649 *dirty*; unprotected, unguarded, unchaperoned; deserted; unattended, left alone, home alone; unheeded 860 *unwanted*; disregarded, ignored, out in the cold; overlooked, omitted; unnoticed, unmarked 444 *invisible*; shelved, pigeonholed, put aside, mothballed, on the back-burner 136 *late*; unread, unexplored; skimped, perfunctory 726 *uncompleted*; hid under a bushel.

Vb. *neglect*, omit; pass over; lose sight of, overlook 456 *be inattentive*; leave undone, leave half-done, leave loose ends, do by halves 726 *not complete*, botch, bungle 695 *be clumsy*; skimp, scamp 204 *shorten*; skip; skate over, gloss over 525 *conceal*.

disregard, ignore, pass over, give the go-by, dodge, shirk 620 *avoid*; let pass connive at, take no notice 734 *be lax*; pay no attention to, turn a blind eye to, dismiss 439 *be blind*; excuse, overlook 909 *forgive*; discount 483 *underestimate*; pass by 282 *deviate*; turn one's back on, slight, cold-shoulder, cut, cut dead, send to Coventry 885 *be rude*; turn a deaf ear to 416 *be deaf*; take lightly, not take seriously, not trouble one's head about 860 *be indifferent*; have no time for, laugh off, pooh-pooh 922 *hold cheap*; leave out in the cold 57 *exclude*; leave to their own devices, leave in the lurch, desert, abandon 621 *relinquish*.

be neglectful, doze, nod 679 *sleep*; be off one's guard; be caught napping, oversleep; be caught with one's pants *or* trousers down 508 *not expect*; procrastinate, put off until tomorrow, let slide, let slip, let the grass grow under one's feet 677 *not act*; take it easy, coast 679 *be inactive*; shelve, pigeonhole, lay aside, mothball, put on the back-burner, put aside.

459 Enquiry
N. *enquiry*, asking, questioning (**see** *interrogation*); challenge (**see** *question*); asking about 524 *information*; close enquiry, witch-hunt (**see** *search*); inquisition, examination, investigation; checkup, medical; inquest, post mortem, autopsy, audit, trial 959 *legal trial*; public enquiry; commission of enquiry, working party (**see** *enquirer*); census, canvass, survey, market, research; poll, public opinion poll, Gallup p. (tdmk), straw p. *or* vote 605 *vote*; probe, test, means t., check, spot c., trial run 461 *experiment*; review, scrutiny 438 *inspection*; IQ test; introspection; personality testing, Rorschach *or* inkblot test; research 536 *study*; analysis, dissection; exploration, reconnaissance, recce, reconnoitre, survey 484 *discovery*; discussion, canvassing, consultation 584 *conference*; scientific enquiry 449 *philosophy*.

interrogation, questioning; forensic examination, leading question, cross-examination; quiz, brains trust; catechism; inquisition, third degree, grilling; dialogue; question time, Prime Minister's question t.

question, question mark, interrogation m. 547 *punctuation*; query; questions, questionnaire 87 *list*; question paper, examination p.; Parliamentary question; challenge; trick question, catch, loaded q.; indirect question, feeler, leading question; rhetorical q.; moot point; point at issue 452 *topic*; crucial question, burning q., sixty-four-thousand-dollar q.; vexed question, controversy, bone of contention 475 *argument*; problem, brain-teaser, poser, mind-boggler, unsolved mystery 530 *enigma*.

exam, examination, oral e., viva voce e., viva; interview, audition 415 *hearing*; practical examination, written e., multiple choice e.; test, series of tests, battery; intelligence test, IQ test;

11-plus, qualifying examination, entrance e., common entrance, matriculation; Certificate of Secondary Education, CSE, 16-plus, General Certificate of Education, GCE, General Certificate of Secondary Education, GCSE; 'O' level, 'A' level, 'S' level, 'A/S' level; 'O' grade, Standard g., Higher, SYS, baccalaureate; prelims, pre-Meds, Responsions; tripos, Moderations, Mods., Greats, finals, degree exams; doctorate examination, bar e.; degree level, pass 1., honours 1.

search, probe, investigation, enquiry; quest, hunt, witch-h., treasure h. 619 *pursuit*; house-to-house search; frisking, skin-search, strip-search; rummaging, turning over; exploration, excavation, dig; speleology, potholing; searchparty; search warrant.

police enquiry, investigation, criminal i., detection 484 *discovery*; detective work, shadowing, tailing, house-watching; grilling, third degree; Criminal Investigation Department, CID, Federal Bureau of Investigation, FBI, Interpol; secret police, Gestapo.

secret service, espionage, counter-e., spying, intelligence, MI5, CIA, KGB; informer, spy, operative, mole, sleeper, spook, 007, undercover agent, secret a., cloak-and-dagger man; double agent, inside a.; counterspy; spy ring.

detective, investigator, criminologist; plain-clothes man; enquiry agent, private detective, private investigator, private eye; hotel detective, store d.; amateur detective; Federal agent, FBI a., G-man, CID man; tec, sleuth, bloodhound, gumshoe, dick, snooper, nose, spy 524 *informer*; graphologist, handwriting expert; Sherlock Holmes; forensic expert.

enquirer, investigator; journalist 529 *news reporter*; student, seeker for truth; search party; water diviner 484 *detector*; prospector, gold-digger; talent scout; scout, spy, surveyor, reconnoitrer; inspector; checker screener, scrutineer, censor, ombudsperson 480 *estimator*; scanner, examiner, board of examiners; tester, test pilot, researcher, research worker, analyst, dissector 461 *experimenter*; market researcher, sampler, pollster, canvasser; explorer 268 *traveller*.

questioner, cross-q., cross-examiner, interrogator, inquisitor, Grand I.; interviewer; challenger, heckler; question *or* quiz master.

Adj. *enquiring*, curious, prying, nosy 453 *inquisitive*; quizzing, quizzical; interrogatory, interrogative; examining, inquisitional; probing, poking, digging, investigative; testing, searching, fact-finding, exploratory, empirical, tentative 461 *experimental*; analytic, diagnostic.

Vb. *enquire*, ask 491 *not know*; demand 761 *request*; canvass, query, bring in question 475 *argue*; ask for, look for, enquire for, seek (**see** *search*); hunt for 619 *pursue*; enquire into, make

enquiries, probe, delve into, dig i., sound, look into, investigate, throw open to enquiry, hold *or* conduct an enquiry, call in Scotland Yard; try, hear 959 *try a case*; review, overhaul, audit, scrutinize, monitor, screen; analyse, dissect, sift; research 536 *study*; examine 449 *meditate*; check, check on; take the temperature, put a toe in the water, take soundings; follow up an enquiry, pursue an e., get to the bottom of, fathom, X-ray 438 *scan*; ferret out, nose out; peer, peep, peek, snoop, spy, pry, nose around 453 *be curious*; survey, reconnoitre, case, sus out; explore, feel one's way 461 *be tentative*; test, try, sample, taste 461 *experiment*.

interrogate, ask questions; question; cross-question, cross-examine, badger, challenge, heckle; interview, hold a viva; examine, subject to questioning, sound out, probe, quiz, catechize, grill, give the third degree; put to the question 963 *torture*; pump, pick one's brains; move the question, put the q., pop the q.; pose, propose a question; frame a q., raise a q., moot, postulate a question.

search, seek, look for; conduct a search, rummage, ransack, comb; scrabble, forage, fossick, root about; scour, clean out, turn over, rake o., pick o., turn out, turn inside out, rake through, rifle t., go t., search t., look into every nook and corner *or* cranny; look high and low; sift through, winnow, go over with a fine-tooth comb; pry into, peel t., peep i., overhaul, frisk, strip-search, skin-search, go over, search one's pockets, search for, feel for, grope for, hunt for, drag for, fish, fish for, dig for; leave no stone unturned, explore every avenue 682 *exert oneself*; cast about, seek a clue, follow the trail 619 *pursue*; probe, explore, go in quest of 461 *be tentative*; dig, excavate, prospect, embark on a treasure-hunt.

460 Answer

N. *answer*, reply, response; reaction; answer by return of post, acknowledgment, return 588 *correspondence*; official reply; returns, results 548 *record*; feedback 524 *information*; echo 106 *repetition*; password 547 *identification*; keyword, open sesame; answering back, backchat, repartee; retort, counterblast, riposte 714 *retaliation*; give and take, question and answer, dialogue, discussion 584 *interlocution*; last word, final answer; Parthian shot; clue, key, right answer, explanation 520 *interpretation*; solution 658 *remedy*; oracle 530 *enigma*.

rejoinder, counterstatement, reply, counterblast, rebuttal; defence, reply; refutation, contradiction 533 *negation*, 467 *counterevidence*; countercharge, counterclaim.

respondent, defendant; answerer, responder,

replier, correspondent; examinee; candidate, applicant, entrant, sitter, examinee 716 *contender.*

Vb. *answer,* reply, reply by return of post, reply to an invitation, RSVP, write back, acknowledge, respond, echo; answer back, retort, riposte 714 *retaliate;* say in reply, rejoin, rebut, counter 479 *confute;* field; parry 620 *avoid;* contradict 533 *negate;* defend; get the right answer, solve the riddle 520 *interpret;* settle, decide 480 *judge;* suit the requirements, suit one down to the ground 642 *be expedient;* answer to, correspond to 12 *correlate.*

461 Experiment

N. *experiment,* practical e., scientific e., controlled e.; experimentalism, experimentation, experimental method, verification, verification by experiment; exploration, probe; analysis, examination 459 *enquiry;* object lesson, proof 478 *demonstration;* assay 480 *estimate;* testability; check, test, crucial t., acid t., test case; probation; double-blind test; practical test, trial, trials, try-out, trial run, practice r., dry r., test flight 671 *attempt;* audition, voice test; pilot scheme.

empiricism, speculation, guesswork, guesstimation 512 *conjecture;* tentativeness; experience, practice, rule of thumb, trial, trial and error, hit and miss; random shot, shot in the dark, leap in the d., gamble 618 *gambling;* instinct 476 *intuition;* sampling, random sample, straw vote; feeler 459 *question;* straw to show which way the wind is blowing, kite-flying, toe in the water, trial balloon.

experimenter, experimentalist, empiricist, researcher, research worker, analyst, vivisector; assayer, chemist; tester; test driver, test pilot; speculator, prospector; prober, explorer.

testing agent, criterion, touchstone; standard, yardstick 465 *gauge;* breathalyser, sniffer torch; control; indicator, reagent, litmus paper, retort, test tube; proving ground, wind tunnel; simulator, flight s., test track; laboratory.

Adj. *experimental,* analytical, probationary; provisional, tentative 618 *speculative;* trial, exploratory 459 *enquiring;* empirical; in the experimental stage 474 *uncertain.*

Vb. *experiment,* experimentalize; put to the proof; assay, analyse; research; experiment upon, vivisect, make a guinea pig of, practise upon; test, put to the t., run a t. on, put through a battery of tests 459 *enquire;* give something a try; try out, give a trial to 671 *attempt.*

be tentative, feel one's way, proceed by trial and error; feel 378 *touch;* grope, fumble; get the feel of 536 *learn;* put out a feeler, dip a toe in, put a toe in the water, fly a kite, feel the pulse,

consult the barometer, take the temperature, see how the land lies, see how the wind blows; fish for, angle for, cast one's net; wait and see, see what happens; try it on, see how far one can go; try one's fortune, try one's luck, speculate 618 *gamble;* venture, explore, prospect 672 *undertake;* probe, sound 459 *enquire.*

462 Comparison

N. *comparison,* comparing, likening; juxtaposition 202 *contiguity;* comparability, points of comparison, analogy, parallel, likeness, similitude 18 *similarity;* identification 13 *identity;* antithesis 14 *contrariety;* contrast 15 *differentiation;* simile, allegory 519 *metaphor;* criterion, pattern, model, check list, control 23 *prototype.*

Adj. *compared,* compared with, in comparison with, likened, measured against, contrasted; comparative, comparable, analogical; relative, correlative; allegorical, metaphorical 519 *figurative.*

Vb. *compare,* collate, confront; set side by side, bring together; draw a comparison 18 *liken,* 13 *identify;* parallel; contrast 15 *differentiate;* compare and contrast 463 *discriminate;* match, pair, balance 28 *equalize;* view together, check with 12 *correlate;* draw a parallel; compare to, compare with; compare notes.

463 Discrimination

N. *discrimination,* distinction 15 *differentiation;* discernment, discretion, connoisseurship 480 *judgment;* insight, perception, acumen, flair 498 *intelligence;* appreciation, critique 480 *estimate;* sensitivity 494 *accuracy;* sensibility 819 *moral sensibility;* tact, delicacy, kid gloves, refinement 846 *good taste;* timing, sense of t.; nicety, particularity 862 *fastidiousness;* sublety, hair-splitting 475 *reasoning;* sorting out 62 *sorting;* selection 605 *choice;* nuance 15 *difference.*

Adj. *discriminating,* discriminative, selective, judicious, discerning, discreet; sensitive 494 *accurate;* fine, delicate, nice, particular 862 *fastidious;* thoughtful, tactful 513 *imaginative;* tasting, appraising, critical 480 *judicial;* distinguishing 15 *distinctive.*

Vb. *discriminate,* distinguish 15 *differentiate;* compare and contrast 462 *compare;* sort out, sieve, sift; separate, separate the sheep from the goats, winnow, sort the wheat from the chaff 46 *set apart;* pick out 605 *select;* exercise discretion, make a distinction, make an exception, draw the line 468 *qualify;* make a value judgment 480 *judge;* have a feel for, have an eye *or* an ear for; know what's what, know how many beans make five, know one's way about, know one's stuff, know a hawk from a handsaw 490 *know.*

464 Indiscrimination

N. *indiscrimination*, lack of discrimination, promiscuity 79 *generality*; lack of judgment, simplicity, naiveté; obtuseness 499 *unintelligence*; indiscretion 857 *rashness*; imperceptivity 439 *blindness*; insensitiveness, insensibility; lack of refinement, coarseness, vulgarity 847 *bad taste*.

Adj. *indiscriminate*, unsorted; undistinguished, undifferentiated, same for everybody 16 *uniform*; random, unaimed, undirected; confused, undefined, unmeasured 474 *uncertain*; promiscuous, haphazard, wholesale, blanket, global 79 *general*.

indiscriminating, unselective, undiscerning, uncritical 499 *unintelligent*; imperceptive, obtuse; tactless, insensitive, unimaginative 820 *impassive*; unrefined, tasteless, coarse 847 *vulgar*; indiscreet, ill-judged 857 *rash*; tone-deaf 416 *deaf*; colour-blind 439 *blind*; inaccurate 495 *inexact*.

465 Measurement

N. *measurement*, quantification; mensuration, surveying; geodetics, geodesy; dose, dosage 26 *finite quantity*; rating, valuation, evaluation; appraisal, assessment, appreciation, estimation 480 *estimate*; calculation, computation, reckoning 86 *numeration*; gauging; checking, check; reading; trigonometry; second, degree, minute, quadrant 247 *angular measure*.

geometry, plane g., planimetry; solid geometry, stereometry; altimetry, hypsometry; Euclidean geometry, non-Euclidean g.; geometer.

metrology, dimensions, length, breadth, height, depth, thickness 195 *size*; weights and measures, avoirdupois, metric system, unit of measurement; weights 322 *weighing*; axle load; linear measure 203 *long measure*; measure of capacity, volume, cubic contents 183 *measure*; liquid measure, gill, pint, imperial p., quart, gallon, imperial g.; barrel, pipe, hogshead 194 *vessel*; litre; apothecaries' fluid measure, minim, dram; dry measure, peck, bushel, quarter; unit of energy, ohm, watt 160 *electricity*; horse power 160 *energy*; candle-power 417 *light*; decibel, sone.

gauge, measure, scale, graduated s.; time scale 117 *chronometry*; balance 322 *scales*; vernier, micrometer; footrule; yardstick, metre bar; yard measure, tape m., measuring tape, metal rule; chain, link, pole, perch, rod; lead, log, log-line; echo sounder; ruler, slide rule; straightedge, T-square, try s., set sq.; dividers, callipers, compass, protractor; sextant, quadrant 269 *sailing aid*; theodolite; astrolabe 321 *astronomy*; index, Plimsoll line, Plimsoll mark, bench m. 547 *indication*; high-water mark, tidemark, floodmark,

water line 236 *limit*; axis, coordinate; rule of thumb, standard, criterion, norm 23 *prototype*; milestone 547 *signpost*.

meter, measuring instrument; altimeter; bathometer 211 *depth*; thermometer 379 *thermometry*; barometer, anemometer; dynamometer; hygrometer, fluviometer; gas etc. meter; speedometer, tachometer, tachymeter, tachograph, spy-in-the-cab, odometer, milometer 277 *velocity*; cyclometer, pedometer 267 *land travel*; metronome, time switch, parking meter 117 *timekeeper*; micrometer; Geiger counter; seismograph.

Adj. *metrical*, mensural; imperial, metric; metrological; dimensional, three-d.; cubic, volumetric, linear, micrometric; cadastral, topographical; geodetic.

Vb. *measure*, mensurate, survey, triangulate; compute, calculate, count, reckon 86 *number*; quantify, take the measurements, measure the length and breadth, measure up; size up, estimate the average 30 *average out*; beat the bounds, pace out; tape, span; calliper, use the dividers; probe, sound, fathom, plumb 313 *plunge*; take soundings, heave the lead; pace, check the speed 117 *time*; balance 322 *weigh*.

gauge, meter, take a reading, read, read off; standardize 16 *make uniform*; grade, mark off, mark out, calibrate 27 *graduate*; reduce to scale, draw to s., map 551 *represent*.

appraise, gauge, value, cost, fix the price of 809 *price*; evaluate, estimate, make an e., form an e.; appreciate, assess, assay 480 *estimate*; form an opinion 480 *judge*; tape, have taped, have the measure of, size up.

mete out, mete, measure out, weigh, weigh out, dole o., allocate, divide, share, share out, portion out 775 *participate*, 783 *apportion*.

SECTION THREE

Materials for reasoning

466 Evidence

N. *evidence*, facts, data, biodata, curriculum vitae, case history; grounds 475 *reasons*; premises 475 *premise*; hearsay 524 *report*; circumstantial evidence 8 *circumstance*; constructive evidence 512 *supposition*; prima facie evidence; proof 478 *demonstration*; corroboration; verification, confirmation 473 *certainty*; 467 *counter-evidence*; fact, relevant f.; document, exhibit, fingerprints, DNA fingerprinting, genetic f. 548 *record*; clue 524 *hint*; symptom, syndrome, sign, sure s. 547 *indication*; mention, reference, quotation, citation, chapter and verse; one's authorities, documentation.

testimony, witness; statement 524 *information*;

admission, confession 526 *disclosure*; one's case, plea 614 *pretext*; word, assertion, allegation 532 *affirmation*; evidence on oath; legal evidence; deposition, affidavit, attestation 532 *oath*; State's evidence, King's *or* Queen's evidence; word of mouth, verbal; documentary evidence; character reference, compurgation 927 *vindication*; case record, dossier 548 *record*; written contract, contract of employment 765 *compact*; deed, testament 767 *security*.

credential, testimonial, chit, character, recommendation, references; seal, signature, countersignature, endorsement, docket, counterfoil; voucher, warranty, warrant, certificate, diploma 767 *security*; ticket, passport, visitor's p., visa 756 *permit*; authority, scripture.

witness, eye w. 441 *spectator*; indicator, informant, telltale, grass, supergrass 524 *informer*; deponent, testifier, swearer, attestor 765 *signatory*; witness to character, referee; sponsor 707 *patron*.

Adj. *evidential*, suggesting, significant 514 *meaningful*; indicative, symptomatic, identifying, diagnostic; deducible, verifiable 471 *probable*; corroborative, confirmatory; damning; presumptive, reliable 473 *certain*; proving, demonstrative, conclusive; factual, documented, well-documented 473 *positive*; well-grounded, well-founded 494 *true*; authoritative 178 *influential*; testified, attested, witnessed; in evidence, on the record.

Vb. *evidence*, show, evince, furnish evidence; show signs of, betray symptoms of, have the makings of; betoken 551 *represent*; breathe of, declare witness to 522 *manifest*; lend colour to 471 *make likely*; tell its own tale, speak for itself, speak volumes; carry weight 178 *influence*; suggest 547 *indicate*; argue, involve 523 *imply*.

testify, witness; take one's oath, swear, be sworn, speak on oath 532 *affirm*; bear witness, take the stand, give testimony, give evidence, witness for *or* against, swear to, vouch for, give one's word; authenticate, validate, give credence, certify 473 *make certain*; attest, subscribe, countersign, endorse, sign; plead, state one's case 475 *argue*; admit, avow, acknowledge 526 *confess*; give a character reference, act as referee.

corroborate, support, buttress 162 *strengthen*; sustain, uphold in evidence, substantiate 927 *vindicate*; bear out, verify; validate, confirm, ratify, establish, make a case for 473 *make certain*; lead evidence; produce one's witnesses; produce the evidence; document, give credence; collect evidence; cite the evidence, refer to a precedent, quote one's authorities, give chapter and verse.

467 Counterevidence

N. *counterevidence*, contraindication 14 *contrariety*; evidence against, defence, rebuttal, rejoinder 460 *answer*; refutation 479 *confutation*; denial 533 *negation*; justification 927 *vindication*; one word against another; counteroath, counterclaim; conflicting evidence, contradictory e.; mitigating evidence 468 *qualification*; hostile witness.

Vb. *tell against*, weigh against, countervail; contravene, run counter, contradict, contraindicate; rebut 479 *confute*; oppose, point the other way 14 *be contrary*; cancel out 182 *counteract*; cut both ways 518 *be equivocal*; lead for the other side; fail to confirm, alter the case; weaken, damage, spoil; undermine, subvert 165 *destroy*; demolish the case, turn the tables, contradict oneself, turn hostile.

Adv. *conversely*, on the other hand; in rebuttal.

468 Qualification

N. *qualification*, specification 80 *speciality*; prerequisite 627 *requirement*; assumption 512 *supposition*; leaven, colouring, tinge; modification 143 *change*; mitigation 177 *moderation*; stipulation, condition, sine qua non 766 *conditions*; limitation 747 *restriction*; proviso, reservation; exception, salvo, escape clause, letout c., penalty clause, exemption 919 *nonliability*; demur, objection, but 704 *opposition*; consideration, concession, allowance; extenuating circumstances; redeeming feature.

Adj. *qualifying*, restricting, limiting; modifying; mitigatory; extenuating, palliative, excusing, weakening, colouring, leavening; contingent, provisional 766 *conditional*; discounting, allowing for, taking into account; saving, excepting, exempting; qualified, not absolute; exceptional, exempted, exempt 919 *nonliable*.

Vb. *qualify*, condition, limit, restrict 747 *restrain*; colour; shade; leaven, alter 143 *modify*; temper, season, palliate, mitigate 177 *moderate*; adulterate 163 *weaken*; excuse 927 *extenuate*; grant, concede, make allowance for, take into account, take cognizance of; lessen 37 *abate*; make exceptions 919 *exempt*; alter the case; insert a qualifying clause; insist on 627 *require*; relax 734 *be lax*; take exception, object, demur, raise an objection 762 *deprecate*.

Adv. *provided*, provided always, with the proviso that, according as, subject to, conditionally, with the understanding that, so *or* as long as; granting, admitting, supposing; allowing for; with a pinch of salt; not absolutely, not invariably; if, if not, unless 8 *if*; though, although, even if.

nevertheless, even so, all the same, for all that, after all; despite, in spite of; but, yet, still, at all events; whether, whether or no.

469 Possibility
N. *possibility*, potentiality; capacity, viability, viableness, workability 160 *ability*; what might be; best one can do, all in one's power, contingency, eventuality, a possibility, chance, off-chance 159 *fair chance*; good chance 137 *opportunity*; bare possibility, ghost of a chance, outside c.; likelihood 471 *probability*; conceivability; practicability; practicableness, feasibility; availability, accessibility; risk of.

Adj. *possible*, potential, hypothetical; able, capable, viable; arguable, reasonable; feasible, practicable, negotiable 701 *easy*; workable, achievable; doable, operable; attainable, approachable, accessible, obtainable, realizable; surmountable; within the bounds *or* realms of possibility; available, still open, not excluded, not too late; conceivable, imaginable; practical; allowable; contingent 124 *future*; on the cards 471 *probable*; liable, tending.

Vb. *be possible*, – feasible etc. adj.; may, might; be a possibility, depend, be contingent, lie within the bounds *or* realms of possibility; stand a chance 471 *be likely*.

make possible, enable; allow 756 *permit*; give the green light, clear the path, smoothe the way, remove the obstacles.

Adv. *possibly*, conceivably; perhaps, perchance, for all one knows; within reach, within one's grasp; may be, could be; if possible, if humanly possible; wind and weather permitting, God willing, Deo volente, D.V.

470 Impossibility
N. *impossibility*, inconceivability etc. adj.; unthinkableness, no chance, no way, not a chance of, not a cat's chance, not a snowball's chance in hell, not a hope 853 *hopelessness*; irrevocability; impasse, deadlock, logjam 702 *obstacle*; impracticability 643 *inexpedience*; unavailability, inaccessibility, sour grapes; impossible task, no go 700 *hard task*.

Adj. *impossible*, not possible; ruled out, excluded; not to be thought of, out of the question, hopeless; unreasonable; incompatible with the facts 495 *erroneous*; inconceivable, unthinkable, unimaginable, unheard of; miraculous 864 *wonderful*; unrealistic 513 *imaginary*.

impracticable, not feasible; unworkable; out of the question, unattainable, insoluble, inextricable, beyond one 700 *difficult*; insuperable; insurmountable, impenetrable, unnavigable, inaccessible, unobtainable, not within one's grasp; elusive.

Vb. *be impossible*, – impracticable etc. adj., have no chance whatever.

make impossible, rule out, exclude; put out of reach, set an impossible task; eat one's hat if 533 *negate*.

attempt the impossible, labour in vain 641 *waste effort*; have nothing to go upon, grasp at shadows, clutch at straws; be in two places at once, square the circle, discover the philosopher's stone, find the elixir of life, find a needle in a haystack; weave a rope of sand, gather grapes from thorns *or* figs from thistles, get blood from a stone, fetch water in a sieve; make bricks without straw, make a silk purse out of a sow's ear, change a leopard's spots; have one's cake and eat it; walk on water, set the Thames on fire.

Adv. *impossibly*, nohow, no way.

471 Probability
N. *probability*, likelihood 159 *chance*; good chance, fair c., sporting c., odds-on c. 469 *possibility*; excellent prospect 511 *prediction*; fair expectation 507 *expectation*; well-grounded hope 852 *hope*; safe bet, sure thing 473 *certainty*; credibility; likely belief 485 *belief*; plausibility, good reason 475 *reasons*; verisimilitude, semblance 445 *appearance*; theory of probability.

Adj. *probable*, likely 180 *liable*; on the cards, in a fair way; to be expected, foreseeable, foreseen; presumptive; promising 507 *expected*; on the horizon, in the wind 155 *impending*; highly possible 469 *possible*.

plausible, specious; to all intents and purposes, to all appearances 445 *appearing*; reasonable 475 *rational*; convincing, persuasive 485 *credible*; well-grounded, well-founded 494 *true*.

Vb. *be likely*, – probable etc. adj.; have a chance, be on the cards, stand a chance, be in with a c., run a good c. 469 *be possible*; bid fair to, be in danger of 179 *tend*; show signs, have the makings of, promise.

make likely, make probable, increase the chances; involve 523 *imply*; entail; put in the way to, promote 703 *aid*; point to 466 *evidence*.

assume, presume, take for granted; conjecture, guess, dare say 512 *suppose*; think likely; count upon 473 *be certain*; gather, deduce, infer 475 *reason*.

Adv. *probably*, presumably; in all probability, in all likelihood, doubtless, as is to be expected, all things considered; very likely, most l., ten to one, by all odds, a pound to a penny; seemingly, apparently, on the face of it, to all intents and purposes, to all appearances; like enough, as likely as not.

472 Improbability

N. *improbability*, doubt, real d. 474 *uncertainty*; little chance, little or no c., chance in a million, off-chance, small c., poor c., slim c., outside c., long shot; not a ghost of a chance, no c., not a hope 470 *impossibility*; long odds, barest of possibilities; pious hopes, forlorn hope, poor prospect 508 *lack of expectation*; rare occurrence, rarity 140 *infrequency*; implausibility, traveller's tale, fisherman's yarn 541 *falsehood*.

Adj. *improbable*, unlikely, more than doubtful, dubious 474 *uncertain*; hard to believe, fishy, unconvincing, implausible; rare 140 *infrequent*; inconceivable 470 *impossible*; incredible, too good to be true.

Vb. *be unlikely*, – improbable, look impossible etc. adj.; have the barest of chances, show little hope, be implausible, not wash, be hard to believe, strain one's credulity 486 *cause doubt*; think unlikely, whistle for 508 *not expect*.

Int. not likely! no fear! no way! not on your life! not on your nelly! not a hope! some hopes!

473 Certainty

N. *certainty*, certain knowledge 490 *knowledge*; certainness, assuredness, sureness; inevitability, inexorability, irrevocability, necessity 596 *fate*; infallibility; reliability, unimpeachability 494 *truth*; unambiguity, unequivocalness; incontrovertibility, irrefutability, indisputability, proof 478 *demonstration*; authentication, ratification, validation; certification, verification, confirmation; attestation 466 *testimony*; check 459 *enquiry*; ascertainment 484 *discovery*; dead certainty, cert, dead c., sure thing, safe bet, cinch, open and shut case, foregone conclusion; fact; matter of fact, fait accompli 154 *event*; settled decision 480 *judgment*.

positiveness, moral certainty; assurance, confidence, conviction, persuasion 485 *belief*; unshakable opinion 485 *opinion*; idée fixe, obsession 481 *bias*; dogmatism; infallibility; self-confidence; pontification, laying down the law.

dogmatist, self-opinionated person; bigot, fanatic, zealot; oracle, knowall, smarty-pants 500 *wiseacre*.

Adj. *certain*, sure, solid, unshakable, well-founded, well-grounded 3 *substantial*; reliable 929 *trustworthy*; authoritative, official 494 *genuine*; factual, historical 494 *true*; authenticated, ascertained, certified, attested, guaranteed, warranted; tested, tried, foolproof 660 *safe*; infallible, unerring 540 *veracious*; axiomatic, dogmatic, taken for granted; self-evident, evident, apparent; unequivocal, unambiguous, unmistakable, clear, clear as day 443 *obvious*;

inevitable, irrevocable, inexorable 596 *fated*; bound, bound to be, in the bag; sure as fate, sure as death; inviolable, safe as houses, safe as the Bank of England 660 *invulnerable*; verifiable, demonstrable.

positive, confident, assured, self-assured, self-confident, certain in one's mind, undoubting, convinced, persuaded, certified, sure; opinionated, self-o; pontificating, oracular 532 *assertive*; dogmatic, doctrinaire 976 *orthodox*; obsessed, bigoted, fanatical 481 *biased*; unshaken, set in one's ways, fixed in one's opinions 153 *unchangeable*; clear-cut; definite, decisive, defined, unambiguous, unambivalent, unequivocal; convincing 485 *credible*; affirmative, categorical, absolute, unqualified, unreserved; conclusive.

undisputed, beyond doubt, beyond all reasonable d., without a shadow of doubt, axiomatic, uncontroversial; unquestioned, undoubted, uncontested, unarguable, undebatable, indubitable, unquestionable, incontrovertible, incontestable, unimpeachable, undeniable, irrefutable.

Vb. *be certain*, – sure etc. adj.; leave no doubt, be clear as day, be plain as the nose on your face, stand to reason, be axiomatic; be positive, be assured, satisfy oneself, convince o., feel sure, be clear in one's mind, have no doubts; know for certain 490 *know*; stick to one's guns, have made up one's mind, dismiss all doubt; depend on it, rely on, bank on, trust in, swear by; put one's shirt on, lay one's bottom dollar.

dogmatize, pontificate, lay down the law 532 *affirm*; know all the answers.

make certain, certify, authenticate, ratify, seal, sign 488 *endorse*; guarantee, warrant, assure; finalize, settle, decide 480 *judge*; remove doubt, persuade 485 *convince*; make sure, ascertain, check, run a check, double-check, verify, confirm, confirm in writing, clinch 466 *corroborate*; reassure oneself, take a second look, do a double take; insure against 660 *safeguard*; reinsure 858 *be cautious*; ensure, make inevitable 596 *necessitate*.

Adv. *certainly*, definitely, for sure, to be sure, no doubt, doubtless, indubitably, as sure as anything, as sure as eggs is eggs, as sure as God made little green apples, as night follows day, of course, as a matter of c., no question; no two ways about it, no ifs or buts; without fail, sink or swim, rain or shine, come hell or high water, come what may, whatever happens.

474 Uncertainty

N. *uncertainty*, doubtfulness, dubiousness; ambiguity, ambivalence 518 *equivocalness*; vagueness, haziness, obscurity 418 *darkness*; mist, haze, fog 423 *opacity*; grey area; yes and no, don't know, floating voter, vacillation, indeterminacy, borderline case; indefiniteness, roving commission; query, question mark 459 *question*; open question, anybody's guess, a matter of tossing a coin; nothing to go on, guesswork, guestimate 512 *conjecture*; contingency 159 *chance*; gamble, toss-up, wager 618 *gambling*; leap *or* shot in the dark, bow at a venture, pig in a poke, blind date; something or other, this or that.

dubiety, 486 *doubt*; open verdict, a verdict of not proven; suspense, waiting 507 *expectation*; doubt, indecision, hesitancy, shilly-shallying, vacillation 317 *fluctuation*; seesaw, floating vote 601 *irresolution*; bafflement, quandary; dilemma, cleft stick, Morton's fork.

unreliability, fallibility 495 *error*; precariousness, unstable condition, touch and go 661 *danger*; untrustworthiness, treacherousness; variability, changeability 152 *changeableness*; unpredictability, unexpectedness 508 *lack of expectation*; fickleness, capriciousness; slipperiness; lack of security, no guarantee, no collateral, gentleman's agreement, handshake deal.

Adj. *uncertain*, unsure, doubtful, dubious; chancy, risky 661 *unsafe*; treacherous (**see** *unreliable*); subject to chance, at the mercy of events; sporadic 140 *infrequent*; fluid; contingent, depending on 766 *conditional*; unpredictable, unforeseeable 508 *unexpected*; indeterminate, undefined; random; indecisive, undecided, vacillating, in suspense; in question, under enquiry; open to question, questionable; arguable, debatable, disputable, controvertible, controversial; suspicious 472 *improbable*; problematical, hypothetical, speculative; undefinable, borderline, grey-area, marginal; ambiguous 518 *equivocal*; paradoxical 477 *illogical*; oracular, enigmatic, cryptic, obscure 517 *puzzling*; vague, hazy, misty, cloudy 419 *shadowy*; mysterious, veiled 523 *occult*; unresolved, unexplained 517 *unintelligible*; perplexing, bewildering.

unreliable, undependable, untrustworthy; treacherous 930 *dishonest*; unsteady, unstable, variable, vacillating, changeable 152 *changeful*; unpredictable, unforeseeable; fickle 604 *capricious*; fallible, open to error 495 *erroneous*; precarious, touch and go.

doubting, in doubt, doubtful, dubious, full of doubt, riddled with d., plagued by uncertainty; agnostic, sceptical; sitting on the fence, hedging one's bets, in two minds; in suspense, openminded; distrustful, mistrustful 858 *cautious*; uncertain, diffident; hesitant, undecided, wavering, vacillating, unsure which way to jump 601

irresolute; unable to say; baffled 517 *puzzled*; in a cleft stick, on the horns of a dilemma; disorientated; clueless 491 *ignorant*.

Vb. *be uncertain*, be contingent, lie in the lap of the gods; hinge on, be dependent on 157 *depend*; be touch and go, hang by a thread, tremble in the balance; be open to question, be ambiguous 518 *be equivocal*; have one's doubts 486 *doubt*; wait and see 507 *await*; have a suspicion, suspect, wonder, wonder whether; dither, be in two minds, hover, float, be a don't know, sit on the fence, sway, seesaw, waver, teeter, vacillate, shilly-shally, falter, pause, hesitate 601 *be irresolute*; demur; flounder; be in the dark, have nothing to go on, grope 461 *be tentative*; cast about, lose the thread, miss one's way, get lost 282 *stray*; lose the scent, lose track of; not know which way to turn, be at one's wits' end, be at a loss, not know what to make of, be in a dilemma, be in a quandary; wouldn't swear, could be wrong.

puzzle, perplex, confuse, daze, bewilder, baffle, boggle the mind, nonplus, flummox, stump, floor 727 *defeat*; mystify, keep one guessing; bamboozle; fox, throw off the scent 495 *mislead*; plague or riddle with doubt 486 *cause doubt*; make one think.

Adv. *in suspense*, in a state of uncertainty, on the horns of a dilemma, in a maze, in a daze.

SECTION FOUR

Reasoning processes

475 Reasoning

N. *reasoning*, force of argument; reason, discursive r.; lateral thinking 476 *intuition*; sweet reason, reasonableness, rationality; dialectics, logic; logical process, logical sequence, inference, generalization; distinction 463 *discrimination*; deductive reasoning, deduction; inductive reasoning, empirical reasoning; rationalism, dialectic 449 *philosophy*; modern maths 86 *mathematics*; simple arithmetic.

premise, postulate, basis of reasoning; principle, general p., first p.; lemma, starting point; assumption, stipulation 512 *supposition*; axiom, self-evident truth 496 *maxim*; datum, data; hypothesis.

argument, discussion, symposium, dialogue; exchange of views, cut and thrust; disputation, controversy, debate 489 *dissent*; set *or* formal argument plea, pleading; thesis, case; reasons, submission; defence; polemics; war of words, paper war 709 *quarrel*; propaganda, pamphleteering 534 *teaching*; controversialism, argumentativeness, hair-splitting, logic-chopping, contentiousness, wrangling, jangling 709 *dissension;* sophism 477 *sophistry;* legal argument, pleadings 959 *litigation.*

reasons, grounds; arguments, pros and cons; case, good c., case to answer; sound argument, conclusive argument 478 *demonstration;* point, valid p., point well taken.

Adj. *rational,* clear-headed, reasoning, reasonable; rationalistic, logical; cogent, acceptable, admissible, to the point, pointed, well-grounded, well-argued 9 *relevant;* sensible, fair 913 *just;* analytic; consistent, systematic, methodological; dialectic, discursive, deductive, inductive, axiomatic 473 *certain;* tenable 469 *possible.*

Vb. *be reasonable* 471 *be likely;* stand to reason, follow, hang together, hold water; appeal to reason; listen to reason, be guided by r.; yield to argument; admit, concede; have a case, have a case to be answered, have logic on one's side.

reason, philosophize 449 *think;* syllogize, rationalize; apply reason, bring reason to bear, use one's grey matter, put two and two together; infer, deduce, induct; explain 520 *interpret.*

argue, argufy, argy-bargy, bandy arguments, cut and thrust; hold a symposium; exchange opinions, have an exchange of views, discuss; debate, dispute; quibble, split hairs, chop logic; argue the case, argue the point; stick to one's guns; work an argument to death 532 *emphasize;* put one's case, plead; pamphleteer 534 *teach;* take up the case, defend; attack; cross swords, take up a point with, join issue, demur, cavil 489 *dissent;* analyse, pull to pieces; outargue; have words, have a confrontation, wrangle; answer back, make a rejoinder 460 *answer;* start an argument, move a motion, open a discussion *or* debate.

postulate, posit, stipulate, lay down, assume 512 *suppose;* take for granted, refer to first principles.

476 Intuition: absence of reason

N. *intuition,* instinct, association, Pavlovian response, automatic reaction, gut r., knee-jerk r. 450 *absence of thought;* sixth sense, extrasensory perception, ESP; telepathy; insight, second sight, clairvoyance 984 *psychics;* id, subconscious; intuitiveness; divination; inspiration, presentiment, impulse 818 *feeling;* feminine logic; rule of thumb; hunch.

Adj. *intuitive,* instinctive, impulsive; devoid of logic 477 *illogical;* impressionistic, subjective; involuntary 609 *spontaneous;* subconscious 447 *psychic;* beyond reason; inspirational, inspired, clairvoyant, ESP, telepathic.

Vb. *intuit,* know by instinct, have a sixth sense; sense, feel in one's bones, have a funny feeling, have a hunch; have a gut reaction, react instinctively; play it by ear, go by impressions, rely on intuition, dispense with reason, use feminine logic; use guesswork, work on a hunch.

477 Sophistry: false reasoning

N. *sophistry,* illogicalness, illogic; feminine logic 476 *intuition;* sophistical reasoning; false r., rationalization; double think, self-deception; mental reservation 525 *concealment;* equivocation, blinding with science, casuistry; subtlety, over-subtlety; hair-splitting, logic-chopping; claptrap, mere words 515 *empty talk;* quibbling; chicanery, subterfuge; evasion 614 *pretext.*

sophism, a sophistry, specious argument; illogicality, fallacy; loose thinking, sloppy t.; solecism, flaw in the argument; begging the question, circular reasoning; non sequitur, irrelevancy, contradiction in terms; weak case.

Adj. *illogical,* contrary to reason, irrational, unreasonable; unreasoned, arbitrary; fallacious, fallible; contradictory, self-c., inconsistent, incongruous; unwarranted, invalid, untenable, unsound; unfounded, ungrounded, groundless; irrelevant, inconsequent, inconsequential; incorrect, unscientific, false 495 *erroneous.*

poorly reasoned, unrigorous, inconclusive; unproved; weak, feeble; flimsy; loose, woolly, muddled, confused.

Vb. *reason badly,* argue in a circle, beg the question, fail to get to the point, not see the wood for the trees, strain at a gnat and swallow a camel; not have a leg to stand on; talk at random.

sophisticate, mislead 535 *misteach;* mystify, quibble, cavil, split hairs 475 *argue;* equivocate 518 *be equivocal;* dodge, shuffle, fence; not come to the point, beat about the bush 570 *be diffuse;* evade 667 *elude;* draw a veil over, varnish, gloss over, whitewash; colour 552 *misrepresent;* pervert, misapply 675 *misuse;* pervert reason, twist the argument, torture logic; prove that white is black.

478 Demonstration

N. *demonstration,* documentation, authentication 466 *evidence;* proven fact 494 *truth;* proof; conclusive proof; conclusiveness 473 *certainty;* verification, ascertainment 461 *experiment;* deduction, inference, argument, triumph of a. 475 *reasoning;* exposition, clarification 522 *manifestation;* burden of proof, onus.

V. *demonstrate,* prove; show, evince 522 *manifest;* justify 927 *vindicate;* bear out 466 *corrobor-*

ate; produce the evidence, document, provide documentation, substantiate, establish, verify 466 *evidence;* infer, deduce, draw, draw a conclusion 475 *reason;* settle the question, satisfy 473 *make certain;* make out a case, prove one's point, clinch an argument, have the best of an a., win an a. 485 *convince.*

be proved, prove to be true, stand to reason 475 *be reasonable;* stand up to investigation, hold water, hold good 494 *be true.*

Adv. *of course,* undeniably, without doubt; as already proved.

479 Confutation

N. *confutation,* refutation, disproof, invalidation; conviction 961 *condemnation;* rebuttal, rejoinder, clincher, knock-down argument; last word, retort, repartee 839 *witticism;* contradiction, denial, denunciation 533 *negation;* exploded argument.

Vb. *confute,* refute, disprove, invalidate; rebut, rejoin, retort, have an answer, explain away; deny, contradict 533 *negate;* give the lie to, force to withdraw; prove the contrary, show the fallacy of; cut the ground from under, leave someone without a leg to stand on; confound, rout, silence, reduce to s., stop the mouth, shut up, floor, gravel, nonplus; condemn one out of his own mouth; show up, expose; convict 961 *condemn;* defeat one's logic; blow sky-high, shoot full of holes, puncture, riddle, destroy, explode, demolish one's arguments, drive a coach and horses through, knock the bottom out of 165 *demolish;* have, have in one's hand, have one on the hip; overthrow, squash, crush, overwhelm 727 *defeat;* riddle the defence, outargue, have the better of the argument, get the better of, score off; parry, avoid the trap; stand, stand up to argument; dismiss, override, sweep aside, brush a.; brook no denial, affirm the contrary 532 *affirm.*

SECTION FIVE

Results of reasoning

480 Judgment: conclusion

N. *judgment,* judging (**see** estimate); good judgment, discretion 463 *discrimination;* bad judgment, lack of discretion 464 *indiscrimination;* arbitration, umpirage; verdict, finding; sentence, tariff 963 *punishment;* summing-up, pronouncement; act of judgment, decision, adjudication, award; order, court order, ruling, fatwa, order of the court 737 *decree;* decree nisi; decree absolute; judgment in appeal, irrevocable decision; settled decision; final judgment, conclusion, result, upshot; moral 496 *maxim;*

value judgment 476 *intuition;* reasoned judgment, deduction, inference, corollary 475 *reasoning;* wise judgment, j. of Solomon 498 *wisdom;* fair judgment, unclouded eye 913 *justice;* vox populi, voting, referendum, plebiscite, poll 605 *vote.*

estimate, estimation, view 485 *opinion;* assessment, valuation, evaluation, calculation 465 *measurement;* consideration, comparing, contrasting 462 *comparison;* appreciation, appraisal, appraisement 520 *interpretation;* criticism, constructive c. 703 *aid;* destructive criticism 702 *hindrance;* critique, crit, review, notice, press n., comment, comments, observations, remarks, profile 591 *article;* summing-up; survey 438 *inspection;* favourable report 923 *approbation;* unfavourable report, censure 924 *disapprobation.*

estimator, judge, adjudicator; arbitrator, umpire, referee; surveyor, valuer, valuator; inspector, inspecting officer, reporter, examiner, ombudsman, ACAS (= Advisory, Conciliation and Arbitration Service) 459 *enquirer;* counsellor 691 *adviser;* censor, critic, reviewer 591 *dissertator;* commentator, observer 520 *interpreter;* juror, assessor 957 *jury;* voter, elector 605 *electorate.*

Adj. *judicial,* judicious 463 *discriminating;* shrewd 498 *wise;* unbiased, dispassionate 913 *just;* arbitral; judicatory, conclusive; sententious.

Vb. *judge,* sit in judgment, hold the scales; arbitrate, referee, umpire; hear, try, hear the case, try the cause; uphold an objection, disallow an o.; rule, pronounce; find, find for, find against; decree, award, adjudicate; decide, settle, conclude; confirm, make absolute; pass judgment, deliver j.; sentence, pass s., doom 961 *condemn;* agree on a verdict, return a v., bring in a v.; sum up.

estimate, form an e., make an e., measure, calculate, make 465 *gauge;* value, evaluate, appraise; rate, rank; sum up, size up; conjecture, guess 512 *suppose;* take stock 808 *account;* consider, weigh, ponder, weigh the pros and cons, take everything into consideration 449 *meditate.*

Adv. *sub judice,* under investigation, under trial, under sentence.

481 Misjudgment. Prejudice

N. *misjudgment,* miscalculation, misreckoning, misconception, wrong impression 495 *error;* loose thinking, sloppy t. 495 *inexactness;* bad judgment, poor j. 464 *indiscrimination;* fallibility, gullibility 499 *unintelligence;* misconstruction 521 *misinterpretation;* wrong verdict, miscarriage of justice 914 *injustice;*

overvaluation 482 *overestimation*; undervaluation 483 *underestimation*; autosuggestion, self-deception, self-delusion, wishful thinking 542 *deception*; fool's paradise 513 *fantasy*; false dawn 509 *disappointment*.

prejudgment, foregone conclusion 608 *predetermination*; preconception, mind made up; preconceived idea; idée fixe, obsession, hang-up, fixation, bee in the bonnet, monomania 503 *personality disorder*.

prejudice, predilection; partiality, favouritism 914 *injustice*; penchant, bias, biased judgment, warped j., jaundiced eye; blind spot, blind side, tunnel vision, mote in the eye, beam in the e. 439 *blindness*; onesidedness, party spirit 708 *party*; partisanship, clannishness, cliquishness, esprit de corps; parochialism, provincialism, insularity; 978 *sectarianism*; gung-ho attitude, chauvinism, xenophobia, my country right or wrong; snobbishness, class war, class prejudice, classism, postcode discrimination; ageism, granny-bashing; ableism; fattism; heightism, sizeism; sexism, sex prejudice, sex discrimination, gender d.; male chauvinism, glass ceiling; heterosexism, homophobia; xenophobia, race prejudice, racialism, racism; colour prejudice, colour bar, apartheid, segregation, discrimination 57 *exclusion*; intolerance, persecution, anti-Semitism 888 *hatred*.

narrow mind, narrow-mindedness, small-m.; insularity, parochialism, provincialism; closed mind, one-track m., tunnel vision; onesidedness; legalism, pedantry 735 *severity*; intolerance, dogmatism 473 *positiveness*; bigotry, fanaticism 602 *opinionatedness*; pedant, stickler 862 *perfectionist*; faddist 504 *crank*; zealot, bigot, fanatic 473 *dogmatist*; racialist, racist, white supremacist; chauvinist, sexist.

bias, unbalance, disequilibrium 29 *inequality*; warp, bent, slant, liability, penchant 179 *tendency*; angle, point of view 485 *opinion*; mind made up (**see** *prejudgment*).

Adj. *misjudging*, misconceiving, misinterpreting etc. vb.; miscalculating, in error, out 495 *mistaken*; fallible, gullible 499 *foolish*; wrong, wrong-headed; unseeing 439 *blind*; myopic, purblind, short-sighted 440 *dimsighted*; misguided, superstitious 487 *credulous*; subjective, unrealistic, visionary, impractical; crankish, faddy, faddish, whimsical 503 *crazy*; besotted, infatuated 887 *enamoured*; haunted, obsessed, hung up, eaten up with.

narrow-minded, petty-m., narrow, hidebound; short-sighted, tunnel-visioned; parochial, provincial, insular; pedantic, donnish 735 *severe*; legalistic, literal, literal-minded, unimaginative, matter-of-fact; hypercritical, over-scrupulous, picky, fussy 862 *fastidious*; stiff, unbending 602

obstinate; dictatorial, dogmatic 473 *positive*; opinionated, opinionative; self-opinioned, self-conceited 871 *proud*.

biased, warped, twisted, swayed; jaundiced, prejudiced; snobbish, clannish, cliquish; partisan, one-sided, party-minded 978 *sectarian*; nationalistic, chauvinistic, gung-hoish, jingoistic, xenophobic; racist, racialist; sexist, ageist; classist; class-prejudiced, colour-p.; predisposed, preconceived; prejudging 608 *predetermined*; discriminatory 914 *unjust*; intolerant 735 *oppressive*; bigoted, fanatic 602 *obstinate*; blinded 439 *blind*.

Vb. *misjudge*, miscalculate, miscount 495 *blunder*; not take into account, reckon without; undervalue, minimize 483 *underestimate*; overestimate, overvalue 482 *overrate*; guess wrong, come to the wrong conclusion, misconceive 521 *misinterpret*; overreach oneself, overplay one's hand; get the wrong end of the stick 695 *act foolishly*; not see the wood for the trees; not see beyond one's nose 499 *be foolish*; fly in the face of facts 477 *reason badly*.

prejudge, judge beforehand, make up one's mind in advance 608 *predetermine*; prejudice the issue, precondemn; preconceive, presuppose, presume 475 *postulate*; jump to conclusions 857 *be rash*.

bias, warp, twist, bend; jaundice, prejudice; predispose 178 *influence*.

be biased, – prejudiced etc. adj.; be one-sided, see one side only, show favouritism, favour one side 914 *do wrong*; lean, favour, take sides, have a down on, have it in for, hold it against one, be unfair, discriminate against 735 *oppress*; lose one's sense of proportion; suffer from tunnel vision, blind oneself to, have a blind side, have a blind spot 439 *be blind*.

482 Overestimation

N. *overestimation*, overestimate, overenthusiasm, overvaluation 481 *misjudgment*; overstatement 546 *exaggeration*; boasting 877 *boast*; ballyhoo, hype, buildup, overkill 528 *publicity*; overpraise, panegyric, gush, hot air 515 *empty talk*; storm in a teacup, much ado about nothing; megalomania, vanity 871 *pride*; overconfidence 857 *rashness*; egotism 932 *selfishness*; overoptimism; defeatism 853 *hopelessness*; optimist 852 *hope*; pessimist, prophet of doom, doom-watcher, doomster, Jonah, defeatist; exaggerator, puffer, barker, advertiser, promoter 528 *publicizer*.

Adj. *optimistic*, upbeat, sanguine, overconfident; overpitched; overenthusiastic, raving.

Vb. *overestimate*, overrate, count all one's geese swans; overvalue, overprice, set too high a value on 811 *overcharge*; rave, idealize, overpraise, think too much of; make too much of 546 *exaggerate*; overemphasize, overstress, overdo, play up, overpitch, inflate, magnify 197 *enlarge*; boost, puff, panegyrize, hype 923 *praise*; attach too much importance to, make mountains out of molehills; maximize, make the most of; whitewash, paper over the cracks.

483 Underestimation
N. *underestimation*, underestimate, undervaluation, minimization; conservative estimate, modest calculation 177 *moderation*; depreciation 926 *detraction*; understatement, litotes, meiosis; euphemism 950 *prudery*; self-depreciation, self-effacement, overmodesty 872 *humility*; false modesty, mock m., irony 850 *affectation*; pessimism 853 *hopelessness*; pessimist, minimizer, cynic 926 *detractor*.

Vb. *underestimate*, underrate, undervalue, underprice; mark down, discount 812 *cheapen*; depreciate, underpraise, run down, cry d., disparage 926 *detract*; slight, pooh-pooh 922 *hold cheap*; not do justice to, do less than justice 481 *misjudge*; understate; play down, soft-pedal; shrug off 458 *disregard*; make little of, minimize; make light of, set no store by, think too little of 922 *despise*.

484 Discovery
N. *discovery*, finding; invention; exploration, archaeology, speleology, potholing; excavation 459 *search*; detection 438 *inspection*; radiolocation 187 *location*; water divining; exposure, revelation 522 *manifestation*; illumination, realization, disenchantment; hitting upon, serendipity; strike, find, lucky f., treasure trove; eye-opener 508 *lack of expectation*; open sesame 263 *opener*.

detector, probe; space p., spy satellite 276 *spaceship*; asdic, sonar; early warning system; radar, radar trap, speed trap; breathalyser, breath test, sniffer torch; finder 442 *telescope*; lie detector; Geiger counter 465 *meter*; metal detector; divining rod; water diviner; talent scout; discoverer, inventor; explorer 268 *traveller*; archaeologist, speleologist, potholer 459 *enquirer*; prospector 461 *experimenter*; gastroscope, auriscope, ophthalmoscope, colposcope 658 *diagnostic*.

Vb. *discover*, invent, explore; find out; strike, hit, hit upon; come upon, happen on, stumble on; meet, encounter 154 *meet with*; tumble to, awake to, see the truth, see the light, see in its true colours 516 *understand*; find, locate 187 *place*; recognize, identify 490 *know*; unearth, uncover, bring to light 522 *manifest*; elicit, worm out, ferret o., nose o., sniff o., smell o. 459 *search*; get wind of 524 *be informed*.

detect, find a clue, be on the track, be getting warm, see daylight; put one's finger on the spot, hit the nail on the head; discern, perceive, notice, spot, catch sight of 438 *see*; sense, trace; smell a rat; nose, scent out; follow, tail, trail, trace, track down 619 *hunt*.

Int. eureka! got it!

485 Belief
N. *belief*, suspension of disbelief; credence, credit; assurance, conviction, persuasion; dependence on, trust, faith; religious belief 973 *religious faith*; implicit belief, firm b., unshakable b. 473 *certainty*; obsession, self-conviction; expectation 852 *hope*; folklore; popular belief, public opinion; one's word of honour 929 *probity*.

creed, credo, what one believes; dogma 976 *orthodoxy*; precepts, principles, tenets, articles; catechism, articles of faith; rubric, canon, rule 496 *maxim*; declaration of faith, confession of faith 526 *disclosure*; doctrine, system, school.

opinion, sentiment, mind, view; point of view, viewpoint, stand, position, attitude, angle 438 *view*; impression 818 *feeling*; conception, thought 451 *idea*; thinking, way of thinking, outlook on life 449 *philosophy*; assumption, presumption, principle 475 *premise*; theory, hypothesis 512 *supposition*; surmise, guess 512 *conjecture*; conclusion 480 *judgment*.

Adj. *credible*, plausible, believable, tenable, reasonable 469 *possible*; likely, to be expected 471 *probable*; reliable, trustworthy, trusty; persuasive, convincing 178 *influential*; trusted, believed; held, maintained; accepted, credited, accredited.

creedal, taught, doctrinal, dogmatic, confessional; canonical, orthodox, authoritative, accredited, ex cathedra; of faith, accepted on trust; sacrosanct, unquestioned, God-given; undeniable, absolute, unshakable 473 *undisputed*.

Vb. *believe*, be a believer; credit, put faith in; hold, hold to be true; maintain, declare 532 *affirm*; believe religiously, perceive as true, take for gospel; take on trust, take on credit; buy, swallow, swallow whole 487 *be credulous*; have no doubt, know for certain, be convinced, be sold on; rest assured, be easy in one's mind about, be secure in the belief, believe implicitly; have confidence in, trust, rely on, depend on, take one at his *or* her word; give one credit for, pin one's faith on, pin one's hopes on; have faith in, believe in, swear by, reckon on, count on, bank on; come to believe, be converted; realize 484 *discover*; take as proven.

be of the opinion that, opine, think, conceive,

fancy; have a hunch, surmise, guess 512 *suppose*; suspect, be under the impression, have the i. 818 *feel*; deem, assume, presume, take it, hold; get hold of an idea, get it into one's head; have views, have a point of view, view as, take as, regard as, consider as, look upon as, set down as; cherish an opinion; express an opinion; hazard an o. 532 *affirm*; change one's mind 603 *recant*.

convince, make believe, assure, persuade, satisfy; bring home to 478 *demonstrate*; make confident, restore one's faith; convert, win over, bring o., bring round, wean from; evangelize, spread the gospel; propagandize, indoctrinate, din into 534 *teach*; cram down one's throat; sell an idea to, put over, put across; gain one's confidence, sway one's belief 178 *influence*, mesmerize, hypnotize.

be believed, be widely b., be received, gain wide acceptance; go down well, be swallowed; find willing ears; carry conviction; find credence, pass for truth.

486 Unbelief. Doubt

N. *unbelief*, disbelief, incredulity, discredit; disagreement 489 *dissent*; agnosticism; denial 533 *negation*; want of faith; misbelief 977 *heresy*; atheism 974 *irreligion*; derision, scorn, mockery 851 *ridicule*; loss of faith, lapse of f., crisis of conscience, retraction 603 *recantation*; incredibility 472 *improbability*.

doubt 474 *dubiety*; hesitation, wavering, vacillation, shilly-shallying, uncertainty; misgiving, distrust, mistrust; suspiciousness, scepticism, agnosticism; reserve, reservation, second thoughts 468 *qualification*; demur, objection 704 *opposition*; scruple, qualm, suspicion 854 *nervousness*.

unbeliever, disbeliever; heathen, infidel 977 *heretic*; atheist; sceptic, agnostic; doubter, doubting Thomas; dissenter 489 *dissentient*; retractor, recanter 603 *tergiversator*; denier 533 *negation*; cynic, pessimist; scoffer, mocker, scorner 926 *detractor*.

Vb. *disbelieve*, be incredulous, find hard to believe, explain away, discredit, greet with scepticism, withhold assent, disagree 489 *dissent*; not fall for, not buy; mock, scoff at 851 *ridicule*; deny, deny outright 533 *negate*; refuse to admit, ignore; retract, lapse 603 *recant*.

doubt, half-believe 474 *be uncertain*; demur, object, cavil, question, scruple, boggle, have reservations 468 *qualify*; pause; hesitate, waver 601 *be irresolute*; distrust, mistrust, suspect, have fears 854 *be nervous*; shy at; be sceptical, doubt the truth of, take leave to doubt; not trust, set no store by; have one's doubts, take with a pinch of salt, harbour doubts, cherish scruples;

entertain suspicions, smell a rat; hold back, not go all the way with one 598 *be unwilling*.

cause doubt, cast d., raise questions; cast a shadow over, render suspect; call in question, discredit 926 *defame*; shake, shake one's faith, undermine one's belief; pass belief 472 *be unlikely*; keep one guessing 517 *be unintelligible*.

487 Credulity

N. *credulity*, credulousness; simplicity, gullibility, naiveté; blind faith 612 *persuadability*; self-delusion, self-deception, wishful thinking 481 *misjudgment*; superstition, superstitiousness; sucker, mug 544 *dupe*.

Adj. *credulous*, believing, persuadable, amenable; easily taken in, easily deceived, easily duped; unworldly; naive, simple, unsophisticated, green; overcredulous; infatuated; confiding, trustful, unsuspecting.

Vb. *be credulous*, be easily persuaded; kid oneself, fool o.; suspend one's judgment 477 *reason badly*; follow implicitly, believe every word, fall for, buy it, take on trust, take for granted, take for gospel 485 *believe*; accept 299 *absorb*; rise to the bait, swallow, swallow hook, line and sinker 544 *be duped*; run away with an idea *or* a notion, rush *or* jump to a conclusion; be superstitious, touch wood, keep one's fingers crossed; think the moon is made of green cheese, not hear a word against.

488 Assent

N. *assent*, yes, aye, uh-huh, yea, amen; hearty assent; welcome; agreement, concurrence 758 *consent*; acceptance, agreement in principle 597 *willingness*; acquiescence 721 *submission*; acknowledgment, admission, clean breast, plea of guilty 939 *penitence*; confession; declaration of faith, profession 532 *affirmation*; sanction, nod, OK, imprimatur, thumbs up, go-ahead, green light 756 *permission*; approval 923 *approbation*; corroboration 466 *evidence*; confirmation, verification 478 *demonstration*; ratification; authentication, certification, endorsement, seal, signature, mark, cross; visa, passport, pass 756 *permit*; stamp, rubber s. 547 *label*; support 703 *aid*.

consensus, same mind 24 *agreement*; concordance, harmony, unison 710 *concord*; unanimity, common consent; universal agreement; popular belief, public opinion; single voice; likemindedness, same wavelength, two minds with but a single thought 18 *similarity*; mutual understanding, bargain 765 *compact*.

assenter, follower 83 *conformist*; fellow traveller, ally 707 *collaborator*; yes-man 925 *flatterer*; the ayes; upholder, supporter, active s., abettor 703 *aider*; seconder 707 *patron*; subscriber, endorser 765 *signatory*; consenting party, covenanter.

Adj. *assenting*, concurring, party to 24 *agreeing*; aiding and abetting, supporting, collaborating 706 *cooperative*; likeminded, sympathetic, on the same wavelength, welcoming 880 *friendly*; unanimous, with one voice, in chorus; acquiescent 597 *willing*; granting 756 *permitting*; sanctioning, ratificatory; not opposed, conceding.

Vb. *assent*, concur, agree with 24 *accord*; welcome, acclaim 923 *applaud*; have no reservations 473 *be certain*; accept, agree in principle, like the idea, buy it; not deny, concede, own, acknowledge, grant, allow 475 *be reasonable*; plead guilty, avow 526 *confess*; signify assent, nod, say aye, say yes, raise one's hand in assent, agree to, give one's assent, go along with 758 *consent*; sanction 756 *permit*; ratify (**see** *endorse*); agree with, see eye to eye, be on the same wavelength; echo, say amen, say hear hear; back up; be a yes-man, rubber-stamp 925 *flatter*; side with 708 *join a party*; collaborate 706 *cooperate*; tolerate (**see** *acquiesce*); agree upon, come to an understanding, have a mutual agreement 765 *contract*.

acquiesce, accept, abide by 739 *obey*; tolerate, put up with, suffer, bear, endure, wear it; sign on the dotted line, toe the l. 721 *submit*; yield, defer to, withdraw one's objections; let the ayes have it, allow 756 *permit*; let it happen, look on 441 *watch*; go with the stream *or* crowd, float with the current, join in the chorus, follow the fashion *or* trend, run with the pack, jump on the bandwagon 83 *conform*.

endorse, second, support, back up, vote for, give one's vote to 703 *patronize*; subscribe to, attest 547 *sign*; rubber-stamp, ratify, sanction, authorize 758 *consent*; authenticate 473 *make certain*; countersign.

Int. amen! hear, hear! aye, aye! well said! you can say that again! how right you are! I couldn't agree more! yes indeed! yes! absolutely!

489 Dissent

N. *dissent*, agreement to disagree *or* differ; dissidence, difference 704 *opposition*; difference of opinion, a vote against, disagreement, controversy 709 *dissension*; faction 708 *party*; disaffection 829 *discontent*; dissatisfaction, disapproval 924 *disapprobation*; repudiation 607 *rejection*; protestantism, nonconformism, schism 978 *sectarianism*; alternative life style, alternative medicine, alternative birth 84 *nonconformity*; withdrawal, secession 621 *relinquishment*; walkout 145 *strike*; reluctance 598 *unwillingness*; recusancy 738 *disobedience*; noncompliance 769 *nonobservance*; denial 760 *refusal*; contradiction

533 *negation*; recantation, retraction 603 *change of mind*; doubtfulness 486 *doubt*; demur, objection, reservation 468 *qualification*; protest; challenge 711 *defiance*; passive resistance 738 *sedition*.

dissentient, objector, critic 926 *detractor*; interrupter, heckler, obstructor; dissident, dissenter, protester; sectary 978 *sectarian*; separatist, seceder 978 *schismatic*; rebel 738 *revolter*; dropout 84 *nonconformist*; grouser 829 *malcontent*; odd man out, minority; splinter group, breakaway party, cave, faction 708 *party*; the noes, the opposition 704 *opposition*; conscientious objector, peace women, CND, green party, ecowarrior 705 *opponent*; agitator, revolutionary, contra 149 *revolutionist*.

Adj. *dissenting*, differing, dissident 709 *quarrelling*; agnostic, sceptical; separatist, schismatic 978 *sectarian*; non-conformist 84 *unconformable*; malcontent, dissatisfied 829 *discontented*; recanting; not consenting; noncompliant 769 *nonobservant*; loath, reluctant 598 *unwilling*; obstructive; challenging 711 *defiant*; resistant 704 *opposing*.

Vb. *dissent*, differ, agree to d. 25 *disagree*; beg to differ, pick a bone with, take one up on 479 *confute*; demur, object, raise objections, have reservations, cavil, boggle; protest, raise one's voice against, demonstrate a. 762 *deprecate*; resist 704 *oppose*; challenge 711 *defy*; show reluctance 598 *be unwilling*; withhold assent, say no, shake one's head, not wear it 760 *refuse*; shrug one's shoulders, wash one's hands of it 860 *be indifferent*; disallow 757 *prohibit*; negative, contradict 533 *negate*; repudiate, hold no brief for; look askance at, not hold with 924 *disapprove*; secede, form a breakaway party, form a splinter group, withdraw 621 *relinquish*; recant, retract 603 *apostatize*; argue, wrangle, bicker 709 *quarrel*.

Adv. *no*, on the contrary, no way; in the negative.

Int. God forbid! not on your life! not on your nelly! over my dead body! tell that to the marines! not likely!

490 Knowledge

N. *knowledge*, ken; knowing, cognition, cognizance, recognition, realization, apprehension, comprehension, perception, understanding, grasp, mastery 447 *intellect*; conscience, consciousness, awareness; insight 476 *intuition*; precognition 510 *foresight*; illumination 975 *revelation*; enlightenment 498 *wisdom*; learning, lore (**see** *erudition*); folklore; occult lore 983 *sorcery*; education, background; experience, practical e., hands-on e., acquaintance, nodding a., acquaintanceship, familiarity, intimacy; private knowledge, being in the know, sharing the secret 524 *information*; public knowledge, common knowledge, open secret 528 *publicity*; omniscience; intimation, glimpse, glimmering, inkling, suggestion 524 *hint*; suspicion, scent; self-knowledge, introspection; detection, clue 484 *discovery*; expert knowledge, specialization savoir-faire, savvy, know-how, expertise 694 *skill*; smattering 491 *sciolism*; epistemology.

erudition, lore, wisdom, scholarship, letters, literature 536 *learning*; acquired knowledge, general k., practical k.; professional k., encylopaedic k., universal k.; profound learning; smattering, dilettantism 491 *sciolism*; reading, wide r.; learning by rote, book-learning, bookishness, bibliomania; pedantry, donnishness; information; mine of information, store of knowledge, encyclopaedia 589 *library*.

culture, letters 557 *literature*; the humanities, the arts, the visual a.; education, instruction 534 *teaching*; literacy, numeracy; liberal education, scientific e.; self-education, self-instruction; civilization; attainments, accomplishments, proficiency, mastery.

science, natural s., the life sciences; natural philosophy; scientific knowledge; applied science, technology, computer science; ologies and isms.

Adj. *knowing*, all-k., encyclopaedic, comprehensive, omniscient 498 *wise*; cognizant, cognitive 447 *mental*; conscious, aware, mindful of 455 *attentive*; alive to, sensible of 819 *impressible*; experienced, competent, no stranger to, at home with, acquainted, familiar with, au fait with 610 *habituated*; intimate, privy to, wise to, on to, in the know, in on 524 *informed*; fly, canny, shrewd 498 *intelligent*; conversant, practised, versed in, proficient 694 *expert*; having hands-on experience.

known, perceived, seen, heard; ascertained, verified 473 *certain*; discovered, explored; noted, celebrated, famous 866 *renowned*; no secret, open s., public; familiar, intimate, dear; hackneyed, stale, trite; proverbial, household, commonplace 610 *usual*; prevalent 79 *general*; memorized, learnt off 505 *remembered*.

Vb. *know*, savvy; ken; have a nodding acquaintance with, be acquainted; apprehend, conceive, catch, grasp, twig, click, have, take in, get 516 *understand*; comprehend, master; come to know, latch on, get the hang of, get into one's head, realize; get to know, acquaint oneself, familiarize o., become au fait with; know again, recognize; be conscious of, be aware, be cognizant 447 *perceive*; discern 463 *discriminate*; perceive 438 *see*; know well, know full w., be thoroughly acquainted with, see through, read one like a book, have one's measure, have one

taped, have one sized up, know inside out; know down to the ground, know from A to Z, know like the back of one's hand; know for a fact 473 *be certain*; know of, have knowledge of, know something; be in the know, be in the secret, have the lowdown 524 *be informed*; know by heart, know by rote 505 *memorize*; know backwards, have it pat, have at one's finger tips, be master of, know one's stuff 694 *be expert*; have a little knowledge of 491 *not know*; know by experience; get the picture, see the light; know all the answers, be omniscient; know what's what, see one's way, know one's way about 498 *be wise*.

be known, become k., come to one's knowledge, be brought to one's notice, come to one's ears; be a well-known fact, be public knowledge, be an open secret, be no secret 528 *be published*.

491 Ignorance

N. *ignorance*, no news, no word of; unawareness, unconsciousness 375 *insensibility*; incognizance, nonrecognition, nonrealization; incomprehension, incapacity, backwardness 499 *unintelligence*; inappreciation, Philistinism 439 *blindness*; obstacle to knowledge, superstition 495 *error*; crass ignorance; lack of knowledge; lack of education, no schooling; blank mind, tabula rasa; unfamiliarity, inexperience, greenness, rawness; gaucherie, awkwardness; inexpertness, amateurishness 695 *unskilfulness*; innocence, simplicity, naivety 699 *artlessness*; nothing to go on, no lead, lack of information, general ignorance, anybody's guess, bewilderment 474 *uncertainty*; moral ignorance, unwisdom 499 *folly*; darkness, benightedness, unenlightenment; savagery, heathenism, paganism 982 *idolatry*; Age of Ignorance, Dark Ages; imperfect knowledge, semi-ignorance **(see** *sciolism***)**; ignorant person, illiterate 493 *ignoramus*; layman, autodidact, amateur, no expert 697 *bungler*; obscurantist; Philistine.

unknown thing, obstacle to knowledge; unknown quantity, matter of ignorance; prehistory 125 *antiquity*; sealed book, closed b., Greek; Dark Continent, terra incognita, unknown country, unexplored ground, virgin soil, lion country; frontiers of knowledge; dark horse, wild card, enigma, mystery 530 *secret*; unidentified flying object, UFO; unidentified body; unknown person, mystery p., Mr *or* Miss X., anonymity 562 *no name*.

sciolism, smattering, smatter, a little learning; glimmering, glimpse, half-glimpse 524 *hint*; vagueness, half-knowledge 495 *inexactness*; unreal knowledge 495 *error*; superficiality 212 *shallowness*; dilettantism, dabbling; affectation of knowledge, pedantry, quackery, charlatanism, bluff 850 *affectation*, smatterer 493 *dabbler*.

Adj. *ignorant*, unknowing; uncomprehending; unwitting; unaware, unconscious, oblivious 375 *insensible*; unfamiliar with, not au fait with, unacquainted, a stranger to, not at home with; in the dark (**see** *uninstructed*); mystified 474 *uncertain*; clueless, with nothing to go on; blindfolded 439 *blind*; groping 461 experimental; amateurish, inexpert, ham 695 *unskilful*; unversed, inexperienced, uninitiated, green, raw, wet behind the ears; innocent of, guiltless 935 *innocent*; naive, simple, unworldly 699 *artless*; unenlightened, benighted; savage, uncivilized; pagan, heathenish; backward, dull, dense, dumb 499 *unintelligent*; empty-headed, foolish 499 *unwise*; half-baked, out of touch, behind the times 125 *retrospective*; wilfully ignorant, indifferent 454 *incurious*.

uninstructed, uninformed, kept in the dark; ill-informed, vague about 474 *uncertain*; untaught, untutored, untrained; illiterate, innumerate, uneducated; uncultivated, uncultured, lowbrow; unscholarly, unread, Philistine; dense, dumb (**see** *ignorant*).

unknown, unbeknown, untold, unheard; unspoken, unsaid, unvoiced, unuttered; unseen 444 *invisible*; hidden, veiled 525 *concealed*; unrecognized 525 *disguised*; unperceived; unexplained 517 *unintelligible*; dark, enigmatic, mysterious 523 *occult*; strange, new, new-fangled, unfamiliar, unprecedented; unnamed 562 *anonymous*; unidentified, unclassified, uninvestigated 458 *neglected*; undiscovered, unexplored, uncharted, untravelled, unplumbed, unfathomed; untried, untested; virgin, novel 126 *new*; unforeseeable, unpredictable 124 *future*; unheard of, obscure 639 *unimportant*.

dabbling, unqualified; shallow, superficial, dilettante.

Vb. *not know*, be ignorant, be in the dark, have nothing to go on, have no lead; be unacquainted, not know from Adam; be green, be wet behind the ears, know no better; cannot say; not know the half of, have no conception, have no notion, have no clue, have no idea, have not the remotest i., not have the foggiest, not have an inkling, be reduced to guessing 512 *suppose*; know nothing of, not hear 416 *be deaf*; not see, suffer from tunnel vision 439 *be blind*; be at a loss, be stumped, not know what to make of 474 *be uncertain*; not know the first thing about, have to start at the bottom 695 *be unskilful*; not know chalk from cheese; misunderstand 517 *not understand*; misconstrue 481 *misjudge*; half know, know a little, have a smattering, dabble in; suspect 486 *doubt*; ignore

458 *disregard*; profess ignorance, shrug one's shoulders, not want to know 860 *be indifferent*; grope, fumble 461 *be tentative*.

492 Scholar

N. *scholar*, savant(e), learned person, erudite p., educated p., man *or* woman of learning, man *or* woman of letters, bookman, bookwoman, bibliophile; don, reader, professor, pedagogue 537 *teacher*; pedant, bookworm, bluestocking; encyclopaedist; mine of information, walking encyclopaedia, talking dictionary; student, serious student 538 *learner*; degree-holder, graduate, diploma-holder; academic circles, academia, groves of academe; professoriate.

intellectual, academic, scholastic; genius, gifted child, prodigy 500 *sage*; know-all, brainbox; highbrow, egghead, bluestocking, intelligentsia, literati, illuminati, intellectual snob; academician.

collector, connoisseur, dilettante 846 *people of taste*; bibliophile, book-collector; librarian, curator 749 *keeper*; antiquary 125 *antiquarian*; numismatist, phillumenist, philatelist, stamp-collector 504 *enthusiast*; lexicographer, philologist 557 *linguist*.

493 Ignoramus

N. *ignoramus*, illiterate, lowbrow; philistine; duffer, thickhead, numskull, bimbo 501 *dunce*; bonehead, blockhead, goof, goose, bungler 501 *fool*; greenhorn, novice, raw recruit 538 *beginner*; simpleton 544 *dupe*.

dabbler, dilettante; quack, charlatan 545 *impostor*.

494 Truth

N. *truth*, verity, rightness; basic truth; truism, platitude 496 *axiom*; accordance with fact; truth of the matter, honest truth, plain t., simple t.; gospel, Holy Writ, Bible 975 *revelation*; facts, lowdown, the heart of the matter; actuality; factualness, fact, matter of f. 3 *substantiality*; home truth, candour, frankness 929 *probity*; naked truth, unvarnished t.; the t., the whole t. and nothing but the t.; truthfulness 540 *veracity*; appearance of truth, verisimilitude 471 *probability*.

authenticity, validity, realness, genuineness; the real McCoy, the real thing, the genuine article, it 13 *identity*; no illusion, not a fake 21 *no imitation*.

accuracy, attention to fact; verisimilitude, local colour, realism, 'warts and all'; fidelity, high f., exactitude, exactness, preciseness, precision, mathematical p., clockwork p.; micrometry 465 *measurement*; mot juste, hitting the nail on the head, aptness 24 *adaptation*;

meticulousness, punctiliousness 455 *attention*; letter of the law, acting according to the book 735 *severity*; literalness 514 *meaning*; true report, the very words, a verbatim account 540 *veracity*; chapter and verse, facts, statistics 466 *evidence*.

Adj. *true*, correct, right, so; real, tangible 3 *substantial*; actual, factual, historical; well-grounded, well-founded, well-thought-out; well-argued, well-taken; literal, truthful 540 *veracious*; true to the facts, true to scale, true to the letter, according to the book (**see** *accurate*); unquestionable 473 *undisputed*; reasonable 475 *rational*; true to life, true to nature, faithful, verbatim; realistic; unromantic, down to earth; candid, honest, warts and all.

genuine, authentic, bona fide, valid, guaranteed, authenticated, official; sound, solid, reliable, honest 929 *trustworthy*; natural, pure, sterling, hallmarked; fair dinkum; true-born; rightful, legitimate; unadulterated, unvarnished, uncoloured, straight from the shoulder, undisguised, undistorted, unexaggerated.

accurate, exact, precise, definite, defined; well-adjusted, well-pitched, high-fidelity, dead-on 24 *adjusted*; well-aimed, direct, straight, dead-centre 281 *directed*; unerring, undeviating; constant, regular 16 *uniform*; punctual, right, correct, true, spot on, on the button, on the mark; infallible; close, faithful; fine, nice, delicate, sensitive; micrometric; mathematically exact, scientifically e.; scrupulous, punctilious, meticulous, strict, severe 455 *attentive*; word for word, verbatim, literal; literal-minded, just so 862 *fastidious*.

Vb. *be true*, be so, be just so, be the case, happen, exist 1 *be*; hold, hold true, hold good, hold water, wash, stand the test, ring true; conform to fact, prove true, hold together; speak the truth, omit nothing 540 *be truthful*; seem real, copy nature 551 *represent*; square, set, trim 24 *adjust*; substantiate 466 *corroborate*; prove 478 *demonstrate*; be right, be correct, have the right answer; get at the truth, hit the nail on the head, hit the mark, be spot on 484 *detect*.

Adv. *truly*, undeniably, indubitably, certainly, undoubtedly, really, genuinely, indeed; as a matter of fact 1 *actually*; to tell the truth 540 *truthfully*; strictly speaking, sic, literally, to the letter, word for word, verbatim; exactly, accurately, precisely, right, to an inch, to a nicety, to a turn, to a T, just right, spot on; in every detail, in all respects, tout à fait.

495 Error

N. *error*, erroneousness, wrongness, unsoundness; silliness 497 *absurdity*; untruth, falsity; straying from the truth, inexactitude 282 *deviation*; inaccuracy, fallacy, self-contradiction 477 *sophism*; unorthodoxy 977 *heterodoxy*; old wives' tales, superstition, popular misconception 491 *ignorance*; fallibility 481 *misjudgment*; mistaken belief, wishful thinking, doublethink, self-deception; misunderstanding, misconception, misconstruction, cross-purposes 521 *misinterpretation*; falseness, untruthfulness 541 *falsehood*; illusion, hallucination, mirage 440 *visual fallacy*; false pregnancy, pseudocyesis; false light, false dawn 509 *disappointment*; delusion 503 *mental disorder*; dream 513 *fantasy*; false impression; prejudice 481 *bias*.

inexactness, inexactitude, inaccuracy, imprecision, nonadjustment; faultiness; looseness, laxity, generalization 79 *generality*; loose thinking, sloppy t. 477 *sophistry*; carelessness 458 *negligence*; mistiming 118 *anachronism*; misinformation 552 *misrepresentation*; misquotation (**see** *mistake*); malapropism 565 *solecism*.

mistake, miscalculation 481 *misjudgment*; blunder, botch-up 695 *bungling*; mistaken identity, own goal, friendly fire; wrong address; glaring error, bloomer, clanger, howler, gaffe, bull, Irish b. 497 *absurdity*; oversight 456 *inattention*; bungle, foul-up, louse-up, screw-up, balls-up, cock-up, boo-boo, slip-up, boob, goof, blooper; fluff, muff; leak, slip, slip of the pen, slip of the tongue, spoonerism 565 *solecism*; typist's error; typographical error, printer's e., misprint, typo, literal, erratum, corrigendum; human error, computer e.; inadvertency; bad tactics, faux pas; solecism 847 *bad taste*; blot, flaw 845 *blemish*.

Adj. *erroneous*, erring, wrong; in error (**see** *mistaken*); unfactual, unhistorical, mythical 2 *unreal*; aberrant; wide of the mark, wide of the truth, devoid of t. 543 *untrue*; unsound, unscientific, unreasoned, cock-eyed, ill-reasoned, self-contradictory 477 *illogical*; implausible 472 *improbable*; unsubstantiated, uncorroborated, unfounded, ungrounded, groundless, disproved; exploded, discredited 924 *disapproved*; fallacious, misleading; unauthentic, apocryphal; perverted, unorthodox, heretical; untruthful, lying 541 *false*; flawed, fake, simulated, bogus 542 *spurious*; hallucinatory, illusive, illusory, delusive, deceptive; unrealistic, fantastical 513 *imaginary*; wild, crackpot 497 *absurd*; fallible, perverse, prejudiced 481 *biased*; superstitious 491 *ignorant*.

mistaken, misunderstood, misconceived; misrepresented, perverted; misinterpreted, misconstrued, misread, misprinted; miscalculated, misjudged; in error, misled, misguided; misinformed, ill-informed, deluded 491 *uninstructed*; slipping, blundering 695 *clumsy*; straying, wandering; wide, misdirected, off-target, off-beam, out to lunch 25 *unapt*; at fault, cold, off the scent, off the track, off the beam, wide of the mark, on the wrong tack, on the wrong scent, off the rails, at sea 474 *uncertain*.

inexact, inaccurate; loose; broad, generalized 79 *general*; incorrect, misreported, garbled; imprecise, erratic, wild, hit-or-miss; wildly out, maladjusted; untuned, out of tune, out of gear; out of synch, unsynchronized, slow, losing, fast, gaining; uncorrected, unrevised; faulty, full of holes, flawed, botched, mangled 695 *bungled*; misprinted, misread, mistranslated.

Vb. *err*, commit an error, go wrong, stray from the straight and narrow, mistake, make a m.; labour under a misapprehension, bark up the wrong tree, be on the wrong scent; be in the wrong, be mistaken; delude oneself, suffer hallucinations 481 *misjudge*; be misled, be misguided; receive a wrong impression, get hold of the wrong end of the stick, be at cross-purposes, misunderstand, misconceive, misapprehend, get it wrong 517 *not understand*; miscount, misreckon 482 *overrate*, 483 *underestimate*; go astray 282 *stray*; gain, be fast 135 *be early*; lose, be slow, stop 136 *be late*.

blunder, trip, stumble, miss, fault 695 *be clumsy*; slip, slip up, drop a brick, drop a clanger, boob, goof, foul up, screw up, mess up, make a hash of; commit a faux pas, put one's foot in it; betray oneself, give oneself away 526 *disclose*; blot one's copybook, blot, flaw; fluff, muff, botch, bungle; blow it 728 *fail*; play into one's hands 695 *act foolishly*; miscount, miscalculate 481 *misjudge*; misread, misquote, misprint, misapprehend, mistranslate 521 *misinterpret*.

mislead, misdirect 282 *deflect*; misinform, lead astray, pervert; beguile, lead one a dance, lead one up the garden path 542 *deceive*; give a false impression, create a false i., falsify, garble 541 *dissemble*; gloss over, whitewash, cover up 525 *conceal*.

496 Maxim

N. *maxim*, adage, saw, proverb, byword, aphorism; dictum, tag, saying, stock s., common s., truth; epigram, mot 839 *witticism*; wise maxim; truism, cliché, commonplace, platitude, banality, hackneyed saying, trite remark, statement of the obvious, bromide; motto, watchword, slogan, catchword; formula, mantra; text, canon, sutra, rule, golden r. 693 *precept*; gloss, comment, note, remark, observation 520 *commentary*; moral, edifying story, fable, cautionary tale 590 *narrative*.

axiom. self-evident truth, truism; principle, postulate, theorem, formula; Sod's Law, Murphy's Law.

Adj. *aphoristic*, proverbial, moralizing, holier than thou 498 *wise*; epigrammatic, pithy 839 *witty*; snappy 569 *concise*; enigmatic 517 *puzzling*; common, banal, trite, corny, hackneyed, platitudinous, clichéd, commonplace, stock 610 *usual*; axiomatic.

Adv. *proverbially*, as the saying goes, as they say, as the old adage has it, to coin a phrase; in a nutshell; epigrammatically, by way of moral.

497 Absurdity

N. *absurdity*, height of a., height of nonsense, absurdness 849 *ridiculousness*; inconsequence 10 *irrelevance*; false logic 477 *sophistry*; foolishness, silliness, silly season 499 *folly*; senselessness, futility, fatuity 641 *lost labour*; nonsense verse, doggerel; talking through one's hat; rot, rubbish, nonsense, stuff and nonsense, gibberish, jargon, twaddle 515 *silly talk*; Irish bull, malapropism, howler 495 *mistake*; limerick 839 *witticism*; pun, play upon words 518 *equivocalness*; riddle, riddle-me-ree 530 *enigma*; anticlimax, bathos, descent from the sublime to the ridiculous.

foolery, antics, capers, fooling about, horsing around, silliness, tomfoolery, shenanigans, high jinks, skylarking 837 *revel*; vagary, whimsy, whimsicality 604 *whim*; extravagance, extravaganza; escapade, scrape 700 *predicament*; practical joke, monkey trick, piece of nonsense; drollery 849 *ridiculousness*; clowning, buffoonery, burlesque, parody, caricature 851 *ridicule*; farce, mummery, pretence 850 *affectation*; showing off 875 *ostentation*.

Adj. *absurd*, ludicrous, laughable, risible, farcical, comical, grotesque 849 *ridiculous*; rash, silly, asinine, idiotic, cock-eyed, moronic, tomfool 499 *foolish*; nonsensical, senseless 515 *meaningless*; preposterous, without rhyme or reason 477 *illogical*; wild; pretentious 850 *affected*; frantic 503 *frenzied*; mad, crazy, crackpot, harebrained 495 *erroneous*; fanciful, fantastic 513 *imaginative*; futile, fatuous 641 *useless*; punning 518 *equivocal*.

Vb. *be absurd*, play the fool, play the clown, act like a fool, behave like an idiot 499 *be foolish*; fool, fool about, lark about, muck a., horse a., monkey around, play practical jokes 837 *amuse oneself*; be a laughingstock 849 *be ridiculous*; clown, clown about, parody, caricature, mimic, guy, make a fool of 851 *ridicule*; talk rot, talk nonsense, talk through one's hat, talk gibberish 515 *mean nothing*; rave 503 *be insane*.

498 Intelligence. Wisdom

N. *intelligence*, powers of thought, intellectualism 447 *intellect*; brains, brain, grey matter, head, loaf, upper storey, upstairs, noddle; nous, wit, common sense; understanding, sense, good s., horse s., savvy, gumption, knowhow; wits, sharp w., ready w., quick thinking; ability, capacity, mental c., mental grasp; calibre, mental c., intelligence quotient, IQ; high IQ, Mensa, forwardness, brightness; braininess, cleverness 694 *aptitude*; mental gifts, giftedness, brilliance, talent, genius; ideas, inspiration, sheer i. 476 *intuition*; brainwave, bright idea 451 *idea.*

sagacity, judgment, sound j., discretion, discernment 463 *discrimination*; perception, perspicacity, clear thinking, clear-headedness; acumen, sharpness, acuteness, acuity, penetration; shrewdness; level-headedness, balance 502 *sanity*; prudence, forethought, farsightedness 510 *foresight*; craftiness 698 *cunning*; worldly wisdom; vigilance, alertness, awareness 457 *carefulness*; tact, statesmanship, strategy 688 *tactics.*

wisdom, sapience; profundity of thought 449 *thought*; breadth of mind; experience, lifelong e.; soundness; mental balance, enlightenment.

Adj. *intelligent,* brainy, clever, forward, bright, bright as a button; brilliant, scintillating, talented 694 *gifted*; capable, able 694 *skilful*; apt, ready, quick, quick on the uptake; receptive; acute, sharp, sharp as a needle, sharpwitted, quick-w., nimble-w.; aware, on one's toes, streetwise, with it 455 *attentive*; astute, shrewd, fly, smart, canny, not born yesterday, all there, on the ball; knowing, sophisticated, worldly-wise; too smart for one's own good, too clever by half; sagacious, prudent, watchful 457 *careful*; farseeing, farsighted 510 *foreseeing*; discerning 463 *discriminating*; penetrating, perspicacious, clear-headed; politic, statesmanlike.

wise, sage, sagacious, sapient; thinking, reflecting 449 *thoughtful*; reasoning 475 *rational*; knowledgeable; highbrow, intellectual, profound, deep; sound, sensible, reasonable 502 *sane*; not born yesterday, experienced; levelheaded; judicious 913 *just*; enlightened, prudent, tactful, politic 698 *cunning*; wise as a serpent, wise as an owl, wise as Solomon, like a Daniel come to judgment; well-advised, wellconsidered, well-judged.

Vb. *be wise,* – intelligent etc. adj.; use one's head, use one's loaf or noddle, use one's intelligence; have a fund of wisdom 490 *know*; have brains, have plenty of grey matter, have a head on one's shoulders, have one's wits about one, know how many beans make five, see with half an eye, see at a glance; have one's head screwed on the right way, know a thing or two, know what's what, know the score; be up on, be in the know, be au courant; show foresight 510 *foresee*; know which side one's bread is buttered on, be prudent, take care 858 *be cautious*; have

sense, listen to reason 475 *be reasonable*; be politic 623 *plan*; have tact 698 *be cunning*; learn from one's mistakes, come to one's senses.

499 Unintelligence. Folly

N. *unintelligence,* lack of intelligence, want of intellect 448 *absence of intellect*; feeblemindedness, low IQ, low mental age, brain damage, dementia, mental deficiency; mental handicap, arrested development, retardation, backwardness; imbecility, idiocy; stupidity, slowness, dullness, obtuseness, thickheadedness, denseness; oafishness; no head for; incapacity, incompetence 695 *unskilfulness*; gullibility 481 *misjudgment*; inanity, vacuity, vacuousness, superficiality 212 *shallowness.*

folly, foolishness, eccentricity 849 *ridiculousness*; tomfool idea, tomfoolery, act of folly 497 *foolery*; giddiness 456 *inattention*; irrationality, illogic 477 *sophistry*; indiscretion, tactlessness; fatuity, fatuousness, pointlessness; wild-goose chase 641 *lost labour*; silliness; idiocy, lunacy, utter folly; recklessness, wildness 857 *rashness*; infatuation 481 *misjudgment*; puerility, childishness 130 *nonage*; second childhood, senility, dotage, senile dementia 131 *old age*; drivelling, babbling, maundering, wandering.

Adj. *unintelligent,* unintellectual, low-brow; talentless, no genius; incompetent 695 *clumsy*; dull; subnormal, ESN, mentally handicapped, having a learning disability, mentally disadvantaged, mentally deficient; backward, retarded, feeble-minded, moronic, cretinous, imbecile 503 *mentally disordered*; deficient, wanting, not all there, vacant, not quite the full pound note, not right in the head; limited, weak, weak in the upper storey; slow, slow on the uptake, slow to learn; stupid, obtuse, dense, thick, gormless, bovine, blockish, oafish, doltish; dumb, dopey, dim, dim-witted, dull-w., slow-w., half-w.; pig thick or ignorant, dead from the neck up, thick as two short planks; thick-skulled, boneheaded, muddle-h.; cracked, barmy 503 *crazy*; unteachable; muddled, addled.

foolish, silly, idiotic, imbecile, asinine; nonsensical, senseless, fatuous, futile, inane 497 *absurd*; ludicrous, laughable, risible 849 *ridiculous*; like a fool, like an idiot 544 *gullible*; inexperienced 491 *ignorant*; tactless, impolitic; soft, wet, soppy, sappy, gormless; goofy, dopey; puerile, infantile; gaga, senile, away with the fairies; besotted, doting; spoony 887 *enamoured*; dazed, fuddled, maudlin 949 *drunk*; babbling, burbling, drivelling, maundering, wandering; mindless (**see** *unintelligent*); bird-witted, feather-brained, crack-b., scatter-b., hare-b. 456

light-minded; eccentric, unstable, wild, madcap, scatty, nutty, dotty, daft 503 *crazy*.

unwise, unenlightened; unintellectual; irrational 477 *illogical*; indiscreet 464 *indiscriminating*; injudicious; short-sighted 439 *blind*; unteachable; thoughtless; impatient 680 *hasty*; foolhardy, reckless 857 *rash*; unbalanced; unreasonable; unseemly, improper 643 *inexpedient*; ill-considered, ill-advised, ill-judged 495 *mistaken*.

Vb. *be foolish*, maunder, dote, drivel, babble, burble, wander, talk through one's hat 515 *mean nothing*; go haywire, lose one's wits, take leave of one's senses, go off one's head, go off one's rocker 503 *be insane*; have no sense, not have the sense one was born with; not see farther than one's nose, not see the wood for the trees; never learn; invite ridicule, look like a fool, look foolish 849 *be ridiculous*; make a fool of oneself, play the fool, act the f., act the giddy goat 497 *be absurd*; burn one's fingers 695 *act foolishly*; go on a fool's errand 641 *waste effort*; miscalculate 481 *misjudge*.

500 Sage

N. *sage*, nobody's fool; learned person 492 *scholar*; wise man, wise woman, statesman *or* -woman; elder statesman *or* -woman, consultant, authority 691 *adviser*; expert 696 *proficient person*; genius, master mind; master, mentor, guide, guru, pundit 537 *teacher*; seer, prophet 511 *oracle*; yogi 945 *ascetic*; leading light, shining l., luminary; mahatma; doctor, thinker; egghead, boffin, highbrow, blue stocking 492 *intellectual*; wizard, witch doctor 983 *sorcerer*; magus, Magi, wise men from the East; Solomon, Daniel, Daniel come to judgment, learned judge; Grand Old Man.

wiseacre, wise guy, know-all, smarty-pants, smart ass 873 *vain person*; smart alec, clever dick.

501 Fool

N. *fool*, silly f., tomfool 504 *madman*; buffoon, clown, comic, jester, zany 594 *entertainer*; perfect fool, complete idiot, big girl's blouse, geek, ninny, nincompoop, ass, jackass, donkey, goose, cuckoo; zombie, idiot, born fool; cretin, moron, imbecile; half-wit, dimwit, silly, sillybilly, twerp; stooge, butt 851 *laughingstock*; fathead, pinhead, muddle-head, incompetent, twit, clot, wally, plonker, nerd 697 *bungler*; birdbrain, featherbrain, bimbo, dingbat; flibbertigibbet; crackpot, eccentric 504 *crank*; babbler, burbler, driveller; dotard 133 *old man*.

ninny, simpleton, Simple Simon; charley; nincompoop, juggins, muggins, booby, sap, big

stiff, dope, jerk, gowk, galoot, goof; greenhorn 538 *beginner*; wet, weed, drip, milksop, wimp 163 *weakling*; sucker, mug 544 *dupe*.

dunce, dullard; blockhead, wooden-head, numskull, duffer, dummkopf, dolt, dumb cluck, bimbo, himbo 493 *ignoramus*; fat-head, bonehead, pinhead, blockhead, dunderhead, nitwit, dimwit; chump, clot, clod.

502 Sanity

N. *sanity*, saneness, soundness of mind; rationality, reason; balance of the mind, mental equilibrium; common sense; coherence 516 *intelligibility*; lucidity, lucid moment; proper mind, right m., senses; sound mind.

Adj. *sane*, of sound mind, all there; compos mentis, in one's right mind, in possession of one's faculties, with all one's wits about one; rational, reasonable 498 *intelligent*; coherent 516 *intelligible*, lucid, clear-headed.

503 Insanity: mental disorder

N. *mental disorder*, insanity, lunacy, madness, certifiability; mental illness; mental instability; mental derangement, unsound mind, delirium, brain damage; CJD, Creutzfeldt-Jakob disease, Creutzfeldt-Jakob disease NU, Kuru, persistent vegetative state, PVS, Alzheimer's disease, softening of the brain 131 *age*; dementia, senile d., psychiatry, clinical psychology 447 *psychology*; psychotherapy 658 *therapy*; psychoanalyst, analyst, psychiatrist, shrink 658 *doctor*.

psychosis, paranoia, delusions, hallucinations; catatonia, schizophrenia; confusion; melancholia 834 *melancholy*; clinical depression, manic d., mania, megalomania,

learning disability, special needs, learning difficulty, mental handicap, mental deficiency, idiocy, imbecility, cretinism, feeblemindedness; Down's syndrome, mongolism; Asperger syndrome, autism 84 *abnormality*.

personality disorder, psychopathology, psychopathy, maladjustment; split personality, dual p.; persecution mania; kleptomania; nymphomania, satyriasis; inferiority c.

neurosis, psychoneurosis, anxiety neurosis, nerves, nervous disorder; hysteria; nervous breakdown, brainstorm; shell-shock, combat fatigue; obsession, compulsion, phobia, claustrophobia, agorophobia 854 *phobia*; hypochondria; depression, depressed state, blues.

frenzy, furore; ecstasy; raving, hysteria; distraction 456 *abstractedness*; incoherence 517 *unintelligibility*; delirium tremens, DTs; epilepsy, fit, epileptic f., epileptic frenzy, paroxysm 318 *spasm*.

eccentricity, craziness, crankiness; queerness, oddness, weirdness; oddity, twist, quirk, kink, craze, fad 84 *abnormality*; a screw loose, bats in the belfry; fixation, hang-up; obsession, infatuation, bee in one's bonnet 604 *whim*.

mental hospital, psychiatric h., psychiatric unit, mental institution; mental home, madhouse, lunatic asylum, Bedlam; loony-bin, nuthouse, bughouse, funny farm; locked ward, padded cell 658 *hospital*.

person with a learning disability, mentally-handicapped person, idiot, congenital i., natural, cretin, moron 501 *fool*.

Adj. *mentally disordered*, insane, mad, lunatic, of unsound mind, not in one's right m., non compos mentis, out of one's mind, deranged, demented; certifiable, mental; psychologically abnormal, mentally disturbed, mentally ill, of diseased *or* disordered *or* distempered mind; unbalanced; brain-damaged; raving mad, stark staring mad, mad as a hatter, mad as a March hare, off one's rocker (*see frenzied*); gaga, loony, certified; locked up, put away.

having a learning disability, imbecile, moronic, cretinous, defective, feebleminded, subnormal; autistic.

psychotic, paranoiac, paranoid, schizophrenic, schizoid; manic, maniacal; catatonic, depressive, clinically depressed 834 *melancholic*; hyperactive.

neurotic, hypochondriac; kleptomaniac; nymphomaniac, claustrophobic, agoraphobic.

maladjusted, psychopathic, psychopathological.

crazy, bewildered, wandering, bemused, pixilated, moidered 456 *abstracted*; not all there, not right in the head; off one's head *or* one's nut, off one's trolley, round the bend *or* the twist, up the pole; crazed, demented, driven mad, maddened (*see frenzied*); unhinged, unbalanced, off one's rocker; deluded; infatuated, possessed; besotted 887 *enamoured*; drivelling, gaga, in one's second childhood, away with the fairies; touched, wanting; idiotic, scatterbrained, crack-brained 499 *foolish*; crackers, cracked, scatty, screwy, nutty, nutty as a fruit cake, nuts, bananas, batty, bats, cuckoo, barmy, bonkers, meshuga; daft, dippy, loony, loopy, goofy, potty, dotty; cranky, wacky, flaky, eccentric, erratic, funny, queer, odd, peculiar 84 *abnormal*; crotchety, whimsical 604 *capricious*; dizzy, giddy 456 *light-minded*.

frenzied, rabid, maddened; furious, foaming at the mouth 891 *angry*; wild, distraught 825 *suffering*; possessed; frantic, frenetic, demented, like one possessed, out of one's mind, beside oneself, uncontrollable; berserk, seeing red, running amok, running wild 176 *violent*; having fits; hysterical, delirious, hallucinating, raving, rambling, wandering, incoherent, fevered.

Vb. *be insane*, – mad, – crazy etc. adj.; have bats in the belfry, have a screw loose; drivel 499 *be foolish*; ramble, wander; babble, rave; foam at the mouth; be delirious, see things.

go mad, go off one's head, go off one's rocker *or* nut, go crackers, lose one's marbles, go out of one's mind, crack up; go berserk, run amok, see red, foam at the mouth, lose one's head 891 *get angry*.

make mad, drive m., drive insane, madden; derange; send one off his head *or* out of his mind; send round the bend *or* the twist, drive up the wall; turn one's brain; blow one's mind 821 *excite*; unhinge, unbalance, send off one's rocker; infuriate, make one see red 891 *enrage*; possess; go to one's head, turn one's h.

504 Madman

N. *madman*, madwoman, lunatic; raving lunatic, maniac; screwball, nut, nutcase, loon, loony, kook, meshuggenah.

psychotic, paranoiac, schizoid, schizophrenic, manic depressive; megalomaniac; catatonic.

neurotic, hysteric; neuropath; hypochondriac; obsessive; phobic, claustrophobic, agoraphobic; depressive, melancholic; kleptomaniac, pyromaniac.

the maladjusted, psychopath, psycho, psychopathic personality, sociopath, unstable personality, aggressive p., antisocial p.; dipsomaniac 949 *drunkard*; dope addict, dope fiend, junkie; drug addict 949 *drug-taking*; crank, crackpot, nut, nutter, crackbrain; eccentric, oddball 851 *laughingstock*; freak 84 *nonconformist*; fanatic, extremist, lunatic fringe.

enthusiast, zealot; devotee, aficionado, addict, freak, buff, anorak, train-spotter, geek, big; fan, supporter 707 *patron*; connoisseur, fancier 846 *people of taste*; fitness freak, radio ham, balletomane, opera buff, film b.; bibliophile 492 *collector*.

SECTION SIX

Extension of thought

505 Memory

N. *memory*, good m., retentiveness; photographic m.; tribal m., atavism.

remembrance, recollection, recall, total r.; commemoration, evocation, mind's eye; recapitulation 106 *repetition*; memorization, remembering, learning by heart, committing to memory, learning by rote 536 *learning*; reminiscence, retrospection, review, retrospect, hindsight; flashback, recurrence, voice from the past; déjà vu 984 *psychics*; afterthought 67 *sequel*; nostalgia, regrets 830 *regret*; memorabilia, memoirs, reminiscences, recollections; place in history 866 *famousness*; memoranda.

reminder, memorial, testimonial, commemoration; souvenir, keepsake, relic, memento, autograph; trophy, bust, statue 548 *monument*; prompter; testifier 466 *witness*; memorandum, memo, chit, note, notebook, memo pad, aide-mémoire, diary, engagement d., Filo fax (tdmk); personal organizer, telephone book; album, autograph a., photograph a., scrapbook, commonplacebook, promptbook; leading question, prompt, prompting, suggestion, cue 524 *hint*; mnemonic, aid to memory, knotted handkerchief.

Adj. *remembered*, recollected etc. vb.; retained, not forgotten, green, fresh, fresh in one's memory, of recent memory, as clear as if it were yesterday; uppermost in one's thoughts; of blessed memory, missed, regretted; memorable, unforgettable; haunting, persistent, undying; deep-rooted, indelible, inscribed upon the mind, stamped on one's memory; got by heart, memorized 490 *known*.

remembering, mindful, keeping in mind; evocative, commemorative 876 *celebratory*; reminiscent, recollecting; living in the past, dwelling upon the past, nostalgic; haunted; recalling, reminding, mnemonic, prompting, suggesting.

Vb. *remember*, bring to m., call to m.; recognize, know again 490 *know*; recollect; not forget, bottle up 778 *retain*; hold in mind; enshrine in one's memory, store in one's mind, cherish the memory; never forget, be unable to f.; recall, call to mind, return to thoughts of, think of; reflect, review, think back, muse upon, keep in mind 455 *be mindful*; recapture, hark back, cast one's mind b.; conjure up, rake up the past, reminisce; live in the past; reopen old wounds, recapture old times; remind oneself, make a note of, tie a knot in one's handkerchief; rack one's brains, tax one's memory.

remind, jog one's memory, refresh one's m.; renew one's m.; put one in mind of, take one back; drop a hint, cue, prompt, suggest 524 *hint*; not allow one to forget, haunt; not let sleeping dogs lie, fan the embers, keep the wounds open 821 *excite*; turn another's mind back, make one think of, awake memories of; commemorate, keep the memory green, toast 876 *celebrate*; recount, recapitulate 106 *repeat*.

memorize, commit to memory; get by heart, learn by rote 536 *learn*; fix in one's memory, implant in one's m., impress on one's m., engrave on the m., hammer into one's head, din into one's h.; cram the mind with.

be remembered, linger in the memory, stick in the mind, make a lasting impression; recur 106 *reoccur*; flash across one's mind, ring a bell; run

in one's mind, haunt one's t. or mind, be at the back of one's mind, lurk in one's mind, make history; live on 115 *be eternal*.

Adv. *in memory*, in memory of, to the memory of, as a memorial to, in memoriam, lest we forget; by heart, by rote, from memory.

506 Oblivion

N. *oblivion*, blankness, no recollection, no memory; obliviousness, forgetfulness, absent-mindedness 456 *abstractedness*; loss of memory, amnesia, blackout, total blank, mental block; insensibility of the past; dim memory, hazy recollection; short memory, poor m., defective m., failing m., faulty m., false memory syndrome; lapse of memory, memory like a sieve; effacement 550 *obliteration*; Lethe, waters of oblivion; good riddance.

amnesty, letting bygones be bygones, burial of grievances, burial of the hatchet, shaking of hands; pardon, free p., absolution 909 *forgiveness*.

Adj. *forgotten*, clean f., beyond recall; not missed; unremembered; in limbo 458 *neglected*; misremembered etc. vb., on the tip of one's tongue; in the recesses of one's mind, gone out of one's head; buried, suppressed; out of mind, over and done with, dead and buried, sunk in oblivion, amnestied.

forgetful, forgetting, oblivious; sunk in oblivion; unconscious of the past; unable to remember, suffering from amnesia, amnesic; unmindful, heedless, mindless 458 *negligent*; absent-minded 456 abstracted; conveniently forgetting 918 *undutiful*.

Vb. *forget*, clean f., not remember, have no recollection of; not give another thought to, think no more of; suppress the memory, consign to oblivion, be oblivious; amnesty, let bygones be bygones, bury the hatchet 909 *forgive*; break with the past; suffer from amnesia, lose one's memory, remember nothing; misremember; be forgetful, have a poor memory, need reminding; lose sight of, leave behind, overlook; be absent-minded, fluff one's notes 456 *be inattentive*; forget one's lines, dry; have a memory like a sieve, go in one ear and out of the other, forget one's own name; have on the tip of one's tongue, not quite recall, draw a blank.

be forgotten, slip one's memory; sink into oblivion, be consigned to o.; become passé, be overlooked.

507 Expectation

N. *expectation*, state of e., expectancy 455 *attention*; contemplation 617 *intention*; confidence, trust 473 *certainty*; presumption 475 *premise*;

foretaste 135 *anticipation*; eager expectation 859 *desire*; breathless expectation 852 *hope*; waiting, suspense 474 *uncertainty*; dread, feelings of doom, doom watching, apprehension, apprehensiveness 854 *fear*; anxiety 825 *worry*; expectance, one's expectations 471 *probability*; prospect, lookout, outlook, forecast 511 *prediction*; contingency 469 *possibility*; destiny 596 *fate*; unfulfilled expectation 509 *disappointment*; what is expected, the usual thing 610 *practice*.

Adj. *expectant*, expecting, in expectation, in hourly e.; in suspense, on the waiting list, on the short l., on the short leet; sure, confident 473 *certain*; anticipatory, anticipating, banking on, putting all one's money on; presuming, taking for granted; predicting 510 *foreseeing*; forewarned, forearmed, ready 669 *prepared*; waiting, waiting for, awaiting; on the lookout, keeping cave, on the watch for, standing by, on call 457 *vigilant*; keyed up 821 *excited*; on tenterhooks, on the rack, in agonies of expectation, agog; hopeful, sanguine 852 *hoping*; dreading, anxious 854 *nervous*; doom-watching 853 *hopeless*; expecting a baby, expecting a happy event, parturient 167 *fertilized*.

expected, long e.; up to expectation, as one expected; anticipated, presumed, predicted, on the cards, foreseen 471 *probable*; prospective, future, on the horizon 155 *impending*; promised, intended, in prospect; longed for 859 *desired*; dreaded, feared 854 *frightening*.

Vb. *expect*, look for, face the prospect; have in mind; calculate 480 *estimate*; forecast 510 *foresee*; see it coming 865 *not wonder*; think likely, presume 471 *assume*; bank on, count upon, put one's money on 473 *be certain*; count one's chickens before they are hatched 509 *be disappointed*; anticipate 669 *prepare oneself*; look out for, watch out f., be waiting f., be ready f. 457 *be careful*; stand by, be on call; hang around (**see** *await*); dread, doomwatch 854 *fear*; look forward to, hope for 852 *hope*, 859 *desire*.

await, be on the waiting list; stand and wait, watch and pray 136 *wait*; queue up, line up, mark time, bide one's t.; stand by, hold oneself ready, be on call; keep one waiting; have in store for, be in store for.

Adv. *expectantly*, in suspense, with bated breath, on edge, on the edge of one's chair.

508 Lack of expectation

N. *lack of expectation*, false expectation 509 *disappointment*; resignation, no hope 853 *hopelessness*; apathy 454 *incuriosity*; unpreparedness 670 *nonpreparation*; unexpectedness, unforeseen contingency; miscalculation 495 *error*; surprise; the unexpected, the unforeseen, surprise packet; windfall, gift from the gods, something

to one's advantage 615 *benefit*; shock, nasty s., jolt; blow, sudden b.; bolt from the blue, thunderbolt, thunderclap, bombshell; revelation, eye-opener; culture shock; reversal; amazement 864 *wonder*.

Adj. *unexpected*, unanticipated, unlooked for; unpredicted, unforeseen; unheralded, unannounced; without warning; astounding, mind-boggling, eye-opening, staggering, amazing 864 *wonderful*; shocking, startling 854 *frightening*; sudden 116 *instantaneous*; like a bombshell, like a thunderbolt, like a bolt from the blue, dropped from the clouds; unbargained for, uncatered for 670 *unprepared*; contrary to expectation; beyond one's wildest dreams, unprecedented 84 *unusual*; freakish 84 *abnormal*; unaccountable 517 *puzzling*.

unexpecting, unexpectant, unsuspecting, off guard 456 *inattentive*; uninformed 491 *ignorant*; not forewarned; surprised, disconcerted, taken by surprise, taken aback, caught napping, caught with one's pants *or* trousers down, caught on the hop, on the wrong foot 670 *unprepared*; astonished, amazed, thunderstruck, dumbfounded, gobsmacked, dazed, stunned 864 *wondering*; startled, jolted, shocked; without expectations.

Vb. *not expect*, not look for, think unlikely, not foresee 472 *be unlikely*; not hope for 853 *despair*; be caught out, fall into the trap; be taken aback, be taken by surprise, be caught with one's pants *or* trousers down, not bargain for 670 *be unprepared*; get a shock, start, jump out of one's skin; have one's eyes opened; look surprised, goggle, stare, gawp.

surprise, take by s., spring something on one, catch, trap, ambush 542 *ensnare*; catch unawares, catch napping, catch off one's guard, catch with one's pants *or* trousers down; startle, make one jump, give one a turn, make one jump out of one's skin; take aback, leave speechless, stagger, stun; take one's breath away, knock one down with a feather, bowl one over, strike one all of a heap; be one in the eye for 509 *disappoint*; give one a surprise, pull out of the hat; astonish, amaze, astound, dumbfound 864 *be wonderful*; shock, electrify 821 *impress*; flutter the dovecotes, set the cat among the pigeons, let all hell loose 63 *derange*; drop from the clouds, come out of the blue; fall upon, spring u., pounce on; steal upon, creep up on; come up from behind, appear from nowhere.

509 Disappointment

N. *disappointment*, sad d., bitter d., cruel d.; regrets 830 *regret*; frustration, bafflement; blighted hopes 853 *hopelessness* false expectation 482 *overestimation*; bad news 529 *news*;

not what one expected, disenchantment, disillusionment 829 *discontent*; miscalculation 481 *misjudgment*; mirage, trick of the light, false dawn, fool's paradise; shock, blow, setback, double whammy, balk 702 *hitch*; nonfulfilment 726 *noncompletion*; bad luck, slip 'twixt the cup and the lip 731 *misfortune*; one in the eye for, letdown 872 *humiliation*; damp squib 728 *failure*.

Adj. *disappointed*, expecting otherwise 508 *inexpectant*; frustrated, thwarted, balked 702 *hindered*; baffled, foiled 728 *defeated*; crestfallen, chagrined, humiliated; disgruntled, dischuffed, soured 829 *discontented*; sick with disappointment 853 *hopeless*; let down; refused, turned away.

disappointing, unsatisfying, unsatisfactory 636 *insufficient*; not up to expectation 829 *discontenting*; abortive 728 *unsuccessful*.

Vb. *be disappointed*, – unsuccessful etc. adj.; try in vain 728 *fail*; have hoped for something better, not realize one's expectations 307 *fall short*; expect otherwise, be let down, be left in the lurch, be jilted, laugh on the wrong side of one's face, be crestfallen, look blue; be sick with disappointment.

disappoint, not come up to expectations 307 *fall short*; dash one's hopes; burst the bubble, disillusion; let one down, leave one in the lurch, not come up to scratch; balk, foil, thwart, frustrate 702 *hinder*; amaze, dumbfound, boggle one's mind 508 *surprise*; betray, play one false 930 *be dishonest*; jilt; dash the cup from one's lips, leave unsatisfied, spoil one's pleasure, dissatisfy, turn away 607 *reject*.

510 Foresight

N. *foresight*, anticipation, foretaste; foreknowledge, second sight, clairvoyancy; premonition, presentiment, foreboding, forewarning 511 *omen*; prognosis, prognostication 511 *prediction*; foregone conclusion 473 *certainty*; programme, prospectus 623 *plan*; forward planning, forethought, vision, longsightedness 498 *sagacity*; premeditation 608 *predetermination*; prudence, providence 858 *caution*; provision 669 *preparation*.

Adj. *foreseeing*, prospective, prognostic, predictive 511 *predicting*; clairvoyant, second-sighted, prophetic; far-sighted, sagacious 498 *wise*; provident, prudent 858 *cautious*; anticipatory 507 *expectant*.

Vb. *foresee*, divine, prophesy, forecast 511 *predict*; forewarn 664 *warn*; see *or* peep *or* pry into the future, look into one's crystal ball, read one's palm, have second sight; be forewarned, know in advance 524 *be informed*; look ahead, see it coming, scent, feel in one's bones; look

for 507 *expect*; be prepared, anticipate, forestall 135 *be early*; make provision 669 *prepare*; surmise, make a good guess 512 *suppose*; forejudge 608 *predetermine*; plan ahead 623 *plan*; look to the future, have an eye to the f., see how the cat jumps, see how the wind blows 124 *look ahead*; have an eye on the main chance 498 *be wise*; feel one's way, keep a sharp lookout 455 *be attentive*; lay up for a rainy day 633 *provide*; take precautions, provide against 858 *be cautious*.

511 Prediction

N. *prediction*, foretelling, forewarning, prophecy; apocalypse 975 *revelation*; forecast; prognostication, prognosis; presentiment, foreboding 510 *foresight*; 1984 (book); programme, prospectus, forward planning 623 *plan*; announcement, advance notice 528 *publication*; warning, preliminary w., warning shot 665 *danger signal*; prospect 507 *expectation*; shape of things to come, horoscope, fortune, palm-reading, palmistry, crystal-gazing.

divination, clairvoyancy; augury; soothsaying; astrology, horoscopy, casting nativities; fortune-telling, palmistry; crystal gazing; casting lots; dowsing 484 *discovery*.

omen, portent, writing on the wall; symptom, syndrome, sign 547 *indication*; forewarning, caution 664 *warning*; harbinger, herald 529 *messenger*; ominousness, portentousness, gathering clouds, signs of the times 661 *danger*; luckbringer, black cat, horseshoe 983 *talisman*; portent of bad luck, broken mirror, spilt salt, shooting star, walking under a ladder; bird of ill omen, owl, raven.

oracle, consultant 500 *sage*; meteorologist, weatherman *or* woman; doom merchant, doomster, doomwatcher, Cassandra 664 *warner*; prophet, prophetess, seer, futurologist, forecaster; soothsayer 983 *sorcerer*; clairvoyant, medium 984 *occultist*; Delphic oracle; Sibyl; Nostradamus; cards, tarot c., dice; crystal ball, tea leaves, palm.

diviner, water d., dowser; tipster 618 *gambler*; astrologer; fortune-teller, palmist, crystal-gazer.

Adj. *predicting*, predictive, foretelling; clairvoyant 510 *foreseeing*; fortune-telling; weather-forecasting; prophetic, apocalyptic; oracular; foreboding; heralding 66 *precursory*; ominous, portentous; auspicious, promising, favourable 730 *prosperous*; inauspicious, sinister 731 *adverse*.

Vb. *predict*, forecast, make a prediction, make a prognosis; foretell, prophesy, forebode, bode, augur, spell; foretoken, presage, portend; foreshow, foreshadow, prefigure, shadow forth, forerun, herald, be harbinger, usher in 64 *come before*; point to, betoken, typify, signify

547 *indicate*; announce, give notice, notify 528 *advertise*; forewarn, give warning 664 *warn*; look black, look ominous, lour, menace 900 *threaten*; promise, augur well, bid fair to, give hopes of, hold out hopes, build up h., raise expectations, excite e.

divine, auspicate, haruspicate; read the entrails, take the auspices, take the omens; soothsay, vaticinate; cast a horoscope, cast a nativity; cast lots 618 *gamble*; tell fortunes; read the future, read the signs, read the stars; read the cards, read one's hand, read one's palm.

SECTION SEVEN

Creative thought

512 Supposition

N. *supposition*, notion 451 *idea*; fancy; pretence, pretending 850 *affectation*; presumption, assumption, presupposition, postulation, postulate 475 *premise*; condition, stipulation, sine qua non 766 *conditions*; proposal, proposition 759 *offer*; submission 475 *argument*; hypothesis, working h., theory; thesis; basis of supposition, datum 466 *evidence*; association of ideas 449 *thought*; supposability, conjecturability 469 *possibility*.

conjecture, guess, surmise, suspicion; bare supposition, vague suspicion, rough guess, crude estimate, guesstimate; shrewd idea 476 *intuition*; guesswork, guessing, speculation; gamble, shot, shot in the dark 618 *gambling*.

Adj. *supposed*, conjectured etc. vb.; assumed, presumed, taken as read, postulated; proposed, mooted 452 *topical*; given, granted, granted for the sake of argument; putative, presumptive; so-called, quasi; not real 2 *unreal*; alleged.

Vb. *suppose*, just s., fancy; think, conceive, take into one's head, get into one's head 485 *opine*; surmise, conjecture, guess, hazard a g., make a g.; suppose so, dare say; presume, assume, presuppose; posit; take for granted, take it, postulate 475 *reason*; speculate, have a theory, theorize 449 *meditate*; rely on supposition 618 *gamble*.

propound, propose 759 *offer*; put on the agenda, moot, move, propose a motion, postulate 761 *request*; put a case, submit, make one's submission 475 *argue*; put forth, make a suggestion, venture to say, put forward a notion, throw out an idea, throw something into the melting-pot 691 *advise*; suggest.

513 Imagination

N. *imagination*, vivid i., fertile i., wild i.; imaginativeness, creativeness; inventiveness, creativity 21 *originality*; ingenuity, resourcefulness 694 *skill*; fancifulness, fantasy, stretch of the imagination; understanding, insight, empathy, sympathy 819 *moral sensibility*; poetic imagination, ecstasy, inspiration, fancy, the mind's eye, recollection, recollection in tranquillity, visualization, image-building, imagery, word-painting; artistry, creative work.

ideality, conception 449 *thought*; idealization; mental image, projection 445 *appearance*; concept, image, conceit, fancy, notion 451 *idea*; whim, whimsy 497 *absurdity*; vagary 604 *caprice*; figment, f. of the imagination, fiction 541 *falsehood*; work of fiction, story 590 *novel*; science fiction, space odyssey, steam punk, cyberpunk; fairy tale; flight of fancy, uncontrolled imagination, romance, fantasy, extravaganza, rhapsody 546 *exaggeration*; poetic licence 593 *poetry*; skiamachy.

fantasy, wildest dreams; vision, dream, nightmare, night terror; Jabberwocky 84 *rara avis*; bogey, phantom 970 *ghost*; shadow, vapour 419 *dimness*; mirage 440 *visual fallacy*; delusion, hallucination, chimera 495 *error*; reverie, day dream, brown study 456 *abstractedness*; trance, somnambulism 375 *insensibility*; delirium 503 *frenzy*; autosuggestion; wishful thinking 477 *sophistry*; make believe, vapourware, golden dream, pipe d. 859 *desire*; romance, stardust; romanticism, escapism, idealism, Utopianism; Utopia, Erewhon; promised land, El Dorado, the end of the rainbow; Happy Valley, Fortunate Isles, Isles of the Blest; land of Cockaigne, Ruritania, Shangrila, Atlantis, Lyonesse, Middle Earth, Narnia, San Serif; fairyland, wonderland; cloud-cuckoo-land, dream 1., dream world, castles in Spain, castles in the air; pie in the sky, good time coming, millennium 124 *future state*; idle fancy, myth 543 *fable*; fantasy fiction; fantasy game, fantasy football.

visionary, seer 511 *diviner*, dreamer, day-d.; fantasist; idealist, Utopian 901 *philanthropist*; escapist; romantic, romancer, romanticist, rhapsodist, myth-maker; creative worker 556 *artist*.

Adj. *imaginative*, creative, lively, original, inventive, fertile, ingenious; resourceful 694 *skilful*; romancing, romantic; high-flown, rhapsodical, carried away; poetic, fictional; Utopian, idealistic; rhapsodic, enthusiastic; dreaming, daydreaming, in a trance; extravagant, grotesque, bizarre, fantastical, unreal, whimsical, airy-fairy, preposterous, impractical, Heath Robinson 497 *absurd*; visionary.

imaginary, unreal, unsubstantial 4 *insubstantial*; notional, chimerical, illusory 495 *erroneous*; dreamy, visionary, not of this world, of another world, ideal; vaporous 419 *shadowy*; fictitious, fabulous, fabled, legendary, mythological 543 *untrue*; fanciful, fancied, imagined, fabricated;

thought-up, dreamed-up; hypothetical; pretended, make-believe.

Vb. *imagine*, fancy, dream; think of, think up, conjure up, dream up; make up, devise, invent, originate, create, have an inspiration 609 *improvise*; coin, hatch, concoct, fabricate 164 *produce*; visualize, envisage, see in the mind's eye 438 *see*; conceive, form an image of; picture to oneself; paint, write a pen portrait of, conjure up a vision, capture, recapture 551 *represent*; use one's imagination, give reins to one's i., run riot in imagination 546 *exaggerate*; pretend, make-believe, daydream 456 *be inattentive*; build castles in the air, build castles in Spain; see visions, dream dreams; fantasize, idealize, romanticize, fictionalize, rhapsodize 546 *exaggerate*; enter into, empathize, sympathize 516 *understand*.

4.2
Communication of Ideas

SECTION ONE

Nature of ideas communicated

514 Meaning

N. *meaning*, substance, essence, spirit, sum and substance, gist, pith, nitty-gritty; contents, text, matter, subject m. 452 *topic*; semantic content, sense, drift, tenor, purport, import, implication; relevance, bearing; meaningfulness, context; semantics.

connotation, denotation, signification, significance, reference, application; construction 520 *interpretation*; context; derivation, etymology 156 *source*; semantic field, comprehension; extended meaning, core m.; leading sense; specialized meaning, idiom 80 *speciality*; usage, accepted meaning 610 *practice*; single meaning 516 *intelligibility*; double meaning, ambiguity 518 *equivocalness*; many meanings, polysemy; same meaning; synonym, synonymousness, synonymity, equivalence 13 *identity*; opposite meaning, antonym, antonymy 14 *contrariety*; contradictory meaning, countersense; changed meaning, semantic shift; level of meaning, literal meaning, literality 573 *plainness*; metaphorical meaning 519 *metaphor*; hidden meaning, esoteric sense 523 *latency*; constructive sense, implied s., no sense 497 *absurdity*.

Adj. *meaningful*, significant, of moment 638 *important*; substantial, pithy, meaty, full of meaning, packed with m., pregnant; meaning etc. vb.; importing, purporting indicative; telling 516 *expressive*; pointed, epigrammatic 839 *witty*; suggestive.

semantic, semiological, philological, etymological 557 *linguistic*; connotational, connotative; denotational, denotative; literal, verbal 573 *plain*; metaphorical 519 *figurative*; univocal, unambiguous 516 *intelligible*; polysemous, ambiguous 518 *equivocal*; synonymous, homonymous 13 *identical*; tantamount, equivalent 18 *similar*; tautologous 106 *repeated*; antonymous 14 *contrary*; idiomatic 80 *special*; paraphrastic 520 *interpretive*; obscure 568 *unclear*; clear; implied, constructive 523 *tacit*; nonsensical 497 *absurd*; without meaning 515 *meaningless*.

Vb. *mean*, mean something; convey a meaning, get across 524 *communicate*; symbolize 547 *indicate*; signify, denote, connote; purport; point to, add up to, boil down to, spell, involve 523 *imply*; convey, express, declare, assert 532 *affirm*; bespeak, tell of, speak of, breathe of, savour of, speak volumes 466 *evidence*; be getting at, be driving at, have in mind; be synonymous, have the same meaning; say it in other words, put it another way; mean the same thing, be the same thing in the end.

515 Lack of meaning

N. *lack of meaning*, meaninglessness, nonsignificance 639 *unimportance*; inanity, emptiness, triteness; truism, platitude, cliché 496 *maxim*; mere words, empty w.; illogicality 477 *sophistry*; invalidity, dead letter; illegibility, scribble, scribbling, scrawl 586 *script*; daub 552 *misrepresentation*; empty sound, strumming; sounding brass, tinkling cymbal 400 *loudness*; jargon, rigmarole, gobbledygook, galimatias, psychobabble; abracadabra, hocus-pocus, mumbo jumbo; gibberish, gabble, double dutch, Greek, Babel 517 *unintelligibility*; incoherence, raving, delirium 503 *frenzy*; double-talk.

silly talk, nonsense 497 *absurdity*; stuff and nonsense, balderdash, rubbish, load of r., rot, tommyrot, pants; drivel, twaddle, fiddle-faddle, bosh, tosh, tripe, piffle, bilge, bull.

empty talk, sweet nothings; wind, gas, hot air, verbiage 570 *diffuseness*; rant, bombast 877 *boasting*; blether, blather, blah-blah, flimflam; guff, pi-jaw, eyewash, claptrap, poppycock 543 *fable*; humbug 541 *falsehood*; moonshine, malarkey, hokum, bunkum, bunk, boloney, hooey; flannel, flummery, blarney 925 *flattery*; sales talk, patter, sales p., spiel; talk, chatter, prattle, prating, yammering, babble, gabble, jabber, jabber jabber, jaw, yackety yack, yak yak, rhubarb rhubarb 581 *chatter*.

Adj. *meaningless*, nonsensical 497 *absurd*; senseless; unexpressive, insignificant, inane, empty, trivial, trite 639 *unimportant*; fatuous, piffling; waffling; incoherent, raving, gibbering 503 *frenzied*.

Vb. *mean nothing*, make no sense, be irrelevant; scribble, daub, talk bunkum 497 *be absurd*; babble, prattle, prate, gabble, gibber, jabber, yak 581 *be loquacious*; talk double dutch, talk gibberish; rant 546 *exaggerate*; rave, drivel, blether, waffle, talk hot air; not mean what one says; be Greek to, pass over one's head 474 *puzzle*.

516 Intelligibility

N. *intelligibility*, cognizability; explicability; comprehensibility; readability, legibility; clearness, clarity, coherence, limpidity, lucidity 567 *perspicuity*; precision, unambiguity 473 *certainty*; simplicity, straightforwardness, plain speaking, plain speech, plain words, plain English, no gobbledygook; simplification 701 *facility*.

Adj. *intelligible*, understandable, comprehensible; coherent 502 *sane*; audible, recognizable, distinguishable, unmistakable; cognizable 490 *known*; unambiguous, unequivocal 514 *meaningful*; explicit; distinct, clear-cut, precise 80 *definite*; articulate, eloquent; plain-spoken, downright, forthright 573 *plain*; straightforward, simple 701 *easy*; obvious, self-explanatory; explained, simplified; clear, limpid 422 *transparent*; lucid; readable, legible, decipherable, crystal clear, plain as a pikestaff 443 *visible*.

expressive, telling, meaningful, informative, striking, vivid, graphic, emphatic; illustrative, explicatory 520 *interpretive*.

Vb. *be intelligible*, – clear, – easy etc. adj.; be readable, be an easy read, read easily; make sense, add up 475 *be reasonable*; tell its own tale, speak for itself, be self-explanatory 466 *evidence*; have no secrets 443 *be visible*; be understood, come over, get across, sink in, dawn on; clarify, clear up, open one's eyes, elucidate 520 *interpret*; simplify.

understand, comprehend, apprehend 490 *know*; master 536 *learn*; have, hold, retain 505 *remember*; have understanding 498 *be wise*; see through, penetrate, fathom, get to the bottom of 484 *detect*; spot, descry, discern, distinguish, make out, see at a glance, see with half an eye 438 *see*; recognize, make no mistake 473 *be certain*; grasp, get hold of, be on to it, cotton on to, dig; get the hang of, take in, register; be with one, follow, savvy; collect, get, catch on, latch on to, twig; catch one's drift, get the idea, get the picture; realize, get wise to, tumble to, rumble; have one's eyes opened, see the light, see through, see it all; get to know, get the hang of.

517 Unintelligibility

N. *unintelligibility*, incomprehensibility, unaccountability, inconceivability; inexplicability; difficulty 474 *uncertainty*; obscurity 568 *imperspicuity*; ambiguity 518 *equivocalness*; mystification 515 *lack of meaning*; incoherence 503 *mental disorder*; double dutch, gibberish; jargon, psychobabble, foreign tongue, idiolect 560 *dialect*, *slang*; stammering 580 *speech defect*; undecipherability, illegibility; scribble, scrawl 586 *lettering*; inaudibility 401 *faintness*; Greek, sealed book 530 *secret*; paradox, knotty point, riddle 530 *enigma*; mysterious behaviour, Sphinx-like attitude.

Adj. *unintelligible*, incomprehensible, inconceivable, inexplicable, unaccountable; unrecognizable, as Greek to one, like double Dutch 491 *unknown*; unfathomable, inscrutable, impenetrable; blank, poker-faced, expressionless 820 *impassive*; inaudible 401 *muted*; illegible, scrawly, scribbled, undecipherable; undiscernible 444 *invisible*; arcane 523 *occult*; cryptic; esoteric 80 *private*; Sphinx-like, enigmatic.

puzzling, complex 700 *difficult*; hard, beyond one, over one's head, recondite, abstruse, elusive; sphinxian, enigmatic, mysterious 523 *occult*; nebulous, obscure 419 *shadowy*; clear as mud, clear as ditch water 568 *unclear*; ambiguous 518 *equivocal*; paradoxical 508 *unexpected*; fishy, strange, odd 84 *abnormal*; unexplained, insoluble, unsolvable.

inexpressible, unspeakable, untranslatable; unpronounceable, unutterable, ineffable; incommunicable, indefinable.

puzzled, mystified, out of one's depth, flummoxed, stumped, baffled, perplexed, nonplussed 474 *uncertain*.

Vb. *be unintelligible*, – puzzling, – inexpressible etc. adj.; be hard, be difficult, make one's head ache *or* swim 474 *puzzle*; talk in riddles 518 *be equivocal*; talk double dutch, talk gibberish 515 *mean nothing*; speak badly 580 *stammer*; write badly, scribble, scrawl; keep one guessing 486 *cause doubt*; perplex; require explanation, have no answer, need an interpreter; go over one's head; elude one's grasp, escape one; pass comprehension, baffle understanding.

not understand, not get it, not grasp it; find unintelligible, not make out, not know what to make of, make nothing of, make neither head nor tail of, be unable to account for; puzzle over, rack one's brains over, be floored by, be stumped by, give up; be out of one's depth 491 *not know*; be at sea 474 *be uncertain*; have no grasp of 695 *be unskilful*; have a blind spot 439 *be blind*; be on different wavelengths, be at cross-purposes 495 *blunder;* get one wrong 481 *misjudge.*

518 Equivocalness

N. *equivocalness,* ambiguity, ambivalence 517 *unintelligibility;* vagueness 474 *uncertainty;* newspeak, doubletalk, weasel word 515 *lack of meaning;* conundrum, riddle 530 *enigma;* prevarication; equivocation, white lie 543 *untruth;* quibble, quibbling 477 *sophistry;* wordplay, play upon words; pun, double entendre 839 *witticism;* faux ami, confusible; anagram, acrostic; synonymy, homonymy; homonym, homophone 18 *analogue.*

Adj. *equivocal,* ambiguous, ambivalent; two-edged; left-handed, back-h.; equivocating, prevaricating; evasive; anagrammatic.

Vb. *be equivocal,* cut both ways; play upon words, pun; have two meanings; speak with two voices 14 *be contrary;* fudge, waffle, stall, not give a straight answer, beat about the bush, sit on the fence 620 *avoid;* equivocate, prevaricate.

519 Metaphor: figure of speech

N. *metaphor,* mixed m.; transference; allusion; extended metaphor, allegory; fable, parable 534 *teaching;* symbol; symbolism, figurativeness, imagery 513 *imagination;* simile, likeness 462 *comparison;* personification.

trope, figure of speech, turn of s., flourish; manner of speech; irony, sarcasm 851 *satire;* rhetorical figure 574 *ornament;* metonymy, antonomasia, synecdoche, transferred epithet; anaphora; litotes 483 *underestimation;* hyperbole; stress, emphasis; circumlocution, euphuism, euphemism, dysphemism 850 *affectation;* anacoluthon, colloquialism 573 *plainness;* contrast, antithesis 462 *comparison;* metathesis 221 *inversion;* paradox, epigram, paronomasia, wordplay 518 *equivocalness.*

Adj. *figurative,* metaphorical, allusive, symbolical, allegorical; parabolical; euphemistic 850 *affected;* hyperbolic 546 *exaggerated;* flowery.

520 Interpretation

N. *interpretation,* explanation, explication, exposition; elucidation, clarification, illumination; illustration, exemplification 83 *example;* solution, key, clue 460 *answer;* decipherment, decoding, cracking 484 *discovery;* construction, reading; allegorization 519 *metaphor;* accepted reading, vulgate; alternative reading, variant r.; criticism, textual c., literary c., practical c., appreciation 557 *literature;* critique, review, notice 480 *estimate;* insight.

commentary, comment, editorial c., gloss, footnote; caption, legend 563 *phrase;* motto; annotation, notes, marginalia; exposition 591 *dissertation;* critical edition, variorum; glossary, lexicon 559 *dictionary.*

translation, version, rendering, free translation; literal translation; key, crib; paraphrase; précis, abridgment; adaptation; decoding, decipherment.

interpreter, explainer, exponent, expounder 537 *teacher,* 973 *religious teacher;* demythologizer; editor, copy e. 528 *publicizer;* textual critic; emender, emendator; commentator, annotator; glossarist, critic, reviewer; medium 984 *spiritualism;* translator, paraphraser; cryptographer, encoder; code-breaker; decoder; cryptanalyst, cryptologist; lip-reader; spokesman, mouthpiece; public relations officer, PR consultant, press officer, spin-doctor 524 *informant;* executant, performer 413 *musician;* player 594 *actor.*

guide, precedent 83 *example;* light, guiding l., star, guiding s.; courier 690 *director;* demonstrator 522 *exhibitor.*

Adj. *pb0767$403terpretative,* interpretive, constructive; explanatory, explicatory, elucidatory; expository 557 *literary;* defining; illuminating, illustrative, exemplary; glossarial, annotative, editorial; lip-reading; mediumistic; literal; faithful; free 495 *inexact.*

Vb. *interpret,* define, clarify; explain, expound, elucidate 516 *be intelligible;* illustrate 83 *exemplify;* demonstrate 522 *show;* act as guide; comment on, edit, write notes for, add footnotes to, annotate, gloss; read, spell out; construe, put a construction on, understand by, make sense of; illuminate, throw light on; enlighten 524 *inform;* deduce, infer 475 *reason;* act as interpreter, be spokesman *or* -woman *or* -person 755 *deputize;* put a spin on, spin-doctor.

translate, render, do into, turn i.; re-word, paraphrase; abridge, précis, adapt; transliterate, transcribe; encode; lip-read.

decipher, crack, decode; read, spell out, puzzle o., make o., work o.; piece together, find the sense of; solve, resolve, unravel, disentangle, read between the lines.

Adv. *in plain words,* in plain English; by way of explanation; that is, i.e.; in other words, to put it another way, to wit, namely, viz.; to explain.

521 Misinterpretation

N. *misinterpretation,* misunderstanding, misconstruction, misapprehension, wrong end of the stick; cross-purposes, different wavelengths, crossed lines 495 *mistake;* mistranslation, misconstrue; wrong interpretation, false construction; false reading; dark glasses, rose-coloured spectacles; falsification 552 *misrepresentation;*

travesty 851 *ridicule*; misapplication 565 *solecism*.

Vb. *misinterpret*, misunderstand; get wrong, get one wrong, get hold of the wrong end of the stick 495 *blunder*; misread, misspell 495 *err*; mistranslate, misconstrue, put a false sense or construction on; give a twist or turn, strain the sense; twist, twist the words 246 *distort*; equivocate, play upon words 518 *be equivocal*; read into, write i. 38 *add*; misquote; garble 552 *misrepresent*; parody, caricature; misrepresent 926 *defame*.

SECTION TWO

Modes of communication

522 Manifestation

N. *manifestation*, revelation, unfolding, discovery, daylight, exposure 526 *disclosure*; expression; proof 466 *evidence*; presentation; sign, token 547 *signal*; symptom, syndrome 511 *omen*; press conference, prerelease, preview 438 *view*; demonstration, exhibition; display, showing off 875 *ostentation*; proclamation 528 *publication*; candour; conspicuousness 443 *visibility*; apparition, vision, materialization 445 *appearance*; séance 984 *occultism*; incarnation.

exhibit, specimen, sample 83 *example*; piece of evidence, quotation, citation 466 *evidence*; model, mock-up 551 *image*; show piece, museum p., collector's item, antique, curio; display, show, dress s., mannequin parade 445 *spectacle*; scene 438 *view*; exhibition hall, exhibition centre, showplace, showroom, showcase, placard, hoarding, bill 528 *advertisement*; sign 547 *label*; shop window, museum, gallery 632 *collection*; exhibition, exposition; fair 796 *market*.

exhibitor, advertiser, publicist, promotion manager 528 *publicizer*; displayer, demonstrator; showman; impresario 594 *stage manager*; exhibitionist; model, male m., mannequin; flaunter.

Adj. *manifest*, apparent, ostensible 445 *appearing*; plain, clear, defined 80 *definite*; explained, plain as a pikestaff, plain as the nose on one's face, clear as daylight 516 *intelligible*; unconcealed, showing 443 *visible*; conspicuous, noticeable, notable, prominent, pronounced, signal, marked, striking, in relief, in the foreground, in the limelight 443 *obvious*; open, evident; gross, crass, palpable; self-evident, written all over one, for all to see, unmistakable, recognizable, identifiable, incontestable, staring one in the face 473 *certain*; public, famous, notorious, infamous; catching the eye, eye-catching, gaudy 875 *showy*; arrant, glaring, stark staring, flagrant, loud, on the rooftops, shouting from the r.

shown, manifested etc. vb.; declared, divulged, made public; unconcealed, overt, explicit, in the open, public; showing, featured, on show, on display, on view, on 443 *visible*; exhibited, shown off; brought forth, produced; mentioned, brought to one's notice; adduced, cited, quoted; confronted, brought face to face; worn, sported, paraded; unfurled, flaunted, waved, brandished; naked and unashamed; advertised, publicized, promoted 528 *published*; expressible, producible, showable.

Vb. *manifest*, reveal, divulge, give away, betray 526 *disclose*; evince, betoken, show signs of 466 *evidence*; bring to light, unearth 484 *discover*; explain, make plain, make obvious 520 *interpret*; expose, lay bare, unroll, unfurl, unsheathe 229 *uncover*; open up, throw open, lay o. 263 *open*; elicit, draw forth, drag out 304 *extract*; invent, bring forth 164 *produce*; bring out, shadow forth, body f.; incorporate, incarnate, personify; typify, symbolize, exemplify 547 *indicate*; point up, accentuate, enhance, develop 36 *augment*; throw light on; highlight, spotlight, throw into relief 532 *emphasize*; express, formulate 532 *affirm*; bring, bring up, make reference to, mention, cite, quote; bring to the fore, place in the foreground; bring to notice, produce, trot out, come out with, proclaim, publicize, promote 528 *publish*; show for what it is (see *show*).

show, exhibit, display; set out, put on display, put on show, put on view, expose to v., offer to the v., set before one's eyes; flourish 317 *brandish*; sport 228 *wear*; flaunt, parade 875 *be ostentatious*; make a show of, affect 850 *be affected*; present, feature, enact 551 *represent*; put on, stage, release 594 *dramatize*; televise, screen, film; stage an exhibition, put on show or display, hang (a picture); show off, set o., model (garments); put one through his paces; demonstrate 534 *teach*; show round, show over, give a guided tour, point out, draw attention to, bring to notice 547 *indicate*; confront, force a confrontation, bring face to face, bring eyeball to eyeball; reflect, image, mirror, hold up the mirror to 20 *imitate*; tear off the mask, show up, expose 526 *disclose*.

be plain, – explicit etc. adj.; show one's face, unveil, unmask; show one's true colours, have no secrets, make no mystery, not try to hide, wear one's heart on one's sleeve; have no shame, wash one's dirty linen in public; speak one's mind, speak out, tell to one's face, make no secret of, give straight from the shoulder, make no bones about 573 *speak plainly*; speak for itself, tell its own story, require no explanation 516 *be intelligible*; be obvious, stand to reason, go without saying 478 *be proved*; be conspicuous, be as plain as the nose on one's face, stand out, stand out a mile 443 *be visible*; show the flag, be seen, show up, show up well, hold the stage, be in the limelight, have the spotlight on one, stand in full view 455 *attract notice*; loom large, stare one in the face; appear on the horizon, rear its head, show its face, transpire, emanate, come to light 445 *appear*.

523 Latency
N. *latency*, insidiousness; dormancy, potentiality 469 *possibility*; esotericism; occultness, mysticism; hidden meaning; symbolism, allegory 519 *metaphor*; implication, mystery 530 *secret*; inmost recesses 224 *interiority*; dark 418 *darkness*; shadowiness 419 *dimness*; imperceptibility 444 *invisibility*; more than meets the eye; deceptive appearance, hidden fires, hidden depths; iron hand in a velvet glove; slumbering volcano, sleeping dog, sleeping giant 661 *danger*; dark horse, mystery man; red under the bed, nigger in the woodpile, snake in the grass, mole 663 *pitfall*; manipulator, puppeteer, hidden hand, wirepuller, strings, friends in high places, friend at court, power behind the throne, éminence grise 178 *influence*; old-boy network, networking; subconscious; subliminal influence, subliminal advertising; something rotten; innuendo, insinuation, suggestion 524 *hint*; sealed lips 582 *taciturnity*; undercurrent, undertone, aside 401 *faintness*; clandestineness, secret society, cabal, intrigue 623 *plot*; code, cryptography.

Adj. *latent*, lurking, skulking 525 *concealed*; dormant, sleeping 679 *inactive*; passive 266 *quiescent*; in abeyance 175 *inert*; undeveloped 469 *possible*; unsuspected; subconscious, subliminal, underlying; in the background, behind the scenes, backroom, undercover; unmanifested, unseen, undetected, unexposed 444 *invisible*; arcane, impenetrable 517 *unintelligible*; sequestered 883 *secluded*; undiscovered, unexplored.

tacit, unsaid, unspoken, unpronounced, unexpressed, unvoiced, unmentioned, unarticulated, untold of, unsung; undivulged, unproclaimed, unprofessed, undeclared; unwritten, unpublished; understood, implied, inferred, implicit, between the lines; allusive.

occult, mysterious, mystic; symbolic, allegorical 519 *figurative*; cryptic, esoteric; veiled, masked, covert; clandestine, secret; insidious 930 *perfidious*; underhand 525 *stealthy*; undiscovered, hush-hush, top-secret; off the record 80 *private*; cryptographic 525 *disguised*.

Vb. *lurk*, hide, be latent, lie dormant, be a stowaway; burrow, stay underground; lie hidden; lie low, lie doggo; evade detection, escape recognition; act behind the scenes; creep, slink; pull the strings, stage-manage, underlie, be at the bottom of 156 *cause*; smoulder; be subliminal.

imply, insinuate, whisper, murmur, suggest 524 *hint*; understand, infer, allude; connote, carry a suggestion, involve, spell 514 *mean*.

524 Information
N. *information*, informatics; information technology, IT, computerized information, Internet, the Net, World Wide Web, website, information superhighway; data base, viewdata 86 *data processing*; customer service; mailing list, distribution l. 588 *correspondence*; hearsay, word of mouth; enlightenment, instruction, briefing 534 *teaching*; thought-transference; communication; mass media 528 *the press*, 531 *broadcasting*; notification, announcement, intimation, warning, advice, notice, mention, tip, tip-off (**see** *hint*); newspaper announcement, hatch, match and dispatch, obit, small ad, advertisement, circular 528 *publicity*; common knowledge, gen, info; background, facts, the goods; credit-rating, black information, white i.; documentary 494 *truth*; material, literature 589 *reading matter*; inside information, king's or queen's evidence, dope, lowdown, undisclosed source, confidence 530 *secret*; scoop; the know 490 *knowledge*; file, dossier 548 *record*; word, report, intelligence; item of news 529 *news*; wire, telegram, telemessage, telex, cable, cablegram 529 *message*; communicativeness; leak, disinformation 526 *disclosure*.

report, review, annual report; paper, Green Paper, White P., Black P.; account, eyewitness a. 590 *narrative*; statement, return, annual r., tax r. 86 *statistics*; specification, estimates 480 *estimate*; progress report, confidential r.; dispatch, bulletin, communiqué, handout, press release 529 *news*; presentation, case; petition 761 *entreaty*; round robin 762 *deprecation*; letters, letters to the editor, dispatches 588 *correspondence*.

hint, gentle h., whisper, aside 401 *faintness*; intimation; broad hint, signal, nod, a nod is as good as a wink to a blind horse, wink, look, nudge, kick, kick under the table, gesticulation 547 *gesture*; prompt, cue 505 *reminder*; suggestion; caution 664 *warning*; tip, tip-off (**see** *information*); word in the ear, word to the wise; insinuation, innuendo; clue, symptom 520 *interpretation*; sidelight, glimpse, inkling; suspicion, inference.

informant, teller; spokesman or -woman or -person 579 *speaker*; mouthpiece, representative 754 *delegate*; announcer, radio a., television a., weather-forecaster, weatherman or -woman 531 *broadcaster*; notifier, advertiser, promoter 528 *publicizer*; harbinger, herald 529 *messenger*; testifier 466 *witness*; one in the know, authority, source; quarter, channel, circle, grapevine; chattering classes; pander, go-between, contact 231 *intermediary*; informed circles, information centre; news agency, wire service, Reuter, TASS 528 *the press*; communicator, correspondent, special c., reporter, newshound, chequebook journalist, commentator, columnist, gossip writer 529 *news reporter*; tipster 691 *adviser*; guide; little bird.

informer, spy, spook, snoop, sleuth 459 *detective*; undercover agent, inside a., mole; stool pigeon, nark, copper's n., snitch, sneak, nose, squealer, whistle-blower, grass, supergrass; eavesdropper, telltale, talebearer, clype, tattler, tattletale, gossip 581 *chatterer*.

guidebook, Baedeker; travelogue; handbook, book of words, manual, vade mecum, ABC, A-Z; timetable, Bradshaw; roadbook, itinerary, route map, chart, plan 551 *map*; gazetteer 589 *reference book*; nautical almanac; telephone directory, phone book, Yellow Pages; index, catalogue 87 *directory*; courier 520 *guide*.

Adj. *informative*, communicative, newsy; instructive, documentary 534 *educational*; oral, verbal, spoken; explicit; indiscreet 581 *loquacious*.

informed, well-i., kept i., au fait; posted, primed, briefed, instructed 490 *knowing*; au courant, genned-up, clued-up, wised-up; in the know, in on, in the picture, sussed, up to speed; brought up to date.

Vb. *inform*, certify, advise, beg to a.; intimate, impart, convey (**see** *communicate*); apprise, acquaint, have one know, give to understand; give one the facts, brief, instruct 534 *teach*; let one know, put one in the picture, fill one in on; enlighten 534 *educate*; point out, direct one's attention 547 *indicate*; insinuate (**see** *hint*); confide, mention privately; put one wise, put right, correct, disabuse, disillusion; be specific, state, name, signify 80 *specify*; mention, mention en passant, refer to, touch on, speak of 579 *speak*; gossip, spread rumours; be indiscreet, open one's mouth, let the cat out of the bag, blurt out, talk 581 *be loquacious*; leak information, give disinformation, break the news, reveal 526 *disclose*; tell, clype, blab, split, grass, snitch, squeal, blow the gaff 526 *confess*; rat, turn Queen's evidence, turn State's e.; betray one, blow the whistle on, sell one down the river; tell tales, tell on, clype on; inform against, shop, denounce 928 *accuse*.

communicate, transmit, pass on, pass on information; dispatch news 588 *correspond*; report, cover, make a report, submit a r.; report progress, keep posted; get through, get across, put it over; contact, get in touch; convey, bring

word, send w., leave w., write 588 *correspond*; beam; send a message, speak, semaphore 547 *signal*; wire, telegraph, send a telemessage, send a singing telegram, send a kissogram, etc., telex, radio; telephone, phone, call, dial, ring, ring up, give one a ring *or* a tinkle *or* a buzz; disseminate, broadcast, telecast, televise; announce, notify, give notice, serve n. 528 *advertise*; give out, put out, carry a report, issue a press notice *or* release, publicize 528 *publish*; retail, recount, narrate 590 *describe*; commune 584 *converse*; swap news, exchange information, pool one's knowledge.

hint, drop a h., suggest, throw out a suggestion; put an idea in one's head; prompt, give the cue 505 *remind*; caution 664 *warn*; tip off 691 *advise*; wink, tip the wink; nudge 547 *gesticulate*; insinuate, breathe, whisper, say in one's ear, touch upon, just mention, mention in passing *or* en passant, say by the way, let fall, imply, allude, leave one to gather, intimate.

be informed, be in possession of the facts 490 *know*; have it on good authority; keep one's ear to the ground, hear it on the grapevine, be a fly on the wall, overhear 415 *hear*; be told by a little bird, get wind of; have a line on, have the dope, have the gen *or* info.

525 Concealment

N. *concealment*, confinement, purdah 883 *seclusion*; hiding 523 *latency*; covering up; cache 527 *hiding-place*; disguise, camouflage 542 *deception*; masquerade, anonymity, incognito 562 *no name*; smoke screen 421 *screen*; reticence, reserve; mental reservation, ulterior motive, hidden agenda; evasion, evasiveness 518 *equivocalness*; misinformtion, disinformation; white lie; subterfuge 542 *trickery*; suppression, D notice, Official Secrets Act; cover-up 543 *untruth*; deceitfulness, dissimulation 541 *duplicity*.

secrecy, secretness, mystery 530 *secret*; seal of secrecy, hearing in camera; secret society, clandestineness, secretiveness, furtiveness, stealthiness; underhand dealing 930 *improbity*; conspiracy 623 *plot*; cipher, code 517 *unintelligibility*.

Adj. *concealed*, crypto-, hidden, closet; hiding, in ambush; confined; mysterious, recondite, arcane 517 *unintelligible*; cryptic 523 *occult*; private 883 *secluded*; confidential, off the record; secret, top secret, restricted, hush-hush; unrevealed, ex-directory; undisclosed; unsigned, unnamed 562 *anonymous*; covert, behind the scenes; covered; hooded, masked, veiled, eclipsed; smothered, stifled, suppressed, clandestine, undercover, underground, subterranean 211 *deep*.

disguised, camouflaged; incognito 562 *anonymous*; unrecognizable 491 *unknown*; masked 421 *screened*; codified, cryptographic 517 *unintelligible*.

stealthy, silent, furtive, catlike, on tiptoe; prowling, skulking, loitering, lurking; clandestine, hugger-mugger, conspiratorial, cloak-and-dagger; hole-and-corner, backdoor, underhand, surreptitious 930 *dishonest*.

reticent, reserved, shy, self-contained, withdrawn; noncommittal, uncommunicative, uninformative, cagey, evasive; vague, studiously v.; keeping one's own counsel, discreet, silent 582 *taciturn*; tight-lipped, poker-faced; close, secretive, buttoned-up, close as an oyster, clamlike; in one's shell 883 *unsociable*.

Vb. *conceal*, hide, hide away, plank, secrete, ensconce, confine, keep in purdah 883 *seclude*; stow away, lock up, seal up, bottle up 632 *store*; hide underground, bury 364 *inter*; put out of sight, sweep under the carpet, cover up, paper over, whitewash 226 *cover*; gloss over; blot out 550 *obliterate*; slur over, not mention 458 *disregard*; smother, stifle 165 *suppress*; veil, muffle, mask, disguise, camouflage; shroud, draw a veil over 421 *screen*; obscure, eclipse 418 *darken*; obfuscate 419 *bedim*; go incognito, masquerade 541 *dissemble*; encode.

keep secret, keep it dark, keep under wraps, keep close, keep under one's hat; look blank, look poker-faced, give nothing away, keep a straight face, keep mum, keep one's mouth shut, hold one's tongue, not breathe a word, not utter a syllable, not talk, keep one's counsel, make no sign 582 *be taciturn*; be discreet, neither confirm nor deny, make no comment; keep back, reserve, withhold, keep it to oneself, let it go no further; hush up, cover up, suppress; keep a low profile, keep in the background, stay in the shadows; let not one's right hand know what one's left hand does; blindfold, bamboozle, keep in the dark 542 *deceive*.

be stealthy, – furtive, – evasive etc. adj.; hugger-mugger, conspire 623 *plot*; snoop, sneak, slink, creep; glide, steal, steal along, steal by, steal past; tiptoe, go on t., pussyfoot; prowl, skulk, loiter; lie doggo 523 *lurk*; dodge 620 *avoid*.

Adv. *secretly*, hugger-mugger; confidentially, sotto voce, with bated breath; entre nous, between ourselves, between you and me and the gatepost; aside, to oneself; not for publication, privately, in private, in camera, behind closed doors, anonymously, incognito.

stealthily, furtively, like a thief in the night; under cloak of darkness; underhand, by the back door, in a hole-and-corner way, under-the-counter; on the sly, on the quiet, on the QT.

526 Disclosure

N. *disclosure*, revelation, apocalypse; daylight, cold light of day; discovery, uncovering; unwelcome discovery, disillusionment 509 *disappointment*; denouement; lid off, exposé, divulgence 528 *publication*; exposure, showing up 522 *manifestation*; telling all, explanations, showdown; communication, leak, indiscretion 524 *hint*; betrayal, giveaway; tell-tale sign; State's evidence, Queen's e. 603 *change of mind*; acknowledgment, admission, avowal, confession, coming clean; confessional 939 *penitence*; clean breast, whole truth, cards on the table 494 *truth*.

Vb. *disclose*, reveal, expose, take the wraps off, disinter 522 *manifest*; bare, lay b., strip b., denude; unfold, unroll, unfurl, unpack, unwrap 229 *uncover*; unveil, lift the veil, raise the curtain, let some light in; break the seal, unclose 263 *open*; lay open, open up 484 *discover*; catch out 484 *detect*; not hide; make known, give away, betray, blow one's cover; unmask, tear off the mask; expose oneself, betray o., give oneself away 495 *blunder*; declare oneself, drop the mask; show oneself in one's true colours, show for what it is, debunk; disabuse, set right, undeceive, disillusion, open the eyes 524 *inform*; take the lid off, unleash, let the cat out of the bag (**see** *divulge*).

divulge, declare, bring into the open, express, vent, give vent to 579 *speak*; ventilate, air, canvass, publicize 528 *publish*; tell all, let on, blurt out, blow the gaff, talk out of turn, spill the beans, let the cat out of the bag, give the show or the game away; speak of, talk, utter, breathe; let out, leak 524 *communicate*; let drop, let fall 524 *hint*; come out with, spit it out 573 *speak plainly*; get it off one's chest, unburden oneself; confide, let one into the secret, open one's mind or heart to; declare one's intentions, show one's hand, put one's cards on the table; report, tell, tell tales out of school, tell on, clype, name names 928 *accuse*; split, squeal, blab, grass 524 *inform*; rat.

confess, admit, avow, acknowledge; concede, grant, allow, own 488 *assent*; own up, cough up; plead guilty; talk, sing, sing like a canary; come out with, come across with, come clean, tell all, speak the truth 540 *be truthful*; make a clean breast of it, go to confession; turn Queen's evidence 603 *tergiversate*.

be disclosed, come out, break 445 *appear*; come to light 478 *be proved*; show the cloven hoof, show its face, show its true colours, stand revealed 522 *be plain*; transpire, become known, become public knowledge 490 *be known*; leak out 298 *emerge*; show 443 *be visible*; show through; come as a revelation, break through the clouds, come with a blinding flash, flash on the mind 449 *dawn upon*; give oneself away, there speaks . . .

527 Hiding. Disguise
N. *hiding-place*, hide, hideout, hideaway, hidey-hole, priesthole, safe house 662 *refuge*; lair, den 192 *retreat*; cache, secret place, oubliette; crypt, vault 194 *cellar*; closet, secret drawer, hidden panel, safe place, safe, safe deposit 632 *storage*; recess, corner, nook, cranny, niche, holes and corners, secret passage, underground p.; cover, underground 662 *shelter*; inmost recesses 224 *interiority*.

ambush, spider's web 542 *trap*; catch 663 *pitfall*; stalking horse, Trojan h., decoy, stool pigeon 545 *impostor*; agent provocateur 663 *troublemaker*.

disguise, blind, masquerade 542 *deception*; camouflage 20 *mimicry*; veneer 226 *covering*; mask, visor, veil, domino 228 *cloak*; fancy dress; smoke screen, cover 421 *screen*.

Vb. *ambush*, set an a., lie in wait 523 *lurk*; set a trap for 542 *ensnare*; waylay.

528 Publication
N. *publication*, dissemination 526 *disclosure*; proclamation; edict; beat of drum, flourish of trumpets 400 *loudness*; press conference, press release, advance publicity (**see** *advertisement*); notification, public notice, official bulletin; announcement, press a.; pronouncement, manifesto, programme, platform; the media, meeja, mass m.; publishing, book trade, book-selling 589 *book*; broadcasting, narrowcasting, televising 531 *telecommunication*; broadcast, telecast, newscast 529 *news*; kite-flying; circulation, circular, encyclical.

publicity, limelight, spotlight, public eye; common knowledge 490 *knowledge*; open discussion, seminar, ventilation; canvassing; blatancy 522 *manifestation*; open secret; notoriety, fame 866 *famousness*; currency, wide c.; circulation, wide c.; readership, audience, viewership; viewing figures, listening f., ratings; public relations, PR, promotion, sales p., propaganda, party political broadcast, soundbite, gesture politics; photocall, photo-opportunity, display, showmanship, salesmanship, window dressing 875 *ostentation*; sensationalism, ballyhoo, hype 546 *exaggeration*; publicization, advertising, skywriting; medium of publicity, television, radio 531 *broadcasting*; public address system, loudspeaker, loud hailer 415 *hearing aid*; public comment, journalism,

reporting the media, meeja, rapportage, coverage, report notice, write-up (**see** *the press*); investigative journalism 459 *enquiry*, newsreel, newsletter, news round-up 529 *news*; sounding board, correspondence column, open letter, letters to the editor; editorial 591 *article*; pulpit, platform, hustings, soapbox; printing press 587 *print*; blaze of publicity, letters a foot high; name in lights.

advertisement, notice, insertion, advert, ad, small a., classified a., advertorial; personal column; agony column; headline, banner h., streamer; puff, blurb, buildup, hype, ballyhoo; promotional literature, unsolicited mail, handout, handbill; bill, poster, flyer 522 *exhibit*; billboard, hoarding, placard, sandwich board; display b., notice b., bulletin b.; yellow pages; advertising copy, slogan, jingle; plug, teaser, trailer, commercial 531 *broadcasting*; hard sell, soft s., subliminal advertising; cold-calling.

the press, fourth estate, Fleet Street, the papers; newspaper, newssheet, freesheet, paper, rag, tabloid, comic; underground press, gutter p., yellow p., tabloid p.; organ, journal, daily paper, daily, quality d., broadsheet, heavy; morning paper, evening p., Sunday p., local p.; issue, edition, stop-press e., sports e., extra; magazine section, supplement, colour s.; insert, leaflet, hand-bill, pamphlet, brochure, newsletter.

journal, review, magazine, glossy m., specialist m., women's m., male-interest m., pulp m.; part-work, periodical, serial, daily, weekly, monthly, quarterly, annual; gazette, trade journal, house magazine, trade publication 589 *reading matter*.

publicizer, notifier, announcer; herald, trumpet 529 *messenger*; proclaimer, crier, town crier; barker, tout; bill sticker, bill poster, sandwichman; demonstrator, promoter, publicist, publicity agent, press a., advertising a.; adman, advertiser, hidden persuader; copywriter, blurb writer, commercial artist, public relations officer, PRO, image-maker, propagandist, pamphleteer 537 *preacher*; printer, publisher 589 *book-person*; reporter, journalist, investigative j., chequebook j. 529 *news reporter*.

Adj. *published*, in print 587 *printed*; in the news, public 490 *known*; broadcast, on the air; on television; multi-media.

Vb. *publish*, make public; report, cover, write up; bring into the open, reveal 526 *divulge*; highlight, spotlight 532 *emphasize*; radio, broadcast, narrowcast, tape, telecast, televise, relay, diffuse 524 *inform*; spread, circulate, distribute, disseminate, circularize; canvass, ventilate, discuss 475 *argue*; pamphleteer, propagate, propagandize 534 *teach*; use the press 587 *print*; syndicate, serialize, edit, subedit, sub; issue, release, get out, put o., give o., send forth, lay before the public; bring to public notice, let it be known; spread a rumour, fly a kite; spread abroad; talk about, pass round, put about, bandy a.; voice, broach, talk of, speak of, utter, emit 579 *speak*.

proclaim, announce, herald, notify; pronounce, declare, go on record 532 *affirm*; make one's views public, make a proclamation, issue a public statement; publish a manifesto; noise, trumpet, blaze abroad, declaim, shout from the rooftops; beat the big drum, announce with a flourish of trumpets.

advertise, publicize; place an ad, bill, post, put up a poster; tell the world, put on the map, headline; make a cynosure of, put in lights, spotlight, build up, promote; make much of, feature; sell, boost, puff, hype up, write up, extol, rave about 482 *overrate*; plug 106 *repeat*.

be published, become public, come out; hit the headlines, make the front page; become the talk of the town, circulate, pass from mouth to mouth, go the rounds, get about, be bruited abroad, spread like wildfire, find a publisher, see oneself in print, get printed, get into the papers; sell well, go like a best-seller become a blockbuster 793 *be sold*.

529 News

N. *news*, good n., no news is good n.; bad news 509 *disappointment*; tidings, glad t.; gospel, evangel 973 *religion*; dispatches, diplomatic bag; intelligence, report, dispatch, word, intimation, advice; titbit 524 *information*; bulletin, communiqué, handout, press release; newspaper report, press notice; news item, news flash, soundbite 531 *broadcast*; latest news, stop-press n.; sensation, scoop, exclusive; old news, stale n.; copy, filler; yarn, story, tall s.; newscast, news-reel 528 *publicity*; news value, newsworthiness.

rumour, unconfirmed report; hearsay, gossip, talk, talk of the town, tittle-tattle 584 *chat*; scandal 926 *calumny*; whisper, buzz, noise; false report, hoax; grapevine, bush telegraph.

message, word of mouth, word, tip 524 *information*; communication 547 *signal*; wireless message, cable, telegram, telemessage, wire, fax, electronic mail 531 *telecommunication*; postcard, pc, note, letters, dispatches 588 *correspondence*; 531 *postal communications*; ring, phone call, buzz, tinkle; errand 751 *commission*.

news reporter, newspaperman *or* -woman, reporter, cub r., journalist, correspondent, legman, stringer 589 *author*; gentleman *or* lady of the press, pressman *or* -woman, press representative 524 *informant*; newsreader, newscaster 531

broadcaster; chequebook journalist, muckraker, scandalmonger.

messenger, forerunner 66 *precursor*; harbinger 511 *omen*, announcer, town crier 528 *publicizer*; ambassador, spokesman *or* -woman *or* -person 754 *envoy*, apostle, emissary; herald; go-between, pander, contact, contact man *or* woman 231 *intermediary*.

courier, runner, Queen's Messenger, express m., dispatch rider, delivery-man *or* -woman; postman *or* -woman 531 *postal communications*; telegraph boy *or* girl, messenger b. *or* girl, errand b. *or* girl, office b. *or* girl; call-boy, bellhop, page, buttons, commissionaire; carrier pigeon 273 *carrier*; Mercury.

530 Secret

N. *secret*, esotericism; mystery 984 *occultism*; confidential information, sealed orders, top-secret-file, state secret, affairs of state; confidential communication; sphinx, man *or* woman of mystery, enigmatic personality, Gioconda smile, inscrutable s.; Mr X 562 *no name*; dark horse, unknown quantity; unknown warrior; skeleton in the cupboard; sealed book; unknown country, terra incognita 491 *unknown thing*.

enigma, mystery, puzzle, Chinese p., Rubik's cube (tdmk), Rubik's magic (tdmk); problem, poser, brain-teaser; hard nut to crack, vexed question; cipher, code, cryptogram, hieroglyphics 517 *unintelligibility*; word-puzzle, anagram, acrostic, crossword; riddle, riddle-me-ree, conundrum; charade; intricacy, labyrinth, maze 61 *complexity*.

531 Communications

N. *telecommunication*; teleinformatics; long-distance communication, telephony, telegraphy, radio *or* wireless t.; signalling, semaphore, morse 547 *signal*; cable, cable-gram, telegram, telemessage, wire, fax, electronic mail, e-mail, spam, voicemail 529 *message*; bush telegraph, grapevine; radar 484 *discovery*; telex, teleprinter, tape machine, ticker; teleconferencing; video-conferencing; intercom, walkie-talkie, bleeper, bleep, pager; microphone 400 *megaphone*; headset 415 *hearing aid*; telephone, radio t., cellular t., cellphone, cordless telephone, car t., mobile phone, mobile, mobe, Vodafone (tdmk), videophone; line, party 1., hot.; extension; telephone exchange, switchboard; call centre, customer service; telesales; telephonist, telephone receptionist, wireless operator, radio ham, telegrapher; tone dialling pulse d.

postal communications, postal services, GPO; post, first class p., second class p., mail, snail m., letters 588 *correspondence*; air letter, aerogramme, surface mail, sea m., air m.; parcel post, registered p., recorded delivery, express d., red star d.; postcode, postage stamp, first-class s., second class s., definitive stamp, commemorative s.; pillarbox, postbox, letter-box; post office, sorting o., mailbag; postmaster *or* -mistress, postman *or* -woman 529 *messenger*; pigeon post; diplomatic bag, dispatch box.

broadcasting, the media, meeja 528 *publicity*; broadcasting authority, BBC, Beeb, Auntie; IBA, ITA; independent television *or* radio; commercial t. *or* r., local t. *or* r., cable t. *or* r., satellite t., pirate r., Citizens' Band r., CB r.; transmitter, booster, communications satellite; aerial, antenna; radio waves, wave lengths, modulation, AM, FM 417 *radiation*; radio station, television channel, network; wireless, radio, cellular r., mobile r., steam r., cat's whisker, crystal set; radiopaging; portable, transistor, tranny *or* trannie, ghetto blaster, personal stereo; television cable t., digital t., telly, TV, the box, gogglebox, small screen, talking head; colour television, black-and-white t., monochrome t.; closed-circuit t. 442 *camera*; videorecorder, videocassette, videocassette recorder, VCR, video, videotape, video nasty, video game 549 *recording instrument*; Teleprompter (tdmk), autocue; teletext, Ceefax (tdmk), Oracle (tdmk), Prestel (tdmk) 524 *information*; Open University; radio listener 415 *listener*; viewer, televiewer, TV addict 441 *spectator*.

broadcast, outside b., telecast, transmission, relay, live r. 528 *publication*; recording, repeat, transcription 548 *record*; programme, request p., phone-in, telethon, quiz, chat show, music 837 *amusement*; news, newsflash, soundbite, news roundup 529 *news*; time signal, pips; talk, feature, documentary 524 *report*; series, soap opera, situation comedy, sitcom, saga, docudrama, faction 594 *drama*; cartoon, film 445 *cinema*; commercial, commercial break 528 *advertisement*.

broadcaster, announcer, commentator, talking head, newsreader, newscaster 524 *informant*; presenter, frontman *or* -woman, anchorman *or* -woman, linkman *or* -woman, compere, question master; disc jockey, DJ, deejay, shock jock; media personality 866 *person of repute*.

532 Affirmation

N. *affirmation*, saying, dictum 496 *maxim*; statement; submission, thesis 512 *supposition*; expressed opinion, conclusion 480 *judgment*; voice, suffrage, ballot 605 *vote*; expression, formulation; written statement, mission s., prepared text; one's position, one's stand *or* stance; declaration, profession; allegation 928 *accusation*; assertion, ipse dixit, say-so; averment;

admission, confession, avowal 526 *disclosure*; corroboration, confirmation, assurance, one's word, warrant 466 *testimony*; insistence, vehemence, peremptoriness 571 *vigour*; stress, accent, emphasis, protesting too much; observation 579 *speech*; comment, criticism 480 *estimate*; assertiveness, self-assertion, pontification 473 *positiveness*.

oath, swearing, swearing on the Bible, statement on oath, deposition, affidavit 466 *testimony*; promissory oath, word of a gentleman, word of honour, pledge, promise, warrant, guarantee 764 *promise*.

Adj. *affirmative*, affirming, professing etc. vb.; not negative 473 *positive*; declaratory; pronouncing; unretractable 473 *undisputed*; committed, promised; earnest; solemn, sworn, formal.

assertive, telling; assured, dogmatic, pontificating, confident, self-assured 473 *positive*; pushing, trenchant, incisive, pointed, decisive; peremptory, categorical, absolute, brooking no denial, emphatic, insistent; vehement; making no bones, blunt, outspoken, strongly-worded, straight from the shoulder 573 *plain*.

Vb. *affirm*, state, express, formulate, set down; declare, pronounce, deliver, enunciate 528 *proclaim*, 579 *orate*; give expression to, voice 579 *speak*; remark, comment, observe, say; state with conviction, be bound, dare swear 485 *opine*; mean what one says, vow, protest; make a statement, make a verbal, assert; maintain, hold, contend 475 *argue*; make one's point 478 *demonstrate*; urge 512 *propound*; put one's case, put forward, submit; appeal, claim 761 *request*; allege, aver; bear witness 466 *testify*; certify, confirm, warrant, guarantee 466 *corroborate*; commit oneself, go as far as; pledge; hold out 759 *offer*; profess, avow; admit 526 *confess*; abide by, stick to one's guns 599 *stand firm*; speak up, speak out, put it bluntly, make no bones about 573 *speak plainly*; brook no denial, shout, shout down; lay down the law, pontificate 473 *dogmatize*; get on one's soapbox, hold the floor, have one's say, have the last word.

swear, take one's oath; attest, confirm by o. 466 *corroborate*; cross one's heart; kiss the book, swear on the Bible.

emphasize, stress, lay stress on, accent, accentuate; underline, italicize, dot the i's and cross the t's, put in bold letters; raise one's voice, speak up, shout, thunder, roar, bellow, fulminate 400 *be loud*; bang one's fist down, thump the table; urge; insist 737 *command*; drive home, impress on, din in, rub in; plug, dwell on, labour 106 *repeat*; highlight, enhance, point up.

533 Negation

N. *negation*, negative, nay, no; denial 760 *refusal*; disbelief 486 *unbelief*; disagreement 489 *dissent*; rebuttal, appeal 460 *rejoinder*; refutation 479 *confutation*; emphatic denial, contradiction, gainsaying; challenge 711 *defiance*; demurrer 468 *qualification*; protest 762 *deprecation*; repudiation, disclaimer, dissociation 607 *rejection*; abnegation, renunciation 621 *relinquishment*; abjuration 603 *recantation*; negativism, negative attitude, noncorroboration; contravention 738 *disobedience*; cancellation, invalidation, nullification, revocation.

Adj. *negative*, denying, negating, contradictory 14 *contrary*; contravening 738 *disobedient*; protesting, abnegating, renunciatory; denied, disowned, dissociated.

Vb. *negate*, negative; contravene 738 *disobey*; deny, gainsay, give the lie to, belie, contradict; eat one's hat if 470 *make impossible*; repudiate, disclaim, disown 607 *reject*; refuse to corroborate; hold no brief for 860 *be indifferent*; demur, object 468 *qualify*; disagree 489 *dissent*; dissociate oneself 704 *oppose*; impugn, question, call in q., express doubts, refute, rebut, disprove 479 *confute*; protest, appeal against 762 *deprecate*; challenge 711 *defy*; thwart 702 *obstruct*; say no, decline, shake one's head, disallow 760 *refuse*; not allow 757 *prohibit*; revoke, invalidate, nullify 752 *abrogate*; abnegate, renounce 621 *relinquish*; abjure, forswear, swear off 603 *recant*; go back on one's word, do a U-turn 603 *tergiversate*.

534 Teaching

N. *teaching*, pedagogy, pedagogics, tutoring; education, schooling; tutelage; direction, guidance, instruction, edification; dictation; chalk and talk; programmed instruction, direct method, immersion m., induction 475 *reasoning*; tuition, preparation, coaching, cramming; seminar, teach-in, workshop, tutorial; initiation, introduction; training, discipline, drill 682 *exercise*; inculcation, indoctrination, preaching; propagandism; conversion; conditioning, brainwashing; pamphleteering, propaganda, agitprop 528 *publicity*.

education, liberal e. 490 *culture*; classical education, scientific e., technical e.; moral training; technical training, technological training, vocational t.; coeducation, progressive education, Froebel system, Froebelism, kindergarten method, Montessori system; elementary education, grounding; nursery education, preschool e., primary e., secondary e., further e., higher e., tertiary e., university e., adult e.; day release, block r.; sandwich course, refresher c.; advanced studies, postgraduate s.; remedial education; physical education, PE.

curriculum, National Curriculum, course of study 536 *learning*; core curriculum, common core; ABC, the three R's 68 *beginning*; foundation course, access c.; set books, prescribed text; module, project, exercise, homework, prep; Open University course, correspondence c., in-service c.

lecture, talk, illustrated t., documentary 531 *broadcasting*; reading, discourse; sermon, homily 579 *oration*; lesson, parable.

Adj. *educational*, pedagogic, tutorial; scholastic, scholarly, academic; instructional, informational; audiovisual, instructive 524 *informative*; educative, didactic, doctrinal; edifying, moralizing, primary, secondary etc. n.; single-sex, coeducational, comprehensive, all-ability, all-in; set, streamed, creamed, mixed-ability; extramural, intramural; extracurricular; redbrick, Oxbridge, Ivy League; cultural.

Vb. *educate*, edify (**see** *teach*); rear, nurture, bring up, develop, form, mould, shape, lick into shape; send to school, tutor, teach, school; ground, coach, cram, prime 669 *prepare*; guide 689 *direct*; instruct 524 *inform*; enlighten; sharpen the wits, open the eyes; stuff with knowledge, cram with facts; impress on the memory, din in, inculcate, indoctrinate, imbue, impregnate, infuse, instil, infix, implant, engraft, sow the seeds of.

teach, give lessons, take a class, lecture, deliver lectures; tutor, give tutorials, hold seminars; dictate, read out; preach, harangue, sermonize, pontificate; discourse, hold forth; moralize; expound 520 *interpret*; indoctrinate; pamphleteer, disseminate propaganda, condition, brainwash 178 *influence*.

train, coach 669 *prepare*; take on, take in hand, initiate, tame 369 *break in*; foster, cultivate; inure, keep one's nose to the grindstone; drill, exercise, practise, familiarize, accustom, groom one for 610 *habituate*; show one the ropes; make fit, qualify; house-train, teach manners, teach etiquette.

535 Misteaching

N. *misteaching*, misdirection; a case of the blind leading the blind; misinformation, disinformation 552 *misrepresentation*; propaganda, brainwashing 541 *falsehood*; perversion 246 *distortion*; false logic.

536 Learning

N. *learning*, lore, scholarship, attainments 490 *erudition*; tutelage, apprenticeship, initiation 669 *preparation*; basic training, basics, first steps, teething troubles 68 *beginning*; teachability 694 *aptitude;* self-improvement; culture, cultivation; self-c.

study, studying; application, studiousness; cramming, swotting, grind, mugging up, burning the midnight oil; studies, course of s., lessons, class, classwork, deskwork; homework, prep, preparation; revision, refresher course, further reading, further study; crash course; perusal, reading 455 *attention;* research, research work, field w., investigation 459 *enquiry;* learning curve.

learning difficulty, learning disability, dyslexia, dysgraphia, dyscalculia, attention deficit disorder; dyspraxia, mental retardation; person with learning difficulties, person with learning disabilities.

Adj. *studious,* academic, bookish, well-read, scholarly, erudite, learned, scholastic 490 *knowing;* diligent 678 *industrious;* receptive, teachable, self-taught, immersed in one's books 455 *attentive.*

Vb. *learn,* pursue one's education, go to school, attend college, take lessons, sit at the feet of, take a course; acquire knowledge, glean information, drink in, cram oneself with facts, know one's f. 490 *know;* apprentice oneself, learn one's trade, serve an apprenticeship, article oneself 669 *prepare oneself;* train, practise, exercise 610 *be wont;* learn the basics, get the feel of, get the hang of, master; get by heart, learn by rote 505 *memorize;* finish one's education, graduate.

study, apply oneself, burn the midnight oil; do, take up; research into 459 *enquire;* specialize, major in; swot, cram, mug, get up; revise, go over, run over, brush up, take a refresher course; read, peruse, pore over, wade through; thumb, browse, skip, flip through, turn the leaves, dip into; be studious, be bookish, always have one's nose in a book; bury oneself in one's books, become a polymath.

Adv. *studiously,* at one's books; under training, in articles.

537 Teacher

N. *teacher,* mentor 520 *guide;* minister 986 *pastor;* guru 500 *sage;* instructor, educator; tutor, crammer, coach; governor, governess, nursemaid 749 *keeper;* educationist, educationalist, pedagogue; pedant 500 *wiseacre;* dominie, beak, schoolmarm; master *or* mistress, school teacher, supply t., class t., form t.; house master *or* mistress; assistant teacher, deputy head, head teacher, head, headmaster *or* -mistress, principal, rector; pupil teacher, trainee t., proctor; dean, don, fellow; lecturer, demonstrator, exponent 520 *interpreter;* reader, professor,

Regius p., professor emeritus; consultant 691 *adviser;* teaching staff, faculty, professoriate.

trainer, personal t., instructor; coach, team c., life c.; choirmaster; dancing-master *or* mistress; animal trainer; breaker-in, lion-tamer 369 *breeder.*

preacher, lay p. 986 *pastor;* pulpiteer; hot gospeller, evangelist; apostle, missionary; prophet.

538 Learner

N. *learner,* disciple, follower; proselyte, convert, initiate; mature student; self-taught person; do-it-yourself fan; swot, mugger, bookworm 492 *scholar;* pupil, scholar, schoolboy *or* -girl, student; day pupil, boarder; sixth-former; schoolfellow, schoolmate, classmate, fellow student; gifted child, high flier; slow learner, late developer, under-achiever, remedial pupil; school-leaver; old boy, old girl, former pupil.

beginner, novice, debutant; new boy *or* girl, tyro, greenhorn, tenderfoot, neophyte; rabbit, amateur 987 *lay person;* raw recruit, rookie; colt, cadet, trainee, apprentice, articled clerk; probationer, L-driver, examinee.

student, university s., college s.; undergraduate, undergrad, freshman, fresher, sophomore; former student, alumnus, alumna; foundationer, exhibitioner; scholarship-holder, bursary-h., Rhodes Scholar; honours student; graduand, graduate, post-g., fellow; mature student, research worker.

class, form, grade, remove; set, band, stream; age group; house; lower form, upper f.; workshop; seminar.

539 School

N. *academy,* institute, educational i.; college, lycée, gymnasium, senior secondary school; conservatoire, ballet school, art s., academy of dramatic art; finishing school; correspondence college; university, campus; Open University; redbrick university, Oxbridge, varsity; sixth-form college, FE c., college of further *or* higher education; polytechnic, poly; alma mater, old school, groves of academe.

school, nursery s., crèche, playgroup, kindergarten; infant school; private school, independent s., public s., state-aided s., state s.; preparatory school, prep s., crammer; primary school, middle s., secondary s., high s., secondary modern s., grammar s., senior secondary s.; comprehensive s., sixth form college, FE c.; boarding school, day s.; night s., evening classes; Sunday s.; special s.; approved school, List D s.; reform s., Borstal; remand home, detention centre; catchment area, parents' charter.

540 Veracity

N. *veracity*, truthfulness; truth, the whole truth and nothing but the truth, fidelity, verisimilitude, realism, exactitude 494 *accuracy*; candour; honour bright, scout's honour, no kidding; honesty, sincerity 929 *probity*; ingenuousness 699 *artlessness*; plain speaking, speaking straight from the shoulder 573 *plainness*; plain words, words of one syllable, home truth, honest truth 494 *truth*; clean breast 526 *disclosure*.

Adj. *veracious*, truthful 494 *true*; as good as one's word, reliable 929 *trustworthy*; factual, ungarbled, unembroidered, exact, just 494 *accurate*; full 570 *diffuse*; ingenuous 699 *artless*; bona fide; unaffected, unpretentious, open, above-board; frank, candid; blunt, forthright, outspoken, straightforward, straight from the shoulder, honest to God 573 *plain*; honest, sincere, on the level 929 *honourable*.

Vb. *be truthful*, tell the truth, tell the truth and shame the devil, tell the whole truth and nothing but the truth, stick to the facts, play it according to the letter 494 *be true*; mean it; weigh one's words 834 *be serious*; speak one's mind, keep nothing back 522 *show*; come clean, make a clean breast of it; appear in one's true colours 526 *disclose*; be prophetic 511 *predict*.

541 Falsehood

N. *falsehood*, falseness, spuriousness, falsity; treachery, bad faith 930 *perfidy*; untruthfulness, mendacity, deceitfulness; lie, terminological inexactitude; lying, pathological l., perjury 543 *untruth*; fabrication, fiction; faking, forgery, falsification 542 *deception*; invention 513 *imagination*; prevarication, equivocation, ambivalence, evasion, double-talk 518 *equivocalness*; economy of truth, whitewashing, cover-up, overstatement 546 *exaggeration*; perversion 246 *distortion*; misrepresentation; humbug, bunkum, boloney, hooey, rubbish, bull, flim-flam 515 *empty talk*; cant, eyewash, hogwash (**see** *duplicity*), blarney.

duplicity, double life, double-dealing 930 *improbity*; guile 542 *trickery*; front, facade, mask, show, window-dressing, fanfaronade 875 *ostentation*; pretence, hollow p., bluff, act, fake, counterfeit, imposture 542 *sham*; hypocrisy; playacting, dissimulation, dissembling, insincerity, tongue in cheek, cant; lip service, cupboard love; false piety; outward show, crocodile tears; Judas kiss; fraud, sting, diplomatic illness; cheating, sharp practice; collusion, nod and a wink; put-up job, frame-up; quackery, charlatanism 850 *pretension*.

Adj. *false*, not true; imagined, made-up; untruthful, lying, mendacious 543 *untrue*; perfidious, treacherous, perjured; disingenuous, dishonest; falsified, garbled; touched up; overdone; imitation, simulated, counterfeit, fake, phoney, sham, pseudo, quack, bogus 542 *spurious*; cheating, deceptive, deceitful, fraudulent; fiddled, fixed, engineered, rigged, packed; trumped up.

hypocritical, insincere, diplomatic, put on, imitated, pretended, simulated, economical with the truth, feigned; make-believe, play-acting; two-faced, shifty, sly, treacherous, double-dealing, designing, Machiavellian 930 *perfidious*; sanctimonious; plausible, smooth, smooth-tongued, oily; creepy, goody-goody; mealy-mouthed, euphemistic 850 *affected*.

Vb. *be false*, – perjured, – forsworn etc. adj.; perjure oneself, bear false witness, swear that black is white; lie, tell lies, lie in one's teeth *or* one's throat; swing the lead, malinger; stretch the truth, tell a tall story 546 *exaggerate*; tell a white lie, fib, tell a fib, tell a whopper; invent, make believe, make up, romance 513 *imagine*; put a false construction on 521 *misinterpret*; garble, doctor, tamper with, falsify 246 *distort*; misquote, misinform, cry wolf 535 *misteach*; play false; run with the hare and hunt with the hounds, have a foot in both camps; break faith, betray 603 *tergiversate*.

dissemble, dissimulate, disguise 525 *conceal*; simulate, counterfeit 20 *imitate*; put on, assume, affect, dress up, play-act, play a part, go through the motions, make a show of 594 *act*; feign, pass off for, sham, pretend, be under false pretences, sail under false colours; malinger 542 *deceive*; be less than honest, say one thing and mean another; keep something back, fail to declare; fudge the issue, prevaricate, beat about the bush, dodge.

fake, fudge, fabricate, forge, plagiarize, counterfeit 20 *imitate*; get up, trump up, frame; manipulate, fiddle, fix, wangle, rig, pack (a jury); spin, weave, cook, cook up, concoct, hatch, invent 623 *plot*; touch-up, embroider; gloss over.

542 Deception

N. *deception*, kidding, kidology, tongue in cheek; self-deception, wishful thinking 487 *credulity*; fallacy 477 *sophistry*; illusion, delusion, hallucination; deceptiveness; false appearance, mockery, mirage, will-o'-the-wisp 440 *visual fallacy*; false show, meretriciousness, paint (**see** *sham*); feet of clay; bubble 4 *insubstantiality*; falseness, deceit, quackery, imposture, lie, terminological inexactitude, pious fraud 541 *falsehood*; deceitfulness, guile, craft, artfulness 698 *cunning*; hypocrisy, insincerity 541 *duplicity*;

treachery, betrayal 930 *perfidy*; machination, hanky-panky, jiggery-pokery, monkey business, wheeler-dealing, collusion 623 *plot*; fraudulence, cozenage, cheating, cheat, diddling; cheat 545 *deceiver*.

trickery, dupery, swindling, skulduggery, shenanigan; sharp practice, wheeler-dealing, chicanery, pettifoggery; swindle, ramp, racket, wangle, fix, fiddle, diddle, swizzle, swiz, sell, fraud, cheat; cardsharping; trick, dirty t., bag of tricks, tricks of the trade, confidence trick, con trick, fast one, wiles, ruse, shift, dodge, artful d., blind, feint 698 *stratagem*; wrinkle 623 *contrivance*; bait, gimmick, diversion, red herring, smoke screen, hoax, bluff, spoof, leg-pull; game, sport, joke, practical j., rag 839 *witticism*; April fooling.

sleight, sleight of hand, legerdemain, conjuring, hocus-pocus, illusion, ventriloquism; juggling, three-card trick; magic 983 *sorcery*.

trap, deathtrap 527 *ambush*; catch 530 *enigma*; plant, frame-up; snare, gin, man trap; net, meshes, web; blind, decoy, decoy duck, bait, lure, sprat to catch a mackerel; baited trap, mouse t., flypaper, birdlime; booby trap, mine, tripwire, pit 663 *pitfall*; car bomb, letter b., parcel b.; trapdoor, sliding panel, false bottom 530 *secret*; poisoned apple, Trojan horse, Greek gift; honey trap.

sham, false front, veneer 541 *duplicity*; lip service, tokenism; make-believe, pretence 850 *affectation*; whitewash, gloss; whited sepulchre, man of straw, paper tiger; wolf in sheep's clothing 545 *impostor*; dummy, scarecrow, tattie bogle; imitation, simulacrum, facsimile 22 *copy*; mockery; counterfeit, forgery, fake; masquerade, mummery, mask, veil, cloak, disguise, borrowed plumes, false colours 525 *concealment*; imitation ware, tinsel, paste.

Adj. *spurious*, false, faked, fake; sham, counterfeit 541 *false*; trumped-up, pretended; make-believe, mock, ersatz, bogus, phoney; pseudo-, so-called; cosmetic; artificial, simulated, man-made, plastic, paste, cultured, imitation; shoddy, rubbishy 641 *useless*; tinsel, meretricious, flash, gaudy, pasteboard 330 *brittle*; whitewashed, varnished.

Vb. *deceive*, delude; beguile, sugar the pill, gild the p., give a false impression, belie; let down 509 *disappoint*; pull the wool over one's eyes, blindfold 439 *blind*; kid, bluff, bamboozle, hoodwink, hoax; throw dust in the eyes, create a smoke screen, lead up the garden path 495 *mislead*; spoof, mystify 535 *misteach*; play false, leave in the lurch, betray, two-time, double-cross 930 *be dishonest*; steal a march on 135 *be early*; pull a fast one, take one for a ride, outsmart 698 *be cunning*; trick, dupe; cheat, cozen,

con, swindle, sell, rook, do; diddle, do out of, bilk, fleece, rip off, shortchange, obtain money by false pretences 788 *defraud*; juggle, conjure, palm off, foist o.; fob, fob off with; live on one's wits, try it on; tinker with, fiddle, wangle, fix; load the dice, mark the cards; counterfeit 541 *fake*.

fool, make a fool of, make an ass of make a wally of, make one look silly; mock, make fun of 851 *ridicule*; play tricks on, play practical jokes on, pull one's leg, have one on, make an April fool of, play a joke on 497 *be absurd* throw over, jilt; take in, have, have on, put on, dupe, bull, victimize, gull, outwit, outsmart; trick, trap, catch out, take advantage of, manipulate, twist round one's little finger; kid, spoof, bamboozle, string along, lead one on (**see** *deceive*); cajole, wheedle, get round; play fast and loose with, leave in the lurch, leave one holding the baby 509 *disappoint*; send on a fool's errand, send on a wild-goose chase 495 *mislead*; make one an applepie bed.

ensnare, snare, trap, set a trap for, lay a trap for; entangle, net; trip, trip up, catch, catch out, hook; bait, bait the trap, bait the hook, lure, decoy, lead astray, entice, inveigle 612 *tempt*; lie in wait, waylay 527 *ambush*; nab, nick, kidnap, shanghai, hijack, take hostage 788 *steal*.

543 Untruth

N. *untruth*, more than the truth, lie, downright l., barefaced l.; white lie, fib, diplomatic excuse, whopper; false statement, terminological inexactitude; breach of promise 930 *perfidy*; perjury; pack of lies, tissue of l., trumped-up story, frame-up 466 *evidence*; fabrication, invention 513 *ideality* (**see** *fable*); false excuse; misinformation, disinformation; misrepresentation, perversion 246 *distortion*; gloss, varnish, falsification 521 *misinterpretation*; disingenuousness, economy of truth.

fable, invention, fiction, story, tale 590 *narrative*; tall story, shaggy dog story, fisherman's yarn, traveller's tale 546 *exaggeration*; fairy tale, nursery t., romance, tale, yarn, story, cock-and-bull s., all my eye and Betty Martin 497 *absurdity*; claptrap, gossip, guff, bull; old wives' tales; myth; moonshine, farce, mare's nest, sell, swiz, hoax, humbug, flummery 515 *empty talk*.

Adj. *untrue*, lying, mendacious 541 *false*; trumped-up, framed, cooked, fixed, hatched, concocted; mythological, fabulous; unfounded, ungrounded, empty; fictitious, imagined, hallucinatory, make-believe; artificial, synthetic, simulated; phoney, bogus, so-called 542 *spurious*; perjured, forsworn 930 *perfidious*.

Vb. *be untrue*, not hold water, not stand up in court, be wide of the mark; not ring true 472 *be* *unlikely;* lie, be a liar 541 *be false;* spin a yarn, tell a tall story, draw the long bow 546 *exaggerate;* make-believe 513 *imagine;* be phoney, pretend, sham, counterfeit, forge, falsify 541 *dissemble.*

544 Dupe

N. *dupe,* fool, April f. 851 *laughingstock;* Simple Simon; easy prey, sitting duck, soft touch, soft mark, pushover, cinch; fair game, victim, schlemiel, fall guy, patsy, stooge, mug, sap, sucker, schmuck, schnook, dude, greenhorn, innocent 538 *beginner;* puppet, cat's-paw, pawn 628 *instrument;* admass.

Vb. *be duped,* be had, be done, be taken in; be sold a pup, be sold a pig in a poke, be diddled; fall for walk into the trap, rise, nibble, swallow the bait, swallow hook line and sinker; get taken for a ride; carry the can; catch a Tartar 508 *not expect.*

545 Deceiver

N. *deceiver,* leg-puller; practical joker; dissembler; whited sepulchre, false friend, fair-weather f.; rat, two-timer, double-crosser, double agent; traitor, Judas 938 *knave;* seducer 952 *libertine;* serpent, snake in the grass, joker in the pack 663 *troublemaker;* plotter, Guy Fawkes, intriguer, conspirator 623 *planner;* counterfeiter, forger.

liar, pathological l.; fibber, storyteller; romancer; yarn-spinner; fabricator.

impostor, shammer, malingerer, adventurer, carpetbagger; usurper; cuckoo in the nest 59 *intruder;* wolf in sheep's clothing; pretender, charlatan, quack, mountebank; fake, fraud, con man, humbug; pseud, pseudo, phoney; masquerader.

trickster, hoaxer, spoofer, hood-winker, bamboozler; cheat, cozener; sharper, cardsharp; shyster; fraudster, swindler, bilker, diddler, shark 789 *defrauder;* twister, rogue 938 *knave;* confidence trickster, con man; decoy, decoy duck, agent provocateur; fiddler, manipulator, rigger, fixer.

546 Exaggeration

N. *exaggeration,* overemphasis, inflation, magnification, enlargement 197 *expansion;* straining; extravagance, exaggerated lengths, gilding the lily, extremes, immoderation, extremism; overkill; excess, excessiveness, feeding frenzy; violence 943 *intemperance;* inordinacy, exorbitance, overdoing it, piling it on; overacting, histrionics 875 *ostentation;* sensationalism, ballyhoo, hype 528 *publicity;* overstatement, hyperbole 519 *trope;* embroidery 38 *addition;* disproportion 246 *distortion;* caricature, burlesque 851

satire; exacerbation 832 *aggravation;* big talk, 877 *boasting;* grandiloquence 574 *grandiloquence;* overpraise, chauvinism 481 *prejudice;* tall story 543 *fable;* flight of fancy, stretch of the imagination 513 *imagination;* fuss, storm in a teacup, much ado about nothing 318 *commotion.*

Vb. *exaggerate,* maximize, magnify, expand, inflate, blow up, blow up out of all proportion 197 *enlarge;* overamplify, overelaborate; add to, pile up, pile it on 38 *add;* touch up, enhance, heighten, add a flourish, touch up, embroider, varnish 844 *decorate;* lay it on thick or with a trowel, depict in glowing terms, overvalue; overdo, overcolour; overemphasize; overpraise, puff, hype up, oversell; make too much of 925 *flatter;* stretch, strain, labour 246 *distort;* caricature 851 *satirize;* go to all lengths, gild the lily, not know when to stop, protest too much; overact, dramatize, out-Herod Herod; talk big, bull 877 *boast;* run riot, go to extremes; draw the long bow, overshoot the mark, overstep the m., go too far 306 *overstep;* spin a yarn, tell a tall tale; make mountains out of molehills, make a storm in a tea cup; exacerbate 832 *aggravate;* overcompensate, lean over backwards.

SECTION THREE

Means of communicating ideas

547 Indication

N. *indication,* signification, meaning 514 *connotation;* notification 524 *information;* symbolization, symbolism 551 *representation;* symbol; rune, hieroglyph 530 *enigma;* cross; pentacle 983 *talisman;* image, type, figure; token, emblem, figurehead (**see** *badge*); symptom, syndrome, sign 466 *evidence;* tell-tale sign, blush 526 *disclosure;* nudge, wink, kick 524 *hint* (**see** *gesture*); kite-flying, straw in the wind, sign of the times 511 *omen;* clue, scent, whiff, trace 484 *discovery;* noise, footfall 398 *sound;* semiology, semiotics; pointer, finger, forefinger, index finger (**see** *indicator*); guide, index, thumb i. 87 *directory;* key 520 *interpretation;* marker, mark; blaze; nick, scratch 260 *notch;* stamp, print, impression; stigma, stigmata; tattoo mark; scar 845 *blemish;* wrinkle, line, score, stroke; note, catchword (**see** *punctuation*); legend, caption 590 *description;* inscription, epitaph; motto, cipher, monogram.

identification, naming 561 *nomenclature,* 77 *classification;* brand, earmark, trademark, imprint (**see** *label*); name and address; autograph, signature, hand 586 *script;* fingerprint, footprint, spoor, track, trail, scent 548 *trace;* dental record; genetic fingerprinting, DNA f.;

password, open sesame, watchword, shibboleth; markings, colouring, characteristic, trait, lineament, outline, form, shape 445 *feature*; personal characteristic, mannerism, idiolect; mole, scar, birthmark, strawberry mark 845 *blemish*.

gesture, gesticulation, sign language; deaf-and-dumb language; sign 524 *hint*; pantomime, dumb show, charade, mime; body language, kinesics; demeanour, tone of one's voice 445 *mien*; motion, move; tic, twitch 318 *spasm*; shrug, shrug of the shoulders; raising of the eyebrows, nod, beck, wink, flicker of the eyelash, batting of the eyelids *or* eyelashes, twinkle, glance, ogle, leer, grimace 438 *look*; smile, laugh 835 *laughter*; touch, kick, kick under the table, nudge, jog, dig in the ribs 279 *knock*; hug; squeeze of the hand, handshake, grip; push, shove 279 *impulse*; pointing, signal, waving, wave, hand-signal, wave of the hand, Mexican wave; raising one's hand; drumming one's fingers, tapping one's foot, stamp of the foot 822 *excitable state*; clenching one's teeth, gritting one's t. 599 *resolution*; gnashing *or* grinding one's teeth; wringing one's hands, tearing one's hair 836 *lamentation*; clenched fist 711 *defiance*; V-sign, flag-waving 876 *celebration*; clapping, cheer 923 *applause*; hissing, hooting, booing, catcall, Bronx cheer, raspberry 924 *disapprobation*; two-finger gesture, Harvey Smith salute; stuck-out tongue 878 *sauciness*; frown, scowl 893 *sullenness*; pout, moue, pursing of the lips 829 *discontent*.

signal 529 *message*; sign, symptom, syndrome 522 *manifestation*; flash, rocket; railway signal, smoke s., heliograph, semaphore, tick-tack; telegraph, morse 531 *telecommunication*; flashlamp, signal lamp 420 *lamp*; warning light, beacon 379 *fire*; red flag, warning light, red l., Belisha beacon, green light, all clear 420 *signal light*; alarum, alarm, fire a., burglar a., warning signal, distress s., SOS 665 *danger signal*; whistle, police w.; siren, hooter; bleeper, bleep, pager; buzzer, knocker, doorknocker 414 *gong*; bell, doorbell, alarm bell; church bells, angelus, carillon; time signal, pip, dinner gong, dinner bell 117 *chronometry*; passing bell, knell, muffled drum 364 *obsequies*.

indicator, index, pointer, arrow, needle; arm, finger, index-f.; hand, hour h., minute h. 117 *timekeeper*; Plimsoll line 465 *gauge*; traffic indicator, trafficator; direction finder, radar; cursor, white line, cat's-eyes (tdmk) 305 *traffic control*; weathercock, wind sock 340 *weather*.

signpost, fingerpost; milestone, waymark; lighthouse, buoy 662 *safeguard*; compass 269 *sailing aid*; lodestar, guiding star, Southern Cross 321 *star*; landmark; cairn 253 *earthwork*; benchmark.

call, hue-and-cry 528 *publication*; shout, hail; call to prayer, church bell 981 *worship*; summons 737 *command*; call for help, cry of help, distress call, Mayday; bugle, trumpet; reveille, rally; last post; peal, flourish; drum, drumbeat, drum-roll, tattoo 403 *roll*; call to arms, fiery cross; battle cry, war c., rallying c.

badge, token, emblem, symbol, sign, totem (**see** *indication*); insignia (**see** *heraldry*); markings; throne, sceptre, orb, crown 743 *regalia*; badge of office, robes of o., Black Rod, mace 743 *badge of rule*; pips, stripes, epaulette 743 *badge of rank*; medal, cross, Victoria Cross, George C., Iron C., Croix de Guerre; order, star, garter, sash, ribbon 729 *decoration*; badge of merit, laurels, wreath 729 *trophy*; colours, blue, half-b., cap; favour, rosette; black armband, widow's weeds 228 *clothing*.

heraldry, armory, blazonry; heraldic register, Roll of Arms; armorial bearings, coat of arms, blazon; achievement, funereal a., hatchment; shield, escutcheon; crest, torse, wreath, helmet, crown, coronet, mantling, lambrequin; supporters, motto; field, quarter, dexter, sinister, chief, base; charge, device, bearing; ordinary, fess, bar, label, pale, bend, bend sinister, chevron, pile, saltire, cross; canton; inescutcheon, bordure, lozenge, fusil, gyron, flanches; marshalling, quartering, impaling, dimidiation; differencing; fess point, honour p., nombril p.; animal charge, lion, lion rampant, lion couchant, unicorn, griffin, cockatrice, eagle, falcon, martlet; floral charge, Tudor rose, cinquefoil, trefoil, planta genista; badge, rebus, antelope, bear and ragged staff, portcullis; national emblem, rose, thistle, leek, daffodil, shamrock, lilies, fleur-de-lis; device, national d., lion and unicorn, spread eagle, bear, hammer and sickle, triskelion; swastika, fylfot; skull and crossbones; heraldic tincture, colour, gules, azure, vert, sable, purpure, tenné, murrey; metal, or, argent; fur, ermine, ermines, erminois, pean, vair, potent; heraldic personnel, College of Arms, Earl Marshal, King of Arms, Lord Lyon K. of A.; herald, herald extraordinary, pursuivant, Bluemantle, Rouge Croix, Rouge Dragon, Portcullis.

flag, ensign, white e., blue e.; red ensign, Red Duster; jack, pilot j., merchant j.; flag of convenience; colours, ship's c., regimental c., King's Colour, Queen's C.; guidon, standard, vexillum, labarum, banner, gonfalon; bannerette, bannerol, banderole, oriflamme; pennon, streamer, pennant, swallowtail, triple tail; pendant, broad p., burgee; bunting; Blue Peter, yellow flag; white flag 721 *submission*; eagle, Roman e.; tricolour; Union Jack; Stars and Stripes, Old Glory, star-spangled banner; Red

Flag; black flag, pirate f., Jolly Roger, skull and crossbones; parts of a flag, hoist, fly, canton; flagpole, flagstaff.

label, tattoo, caste mark (**see** *identification*); ticket, bus t., raffle t., cloakroom t., bill, docket, chit, counterfoil, stub, duplicate; counter, chip; mark, countermark; luggage label, sticky l., sticker; tie-on label, tab, tag; name badge, name tape, nameplate, signboard; number-plate, cherished n.; sign, inn s., barber's pole, three balls 522 *exhibit*; brass plate, trademark, logotype, logo, hallmark; earmark, brand; electronic tag; dunce's cap; seal, signet, stamp, impression; letterhead, masthead, caption, heading, title, headline, superscription, rubric; imprint, colophon, watermark; bookplate, name, name and address, personal details; card, visiting c.; birth certificate, marriage c., death c., identification papers, identity card, identification tag, passport, pass, pet passport, animal p., 756 *permit*; endorsement 466 *credential*, swipe card, PIN, pin number, signature, autograph, cipher, mark, cross, initials, monogram; fingerprint, thumbprint, footprint 548 *trace*; genetic fingerprint.

punctuation, punctuation mark, point, stop, full s., period; comma, colon, semi-colon; inverted commas, quotation marks, quotes, air q., apostrophe; exclamation mark, question-mark, query; parentheses, brackets, square b., crotchet, crook, brace; hyphen, hyphenation; en rule, em r., dash, swung d., dot, caret, omission mark, ellipsis, blank; asterisk; dagger, grave accent, acute a., circumflex a.; diaeresis, cedilla, tilde; macron, breve, umlaut; paragraph; plus sign, minus s., multiplication s., division s., equals s., decimal point; italics 587 *print-type*.

Adj. *heraldic*, emblematic; crested, armorial, blazoned, emblazoned etc. vb.; paly, barry; dexter, sinister; gules, azure, vert, purpure, sable, tenné, murrey, or, argent, ermine; fleury, semé, pommé; rampant, gardant, regardant, couchant, statant, sejant, passant.

Vb. *indicate*, point 281 *point to*; point out, exhibit 522 *show*; blazon; delineate, demarcate, mark out, blaze, signpost; register 548 *record*; name, give a name to, identify, classify 80 *specify*; index, supply references, refer; point the way, show the w., guide 689 *direct*; signify, denote, connote, suggest, imply, involve, spell, bespeak, argue 514 *mean*; symbolize, typify, betoken, stand for, be the sign of 551 *represent*; declare 532 *affirm*; highlight 532 *emphasize*; show signs of, bear the stamp of, give evidence of, witness to 466 *evidence*; smack of, smell of, hint at 524 *hint*; reveal 526 *disclose*; herald, prefigure, forebode, presage 511 *predict*.

mark, mark off, mark out, demarcate, delin-

eate, delimit 236 *limit*; label, ticket, docket, tag, tab; earmark, designate; annotate, score, underline; number, letter, page, paginate, index; tick, tick off; nick, scribe 260 *notch*; chalk, chalk up; scratch, scribble, cover 586 *write*; blot, stain, blacken 649 *make unclean*; scar, disfigure 842 *make ugly*; punctuate, dot, dash, cross, cross out, asterisk; put one's mark on, leave fingerprints *or* footprints; blaze, brand, earmark, burn in; electronically tag; tattoo 263 *pierce*; stamp, seal, punch, impress, emboss; imprint, overprint 587 *print*; etch 555 *engrave*; emblazon, blazon.

sign, autograph, write one's signature, inscribe; subscribe, undersign; initial; put one's cross.

gesticulate, mime, mimic, suit the action to the word 20 *imitate*; wave one's hands, talk with one's h.; wave 318 *agitate*; wave to, hold out one's hand 884 *greet*; stamp 923 *applaud*; wave one's arms, gesture, motion, sign; point, beckon, raise one's hand, bat one's eye-lashes 455 *attract notice*; nod, wink, shrug; jog, nudge, kick, poke, prod, dig in the ribs, clap on the back; look, look volumes, look daggers, glance, leer, ogle 438 *gaze*; twinkle, smile 835 *laugh*; raise one's eyebrows, wag one's finger, shake one's head, purse one's lips 924 *disapprove*; wring one's hands, tear one's hair 836 *lament*; grit one's teeth, clench one's t. 599 *be resolute*; gnash one's teeth 891 *be angry*; snap, bite; grimace, pout, scowl, frown 829 *be discontented*; shrug one's shoulders, curl one's lip 922 *despise*; shuffle, pat, stroke 889 *caress*.

signal, send a s., send smoke s., speak 524 *communicate*; tap out a message, semaphore, heliograph; flag down, thumb; wave on; unfurl the flag, fly the f., dip the f., salute; alert, sound the alarm, cry help, send an SOS, dial 999 665 *raise the alarm*; beat the drum, sound the trumpets; fire a warning shot 664 *warn*.

548 Record

N. *record*, recording, documentation; historical record, memoir, chronicle, annals, history 590 *narrative*; case history, case notes, curriculum vitae 590 *biography*; photograph, portrait, sketch 551 *representation*; file, dossier, rogues' gallery; public record, gazette, official journal, Hansard, official report, official publication, blue book, White Paper; minutes, transactions; notes, annotations, marginalia, jottings, cuttings, press c.; memorabilia, memorandum, memo 505 *reminder*; reports, annual report, returns, tax r., statements 524 *report*; tally, score-sheet, scoreboard; document; voucher, certificate, diploma, charter 466 *credential*; birth certificate, death c., marriage c., marriage lines

767 *title deed*; copy, spare c., carbon c., Xerox (tdmk) 22 *duplicate*; records, files, archives, papers, correspondence; record, book, roll, register, registry; notebook, memo pad, logbook, log, diary, journal, commonplace book, scrapbook, album; ledger, cashbook, chequebook; catalogue, index, waiting list 87 *list*; card, index c., microfilm, microfiche 196 *miniature*; tape, computer t. 86 *data processing*; magnetic tape, pressing 414 *gramophone*; inscription, legend, caption, heading 547 *indication*; graffiti 586 *script*.

monument, memorial, war m. 505 *reminder*; mausoleum 364 *tomb*; statue, bust 551 *image*; brass, tablet, inscription 364 *obsequies*; pillar, memorial arch, obelisk, monolith; national monument, ancient m., cromlech, dolmen, menhir, megalith 125 *antiquity*; cairn, barrow 253 *earthwork*.

trace, vestige, relic, remains 41 *leavings*; track, tracks, footstep, footprint, footmark, hoofmark, clawmark, tread; spoor; scent, smell; wake, wash, trail, vapour t.; furrow, swathe, path; scuffmark, skidmark, tyremark, fingermark 547 *indication*; fingerprint, dabs 466 *evidence*; mark, tidemark, stain, scar, scratch, weal 845 *blemish*.

Vb. *record*, tape-record, telerecord, tape, videotape, video; store in a database, input, film 551 *photograph*; paint 551 *represent*; document, put *or* place on record; docket, file, index, catalogue; inscribe, carve; take down, note down, set down in black and white, commit to writing 586 *write*; capture on film, preserve for posterity; log, write down, jot d.; note, make a note of; take minutes of, minute; chronicle 590 *describe*.

register, mark up, chalk up, cross off, notch up, score; tabulate, enrol 87 *list*; enter 808 *account*; reserve, put on the waiting l.; inscribe, log.

549 Recorder

N. *recorder*, registrar, record-keeper, archivist; Master of the Rolls; amanuensis, stenographer, scribe; secretary; writer, clerk, filing c., bookkeeper 808 *accountant*; photographer, cameraman 551 *photography*; Record Office; Recording Angel.

chronicler, annalist, diarist, historian, historiographer, biographer, autobiographer; archaeologist 125 *antiquarian*; reporter, journalist.

recording instrument, recorder, tape r., videotape r., VTR, videocassette recorder, VCR; record, disc, compact d., laser d. 414 *gramophone*; dictaphone, teleprinter, tape machine 531 *telecommunication*; cash register, till, checkout; turnstile; speedometer, tachograph 465 *gauge*; flight recorder, black box; time-

recorder, stopwatch 117 *timekeeper*; hygrometer; anemometer; camera, speed c.; photocopier, Xerox (tdmk); pen, pencil, Biro (tdmk) 586 *stationery*.

550 Obliteration

N. *obliteration*, wiping out etc. vb.; erasure, effacement; defacement; deletion; crossing out, cancellation; annulment, 752 *abrogation*; oblivion 506 *amnesty*; blot 649 *dirt*; clean sweep 149 *revolution*; rubber, eraser.

Vb. *obliterate*, remove the traces, cover, cover up 525 *conceal*; deface; efface; eliminate, erase, scratch out, rub o.; expunge, wipe out; blot out; wipe off, wash o.; brush o.; cancel, delete; cross out, score o., censor, blue-pencil; raze 165 *demolish*; cover 364 *inter*; submerge 311 *lower*; drown 399 *silence*.

551 Representation

N. *representation*, personification, incarnation, embodiment, bodying forth; typifying, typification, symbolization 547 *indication*; diagram, hieroglyphics, runes 586 *writing*; presentation; impersonation; enactment, performance; role-playing, psychodrama 658 *therapy*; mimicry, charade, mime, dumb show 20 *imitation*; depiction, characterization 590 *description*; delineation, drawing, illustration, artwork, graphics 553 *painting*; creation, work of art 164 *product*; impression, likeness, identikit, Photofit (tdmk), E-fit, electronically generated picture 18 *similarity*; exact likeness, double, spitting image, look-alike, facsimile 22 *duplicate*; tracing 233 *outline*; reflection (**see** *image*); portrayal; striking likeness, realism 553 *picture*; bad likeness 552 *misrepresentation*; reproduction, copy, Xerox (tdmk), lithograph; etching 555 *engraving*; design, blueprint, draft, cartoon, sketch, outline 623 *plan*.

image, spitting i. 22 *duplicate*; mental image, after-image 451 *idea*; reflected image, hologram, silhouette 417 *reflection*; pixel; magic eye, autostereogram; visual aid 445 *spectacle*; idol, graven image 982 *idolatry*; icon; cherub; statue, colossus; statuette, bust, torso, head 554 *sculpture*; effigy, figure, figurine, figurehead; gargoyle; wax figure, waxwork; dummy, tailor's d., manikin; model; doll, china d., rag d., Cabbage Patch (tdmk) d., Cindy (tdmk) d., golliwog; teddy bear; marionette, puppet, finger p., glove p.; snowman, gingerbread man; scarecrow, tattie bogle, guy, Guy Fawkes; robot, Dalek, automaton; type, symbol.

art, architecture 243 *formation*; fine arts; graphic art 553 *painting*; plastic art 554 *sculpture*; classical art, Byzantine a., Renaissance a., Baroque, Rococo; art nouveau, art deco, modern art, abstract art; Surrealism, Expressionism 553 *school of painting*; op art, pop a.; kitsch, camp, high c. 847 *bad taste*; aestheticism, functionalism, De Stijl, Bauhaus; functional art, commercial a.; useful arts; decorative a. 844 *ornamental art*; the minor arts, illumination, calligraphy, weaving, tapestry, collage, embroidery, pottery.

photography, radiography, scanning; time-lapse photography, aerial p., telephotography, microphotography, macrophotography; cinematography 445 *cinema*; photograph, photo, picture, snapshot, snap; plate, film; exposure, negative, print, sepia p., colour p., slide, transparency; frame, still; reel, spool, cassette; filmstrip, microfilm, microfiche, movie, home m. 445 *film*; hologram; radiograph, X-ray, scan 417 *radiation*; photocopy, Xerox (tdmk) 22 *copy*; shot, close-up, mug shot, pan, zoom, fade; lens 442 *camera*; cameraman, photographer, lensman, paparazzo; radiographer.

map, chart, plan, town p., outline 86 *statistics*; sketch map, relief m., survey m., Ordnance S. m., road m., star m.; Admiralty chart; ground plan, elevation; projection, Mercator's p.; atlas; globe; map-making, cartography, computerized c.

Vb. *represent*, stand for, denote, symbolize 514 *mean*; typify, embody, body forth, personify; act the part of, assume the role of, role-play; impersonate, pose as 542 *deceive*; pose, model, sit for 23 *be an example*; enact 594 *dramatize*; suggest; reflect, hold the mirror up to nature; mimic, mime, copy 20 *imitate*; depict, characterize 590 *describe*; delineate, draw, picture, portray; illustrate 553 *paint*; catch a likeness, capture; carve, cast 554 *sculpt*; cut 555 *engrave*; mould, shape 243 *form*; fashion upon; design, draft, sketch out, rough o., block o. 623 *plan*; make a diagram, construct a figure, describe a circle 233 *outline*; sketch; map, chart, survey, plot.

photograph, photo, take a p. *or* a picture; snap; take, shoot, film; X-ray, scan; expose, develop, process, print, enlarge, blow up, reduce.

552 Misrepresentation

N. *misrepresentation*, not a true picture 19 *dissimilarity*; false light 541 *falsehood*; bad likeness, poor 1. 914 *injustice*; travesty, parody 546 *exaggeration*; caricature; flattering portrait 925 *flattery*; nonrepresentational art 551 *art*; daub, botch; distorted image 246 *distortion*; misinformation, disinformation.

Vb. *misrepresent*, give a twist *or* turn, tone down 925 *flatter*; overdramatize 546 *exaggerate*; gild the lily, overembellish, caricature; parody, daub, botch, lie 541 *be false*.

553 Painting

N. *painting*, graphic art, colouring, illumination; daubing, finger painting; washing, colourwashing, tinting, touching up; depicting, drawing, sketching 551 *representation*; artistry, composition, design, technique, draughtsmanship, brushwork; line, perspective, golden section; treatment, tone, values, atmosphere, ambience; highlight, local colour, shading, contrast; monotone, monochrome, polychrome 425 *colour*; black and white, chiaroscuro, grisaille.

art style, style of painting, grand style, grand manner 243 *form*; intimate style, genre painting (**see** *art subject*); pasticcio, pastiche; trompe l'oeil; iconography, portrait-painting, portraiture; scenography, scene painting, sign p., poster p., miniature p.; oil painting, watercolour, tempera, gouache; fresco painting, mural p., encaustic p., impasto, secco.

school of painting, the Primitives, Byzantine school, Renaissance s., Sienese s., Florentine s., Venetian s., Dutch s., Flemish s., French s., Spanish s.; Mannerism, Baroque, Rococo, Pre-Raphaelitism, Neo-Classicism, Realism, Romanticism, Impressionism, Post-Impressionism, Neo-I., Pointillism, Symbolism, Fauvism, Dada, Cubism, Expressionism, Die Brücke, Der Blaue Reiter, Vorticism, Futurism, Surrealism, Abstract Expressionism, Tachism, action painting; minimal art, Minimalism, Conceptualism;

art subject, modernism 551 *art*; landscape, seascape, skyscape, cloudscape; scene, prospect, diorama, panorama 438 *view*; interior, conversation piece, still life, pastoral, nocturne, nude.

picture, pictorial equivalent 551 *representation*; tableau, mosaic, tapestry; collage, montage, photomontage; frottage, brass rubbing; painting, pastiche; icon, triptych, diptych, panel; fresco, mural, wall painting, poster; canvas, daub; drawing, line d.; sketch, outline, cartoon; oil painting, oleograph, gouache, watercolour, aquarelle, pastel, wash drawing, pen-and-ink d., pencil d., charcoal d.; design, pattern, doodle; cartoon, chad, caricature, silhouette; miniature, vignette, thumbnail sketch, illuminated initial; old master, masterpiece; study, portrait, full-length p., half-l. p., kit-cat, head, profile, full-face portrait; studio portrait, snap, Polaroid (tdmk), pin-up 551 *photography*; rotogravure, photogravure, chromolithograph, reproduction, photographic r., halftone; aquatint, woodcut 555 *engraving*; print, plate; illustration, fashion plate, picture postcard, cigarette card, tea c., stamp, transfer, scrap, sticker; picture book, illustrated b., scrapbook, photograph album, illustrated work 589 *book*.

Adj. *painted*, graphic, pictorial, scenic,

picturesque, decorative 844 *ornamental*; pastel, in paint, in oils, in watercolours, in tempera; linear, black-and-white, chiaroscuro, shaded, stippled, sfumato; grisaille 429 *grey*; painterly, paintable.

Vb. *paint*, wash 425 *colour*; tint, touch up; lay on the colour 226 *coat*; slap on paint; paint a picture, do a portrait, portray, draw, sketch, limn, cartoon 551 *represent*; illuminate; do in oils *or* watercolours *or* tempera, do in black-and-white; ink, chalk, crayon, pencil, stencil, shade, stipple; block in.

554 Sculpture

N. *sculpture*, plastic art 551 *representation*; modelling 243 *formation*; carving, stone cutting, wood carving; moulding; paper modelling, origami; rock carving; toreutics 844 *ornamental art*; constructivism 553 *school of painting*; kinetic art; statuary; statue; statuette, figurine, bust, torso, head; model, cast, plaster c., death mask, waxwork 551 *image*; ceramics 381 *pottery*; medallion, cameo, intaglio; relief, bas-relief; stone, marble; bronze, clay, modelling c., wax, Plasticine (tdmk), papier-mâché.

Vb. *sculpt*, sculpture, rough-hew 243 *form*; cut, carve, whittle, chisel, chip; chase, engrave, emboss; model, mould, cast.

555 Engraving. Printing

N. *engraving*, etching, line engraving, plate e., steel e., copper e.; photogravure, photoengraving; zincography, cerography, glyptography, gem cutting, gem engraving; glass engraving; mezzotint, aquatint; wood engraving, xylography, lignography, woodcut; linoprinting, linocut; scraperboard; silverpoint; dry-point; steel plate, copper p.; stone, block, wood-b.; chisel, graver, burin, burr, needle, dry-point, etching-p., style.

printing, type-p., typography 587 *print*; laser printing; plate printing, copper-plate p., intaglio p.; lithography, photolithography, photogravure, chromolithography, colour printing; fabric printing, batik; silk-screen printing, stereotype; impression.

Vb. *engrave*, grave, cut; etch, stipple, scrape; bite, bite in, eat in; sandblast; impress, stamp; lithograph 587 *print*.

556 Artist

N. *artist*, craftsman *or* -woman 686 *artisan*; architect 164 *producer*; art-master *or* mistress, designer, graphic d., draughtsman *or* -woman; dress-designer, couturier; drawer, sketcher, delineator; caricaturist, cartoonist; illustrator, commercial artist; painter, colourist; pavement artist, scene-painter, sign-p.; oil-painter, water-

colourist, pastellist; miniaturist; portrait painter, landscape p., marine p., genre p., still-life p.; Academician, RA, old master, primitive; Pre-Raphaelite, Impressionist, Fauve, Dadaist, Cubist, Vorticist, Surrealist, action painter, Minimalist 553 *school of painting*; art historian.

557 Language

N. *language*, tongue, speech, idiom, parlance, talk, dialect; spoken language, living l.; patter, lingo 560 *dialect*; idiolect; mother tongue, native t.; vernacular, common speech, vulgar tongue; colloquial speech, English as she is spoken 579 *speech*; Queen's English; correct speech, idiomatic s., slang; jargon, vulgarism; Estuary English; lingua franca, pidgin English, sign language 547 *gesture*; Basic English; Esperanto; official language, Mandarin, Hindi; Received Pronunciation, Standard English, BBC English; officialese 560 *neology*; machine language 86 *data processing*; dead language, Latin, Greek, Sanskrit; metalanguage; Babel, babble 61 *confusion*.

literature, creative writing, belles lettres; letters, classics, humanities; literary genre, fiction, metafiction, faction, non-fiction 590 *narrative, description*; lyricism, poetry 593 *poem*; plays 594 *drama*; criticism 480 *estimate*; literary criticism 520 *interpretation*; literary movement, Classicism, Neo-classicism, Sturm und Drang, Romanticism, Symbolism, Idealism, Expressionism, Surrealism, Realism, Naturalism; literary history; Golden Age, Silver A., Augustan A., Classical A. 110 *era*.

linguist, philologist, etymologist, lexicographer; semanticist; grammarian 564 *grammar*; phonetician.

Adj. *linguistic*, philological, etymological, grammatical, morphological; lexicographical, lexicological, semantic; monosyllabic; inflected; written, literary, standard; spoken, living, idiomatic; vulgar, colloquial, vernacular, slangy, jargonistic 560 *dialectal*; current, common, demotic; bilingual, multilingual.

literary, written, polished; humanistic; classical, romantic, naturalistic, surrealistic, futuristic, decadent; learned; formal; critical 520 *interpretive*.

558 Letter

N. *letter*, sign, symbol, character 586 *writing*; alphabet, ABC; International Phonetic Alphabet, IPA; Chinese character; pictogram, cuneiform, hieroglyph 586 *lettering*; ogham alphabet, runic a., futhorc; Greek alphabet, Roman a., Cyrillic a., Hebrew a., Arabic a.; Pinyin; Devanagari; runic letter, rune, wen; lettering, Gothic, italic; ampersand; capital letter, cap, upper case;

small letter, lower case, minuscule; block letter, uncial; cursive; printed letter, letterpress, type, bold t. 587 *print-type*.

spelling, misspelling; orthography; spelling check, spell-check; phonography; spelling game, spelling bee; transliteration 520 *translation*.

Vb. *spell*, spell out, read, syllabify; alphabetize; transliterate; form letters 586 *write*; initial 547 *sign*.

559 Word

N. *word*, term 561 *name*; phoneme, syllable 398 *speech sound*; synonym 13 *identity*; homonym, homograph, homophone, palindrome, pun, weasel word 518 *equivocalness*; antonym 14 *contrariety*; etymon, root, back-formation; folk etymology; derivation, derivative, doublet; morpheme, stem, inflexion; part of speech 564 *grammar*; diminutive, intensive; contraction, abbreviation, acronym, portmanteau word 569 *conciseness*; cliché, catchword, vogue word, buzz w., nonce w., neologism, loan w. 560 *neology*; rhyming word; four-letter word 573 *plainness*; swearword, oath 899 *malediction*; hard word, long word, polysyllable; short word, monosyllable, word of one syllable; verbiage, wordiness, verbal diarrhoea, loquacity, verbosity 570 *pleonasm*.

dictionary, rhyming d., reverse word d., monolingual d., learners' d., school d., illustrated d., bilingual d., multilingual d.; lexicon, wordbook, word list, glossary, vocabulary; thesaurus 632 *store*; concordance.

Adj. *verbal*, literal; etymological, lexical; philological, lexicographical; derivative, conjugate, cognate; synonymous; verbose.

Adv. *verbally*, verbatim, word for word.

560 Neology

N. *neology*, neologism 126 *newness*; coinage, new word, nonce w., vogue w., buzz w., catch phrase, cliché; borrowing, loan word; newfangled expression, slang e.; technical language, jargon, technical term, psychobabble, technospeak; barbarism, hybrid; corruption, dog Latin, novelese, journalese, officialese, telegraphese; baby talk; gobbledygook, newspeak, doubletalk; archaism; malapropism 565 *solecism*; word-play, spoonerism 839 *witticism*.

Adj. *dialect*, idiom, lingo, patois, vernacular 557 *language*; idiolect, burr, brogue, accent 577 *pronunciation*; cockney, Geordie, Doric, broad Scots, Lallans; broken English, pidgin E., pidgin; lingua franca, hybrid language; Briticism, Strine, Franglais; anglicism, Americanism, Hibernicism, Irishism.

slang, vulgarism, colloquialism; jargon,

psychobabble, technospeak, argot, cant, patter; Romany; thieves' Latin, rhyming slang; Billingsgate 899 *scurrility*; gobbledygook 515 *empty talk*.

dialectal, vernacular; Doric, cockney, broad; local; colloquial; nonstandard, slangy, cant; jargonistic, journalistic.

561 Nomenclature

N. *nomenclature*, naming etc. vb.; eponymy; terminology; description, designation, appellation, denomination; addressing, roll-call 583 *allocution*; christening, baptism 988 *Christian rite*; study of place names, toponymy.

name, first name, forename, Christian name; middle name(s), surname, family name, patronymic, matronymic; maiden name, married n.; appellation, moniker; nickname, pet name, diminutive; sobriquet, epithet, description; handle, style 870 *title*; heading, caption 547 *indication*; designation; name and address, signature 547 *label*; term, technical t., trade name 560 *neology*; namesake, synonym, eponym; pen name, pseudonym 562 *misnomer*; noun, proper n. 564 *part of speech*.

Adj. *named*, called etc. vb.; entitled, christened; known as, alias, under the name of; so-called, soi-disant, self-styled; named after, eponymous.

Vb. *name*, call, christen, baptize 988 *perform ritual*; give one's name to; nickname, dub; address, sir; entitle, style, term 80 *specify*; call by name, call the roll, call out the names, announce.

562 Misnomer

N. *misnomer*, malapropism 565 *solecism*; false name, alias, assumed title; nom de guerre, nom de plume, pen name; stage name, pseudonym; nickname, pet name 561 *name*.

no name, anon, certain person, so-and-so, what's his name, what's his face; N or M, Miss X, A. N. Other; what d'you call it, thingummy, thingummyjig, thingamabob, whatsit, oojakapivvy; this or that; and co., etc.; some, any, what-have-you.

Adj. *anonymous*, unknown, faceless, nameless; incognito, unnamed, unsigned; a certain, certain, such; some, any, this or that.

Vb. *misname*, misterm, mistitle; nickname; assume an alias, go under a false name; be anonymous; write under an assumed name, pass oneself off as 541 *dissemble*.

563 Phrase

N. *phrase*, form of words; collocation; expression; idiom, mannerism 80 *speciality*; fixed expression; set phrase; euphemism, metaphor; catch phrase, slogan; hackneyed expression, cliché, commonplace 610 *habit*; saying, proverb, motto, moral, epigram, adage 496 *maxim*; epitaph 364 *obsequies*; inscription, legend, caption 548 *record*; empty phrases, words, empty w., compliments 515 *empty talk*; terminology 561 *nomenclature*; phraseology, phrasing, diction, wording, turn of phrase; well-turned phrase; circumlocution 570 *diffuseness*; paraphrase 520 *translation*; epigrammatist.

Vb. *phrase*, word, verbalize, voice, articulate, syllable; reword, rephrase 520 *translate*; express, formulate, put in words, clothe in w., find words for, state 532 *affirm*; sloganize, talk in clichés; put words together, turn a sentence, round a period 566.

564 Grammar

N. *grammar*, comparative g., philology; analysis, parsing, construing; accidence, inflection, case, declension; conjugation, mood, voice, tense; number, gender; punctuation; pointing 547 *punctuation*; syntax, word order, ellipsis, bad grammar 565 *solecism*; good grammar, grammaticalness, Standard English, good E.

part of speech, substantive, noun, common n., proper n., collective n.; pronoun; adjective; verb, reflexive v., transitive v., intransitive v.; adverb, preposition, conjunction, interjection; subject, object, direct o., indirect o.; predicate, copula, complement; article, definite a., indefinite a., particle, affix, suffix, infix, prefix; inflexion, case-ending; formative, morpheme, semanteme; diminutive, intensive, augmentative.

Adj. *grammatical*, correct; syntactic, inflectional; irregular, anomalous; masculine, feminine, neuter; singular, dual, plural; substantival, adjectival, attributive, predicative; verbal, adverbial; participial; prepositional; conjunctive; comparative, superlative.

565 Solecism

N. *solecism*, bad grammar, incorrectness, misusage; faulty syntax; barbarism 560 *neology*; malapropism, slip of the pen, slip of the tongue; mispronunciation, dropping one's aitches 580 *speech defect*; misspelling.

566 Style

N. *style*, fashion, mode, tone, manner, vein, strain, idiom; idiosyncrasy, mannerism 80 *speciality*; mode of expression, diction, phrasing, phraseology 563 *phrase*; idiolect, vocabulary; literary style, command of language *or* idiom, raciness, power 571 *vigour*; feeling for words; literary charm, grace 575 *elegance*; word

power; vernacular s. 573 *plainness*; elaborate style 574 *ornament*.

Adj. *stylistic*, mannered, literary; elegant, ornate, rhetorical; expressive, eloquent, fluent; racy, idiomatic; plain, perspicuous, forceful.

567 Perspicuity

N. *perspicuity*, perspicuousness, clearness, clarity, lucidity, limpidity 422 *transparency*; lucid prose 516 *intelligibility*; directness 573 *plainness*; definition, definiteness, exactness 494 *accuracy*.

568 Imperspicuity

N. *imperspicuity*, obscurity, obfuscation 517 *unintelligibility*; fogginess 423 *opacity*; abstraction, abstruseness; complexity, involved style 574 *ornament*; purple prose, hard words, Johnsonese 700 *difficulty*; imprecision, impreciseness, vagueness 474 *uncertainty*; inaccuracy 495 *inexactness*; ambiguity 518 *equivocalness*; mysteriousness 530 *enigma*; profundity 211 *depth*; ellipsis 569 *conciseness*; verbiage 570 *diffuseness*.

Adj. *unclear*, not transparent, muddied, clear as mud, cloudy 423 *opaque*; obscure 418 *dark*; mysterious, enigmatic 517 *unintelligible*; abstruse, profound 211 *deep*; allusive, indirect 523 *latent*; vague, imprecise, indefinite 474 *uncertain*; ambiguous 518 *equivocal*; muddled, confused, tortuous, convoluted, involved 61 *complex*; hard, Johnsonian 700 *difficult*.

569 Conciseness

N. *conciseness*, succinctness, brevity; pithiness 496 *maxim*; aphorism, epigram, clerihew 839 *witticism*; economy of words, terseness, words of one syllable, laconicism; compression, telegraphese; overconciseness; ellipsis, abbreviation, contraction 204 *shortening*; epitome, précis, outline, brief sketch 592 *compendium*; compactness, portmanteau word; clipped speech, monosyllabism 582 *taciturnity*; nutshell.

Adj. *concise*, brief, not long in telling, short and sweet 204 *short*; laconic, monosyllabic, sparing of words 582 *taciturn*; succinct; crisp, brisk, to the point; trenchant, mordant, incisive; terse, curt, brusque; condensed, tight-knit, compact; pithy, neat, exact, epigrammatic; elliptic, telegraphic, contracted, compressed; summary, cut short, abbreviated, truncated.

Vb. *be concise*, – brief etc. adj.; need few words, not beat about the bush, pull no punches, come straight to the point, cut the cackle, cut a long story short, get down to brass tacks, talk turkey; telescope, compress, condense, contract, abridge, abbreviate, truncate 204 *shorten*; summarize; be short with, be curt with, cut short, cut off; waste no words.

Adv. *concisely*, in brief, in short, in a word, in

a nutshell; to put it succinctly, to cut a long story short; to sum up.

570 Diffuseness

N. *diffuseness,* verboseness etc. adj.; profuseness, copiousness; amplification 197 *expansion;* expatiation, minuteness, blow-by-blow account; productivity 171 *productiveness;* inspiration, vein, flow, outpouring; abundance, superabundance, exuberance, redundancy 637 *redundance;* richness, verbosity, wordiness, verbiage; fluency, verbal diarrhoea 581 *loquacity;* long-windedness, prolixity, epic length; repetitiveness, reiteration 106 *repetition;* twice-told tale 838 *tedium;* gush, rigmarole, waffle, blah 515 *empty talk;* effusion, tirade, harangue, sermon, speeches 579 *oration;* superfluity, redundancy 637 *redundance;* tautology; circumlocution, periphrasis; beating about the bush 518 *equivocalness;* padding, filler 40 *extra;* digression 10 *irrelevance.*

Adj. *diffuse,* verbose, nonstop, in love with one's own voice 581 *loquacious;* profuse, copious, ample, rich; fertile, abundant, superabundant, voluminous, scribacious 171 *prolific;* fluent; exuberant, overflowing 637 *redundant;* expatiating, detailed, minute; gushing, effusive; windy, turgid, bombastic; polysyllabic, redundant, excessive, repetitious, repetitive; tautological; padded out.

prolix, long-winded, wordy, prosy; spun out, long-drawn-out; boring 838 *tedious;* lengthy, epic, never-ending, going on and on 203 *long;* discursive, digressing, episodic; rambling, wandering; loose-knit, incoherent; desultory, waffling, pointless 10 *irrelevant;* indirect, circumlocutory, periphrastic, round-about.

Vb. *be diffuse,* – prolix etc. adj.; expatiate, amplify, particularize, detail, go into detail, expand, enlarge upon; descant, discourse at length; repeat; pad out, draw o., spin o., protract 203 *lengthen;* gush, be effusive 350 *flow;* let oneself go, rant, rant and rave, harangue 579 *orate;* have swallowed the dictionary; launch out on, spin a long yarn 838 *be tedious;* blether on, rabbit on, go on and on 581 *be loquacious;* wander, waffle, digress 282 *deviate;* ramble, drivel, beat about the bush, not come to the point 518 *be equivocal.*

Adv. *diffusely,* on and on, ad nauseam.

571 Vigour

N. *vigour* 174 *vigorousness;* power, strength, vitality, drive, force, forcefulness, oomph, go, get-up-and-go 160 *energy;* vim, punch, pep, guts, smeddum; verve, élan, panache, vivacity, liveliness, gusto, pizzazz, raciness; spirit, fire, ardour, glow, warmth, fervour, vehemence, enthusi-

asm, passion 818 *feeling;* stress, underlining, emphasis 532 *affirmation;* gravity, weight; impressiveness; declamation 574 *grandiloquence;* rhetoric 579 *eloquence.*

Adj. *forceful,* powerful, strenuous 162 *strong;* energetic, peppy, zingy, punchy 174 *vigorous;* racy; bold, dashing, spirited, vivacious 819 *lively;* fiery, ardent, enthusiastic, impassioned 818 *fervent;* vehement, emphatic, insistent, positive 532 *affirmative;* grave, sententious, strongly-worded, pulling no punches 834 *serious;* heavy, meaty, solid; weighty, forcible, cogent 740 *compelling;* vivid, graphic, effective; inspired 579 *eloquent.*

572 Feebleness

N. *feebleness* 163 *weakness;* ineffectiveness, flatness, staleness, vapidity 387 *insipidity;* jejuneness, poverty, thinness; enervation, flaccidity; anticlimax.

Adj. *feeble,* weak, thin, flat, vapid, insipid 387 *tasteless;* wishy-washy, watery, wersh; sloppy, sentimental, schmaltzy, novelettish; meagre, jejune, exhausted, spent; wan, colourless, bald 573 *plain;* languid, flaccid, nerveless, emasculated; uninspired, unimpassioned; ineffective, prosaic, uninspiring; monotonous, pedestrian, dull, dry, boring 838 *tedious;* hackneyed, platitudinous, stale; inane, empty, pointless; juvenile, childish; limping; lame, unconvincing 477 *poorly reasoned;* limp, loose, lax, inexact; poor, trashy 847 *vulgar.*

573 Plainness

N. *plainness,* naturalness, simplicity 699 *artlessness;* austerity, severity, baldness, spareness, bareness, starkness; matter-of-factness, plain English 516 *intelligibility;* home truths 540 *veracity;* homespun, vernacular, common speech, vulgar parlance; unaffectedness 874 *modesty;* bluntness, frankness, speaking straight from the shoulder, mincing no words, coarseness, four-letter word.

Adj. *plain,* simple 699 *artless;* austere severe; bald, spare, stark, bare, unfussy, bog standard, no-frills, vanilla, without bells and whistles; neat 648 *clean;* pure, unadulterated 44 *unmixed;* unadorned, unvarnished, unembellished 540 *veracious;* played down; unassuming, unpretentious 874 *modest;* chaste, restrained; unaffected, honest, natural, straightforward; homely, homey, homespun; prosaic, sober 834 *serious;* workaday, everyday, commonplace 610 *usual;* uninspired.

Vb. *speak plainly,* call a spade a spade, use plain English 516 *be intelligible;* moderate one's language; say outright, tell it like it is, spell it out, tell one straight *or* to his *or* her face; not mince words, speak straight from the shoulder, not beat about the bush, come to the point, come down to brass tacks, talk turkey.

574 Ornament
N. *ornament*, embellishment, colour, decoration, embroidery, frills, flourish 844 *ornamentation*; floridness, floweriness, flowers of speech, arabesques 563 *phrase*; euphuism; preciousness, euphemism; rhetoric, purple patch *or* passage; figure of speech 519 *trope*; alliteration, assonance; paralipsis, aposiopesis; inversion, chiasmus; zeugma; metaphor, simile, antithesis.

grandiloquence, high tone 579 *eloquence*; declamation, rhetoric 571 *vigour*; overstatement, extravagance, hyperbole 546 *exaggeration*; turgidity; pretentiousness, affectation, pomposity 875 *ostentation*; talking big 877 *boasting*; highfalutin, bombast, rant 515 *empty talk*; Johnsonese, long words.

Adj. *ornate*, beautified; rich, luxuriant, florid, flowery; precious, euphuistic, euphemistic; pretentious 850 *affected*; meretricious, flashy, flamboyant, frothy 875 *showy*; alliterative 519 *figurative*; stiff, stilted; pedantic, long-worded, Latinate, Johnsonian.

Vb. *ornament*, beautify, grace, adorn, enrich, gild 844 *decorate*; charge, overlay; elaborate, smell of the lamp, overelaborate, overembellish, gild the lily.

575 Elegance
N. *elegance*, style, grace, gracefulness 841 *beauty*; refinement, taste 846 *good taste*; propriety; classicism; harmony, euphony, balance, proportion 245 *symmetry*; rhythm, ease, fluency, felicity, the right word in the right place, the mot juste; neatness, polish, finish; well-turned phrase; flourish.

Adj. *elegant*, majestic, stately 841 *beautiful*; graceful; stylish 846 *tasteful*; dignified; expressive; unaffected 573 *plain*; unlaboured, fluid, fluent, rhythmic, mellifluous, euphonious; harmonious, balanced, well-proportioned 245 *symmetrical*; neat, felicitous, happy, right, neatly put, well-turned; artistic; polished, finished, soigné; flawless 646 *perfect*; classic, classical, Attic, Ciceronian, Augustan.

576 Inelegance
N. *inelegance*, awkwardness, roughness, uncouthness 699 *artlessness*; coarseness 647 *imperfection*; harshness; stiltedness 326 *hardness*; unwieldiness; impropriety, barbarism; vulgarity 847 *bad taste*; artificiality 850 *affectation*; lack of style; anti-chic; turgidity, pomposity 574 *grandiloquence*.

Adj. *inelegant*, ungraceful, graceless 842 *ugly*;

unpolished, unrefined 647 *imperfect*; coarse, crude, barbarous 699 *artless*; tasteless 847 *vulgar*; meretricious; turgid; forced, laboured, artificial; jarring, grating; insensitive; harsh; halting, unfluent; clumsy, awkward, gauche; wooden, stiff, stilted 875 *formal*.

577 Voice
N. *voice*, vocal sound; speaking voice 579 *speech*; singing voice; tongue, vocal organs, vocal cords; lungs, bellows; larynx, voice box; phoneme, vowel, diphthong; open vowel, closed v., voiced consonant, syllable 398 *speech sound*; articulation; utterance, enunciation, delivery, articulation; exclamation, ejaculation, gasp; mutter, whisper, stage w., aside 401 *faintness*; tone of voice, accents, timbre, pitch, tone, intonation, modulation.

pronunciation, articulation, elocution, enunciation, inflection, accentuation, stress, emphasis; accent; broad accent; foreign a.; burr, brogue, drawl, twang 560 *dialect*; trill; aspiration, glottal stop; nasality; lisping, stammer 580 *speech defect*; mispronunciation 565 *solecism*.

Vb. *voice*, pronounce, verbalize, put into words 579 *speak*; mouth, give tongue, give voice, express, utter, enunciate, articulate; vocalize; inflect, modulate; breathe, aspirate, sound one's aitches; trill, roll, burr, roll one's r's; accent, stress 532 *emphasize*; raise the voice, lower the v., whisper, stage-w., make an aside, speak sotto voce; exclaim, ejaculate, rap out 408 *cry*; drone, intone, chant, warble, carol, hum 413 *sing*; bellow, shout, roar, vociferate, use one's voice 400 *be loud*; mispronounce, lisp, drawl, swallow one's consonants, speak thickly 580 *stammer*.

578 Voicelessness
N. *voicelessness*, no voice, loss of v.; difficulty in speaking, dysphonia, inarticulation; thick speech, hoarseness, huskiness, raucousness; muteness 399 *silence*; dumbness, mutism, deaf-m.; childish treble, falsetto; breaking voice; sob, sobbing; undertone, aside, low voice, muffled tones, whisper, bated breath 401 *faintness*; surd, unvoiced consonant; sign language, deaf and dumb language 547 *gesture*; meaningful look; body language, kinesics.

Adj. *voiceless*, aphonic, dysphonic; unvoiced, surd; breathed, whispered, muffled, low-voiced, inaudible 401 *muted*; mute, dumb, deaf and dumb; speechless, at a loss for words; inarticulate, tongue-tied; silent, mum 582 *taciturn*; silenced, gagged; croaking, hoarse as a raven 407 *hoarse*; breathless.

Vb. *be mute*, keep mum 582 *be taciturn*; be

silent, keep quiet, hold one's tongue 525 *keep secret*; bridle one's tongue, dry up, shut up, ring off, hang up; lose one's voice, be struck dumb, lose the power of speech; make sign language, exchange meaningful glances 547 *gesticulate*; have difficulty in speaking 580 *stammer*.

make mute, strike dumb, dumbfound, take one's breath away, rob one of words; stick in one's throat, choke on; muffle, hush, deaden 401 *mute*; shout down, make one inaudible, drown one's voice; muzzle, gag, stifle 165 *suppress*; stop one's mouth, reduce one to silence, shut one up, cut one short, hang up on; still, hush, put to silence 399 *silence*.

579 Speech

N. *speech*, faculty of s., gift of s., tongue, lips 577 *voice*; parlance 557 *language*; word of mouth, personal account 524 *report*; spoken word, accents, tones 559 *word*; discourse, colloquy, conversation, talk, chat, rap, palaver, prattle, chinwag 584 *interlocution*; address; fluency, talkativeness, volubility 581 *loquacity*; prolixity; elocution, voice production; articulation, utterance, delivery, enunciation 577 *pronunciation*; ventriloquism; sign language, eye l., meaningful glance *or* look 547 *gesture*; body language; speech, dictum, utterance, remark, observation, comment, interjection 532 *affirmation*; fine words 515 *empty talk*; spiel, patter 542 *trickery*.

oration, speech; one's say, a word in edgeways; public speech, formal s., discourse, disquisition, address, talk; welcoming address 876 *celebration*; panegyric, eulogy; valedictory, funeral oration 364 *obsequies*; after-dinner speech, toast, vote of thanks; broadcast, commentary 534 *lecture*; recitation, recital, reading; set speech, declamation; sermon, homily, exhortation; harangue, ranting, tub-thumping, tirade, diatribe, invective; monologue 585 *soliloquy*; written speech, dictation, paper, screed 591 *dissertation*; preamble, prologue, foreword, narration, account, digression, peroration.

oratory, art of speaking, rhetoric, public speaking, stump oratory, tub-thumping; speechmaking, speechifying; declamation, rhetoric, elocution, ranting, rant; vituperation, invective; soapbox; Hyde Park Corner.

eloquence, gift of the gab, fluency, articulacy; blarney; way with words, word power 566 *style*; power of speech; grandiloquence; elocution, good delivery; peroration, purple passage.

speaker, utterer; talker, prattler, gossiper 581 *chatterer*; conversationalist; speechifier, speechmaker, speech-writer, rhetorician, elocutionist; orator, public speaker, after-dinner s., toast-master *or* -mistress; improviser, adlibber; declaimer, ranter, soap-box orator, tubthumper, haranguer 738 *agitator*; lecturer; pulpiteer 537 *preacher*; presenter, announcer 531 *broadcaster*; narrator, chorus 594 *actor*; mouthpiece, spokesman *or* -woman, spokesperson 754 *delegate*; advocate, pleader, mediator 231 *intermediary*; salesman *or* -woman, salesperson, rep 793 *seller*; Cicero.

Adj. *speaking*, talking; with a tongue in one's head, vocal; bilingual, polyglot; articulate, fluent, talkative 581 *loquacious*; oral; well-spoken, soft-s.; audible, spoken, verbal; elocutionary.

eloquent, spellbinding, silver-tongued; smooth-t. 925 *flattering*; elocutionary, oratorical; grandiloquent, declamatory 571 *forceful*; tub-thumping, fire-and-brimstone, ranting, rousing 821 *exciting*.

Vb. *speak*, mention, say; utter, articulate 577 *voice*; pronounce, declare 532 *affirm*; let out, blurt out, come clean, tell all 526 *divulge*; whisper, breathe 524 *hint*; talk 584 *converse*; give utterance, deliver oneself of; break silence, open one's mouth *or* lips, find one's tongue; pipe up, speak up, raise one's voice; give tongue, rattle on, gossip, prattle, chatter, rap 581 *be loquacious*; patter, give a spiel, jabber, gabble; sound off, speak one's mind, tell a thing or two, have one's say, expatiate 570 *be diffuse*; trot out, reel off, recite; read, read aloud, read out, dictate; have a tongue in one's head, speak for oneself; use sign language 547 *gesticulate*.

orate, speechify; declaim, deliver a speech; hold forth, spout, be on one's hind legs; take the floor *or* the stand, rise to speak; preach, harangue; lecture, address 534 *teach*; perorate, mouth, rant, rail, sound off, tub-thump; spellbind, hold enthralled, be eloquent, have the gift of the gab, have kissed the Blarney Stone, 925 *flatter*; talk to oneself 585 *soliloquize*; speak off the top of one's head, ad-lib 609 *improvise*.

580 Speech defect

N. *speech defect*, aphasia, loss of speech, aphonia; paraphasia, paralalia; idiolalia; stammering, stammer, stutter, lallation, lisp; sigmatism 406 *sibilation*; dysphonia, speech impediment, hesitation, drawl, slur; indistinctness, inarticulateness, thick speech, cleft palate; burr, brogue 560 *dialect*; accent, twang, nasal t. 577 *pronunciation*; affectation, plum in one's mouth, marble in one's m., Oxford accent, haw-haw 246 *distortion*; speech therapy.

Vb. *stammer*, stutter, trip over one's tongue; drawl, hesitate, falter, quaver, hem and ha, hum and haw; um and ah, mumble, mutter; lisp; splutter; speak through the nose, drone;

clip one's words, swallow one's w., gabble, slur; mispronounce.

581 Loquacity

N. *loquacity*, loquaciousness, garrulity, talkativeness, communicativeness, yak, yacketyyack; volubility, runaway tongue, flow of words, fluency 570 *diffuseness*; verbosity, wordiness, prolixity; running on, spate of words, logorrhoea, verbal diarrhoea, inexhaustible vocabulary; patter, spiel, gab, gift of the g. 579 *eloquence*.

chatter, chattering, gossiping, gabble, jabber, rap, palaver, jaw-jaw, yackety-yack; clack, cackle, babble, prattle; small talk, gossip, idle g., tittle-tattle; waffle, blether, gush, guff, gas, hot air 515 *empty talk*.

chatterer, chatterbox; gossip, tittle-tattler 529 *news reporter*; haverer, ranter; preacher, sermonizer; windbag, gas-bag, conversationalist; chattering classes.

Adj. *loquacious*, talkative, garrulous, gossiping, tattling, tittle-tattling, yakking; communicative, rapping, chatty, gossipy, newsy 524 *informative*; gabbing, babbling, gabbling, gabby, gassy, windy, verbose, long-winded 570 *prolix*; nonstop, voluble, going on and on, fluent, glib; conversational.

Vb. *be loquacious*, – talkative etc. adj.; have a long tongue, chatter, rattle, go on and on, run on, bang on, reel off, talk nineteen to the dozen; gossip, tattle 584 *converse*; clack, gabble, jabber 515 *mean nothing*; talk, jaw, yak, go yackety-yack, gab, prate, gas, waffle, haver, blether, twitter, ramble on, rabbit on; rap; drone, drivel; launch into speech, start talking, give tongue, shoot; have one's say, talk at length; expatiate, spout 570 *be diffuse*; talk down; filibuster, stonewall; talk one's head off, talk the hind leg off a donkey; talk shop, bore 838 *be tedious*; engage in conversation, buttonhole; monopolize the conversation, hold the floor, not let one get a word in edgeways, never stop talking.

582 Taciturnity

N. *taciturnity*, incommunicativeness, reserve, reticence 525 *secrecy*; few words, brusqueness, curtness, gruffness 885 *rudeness*; muteness 578 *voicelessness*; economy of words; no orator; person of few words; clam; Trappist.

Adj. *taciturn*, mute, mum 399 *silent*; sparing of words, monosyllabic, short, curt, laconic, brusque, gruff 569 *concise*; not talking, incommunicative; withdrawn, reserved, keeping oneself to oneself, guarded, with sealed lips 525 *reticent*; close, tight-lipped; not to be drawn, keeping one's counsel, discreet 858 *cautious*; inarticulate, tongue-tied 578 *voiceless*.

Vb. *be taciturn*, – laconic etc. adj.; spare one's words 569 *be concise*; not talk, say nothing, have little to say; observe silence, make no answer; not be drawn, refuse comment, neither confirm nor deny; keep one's counsel 525 *keep secret*; hold one's tongue, put a bridle on one's t., keep one's mouth *or* one's trap shut; fall silent, relapse into s., pipe down, dry up 145 *cease*; be speechless, lose one's tongue 578 *be mute*; waste no words on, save one's breath to cool one's porridge; not mention, leave out, pass over, omit 458 *disregard*.

Int. hush! sh! shut up! mum's the word! no comment! a word to the wise!

583 Allocution

N. *allocution*, apostrophe; address, lecture, talk, speech, pep talk, sermon 579 *oration*; greeting, salutation; invocation, appeal, interjection, buttonholing, word in the ear, aside.

Vb. *speak to*, address, talk to, lecture to; turn to, direct one's words at, appeal to, pray to; sir; approach, accost; hail, call to, salute, say good morning 884 *greet*; pass the time of day, parley with 584 *converse*; take aside, buttonhole.

584 Interlocution

N. *interlocution*, parley, colloquy, converse, conversation, talk, chat, rap, cybertalk; dialogue, question and answer; exchange, repartee, banter, badinage; slanging match 709 *quarrel*; confab, social intercourse 882 *fellowship*; commerce, communion, communication, intercommunication 524 *information*; tête-à-tête.

chat, chinwag, natter; chit-chat, talk, small t., rap; gossip; tattle, tittle-tattle, tongue-wagging 581 *chatter*; fireside chat, cosy chat, tête-à-tête, heart-to-heart.

conference, colloquy, talks, parley, pow-wow; discussion, debate, forum, focus group, quality circle, symposium, seminar, teach-in, talk-in, controversy; exchange of views, high-level talks, summit meeting, summit conference, summit; negotiations, bargaining 765 *treaty*; conclave, convention, meeting, gathering 74 *assembly*; working lunch; reception 882 *social gathering*; audience, interview; consultation, huddle, council, war c., family c., round-table conference 691 *advice*.

Vb. *converse*, parley, talk together (**see** *confer*); pass the time of day, exchange pleasantries; draw one out; buttonhole, engage in conversation, carry on a c., join in a c., butt in, put in a word, bandy words, exchange w.; chat, have a chat *or* a natter *or* a good talk; be drawn out 579 *speak*; natter, chinwag, chew the fat, rap, gossip, tattle 581 *be loquacious*; commune with; be closeted with; whisper together, talk tête-à-tête, go into a huddle, indulge in pillow talk.

confer, talk it over, sit in council *or* in conclave, sit in committee, hold a council of war, pow-wow; discuss, debate 475 *argue*; parley, negotiate, hold talks, hold a summit, get round the table; consult with 691 *consult*.

585 Soliloquy

N. *soliloquy*, monologue; stream of consciousness; apostrophe; aside; one-man *or* one-woman show.

Vb. *soliloquize*, say to oneself, make an aside, think aloud; apostrophize; talk to the wall, address an empty house, have an audience of one.

586 Writing

N. *writing*, creative w., literary composition, authorship, journalism 590 *description*; literary output 557 *literature*; script, copy, works, books 589 *reading matter*; pen-pushing, hackwork, Grub Street; paperwork 548 *record*; copying, transcribing, transcription, rewriting, editing; holography; handwriting; longhand, shorthand, stenography; speedwriting, typewriting, typing 587 *print*; braille; cipher, code 530 *secret*; hieroglyphics; sign-writing, skywriting 528 *advertisement*; inscribing, carving; graphology.

lettering, stroke of the pen, up-stroke, down-s.; line, dot, point; flourish, scroll; handwriting; calligraphy, penmanship; fair hand; script, italic, copperplate; printing, block letters; scribble, scrawl; letters, characters, alphabet 558 *letter*; runes, pictogram, hieroglyph; palaeography.

script, written matter, illuminated address; calligraph; writing, screed, scrawl, scribble; manuscript, MS; original, one's own hand, autograph, holograph; signature; copy, transcript, transcription, fair copy 22 *duplicate*; typescript, stencil; newsprint; printed matter; letter, epistle, written reply 588 *correspondence*; inscription, graffito 548 *record*; superscription, caption, heading; illuminated letters.

stationery, writing materials, pen and paper, pen and ink; pen, quill-p., fountain p., cartridge p., felt-tip p., ballpoint p., Biro (tdmk); nib; stylo; pencil, propelling p., lead p., coloured p.; crayon, chalk; papyrus, parchment, vellum; foolscap 631 *paper*; writing paper, notepaper, lined p., blank p., notebook, pad, jotter; slate, blackboard; inkstand, inkwell; pencil sharpener, penknife; blotting paper, blotter; typewriter, ribbon, daisy wheel; stencil.

stenographer, shorthand writer, typist, shorthand t., stenotypist, audiotypist, secretary, personal s., personal assistant, PA, Girl Friday.

Adj. *written*, inscribed, in black and white; in writing, in longhand, in shorthand; handwritten, manuscript, signed; penned, pencilled, scrawled, scribbled etc. vb.; copybook, copperplate; italic, calligraphic; hieroglyphic, lettered, alphabetic; runic, roman, italic 558 *literal*; upright, sloping, bold, spidery.

Vb. *write*, form characters, inscribe; letter, block, print; write well; write badly, scribble, scrawl; put in writing, confirm in writing, set down in black and white, commit to paper, write down, jot d., note 548 *record*; transcribe, copy out, make a fair copy, rewrite, write out; take down, take dictation, take down in shorthand, type, key; take down longhand, write in full; draft; compose; pen, pencil, dash off; write letters 588 *correspond*; write one's name 547 *sign*; take pen in hand, put pen to paper; be an author.

587 Print

N. *print*, printing, laser p., typing, typewriting 586 *writing*; typography, lithography, litho, photolithography, photolitho 555 *printing*; photocopying 551 *photography*; photocomposition, phototypesetting, computer typesetting, cold type; composition, typesetting, make-up; monotype, linotype, stereotype, electrotype; impression, printout; proof, galley p., bromide, page proof, revise; proofcopy.

print-type, type, stereotype, plate; flong, matrix; broken type, pie; upper case, lower c., capitals, small c., caps; fount, face, typeface, boldface, bold, clarendon, lightface, old face, bastard type; roman, italic, Gothic, black letter 558 *letter*; body, bevel, shoulder, shank, beard, ascender, descender, serif, sanserif; lead, rule, en, em; space, hairspace, quad; type bar, slug, logotype.

press, printing p., printing works, printers; composing room; machining r.; handpress, flatbed, platen press, rotary press, Linotype (tdmk), Monotype (tdmk), offset press.

Adj. *printed*, in print 528 *published*; cold-type, hot-metal; set, composed, machined etc. vb.; in type, in italic, in bold, in roman; typographic; leaded, spaced, justified; solid, tight, crowded.

Vb. *print*, stamp; typeset, key, compose, photocompose; align, register, justify; set up in type, make ready, impose, machine, run off, pull off, print off; collate, foliate; paginate, lithograph, litho, offset, stereotype; put to bed; proofread; bring out 528 *publish*.

588 Correspondence

N. *correspondence*, barrage of c., exchange of letters, backlog of correspondence; communication 524 *information*; mailing list, distribution

1.; letters, mail, post, postbag 531 *postal communications*; letter, epistle, missive, dispatch, bulletin; love letter, billet doux, greetings card, Christmas c., Easter c., birthday c., Valentine 889 *endearment*; postcard, pc, picture p., card, letter c., notelet; air letter, aerogramme, air mail, sea m.; business letter, bill, account, enclosure; open letter 528 *publicity*; unsolicited mail, junk m., circular, round robin, chain letter, begging 1.; note, line, chit; answer, acknowledgment; envelope, cover, stamp, seal; postcode.

correspondent, letter writer, penfriend, penpal, poison pen; foreign correspondent, contributor 529 *news reporter*.

Vb. *correspond*, correspond with, exchange letters, maintain *or* keep up a correspondence, keep in touch with 524 *communicate*; write to, send a letter to, drop a line; report 524 *inform*; deal with one's correspondence, catch up on one's c., acknowledge, reply, write back, reply by return 460 *answer*; circularize 528 *publish*.

589 Book

N. *book*, title, volume, tome, roll, scroll, document; codex, manuscript, MS; script, typescript; published work, publication, best-seller, potboiler, blockbuster; sleeper, remainder; standard work, classic, definitive work, collected works; major work, monumental w., magnum opus; slim volume; booklet; illustrated work, picture book, coffee-table b. 553 *picture*; magazine, periodical, rag 528 *journal*; brochure, pamphlet, leaflet 528 *the press*; bound book, cased book, hardback, softback, limpback, paperback (**see** *edition*).

reading matter, printed word, written w. 586 *writing*; forms, papers, bumf, literature, 548 *record*; circular, junk mail; script, copy; text, the words, libretto, lyrics, scenario, screenplay, book of words; proof, revise, pull; writings, prose literature 593 *prose*; poetical literature 593 *poetry*; classical literature, serious 1., light 1. 557 *literature*; books for children, children's books, juveniles; history, biography, travel 590 *description*; work of fiction 590 *novel*; biographical work, memoirs, memorabilia 590 *biography*; addresses, speeches 579 *oration*; essay, tract, treatise 591 *dissertation*; piece, occasional pieces 591 *article*; miscellanea, marginalia, jottings, thoughts, pensées; poetical works 593 *poem*; selections, flowers 592 *anthology*; dedicatory volume, Festschrift; early works, juvenilia; posthumous works, literary remains; complete works, oeuvre, corpus; newspaper, magazine 528 *journal*; issue, number, back n.; fascicle, part, instalment, serial, sequel, prequel.

reference book, encyclopaedia, cyclopaedia 490

erudition; lexicon, thesaurus 559 *dictionary*; biographical dictionary, dictionary of quotations, rhyming dictionary, dictionary of reverse words, technical dictionary, gazetteer, yearbook, annual 87 *directory*; calendar 117 *chronology*; guide 524 *guidebook*; notebook, diary, album 548 *record*; bibliography, reading list.

edition, impression, issue, run; series, set, collection, library; bound edition, library e., de luxe e., school e., trade e., standard e., definitive e., omnibus e., complete e., collected e., complete works; first edition, new e., revised e.; reissue, reprint; illustrated edition, special e., limited e., expurgated e.; critical e., annotated e., variorum e.; adaptation, abridgment 592 *compendium*; quarto, folio; layout, format; house style; front matter, prelims, preface, prefatory note; dedication, acknowledgments; title, half-t.; flyleaf, title page, endpaper, colophon 547 *label*; contents, errata, corrigenda, addenda; back matter, appendix, supplement, index, thumb i., bibliography; caption, heading, headline, running h.; footnote; guide word, catchword; margin; gutter; folio, page, leaf, recto, verso; sheet, forme, signature; chapter, section; inset; plate, print, illustration, halftone, line drawing 553 *picture*.

bookbinding, binding, spiral b., perfect b., stitching, casing; case, slip c., cover, jacket, dust j. 226 *wrapping*; boards 631 *paper*; cloth, limp c., linen, scrim, buckram, leather, pigskin, calf, morocco, vellum, parchment; spine, headband; tooling, gilding, marbling.

library, national library, public 1., local 1., reference 1., mobile 1., lending 1., circulating 1.

bookperson, man *or* woman of letters, bluestocking; reader, bookworm 492 *scholar*; bibliophile, book lover, book collector, bibliographer; librarian; stationer, bookseller, antiquarian b., secondhand b., publisher; editor, book reviewer, critic, reviewer 480 *estimator*.

author, authoress, writer, creative w., wordsmith; man *or* woman of letters; fiction-writer, novelist, crime writer, historian, biographer, essayist 591 *dissertator*; prose writer; verse writer 593 *poet*; playwright, librettist, script writer 594 *dramatist*; freelance; copywriter 528 *publicizer*; pressman *or* -woman, journalist 529 *news reporter*; editor; subeditor, copy editor, contributor, correspondent, special c., war c., sports c., columnist, gossip writer, diarist; agony aunt; scribbler, penpusher, hack, Grub Street h.; ghost writer.

590 Description

N. *description*, account, detailed a.; statement, exposé, summary 524 *report*; brief, abstract, inscription, caption, subtitle, legend 592 *com-*

pendium; narration, relation, recital, version (**see** *narrative*); documentary account; specification, characterization, details, particulars 87 *list*; portrayal, delineation, depiction; portrait, word p., sketch, character s., profile; case history 548 *record*; faction, documentary drama, docudrama; picture, true p., realism; travelogue 524 *guidebook*; vignette, cameo, thumbnail sketch, outline; idyll, parody 851 *satire*; epitaph 364 *obsequies*.

narrative, storyline, plot, subplot, scenario 594 *stage play*; episode 154 *event*; dénouement 725 *completion*; dramatic irony, comic relief; catharsis; stream of consciousness; fantasia 513 *fantasy*; fiction, faction, story, tale, romance, fairytale, folk tale; tradition, legend, myth, saga, river s., soap opera, serial, epic; ballad 593 *poem*; allegory, parable, cautionary tale; yarn 543 *fable*; anecdote, reminiscence 505 *remembrance*; annals, chronicle, history, historiography 548 *record*.

biography, real-life story, human interest; life, curriculum vitae, cv, biodata, life story *or* history; experiences, adventures, fortunes; hagiology, hagiography, martyrology; obituary, obit; autobiography, confessions, memoirs 505 *remembrance*; diary, journals 548 *record*; letters 588 *correspondence*.

novel, fiction; roman fleuve; anti-novel, metafiction; historical novel, novelization; short story, novelette, novella; light reading, bedside r. 589 *reading matter*; romance, love story, fairy s., adventure s., Western, science fiction, sci-fi, cyberpunk; gothic novel, ghost story; picaresque novel; crime story, detective s., spy s., whodunit, whydunit; cliffhanger, thriller, horror story, shocker, bodice ripper, penny dreadful, horror comic; sex-and-shopping novel; Aga saga; paperback, pulp literature, airport fiction; potboiler, trash; popular novel, blockbuster, best-seller 589 *book*.

Adj. *descriptive*, graphic, colourful, vivid; well-drawn, sharp; true-to-life, realistic, real-life, photographic, impressionistic, evocative, emotive, full, detailed 570 *diffuse*; documentary.

Vb. *describe*, delineate, draw, picture, depict, paint 551 *represent*; evoke, bring to life, capture; characterize, detail; sketch 233 *outline*; relate, recount, recite, report, give an account 524 *communicate*; write, write about 548 *record*; narrate, tell, spin a yarn, unfold a tale; make a story out of; recapitulate 106 *repeat*; reminisce, relive the past 505 *retrospect*.

591 Dissertation

N. *dissertation*, treatise, tract, exposition, summary 592 *compendium*; theme, thesis 475 *argu-*

ment; disquisition, essay, examination, survey 459 *enquiry*; discourse, discussion; paper, monograph, study; homily, sermon 534 *lecture*, commentary.

article, news a., column; leader, editorial; essay; literary composition; comment, review, rave r., notice, critique, criticism, write-up 480 *estimate*.

dissertator, essayist; pamphleteer, publicist 528 *publicizer*; editor, leader writer, writer, contributor 589 *author*; reviewer, critic, commentator, pundit 520 *interpreter*.

Vb. *dissertate*, treat, handle, write about, deal with; discourse upon 475 *argue*; develop a thesis; go into, go into in depth, conduct an in-depth-enquiry, survey; set out, discuss, ventilate, air one's views; criticize, comment upon; write an essay, write a treatise, do a paper, write an article, do a piece; annotate, commentate 520 *interpret*.

592 Compendium

N. *compendium*, epitome, resumé, summary, brief; contents, heads, analysis; abstract, sum and substance, gist, drift; consolidation, digest, pandect; multum in parvo, précis; aperçu, conspectus, synopsis, bird's-eye view, survey; review, recapitulation, recap; rundown, runthrough; draft, minute, note 548 *record*; sketch, thumbnail s., outline, brief o., skeleton; blueprint 623 *plan*; syllabus, prospectus, brochure 87 *list*; abridgment, abbreviation, concise version 204 *shortening*; contraction, compression 569 *conciseness*.

anthology, treasury, flowers, gems; selections, extracts 589 *textbook*; collection, compilation, miscellany; ephemera; gleanings; cuttings, album, scrapbook, sketchbook, commonplace book.

Vb. *abstract*, sum up, resume, summarize, run over; epitomize, make a synopsis of, reduce, abbreviate, abridge 204 *shorten*; capsulize, encapsulate; docket 548 *record*; condense, pot, give an out-line 569 *be concise*; compile 87 *list*; collect 74 *bring together*; conflate 50 *combine*; excerpt, select; sketch out 233 *outline*.

593 Poetry. Prose

N. *poetry*, poesy, balladry; versification (**see** *prosody*); poetic art, poetics; verse, rhyme; poetic licence; poetic inspiration, muse, Muses.

poem, versification, piece of verse, lines, verses, stanzas, strains; narrative verse, heroic poem, epic, dramatic poem, dramatic monologue, verse drama; light verse, lyric verse; comic verse, nonsense v., limerick; ode; dirge, elegy; idyll; occasional poem; song, shanty, lay, ballad 412 *vocal music*; war-song, marching song; love song, drinking s., collected poems 592 *anthology*; cycle, sequence.

doggerel, jingle, ditty, nursery rhyme; nonsense verse, comic v.; clerihew, limerick; burlesque.

verse form, sonnet, sestet, Petrarchan *or* Italian sonnet, Shakespearean *or* English s.; ballade, rondeau, virelay, triolet, villanelle, bouts rimés; burden, refrain, envoi; couplet, distich, sloka; haiku, tanka; triplet, tercet, terza rima, quatrain, ghazal; sestina, rhyme royal, ottava rima, Spenserian stanza; accentual verse, syllabic v., metrical v., blank v.; concrete poetry; Sapphics, Alcaics; limping iambics, scazon; free v., vers libre; verse, versicle, stanza, stave, laisse, strophe, antistrophe; stichomythia; broken line, half l., hemistich. See *prosody*.

prosody, versification, metre; scansion; rhyme, masculine r., feminine r., internal r., eye r.; rhyme scheme; assonance, alliteration; cadence, rhythm; metrical unit, foot; iamb, trochee, spondee, pyrrhic; dactyl, anapaest; tetrameter, pentameter, hexameter, heptameter, octameter; iambic pentameters, blank verse; alexandrine, heroic couplet; beat, stress, accent; elision; caesura.

poet, poet laureate; Lake poet, Georgian p., Metaphysical p., beat p., modern p.; versemonger, poetaster; versifier, rhymer, bard, minstrel, balladeer, troubadour, Meistersinger, epic poet, lyric p., dramatic p., elegiac p.; sonneteer, ballad-monger; songwriter, librettist.

prose, prose poem; piece of prose, prose composition, prosaicness, prose-writing, everyday language 573 *plainness*; prose writer 589 *author*.

Adj. *poetic*, poetical; Parnassian, satiric; elegiac, lyrical, lyric, rhyming, jingling, etc. vb.; doggerel, prosodic, metrical, measured, rhythmic, scanning; iambic.

prosaic, pedestrian, uninspired, unpoetical, in prose, matter-of-fact 573 *plain*.

Vb. *poetize*, scan; rhyme; versify, put into verse; write poetry, compose an epic, write a lyric, write a sonnet; make up a limerick; celebrate in verse; lampoon 851 *satirize*.

594 Drama. Ballet

N. *drama*, the theatre, the stage, the boards, the footlights; theatreland, Broadway, West End; silver screen, Hollywood 445 *cinema*; show business, show biz, dramatic entertainment, straight drama, legitimate theatre, live t.; intimate t., theatre in the round, total theatre, alternative t., street t., the Fringe, off-off-Broadway; repertory, rep; theatricals, amateur dramatics, dressing-up; masque, charade, dumb show, puppetry, tableau, t. vivant 551 *represen-*

tation; tragic mask, comic m., sock, buskin; Thespis.

dramaturgy, dramatic form 590 *narrative*; dramatic unities; dramatization, theatricals, dramatics; melodramatics, histrionics; theatricality, staginess; good theatre, bad t., good cinema, good television; play writing, script w., libretto w.; stagecraft; action, plot, subplot 590 *narrative*; characterization 551 *representation*; production, new p.; revival; auditions, casting; walkthrough, rehearsal, dress r.; direction, stage management; continuity; staging, stage directions; choreography; dialogue, soliloquy, stage whisper, aside, cue; entrance, exit (**see** *acting*); rising of the curtain, prologue, chorus; act, scene, opening s., coup de théâtre, deus ex machina, alarums and excursions; curtain, drop of the c., blackout; finale, final curtain, epilogue; curtain call, encore; interval, intermission, break; enactment, performance, command p., première, preview, first night, gala n.; matinée, first house, second h.; one-night stand, road show; sell-out, hit, smash h., box-office h., long run; flop.

stage play, play, drama, work; show, libretto, scenario, script, text, prompt book; part, lines 579 *speech*; dramatic representation 551 *representation*; five-act play, one-act p., playlet; sketch, skit; double bill; curtain-raiser, monologue, duologue, two-hander; masque, mystery play, miracle play, morality p., passion p., Oberammergau; commedia dell'arte; No, Kabuki; Greek drama, trilogy, tetralogy, cycle; poetic drama, verse d.; melodrama, gothic drama, blood and thunder; tragedy; tragicomedy, comedy, comedy of manners, Restoration comedy; situation comedy, sit-com; kitchen-sink drama, theatre of the absurd, t. of cruelty; black comedy, farce, slapstick, burlesque 849 *ridiculousness*; pantomime, panto, musical comedy, musical, light opera, comic o., grand opera 412 *vocal music*; television play 531 *broadcast*; screenplay 445 *cinema*; mime, puppet show, Punch and Judy show.

stage show 445 *spectacle*; live show; ice show, circus 837 *amusement*; variety, music hall, vaudeville; review, revue, intimate r., late-night r.; Follies, leg show, strip s.; floor show, cabaret; song and dance, act, turn; star turn; tableau.

ballet, dance, ballet dancing 837 *dancing*; choreography; classical ballet, modern dance; toe dance 837 *dance*; solo, pas seul, pas de deux; chassé, glissade; arabesque; fouetté, plié, pirouette 315 *rotation*; pas de chat, entrechat, jeté 312 *leap*.

stage set, set, setting, décor, scenery, scene 445 *spectacle*; drop curtain, backdrop, backcloth; screen, wings; background, foreground, front stage, upstage, down stage, stage, boards; apron, proscenium, proscenium arch, apron stage, picture-frame stage; stage in the round, curtain; prompt box (**see** *theatre*); properties, props, costume; make-up, grease-paint.

theatre, amphitheatre, stadium 724 *arena*; circus, hippodrome; fleapit, picture house, movie theatre 445 *cinema*; theatre in the round, open-air t.; pavilion; big top; playhouse, opera house, music hall, vaudeville theatre, variety t.; night club, cabaret; stage, boards, proscenium, wings, flies; dressing room, green r.; footlights, spotlight, limelight, houselights; auditorium, orchestra; seating, stalls, front s., back s., orchestra s., front rows; pit, box, circle, dress c., upper c., gallery, balcony, gods; front of house, foyer, box office, stage door.

acting, impersonation; interpretation, improvisation, pantomime, miming, taking off 20 *mimicry*; histrionics, play-acting, the Method; hamming, barn-storming; overacting, camping it up, staginess, theatricality; repertoire; character, personage, role; leading role; part, fat p.; vignette, cameo; supporting part, bit p.; speaking p.; walk-on p.; stock part, stereotype, ingenue, heavy father, injured husband, merry widow, stage villain. stage Irishman; principal boy *or* girl; Harlequin, Columbine, Pierrot, pantomime dame; hero, heroine, antihero; stage fever; stage fright, first-night nerves.

actor, actress, Thespian, luvvy, mimic, mime 20 *imitator*; mummer, play-actor, player, strolling p., trouper, ham; rep player, character actor; actor-manager, star, star of stage and screen, film star, starlet, tragedian, tragedienne; comedian, comedienne, comedy actor *or* actress; opera singer, prima donna, diva; ballet dancer, ballerina, prima b., protagonist, lead, leading man, leading lady, juvenile lead, understudy, stand-in, body double; extra, bit player; chorus, gentlemen *or* ladies of the chorus; corps de ballet, troupe, company, repertory c., dramatis personae, characters, cast.

entertainer, performer, artiste, artist, drag a., striptease a.; impressionist, impersonator,

female i.; troubadour, minstrel; busker; crooner, pop singer 413 *vocalist*; comic, stand-up c., comedian, comedienne 839 *humorist*; ventriloquist, fire-eater, juggler; ropewalker, acrobat 162 *athlete*; clown; pierrot, Punch, hoofer, dancer, show girl, chorus g., cancan dancer, belly d., gogo d.; dancing girl.

stage manager, producer, director, actor manager, business m., press agent *or* officer; impresario, showman; backer, sponsor, angel.

dramatist, playwright, scenario writer; script w., librettist; choreographer.

playgoer, theatregoer, operagoer; film fan, opera buff, balletomane 504 *enthusiast*; first-nighter; stage-door Johnny; audience, house, packed h., full h., sell-out; stalls, pit, gods, gallery; dramatic critic, play *or* film reviewer.

Adj. *dramatic*, theatrical, stagy; operatic, balletic, Terpsichorean, choreographic; live, legitimate; Thespian; histrionic, camp; tragic, comic, tragicomic; farcical, burlesque, knockabout, slapstick 849 *funny*; melodramatic, sensational, horrific, blood and thunder 821 *exciting*; avant-garde; released, showing, running 522 *shown*; dramatized; camped up; barnstorming; on the stage; stagestruck, film-struck.

Vb. *dramatize*, write plays, write for the stage; make a play of, adapt for the stage *or* for radio; stage, mount, produce, direct, stage-manage; cast; star, feature; present, put on, release 522 *show*; open, raise *or* ring up the curtain.

act, go on the stage, tread the boards; face the cameras; perform, enact, play, playact, do a play; impersonate; take the part; mime, take off 20 *imitate*; create a role, play a part, play the lead; play opposite, support; star, co-star, get one's name in lights, steal the show, upstage, take all the limelight; play to the gallery, ham, camp it up, send up, barnstorm, overact 546 *exaggerate*; underact, throw away; walk on; understudy, stand in 150 *substitute*; rehearse, say one's lines, cue in; fluff, forget one's lines, dry; ad-lib, gag; take a curtain call, do an encore, receive a standing ovation.

Volition: the exercise of the will

5.1
Individual Volition

SECTION ONE

Volition in general

595 Will

N. *will*, volition; disposition, inclination, mind, cast of mind, fancy, preference 597 *willingness*; act of will; strength of will, willpower, determination, firmness of purpose, 599 *resolution*; self-control 942 *temperance*; purpose 617 *intention*; decision 608 *predetermination*; one's own sweet will 932 *selfishness*; iron will, wilfulness 602 *obstinacy*; whimsicality 604 *caprice*; free will, self-determination 744 *independence*; free choice, option, discretion 605 *choice*; voluntariness, spontaneousness, spontaneity 597 *voluntary work*.

Adj. *volitional*, willing; unprompted, unasked, unbidden, freewill, spontaneous, original 597 *voluntary*; discretionary, optional; self-willed, iron-willed, wayward, wilful 602 *obstinate*; arbitrary, autocratic, dictatorial 735 *authoritarian*; independent; determined, hell-bent 599 *resolute*; intentional, willed, intended 608 *predetermined*.

Vb. *will*, exercise the will; impose one's will, have one's way, have it all one's own w. 737 *command*; do what one chooses, do as one likes 744 *be free*; be so minded, have a mind to, see fit, think f., think best 605 *choose*; determine 617 *intend*; wish 859 *desire*; have a mind of one's own, be independent, go one's own way, do as one chooses, be one's own man *or* woman; exercise one's discretion, judge for oneself 480 *judge*; take the responsibility, take it upon oneself; be hell-bent on, take the law into one's own hands, take the bit between one's teeth 602 *be obstinate*; know one's own mind 599 *be resolute*; volunteer, offer, do of one's own accord, do without prompting 597 *be willing*.

596 Necessity

N. *necessity*, stern n., no alternative, no escape, no option, zero o., Hobson's choice 606 *no choice*; last shift, last resort 700 *predicament*; inevitability, the inevitable, inescapability, sure thing, what must be 155 *destiny*; determinism, fatalism 608 *predetermination*; pressure of events, pressure of work, force of circumstances, c. beyond one's control, act of God, fatality 154 *event*; no freedom 745 *subjection*; law of nature; superior force 740 *compulsion*; logical necessity, necessary conclusion, proof 478 *demonstration*; force of law 953 *law*; obligation, conscience 917 *duty*; indispensability, sine qua non, a necessity, a must, matter of life and death 627 *requirement*; want, lack 801 *poverty*; involuntariness, reflex action; instinct, impulse, blind i. 476 *intuition*.

fate, inexorable f., lot, portion; weird, karma, kismet; doom, die, predestination, destiny; book of fate, God's will, will of Allah; fortune, wheel of f., 159 *chance*; stars, planets, astral influence; Dame Fortune, the Fates; Destinies; Weird S., Lachesis, Clotho, Atropos.

Adj. *necessary*, indispensable, essential, vital, important, requisite 627 *required*; imperative; overriding, irresistible; compulsory, mandatory, binding 917 *obligatory*; necessitated, inevitable, unavoidable, inescapable, inexorable, life-and-death 473 *certain*; sure thing, leaving no choice, deterministic.

involuntary, instinctive 476 *intuitive*; unpremeditated, unintended 618 *unintentional*; unconscious, subliminal, unthinking, gut, unwitting, blind, impulsive 609 *spontaneous*; under a spell 983 *bewitched*; conditioned, reflex, automatic, mechanical.

fated, karmic, fatal; predestined, preordained 608 *predetermined*; doomed, precondemned 961 *condemned*.

Vb. *be forced*, compelled etc. adj.; incur the necessity; submit to the n. 721 *submit*; be fated, bow to fate, dree one's weird; be cornered, be driven into a corner, be pushed to the wall 700 *be in difficulty*; be faced with a sine qua non, have no choice, have no option, have zero o., needs must; make a virtue of necessity; be unable to help it.

necessitate, dictate, impose, oblige 740 *compel*; bind by fate, destine, doom, foredoom, predetermine 155 *predestine*; brook no denial, not take no for an answer; leave no choice, face with a sine qua non, impose the necessity, drive into a corner, bulldoze; demand 627 *require*.

597 Willingness

N. *willingness*, voluntariness, volunteering; spontaneousness 609 *spontaneity*; free choice, option 605 *choice*; disposition; inclination, fancy, leaning, bent, bias, penchant, propensity 179 *tendency*; facility 694 *aptitude*; predisposition, readiness, right mood, receptive frame of mind; acquiescence 488 *assent*; compliance 758 *consent*; cheerful consent, alacrity, gameness, eagerness, enthusiasm; initiative, impatience, over-eagerness; dedication, sacrifice 931 *disinterestedness*; helpfulness 706 *cooperation*; loyalty 739 *obedience*; pliancy, putty in one's hands, docility, tractability 612 *persuadability*; submissiveness 721 *submission*; obsequiousness 879 *servility*.

voluntary work, voluntary service 901 *philanthropy*; honorary employment, unpaid labour, labour of love, self-appointed task.

volunteer, unpaid worker, willing horse; no slouch; do-gooder 901 *philanthropist*.

Adj. *willing*, ungrudging, acquiescent 488 *assenting*; compliant, game for; in the mood, feeling like, receptive, inclined, disposed, well-d., predisposed, amenable; cordial; happy, pleased, glad, delighted; ready 669 *prepared*; ready and willing, prompt, quick 678 *active*; forward; eager, enthusiastic, dedicated, overeager, impatient, raring to go; doing one's best; helpful 706 *cooperative*; docile, biddable, easy-going 24 *agreeing*; submissive 721 *submitting*; obsequious 879 *servile*; desirous, dying to.

voluntary, unprompted, unsought, unasked, unbidden 609 *spontaneous*; unsolicited, uncalled for, self-imposed; beyond the call of duty; discretionary, optional 605 *chosen*; volunteering, on one's own initiative, off one's own bat, of one's own free will; gratuitous, honorary, unpaid 812 *uncharged*.

Vb. *be willing*, – ready etc. adj.; have half a mind to; feel like, have a fancy to, have a good mind to 595 *will*; agree, acquiesce 488 *assent*; show willing, be ready and waiting, comply 758 *consent*; be found willing 739 *obey*; try, do one's best 671 *attempt*; go out of one's way to, lean over backwards; collaborate 706 *cooperate*; meet halfway; jump at, leap at; can't wait, be burning

to, be thrilled at the idea; not hesitate; volunteer, sacrifice oneself 759 *offer oneself*.

Adv. *willingly*, with a will, with relish, cordially; voluntarily, spontaneously, without being asked; like a shot, at the drop of a hat; with open arms, with all one's heart, heart and soul, with a good grace, without demur, nothing loath; gladly, with pleasure.

598 Unwillingness

N. *unwillingness*, disinclination, reluctance; disagreement 489 *dissent*; demur, objection 468 *qualification*; protest 762 *deprecation*; recalcitrance 704 *opposition*; rejection 760 *refusal*; unhelpfulness, noncooperation 702 *hindrance*; dissociation; faintheartedness, lack of zeal 860 *indifference*; backwardness 278 *slowness*; hesitation 858 *caution*; scruple, repugnance 861 *dislike*; recoil, aversion; bashfulness 874 *modesty*; noncompliance 738 *disobedience*; refractoriness; grudging service; unreliability 474 *uncertainty*; shelving, postponement, procrastination, laziness 679 *sluggishness*; neglect, remissness 458 *negligence*.

Adj. *unwilling*, indisposed, loath, reluctant, averse; not prepared, not so minded, not in the mood, not feeling like; unconsenting, opposed; demurring; regretful, with regret 830 *regretting*; hesitant 858 *cautious*; shy, bashful 874 *modest*; unenthusiastic, half-hearted, lukewarm; backward; uncooperative; recalcitrant; perfunctory, remiss 458 *negligent*; grudging; unspontaneous, forced, begrudged, with bad grace.

Vb. *be unwilling*, – reluctant etc. adj.; not have the heart to, not stomach 861 *dislike*; disagree, boggle, scruple 489 *dissent*; object, demur, protest 762 *deprecate*; resist 704 *oppose*; reject, give the thumbs down, give the red light 760 *refuse*; recoil, blench, fight shy, duck, shirk 620 *avoid*; drag one's feet, hold back, hesitate, tread warily, hang fire, go slow 278 *move slowly*; not play ball, abstain 702 *obstruct*; grudge, begrudge, turn up one's nose; force o.; have regrets 830 *regret*; tear oneself away 296 *depart*.

599 Resolution

N. *resolution*, sticking point, resoluteness, determination, grim d.; zeal, ardour, earnestness, seriousness; resolve, mind made up, decision 608 *predetermination*; drive, vigour 174 *vigorousness*; energy; concentration, iron will, willpower 595 *will*; strength of character, self-control, self-restraint, self-possession; tenacity 600 *perseverance*; aplomb, mettle, daring, dash, élan 712 *attack*; guts, pluck, spunk, grit, backbone, spirit; fortitude, stiff upper lip, gritted teeth, moral fibre 855 *courage*; single-mindedness, commitment, total c., devotedness, devotion, dedication; reliability, staunchness, steadiness, constancy, firmness 153 *stability*; insistence, pressure 740 *compulsion*; sternness, relentlessness, ruthlessness, inexorability, implacability 906 *pitilessness*; inflexibility, steeliness 326 *hardness*, iron, steel, rock; clenched teeth, hearts of oak, bulldog breed 600 *stamina*.

Adj. *resolute*, resolved, made up, determined 597 *willing*; desperate, stopping at nothing, all out; serious, earnest, concentrated; intent upon, set u., bent u.; insistent, pressing, urgent, driving, forceful, energetic, heroic 174 *vigorous*; firm, staunch, reliable, constant 153 *unchangeable*; iron-willed, strong-w., strong-minded, decisive, unbending, immovable, unyielding, inflexible, uncompromising, intransigent 602 *obstinate*; stern, grim, inexorable, implacable, relentless, ruthless, merciless 906 *pitiless*; iron, steely; undaunted, nothing daunted; steadfast, unwavering, unshaken, unshakable, unflinching, game, tenacious; indomitable; steeled, armoured, proof; self-controlled, self-restrained 942 *temperate*; self-possessed, self-reliant, self-confident; purposeful, single-minded, whole-hearted, committed, devoted, dedicated.

Vb. *be resolute*, – determined etc. adj.; steel oneself, brace o.; clench one's teeth, grit one's t. (**see** *stand firm*); make up one's mind, take a resolution, will, resolve, determine, purpose 617 *intend*; decide, fix, seal, conclude, finish with 69 *terminate*; take on oneself, accept responsibility 595 *will*; know one's own mind, insist, press, urge, not take no for an answer 532 *emphasize*; cut through, override, put one's foot down, stand no nonsense; mean business, stick at nothing, not stop at trifles, go to all lengths, go to any length, push to extremes; go the whole hog, see it through 725 *carry through*; face the odds, take on all comers, 661 *face danger*; bell the cat, outface, dare 711 *defy*; endure, go through fire and water 825 *suffer*; face the issue, bring to a head, take the bull by the horns; take the plunge, cross the Rubicon, burn one's boats, burn one's bridges, throw down the gauntlet, nail one's colours to the mast; be single-minded, set one's heart on, take up, go in for, take up in earnest, devote or dedicate oneself, commit oneself, give oneself to, give up everything for; set to, buckle to, go to it, put one's shoulder to the wheel, put one's heart into, grapple, strain 682 *exert oneself*.

stand firm, not be moved, dig one's toes *or* heels in, stand one's ground, stay put; not budge, not yield, not compromise, not give an inch; never despair, stand fast, hold out 600 *persevere*; be hell-bent on, bear the brunt, have what it takes, fight on, soldier on, stick it out,

grin and bear it, endure 825 *suffer*; fight to the death, die with one's boots on; go down with colours flying.

600 Perseverance

N. *perseverance*, persistence, tenacity, pertinacity, stubbornness 602 *obstinacy*; staunchness, constancy, steadfastness 599 *resolution*; single-mindedness, commitment, singleness of purpose, concentration 455 *attention*; sedulousness, application, tirelessness, indefatigability, assiduousness, industriousness 678 *assiduity*; doggedness, plodding, hard work 682 *exertion*; endurance, patience, fortitude 825 *suffering*; maintenance 146 *continuance*; ceaselessness 144 *permanence*; repeated efforts, unflagging e. 106 *repetition*.

stamina, endurance, staying power, indefatigability, fortitude 162 *strength*; grit, true g., backbone, gameness, guts, gutsiness, pluck; bulldog courage 855 *courage*.

Vb. *persevere*, persist, keep at it, not take no for an answer, hold out for; not despair, never d., never say die, never give up hope, hope on 852 *hope*; endure, have what it takes, come up for more 825 *suffer*; try, keep on trying, try and try again, renew one's efforts 671 *attempt*; maintain, keep up, follow up 146 *sustain*; plod, slog away, peg a., plug a., hammer away at, work at 682 *work*; continue, go on, keep on, keep the pot boiling, keep the ball rolling, rally, keep going; not let go, cling, hold fast, maintain one's grip, hang on like grim death 778 *retain*; hang on, stick it out, sweat it out, stay the course, stick with it, see it through, stay till the end; be in at the death, survive 41 *be left*; maintain one's ground, not budge, dig in one's heels, grit one's teeth 602 *be obstinate*; stick to one's guns, hold out, hold out to the last, die at one's post 599 *stand firm*; work till one drops, die with one's boots on, die in harness; spare no pains, move heaven and earth 682 *exert oneself*; bring to conclusion, see the end of, complete 725 *carry through*.

601 Irresolution

N. *irresolution*, faintheartedness, squeamishness, loss of nerve, spinelessness, no backbone, no grit 856 *cowardice*; nonperseverance, broken promise 603 *change of mind*; indecision, uncertainty, doubt, floating vote 474 *dubiety*; hesitation; inconstancy, fluctuation, vacillation, variability, blowing hot and cold 152 *changeableness*; levity, fickleness, whimsicality, irresponsibility 604 *caprice*; passivity 679 *inactivity*; compromise 734 *laxity*; lukewarmness, apathy 860 *indifference*; weak will 163 *weakness*; suggestibility 612 *persuadability*; pliancy, putty in one's hands, obsequiousness 879 *servility*; submissiveness.

Adj. *irresolute*, undecided, indecisive, of two minds, wavering, vacillating; unable to make up one's mind, stalling, undetermined, unresolved, uncertain 474 *doubting*; hesitating 598 *unwilling*; faint-hearted; lukewarm 860 *indifferent*; infirm of purpose 474 *unreliable*; characterless; compromising, weak-willed, weak-kneed, spineless 163 *weak*; flexible, pliant, putty-like 327 *soft*; inconstant, variable; whimsical, mercurial, not to be pinned down, grasshopper-like 604 *capricious*; restless, unsteady; uncommitted, giddy; superficial 456 *inattentive*.

Vb. *be irresolute*, – undecided etc. adj.; back away, shy, shirk 620 *avoid*; shilly-shally 518 *be equivocal*; fluctuate, vacillate, seesaw, waver, sway, hover, teeter, stall, dither 317 *oscillate*; not know one's own mind, blow hot and cold, back and fill, hum and haw, be in two minds, go round in circles, not know what to do, be at one's wits' end 474 *be uncertain*; leave in suspense, delay, put off a decision, put off until tomorrow 136 *put off*; dilly-dally 136 *wait*; debate, balance, weigh up the pros and cons, seesaw 475 *argue*; have second thoughts, hesitate 858 *be cautious*; falter, not persevere, give up 621 *relinquish*; make a compromise, take half measures 770 *compromise*; yield, give way 721 *submit*; change sides.

602 Obstinacy

N. *obstinacy*, mind of one's own; determination, will, single-mindedness 599 *resolution*; doggedness, tenacity, bulldog t., pertinacity 600 *perseverance*; stubbornness, obduracy, obdurateness; pigheadedness; inflexibility, immovability, toughness 326 *hardness*; intransigence, hard line, hard core, no compromise; constancy, irreversibility, fixity 153 *stability*; stiff neck; incorrigibility 940 *impenitence*; intractability, mulishness, dourness, sulkiness 893 *sullenness*; perversity, wrongheadedness, cussedness, bloody-mindedness.

opinionatedness, dogmatism, bigotry, zealotry; intolerance, fanaticism 735 *severity*; ruling passion, obsession, idée fixe 481 *bias*; old school.

Adj. *obstinate*, stubborn, obdurate; pigheaded, mulish; pertinacious, unyielding, firm, determined 599 *resolute*; dogged, bulldog-like, tenacious; adamant, inflexible, unbending; obdurate, hard-nosed, hardened, case-h.; uncompromising, hard-core, intransigent; unrelenting, immovable 153 *unchangeable*; inexorable, implacable; set in one's ways, hidebound; impervious; opinionated, dogmatic, pedantic

473 *positive*; obsessed, bigoted, fanatical 481 *biased*; dour, grim 893 *sullen*; stiff-necked; perverse, incorrigible, bloody-minded, plain cussed; persistent, incurable, chronic 113 *lasting*.

wilful, self-willed, pig-headed, bull-headed, mulish, wayward; headstrong, perverse; unruly, refractory; unmanageable, intractable, uncontrollable 738 *disobedient*; incorrigible.

Vb. *be obstinate*, – stubborn etc. adj.; persist 600 *persevere*; brazen it out 940 *be impenitent*; stick to one's guns, dig in one's heels, stand out, not budge, stay put 599 *stand firm*; insist, brook no denial, not take no for an answer; must have one's way; not change one's mind 473 *dogmatize*; stay in a rut, cling to custom 610 *be wont*; not listen, stop up one's ears, take no advice, take the bit between one's teeth, damn the consequences 857 *be rash*; not yield to treatment, become chronic 113 *last*.

603 Tergiversation: Change of mind

N. *change of mind*, tergiversation, better thoughts; afterthought, second thoughts 67 *sequel*; change of allegiance, conversion; new resolve; break with the past, repentance 939 *penitence*; revulsion 280 *recoil*; backsliding; shifting ground, change of direction 282 *deviation*; reversal, back-pedalling, veering round, about-face, about-turn, U-turn, volte-face, looking back 286 *return*; apostasy, turning renegade *or* traitor, defection, desertion 918 *undutifulness*; ratting, going over, treachery 930 *perfidy*; secession; abandonment 621 *relinquishment*; change of mood.

recantation, eating one's words, retraction, withdrawal, apology; renunciation, forswearing; disclaimer, denial 533 *negation*; revocation.

recanter, tergiversator, turncoat, rat; back-pedaller; opportunist, timeserver, Vicar of Bray 518 *equivocalness*; double-dealer, two-faced person 545 *deceiver*; jilt; apostate, renegade; traitor, Judas, betrayer 938 *knave*; quisling, fifth columnist, collaborationist 707 *collaborator*; deserter, defector, quitter, ratter; grass 524 *informer*; strike-breaker, blackleg, scab; seceder 978 *schismatic*; runaway; backslider 904 *offender*; convert.

Vb. *change one's mind*, tergiversate, think again, think better of it 601 *be irresolute*; change one's tune, shift one's ground 152 *vary*; get cold feet, back out, scratch, withdraw 753 *resign*; back down, crawl 872 *be humbled*; apologize (**see** *recant*); change round, swerve, tack, veer round, do a U-turn, backpedal, wheel about 282 *turn round*; turn one's back on 286 *turn back*; turn over a new leaf, repent 939 *be penitent*;

reform, mend one's ways 654 *get better*; back-slide 657 *relapse*; ditch, jilt, throw over, desert, walk out on 918 *fail in duty*; turn against.

apostatize, turn one's coat, change sides, change one's allegiance, turn renegade *or* traitor; switch over, join the opposition, cross over, cross the floor, go over, desert, defect; blackleg, rat; betray, collaborate 930 *be dis-honest*; be off with the old love, follow the rising star.

recant, unsay, eat one's words, eat one's hat; eat humble pie, apologize; take back, go back on, backpedal, backtrack, do a U-turn; withdraw 769 *not observe*; retract, disclaim, repudiate, deny 533 *negate*; renounce, abjure, forswear, recall, revoke, rescind 752 *abrogate*.

604 Caprice

N. *caprice*, capriciousness, arbitrariness; whimsicality, freakishness; faddishness; inconsistency 25 *disagreement*; fitfulness, changeability, variability, fickleness, unreliability, levity, giddiness, irresponsibility 152 *changeableness*; inconstancy, coquettishness, flirtatiousness.

whim, whimsy, caprice, fancy; passing fancy, impulse 609 *spontaneity*; vagary, humour, mood, fit, bee in the bonnet, quirk, kink, fad, craze, freak, idiosyncrasy 503 *eccentricity*; escapade, prank; coquetry, flirtation.

Adj. *capricious*, whimsical, fanciful, fantastic; eccentric, temperamental, crotchety, freakish, fitful; mad 503 *crazy*; mischievous, wayward, perverse; faddy; arbitrary, unreasonable; fretful, moody, contrary 892 *irascible*; refractory 602 *wilful*; erratic, uncertain, unpredictable 508 *unexpected*; volatile, mercurial, skittish, giddy, frivolous 456 *light-minded*; inconsistent, inconstant, variable; irresponsible, unreliable, fickle, feckless; coquettish.

Vb. *be capricious*, – whimsical etc. adj.; take it into one's head, have a sudden fancy for; chop and change, blow hot and cold 152 *vary*; be fickle; vacillate 601 *be irresolute*; flirt.

605 Choice

N. *choice*, election 463 *discrimination*; picking and choosing, finickiness 862 *fastidiousness*; picking out, selection; co-option, adoption; nomination, appointment 751 *commission*; option; freedom of choice, discretion, pick; decision 480 *judgment*; third way; preference, predilection, partiality, inclination, leaning, bias 179 *tendency*; taste 859 *liking*; availability 759 *offer*; selection, short list; short leet; alternative, embarras de choix, alternative medicine, alternative energy; difficult choice, dilemma 474 *dubiety*; limited choice, no real alternative; Hobson's c., zero option; nothing for it but 606

no choice; preferability, desirability; favour, fancy, first choice, top seed; selection, excerpts; the best of; literary selection 592 *anthology*; deselection.

vote, voice 485 *opinion*; representation, proportional r.; cumulative vote, transferable v., single transferable v.; majority vote, first past the post; one man one vote, OMOV; alternative voting; additional member system, casting v.; ballot, secret b.; postal vote; vote of confidence; vote of no confidence, blackballing, vote-counting, show of hands, division, poll, straw p., plebiscite, referendum; suffrage, universal s.; franchise, votes for women, women's suffrage, suffragettism; electoral system, ballot box, vox populi; polling, counting heads; straw vote, Gallup poll (tdmk), Mori p. (tdmk), opinion p.; election, general e.; by-election; local election, local-government e.; primary; polls, voting, electioneering, whistle-stop tour, canvassing, doorstepping, polling, hustings, candidature; return; psephology, psephologist; suffragette.

electorate, voters, elector, electoral college; quorum; electoral roll; constituent, constituency, marginal c.; borough, pocket b., rotten b.; polling booth, ballot box, voting paper; ticket, manifesto.

Adj. *chosen*, well-c.; select, choice, hand-picked 644 *excellent*; seeded 62 *arranged*; elect, designate; elected; adopted, selected; deselected; on approval, on an appro; favourite, pet; God's own; by appointment.

Vb. *choose*, make one's choice, make one's bed; shop around, be choosy, be picky; exercise one's discretion, accept, opt for, take up an option; elect, co-opt, adopt; favour, fancy; incline, lean, have a bias 179 *tend*; prefer, have a preference; think it best to, make up one's mind 480 *judge*; settle on, fix on, plump fur; take sides, back, support, embrace, espouse, throw in one's lot with 703 *patronize*.

select, pick, single out; pass 923 *approve*; nominate, appoint 751 *commission*; designate, detail, mark out; preselect, earmark, reserve 46 *set apart*; recommend, put up, propose, second 703 *patronize*; cull; glean, winnow, sift 463 *discriminate*; separate; skim off, cream, pick the best; take one's pick, cherry-pick, pick and choose 862 *be fastidious*.

vote, have a v., have a voice, have a say; be enfranchised, be on the electoral roll; poll, go to the polls; cast a vote, register one's v., raise one's hand; vote for, elect, return; deselect, vote with one's feet 607 *reject*; electioneer, canvass; stand 759 *offer oneself*; put to the vote, hold a referendum; count heads, count noses, count straws; hold an election, go to the country, appeal to the electorate, ask for a vote of confidence.

606 Absence of choice

N. *no choice*, Hobson's c., no alternative, zero option 596 *necessity*; any, the first that comes 464 *indiscrimination*; neutrality; no difference, six of one and half a dozen of the other, 'a plague on both your houses' 28 *equality*.

Vb. *be neutral*, take no sides, not vote, be a don't know, abstain; sit on the fence 601 *be irresolute*; not know.

have no choice, have no alternative, have Hobson's choice; have zero option; take it or leave it, make a virtue of necessity, make the best of a bad job 596 *be forced*; have no say.

Adv. *neither*, neither . . . nor.

607 Rejection

N. *rejection*, nonacceptance; repudiation, denial 533 *negation*; rebuff, frozen mitt, cold shoulder 760 *refusal*; spurning, kick, more kicks than ha'pence, more bricks than bouquets; electoral defeat; elimination 300 *ejection*; exemption 57 *exclusion*; discarding, deselection, disemployment 674 *nonuse*; reject, wallflower; no-hoper, lost cause.

Vb. *reject*, decline, say no to, draw the line at, rebuff, repulse, spurn, dismiss out of hand 760 *refuse*; send back; pass over, ignore 458 *disregard*; vote against; scrap, discard, deselect, ditch, junk, throw aside, lay a., give up 674 *stop using*; disallow, revoke 752 *abrogate*; set aside; expel, cast out, throw o., chuck o., sling o., kick o., fling o. 300 *eject*; kick upstairs; sort out 44 *eliminate*; exempt 57 *exclude*; blackball, cold-shoulder, hand the frozen mitt to, turn one's back on, give the brush-off 885 *be rude*; disclaim, deny 533 *negate*; abnegate, repudiate; disdain, deride 851 *ridicule*; turn up one's nose at, sniff at, look a gift horse in the mouth 922 *hold cheap*; opt out.

608 Predetermination

N. *predetermination*, predestination 596 *necessity*; preordination 155 *destiny*; decree 595 *will*; premeditation; prearrangement 669 *preparation*; order of the day, order paper, agenda 622 *business*; frame-up, put-up job, packed jury 623 *plot*; closed mind 481 *prejudice*; foregone conclusion.

Adj. *predetermined*, decreed, premeditated etc. vb.; predestined, preordained; deliberate, aforethought; with a motive, studied, calculated, measured; weighed, considered, advised; devised, controlled, contrived 623 *planned*; put-up, framed, stacked, packed, prearranged 669 *prepared*.

Vb. *predetermine*, predestine, preordain; premeditate, preconceive; agree beforehand; fix; contrive, arrange, prearrange 623 *plan*; frame, put up, pack a jury, stack the cards 541 *fake*.

609 Spontaneity

N. *spontaneity*, ad hoc measures, improvisation; extemporization, ad-libbing, impromptu thinking on one's feet 670 *nonpreparation*; involuntariness, reflex, automatic r.; impulsiveness, impulse, blind i., instinct 476 *intuition*; spur of the moment; snap decision; burst of confidence 526 *disclosure*; inspiration, sudden thought, hunch, flash 451 *idea*.

Adj. *spontaneous*, off-the-cuff, ad hoc, improvised, ad-libbing, extemporaneous, extemporary, sudden, snap; makeshift; impromptu, unpremeditated, unrehearsed 618 *unintentional*; unprompted, unmotivated, unprovoked; instinctive, involuntary, automatic, knee-jerk; impulsive.

Vb. *improvise*, extemporize, think on one's feet, vamp, ad-lib 670 *be unprepared*; obey an impulse, act on the spur of the moment 604 *be capricious*; blurt, come out with, say whatever comes into one's head, have a sudden brainwave; rise to the occasion.

Adv. *extempore*, impromptu, ad hoc, on the spur of the moment, off the cuff, off the top of one's head.

610 Habit

N. *habit*, disposition; force of habit; second nature; occupation; addiction, confirmed habit, constitutional; trait, idiosyncrasy; knack, trick, mannerism; instinct, leaning 179 *tendency*; bad habit; usage, custom, old c., mores; use, wont 146 *continuance*; inveteracy; tradition, law, precedent; way, ways, the old w.; lifestyle, way of life; beaten track, tramlines, groove, rut; fixed ways, daily round, daily grind, regularity 141 *periodicity*; routine, drill, system 60 *order*; usual suspects; red tape, bureaucracy, conventionalism, traditionalism, conservatism, old school 83 *conformity*.

practice, common p., matter of course; conventionality 83 *conformity*; mores, behaviour patterns; institution, ritual, observance 988 *rite*; religious observance; mode, vogue, craze, in-thing; order of the day 848 *fashion*; convention, protocol, unwritten law, done thing, the usual thing; recognized procedure, drill; form, good f. 848 *etiquette*; manners, table m., eating habits; rules and regulations, house rules, standing order, routine 688 *conduct*.

habituation, training, indoctrination 534 *teaching*; inurement, hardening; naturalization, acclimatization; conditioning, reflex, conditioned r., drill, routine.

habitué, creature of habit, addict; traditionalist, conventionalist 83 *conformist;* regular, client 792 *purchaser;* frequenter, devotee, fan, groupie, camp follower 504 *enthusiast.*

Adj. *habitual,* customary; routine; conventional, traditional 976 *orthodox;* inveterate, time-honoured; habit-forming; ingrained, dyed-in-the-wool, bred in the bone 5 *intrinsic;* rooted, deep-r., deep-seated; imbued, soaked, permeated.

usual, accustomed, wonted, traditional; in character, natural; household, familiar, well-known 490 *known;* unoriginal, hackneyed; banal, commonplace, common, ordinary 79 *general;* set, stock, stereotyped 83 *typical;* widespread 79 *universal;* monthly, daily, everyday 139 *frequent;* practised, done; acknowledged, received, accepted, understood; established, official, hallowed by custom; de rigueur 740 *compelling;* invariable 153 *unchangeable;* in, in vogue 848 *fashionable.*

habituated, in the habit of, accustomed to, given to, addicted to; devoted to, wedded to; used to, familiar with, conversant w., au fait w., at home in 490 *knowing;* inveterate, confirmed; practised, inured, seasoned, incorrigible, hardened 669 *prepared;* broken in, trained, tame 369 *tamed;* naturalized, acclimatized.

Vb. *be wont,* be used to, be a creature of habit; haunt, frequent; make a habit of, take up, embrace, go in for; be set in one's ways, be in a rut, stick in a groove, become a habit, catch on, grow on one, take hold of o.; stick; take root; be the rule, obtain, hold good 178 *prevail;* acquire the force of custom.

habituate, accustom oneself, get used to, get into the way of, get the knack of, get the feel of, get the hang of, warm up, get into one's stride; take to, acquire the habit; get into a habit, catch oneself doing; keep one's hand in, practise 106 *repeat;* accustom, inure, season, train; domesticate, tame 369 *break in;* naturalize, acclimatize; imbue 534 *teach;* condition, brainwash 178 *influence.*

611 Desuetude

N. *desuetude,* discontinuance, disuse 674 *nonuse;* rust, decay 655 *deterioration;* rustiness, lack of practice 695 *unskilfulness;* discarded custom; 550 *obliteration;* weaning 134 *adultness;* not the thing, not etiquette, unconventionality 84 *nonconformity;* inexperience, unfamiliarity 491 *ignorance.*

Adj. *unwonted,* not customary, not done; not de rigueur; unfashionable, bad form, non-U 847 *vulgar;* out of fashion, old hat, defunct

125 *past;* discarded 674 *disused;* unconventional 84 *unconformable;* untraditional, unprecedented,

unhabituated, unaccustomed, not in the habit of 769 *nonobservant;* untrained, undomesticated; unfamiliar, inexperienced, new, raw, fresh, callow, green 491 *uninstructed;* weaned; out of the habit, rusty 695 *unskilful.*

Vb. *disaccustom,* wean from, cure of 656 *cure;* break a habit, kick the h.; dry out; wean oneself from, outgrow; give up, throw off, slough off, shed.

612 Motive

N. *motive,* cause of action, what is behind it; rationale, reasons, grounds 156 *reason why;* motivation, driving force, impetus, mainspring, what makes one tick, what turns one on 156 *causation;* intention 617 *objective;* ideal, principle, guiding p.; aspiration 852 *hope;* ambition 859 *desire;* calling, call 622 *vocation;* conscience, dictate of c., personal reasons, ulterior motive, hidden agenda 932 *selfishness;* impulse.

inducement, pressure, urgency, insistence; lobbying 178 *influence;* indirect influence; provocation, urging, incitement, encouragement, incitation, instigation, prompting; support, abetment 703 *aid;* solicitation, invitation 761 *request;* temptation, enticement, carrot, allurement, seduction, seductiveness, fascination, charm, charm offensive, sex appeal, it, attractiveness, magnetism 291 *attraction;* blandishment 925 *flattery;* coaxing, wheedling 889 *endearment;* persuasion, persuasiveness, salesmanship, sales talk, spiel, patter 579 *eloquence;* pep talk, rallying cry 547 *call;* exhortation 534 *lecture;* pleading, advocacy 691 *advice;* propaganda, agitprop; advertising, sales promotion, soft sell, hard s. 528 *advertisement;* promises, election p.; bribery, b. and corruption, graft, palm-greasing, back-scratching 962 *reward;* honeyed words, winning ways.

persuadability, docility, tractability, willingness; pliancy, pliability, putty in one's hands 327 *softness;* susceptibility, impressibility; credulousness 487 *credulity.*

incentive, inducement; stimulus, fillip, tickle, prod, spur, goad, lash, whip; rod, big stick, crack of the whip 900 *threat;* energizer, tonic, carrot, carrot and stick, jam tomorrow, sop, sop to Cerberus 174 *stimulant;* charm 983 *spell;* attraction, magnet; lure, decoy, decoy duck, bait 542 *trap;* come-on, loss leader, special offer; profit 771 *gain;* cash, gold 797 *money;* pay, salary, perks, pay increase, increment, rise, raise, bonus 804 *payment;* donation, handout, freebie 781 *gift;* gratuity, tip, bribe, hush money, slush fund 962 *reward;* forbidden fruit;

tempting offer, offer one cannot refuse 759 *offer.*

motivator, prime m. 156 *cause*; manipulator, wire-puller 178 *influence*; manoeuvrer, tactician, strategist 623 *planner*; instigator, prompter; inspirer; aider and abettor 703 *aider*; agent provocateur 545 *deceiver*; tempter, seducer; seductress, temptress, vamp, femme fatale, siren; Circe, Lorelei; hypnotizer, hypnotist; orator, rhetorician 579 *speaker*; advocate; wheedler 925 *flatterer*; advertiser, promotion manager, propagandist 528 *publicizer*; ringleader 690 *leader*; firebrand, rabble-rouser 738 *agitator*; lobbyist, lobby, pressure group, ginger g.

Vb. *motivate*, move, actuate, manipulate 173 *operate*; work upon, play u., act u., operate u. 178 *influence*; weigh, count, be a consideration, sway 178 *prevail*; call the tune, override 34 *predominate*; work on the feelings, appeal, challenge, shame into; infect, inject with, infuse into 534 *educate*; interest, intrigue 821 *impress*; charm, fascinate, captivate, hypnotize, spellbind 983 *bewitch*; turn on; pull 291 *attract*; push 279 *impel*; force, enforce 740 *compel*; bend, incline, dispose; predispose, prejudice 481 *bias*; predestine 608 *predetermine*; lead, direct 689 *manage*; lead astray 495 *mislead*; give a lead, set the fashion, be a trend-setter, set an example, set the pace 283 *precede.*

incite, energize, galvanize, stimulate 174 *invigorate*; encourage, cheer on, act as cheer-leader, root for 855 *give courage*; inspire, animate, provoke, rouse, rally 821 *excite*; evoke, call forth, challenge; exhort, invite, urge, exert pressure, bring pressure to bear on, lobby; nag, needle, goad, prod, jog, jolt; spur, prick; whip, lash, flog; spur on, egg on; drive, hurry up 680 *hasten*; instigate, prompt, put up to; abet, aid and a. 703 *aid*; start, kindle 68 *initiate.*

induce, instigate, bring about 156 *cause*; persuade, carry with one 485 *convince*; prevail upon, talk into, push i., drive i., nag i., bully i., browbeat (**see** *motivate*); twist one's arm 740 *compel*; wear down, soften up; get round, bring r., talk r. 147 *convert*; bring over, win o., procure, enlist, engage; talk over, sweet-talk into, coax into, cajole 925 *flatter*; entice, seduce.

tempt, lead into temptation; entice, hold out a carrot to, dangle before one's eyes, make one's mouth water; tantalize, tease; allure, lure, inveigle 542 *ensnare*; coax, wheedle.

bribe, offer an inducement, hold out a carrot 759 *offer*; suborn, seduce, corrupt; square, buy off; oil, grease the palm, give a sop to Cerberus; tip 962 *reward.*

613 Dissuasion

N. *dissuasion*, caution 664 *warning*; discouragement, setback 702 *hindrance*; deterrence 854 *intimidation*; objection, expostulation, remonstrance, reproof, admonition 762 *deprecation*; rebuff 715 *resistance*; disincentive; health warning; deterrent, red light 665 *danger signal*; contraindication; cold water, damper, wet blanket; killjoy, spoilsport.

Vb. *dissuade* persuade against, convince to the contrary, talk out of 479 *confute*; caution 664 *warn*; remonstrate; expostulate, protest against 762 *deprecate*; make one stop in one's tracks, give one pause 486 *cause doubt*; head off, steer one away from, turn one aside 282 *deflect*; keep back; disenchant, disillusion, disincline; set against, turn a., put off, repel; dishearten, discourage; throw cold water on, dampen, quench, cool, damp the ardour, be a wet blanket; take the edge off 257 *blunt.*

614 Pretext

N. *pretext*, ostensible motive, alleged m., reason given; statement, allegation, profession, claim 532 *affirmation*; plea, excuse, defence, apology, rationale, justification 927 *vindication*; alibi 667 *means of escape*; peg to hang something on 218 *prop*; shallow pretext, lame excuse, quibble 477 *sophism*; proviso 468 *qualification*; subterfuge 698 *stratagem*; pretence, Bunbury, previous engagement, diplomatic illness 543 *untruth*; blind, red herring, dust thrown in the eyes; stalking horse, smoke screen, cloak, cover 421 *screen*; apology for, pale imitation of; colour, guise 445 *appearance*; bluff.

Adj. *ostensible*, alleged, pretended; seeming.

Vb. *plead*, allege, claim, give as one's reason *or* rationale, profess 532 *affirm*; make one's pretext, make a plea of 475 *argue*; make excuses, offer an excuse, excuse oneself, defend o. 927 *justify*; gloss over; shelter behind, use as a stalking horse; make capital out of, cash in on 137 *profit by*; find a loophole, wriggle out of 667 *escape*; bluff; varnish, colour; blind, throw dust in the eyes, draw a red herring across.

615 Good

N. *good*, one's g., what is good for one; advantage, benefit; the best; common good; lesser evil, utilitarianism 642 *good policy*; well-being, welfare 730 *prosperity*; riches 800 *wealth*; luck, good l., fortune, good f.; happy days, happy ending 824 *happiness*; blessing, world of good; well-wishing.

benefit, something to one's advantage, advantage, interest; convenience; crop, harvest, return 771 *acquisition*; profit, increment, gain; edification, betterment 654 *improvement*; boon

781 *gift*; good turn; favour, blessing, blessing in disguise; turn-up for the book, godsend, windfall, legacy, piece of luck, treasure trove, find, prize; good thing.

Adj. *good*, goodly, fine; blessed, happy; advantageous, heaven-sent 644 *beneficial*; worthwhile 644 *valuable*; helpful 706 *cooperative*; praiseworthy, commendable, recommended 923 *approved*; edifying, moral 933 *virtuous*; pleasure-giving 826 *pleasurable*.

Vb. *benefit*, do good, help, avail, be of service; edify, advantage, profit; repay 771 *be profitable*; do one a power of good 654 *make better*; turn out well, be all for the best, come right in the end.

flourish, thrive, do well, be on top of the world, be on the crest of a wave; rise, rise in the world 730 *prosper*; arrive 727 *succeed*; benefit by, gain by, be the better for, improve 654 *get better*; turn to good account, cash in on 137 *profit by*; make a profit 771 *gain*; make money 800 *get rich*.

Adv. *well*, satisfactorily, favourably, profitably, happily, healthily, not amiss, all to the good; to one's advantage, to one's benefit, for the best, in one's best interests; in fine style, on the up and up.

616 Evil

N. *evil*, wickedness, iniquity, mischievousness, injuriousness, disservice, injury, putting the boot in, dirty trick; wrong, injury, outrage 914 *injustice*; crying shame, shame, abuse; curse, scourge, poison, pest, plague, sore, running s. 659 *bane*; ill, ills that flesh is heir to, Pandora's box; sad world, vale of tears; trouble, troubles 731 *adversity*; affliction, misery, distress 825 *suffering*; grief, woe 825 *sorrow*; unease, malaise, angst, discomfort 825 *worry*; nuisance 827 *annoyance*; hurt, bodily harm, wound, bruise, cut, gash 377 *pain*; blow, mortal b., death b., buffet, stroke 279 *knock*; outrageous fortune, slings and arrows, calamity, bad luck 731 *misfortune*; casualty, accident 154 *event*; fatality 361 *death*; catastrophe 165 *ruin*; tragedy, sad ending 655 *deterioration*; mischief, devilry, harm, damage 772 *loss*; ill effect, bad result; disadvantage 35 *inferiority*; drawback, fly in the ointment 647 *defect*; setback 702 *hitch*; indigence 801 *poverty*; sense of injury, grievance 829 *discontent*; vindictiveness 910 *revengefulness*.

Adj. *evil*, wicked, iniquitous 934 *vicious*; black, foul, shameful 914 *wrong*; bad, too bad 645 *damnable*; unlucky, inauspicious, sinister 731 *adverse*; insidious, injurious, prejudicial, disadvantageous 645 *harmful*; troublous 827 *distressing*; fatal, fell, mortal, deathly 362 *deadly*; ruinous, disastrous 165

destructive; catastrophic, calamitous, tragic 731 *unfortunate*; all wrong, awry, out of joint, out of kilter.

Adv. *amiss*, wrong, awry, sour.

SECTION TWO

Prospective volition

617 Intention

N. *intention*, intent, meaning; deliberateness; calculation, calculated risk 480 *estimate*; purpose, determination, predetermination, resolve 599 *resolution*; mind 447 *intellect*; criminal intent 936 *guilt*; good intentions 897 *benevolence*; view, prospect; proposal; design 623 *plan*; enterprise 672 *undertaking*; ambition 859 *desire*; decision 480 *judgment*; ultimatum 766 *conditions*; bid, bid for 671 *attempt*; destination 69 *end*.

objective, destination, object, end, end in view, aim, mission statement; axe to grind; butt, target, bull's-eye 225 *centre*; tape, winning post 295 *goal*; Mecca 76 *focus*; quarry, game, prey 619 *chase*; prize, crown, wreath, laurels 729 *trophy*; dream, aspiration, vision 513 *ideality*; heart's desire, Promised Land, El Dorado, land flowing with milk and honey, pot *or* crock of gold at the end of the rainbow, Holy Grail 859 *desired object*.

Vb. *intend*, propose; have in mind, have in view, have an eye to, contemplate, think of; study, meditate; reckon on, calculate, look for 507 *expect*; foresee the necessity of 510 *foresee*; have a mind to, mean to, have every intention 599 *be resolute*; resolve, determine, premeditate 608 *predetermine*; project, design, plan for 623 *plan*; intend for, destine f. 155 *predestine*; earmark 547 *mark*; put aside for, reserve f.; intend for oneself (**see** *aim at*).

aim at, make one's target; go after, go all out for, work towards, strive after 619 *pursue*; try for 671 *attempt*; be after, have an eye on, have designs on, promise oneself, aspire to; take aim, zero in on, focus on, point at, level at, train one's sights on, aim high, hitch one's wagon to a star 281 *aim*.

Adv. *purposely*, on purpose, in cold blood, deliberately, intentionally; knowingly, wittingly; with forethought, with malice aforethought; in order to; with the intention of, with a view to, with the object of, by design, as planned, according to plan, as arranged.

618 Nondesign. Gamble

N. *nondesign*, indeterminacy; involuntariness, instinct 609 *spontaneity*; coincidence; accident, fluke, luck; good luck, windfall, stroke of luck;

bad luck, hard 1. 616 *evil*; lottery, luck of the draw (**see** *gambling*); potluck; wheel of Fortune 596 *fate*.

gambling, risk-taking; flier, risk, hazard, Russian roulette 661 *danger*; gamble, potluck 159 *chance*; venture, speculation, flutter 461 *experiment*; shot, shot in the dark, leap in the d., pig in a poke, blind bargain 474 *uncertainty*; bid, throw; toss of a coin, turn of a card; wager, bet, stake, ante; dice, die; element of risk, game of chance; bingo; fruit machine, gaming m., one-armed bandit; roulette, rouge et noir 837 *gambling game*; betting, turf, horse-racing, dog-r. 716 *racing*; football pool, treble chance, pools; draw, lottery, National Lottery, Scratch card, raffle, tombola, sweepstake, premium bond.

gaming-house, gambling den; betting shop, bookie's, bookmaker's, turf accountant's; casino, pool room, bingo hall, amusement arcade; racecourse, turf; tote.

stock exchange, exchange, share shop, bucket shop.

gambler, gamester, player, better, backer, punter; turf accountant, bookmaker, bookie, tout, tipster; risk-taker; venture capitalist, adventurer, entrepreneur 672 *undertaking*; speculator; bear, bull, stag; arbitrageur.

Adj. *unintentional*, inadvertent, unintended, unmeant 596 *involuntary*; unpremeditated; accidental, coincidental 159 *casual*.

speculative, experimental 474 *uncertain*; hazardous, risky, chancy, dicey; risk-taking, adventurous, enterprising.

Vb. *gamble*, do the pools; bet, stake, wager; call one's hand; play for high stakes; take bets, offer odds, make a book; back, punt; cover a bet; play the market, speculate, arbitrage, have a flutter 461 *experiment*; run a risk, take risks, push one's luck, tempt Providence; buy a pig in a poke 857 *be rash*; venture, chance it, chance one's arm, tempt fortune, tempt fate, try one's luck, trust to chance; raffle, draw lots, cut straws, cut for aces, spin a coin, toss up.

619 Pursuit

N. *pursuit*, pursuance, follow-up 65 *sequence*; seeking, looking for, quest 459 *search*; hunting, tracking, spooring, trailing, tailing, dogging, poaching, lamping, hounding, persecution, witch-hunt; affairs 622 *business*.

chase, run; steeplechase, paperchase 716 *racing*; hunt, hunting, hounding, hue and cry, tally-ho; beat, drive; shooting, gunning, hunting, shooting and fishing 837 *sport*; blood sport, fox hunt, stag h.; big-game h., lion h., tiger h.; elephant h., boar h.; pigsticking; stalking, deer s.; hawking, fowling, falconry; fishing, angling, fly fishing, coarse f., sea f.; inshore f., deep-sea

f., whaling; beagling, coursing, ratting, trapping, ferreting, rabbiting, mole-catching; fishing tackle, rod and line, bait, fly, fly-tying; fowling-piece 723 *firearm*; fishtrap, rat-trap 542 *trap*; manhunt, dragnet; game, quarry, prey, victim 617 *objective*; catch 771 *acquisition*.

hunter, quester, seeker, searcher 459 *enquirer*; search party; pursuer, tracker, trailer, sleuth, tail, shadow; huntsman, huntress; beater; Diana; sportsman, sportswoman, sportsperson 837 *player*; gun, shot, marksman *or* -woman; head-hunter 362 *killer*; big-game hunter, fox h., deer stalker; poacher, guddler, trout-tickler; trapper, rat-catcher, rodent officer, mole-catcher; bird catcher, fowler, falconer, hawker; fisherman; angler; shrimper; trawler, trawlerman, whaler; pack, hounds; hound, foxhound, otterhound, bloodhound 365 *dog*; hawk 365 *bird*; beast of prey, man-eater 365 *mammal*; mouser 365 *cat*.

Vb. *pursue*, seek, look for, cast about for; be gunning for, hunt for, fish for, dig for 459 *search*; send out a search party; stalk; shadow, dog, track, trail, sleuth, tail, dog one's footsteps, follow the scent 284 *follow*; scent out 484 *discover*; witch-hunt, harry, persecute 735 *oppress*; chase, give c., hunt; raise the hunt, raise the hue and cry; mark as one's prey, make one's quarry 617 *aim at*; run after, set one's cap at, throw oneself at, woo 889 *court*; be after; pursue one's own interests 622 *busy oneself*; follow up.

hunt, go hunting, go big-game h., go shooting, ride to hounds; go fishing, fish, angle, fly-fish; trawl; whale; shrimp; net, catch 542 *ensnare*; mouse; stalk, deer-s., fowl, hawk; course; flush, beat; set snares, poach, guddle.

620 Avoidance

N. *avoidance*, prevention 702 *hindrance*; abstinence, abstention 942 *temperance*; forbearance, refraining 177 *moderation*; nonintervention, noninvolvement; evasiveness 518 *equivocalness*; evasive action, dodge, duck, sidestep; delaying action; evasion, flight 667 *escape*; shrinking 854 *fear*; shunning, wide berth, safe distance 199 *distance*; shirking 458 *negligence*; nonattendance 190 *absence*; escapism.

avoider, abstainer; dodger, evader, tax e., moonlighter, bilker; welsher 545 *trickster*; shrinker, quitter 856 *coward*; shirker, skiver, slacker, sloucher, leadswinger 679 *idler*; skulker; draft-dodger, truant, deserter 918 *undutifulness*; runaway, fugitive, escapee 667 *escaper*; escapist, dreamer 513 *visionary*; head in the sand, ostrich.

Vb. *avoid*, not go near, keep off, keep away; bypass, circumvent 282 *deviate*; turn aside, look the other way, turn a blind eye, cold-shoulder;

stand apart, have no hand in, play no part in, not soil one's fingers, keep one's hands clean, wash one's hands of, shun, eschew, leave, let alone, have nothing to do with, not touch with a bargepole; give a miss, give the go-by; fight shy, back away, draw back 290 *recede*; hold off, stand aloof, keep one's distance, keep a respectful d., keep at arm's length, give a wide berth; keep out of the way, keep clear, stand c., get out of the way; forbear; refrain, abstain, forswear; hold back, hang b., balk at 598 *be unwilling*; pass the buck, get out of; cop out, funk, shirk 458 *neglect*; shrink, flinch, jib, refuse, shy; take evasive action, lead one a dance, draw a red herring, throw dust in one's eyes, throw one off the scent, play hide-and-seek; sidestep, dodge, duck; deflect, ward off; duck the issue, fudge the i., get round, obviate, skirt round, fence, hedge, pussyfoot 518 *be equivocal*; evade, escape, give one the slip 667 *elude*; hide 523 *lurk*; bury one's head in the sand, be ostrich-like; deny 533 *negate*.

run away, desert, play truant, jump bail, take French leave, go AWOL 918 *fail in duty*; abscond, welsh, flit, elope 667 *escape*; absent oneself 190 *be absent*; withdraw, retire, retreat, beat a r., turn tail, turn one's back 282 *turn round*; flee, flit, fly, take to flight, run for one's life; make off, slope o., bolt, run, run for it, cut and run, show a clean pair of heels, take to one's h., beat it, make oneself scarce, scoot, scram, skedaddle 277 *move fast*; slip the cable, break away 296 *decamp*; shake the dust from one's feet, steal away, sneak off, slink o., scuttle, do a bunk.

621 Relinquishment

N. *relinquishment*, abandonment; leaving, evacuation 296 *departure*; desertion, truancy, defection 918 *undutifulness*; withdrawal, secession 978 *schism*; walk-out 145 *strike*; cop-out 620 *avoidance*; yielding, giving up; abnegation, renunciation 779 *nonretention*; abdication, retirement 753 *resignation*; disuse 674 *nonuse*; discontinuance 611 *desuetude*; cancellation, annulment 752 *abrogation*;

Vb. *relinquish*, drop, let go, leave hold of; surrender, resign, give up, yield; waive, forgo; cede, hand over, transfer 780 *assign*; forfeit 772 *lose*; renounce, abnegate, recant, change one's mind 603 *tergiversate*; not proceed with, drop the idea, forget it 506 *forget*; wean oneself 611 *disaccustom*; forswear, abstain 620 *avoid*; shed, slough, cast off, divest; drop, discard, get rid of, jettison, write off 674 *stop using*; lose interest, have other fish to fry 860 *be indifferent*; abdicate, back down, scratch, stand down, withdraw, retire, drop out 753 *resign*; jack it in, give

in, throw in the sponge *or* the towel, throw in one's hand 721 *submit*; leave, quit, move out, vacate, evacuate 296 *depart*; forsake, abandon, run out on, leave stranded, quit one's post, desert 918 *fail in duty*; play truant 190 *be absent*; down tools, strike, come out 145 *cease*; walk out, secede; throw over, ditch, jilt, break it off, go back on one's word 542 *deceive*; pass on to the next, shelve, postpone 136 *put off*; annul, cancel 752 *abrogate*.

622 Business

N. *business*, affairs, business interests, irons in the fire; occupation, concern; business on hand, case, agenda 154 *affairs*; enterprise, venture, undertaking, pursuit 678 *activity*; office routine, daily round 610 *practice*; daily work; business circles, business world, City, world of commerce; technology, industry, light i., heavy i., sunrise i., commerce, e-commerce, m-c., dot c., e-business, m-b., big business; multinational, business company 708 *corporation*; cottage industry; industrialism, industrialization, industrial arts, manufacture 164 *production*; trade, craft, handicraft; guild, union, chamber of commerce, business association 706 *association*; employment, work, black economy, grey e..

vocation, calling, life work, mission; life, lifestyle, walk of life, career, chosen career, labour of love; living, livelihood, daily bread, one's bread and butter; profession, métier, craft, trade; line, line of country (**see** *function*); ministry; cloth, veil, habit 985 *the church*; military profession, arms 718 *war*; naval profession, sea; legal profession 953 *law*; teaching profession, education 534 *teaching*; medical profession, medicine, practice; industry, commerce 791 *trade*; diplomatic service, civil s., administration 689 *management*; public service, public life; social service 901 *sociology*.

job, chores, odd jobs, work, task, exercise 682 *labour*; duty, charge, commission, mission, errand; employ, service, employment, self-employment; hours of work, working day, working week, man-hour; occupation, situation, position, appointment, post, office; full-time job, permanency; temporary job, part-time j., freelance work; situation wanted; situation vacant, opening, vacancy; labour exchange, employment agency, Job Centre, Department of Employment.

function, capacity, office, duty; area of interest, realm, province, domaine, orbit, sphere; scope, field, terms of reference 183 *range*; department, line, line of country; role, part; business, job; responsibility, brief, concern, care, lookout, baby, pigeon.

Vb. *employ*, busy, occupy, take up one's time,

fill one's t.; give employment, engage, recruit, hire, enlist, appoint, post 751 *commission*; take on, take on the payroll 804 *pay*; offer a job to, fill a vacancy, staff.

busy oneself, work, work for 742 *serve*; have a career, be employed, be self-employed, be freelance, work from home, do a job, hold down a j., earn, earn one's living; earn an honest crust, turn an honest penny, keep the wolf from the door 771 *acquire*; take on a job, apply for a j.; be up and doing, bustle 678 *be busy*; concern oneself with, make it one's business, take a hand in 678 *meddle*; work at, ply; engage in, turn one's hand to, take up, engage in, go in for; have one's hands full, take on oneself, bear the burden, assume responsibility, bear the brunt, take on one's shoulders 917 *incur a duty*; work with one's hands, work with one's brains; pursue one's hobby 837 *amuse oneself.*

function, work, go 173 *operate*; fill a role, play one's part, carry on; officiate, act, discharge one's duties, serve as, do duty for, perform the duties, do the work of; substitute, stand in for 755 *deputize*; hold office, hold down a job, have a brief.

do business, transact, negotiate 766 *make terms*; ply a trade, follow a career; have a business, engage in, carry on a trade, keep shop; do business with, deal w., enter into trade relations 791 *trade*; transact business, go about one's business; pursue one's vocation, earn one's living (**see** *busy oneself*); be self-employed, work from home, run a cottage industry, freelance, set up in business, go into b.

623 Plan

N. *plan*, scheme, design; planning, geomancy, feng shui; organization, systematization, rationalization, centralization 60 *order*; programme, project, proposal 617 *intention*; proposition, suggestion, motion, resolution (**see** *policy*); master plan, five-year p., ground p., scale drawing, blueprint 551 *map*; diagram, flow chart 86 *statistics*; sketch, outline, draft, first d., schedule; skeleton; model, pattern, pilot scheme 23 *prototype*; drawing board, planning office.

policy, forethought 510 *foresight*; statesmanship 498 *wisdom*; course of action, procedure, strategy 688 *tactics*; approach, attack 624 *way*; steps, measures 676 *action*; proposed line of action, programme, prospectus, platform, outline, ticket, slate; party line; formula 81 *rule*; schedule, agenda, order of the day, any other business, AOB 622 *business.*

contrivance, expedient, resource, recourse, resort, last r., card, trump c., card up one's sleeve 629 *means*; recipe; loophole, escape clause, way out, alternative, artifice, device, gimmick, dodge, ploy, flag of convenience 698 *stratagem*; wangle, fiddle; trick 694 *skill*; stunt; inspiration, brainwave, brainstorm, happy thought, bright idea; notion, invention; tool, weapon, contraption, gadget, gizmo 628 *instrument*; improvisation 609 *spontaneity*; feat, tour de force; bold move, masterstroke 676 *deed.*

plot, intrigue; web of intrigue; cabal, conspiracy, inside job, insider trading *or* dealing; scheme, racket, game 698 *stratagem*; frame-up, put-up job, fit-up, machination; manipulation, wire-pulling 612 *motive.*

planner, inventor, originator, deviser; proposer; founder, author, architect, designer, town-planner; backroom boy, boffin 696 *expert*; brains, mastermind; organizer, systems analyst; strategist, tactician; statesman *or* -woman, politician; wheeler-dealer, axe-grinder; plotter, intriguer; conspirator 545 *deceiver.*

Adj. *planned*, under consideration, at the planning stage, on the stocks, strategic, tactical.

Vb. *plan*, form a p.; make a plan, draw up, design, draft, blueprint; frame, shape 243 *form*; project, plan out, sketch o., map o., lay o., design a prototype; draw up a programme, lay the foundation; shape a course, mark out a c.; organize, systematize, rationalize; schedule, draw up a s., phase; invent, think up 484 *discover*; conceive a plan 513 *imagine*; devise, engineer, hatch, concoct; prearrange 608 *predetermine*; calculate, think ahead, look a. 498 *be wise*; follow a plan, work to a schedule; have an axe to grind.

plot, scheme, have designs, be up to something, wheel and deal; manipulate, pull strings 178 *influence*; conspire, intrigue; cook up; hatch a plot 698 *be cunning*; undermine; work against; frame 541 *fake*.

624 Way

N. *way*, route 267 *itinerary*; manner, guise; fashion, style 243 *form*; method, mode, line, approach, address, attack; procedure, process, way of, way of doing things, modus operandi 688 *tactics*; operation, treatment; routine 610 *practice*; technique, know-how 694 *skill*; gait 265 *motion*; progress 285 *progression*; primrose path; way of life, lifestyle.

access, right of way, communications; way to 289 *approach*; entrance, door 263 *doorway*; side-entrance, back-e., tradesman's e.; drive, driveway, gangway; porch, hall, hallway, corridor, vestibule 194 *lobby*; way through, pass, passageway 305 *passage*; intersection, junction, crossing; zebra crossing, pedestrian c., pelican c. 305 *traffic control*; strait, sound 345 *gulf*; channel, fairway, canal 351 *conduit*; lock, stile, turnstile, tollgate; stairs, flight of s., stairway, ladder 308 ascent.

bridge, brig; footbridge, flyover, road bridge, aqueduct; suspension bridge, swing b., Bailey b.; humpback b.; viaduct, span; railway bridge; pontoon bridge, floating b., transporter b.; drawbridge; causeway, stepping-stone, gangway, gangplank, catwalk, duckboards; ford, ferry 305 *passage*; way under, subway, underpass 263 *tunnel*; isthmus.

route, direction, way to *or* from, course, march, tack, track; trajectory, orbit; carriageway, lane, bus l. 305 *traffic control*; air lane, sea-l., seaway, fairway, waterway 351 *conduit*; short cut, bypass; detour; line of communication.

path, pathway, footpath, pavement, sidewalk; towpath, bridlepath; lane, track, sheep t., trail, heritage t.; right of way, public footpath; walk, promenade, esplanade, front, avenue, drive, boulevard, mall; pedestrian precinct, arcade, colonnade, aisle, cloister, ambulatory; racetrack, running track, speed t. 724 *arena*; fairway, runway.

road, high r., highway, Queen's h., highways and byways; main road, A road, minor r., B r., dirt r., cinder track; side road; toll road, turnpike, route nationale; thoroughfare, trunk r., artery, bypass, ring road; motorway, M-way, autoroute, autobahn, autostrada; expressway, throughway, clearway; sliproad, fast lane; crossroads, junction, T-junction, turn-off; intersection, roundabout, cloverleaf; crossing, pedestrian c., zebra c, pelican c. 305 *traffic control*; roadway, carriageway, dual c.; central reservation, crash barrier; cycle track, cycleway; street, high s., one-way s., side s., back s.; alleyway, wynd, alley, blind a., cul de sac; close, avenue 192 *housing*; pavement, sidewalk, kerb; paving, cobbles, setts, paving stone, flagstones; hard shoulder, verge; macadam, tarmac, asphalt, road metal; surface.

railway, railroad, line; permanent way, track, lines, railway l., electrified l., main line, branch l.; tramlines, tramway; monorail; funicular; overhead railway, elevated r., underground r., electric r., subway, tube, metro 274 *train*; light railway, narrow gauge, standard g.; junction, crossover, level crossing, tunnel, cutting, embankment; siding, marshalling yard, goods y., shunting y.; station, halt; platform 145 *stopping place*; signal; rails, points, sleepers.

Adv. *via*, by way of, in transit.

625 Middle way

N. *middle way*, middle course, middle of the road; balance, golden mean, happy medium 30 *average*; halfway, halfway house, midstream 30

middle point; half tide; neutrality 177 *moderation*; half measures 601 *irresolution*; mutual concession 770 *compromise*.

moderate, nonextremist, wet, Girondist, Menshevik; neutral, don't know; Laodicean.

Adj. *neutral*, impartial 913 *just*; uncommitted, unattached, free-floating, don't know; detached 860 *indifferent*; moderate, wet, nonextreme, middle-of-the-road 225 *central*; sitting on the fence, lukewarm, half-and-half, shilly-shallying 601 *irresolute*; neither one thing nor the other, grey.

626 Circuit

N. *circuit*, roundabout way, circuitous route, scenic r., bypass, detour, ring road, loop, diversion; orbit, round, lap 314 *circuition*; circumference 250 *circle*.

Adj. *roundabout*, circuitous, indirect, meandering; circumlocutory 570 *diffuse*; skirting.

Vb. *circuit*, lap, beat the bounds, go round, make a circuit, loop the loop 314 *circle*; make a detour, go a roundabout way, go out of one's way 282 *deviate*; short-circuit 620 *avoid*; encircle, encompass 230 *surround*; skirt.

Adv. *round about*, round the world, in a roundabout way, circuitously, indirectly, from pillar to post.

627 Requirement

N. *requirement*, essential, sine qua non, a must 596 *necessity*; needs, necessities; indent, order, requisition, shopping list; stipulation, prerequisite; need 636 *insufficiency*; gap, lacuna 190 *absence*; demand, call for, run on, seller's market, bearish m., bullish m. 792 *purchase*; consumption, input, intake; shortage 307 *shortfall*; slippage; balance due, what is owing 803 *debt*; claim 761 *request*; ultimatum, injunction 737 *command*.

needfulness, necessity for, indispensability, desirability; necessitousness, want, breadline, poverty level 801 *poverty*; exigency, urgency, emergency 137 *crisis*; matter of life and death 638 *important matter*; bare minimum.

Adj. *required*, requisite, prerequisite, needful, needed; necessary, essential, vital, indispensable; called for, in demand 859 *desired*.

necessitous, in want, in need, feeling the pinch, on the breadline, in the poverty trap; lacking, deprived of; destitute 801 *poor*; starving 636 *underfed*; disadvantaged.

Vb. *require*, need, have need of, want, lack 636 *be unsatisfied*; be without, feel the need for, have occasion for; have a vacancy for; miss; crave 859 *desire*; cry out f.; claim, put in a claim for, apply for 761 *request*; find necessary, be unable to do without, must have; create a need, necessitate; make demands 737 *demand*; order, tele-order, indent, requisition; reserve, book.

628 Instrumentality

N. *instrumentality*, operation 173 *agency*; occasion 156 *cause*; result 157 *effect*; pressure 178 *influence*; efficacy 160 *power*; services 703 *aid*; intervention, interference 678 *activity*; medium 629 *means*; use; instrumentation, mechanization, automation, computerization 630 *machine*.

instrument, hand, organ, sense o.; amanuensis, scribe, lackey, slave 742 *servant*; agent, midwife, medium, help, assistant 703 *aider*; go-between, pander 720 *mediator*; catalyst; vehicle; pawn; robot 630 *machine*; cat's paw, stooge, puppet, creature 707 *auxiliary*; weapon, implement, appliance, lever 630 *tool*; magic ring, Aladdin's lamp 983 *spell*; key, skeleton k., master k., passkey 263 *opener*; open sesame, watchword, password, slogan, shibboleth, passport 756 *permit*; stepping-stone 624 *bridge*; highway 624 *road*; controls; device, gadget, gizmo 623 *contrivance*.

Adj. *instrumental*, working 173 *operative*; manual; automatic, computerized, electronic, push-button 630 *mechanical*; effective 160 *powerful*; conducive; applied; serviceable, promoting, assisting, helpful 703 *aiding*; functional.

Vb. *be instrumental*, work, act 173 *operate*; perform 676 *do*; serve, work for, lend oneself *or* itself to; help, assist 703 *aid*; advance, promote 703 *patronize*; have a hand in 775 *participate*; be to blame for 156 *cause*; be the creature of, be a cat's paw, pull another's chestnuts out of the fire; use one's influence, pull strings 178 *influence*.

Adv. *through*, per, by the hand of, by means of, with the help of, thanks to.

629 Means

N. *means*, ways and m., wherewithal; power, capacity 160 *ability*; conveniences, facilities; appliances, tools, tools of the trade, bag of tricks 630 *tool*; technology, new t., high t., high tech, third wave 490 *knowledge*; technique, know-how 694 *skill*; equipment, supplies, ammunition 633 *provision*; resources, raw material 631 *materials*; nuts and bolts 630 *machine*; workforce, manpower 686 *personnel*; cash flow 797 *money*; capital, working c. 628 *instrument*; assets, stock-in-trade 777 *property*; stocks and shares, investments; revenue, income; borrowing capacity; reserves, something in reserve, shot in one's locker, card up one's sleeve, two strings to one's bow 662 *safe-guard*; method, measures, steps 624 *way*; expedient, device, resort, recourse 623 *contrivance*; last resort.

Adv. *by means of*, with, by, using, through; with the aid of; by dint of.

630 Tool

N. *tool*, precision t., machine t., hand t, implement 628 *instrument*; apparatus, appliance, utensil; weapon, arm 723 *arms*; device, contraption, gadget, gizmo 623 *contrivance*; doodah, thingummy, whatsit; screw, screwdriver, drill, electric d. 263 *perforator*; wrench, monkey w., pipe w., mole w., Stillson (tdmk), spanner; pliers, pincers, tweezers 778 *pincers*; chisel, wedge, knife, Stanley (tdmk) k. 256 *sharp edge*; rope 47 *cable*; peg, nail 217 *hanger*, 218 *support*; leverage, lever, jemmy, crowbar, jack 218 *pivot*; grip, haft, shaft, tiller, helm, rudder 218 *handle*; pulley, sheave 250 *wheel*; switch, stopcock; trigger; pedal, pole, punt-p. 287 *propulsion*; ram 279 *hammer*; prehistoric tool, flint; tools of the trade, tool-kit, do-it-yourself k., bag of tricks.

machine, machinery, mechanism, works; clockwork, wheels within wheels; nuts and bolts 58 *component*; spring, mainspring, hairspring; gears, gearing, bevel gears, syncromesh, automatic gear change; motor, engine, internal combustion e., lean-burn e., diesel e., steam e.; turbine, dynamo 160 *sources of energy*; servomechanism, servomotor; robot, automaton; computer 86 *data processing*.

equipment, gear, tackle; outfit, kit; furnishing; trappings, accoutrement 228 *dress*; utensils, impedimenta, paraphernalia, chattels 777 *property*; wares, stock-in-trade 795 *merchandise*; plant 687 *workshop*.

machinist, operator, operative; driver; engineer, technician, mechanic, fitter; craftsman, skilled worker 686 *artisan*.

Adj. *mechanical*, mechanized, motorized, powered, power-driven; labour-saving, automatic 628 *instrumental*; automated, computerized, electronic.

631 Materials

N. *materials*, resources 629 *means*; material, stuff; raw material; meat, fodder 301 *food*; ore, mineral, metal, pig-iron, ingot; clay, adobe, china clay, potter's c., gypsum 344 *soil*; glass 422 *transparency*; plastic, polythene, polyethylene, polypropylene, polystyrene, polyvinyl chloride, PVC, polytetrafluoroethylene, latex, celluloid, fibreglass; rope, yarn, wool 208 *fibre*; leather, hide 226 *skin*; timber 366 *wood*; rafter, board 218 *beam*; plank, plywood, lath; stuffing 227 *lining*; cloth, fabric 222 *textile*.

building material, building block, breeze b.,

brick 381 *pottery*; bricks and mortar, lath and plaster, wattle and daub; thatch, slate, tile 226 *roof*; stone, marble, granite, flint, ashlar, masonry; rendering 226 *facing*; cement, concrete, reinforced c., flag, cobble 226 *paving*; gravel, tarmac, asphalt 624 *road*.

paper, pulp, newsprint; card, art paper, cartridge p., carbon p., tissue p., crepe p., tracing p., cellophane; papier mâché, cardboard, pasteboard; sheet, foolscap, quarto, imperial, A1, A2, A3, A4, A5; quire, ream; notepaper 586 *stationery*.

632 Store

N. *store*, mass, heap, load, stack, stockpile, mountain, butter m., lake, wine l., buildup 74 *accumulation*; packet, bundle, bagful, bucketful 26 *quantity*; harvest, crop, vintage, mow 771 *acquisition*; haystack, haycock, hayrick; stock, stock-in-trade 795 *merchandise*; assets, capital, holding, investment 777 *property*; fund, reserves, something in reserve, backlog; savings, savings account, nest egg; deposit, hoard, treasure; buried treasure, cache 527 *hiding-place*; bottom drawer, hope chest, trousseau 633 *provision*; pool, kitty; appeal fund; quarry, mine, gold-m.; natural resources, mineral deposit, coal d.; coalfield, gasfield, oilfield; coal mine, colliery, working, shaft; coalface, seam, lode; vein; well, oil w., gusher; fountain, fount 156 *source*; supply, stream; tap, pipeline, artesian well 341 *irrigator*; milch cow, the goose that lays the golden eggs, cornucopia, abundance 635 *plenty*.

storage, stowage, gathering, garnering 74 *accumulation*; conservation, bottling 666 *preservation*; safe deposit 660 *protection*; stabling, warehousing; mountain, butter m., lake, wine l.; storage space, shelf-room, space, accommodation 183 *room*; boxroom, loft; hold, bunker 194 *cellar*; storehouse, storeroom, stockroom; warehouse, goods shed; depot, dock, wharf 192 *stable*; magazine, arsenal, armoury, gunroom; treasure house 799 *treasury*; exchequer, strongroom, vault, coffer, moneybox, moneybag, till, safe, night s., bank; blood b., sperm b.; data b. 86 *data processing*; store of memories 505 *memory*; hive, honeycomb; granary, garner, barn, silo; water tower, reservoir, cistern, tank, gas-holder, gasometer; battery, garage, petrol station, gas s., filling s., petrol pump; dump, sump, drain, cesspool, sewage farm 649 *sink*; pantry, larder, buttery, stillroom 194 *chamber*; cupboard, shelf 194 *cabinet*; refrigerator, fridge, deep freeze, freezer, fridge-freezer; portmanteau, holdall, packing case 194 *box*; container, holder, quiver 194 *receptacle*.

collection, set, complete s.; archives, file 548 *record*; portfolio 74 *accumulation*; museum 125 *antiquity*; gallery, art g., art museum; library, thesaurus 559 *dictionary*; menagerie, aquarium 369 *zoo*; waxworks, Madame Tussaud's; exhibition 522 *exhibit*; repertory, repertoire, bag of tricks.

Vb. *store*, stow, pack, bundle 193 *load*; roll up, fold up; lay up, stow away, mothball; dump, garage, stable, warehouse; gather, harvest, reap, mow, pick, glean 370 *cultivate*; stack, heap, pile, amass, accumulate 74 *bring together*; stock up, stock up one's cupboards *or* larder, lay in, bulk-buy, panic buy, stock-pile, pile up, build up; take on, take in, fuel; fill, fill up, top up, refill, refuel 633 *replenish*; put by, save, keep, hold, file, hang on to 778 *retain*; bottle, pickle, conserve 666 *preserve*; leave, set aside, put a., lay by, put b., reserve; bank, deposit, invest; hoard, treasure; bury, stash away, secrete 525 *conceal*; husband, save up, salt away, make a nest egg, prepare for a rainy day 814 *economize*; equip oneself, put in the bottom drawer 669 *prepare oneself*; pool, put in the kitty.

633 Provision

N. *provision*, furnishing, equipment; catering; service, delivery, distribution; self-service; procuring; feeding, entertainment, bed and breakfast, board and lodging, maintenance; assistance, lending 703 *subvention*; supply, food s., water s., feed; pipeline 272 *transference*; commissariat, provisioning, supplies, stores, rations, iron r., reserves 632 *store*; refill, filling-up 54 *plenitude*; food, provender 301 *provisions*, helping, portion 301 *meal*; grist to the mill, fuel to the flame; produce 164 *product*; budgeting.

caterer, purveyor, hotelier, hotelkeeper, hotel manager, restaurateur, head waiter, maître d'hôtel; innkeeper, landlord, landlady, licensee, mine host, publican; housekeeper, housewife; cook, chef, pastrycook, confectioner.

Vb. *provide*, afford, offer, lend 781 *give*; equip, furnish, arm, man, fit out, kit o. 669 *make ready*; supply; yield 164 *produce*; cater, purvey; procure, pander, pimp; service, service an order, meet an o. 793 *sell*; distribute, deliver, deliver the goods; hand out, hand round, serve, serve up, dish up; feed, do for, board, put up, maintain, keep, clothe; stock; budget, make provision, make due p.; provide for oneself, do for o.; stock up, lay in a stock 632 *store*; fuel; forage, water.

replenish, reinforce, top up, refill 54 *fill*; restock, refuel.

634 Waste

N. *waste*, wastage; leakage; depletion, exhaustion, drainage 300 *voidance*; dissipation 75 *dispersion*; evaporation 338 *vaporization*; melting 337 *liquefaction*; damage 772 *loss*; wear and tear, built-in obsolescence 655 *deterioration*; wastefulness, improvidence, lavishness, extravagance, overspending, squandering; overproduction 637 *superfluity*; misapplication, frittering away; vandalism, sabotage 165 *destruction*; waste product, litter, refuse 641 *rubbish*.

Adj. *wasteful*, extravagant, uneconomic 815 *prodigal*; time-consuming; damaging 165 *destructive*.

Vb. *waste*, deplete, drain 300 *empty*; dissipate, scatter; abuse, overwork, overfish, overgraze; wear out, erode, damage 655 *impair*; misapply, fritter away, cast pearls before swine; make no use of 674 *not use*; labour in vain 641 *waste effort*; be extravagant, overspend, squander, throw away, pour down the drain, throw out the baby with the bath water 815 *be prodigal*; be careless, spill; be destructive, destroy, sabotage, vandalize; be wasted, decay 37 *decrease*; leak; melt, melt away 337 *liquefy*; evaporate 338 *vaporize*; run to seed 655 *deteriorate*; go down the drain.

635 Sufficiency

N. *sufficiency*, elegant s., right amount; right number, quorum; adequacy, enough; assets, competence, living wage; subsistence farming; self-sufficiency; exact requirement, no surplus; breadline; minimum, bare minimum, least one can do; full measure; fulfilment 725 *completion*; one's fill.

plenty, horn of p., cornucopia 171 *abundance*; showers of, flood, spate, oceans, streams 350 *stream*; lots, lashings, oodles, galore 32 *great quantity*; copiousness 54 *plenitude*; affluence, riches 800 *wealth*; fat of the land, luxury, groaning board, feast, banquet 301 *feasting*; orgy, profusion 815 *prodigality*; richness, fat; fertility, productivity, luxuriance, lushness 171 *productiveness* harvest, rich h., vintage h., bumper crop; bonanza, endless supply; more than enough, too much, superabundance, embarras de choix, embarras de richesses 637 *redundance*.

Adj. *sufficient*, sufficing; self-sufficient 54 *complete*; enough, adequate, competent; enough to go round; satisfactory; up to the mark; just right, not too much not too little; only just enough.

plentiful, plenteous, ample, enough and to spare, more than enough 637 *superfluous*; lavish 813 *liberal*; without stint, unsparing, inexhaustible 32 *great*; luxuriant, riotous, lush, fertile, fat 171 *prolific*; profuse, abundant, copious, overflowing 637 *redundant*; rich, opulent, affluent 800 *moneyed*.

filled, full up, chock-full, chock-a-block, replete, satiated, had it up to here, ready to burst 863 *sated*; satisfied; teeming, overflowing with.

Vb. *suffice*, be enough, do. just do, do and no more, serve; qualify, make the grade 727 *be successful*; pass, pass muster, measure up to, meet requirements, fill the bill; rise to the occasion; stand up to, take the strain 218 *support*; do what is required 725 *carry out*; satisfy 828 *content*; more than satisfy, satiate; make adequate provision 633 *provide*.

abound, proliferate, teem, swarm, bristle with, crawl w. 104 *be many*; riot, luxuriate 171 *be fruitful*; flow, shower, snow, pour, stream, sheet 350 *rain*; brim, overflow, flow with milk and honey 637 *superabound*.

have enough, be satisfied 828 *be content*; eat one's fill 301 *eat*; drink one's fill 301 *drink*; be sated, be chock-full, have had enough, have had it up to here, have had one's bellyful, be fed up 829 *be discontented*; have the means 800 *afford*.

Adv. *enough*, sufficiently, amply, to the full, to one's heart's content; on tap, on demand; abundantly.

636 Insufficiency

N. *insufficiency*, not enough, drop in the bucket; nonsatisfaction 829 *discontent*; inadequacy, incompetence; minginess, nothing to spare, too few; deficiency, imperfection 647 *defect*; deficit 55 *incompleteness*; nonfulfilment 726 *noncompletion*; half measures, failure, weakness, slippage 307 *shortfall*; bankruptcy 805 *insolvency*; subsistence level, breadline, poverty level, pittance, dole, mite; stinginess, meanness 816 *parsimony*; short commons, iron rations, starvation r., half r.; austerity, Spartan fare, starvation diet, bread and water 945 *asceticism*; malnutrition, vitamin deficiency 651 *disease*.

scarcity, scarceness, paucity 105 *fewness*; dearth, seven lean years; drought, famine, starvation; shortage 307 *shortfall*; slippage; power cut 37 *decrease*; short supply, seller's market, bearish m.; scantiness, meagreness; deprivation 801 *poverty*; lack, want, need 627 *needfulness*.

Adj. *insufficient*, disappointing 829 *discontenting*; inadequate, not enough, too little; scant, scanty, skimpy, slender; deficient, light on, low on, lacking 55 *incomplete*; wanting, poor 35 *inferior*; incompetent, unequal to, not up to it 695 *unskilful*; weak, thin, watery, wersh, jejune, unnourishing 4 *insubstantial*; niggardly, miserly; stingy 816 *parsimonious*.

unprovided, unfurnished, ill-equipped; bare; unfilled, unsated 829 *discontented*; unprovided for, unaccommodated; lacking in, hard up 801 *poor*; undercapitalized, underfinanced, understaffed, undermanned, shorthanded, unavailable, off the menu, off 190 *absent*.

underfed, undernourished; half-starved, on short commons; famished, starved, starving ravening, ravenous 946 *fasting*; skin and bone, anorexic, emaciated.

scarce, rare 140 *infrequent*; sparse 105 *few*; in short supply, at a premium, hard to get, hard to come by, not to be had for love or money, not to be had at any price, unavailable, unobtainable, out of season, out of stock.

Vb. *not suffice*, be insufficient, – inadequate etc. adj.; not meet requirements 647 *be imperfect*; want, lack; fail 509 *disappoint*; fall below 35 *be inferior*; come short, default 307 *fall short*; run out, dry up; paper over the cracks 726 *not complete*.

be unsatisfied, ask for more, come again, take a second helping; feel dissatisfied; spurn an offer, reject; miss, feel the lack, stand in need of; be a glutton for, be unable to have enough of 947 *gluttonize*.

637 Redundance

N. *redundance*, redundancy, overspill, overflow; superabundance; embarras de richesses, avalanche, spate 32 *great quantity*; too many, mob 74 *crowd*; saturation, saturation point 54 *plenitude*; excess 634 *waste*; excessiveness, exorbitance, extremes, too much 546 *exaggeration*; overdoing it, overstretching oneself, overextension, too many irons in the fire 678 *overactivity*; officiousness, red tape; overpraise, overoptimism 482 *overestimation*; overweight; overload, last straw 322 *gravity*; lion's share; overindulgence 943 *intemperance*; plethora, congestion 863 *satiety*; more than enough; glut; obesity 651 *disease*.

superfluity, more than is needed, luxury; frills, luxuries, nonessentials; overkill, duplication; something over, bonus, spare cash, money to burn 40 *extra*; margin, overlap, excess, surplus, balance 41 *remainder*; superfluousness, accessory, fifth wheel, parasite 641 *uselessness*; padding; tautology 570 *diffuseness*; redundancy; overmanning 678 *activity*; too much of a good thing, embarras de richesses, glut, drug on the market; surfeit, overdose 863 *satiety*.

Adj. *redundant*, one too many, one over the eight 104 *many*; overmuch, overabundant, excessive, immoderate 32 *exorbitant*; overdone, overflowing, overfull, running over, brimming

over 54 *full*; flooding; snowed under, overwhelmed; cloying; replete, stuffed, overfed; overstretched; overloaded; congested.

superfluous, redundant, supernumerary; needless, unnecessary, uncalled for 641 *useless*; excessive; luxurious; surplus, extra, over and above 41 *remaining*; spare 38 *additional*; de trop, on one's hands, left over, going begging 860 *unwanted*; dispensable, expendable.

Vb. *superabound*, luxuriate 635 *abound*; run riot 171 *be fruitful*; bristle with, swarm w., teem w., hotch w., crawl w.; overflow, brim over, burst at the seams 54 *be complete*; flood, inundate, burst its banks, deluge, overwhelm 350 *flow*; engulf 299 *absorb*; know no bounds, spread far and wide 306 *overstep*; overlap 183 *extend*; saturate 341 *drench*; stuff, gorge, cram 54 *fill*; congest, choke, suffocate; overdose, glut, cloy, satiate, sate; pamper oneself, overindulge o., overeat, overdrink 943 *be intemperate*; oversubscribe, do more than enough; oversell, flood the market; overstock; overdo, go over the top, overstep the mark, pile it on, lay it on thick, lay it on with a trowel 546 *exaggerate*; overload, overburden; overcharge; lavish upon 813 *be liberal*; be lavish, make a splash 815 *be prodigal*; roll in, stink of 800 *be rich*.

be superfluous, – redundant etc. adj.; go begging, remain on one's hands 41 *be left*; have time on one's hands 679 *be inactive*; do twice over, duplicate; carry coals to Newcastle, gild the lily, teach one's grandmother to suck eggs; labour the obvious, take a sledgehammer to crack a nut, break a butterfly on a wheel, hold a candle to the sun; exceed requirements.

638 Importance

N. *importance*, priority, urgency 64 *precedence*; paramountcy, supremacy 34 *superiority*; essentialness; import, consequence, significance, weight, weightiness, gravity, seriousness; substance, moment 3 *substantiality*; interest, consideration, concern 622 *business*; notability, memorability, mark, prominence, distinction, eminence 866 *repute*; influence 866 *prestige*; size, magnitude 32 *greatness*; rank; value, merit 644 *goodness*; stress, emphasis.

important matter, vital concern, hot-button issue, bottom line, crucial moment, turning point 137 *crisis*; be-all and end-all; no joke, no laughing matter, matter of life and death; big news 529 *news*; exploit 676 *deed*; landmark, milestone; red-letter day, great d. 876 *special day*.

chief thing, what matters, the thing, great t., main t.; supreme issue, crux 452 *topic*; fundamentals, bedrock, nitty-gritty; nuts and bolts, sine qua non 627 *requirement*; priority 605 *choice*; substance 5 *essential part*; highlight; cream, crème de la crème, pick 644 *elite*; keynote, cornerstone, mainstay, linchpin, kingpin; head, spearhead; sum and substance, heart of the matter, heart, core, kernel, nucleus, nub 225 *centre*; hub 218 *pivot*; chief hope, trump card, main chance.

bigwig, personage, notable, personality, heavyweight, somebody 866 *person of repute*; local worthy, pillar of the community; great man *or* woman, VIP, brass hat; his *or* her nibs, big gun, big shot, big noise, big wheel, big white chief, Mr Big; leading light; kingpin; prima donna, star, lion, catch 890 *favourite*; head, chief, godfather, Big Brother 34 *superior*; the greatest 644 *exceller*; grandee 868 *aristocrat*; magnate, mogul, mandarin; baron, tycoon 741 *autocrat*; captains of industry, big battalions, top brass, top people, establishment 733 *authority*; superpower 178 *influence*.

Adj. *important*, weighty, grave, serious; pregnant; of consequence, of importance, of concern; considerable; world-shattering, earth-shaking, momentous, critical, fateful 137 *timely*; chief, capital, cardinal, staple, major, main, paramount 34 *supreme*; crucial, essential; pivotal, hot-button 225 *central*; basic, fundamental, bedrock, radical, grass-roots; primary, prime, foremost, leading; worthwhile, not to be sneezed at 644 *valuable*; necessary, vital, indispensable, key 627 *required*; significant, telling; imperative, urgent, high-priority; high-level; hush-hush 523 *latent*; high, grand, noble 32 *great*.

notable, memorable, signal, unforgettable 505 *remembered*; first-rate, A1, outstanding, superior; top-rank, top-flight 644 *excellent*; conspicuous, prominent, eminent, distinguished, exalted, august 866 *noteworthy*; imposing 821 *impressive*; formidable, powerful 178 *influential*; newsworthy, front-page; eventful, world-shattering, earth-shaking, epoch-making.

639 Unimportance

N. *unimportance*, inconsequence, insignificance 35 *inferiority*; immateriality, lack of substance 4 *insubstantiality*; nothingness; pettiness 33 *smallness*; triviality; worthlessness 812 *cheapness*; uselessness 641 *uselessness*; irrelevance, red herring 10 *unrelatedness*.

trifle, inessential, triviality; nothing, mere n., no great matter, secondary matter, nothing of note, matter of indifference, not the end of the world; no great shakes, nothing to speak of, nothing to write home about, nothing to worry about, storm in a teacup 482 *overestimation*; bagatelle, tinker's cuss, fig, damn, toss, straw, chaff, pin, button, feather, dust; tuppence,

small change, small beer; paltry sum, peanuts, chickenfeed, flea-bite; pinprick, scratch; nothing to it, child's play 701 *easy thing*; peccadillo; trifles, trivia, minutiae, petty detail 80 *particulars*; whit, jot, the least bit, drop in the ocean 33 *small quantity*; cent, brass farthing 33 *small quantity*; nonsense.

bauble, toy 837 *plaything*; geegaw, doodad, knick-knack, bric-a-brac, novelty, trinket; tinsel, trumpery, frippery, trash, gimcrack.

nonentity, nobody, nonperson; man of straw 4 *insubstantial thing*; figurehead, cipher, sleeping partner; lightweight, small beer; small fry, small game; other ranks, lower orders 869 *commonalty*; second fiddle 35 *inferior*; underling; pawn in the game, cat's paw, stooge, puppet 628 *instrument*; poor relation 801 *poor person*.

Adj. *unimportant*, immaterial 4 *insubstantial*; inconsequential, of no consequence, of no great weight; insignificant 515 *meaningless*; inessential, nonessential, fringe; unnecessary, expendable; small, petty, trifling, paltry 33 *inconsiderable*; negligible, inappreciable, not worth considering; weak, measly; obscure; beneath contempt 922 *contemptible*; jumped-up, no-account, tinpot; low-level, secondary, minor, subsidiary, peripheral 35 *inferior*.

trivial, trifling, piffling, piddling; pettifogging, nit-picking; footling, frivolous, puerile, childish 499 *foolish*; airy 4 *insubstantial*; superficial 212 *shallow*; slight 33 *small*; lightweight 323 *light*; parish-pump, small-time; twopenny-halfpenny, one-horse, second-rate, third-r.; grotty, rubbishy, trashy, tawdry, shoddy, gimcrack 645 *bad*; two-a-penny 812 *cheap*; worthless, valueless 641 *useless*; not worth a second thought 922 *contemptible*; token, nominal, symbolic; mediocre, nondescript, eminently forgettable; commonplace, ordinary, uneventful 610 *usual*.

640 Utility

N. *utility*, use, usefulness; employability, serviceability, handiness 628 *instrumentality*; efficacy, efficiency 160 *ability*; adequacy 635 *sufficiency*; applicability, suitability 642 *good policy*; availability 189 *presence*; service, avail, help; value, worth, merit 644 *goodness*; virtue, function, capacity, potency, clout 160 *power*; advantage, commodity; profitability, bottom line, earning capacity, productivity 171 *productiveness*; profit, mileage 771 *gain*; convenience, benefit, common weal, public good 615 *good*; utilitarianism, functionalism; employment, utilization 673 *use*.

Adj. *useful*, of use, helpful, of service 703 *aiding*; sensible, practical, applied, functional; versatile, multipurpose, all-purpose, of all work;

practicable, convenient, expedient 642 *advisable*; at hand, available, on tap; serviceable, fit for, good for, applicable; ready for use, operative, on stream, usable, employable; valid, current; able, competent, efficacious, effective, effectual, efficient 160 *powerful*; conducive; adequate 635 *sufficient*; pragmatic, utilitarian.

profitable, paying, remunerative 771 *gainful*; beneficial, advantageous, to one's advantage, edifying, worthwhile 615 *good*; worth one's salt, worth one's keep, worth one's weight in gold, invaluable, priceless 644 *valuable*.

find useful, find a use for, make use of, utilize 673 *use*; turn to good account, make capital out of 137 *profit by*; reap the benefit of 771 *gain*; be the better for 654 *get better*.

641 Inutility

N. *uselessness*; inutility, superfluousness 637 *superfluity*; futility, inanity; worthlessness; inadequacy 636 *insufficiency*; inefficacy, ineffectualness, inability 161 *impotence*; inefficiency, incompetence, ineptitude 695 *unskilfulness*; unserviceableness, unfitness 643 *inexpedience*; inapplicability, no benefit 172 *unproductiveness*; unhelpfulness.

lost labour, wasted effort 728 *failure*; game not worth the candle; waste of breath, waste of time, dead loss; labours in vain, wild-goose chase, fool's errand; labour of Sisyphus.

rubbish, trash, load of old rubbish; waste, refuse, lumber, junk, scrap, litter; wastage, bilge, wastepaper; scourings, sweepings, shavings 41 *leavings*; chaff, husks, bran; scraps; crumbs; offal, carrion; dust, muck, debris, slag, clinker, dross, scum 649 *dirt*; peel, orange p., banana skin, dead wood, stubble, weeds; rags and bones, old clothes, cast-offs; reject; midden, rubbish heap, tip, slag heap, dump.

Adj. *useless*, functionless, purposeless, pointless; naff; futile 497 *absurd*; unpractical, impracticable, unworkable, no go; nonfunctional 844 *ornamental*; redundant; expendable, dispensable; unfit, inapplicable 643 *inexpedient*; fit for nothing, unusable, unemployable; inefficient, incompetent 695 *unskilful*; unable, ineffective, feckless, ineffectual 161 *impotent*; nonfunctioning, inoperative, dud, kaput; invalid; out of order; broken down, worn out, hors de combat, past it, obsolete; hopeless, vain.

profitless, loss-making, unprofitable, wasteful, ill-spent; vain, abortive 728 *unsuccessful*; nothing to show for; unrewarding, thankless; fruitless; valueless; not worth the effort, not worth the paper it is written on 645 *bad*; unsaleable, dear at any price 811 *dear*.

make useless, disqualify, unfit, disarm, render harmless, take the sting out of 161 *disable*; cas-

trate, emasculate 161 *unman*; cripple, lame, clip the wings 655 *impair*; put out of commission, lay up 679 *make inactive*; sabotage, throw a spanner in the works, put a spoke in one's wheel, cramp one's style 702 *obstruct*; take to pieces, break up 46 *disunite*; deface.

waste effort, labour the obvious; waste one's breath, waste one's time, talk to a brick wall, beat one's head against a b. w.; preach to the converted 637 *be superfluous*; be on a hiding to nothing, get nowhere, labour in vain; flog a dead horse, beat the air, tilt at windmills; cry for the moon 470 *attempt the impossible*.

642 Good policy

N. *good policy*, expediency, expedience; right answer, advisability, desirability, worthwhileness, suitability 640 *utility*; fitness, propriety 915 *dueness*; proper time, opportunity 137 *occasion*; convenience, pragmatism, utilitarianism, opportunism; profit, advantage 615 *benefit*; facilities.

Adj. *advisable*, commendable; as well to, better to, desirable; fitting, seemly, proper 913 *right*; well-timed, opportune 137 *timely*; prudent, politic, judicious 498 *wise*; expedient, advantageous; practical, pragmatic; applicable.

Vb. *be expedient*, not come amiss, come in useful, suit the occasion; be to the purpose, help 703 *aid*; forward, advance, promote; have the desired effect, produce results; work, do, serve, be better than nothing, deliver the goods, fill *or* fit the bill 635 *suffice*; achieve one's aim 727 *succeed*; fit, be just the thing 24 *accord*; profit, advantage, benefit 644 *do good*.

643 Inexpedience

N. *inexpedience*, inexpediency; not the answer, lack of planning; inadvisability, undesirability; unsuitability, unfitness 25 *inaptitude*; impropriety, unfittingness, unseemliness 916 *undueness*; wrongness 914 *wrong*; inopportuneness 138 *untimeliness*; inconvenience, disadvantage; mixed blessing, two-edged weapon, last resort 596 *necessity*.

Adj. *inexpedient*, better not, as well not to, inadvisable, undesirable, not recommended; ill-advised, impolitic, imprudent, injudicious 499 *unwise*; inappropriate, unfitting, out of place, unseemly; improper; unfit, inadmissible, unsuitable, unhappy, inept 25 *unapt*; unseasonable, inopportune, untimely 138 *ill-timed*; unsatisfactory 636 *insufficient*; inconvenient; detrimental, disadvantageous; unhealthy, unwholesome 653 *insalubrious*; unprofitable 641 *useless*; unhelpful; untoward 731 *useless*; awkward 695 *clumsy*; cumbersome.

644 Goodness

N. *goodness,* soundness 650 *health;* virtuosity 694 *skill;* quality, vintage; good points, redeeming feature; merit, desert, claim to fame; excellence, eminence; virtue, worth, value 809 *price;* pricelessness; flawlessness 646 *perfection;* quintessence 1 *essence.*

elite, chosen few; pick, prime, flower; cream, crème de la crème, salt of the earth, pick of the bunch, meritocracy; crack troops; top people 638 *bigwig;* charmed circle, top drawer, upper crust, aristocracy, Sloane Rangers 868 *upper class;* titbit, prime cut, pièce de résistance; plum, prize 729 *trophy.*

exceller, nonpareil; prodigy, gifted child, genius; superman, wonderwoman, wonder, wonder of the world 864 *prodigy;* Admirable Crichton 646 *paragon;* one in a thousand, one in a million, treasure; jewel, pearl, ruby, diamond 844 *gem;* gem of the first water, pure gold, chef-d'oeuvre, pièce de résistance, collector's item, museum piece 694 *masterpiece;* record-breaker, best-seller, chart-topper, best ever, last word in, ne plus ultra, best thing since sliced bread; bee's knees, cat's whiskers, cat's pyjamas; the goods, winner, corker, humdinger, wow, knockout, hit, smash h.; smasher, charmer 841 *a beauty;* star, idol 890 *favourite;* best of its kind, the tops, the greatest, top of the pops; top-notcher, top seed, first-rater; cock of the walk, toast of the town, Queen of the May; champion, title-holder, world-beater, prizewinner 727 *victor.*

Adj. *excellent,* fine, braw; exemplary; good, good as gold 933 *virtuous;* above par, preferable, better 34 *superior;* very good, first-rate, ace, A1, alpha plus; prime, quality, fine, superfine; God's own, superlative, in a class by itself; all-star, of the first water, rare, vintage, classic 646 *perfect;* choice, select, hand-picked, exquisite, recherché 605 *chosen;* exclusive, pure 44 *unmixed;* worthy, meritorious; admired, admirable, estimable, praiseworthy, creditable; famous, great; lovely 841 *beautiful;* glorious, dazzling, splendid, splendiferous, magnificent, marvellous, wonderful, terrific, sensational, superb, cool, wicked, def, awesome, phat.

super, superduper, fantastic, way-out, fabulous, fab, groovy, brill, magic, wizard, wizzo; spot-on, bang-on; top-notch, top-flight (**see** *best*); lovely, glorious, gorgeous, heavenly, out of this world 32 *prodigious;* smashing, stunning, spiffing, ripping, topping, swell, great, grand, famous, capital, dandy, bully, hunky-dory; scrumptious, delicious, juicy, plummy, jammy 826 *pleasurable.*

best, optimum, A1, champion, tiptop, top-notch, ace; first-rate, crack; second to none 34

supreme; unequalled, unparalleled, unmatched, peerless, unbeatable, unsurpassable 646 *perfect;* best-ever, record, record-breaking, best-selling, chart-topping.

valuable, invaluable, inestimable, priceless, costly, rich 811 *of price;* rare, precious, worth its weight in gold, worth a king's ransom; sterling, gilt-edged, blue-chip.

beneficial, wholesome, healthy, salutary; edifying, worthwhile, advantageous, profitable 640 *useful;* favourable, propitious 730 *prosperous.*

not bad, tolerable, so-so, passable, respectable, fair; all right, okay, OK; indifferent, middle-of-the-road, middling, mediocre, ordinary, fifty-fifty, average 30 *median.*

Vb. *be good* – sound etc. adj.; have merit, deserve well 915 *deserve;* stand the test, pass muster 635 *suffice;* equal the best 28 *be equal;* excel, transcend, take the prize 34 *be superior.*

do good, have a good effect, improve, edify; do a world of good; be the making of, make a man of 654 *make better;* help 615 *benefit;* do a favour, do a good turn.

645 Badness

N. *badness,* obnoxiousness, nastiness, beastliness, foulness, grossness, rottenness; unworthiness, worthlessness; second-rateness, inferiority; flaw 647 *imperfection;* shoddiness 641 *uselessness;* unsoundness, decay, corruption 655 *deterioration;* disruption; morbidity 651 *disease;* harmfulness, hurtfulness, ill, hurt, harm, injury, detriment, damage, mischief 616 *evil;* noxiousness, poisonousness, deadliness, virulence 653 *insalubrity;* poison, blight, canker, cancer 659 *bane;* pestilence, sickness 651 *plague;* contamination, plague spot, trouble s., hotbed 651 *infection;* affair, scandal 867 *slur;* abomination, filth 649 *uncleanness;* sewer 649 *sink;* bitterness; painfulness, sting, ache, pang, thorn in the flesh 377 *pain;* angst, anguish 825 *suffering;* maltreatment, oppression, persecution; unkindness, cruelty, malignancy, spitefulness, spite 898 *malevolence;* depravity, vice 934 *wickedness;* sin 936 *guilt;* bad influence, evil genius; ill wind; black magic, evil eye, hoodoo, jinx, gremlin 983 *sorcery;* curse 899 *malediction;* snake in the grass 663 *troublemaker.*

Adj. *bad,* vile, base, evil; gross, black; irredeemable; poor, mean, wretched, grotty, gungy, gruesome, measly, low-grade, second-rate, execrable, awful 35 *inferior;* worthless, shoddy, tacky, naff, crummy, ropy, punk, pathetic 641 *useless;* unsatisfactory, faulty, flawed 647 *imperfect;* incompetent, inefficient; mangled, spoiled 695 *bungled;* scruffy, filthy, mangy, manky 649 *dirty;* foul; gone bad, rank, tainted; corrupt, decaying, rotten to the core;

infected, poisoned, septic 651 *diseased*; incurable; depraved, vicious, villainous, accursed 934 *wicked*; heinous, sinful 936 *guilty*; mean, wrongful, unjust 914 *wrong*; sinister 616 *evil* (**see** *harmful*); contemptible; shameful, scandalous, disgraceful 867 *discreditable*; lamentable, deplorable, grievous, heavy, burdensome; too bad 827 *annoying*.

harmful, hurtful, injurious, damaging, detrimental, prejudicial, disadvantageous 643 *inexpedient*; deleterious, corrosive, destructive; pernicious, fatal 362 *deadly*; disastrous, ruinous, calamitous 731 *adverse*; degenerative, noxious, malign, malignant, unhealthy, unwholesome; infectious 653 *insalubrious*; polluting, poisonous, risky 661 *dangerous*; sinister, ominous, dire, dreadful, accursed, devilish 616 *evil*; mischievous, spiteful, malicious, malevolent, ill-disposed; mischief-making; inhuman 898 *cruel*; outrageous, rough, harsh, intolerant, persecuting 735 *oppressive*; monstrous 32 *exorbitant*.

not nice, obnoxious, nasty, beastly, horrid, horrific, horrible, terrible, gruesome, grim, ghastly, awful, dreadful, from hell; foul, rotten, lousy, putrid, putrefying, stinking, sickening, revolting, nauseous, nauseating; loathsome, detestable, abominable 888 *hateful*; vulgar, sordid, low, indecent, improper, gross, filthy, pornographic, obscene 951 *impure*; shocking, disgusting, reprehensible, monstrous, horrendous.

damnable, damned, darned, blasted, bloody, confounded, blinking, dratted, blankety-blank; execrable, accursed, cursed, hellish, infernal, devilish, diabolical.

Vb. *harm.* do h., do one a mischief; disagree with, make one ill, make one sick; injure, damage, pollute 655 *impair*; corrupt 655 *pervert*; play havoc with 63 *derange*; do no good; have a deleterious effect on; molest; plague; land one in trouble, queer one's pitch, do for; be unkind 898 *be malevolent*.

ill-treat, maltreat, abuse 675 *misuse*; ill-use, put upon, tyrannize, trample on, victimize, prey upon; persecute 735 *oppress*; wrong, distress 827 *torment*; outrage, violate, force; savage, maul, bite, scratch, tear 655 *wound*; stab 263 *pierce*; batter, bruise, buffet 279 *strike*; crucify 963 *torture*; take one's spite out on; crush 165 *destroy*.

Adv. *badly*, amiss, wrong, ill.

646 Perfection

N. *perfection*, sheer p.; finish; the ideal; immaculateness, faultlessness, flawlessness, mint condition; correctness, irreproachability; impeccability, infallibility; transcendence 34 *superiority*; quintessence, essence; peak, zenith,

pinnacle 213 *summit*; height of perfection, acme of p.; ne plus ultra, last word; chef d'oeuvre, flawless performance 694 *masterpiece*.

paragon, nonpareil, flower, prince of 644 *exceller*; ideal, knight in shining armour, saint, plaster s.; classic, pattern of perfection, model, shining example 23 *prototype*; superman, superwoman, wonderwoman, demigod 864 *prodigy*.

Adj. *perfect*, perfected, finished; just right, ideal, flawless, faultless, impeccable, infallible, correct, irreproachable; immaculate, spotless, blemish-free, without a stain; uncontaminated, pure 44 *unmixed*; sound as a bell, right as rain, in perfect condition; one hundred per cent, A1; complete 52 *intact*; consummate, unsurpassable 34 *supreme*; brilliant, masterly 694 *skilful*; model, classical.

undamaged, safe and sound, unhurt, unscathed, no harm done; unmarked; without blemish, unspoilt; without loss, intact; in the pink 650 *healthy*.

Vb. *perfect*, consummate, bring to perfection; put the finishing touch 213 *crown*; complete, leave nothing to be desired 725 *carry through*.

647 Imperfection

N. *imperfection*, imperfectness; room for improvement; faultiness, erroneousness, fallibility 495 *error*; patchiness, unevenness, curate's egg 17 *nonuniformity*; defectiveness, bit missing 55 *incompleteness*; deficiency, inadequacy 636 *insufficiency*; unsoundness 661 *vulnerability*; failure, weakness 307 *shortfall*; second best, third rate, makeshift 150 *substitute*; mediocrity; adulteration 43 *mixture*.

defect, fault 495 *error*; flaw, rift, leak, loophole, crack lacuna 201 *gap*; deficiency, limitation 307 *shortfall*; kink, foible, screw loose 503 *eccentricity*; weak point, soft spot, tragic flaw, chink in one's armour, Achilles' heel 661 *vulnerability*; feet of clay, weak link in the chain 163 *weakness*; stain, blot, spot, smudge 845 *blemish*; snag.

Adj. *imperfect*, not quite right, less than perfect, fallible, uneven, patchy, good in parts, like the curate's egg 17 *nonuniform*; faulty, botched 695 *bungled*; flawed, cracked; leaky; wobbly, rickety 163 *flimsy*; unsound 661 *vulnerable*; shop-soiled, tainted, stained, spotted, marked, scratched; below par, off form; unfit, not good enough, not up to the mark, inadequate, deficient, wanting, lacking 636 *insufficient*; defective 55 *incomplete*; broken 53 *fragmentary*; crippled; half-finished 55 *unfinished*; perfunctory 456 *inattentive*; warped, twisted, distorted 246 *deformed*; mutilated, maimed, lame 163 *weakened*; undeveloped, makeshift, jerry-built, rough and ready, provisional 150 *substituted*;

second-rate, third-rate 35 *inferior*; no great
shakes, nothing to boast of, nothing to write
home about.

Vb. *be imperfect*, fall short of perfection, be
flawed; not bear inspection, not pass muster,
fail the test, dissatisfy 636 *not suffice*; not make
the grade 924 *incur blame*; have feet of clay.

648 Cleanness

N. *cleanness*, immaculateness 950 *purity*; freshness, whiteness; spit and polish; cleanliness,
daintiness 862 *fastidiousness*.

cleansing, clean, spring-cleaning, dry-c.; washing, cleaning up, mopping up, washing up, wiping up, scrubbing; refining, purification;
purgation; washing out, flushing, dialysis; purging, enema, defecation 302 *excretion*; airing, ventilation, fumigation 338 *vaporization*;
deodorization 395 *inodorousness*; sterilization,
disinfection, decontamination, delousing; sanitation, drainage, sewerage, plumbing 652
hygiene; water closet, flush 649 *latrine*.

ablutions, washing; hygiene, oral h.; douche,
flush; wash, lick and a promise; soaking, bathing, dipping; soaping, lathering, scrubbing,
sponging, rinsing, shampoo; dip 313 *plunge*;
bath, tub; bathtub, hipbath, bidet; washbasin,
wash-hand basin, washstand; Turkish b., sauna,
Jacuzzi (tdmk), hot tub; shower; bathroom,
washroom, public baths; swimming bath, swimming pool; wash, laundry; washtub, washboard, dolly; copper, boiler, washing machine,
washer, twin tub, launderette.

cleanser, purifier; disinfectant, carbolic,
deodorant; detergent, soap, soap flakes; washing powder, soap p., washing-up liquid, water,
soap and w., shampoo; mouth wash, gargle;
cleansing cream; toothpaste; pumice stone; furniture polish, boot p., blacking; wax, varnish;
whitewash, paint; blacklead; aperient 658 *purgative*.

cleaning utensil, broom, besom, mop, sponge,
swab, scourer; loofah; duster, feather d.; brush,
scrubbing b., nailbrush, toothbrush, toothpick,
dental floss; comb, hair brush, clothes b.; dust-
pan and brush, waste bin, dustbin, wastepaper
basket, litter bin, waste disposal unit, com-
pactor; poop-scoop; carpet sweeper, vacuum
cleaner, Hoover (tdmk); doormat, foot-scraper;
pipe cleaner, windscreen wiper; sieve, riddle;
filter; dishwasher.

cleaning cloth, duster; dishcloth, tea towel;
wash-leather; chamois, shammy; face f., face-
cloth, towel, bath t., hand t.; handkerchief,
paper h., tissue; toilet tissue, toilet paper, lavatory p., toilet roll.

cleaner, laundryman, laundress, washer-
woman; washer-up, dish-washer; charwoman,

char, charlady, cleaner, help, daily help, daily,
home help; Mrs Mop; dustman, refuse collector; lavatory attendant, sanitary engineer; chimneysweep, window cleaner; bootblack.

Adj. *clean*, dirt-free; snowy 427 *white*;
polished, clean, shining 417 *undimmed*; cleanly;
fresh; bright as a new pin, fresh as a daisy;
cleaned, scrubbed, polished etc. vb.; cleaned
up, laundered; spruce, spick and span, well-
groomed 60 *orderly*; deodorized, disinfected,
hygienic, sterilized; purified, immaculate, spotless, clean as a whistle 646 *perfect*; ritually clean,
kosher 301 *edible*.

Vb. *clean*, spring-clean, clean up, clear up;
groom, valet, spruce; wash, wipe, wipe clean,
wash up, sponge, mop, mop up, swab, wash
down; scrub, scour; scrape 333 *rub*; do the washing, launder; bleach, dry-clean; soap, lather,
shampoo; bathe, dip, dunk, rinse, swill down,
sluice, douche, shower 341 *drench*; dust, sweep,
sweep up, beat, vacuum, hoover; brush, brush
up; buff, polish; blacklead 417 *make bright*;
whitewash 427 *whiten*; erase 550 *obliterate*;
clean out, clear out, make a clean sweep 300
eject.

purify, purge, clean up; bowdlerize, censor,
blue-pencil, expurgate; elevate 654 *make better*;
cleanse, freshen, ventilate, deodorize, fumigate;
desalinate; decontaminate, disinfect, sterilize,
chlorinate, pasteurize 652 *make sanitary*; refine,
distil, clarify, skim, scum, decarbonize; strain,
filter, percolate, leach; sift, sieve; dialyse, catheterize, clean out, wash o., drain.

649 Uncleanness

N. *uncleanness*, uncleanliness; soiling, dirtiness
(**see** *dirt*); muckiness; scruffiness, grottiness,
filthiness; lousiness; squalor; untidiness, sluttishness, slovenliness 61 *disorder*; stink 397
stench; pollution, defilement; corruption, taint,
putrefaction 51 *decomposition*; contamination
651 *infection*; unwashed body.

dirt, filth, stain, blot; crud, yuk, gunge, gunk,
muck, mud, sludge, slime; bog 347 *marsh*;
dung, droppings, ordure, faeces 302 *excrement*;
snot, mucus; dust, mote 332 *powder*; cobweb,
grime, smut, smudge, soot, smoke; grounds,
dregs; scourings 41 *leavings*; sediment, deposit,
precipitate, residuum, fur; scum, dross, froth;
ashes, cinders, ash; drainage, sewerage; slough;
scurf, dandruff; tartar, plaque; pus, matter,
refuse, garbage, litter 641 *rubbish*; rot, rust, mildew, mould, fungus 51 *decay*; vermin.

latrine, privy, heads, jakes, bog, john, loo;
closet, earth c., water closet, WC; cloakroom,
powder room, rest r., washroom, lavatory,
toilet; urinal, public convenience, comfort
station, Ladies, Gents; toilet bowl, lavatory b.,

commode, bedpan, chamber pot, potty 302 *defecation*.

sink, kitchen sink, draining board; cesspit,
cesspool, sump, septic tank; gutter, sewer 351
drain; dunghill, midden, tip, rubbish heap,
dust-h., compost-h.; dustbin, trashcan 194 *vessel*; pigsty; slum, spittoon.

dirty person, sloven, slattern, slut; litterbug, litter lout; street arab; scavenger 648 *cleaner*; pig,
ratbag, fleabag.

Adj. *unclean*, smutty, obscene, corrupt 951
impure; coarse, unpurified; septic, festering; non-
sterile 653 *infectious*; sordid, squalid, slummy,
insanitary, unhygienic 653 *insalubrious*; foul,
offensive, nasty, grotty, manky, yukky; disgusting, repulsive 645 *not nice*; nauseous,
nauseating, stinking, ponging; uncleanly;
grubby, scruffy, scabby, mangy; flea-ridden,
lousy, crawling; faecal, rotting, tainted, high;
flyblown, maggoty.

dirty, filthy; dusty, grimy, sooty, smoky,
fuggy; polluted, littered; untidy, unkempt, slatternly, sleazy, slovenly, sluttish, bedraggled;
unwashed; black, dingy, tarnished, stained,
soiled; greasy, oily; caked, matted, muddied;
messy, mucky, muddy, slimy 347 *marshy*; turbid; furred up, scummy; musty, fusty, cob-
webby; mouldy, rotten 655 *dilapidated*.

Vb. *be unclean*, – dirty etc. adj.; collect dust,
foul up, clog; rust, mildew, moulder, rot, go
bad, go off 51 *decompose*; smell 397 *stink*.

make unclean, foul, dirty, soil; stain, blot,
sully, tarnish; muck up, make a mess, untidy 61
be disordered; besmirch, smudge, blur, smoke
419 *bedim*; spot; streak, smear, besmear, grease;
cake, clog, muddy, bespatter, splash; taint,
infect, pollute, contaminate 655 *impair*; defile,
profane, desecrate.

650 Health

N. *health*, rude h., good h.; healthiness, iron
constitution, health and strength 162 *vitality*;
fitness, good condition, pink of c.; bloom, rosy
cheeks, ruddy complexion; well-being, physical
w.; soundness; clean bill of health; health
warning.

Adj. *healthy*, wholesome, sanitary 652 *salubrious*; in good health, bursting with h., blooming,
ruddy, rosy; lusty, bouncing, strapping, hale,
hearty, hale and hearty, sound, fit, well, full of
beans 174 *vigorous*; robust, hardy, strong, vigorous 162 *stalwart*; fighting fit, in peak condition,
in tip-top c., in the pink, in good nick, in good
shape, in fine fettle; feeling great; sound in
wind and limb, sound as a bell, fit as a fiddle, fit
as a flea, strong as a horse, A1; a picture of
health, feeling good; getting well, convalescent,
on the mend, on the up and up, up and about.

Vb. *be healthy*, – well etc. adj.; look after oneself, take care of o.; feel fine, bloom, thrive,
flourish, enjoy good health; be in the pink, have
never felt better; wear well, be well-preserved;
keep fit, keep well, have a clean bill of health.

get healthy, – fit etc. adj.; recuperate, return to
health, recover one's health, get the colour
back in one's cheeks; mend, convalesce, get
back on one's feet, take a fresh lease of life,
become a new man *or* woman 656 *revive*.

651 III health. Disease

N. *ill health*, poor h., delicate h.; weak constitution; unhealthiness, weakliness, infirmity,
debility 163 *weakness*; seediness; indisposition;
allergy; chronic ill health, invalidism, val-
etudinarianism, hypochondria; nerves 503 *neurosis*; health warning.

illness, loss of health 655 *deterioration*; affliction, disability, handicap, infirmity 163 *weakness*; sickness, indisposition, ailment,
complaint, virus, complication; condition, history of; bout of sickness, attack; spasm, stroke,
seizure, apoplexy, fit; shock; poisoning, food p.;
nausea, queasiness, vomiting; dizziness, vertigo; headache, migraine 377 *pain*; symptom,
syndrome 547 *indication*; temperature, feverishness, fever, ague, shivers, shakes 318 *spasm*;
hypothermia, hyperthermia, pyrexia; delirium
503 *frenzy*; breakdown, collapse; fainting 375
insensibility; prostration, coma; terminal disease, fatal illness 361 *decease*.

disease, malady, disorder; epidemic disease,
endemic d.; infectious d., contagious d., communicable d., notifiable d., debilitating d., killer
d.; congenital d., occupational d., industrial d.;
alcoholism, drug addiction; obesity; malnutrition, anorexia nervosa, bulimia n., avitamin-
osis, kwashiorkor, beri-beri, pellagra, rickets,
scurvy; degenerative disease, wasting d.,
atrophy; trauma; organic disease; neurological
d., nervous d., epilepsy; heart d., cardiac d.; dia-
betes; venereal d.; cancer; respiratory disease;
gastro-intestinal d.; virus; bacterial d., fibrosis;
brain disease, ME, myalgic encephalomyelitis;
Gulf War Syndrome, desert fever; post-trau-
matic stress disorder; 503 *mental disorder*.

plague, pest, scourge 659 *bane*; pestilence,
infection, contagion; epidemic; bubonic p.,
Black Death.

infection, contagion, bug, super-bug, pollution; infectiousness, contagiousness 653 *insalubrity*; suppuration, festering, purulence;
gangrene; toxicity, sepsis, poisoning 659 *poison*;
vector, carrier, host; parasite, worm, toxocara
canis 659 *bane*; virus, parvovirus, retrovirus,
lentivirus, bacillus, bacteria, germ, pathogen;
Coxsackie virus; blood-poisoning, toxaemia,

septicaemia; necrotizing fasciitis, flesh-eating bug; food-poisoning, botulism; E coli, E coli 0157, campylobacter, heliobacter pylorus; gastroenteritis, cholera; parasitical disease, toxocariasis, toxoplasmosis, bilharzia (**see** *tropical disease*); infectious disease, common cold, influenza, flu, Asian f., bird f.; diphtheria, pneumonia, viral p.; infective hepatitis; tuberculosis, consumption; measles, German measles, rubella; whooping-cough, pertussis, mumps; chickenpox, smallpox, variola; scarlet fever, scarlatina, roseola; fever, malaria (**see** *tropical disease*); typhus; typhoid; glandular fever, infectious mononucleosis; poliomyelitis, polio; encephalitis, meningitis; sleepy sickness; tetanus, lockjaw; rabies, hydrophobia.

tropical disease, malaria; cholera; yellow fever, blackwater f., Lassa f., dengue; green monkey disease; kala-azar, leishmanrasis; sleeping sickness; bilharzia; hookworm; trachoma, glaucoma, river blindness 439 *blindness*; yaws; leprosy; beri-beri, kwashiorkor.

digestive disorders, indigestion, dyspepsia, liverishness; biliousness, nausea, sickness, vomiting, retching; colic, gripes; stomach ache; stomach upset, tummy u., collywobbles, gippy tummy, irritable bowel syndrome, diarrhoea, diarrhoea and vomiting, D and V, travellers' d., dreaded lurgy, Montezuma's revenge; the runs, the trots 302 *defecation*; gastroenteritis; dysentery, cholera, typhoid; food poisoning, botulism; flatulence, wind, belching 300 *voidance*; acidosis, heartburn; hiatus hernia; ulcer, peptic u., gastric u., duodenal u.; gastritis, enteritis, colitis, peritonitis, appendicitis; cancer of the stomach; jaundice, hepatitis, cirrhosis, cystitis, nephritis; gallstones, haemorrhoids, piles; constipation; cancer of the bowel.

respiratory disease, cough, cold, common c., coryza; sore throat, catarrh, rhinitis, allergic r., sinusitis, adenoids, tonsilitis, pharyngitis; laryngitis, tracheitis, croup, bronchitis; emphysema, asthma; pleurisy, pneumonia, legionnaire's disease; pneumoconiosis, silicosis, asbestosis; diphtheria; whooping cough; lung cancer; smoker's cough; cystic fibrosis; tuberculosis, consumption.

cardiovascular disease, cardiac d.; angina; chest-pain; bradycardia, tachycardia; palpitation; heart murmur; enlarged heart; heart condition, bad heart, weak h., heart trouble; congenital heart disease, hole in the heart; rheumatic heart disease, coronary h. d.; heart failure, cardiac arrest; heart attack, coronary thrombosis, coronary; cerebral thrombosis, brain haemorrhage, stroke; blood pressure, hypertension; hypotension, high b. p., low b. p.; vascular disease, atheroma, aneurysm;

arteriosclerosis; phlebitis, varicose veins; thrombosis, coronary t., embolism, pulmonary e., infarction, myocardial i.

blood disease, anaemia, aplastic a., pernicious a., sickle-cell a, thalassaemia; leukaemia, Hodgkin's disease; haemophilia, AIDS; haemorrhage.

cancer, neoplasm, growth; primary g., secondary g., tumour, benign t., innocent t.; malignant t., cancerous growth; carcinoma, sarcoma, melanoma.

skin disease, skin lesion; mange; yaws; leprosy; erythema, prickly heat; erysipelas; impetigo, herpes, herpes zoster, shingles; dermatitis, eczema; serpigo, ringworm; pruritis, itch 378 *formication*; hives, urticaria, nettlerash; thrush; athlete's foot; rash, eruption, acne, rosacea, spots, blackheads; pustule, papula, pimple; goitre, cyst, blister, wart, verruca 253 *swelling*; macula, mole, freckle, birthmark, pockmark 845 *blemish*; skin cancer, melanoma.

venereal disease, VD, sexually-transmitted disease, social d., pox; syphilis, gonorrhoea, the clap; herpes.

ulcer, ulceration, gathering, festering, purulence; inflammation, lesion 655 *wound*; scald, burn, first-degree b.; sore, boil, abscess, fistula; cyst; chilblain, corn 253 *swelling*; gangrene.

rheumatism, rheumatics; rheumatic fever; fibrositis; frozen shoulder, tennis elbow, housemaid's knee, pulled muscle; arthritis, rheumatoid a.; gout 377 *pang*; osteoarthritis; lumbago, sciatica; slipped disc.

nervous disorders, nervous breakdown 503 *psychopathy*; brain tumour; cerebral haemorrhage, stroke, seizure; general paralysis, atrophy 375 *insensibility*; partial paralysis, paresis; cerebral palsy, spasticity; tic 318 *spasm*; petit mal, grand mal, epilepsy; poliomyelitis, polio; spina bifida; Parkinson's disease; Huntington's chorea, St Vitus's dance; multiple sclerosis, MS; muscular dystrophy.

animal disease, distemper, foot-and-mouth disease, swine fever, swine vesicular disease; BSE, bovine spongiform encephalopathy, mad cow disease, myxomatosis; rinderpest, murrain; anthrax, sheeprot, bloat; liver fluke, worms; megrims, staggers; glanders, farcy, sweeny, spavin, thrush; Newcastle disease, fowl pest; psittacosis; hard pad, Kennel cough; mange; rabies; parapox.

sick person, patient, in-p., out-p.; stretcher case, hospital c.; mental case 504 *madman*; invalid, chronic i.; valetudinarian, hypochondriac, malingerer, leadswinger, martyr to ill health; consumptive, asthmatic, bronchitic, dyspeptic, diabetic; haemophiliae, bleeder; person with AIDS, PWA; insomniac; addict, alcoholic; spastic, arthritic, paralytic; paraplegic, disabled person; crock, old c., cripple 163 *weakling*.

Adj. *unhealthy*, sickly; infirm, weakly 163 *weak*; delicate, of weak constitution, in poor health, out of kilter, in poor condition; anorexic, malnourished 636 *underfed*; peaky, emaciated, skin and bones; sallow, pale, anaemic 426 *colourless*; bilious 434 *green*; jaundiced 433 *yellow*.

sick, ill, unwell, indisposed, out of sorts, under the weather, off-colour, below par, one degree under, out of kilter; queasy, nauseated, green around the gills; in a bad way, poorly, seedy, squeamish, groggy, grotty, queer, ailing; sickening for; feverish, headachy, off one's food, off one's oats; confined, laid up, bedridden, on one's back, in bed, in hospital, on the sick list, invalided, hospitalized; run down, exhausted 684 *fatigued*; taken ill, taken bad; prostrate, collapsed; in a coma 375 *insensible*; on the danger list, in intensive care; critical, serious; chronic, incurable, inoperable; terminally ill 361 *dying*.

diseased, pathological; infected, contaminated, tainted, rotten, gangrenous; morbid, pathogenic; iatrogenic; psychosomatic 447 *mental*; infectious, contagious; poisonous, festering, purulent 653 *toxic*; degenerative, consumptive, tubercular; diabetic, hydrocephalic; anaemic; bloodless, leukaemic, haemophilic; arthritic, rheumatic, rheumatoid; palsied, paralysed, spastic, epileptic; leprous; cancerous, oncogenic, carcinogenic; syphilitic, venereal; swollen, oedematous; gouty; bronchial, bronchitic, asthmatic; allergic; pyretic, febrile, fevered, shivering, feverish, delirious; ulcerated, inflamed; erythematous, erysipelatous.

Vb. *be ill*, – sick etc. adj.; enjoy poor health; ail, suffer, undergo treatment; have a complaint *or* an affliction; be a chronic invalid; not feel well, complain of; feel queer etc. adj., come over all queer; feel sick 300 *vomit*; sicken, fall sick, fall ill; become infected, catch a bug, contract a disease; go down with; be seized, be stricken, be taken bad, not feel so good; have a stroke, collapse; be laid up, take to one's bed; be invalided out; go into a decline; fail, sink, weak 163 *be weak*.

652 Salubrity
N. *salubrity*, healthiness, state of health; well-being 650 *health*; salubriousness, wholesomeness; fresh air.

hygiene, sanitation, cleanliness 648 *cleanness*; cordon sanitaire 660 *protection*; pasteurization; antisepsis, sterilization, disinfection, chlorination.

Adj. *salubrious*, healthful, healthy, whole-

some; pure, fresh 648 *clean*; ventilated; hygienic, sanitary, disinfected, chlorinated, pasteurized, sterilized, aseptic, antiseptic; good for, salutary, what the doctor ordered 644 *beneficial*; nutritious; body-building, health-giving.

make sanitary, disinfect, boil, sterilize, chlorinate, pasteurize; put in quarantine; ventilate 340 *aerate*; decontaminate 648 *purify*; cleanse 648 *clean*.

653 Insalubrity
N. *insalubrity*, unhealthiness, unwholesomeness; uncleanliness, lack of hygiene, dirty habits 649 *uncleanness*; slum; bad air, fug, smog; infectiousness, contagiousness; sewer 649 *sink*; contagion 651 *infection*; pollution, radioactivity, fallout; poisonousness 659 *bane*.

Adj. *insalubrious*, unwholesome, unhealthy; insanitary, unhygienic 649 *unclean*; noxious; injurious 645 *harmful*; radioactive, carcinogenic; verminous, rat-infested, flea-ridden, fly-blown; stagnant, polluted, undrinkable, inedible; unnutritious; stale, gone bad, gone off; unventilated; stuffy; overheated, underheated.

infectious, pathogenic; infective, germ-carrying; contagious, catching, communicable; pestilent, plague-stricken; epidemic, pandemic, endemic; infected 649 *dirty*.

toxic, poisonous, germ-laden; venomous, poisoned; festering, septic, purulent, suppurating; lethal 362 *deadly*.

654 Improvement
N. *improvement*, betterment, amelioration, kaizen, uplift, regeneration; good influence, the making of 178 *influence*; a turn for the better, change for the b., sea change, transfiguration 143 *transformation*; conversion, new leaf 939 *penitence*; revival, recovery economic r., green shoots 656 *restoration*; evolution; enrichment; advance, progress 285 *progression*; promotion, rise, lift; upturn, upward mobility, upswing 310 *elevation*; enhancement 36 *increase*.

amendment, mending etc. vb.; renovation 656 *repair*; reorganization 62 *arrangement*; reformation, reform; rectification; correction, revision, red ink, blue pencil; emendation, revised edition, new e., improved version 589 *edition*; revise, proof; second thoughts, review; polish, finishing touch 725 *completion*.

reformer, repairer, restorer 656 *mender*; emender, corrector, editor, proofreader, reviser; progressive, gradualist, Fabian 625 *moderate*; liberal, radical, feminist, masculinist; extremist, revolutionary 738 *agitator*; socialist, communist, Marxist, Red; reformist; idealist, Utopian

513 *visionary*; sociologist, social worker 901 *philanthropist*.

Adj. *improving*, reformatory, remedial; reforming, progressive, radical; civilizing, cultural; idealistic, perfectionist, Utopian, perfectionist 862 *fastidious*.

Vb. *get better*, improve, mend, take a turn for the better, turn the corner; pick up, rally, revive, recover 656 *be restored*; make progress, make headway, advance, develop, evolve 285 *progress*; mellow, ripen 669 *mature*; bear fruit 171 *be fruitful*; rise 308 *ascend*; graduate 727 *succeed*; rise in the world, prosper; better oneself, be upwardly mobile, mend one's ways, reform, turn over a new leaf, go straight 939 *be penitent*; improve oneself, learn by experience 536 *learn*.

make better, better, improve, refine, ameliorate, reform; make improvements, improve upon, polish, enrich, enhance; work a miracle on, do one a power of good 644 *do good*; improve out of all recognition, transfigure 147 *transform*; make, be the making of, have a good influence, leaven 178 *influence*; uplift, regenerate; refine, elevate, sublimate 648 *purify*; civilize, socialize, teach manners; mend 656 *repair*; restore 656 *cure*; revive, infuse fresh blood into 685 *refresh*; forward, advance, upgrade 285 *promote*; foster, encourage, hype, bring to fruition 669 *mature*; make the most of, get the best out of 673 *use*; develop, open up; tidy up, make shipshape, neaten 62 *arrange*; spruce up, freshen up 648 *clean*; do up, vamp up, rationalize; renovate, refurbish, renew, give a face lift; bring up to date 126 *modernize*; touch up 841 *beautify*; improve on nature, gild the lily, make up, titivate 843 *primp*; embellish, adorn, ornament 844 *decorate*.

rectify, put right, set right, straighten, straighten out 24 *adjust*; mend, patch 656 *repair*; correct, debug, decontaminate, blue-pencil, proofread; revise, edit, subedit, amend, emend; rewrite, redraft; remould, refashion, remodel, reform; reorganize 62 *regularize*; streamline, finetune, rationalize; review; have second thoughts.

655 Deterioration

N. *deterioration*, debasement; cheapening, devaluation; retrogression, losing ground 286 *regression*; decline, ebb 37 *decrease*; twilight, fading 419 *dimness*; falling off, downturn, slump, depression, recession; impoverishment 801 *poverty*; exhaustion 634 *waste*; corruption, perversion, prostitution, depravation, degeneration, degeneracy, decadence, depravity 934 *wickedness*; downward course, primrose path 309 *descent*; setback 657 *relapse*.

dilapidation, collapse, ruination 165 *destruc-*

tion; planning blight; inner city deprivation, disrepair, neglect 458 *negligence*; slum 801 *poverty*; ravages of time, wear and tear, erosion, corrosion, rust, rot, canker, corruption, putrefaction, cancer, concrete cancer 51 *decay*; mouldiness, mildew 659 *blight*; decrepitude, senility 131 *old age*; atrophy 651 *disease*; ruin, wreck.

impairment, spoiling 675 *misuse*; detriment, damage, spoilage, waste 772 *loss*; discoloration; pollution, contamination, defilement 649 *uncleanness*; adulteration; ruination, demolition 165 *destruction*; injury, mischief, harm; disablement, crippling, laming, nobbling, disabling, mutilation, weakening 163 *weakness*; sprain, strain, pulled muscle, dislocation; sabotage.

wound, injury, trauma; sore, running s. 651 *ulcer*; laceration, lesion; cut, gash, incision, abrasion, nick, scratch 46 *scission*; stab, prick, jab, puncture; contusion, bruise, bump, discoloration, black eye, shiner, cauliflower ear 253 *swelling*; burn, scald; rupture, hernia; broken bones, fracture; scar, mark, scab.

Adj. *dilapidated*, the worse for wear, falling to pieces, in disrepair, in ruins; broken, kaput, cracked, leaking; battered, weather-beaten, storm-tossed; decrepit, ramshackle, tottery, wonky, shaky, rickety, tumbledown, run-down, on its last legs 163 *weakened*; condemned; worn, well-w., frayed, shabby, tatty, dingy, in tatters, in rags, out-at-elbows; worn out, done for 641 *useless*; seedy, down at heel, down and out 801 *poor*; rusty, rotten, mildewed, mouldering, moth-eaten, dog-eared.

Vb. *deteriorate*, worsen, get worse, go from bad to worse, take a turn for the worse; slip, slide, go downhill; have seen better days; fall off, slump, decline, wane, ebb, sink, fail 37 *decrease*; revert 286 *regress*; lapse; degenerate, let oneself go, go to pieces, run to seed; tread the primrose path, go to the bad 934 *be wicked*; disintegrate, fall apart, collapse, break down, fall, totter, droop 309 *tumble*; contract, shrink 198 *become small*; wear out, age; fade, wither, wilt, shrivel, perish, crumble, moulder, mildew; go to rack and ruin; weather, rust, rot, decay 51 *decompose*; spoil, go flat, go off, go sour, turn 391 *be unpalatable*; go bad, smell, pong 397 *stink*; corrupt, putrefy, rankle, fester, suppurate 51 *decompose*; sicken 651 *be ill*; make things worse, jump from the frying pan into the fire.

pervert, deform, warp, twist 246 *distort*; prostitute 675 *misuse*; deprave 951 *debauch*; corrupt 934 *make wicked*; lower, degrade, debase 311 *abase*; brutalize, dehumanize; brainwash.

impair, damage, make inoperative, hurt, injure 645 *harm*; mess up, muck up 63 *jumble*;

play havoc with 63 *derange*; disorganize; spoil, mar, botch, cock up, make a balls-up of 695 *be clumsy*; tinker, tamper, meddle with, fool w., monkey w. 678 *meddle*; deteriorate; degrade, devalue, debase 812 *cheapen*; stain; scar, mark; deface, disfigure, deform, warp 246 *distort*; mutilate, maim, lame, cripple 161 *disable*; cramp, hamper 702 *hinder*; castrate 161 *unman*; curtail; adulterate; deactivate 679 *make inactive*; subvert, sap, undermine, demoralize 163 *weaken*; erode, corrode, rust, rot, mildew 51 *decompose*; blight, blast; ravage, rape, waste, scorch; vandalize, wreck, ruin 165 *destroy*; crumble 332 *pulverize*; dilapidate, wear out; exhaust, deplete, drain; infect, contaminate; taint, pollute 649 *make unclean*; defile, desecrate, profane 980 *be impious*.

wound, draw blood; tear, lacerate, slit, mangle, rip 46 *disunite*; maul, savage, traumatize; black one's eye, bloody one's nose; bite, scratch, claw; slash, gash, hack, incise 46 *cut*; scarify, score 262 *groove*; nick 260 *notch*; sting, prick, stab, puncture 263 *pierce*; bruise, contuse; crush, grind 332 *pulverize*; chafe 333 *rub*; smash 46 *break*; graze, wing.

656 Restoration

N. *restoration*, giving back 787 *restitution*; redress, amends, reparation 941 *atonement*; retrieval, recovery; re-establishment, recall, replacement, reinstatement; rehabilitation; reclamation, gentrification, recycling; rescue, salvage, redemption, ransom, salvation 668 *deliverance*; reconstitution, rebuilding, reformation, reconstruction, reorganization; readjustment; remodelling 654 *amendment*; resumption.

repair, reparation, repairs, running r., service, servicing, renovation, renewal, reconditioning; overhauling, DIY; rectification, emendation; restoration, mending, invisible m., darning, patching; cobbling, tinkering etc. vb.; reinforcement; new look, face-lift 843 *beautification*.

revival, recovery 685 *refreshment*; renewal, reawakening, resurgence, rally, comeback; economic recovery, green shoots, economic miracle, boom 730 *prosperity*; reactivation, resuscitation, rejuvenation; face-lift, new look; rebirth, renaissance; regeneration; new life, resurrection.

recuperation, recovery, pulling through, rallying, perking up, taking a turn for the better, turning the corner, cure; healing, mending; healing over; convalescence 658 *remedy*; easing 831 *relief*; curability; recovering alcoholic.

mender, repairer, renovator, painter, decorator, interior d., DIYer; mechanic; restorer;

cobbler, shoe-repairer; plumber, handyman; healer, bone-setter, osteopath 658 *doctor*.

Vb. *be restored*, recover, come round, come to, revive, pick up, rally 685 *be refreshed*; pull through, get over, get well, convalesce, recuperate; turn the corner 654 *get better*; weather the storm, survive, live through; come to life again, arise from the dead, return from the grave; reappear, make a comeback, take on a new lease of life; be oneself again, bounce back, snap out of it, come up smiling; pick oneself up, find one's feet again; return to normal, get back to n.

restore, give back, hand b., yield up 787 *restitute*; make amends 941 *atone*; replace; recall, reappoint, reinstall, re-establish, rehabilitate; reconstitute, reconstruct, reform, reorganize 654 *make better*; renovate, renew, rebuild, remake, redo; overhaul, service, refit, refurbish, make like new 126 *modernize*; make whole; reclaim; recycle; build up one's strength 162 *strengthen*; rally, reassemble 74 *bring together*; redeem, rescue, salvage 668 *deliver*.

revive, revitalize, resuscitate, regenerate, resurrect, rekindle; breathe fresh life into, give a new lease of life, rejuvenate; freshen 685 *refresh*.

cure, heal, make well, cure of, break of; nurse; bandage, put a plaster on, nurse through, work a cure, snatch from the grave, restore to health, set on one's feet again; set (a bone); heal over; knit together; right itself.

repair, do repairs; amend, emend, right, set to rights, put right, put back into operation, remedy, sort 654 *rectify*; overhaul, DIY, mend, fix; cobble, resole, heel; recover, resurface, thatch 226 *cover*; reline 227 *line*; darn, patch, fill (teeth); make over, do up, touch up, freshen up, retouch, revamp, fill in the cracks, paper over; seal, plug a hole 350 *staunch*; caulk 264 *close*; splice, bind 45 *tie*; piece together, reassemble, cannibalize 45 *join*; give a face-lift, upgrade, gentrify, refurbish, recondition, renovate, renew, remodel, reform.

retrieve, get back, recover, regain, retake, recapture; find again, reclaim, claim back, compensate oneself 31 *recoup*; make up for, make up time, make up leeway.

657 Relapse

N. *relapse*, lapse, falling back; throwback, return 148 *reversion*; retrogression 286 *regression*; sinking, falling off, fall 655 *deterioration*; back-sliding; reinfection, recurrence, fresh outbreak.

Vb. *relapse*, slip back, slide b., sink b., fall b., lose ground; return, retrogress 286 *regress*; degenerate 655 *deteriorate*; backslide, lapse, fall from grace 603 *apostatize*; revert to 148 *revert*; have a relapse, suffer a recurrence.

658 Remedy

N. remedy, succour, help 703 *aid*; oil on troubled waters 177 *moderator*; corrective 654 *amendment*; redress, amends 787 *restitution*; expiation 941 *atonement*; cure 656 *recuperation*; healing quality *or* property; sovereign remedy, specific, answer, solution; prescription, recipe, formula, nostrum; quack remedy, patent medicine; panacea, cure-all, elixir.

medicine, pharmacopoeia; herbal remedy; medicinal herb; balm, balsam; medication, medicament, patent medicine, proprietary drug, generic d., ethical d.; placebo; pill, bolus, tablet, capsule, caplet, lozenge; draught, potion, elixir; infusion; dose, booster d.; drops, drip; injection, jab, shot; preparation, mixture, powder, linctus; plaster (**see** *surgical dressing*); spray, inhaler.

diagnosis, symptom, syndrome; e-health; sample, urine s., semen s.; battery of tests, test, laboratory t., lab t., blood t., serotests, sputum t., stool t., eye t., hearing t.; breath test; pregnancy t.; amniocentesis, alphafetoprotein test, chorionic villus sampling; cervical smear, smear test, Pap t, liquid-based cytology; mammogram, angiogram, arteriogram, cardiogram, ECG, lymphogram, pyelogram, venogram; radiograph; chest X-ray; barium meal, barium enema; ultrasound, screening, scanning, CAT s.; body s., brain s., EEG; MRI magnetic resonance imaging; biopsy, cone b.; stethoscope, bronchoscope, ophthalmoscope, auriscope; endoscope, colposcope, ureteroscope, bronchoscopy, colonoscopy, endoscopy, gastroscopy, laparoscopy; forensic test; DNA fingerprinting, genetic f.

prophylactic, preventive; cordon sanitaire, quarantine 652 *hygiene*; prophylaxis, immunization, inoculation, vaccination, chemoprevention; vaccine, triple v., BCG, TAB; quinine; antisepsis, disinfection, sterilization; antiseptic, disinfectant, iodine, carbolic, boric acid, boracic a.; bactericide, germicide, insecticide 659 *poison*; fumigant; fluoridation, fluoride.

antidote, counterirritant, antihistamine; antiserum, antitoxin; antiemetic; febrifuge, quinine; vermifuge, anthelmintic; antigen, antibody, interferon; antibiotic; immunosuppressant; antispasmodic, anticonvulsant; sedative; anticoagulant; antacid, analgesic, painkiller.

purgative, purge, cathartic, laxative, aperient; castor oil, Epsom salts, health s.; senna pods; cascara, milk of magnesia; diuretic; expectorant, emetic, nauseant, ipecacuanha; carminative, digestive, liquorice, dill water; douche, enema.

tonic, restorative; tonic wine; reviver, refresher, pick-me-up 174 *stimulant*; caffeine, nicotine, alcohol; spirits, smelling salts, sal volatile; infusion, tisane, herb tea; betel nut, ginseng, royal jelly; vitamin tablet, iron pill.

drug, medicinal drug; wonder drug; antibiotic, sulphonamide; penicillin, aureomycin, streptomycin, insulin, cortisone; hormone, steroid; progesterone, oestrogen; HRT; Viagra; contraceptive pill 172 *contraception*; tamoxifen; analgesic, aspirin, codeine, paracetamol, 375 *anaesthetic*; tranquillizer, diazepam, Valium (tdmk), temazepan, antidepressant, Prozac (tdmk), sedative; barbiturate, sleeping pill; narcotic, dope, morphia, morphine, opium, cocaine, heroin; stimulant 949 *drug-taking*; AZT; Aricept; Ritalin.

balm, balsam oil, emollient 177 *moderator*; salve, ointment; cream 843 *cosmetic*; lanolin, liniment, embrocation; lotion, wash; eyewash.

surgical dressing, dressing, lint, gauze; swab; bandage, sling, splint, cast, plaster of Paris; tourniquet; fingerstall; patch; plaster, sticking p., Elastoplast (tdmk), Band-Aid (tdmk) corn plaster; fomentation, poultice, compress; tampon; pessary, suppository.

medical art, therapeutics; medical advice, medical practice; medical care, managed c., primary c., integrated c., triage; telemedicine; homeopathy, naturopathy; medicine, clinical m., preventive m., fringe m., alternative m., complementary m., holistic m., unorthodox m., folk m.; iridology, reflexology, radiesthesia; acupuncture, acupressure; radiography, radiology, tomography; diagnosis, prognosis; healing, laying on of hands, faith healing, Christian Science; sexology, gynaecology, midwifery 167 *obstetrics*; gerontology, geriatrics, paediatrics; orthopaedics, orthotics, ophthalmology, orthoptics, neurology, dermatology, ear, nose and throat, ENT, cardiology, oncology; nuclear medicine; radiotherapy; psychopathology, bacteriology, microbiology, virology, immunology; pharmaceutics, pharmacology; veterinary medicine.

surgery, general surgery, keyhole s., telesurgery, laser surgery, brain s., heart s., cardiac s., angioplasty, balloon a., open-heart s., by-pass s., transplant s., xenotransplantation; plastic surgery, cosmetic s., nip-and-tuck, rhinoplasty, prosthesis, prosthetics; liposuction; chiropractic; operation, surgical o., op.; phlebotomy, venesection, somnoplasty; tranfusion; dialysis; D and C, dilatation and curettage, transplant; cauterization; amputation, trephination, trepanning, lobotomy, tonsillectomy, appendicectomy, appendectomy, colostomy, laparotomy; mastectomy, radical m., lumpectomy; hysterectomy; vasectomy; dentistry, extracting, filling.

therapy, therapeutics; medical care treatment,

medical treatment, clinical t.; nursing, bedside manner; first aid, aftercare; cure, faith c.; hydrotherapy; thalassotherapy; regimen; bone-setting, orthopaedics, osteopathy, osteotherapy; hypnotherapy; hormone therapy, HRT, HRT patch; immunotherapy; chemotherapy; gene therapy; physiotherapy, occupational therapy; radiotherapy; heat treatment; electrotherapy, ECT, shock treatment; clinical psychology; child psychology; psychotherapy, psychiatry, psychoanalysis, counselling, genetic c. 447 *psychology*; group therapy, behaviour t., cognitive behaviour t., aversion t., Gestalt t., primal t.; acupuncture, acupressure; catheterization; intravenous injection, dripfeed; fomentation, poulticing.

alternative therapy, complementary therapy, supplementary t., homeopathy, holistic medicine; folk m., traditional m., fringe m., herbal m., ayurveda, ayurvedic medicine; acupuncture, acupressure, shiatsu; osteopathy, chiropractic manipulative therapy; faith healing, laying on of hands; relaxation therapy, autogenic t., autogenics, autogenic training; meditations; aromatherapy, crystal healing, crystal therapy; reflexology; iridology; kinesiology.

hospital, infirmary, general hospital, hospital trust, hospital manager; maternity h., children's h.; 503 *mental hospital*; dispensary, clinic, antenatal c.; nursing home, convalescent h.; hospice; hospital ship, hospital train; stretcher, ambulance; ward, hospital w., casualty w., isolation w., sick bay, sickroom, sick-bed; hospital bed; bed-blocking; oxygen tent, iron lung; respirator, life-support system, heart-lung machine, kidney m.; incubator, intensive care unit; X-ray machine, scanner, body s., brain s., head s., CAT s.; first-aid station; casualty department, crash team; operating theatre, operating table; consulting room, surgery, clinic, one-stop c., community health centre; sanatorium, spa, hydro; pump room, baths, hot springs, thermae.

doctor, physician; quack; veterinary surgeon, vet, horse-doctor; herbalist; faith healer, Christian Scientist; homeopath, naturopath; acupuncturist; hakim, barefoot doctor, flying d.; witchdoctor, medicine man 983 *sorcerer*; medic, medical student; houseman, intern, registrar; medical practitioner, general p., GP, family doctor; locum tenens, locum; clinician, therapeutist; surgeon, general s., plastic s.; dot com doctor, neurosurgeon; medical officer, environmental health o., sanitary inspector; medical adviser, consultant, specialist; diagnostician, pathologist; alienist, psychiatrist, psychoanalyst, shrink, neurologist, radiographer; physiotherapist, occupational therapist, speech t.;

paediatrician, geriatrician; obstetrician, midwife; gynaecologist; sexologist; dermatologist, haematologist; biochemist, microbiologist; radiotherapist; orthopaedist, orthotist, osteopath, chiropractor, podiatrist, chiropodist; ophthalmologist, optician, ophthalmic optician, oculist, orthoptist; aurist; dentist, dental surgeon, orthodontist; dietician; medical profession, private medicine, Harley Street, National Health Service; Red Cross, St. John Ambulance; Hippocratic oath.

druggist, apothecary, chemist, pharmacist; dispenser, pharmacologist; chemist's, pharmacy.

nurse, male n., student n., staff n.; charge n., sister, night s., ward s., theatre s., nursing officer, senior n. o.; matron; state-enrolled nurse, SEN; state-registered nurse, SRN; special nurse, day n., night n.; district nurse, community n.; health visitor; nursing auxiliary, ward-orderly, ambulanceman; almoner, hospital social worker 901 *sociology*; caring profession; Florence Nightingale, lady with a lamp, ministering angel.

Adj. *remedial*, corrective, curative, restorative; helpful 644 *beneficial*; therapeutic, medicinal, healing, curing; soothing, emollient, palliative; anodyne, analgesic, narcotic, hypnotic, anaesthetic 375 *insensible*; digestive; purging; cathartic, emetic, laxative; antidotal; prophylactic, disinfectant, antiseptic; antipyretic, febrifugal; tonic; nutritional.

medical, pathological, homeopathic, herbal; surgical, rhinoplastic, orthopaedic, orthotic; obstetric, obstetrical; clinical; operable, curable.

Vb. *remedy*, fix, put right, correct 656 *restore*; help 703 *aid*; treat, heal; soothe 831 *relieve*.

doctor, practise medicine; treat, prescribe; attend 703 *minister to*; tend, nurse; give first aid, give the kiss of life 656 *revive*; hospitalize, medicate; inject, give a jab, give a shot; dress, bandage, put a plaster on; apply a tourniquet 350 *staunch*; poultice, plaster; set, put in splints; drug, anaesthetize; operate, amputate; trepan, trephine; curette; cauterize; bleed, phlebotomize; transfuse; manipulate; extract, pull, fill; immunize, vaccinate, inoculate; sterilize.

659 Bane

N. *bane*, curse, plague; scourge, ruin 616 *evil*; malady 651 *disease*; bad habit, besetting sin 934 *vice*; hell, affliction 731 *adversity*; woe, funeral 825 *sorrow*; cross, cross to bear, trial; bore 838 *tedium*; bugbear, bête noire 827 *annoyance*; burden, imposition, white elephant; thorn in the flesh, stone round one's neck; stress, strain, perpetual worry, constant anxiety, angst, torment, nagging pain 825 *worry*; running sore 651 *ulcer*; bitterness 393 *sourness*; bite, sting, poison dart, fang, nettle 256 *sharp-point*; trouble spot, hornet's nest 663 *pitfall*; viper, adder, serpent 365 *reptile*; snake, shake in the grass 663 *troublemaker*; parasite, tapeworm 365 *insect, creepy-crawly*; mosquito, mozzie, wasp; locust 168 *destroyer*; oppressor 735 *tyrant*.

blight, rot, dry r., wet r.; mildew, mould, rust, fungus; moth, woodworm, canker, cancer 51 *decay*; nuclear winter visitation 651 *plague*; frost 380 *coldness*, drought 342 *desiccation*.

poison, poisonousness, virulence, venomousness, toxicity; pollution; bacteria, salmonella, bacillus, germ, virus 651 *infection*; teratogen, carcinogen, oncogene; biological weapon; venom, toxin; deadly poison, snake p., rat p., *slung* pellets; germicide, insecticide, carburfuran, organo-phosphates;, pesticide; fungicide, herbicide, weed-killer, defoliant, dioxin, paraquat, derris, DDT; hemlock, arsenic, strychnine, cyanide, prussic acid, vitriol; asphyxiant, poison gas, nerve g., mustard gas, tear g., CS gas; carbon monoxide, carbon dioxide; CFC, chlorofluorocarbon; miasma, sewer gas 653 *insalubrity*; atmospheric pollution, acid rain, smog; lead pollution; uranium, plutonium; radioactivity, nuclear fallout, strontium 90 417 *radiation*; heroin 658 *drug*, 949 *drug-taking*; lethal dose, overdose; toxicology.

poisonous plant, hemlock, deadly nightshade, belladonna, datura, henbane, monkshood, aconite, hellebore; nux vomica, upas tree.

660 Safety

N. *safety*, safeness, security; immunity; safety in numbers 104 *multitude*; secure position, safe job; social security, welfare state 901 *sociology*; safe distance, wide berth 620 *avoidance*; all clear, coast c.; guarantee, warrant 473 *certainty*; sense of security, assurance, confidence 855 *courage*; safety valve 667 *means of escape*; rescue 668 *deliverance*.

protection, conservation 666 *preservation*; insurance, surety 858 *caution*; patronage, care, sponsorship, good offices, auspices, aegis, fatherly eye 703 *aid*; protectorate, guardianship, wardenship, wardship, tutelage, custody, protective c., care in the community, community care, caring profession; surrogacy 747 *restraint*; safekeeping, keeping, charge, safe hands; ward, watch, electronic surveillance, Big Brother, vetting, positive v. 457 *surveillance*; safeguard, precaution, security system, alarm s., preventive measure 713 *defence*; immunization, prophylaxis, quarantine, cordon sanitaire 652 *hygiene*; cushion, buffer; screen, cover; sun screen, suntan cream, sun protection factor, protection f.; umbrella 662 *shelter*; deterrent 723 *weapon*; safe-conduct, passport, pass 756

permit; escort, convoy, guard 722 *armed force*; defence, bastion, bulwark, tower of strength 713 *defences*; haven, sanctuary, asylum 662 *refuge*; anchor 662 *safeguard*; moat, ditch, palisade, stockade 235 *fence*; shield, breastplate, armour plate 713 *armour*; human shield.

protector, protectress, guardian; guardian angel, patron saint, liege lord, feudal 1., fairy godmother 707 *patron*; defender, preserver, shepherd; bodyguard, minder, lifeguard, strongarm man, bouncer; vigilante 713 *defender*; custodian, curator, warden; warder, guard, security g., coastguard; chaperon, duenna, governess, nursemaid, nanny, baby-sitter, au pair, care assistant, buddy, carer, minder 749 *keeper*; lookout, watch, watchman, night w. 664 *warner*; firewatcher, fire fighter, fireman; policeman or -woman, police constable, community policeman, police sergeant, sheriff; copper, cop 955 *police*; private eye 459 *detective*; sentry, sentinel, garrison, security forces 722 *soldiery*; watchdog, guard dog, police d. 365 *dog*; Cerberus 457 *surveillance*.

Adj. *safe*, secure, sure; safe and sound, spared 666 *preserved*; intact, unharmed 646 *undamaged*; garrisoned, well-defended; insured; immunized, vaccinated, inoculated; disinfected; in safety, on sure ground, home and dry, on home ground, on the home stretch, on terra firma; in harbour; out of the wood, out of danger, out of harm's way; clear, in the clear, sheltered, shielded, screened, protected etc. vb.; under the protection of, under the wing of; in safe hands, in custody, behind bars, under lock and key 747 *imprisoned*; reliable, guaranteed; harmless 615 *good*.

invulnerable, immune, impregnable, sacrosanct; unassailable, unbreakable; tenable 162 *strong*; proof, foolproof; weatherproof, waterproof, showerproof, leakproof, gasproof, fireproof, bulletproof, bombproof, shatterproof; seaworthy, airworthy; shrink-wrapped, vacuum sealed, hermetically s.; armoured.

Vb. *be safe*, – invulnerable etc. adj.; reach safety; come through, save one's bacon 667 *escape*; land on one's feet, keep one's head above water, weather the storm, ride it out; bear a charmed life, have nine lives; have a roof over one's head; be under cover 523 *lurk*; keep a safe distance, give a wide berth 620 *avoid*.

safeguard, keep safe, guard, protect; stand surety for, go bail for 713 *defend*; shield; grant asylum, afford sanctuary; keep, conserve 666 *preserve*; hoard 632 *store*; keep in custody 747 *imprison*; ward, watch over, care for, mother, take under one's wing; nurse, foster, cherish; have charge of, keep an eye on, chaperon 457 *look after*; hide, put in a safe place 525 *conceal*;

cushion, cocoon 218 *support*; insulate; cover, shade 421 *screen*; keep under cover, garage, lock up; take in, house, shelter; enfold, make safe, secure, fortify 162 *strengthen*; entrench, fence in, fence round 232 *circumscribe*; arm, armour; shepherd, convoy, escort; flank, support; garrison, mount guard; immunize, inoculate, vaccinate; pasteurize, chlorinate, fluoridate, fluoridize, disinfect; give assurances, warrant, guarantee 473 *make certain*; keep order, police, patrol.

661 Danger

N. *danger*, peril; dangerousness, perilousness, shadow of death, jaws of d., lion's mouth, dragon's lair; dangerous situation, parlous state, dire straits, forlorn hope 700 *predicament*; emergency 137 *crisis*; jeopardy, risk, hazard, banana skin, precariousness, razor's edge 474 *uncertainty*; black spot, snag 663 *pitfall*; trap, death t. 527 *ambush*; endangerment, imperilment, hazarding, dangerous course; daring, overdaring 857 *rashness*; venture 672 *undertaking*; leap in the dark 618 *gambling*; slippery slope, road to ruin 655 *deterioration*; sword of Damocles, menace 900 *threat*; cause for alarm, rocks ahead, storm brewing, gathering clouds, gathering storm 665 *danger signal*; narrow escape, close shave, near thing 667 *escape*.

vulnerability, danger of 180 *liability*; security risk; exposure, nakedness, defencelessness, naivety 161 *helplessness*; insecurity 152 *changeableness*; easy target, sitting duck; chink in the armour, Achilles' heel 163 *weakness*; soft underbelly 327 *softness*; feet of clay, human error, tragic flaw, fatal f. 647 *imperfection*; weaker brethren, weaker sex.

Adj. *dangerous*, perilous, fraught with danger, treacherous, beset with perils; risky, hazardous, venturesome, dicey, dodgy, chancy 618 *speculative*; serious, nasty, critical; at stake; menacing, ominous, foreboding, alarming; toxic, poisonous 645 *harmful*; unhealthy, infectious 653 *insalubrious*; inflammable, flammable, explosive, radioactive.

unsafe, slippery, treacherous, untrustworthy 474 *unreliable*; insecure, precarious, dicky; unsteady; shaky, tottering, crumbling, ramshackle, rickety, frail 655 *dilapidated*; jerry-built, gimcrack, crazy 163 *weak*; built on sand; critical, touch and go, hanging by a thread, trembling in the balance, teetering on the edge, on the edge, on the brink, on the verge.

vulnerable, in danger of 180 *liable*; exposed, naked, bare 229 *uncovered*; undefended, unprotected, at the mercy of; shelterless, helpless; unguarded, unescorted; unsupported, out on a limb; off one's guard 508 *inexpectant*.

endangered, in danger, in peril etc. n.; in a bad way; on the rocks, on slippery ground, on thin ice; in a tight corner, surrounded, trapped, under fire; in the lion's den, be thrown to the lions, on the razor's edge; out of the frying pan into the fire; between the devil and the deep blue sea, between Scylla and Charybdis; on the run, not out of the wood; at bay, with one's back to the wall, awaiting execution 961 *condemned*.

Vb. *be in danger*, run the risk of 180 *be liable*: enter the lion's den, walk into a trap, tread on dangerous ground, skate on thin ice, get out of one's depth, sail too near the wind, play with fire, sit on a powder barrel, sleep on a volcano; lean on a broken reed, feel the ground give way, be up against it, have to run for it; hang by a thread, tremble in the balance, hover on the brink, teeter on the edge 474 *be uncertain*.

face danger, dice with death, have one's back to the wall; take one's life in one's hands 855 *be courageous*; lay oneself open to; bell the cat, look danger in the face, look down a gun barrel; face heavy odds, have the odds against one; engage in a forlorn hope, be on a hiding to nothing, tempt providence, court disaster; take a tiger by the tail, put one's head in the lion's mouth 857 *be rash*; run the gauntlet, come under fire; take a chance, stick one's neck out 618 *gamble*.

endanger, be dangerous, spell danger, expose to d., put at risk, put in jeopardy; imperil, jeopardize; risk 618 *gamble*; run on the rocks, drive dangerously, drive without due care and attention, put one in fear of his *or* her life; loom, forebode, bode ill, menace 900 *threaten*.

662 Refuge. Safeguard

N. *refuge*, sanctuary, asylum, retreat, safe house; traffic island, zebra crossing, pedestrian crossing, pelican c., green man; last resort, bolthole, burrow; trench, dugout, air-raid shelter, fallout s.; earth, hole, den, lair; hearth 192 *home*; sanctum 194 *chamber*; cloister, ivory tower 192 *retreat*; sanctum sanctorum, temple; bastion; stronghold 713 *fort*; keep; secret place 527 *hiding-place*; tower of strength, mainstay 218 *prop*.

shelter, cover, roof, roof over one's head; earth, hole; fold, sheepfold; lee; windbreak, hedge 235 *fence*; camp, stockade 235 *enclosure*; shield; fireguard, fender, bumper, mudguard, windscreen 421 *screen*; umbrella, oilskins; sunglasses, goggles, ear muffs, ear plugs; shinguard, pads; protective clothing, overalls; haven, harbour, port; harbourage, anchorage, quay, jetty, marina, dock 192 *stable*; halfway house, sheltered housing; old people's home, children's home, dog's h., hospice, Welfare State.

safeguard, protection 660 *safety*; precautions 702 *hindrance*; crush barrier, guardrail, railing; mail 713 *armour*; arms, deterrent, Star Wars, SDI 723 *weapon*; respirator, gas mask; air-bag, dead man's handle, safety catch, safety valve; crash helmet, safety h. 228 *headgear*; seat belt, safety b., safety harness; ejector-seat, parachute; safety net; lifeboat, rubber dinghy, life raft; life belt, life jacket, lifeline, breeches buoy; reins, brake 748 *fetter*; bolt, lock 264 *stopper*; ballast; breakwater, sea wall, embankment; lighthouse, lightship 269 *sailing aid*; spare parts 40 *extra*.

Vb. *seek refuge*, take refuge; take to the hills; shelter under the wing of, pull the blankets over one's head; seek political asylum; clasp the knees of, hide behind the skirts of; reach safety, find shelter; let down the portcullis, raise the drawbridge, batten down the hatches.

663 Pitfall: source of danger

N. *pitfall*, pit, trap for the unwary, banana skin, catch, Catch-22; snag 702 *obstacle*; booby trap, death t., minefield 542 *trap*; lying in wait 527 *ambush*; sleeping dog; thin ice; quagmire 347 *marsh*; quicksands; reef, coral r., rock; chasm, abyss, crevasse, precipice 209 *high land*; rapids, crosscurrent, undertow 350 *current*; vortex, maelstrom, whirlpool 350 *eddy*; tidal wave, flash flood; volcano 383 *furnace*; dynamite, time bomb, powder keg 723 *explosive*; trouble spot 661 *danger*; hotbed 651 *infection*; hornet's nest, hazard 659 *bane*.

troublemaker, mischiefmaker, agent provocateur 738 *agitator*; ugly customer, vandal, delinquent 904 *ruffian*; nigger in the woodpile, snake in the grass, viper in the bosom; a wolf in sheep's clothing; yellow peril.

664 Warning

N. *warning*, caution, caveat; example, lesson, object l.; notice, advance n. 524 *information*; word, word in the ear, word to the wise, tip, tip-off, wink, nudge 524 *hint*; whistle-blowing 528 *publication*; final warning, final notice, ultimatum 737 *demand*; admonition, admonishment 924 *reprimand*; deterrent 613 *dissuasion*; warning shot, s. across the bows; foreboding, premonition 511 *prediction*; warning voice 917 *conscience*; alarm, siren, foghorn, red alert 665 *danger signal*; stormy petrel, bird of ill omen 511 *omen*; gathering cloud, war cloud 661 *danger*; writing on the wall, symptom, sign 547 *indication*; death knell 364 *obsequies*; beacon.

warner, prophet, Cassandra 511 *diviner*; signaller; lighthouse-keeper; watchman, lookout, security man *or* woman, watch 457 *surveillance*;

scout, spy; picket, sentinel, sentry 660 *protector*; advanced guard, rearguard; watchdog.

Vb. *warn*, caution; give fair warning, give notice, notify 524 *inform*; drop a hint, tip off, blow the whistle on 524 *hint*; admonish 924 *reprove*; forewarn 511 *predict*; forearm, put someone on their guard, alert 669 *prepare*; lour, menace 900 *threaten*; issue a caveat; sound the alarm 665 *raise the alarm*.

665 Danger signal

N. *danger signal*, warning; writing on the wall, evil omen 511 *omen*; gale warning; alarm bell, burglar alarm, fire alarm, foghorn, motor horn, bicycle bell, police whistle; alarm, curfew, siren, red alert; war cry, battle c., rallying cry; fiery cross; warning light, red l., beacon; red flag, SOS 547 *signal*.

false alarm, cry of 'wolf', scare, hoax; hoax call; bad dream 854 *intimidation*; flash in the pan 4 *insubstantiality*; scaremonger 854 *alarmist*.

Vb. *raise the alarm*, sound the a., give the a., dial 999, alert, arouse, scare, startle 854 *frighten*; sound one's horn, honk, toot; turn out the guard, call the police, raise a hue and cry, cry blue murder 528 *proclaim*; give a false alarm, cry wolf, cry too soon; sound a warning, toll, knell.

666 Preservation

N. *preservation*, safekeeping; safe conduct 660 *protection*; saving, salvation 668 *deliverance*; conservation, conservancy; conservation of the environment, ecotage, tree-hugging, tree-house, twigloo; energy-saving, energy audit; perpetuation 144 *permanence*; support 633 *provision*; self-preservation 932 *selfishness*; game reserve, nature r., bird sanctuary, conservation area, green belt, listed building; protected species; taxidermy, mummification, embalming 364 *interment*; cold storage, deep-freezing, freeze-drying 382 *refrigeration*; UHT, dehydration 342 *desiccation*; canning, processing; preventive medicine, quarantine, cordon sanitaire.

preserver, life-saver, saviour, rescuer, deliverer 668 *deliverance*; preservative, ice, formaldehyde; camphor, mothball; pickle, marinade, brine 389 *condiment*; freezer 384 *refrigerator*; Thermos flask (tdmk); canning factory, bottling plant; safety device, seat belt, airbag, gas mask 662 *safeguard*; incubator, respirator, iron lung, life support system; embalmer, mummifier; canner, bottler; preservationist, conservationist, environmentalist, green; green peace movement, green m; ecowarrior, tree-hugger.

Adj. *preserved*, well-p., long-life; frozen, on

ice; pickled, marinated, salted, canned, bottled; mummified, embalmed; mothballed; conserved, protected 660 *safe*.

Vb. *preserve*, conserve, freeze, freeze-dry, keep on ice 382 *refrigerate*; embalm, mummify, stuff; pickle, salt 388 *season*; marinate; cure, smoke, kipper, dehydrate 342 *dry*; bottle, tin, can, process; protect, varnish, creosote, waterproof; maintain, keep in good repair, service 656 *repair*; prop up, shore up 218 *support*; sustain; keep safe; hold 778 *retain*; prolong; save, rescue 668 *deliver*.

667 Escape

N. *escape*, leak, leakage; extrication, delivery, rescue 668 *deliverance*; riddance, good r. 831 *relief*; getaway, breakout; decampment, flight, flit, moonlight f., French leave 296 *departure*; withdrawal, retreat, hasty r. 286 *regression*; disappearing trick 446 *disappearance*; elopement; evasion, truancy, bunking off, tax-dodging black economy, moonlighting 620 *avoidance*; narrow escape, close shave, narrow squeak, near thing 661 *danger*; let-off, discharge, reprieve 960 *acquittal*; setting free 746 *liberation*; immunity, exemption 919 *nonliability*; escapology, escapism.

means of escape, exit, emergency e., way out, back door, secret passage 298 *egress*; ladder, fire escape, escape hatch; drawbridge 624 *bridge*; vent, safety valve 662 *safeguard*; dodge; loophole, escape clause, technicality, let-out.

escaper, escapee, runaway; truant, escaped prisoner, prison-breaker; fugitive, refugee; survivor; escapist; escapologist, Houdini.

Vb. *escape*, find or win freedom 746 *achieve liberty*; make good one's escape, make a getaway, vamoose, break gaol, break out of prison; abscond, jump bail, flit, elope, skip, take flight, take French leave, go AWOL 620 *run away*; steal away, sneak off, duck and run, make oneself scarce, beat a hasty retreat 296 *decamp*; slip through, break t., break out, break loose, break away, get free, break one's chains, go over the wall, slip one's lead, shake one's yoke; get out, bluff one's way o., sneak o. 298 *emerge*; get away, slip through one's fingers; get off, get off lightly, secure an acquittal, go scot-free; get off on a technicality, save one's bacon, weather the storm, survive; get away with it, secure exemption, wriggle out of 919 *be exempt*; rid oneself, be well rid of; leak.

elude, evade, welsh, abscond, dodge 620 *avoid*; lie low 523 *lurk*; give one the slip, shake off, throw off the scent, throw dust in one's eye, draw a red herring, give one a run for one's money; escape notice, be found to be missing 190 *be absent*.

668 Deliverance

N. *deliverance*, delivery, extrication 304 *extraction*; riddance 831 *relief*; liberation, rescue, lifesaving; salvage, retrieval 656 *restoration*; salvation, redemption 965 *divine function*; ransom, buying off 792 *purchase*; release, amnesty; discharge, reprieve 960 *acquittal*; day of grace, respite 136 *delay*; truce; way out, let-out 667 *escape*; dispensation, exemption 919 *nonliability*.

Vb. *deliver*, save, rescue, come to the r., save by the bell, snatch from the jaws of death, throw a lifeline; get one out of 304 *extract*; extricate; untie, unbind 46 *disunite*; rid, save from 831 *relieve*; release; free, set free 746 *liberate*; let one off, get one off 960 *acquit*; deliver oneself 667 *escape*; save one's skin, rid oneself, get rid of; snatch a brand from the burning, be the salvation of; redeem, ransom, buy off 792 *purchase*; salvage, retrieve, recover; spare, excuse, dispense from 919 *exempt*.

669 Preparation

N. *preparation*, preparing, making ready; premedication; clearing the decks; preliminaries, priming; mobilization 718 *war measures*; trial run, trial, trials 461 *experiment*; practice, rehearsal, dress r.; brief, briefing; training 534 *teaching*; prep, homework 536 *learning*; spadework 682 *labour*; groundwork, foundation 218 *basis*; planning, first draft, outline, blueprint, prototype, pilot scheme 623 *plan*; advance factory; prearrangement, premeditation 608 *predetermination*; consultation 691 *advice*; precautions 510 *foresight*; bottom drawer, nest egg 632 *store*.

ripening, maturation, bringing to a head; seasoning, acclimatization; brewing, hatching, gestation, incubation 167 *propagation*; nurture; cultivation, tillage, sowing, planting 370 *agriculture*; bloom, efflorescence; fruition 725 *completion*.

Adj. *preparatory*, preparing etc. adj.; precautionary, preliminary 64 *preceding*; provisional, stopgap 150 *substituted*; marinating, brewing, cooking, brooding, hatching, incubating, maturing; in embryo; in preparation, afoot, on the stocks, in store, in the offing, forthcoming 155 *impending*; under consideration, at the committee stage, mooted 623 *planned*; under training.

prepared, ready, alert 457 *vigilant*; made ready, in readiness, at the ready; mobilized, standing by, on call; all set, ready to go, raring to go; teed up, keyed up, psyched up, spoiling for; trained, qualified, well-prepared, practised, in practice, at concert pitch, word-perfect; primed, briefed, instructed 524 *informed*; forewarned, forearmed; saddled; battened down; groomed, in one's best bib and tucker, dressed to kill, in full war-paint; accoutred, armed, in harness, armed to the teeth; rigged, rigged out, equipped, furnished, fully f., well-appointed, provided; in store, in hand; in reserve, to hand, ready for use; ready for anything; in working order, operational.

matured, ripened, cooked, hatched etc. vb.; ripe, mellow, mature, seasoned, weathered, hardened; tried, experienced, veteran 694 *expert*; adult, full-grown, full-fledged 134 *grown-up*; out, in flower, florescent, flowering, fruiting; overripe; elaborated, worked up, laboured, smelling of the lamp; perfected 725 *completed*.

ready-made, ready-mixed, cut and dried, ready to use, ready-to-wear, off the peg; prefabricated; processed, oven-ready; precooked, instant.

Vb. *prepare*, take steps, take measures; make preparations, make ready, pave the way, show the w., bridge, build a b., lead up to, pioneer 64 *come before*; choose one's ground, lay the foundations, do the groundwork, provide the basis; soften up; prepare the ground, sow the seed 370 *cultivate*; set to work, address oneself to 68 *begin*; cut out, block o.; sketch, outline, blueprint 623 *plan*; plot, prearrange 608 *predetermine*; prepare for, forearm, insure, take precautions, prepare for a rainy day; anticipate 507 *expect*.

make ready, set in order, make operational; batten down the hatches; put in commission; put one's house in order, put in working order, bring up to scratch, wind up, tune, adjust 62 *arrange*; set the stage; clear the decks; mobilize 74 *bring together*; whet the knife, shuffle the cards, tee up; set, cock, prime, load; warm up, crank up, rev up, get into gear; equip, man; fit out, furnish, kit out, rig out, dress; arm 633 *provide*; rehearse, drill, groom, exercise, lick into shape 534 *train*; inure, acclimatize 610 *habituate*; coach, brief, bring one up to date 524 *inform*.

mature, mellow, ripen, bring to fruition 646 *perfect*; force, bring on 174 *invigorate*; bring to a head 725 *climax*; brew 301 *cook*; gestate, hatch, incubate, breed 369 *breed stock*; grow, farm 370 *cultivate*; nurture; elaborate, work out 725 *carry through*; season, weather, smoke, dry, cure; temper, harden, season.

prepare oneself, brace o.; serve an apprenticeship; study, brief oneself, do one's homework; train, exercise, go for the burn, rehearse, practise 536 *learn*; gird up one's loins, roll up one's sleeves; limber up, warm up, gear oneself up; psych oneself up, flex one's muscles; buckle on one's armour, take up one's sword, take sword in hand, shoulder arms; be prepared, get ready for action, stand by, hold oneself in readiness, keep one's powder dry.

Adv. *in preparation*, in hand, in train, under way, under construction.

670 Nonpreparation

N. *nonpreparation*, potluck; unpreparedness, unreadiness; want of practice, rustiness; unfitness; rawness, immaturity, greenness, unripeness 126 *newness*; belatedness 136 *lateness*; neglect 458 *negligence*; hastiness; improvisation 609 *spontaneity*; imperfection 55 *incompleteness*.

undevelopment, virgin soil; untilled ground 458 *negligence*; raw material, unlicked cub, rough diamond; late developer; rough copy; embryo, abortion.

Adj. *unprepared*, not ready, behindhand 136 *late*; unorganized; unpremeditated, without preparation, ad hoc, ad lib, extemporized, improvised, impromptu, snap, off the top of one's head, off the cuff 609 *spontaneous*; careless 458 *negligent*; overhasty 680 *hasty*; unguarded, with one's trousers down 661 *vulnerable*; caught unawares, taken off guard, caught napping, on the wrong foot 508 *inexpectant*; at sixes and sevens; scratch, untrained 491 *uninstructed*; unrehearsed 611 *unhabituated*; untilled, virgin.

immature, half-grown, unripe, green, underripe; unseasoned; unfledged, callow, wet behind the ears; adolescent, juvenile, childish, puerile, boyish, girlish 130 *young*; undeveloped, half-baked, raw 647 *imperfect*; underdeveloped, backward, retarded 136 *late*; unhatched, unborn, embryonic, rudimentary 68 *beginning*; half-formed, unformed, roughhewn, uncut, unpolished, half-finished, unfinished; premature, abortive, at half-cock 728 *unsuccessful*; untrained, apprentice 695 *unskilled*; crude; forced.

uncooked, raw, rare, underdone; cold; ungarnished.

unequipped, unrigged, undressed 229 *uncovered*; unfurnished, ill-provided 307 *deficient*; unfitted, unqualified.

Vb. *be unprepared*, – unready etc. adj.; want practice; make no preparations, offer potluck, extemporize 609 *improvise*; live from day to day, take one day at a time, let tomorrow take care of itself; be premature, go off at half-cock 135 *be early*; take no precautions, drop one's guard 456 *be inattentive*; catch unawares 508 *surprise*.

Adv. *unreadily*, extempore, off the cuff, ad hoc.

671 Attempt

N. *attempt*, essay, bid; step, move, gambit 676 *deed*; endeavour, effort 682 *exertion*; tackle, try, some attempt; good try; valiant effort; one's level best, best one can do; catch-as-catch-can; determined effort, dead s. 712 *attack*; trial, probation 461 *experiment*; go at, shot at, stab at, crack at, bash at; first attempt, first go, first shot, first offence, first strike 68 *debut*; final attempt, swan song, last bid, last throw; venture; speculation; aim, goal 617 *objective*; straining after, high endeavour.

Vb. *attempt*, essay, try; seek to, aim, make it one's a. 617 *intend*; angle for, fish for, seek 459 *search*; offer, bid, make a b.; make an attempt, make shift to, make the effort, do something about, not just stand there; endeavour, struggle, strive, try hard, try and try again 599 *be resolute*; do one's best, do one's damnedest, go all out, redouble one's efforts 682 *exert oneself*; push hard, strain, sweat 682 *work*; tackle, take on, try one's hand at, have a go, give it a try, give it a whirl, have a shot at, have a crack at, have a stab at 672 *undertake*; take the bull by the horns; chance one's arm, try one's luck, venture, speculate 618 *gamble*; put out a feeler, dip in a toe, put a toe in the water, fly a kite 461 *be tentative*; bite off more than one can chew; die in the attempt 728 *fail*.

Int. here goes! nothing venture, nothing gain.

672 Undertaking

N. *undertaking*, job, task, assignment; self-imposed task, labour of love, pilgrimage 597 *voluntary work*; contract, engagement, obligation 764 *promise*; operation, exercise; programme, project, design 623 *plan*; tall order, big undertaking 700 *hard task*; enterprise, quest, search, adventure 459 *enquiry*; venture, speculation 618 *gambling*; occupation, matter in hand 622 *business*; campaign 671 *attempt*.

Adj. *enterprising*, pioneering, adventurous, venturesome, daring; go-ahead, go-go, progressive, innovative; opportunist, with an eye to the main chance; ambitious.

Vb. *undertake*, engage in, apply oneself to, address o. to, take up, go in for, devote oneself to; venture on, take on, tackle 671 *attempt*; go about, take in hand, turn *or* put *or* set one's hand to; set going 68 *initiate*; proceed to, embark on, launch into, plunge into, fall to, set to, get one's head down, buckle to, put one's best foot forward, set one's shoulder to the wheel, set one's hand to the plough 68 *begin*; grasp the nettle 855 *be courageous*; assume responsibility, take charge of 689 *manage*; execute 725 *carry out*; set up shop, have irons in the fire

622 *busy oneself*; shoulder, take on one's shoulders, take upon oneself 917 *incur a duty*; commit oneself 764 *promise*; get involved, let oneself in for, volunteer 597 *be willing*; take on too much, bite off more than one can chew, have too many irons in the fire 678 *be busy*.

673 Use

N. *use*, utilization, exploitation; employment, application, appliance; exercise 610 *practice*; usage; treatment, proper treatment 457 *carefulness*; ill-treatment; misuse; abuse; wear, wear and tear 655 *dilapidation*; exhaustion, consumption 634 *waste*; reuse, recycling; usefulness, benefit, service 642 *good policy*; practicality, applicability 640 *utility*.

Adj. *used*, applied, employed etc. vb.; in service, in use, in constant u., in practice; used up, consumed, worn, thread-bare, down-at-heel, second-hand, well-used, well-thumbed, dog-eared, well-worn 655 *dilapidated*; beaten, well-trodden 490 *known*; hackneyed, stale; available, usable, employable, utilizable, convertible 640 *useful*; at one's service, consumable, disposable.

Vb. *use*, employ, exercise, practise, put into practice, put into operation; apply, exert, bring to bear, administer; spend on, give to, devote to, dedicate to; assign to, allot; utilize, make use of, convert, convert to use 640 *find useful*; reuse, recycle, exploit, get a lot of mileage out of, use to the full, get the best out of, make the most of, maximize, exhaust the possibilities; milk, drain 304 *extract*; put to good use, turn to good account, capitalize on, make capital out of, use to advantage, profit by; play on, trade on, cash in on; play off against; make a pawn *or* cat's-paw of, take advantage of; put to use, wear, wear out, use up, consume 634 *waste*; work, manipulate 173 *operate*; wield, ply, brandish; overwork, tax 684 *fatigue*.

avail oneself of, take up, adopt, try; resort to, have recourse to, fall back on, turn to, draw on; impose on, presume on; press into service, enlist in one's s.

dispose of, have at one's disposal, control, have at one's command, do what one likes with; allot, assign 783 *apportion*; requisition; call into play, set in motion, set going, deploy 612 *motivate*; enjoy 773 *possess*; consume, expend, absorb, use up 634 *waste*.

674 Nonuse

N. *nonuse*, abeyance, suspension 677 *inaction*; nonavailability 190 *absence*; stagnation, unemployment 679 *inactivity*; abstinence 620 *avoidance*; disuse, obsolescence 611 *desuetude*; redundancy, dismissal 300 *ejection*; surrender, throwing in the towel 621 *relinquishment*; with-

drawal, cancellation 752 *abrogation*; unsuitability 643 *inexpedience*; uselessness, write-off
641 *uselessness*.

Adj. *disused*, derelict, discarded, cast-off, jetti-
soned, scrapped, written off; sacked, discharged, laid off etc. vb.; laid up, mothballed,
put on the back burner, out of commission, rust-
ing; in limbo 458 *neglected*; worn out; on the
shelf, retired; out of use, superseded, superannuated, obsolete, discredited 127 *antiquated*.

Vb. *not use*, not utilize, hold in abeyance; not
touch, have no use for; abstain, forbear, hold
off, do without 620 *avoid*; dispense with;
reserve, keep in hand 632 *store*.

stop using, leave off 145 *cease*; outgrow 611 *disaccustom*; lay up, put in mothballs, put on the
back burner, put out of commission; have done
with, lay aside, put on the shelf; pension off,
put out to grass; discard, dump, ditch, scrap,
write off; jettison, throw away, throw overboard 300 *eject*; slough, cast off; give up, relinquish, resign 779 *not retain*; suspend, withdraw,
cancel 752 *abrogate*; discharge, lay off, pay off,
make redundant 300 *dismiss*; drop, supersede,
replace 150 *substitute*.

675 Misuse

N. *misuse*, abuse, wrong use, alcohol abuse,
drug a., substance a., steroid a., solvent a.; misapplication; mismanagement, maladministration 695 *bungling*; misappropriation,
malpractice 788 *peculation*; perversion 246 *distortion*; prostitution, violation; desecration 980
impiety; malapropism 565 *solecism*; pollution
649 *uncleanness*; overuse, overgrazing, overfish-
ing; extravagance 634 *waste*; misusage, mishandling, mistreatment, maltreatment, ill-
treatment.

Vb. *misuse*, abuse; use wrongly, misemploy,
put to bad use, misdirect; manipulate, misappropriate 788 *defraud*; violate, desecrate, take in
vain 980 *profane*; prostitute 655 *pervert*; pollute
649 *make unclean*; do violence to 176 *force*; take
advantage of, exploit 673 *use*; manhandle,
knock about 645 *ill-treat*; maltreat 735 *oppress*;
misgovern, misrule, mishandle, mismanage
695 *be unskilful*; squander, fritter away 634
waste; misapply, use a sledgehammer to crack a
nut 641 *waste effort*.

SECTION THREE

Voluntary action

676 Action

N. *action*, doing, performance; steps, measures,
move 623 *policy*; transaction, enactment, commission; execution, accomplishment 725 *completion*; procedure, routine 610 *practice*;
behaviour 688 *conduct*; movement, play, swing
265 *motion*; operation, working, interaction 173
agency; force, pressure 178 *influence*; work,
labour 682 *exertion*; militancy, activeness;
effort, endeavour, campaign, crusade, battle
671 *attempt*; implementation, administration,
handling 689 *management*.

deed, act; action, piece of the a., exploit, feat,
achievement 855 *prowess*; crime; stunt, tour de
force, stroke of genius 875 *ostentation*; gesture,
measure, step, move 623 *policy*; manoeuvre 688
tactics; stroke, blow, coup, coup d'état 623 *contrivance*; job, task, operation, exercise 672 *undertaking*; proceeding, transaction, deal, doings,
dealings 154 *affairs*; work, handiwork.

doer, man or woman of action, go-getter, activist, movers and shakers 678 *busy person*; practical person; achiever; hero, heroine 855 *brave
person*; practitioner 696 *expert*; stunt man or
woman, player 594 *actor*; executant, performer;
perpetrator, committer; mover, controller,
manipulator 612 *motivator*; operator 686 *agent*;
contractor, undertaker, entrepreneur, intrapreneur; campaigner, canvasser; executor, executive, administrator, manager 690 *director*; hand,
workman, operative 686 *worker*.

Vb. *do*, act, perform, get in on the act; be in
action, come into operation 173 *operate*; militate, act upon 178 *influence*; manipulate 612
motivate; use tactics, manoeuvre 698 *be cunning*;
do something, lift a finger; proceed, proceed
with, get on with, get going, move, take action,
take steps; try 671 *attempt*; tackle, take on 672
undertake; adopt a measure, enact, legislate 953
make legal; do the deed, perpetrate, commit,
achieve, accomplish, complete, been there
done that 725 *carry through*; do the needful,
take care of, dispatch, execute, implement, fulfil, put into practice 725 *carry out*; do great
deeds, make history, win renown 866 *have a
reputation*; practise, exercise, carry on, discharge, prosecute, pursue, wage, ply, ply one's
trade, employ oneself 622 *busy oneself*; officiate,
do one's stuff 622 *function*; transact, proceed
622 *do business*; administer, administrate, manage, control 689 *direct*; have to do with 688 *deal
with*; sweat, labour, campaign, canvass 682
work; exploit 673 *use*; have a hand in, be active
in, play a part in 775 *participate*; deal in, have a
finger in, get mixed up in 678 *meddle*; conduct
oneself, indulge in 688 *behave*.

677 Inaction

N. *inaction*, nothing doing, inertia 175 *inertness*;
impotence; failure to act, neglect 458 *negligence*;
abstention, refraining 620 *avoidance*; passive
resistance 711 *defiance*; suspension, abeyance,

dormancy 674 *nonuse*; deadlock, stalemate, logjam, gridlock 145 *stop*; immobility, paralysis, impassivity 375 *insensibility*; passivity, stagnation, vegetation, doldrums, stillness, quiet, calm 266 *quiescence*; time on one's hands, idle hours 681 *leisure*; rest 683 *repose*; nonemployment, underemployment, unemployment, joblessness; no work, sinecure; loafing, idleness, indolence, twiddling one's thumbs 679 *inactivity*; Fabian policy, Fabian tactics 136 *delay*; lack of progress 655 *deterioration*; non-interference, nonintervention 860 *indifference*; head in the sand, defeatism 856 *cowardice*.

Adj. *nonactive*, inoperative, idle, suspended, in abeyance 679 *inactive*; passive, dull, sluggish 175 *inert*; unoccupied, leisured 681 *leisurely*; do-nothing, unprogressive, ostrich-like; Fabian, cunctative, delaying, procrastinating; stationary, motionless, immobile, becalmed 266 *quiescent*; cold, extinct; not stirring, without a sign of life, dead-and-alive 361 *dead*; laid off, unemployed, jobless, out of work, on the dole, without employment; incapable of action 161 *impotent*; benumbed, paralysed 375 *insensible*; apathetic, phlegmatic 820 *impassive*.

Vb. *not act*, hang fire 598 *be unwilling*; refrain, abstain, pass the buck 620 *avoid*; look on, stand by 441 *watch*; let the world go by, wait and see, bide one's time 136 *wait*; procrastinate 136 *put off*; let things take their course, laissez-faire, let sleeping dogs lie, let well alone; hold no brief for, stay neutral, not take sides, sit on the fence 860 *be indifferent*; do nothing, turn a blind eye 458 *disregard*; sit tight, not move, not budge, not lift a finger, not even attempt 175 *be inert*; rest on one's oars, rest on one's laurels; drift, slide, coast, free-wheel; have no hope 853 *despair*; let pass, let go by, leave alone, let a., give it a miss 458 *neglect*; stay still, keep quiet 266 *be quiescent*; sit back, relax 683 *repose*; have no function, have nothing to do, kick one's heels, twiddle one's thumbs, sit on one's hands; pause, desist 145 *cease*; rust, lie idle, stay on the shelf, lie fallow 674 *not use*; have no life, lie dead 361 *die*.

678 Activity

N. *activity*, activeness, activism, militancy 676 *action*; scene; interest, active i. 775 *participation*; social activity, group a. 882 *sociability*; activation 612 *motive*; excitation 174 *simulation*; agitation, movement, mass m. 738 *sedition*; life, stir 265 *motion*; nimbleness, briskness, smartness, alacrity, promptitude 597 *willingness*; readiness 135 *punctuality*; quickness, dispatch, expedition 277 *velocity*; spurt, burst, fit 318 *spasm*; hurry, flurry, hurry-skurry, hustle, bustle 680 *haste*; hussle, fuss, bother, botheration, ado, to-do,

tumult, frenzy 61 *turmoil*; whirl, scramble, mad s., rat race, maelstrom 315 *vortex*; drama, much ado, thick of things, thick of the action, the fray; plenty to do, a piece of the action, irons in the fire 622 *business*; call on one's time; pressure of work, no sinecure; hum, hive of industry 687 *workshop*.

restlessness, fiddling; fidgets, fidgetiness 318 *agitation*; fret 503 *frenzy*; energy, dynamism, aggressiveness, militancy, enterprise, initiative, push, drive, go, get-up-and-go, pep 174 *vigorousness*; vivacity, spirit, animation, liveliness, vitality 360 *life*; watchfulness, wakefulness, vigilance 457 *carefulness*; sleeplessness, insomnia.

assiduity, application, concentration, intentness 455 *attention*; industriousness, industry, laboriousness; determination, earnestness, empressement 599 *resolution*; tirelessness, indefatigability 600 *perseverance*; studiousness, painstaking, diligence; whole-heartedness, devotedness.

overactivity, overextension, overexpansion, excess 637 *redundance*; Parkinson's law; displacement activity; chasing one's own tail 641 *lost labour*; song and dance 318 *commotion*; hyperthyroidism, overexertion; officiousness, interference, finger in every pie.

busy person, new broom, enthusiast, hustler, jet-setter; workaholic 686 *worker*; factotum, jack-of-all-trades, maid-of-all-work, galley slave, Trojan; eager beaver, busy bee, workhorse, willing horse; man *or* woman of action, activist, militant 676 *doer*; live wire, human dynamo; powerhouse, whiz kid, go-getter, pusher, careerist.

meddler, stirrer, interferer, trouble-maker, nosy parker, busybody; back-seat driver 691 *adviser*.

Adj. *active*, stirring, kicking 265 *moving*; going, working, incessant; expeditious; able, able-bodied, abled 162 *strong*; quick, brisk, nippy, spry, smart 277 *speedy*; nimble, energetic, forceful, proactive 174 *vigorous*; pushing, go-getting, up-and-coming 672 *enterprising*; frisky, sprightly, mettlesome, live, alive and kicking, full of beans, animated, bright-eyed and bushy-tailed, vivacious 819 *lively*; eager 818 *fervent*; enthusiastic, zealous, prompt, on one's toes 597 *willing*; awake, alert, watchful, wakeful, on the qui vive 457 *vigilant*; sleepless, restless, feverish, fretful, tossing, fidgety, jumpy, nervy, like a cat on hot bricks, like a hen on a hot griddle; frantic 503 *frenzied*; hyperactive, overactive 822 *excitable*; involved; aggressive, militant, up in arms 718 *warlike*.

busy, bustling, humming, lively, eventful; coming and going, rushing to and fro; up and doing, stirring, astir, afoot, on the move, on the go, on the trot, in full swing; rushed off one's feet, hard at it, up to one's eyes; at work, at one's desk; occupied, fully o., employed; busy as a bee.

industrious, studious, sedulous, assiduous; hardworking; slogging 682 laborious; tireless, indefatigable, burning the candle at both ends, efficient, workman-like.

Vb. be active, interest oneself in, join in 775 participate; be stirring, rush to and fro 265 move; run riot 61 rampage; rouse oneself, bestir o., stir one's stumps, rub the sleep from one's eyes, be up and doing; hum, thrive 730 prosper; make progress 285 progress; keep moving, keep on the go, keep the pot boiling 146 go on; push, shove, thrust, drive 279 impel; elbow one's way, thrust oneself forward 174 be vigorous; rush, surge 350 flow; roar, rage, bluster 352 blow; explode, burst; dash, fly, run 277 move fast; make the effort, do one's best 671 attempt; take pains 455 be attentive; buckle to, put one's shoulder to the wheel, put one's hand to the tiller 682 exert oneself; persist, beaver away 600 persevere; polish off, dispatch, make short work of, not let the grass grow under one's feet; rise to the occasion, work wonders 727 be successful; jump to it, show willing, make things hum 676 do; be on one's toes, anticipate 457 be careful; seize the opportunity, take one's chance, take the bull by the horns 137 profit by; assert oneself, not take it lying down, be up in arms, react, react sharply, show fight 711 defy; protest, agitate, demonstrate, kick up a shindy, raise the dust 762 deprecate; be busy, keep b.; have irons in the fire 622 busy oneself; be always on the go, bustle, hurry, hassle, scurry 680 hasten; live in a whirl, join the rat race, run round in circles; chase one's own tail 641 waste effort; not know which way to turn 700 be in difficulty; have one's hands full, be rushed off one's feet, have not a moment to spare or to call one's own, have no time to lose, burn the midnight oil, burn the candle at both ends; stamp with impatience 822 be excitable; have other fish to fry 138 be engaged; slave, slog 682 work; never stop, improve the shining hour.

meddle, intervene, interfere, be officious, not mind one's own business, have a finger in every pie; pry into, poke one's nose in, shove one's oar in, butt in 297 intrude; pester, bother, annoy 827 trouble; be bossy, boss, boss one around, tyrannize 735 oppress; tinker, tamper.

Adv. actively, on the go, on one's toes; full tilt, full belt, whole hog, like a bomb, on all cylinders; with might and main, for all one is worth, for dear life, as if one's life depended on it.

679 Inactivity

N. inactivity, inactiveness 677 inaction; inertia, torpor 175 inertness; lull, suspension 145 cessation; immobility, stillness, slack period, doldrums, morgue 266 quiescence; logjam, putting off till tomorrow, stagnation 655 deterioration; rustiness 674 nonuse; slump, recession 37 decrease; unemployment, shutdown; absenteeism 598 unwillingness; procrastination, laissez-faire, mañana 136 delay; idleness, indolence, loafing.

sluggishness, lethargy, laziness, indolence, sloth; dawdling 278 slowness; debility 163 weakness; lifelessness; languor, listlessness 820 moral insensibility; stupor, torpor 375 insensibility; apathy 860 indifference; phlegm, impassivity 823 inexcitability; supineness, line of least resistance 721 submission.

sleepiness, tiredness, weariness, lassitude 684 fatigue; drowsiness, heaviness, nodding; yawning; tired eyes, heavy lids, sand in the eyes; dreaminess 513 fantasy.

sleep, slumber, kip, bye-byes; beauty sleep; sleep of the just; drowse; nap, catnap, forty winks, shut-eye, snooze, doze, siesta 683 repose; hibernation; unconsciousness, coma, oblivion, trance, catalepsy, hypnosis 375 insensibility; sleepwalking, somnambulism; sleepy sickness 651 disease; dreams; Land of Nod.

soporific, sleeping draught, nightcap; sleeping pill, sedative, barbiturate; opiate, opium, morphine 375 anaesthetic; lullaby, cradlesong, bed-time story.

idler, drone, lazybones, loafer, sloucher, couch potato, mouse p., sluggard; slacker, skiver, clock-watcher; sleepyhead; dawdler 278 slowcoach; hobo, bum, tramp 268 wanderer; mendicant 763 beggar; parasite, cadger, sponger, scrounger, moocher, freeloader; layabout, good-for-nothing, ne'er-do-well; drifter, free-wheeler; lotus-eater; passenger, sleeping partner; idle rich, Sloane Ranger, leisured classes; dreamer.

Adj. inactive, motionless, stationary, at a standstill, still 266 quiescent; suspended, discontinued, not working, not operating, not in use, laid up, out of commission 674 disused; inanimate, lifeless 175 inert; torpid, unconscious, drugged 375 insensible; sluggish, rusty 677 nonactive; listless, lackadaisical 834 dejected; tired, faint, languid, languorous 684 fatigued; dull, heavy, leaden, lumpish, stolid 820 impassive; unresisting, supine, submissive 721 submitting; uninterested 454 incurious; apathetic 860 indifferent; lethargic 823 inexcitable; nonparticipating, sleeping 190 absent; idle, unoccupied 681 leisurely; on strike, out, locked o.

lazy, bone-l.; slothful, sluggish, workshy, indolent, idle, bone-idle, parasitical; idling, loafing 681 *leisurely*; dawdling 278 *slow*; tardy, procrastinating 136 *late*; slack 458 *negligent*.

sleepy, ready for bed, tired 684 *fatigued*; half-awake, half-asleep; somnolent, heavy-eyed; drowsy, dozy, dopey, groggy, nodding, yawning; napping, dozing; asleep, dreaming, snoring, fast asleep, sound a., dead to the world; unconscious, out, out cold; dormant, hibernating, comatose; in dreamland, in the land of Nod, in the arms of Morpheus, in bed.

Vb. *be inactive*, do nothing, relax, hang out; rust, stagnate, vegetate, veg, smoulder, hang fire 677 *no act*; let the grass grow under one's feet, let the world go by, delay 136 *put off*; not bother, take it easy, let things go, laissez-faire 458 *be neglectful*; hang about, kick one's heels 136 *wait*; slouch, lag, loiter, dawdle 278 *move slowly*; dally, drag one's feet 136 *be late*; stand, sit, lie, loll, lounge, laze, rest, take it easy 683 *repose*; lie down on the job, slack, skive, shirk 620 *avoid*; not work, fold one's arms, sit around; have nothing to do, loaf, idle, mooch about, moon a., while away the time, kill t., sit on one's hands, twiddle one's thumbs; waste time, trifle, dabble, fritter away the time, piddle, potter 641 *waste effort*; come to a standstill 278 *decelerate*; dilly-dally, hesitate 474 *be uncertain*; droop, faint, fail, languish, slacken 266 *come to rest*; slump 37 *decrease*; be still, be hushed 266 *be quiescent*; discontinue, stop, come to an end 145 *cease*; strike, come out, take industrial action.

sleep, slumber, snooze, nap, catnap; hibernate; sleep like a log, sleep like a top, sleep the sleep of the just; dream; snore, drive pigs to market; go to sleep, nod off, drop off, fall asleep, take a nap, have a kip, have forty winks; close one's eyes, feel sleepy, yawn, nod, doze, drowse; go to bed, turn in, doss down, kip d., shake d., hit the hay; settle down, bed d.

make inactive, put to sleep; send to sleep, lull, rock, cradle; soothe 177 *assuage*; deaden, paralyse, benumb, anaesthetize, dope, drug 375 *render insensible*; cramp, immobilize 747 *fetter*; lay up, put out of commission 674 *stop using*; dismantle 641 *make useless*; lay off 300 *dismiss*.

680 Haste

N. *haste*, hurry, scurry, hurry-scurry, hustle, bustle, hassle, flurry, whirl, scramble 678 *activity*; flap, flutter, fidget, fuss 318 *agitation*; rush, rush job 670 *nonpreparation*; feverish haste, tearing hurry, race against time, no time to lose 136 *lateness*; immediacy, urgency 638 *importance*; push, drive, expedition, dispatch 277 *velocity*; hastening, acceleration, forced march, dash 277

spurt; precipitateness, impetuosity 857 *rashness*; hastiness, impatience 822 *excitability*; the more haste the less speed.

Adj. *hasty*, impetuous, impulsive, hotheaded 857 *rash*; feverish, impatient; pushing, shoving, elbowing; boisterous, furious 176 *violent*; precipitate, headlong, breakneck 277 *speedy*; without delay; hastening, making speed; in haste, in all h., hotfoot, running, racing; in a hurry, unable to wait, pressed for time, hard-pressed, driven; done in haste, hurried, scamped, slapdash, cursory 458 *negligent*; rough and ready, forced, rushed, rush, last-minute 670 *unprepared*; rushed into, railroaded; stampeded; allowing no time, brooking no delay, urgent, immediate 638 *important*.

Vb. *hasten*, expedite; urge, drive, stampede, spur, goad, whip, lash, flog 612 *incite*; bundle off, hustle away; rush, allow no time, railroaded, brook no delay; be hasty, be precipitate, rush headlong 857 *be rash*; haste, make haste; race, run, dash off, tear off 277 *move fast*; make up for lost time, overtake 277 *outstrip*; spurt, dash, make a forced march 277 *accelerate*; hurry, scurry, hustle, bustle, fret, fume, fidget, rush to and fro, dart to and fro 678 *be active*; be in a hurry, have no time to spare, have no time to lose, act without ceremony, cut short the preliminaries, brush aside; cut corners, rush one's fences; rush through, dash through, make short work of; be pressed for time, work against time *or* to a deadline, work under pressure, think on one's feet; do at the last moment 136 *be late*; lose no time, lose not a moment, make every minute count; hasten away, cut and run, make oneself scarce, not be seen for dust 296 *decamp*.

Int. hurry up! be quick! buck up! look lively! look sharp! get a move on! step on it! quick march! at the double!

681 Leisure

N. *leisure*, spare time, free t.; idle moments; time on one's hands, time to kill; sinecure; idleness, breathing space, off duty, time off, day off, holiday, half-h., break, gap year, vacation, leave, sabbatical, furlough 679 *inactivity*; time to spare, no hurry, ample time, all the time in the world; rest, ease, relaxation 683 *repose*; redundancy, retirement 753 *resignation*.

Adj. *leisurely*, unhurried 278 *slow*; at one's convenience, in one's own time, at any odd moment; leisured, at leisure, unoccupied 683 *reposeful*; at a loose end; off duty, on holiday, on vacation, on leave, on furlough, on sabbatical; retired, in retirement, redundant; labour-saving.

682 Exertion

N. *exertion*, effort, struggle 671 *attempt*; strain, stress, might and main; tug, pull, stretch, heave, lift, throw; drive, force, pressure, applied energy 160 *energy*; ergonomics; ado, hassle, trouble, the hard way; muscle, elbow grease, sweat of one's brow; pains 678 *assiduity*; overwork 678 *overactivity*.

exercise, practice, drill, training, work-out, the bar (ballet) 669 *preparation*; physical education, PE, keeping fit, jogging, jarming, cycling, constitutional, daily dozen; gymnastics 162 *athletics*; weight-lifting, body-building; yoga, isometrics, eurhythmics, callisthenics, aerobics, step, games, sports, races 837 *sport*.

exercise equipment, exercise bike, rowing machine, stepper, treadmill, multi-gym, weights.

labour, industry, work, hard w., long haul; spadework, donkeywork; legwork; manual labour, sweat of one's brow; housework, chores, daily grind, toil, drudgery, slavery, sweat, fag, grind, strain, treadmill, grindstone; hack work; bull; hard labour 963 *penalty*; forced labour, fatigue, spell of d. 917 *duty*; piecework, taskwork, homework, out-work; task, chore, job, operation, exercise 676 *deed*; shift, stint, stretch, bout, spell of work 110 *period*; job of work, stroke of w., hand's turn; working life, working week, working day, man-hours, woman-h.

Adj. *labouring*, horny-handed; working, drudging, etc. vb.; on the go, hard at it 678 *busy*; hardworking, laborious 678 *industrious*; slogging, plodding; strenuous, energetic 678 *active*; painstaking.

laborious, backbreaking; gruelling, punishing, unremitting, exhausting, weary, wearisome, painful, burdensome; heroic, Herculean; arduous, hard, heavy, uphill 700 *difficult*; hardfought, hard-won; thorough, painstaking, laboured; effort-wasting 641 *useless*.

Vb. *exert oneself*, apply oneself, put one's best foot forward, make an effort, try 671 *attempt*; struggle, strain, strive, sweat blood; trouble oneself, put oneself out, bend over backwards; spare no effort, turn every stone, leave no stone unturned, do one's utmost, try one's best, use one's best endeavours, do all one can, go to any lengths, move heaven and earth; go all out, pull out all the stops, put one's heart and soul into it, put one's back into it, strain every nerve 678 *be active*; force one's way, elbow one's way, drive through, wade t.; hammer at, slog at 600 *persevere*; take action 676 *do*.

work, labour, toil, drudge, grind, slog, sweat, work up a sweat, work up a lather; sweat blood; pull, haul, tug, shove, hump, heave, ply the oar; dig, lumber; get down to it, set to, roll up one's sleeves 68 *begin*; keep at it, plod 600 *persevere*; work hard, work overtime, moonlight, work all hours, be firing on all cylinders, burn the midnight oil 678 *be busy*; slave away, beaver away, work one's fingers to the bone, work like a galley slave, work like a horse, work like a Trojan; work oneself to death; overdo it; work for, serve 703 *minister to*; put to work, tax 684 *fatigue*.

683 Repose

N. *repose*, rest 679 *inactivity*; restfulness, ease, comfort 376 *euphoria*; peace and quiet, tranquillity 266 *quiescence*; happy dreams 679 *sleep*; relaxation, breathing space, breather 685 *refreshment*; pause, respite, let-up, recess, break 145 *lull*; interval; holiday, vacation, leave, furlough, day off, sabbatical, sabbatical year 681 *leisure*; day of rest, Sabbath, Lord's day.

Adj. *reposeful*, restful, relaxing; carefree, relaxed, laid-back, at ease 828 *content*; peaceful, quiet 266 *tranquil*; leisured, holiday 681 *leisurely*.

Vb. *repose*, rest, take a rest, take it easy, take one's ease, sit back, put one's feet up; recline, lie down, loll, lounge, laze, sprawl 216 *be horizontal*; perch, roost 311 *sit down*; go to bed, kip down, go to sleep 679 *sleep*; relax, unwind, unbend; take a breather 685 *be refreshed*; slack off, let up, slow down; rest on one's oars 266 *come to rest*; take time off or out.

684 Fatigue

N. *fatigue*, tiredness, weariness, lassitude, languor, lethargy; exhaustion, collapse, prostration; strain, stress, mental fatigue, overwork, burnout, karoshi 682 *exertion*; donor fatigue, compassion f., disaster f.

Adj. *fatigued*, tired, ready for bed 679 *sleepy*; asleep on one's feet, tired out, exhausted, spent; done, done up, done in, pooped, fagged out, knocked up, washed out, worn to a frazzle; stressed, strained, overworked, overtired, burned out, stressed out; dog-tired, bone-weary, tired to death, ready to drop, on one's last legs, all in, dead beat, whacked, knackered, flaked out, flat o.; more dead than alive, prostrate; stiff, aching, sore, footsore, walked off one's feet; heavy-eyed, hollow-e.; tired-looking, haggard, worn; drooping, flagging.

Vb. *be fatigued*, - fagged etc. adj.; tire oneself out, overdo it, overtax one's strength; get weary, ache in every muscle or limb, gasp, pant, puff, blow, grunt 352 *breathe*; languish, droop, drop, sink, flag, fail 163 *be weak*; stagger, faint, swoon, feel giddy; yawn, nod, drowse 679 *sleep*;

succumb, drop, collapse, flake out, crack up, pack up; be at the end of one's tether; can go no further; overwork, need a rest, need a break; be burned out.

fatigue, tire, tire out, wear, wear out, exhaust, do up, fag, whack, knock up, prostrate; wind; tax, strain, stress, overwork, overtax, overtask, overburden, overstrain, burn out; enervate, drain, take it out of; tire to death, weary 838 *be tedious*.

685 Refreshment

N. *refreshment*, breather, breath of air 683 *repose*; break, recess 145 *lull*; recreation, recuperation 656 *restoration*; revival; easing 831 *relief*; refresher, reviver, stimulant, refreshments.

Adj. *refreshing*, thirst-quenching; comforting; bracing, reviving.

Vb. *refresh*, freshen, freshen up 648 *clean*; air, fan, ventilate 340 *aerate*; cool, cool off, cool one down 382 *refrigerate*; brace, stimulate 174 *invigorate*; revive; offer food 301 *feed*.

be refreshed, draw breath, get one's breath back, regain *or* recover one's breath; clear one's head; come to, perk up, get one's second wind, feel like a new man *or* woman; revive 656 *be restored*; mop one's brow, stretch one's legs, refresh oneself, take a breather, sleep it off.

686 Agent

N. *agent*, operator, actor, performer, player, executant, practitioner; perpetrator 676 *doer*; minister, tool 628 *instrument*; functionary 741 *officer*; representative 754 *delegate*; spokesman 755 *deputy*; proxy 150 *substitute*; executor, executrix, executive, administrator, dealer; middleman 794 *merchant*.

worker, voluntary w. 597 *volunteer*; social worker 901 *philanthropist*; freelance, self-employed person; home-worker, teleworker; organization man 83 *conformist*; trade unionist 775 *participator*; toiler, drudge, dogsbody, fag, hack; flunkey, menial, factotum, maid-of-all-work, domestic servant 742 *servant*; hewer of wood and drawer of water, beast of burden 742 *slave*; professional person, business man, business woman, career w., executive, bread-winner, salary e., wage earner, wage slave, employee; boffin; clerical worker, desk w., white-collar w., black-coat w.; office w., girl Friday, man Friday; shop assistant 793 *seller*; charwoman, dustman 648 *cleaner*; labourer, casual l., agricultural l., farm worker 370 *farmer*; piece-worker, manual w., blue-collar w.; working man *or* woman, working girl, workman, hand, operative, factory worker, factory hand; navvy, roadman; ganger, plate-layer; docker, stevedore, packer; porter.

artisan, tradesman; skilled worker, semi-skilled w., master 696 *proficient person*; journeyman, apprentice 538 *learner*; craftsman *or* -woman, potter, turner, joiner, cabinet-maker, carpenter, carver, woodworker, cooper; wheel-wright; coach-builder; shipwright, boatbuilder; builder, architect, master mason, mason, house-builder, bricklayer, plasterer, tiler, thatcher; painter, decorator; forger, metalworker, smith, blacksmith, tinsmith, goldsmith, silversmith, gunsmith, locksmith; tinker, knife-grinder; collier, miner, face-worker, steelworker, foundryman; mechanic, machinist, fitter; engineer, civil e., mining e., computer e., television e.; plumber, welder, electrician, gas-fitter; weaver, spinner, tailor, needlewoman 228 *clothier*; watchmaker, clockmaker; jeweller; glass-blower.

personnel, staff, force, company, team, gang, squad, crew; dramatis personae 594 *actor*; work-people, hands, men, payroll; labour; workforce, labour force, manpower, human resources, liveware, peopleware.

687 Workshop

N. *workshop*, studio; workroom, study, den, library; laboratory; works, factory; workshop, yard; mill, loom; sawmill, paper mill; foundry, metalworks; steelyard, steelworks, smelter; blast furnace, forge, smithy 383 *furnace*; power station, gasworks 160 *energy*; quarry, mine 632 *store*; colliery, coalmine, pit, coalface; tin mine; mint; arsenal, armoury; dockyard, shipyard, slips; wharf, dock 192 *stable*; construction site, building s.; refinery, distillery, brewery, shop, shopfloor, bench, production line; nursery 370 *farm*; dairy, creamery 369 *stock farm*; kitchen, laundry; office, workstation, bureau.

688 Conduct

N. *conduct*, behaviour, deportment; bearing, comportment, carriage; demeanour, attitude, posture 445 *mien*; aspect, look 445 *appearance*; tone of voice, delivery 577 *voice*; motion, action, gesticulation 547 *gesture*; mode of behaviour, fashion, style; manner, guise, air; poise, savoir-faire, dignity, presence; breeding, graciousness, good manners 884 *courtesy*; ungraciousness, boorishness, rudeness, bad manners 885 *discourtesy*; pose, role-playing 850 *affectation*; outlook 485 *opinion*; mood 818 *feeling*; good behaviour 933 *virtue*; misbehaviour, misconduct 934 *wickedness*; past behaviour, track record, history; reward of conduct, deserts 915 *dueness*; way of life, ethos, morals, principles, ideals, customs, mores, manners, lifestyle 610 *habit*; line of action 623 *policy*; career, course, race, walk, walk of life 622 *vocation*;

observance, routine 610 *practice*; procedure, process, method, modus operandi 624 *way*; organization, orchestration, treatment, handling, manipulation, direction, masterminding 689 *management*; gentle handling, kid gloves, velvet glove 736 *leniency*; rough handling, putting the boot in, jackboot, iron hand 735 *severity*; dealings, transactions 154 *affairs*; deeds 676 *deed*; behaviourism.

tactics, strategy, campaign, plan of c., logistics; programme 623 *plan*; line, party 1. 623 *policy*; politics, diplomacy, statesmanship 733 *governance*; lifemanship, gamesmanship, one-upmanship 698 *cunning*; brinkmanship, generalship, seamanship 694 *skill*; jockeying for position; tactical advantage, vantage ground 34 *advantage*; playing for time 136 *delay*; manoeuvre; move, gambit 676 *deed*; stratagem.

Vb. *behave*, act 676 *do*; behave well, mind one's p's and q's, play the game 933 *be virtuous*; behave badly, break all the rules, misbehave, try it on 934 *be wicked*; keep out of mischief, be on one's best behaviour, keep a low profile; gesture 547 *gesticulate*; posture, pose, affect 850 *be affected*; conduct oneself, behave o., acquit o., comport o.; set an example; conduct one's affairs 622 *busy oneself*; follow a course, steer a c. 281 *steer for*; paddle one's own canoe, be master of one's own ship, shift for oneself 744 *be free*; employ tactics; behave towards, treat.

deal with, have on one's plate, have to do with 676 *do*; handle, manipulate 173 *operate*; carry on, conduct, run 689 *manage*; see to, cope with, do the needful; transact, enact, execute, dispatch, carry through, put into practice 725 *carry out*; work out 623 *plan*; work at, work through, wade t. 682 *work*; go through, read 536 *study*.

689 Management

N. *management*, conduct of affairs, running handling; managership, agency 751 *commission*; care, charge, control 733 *authority*; superintendence, oversight 457 *surveillance*; art of management, tact 694 *skill*; business management, work study, management s., time and motion s.; organization, masterminding, decision-making, adhocracy 623 *policy*, housekeeping, husbandry, economics; the economy, national e., stakeholder e.; political economy; statesmanship; government 733 *governance*; ménage, regime; regulation, law-making 953 *legislation*; reins of government, ministry, cabinet; administration; bureaucracy.

directorship, direction, responsibility, control 737 *command*; dictatorship, leadership, premiership, chairmanship, captaincy 34 *superiority*; guidance.

Vb. *manage*, organize; influence; handle, conduct, run, carry on; administer; supervise, superintend, oversee, caretake 457 *invigilate*; have charge of; hold the purse strings, hold the reins 612 *motivate*; *keep order, police*; *legislate*; *control, govern, rule.*

direct, lead; boss, dictate 737 *command*; be in charge, head up, wear the trousers; hold office; mastermind, have overall responsibility; assume command; preside, take the chair, be in the chair; head, captain, skipper; steer, take the helm, show the way 547 *indicate*; guide, conduct, compère; channel.

690 Director

N. *director*, governing body 741 *governor*; steering committee, quango, select committee; cabinet, inner c. 692 *council*; board of directors, board, chair; staff, top brass, VIPs, management; manager, controller; legislator; employer, boss 741 *master*; headman, chief, head of state 34 *superior*; principal, head, headmaster *or* -mistress, rector, moderator, dean, vice-chancellor, chancellor; president; chairperson, chairman, chairwoman, speaker, presiding officer; premier, prime minister, first minister, captain, skipper; master 270 *mariner*; pilot 520 *guide*; director of studies 537 `*teacher*.

leader, judge (Old Testament) 741 *governor*; messiah; ayatollah, guru; leader of the House, leader of the opposition; spearhead, centre forward; shepherd, drover 369 *herdsman*; bellwether; pace-maker, pacesetter, master of ceremonies, MC; high priest; chorus-leader; conductor, leader of the orchestra, first violin; drum major; Führer, Duce 741 *autocrat*; ringleader; captain.

manager, man *or* woman in charge, key person, kingpin 638 *bigwig*; administrator, executive, executor 676 *doer*; statesman *or* -woman, politician; house-keeper, chatelaine, housewife, house husband; steward, bailiff, farm manager, agent, factor 754 *consignee*; superintendent, supervisor, inspector, overseer, foreman *or* -woman, ganger, gaffer; warden, matron, senior nursing officer; party manager, whip, chief whip; custodian, caretaker, curator 749 *keeper*; master of hounds; ringmaster; compère.

official, office-bearer; steward; shop steward; MP, Member of Parliament, constituency MP, public servant, civil s., apparatchik; minister, cabinet m., secretary of state, secretary-general; permanent secretary, bureaucrat, Eurocrat, Euro-MP; magistrate 733 *position of authority*; commissioner, prefect; consul, praetor; first secretary; alderman, mayor 692 *councillor*; party official.

691 Advice

N. *advice*, word of a., piece of a., counsel; words of wisdom, counselling, marriage c., debt c. 658 *therapy*; criticism 480 *estimate*; didacticism, prescription 693 *precept*; caution 664 *warning*; recommendation, proposition, proposal, motion 512 *supposition*; suggestion; tip, word to the wise 524 *hint*; guidance, briefing, instruction 524 *information*; taking counsel, consultation, huddle, heads together, tête-à-tête, powwow, parley 584 *conference*.

adviser, counsellor, consultant, troubleshooter; referee, arbiter, arbitrator 480 *estimator*; advocate, prompter 612 *motivator*; medical adviser, therapist 658 *doctor*; legal adviser, advocate, counsel 958 *lawyer*; guide, mentor, confidant(e) 537 *teacher*; Dutch uncle; oracle, wise man 500 *sage*; backseat driver; public enquiry, consultative body 692 *council*.

Vb. *advise*, give advice, counsel; recommend, prescribe, advocate, commend; propose, move, submit, suggest 512 *propound*; prompt 524 *hint*; urge, exhort 612 *incite*; advise against 613 *dissuade*; admonish 664 *warn*.

consult, seek advice, refer; call in, call on; refer to arbitration, ask for a second opinion, hold a public enquiry; confide in, be closeted with; take advice; take one's cue from, follow advice; sit in conclave, put heads together, hold a council of war, have a powwow with, parley, sit round a table.

692 Council

N. *council*, round table; council chamber, board room; court 956 *tribunal*; Privy Council; ecclesiastical council, Bench of Bishops; vestry; cabinet; panel, quango, think tank, board, advisory b., consultative body, Royal Commission; assembly, conventicle, congregation 74 *assembly*; conclave, convocation 985 *synod*; convention, congress, meeting, top-level m., summit; League of Nations, UNO, Security Council; municipal council, county c., regional c., district c., town c., parish c.; community c; soviet; council of elders; sitting, session, séance.

parliament, European P., Mother of Parliaments, Westminster, Upper House, House of Lords, Lower House, House of Commons; senate, senatus; legislative assembly; Reichsrat, Reichstag; States-General, National Assembly, Chambre des Députés, Bundesrat, Bundestag; Supreme Soviet; Congress, Senate; House of Representatives; quorum.

councillor, privy councillor; senator, peer; Lords Spiritual, L. Temporal; representative, deputy, congressman *or* – woman, member of Parliament, MP, constituency list, Euro-MP 754 *delegate*; backbencher, parliamentarian; mayor, alderman 690 *official*.

693 Precept

N. *precept*, firm advice 691 *advice*; direction, instruction, injunction, charge 737 *command*; commission 751 *mandate*; order, writ 737 *warrant*; prescription, ordinance, regulation 737 *decree*; canon, form, formula, formulary; guidelines 81 *rule*; principle, rule, golden r., moral 496 *maxim*; recipe, receipt 658 *remedy*; commandment, statute, enactment, act, code, penal c. 953 *legislation*; tenet, article, set of rules, constitution; ticket, party line; Ten Commandments, Twelve Tables; canon law, common l., unwritten l. 953 *law*; habit and repute, convention 610 *practice*.

694 Skill

N. *skill*, skilfulness, dexterity, handiness, ambidexterity; style 575 *elegance*; deftness, adroitness; ease 701 *facility*; proficiency, competence; faculty, capability, capacity 160 *ability*; versatility; adaptability, flexibility; mastery, wizardry, virtuosity, excellence, prowess 644 *goodness*; strong point, métier, forte; attainment, accomplishment, skills; seamanship, airmanship, horsemanship, marksmanship; experience, expertise, professionalism; specialism; know-how, technique 490 *knowledge*; deft fingers; craftsmanship, art, artistry; finish, execution 646 *perfection*; ingenuity, resourcefulness, craft, craftiness 698 *cunning*; cleverness, sharpness, worldly wisdom; savoir-faire, finesse 463 *discrimination*; feat of skill, trick, dodge 623 *contrivance*; sleight of hand.

aptitude, innate ability, good head for; bent, natural b. 179 *tendency*; faculty, endowment, gift, flair; knack, green fingers; talent, natural t., genius, genius for; aptness, fitness.

masterpiece, chef-d'oeuvre, a beauty, a creation; pièce de résistance, masterwork, magnum opus; stroke of genius, masterstroke, coup, feat, exploit, hat trick 676 *deed*; smash hit; tour de force, ace, trump 644 *exceller*; work of art, objet d'art, collector's piece *or* item.

Adj. *skilful*, good, good at, top-flight, top-notch, first-rate, ace 644 *excellent*; skilled, crack; handy, dexterous, ambidextrous, deft, slick, adroit, agile, nimble; nimble-fingered, green-f.; sure-footed; cunning, clever, quick, quick-witted, shrewd, smart, ingenious 498 *intelligent*; politic, diplomatic, statesman-like 498 *wise*; flexible, resourceful; versatile; sound, able, competent; wizard, masterly, accomplished.

gifted, of many parts, talented, endowed, well-e.

expert, experienced, veteran, seasoned, tried,

versed in, up in, well up in, au fait; skilled, trained, practised, well-p. 669 *prepared*; finished, specialized 669 *matured*; proficient, qualified, competent, up to the mark; professional.

Vb. *be skilful*, – deft etc. adj.; be good at, do well 644 *be good*; shine, excel 34 *be superior*; have a gift for, show aptitude, show a talent for; have the knack; be on form, be in good f., have one's eye *or* hand in, play one's cards well, not put a foot wrong, know what one is about; live by one's wits, know all the answers, know what's what, have one's wits about one 498 *be wise*.

be expert, be at the top of one's profession, be good at one's job, be a top-notcher, know one's stuff *or* one's onions, have the know-how; have experience, be an old hand, know the ropes, know all the ins and outs, know backwards; display one's skill.

Adv. *skilfully*, craftily, artfully etc. adj.; well, with skill, with aplomb; knowledgeably, expertly; faultlessly, as to the manner born.

695 Unskilfulness

N. *unskilfulness*, lack of practice, rustiness 674 *nonuse*; inexperience, inexpertness 491 *ignorance*; inability, incompetence, inefficiency; lack of proficiency; clumsiness, awkwardness, gaucherie (**see** *bungling*); backwardness, slowness 499 *unintelligence*; booby prize, wooden spoon.

bungling, botching, half-measures, pale imitation, travesty 726 *noncompletion*; bungle, botch, dog's breakfast, pig's ear, cock-up, balls-up, shambles; off day, poor show, bad job, flop 728 *failure*; hamhandedness, dropped catch, butterfingers, fumble, muff, fluff, miss, mishit, slice, misfire, own goal, friendly fire 495 *mistake*; tactlessness, heavy-handedness, indiscretion 464 *indiscrimination*; mishandling, misapplication 675 *misuse*; too many cooks; mismanagement, misrule, misgovernment, maladministration 481 *misjudgment*; wild-goose chase 641 *lost labour*.

Adj. *unskilful*, talentless, unendowed, unaccomplished; unversatile 679 *inactive*; unfit, inept 25 *unapt*; unable, incapable 161 *impotent*; incompetent, inefficient, ineffectual; unpractical, unbusinesslike, stupid, foolish 499 *unwise*; feckless; not up to scratch, failed 728 *unsuccessful*; inadequate 636 *insufficient*.

unskilled, raw, green, undeveloped 670 *immature*; uninitiated, under training, untrained, apprentice, half-skilled, semi-s. 670 *unprepared*; unqualified, inexpert, inexperienced, ignorant, unversed 491 *uninstructed*; nonprofessional, ham, amateurish, amateur, self-taught; unsound, quack.

clumsy, awkward, uneasy, gauche, gawky, boorish, uncouth 885 *discourteous*; stuttering; tactless, indiscreet 464 *indiscriminating*; bumbling, bungling; maladroit, all thumbs, butterfingered; cack-handed, heavy-h., ham-h., heavy-footed; ungainly, lumbering, hulking, gangling, shambling; out of practice, out of training 611 *unhabituated*; slovenly, slatternly, slapdash 458 *negligent*; fumbling, groping, tentative 461 *experimental*; graceless 576 *inelegant*; top-heavy, lopsided 29 *unequal*; cumbersome, ungainly.

bungled, botched, messed up, fouled up, screwed up, mismanaged, mishandled etc. vb.; ill-considered; ill-prepared 670 *unprepared*; ill-contrived, ill-devised, cobbled together; crude, rough and ready, inartistic, amateurish, jerry-built, slapdash, perfunctory 458 *neglected*; half-baked 726 *uncompleted*.

Vb. *be unskilful*, – inept, unqualified etc. adj.; not know how 491 *not know*; show one's ignorance, be handless, be clueless, on the wrong way about it; paper over the cracks 726 *not complete*; burn one's fingers, catch a Tartar 508 *not expect*; mismanage, misgovern; misapply 675 *misuse*; misdirect 495 *blunder*; forget one's words, fluff one's lines, miss one's cue 506 *forget*; ham; go rusty, get out of practice 611 *disaccustom*.

act foolishly, not know what one is about, cut one's own throat, cut off one's nose to spite one's face, throw out the baby with the bath water, make a fool of oneself, make an ass of oneself, lose face, be left with egg all over one's face 497 *be absurd*; bite the hand that feeds one, kill the goose that lays the golden eggs; spoil the ship for a ha'porth of tar; bring one's house about one's ears, knock one's head against a brick wall, put the cart before the horse; have too many eggs in one basket; bite off more than one can chew, have too many irons in the fire; put a square peg in a round hole, put new wine into old bottles 495 *blunder*; labour in vain 470 *attempt the impossible*; go on a fool's errand 641 *waste effort*; strain at a gnat and swallow a camel.

be clumsy, lumber, bumble, galumph, hulk, get in the way, be de trop, stand in the light; trip, trip over, stumble, blunder, boob; not look where one is going 456 *be inattentive*; stutter 580 *stammer*; fumble, grope, flounder 461 *be tentative*; muff, fluff; slice, mishit, misthrow, misfire; spill, slop, drop, drop a catch, drop a sitter 311 *let fall*; catch a crab; let the cat out of the bag, bungle, drop a brick, put one's foot in it, make a faux pas, get egg on one's face 495 *blunder*; botch, spoil, mar, blot 655 *impair*; fool with 678 *meddle*; make a mess of it, make a hash of it

728 *miscarry*; do a bad job, make a poor fist at 728 *fail*.

696 Proficient person

N. *proficient person*, sound player, expert, adept, dab hand, dabster; do-it-yourself type, all-rounder, Jack of all trades, handyman, admirable Crichton 646 *paragon*; Renaissance man, person of many parts; maître, master, past m., graduate, cordon bleu; intellectual, mastermind 500 *sage*; genius, wizard, gifted child 864 *prodigy*; magician; maestro, virtuoso; bravura player 413 *musician*; prima donna, first fiddle, top sawyer, prize-winner, gold-medallist, champion, title-holder, cup-h., dan, black belt, ace 644 *exceller*; picked man, capped player, star p., seeded p., white hope; crack shot; acrobat, gymnast 162 *athlete*.

expert, professional, pro, specialist, authority, doyen, professor 537 *teacher*; pundit, guru, walking encyclopaedia 492 *scholar*; veteran, old hand, old stager, old dog, old soldier, warhorse, sea dog; practised hand, practised eye; man *or* woman of the world, businessman *or* – woman, career woman, careerist; tactician, strategist, politician; diplomat, diplomatist; artist, craftsman *or* -woman; technician, skilled worker 686 *artisan*; experienced hand, right person for the job, key man *or* -woman; consultant 691 *adviser*; boffin 623 *planner*; cognoscente, connoisseur.

697 Bungler

N. *bungler*, failure 728 *loser*; one's despair; incompetent, botcher; bumbler, blunderer; fumbler, muffer, butterfingers; clumsy 1.; hulk, bull in a china shop; duffer, buffoon, booby, galoot, clot, clod, hick, oaf, ass, plonker, big girl's blouse 501 *fool*; slob, sloven, slattern 61 *slut*; hack, dauber; poor shot; amateur, ham; Jack of all trades and master of none; novice, greenhorn, raw recruit 538 *beginner*; landlubber; fish out of water, square peg in a round hole 25 *misfit*.

698 Cunning

N. *cunning*, craft 694 *skill*; know-how; resourcefulness, inventiveness, ingenuity 513 *imagination*; guile, gamesmanship, cunningness, craftiness, artfulness, subtlety, wiliness, slyness; stealthiness, stealth 523 *latency*; cageyness 525 *concealment*; slipperiness; sleight of hand, cheating, monkey business 542 *deception*; double-dealing, imposture 541 *duplicity*; wheeling and dealing, manoeuvring 688 *tactics*; diplomacy, Machiavellism, realpolitik; gerrymandering 930 *improbity*; underhand dealing, under-the-counter dealing, sharp practice.

stratagem, ruse, wile, artifice, device, ploy, dodge 623 *contrivance*; machination, game, little g. 623 *plot*; subterfuge, evasion; excuse 614 *pretext*; white lie; cheat 542 *deception*; trick, old t., box of tricks, tricks of the trade, rules of the game 542 *trickery*; feint; ambush, Greek gift, Trojan horse, stalking h. 542 *trap*; ditch, pit 663 *pitfall*; Parthian shot; web of cunning, web of deceit; blind, dust thrown in the eyes, red herring; thin end of the wedge, manoeuvre, move 688 *tactics*.

slyboots, artful dodger, wily person, serpent, snake, fox; fraud, wolf in sheep's clothing, double-crosser 545 *deceiver* cheat, sharper 545 *trickster*; juggler; smoothie 925 *flatterer*; Machiavelli, intriguer, plotter, schemer 623 *planner*; strategist, tactician, manoeuvrer, wheeler-dealer.

Adj. *cunning*, crafty, disingenuous, artful, sly, wily, subtle; tricksy; scheming, plotting, intriguing, Machiavellian; knowing, fly, slick, smart, sophisticated, urbane; canny, pawky, sharp, astute, shrewd, acute; too clever for, too clever by half, too smart for his *or* her own good, up to everything, not to be caught napping, no flies on, not born yesterday 498 *intelligent*; not to be drawn, cagey 525 *reticent*; experienced 694 *skilful*; resourceful, ingenious; tactical; insidious 930 *perfidious*; shifty, slippery 518 *equivocal*; deceitful, crooked, devious 930 *dishonest*.

Vb. *be cunning*, – sly etc. adj.; dodge, juggle, manoeuvre, jockey, double-cross; intrigue, scheme, weave a plot, have an ulterior motive, have an axe to grind, have an eye to the main chance 623 *plot*; contrive, wangle, devise 623 *plan*; monkey about with, gerrymander; pull a fast one, steal a march on, trick, cheat 542 *deceive*; sweet-talk 925 *flatter*; play for time; be too clever for, be one up on, outsmart, outwit, go one better, know a trick worth two of that 306 *outdo*; be too quick for, snatch from under one's nose, pip at the post; waylay, dig a pit for, undermine, bait the trap 527 *ambush*; get one's foot in the door; have a card up one's sleeve, have a shot in one's locker; know all the answers, live by one's wits.

699 Artlessness

N. *artlessness*, simplicity, simple-mindedness; naivety, ingenuousness, guilelessness 935 *innocence*; inexperience, unworldliness; unaffectedness, unsophistication, naturalness 573 *plainness*; sincerity, candour, frankness; truth, honesty 929 *probity*.

Adj. *artless*, without artifice; unstudied; uncomplicated, uncontrived 44 *simple*; unadorned, unvarnished 573 *plain*; native, natural, unartificial, homespun, homemade; do-it-yourself 695 *unskilled*; in a state of nature, primitive; unsophisticated, ingenuous, naive, childlike 935 *innocent*; green, unworldly, simpleminded, callow, wet behind the ears; guileless, unsuspicious, confiding; unaffected 609 *spontaneous*; candid, frank, open, undissembling, straightforward 540 *veracious*; true, honest, sincere 929 *honourable*; above-board, on the level; transparent; shy, unassuming, unpretentious 874 *modest*.

Vb. *be artless*, – natural etc. adj.; have no guile 935 *be innocent*; have no affectations; wear one's heart upon one's sleeve; look one in the face, look one straight in the eyes, call a spade a spade, say what is in one's mind, speak one's mind 573 *speak plainly*; not mince one's words 540 *be truthful*.

SECTION FOUR

Antagonism

700 Difficulty

N. *difficulty*, hardness, arduousness, laboriousness 682 *exertion*; impracticability, no go, nonstarter 470 *impossibility*; intricacy, perplexity, inextricability, involvement 61 *complexity*; complication 832 *aggravation*; obscurity, impenetrability 517 *unintelligibility*; inconvenience, awkwardness 643 *inexpedience*; difficult terrain, rough ground, hard going, bad patch 259 *roughness*; quagmire, slough 347 *marsh*; knot, Gordian k. 251 *coil*; problem, thorny p., crux, hard nut to crack, poser, teaser, puzzle, the sixty-four-thousand-dollar question, headache 530 *enigma*; impediment, handicap, obstacle, snag, rub, where the shoe pinches 702 *hindrance*; teething troubles 702 *hitch*; maze, crooked path 251 *convolution*; cul-de-sac, dead end, impasse, no-go area, blank wall 264 *closure*; deadlock, standstill, logjam, stoppage 145 *stop*; stress, brunt, burden 684 *fatigue*; trial, ordeal, temptation, tribulation, vexation 825 *suffering*; trouble, sea of troubles 731 *adversity*; difficult person, handful, one's despair, hot potato.

hard task, test, trial of strength; Herculean task, superhuman t., thankless t., never-ending t., Sisyphean labour; work cut out, hard row to hoe, hard furrow to plough, no picnic; handful, tall order, tough assignment, impossible task, hard work, uphill struggle 682 *labour*.

predicament, embarrassment, delicate situation; quandary, dilemma, cleft stick; catch-22 situation; fix, jam, hole, scrape, hot water, trouble, fine kettle of fish, pickle, stew, soup, imbroglio, mess, muddle; straits, pretty pass; slippery slope, sticky wicket, tight corner, painting oneself into a corner, diplomatic incident, ticklish situation, tricky s., hot seat 661 *danger*; emergency 137 *crisis*.

Adj. *difficult*, hard, tough, formidable; steep, arduous, uphill; inconvenient, onerous, burdensome, irksome 682 *laborious*; exacting, demanding; insuperable, impracticable 470 *impossible*; problematic; delicate, ticklish, tricky; unwieldy, unmanageable; intractable, refractory 738 *disobedient*; recalcitrant, stubborn, unyielding, perverse 602 *obstinate*; ill-behaved, naughty 934 *wicked*; perplexing, obscure 517 *unintelligible*; knotty, complex, complicated, inextricable, labyrinthine 251 *intricate*; impenetrable, impassable, unnavigable; thorny, rugged, craggy 259 *rough*; sticky, critical 661 *dangerous*.

in difficulties, hampered 702 *hindered*; labouring under difficulties; in a quandary, in a dilemma, in a cleft stick, between two stools, between Scylla and Charybdis, between the devil and the deep blue sea 474 *doubting*; baffled, clueless, nonplussed 517 *puzzled*; in a jam, in a fix, on the hook, up a gum tree, up the creek, in a spot, in a hole, in a scrape, in hot water, in the soup, in a pickle; in deep water, out of one's depth, under fire, not out of the wood, in danger, on the danger list, on a hit list, in the hot seat 661 *endangered*; worried, beset with difficulties 825 *suffering*; under pressure, up against it, in a catch-22 situation, hard pressed, sore p., hard put to it, driven to extremities; in dire straits, in distressed circumstances; left holding the baby, left in the lurch; at one's wits end, at the end of one's tether, cornered, at bay, with one's back against the wall; stuck, stuck fast, aground.

Vb. *be difficult*, – hard etc. adj.; complicate matters 63 *bedevil*; put one on the spot, inconvenience, bother, irk, try one's patience, lead one a merry dance, be a thorn in one's flesh, be one's bête noire, go against the grain 827 *trouble*; present difficulties, set one a problem, pose, perplex, baffle, nonplus, stump 474 *puzzle*; hamper, obstruct 702 *hinder*; make things worse 832 *aggravate*; lead to an impasse, create deadlock 470 *make impossible*.

be in difficulty, have a problem; tread on eggs 461 *be tentative*; have one's hands full 678 *be busy*; not know which way to turn, be at a loss 474 *be uncertain*; have difficulties, have one's work cut out, be hard put to it, have trouble with; run into trouble, strike a bad patch; be asking for trouble, fish in troubled waters; let oneself in for, cop it, catch it, catch a packet, catch a Tartar, have a tiger by the tail, stir up a hornet's nest; have a hard time of it 731 *have trouble*; bear the brunt, feel the pinch 825 *suffer*;

sink under the burden 684 *be fatigued*; bring it on oneself, make heavy weather of, flounder; come unstuck 728 *miscarry*; do it the hard way, swim upstream, fight 716 *contend*; live dangerously 661 *face danger*; labour under difficulties, be disadvantaged, labour under a disadvantage, have one hand tied behind one's back, be handicapped by.

Adv. *with difficulty*, with much ado; the hard way, uphill, against the stream, against the wind, against the grain; in the teeth of; at a pinch.

701 Facility

N. *facility*, easiness, ease, convenience, comfort; flexibility, pliancy 327 *softness*; capability, capacity, feasibility 469 *possibility*; comprehensibility 516 *intelligibility*; facilitation, easing, making easy, simplification, smoothing disentanglement 746 *liberation*; free hand, full scope, blank cheque, clean slate 744 *scope*; facilities, provision for 703 *aid*; leave 756 *permission*; simplicity, no complication 44 *simpleness*; straightforwardness, no difficulty, no competition; an open-and-shut case; no friction, easy going, calm seas 258 *smoothness*; fair wind, clear coast, clear road 137 *opportunity*; straight road.

easy thing, no trouble, no sweat, a pleasure, child's play, kid's stuff; soft option, short work, light work, cushy number, sinecure 679 *inactivity*; picnic, doddle 837 *amusement*; peanuts, piece of cake, money for jam *or* old rope; easy money, fast buck; smooth sailing, plain s., easy ride; nothing to it, easy target, sitting duck; easy meat, soft touch; pushover, walkover 727 *victory*; cinch, sure thing, dead cert 473 *certainty*.

Adj. *easy*, facile, undemanding, cushy; effortless, painless; light; uncomplicated 44 *simple*; not hard, not difficult, easy as pie, easily done, no sooner said than done; as easy as falling off a log, as simple as ABC; feasible 469 *possible*; facilitating 703 *aiding*; downhill, with the current, with the tide, with the crowd; convenient 376 *comfortable*; approachable, within reach, within easy reach 289 *accessible*; open to all 263 *open*; comprehensible 516 *intelligible*.

tractable, manageable 597 *willing*; submissive 721 *submitting*; yielding, malleable, pliant 327 *flexible*; manoeuvrable.

Vb. *be easy*, – simple etc. adj.; be trouble-free, require no effort, present no difficulties, give no trouble, make no demands; be one's for the asking; be easily solved, have a simple answer 516 *be intelligible*; go like clockwork.

do easily, have no trouble; make light of, make no bones about, make short work of, do it standing on one's head, do it with one hand

tied behind one's back; have it all one's own way, carry all before one, have it in the bag, hold all the trumps, win hands down, have a walk-over 727 *win*; sail home, coast h., freewheel; be at ease, be at home, be in one's element, take in one's stride, take to like a duck to water; not strain oneself, drift with the tide, swim with the stream 721 *submit*; take the easy way out, take the line of least resistance.

facilitate, ease, make easy; iron out 258 *smooth*; oil 334 *lubricate*; explain, gloss, simplify 520 *interpret*; enable; make way for, allow 756 *permit*; put one in the way of 469 *make possible*; help, speed, accelerate, expedite 703 *aid*; clear the way, blaze a trail 64 *come before*; pave the way, bridge the gap; make an opening for 744 *give scope*.

disencumber, free, set free, liberate, unshackle, unfetter 668 *deliver*; clear, clear the ground, weed, clear away, unclog 648 *clean*; derestrict, cut through red tape; disentangle, extricate; untie 46 *disunite*; cut the knot, cut the Gordian k. 46 *cut*; ease, lighten, unload, unhamper, unburden, ease the burden, alleviate, obviate 831 *relieve*.

Adv. *easily*, smoothly, like clockwork; swimmingly; effortlessly, with one's eyes closed, with one hand tied behind one's back, just like that; without a hitch.

702 Hindrance

N. *hindrance*, let or h., impediment; inhibition, block; stalling, thwarting, obstruction, frustration; hampering, shackling, clogging etc. vb.; blockage, logjam, blocking, bed-blocking 264 *closure*; blockade, siege 712 *attack*; limitation, restriction, control, squeeze 747 *restraint*; arrest 747 *detention*; check, retardation, deceleration 278 *slowness*; drag 333 *friction*; interference, meddling 678 *overactivity*; interruption, interception, intervention 231 *interjacency*; obtrusion 303 *insertion*; objection 762 *deprecation*; obstructiveness, picketing, secondary p., sabotage 704 *opposition*; lockout 182 *counteraction*; defence 715 *resistance*; discouragement, disincentive 613 *dissuasion*; hostility 924 *disapprobation*; blacking, boycott 620 *avoidance*; forestalling, prevention; prophylaxis 652 *hygiene*; sterilization, birth control 172 *contraception*; ban, embargo, no-no 757 *prohibition*; nuisance value.

obstacle, impediment, hindrance, nuisance, drawback, inconvenience, handicap 700 *difficulty*; hazard; bottleneck, blockage, road block, contraflow, traffic jam, logjam; a hindrance, wheel clamp, tie, tether 47 *bond*; previous engagement 138 *untimeliness*; red tape, regulations; snag, block; stumbling block, tripwire, hurdle, hedge, ditch, moat; water-jump; something in the way, barrier, bulkhead, wall, brick w., stone w., sea w., dam, weir, dike, embankment 662 *safeguard*; bulwark, buffer, parapet, portcullis, barbed wire 713 *defences*; fence, blockade 235 *enclosure*; curtain, iron c., bamboo c. 231 *partition*; stile, gate, turnstile, tollgate; crosswind, headwind, crosscurrent; impasse, deadlock, stalemate, vicious circle, catch-22; cul-de-sac, blind alley, dead end, blank wall.

hitch, unexpected obstacle, snag, catch; contretemps; teething troubles; technical hitch, breakdown, engine failure; puncture, flat; leak, burst pipe; fuse, short circuit; stoppage, holdup, setback 145 *stop*; something wrong, computer malfunction, screw loose, spanner in the works, fly in the ointment.

encumbrance, handicap; drag, shackle, chain 748 *fetter*; trammels; impedimenta, cross, millstone, albatross round one's neck, weight on one's shoulders, dead weight 322 *gravity*; burden, overload, last straw; onus, Old Man of the Sea; family commitments; mortgage, debts 803 *debt*.

Adj. *hindered*, waterlogged, handicapped, disadvantaged, encumbered, burdened with, lumbered w., saddled w., stuck w.; frustrated, thwarted, stymied etc. vb.; up against a brick wall; held up, delayed, stuck, becalmed, fogbound, snowbound, snowed-up 747 *restrained*; stopped, prevented 757 *prohibited*; heavy-laden, overburdened 684 *fatigued*; marooned, stranded, left high and dry, up the creek.

Vb. *hinder*, hamper, obstruct, impede; delay, use Fabian tactics; inconvenience 827 *trouble*; upset 63 *derange*; trip up, get under one's feet; entangle 542 *ensnare*; get in the way; come between, intervene, interpose 678 *meddle*; intercept, head off, undermine, stop one in the act, cut the ground from under one's feet, pull the rug from under one's f.; nip in the bud, stifle, choke; gag, muzzle 578 *make mute*; suffocate, repress 165 *suppress*; quell; hamper, burden, encumber; hang like a millstone round one's neck 322 *weigh*; load with, saddle w. 193 *load*; handicap; shackle, trammel, tie one's hands, tie hand and foot 747 *fetter*; put under house arrest, put under curfew; restrict 236 *limit*; check, brake, be a drag on, hold back 747 *restrain*; hold up, slow down, set one back 278 *retard*; lame, cripple, hobble, hamstring, paralyse 161 *disable*; wing 655 *wound*; clip the wings, cramp the style of, take the wind out of one's sails; deter 854 *frighten*; damp down, throw cold water on.

obstruct, intervene, interfere 678 *meddle*; obtrude 297 *intrude*; stymie, snooker, stand in the way 231 *lie between*; buzz, jostle, crowd,

elbow, squeeze; sit on one's tail 284 *follow*; stop, intercept, occlude, stop up, block, block up, wall up 264 *close*; jam, jam tight, foul up, cause a stoppage, bring to a standstill; bind 350 *staunch*; dam, dam up; divert 495 *mislead*; fend off, stave off; barricade 235 *enclose*; fence, hedge in, blockade 232 *circumscribe*; deny access, keep out 57 *exclude*; prevent, inhibit, ban, bar, debar 757 *prohibit*.

be obstructive, make it hard for, play up 700 *be difficult*; put off, stall, stonewall; not play ball 598 *be unwilling*; baffle, foil, stymie, balk, be a dog in the manger; counter 182 *counteract*; thwart, frustrate; object, raise objections 704 *oppose*; interrupt, heckle, barrack; shout down 400 *be loud*; take evasive action 620 *avoid*; filibuster 581 *be loquacious*; play for time, use Fabian tactics, protract; strike 145 *halt*; picket; sabotage, throw a spanner in the works, gum up the works, spike the guns, put a spoke in one's wheel; take the wind out of one's sails.

703 Aid

N. *aid*, assistance, help, customer service, helping hand, leg-up, lift, boost; succour, rescue 668 *deliverance*; support, backing, seconding, abetment, encouragement; reinforcement; helpfulness 706 *cooperation*; service, ministration; good offices; patronage, auspices, sponsorship, favour 660 *protection*, 178 *influence*; good will, charity 897 *benevolence*; intercession 981 *prayers*; championship; good advice, constructive criticism 691 *advice*; spoonfeeding, featherbedding; first aid, medical assistance 658 *medical art*; favourable circumstances 730 *prosperity*; fair wind; self-help.

subvention, economic aid, monetary help; donation 781 *gift*; charity 901 *philanthropy*; social security, welfare benefit, unemployment b., job-seeker's allowance, sickness benefit, supplementary b., child b.; loan 802 *credit*; subsidy, hand-out, bounty, grant, allowance, expense account; stipend, bursary, scholarship 962 *reward*; maintenance, alimony, aliment, support, keep, upkeep 633 *provision*; dependency culture.

aider, help, helper, assistant, lieutenant, henchman, aide, right-hand man *or* woman, man Friday, girl F., backing group; stand-by, support, mainstay; tower of strength, rock 660 *protector*; district nurse, community n., social worker, Child Support Agency; CSA help-line, help-desk, counsellor 691 *adviser*; good neighbour, Good Samaritan; ally, brother-in-arms 707 *collaborator*; reinforcements 707 *auxiliary*; fairy godmother 903 *benefactor*; sponsor 707 *patron*; abettor.

Adj. *aiding*, helpful, obliging 706 *cooperative*;

kind 897 *benevolent*; supporting, seconding, abetting; supportive, encouraging; of service, of help, of great assistance 640 *useful*; constructive, well-meant; morale-boosting; assistant, auxiliary, subsidiary, ancillary; contributory, assisting 628 *instrumental*.

Vb. *aid*, help, assist, lend a hand, give a helping hand 706 *cooperate*; render assistance; be there for, hold out a hand to, take under one's wing, take in tow, give a lift to; hold one's hand, spoonfeed, featherbed; be kind to, do one a good turn, give a leg up, help a lame duck, help a lame dog over a stile; help one out, tide one over, see one through; oblige, accommodate, lend money to 784 *lend*; put up the money, finance, subsidize; pitch in, chip in, send the hat round; facilitate, boost 285 *promote*; abet, fan the flame 612 *induce*; contribute to, be accessory to; lend support to, boost one's morale, back up, stand by, bolster, prop up 218 *support*; comfort, sustain, hearten, encourage, rally 855 *give courage*; succour, send help to, bail out, help o. 668 *deliver*; step into the breach, reinforce; set one on his *or* her feet 656 *restore*.

patronize, sponsor, back, guarantee, go bail for, stand surety for; recommend, put up for; propose, second; contribute to, subscribe to 488 *endorse*; take an interest in 880 *befriend*; champion, take up the cudgels for, stick up for, stand up f., stand by 713 *defend*; canvass for, root f., vote f. 605 *vote*; bestow one's custom, buy from 792 *purchase*.

minister to, wait on, do for, help, oblige 742 *serve*; give first aid to, nurse 658 *doctor*; squire, valet, mother; be of service to, make oneself useful to; anticipate the wishes of 597 *be willing*; pander to, toady, humour, be a cat's paw to, scratch one's back, suck up to 925 *flatter*; slave, do all one can for, wait hand and foot on, do everything for 682 *work*; be assistant to, make oneself the tool of 628 *be instrumental*.

704 Opposition

N. *opposition*, antagonism, hostility 881 *enmity*; conflict, friction 709 *dissension*; noncooperation 598 *unwillingness*; contrariness, recalcitrance 602 *obstinacy*; counterargument 479 *confutation*; contradiction, denial 533 *negation*; challenge 711 *defiance*; stout opposition, stand 715 *resistance*; infringement 738 *revolt*; going against, siding a., voting a., canvassing a. 924 *disapprobation*; headwind, crosscurrent 702 *obstacle*; cross purposes, tug of war, tug of love, battle of wills; faction, rivalry, emulation, competition 716 *contention*; political opposition, the Opposition, Her Majesty's O., the other side.

opposites, contraries, extremes, opposite poles

14 *contrariety*; rivals, duellists, competitors 716 *contender*; opposite parties, factions, black and white, cat and dog; town and gown, the right and the left, management and workers, Labour and Conservative, Democrat and Republican.

Adj. *opposing*, opposed; in opposition; anti, against, agin; antagonistic, hostile, unfriendly, antipathetic, unsympathetic 881 *hostile*; unfavourable, unpropitious 731 *adverse*; cross, thwarting; contradictory 14 *contrary*; cussed, bloody-minded, bolshie 602 *obstinate*; refractory, recalcitrant 738 *disobedient*; resistant; clashing, conflicting, at variance, at odds with 709 *quarrelling*; militant, up in arms, at daggers drawn; face to face, eyeball to eyeball 237 *frontal*; at opposite extremes 240 *opposite*; rival, competitive 911 *jealous*.

Vb. *oppose*, go against, militate a. 14 *be contrary*; side against, stand a., hold out a., fight a., dig one's heels in, refuse to budge, stand one's ground 715 *resist*; set one's face against, make a dead set a. 607 *reject*; object, kick, protest, protest against 762 *deprecate*; vote against 924 *disapprove*; canvass against, dissociate oneself; contradict, belie 533 *negate*; counter 479 *confute*; work against 182 *counteract*; countermine, thwart, baffle, foil 702 *be obstructive*; be at cross purposes; stand up to, challenge, dare 711 *defy*; vie with, compete with, bid against 716 *contend*.

withstand, confront, face, stand against, stand up to 661 *face danger*; rise against 738 *revolt*; take on, meet, encounter, cross swords with 716 *fight*; struggle against, breast the tide, stem the t., swim against the stream; cope with, grapple w., wrestle w. 678 *be active*; not be beaten 599 *stand firm*; hold one's own, bear the brunt 715 *resist*.

Adv. *in opposition*, against, versus, agin; in conflict with, against the crowd, against the tide, against the wind, against the grain, in the teeth of, in the face of, in defiance of.

705 Opponent

N. *opponent*, opposer, adversary, challenger, antagonist, foe 881 *enemy*; assailant 712 *attacker*; opposing party, opposition p., the opposition, opposite camp; cross benches; objector 489 *dissentient*; resister, dissident 829 *malcontent*; challenger, rival, competitor, combatant, contestant, duellist; entrant, the field, all comers 716 *contender*.

706 Cooperation

N. *cooperation*, helpfulness 597 *willingness*; interaction; duet, tandem; collaboration, joint effort, combined operation; team work, working together, concerted effort; relay race; team spirit, esprit de corps; unanimity, agreement

710 *concord*; clannishness, party spirit, cliquishness, partisanship; connivance, collusion, abetment 612 *inducement*; conspiracy 623 *plot*; complicity, participation, worker p.; sympathy 880 *friendliness*; fraternity, sorority, solidarity, fellowship, freemasonry, fellow feeling, comradeship, fellow-travelling; common cause, mutual assistance, networking, back-scratching, aiding and abetting; reciprocity, give and take, mutual concession 770 *compromise*.

association, co-ownership, partnership 775 *participation*; nationalization 775 *joint possession*; pool, kitty; affiliation 78 *inclusion*; tie-up 9 *relation*; combination 45 *union*; solidarity 52 *whole*; unification 88 *unity*; amalgamation, fusion, merger; coalition, alliance, league, federation, confederacy, umbrella organization; united front 708 *political party*; an association, fellowship, club, fraternity, sorority 708 *community*; set, clique, coterie, cell 708 *party*; workers' association, trade union, chapel; business association, company, joint-stock c., syndicate, combine consortium, trust, cartel, ring 708 *corporation*; workers' cooperative, commune 708 *community*.

Adj. *cooperative*, helpful 703 *aiding*; collaborating, married, associating, associated, in league, back-scratching, hand in glove with; bipartisan; federal 708 *corporate*.

Vb. *cooperate*, collaborate, work together, pull t., work as a team; hunt in pairs, run in double harness; team up, join forces, pool resources, go into partnership 775 *participate*; show willing, play ball, reciprocate, respond; join in, take part, enter into, pitch in; rally round 703 *aid*; stand shoulder to shoulder, stand by each other, sink or swim together; be in league with, be in cahoots with, make common cause with; network, band together, gang up, associate, ally; coalesce, merge, unite; combine, make common cause, club together; conspire 623 *plot*; collude, connive, negotiate 766 *make terms*.

707 Auxiliary
N. *auxiliary*, reinforcement; back-up; second line 722 *soldiery*; paramedic, auxiliary nurse; assistant, helper 703 *aider*; right-hand man; adjutant, lieutenant, aide-de-camp; amanuensis, secretary, girl Friday; dogsbody 742 *servant*; acolyte; best man, bridesmaid; henchman, follower 742 *dependant*; disciple, adherent 978 *sectarian*; loyalist, flunkey, stooge, cat's-paw, puppet 628 *instrument*; shadow.

collaborator, cooperator, co-author, co-worker, fellow w.; team-mate; fellow traveller, fifth column, fifth columnist, quisling, traitor, mole, conspirator, conniver.

colleague, associate, fellow-worker, peer, brother, sister; co-director, partner 775 *participator*; comrade, companion, boon c., playmate, alter ego, faithful companion; mate, chum, pal, buddy, oppo, crony 880 *friend*; helpmate, better half 894 *spouse*; stalwart; ally, confederate; accomplice, accessory, abettor, aider and abettor, fellow conspirator, partner in crime.

patron, guardian angel 660 *protector*; champion, friend at court; supporter, sponsor, backer, angel, guarantor; fan 887 *lover*; good friend, friend in need, deus ex machina; fairy godmother, rich uncle, sugar daddy 903 *benefactor*; promoter, founder; customer, client 792 *purchaser*.

708 Party
N. *party*, group, class 77 *classification*; denomination, church 978 *sect*; faction, cabal, cave, splinter group, breakaway movement 489 *dissentient*; circle, inner c., charmed c., kitchen cabinet; set, clique, in-crowd, coterie; caucus; committee, quango, club, cell, cadre; ring, closed shop; eight, eleven, fifteen; crew, team, complement 686 *personnel*; troupe, company 594 *actor*; gang, outfit 74 *band*; side, camp.

political party, right, left, centre; Conservative, Tories, Unionists, National Front; Liberals, Radicals, Whigs; Socialists, Labour, New Labour; LibLab, Social Democrats, SDP; Democrats, Republicans; Nationalists, Scottish N., SNP; Ecologists, Greens; Militant Tendency, Workers' Revolutionary Party, International Socialists, Trotskyists, Marxists, Communists, Bolsheviks, Mensheviks; Fascists, Nazis; coalition, popular front, bloc; comrade; socialist, Fabian; anarchist 738 *revolter*; right-winger, true blue; left-winger, leftist, leftie, pinko; populist, democrat; moderate; wet, dry; fundamentalist, fundie; party worker, canvasser, party member, politician; militant, activist 676 *doer*.

society, partnership, coalition, combination, combine 706 *association*; league, alliance; federation, confederacy; cooperative, union, EEC, European Community, E. union, euroland, Common Market, free trade area; club 76 *focus*; secret society, Freemasonry, lodge, cell; trades union; chapel; youth movement, Boy Scouts, Cubs, Rovers, Rangers, Girl Guides, Brownies; Women's Institute, Mother's Union; fellow, associate, member; party m., paid-up m., card-carrying m.; trade unionist.

community, fellowship, brotherhood, congregation, fraternity, sorority, sisterhood; clique, coterie; guild; race, tribe, clan, sect 11 *family*; order 77 *classification*; social class 371 *social group*; state, nation.

corporation, body; company, joint-stock c.,

limited liability c., public limited c., dot com c., holding c.; multinational c.; firm, concern; partnership; business house; establishment, organization, institute; trust, combine, monopoly, cartel, syndicate, conglomerate 706 *association*; trade association, chamber of commerce, guild, cooperative society; consumers' association.

Vb. *join a party*, subscribe; join, swell the ranks, become one of, become a member, take out membership; sign on, enlist, enrol oneself, get elected; align oneself, side with, range oneself with, team up w. 706 *cooperate*; associate, ally.

709 Dissension

N. *dissension*, disagreement 489 *dissent*; noncooperation 704 *opposition*; disharmony, jar, jangle, jarring note, discordant n. 411 *discord*; wrangling, quarrelling, bickering, sniping, cat-and-dog life; differences, odds, variance, friction, tension, unpleasantness, scenes; hostility 888 *hatred*; disunity, internal dissension, muttering in the ranks, house divided against itself 25 *disagreement*; rift, cleavage, parting of the ways, separation 294 *divergence*; split 978 *schism*; cross purposes 481 *misjudgment*; breach, rupture, severance of relations; declaration of war, open war 718 *war*.

quarrelsomeness, factiousness, litigiousness; aggressiveness, combativeness, pugnacity, belligerence, warlike behaviour 718 *bellicosity*; provocativeness, inviting trouble, trailing one's coat 711 *defiance*; contentiousness 716 *contention*; rivalry 911 *jealousy*; apple of discord.

quarrel, feud, blood f., vendetta 910 *revenge*; war 718 *warfare*; strife 716 *contention*; conflict, clash 279 *collision*; legal battle 959 *litigation*; controversy, dispute, wrangle, argy-bargy; paper war 475 *argument*; words, war of w., raised voices, stormy exchange, confrontation, altercation, set-to, slanging match 899 *scurrility*; spat, tiff, squabble, wrangle, barney, hassle, squall, storm in a teacup; rumpus, dustup, disturbance, hubbub, racket, row, shindig, stramash, commotion, scrimmage, fracas, brawl, fisticuffs, breach of the peace 61 *turmoil*; gang warfare, street fighting, riot 716 *fight*.

Adj. *quarrelling*, clashing, conflicting 14 *contrary*; on bad terms, feuding, at odds, at loggerheads, at variance, at daggers drawn, up in arms 881 *hostile*; divided, factious, schismatic 489 *dissenting*; mutinous, rebellious 738 *disobedient*; cantankerous 892 *irascible*; litigious; quarrelsome, bellicose 718 *warlike*; pugnacious, combative, spoiling for a fight, trailing one's coat, inviting trouble, asking for it, belligerent, aggressive, militant; argumentative, contentious, disputatious, wrangling.

Vb. *quarrel*, clash, conflict 279 *collide*; cross swords with, be at one another's throats; be at cross purposes, be at variance, have differences, have a bone to pick 15 *differ*; fall out, go one's separate ways, part company, split, break with; break away; break off relations, break off diplomatic r., declare war 718 *go to war*; go to law, take it to court 959 *litigate*; squabble, row with, go at it hammer and tongs, brawl; have a feud with, carry on a vendetta 910 *be revengeful*.

make quarrels, pick q., pick a fight; look for trouble, ask for it, be spoiling for a fight, trail one's coat, challenge 711 *defy*; rub up the wrong way, tread on one's toes, get up one's nose, provoke 891 *enrage*; have a bone to pick; estrange, set at odds, set at variance, set by the ears; sound a discordant note 411 *discord*; sow dissension, stir it, make mischief, make trouble, kick up a shindy, disturb the peace; put the cat among the pigeons; come between, drive a wedge b. 46 *sunder*; widen the breach, fan the flame 832 *aggravate*; set against.

710 Concord

N. *concord*, harmony 410 *melody*; unison, unity, duet 24 *agreement*; unanimity, bipartisanship 488 *consensus*; understanding, mutual u., rapport; solidarity, team spirit 706 *cooperation*; reciprocity 12 *correlation*; sympathy, fellow feeling 887 *love*; compatibility, coexistence 880 *friendship*; détente, reunion, reconciliation, conciliation, peacemaking 719 *pacification*; arbitration 720 *mediation*; entente cordiale, happy family, picture of content, the best of friends, sweetness and light, love and peace 717 *peace*; goodwill, honeymoon period.

Vb. *concord* 410 *harmonize*; bring into concord 719 *pacify*; agree 24 *accord*; hit it off, see eye to eye, play a duet, chime in with, pull together 706 *cooperate*; reciprocate, respond, run parallel 181 *concur*; fraternize 880 *be friendly*; keep the peace, remain at peace 717 *be at peace*.

711 Defiance

N. *defiance*, dare, daring, challenge, gage, gauntlet, hat in the ring; bold front, belling the cat, brave face 855 *courage*; war dance, war cry, war whoop, war song, battle cry, declaration of war 900 *threat*; brazenness 878 *insolence*; demonstration, display, bravura 875 *ostentation*.

Adj. *defiant*, defying, challenging, provocative; in-your-face, belligerent, bellicose, militant 718 *warlike*; saucy, insulting 878 *insolent*; mutinous, rebellious 738 *disobedient*; greatly daring 855 *courageous*; stiff-necked 871 *proud*; reckless, trigger-happy 857 *rash*.

Vb. *defy*, challenge, take one up on 489 *dis-*

sent; stand up to 704 *oppose*; caution 664 *warn*; throw in one's teeth, throw down the gauntlet, throw one's hat in the ring; demand satisfaction, call out, send one's seconds; dare, outdare, beard; brave, run the gauntlet 661 *face danger*; laugh to scorn, laugh in one's face, laugh in one's beard, set at naught, snap one's fingers at 922 *hold cheap*; bid defiance to, set at d., hurl d.; call one's bluff, double the bid; show fight, bare one's teeth, show one's fangs, double one's fist, clench one's f., shake one's f. 900 *threaten*; refuse to bow down to 871 *be proud*; look big, throw out one's chest, beat one's c., show a bold front; wave a banner 317 *brandish*; march, demonstrate, hold a demonstration, stage a sit-in, not be moved; cock a snook 878 *be insolent*; ask for trouble 709 *make quarrels*; crow over, shout 727 *triumph*; crow, bluster, brag 877 *boast*.

Adv. *defiantly*, challengingly, in defiance of, in one's teeth, to one's face, under the very nose of; in open rebellion.

Int. do your worst! come on if you dare!

712 Attack

N. *attack*, hostile a., best method of defence; pugnacity, combativeness, aggressiveness 718 *bellicosity*; belligerence, aggression, unprovoked a. 914 *injustice*; stab in the back; mugging, assault, assault and battery, grievous bodily harm 176 *violence*; armed attack, offensive, charm o., drive, push, thrust, pincer movement 688 *tactics*; dead set at; onslaught, onset, rush, charge; sally, sortie, breakthrough; counter-attack 714 *retaliation*; shock tactics, blitzkrieg, surprise; infringement 306 *overstepping*; invasion, incursion, overrunning 297 *ingress*; raid, ram r., foray 788 *brigandage*; blitz, air raid; taking by storm, boarding; siege, blockade 230 *surroundings*.

terror tactics, guerrilla warfare, sniping, war of attrition, war of nerves 854 *intimidation*; shot across the bows; bloodbath 362 *slaughter*; laying waste.

bombardment, cannonade, barrage, strafe, blitz; broadside, volley, salvo; bomb-dropping, bombing, saturation b.; firing, shooting, gun-fire, fusillade, cross-f.; anti-aircraft fire, flak; sniping.

attacker, assailant, aggressor, mugger; storm troops, strike force; fighter pilot, bomber 722 *armed force*; sniper; terrorist, guerrilla; invader, raider; besieger.

Vb. *attack*, be spoiling for a fight; start a fight, declare war 718 *go to war*; strike the first blow, open fire on, fire the first shot; assault, go for, set on, pounce upon, fall u., pitch into, sail i.; attack tooth and nail, savage, maul, draw

blood 655 *wound*; launch out at, let fly at, let one have it, lay into, tear into, lace into, round on; take by surprise, blitz, overwhelm; invade 306 *encroach*; raid, foray, overrun, infest; take the offensive; make a sortie; board, grapple; take by storm, capture 727 *overmaster*; ravage, make havoc; harry, drive 619 *hunt*; take up the cudgels 716 *fight*.

besiege, lay siege to, beleaguer, surround, beset, blockade 235 *enclose*.

strike at, raise one's hand against; lay about one, swipe, flail, hammer 279 *strike*; go berserk; run amok; lash out at; beat up, mug; lunge; grapple with, fight hand to hand, cut and thrust; push, butt, thrust, poke at, thrust at; stab, spear, lance, bayonet, run through, cut down 263 *pierce*; lay low, bring down 311 *abase*.

fire at, shoot at; fire a shot at, take a potshot, snipe, pick off 287 *shoot*; shoot down; torpedo; strafe, bombard, blitz, shell, pepper; bomb, drop b.; open fire; rake; take aim, pull the trigger, level, draw a bead on 281 *aim*.

713 Defence

N. *defence*, the defensive, self-defence 715 *resistance*; art of self-defence, boxing 716 *pugilism*; judo, jujitsu, karate 716 *wrestling*; parry, warding off 182 *counteraction*; defensiveness 854 *nervousness*; guard; self-protection 660 *protection*; a defence, rampart, bulwark, screen, buffer, fender, bumper, bull bars 662 *safeguard*.

defences, lines, entrenchment; earthwork, embankment, mound; boom; wall, barricade, fence 235 *barrier*; palisade, paling, stockade; moat, ditch, dike; trench, dugout; tripwire, booby trap 542 *trap*; barbed wire; spike; anti-tank obstacles, Maginot Line, Siegfried L., Hadrian's Wall, Antonine W., Great Wall of China; air raid shelter, fallout s., bunker 662 *shelter*; barrage, anti-aircraft fire, flak; barrage balloon; minefield, mine; smokescreen 421 *screen*.

fortification (see *fort*); bulwark, rampart, wall; parapet, battlement, emplacement; escarp; bastion; outwork; buttress, abutment.

fort, fortress, stronghold, fastness; citadel, capitol, acropolis 662 *refuge*; castle, keep, tower, turret; portcullis, drawbridge; gate, postern; Martello tower, pillbox; laager, encampment 235 *enclosure*; Roman camp.

armour, panoply; mail, chain m.; breastplate; cuirass; hauberk, coat of mail, corslet; helmet, casque, visor, beaver; steel helmet, tin hat; bearskin 228 *headgear*; gauntlet; shield, buckler; protective clothing, riot shield, gas mask 662 *safeguard*.

defender, champion; patron 703 *aider*; knight errant; loyalist, patriot; bodyguard, lifeguard 722 *soldier*; watch, sentry, sentinel; vigilante;

patrol, patrolman; security man *or* woman; garrison, picket, guard, escort, rearguard; Home Guard, Territorials, Territorial Army, militia, thin red line 722 *soldiery*; fireman; Civil Defence; guardian, warden 660 *protector*; warder, custodian 749 *keeper*.

Vb. *defend*, guard, protect, keep, watch 660 *safeguard*; fence, hedge 232 *circumscribe*; barricade 235 *enclose*; block 702 *obstruct*; cushion, pad, shield, curtain, cover 421 *screen*; cloak 525 *conceal*; arm 669 *make ready*; armour, reinforce, fortify 162 *strengthen*; entrench, dig in 599 *stand firm*; stand in front, stand by; garrison, man, stop the gap; plead for, hold a brief for, argue for, take up the cause of, champion 927 *vindicate*; fight for, take up arms for, take up the cudgels for, rescue.

714 Retaliation

N. *retaliation*, reprisal 910 *revenge*; requital, recompense, comeuppance 962 *reward*; deserts, just deserts 915 *dueness*; punitive action, poetic justice, retribution, Nemesis 963 *punishment*; reaction, boomerang, backlash 280 *recoil*; counterstroke, counterblast, counterplot, countermine 182 *counteraction*; counterattack, sally, sortie 712 *attack*; recrimination, answering back, rispote, retort 460 *rejoinder*; heaping coals of fire; reciprocation, like for like, tit for tat, quid pro quo, measure for measure, blow for blow, an eye for an eye and a tooth for a tooth, a taste of one's own medicine, a Roland for an Oliver, biter bit, a game at which two can play; what is coming to one; deterrent 854 *intimidation*.

Vb. *retaliate*, exact compensation 31 *recoup*; take reprisals 963 *punish*; counter, riposte; pay off old scores, square the account, be quits, get even with, get upsides with, get one's own back 910 *avenge*; teach one a lesson; reciprocate, give and take, return like for like; return the compliment, give as good as one got, pay one in his own coin, get one's pound of flesh; retort, cap, answer back 460 *answer*; round on, kick back, hit b., not take it lying down 715 *resist*; turn the tables on, hoist one with his *or* her own petard, make one laugh on the other side of his face, make one take back his *or* her own words, have the last laugh.

715 Resistance

N. *resistance*, stand, brave front 704 *opposition*; intractability 602 *obstinacy*; objection, demur 468 *qualification*; recalcitrance, protest 762 *deprecation*; noncooperation, passive resistance, civil disobedience; rising, insurrection, backlash 738 *revolt*; self-defence 713 *defence*; repulsion, rebuff 760 *refusal*.

Adj. *resisting*, opposing; protesting, reluctant 598 *unwilling*; recalcitrant, mutinous 738 *disobedient*; stubborn 602 *obstinate*; unyielding, indomitable; resistant, tough, proofed, bulletproof, waterproof, showerproof.

Vb. *resist*, offer resistance, stand against 704 *withstand*; obstruct 702 *hinder*; challenge, stand out against 711 *defy*; confront 661 *face danger*; struggle against, contend with, stem the tide 704 *oppose*; kick against the pricks, protest 762 *deprecate*; demur, object 468 *qualify*; down tools, vote with one's feet, walk out, come out 145 *cease*; call out 145 *halt*; mutiny, rise, not take it lying down 738 *revolt*; make a stand, fight off, keep at arm's length, keep at bay, hold off; make a fight of it 716 *contend*; hold out, not submit, stand one's ground, not give way 599 *stand firm*; endure 825 *suffer*; repel, rebuff 760 *refuse*; resist temptation, not be tempted.

716 Contention

N. *contention*, strife, tussle, conflict, clash, running battle 709 *dissension*; combat, fighting, war 718 *warfare*; debate, dispute, controversy, polemics, ink-slinging 475 *argument*; altercation, words, war of w. 709 *quarrel*; bone of contention; competition, rivalry, price war, emulation 911 *jealousy*; competitiveness, gamesmanship, survival of the fittest, rat race; turf war; cut-throat competition, war to the knife, no holds barred; sports, athletics 837 *sport*.

contest, trial, trial of strength, marathon, pentathlon, decathlon, tug-of-war, tug of love 682 *exertion*; tussle, struggle 671 *attempt*; needle match; nothing in it, close finish, photo f. 200 *short distance*; competition, free-for-all; pro-am, knockout competition, tournament; prize competition, stakes, Ashes; match, Test m.; rally; event, handicap, run-off; heat, final, semifinal, quarterfinal, Cup tie, Cup final; set, game, rubber; sporting event, wager, bet 837 *sport*; field day 837 *amusement*; Derby day (**see** *racing*); athletics, gymnastics; gymkhana, horseshow, rodeo; games. Highland Games, Commonwealth G., Olympic G., Olympics; Wimbledon, Wembley, Lord's 724 *arena*.

racing, races, race, foot r., flat r., sprint; racewalking, road race, marathon, fun run; long-distance race, cross-country r., orienteering; slalom, obstacle race; hare and hounds r., treasure hunt; sack race, egg and spoon r.; relay r., team r.; the Turf, horse racing, sport of kings; the Derby, the Oaks; point-to-point, steeplechase, hurdles, sticks 312 *leap*; motor race, motor rally, dirt-track racing, stockcar r., speedway, motocross; cycle race, Tour de France, cyclocross; dog racing, the dogs; boat race, yacht r.; regatta, eights, Ascot, racecourse, track, stadium 724 *arena.*

pugilism, noble art of self-defence, boxing, sparring, jabbing, socking, slugging, pummeling, lambasting, fisticuffs; fighting, prize f.,; target boxing, kick-boxing; boxing match, prizefight; round, bout; the ring, the fancy 837 *sport.*

wrestling, jujitsu, judo, aikido, karate, kyoku-shinkai, taekwondo, kungfu, ninjutsu; all-in wrestling, catch-as-catch-can, no holds barred; catch, hold; wrestle, grapple, wrestling match.

duel, affair of honour, seconds out; jousting, tilting, tournament; fencing, iaido, swordplay, kendo; hand-to-hand fighting; bullfight; cockfight; bullring, cockpit, lists 724 *arena.*

fight, hostilities, blow-up, appeal to arms 718 *warfare;* battle royal, free fight, free-for-all, showdown, rough and tumble, roughhouse, horseplay, shindig, stramash, scuffle, scrum, scrimmage, scramble, dogfight, mêlée, fracas, uproar, rumpus, ruction 61 *turmoil;* gang warfare, street fight, riot, brawl, broil 709 *quarrel;* fisticuffs, blows, hard knocks; give and take, cut and thrust; affray, set-to, tussle; running fight, hand-to-hand fighting; combat, fray, clash, conflict 279 *collision;* encounter, dustup, scrap, brush; skirmish; engagement, action, pitched battle, stand-up fight, shoot-out 718 *battle;* campaign, struggle; war to the knife, fight to the death; Armageddon.

contender, fighter, gladiator; duellist; candidate, entrant, examinee; competitor, rival; challenger, front runner, favourite, top seed; the field, all comers; contestant; racer, runner, marathoner 162 *athlete;* sprinter.

Vb. *contend,* combat, strive, struggle, battle, fight, tussle, wrestle, grapple 671 *attempt;* oppose, put up a fight 715 *resist;* argue for, stick out for, insist 532 *emphasize;* contest, compete, challenge, stake, wager, bet; play, play against, match oneself, vie with, race, run a race; emulate, rival; outrival 306 *outdo;* enter, enter for, take on, enter the lists, descend into the arena, take up the challenge, pick up the gauntlet; cross swords with; take on, grapple with, lock horns w. 712 *strike at;* have a hard fight, fight to a finish.

fight, scuffle, row, scrimmage, scrap, set to; pitch into, sail i. 712 *attack;* lay about one 712 *strike at;* mix it, join in the mêlée; square up to, come to blows, exchange b., put up one's fists; box, spar, pummel, jostle, hit, kick, scratch, bite 279 *strike;* quarrel; duel; encounter, have a brush with, scrap w., skirmish; take on, engage, fight a pitched battle; come to grips, close with, grapple, lock horns; fence, cross swords; fight hand to hand, combat, campaign, fight the

good fight 718 *wage war;* fight it out, fight to the last man 599 *be resolute.*

717 Peace

N. *peace,* peacefulness, peace and quiet, a quiet life, the line of least resistance 266 *quiescence;* harmony 710 *concord;* peacetime; law and order 60 *order;* truce, armistice 145 *lull;* peace dividend; coexistence; neutrality, nonalignment; noninvolvement 860 *indifference;* non-intervention 620 *avoidance;* peaceableness, nonaggression 177 *moderation;* cordial relations 880 *friendship;* pacifism, peace at any price, peace in our time, nonviolence; disarmament, peacemaking, peace process 719 *pacification;* pipe of peace; peace treaty, burial of the hatchet 506 *amnesty.*

pacifist, man *or* woman of peace, peace women, peace-lover, peacemonger, dove; peace camp, CND 177 *moderator;* neutral, noncombatant; passive resister, conscientious objector, conchie; peacemaker 720 *mediator.*

Adj. *peaceful,* quiet, halcyon 266 *tranquil;* bloodless; harmless, dovelike 935 *innocent;* easy-going 884 *amiable;* uncompetitive; peaceable, law-abiding, peace-loving, pacific, unaggressive, pacifist, nonviolent; unarmed, noncombatant; passive, submissive 721 *submitting;* peacemaking, conciliatory; without enemies, at peace; not at war, neutral; postwar, prewar, interwar; peacetime.

Vb. *be at peace,* stay at p., observe neutrality, keep out of trouble; mean no harm, forget one's differences, be pacific 935 *be innocent;* keep the peace, make p. 720 *mediate;* beat swords into plough-shares, make the lion lie down with the lamb, smoke the pipe of peace.

718 War

N. *war,* arms, the sword; ground war., air w., cold w., armed neutrality; paper war, war of words, polemic 709 *quarrel;* war of nerves, sabre-rattling, gunboat diplomacy 854 *intimidation;* uneasy peace, phoney w.; armed intervention, police action; civil w., war of revolution, war of independence; wars of religion, holy war, crusade; war of expansion; all-out war; world w., total w., blitzkrieg, atomic war, nuclear w.; war of attrition, war to the death, no holds barred; war to end all wars, Armageddon; the panoply of war, martial music; call to arms, bugle call 547 *call;* battle cry, rallying cry, Mars.

belligerency, state of war; declaration of war, militancy, hostilities; wartime.

bellicosity, war fever; pugnacity, combativeness, aggressiveness, hawkishness, militancy 709 *quarrelsomeness;* militarism, expansionism;

jingoism, chauvinism, gung-ho 481 *prejudice.*

war measures, war preparations, arming 669 *preparation;* call to arms, clarion call, fiery cross 547 *call;* war effort, war work, call-up, rally, mobilization, recruitment, conscription, national service, military duty; volunteering, doing one's duty, for king *or* queen and country, joining up, enlisting.

warfare, war, open w., warpath, waging w.; bloodshed, battles, sieges 176 *violence;* fighting, campaigning, soldiering, active service; military s., naval s., air s.; bombing, saturation b. 712 *bombardment;* raiding; besieging, blockading 235 *enclosure;* aerial warfare, naval w., chemical w., gas w., germ w., atomic w., nuclear w.; economic w., blockade, attrition, scorched earth policy; psychological warfare, propaganda; offensive warfare 712 *attack;* defensive warfare 713 *defence;* trench w., desert w., jungle w.; bush-fighting, guerrilla warfare, sniping; campaign, expedition; operations; incursion, invasion, raid; order, orders 737 *command;* battle cry; plan of campaign, strategy 623 *plan.*

battle, pitched b., battle royal 716 *fight;* line of battle, array; line, firing l., front l., front, battle f., battle station; armed conflict, action, scrap, skirmish, brush, collision, clash, shoot-out; offensive, blitz 712 *attack;* defensive battle, stand 713 *defence;* engagement, naval e., sea fight, air f., dogfight; battlefield, theatre of war 724 *battleground.*

Adj. *warring,* on the warpath; campaigning, battling etc. vb.; at war; belligerent, aggressive, bellicose, militant, mobilized, under arms, in the army, at the front, on active service; militant, up in arms; armed, sword in hand 669 *prepared;* arrayed, embattled; engaged, at loggerheads 709 *quarrelling;* on the offensive.

warlike, militaristic, bellicose, hawkish, militant, aggressive, belligerent, pugnacious, pugilistic, combative; war-loving, warmongering; bloodthirsty, war-fevered; military, paramilitary, martial, battle-scarred.

Vb. *go to war,* resort to arms; declare war, open hostilities, let slip the dogs of war; appeal to arms, unsheathe the sword, throw away the scabbard, whet the sword, take up the cudgels 716 *fight;* fly to arms, rise, rebel 738 *revolt;* raise one's banner, call to arms, send round the fiery cross; arm, militarize, mobilize, put on a war footing; rally, call up, call to the colours, recruit, conscript; join the army, join up, enlist; make w., go on the warpath, march to war, engage in hostilities, war against; open a campaign; go on active service, take the offensive, invade 712 *attack;* act on the defensive 713 *defend;* march, countermarch; blockade, besiege

230 *surround;* shed blood, put to the sword 362 *slaughter;* ravage, burn, scorch; give battle; cross swords with, take issue with; join battle, engage, stage a shoot-out, call for a show-down, combat, confront, fight it out 716 *fight;* beat the drum, go over the top; open fire 712 *fire at.*

719 Pacification

N. *pacification,* pacifying, peacemaking; conciliation, appeasement, mollification 177 *moderation;* reconciliation, reconcilement, détente, rapprochement; accommodation, adjustment 24 *agreement;* good offices 720 *mediation;* peace process, peace talks; entente, understanding, peace treaty, nonaggression pact, SALT 765 *treaty;* truce, armistice, cease-fire 145 *lull;* disarmament, CND, peace movement, demobilization, disbanding; nuclear-free zone, peace camp.

peace offering, appeasement 736 *leniency;* dove of peace, olive branch, overture, hand of friendship, outstretched hand 880 *friendliness;* flag of truce, white flag, pipe of peace 717 *peace;* blood money, compensation 787 *restitution;* plea for peace 506 *amnesty.*

Vb. *pacify,* make peace; allay, tranquillize, mollify, soothe 177 *assuage;* smooth one's ruffled feathers, pour balm into one's wounds, heal 656 *cure;* hold out the olive branch, hold out one's hand, coo like a dove 880 *be friendly;* conciliate, propitiate, disarm, reconcile, placate, appease, satisfy 828 *content;* pour oil on troubled waters 266 *bring to rest;* restore harmony 410 *harmonize;* win over, meet halfway 770 *compromise;* settle differences; bring together 720 *mediate;* grant peace 766 *give terms;* keep the peace 717 *be at peace.*

make peace, stop fighting, cry quits, break it up 145 *cease;* bury the hatchet, let bygones be bygones, forgive and forget 506 *forget;* shake hands, make it up, make friends, kiss and make up, patch up a quarrel, come to an understanding, agree to differ; lay down one's arms, sheathe the sword, put up one's sword, beat swords into ploughshares; make a truce, suspend hostilities, demilitarize, disarm, demobilize; smoke the pipe of peace.

720 Mediation

N. *mediation,* good offices, mediatorship, intercession; umpirage, refereeship, arbitration; intervention, stepping-in, diplomacy; parley, negotiation 584 *conference.*

mediator, mutual friend, middleman, matchmaker, marriage bureau, dating agency, introduction a., computer dating, lonely hearts column; go-between, pander, Pandarus, negotiator 231 *intermediary;* arbitrator, umpire, referee

480 *estimator;* diplomat, diplomatist, representative, agent, spokesperson 754 *delegate;* peace movement, peace-keeping force 177 *moderator;* pacifier, troubleshooter, ombudsman, ACAS; marriage guidance counsellor, family conciliation service 691 *adviser;* peace-maker.

Vb. *mediate,* intervene 678 *meddle;* step in, interpose; proffer one's good offices, intercede for, propitiate; run messages for, be a go-between, act as a pander for; bring together, negotiate, act as agent; arbitrate, umpire 480 *judge.*

721 Submission

N. *submission,* submissiveness 739 *obedience;* subservience 745 *servitude;* acquiescence, compliance, consent 488 *assent;* supineness, peace at any price, line of least resistance, nonresistance, passiveness, resignation, fatalism 679 *inactivity;* yielding, giving way, giving in, white flag, capitulation, surrender, unconditional s. 621 *relinquishment;* deference 872 *humility;* homage 739 *loyalty;* genuflexion, prostration 311 *obeisance.*

Adj. *submitting,* surrendering etc. vb.; meek, unresisting, law-abiding 717 *peaceful;* submissive 488 *obedient;* fatalistic, resigned, acquiescent 488 *assenting;* pliant, accommodating, malleable 327 *soft;* crawling, cringing, supine, prostrate; boot-licking, bowing and scraping; kneeling, on bended knees, sycophantic, Uriah Heepish, toadying 872 *humble.*

Vb. *submit,* yield, give in; defer to; bow to, make a virtue of necessity, admit defeat 728 *be defeated;* be resigned 488 *acquiesce;* accept 488 *assent;* shrug one's shoulders 860 *be indifferent;* withdraw, make way for, draw in one's horns 286 *turn back;* not contest 679 *be inactive;* stop fighting, have no fight left, have all the fight knocked out of one, give up, cry quits, have had enough, throw up the sponge, throw in the towel, surrender, hold up one's hands, show the white flag, ask for terms; surrender, capitulate; throw oneself on another's mercy; give oneself up, throw down one's arms, hand over one's sword, hang up one's sword, haul down the flag, strike one's colours.

knuckle under, succumb, cave in, collapse; show no fight, take the line of least resistance, bow before the inevitable, bow before the storm; be submissive, bow one's neck to the yoke, do homage 745 *be subject;* take one's medicine, swallow the pill 963 *be punished;* eat humble pie, eat dirt 872 *be humble;* take it, take it from one, take it lying down, grin and bear it, stomach, put up with 825 *suffer;* bend, bow, kneel, kowtow, toady, crouch, cringe, crawl, bow and scrape 311 *stoop;* grovel, lick the dust,

lick the boots of, kiss the rod; fall on one's knees, throw oneself at the feet of, clasp someone's knees, beg for mercy, cry *or* howl for m.

722 Combatant. Army. Navy. Air Force

N. *combatant,* fighter 716 *contender;* aggressor, assailant, mugger 712 *attacker;* besieger, storm-troops; belligerent, fighting man, man-at-arms, warrior, brave; bodyguard 713 *defender;* gunman, strongarm man, hitman 362 *killer;* bully, rough, rowdy, bovver boy, boot boy 904 *ruffian;* duellist; swordsman, fencer; gladiator 162 *athlete;* fighting cock; bull-fighter, toreador, matador, picador; wrestler, jujitsuist, judoist, karate expert 716 *wrestling;* competitor 716 *contender;* jouster, knight; wrangler; barrister, advocate 959 *litigant.*

pugilist, boxer, champion, champ, sparring partner; flyweight, bantam-weight, featherweight, welterweight, middleweight, cruiserweight, heavy-weight; slogger, pummeler 716 *pugilism.*

militarist, jingoist, chauvinist, gung-ho, expansionist, militant, warmonger, hawk; crusader; Samurai; mercenary; soldier of fortune; freebooter, pirate, buccaneer 789 *robber.*

soldier, army man, military man, regular; soldiery, troops (**see** *armed force*); old campaigner, veteran, Chelsea pensioner; fighting man, warrior, brave; man-at-arms, redcoat, legionnaire, centurion; standard-bearer, colour sergeant, ensign; sniper; territorial, Home Guard, militiaman; yeomanry, yeoman; irregular troops; raider, guerrilla, partisan, freedom fighter; resistance fighter, Maquis; guards 660 *protector;* enlisted man; reservist; volunteer; mercenary; conscript, recruit, rookie; serviceman, Tommy, Jock, GI, Anzac, sepoy, Gurkha; female warrior, Amazon, Boadicea; Valkyrie; Wren, WRAF, WRAC.

soldiery, cannon fodder, gallant company, heroes; rank and file, other ranks; private, common soldier, man-at-arms; archer, crossbowman; spearman, pike-man, halberdier, lancer; musketeer, fusilier, rifleman, grenadier; bombardier, gunner, artilleryman; sapper, engineer; signalman; corporal, sergeant, lieutenant 741 *army officer.*

army, host; legion; cohorts, big battalions; horde 104 *multitude;* National Guard, Home G.; militia, yeomanry; vigilantes; regular army, standing a., professional a., mercenary a., territorial a., draft; the services, armed forces.

armed force, forces, troops, ground t., contingents, men, personnel; armada; guards; Household Cavalry, Life Guards, crack troups; reconnaissance party, expeditionary force, flying column; paratroops, Commandos, task force, raiding party, guerrilla force; combat troops, field army, line, thin red 1., front 1.; vanguard, rearguard; reserves, recruits, reinforcements, draft, levy 707 *auxiliary*; detachment, party, detail; patrol; sentry; garrison, army of occupation.

formation, line; legion; column, file; unit, detachment, corps, division, armoured d.; brigade, light b.; battery; regiment, cavalry r., squadron, troop; battalion, company, platoon, section, squad, detail, party 74 *band*.

infantry, foot regiment, infantryman, foot soldier; light infantry.

cavalry, yeomanry; cavalry regiment; horseman; mounted troops, mounted police, cavalryman, yeoman; trooper; knight; man-at-arms, hussar, dragoon; Cossack; armoured car; tank, Panzer; charger.

navy, admiralty; senior service, sail; fleet arm, armada; fleet, flotilla, squadron; argosy; merchant marine.

naval man, admiral, Sea Lord 741 *naval officer*; sailor 270 *mariner*; able seaman, rating; cabin boy; swabbie; marine, limey; submariner 270 *nautical personnel*; Royal Navy, RN, WRNS; Royal Marines; Royal Naval Reserve, RNR.

warship, galleon 275 *ship*; pirate ship; man-o'-war, ship of the line, battleship, dreadnought; cruiser; frigate, corvette; gunboat, E-boat; destroyer; fire ship, minesweeper; submarine, nuclear s., U-boat; Q-ship; aircraft carrier; landing craft, troopship; hospital s.; flagship.

air force, RAF, WRAF; flying corps; fleet air arm; squadron, flight, group, wing; warplane 276 *aircraft*; battle plane, bomber, fighter; troop-carrier; Zeppelin, barrage balloon 276 *airship*; paratroopers; ground staff; fighter pilot, navigator, observer, air crew.

723 Arms

N. *arms* (**see** *weapon*); armament, munitions; armaments, arms race; nuclear deterrent, Star Wars, Strategic Defence Initiative, SDI 713 *defence*; gun-running; ballistics, rocketry, missilery, gunnery, musketry, archery.

arsenal, armoury, gun room; magazine, powder keg; caisson; cartridge belt, bandolier; quiver; scabbard, sheath; holster 194 *receptacle*.

weapon, deterrent; conventional weapon, nuclear w.; secret weapon, death ray, laser; germ warfare, chemical w.; poison gas, mustard g., nerve g. 659 *poison*; teeth, claws, nails 256 *sharp point*.

missile weapon, javelin, harpoon, dart; lasso; boomerang; arrow, poisoned a., shaft, bolt; arrowhead, barb; stone, brick; shot, ball, bullet, pellet, shell, shrapnel, rocket, MIRV (**see** *ammunition*); bow, longbow, crossbow, cata-

pult, sling; blowpipe; bazooka, rocket-thrower; cruise missile, guided m., ballistic m., ICBM, intercontinental ballistic missile, surface-to-air m., Exocet (tdmk) 287 *missile*; Star Wars.

club, mace, hammer; battering ram 279 *ram*; bat, staff, stave, stick, switch; life-preserver, bludgeon, truncheon, cudgel, shillelagh, sandbag, knuckle-duster, cosh, bicycle chain, blunt instrument.

spear, harpoon, gaff; lance, javelin, pike, assegai; halberd 256 *sharp point*.

axe, battleaxe, tomahawk, hatchet, halberd, poleaxe, chopper 256 *sharp edge*.

sidearms, sword; broadsword, claymore; cutlass, swordstick; sabre, scimitar; blade, trusty b.; rapier; épée, foil; dagger, bayonet, dirk, skean, skean-dhu, poniard, dudgeon, stiletto 256 *sharp point*; machete, kukri, kris, parang, panga; knife, bowie k., flick k. 256 *sharp edge*.

firearm, small arms, hand gun; matchlock, flintlock, fusil, musket; blunder-buss, carbine; rifle, Winchester; fowling piece, shotgun, sawn-off s., double-barrelled g., elephant g.; Enfield rifle, bore, calibre; muzzle; trigger, lock; magazine; breech, butt; sight, ramrod.

pistol, duelling p.; six-shooter, colt, revolver, repeater, rod, shooting iron, automatic.

gun, guns, cannonry, artillery; battery, broadside; cannon, bombard, carronade; mortar; field gun; great gun; Big Bertha; howitzer, minethrower, trench gun; anti-aircraft gun; Bofors gun, bazooka; Gatling gun, Lewis gun, machine g., Bren g., submachine g., tommy g.; flamethrower; caisson; gun emplacement, rocket site, launching pad, silo.

ammunition, live a., ammo; round of ammunition; shot, grape s., buckshot; cannonball, bullet, soft-nosed b., dumdum b., rubber b., plastic b., baton round; projectile 287 *missile*; slug, stone, pellet; shell, shrapnel; flak, ack-ack; wad, cartridge; spent cartridge, dud; blank cartridge, blank; cartridge belt, cartridge case.

explosive, gunpowder; saltpetre, high explosive, lyddite, melinite, cordite, gun cotton, dynamite, gelignite, TNT, nitroglycerine; cap, detonator, fuse; priming, charge, warhead, atomic w.; fissionable material; fireworks.

bomb, shell, bombshell; grenade, hand g., Molotov cocktail; megaton bomb, atom b., A-bomb, nuclear b., hydrogen b., H-bomb; neutron b., enhanced radiation b.; mushroom cloud, fallout; block-buster; cluster bomb, fragmentation b.; firebomb, incendiary bomb, napalm b.; letter bomb, nail b.; mine, landmine; booby trap 542 *trap*; depth charge, torpedo; flying bomb, doodlebug; time bomb.

724 Arena

N. *arena*, field; ground, terrain; centre, scene, stage, theatre; hustings, platform, floor; amphitheatre, coliseum, stadium, stand, grandstand; campus, parade ground, training g.; forum, marketplace 76 *focus*; hippodrome, circus, course, racecourse, turf; racetrack, track, running t., cinder t., indoor t., dog t.; ring, bullring, boxing r., ropes; rink, skating r., ice r.; gymnasium, gym, exercise room, work-out r.; range, shooting r., rifle r., butts; playground, beach, swimming complex, lido, marina, pier, fairground 837 *pleasure ground*; leisure centre, recreation ground, playing field, football f., pitch, cricket p.; court, tennis c., badminton c., squash c.; putting green, bowling g., bowling alley, skittle a.; snooker club; beargarden; chessboard; bridge table; snooker t., pool t.; auction room.

battleground, battlefield, field of conflict, scene of action; theatre of war, combat zone, no-go area; front, front line, firing l., trenches, no-man's-land; disputed territory 718 *battle*.

SECTION FIVE

Results of action

725 Completion

N. *completion*, finish, termination, conclusion, end of the matter 69 *end*; terminus 295 *goal*; issue, upshot 154 *event*; result, end r., final r., end product 157 *effect*; fullness 54 *completeness*; fulfilment 635 *sufficiency*; maturity, maturation, fruition, readiness; consummation, culmination, ne plus ultra 646 *perfection*; exhaustiveness, thoroughness 455 *attention*; elaboration, rounding off, finishing off, mopping up, winding up; topping out; top, crown 213 *summit*; missing link 627 *requirement*; last touch, crowning glory, final stroke, coup de grace; the icing on the cake, achievement, fait accompli, finished product; boiling point, danger p., breaking p., last straw 236 *limit*; climax, payoff; resolution, solution, dénouement, catastrophe, last act, final curtain, swansong, finale, finis 69 *finality*; execution, implementation, accomplishment, achievement.

Adj. *completed*, full 54 *complete*; accomplished etc. vb.; elaborate 646 *perfect*; sewn up, buttoned up, in the can, in the bag, under one's belt, secured 727 *successful*.

Vb. *carry through*, follow t., follow up; drive home, clinch, seal, set the seal on; clear up, mop up, wipe up, finish off, polish off; dispose of, dispatch; complete, consummate, put the finishing touch, put the icing on the cake, top out 54 *make complete*; elaborate, hammer out, work o. 646 *perfect*; ripen, bring to a head, bring to the boil 669 *mature*; sit out, see out, see it through; get through, get shot of, dispose of, bring to its close drive a nail into the coffin 69 *terminate*; set at rest 266 *bring to rest*.

carry out, see through, effect, enact 676 *do*; dispatch, execute, discharge, implement, realize, bring about, accomplish, fulfil, consummate, achieve 727 *succeed*; make short work of; leave no loose ends, leave no stone unturned, not do by halves, go the whole hog, be in at the death; deliver the goods, bring home the bacon, be as good as one's word, fill the bill.

climax, cap, crown all 213 *crown*; culminate, peak, reach its peak; reach the zenith, reach a climax, scale the heights, conquer Everest; have an orgasm, come; reach boiling point, come to a crisis; reach the limit, put the lid on; come to fruition, achieve one's goal 295 *arrive*.

726 Noncompletion

N. *noncompletion*, neglect 458 *negligence*; nonfulfilment 636 *insufficiency*; deficit 307 *shortfall*; lack 55 *incompleteness*; immaturity 670 *undevelopment*; never-ending task, painting the Forth Bridge, a woman's work, Sisyphean labour, going round in circles, recurring decimal 71 *continuity*; superficiality, a lick and a promise 456 *inattention*; work undone, job half-done, loose ends; no result, drawn game, draw; stalemate, deadlock.

Adj. *uncompleted*, fragmentary 55 *incomplete*; unaccomplished; unrealized, half-done, half-finished, scamped 458 *neglected*; unripe 670 *immature*; superficial; left hanging, left in the air; lacking finish, not worked out, not thought through, sketchy 647 *imperfect*; unprocessed.

Vb. *not complete*, leave undone, leave in the air, leave hanging 458 *neglect*; skip, skive, scamp, do by halves, scotch the snake not kill it 655 *wound*; give up, not follow through; fall out, drop o., not stay the course; fall short of one's goal, fall down on 728 *fail*; defer, postpone.

727 Success

N. *success*, sweet smell of s., coming up roses, glory 866 *famousness*; happy ending; success story, progress 285 *progression*; breakthrough, quantum leap; one's day, landing on one's feet, run of luck, good fortune 730 *prosperity*; lead 34 *advantage*; flash in the pan; feat, achievement 676 *deed*; accomplishment, goal 725 *completion*; a success, feather in one's cap, triumph, hit, smash h., box-office h., top of the charts, charttopper, best-seller, sell-out, howling success, succès fou, rave reviews; good shot 694 *skill*;

beginner's luck, lucky stroke, fluke 618 *nondesign*; hat trick, stroke of genius, coup, tour de force, masterstroke 694 *masterpiece*; trump, trump card; pass, qualification.

victory, beating, licking, trouncing 728 *defeat*; conquest; taking by storm 712 *attack*; the best of it; win, game, set and match; outright win, checkmate; narrow win, Pyrrhic victory; runaway victory, love game, walkover, pushover, picnic 701 *easy thing*; crushing victory, slam, grand s.; knockout, KO; upper hand, whip h., advantage, edge, pole position; triumph, ovation, standing o., bouquets.

victor, winner, champion, medallist, prizewinner, dux, first, double f. 644 *exceller*; winning side, the winners; conquering hero; conqueror, vanquisher; master *or* mistress of the field, master *or* mistress of the situation; a success, man *or* woman to watch, whiz kid, rising star 730 *prosperous person*.

Adj. *successful*, effective, efficacious; fruitful 640 *profitable*; felicitous 694 *skilful*; foolproof; home and dry 725 *completed*; prizewinning, victorious, world-beating, chart-topping 644 *excellent*; winning, leading; on top, in the ascendant, rising, on the up and up, going places, sitting pretty 730 *prosperous*; triumphant; triumphal, victorious; crowned with success, flushed with victory.

Vb. *succeed*, succeed in, effect, accomplish, achieve; be successful, make out, win one's spurs; make a success of, make a go of, make short work of, rise to the occasion; make good, rise, do well, pull oneself up by one's bootstraps, become a self-made man *or* woman, get promotion, work one's way up the ladder, come to the top 730 *prosper*; pass, make the grade, qualify, graduate, come off well, land on one's feet, give a good account of oneself, come well out of it, come off with flying colours, come out on top, have the best of it 34 *be superior*; advance, break through, make a breakthrough 285 *progress*; reach one's goal, obtain one's objective; pull it off, bring it off, be as good as one's word, bring home the bacon; have a success, score a s., make the big time, make a hit, top the charts, make a kill, go over big; hit the jackpot, break the bank; score a point, win a p., carry a p.; carry the day; arrive, be a success, make one's mark, click.

be successful, do the trick, fill the bill; turn up trumps, rise to the occasion; do the job, do wonders, do marvels, work miracles; work, work like magic, act like a charm 173 *operate*; take effect 178 *influence*; pay off, pay dividends, bear fruit 171 *be fruitful*; hit it, hit the nail on the head, find the mot juste; play one's hand well, not put a foot wrong, never go w., not be

wrong-footed; keep on the right side of; have the ball at one's feet, hold all the trumps; have the world in his *or* her hand; be irresistible, not know the meaning of failure, brush obstacles aside 701 *do easily*; not know when one is beaten, land on one's feet, come up smiling, come up smelling of roses 599 *be resolute*; hold one's own 599 *stand firm*.

triumph, have one's day, be crowned with success, wear the laurels of victory 876 *celebrate*; crow, crow over 877 *boast*; score, score off, be one up on; triumph over difficulties, manage, make it, win through; overcome obstacles; find a loophole, find a way out, find a way round 667 *escape*; make headway against, stem the tide, weather the storm 715 *resist*; reap the fruits 771 *gain*.

overmaster, be too much for, be more than a match for 34 *be superior*; master, overcome, overpower, overthrow, overturn, override 306 *outdo*; have the advantage, seize the a., prevail 34 *predominate*; have one on the hip, have someone where one wants him *or* her, have one by the short hairs; have at one's mercy; checkmate, trump; conquer, vanquish, quell, subdue, subject, suppress, put down, crush 745 *subjugate*; capture, take by s.

defeat, discomfit, dash, put another's nose out of joint, settle one's hash, cook one's goose; repulse, rebuff 292 *repel*; best, be too good for, get the better of, get the upper hand, get the whip h. 34 *be superior*; worst, outplay, outpoint, outflank, outmanoeuvre, outclass, outwit, outshine 306 *outdo*; disconcert, cut the ground from under one's feet, lay by the heels 702 *obstruct*; baffle, nonplus 474 *puzzle*; knock spots off, wipe the floor with; beat, lick, thrash, trounce, crush, give a drubbing, trample underfoot, beat hollow, rout, put to flight, scatter 75 *disperse*; silence, put the lid on 165 *suppress*; flatten, knock the stuffing out of, put out for the count, knock out; knock for six, hit for s.; bowl out; drive to the wall, check, put in check 661 *endanger*; put an end to, wipe out, do for, settle, fix, dish 165 *destroy*; sink; break, bankrupt, beggar 801 *impoverish*.

win, win the battle, carry the day, achieve victory, defeat the enemy; be victorious, claim the victory; come off best, come off with flying colours; win hands down, carry all before one, have it all one's own way, romp home, have a walkover, walk off with, waltz away with, walk it 701 *do easily*; win on points, win by a short head, win by a whisker, scrape home; win the last battle, win the last round; win the match, take the prize, gain the palm, wear the laurel wreath; become champion, beat all comers, sweep the board, rule OK 34 *be superior*.

728 Failure

N. *failure*, lack of success; no luck, off day 731 *misfortune*; nonfulfilment 726 *noncompletion*; frustration 702 *hindrance*; vain attempt, abortive a., wild-goose chase, futile effort, no result 641 *lost labour*; bungle 695 *bungling*; abortion, miscarriage 172 *unproductiveness*; damp squib, washout, fiasco, flop; slip, omission, faux pas 495 *mistake*; no go, halt 145 *stop*; engine failure, electrical fault, computer f., machine malfunction, gremlin, bug, breakdown 702 *hitch*; collapse, fall 309 *descent*; losses 772 *loss*; bankruptcy 805 *insolvency*.

defeat, bafflement 474 *uncertainty*; deadlock, stalemate 145 *stop*; repulse, rebuff, bloody nose, check, reverse; checkmate; the worst of it, discomfiture, stick, flak, beating, drubbing, hiding, licking, thrashing, trouncing; retreat; flight 290 *recession*; stampede; rout, landslide; fall, downfall, collapse, débâcle; lost cause, losing battle; deathblow, nail in the coffin, quietus; Waterloo.

loser, also-ran, nonstarter; has-been, dud, failure, flop, no-hoper, lemon; born loser 731 *unlucky person*; underdog 35 *inferior*; dropout 25 *misfit*; bankrupt 805 *nonpayer*; losing side.

Adj. *unsuccessful*, vain, fruitless; dud, misfired; miscarried, stillborn, aborted, abortive; ditched; manqué, failed, bombed, ploughed; flunked; out of one's depth, losing one's grip 474 *uncertain*.

defeated, beaten, bested, worsted, done for; baffled, thwarted, foiled 702 *hindered*; dashed, discomfited, hoist with one's own petard; outmanoeuvred, outplayed, outvoted; outwitted, outclassed, outshone 35 *inferior*; thrashed, licked; on the losing side, out of the running; in retreat; routed, put to flight; sunk; overthrown, had it, knocked out, kaput, brought low, fallen; captured.

Vb. *fail*, have no success; be unsuccessful, – beaten etc. adj.; bomb, flop; flatline; fall down on, botch, bungle 495 *blunder*; flunk, not make the grade, be found wanting 636 *not suffice*; miss the boat 138 *lose a chance*; go wide, miss, hit the wrong target, fall between two stools, miss an opportunity 282 *deviate*; get nothing out of it, get no change out of it, draw a blank, back the wrong horse, return empty-handed, labour in vain, have shot one's bolt 641 *waste effort*; kiss goodbye to 772 *lose*; overreach oneself, bite off more than one can chew, come a cropper, fall, collapse, slide 309 *tumble*; break down, malfunction, come to pieces, fall to bits, come unstuck; falter, stall, seize up, pack up, conk out; stop, come to a dead stop, come up against a blank wall, come to a dead end; stick, get bogged down 145 *cease*; come to a sticky end, come to a bad e. 655 *deteriorate*; go on the rocks, run aground, be left high and dry, make a loss, crash, go bust, go bankrupt 805 *not pay*.

miscarry, be stillborn, abort; misfire; crash 309 *tumble*; not come off, come to naught, come to nothing, go by the board; fall flat, come to grief; blow up, go up in smoke; flop, bomb, prove a fiasco; go wrong, go awry, gang agley, take a turn for the worse, take an ugly turn; do no good, make things worse 832 *aggravate*.

be defeated, lose, lose out, suffer defeat, take a beating, lose the day, lose the battle, lose the match; lose the election, concede defeat, lose one's seat, lose the vote, be outvoted; lose by a whisker, get pipped at the post; be in a catch-22 situation; be on a hiding to nothing; get the worst of it, come off second best, go off with one's tail between one's legs, lick one's wounds; be taken to the cleaner's; lose hands down, come in last; bite the dust; fall; be captured, fall a prey to; retreat, lose ground 290 *recede*; take to flight 620 *run away*; admit defeat, had enough, cry quits 721 *submit*; have not a leg to stand on, have the ground cut from under one's feet; go to the wall.

729 Trophy

N. *trophy*, spoils of war, captives 790 *booty*; scalp, battle, scars, wounds 655 *wound*; memorial, war m., memento 505 *reminder*; triumphal arch 548 *monument*; triumph, ovation, standing o. 876 *celebration*; plum, glittering prizes; benefit match; prize, consolation p., booby p., wooden spoon 962 *reward*; sports trophy, Ashes, cup, shield; award, Oscar a., Tony a., Emmy a., golden disc, laurels, crown, garland, wreath, palm of victory; pat on the back; bouquet; feather in one's cap.

decoration, battle honours, spurs 866 *honours*; citation, mention in dispatches; rosette, ribbon, sash, cordon bleu; blue, oar, cap; medal, cross, garter, order; service stripe, long-service medal, war m., campaign m.; Victoria Cross, VC, Military C., Croix de Guerre, Iron Cross; Distinguished Service Cross, Congressional Medal, Medal of Honour; George Cross, Legion of Honour, civic crown; honours list.

730 Prosperity

N. *prosperity*, thriving, health and wealth; well-being, welfare; social inclusion; economic prosperity, booming economy, boom; roaring trade, seller's market, bullish m., luxury, affluence, Easy Street 800 *wealth*; golden touch, Midas t.; fleshpots, fat of the land, milk and honey 635 *plenty*; auspiciousness, good fortune; bonanza, winning streak, luck, run of l., good l., break, lucky b., lucky gamble, lucky shot, luck of the draw 159 *chance*.

palmy days, heyday, prime, peak, zenith, halcyon days, summer, fair weather, Indian summer; life of Riley, place in the sun, clover, velvet, bed of roses, roses all the way 376 *euphoria*; Golden Age 824 *happiness*.

prosperous person, man *or* woman of substance, man *or* woman of property, fat cat 800 *rich person*; whiz kid; entrepreneur, nouveau riche, profiteer; celebrity.

Adj. *prosperous*, thriving, flourishing, booming 727 *successful*; rising, doing well, up and coming, on the up and up, in the ascendant, going up in the world; on the make, profiteering; well set-up, established, well-to-do, well-off, well-heeled, rolling in it, affluent, comfortable, comfortably off 800 *moneyed*; riding on the crest of a wave, buoyant, bullish; fortunate, lucky, born with a silver spoon in one's mouth, born under a lucky star; in clover, on velvet; on easy street, in the money, fat.

palmy, balmy, halcyon, golden, rosy; blissful; providential, favourable, promising, auspicious, propitious, cloudless, clear, fine, fair, set f.; glorious, euphoric.

Vb. *prosper*, thrive, flourish, do well, have a good time of it 376 *enjoy*; bask in sunshine, make hay, live in clover, lie on velvet, have it easy, live on easy street, have it made, live on milk and honey, live on the fat of the land, 'never have had it so good'; be in the money, be rolling in it; be well-heeled, batten on, grow fat; blossom, bloom, flower 171 *be fruitful*; boom, drive a roaring trade, enjoy a seller's market; profiteer 771 *gain*; get on, go far, rise in the world, work one's way up, make it, arrive 727 *succeed*; make money, make a fortune, strike it rich, make one's pile, feather one's nest line one's pockets, 800 *get rich*; run smoothly; go on swimmingly.

have luck, have all the l., have a stroke of l., have a lucky break, have a run of luck; strike lucky, strike oil, be on to a good thing, get on the gravy train; fall on one's feet, bear a charmed life, be born under a lucky star, be born with a silver spoon in one's mouth, have the ball at one's feet.

be auspicious, – propitious etc. adj.; promise well, augur well, set fair; look kindly on, smile on, bless.

Int. good luck! all the best! best of British!

731 Adversity

N. *adversity*, adverse circumstances, misfortune; continual struggle; hardship, hard life, tough time 825 *suffering*; travail 377 *pain*; hard times, hell upon earth, vale of sorrows 616 *evil*;

burden, load, pressure, pressure of the times; ups and downs of life, vicissitude 154 *event*; troubles, sea of t., trials, cares, worries 825 *worry*; wretchedness, misery, despondency, Slough of Despond 834 *dejection*; bitter pill 872 *humiliation*; cross 825 *sorrow*; curse, blight, plague, scourge, infliction, visitation 659 *bane*; bleakness, cold wind, draught, chill, cold, winter 380 *coldness*; gloom 418 *darkness*; ill wind; blow, hard b. 704 *opposition*; setback, check, rebuff, reverse 728 *defeat*; pinch, plight, poor lookout, trouble ahead; trough, bad patch, rainy day 655 *deterioration*; slump, recession, depression 679 *inactivity*; storm clouds, gathering c. 900 *threat*; decline, downfall 165 *ruin*; want, need, distress, extremity 801 *poverty*.

misfortune, bad luck, hard luck, ill luck, a bad hair day, annus horribilis; no luck 728 *failure*; evil star 645 *badness*; raw deal; hard lines; ill hap, mishap, misadventure, contretemps, accident, casualty 159 *chance*; disaster, calamity, catastrophe, the pits.

unlucky person, no-hoper, poor risk; star-crossed lover, plaything of the gods, Jonah; down-and-out 728 *loser*; under-dog 35 *inferior*; lame dog, lame duck 163 *weakling*; scapegoat, victim.

Adj. *adverse*, hostile, ominous, sinister, inauspicious, unfavourable; disadvantageous, antipathetic, bleak, cold, hard; opposed, contrary, opposing; malign 645 *harmful*; ruinous 165 *destructive*; disastrous, calamitous, catastrophic.

unprosperous, in poor shape, out of kilter; not doing well, badly off 801 *poor*; in trouble, up against it, in adverse circumstances, with one's back to the wall, declining, on the wane, on the down grade, on the slippery slope, on the road to ruin; in a bad way, in dire straits.

unfortunate, ill-fated, unlucky, ill-starred, star-crossed; luckless, hapless, poor, wretched, forlorn, miserable, unhappy; stricken, doomed, accursed; out of luck, down on one's luck; born under an evil star; accident-prone.

Vb. *have trouble*, be in t.; have no luck, get more kicks than ha'pence; get more bricks than bouquets; be in for it, go through it, be hard pressed, be up against it, strike a bad patch 825 *suffer*; come to grief 728 *miscarry*; feel the pinch, feel the draught, fall on evil days, have seen better d. 801 *be poor*; go downhill, go down in the world, decline 655 *deteriorate*; sink 313 *founder*; come to a bad end 728 *fail*; go to rack and ruin, go to the dogs 165 *be destroyed*.

732 Averageness

N. *averageness*, mediocrity 30 *average*; golden mean, neither too much nor too little; middle class; suburbia, common man, everyman, man in the street, joe soap 869 *commoner;* hoi polloi

Adj. *middling,* average, mediocre; neither good nor bad, ordinary, commonplace 30 *median;* middle-of-the-road 177 *moderate;* undistinguished, nothing special, fair, fair to middling; so-so, comme ci comme ça, adequate; tolerable, passable, fifty-fifty, much of a muchness; medium, middle, grey 625 *neutral.*

Vb. *be middling,* – mediocre etc. adj.; jog on, manage well enough, never set the Thames on fire, never set the heather on fire.

5.2
Social Volition

SECTION ONE

General social volition

733 Authority

N. *authority,* power; powers that be, 'they', the Establishment, ruling classes, Big Brother 741 *master;* the Government, the Administration, Whitehall 690 *director;* right, divine r., prerogative, royal p.; law, rightful power; legislative assembly 692 *parliament;* regency, committee 751 *commission;* office, place; portfolio 955 *jurisdiction;* power behind the throne 178 *influence;* credit; leadership 689 *directorship;* ascendance, supremacy 34 *superiority;* pride of place, seniority, priority 64 *precedence;* majesty, royalty, crown 868 *nobility;* authoritativeness.

governance, rule, sway, reins of government, direction, command 689 *directorship;* control; hold, grip, clutches 778 *retention;* domination, control freakery, mastery, whip hand, long arm; ascendancy, dominion, sovereignty, raj, overlordship, presidency, supremacy 34 *superiority;* reign, regency, dynasty; foreign rule, empire 745 *subjection;* imperialism, colonialism, white supremacy, black power; regime, regiment, regimen; state control, paternalism; bureaucracy, apparat, civil service, officialism, beadledom, bumbledom, red tape, bumf; Parkinson's law 197 *expansion.*

despotism, paternalism; tyranny; dictatorship, Caesarism, tsarism, Stalinism; autocracy, absolute monarchy; totalitarianism; police state, rule of terror 735 *brute force.*

government, direction 689 *management;* politics; constitutionalism, rule of law 953 *legality;* misgovernment 734 *anarchy;* theocracy, papal rule, hierocracy, clericalism 985 *ecclesiasticism;* monarchy, constitutional m.; republicanism, federalism; tribal system, tribalism, clan system; patriarchy, matriarchate; feudalism; benevolent despotism, paternalism; aristocracy,

meritocracy, oligarchy, elitism; gynocracy 373 *womankind;* gerontocracy; triumvirate; plutocracy; representative government, parliamentary g., government by the ballot box, party system 708 *political party,* 605 *vote;* democracy, egalitarianism, government of the people, by the people, for the people; demagogy, vox populi; majority rule, one man one vote, proportional representation; pluralism, collectivism, proletarianism; communism, Leninism, Maoism; Bolshevism, Fascism, Nazism; committee rule, sovietism; military government, martial law; mob rule, anarchy; socialism, Fabianism; bureaucracy, technocracy; self-government, autonomy, home rule 744 *independence;* puppet government 628 *instrument;* caretaker government, regency, interregnum; mandate.

position of authority, high office, kingship, tsardom, royalty, regency, protectorship; chieftainship, sheikhdom, emirate, lordship, sultanate, caliphate, governorship, viceroyalty; consulate, consulship, proconsulate, prefecture, tribunate, magistracy; mayoralty, aldermanship; headship, presidency, premiership, chairmanship 689 *directorship;* overlordship, superintendency, inspectorship; mastership; Big Brother; government post, Cabinet seat; seat of government.

political organization, body politic; state, commonwealth; country, realm, kingdom, republic, city state, city; federation, confederation; principality, duchy, archduchy, dukedom; empire, dominion, colony, dependency, protectorate, mandate, mandated territory 184 *territory;* communist bloc, Third World 184 *region;* superpower 34 *superiority;* banana republic 35 *inferiority;* buffer state 231 *interjacency;* province, county 184 *district;* welfare state.

Adj. *authoritative,* empowered, sanctioned, approved, competent; in office, in authority, magisterial, official, ex officio; mandatory, binding, compulsory 740 *compelling;* magistral, masterful, domineering; commanding, lordly, dignified, majestic; overruling, imperious, bossy; peremptory, arbitrary, absolute, autocratic, tyrannical, dictatorial, totalitarian 735 *authoritarian;* powerful 162 *strong;* leading 178 *influential;* pre-eminent, preponderant, predominant, dominant, paramount 34 *supreme;* Big Brotherish.

ruling, reigning; sovereign, on the throne; royal, regal, majestic, kinglike, kingly, queenly, princely, lordly; imperial; magisterial; governing, controlling, dictating etc. vb.

governmental, gubernatorial, political, constitutional; administrative, ministerial, official, bureaucratic, centralized; technocratic; matriarchal, patriarchal; monarchical, feudal, aristocratic, oligarchic, plutocratic, democratic, popular, classless, republican; self-governing, autonomous 744 *independent*; anarchy.

Vb. *rule*, hold sway, reign, reign supreme, wear the crown, wield the sceptre; govern, control 737 *command*; manage, hold the reins, hold office 689 *direct*; be in power, have authority, wield power, exercise authority, exert a., use one's a.; rule absolutely., tyrannize 735 *oppress*; dictate, lay down the law; keep order, police.

take authority, ascend the throne, succeed to the t., take office, assume command; take over the reigns; assume authority, form a government; gain power, take control; seize power, usurp.

dominate, turn the scale, hold all the aces, hold all the cards 34 *predominate*; lord it over, boss, rule the roost, be queen bee, wear the trousers, be in the driving seat, be in the saddle 737 *command*; have the upper hand, have the whip h., call the tune, call the shots 727 *overmaster*; have in one's power, have over a barrel; lead by the nose, twist round one's little finger, have under one's thumb, have one by the short hairs, bend to one's will, hold in the palm of one's hand 178 *influence*; drive 735 *be severe*; dictate, coerce 740 *compel*; hold down, ride roughshod over 745 *subjugate*; override, overrule, have it all one's own way.

734 Laxity: absence of authority

N. *laxity*, slackness, remissness, indifference 458 *negligence*; laissez-faire 744 *scope*; informality, lack of ceremony 769 *nonobservance*; looseness, relaxation, derestriction, loose cannon 746 *liberation*; decentralization 46 *disunion*; indulgence, toleration, licence, permissiveness 736 *leniency*; line of least resistance 721 *submission*; weak will, feeble grasp, weak administration, crumbling power 163 *weakness*; no drive, no push, inertia 175 *inertness*; no control, policy of nonintervention, abdication of authority, surrender of control 753 *resignation*; renunciation 621 *relinquishment*.

anarchy, breakdown of law and order; free-for-all, every man for himself, dog-eat-dog; disorder, disorganization, chaos 61 *turmoil*; anarchism 769 *nonobservance*; mob rule, mob law, lynch l. 954 *lawlessness*.

Adj. *lax*, loose, slack; disorganized; feeble, soft, wet, wimpish 163 *weak*; slipshod, remiss 458 *negligent*; relaxed, informal, free-and-easy; permissive, tolerant, undemanding 736 *lenient*; unassertive.

Vb. *be lax*, give one his *or* her head, give rope enough 744 *give scope*; waive the rules, stretch a point; tolerate, put up with; laissez-faire, laissez-aller 756 *permit*; let one get away with, not say boo to a goose; spoonfeed, featherbed,

indulge, spoil 736 *be lenient*; make concessions 770 *compromise*; relax 46 *disunite*; lose control, reduce to chaos 63 *derange*.

735 Severity

N. *severity*, rigorousness, strictness, stringency; formalism; rigidity, inflexibility 326 *hardness*; discipline, strong hand, iron h., tight grasp 733 *authority*; rod of iron, heavy hand, zero tolerance, Draconian laws; harshness, rigour, extremity, extremes; letter of the law, pound of flesh; intolerance, rigorism; censorship; puritanism 950 *prudery*; infliction, visitation, inquisition, persecution, exploitation, harassment, oppression; callousness, inclemency, mercilessness, pitilessness; harsh treatment, the hard way, tender mercies, cruelty 898 *inhumanity*; austerity 945 *asceticism*.

brute force, show of force; big battalions, gunboat diplomacy 160 *power*; coercion, bludgeoning 740 *compulsion*; violence; subjugation 745 *subjection*; autocracy, dictatorship 733 *despotism*; tyranny; Fascism, Nazism, totalitarianism; Prussianism, militarism; martial law, iron rule, iron hand, mailed fist, jackboot, bludgeon.

tyrant, petty tyrant; disciplinarian, martinet, sergeant major; militarist, jackboot; hanging judge; heavy father, Dutch uncle; Big Brother, authoritarian, despot, dictator 741 *autocrat*; boss, inquisitor, persecutor; oppressor, bully, taskmaster, slave-driver; bloodsucker; ogre, brute 938 *monster*.

Adj. *severe*, austere, Spartan 945 *ascetic*; strict, rigorous, extreme; straitlaced, puritanical, prudish, old-maidish; donnish, pedagogic, hidebound; formalistic, pedantic; bigoted, fanatical; hypercritical 862 *fastidious*; intolerant, censorious 924 *disapproving*; unbending, stiff-necked, rigid 326 *hard*; hard as nails, hard-headed, hardboiled, flinty, dour; inflexible, obdurate, uncompromising 602 *obstinate*; inexorable, relentless, merciless, unsparing, implacable, unforgiving 906 *pitiless*; heavy, stern, stiff; punitive; stringent, Draconian, drastic, savage.

authoritarian, masterful, domineering, lordly, arrogant, haughty 878 *insolent*; despotic, absolute, arbitrary; totalitarian, Fascist; dictatorial, Big Brotherish, autocratic; undemocratic; coercive, compulsive 740 *compelling*; bossy, nannyish.

oppressive, hard on 914 *unjust*; tyrannical, despotic; tyrannous, harsh, exigent, exacting, extortionate, persecuting, inquisitorial, unsparing; high-handed, overbearing, domineering; heavy-handed, Draconian, brutal, ogreish 898 *cruel*.

Vb. *be severe*, – harsh, – strict etc. adj., be cruel to be kind; bear hard on; keep a tight rein on 747 *restrain*; be down on, have a down on; come down on, come down like a ton of bricks, crack down on, stamp on, put a stop to, clamp down on 165 *suppress*; persecute, hunt down 619 *pursue*; ill-treat, mishandle, abuse 675 *misuse*; get tough with, pull no punches; take off the gloves, rule with an iron hand, inflict; mete out stern punishment; have one's pound of flesh; harden one's heart, show no mercy, take Draconian measures 906 *be pitiless*; give no quarter, put to the sword 362 *slaughter*.

oppress, tyrannize, play the tyrant, be despotic, abuse one's authority; domineer, lord it; overawe, intimidate, terrorize 854 *frighten*; bludgeon 740 *compel*; boss around, put upon; bully, be always on one's back, harass, plague, hassle 827 *torment*; persecute, victimize 898 *be malevolent*; break, crush the spirit, take the heart out of, tame 369 *break in*; tax 684 *fatigue*; overtax, exploit, extort, suck, squeeze, grind, grind the faces of the poor; trample, tread down, tread underfoot, stamp on, hold down 165 *suppress*; enslave 745 *subjugate*; ride roughshod, inflict injustice 914 *do wrong*; rule with an iron hand, rule with a rod of iron; take Draconian measures; whip, scourge, put the screws on 963 *torture*; shed blood 362 *murder*; be heavy, weigh on, burden, crush 322 *weigh*.

736 Leniency

N. *leniency*, lenience; mildness, gentleness, tenderness; forbearance, easygoingness, long-suffering 823 *patience*; pardon 909 *forgiveness*; quarter, mercy, lenity, clemency, mercifulness, compassion 905 *pity*; humanity, kindness 897 *benevolence*; indulgence, toleration; moderation; light rein, velvet glove, kid gloves.

Adj. *lenient*, soft, gentle, mild; indulgent, tolerant; moderate, easy, easy-going, undemanding 734 *lax*; longsuffering 823 *patient*; clement, merciful; tender 905 *pitying*.

Vb. *be lenient*, make few demands; go easy, handle with kid gloves 177 *moderate*; featherbed, spoonfeed, spoil, indulge, play the fond parent, humour 889 *pet*; stretch a point; forbear 823 *be patient*; pity, spare, give quarter 905 *show mercy*; pardon 909 *forgive*; relax.

737 Command

N. *command*, royal c., summons; commandment, ordinance; injunction; imposition; dictation, bidding, behest; dictum, say-so 532 *affirmation*; charge, commission, appointment 751 *mandate*; instructions, manifesto, rules, regulations, code of practice; brief 524 *information*; directive, order, order of the day, marching orders; word of command, word; beck, nod, sign 547 *gesture*; signal, bugle call, trumpet c. 547 *call*; whip, three-line w.; dictate 740 *compulsion*; ban, embargo; counterorder 752 *abrogation*.

decree, edict, ipse dixit; law, canon, prescript 693 *precept*; bull, papal decree; circular, encyclical; ordinance; decree nisi, decree absolute; decision 480 *judgment*; enactment, act 953 *legislation*; plebiscite, manifesto, electoral mandate 605 *vote*; dictate, diktat.

demand, claim, requisition 761 *request*; notice, warning n., final n., final demand, ultimatum; blackmail 900 *threat*; imposition, exaction, levy, tax demand 809 *tax*.

warrant, search w., authorization, written authority, passport 756 *permit*; writ, summons, subpoena, citation, habeas corpus 959 *legal process*.

Adj. *commanding*, imperative, categorical, dictatorial; mandatory, obligatory, peremptory, compulsive 740 *compelling*; authoritative; decisive, conclusive, final; demanding, insistent, hectoring.

Vb. *command*, bid, invite; order, tell, issue a command, give an order, lay down the law; signal, call, nod, beck, motion, sign, make a s. 547 *gesticulate*; wink, give a cue, tip the wink 524 *hint*; direct, give a directive, instruct, brief, circularize; rule, lay down, enjoin; give a mandate, charge, call upon 751 *commission*; impose, lay upon, set a task, make obligatory 917 *impose a duty*; detail; call together, rally, convene 74 *bring together*; send for, summon; cite, subpoena, issue a writ 959 *litigate*; remand; dictate, take a strong line, put one's foot down 740 *compel*; countermand 752 *abrogate*; lay an embargo, ban, impose a ban, taboo, declare t., proscribe 757 *prohibit*.

decree, promulgate 528 *proclaim*; declare, say so, lay down the law 532 *affirm*; signify one's will and pleasure, prescribe, ordain 608 *predetermine*; enact, pass a law, legislate, decriminalize 953 *make legal*; pass judgment, give j., give a ruling 480 *judge*.

demand, require, requisition 627 *require*; order, indent 761 *request*; make demands on, send a final demand, issue a final warning, give final notice, present an ultimatum, demand with threats, blackmail 900 *threaten*; present one's claim, make claims upon, demand payment, dun, sue, bill, invoice; charge 809 *price*; exact, levy 809 *tax*.

738 Disobedience

N. *disobedience*, indiscipline, recalcitrance, refractoriness 598 *unwillingness*; naughtiness, misbehaviour, mischief-making, monkey tricks; delinquency 934 *wickedness*; insubordination, mutinousness, mutineering; defiance; noncompliance 769 *non-observance*; disloyalty, defection, desertion 918 *undutifulness*; infraction, infringement, criminality, crime, sin 936 *guilty act*; civil disobedience, passive resistance 715 *resistance*; conscientious objection 704 *opposition*; obstructionism 702 *hindrance*; seditiousness; wildness 954 *lawlessness*.

revolt, mutiny; strike; faction 709 *dissension*; breakaway, secession 978 *schism*; defection 603 *change of mind*; restiveness 318 *agitation*; sabotage 165 *destruction*; breach of the peace, riot, street r., rioting, gang warfare, street-fighting, tumult 61 *turmoil*; rebellion, insurrection, rising, uprising, intifada 176 *outbreak*; putsch, coup d'état; resistance movement, insurgency 715 *resistance*; subversion 149 *revolution*; terrorism 954 *lawlessness*; civil war 718 *war*; anarchy; regicide, tyrannicide 362 *homicide*.

sedition, seditiousness; intrigue 623 *plot*; agit-prop, subversion, infiltration, fifth-columnism; spying, espionage, underground activities 523 *latency*; terrorism, anarchism, nihilism; treason, high t., lese-majesty 930 *perfidy*.

revolter, mutineer, rebel; demonstrator, striker, picketer 705 *opponent*; secessionist, seceder, splinter group, rebel g. 978 *schismatic*; dissident 829 *malcontent*; blackleg, scab 84 *nonconformist*; maverick, lone wolf; seditionary, seditionist; traitor, Quisling, fifth columnist, infiltrator, spy, industrial spy 603 *tergiversator*; insurrectionist, insurgent; guerrilla, urban g., partisan; resistance, underground, Maquis; Black Panther, Black Muslim, Rastafarian; Provisional, Provo; extremist, Jacobin, Bolshevist, Trotskyist, red 149 *revolutionist*; counter-revolutionary, reactionary, monarchist, White Russian, terrorist, anarchist, nihilist; mafia.

agitator, agent provocateur; agitprop, protester, demonstrator, marcher; soap-box orator, tub-thumper, ranter, rabble-rouser; firebrand, mischief-maker 663 *troublemaker*; seditionist; ringleader.

rioter, street r., urban guerrilla, bovver boy, boot boy, brawler, rowdy 904 *ruffian*; saboteur, Luddite.

Adj. *disobedient*, undisciplined; naughty, mischievous, misbehaving; unbiddable, difficult, self-willed, wayward, unruly, unmanageable 176 *violent*; intractable, ungovernable 598 *unwilling*; insubordinate, mutinous, rebellious, bolshie, bloody-minded; contrary 704 *opposing*; nonconformist 84 *unconformable*; uncompliant 769 *nonobservant*; recalcitrant 715 *resisting*; challenging 711 *defiant*; refractory, perverse 602 *obstinate*; subversive, revolutionary, reactionary; seditious; traitorous, treasonous; untamed.

Vb. *disobey*, be disobedient, misbehave, get into mischief; flout authority, not comply with

769 *not observe*; not do as one is told, disobey orders, show insubordination 711 *defy*; defy the whip; cock a snook, snap one's fingers, fly in the face of 704 *oppose*; break the law, commit a crime 954 *be illegal*; violate, infringe, transgress, trespass 306 *encroach*; kick, chafe, fret, champ at the bit, play up; kick over the traces, take the bit between one's teeth, bolt, take French leave, go AWOL, go walkabout, take the law into one's own hands, be a law unto oneself.

revolt, rebel, mutiny; down tools, strike, take industrial action, come out 145 *cease*; sabotage 702 *obstruct*; undermine, work underground; secede, break away; betray 603 *tergiversate*; agitate, demonstrate, protest 762 *deprecate*; create, create a row, kick up a stink, raise Cain, start a riot, stage a revolt, lead a rebellion 715 *resist*; rise up, rise in arms, throw off the yoke, throw off one's shackles, overthrow.

739 Obedience

N. *obedience*, compliance 768 *observance*; meekness, biddability, tractability, pliancy, malleability 327 *softness*; willingness; nonresistance, submissiveness, acquiescence 721 *submission*; passiveness 679 *inactivity*; dutifulness, discipline 917 *duty*; deference, obsequiousness; slavishness 879 *servility*; tameness, docility.

loyalty, constancy, devotion, fidelity, faithfulness, good faith 929 *probity*; allegiance, fealty.

Adj. *obedient*, compliant, cooperating, conforming 768 *observant*; loyal, faithful, steadfast, constant; devoted, dedicated, sworn; submissive 721 *submitting*; law-abiding 717 *peaceful*; amenable, docile; good, well-behaved; daughterly; acquiescent, passive 679 *inactive*; meek, sheep-like, biddable, like putty in one's hands, dutiful; at one's beck and call, on a string, on a lead, puppet-like, under one's thumb, under control; disciplined, regimented 917 *obliged*; trained, manageable, tame; obsequious 879 *servile*.

Vb. *obey*, comply, act upon 768 *observe*; do the needful, sign on the dotted line, toe the l., come to heel 83 *conform*; assent 758 *consent*; listen, heed, obey orders, do as one is told; put oneself at one's service 597 *be willing*; obey the whip, follow the party line; do one's bidding, wait upon, follow, follow like a sheep, follow to the world's end 742 *serve*; be loyal, bear allegiance, pay homage 768 *keep faith*; pay tribute 745 *be subject*; make oneself useful, do sterling service 703 *minister to*; defer to, be submissive 721 *submit*.

740 Compulsion

N. *compulsion*, needs must 596 *necessity*; law of nature 953 *law*; act of God; moral compulsion

917 *conscience*; Hobson's choice 606 *no choice*; carrot and stick; coercion, regimentation; arm-twisting, blackmail 900 *threat*; sanctions 963 *penalty*; constraint, duress, force, physical f.; big stick, strongarm tactics 735 *brute force*; force-feeding; pressgang, conscription, call-up, draft 718 *war measures*; extortion; slavery, forced labour.

Adj. *compelling*, compulsive, of necessity, unavoidable, inevitable 596 *necessary*; imperative 737 *commanding*; compulsory, mandatory, binding 917 *obligatory*; urgent, pressing; coercive; forceful, cogent.

Vb. *compel*, constrain, coerce 176 *force*; enforce, put into force; dictate, necessitate, oblige, bind; order 737 *command*; impose 917 *impose a duty*; make one, leave no option; leave no escape, pin down, tie d.; impress, draft, conscript; drive, dragoon, regiment, discipline; force one's hand, apply pressure, bulldoze, steamroller, railroad, stampede, pressgang, bully into; bludgeon 735 *oppress*; take by force, requisition, commandeer, extort, exact, wring from, drag f. 786 *take*; apply pressure, lean on, squeeze, take the gloves off, turn the heat on, put the screws on, twist one's arm 963 *torture*; blackmail, hijack, hold to ransom 900 *threaten*; be peremptory, insist, make a point of, press, urge 532 *emphasize*; brook no denial, not take no for an answer 532 *affirm*; force upon, ram down one's throat, inflict, foist, fob off on; force-feed; hold back 747 *restrain*.

Adv. *by force*, under pressure, under protest, under duress; forcibly, willynilly, at gunpoint, at knifepoint.

741 Master

N. *master*, mistress; master *or* mistress of, captor, possessor 776 *owner*; sire, lord, lady, dame; liege, lord, overlord; protector 707 *patron*; seigneur, lord *or* lady of the manor, squire, laird 868 *aristocrat*; lord and master, man of the house 372 *male*; lady of the house, landlady 373 *lady*; senator; sir, madam 870 *title*; patriarch, matriarch 169 *parentage*; senior, head, principal, provost 34 *superior*; schoolmaster *or* -mistress 537 *teacher*; president, chairman *or* -woman, chairperson, speaker 690 *director*; employer, captain of industry, boss, governor, guvnor, guv 690 *manager*; leader, duce, führer (**see** *autocrat*); bigwig; ruling class, ruling party, vested interest, the Establishment; the authorities, the powers that be, 'them', Big Brother, Westminster, the Government, Whitehall, White House, Pentagon, Kremlin 733 *government*.

autocrat, absolute ruler, despot, tyrant, dictator, duce, führer, Big Brother; tycoon, boss,

shogun, VIP, big gun, big shot 638 *bigwig*; petty tyrant, tin god, little Hitler 690 *official*.

sovereign, crowned head, anointed king *or* queen; Majesty, Highness, Royal H., Excellence; dynasty, house, royal line, royal blood; royalty, monarch, king, queen, rex, regina; divine king, Pharaoh; emperor, empress; Caesar, Kaiser, Kaiserin, Tsar or Czar, Tsarina *or* Czarina, Tsarevitch *or* Czarevich; prince, princess, Infante, Infanta, Dauphin, Prince of Wales, Crown Prince *or* Princess, King of Kings, Shah; khan; Mikado; Mogul, Sultan, Sultana; pope, pontiff, Dalai Lama, Aga Khan; caliph.

potentate, ruler; chief, chieftain, headman, sheikh; prince, princeling, rajah, rani, maharajah, maharani; emir, sherif; nawab, begum; archduke, duke, duchess; Elector, Electress; regent, Prince Regent.

governor, military g., High Commissioner, Governor-General, Crown Representative, viceroy, vicereine, khedive; proconsul; grand vizier, bey, pasha, bashaw; ecclesiastical governor, Prince Bishop; patriarch, archbishop, cardinal 986 *ecclesiarch*; ayatollah 690 *leader*.

officer, person in authority; functionary, mandarin, nabob, bureaucrat, apparatchik 690 *official*; civil servant, public s. 742 *servant*; commissar; prime minister, premier, grand vizier, chancellor, vice-c., Pooh-bah; constable, marshal, warden; mayor, lord m., lady m., mayoress, alderman, provost, bailie, city father, councillor; dignitary, local worthy 866 *person of repute*; sheriff, bailiff; justice of the peace, judge; magistrate, chief m., president, doge; consul; prefect, district officer; commissioner, deputy c.; headman; mace-bearer, beadle; sexton, verger 986 *church officer*; party official, whip, chief whip; powers that be.

naval officer, Sea Lord; admiral, vice a., rear-a., commodore, captain, commander, lieutenant-c., lieutenant, sub-l., petty officer, leading seaman.

army officer, staff, High Command, staff officer, brass hat; commissioned officer; marshal, field m., commander-in-chief, general, lieutenant-g., major-g.; brigadier, colonel, lieutenant-c., major, captain, lieutenant, second l., subaltern; ensign; warrant officer, noncommissioned o., NCO, sergeant major, regimental s. m., staff s., colour s., sergeant, corporal, lance corporal; adjutant, aide-de-camp, quartermaster; war minister, warlord, commanding officer, commander, commandant.

air officer, air marshal, air commodore, group captain, wing commander, squadron leader, flight lieutenant, flying officer, pilot o., warrant o., flight sergeant 722 *air force*.

742 Servant

N. *servant*, public s., civil s. 690 *official*; fag, slave; general servant, factotum, skivvy, maid-of-all work, chief cook and bottle washer 678 *busy person*; humble servant, menial; orderly, attendant; verger 986 *church officer*; subordinate, underling 35 *inferior*; subaltern, helper, assistant, right-hand man, girl Friday 703 *aider*; mercenary, hireling, employee, hand, hired man; oddjob man, handyman, worker, labourer; hewer of wood and drawer of water, hack, drudge, dogsbody; farmhand 370 *farmer*; shepherd, cowherd, milkmaid 369 *herdsman*; shop assistant, salesperson 793 *seller*; steward, stewardess, air hostess, cabin personnel, cabin boy; waiter, waitress, head waiter, wine w.; bartender, barman, barmaid, pot boy, tapster 192 *tavern*; stableman, ostler, groom, stable boy *or* lad, postilion; errand boy, messenger, runner 529 *courier*; doorman, commissionaire, janitor, concierge 264 *doorkeeper*; porter, night p.; caddy; callboy, page boy, bellboy, bellhop, buttons; boots, sweeper 648 *cleaner*; caretaker, house-minder, house-sitter, housekeeper; help, daily, daily help, char, charwoman, cleaning lady; universal aunt; baby-sitter, baby-minder; nurse, nursemaid, nanny 749 *keeper*; companion, confidante.

domestic, domestic servant, general s., manservant, man, serving m.; footman, flunkey, lackey; servant girl, maid, maid-servant, handmaid, parlour maid, housemaid, chambermaid; maid of all work, tweeny, skivvy, slavey; kitchen maid, scullery m., dairy m., laundry m.; scullion, washer-up, dishwasher, housekeeper; butler, cook; steward, governess, tutor, nurse, nanny, nursemaid; personal servant, page, valet, gentlemen's gentleman, batman; lady's maid, waiting woman; mother's help, ayah, amah, au pair, doula; scout, bed-maker; gardener, under- g., groom; coachman, chauffeur 268 *driver*.

retainer, follower, train, cortege 67 *retinue*; court, courtier; attendant, usher, gillie; bodyguard, henchman, squire, page, train-bearer; majordomo, chamberlain, equerry, steward, bailiff; chatelaine, housekeeper, butler, cup-bearer; chaplain, beadsman; lady's maid, lady-in-waiting, companion, confidante; governess, nurse, nursemaid, mother's help, nanny 749 *keeper*.

dependant, hanger-on, parasite, satellite, camp follower, groupie, creature, jackal 284 *follower*; stooge, puppet 628 *instrument*; minion, lackey, flunkey; henchman, vassal; apprentice, protégé(e), ward, charge.

subject, national, citizen, patrial 191 *native*; liege, vassal; people, citizenry 869 *commonalty*.

slave, bondman, bondmaid, slave girl; serf, villein; galley slave, wage s., sweated labour 686 *worker*; eunuch; chattel, puppet, pawn; captive, chaingang 750 *prisoner*.

Adj. *serving*, ministering 703 *aiding*; in service, in domestic s., menial; working, in employment, on the payroll; on the staff; at one's beck and call 739 *obedient*; in servitude, in slavery, in captivity 745 *subject*.

Vb. *serve*, be in service, wait upon, wait on hand and foot 703 *minister to*; live in 89 *accompany*; follow 739 *obey*; tend, squire, valet; char, do chores, do housework, clean for, do for, oblige; fag for, do service; be part of the workforce, work for 622 *function*.

743 Badge of rule

N. *regalia*, insignia of royalty; crown, orb, sceptre; coronet, tiara, diadem; sword of state 733 *authority*; coronation robes, royal robe; ermine, royal purple; throne, seat of kings; ensign 547 *flag*; royal standard, royal arms 547 *heraldry*; lion, eagle, fleur-de-lis; Prince of Wales's feathers.

badge of rule, badge of office, chain of o.; emblem of authority, staff, wand, verge, rod, Black Rod, baton, truncheon, gavel; signet, seal, privy s., keys, ring; sword of state, sword of justice, mace; crosier; woolsack, chair, bench; triple crown, mitre, bishop's hat, cardinal's hat., biretta; bishop's apron, gaiters 989 *canonicals*; judge's cap, black c. 961 *condemnation*; robe, mantle, toga.

badge of rank, sword, belt, sash, spurs, cocked hat, epaulette, tab 547 *badge*; uniform; brass, star, pips, crown, gold braid; chevron, stripe, anchor, armlet; garter, order 729 *decoration*.

744 Freedom

N. *freedom*, liberty; freedom of action; free will 595 *will*; free speech, freedom of the press, academic f., the four freedoms; civil rights, equal r. 915 *dueness*; privilege, prerogative, exemption, immunity, diplomatic i. 919 *nonliability*; liberalism; licence, poetic l.; free love 951 *illicit love*; laissez-faire, nonintervention; neutralism 860 *indifference*; nonalignment, cross benches; isolationism; emancipation 746 *liberation*; women's liberation, women's lib; gay l.; enfranchisement.

independence, freedom of action; freedom of choice 605 *choice*; floating vote, don't know; freedom of thought, emancipation 84 *nonconformity*; bachelorhood 895 *celibacy*; self-expression, individuality 80 *speciality*; self-determination, national status 371 *nation*; autonomy, self-regulation, self-government, self-rule, home r.; self-sufficiency 635 *sufficiency*; freehold 777 *property*; independent means, private means.

scope, free play, full p. 183 *range*; swing, rope; manoeuvrability, leverage; field, room, lebensraum, living space, elbowroom, room to swing a cat, wide berth, leeway, margin, clearance 183 *room*; latitude, liberty; permissive society; informality; fling, licence, excess 734 *laxity*; one's head, one's own way, nothing in one's way; a free hand, ball at one's feet 137 *opportunity*; the run of, free hand, blank cheque, carte blanche; free-for-all, free enterprise, free trade, free port, free market.

free person, freeman, citizen, free c., patrial; freedman, freedwoman; ex-convict; escapee 667 *escaper*; free agent, freelance, free spirit; independent, cross-bencher; neutral 625 *moderate*; free-trader; freethinker, libertarian, bohemian, individualist, eccentric 84 *non-conformist*; loose cannon.

Adj. *free*, freeborn, enfranchised; heart-whole, fancy-free, unattached; scot-free 960 *acquitted*; on the loose, at large; released, freed; free as air, free as the wind, free as a bird; foot-loose, go-as-you-please; privileged; exempt; immune; free-speaking 573 *plain*; free-thinking, emancipated, broadminded; independent, uninfluenced 913 *just*; free and easy 882 *sociable*; loose, licentious, unbridled, at leisure, retired; relaxed, at ease 681 *leisurely*; free of cost, gratis, freebie, on the house, for free, unpaid for 812 *uncharged*; going begging 860 *unwanted*; free for all, unreserved, vacant, unoccupied, up for grabs 289 *accessible*.

independent, uncontrolled; unilateral 609 *spontaneous*; unforced, uninfluenced; unattached 860 *indifferent*; uncommitted, uninvolved; unaffiliated 625 *neutral*; isolationist 883 *unsociable*; unconquered, unbowed, irrepressible; autonomous, self-governing, self-sufficient, self-supporting, self-contained, self-motivated; self-reliant; anarchic; self-employed, one's own boss, freelance; unofficial, cowboy, wildcat; free-minded, free-spirited, maverick; single, bachelor; individualistic, unconventional 84 *unconformable*; breakaway 489 *dissenting*.

Vb. *be free*, enjoy liberty; go free, save oneself 667 *escape*; take French leave 738 *disobey*; have the run of, have the freedom of, range, have scope, have room to swing a cat, have room to breathe, have a free hand, have elbowroom; have plenty of rope, have one's head; feel at home, make oneself at home; feel free, let oneself go, let it all hang out, let one's hair down 683 *repose*; have one's fling, have one's way, have it one's own w., cut loose, drop out, follow one's bent, do one's own thing; go as you please, roam 282 *stray*; go one's own way, go it

alone, be one's own boss, shift for oneself, fend for oneself, paddle one's own canoe, stand alone; have a will of one's own 595 *will*; be independent, call no man master, be one's own man; stand up for one's rights, defy the whip 711 *defy*; stand on one's own feet, be self-sufficient; take liberties, make free with, go too far, presume on 878 *be insolent*; dare, make bold to.

give scope, give one his *or* her head, allow full play, give free rein to, allow enough rope 734 *be lax*; give a free hand, not cramp one's style, give the run of 701 *facilitate*; release, set free 746 *liberate*; live and let live, laissez-aller, laissez-faire.

745 Subjection

N. *subjection*, subordination; inferior rank, inferior status 35 *inferiority*; dependence, tutelage, guardianship, wardship, apron strings, leading s.; apprenticeship 536 *learning*; mutual dependence, symbiosis 12 *correlation*; allegiance; subjugation, conquest; loss of freedom, disfranchisement, bondage, enslavement 721 *submission*; constraint 747 *restraint*; oppression 735 *severity*; yoke 748 *fetter*; slavishness 879 *servility*.

servitude, slavery; captivity, bondage, yoke; serfdom.

Adj. *subjected*, dominated etc. vb.; subjugated, overwhelmed 728 *defeated*; subdued; taken prisoner, in chains 747 *restrained*; discriminated against, disadvantaged, disfranchised; colonized, reduced to slavery, sold into s.; in harness 742 *serving*; under the yoke, under the heel; oppressed, brought to one's knees, downtrodden; treated like dirt, henpecked, browbeaten; the sport of, the plaything of, kicked around like a football; brought to heel, quelled; eating out of one's hand, like putty in one's hands, submissive 721 *submitting*; subservient, slavish 879 *servile*.

subject, satellite; tributary; liege, vassal, feudal 739 *obedient*; subordinate, of lower rank, junior, cadet 35 *inferior*; dependent, in chancery; tied to one's apron strings; subject to, liable to, exposed to 180 *liable*; a slave to 610 *habituated*; in the hands of, in the clutches of, under the control of, in the power of, at the mercy of, under the sway of, under one's thumb; not able to call one's soul one's own; puppet-like, like a puppet on a string; having no say in; parasitical, hanging on 879 *servile*; in the pay of; mortgaged 917 *obliged*.

Vb. *be subject*, pay tribute 739 *obey*; obey the whip; depend on 35 *be inferior*; be a doormat, let oneself be trampled on, let oneself be kicked around, be the stooge of; serve, be a slave; lose one's independence 721 *submit*; sacrifice one's freedom, have no will of one's own, be unable to stand on one's own two feet, be a cat's-paw, be a tool 628 *be instrumental*.

subjugate, subdue 727 *overmaster*; colonize, annex; take captive, drag at one's chariot wheels 727 *triumph*; take, capture, lead captive, sell into slavery; fetter, bind, hold in bondage 747 *imprison*; disfranchise; trample on, tread on, treat like dirt, treat like scum 735 *oppress*; keep under, hold down, repress, sit on, stamp out 165 *suppress*; enthral, captivate 821 *impress*; enchant 983 *bewitch*; dominate, lead by the nose 178 *influence*; tame, quell 369 *break in*; have eating out of one's hand, bring to heel, bring to his *or* her knees, have at one's beck and call; make one's plaything, make a stooge of, do what one likes with 673 *dispose of*.

746 Liberation

N. *liberation*, setting free, release, discharge 960 *acquittal*; abreaction, catharsis 818 *feeling*; unravelling, disentanglement, extrication, disinvolvement 46 *separation*; riddance, good r. 831 *relief*; rescue, redemption, salvation 668 *deliverance*; emancipation, enfranchisement; parole, bail; liberalization, relaxation (of control); derationing, deregulation 752 *abrogation*; demobilization 75 *dispersion*; absolution 909 *forgiveness*; acquittance.

Vb. *liberate*, rescue, save 668 *deliver*; pardon 909 *forgive*; discharge, absolve, let off the hook 960 *acquit*; make free, emancipate; enfranchise, give the vote; grant equal rights; introduce positive discrimination, adopt a policy of affirmative action, release, free, set free, set at liberty, let out; bail, parole 766 *give terms*; unfetter, unshackle, unchain; unlock 263 *open*; loosen, unloose, loose, unbind, untie, disentangle, extricate, disengage, clear; unstop, unplug, uncork; unleash, let off the lead; let loose, turn adrift; give play to, give free rein 744 *give scope*; give vent to 300 *empty*; leave hold, let go 779 *not retain*; relax 734 *be lax*; lift 831 *relieve*; decontrol, deregulate, deration 752 *abrogate*; demobilize, disband 75 *disperse*; unyoke, unharness, unload 701 *disencumber*.

achieve liberty, gain one's freedom; free oneself, shake oneself free; stand on one's own two feet; break loose, burst one's bonds, throw off the yoke, cast off one's shackles, throw off one's ball and chain, slip the collar, kick over the traces, get away 667 *escape*.

747 Restraint

N. *restraint*, self-r., self-control 942 *temperance*; reserve, shyness, inhibitions; suppression, repression, coercion, constraint, straitjacket 740 *compulsion*; cramp, check, obstacle, stumbling-block 702 *hindrance*; curb, drag, brake,

clamp, bridle 748 *fetter*; arrest, retardation, deceleration 278 *slowness*; prevention, veto, ban, bar, embargo 757 *prohibition*; legal restraint, Official Secrets Act, D-notice 953 *law*; control, discipline 733 *authority*; censorship 550 *obliteration*; press laws 735 *severity*.

restriction, limitation 236 *limit*; keeping within limits 232 *circumscription*; speed limit, restricted area; exclusion order, no-go area, curfew; constriction, squeeze 198 *compression*; duress, pressure 740 *compulsion*; control, rationing; restrictive practice, exclusive rights, exclusivity 57 *exclusion*; monopoly, price ring, cartel, closed shop; charmed circle; protectionism, intervention, interventionism, tariff wall; retrenchment, cuts 814 *economy*; economic pressure, freeze, price freeze, price control, credit squeeze; rate-capping; blockade.

detention, custody, protective c. 660 *protection*; arrest, house a., curfew; custodianship, keeping, guarding, keep care, charge, ward; quarantine, internment; remand; captivity, duress; bondage, slavery 745 *servitude*; entombment, burial 364 *interment*; immurement, confinement, solitary c., incarceration, imprisonment; sentence, time, a stretch, bird, lag, porridge; penology, penologist.

Adj. *restraining*, checking etc. vb.; restrictive, conditional; limiting, custodial; cramping, hidebound; unbending, unyielding, strict 735 *severe*; stiff 326 *rigid*; tight 206 *narrow*; confining, close 198 *compressive*; confined, poky; coercive; repressive, inhibiting; monopolistic, protectionist, mercantilist.

restrained, self-controlled 942 *temperate*; pent up, bottled up; reserved, shy; disciplined, controlled, under control 739 *obedient*; kept on a leash, under the thumb; pinned down, kept under 745 *subjected*; on parole 917 *obliged*; protected, rationed; limited, restricted; cramped, hampered, trammelled, shackled 702 *hindered*; tied, bound, gagged; held up, weatherbound, fogbound, snowbound, housebound, bedridden, confined to bed.

imprisoned, confined, detained, kept in; landlocked; entombed, confined; quarantined, in quarantine; interned, in internment; under detention, under house arrest, incommunicado; under arrest, in custody; on remand; behind bars, incarcerated, locked up 750 *captive*; inside, in jug, in clink, in quod, in the slammer, in stir, in the cooler, in a cell; gated, confined to barracks; corralled, penned up, impounded; in irons, fettered, shackled; pilloried, in the stocks; serving a sentence, doing time, doing bird, doing porridge; caged, in captivity, trapped.

Vb. *restrain*, hold back; arrest, check, curb,

rein in, brake, put a brake on, put clamps on, act as a brake 278 *retard*; cramp, clog, hamper 702 *hinder*; bind, tie hand and foot 45 *tie*; call a halt, stop, put a stop to 145 *halt*; inhibit, veto, ban, bar, embargo 757 *prohibit*; bridle, discipline, control 735 *be severe*; subdue 745 *subjugate*; restrain oneself, keep one's cool, keep one's hair *or* shirt on, 823 *keep calm*; grip, hold, pin, keep a tight hold *or* rein on, hold in check 778 *retain*; hold in, keep in, fight back, bottle up, choke back; restrict, tighten, hem in, limit, keep within bounds, cordon off, declare a no-go area, draw the line 232 *circumscribe*; damp down, pour water on 177 *moderate*; hold down, clamp down on, crack down on, keep under, sit on, jump on, repress 165 *suppress*; muzzle, gag, silence 578 *make mute*; censor, black out 550 *obliterate*; debar from, rope off, keep out 57 *exclude*; withhold, keep back, stint; ration, be sparing, cut back, retrench 814 *economize*; resist 704 *oppose*; police, patrol, keep order.

arrest, make an a., apprehend, lay by the heels, catch, cop, nab, collar, pinch, nick, pick up; haul in, run in; fetter, handcuff, put the handcuffs on; take, make a prisoner, take prisoner, capture, lead captive; kidnap, seize, snatch, take hostage; put under arrest, run in, take into custody, clap in jail, hold.

fetter, manacle, bind, pinion, tie up, handcuff, put in irons; pillory, put in the stocks, tether 45 *tie*; shackle, trammel, hobble; chain up, put a ball and chain on.

imprison, confine, immure, quarantine, intern; hold, detain, keep in, gate; keep in detention, keep under arrest, hold incommunicado; cloister 883 *seclude*; entomb, bury 364 *inter*; wall up, seal up; coop up, cage, impound, corral, pen up, box up, shut up, shut in, trap 235 *enclose*; put in a straitjacket; incarcerate, throw into prison, send to p., commit to p., remand, run in; lock up; turn the key on, keep under lock and key, keep behind bars, clap in irons; keep prisoner, keep in captivity, keep in custody; hold hostage.

748 Prison

N. *prison*, prison-house, jail-house, jail, gaol, house of correction; quod, clink, jug, can, stir, slammer, cooler; glasshouse, brig; open prison, prison without bars, halfway house; penitentiary, reformatory, Borstal; boot camp; approved school, List D school, remand home, community h.; assessment centre, detention c.; sin bin; dungeon, oubliette; Bastille, Tower; debtor's prison; Newgate, Wormwood Scrubs, Barlinnie, Holloway; Sing Sing, Alcatraz; criminal lunatic asylum, Broadmoor, Carstairs.

lockup, choky, calaboose, nick, police station;

guardroom, guardhouse; cooler, slammer, peter, cell, prison c., condemned c., Death Row; dungeon, oubliette, torture chamber; prison van, Black Maria; dock, bar; pound, pen, cage, coop, kennel 235 *enclosure*; reserve; stocks, pillory.

prison camp, detention c., internment c., Stalag, Colditz; concentration camp, Belsen, Auschwitz, Buchenwald; labour camp, Gulag; penal settlement *or* colony, Botany Bay, Devil's Island.

fetter, shackle, trammel, bond, chain, ball and c., irons, hobble; manacle, pinion, handcuff; straitjacket; muzzle, gag, bit, bridle, halter; rein, bearing r., check-rein, leading rein, reins, traces; yoke, collar, harness; curb, brake, clamp 702 *hindrance*; lead, tether, rope, leading string, apron strings.

749 Keeper

N. *keeper*, custodian, curator; archivist, record keeper 549 *recorder*; officer in charge; caretaker, house-minder, janitor, concierge, housekeeper; chatelaine, warden, ranger, gamekeeper; guard, escort; garrison 713 *defender*; watchdog, sentry, sentinel, lookout, watchman, night w., security man *or* woman, security officer, watch, house-minder, house-sitter, vigilante, coastguard, lighthouse keeper 660 *protector*; invigilator, tutor, chaperon, duenna, governess, nurse, foster n., wet n., nanny, nursemaid, baby-sitter, baby-minder 742 *domestic*; foster parent, adoptive p., guardian, legal g.; appropriate person; probation officer 901 *philanthropist*.

gaoler, jailer, turnkey, warder, wardress, prison guard, prison officer, screw; prison governor.

750 Prisoner

N. *prisoner*, captive, prisoner of war, POW; ticket-of-leave man; political prisoner, prisoner of conscience; detainee; prisoner at the bar, defendant, accused 928 *accused person*; persistent offender, old lag, jailbird 904 *offender*; guest of Her Majesty; condemned prisoner, convict; lifer; galley slave 742 *slave*; hostage, kidnap victim 767 *security*.

Adj. *captive*, imprisoned, in chains, in irons, behind bars, under lock and key; jailed, in prison, inside 747 *imprisoned*; in custody, under arrest, remanded; under detention, detained at Her Majesty's pleasure; held hostage.

751 Commission: vicarious authority

N. *commission*, vicarious authority; committal, delegation; devolution, decentralization; deputation, legation, mission, embassy 754 *envoy*; regency 733 *authority*; representation, proxy;

card vote; agency, factorage, trusteeship, executorship 689 *management*; clerkship.

mandate, trust, charge 737 *command*; commission, assignment, appointment, office, task, errand, mission; enterprise 672 *undertaking*; nomination, return, election 605 *vote*; posting, translation, transfer 272 *transference*; investment, induction, inauguration, ordination, coronation; power of attorney, written authority, charter, writ 737 *warrant*; diploma 756 *permit*; terms of reference 766 *conditions*; responsibility, care, cure (of souls); ward, charge.

Vb. *commission*, empower, authorize, charge, sanction, charter, license 756 *permit*; post, appoint, detail, assign, nominate; engage, hire, staff 622 *employ*; invest, induct, install, ordain; crown, anoint; commit, turn over to, leave it to; consign, entrust, trust with, grant powers of attorney; delegate, depute, send on a mission, send on an errand, send out, return, elect, give a mandate 605 *vote*.

752 Abrogation

N. *abrogation*, annulment, invalidation; nullification; cancellation, suppression; repeal, revocation, rescinding; abolition, dissolution; repudiation 533 *negation*; recantation; suspension, discontinuance, disuse, undoing 148 *reversion*; counterorder.

deposal, deposition, dethronement; demotion, degradation; disestablishment, discharge, congé, dismissal, sack, redundancy, removal 300 *ejection*; unfrocking 963 *punishment*; ousting, deprivation, divestment 786 *expropriation*.

Vb. *abrogate*, annul, cancel; scrub, wipe out 550 *obliterate*; invalidate, abolish, dissolve, nullify, void, render null and void, declare null and void; quash, set aside, reverse, overrule; repeal, revoke, recall; rescind, tear up; undo 148 *revert*; countermand, counterorder; disclaim, disown, deny 533 *negate*; repudiate, retract 603 *recant*; ignore 458 *disregard*; call off, call a halt 747 *restrain*; suspend, discontinue, write off 674 *stop using*.

depose, dethrone; unseat; divest 786 *deprive*; unfrock; disbar, strike off the register, strike off 57 *exclude*; disestablish; suspend 300 *dismiss*; ease out, edge out, elbow out, oust 300 *eject*; demote, degrade, reduce to the ranks, take down a peg or two, kick upstairs; remove 272 *transfer*.

753 Resignation

N. *resignation*, retirement, retiral; leaving, withdrawal 296 *departure*; pension, compensation, golden handshake 962 *reward*; waiver, surrender, abandonment, abdication, renunciation

621 *relinquishment*; abjuration, disclaimer 533 *negation*; state of retirement 681 *leisure*.

Vb. *resign*, tender one's resignation, hand in one's notice, give n.; hand over, vacate office; apply for the Chiltern Hundreds; stand down, stand aside, make way for; sign off, declare (cricket); scratch, withdraw, back out, give a walkover, retire from the contest, throw in one's hand, surrender, give up 721 *submit*; quit, throw up, chuck it; ask for one's cards; sign away, give a. 780 *assign*; abdicate, abandon, renounce 621 *relinquish*; retire, go into retirement, take early retirement, accept redundancy, be superannuated, be put out to grass; be pensioned off.

754 Consignee

N. *consignee*, committee, steering c., panel, quango 692 *council*; counsellor, team of experts, think tank, brains trust, working party 691 *adviser*; nominee, licensee; trustee, executor 686 *agent*; factor, one's man of business, bailiff, steward 690 *manager*; caretaker, curator 749 *keeper*; representative; legal representative, attorney, counsel, advocate 958 *law agent*; proxy, surrogate 755 *deputy*; negotiator, middleman, broker, stockbroker 231 *intermediary*; underwriter, insurer; purser, bursar 798 *treasurer*; rent collector, tax c., revenue c., income-tax officer; officebearer, secretary of state 741 *officer*; functionary 690 *official*.

delegate, shop steward; nominee, representative; correspondent, special c. 588 *correspondent*; emissary, special messenger 529 *messenger*; delegation, mission.

envoy, emissary, legate, papal nuncio, representative, ambassador, ambassadress, High Commissioner, chargé d'affaires; ambassador at large; diplomatic corps; minister, diplomat; consul, vice-c.; attaché; embassy, legation, mission, consulate, High Commission; diplomatist, negotiator.

755 Deputy

N. *deputy*, surrogate, alternate, proxy; scapegoat, substitute, locum tenens, locum, understudy, stand-in, temp 150 *substitution*; viceroy, vice-president, vice-chairman, vice-chancellor, vice-admiral, vice-captain, vice-consul; vicar; second-in-command, number two 741 *officer*; right-hand man, lieutenant, secretary 703 *aider*; alter ego, power behind the throne, éminence grise 612 *motivator*; caretaker government; heir, heir apparent 776 *beneficiary*; spokesperson, spokesman or woman, mouthpiece, herald 529 *messenger*; second, advocate, champion 707 *patron*; agent, factor, attorney 754 *consignee*.

Vb. *deputize*, act for 622 *function*; act on

behalf of, represent, hold a proxy f., appear for, speak f., answer f., hold a brief f.; hold in trust, be executor 689 *manage*; negotiate, act as go-between for, be broker for, replace, stand in for, understudy, do duty for 150 *substitute*; act as scapegoat.

Special social volition

756 Permission

N. *permission*, liberty 744 *freedom*; leave, sanction, clearance; grant; licence, authorization, warrant; allowance, sufferance, tolerance, indulgence 736 *leniency*; acquiescence 758 *consent*; blessing, approval 923 *approbation*; grace and favour 897 *benevolence*; concession, dispensation, exemption 919 *nonliability*; release 746 *liberation*.

permit, written permission; authority, law 737 *warrant*; commission 751 *mandate*; charter, pass, password; passport, passbook, visa, safe-conduct; ticket, chit; licence, driving l.; free hand, carte blanche, blank cheque 744 *scope*; leave, compassionate l., sick l., leave of absence, furlough, holiday, vacation, sabbatical; parole; clearance, all clear, green light, go-ahead; imprimatur.

Adj. *permitting*, permissive, indulgent, complaisant, laissez-faire, easy-going.

Vb. *permit*, let 469 *make possible*; give permission, grant leave, accord, vouchsafe 781 *give*; nod, say yes 758 *consent*; give one's blessing; sanction 923 *approve*; entitle, authorize, warrant, charter, patent, license, enable; ratify, legalize, decriminalize 953 *make legal*; decontrol; lift a ban, raise an embargo, dispense, release 919 *exempt*; clear, give clearance 746 *liberate*; give the go-ahead, give the all clear, give the green light, tip the wink, let off the hook; recognize, concede, allow 488 *assent*; give one a chance, let one try; leave the way open, open the door to 263 *open*; suffer, tolerate, put up with, brook 736 *be lenient*; connive at, shut one's eyes to, turn a blind eye, wink at 734 *be lax*; laissez-faire, laissez-aller, allow a free hand, give carte blanche, issue a blank cheque 744 *give scope*; permit oneself, allow o., take the liberty.

ask leave, beg l., ask if one may, ask one's blessing; ask to be excused; petition 761 *request*.

757 Prohibition

N. *prohibition*, inhibition, injunction; counterorder; intervention, interference; interdict, veto, ban, embargo, restriction, curfew 747 *restraint*; proscription, taboo; rejection, red

light, thumbs down 760 *refusal*; intolerance 924 *disapprobation*; licensing laws 942 *temperance*; censorship, press laws, repression, suppression 735 *severity*; abolition, cancellation, suspension 752 *abrogation*; blackout 550 *obliteration*; forbidden fruit.

Adj. *prohibited*, forbidden, verboten; barred, banned, under ban; censored, blue-pencilled, blacked-out; contraband, illicit, unlawful, outlawed, against the law 954 *illegal*; taboo; frowned on, not done; unmentionable, unprintable; out of bounds; blackballed, ostracized.

Vb. *prohibit*, forbid; disallow, veto, withhold permission, refuse leave, give the thumbs down, give the red light, forbid the banns 760 *refuse*; withdraw permission, cancel leave; countermand, counterorder, revoke, suspend 752 *abrogate*; prevent 702 *hinder*; restrict, stop 747 *restrain*; ban, taboo, proscribe, outlaw; black; impose a ban, place out of bounds; bar, debar, warn off, shut the door on, blackball, ostracize 57 *exclude*; excommunicate 300 *eject*; repress, stifle, kill 165 *suppress*; censor, blue-pencil 550 *obliterate*; put one's foot down 735 *be severe*; frown on, not countenance, not brook 924 *disapprove*; discourage, crack down on 613 *dissuade*; cramp 232 *circumscribe*; draw the line; intervene, interfere.

758 Consent

N. *consent*, willingness; agreement 488 *assent*; compliance 768 *observance*; accord; acquiescence, acceptance 756 *permission*; sanction, endorsement, ratification, confirmation.

Vb. *consent*, say yes, nod; give consent, give the go-ahead, give the green light, set one's seal on, ratify, confirm 488 *endorse*; sanction, pass 756 *permit*; give one's approval 923 *approve*; tolerate, recognize, allow, connive 736 *be lenient*; agree, fall in with, go along with, accede 488 *assent*; have no objection 488 *acquiesce*; be persuaded, come round; yield, give way 721 *submit*; comply; grant, concede 781 *give*; go halfway to meet 597 *be willing*; do all one is asked 828 *content*; accept, take up an offer, jump at; clinch a deal, seal a bargain 766 *make terms*.

759 Offer

N. *offer*, fair o., proffer; bribe 612 *inducement*; tender, bid, takeover b., green mail, buy-out, merger, proposal; motion, proposition, proposal; approach, overture, advance, invitation; feeler; final offer; present, presentation, offering, sacrifice 781 *gift*; dedication.

Vb. *offer*, proffer, hold out, make an offer, bid, tender; present, lay at one's feet 781 *give*; dedicate, consecrate; sacrifice to; introduce, broach, move, propose, make a proposition, put forward, suggest 512 *propound*; make overtures, leave the door open, keep one's offer open; bribe; invite, send an invitation, ask one in 882 *be hospitable*; hawk, invite tenders, put up for sale 793 *sell*; auction; make a present of 469 *make possible*.

offer oneself, stand, be a candidate, compete, run for, be in the running for, enter 716 *contend*; volunteer, come forward 597 *be willing*; apply, put in for 761 *request*.

760 Refusal

N. *refusal*, nonacceptance, declining, turning down, thumbs down, red light 607 *rejection*; denial, no, nay 533 *negation*; disclaimer, flat refusal 711 *defiance*; repulse, rebuff, slap in the face 292 *repulsion*; withholding 778 *retention*; recalcitrance 738 *disobedience*; noncompliance 769 *nonobservance*; recusancy 598 *unwillingness*; objection, protest 762 *deprecation*; renunciation, abnegation 621 *relinquishment*.

Vb. *refuse*, say no, shake one's head; excuse oneself, send one's apologies; disagree 489 *dissent*; deny, repudiate, disclaim 533 *negate*; decline, turn down, pass up, opt out; spurn 607 *reject*; repulse, rebuff 292 *repel*; turn away 300 *dismiss*; dig one's heels in, be unmoved, harden one's heart 602 *be obstinate*; not hear, not listen, turn a deaf ear 416 *be deaf*; close one's purse; turn one's back on; hang fire, hang back 598 *be unwilling*; beg off, back down; turn from, have nothing to do with, shy at, jib at 620 *avoid*; debar, keep out, shut the door 57 *exclude*; not allow 757 *prohibit*; set one's face against 715 *resist*; oppose 704 *withstand*; kick, protest 762 *deprecate*; not comply 769 *not observe*; grudge, begrudge, withhold, keep from 778 *retain*.

761 Request

N. *request*, asking, first time of a.; canvassing, hawking 793 *sale*; requisition, final demand, last time of asking, ultimatum 737 *demand*; blackmail 900 *threat*; claim, counterclaim 915 *dueness*; consumer demand, seller's market 627 *requirement*; postulate 475 *premise*; proposition, proposal, motion; overture, approach 759 *offer*; bid, application; petition, round robin; prayer, appeal, plea; insistence 740 *compulsion*; cri de coeur; importunity; soliciting, accosting, invitation, temptation; mendicancy, begging, busking, bumming; begging letter, flag day, bazaar, charity performance, benefit match.

entreaty, imploring, begging, beseeching; submission, clasped hands, bended knees; supplication, prayer 981 *prayers*; appeal 583 *allocution*; solemn entreaty, imprecation.

Adj. *supplicatory*, entreating, suppliant, on

bended knees, with folded hands, cap in hand; imploring, beseeching.

Vb. *request*, ask, invite, solicit; make overtures, approach, accost 759 *offer*; woo, pop the question 889 *court*; seek, look for 459 *search*; fish for, angle for; need, call for, clamour f. 627 *require*; crave, make a request, beg a favour, ask a f., have a request to make, make bold to ask, trouble one for 859 *desire*; apply, make application, put in for, bid, bid for, make a bid f.; apply to, call on, appeal to, run to, address oneself to, go cap in hand to; tout, hawk, doorstep, canvass, solicit orders 793 *sell*; petition, press a suit, press a claim, expect 915 *claim*; make demands 737 *demand*; blackmail, put the bite on 900 *threaten*; coax, wheedle, cajole; importune, dun; touch 785 *borrow*; requisition 786 *take*; send an ultimatum 766 *give terms*.

beg, cadge, crave, sponge, freeload; bum; scrounge, mooch; thumb a lift, hitchhike; hold out one's hand, go from door to door, doorstep, knock at doors; appeal for funds, pass the hat, launch an appeal 786 *levy*.

entreat, supplicate, be a suppliant; pray, implore, beseech, appeal, invoke, appeal to, call on 583 *speak to*; address one's prayers to, pray to 981 *offer worship*; kneel to, go down on one's knees, go down on bended knee, fall at one's feet.

762 Deprecation: negative request

N. *deprecation*, dissuasion; plea for mercy; intercession, mediation 981 *prayers*; counterclaim 761 *request*; murmur, complaint 829 *discontent*; exception, demur, expostulation, remonstrance, protest 704 *opposition*; reaction, backlash 182 *counteraction*; tut-tut, raised eyebrows, groans, jeers, sniffs of disapproval 924 *disapprobation*; petition, open letter, round robin; demonstration, march, protest m., hunger m., hunger strike, industrial action, sit-in; noncompliance 760 *refusal*.

Vb. *deprecate*, ask one not to, advise against, have a better idea, make a counterproposal 613 *dissuade*; touch wood, knock on w., cross one's fingers, keep one's fingers crossed; beg off, intercede 720 *mediate*; pray, appeal 761 *entreat*; cry for mercy 905 *ask mercy*; tut-tut, shake one's head, raise one's eyebrows, sniff 924 *disapprove*; remonstrate, expostulate 924 *reprove*; jeer, groan, stamp 926 *detract*; murmur, beef, complain 829 *be discontented*; object, take exception to; demur, jib, kick, squeak, protest against, appeal a., petition a., lobby a., campaign a., raise one's voice a., cry out a. 704 *oppose*; demonstrate, organize a protest march, hold a protest meeting, go on hunger strike; strike, take industrial action, come out, walk o. 145 *cease*.

763 Petitioner

N. *petitioner*, suppliant, supplicant; appealer, appellant; claimant, pretender; postulant, aspirant; solicitor, asker, seeker, enquirer, advertiser; customer, bidder, tenderer; suitor, courter, wooer; canvasser, hawker, tout, barker; dunner; pressure group, ginger g., lobby, lobbyist; applicant, candidate, entrant; competitor 716 *contender*.

beggar, busker, mendicant; tramp, bum 268 *wanderer*; cadger, borrower, moocher, scrounger, hitch-hiker; sponger, freeloader, ligger, parasite 879 *toady*.

SECTION THREE

Conditional social volition

764 Promise

N. *promise*, offer; undertaking, commitment; affiance, betrothal, engagement 894 *marriage*; troth, plight, word, word of honour, vow, marriage v. 532 *oath*; declaration 532 *affirmation*; declared intention 617 *intention*; profession, fair words; assurance, pledge, warranty, guarantee, insurance 767 *security*; bargain, gentlemen's agreement, unwritten a., mutual a. 765 *compact*; covenant, bond, promise to pay 803 *debt*; debt of honour 917 *duty*.

promised, covenanted, guaranteed, secured; bespoke, reserved; betrothed, affianced; committed, bound 917 *obliged*.

Vb. *promise*, say one will 532 *affirm*; hold out, proffer 759 *offer*; make a promise, give one's word, pledge one's w.; vow, take one's oath on it 532 *swear*; vouch for, go bail for, warrant, guarantee, assure, insure, underwrite 767 *give security*; pledge, stake; pledge one's honour, stake one's credit; engage, enter into an engagement 672 *undertake*; make a gentleman's agreement, strike a bargain, sign on the dotted line, shake on it, commit oneself, bind oneself, be bound, covenant 765 *contract*; take on oneself, accept responsibility 917 *incur a duty*; accept a liability, promise to pay, incur a debt of honour 785 *borrow*; plight one's troth, exchange vows 894 *wed*.

take a pledge, demand security 473 *make certain*; put on oath, swear, make one s. 466 *testify*; exact a promise; take one's word 485 *believe*; rely on, expect 473 *be certain*.

Adv. *as promised*, according to contract, as agreed, duly.

765 Compact

N. *compact*, contract, bargain, concordat, agreement, mutual undertaking 672 *undertaking*; gentleman's agreement, unwritten a., debt of honour 764 *promise*; exchange of vows; engagement, betrothal 894 *marriage*; covenant, bond 767 *security*; league, alliance, cartel 706 *cooperation*; pact, understanding 24 *agreement*; private u., something between them; conspiracy 623 *plot*; negotiation 766 *conditions*; deal 770 *compromise*; arrangement, settlement; seal, signature, countersignature; deed of agreement, indenture 767 *title deed*.

treaty, international agreement; Treaty of Rome, Warsaw Pact; peace treaty, nonaggression pact 719 *pacification*; convention, concordat; Geneva Convention.

signatory, signer, countersigner, subscriber, the undersigned; swearer, attestor 466 *witness*; endorser, ratifier; adherent, consenting party 488 *assenter*; covenanter, contractor, contracting party; treaty-maker, negotiator 720 *mediator*.

Adj. *contractual*, bilateral, multilateral; agreed to, negotiated, signed, countersigned, sworn, ratified; covenanted, signed, signed on the dotted line, sealed and delivered.

Vb. *contract*, enter into a contract, engage 672 *undertake*; promise; covenant, strike a bargain, sign a pact, shake hands on, do a deal, clinch a d.; ally 706 *cooperate*; treat, negotiate 791 *bargain*; agree, come to terms 766 *make terms*; conclude, close, settle; indent, execute, sign, sign on the dotted line, subscribe, ratify, attest, confirm 488 *endorse*; insure, underwrite 767 *give security*.

766 Conditions

N. *conditions*, treaty-making, diplomacy, summitry, negotiation, bargaining, collective b.; hard bargaining, trade-off, horse-trading 791 *barter*; formula, terms, terms for agreement; ultimatum, time limit 900 *threat*; part of the bargain, set of terms, basis for negotiation, frame of reference; articles of agreement; provision, clause, escape c., let-out c., proviso, limitation, strings, reservation, exception, small print 468 *qualification*; stipulation, sine qua non, essential clause 627 *requirement*; rule 693 *precept*; terms of reference 751 *mandate*.

Adj. *conditional*, with strings attached, stipulatory, qualificatory, provisory 468 *qualifying*; limiting, subject to terms, contingent, provisional.

Vb. *give terms*, propose conditions; attach strings; hold out for, insist on, make demands 737 *demand*; stipulate, make it a sine qua non 627 *require*; allow no exception 735 *be severe*; insert a proviso, leave a loophole 468 *qualify*; fix the terms, impose the conditions, write the articles, draft the clauses; add a let-out c., write in; keep one's options open, hedge one's bets.

make terms, negotiate, be in treaty, parley, powwow, hold conversations 584 *confer*; deal with, treat w., negotiate w.; make overtures, throw out a feeler 461 *be tentative*; haggle 791 *bargain*; make proposals 759 *offer*; compromise; negotiate a treaty, hammer out a formula, work something out, do a deal 765 *contract*.

Adv. *on terms*, on one's own t.; conditionally, provisionally, subject to, with a reservation.

767 Security

N. *security*, guarantee, warranty, authorization, writ 737 *warrant*; word of honour 764 *promise*; sponsorship, patronage 660 *protection*; surety, bail, parole; gage, pledge, pawn, hostage; stake, deposit, earnest, handsel, token, instalment; colour of one's money, earnest m.; down payment 804 *payment*; indemnity, insurance, underwriting 660 *safety*; transfer of security, mortgage 780 *transfer*; collateral.

title deed, deed, instrument; deed poll; indenture; charter, covenant, bond, bearer b.; receipt, IOU, voucher, counterfoil, certificate, authentication, marriage lines; verification, seal, stamp, signature, endorsement, acceptance 466 *credential*; banknote, treasury note, promissory n., note of hand, bill, treasury bill, bill of exchange; blue chip, giltedged security; portfolio, scrip, share, debenture; insurance policy; will, last will and testament, living will, codicil, certificate of probate; archives 548 *record*.

Vb. *give bail*, go b., bail one out, go surety; take bail, release on bail; hold in pledge, keep in pawn 764 *take a pledge*.

give security, offer collateral, mortgage; pledge, pawn, pop, hock 785 *borrow*; guarantee, act as guarantor, stand surety for, warrant 473 *make certain*; authenticate, verify 466 *corroborate*; execute, endorse, seal, stamp, sign, sign on the dotted line, countersign, subscribe, give one's signature 488 *endorse*; vouch for 764 *promise*; secure, indemnify, insure, assure, underwrite 660 *safeguard*.

768 Observance

N. *observance*, practice; fulfilment 635 *sufficiency*; diligence, conscientiousness; adherence to, attention to; acknowledgment; performance, discharge 676 *action*; compliance 739 *obedience*; conformance 83 *conformity*; fidelity; dependability, reliability 929 *probity*.

Adj. *observant*, practising; heedful, watchful, careful of, attentive to 455 *attentive*; conscientious, diligent, religious, punctilious; meticulous; exact 494 *accurate*; responsible, reliable, dependable 929 *trustworthy*; loyal 739 *obedient*; adhering to, sticking to 83 *conformable*; faithful 929 *honourable*.

Vb. *observe*, heed, respect, regard, have regard to, pay respect to, acknowledge, pay attention to, attend to 455 *be attentive*; keep, practise, adhere to, stick to, cling to, follow, hold by, abide by, be loyal to 83 *conform*; comply 739 *obey*; fulfil, discharge, perform, execute, carry out, carry out to the letter 676 *do*; satisfy 635 *suffice*.

keep faith, be faithful *or* loyal to, discharge one's functions 917 *do one's duty*; honour one's obligations, meet one's o., be as good as one's word, make good one's promise, keep one's p., fulfil one's engagement, be true to the spirit of, stand by; come up to scratch, pay one's debt, pay up 804 *pay*; give one his due.

769 Nonobservance

N. *nonobservance*, informality, indifference 734 *laxity*; inattention, omission 458 *negligence*; nonadherence 84 *nonconformity*; nonperformance; nonfulfilment, shortcoming 726 *noncompletion*; infringement, violation; noncompliance, disloyalty 738 *disobedience*; protest 762 *deprecation*; disregard, discourtesy 921 *disrespect*; breach of faith, repudiation, denial 533 *negation*.

Adj. *nonobservant*, nonpractising, lapsed; nonconforming, blacklegging, nonadhering, nonconformist 84 *unconformable*; inattentive to, disregarding, neglectful 458 *negligent*; informal 734 *lax*; noncompliant 738 *disobedient*; infringing, unlawful 954 *lawbreaking*; disloyal 918 *undutiful*; unfaithful 930 *perfidious*.

Vb. *not observe*, not practise; not conform, not adhere, stand out 84 *be unconformable*; discard 674 *stop using*; set aside 752 *abrogate*; omit, ignore 458 *neglect*; disregard, show no respect for, cock a snook, snap one's fingers at 921 *not respect*; stretch a point 734 *be lax*; violate, do violence to, drive a coach and horses through, ride roughshod over, trample underfoot 176 *force*; transgress 306 *overstep*; not comply with 738 *disobey*; desert 918 *fail in duty*; fail, not qualify, not come up to scratch 636 *not suffice*; break one's word; renege on, go back on, back out, cancel; give the go-by, cut, shirk, dodge, parry, evade, elude 620 *avoid*.

770 Compromise

N. *compromise*, mutual concession, give and take, trade-off, adjustment; commutation; second best, half a loaf 35 *inferiority*; working arrangement 624 *way*; splitting the difference 30 *average*; halfway 625 *middle way*; balancing act, swings and roundabouts.

Vb. *compromise*, find a formula; make mutual

concessions, strike a balance, find a happy medium, steer a middle course, give and take, meet one halfway; live and let live, stretch a point 734 *be lax*; take the mean, go half and half, go Dutch, split the difference 30 *average out*; commute 150 *substitute*; compose differences, go to arbitration; patch up 719 *pacify*; take the good with the bad, take what is offered, make a virtue of necessity, make the best of a bad job; sit on the fence.

SECTION FOUR

Possessive relations

771 Acquisition

N. *acquisition*, getting, winning; earning; acquirement, obtainment, procurement; collection 74 *assemblage*; realization, profit-taking 793 *sale*; encashment 780 *transfer*; fund-raising; exploitation, profiteering; money-grubbing 816 *avarice*; heap, stack, pile, mountain, pool, scoop, jackpot 74 *accumulation*; finding 484 *discovery*; recovery, retrieval, recoupment 656 *restoration*; redemption 792 *purchase*; appropriation; theft 788 *stealing*; inheritance, patrimony; find, windfall, treasure trove; something for nothing, free gift, freebie, giveaway 781 *gift*; legacy, bequest; gratuity, baksheesh 962 *reward*; benefit match, prize 729 *trophy*; gravy 615 *benefit*; easy money 701 *facility*; lucre 797 *money*; plunder 790 *booty*.

earnings, income, earned i., wage, minimum w., salary, screw, pay packet, take-home pay, productivity bonus 804 *pay*; rate for the job, pay scale, differential; fee for service, honorarium; pension, superannuation, compensation, golden handshake; remuneration, emolument 962 *reward*; allowance, expense account; pickings, perquisite, perks, fringe benefits, extras; commission, rake-off 810 *discount*; return, receipts, proceeds, turnover, takings, revenue, taxes 807 *receipt*; harvest, crop, gleanings.

gain, savings 814 *economy*; credit side, profit, net p., capital gain, winnings; dividend, share-out 775 *participation*; usury, interest, high i., compound i., simple i. 36 *increment*; profitable transaction; pay increase, rise, raise 36 *increase*; advantage, benefit.

Adj. *acquiring*, acquisitive, accumulative; on the make, gold-digging, getting, winning 730 *prosperous*.

gainful, paying, money-making, money-spinning, lucrative, remunerative; advantageous 640 *profitable*; fruitful.

Vb. *acquire*, get, come by; earn, gain, obtain, procure; find, strike, come across, come by, pick

up, light upon 484 *discover*; get hold of, get possession of, lay one's hands on, make one's own, annex 786 *appropriate*; win, secure, capture, catch, land, net, bag 786 *take*; pick, glean, fill one's pockets; gather, reap, crop, harvest; derive, draw, tap, milk, mine 304 *extract*; collect, accumulate, heap, pile up 74 *bring together*; scrape together, rake t.; collect funds, launch an appeal, raise, levy, raise the wind; save, save up, hoard 632 *store*; buy, pre-empt 792 *purchase*; reserve, book, engage 135 *be early*; beg, borrow or steal; earn a living, turn an honest penny, keep the wolf from the door 622 *busy oneself*; make money, draw a salary, draw a pension, receive one's wages; have an income, be in receipt of, have a turnover, gross, take 782 *receive*; convert, cash, encash, realize, clear, make; get back, recover, salvage, recycle, regain, redeem, recapture, reconquer 656 *retrieve*; take back, resume, reclaim; recover one's losses 31 *recoup*; recover one's costs, break even, balance the books, practise creative accounting, balance accounts 28 *equalize*; attain, reach; come in for, catch, incur.

inherit, come into, be left, be willed, be bequeathed, fall heir to, come by, come in for, receive a legacy; succeed, succeed to, step into the shoes of, be the heir of.

gain, make a profit, earn a dividend; make; make money, coin m., coin it, line one's pockets 730 *prosper*; make a fortune, make a killing, make one's pile, rake in the shekels, rake it in, turn a pretty penny 800 *get rich*; make a scoop, win, win the jackpot, break the bank; sell at a profit.

be profitable, profit, repay, be worthwhile; pay, pay well; yield 164 *produce*; bring in a return, pay a dividend, show a profit 730 *prosper*.

772 Loss

N. *loss*, deprivation, privation, bereavement; dispossession, eviction 786 *expropriation*; sacrifice, forfeit, lapse 963 *penalty*; dead loss, irretrievable l., perdition 165 *ruin*; depreciation 655 *deterioration*; diminishing returns; setback, check, reverse; loss of profit, loss leader; overdraft, bankruptcy 805 *insolvency*; consumption 806 *expenditure*; nonrecovery, spilt milk, wastage, wear and tear, leakage 634 *waste*; dissipation, evaporation, drain 37 *decrease*; good riddance 746 *liberation*; losing battle 728 *defeat*.

Adj. *lost*, long l., gone, gone for ever; gone by the board, out of sight out of mind, consigned to oblivion 458 *neglected*; vanished, flown out of the window; missing, astray, adrift, mislaid; untraceable, lost, stolen or strayed 190 *absent*; lacking 307 *deficient*; irrecoverable, irretrievable, irredeemable, unsalvageable, nonreturnable, nonrecyclable; spent, gone down the drain, squandered; forfeited.

Vb. *lose*, be unable to find, look in vain for; mislay 188 *misplace*; miss, let slip through one's fingers, kiss *or* say goodbye to 138 *lose a chance*; meet one's Waterloo; squander, throw away 634 *waste*; deserve to lose, forfeit, sacrifice; spill; fritter away, throw good money after bad, sink 806 *expend*; be a loser, draw a blank, burn one's fingers 731 *have trouble*; lose one's bet, pay out; be out of pocket; be set back, incur losses, sell at a loss; be unable to pay, go broke, go bankrupt 805 *not pay*; be overdrawn, be in the red, be minus.

be lost, be missing, be declared m. 190 *be absent*; go down the drain, go down the spout, go up in smoke, go to pot 165 *be destroyed*.

773 Possession

N. *possession*, ownership, proprietorship, lawful possession, enjoyment; occupancy, nine points of the law, bird in the hand; mastery, hold, grasp, grip 778 *retention*; haves and have-nots 776 *possessor*; a possession 777 *property*; tenancy, holding 777 *estate*; tenure, feu, fief; monopoly, ring; preoccupancy, pre-emption, squatting; expectations, inheritance, heritage, patrimony, taking possession, appropriation, laying claim to.

Adj. *possessed*, held etc. vb.; in the possession of, in one's hand, in one's grasp, in the bag; in the bank, to one's name; at one's disposal, on hand; one's own, exclusive; monopolized by, engrossed by, taken up by; booked, reserved, engaged, occupied; included in, attaching.

Vb. *possess*, be possessed of, be the proud possessor of, number among one's possessions, own, have; hold, have and hold, hold in one's grasp, grip 778 *retain*; have at one's command, have absolute disposal of; call one's own, boast of 915 *claim*; contain, include 78 *comprise*; fill, occupy; squat, settle upon, inhabit; enjoy, have for one's own 673 *use*; monopolize, have exclusive rights to, hog, corner the market; get, take possession, make one's own 786 *take*; preoccupy; reserve, engage 135 *be early*.

belong, be vested in, belong to; go with, be included in.

774 Nonownership

N. *nonownership*, nonpossession, vacancy; tenancy, temporary lease; pauperism 801 *poverty*; deprivation 772 *loss*; no-man's-land, debatable territory 190 *emptiness*.

Adj. *unpossessed*, unattached; masterless, ownerless, nobody's, no man's; common; unclaimed; disowned; up for grabs, anybody's;

unoccupied, untenanted; vacant 190 *empty*; abandoned 779 *not retained*; untaken, free, going begging 860 *unwanted*.

775 Joint possession

N. *joint possession*, joint tenancy; joint ownership; common land, common; public property, public domain 777 *property*; condominium 733 *political organization*; joint stock, pool, kitty 632 *store*; cooperative system; nationalization, public ownership, state o., socialism, communism, collectivism; collective farm, collective, commune, kolkhoz, kibbutz 370 *farm*; timesharing.

participation, membership, affiliation 78 *inclusion*; partnership, profit-sharing, time-sharing 706 *association*; Dutch treat, bottle party, byob, share-out; involvement, sympathy; fellow feeling, empathy, sympathetic strike, joint action.

participator, member, partner, joint heir; shareholder, stockholder 776 *possessor*; co-tenant, flat-mate, room-m., housing association; cooperator; trade unionist; collectivist, socialist, communist; commune-dweller, kolkhoznik, kibbutznik; sympathizer, contributor 707 *patron*.

Vb. *participate*, have a hand in, have a say in, join in, pitch in, sit in, be in on, have a finger in the pie 706 *cooperate*; partake of, share in, come in for a s.; share, go shares, go halves, go fifty-fifty, pull one's weight, share and share alike 783 *apportion*; share expenses, go Dutch 804 *defray*.

776 Possessor

N. *possessor*, holder, taker, captor, conqueror; squatter; monopolizer, dog in the manger; occupant, lodger, occupier, incumbent; mortgagee; renter, hirer, lessee, leaseholder, rent-payer; tenantry, tenant; house-owner, owner-occupier, householder, free-holder.

owner, monarch, monarch of all one surveys; master, mistress, proprietor, proprietress, proprietrix; purchaser, buyer 792 *purchaser*; lord, lord *or* lady of the manor, landed gentry, landed interest; squire, laird 868 *aristocracy*; man *or* woman of property, property-holder, shareholder, stockholder, landowner, landlord, landlady; mortgagor; testator, testatrix, bequeather 781 *giver*.

beneficiary, grantee; incumbent 986 *cleric*; legatee; inheritor, successor, successor apparent; next of kin 11 *kinsman*; heir *or* heiress, heir apparent, heir presumptive; crown prince 741 *sovereign*.

777 Property

N. *property*, possession, possessions, one's all; stake; personal property, public p., common p.; church property; chattel, immovables; movables, personal estate, goods and chattels, worldly goods, appurtenances, belongings, paraphernalia, accoutrements, effects, personal e., impedimenta, baggage, bag and baggage, things, gear, what one stands up in; goods, stock 795 *merchandise*; plant, fixtures, furniture.

estate, estate and effects, assets, frozen a., liquid a., assets and liabilities; circumstances, what one is worth, resources 629 *means*; substance, capital, one's money, one's fortune 800 *wealth*; revenue, income 807 *receipt*; valuables, securities, stocks and shares, portfolio; stake, holding, investment; debts; title, interest; living 985 *benefice*; lease, tenure, freehold, copyhold, fee.

lands, land, acres, broad a., acreage, tract, grounds; estate, property, landed p.; real estate, realty; holding, tenure, freehold, copyhold, fief, manor; lordship, domain; plot 184 *territory*; farm, home f., manor f., homestead, plantation, ranch, hacienda; crown lands, common land, common 775 *joint possession*; dependency, dominion 733 *political organization*.

dower, dowry, marriage portion, jointure, marriage settlement; allowance, pin money; alimony, aliment, maintenance, palimony; patrimony, birthright 915 *dueness*; heritage; inheritance, legacy, bequest; heirloom; expectations, entail.

Adj. *proprietary*, branded, patented; landed, feudal, freehold, leasehold, copyhold; hereditary, heritable, entailed; endowed.

Vb. *endow*, endow, bless w. 781 *give*; bequeath; grant, allot 780 *assign*; put in possession, instal 751 *commission*; found.

778 Retention

N. *retention*, prehensility, tenacity; stickiness 354 *viscidity*; tenaciousness, retentiveness, holding on, hanging on, clinging to, handhold, foothold, toehold 218 *support*; beachhead 34 *advantage*; clutches, grip, vice-like g., grasp, hold, firm h., stranglehold, half-nelson; squeeze 198 *compression*; clinch, lock; hug, bear h., embrace, clasp, cuddle 889 *endearment*; keeping in 747 *detention*; finders keepers 760 *refusal*; containment 235 *enclosure*.

pincers, nippers; tweezers, pliers, snub-nosed p., wrench, tongs, forceps, vice, clamp 47 *fastening*; talon, claw, nails 256 *sharp point*; tentacle, hook, tendril 378 *feeler*; teeth, fangs 256 *tooth*; paw, hand, fingers 378 *finger*; fist, clenched f., duke.

Adj. *retentive*, tenacious, prehensile; vice-like,

retaining 747 *restraining*; clinging, adhesive, sticky, gummy, gluey, gooey 48 *cohesive*; firm, unshakable 45 *tied*; tight, strangling.

Vb. *retain*, hold; grab, buttonhole, hold back 702 *obstruct*; hold up, catch, steady 218 *support*; hold on, hold fast, hold tight, keep a firm hold of, maintain one's hold, not let go; cling to, hang on to, freeze on to, stick to, adhere; fasten on, grip, grasp, grapple, clench, clinch, lock; hug, clasp, clutch, embrace; pin, pin down, hold d.; have by the throat, throttle, strangle, keep a stranglehold on, get a half-nelson on, tighten one's grip 747 *restrain*; dig one's nails in, dig one's toes in, hang on like a bulldog, hang on with all one's might, hang on for dear life; keep in, detain 747 *imprison*; contain, keep within limits, draw the line 235 *enclose*; keep to oneself, keep in one's own hands, keep back, keep to one side, withhold 525 *keep secret*; not dispose of 632 *store*; save, keep 666 *preserve*; not part with, keep back, withhold 760 *refuse*.

779 Nonretention

N. *nonretention*, parting with, disposal, alienation 780 *transfer*; selling off 793 *sale*; letting go, leaving hold of, release 746 *liberation*; dispensation; dissolution (of a marriage) 896 *divorce*; abandonment, renunciation 621 *relinquishment*; cancellation 752 *abrogation*; disuse 611 *desuetude*, leak 298 *outflow*; incontinence.

derelict, jetsam, flotsam 641 *rubbish*; cast-off; waif, stray, foundling, orphan, outcast, pariah; down-and-out, vagrant.

Adj. *not retained*, under notice to quit; alienated, disposed of, sold off; left behind 41 *remaining*; dispensed with, abandoned; released; fired, made redundant, given the sack *or* the chop, given the heave-ho; derelict, unclaimed; disowned, divorced, disinherited; for sale 793 *salable*.

Vb. *not retain*, part with, alienate, transfer 780 *assign*; sell off, dispose of 793 *sell*; be open-handed 815 *be prodigal*; free, let go, let slip, unhand, leave hold of, relax one's grip, release one's hold; unlock, unclench 263 *open*; unbind, untie, disentangle 46 *disunite*; forgo, dispense with, do without, spare, give up, waive, abandon, cede, yield 621 *relinquish*; renounce, abjure 603 *recant*; cancel, revoke 752 *abrogate*; lift restrictions, derestrict, raise an embargo, decontrol, deregulate, deration 746 *liberate*; supersede, replace 150 *substitute*; wash one's hands of, turn one's back on, disown, disclaim 533 *negate*; dissolve (a marriage) 896 *divorce*; disinherit, cut off without a penny, cut off with a shilling 801 *impoverish*; marry off 894 *marry*; get rid of, cast off, ditch, jettison, throw overboard 300 *eject*; cast away, abandon, maroon; pension off, put out to grass, invalid out, retire; discharge, give notice to quit, declare redundant, give the heave-ho, ease out, edge out, elbow out, kick o. 300 *dismiss*; lay off; drop, discard 674 *stop using*; withdraw, abandon one's position 753 *resign*; estrange; leak 300 *emit*.

780 Transfer (of property)

N. *transfer*, transmission, consignment, delivery, handover 272 *transference*; settlement; conveyancing; bequeathal; assignment; bequest 781 *gift*; lease, let, rental, hire; buying 793 *sale*; trade, trade-off 791 *barter*; conversion, exchange 151 *interchange*; nationalization, privatization; demutualization, change of hands, changeover 150 *substitution*; devolution, delegation 751 *commission*; succession, inheritance; pawn.

Vb. *assign*, convey; transfer by will; grant, sign away, give a. 781 *give*; let, rent, hire 784 *lease*; sell; negotiate, barter 791 *trade*; change over 150 *substitute*; exchange, convert 151 *interchange*; confer ownership, put in possession, invest with; devolve, delegate, entrust 751 *commission*; give away, marry off 894 *marry*; deliver, transmit, hand over, unload on, pass to, pass the buck 272 *transfer*; pawn 784 *lend*; transfer ownership, nationalize, privatize.

bequeath, will; grant, assign; leave, leave by will, make a bequest, leave a legacy; make a will, make one's last will and testament, put in one's will, add a codicil; leave a fortune.

change hands, be under new management; change places, be transferred, pass, shift; revert to, devolve upon; pass from hand to hand, circulate, go the rounds 314 *circle*.

781 Giving

N. *giving*, bestowal, donation; alms-giving, charity 901 *philanthropy*; liberality; contribution, subscription; prize-giving, presentation, award 962 *reward*; delivery, consignment, conveyance 780 *transfer*; endowment, settlement 777 *dower*; grant, conferment; investment, investiture; bequeathal.

gift, souvenir, memento, keepsake, token; gift token, gift voucher; present, birthday p., Christmas p.; good-luck present, handsel; Christmas box, whip-round, tip, fee, honorarium, baksheesh, gratuity, pourboire, trinkgeld 962 *reward*; token, consideration; bribe, sweetener, douceur, slush fund 612 *inducement*; prize, award, presentation 729 *trophy*; benefit, benefit match, benefit performance; alms, maundy money, dole, charity 901 *philanthropy*; food parcel, free meal; freebie, giveaway; bounty, manna from heaven; largesse, donation, handout; bonus; extras, perks, perquisites, expense

account; grant, allowance, subsidy, aid 703 *subvention*; boon, grace, favour, service, labour of love 597 *voluntary work*; free gift, ex gratia payment; piece of luck, windfall 771 *acquisition*; conscience money 804 *payment*; tribute 809 *tax*; bequest, legacy 780 *transfer*.

offering, dedication, consecration; peace offering, offertory, collection, sacrifice 981 *oblation*; Peter's pence; widow's mite; contribution, subscription, flag day, appeal; stake.

giver, donor, bestower; rewarder, tipper, briber; grantor; presenter, awarder, prize-giver; bequeather; subscriber, contributor; sacrificer 981 *worshipper*; almsgiver, blood donor, kidney d., organ d. 903 *benefactor*; Lady Bountiful, fairy godmother, rich uncle, sugar daddy, Santa Claus, Father Christmas 813 *good giver*; backer, angel.

Adj. *given*, gratuitous, gratis, for nothing, free, freebie, giveaway 812 *uncharged*; concessional.

Vb. *give*, bestow, lend, render; afford, provide; vouchsafe, honour w.; grant, accord 756 *permit*; gift, donate, make a present of; leave 780 *bequeath*; endow; present, award 962 *reward*; confer, bestow upon, invest with; dedicate, consecrate; offer; devote, offer up, sacrifice 981 *offer worship*; make time for; give a present, tip, remember, cross someone's palm with silver; grease the palm 612 *bribe*; bestow alms, give to charity 897 *do good*; give freely, open one's purse, put one's hand in one's pocket, lavish, pour out, shower upon 813 *be liberal*; spare, give away; stand, treat 882 *be hospitable*; give out, dispense, dole out, allot, deal out 783 *apportion*; contribute, subscribe, subsidize, help 703 *aid*; have a whip-round, pass round the hat, launch an appeal; pay one's share or whack, chip in 775 *participate*; part with, fork out, shell o. 804 *pay*; impart 524 *communicate*; pay tribute; yield 621 *relinquish*; hand over, give o., deliver 780 *assign*; commit, entrust 751 *commission*; dispatch 272 *send*.

782 Receiving

N. *receiving*, admittance 299 *reception*; getting 771 *acquisition*; acceptance; inheritance; collection; a receipt, windfall 781 *gift*; toll, tribute, dues, receipts, proceeds, winnings, takings 771 *earnings*; receiving end.

recipient, acceptor, receiver, taker; trustee 754 *consignee*; addressee 588 *correspondent*; buyer 792 *purchaser*; grantee, assignee, licensee, patentee, lessee; legatee, inheritor, heir, successor 776 *beneficiary*; payee, earner, wage-earner; pensioner, old-age p., remittance man 742 *dependant*; winner, prize-w., exhibitioner; one at the receiving end 825 *sufferer*.

receiver, official r., liquidator 798 *treasurer*, payee, collector, debt-c., rent-c., tax-c., publican; income-tax officer, excise o., customs officer; booking clerk.

Vb. *receive*, be given, have from; get 771 *acquire*; collect, take up; gross, net, clear, pocket, be in receipt of, get one's share; accept, take in 299 *admit*; accept from, draw, encash, be paid; have an income, draw a pension; inherit, come into, come in for, be left.

783 Apportionment
N. *apportionment*, assignment, allotment, allocation, earmarking; division, job-sharing, job-splitting, sharing out, parcelling out, divvying up, doing out; shares, distribution, deal; stakeholder economy; dispensing, administration; demarcation, delimitation 236 *limit*; assigned place, seat 27 *degree*.

portion, share, share-out, split; dividend, interim d., final d., divvy, divi; allocation, allotment; lot; proportion, ratio; quota; halves 53 *part*; deal, hand (at cards); modicum, pittance, allowance; ration, iron rations; dose, dosage, measure, dollop, whack, helping, slice, slice of the cake, piece of the action 53 *piece*; rake-off, cut, commission 810 *discount*; stake, ante; task, stint 682 *labour.*

Vb. *apportion*, allot, allocate, earmark; appoint, assign; cast; assign a place, detail, billet; partition, zone; demarcate, delimit 236 *limit*; divide up, subdivide, carve up, split, cut; halve 92 *bisect*; go shares 775 *participate*; share out, divvy up, distribute, spread around; dispense, administer, serve, deal out, dole out, parcel out, dish out 781 *give*; mete out, measure, ration.

Adv. *pro rata*, to each according to his share; proportionately, respectively, each to each; per capita.

784 Lending
N. *lending*, hiring, leasing, farming out; letting, subletting, renting out, lending at interest, on-lending, usury, giving credit 802 *credit*; investment; mortgage, bridging loan; advance, loan; pawnbroking; lease; let, sublet.

pawnshop, pawnbroker's, one's uncle's, pop-shop, hock s.; bank, credit company, building society, International Monetary Fund, IMF, World Bank.

lender, creditor; investor, financier, banker; moneylender, usurer, Shylock; pawnbroker, uncle; mortgagee, lessor, hirer, renter, letter; backer, angel; tallyman; hire-purchase dealer.

Vb. *lend*, loan, on-lend; advance, accommodate, give one a loan 802 *credit*; lend on security, lend on collateral; put up the money, back,

finance; invest, risk one's money, play the stock-market 791 *speculate*.

lease, let, hire out, rent out, farm out; sublet; outsource.

785 Borrowing
N. *borrowing*, touching; request for credit, mortgage 803 *debt*; credit account, credit card, plastic money, plastic; hire purchase, HP, tick, instalment plan, the never-never; pawning; loan, bank loan; forced loan, Morton's fork *or* crutch; infringement, plagiarism, piracy, copying 20 *imitation*; borrowed plumes 542 *deception*.

Vb. *borrow*, cadge from, scrounge from, bum from, mooch from, touch for 761 *request*; mortgage, pawn, pop, hock; provide collateral 767 *give security*; take a loan, exact a forced loan; use a credit card, use plastic money, use plastic; get credit, take on loan, take on credit, take on tick; buy in instalments, buy on hire purchase *or* the never-never 792 *purchase*; ask for credit, apply for a loan, raise a loan, raise the wind; issue debentures; beg, borrow, or steal 771 *acquire*; crib, plagiarize, pirate, infringe 20 *copy*.

786 Taking
N. *taking*, snatching; seizure, capture, rape; taking hold, grasp, apprehension 778 *retention*; taking possession, appropriation, assumption 916 *arrogation*; requisition, earmarking, commandeering, compulsory purchase 771 *acquisition*; exaction, taxation, levy 809 *tax*; taking away, removal 188 *displacement*; stealing; cadging, scrounging, mooching, bumming, touching one for money, abduction, kidnapping, hijacking, piracy; raid; hostage, take, haul, catch, bag, prize, plum 790 *booty*; receipts, takings, winnings, pickings, ill-gotten gains, gleanings 771 *earnings*.

expropriation, dispossession; attachment, foreclosure; eviction 300 *ejection*; takeover, deprivation; hiving off, asset-stripping; disinheritance 780 *transfer*; confiscation; extortion; swindle, rip-off; impounding, sequestration.

rapacity, rapaciousness, avidity, thirst 859 *hunger*; greed, insatiability 816 *avarice*; extortion, blackmail.

taker, appropriator, remover; seizer, snatcher, grabber; raider, pillager, marauder, ransacker, sacker, looter 789 *robber*; kidnapper, hijacker, abductor, press gang; captor, capturer 741 *master*; usurper, extortioner, blackmailer; devourer 168 *destroyer*; bloodsucker, leech, parasite, vampire, harpy, vulture, wolf, shark; beast *or* bird of prey, predator; confiscator, sequestrator 782 *receiver*; expropriator, asset-stripper.

Vb. *take*, accept, be given 782 *receive*; take over, take back; take in, let in 299 *admit*; take up; anticipate 135 *be early*; take hold, fasten on, stick to, clutch, grip, cling 778 *retain*; lay hands upon, seize, snatch, grab, pounce on; snatch at, reach out for, make a long arm; grasp at, clutch at, grab at, make a grab, scramble for, rush f.; capture, rape, storm, take by s. 727 *overmaster*; conquer, captive 745 *subjugate*; catch, overtake, intercept 277 *outstrip*; apprehend, take into custody, make an arrest, run in, nab, nobble, collar, lay by the heels 747 *arrest*; make sure of, fasten, pinion 747 *fetter*; hook, trap, snare, lime 542 *ensnare*; net, land, bag, pocket; gross, have a turnover 771 *acquire*; gather, accumulate, amass, collect 74 *bring together*; cull, pick, pluck; reap, crop, harvest, glean 370 *cultivate*; scrounge, cadge, mooch, bum, ransack 459 *search*; pick up, snap up, snaffle; knock off, help oneself 788 *steal*; pick clean, strip 229 *uncover*; remove; deduct 39 *subtract*; draw off, milk, tap, mine 304 *extract*.

appropriate, take to or for oneself, make one's own, annex; pirate, plagiarize 20 *copy*; take possession, lay claim to, stake one's claim; take over, assume ownership, possess; enter into, come i., succeed 771 *inherit*; instal oneself, seat o. 187 *place oneself*, overrun, occupy, settle, colonize; win, conquer; recover 656 *retrieve*; reclaim 915 *claim*; earmark, commandeer, requisition 737 *demand*; usurp, trespass, squat 916 *be undue*; treat as one's own, make free with; monopolize, hog, engulf, swallow up 299 *absorb*; devour, eat up.

levy, raise, extort, exact, wrest from 304 *extract*; compel to lend 785 *borrow*; exact tribute, extort protection money, raise taxes 809 *tax*; fleece; wring, squeeze dry, squeeze till the pips squeak 735 *oppress*; sequestrate.

take away, remove, shift, unload, disburden 188 *displace*; hive off, relieve of 788 *steal*; escort 89 *accompany*; kidnap, shanghai, pressgang, abduct, take hostage, hijack, carry off; run away w., elope w. 296 *decamp*.

deprive, bereave, orphan, widow; divest, denude, strip 229 *uncover*; unfrock 752 *depose*; dispossess, usurp 916 *disentitle*; oust, elbow out, evict, expel 300 *eject*; confiscate, sequester, foreclose; disinherit, cut out of one's will, cut off with a shilling.

fleece, pluck, skin, shear, clip; strip, denude 229 *uncover*; take to the cleaners, rip off; take one for a ride, swindle, bilk, welsh, con, cheat 542 *deceive*; blackmail, bleed, bleed white, sponge, suck dry; soak, sting; mulct 788 *defraud*; devour, eat out of house and home 301 *eat*; rook, bankrupt, leave one without a penny or cent 801 *impoverish*.

787 Restitution

N. *restitution*, giving back, return, reversion; bringing back, repatriation; reinstatement; rehabilitation 656 *restoration*; ransom, rescue 668 *deliverance*; recuperation, recovery; compensation, repayment, recoupment; refund, reimbursement; indemnity, damages 963 *penalty*; amends, reparation 941 *atonement*.

Vb. *restitute*, make restitution 656 *restore*; return, give back 779 *not retain*; refund, repay, give one one's money back, recoup, reimburse; indemnify, compensate, make it up to; pay compensation, make reparation, make redress, make amends 941 *atone*; repatriate; redeem 668 *deliver*; reinstate, rehabilitate, restore one to favour; recover 656 *retrieve*.

788 Stealing

N. *stealing*, thieving, lifting, robbing etc. vb.; theft, larceny, petty 1.; pilfering, snitching, swiping, nicking, filching, putting one's fingers in the till, pickpocketing, shoplifting, kleptomania; burglary, house-breaking, breaking and entering; safe-breaking, robbery, highway r., robbery with violence, stickup, holdup, bag-snatching, mugging, jumping, smash and grab raid, ram r.; autocrime; poaching, cattle-rustling; rape, abduction, kidnapping, dognapping, hijack, skyjack; body-snatching; cribbing, plagiarism, pirating 20 *imitation*; joyride, auto-theft, twoc 785 *borrowing*; thievery, job, fiddle.

plundering, looting, pillage, sacking ravaging; banditry, outlawry, piracy buccaneering; raiding, foray 712 *attack*

swindling, embezzlement, misappropriation; blackmail, extortion, protection racket; daylight robbery, rip-off moonlighting, tax evasion, black economy, fraud, computer fraud, computer crime, fiddle, swindle, cheating; confidence trick; car clocking.

thievishness, thievery, light-fingeredness, sticky fingers, kleptomania; dishonesty, crookedness 930 *improbity*.

Adj. *thieving*, light-fingered, sticky-fingered; kleptomaniac; larcenous, predatory, raptorial; piratical, buccaneering, raiding, marauding; scrounging, foraging; fraudulent, on the fiddle 930 *dishonest*.

Vb. *steal*, lift, thieve, pilfer, shoplift, help oneself; be light-fingered, be sticky-fingered, pick pockets, have a finger in the till; pick locks, blow a safe; burgle, burglarize, house-break; rob, relieve of; rifle, sack, clean out; swipe, nobble, nick, pinch, pocket, snaffle, snitch, knock off 786 *take*; forage, scrounge; rustle, make off with; abduct, kidnap, shanghai; purloin, filch; walk off with, spirit away; crib, copy, lift, plagiarize, pirate 20 *copy*; smuggle, bootleg, poach, hijack, skyjack.

defraud, embezzle, misappropriate, purloin, fiddle, cook the books, practise creative accounting, obtain money on false pretences; commit a computer crime; con, swindle, cheat, diddle, do out of, bilk 542 *deceive*; rook, gull, dupe; rip off 786 *fleece*.

rob, mug; hold up, stick up; maraud, raid; foray, forage; ransack, rifle; plunder, pillage, loot, sack, despoil, ravage; blackmail, demand money with menaces; extort protection money, screw, squeeze 735 *oppress*.

789 Thief

N. *thief*, den of thieves; crook, Artful Dodger; light fingers, sticky fingers; kleptomaniac, stealer, lifter, filcher, purloiner, pilferer, petty thief, larcenist; sneak thief, shoplifter; pickpocket, cutpurse, bag-snatcher; cattle thief, rustler; burglar, cat b., house-breaker, safe-b., safe-blower, picklock, poacher, bootlegger, smuggler, gun runner, abductor, kidnapper 786 *taker*; hijacker, skyjacker; body-snatcher, resurrectionist; fence, plagiarist, pirate.

robber, forty thieves; brigand, bandit, outlaw, Robin Hood; footpad, highwayman, Dick Turpin, mugger, thug, gangster, racketeer; gunman, hijacker, skyjacker, terrorist; pirate, buccaneer; raider, freebooter, plunderer, pillager, sacker, ravager.

defrauder, embezzler, fiddler, creative accountant, diddler, defaulter, welsher; fraudster, swindler, sharper, cheat, computer criminal, shark, con man 545 *trickster*; forger, counterfeiter.

790 Booty

N. *booty*, spoils; spoils of war, plunder, loot, pillage; find, strike, prize, haul, catch 771 *gain*; pickings, gleanings, stolen goods, swag; contraband; ill-gotten gains, graft, blackmail.

791 Barter

N. *barter*, exchange, fair e., swap 151 *interchange*; payment in kind, traffic, trading, dealing, trade-off, buying and selling; factorage, brokerage, agiotage, jobbing; negotiation, bargaining, hard b., haggling, horse-trading.

trade, trading, exporting 272 *transference*; visible trade, invisible t.; protection, trade restrictions, intervention, interventionism 747 *restriction*; free trade, open market, economic zone, EEC, OPEC 796 *market*; traffic, drug t., white slave t., slave trade; smuggling, black market; retail trade 793 *sale*; capitalism, free enterprise, laissez-faire 744 *scope*; boom and bust 317 *fluctuation*; commerce 622 *business*; private enterprise, private finance initiative, PFI,

privatization, nationalization; private sector, public s.; business venture 672 *undertaking*; speculation 618 *gambling*; transaction, commercial t., deal, business d., bargain, trade-off, negotiation 765 *compact*.

Vb. *trade*, exchange 151 *interchange*; barter, haggle, swap, do a s.; traffic in; vend, buy and sell, export and import; drive a trade, peddle, do business; trade in, deal in, handle; deal in stolen property, fence; turn over 793 *sell*; commercialize, put on a business footing; trade with, do business w., deal w., have dealings w., open an account w.

speculate, venture, risk 618 *gamble*; invest, sink one's capital in, put one's money to work, make one's money work for one; profiteer; deal in the black market, sell under the counter; play the market.

bargain, negotiate, push up, beat down; haggle, argy-bargy 766 *make terms*; bid for, make a takeover bid, propose a merger, act as white knight; raise the bid, outbid 759 *offer*; underbid 483 *underestimate*; stick out for, hold out for, ask for, charge 766 *give terms*; settle for, drive a hard bargain, do a deal, shake hands on, sign on the dotted line 765 *contract*.

792 Purchase

N. *purchase*, buying; buying up, takeover, buyout, green mail, cornering, pre-emption; hire purchase, HP, the never-never, tick 785 *borrowing*; shopping, retail therapy, window s., spending, shopping spree; one-stop shopping, ethical s.; 806 *expenditure*; shopping by post, mail order, teleshopping, tele-ordering, electronic shopping, home s., virtual s., cyber-shopping; consumer demand 627 *requirement*; bid, take-over b. 759 *offer*; buy, purchase on appro, on approval, good buy, bargain, real b.; shopping list, shopping basket, reward card, loyalty c.

purchaser, buyer; consignee; shopper, personal s.; customer, patron, client, clientele, consumer; bidder; bargainer, haggler; share-buyer, bull, stag.

Vb. *purchase*, make a p., complete a p.; buy 771 *acquire*; shop, market, be in the market for, go shopping, purchase by mail order, purchase by tele-ordering, teleshop; get one's money's worth; buy outright, pay cash for, pay on the spot; buy on credit, buy on hire purchase; buy on the never-never, buy on an instalment plan, pay by instalment, buy on tick 785 *borrow*; pay by cheque *or* by Giro, pay by credit card, buy in 632 *store*; buy up; buy out, make a take-over bid, propose a merger, act as a white knight for; buy over, bribe; buy back, redeem; pay for, bear the cost of 804 *defray*; buy oneself in, invest in, sink one's money in 791 *speculate*; rent; bid for 759 *offer*; buy shares.

793 Sale
N. *sale*, selling, putting on sale, putting on the market, marketing, mass m., niche m., telemarketing distribution; disposal 779 *nonretention*; sell-out; clearance sale, stock-taking s., end-of-season s., closing-down s., white s., jumble s., sale of work, charity sale, car boot s., garage s., bazaar; monopoly; auction, sale by a., roup, Dutch auction, good market, market for; boom 730 *prosperity*; salesmanship, sales talk, pitch, sales patter, spiel; hard sell, soft s. 528 *advertisement*; market research 459 *enquiry*; saleability, marketability.

seller, vendor, share-seller, bear; auctioneer; market trader, barrow boy, costermonger, hawker 794 *pedlar*; shopkeeper, dealer 633 *caterer*; wholesaler, retailer 794 *tradespeople*; sales representative, rep, door-to-door salesman, door-stepper; traveller, commercial t., travelling salesman *or* -woman; agent, canvasser, tout; shop assistant, salesman, saleswoman, salesperson; booking clerk, ticket agent; roundsman.

Adj. *salable*, marketable, on sale, for sale; in demand, sought after; on the market, up for sale; bearish, up for grabs; on auction, under the hammer.

Vb. *sell*, make a sale; flog, dispose of; market, put on sale, offer for s., have for s., have on offer, vend; hawk, peddle, push; canvass, tout; put up for sale, auction, auction off, sell by a., bring under the hammer, sell to the highest bidder, knock down to; wholesale; retail, sell under the counter, sell on the black market; turn over one's stock 791 *trade*; sell at a profit 771 *gain*; sell at a loss 772 *lose*; undercut 812 *cheapen*; sell off, remainder; sell up, sell out, wind up 145 *cease*; hold a sale.

be sold, be on sale, come under the hammer 780 *change hands*; sell, have a market, meet a demand, sell well, sell like hot cakes; be a bestseller, be a loss-leader.

794 Merchant
N. *merchant*, guild, chamber of commerce, firm 708 *corporation*; business person, man *or* woman of business; entrepreneur, cyberpreneur, e-preneur, speculator, operator 618 *gambler*; trafficker, fence; importer, exporter; wholesaler; retailer, merchandiser, dealer; middleman, broker, stockbroker; estate agent, house a.; financier, banker 784 *lender*.

tradespeople, tradesman, retailer, middleman, tallyman; shopkeeper 793 *seller*; ironmonger, haberdasher, grocer, greengrocer,

butcher, tobacconist, newsagent 633 *caterer*.

pedlar, seller; hawker, tinker, gipsy, bagman; costermonger, barrow boy; market trader, stallkeeper.

795 Merchandise
N. *merchandise*, line, staple; article, commodity, stock, range 632 *store*; freight, cargo 193 *contents*; wares, goods, consumer durables; perishable goods, dry g., white g., sundries.

796 Market
N. *market*, mart; free trade area. Common Market, EEC, OPEC, free market, economic zone 791 *trade*; black market, black economy, grey e.; grey market; seller's market, buyer's m.; market-place, market cross; street market, flea m., Petticoat Lane; auction room, Christie's, Sotheby's; fair, world f., international f., trade f.; exhibition, exposition, shop window 522 *exhibit*; exchange, corn e., Stock E., bourse; share shop, bucket shop; Wall Street.

emporium, free port; warehouse 632 *storage*; trading centre, trading post; bazaar, arcade, covered market, shopping mall, pedestrian precinct, shopping centre.

shop, retailer's; store, multiple s., department s., chain s.; emporium, bazaar, boutique, bargain basement, supermarket, hypermarket, superstore, cash and carry, warehouse club; trading house; corner shop, convenience store, stall, booth, stand, newsstand, kiosk, barrow, vending machine, slot m.

797 Money
N. *money*, Lsd, pounds, shillings and pence; wealth; lucre, filthy l., root of all evil; currency, unit of currency, decimal c., hard c., soft c.; legal tender; money of account, sterling, pound s.; single currency, europ; precious metal, gold, bullion, gold bar, ingot; silver, ready money, the ready, cash, spot c., hard c., petty c.; change, small c., coppers 33 *small quantity*; pocket money, pin m., allowance; spending money; paltry sum, chickenfeed, peanuts.

shekels, brass, dough, lolly, bread; loot, gravy.

funds, hot money; liquidity, bank account, current a., deposit a., savings a., ISAS, money in the bank, liquid assets; wherewithal, the needful 629 *means*; ready money, the ready, finances, exchequer, cash flow, monies, treasure 633 *provision*; remittance 804 *payment*; capital; reserves, balances; sum of money, amount, figure, sum, round s., lump s.; quid, smacker, oncer, buck; fiver, tenner, pony, monkey, ton, century, grand; mint of money, wads, scads, pile, packet, stacks, heaps, mountains, millions, billions, zillions 32 *great quantity*.

finance, high finance, IMF; financial control, purse strings, almighty dollar; zaitech, cash transaction; money market, Eurodollar m., eurozone, euroland; exchange, stock exchange, Big Bang 796 *market*; exchange rate, bank r., minimum lending r., effective r., sterling effective r.; APR, annual percentage rate; agio, agiotage, snake; floating pound; devaluation, depreciation; strong pound, rallying 654 *improvement*; gold standard; green pound; managed currency, sinking f., inflation; deflation; stagflation; reflation.

coinage, minting, issue; metallic currency, stamped coinage, gold c., silver c., electrum c., copper c., nickel c., billon c., bronze c.; specie, minted coinage, coin, piece, coin of the realm; guinea, sovereign, half s.; pound, quid, nicker; crown, half c., florin, shilling, bob, sixpence, tanner, threepenny bit, penny, bun p., copper, halfpenny, ship h.; farthing; decimal coinage, pound coin, fifty p., twenty p., ten p., five p., two p., one p., half p.; dollar, buck; half dollar, quarter, dime, nickel, jitney, cent; ten-dollar piece, eagle; napoleon, louis d'or; franc, new f.; mark, Deutschmark, guilder, krona, krone, lira, drachma, peseta, escudo, peso, dinar, rupee, rand, yuan, yen, zloty, rouble; obol, talent, shekel, solidus, bezant, ducat, angel, noble, real, pistole, piece of eight; change, small c., groat, bawbee, obolus, centime, sou, pfennig, piastre, kopek, cash 33 *small quantity*; shell money, cowrie, wampum; numismatics, numismatology.

paper money, fiduciary currency; bankroll, wad; note, banknote, treasury note, pound n., five-p. n., ten-p. n., bill, dollar b., greenback, buck, ten-dollar bill; bill of exchange; draft, money order, postal o., cheque, certified c., giro c., traveller's c., Eurocheque, letter of credit; promissory note, note of hand, IOU; standing order, direct debit; scrip, premium bond 767 *security*.

Adj. *monetary*, numismatic; pecuniary, financial, fiscal, budgetary; coined, stamped, minted, issued; fiduciary; gold-based, sterling, solvent 800 *rich*; inflationary, deflationary, floating; devalued, depreciated.

Vb. *mint*, coin, stamp; issue, circulate; forge, counterfeit.

draw money, cash, encash, realize, draw upon, cash a cheque, endorse a c., write a c. 804 *pay*.

798 Treasurer

N. *treasurer*, honorary t.; bursar, purser; cashier, teller, croupier; trustee, steward 754 *consignee*; liquidator 782 *receiver*; bookkeeper 808 *accountant*; banker, financier; keeper of the purse, paymaster, controller, comptroller, Chancellor of the Exchequer, Secretary of the Treasury, Governor of the Bank of England.

799 Treasury

N. *treasury*, exchequer, fisc, public purse; reserves, fund 632 *store*; counting house; bursary; bank, Bank of England, Old Lady of Threadneedle Street; savings bank, Post Office savings b., building society; credit union, coffer, chest 194 *box*; treasure chest, depository 632 *storage*; strongroom, strongbox, safe, safe deposit, cash box, moneybox, piggybank, stocking, mattress; till, cash register, cash desk, slot machine; cash dispenser, automated teller machine, ATM; personal identification number, PIN; box office, gate, turnstile; purse 194 *pocket*; wallet, pocket book, billfold.

800 Wealth

N. *wealth*, lucre, brass 797 *money*; moneymaking, golden touch, Midas t., philosopher's stone; riches, fleshpots 635 *plenty*; luxury 637 *superfluity*; opulence, affluence 730 *prosperity*; ease, comfort, easy street 376 *euphoria*; solvency, credit-worthiness 802 *credit*; substance 3 *substantiality*; independence, competence, self-sufficiency 635 *sufficiency*; high income; gains 771 *gain*; resources, well-lined pockets, capital 629 *means*; liquid assets, bank account, building society a., Post Office savings a.; bottomless purse, goose that lays golden eggs; nest egg 632 *store*; tidy sum, pots of money, pile, heap, mountain, scads, wads, packet, cool million, zillions 32 *great quantity*; fortune; broad acres 777 *property*; bonanza, gold mine; El Dorado, pot of gold, the end of the rainbow, riches of Solomon, king's ransom.

rich person, wealthy p., well-to-do p., man *or* woman of means; baron, tycoon, magnate, moneybags, millionaire, multim., millionairess; Croesus, Midas; moneymaker, fat cat, capitalist, plutocrat, bloated p.; heir, heiress, poor little rich girl 776 *beneficiary*; the haves, the privileged, moneyed class, propertied c., leisured c., the well-to-do, the well-off, the well-heeled, jet set, glitterati 848 *beau monde*; new rich, nouveau riche, self-made man 730 *prosperous person*.

Adj. *rich*, richly endowed, lush, fertile 171 *prolific*; abundant 635 *plentiful*; luxurious, upholstered, plush, ritzy; glittering, glitzy 875 *ostentatious*; wealthy, well-endowed, born in the purple, born with a silver spoon in one's mouth; opulent, affluent 730 *prosperous*; well-off, well-to-do, well-heeled, in easy circumstances, comfortably off, well-paid.

moneyed, propertied, worth a packet, worth millions; made of money, rolling in m., rolling in it, dripping, loaded; stinking rich, filthy r.; rich as Croesus; on easy street, in clover, in funds, in cash, in credit, in the black; well-heeled, flush, in the money; quids in, doing nicely thank you; credit-worthy, solvent.

Vb. *be rich*, have money, have means; be rolling in money, wallow in riches; be in clover, be on easy street, be on velvet, be born in the purple, be born with a silver spoon in one's mouth; be sitting on a goldmine, be raking it in; be flush, be in funds etc. adj.; have money to burn.

afford, have the means, have the wherewithal, be solvent, make both ends meet, keep one's head above water, keep the wolf from the door, keep up with the Joneses 635 *have enough*.

get rich, come into money 771 *inherit*; do all right for oneself 730 *prosper*; make a profit, make money, coin it, rake in the shekels, rake it in, laugh all the way to the bank; make a packet, make a pile, make a bomb, make a fortune, make a mint, make a killing, clean up, feather one's nest, line one's pocket, strike it rich, hit the jackpot, turn up trumps, win the pools, have one's ship come home, find one's Eldorado, find the pot of gold at the end of the rainbow 771 *gain*.

801 Poverty

N. *poverty*, ascetism; financial embarrassment, difficulties, Queer Street 805 *insolvency*; impoverishment, beggary, penury, pennilessness, pauperism, social exclusion, destitution; privation, indigence, neediness, necessity, dire n., need, want, pinch 627 *requirement*; empty larder 636 *scarcity*; wolf at the door, famine 946 *fasting*; empty purse, slender means, straitened circumstances, insufficiency, dire straits, belt-tightening 825 *suffering*; grinding poverty, subsistence level, breadline, poverty line, poverty trap, hand-to-mouth existence; poorness, meagreness, shabbiness, seediness, raggedness; recession, slump, depression 655 *deterioration*; squalor, slum; work-house, poorhouse.

poor person, broken man *or* woman, bankrupt, insolvent 805 *nonpayer*; pauper, indigent, beggar, vagrant, tramp, bum, down-and-out 763 *beggar*; the poor, new poor, the have-nots, the disadvantaged, the underprivileged 869 *lower classes*; Cinderella; poor relation 35 *inferior*.

Adj. *poor*, as poor as a church-mouse; not well-off, badly o., hard up; lowpaid, underprivileged; hard up, impecunious, short of cash, out of pocket, in the red; skint, cleaned out, bust, broke, flat b., stony b., bankrupt, insolvent 805 *nonpaying*; on the breadline, below the poverty line, in the poverty trap, on the dole; impoverished, beggared; deprived, robbed; poverty-

stricken; needy, indigent, in want, in need 627 *necessitous*; homeless; hungry 636 *underfed*; in distress, hard put to it, down at heel, down and out, out at elbow, on one's uppers, on one's beam ends, on the rocks, up against it, not knowing which way to turn 700 *in difficulties*; unable to make both ends meet, unable to pay one's way, unable to keep the wolf from the door; unprovided for, penniless, destitute; down to one's last penny, without a bean, without a cent, without a sou.

Vb. *be poor*, live on a pittance, eke out a livelihood, scratch a living, live from hand to mouth; feel the pinch, fall on hard times, be in dire straits, be on one's uppers, be on the breadline, be below the poverty line, be caught in the poverty trap, have to watch the pennies; sing for one's supper; starve 859 *be hungry*; want, lack 627 *require*; not have a penny, not have two halfpennies to rub together; have no prospects; go broke 805 *not pay*; lose one's money, come down in the world 655 *deteriorate*; go on the dole, claim supplementary benefit.

impoverish, reduce to poverty, leave destitute, beggar, ruin 165 *destroy*; rob, strip 786 *fleece*; disinherit, cut off without a penny 786 *deprive*.

802 Credit

N. *credit*, repute, reputation 866 *prestige*; credit-worthiness, white information; borrowing capacity, tick; letter of credit, credit card, charge card, plastic money, plastic, phonecard, credit note, the black; APR, annual percentage rate (of charge); credits, balances, credit balance 807 *receipt*; unpaid bill, account, budget a., score, tally, bill 808 *accounts*; trading deficit, floating debt 803 *debt*; loan, mortgage.

Vb. *credit*, give *or* furnish c., extend c.; credit one's account; grant, vote; charge to one's account, charge to one's budget a.; sell on tick, take credit, open an account, run up an account, run up a bill 785 *borrow*.

803 Debt

N. *debt*, indebtedness 785 *borrowing*; liability, obligation, commitment; mortgage 767 *security*; debit, charge; debts, bills, hire-purchase debt; national debt, floating d.; debt of honour, unsecured debt 764 *promise*; gearing, leverage; bad debt, write-off 772 *loss*; tally, account; deficit, negative equity, overdraft 307 *shortfall*; insolvency, frozen assets, black information 805 *nonpayment*; deferred payment 802 *credit*; arrears, back pay; foreclosure; debt counselling.

interest, simple i., compound i., usury, pound of flesh; premium, rate of interest, minimum lending rate, discount rate, bank rate.

Vb. *be in debt*, owe, owe money; be debited

with; get credit, overdraw (one's account); get on tick, buy on hire purchase *or* the never-never 785 *borrow*; use a credit card, use a charge card, use plastic money, use plastic, keep an account with, have charged to one's account; charge to one's budget a., run up an a., run into debt; be in the red, be overdrawn; leave one's bills unpaid, bilk, welsh.

804 Payment

N. *payment*, bearing the cost; defraying the cost, paying off, satisfaction, liquidation, clearance, settlement, settlement on account; receipt; cash payment, down p., ready money 797 *money*; EFTPOS, electronic funds transfer at point of sale, Switch card, smart c., swipe c., credit c., plastic; earnest money, deposit; instalment, standing order, direct debit; deferred payment, hire purchase 785 *borrowing*; subscription, tribute 809 *tax*; contribution, whip-round, appeal, collection 781 *offering*; compensation, indemnity 787 *restitution*; remittance 806 *expenditure*.

pay, payout, payoff, pay packet, pay cheque, take-home pay, pay day, wages, salary 771 *earnings*; grant, subsidy 703 *subvention*; salary, pension, annuity, remuneration, emolument, fee, honorarium, bribe 962 *reward*; cut, commission 810 *discount*; contribution, subscription, collection, tribute 809 *tax*; damages, indemnity 963 *penalty*; back pay, compensation, redundancy pay, severance pay, golden handshake, ex gratia payment.

Vb. *pay*, disburse 806 *expend*; contribute 781 *give*; negotiate a trade-off, barter 791 *trade*; pay out, shell o., fork o., dole out, dish out, stump up, cough up; come across, do the needful, put one's hand in one's pocket, open one's wallet; pay a high price, pay an exorbitant price, pay through the nose; pay back, repay, reimburse, compensate 787 *restitute*; grease the palm, cross one's palm with silver 612 *bribe*; pay wages, remunerate, tip 962 *reward*; pay in advance, put money up front, ante up, pay on sight, pay on delivery, C.O.D., pay on demand; pay by cheque *or* by giro; pay by banker's order, pay by standing o., pay by direct debit; pay on the nail, pay cash; honour (a bill), pay up, meet, discharge, get a receipt; settle an account, square accounts with 808 *account*; settle accounts with, settle a score.

defray, pay for, bear the cost, put up funds; pay one's way, pay one's share; foot the bill, pick up the tab, pay the piper; stand a round, treat 781 *give*; go Dutch 775 *participate*.

805 Nonpayment

N. *nonpayment*, default; deduction 963 *penalty*; moratorium, embargo, freeze; refusal to pay,

repudiation 760 *refusal*; tax avoidance, tax evasion, creative accounting, black economy 620 *avoidance*; deferred payment, hire purchase 785 *borrowing*; dishonoured cheque, dud c., bouncing c.

insolvency, inability to pay, failure to meet one's obligations; crash; failure of credit, cash-flow crisis; bankruptcy; nothing in the kitty, overdraft 636 *insufficiency*.

nonpayer, defaulter, embezzler, tax dodger 789 *defrauder*; bilker, welsher, bankrupt.

Adj. *nonpaying*, in arrears; insolvent, bankrupt; up to one's ears in debt; ruined 801 *poor*.

Vb. *not pay*, default; fall into arrears, get behindhand; withhold p., freeze; refuse payment; fiddle one's income tax, practise tax evasion, moonlight, be part of the black economy 930 *be dishonest*; divert, sequester 786 *deprive*; have one's cheque bounce, dishonour; have a cashflow crisis, become insolvent, go bankrupt, go to the wall; sink, fail, go bust, crash, wind up, go into liquidation; welsh, bilk 542 *deceive*, be unable to pay 801 *be poor*.

806 Expenditure

N. *expenditure*, spending, disbursement 804 *payment*; cost of living; outgoings, overheads, costs, expenses, out-of-pocket e., extras, expense account; expense, outlay, investment ethical i., spending spree 815 *prodigality*.

Vb. *expend*, spend; buy 792 *purchase*; lay out, invest, sink money; be out of pocket, incur expenses; afford, stand, bear the cost, defray the c., bankroll, meet charges, disburse, pay out 804 *pay*; draw on one's savings; open one's wallet, put one's hand in one's pocket; donate 781 *give*; spare no expense, go on a spree, do one proud, be lavish 813 *be liberal*; fling money around, splash out, blow, blow one's cash 815 *be prodigal*; use up, consume, get through 634 *waste*.

807 Receipt

N. *receipt*, voucher, counterfoil; credits, revenue, royalty, rents, rates, dues; customs, taxes 809 *tax*; turnover, takings, proceeds, returns, receipts, gross r., net r., box-office r., gate money; income, private i., privy purse; emolument, regular income, pay, half p., salary, wages 771 *earnings*; remuneration 962 *reward*; pension, annuity; allowance, personal a.; pin money, pocket money, spending m.; alimony, aliment, palimony, maintenance; bursary, scholarship 771 *acquisition*; interest, return, rake-off, cut; winnings, profits, gross p., net p., capital gain 771 *gain*; bonus, premium 40 *extra*; legacy, inheritance 777 *dower*.

Vb. see 771 *acquire*, 782 *receive*, 786 *take*.

808 Accounts

N. *accounts*, accountancy, accounting; book-keeping, entry; audit; account, profit and loss a., balance sheet, debit and credit; budgeting, budget, zero-based budgeting; current account, cash a., deposit a., savings a., expense a.; account rendered, statement, bill, invoice 87 *list*; account settled 804 *payment*; reckoning, computation, score, tally, facts and figures 86 *numeration*.

accountant, chartered a., bookkeeper; cashier 798 *treasurer*; auditor; actuary, statistician.

Adj. *accounting*, actuarial, computing, inventorial, budgetary.

Vb. *account*, keep the books, keep accounts; make up an account, budget, prepare a b.; cost, value, write up, write down 480 *estimate*; enter, carry over, debit, credit 548 *register*; prepare a cashflow forecast, prepare a balance sheet, balance accounts; settle accounts, square a., finalize a., wind up a.; prepare a statement, present an account, charge, bill, invoice; practise creative accounting, cook the accounts *or* the books, falsify the a., fiddle, doctor 788 *defraud*; audit, go through the books; take stock.

809 Price

N. *price*, selling p., market p., retail p., wholesale p., discount p., list p.; rate, going r., rate for the job, fee for service; piece rate, flat r.; price control, fixed price 747 *restraint*; value, face v.; worth, what it will fetch; premium, scarcity value; price list, tariff; quoted price, quotation; amount, figure, sum asked for; ransom, fine 963 *penalty*; demand, dues, charge; surcharge, supplement 40 *extra*; rip-off; fare, flat f., hire, rental, rent, ground r.; fee, entrance *or* admission fee; refresher, commission, cut, rake-off; charges, freightage, wharfage; postage; cover charge, service c., corkage.

cost, purchase p.; damage, costs, expenses 806 *expenditure*; running costs, overheads; wage bill, salary b.; legal costs, damages 963 *penalty*; cost of living.

tax, taxes, dues; taxation self-assessment, council tax; Inland Revenue, tax return, tax form, tax demand 737 *demand*; rating, assessment, rateable value; rates, community charge *or* tax, poll tax, capitation tax; water rate; tartan tax; green taxes; stealth tax; levy, toll, duty; imposition; charge; exaction, forced loan, Morton's fork *or* crutch; punitive tax 963 *penalty*; tribute, danegeld, blackmail, protection money, ransom 804 *payment*; ecclesiastical tax, Peter's pence, tithe; national insurance; estate duty, death duty, inheritance tax; direct taxation, income tax, PAYE, surtax, supertax, company tax, corporation t.; capital levy, capital gains tax 786 *expropriation*; tax rebate, tax concession; tax credit, tax break, windfall tax; indirect taxation, excise, customs, tariff; local tax, purchase tax, sales t., value-added tax, VAT, zero-rated goods.

Vb. *price*, cost, assess, value, rate 480 *estimate*; put a price on; place a value on, fix a price for; raise a price, lower a p.; fix the p.; ask a p., charge 737 *demand*.

cost, be worth, fetch, bring in; amount to, come to, mount up to; be priced at, be valued at; bear a price; sell for, go f., set one back, change hands for, realize.

tax, impose a tax; fix a tariff, levy a rate, assess for tax, value; subject to duty, raise taxes, collect t., levy t.

810 Discount

N. *discount*, something off, reduction, rebate, cut; concession, special price; cut price, cut rate, special offer, loss leader 612 *incentive*; bargain price, knock-down p., bargain sale 812 *cheapness*; one's cut, commission, rake-off.

Vb. *discount*, deduct 39 *subtract*; allow a margin, reduce, depreciate, give a rebate; offer a discount; mark down, take off, cut, slash 812 *cheapen*; take a discount, take one's cut, take one's percentage.

811 Dearness

N. *dearness*, costliness, expensiveness; value, pricelessness; scarcity value, rarity; exorbitance, extortion, rack rents, rip-off; overcharge, daylight robbery; bad bargain, high price, fancy p.; cost, high c., pretty penny; ruinous charge; rising costs, sellers' market, bull m., soaring prices; inflation.

Adj. *dear*, high-priced, pricy, expensive, exclusive, ritzy, upmarket; costly, multimillion; extravagant, dearly-bought; dear at the price, overpriced, overpaid; exorbitant, excessive, extortionate; steep, stiff, sky-high; beyond one's means, prohibitive; dear at any price 641 *useless*; rising in price, soaring, mounting, going through the ceiling, inflationary; bullish.

of value, of worth 644 *valuable*; priceless, beyond price, invaluable 640 *useful*; inestimable, worth a king's ransom, worth its weight in gold, worth a fortune; precious, rare, scarce, like gold dust 140 *infrequent*; at a premium, not to be had for love or money.

Vb. *be dear*, cost a lot, cost a packet, cost a pretty penny, be high-priced, hurt one's pocket, make a hole in one's p.; rise in price, harden; go up, appreciate, escalate, soar, go through the ceiling; be out of one's price range, price itself out of the market; prove expensive, cost one dear, cost a fortune, cost the earth.

overcharge, overprice, sell dear, ask too much; profiteer, soak, sting, bleed, skin, extort, charge rack rents, rip off, do, short-change, hold to ransom 786 *fleece*; put up prices, inflate p., mark up; bull, raise the price, raise the bid.

pay too much, pay through the nose, be stung, be ripped off, be had, be done; pay dear, buy a white elephant; achieve a Pyrrhic victory; ruin oneself.

812 Cheapness

N. *cheapness*, inexpensiveness, affordability; good value, value for money, snip, steal, bargain, sale goods, seconds, rejects; low price; cheap rate, off-peak r., off-season r., concessional r., excursion fare, railcard 810 *discount*; reduced price, knock-down p., cut p., bargain p., budget p., competitive p., sale p., giveaway p., rockbottom p., loss leader; peppercorn rent, easy terms; buyers' market, sluggish m.; Dutch auction; falling prices, bearishness; depreciation, fall, slump; deflation; glut, drug on the market 635 *plenty*.

no charge, nominal c. 781 *gift*; gratuitousness, labour of love 597 *voluntary work*; free trade, free port; free entry, free admission, free seats, free pass, free ticket, freebie, complimentary ticket; free quarters, grace and favour; free board, free service, free delivery; everything for nothing.

Adj. *cheap*, inexpensive, reasonable; affordable, within one's means, easy on the pocket; low-budget; substandard; economical, economy, economy size; not dear, worth the money; low-priced, cheap at the price; dirt-cheap, going cheap, going for a song, for peanuts; bargain-rate, bargain-basement, downmarket, cut-price, concessional, sale-price, reduced, r. to clear; marked down, half-price; tourist-class, off-season; two-a-penny; cheapjack, jerry-built; cheapening, bearish, falling; underpaid, underpriced.

uncharged, gratuitous, complimentary, courtesy; gratis, for nothing, for love, for kicks, for the asking; costing nothing, free, scot-f., free of charge, for free, giveaway; zero-rated, untaxed, tax-free, rent-f., post-f.; given away, as a gift 781 *given*; free, gratis and for nothing.

Vb. *be cheap*, – inexpensive etc. adj.; cost little, be economical, be within anyone's reach, be easy on the pocket; be cheap at the price; be bought for a song, go dirt-cheap; cost nothing, be free, be had for the asking; cheapen, get cheaper, fall in price, depreciate.

cheapen, lower the price, reduce the p.; keep cheap, lower one's charges, trim one's prices, mark down, cut, slash; undercharge, let go for a song, give away 781 *give*; beat down, haggle, undercut, undersell.

Adv. *cheaply*, on the cheap; at cost price, at wholesale prices, at a discount, for a song.

813 Liberality

N. *liberality*, bountifulness, munificence, generosity 931 *disinterestedness*; open-handedness, open hand, open purse, hospitality, open house 882 *sociability*; free hand, blank cheque, carte blanche 744 *scope*; lavishness 815 *prodigality*; bounty, largesse 781 *gift*; charity.

good giver, generous g.; donor, blood d., organ d., kidney d.; good tipper; fairy godmother, Lady Bountiful, Father Christmas, Santa Claus, sugar daddy, rich uncle 903 *benefactor*.

Adj. *liberal*, free-spending, open-handed, lavish 815 *prodigal*; bountiful, charitable 897 *benevolent*; hospitable 882 *sociable*; handsome, generous, munificent, slap-up; lordly, princely, royal, right royal; unstinting, unsparing; in liberal quantities, abundant, ample, overwhelming, bounteous, profuse, full, plenteous, overflowing 637 *redundant*.

Vb. *be liberal*, – generous etc. adj.; lavish, shower largesse, shower upon 781 *give*; put one's hand in one's pocket, open one's wallet; give generously, give one's last penny, give the shirt off one's back; pay well, tip w.; keep open house 882 *be hospitable*; do one proud, spare no expense; give carte blanche, give a blank cheque 744 *give scope*; spend freely, not ask for the change, throw money about like water, throw one's money around 815 *be prodigal*.

814 Economy

N. *economy*, thrift, thriftiness, frugality; prudence, care, carefulness; husbandry, good housekeeping, sound stewardship, good management, terotechnology; credit squeeze 747 *restriction*; economy drive, economy measures; time-saving, labour-s., time and motion study, management s.; husbanding of resources, economizing, saving, sparing, pinching, cheese-paring; retrenchment, economies, cuts, cutbacks; savings 632 *store*; conservation, energy-saving.

Adj. *economical*, time-saving, labour-s., energy-s., money-s., cost-cutting; money-conscious, counting every penny 816 *parsimonious*; thrifty, careful, prudent, canny, frugal, cheese-paring, saving, sparing; meagre, Spartan.

Vb. *economize*, be economical, – sparing etc. adj.; husband one's resources, keep costs down, waste nothing, recycle, reuse; keep within one's budget, cut one's coat according to one's cloth, make both ends meet; cut costs, trim expenditure, cut back, make economies, retrench, tighten one's belt; pinch, scrape, look after the pennies 816 *be parsimonious*; save 632 *store*; make one's money work for one.

815 Prodigality

N. *prodigality*, lavishness, profusion, profuseness 637 *redundance*; extravagance; wastefulness, profligacy, dissipation, squandering, spending spree, splurge 634 *waste*; improvidence; misuse of funds 675 *misuse*; money burning a hole in one's pocket.

prodigal, prodigal son, big spender; wastrel, profligate, spendthrift, spendaholic, squanderer.

Adj. *prodigal*, lavish 813 *liberal*; profuse, extravagant, wasteful, squandering, profligate; uneconomic, uneconomical, thriftless, spendthrift, improvident, reckless, dissipated.

Vb. *be prodigal*, blow one's money, blue one's m.; overspend, pour out money, splash money around, throw one's money around, flash pound notes; splurge, go on a spending spree, spend money like water; burn one's money, run through one's savings, exhaust one's resources, spend up to the hilt, splurge out, lash out, blow everything, waste one's inheritance, squander 634 *waste*; burn the candle at both ends, fritter away, throw a., dissipate, scatter to the winds, pour down the drain; not count the cost, have no money sense, think money grows on trees; misspend, throw good money after bad; have no thought for the morrow, overdraw; eat up one's capital; put nothing by, have no nest-egg, have nothing to fall back on, keep nothing for a rainy day.

Int. hang the expense! a short life and a merry one! easy come easy go! you can't take it with you!

816 Parsimony

N. *parsimony*, parsimoniousness; false economy; cheese-paring, scrimping, pinching, scraping, penny-pinching; tightfistedness, niggardliness, meanness, minginess, stinginess, miserliness; uncharitableness; moths in one's wallet 932 *selfishness*.

avarice, cupidity, acquisitiveness, covetousness, green-eyed monster, possessiveness; money-grubbing, itching palm; rapacity, avidity, greed 859 *desire*; mercenariness.

niggard, skinflint, penny pincher, cheeseparer, tightwad, meanie; miser, money-grubber, cadger; hoarder, magpie; Scrooge.

Adj. *parsimonious*, careful 814 *economical*; money-conscious, pennywise, miserly, mean, mingy, stingy, near, close, tight; tight-fisted, close-f. 778 *retentive*; grudging, cheese-paring, ungenerous, uncharitable; sparing, pinching, scraping, scrimping.

avaricious, grasping, monopolistic 932 *selfish*; possessive, acquisitive 771 *acquiring*; hoarding; penny-pinching; miserly; money-grubbing, money-mad, covetous 859 *greedy*; rapacious; mercenary,

Vb. *be parsimonious*, – niggardly etc. adj.; begrudge; stint, skimp; scrape, scrimp, pinch 814 *economize*; fleece; be penny-wise, spoil the ship for a ha'porth of tar; starve oneself, live on a shoestring, live like a pauper; grudge every farthing, haggle 791 *bargain*; sit on, keep for oneself 932 *be selfish*.

Emotion, religion and morality

SECTION ONE

General

817 Affections

N. *affections*, qualities, instincts; passions, feelings, inner f., emotions; nature, disposition 5 *character*; spirit, temper, mettle 5 *temperament*; cast of mind, trait 7 *state*; personality, psychology, psyche, mentality, outlook, inherited characteristics 5 *heredity*; being, innermost b., breast, bosom, heart, soul, core, inmost soul, inner man, cockles of the heart, heart of hearts 5 *essential part*, 447 *spirit*; animus, attitude, frame of mind, state of m., vein, strain, humour, mood; predilection, predisposition, inclinations, turn, bent, bias 179 *tendency*; passion, ruling p.; prejudice; heartstrings 818 *feeling*.

Adj. *with affections*, affected, characterized, formed, moulded, shaped, cast, tempered, framed; imbued with, permeated w., devoured w.; obsessed w., hung up about, ingrained, inborn, inbred, congenital 5 *genetic*; deep-rooted, deep-set, emotional, demonstrative 818 *feeling*.

818 Feeling

N. *feeling*, experience, emotional life, sensation, sense of 374 *sense*; emotion, sentiment; sincerity 540 *veracity*; impulse 609 *spontaneity*; intuition, instinct; responsiveness, response, reaction, fellow feeling, sympathy, involvement, personal i. 880 *friendliness*; vibrations, vibes, bad v., good v.; empathy, appreciation, understanding 490 *knowledge*; impression, deep feeling, deep sense of 819 *moral sensibility*; religious feeling, piety; finer feelings 897 *benevolence*; tender feelings 887 *love*; hard feelings 891 *resentment*; thrill, kick 318 *spasm*; shock, turn 508 *lack of expectation*; pathos 825 *suffering*; catharsis, abreaction; animus, emotionalism 822 *excitability*; sentimentality, romanticism; show of feeling, demonstration, demonstrativeness; expression, facial e., play of features 547 *gesture*; blush, reddening, going pink, flush, hectic f., suffusion; tingling, goose-flesh, creeps, tremor, trembling, nervous tension, quiver, flutter, flurry, palpitation, pulsation, heaving, panting, throbbing 318 *agitation*; ferment 318 *commotion*; lump in one's throat, tears in one's eyes; stoicism, endurance, stiff upper lip 823 *patience*.

warm feeling, glow; cordiality, effusiveness, heartiness; hot head, impatience; unction, earnestness 834 *seriousness*; eagerness, keenness, fervour, ardour, vehemence, enthusiasm, dash, fire 174 *vigorousness*; vigour, zeal 678 *activity*; fanaticism, mania 481 *prejudice*; emotion, passion, ecstasy, inspiration, hwyl, transports of delight 822 *excitable state*.

Adj. *feeling*, sensory 374 *sentient*; spirited, vivacious, lively 819 *sensitive*; sensuous 944 *sensual*; intuitive, sensitive, vibrant, responsive; involved, sympathetic, empathetic; tender-hearted 819 *impressible*; emotional, passionate red-blooded, full of feeling, touchy-feely; unctuous, soulful; intense, tense 821 *excited*; cordial, hearty; gushing, effusive; sentimental, romantic; mawkish, maudlin, schmaltzy, soppy; thrilling, tingling, throbbing.

impressed, affected, influenced; stirred, aroused, moved, touched 821 *excited*; struck, awed, awestruck, over-whelmed, struck all of a heap; imbued with, aflame w., consumed w., devoured by, inspired by; rapt, enraptured, enthralled, ecstatic; lyrical, raving 822 *excitable*.

fervent, fervid, passionate, red-blooded, ardent, tense, intense; eager, breathless, panting, throbbing, pulsating, palpitating; impassioned, vehement, earnest, zealous; enthusiastic, exuberant, happy-clappy, bubbling, bubbly; hot-headed, warm-blooded, impetuous, impatient 822 *excitable*; warm, fiery, glowing, burning, red-hot, flaming, white-hot, boiling 379 *hot*; frenzied; strong, uncontrollable, overwhelming, furious 176 *violent*.

Vb. *feel*, sense, receive an impression, get the

feeling, have a funny feeling, feel in one's bones, have a hunch; entertain feelings, have f., cherish f., harbour f., feel deeply, take to heart 819 *be sensitive*; know the feeling, experience, live, live through, go t., pass t., taste; bear, endure, undergo, smart under 825 *suffer*; sympathize, empathize, share 775 *participate*; respond, react, tingle, warm to, fire, kindle, catch.

show feeling, show signs of emotion; be demonstrative, not hide one's feelings 522 *manifest*; enthuse, go into ecstasies, go into transports of delight 824 *be pleased*; fly into a passion, fly off the handle 891 *get angry*; change colour, colour up; go purple 428 *blacken*; blench, turn pale, go white, look ashen 427 *whiten*; colour, blush, flush, go pink, turn red, turn crimson, go red in the face 431 *redden*; quiver, tremble, shudder, wince; shake, quake 318 *be agitated*; tingle, thrill, vibrate, throb, pulsate, beat faster 317 *oscillate*; palpitate, pant, heave, draw a deep breath 352 *breathe*; reel, lurch, stagger; stutter 580 *stammer*.

819 Sensibility

N. *moral sensibility*, sensitivity, sensitiveness, soul; over-sensitivity, touchiness, prickliness, irritability 892 *irascibility*; thin skin, soft spot, Achilles' heel; sore point, where the shoe pinches 891 *resentment*; susceptibility; finer feelings, sentiments; sentimentality, mawkishness; tenderness, affection 887 *love*; spirit, spiritedness, vivacity, vivaciousness, liveliness, verve 571 *vigour*; emotionalism, over-emotionalism, ebullience, effervescence 822 *excitability*; fastidiousness, finickiness, fikiness, aestheticism 463 *discrimination*; temperament, mood, changeability 152 *changeableness*.

Adj. *impressible*, malleable, plastic, putty-like 327 *soft*; sensible, aware, conscious of, mindful of, awake to, alive to, responsive 374 *sentient*; impressed with, touched, moved, moved to tears, touched to the quick 818 *impressed*; impressionable 822 *excitable*; susceptible; romantic, sentimental; mawkish, maudlin, schmaltzy, soppy, wet, sentimentalizing, gushing; emotional; tender-hearted, soft-h., compassionate 905 *pitying*.

sensitive, sensitized; tingling, sore, raw, tender 374 *sentient*; aesthetic, fastidious 463 *discriminating*; oversensitive, hypersensitive, with one's heart on one's sleeve 822 *excitable*; touchy, irritable, thin-skinned.

lively, vital, vivacious, animated, fun-loving; irrepressible, ebullient, effervescent, bubbly; spirited, high-s.; alert, on one's toes 455 *attentive*; expressive, racy 571 *forceful*.

Vb. *be sensitive*, – sentimental etc. adj.; be

tender-hearted, have a soft heart, take it to heart, weep for, break one's heart for 905 *pity*; tingle 318 *be agitated*.

820 Insensibility

N. *moral insensibility*, insensitiveness; numbness, stupor 375 *insensibility*; inertia 175 *inertness*; lethargy 679 *inactivity*; stagnation, vegetation 266 *quiescence*; woodenness, blockishness, obtuseness, stupidity, dullness; slowness, delayed reaction 456 *inattention*; uninterest 454 *incuriosity*; nonchalance, insouciance, unconcern, lack of care, detachment, apathy 860 *indifference*; phlegm, stolidness, calmness, steadiness, coolness, sangfroid 823 *inexcitability*; aloofness, impassivity; repression, stoicism, stiff upper lip 823 *patience*; inscrutability, poker face, deadpan expression 834 *seriousness*; insensitivity, coarseness, Philistinism 699 *artlessness*; thick skin, rhinoceros hide, elephant h.; frigidity; dourness; unsentimentality, cynicism; callousness 326 *hardness*; lack of feeling, dry eyes, no heart, heart of stone, brutishness, brutality 898 *inhumanity*.

unfeeling person, iceberg, icicle, cold fish; stoic, ascetic; vegetable, stone, block.

Adj. *impassive*, unconscious 375 *insensible*; unsusceptible, insensitive, unimaginative, uninspired; unresponsive, unimpressionable; phlegmatic, stolid, vegetable-like; wooden, blockish; bovine; dull, slow, slow-witted 499 *unintelligent*; unemotional, passionless; proof against, stoical, with stiff upper lip, ascetic, controlled, undemonstrative; aloof, distant, detached 860 *indifferent*; unaffected, calm 266 *tranquil*; steady, unruffled, unshaken, unshockable; imperturbable, without a nerve in one's body; cool; inscrutable, blank, expressionless, deadpan, poker-faced; unseeing 439 *blind*; unhearing 416 *deaf*; unsentimental, cynical; impersonal, dispassionate, reserved, unforthcoming, stony, frigid, frozen, icy, cold; unfeeling, heartless, soulless, inhuman; fancy-free, heart-whole; undemonstrative.

apathetic, unenthusiastic, unambitious; unimpassioned, uninspired, unexcited, unmoved; half-hearted, luke-warm, Laodicean; uninterested 454 *incurious*; insouciant, neglectful 458 *negligent*; spiritless, lackadaisical, couldn't care less; stagnant, bovine, cow-like 266 *quiescent*; sluggish, supine 679 *inactive*; passive 175 *inert*.

thick-skinned, impenetrable, impervious, impermeable; blind to, deaf to, dead to, closed to; obtuse, unimaginative, insensitive, uninspired; callous, insensate, tough, hard, case-hardened, hard-bitten, hard-boiled, inured 669 *matured*; shameless, brazen.

Vb. *be insensitive*, – impassive etc. adj.; have

no feelings; miss the point of, be blind to 439 *be blind*; lack animation, lack spirit; steel oneself, harden one's heart against, be pitiless; feel indifference; feel no emotion, have no finer feelings, be a Philistine; show no regard for 922 *despise*; take no interest 454 *be incurious*; ignore 458 *disregard*; keep a stiff upper lip 942 *be temperate*; stagnate, vegetate 679 *be inactive*; not turn a hair, not bat an eyelid 599 *be resolute*.

821 Excitation

N. *excitation*, rousing, arousal, stirring up, waking up, working up, whipping up; igniting, galvanization, electrification 174 *stimulation*; inspiration, muse, exhilaration, intoxication, headiness; evocation, calling forth; encouragement, animation, incitement, invitation, appeal 612 *inducement*; provocation, irritation; impact 178 *influence*; enchantment 983 *sorcery*; rapture 824 *joy*; sentiment, sob-stuff, pathos; sensationalism; excitement, tension 160 *energy*; perturbation, effervescence, ebullience 318 *agitation*; shock, thrill, kicks 318 *spasm*; ferment, tizzy, flurry, furore 318 *commotion*; fever pitch, orgasm 503 *frenzy*; climax 137 *crisis*, passion, emotion, enthusiasm 818 *feeling*; fuss, hassle, drama 822 *excitable state*; temper, fury, rage 891 *anger*; amazement 864 *wonder*; awe 854 *fear*.

excitant, stimulator, agent provocateur, rabble-rouser, tub-thumper 738 *agitator*; sensationalist, sob sister, muck-raker, chequebook journalist; headline, banner h. 528 *publicity*; fillip, ginger, tonic, pick-me-up 174 *stimulant*; upper, pep pill 949 *drug-taking*; sting, prick, goad, spur, whip, lash, stick, carrot and stick 612 *incentive*; fan; irritant, gadfly.

Adj. *excited*, activated, stimulated, stung etc. vb.; busy, astir, bustling, rushing 678 *active*; ebullient, effervescent, boiling, seething 355 *bubbly*; tense, wrought up, uptight, strung up, keyed up, wound up; feverish; frantic 503 *frenzied*; flushed 379 *hot*; violent 176 *furious*; hot under the collar, hot and bothered; seeing red, wild, mad, livid, fuming, foaming at the mouth, frothing, roaring, raging 891 *angry*; avid, eager, itching, agog, watering at the mouth; tingling 818 *feeling*; flurried, atwitter, all of a flutter, all of a doodah; restless, restive, overexcited, overwrought, distraught, distracted, distrait(e); freaked out, on a high, on a trip, on an ego-trip; beside oneself, hysterical, out of control, uncontrollable, running amok, carried away; turned on, hyped up; crazy about 887 *enamoured*; possessed, impassioned, enthusiastic.

exciting, stimulating, intoxicating, heady, exhilarating, sexy, kicking, mad; provocative, teasing, piquant, tantalizing; spicy, appetizing;

alluring; evocative, emotive, suggestive; cliff-hanging, hair-raising, spine-chilling; thrilling, agitating; moving, affecting, inspiring; rousing, stirring; sensational, dramatic, melodramatic, mind-boggling; gripping.

impressive, imposing, grand, stately; dignified, august, lofty, majestic, regal, royal, kingly, queenly 868 *noble*; awe-inspiring, overwhelming, overpowering; picturesque, scenic; cool, striking, arresting, dramatic; telling, forceful 178 *influential*.

Vb. *excite*, affect, infect 178 *influence*; cheer; touch, move; touch the heart-strings, strike a chord; quicken the pulse, startle, electrify, galvanize; raise to fever pitch 381 *heat*; inflame, set on fire, light the touchpaper 381 *burn*; sting, goad, pique, irritate 891 *enrage*; tease 827 *torment*; cut to the quick; work up, whip up 612 *incite*; enthuse; stir, rouse, arouse, wake, awaken, kindle, turn on (**see** *animate*); touch off, evoke, elicit, summon up, call forth; thrill, exhilarate, intoxicate; send into ecstasies 826 *delight*.

animate, enliven, breathe life into, quicken 360 *vitalize*; revive, resuscitate; inspire; encourage, hearten, buoy up 855 *give courage*; give an edge, put teeth into, whet 256 *sharpen*; urge, nag, egg on, spur, goad, lash 277 *accelerate*; jolt, jog, shake up; buck up, pep up, give a fillip to, stimulate, ginger 174 *invigorate*; cherish, foster, foment 162 *strengthen*; fuel, intensify, fan the flame, blow on the coals, add fuel to the fire, stir the embers.

impress, sink in, leave an impression; project *or* present an image; interest, hold, grip, absorb; intrigue, rouse curiosity, make one sit up; claim attention 455 *attract notice*; affect 178 *influence*; let sink in, bring home to, drive home 532 *emphasize*; penetrate, pierce 516 *be intelligible*; arrest, shake, amaze, astound, stagger 508 *surprise*; stupefy; dazzle; take one's breath away, overwhelm, overpower; upset, unsettle, distress, worry 827 *trouble*.

be excited, lose one's cool, lose control of oneself; flare up, burn 379 *be hot*; sizzle, seethe, simmer, boil, explode 318 *effervesce*; thrill to 818 *feel*; tingle, tremble 822 *be excitable*; quiver, flutter, palpitate, pulsate 318 *be agitated*; squirm, writhe 251 *wriggle*; dance; jump, leap up and down with excitement 312 *leap*; toss and turn.

822 Excitability

N. *excitability*, excitableness, inflammability; instability, emotionalism; hot temper, irritability, touchiness 892 *irascibility*; impatience, impetuosity, recklessness 857 *rashness*; effervescence, turbulence; restlessness, fidgets, nerves, butterflies in the stomach, collywobbles, flap 318 *agitation*.

excitable state, exhilaration, elation, euphoria, intoxication; thrill, trip, high, ecstasy; fever, fret, perturbation, trepidation, bother, fuss, hassle, flurry, whirl 318 *agitation*; ferment, pother, stew; storm, tempest 352 *gale*; effervescence, outburst, explosion, scene, song and dance 318 *commotion*; hysterics, fit, apoplectic f., frenzy; madness 503 *mental disorder*; passion, rage, towering r., fury 176 *violence*; temper, tantrums, rampage 891 *anger*.

Adj. *excitable*, passionate, emotional; inflammable, like tinder, like touchpaper; unstable, impressionable; temperamental, moody, mercurial, volatile 152 *changeful*; fitful 604 *capricious*; restless, nervy, fidgety, edgy, on edge, agitated; nervous, skittish 819 *lively*; irritable, fiery, hot-tempered, hot-headed 892 *irascible*; impatient, trigger-happy 680 *hasty*; impetuous, impulsive, madcap 857 *rash*; tempestuous, turbulent, stormy 176 *violent*; restive; effervescent, seething, boiling; volcanic, explosive; unbalanced; rabid 176 *furious*; feverish, hysterical 503 *frenzied*; like a cat on hot bricks, like a hen on a hot girdle *or* griddle, like a cat on a hot tin roof; tense, electric; elated.

Vb. *be excitable*, – impatient etc. adj.; drum one's fingers, tap one's foot, fret, fume, stamp; shuffle, fidget, champ at the bit; be itching to, be dying to; be on edge, be in a stew, flap 318 *be agitated*; start, jump 854 *be nervous*; be on the verge of a breakdown; have a temper; fume, foam, froth, throw fits, have hysterics 503 *go mad*; throw a tantrum, go wild, run riot, run amok, go berserk, see red; rush about 61 *rampage*; rage, rant; fly into a temper, fly off the handle, explode; kindle; flare up 821 *be excited*.

823 Inexcitability

N. *inexcitability*, imperturbability, calmness, steadiness, composure; coolness, cool, sangfroid, nonchalance; frigidity; tranquillity 266 *quietude*; serenity, placidity 828 *content*; equanimity, poise, equilibrium; self-control 942 *temperance*; stoicism 945 *asceticism*; detachment, dispassionateness 860 *indifference*; staidness, sobriety 834 *seriousness*; lack of fire.

patience, patience of Job; forbearance, endurance, longsuffering, tolerance, stoicism; resignation 721 *submission*.

Adj. *inexcitable*, dispassionate, cold, frigid, impassive; stable 153 *unchangeable*; cool, imperturbable, unflappable; level-headed; composed, controlled; moderate 942 *temperate*; inscrutable, deadpan, poker-faced; unhurried; equable 16 *uniform*; even-tempered, easy-going; staid, sedate, reserved, grave 834 *serious*; placid,

unruffled, calm, peaceful, serene 266 *tranquil*; spiritless, lackadaisical, torpid, passive, vegetable-like 175 *inert*; earthbound 593 *prosaic*.

patient, meek, like patience on a monument, tolerant, longsuffering, forbearing, enduring; stoic, stoical, philosophical, uncomplaining.

Vb. *keep calm*, compose oneself, keep cool, keep a cool head, swallow one's resentment, control one's temper, keep one's cool, not rise to the bait, keep one's hair *or* shirt on; not turn a hair, not bat an eyelid 820 *be insensitive*; relax, not excite oneself, not worry, stop worrying, take things easy, take things as they come 683 *repose*; resign oneself, take in good part, take philosophically, have patience, be resigned 721 *submit*.

be patient, show patience, show forbearance, show restraint, put up with, stand, tolerate, bear, endure, support, suffer, abide; resign oneself, grin and bear it, accept the situation with good grace, put a brave face on it; brook, take, take it from, swallow, digest, stomach, pocket 721 *knuckle under*; turn the other cheek 909 *forgive*; be tolerant, live and let live, condone 736 *be lenient*; turn a blind eye, overlook 734 *be lax*; allow 756 *permit*; not rise to the bait, coexist 770 *compromise*.

tranquillize, steady, moderate, assuage; calm, lull 266 *bring to rest*; cool down, compose 719 *pacify*; set one's mind at rest 831 *relieve*; control, restrain.

SECTION TWO

Personal emotion

824 Joy

N. *joy* 376 *pleasure*; enjoyment, thrill, kick 826 *pleasurableness*; joyfulness 835 *rejoicing*; delight, gladness, rapture, exaltation, exhilaration, transports of delight; abandonment, euphoria, ecstasy; gloating; life of pleasure, joys of life, roses all the way; halcyon days, days of wine and roses.

happiness, felicity, good fortune, well-being, ease, feel-good factor 376 *euphoria*; golden age, age of Aquarius 730 *prosperity*; blessedness, bliss; seventh heaven, cloud nine, nirvana, Paradise, Elysium, the happy hunting-ground in the sky, Garden of Eden, Isles of the Blessed, Arcadia 513 *fantasy*; happy valley, bower of bliss, home sweet home.

enjoyment, gratification, satisfaction, fulfilment 828 *content*; delectation, relish, lip-smacking, zest, gusto; indulgence, luxuriation, wallowing 943 *intemperance*; full life, hedonism,

Epicureanism 944 *sensualism*; merry-making, merriment; fun, treat, excursion, outing 837 *amusement*; feast, bean-feast, thrash; refreshment, good cheer, cakes and ale, beer and skittles 301 *eating*.

Adj. *pleased*, well-p., glad, welcoming; satisfied, happy 828 *content*; gratified, flattered, chuffed, pleased as Punch; over the moon, on top of the world; enjoying, loving it, tickled to death, tickled pink; exhilarated 833 *merry*; euphoric, walking on air, with feet not touching the ground; euphoric, elated, overjoyed 833 *jubilant*; delighted, transported; approving; ravished, in raptures, in transports, in the seventh heaven, on cloud nine; captivated, charmed, enchanted 818 *impressed*; gloating.

happy, happy as a king, happy as a sandboy, happy as a lark, happy as Larry, happy as the day is long, happy as a pig in muck; blithe, joyful, joyous, gladsome 833 *merry*; beaming, smiling 835 *laughing*; radiant, starry-eyed; felicitous, lucky, fortunate 730 *prosperous*; blissful, blessed; in paradise.

Vb. *be pleased*, – glad etc. adj.; hug oneself, congratulate o., purr with pleasure, be like a cat with a dish of cream, be like a dog with two tails, jump *or* dance for joy 833 *be cheerful*; laugh, smile 835 *rejoice*; get pleasure from, get a kick out of, take pleasure in, delight in, rejoice in; go into ecstasies, be in a state of euphoria, rave about 818 *show feeling*; luxuriate in, bask in, wallow; enjoy; have fun 837 *amuse oneself*; gloat; savour, relish, smack one's lips 386 *taste*; take a fancy to, like 887 *love*; think well of 923 *approve*.

825 Suffering

N. *suffering*, heartache, weltschmerz 834 *melancholy*; longing, homesickness, nostalgia 859 *desire*; discontent, weariness 684 *fatigue*; nightmare, waking nightmare, pain, affliction, distress, dolour, anguish, angst, agony, torture, torment, mental t.; twinge, stab, smart, sting, thorn 377 *pang*; painfulness; Passion, Crucifixion, Calvary, martyrdom; rack, the stake 963 *punishment*; purgatory, hell, damnation, eternal d. 961 *condemnation*; bed of nails, bed of thorns 700 *difficulty*; unpleasantness, setback, inconvenience, disagreeableness, discomfort, malaise; the hard way, trial, ordeal; shock, trauma, blow, infliction, visitation, tribulation 659 *bane*; extremity, death's door 651 *illness*; living death, fate worse than death 616 *evil*; evil days, unhappy times.

sorrow, grief, sadness, mournfulness, gloom 834 *dejection*; woe, wretchedness, misery, depths of m.; prostration, despair, despondency, desolation 853 *hopelessness*; unhappi-

ness, tale of woe 731 *adversity*; heavy heart, broken h.; displeasure, dissatisfaction 829 *discontent*; vexation, bitterness, mortification, chagrin, fretting, remorse 830 *regret*.

worry, worrying, worriedness, uneasiness, disquiet, fretting 318 *agitation*; dismay, distress 63 *derangement*; phobia, hang-up, obsession; something on one's mind, weight on one's m., anxiety, concern, solicitude, care; responsibility, load, burden; strain, stress, tension; a worry, worries, business w., cares, cares of the world; trouble, troubles 616 *evil*; bother, annoyance, irritation, bête noire, pest, thorn in the flesh; headache, teaser, puzzle, problem 530 *enigma*.

sufferer, victim, scapegoat, sacrifice; prey; martyr; patient 651 *sick person*.

Adj. *suffering*, ill, indisposed 651 *sick*; writhing, aching, in pain, on a bed of p., in agony, bleeding, harrowed, on the rack, in torment, in hell; inconvenienced, uncomfortable, ill at ease; anguished, distressed, anxious, unhappy about, worried, troubled, apprehensive, dismayed 854 *nervous*; sick with worry, out of one's mind with w., cut up about, in a state 316 *agitated*; discomposed, disconcerted; ill-used, maltreated, abused; longsuffering, downtrodden 745 *subjected*; martyred, victimized, sacrificed; stricken, wounded; heavy-laden, crushed, prostrate 684 *fatigued*; careworn; woeful, woebegone, haggard.

unhappy, infelicitous, unlucky, accursed 731 *unfortunate*; despairing 853 *hopeless*; doomed 961 *condemned*; pitiable, poor, wretched, miserable; sad, melancholy, despondent, disconsolate; cut up, heart-broken, broken-hearted, heavy-h., sick at heart; sorrowful, sorrowing, grieved, grieving, grief-stricken, woebegone 834 *dejected*; sunk in misery, weeping, sobbing, tearful, in tears 836 *lamenting*; disappointed 829 *discontented*; offended, vexed, peeved, miffed, annoyed, pained 924 *disapproving*; piqued, mortified, humiliated 891 *resentful*; sickened, disgusted, nauseated; sorry, remorseful, regretful 830 *regretting*.

Vb. *suffer*, undergo, endure, go through, experience 818 *feel*; bear, put up with, grin and bear it; suffer torments, bleed; hurt oneself, be hurt, do harm to oneself, smart, chafe, ache 377 *feel pain*; wince, flinch, writhe, squirm 251 *wriggle*; take up one's cross, become a martyr, sacrifice oneself; take one's punishment, take it on the chin 599 *stand firm*; have a thin time, have a bad t., go through it, have trouble enough 731 *have trouble*; distress oneself, fuss, hassle, worry, worry to death, fret, be on pins and needles, be on tenterhooks 318 *be agitated*; mind, be upset, take it badly, take it ill, take it to heart; sorrow, grieve, weep, sigh 836 *lament*.

826 Pleasurableness

N. *pleasurableness*, pleasures of, pleasantness, niceness, delectableness, delectability, delightfulness, amenity, sunny side, bright s.; attractiveness, appeal, sex a., it, come-hither look 291 *attraction*; winning ways 925 *flattery*; amiability, winsomeness, charm, fascination, enchantment, witchery, loveliness, sight for sore eyes 841 *beauty*; joyfulness, honeymoon 824 *joy*; a real tonic, a little of what one fancies, a delight, a treat, a joy; novelty, pastime, fun 837 *amusement*; melody, harmony 412 *music*; tastiness, deliciousness 390 *savouriness*; spice, zest, relish, je ne sais quoi; dainty, titbit, sweet 392 *sweetness*; manna in the wilderness, balm 685 *refreshment*; land flowing with milk and honey 635 *plenty*; peace, peace and quiet, tranquillity 266 *quietude*, 681 *leisure*; idyll; pipedream 513 *fantasy*.

Adj. *pleasurable*, pleasant, nice, good; pleasure-giving 837 *amusing*; pleasing, agreeable, gratifying; acceptable, welcome, welcome as the flowers in May; well-liked, to one's taste, to one's liking, just what the doctor ordered; wonderful, marvellous, fabulous, splendid 644 *excellent*; easeful, refreshing 683 *reposeful*; peaceful, quiet 266 *tranquil*; luxurious, voluptuous 376 *sensuous*; genial, warm, sunny; delightful, delectable, delicious, exquisite, choice; luscious, juicy; delicate, tasty 390 *savoury*; sugary 392 *sweet*; dulcet, musical, harmonious 410 *melodious*; picturesque, scenic, lovely 841 *beautiful*; amiable, dear, winning, disarming, endearing; attractive, fetching, appealing, alluring, interesting; seductive, enticing, inviting, captivating; charming, enchanting, bewitching, ravishing; haunting, thrilling, heart-melting, heart-warming 821 *exciting*; homely, cosy; pastoral, idyllic; heavenly, out of this world; beatific, blessed, blissful 824 *happy*.

Vb. *please*, give pleasure, agree with; lull, soothe, calm 177 *assuage*; comfort 833 *cheer*; put at ease, make comfortable 831 *relieve*; give a golden hello to, give a sweetener to, sugar, gild *or* sugar the pill 392 *sweeten*; stroke, pat, pet, baby, coddle, nurse, cuddle 889 *caress*; indulge, pander to 734 *be lax*; charm, interest 837 *amuse*; rejoice, gladden, make happy; gratify, satisfy, leave one walking on air, leave nothing more to be desired 828 *content*; raise to the seventh heaven.

delight, rejoice, exhilarate, elate, elevate, uplift; rejoice one's heart, warm the cockles of one's h., do one's heart good, bring tears of joy *or* happiness; thrill, intoxicate, ravish; transport, turn on, send, send one into raptures *or* ecstasies 821 *excite*; be music to one's ears 925

flatter; take one's fancy, tickle one's f.; tickle one's palate 390 *make appetizing*; regale, refresh; tickle, tickle one to death, titillate; entrance, enrapture; enchant, charm 983 *bewitch*; take one's breath away 821 *impress*; allure, seduce 291 *attract*.

827 Painfulness

N. *painfulness*, harshness, roughness, abuse, child a., sexual a., harassment, sexual h., persecution 735 *severity*; hurtfulness, harmfulness 645 *badness*; disagreeableness, unpleasantness; loathsomeness, hatefulness, beastliness 616 *evil*; grimness 842 *ugliness*; friction, chafing, irritation, ulceration, inflammation, exacerbation 832 *aggravation*; soreness, tenderness 377 *pain*; irritability, inflammability 822 *excitability*; sore point; sore, running s., ulcer, thorn in the flesh, pinprick, where the shoe pinches 659 *bane*; shock 508 *lack of expectation*; unpalatability, disgust, nausea, sickener 391 *unsavouriness*; sharpness, bitterness, bitter pill, gall and wormwood, vinegar 393 *sourness*; affliction, adversity; tribulation, trials and tribulations, ordeal, cross 825 *suffering*; trouble, care 825 *worry*; pathos; sorry sight, sad spectacle, object of pity 731 *unlucky person*; sorrow.

annoyance, vexation, death of, pest, bête noire, curse, plague, pain in the neck 659 *bane*; botheration, hassle, embarrassment 825 *worry*; nuisance, pinprick; burden, drag 702 *encumbrance*; grievance, complaint; hardship, troubles 616 *evil*; last straw, limit, the end; offence, affront, insult, provocation 921 *indignity*; molestation, infestation, persecution, malignity 898 *malevolence*; displeasure, mortification 891 *resentment*; menace, enfant terrible.

Adj. *paining*, hurting, aching, painful, sore, tender; agonizing 377 *painful*; searing, scalding, burning, sharp, shooting, biting, nipping, gnawing, throbbing; caustic, corrosive, vitriolic; harsh, hard, rough, cruel 735 *severe*; grinding, gruelling, punishing, excruciating, extreme; hurtful, harmful, poisonous.

unpleasant, unpleasing, disagreeable; uncomfortable, comfortless, joyless, dreary, dreich, dismal, depressing 834 *cheerless*; unattractive; hideous 842 *ugly*; unwelcome, unacceptable 860 *unwanted*; thankless, unpopular, displeasing; disappointing, unsatisfactory; distasteful, unpalatable, off 391 *unsavoury*; foul, nasty, beastly, horrible, ghastly 645 *not nice*; malodorous, stinking 397 *fetid*; bitter, sharp 393 *sour*; invidious, obnoxious, offensive, objectionable, undesirable, odious, hateful, loathsome, nauseous, slimy, disgusting, revolting, repellent; execrable, accursed 645 *damnable*.

annoying, too bad; troublesome, embarrassing, discomfiting, worrying; bothersome, wearisome, irksome, tiresome, boring 838 *tedious*; burdensome, onerous, oppressive 322 *weighty*; disappointing, unlucky, unfortunate, untoward 731 *adverse*; awkward, unaccommodating, impossible, harassing, hassling; importunate, pestering; trying, irritating, aggravating, provoking, maddening, infuriating; galling, mortifying.

distressing, afflicting, crushing, prostrating, grievous, traumatic; moving, affecting, touching; harrowing, heartbreaking, heart-rending, tear-jerking; pathetic, tragic, tragical, sad, woeful, rueful, mournful, pitiful, lamentable, deplorable; ghastly, grim, dreadful, shocking, appalling, horrifying, horrific 854 *frightening*.

intolerable, insufferable, impossible, insupportable, unbearable 32 *exorbitant*; past enduring, not to be borne; extreme, beyond the limits of tolerance, more than flesh and blood can stand, enough to make a parson swear, enough to try the patience of Job, enough to provoke a saint.

Vb. *hurt*, injure 645 *harm*; pain, cause p. 377 *give pain*; bite, cut, tear, rend 655 *wound*; hurt the feelings, gall, pique, nettle, mortify 891 *huff*; rub up the wrong way, tread on one's corns; cut to the quick, pierce the heart, rend the heartstrings, bring tears to one's eyes, draw tears, grieve, afflict, cause trauma, distress 834 *sadden*; plant a thorn in one's side; corrode, embitter, exacerbate, make matters worse, rub salt in the wound, gnaw, chafe, rankle, fester 832 *aggravate*; offend, aggrieve (**see** *displease*); insult, affront 921 *not respect*.

torment, martyr; harrow, rack, put to the r., break on the wheel 963 *torture*; give the third degree, give one the works; put one through it, put through the hoop, give one a bad time, mal-treat, abuse, bait, bully, rag, bullyrag, persecute 735 *oppress*; be offensive, snap at, bark at 885 *be rude*; importune, dun, doorstep, beset, besiege 737 *demand*; haunt, obsess, annoy; tease, pester, plague, nag, henpeck, badger, worry, try, chivvy, harass, hassle, harry, heckle; molest, bother, vex, provoke, peeve, miff, ruffle, irritate, wind up, needle, sting, chafe, fret, bug, gall, irk, roil, rile 891 *enrage*.

trouble, disquiet, disturb, agitate, discompose, disconcert, discomfit, put one out, upset, incommode 63 *derange*; worry, embarrass, perplex 474 *puzzle*; tire 684 *fatigue*; weary, bore 838 *be tedious*; obsess, haunt, bedevil; weigh upon one, prey on the mind, weigh on the spirits, act as a damper, deject 834 *depress*; infest, get in

one's hair, dog one's footsteps, get under one's feet, get in one's way, thwart 702 *obstruct*.

displease, find no favour 924 *incur blame*; disagree with, grate on, jar on, strike a jarring note, get on one's nerves, set the teeth on edge, go against the grain, give one the pip, give one a pain, get one's goat, get on one's wick, get up one's nose, get under one's skin; disenchant, disillusion 509 *disappoint*; dissatisfy, aggrieve 829 *cause discontent*; offend, shock, horrify, scandalize, disgust, revolt, repel, put one off, turn one off, sicken, nauseate, fill one with loathing, stick in the throat, make one's gorge rise, turn one's stomach, make one sick, make one sick to one's stomach, make one vomit, make one throw up 861 *cause dislike*; make one's hair curl, make one's flesh creep, make one's blood run cold, curdle the blood, make one's hair stand on end, appal 854 *frighten*.

828 Content

N. *content*, contentment, satisfaction, complacency; self-complacency, self-satisfaction, smugness 873 *vanity*; half-smile, purr of content, feel-good factor, ray of comfort; serenity, tranquillity 266 *quietude*; peace of mind, heart's ease 376 *euphoria*; reconciliation 719 *pacification*; snugness, cosiness, comfort, sitting pretty; dreams come true 730 *prosperity*.

Adj. *content*, contented, satisfied 824 *happy*; appeased, pacified 717 *peaceful*; cosy, snug 376 *comfortable*; at ease 683 *reposeful*; smiling 833 *cheerful*, pleased; with nothing left to wish for, having nothing to grumble at 863 *sated*; uncomplaining, with no regrets, without complaints; philosophic, resigned 721 *submitting*; easily pleased, easygoing, easy-osy 736 *lenient*; secure 660 *safe*; untroubled, blessed with contentment.

Vb. *be content* – satisfied etc. adj.; purr with content 824 *be pleased*; rest and be thankful, count one's blessings; be thankful, have much to be thankful for 907 *be grateful*; have all one could ask for, have one's wish, make one's dreams come true, fulfil one's ambition 730 *prosper*; congratulate oneself, rejoice; be at ease, be in one's element, sit pretty 376 *enjoy*; be reconciled 719 *make peace*; get over it, take comfort; rest content; take things as they come, make the best of, have no complaints, have nothing to grumble about, have no regrets; acquiesce 721 *submit*.

content, satisfy, make one's day 826 *please*; meet with approval, go down well, go down a treat; make happy, bless with contentment; grant a boon 781 *give*; make one's dreams come true, comfort 833 *cheer*; bring comfort to; lull, set at ease, set at rest; propitiate, reconcile, conciliate, appease 719 *pacify.*

829 Discontent

N. *discontent,* discontentment; displeasure, pain, dissatisfaction, feel-bad factor 924 *disapprobation;* cold comfort 509 *disappointment;* irritation, chagrin, pique, mortification, bitterness, spleen 891 *resentment;* uneasiness, disquiet 825 *worry;* grief 825 *sorrow;* unrest, state of u., restiveness 738 *disobedience;* agitation 318 *commotion;* finickiness, faddiness, fikiness, hypercriticism, nit-picking 862 *fastidiousness;* querulousness 709 *quarrelsomeness;* chip on one's shoulder, grievance, grudge, complaint 709 *quarrel;* weariness, world-w., weltschmerz, melancholy, ennui 834 *dejection;* sulkiness, sulks, the hump, dirty look, grimace, scowl, frown 893 *sullenness;* groan, curse 899 *malediction;* murmuring, whispering campaign, smear c. 762 *deprecation.*

malcontent, grumbler, grouch, grouser, sniper, complainer, whiner, bleater, bellyacher, Jonah 834 *moper;* plaintiff 763 *petitioner;* faultfinder, nit-picker, critic, censurer; person with a grievance, someone with a chip on their shoulder, angry young man; dissident, dropout 738 *revolter;* seditionist 738 *agitator;* protest meeting, sit-in; conscientious objector.

Adj. *discontented,* displeased, not best pleased; dissatisfied 924 *disapproving;* frustrated 509 *disappointed;* defeated 728 *unsuccessful;* malcontent, dissident 489 *dissenting;* restive 738 *disobedient;* disgruntled, dischuffed, weary, browned off, cheesed o., hacked off, gutted, fed up to the back teeth 838 *bored,* 825 *unhappy;* sad, disconsolate 834 *dejected;* ill-disposed, grudging, jealous, envious; embittered, soured 393 *sour;* peevish, testy, crabbed, crabbit, cross, sulky, sulking, pouting 893 *sullen;* grouchy, grumbling, grousing, whining, swearing 899 *cursing;* protesting; smarting, mortified, insulted, affronted, piqued, vexed, miffed, put out, annoyed 891 *resentful;* fretful, querulous, petulant, complaining; difficult, hard to please, never satisfied, exigent, exacting 862 *fastidious;* fault-finding, critical, hypercritical, censorious; resisting 704 *opposing.*

Vb. *be discontented,* – dissatisfied etc. adj.; carp, criticize, give flak, find fault 862 *be fastidious;* lack, miss 627 *require;* jeer 924 *disapprove;* take offence, take amiss, take ill, take to heart, take on, be offended, be miffed 891 *resent;* get the hump, sulk; look blue, look glum; moan, whine, whinge, winge, bleat, beef, protest, complain, object 762 *deprecate;* bellyache, grumble, grouse, grouch, gripe; wail 836 *lament;* be aggrieved, have a grievance, nurse a grudge,

have a chip on one's shoulder; join the opposition 704 *oppose;* rise up, be up in arms about 738 *revolt;* grudge 912 *envy;* quarrel; not know when one is well off, look a gift horse in the mouth; ask for one's money back, demand a refund, return 607 *reject.*

cause discontent, dissatisfy 636 *not suffice;* leave room for complaint 509 *disappoint;* spoil one's pleasure, get one down 834 *depress;* dishearten, discourage 613 *dissuade;* sour, embitter, disgruntle, dischuff; upset, miff, chafe, niggle, put out of humour, irritate 891 *huff;* mortify 872 *humiliate;* offend, cause resentment 827 *displease;* disgust 861 *cause dislike;* sow the seeds of discontent, make trouble, stir up t., mix it, agitate 738 *revolt.*

830 Regret

N. *regret,* regretfulness; mortification 891 *resentment;* harking back, crying over spilt milk; soul-searching, remorse, contrition, repentance, compunction, qualms, pangs of conscience, regrets, apologies 939 *penitence;* disillusion, second thoughts 67 *sequel;* longing, homesickness, nostalgia 859 *desire;* sense of loss 737 *demand;* matter of regret, pity of it.

Adj. *regretting,* homesick, nostalgic; regretful, remorseful, rueful, conscience-stricken, sorry, apologetic, penitent, contrite 939 *repentant;* disillusioned, sadder and wiser.

Vb. *regret,* rue, deplore, rue the day; curse one's folly, never forgive oneself, blame o., reproach o., kick o., bite one's tongue; wish undone, wring one's hands, cry over spilt milk, spend time in vain regrets 836 *lament;* want one's time over again, sigh for the good old days, fight one's battles over again, relive the past, reopen old wounds, hark back; look back, look over one's shoulder; miss, sadly m., regret the loss; long for, hanker after, be homesick 859 *desire;* express regrets, apologize, be full of remorse, feel contrite, feel remorse, be sorry 939 *be penitent;* ask for another chance 905 *ask mercy;* lament 924 *disapprove;* feel mortified, gnash one's teeth 891 *resent;* have cause for regret, have had one's lesson 963 *be punished.*

831 Relief

N. *relief,* welcome r., rest 685 *refreshment;* easing, alleviation, mitigation, palliation, abatement 177 *moderation;* good riddance; exemption 668 *deliverance;* solace, consolation, comfort, ray of c., crumb of c.; silver lining, break in the clouds 852 *hope;* load off one's mind, sigh of relief 656 *revival;* lulling; soothing, salve 658 *balm;* painkiller, analgesic 375 *anaesthetic;* sedative, tranquillizer.

Vb. *relieve,* ease, soften, cushion; relax, lessen

the strain; temper 177 *moderate*; lift, raise, take off, lighten, relieve the burden, take a load off one's mind 701 *disencumber*; spare, exempt from 919 *exempt*; save 668 *deliver*; console, solace, comfort, bring c.; offer a crumb of c.; cheer up, buck up, encourage, hearten 833 *cheer*; refresh; restore, repair 656 *cure*; put a plaster on, bandage, bind up, apply a tourniquet, poultice, kiss it better 658 *doctor*; calm, soothe, palliate, mitigate, moderate, alleviate 177 *assuage*; smooth the brow, take out the wrinkles, iron out the difficulties 258 *smooth*; lull; kill the pain 375 *render insensible*; take pity on, put one out of one's misery.

832 Aggravation

N. *aggravation*, exacerbation, exasperation, irritation; enhancement, augmentation 36 *increase*; intensification; heightening, deepening, adding to 482 *overestimation*; making worse 655 *deterioration*; complication 700 *difficulty*.

Vb. *aggravate*, intensify 162 *strengthen*; enhance, heighten, deepen; increase 36 *augment*; worsen, make things w., not improve matters 655 *deteriorate*; add insult to injury, rub salt in the wound, rub it in, rub one's nose in it, exacerbate, inflame 821 *excite*; exasperate, irritate 891 *enrage*; add fuel to the flame, fan the embers; complicate, make bad worse, escalate the war, go from bad to worse, jump from the frying pan into the fire.

833 Cheerfulness

N. *cheerfulness*, alacrity 597 *willingness*; optimism, hopefulness 852 *hope*; happiness 824 *joy*; geniality, smiles, good humour; vitality, high spirits, youthful h. s., joie de vivre 360 *life*; light-heartedness, spring in one's step, optimistic outlook 828 *content*; liveliness, sparkle, vivacity, animation, elation, euphoria, exhilaration, elevation 822 *excitable state*; life and soul of the party, party spirit, conviviality 882 *sociability*.

merriment, good cheer; high spirits, gay abandon; jollity, joviality, jocularity, gaiety, glee, mirth, hilarity 835 *laughter*; levity, frivolity 499 *folly*; merry-making, fun, fun and games, amusement; jubilation, jubilee 876 *celebration*.

Adj. *cheerful*, cheery, blithe 824 *happy*; hearty, genial, convivial 882 *sociable*; sanguine, optimistic, rose-coloured; smiling, sunny, bright, beaming, radiant 835 *laughing*; breezy, of good cheer, in high spirits, in a good humour; in good heart, optimistic, upbeat, hopeful, buoyant; irrepressible; carefree, light-hearted, happy-go-lucky; bouncing; pert, jaunty, bright-eyed and bushy-tailed, perky, chirpy, chipper, spry, spirited, peppy, sprightly,

vivacious, animated, vital, sparkling, all lit up, full of beans, on the top of one's form 819 *lively*.

merry, joyful, happy as a sandboy, happy as a king, happy as the day is long, happy as Larry; ebullient, effervescent, bubbly, sparkling, laughter-loving, jocular 839 *witty*; gay, frivolous 456 *light-minded*; playful, sportive, frisky, frolicsome, kittenish 837 *amusing*; roguish, arch, sly; merry-making, mirthful, jovial, jolly, joking, dancing, laughing, singing, drinking; hilarious, uproarious, rip-roaring, rollicking, splitting one's sides, helpless with laughter, tickled pink.

jubilant, overjoyed, gleeful, delighted 824 *pleased*; chuffed, elated, euphoric, flushed, exultant, triumphant, cock-a-hoop, dancing on air 727 *successful*; celebratory.

Vb. *be cheerful*, be in good spirits, be in good humour, be in a good mood, be in good heart; keep cheerful, look on the bright side, keep one's spirits up 852 *hope*; keep one's pecker up, grin and bear it, make the best of it, put a good face upon it 599 *be resolute*; take heart, snap out of it, cheer up, perk up, buck up; brighten up, grow animated, let oneself go, let one's hair down, abandon oneself; radiate good humour, smile, grin from ear to ear, beam, sparkle; dance, sing, carol, lilt, chirrup, chirp, whistle, laugh 835 *rejoice*; whoop, cheer 876 *celebrate*; have fun, frisk, frolic, rollick, romp, gambol, sport, disport oneself, enjoy o., have a good time 837 *amuse oneself*; throw a party, make whoopee 882 *be sociable*.

cheer, gladden, warm the cockles of the heart 828 *content*; comfort, console 831 *relieve*; rejoice the heart, put in a good humour 826 *please*; enliven 821 *animate*; exhilarate, elate 826 *delight*; encourage, uplift, hearten, raise the spirits, buck up, perk up, jolly along, bolster up 855 *give courage*; act like a tonic, put new life into 174 *invigorate*.

834 Dejection. Seriousness

N. *dejection*, joylessness, unhappiness, cheerlessness, dreariness, dejectedness, low spirits, blues, dumps doldrums; dispiritedness, low spirits, feet-bad factor, sinking heart; disillusion 509 *disappointment*; defeatism, pessimism, cynicism, depression, despair, death wish, suicidal tendency 853 *hopelessness*; weariness, oppression, enervation, exhaustion 684 *fatigue*; oppression of spirit, heartache, heaviness, sadness, misery, wretchedness, disconsolateness, dolefulness 825 *sorrow*; despondency, prostration; Slough of Despond, grey dawn; gloom; glumness, long face, face as long as a fiddle; funereal aspect, lacklustre eye; gloom and doom, trouble 825 *worry*.

melancholy, melancholia, depression, clinical d., endogenous d., exogenous d., SAD, seasonal affective disorder, black mood, blues, moping, sighing, sigh; vapours, spleen 829 *discontent*; weariness of life, world-weariness, Weltschmerz, angst, nostalgia, homesickness 825 *suffering*.

seriousness, earnestness; gravity, solemnity, sobriety, demureness, staidness, grimness 893 *sullenness*; primness, humourlessness; straight face, poker f., dead pan; sternness; no laughing matter, no cause for mirth.

moper, complainer, Jonah 829 *malcontent*; sourpuss, crosspatch, bear with a sore head; pessimist, damper, wet blanket, killjoy, spoilsport; Job's comforter, misery, sobersides; death's-head, skeleton at the feast, gloom and doom merchant, doomwatcher, doomster, ecodoomster; hypochondriac, malade imaginaire.

Adj. *dejected*, joyless, dreary, dreich, cheerless, unhappy, sad; gloomy, despondent, downbeat, unhopeful, pessimistic, defeatist, despairing 853 *hopeless*; discouraged, disheartened; dispirited; troubled, worried 825 *suffering*; downcast, downhearted, low, down, down in the mouth, low-spirited, depressed; out of sorts, not oneself, out of spirits; sluggish, listless, spiritless, lackadaisical 679 *inactive*; lacklustre 419 *dim*; crestfallen 509 *disappointed*; browned off, cheesed off, pissed off, hacked off, gutted, sick as a parrot 829 *discontented*; down in the dumps, in the doldrums; sadder and wiser 830 *regretting*; subdued, disillusioned 509 *disappointed*.

melancholic, hypochondriacal; blue, down in the dumps; jaundiced, sour, pensive, deep in thought; melancholy, sad, triste; saddened, cut up, heavy hearted, sick at heart, heart-sick 825 *unhappy*; sorry, rueful 830 *regretting*; mournful, doleful, woeful, tearful 836 *lamenting*; cheerless, joyless, dreary, comfortless; forlorn, miserable, broken up, wretched, disconsolate; self-pitying; moody, sulky 893 *sullen*; dismal, gloomy, morose, glum, sunk in gloom; down in the mouth, woebegone.

serious, sober, sober as a judge, sober-sided, solemn, sedate, stolid, staid, demure, muted, grave, stern, Puritanical 735 *severe*; dour, grim, forbidding 893 *sullen*; unsmiling, inscrutable, straight-faced, po-f., poker-f., deadpan; prim; humourless; unfunny, heavy-going, dull, solid 838 *tedious*.

cheerless, comfortless; uncongenial, unwelcoming; depressing, dreary, dreich, dull 838 *tedious*; dismal, lugubrious, funereal, gloomy, dark, forbidding; drab, grey, sombre; ungenial.

Vb. *be dejected*, become despondent, lose heart, admit defeat 853 *despair*; succumb 728 *be defeated*; languish, sink, droop, sag, wilt, flag, give up 684 *be fatigued*; look downcast, look down in the mouth, look blue, hang one's head, pull a long face, laugh on the wrong side of one's face; mope, brood 449 *think*; take to heart, sulk; eat one's heart out, sigh, grieve 829 *be discontented*; groan 825 *suffer*; weep 836 *lament*.

be serious, keep a straight face, keep one's countenance, maintain one's gravity; look grave; lack humour, not see the joke, have no sense of humour, take oneself seriously, be a bore 838 *be tedious*.

sadden, grieve; turn one's hair grey, break one's heart, pluck at one's heartstrings, make one's heart bleed; draw tears, bring tears to one's eyes, touch the heart, leave not a dry eye 821 *impress*; pain, spoil one's pleasure 829 *cause discontent*; drive to despair; prostrate.

depress, deject, get one down; cause alarm and despondency, dishearten, discourage, dispirit, take the heart out of, unman, unnerve 854 *frighten*; spoil the fun, take the joy out of, cast a shadow, cast a gloom over 418 *darken*; damp, dampen, damp the spirits, put a damper on, be a wet blanket, throw cold water, frown upon 613 *dissuade*; dash one's hopes 509 *disappoint*; weigh heavy on one's heart; make the heart sick, weary 684 *fatigue*; sober 534 *teach*.

835 Rejoicing

N. *rejoicing*, jubilation, exultation 876 *celebration*; congratulations, felicitation, pat on the back, bouquets, self-congratulation, mutual c. 886 *congratulation*; plaudits, clapping, applause, shout, cheers, rousing c., three c., huzza, hurrah, high-five, hosannah, hallelujah 923 *praise*; thanksgiving 907 *thanks*; paean; raptures, elation, euphoria 824 *joy*; revelling 837 *revel*; merrymaking, gay abandon 833 *merriment*.

laughter, risibility; loud laughter, hearty l., shout of laughter, peal of l., shrieks of l., hoots of l., gales of l., cachinnation; derision 851 *ridicule*; laugh, belly l., horse l., guffaw, chuckle, chortle, gurgle, cackle, crow, coo; giggle, snigger, snicker, titter, tee-hee; fit of laughing, the giggles; forced laugh; smile, simper, smirk, grin, broad g., grin from ear to ear, Cheshire cat grin; twinkle, half-smile; humour, sense of h. 839 *wit*; laughableness, laughing matter, comedy, farce 497 *absurdity*.

Adj. *rejoicing*, revelling, cheering, shouting etc. vb.; exultant, elated, euphoric 833 *jubilant*; lyrical, ecstatic 923 *approving*.

laughing, guffawing etc. vb.; splitting one's sides, laughing one's head off, creased, doubled up, convulsed with laughter, dying with l., shrieking with mirth, rolling in the aisles; humorous; mocking; laughable, risible, derisory 849 *ridiculous*; comic, comical, funny, farcical 497 *absurd*.

Vb. *rejoice*, be joyful, jump for j., dance for j., dance, skip 312 *leap*; clap, clap one's hands, throw one's cap in the air, whoop, cheer, huzza, hurrah 923 *applaud*; shout 408 *vociferate*; carol 413 *sing*; sing paeans, shout hosannas, sound the trumpet 923 *praise*; exult, crow 876 *celebrate*; felicitate 886 *congratulate*; give thanks, thank one's lucky stars 907 *thank*; abandon oneself, let oneself go, loosen up, let one's hair down, paint the town red, go mad for joy, dance in the streets; make merry 833 *be cheerful*; have a good time, frolic, frisk 837 *revel*; have a party, go on a spree, celebrate 882 *be sociable*; feel pleased, congratulate oneself, hug o., give oneself a pat on the back, rub one's hands, smack one's lips, gloat 824 *be pleased*; purr, coo, gurgle; sigh for pleasure, cry for joy.

laugh, burst out laughing, crack up, break up, get the giggles, get a fit of the g.; hoot, chuckle, chortle, cackle; giggle, snigger, snicker, titter, tee-hee, ha-ha, haw-haw; laugh at, laugh in one's sleeve *or* one's beard, mock, deride 851 *ridicule*; cachinnate; shake with mirth, fall about, split one's sides, be in stitches, double up, shriek with laughter, hoot with l., roar with l., kill oneself laughing, laugh fit to burst, laugh one's head off.

smile, break into a s., grin, grin from ear to ear, grin like a Cheshire cat; give a half-smile, smirk; twinkle, beam, flash a smile.

Int. cheers! three c.! huzza! hurrah! hooray! hosannah! hallelujah! glory be! hail the conquering hero!

836 Lamentation

N. *lamentation*, lamenting, ululation, wail, groaning, weeping, wailing, keening; weeping and wailing, beating the breast, tearing one's hair, wringing one's hands; mourning 364 *obsequies*; sackcloth and ashes; widow's weeds, crepe, black; Wailing Wall; crying, sobbing, sighing, blubbering, whimpering, whining, snivelling etc. vb.; tears, tearfulness, dolefulness 834 *dejection*; tears of pity 905 *pity*; red eyes, eyes swimming *or* brimming with tears; floods of tears, hysterics; cry, good c.; tear, teardrop; heaving breast, sob, sigh, groan, moan, bawl, boo-hoo.

lament, plaint, dirge, knell, requiem, elegy, swansong, funeral oration 364 *obsequies*; keen, wake 905 *condolence*; howl 409 *ululation*; tears of grief; tale of woe; show of grief, crocodile tears 542 *sham*.

Adj. *lamenting*, crying etc. vb.; in tears, bathed in t.; tearful, lachrymose; red-eyed, with moist eyes; close to tears, on the verge of t., ready to cry; mournful, doleful, lugubrious 825 *unhappy*; woeful, woebegone, wringing one's hands, beating one's breast 834 *dejected*; plaintive, singing the blues; elegiac, dirgelike 364 *funereal*; in mourning, in black, in widow's weeds, in sackcloth and ashes; at half-mast; with a tale of woe; pathetic, pitiful, lamentable, tear-jerking.

Vb. *lament*, grieve, sorrow, sigh, heave a s. 825 *suffer*; deplore 830 *regret*; condole, commiserate 905 *pity*; grieve for, sigh for, weep over, cry o., bewail, bemoan, elegize; sing the dirge, sing a requiem, toll the knell 364 *inter*; mourn, wail, weep and wail, keen; express grief, go into mourning; put on sackcloth and ashes, wring one's hands, beat one's breast, tear one's hair; take on, carry on, take it badly; tell one's tale of woe 829 *be discontented*.

weep, wail, greet; shed tears, burst into t., dissolve in t.; give way to tears, break down, cry, cry like a baby, boo-hoo, bawl, cry one's eyes out; howl, yell, scream, shriek 409 *ululate*; sob, sigh, moan, groan 825 *suffer*; snivel, grizzle, blubber, pule, mewl, whine, whinge, whimper; be on the verge of tears; cry out before one is hurt.

837 Amusement

N. *amusement*, pleasure, delight 826 *pleasurableness*; diversion, divertissement, entertainment, light e., popular e.; dramatic entertainment 594 *drama*; radio, television 531 *broadcasting*; video, video game; pop music, personal stereo, ghetto blaster; karaoke; pastime, hobby, labour of love 597 *voluntary work*; solace, recreation 685 *refreshment*; relaxation 683 *repose*; holiday, Bank h. 681 *leisure*; April Fool's Day, rag day, gala day, red-letter d. 876 *special day*; play, sport, fun, good clean f., high jinks, merriment; do. show, thrash, junket, Gaudy night 876 *celebration*; outing, excursion, jaunt, day out, pleasure trip; treat, Sunday school t., picnic; social gathering, get-together, at-home, conversazione, garden party, bunfight, beanfeast, fête, flower show, gymkhana, jamboree 74 *assembly*; whist drive, bridge party (**see** *card game*); party games (**see** *indoor game*).

festivity, holiday-making, vacationing; visiting 882 *social round*; fun 835 *laughter*; beer and skittles 824 *enjoyment*; social whirl, round of pleasure; high life, night l.; good time; living it up, painting the town red, burning the candle at both ends, a short life and a merry one 943 *intemperance*; festival, fair, funfair, fun of the fair, carnival, fiesta, gala; masque; festivities, fun and games, merrymaking, revels,

Mardi Gras 833 *merriment*; feast day, special d; carousal, wassail 301 *feasting*; conviviality, house-warming, party, bottle p., byob (= bring your own bottle) p. 882 *social gathering*; drinking bout, spree, bender 301 *drinking*; orgy, carouse 949 *drunkenness*; binge, beano, thrash, blowout; barbecue, beanfeast, bunfight, dinner, annual d., banquet 301 *meal*.

revel, rave-up, knees-up, jollification, whoopee, fun, high old time; fun fast and furious, high jinks, spree, junket, junketing; night out, night on the tiles; bonfire; play, game, romp, frolic, lark, skylarking, escapade, antic, prank, rag, trick, monkey t. 497 *foolery*.

pleasure ground, park, theme p., adventure p., deer p., wildlife p., safari p., national p., grouse moor; village green, gardens, pleasure g., winter g. 192 *park*; seaside, Riviera, lido, marina, bathing beach, holiday camp; playground, adventure p., recreation ground, playing field, links, golf course; rink, skating r., ice r.; tennis court, petanque c., bowling green, croquet lawn 724 *arena*; circus, fair.

place of amusement, fairground, funfair, shooting gallery, amusement arcade; skittle alley, bowling a., billiard room, pool r.; concert hall, music h., cinema, movie theatre; theatre, ballroom; dance hall, discothèque, disco; cabaret, night club, strip joint, clip j.; bingo hall, casino 618 *gaming-house*.

sport, outdoor life; sportsmanship, gamesmanship 694 *skill*; sports, field s., track events; games, gymnastics 162 *athletics*, 312 *leap*, 716 *contest*, *racing*, *pugilism*, *wrestling*; weight-lifting, weight-training, pumping iron, going for the burn, outdoor sports, cycling, hiking, rambling, orienteering, trail-running, speed-walking, camping, picnicking; running, jogging, trail-running, speed-walking, race-walking, marathon; riding, pony-trekking; archery, shooting, clay-pigeon s.; hunting, shooting and fishing 619 *chase*; water sports, swimming, bathing, surf-riding, wind-surfing, boardsailing; skin diving, subaqua, water skiing, aqua-planing, boating, rowing, yachting, sailing 269 *aquatics*; rock-climbing, mountaineering 308 *ascent*; exploring, caving, speleology, pot-holing 309 *descent*; winter sports, skiing, snow-boarding, ski-jumping, bobsleighing, tobogganning, skating, ice s., ice hockey; curling; flying, gliding, hang g. 271 *aeronautics*; mind sports.

ball game, bat and ball game; cricket, French c.; baseball, rounders; tennis, lawn t., real t., table t., pingpong; badminton; squash, rackets; handball, volleyball; fives, pelota; netball, basketball; football, Association f., soccer, fantasy football, rugby, Rugby football, R. Union, R. League, rugger; lacrosse, hockey, ice h.; polo,

water polo; croquet, putting, golf, clock g., crazy g.; skittles, ninepins, bowls, petanque, boules, curling; marbles; quoits, deck q., hoop-la; billiards, snooker, pool; bagatelle, pinball, shove ha'penny.

indoor game, parlour g., panel g., party g.; musical bumps, musical chairs, hunt the thimble, hunt the slipper, pass the parcel, postman's knock, kiss in the ring, oranges and lemons, nuts in May; sardines, rabbits, murder; forfeits, guessing game; quiz, twenty questions; charades; parson's *or* minister's cat, I-spy; word game, spelling bee, riddles, crosswords, acrostics, pangrams; paper game, consequences, noughts and crosses, battleships, hangman; darts, dominoes, mah jong, tiddly-winks, jigsaw puzzle.

board game, chess; draughts, checkers, Chinese c., halma; backgammon; Scrabble (tdmk); ludo, snakes and ladders, Monopoly (tdmk), Trivial Pursuit (tdmk), go.

children's games, ring-a-ring-o'-roses; leapfrog, hopscotch, peever 312 *leap*; touch, tag, tig, he, hide-and-seek, follow-my-leader, Simon says, blind man's buff, hares and hounds, cowboys and Indians, cops and robbers.

card game, cards, game of cards, rubber of whist, rubber of bridge; whist, solo w., auction w.; auction bridge, contract b.; nap, napoleon; picquet, cribbage, bezique; rummy, gin r., canasta, hearts, Newmarket, speculation, solitaire, patience; snap, beggar-my-neighbour, old maid, Happy Families; lotto, housey-housey, bingo; vingt-et-un, pontoon, black jack; poker, strip p., stud p.; banker, baccarat, chemin de fer, chemmy.

gambling game, dice g.; roulette, rouge et noir; coin-spinning, heads and tails, raffle, tombola, sweepstake, lottery, National Lottery, scratch card, football pool 618 *gambling*.

dancing, dance, ball; masquerade; fancy dress dance; thé dansant, tea dance, ceilidh, square dance, hoe-down; hop, jam session, disco, rave; disco dancing, breakdancing, body-popping; ballet dancing; tap dancing, clog d., folk d., country d., Scottish c. d., Highland d., Irish d., morris d., old-time d., sequence d., ballroom d.; line dancing; table d., lap d. choreography; eurhythmics, aerobics, step.

dance, war dance, sword d., corroboree; soft-shoe shuffle, cakewalk; clog dance, step d., tap d., toe d.; fan dance, dance of the seven veils, hula-hula; high kicks, cancan; belly dance; flamenco; salsa; country dance, morris d., barn d., square d., sailor's dance, hornpipe; folk dance, polonaise, mazurka, czardas; jig, Irish j.; Highland fling; reel, eightsome r., foursome r., strathspey, Gay Gordons, Petronella, Duke of Perth,

Strip the Willow, Dashing White Sergeant, Sir Roger de Coverley; tarantella, bolero, fandango, galliard, écossaise, gavotte, quadrille, cotillion, minuet, pavane, allemande, schottische, polka; waltz, last w., Viennese w., hesitation w., St Bernard w.; valeta, Lancers; foxtrot, turkey trot, quickstep; Charleston, black bottom, blues, one-step, two-s., Boston t-s., military t-s., paso-doble, tango, rumba, samba, mambo, bossa nova, beguine, conga, conga line, cha-cha; lambada, mosh; boomps-a-daisy, hokey-cokey, Lambeth Walk, Palais Glide; stomp, bop, bebop, shimmy, jive, breakdancing, bodypopping, disco dancing, Lindy-hopping, rock 'n' roll, twist; excuse-me dance, Paul Jones, snowball.

plaything, toy 639 *bauble*; children's toy, rattle, bricks, building b., Meccano (tdmk), Lego (tdmk); Jack-in-the-box, teddy bear, puppet, golliwog, doll, china d., rag d., Cabbage Patch (tdmk) d., Cindy (tdmk) d., Barbie (tdmk), Action Man (tdmk), Power Ranger (tdmk), Teletubbies (tdmk), Furby (tdmk), Pokémon; doll's house, Wendy house, bouncy castle; doll's pram; top, whipping t., yo-yo; marbles; ball, balloon 252 *sphere*; hoop, Hula-Hoop (tdmk), skipping rope, stilts, pogo stick, rocking horse, hobby h., tricycle; roller skates, Roller Blades (tdmk), blades, skateboard, surfboard, snowboard; popgun, airgun, water pistol; toy soldier, tin s., lead s.; model, model aeroplane, clockwork train, model railway; magic lantern, toy theatre 522 *exhibit*; puppet show, marionettes, Punch and Judy 551 *image*; billiard table; cards; domino, tile; draught, counter, chip; tiddly-wink; chess piece, pawn, knight, bishop, castle *or* rook, queen, king.

player, sportsman *or* -woman, sportsperson; competitor 716 *contender*; all-rounder; ballplayer, footballer, forward, striker, winger, defence, sweeper, goal-keeper; cricketer, batsman, fielder, wicket-keeper, bowler; hockey-player, tennis-p.; marksman, archer; shot-putter; gambler; card-player, chess-p.

Adj. *amusing*, entertaining, diverting etc. vb.; fun-making, full of fun 833 *merry*; pleasant 826 *pleasurable*; recreational 685 *refreshing*.

Vb. *amuse*, entertain, divert, tickle, make one laugh, take one out of oneself; tickle the fancy, titillate, please 826 *delight*; enliven 833 *cheer*; raise a smile, convulse with laughter, have them rolling in the aisles, wow, slay, be the death of 849 *be ridiculous*; humour, keep amused, put in a good humour, put in a cheerful mood; give a party, have a get-together, play the host *or* hostess 882 *be hospitable*.

amuse oneself, relax, hang out; kill time, while away the t., pass the t., pursue one's hobby, dabble in; play, play at, have fun, enjoy oneself 833 *be cheerful*; take a holiday, have a break, go on vacation, go on an outing, have a field day, have a ball; disport oneself; take one's pleasure; frolic, romp, gambol, caper, play tricks, play pranks, lark around, fool about, play the fool 497 *be absurd*; jest 839 *be witty*; play cards; game, dice 618 *gamble*; play games, be a fitness freak; live the outdoor life, camp, caravan, take a holiday home, timeshare; picnic; sail, yacht, surf, windsurf, sailboard, fly; hunt, shoot, fish; play golf; ride, trek, hike, ramble; run, jog, race, jump; bathe, swim, dive; skate, roller-skate, ski, toboggan; work out, pump iron.

dance, go dancing; tap-dance, waltz, foxtrot, quickstep, Charleston, tango, rumba, jive, jitterbug, stomp, bop, twist, rock 'n' roll, disco-dance, breakdance, bodypop; whirl 315 *rotate*; cavort, caper, jig about, bob up and down; shuffle, hoof, tread a measure, trip the light fantastic 312 *leap*.

revel, make merry, make whoopee, have a ball, celebrate 835 *rejoice*; drive dull care away, make it a party, have a good time; let oneself go, let one's hair down, let off steam; go on a bender, go on a spree, have a night out, have a night on the tiles, live it up, paint the town red; junket, roister, feast, banquet, carouse, make the rafters ring; go on a binge, go pub-crawling 301 *drink*; drown one's sorrows 949 *get drunk*; sow one's wild oats, burn the candle at both ends; stay up till all hours, go home in the wee sma' hours, never go home till morning, go home with the cows.

838 Tedium

N. *tedium*, ennui, world-weariness, Weltschmerz 834 *melancholy*; lack of interest 860 *indifference*; weariness, languor 684 *fatigue*; tediousness, irksomeness; dryness, stodginess, heaviness; flatness, staleness 387 *insipidity*; stuffiness 840 *dullness*; prolixity 570 *diffuseness*; sameness 16 *uniformity*; monotony 106 *repetition*; time to kill 679 *inactivity*; doodling, thumb-twiddling.

bore, utter b., no fun; drag, bind, chore; beaten track, daily round, rut 610 *habit*; grindstone, treadmill 682 *labour*; boring person, anorak, train-spotter, saddo, dweeb, geek, pain in the neck, pub bore.

Adj. *tedious*, uninteresting, unexciting, unentertaining; slow, dragging, leaden, heavy; dry, arid; flat, stale, insipid 387 *tasteless*; bald 573 *plain*; humdrum, soulless, suburban, depressing, dreary, dreich, stuffy, bourgeois 840 *dull*; stodgy, prosaic, uninspired; long-winded, drawn out 570 *prolix*; soporific, boring, wearisome, tiresome, irksome; wearing; repetitive;

unvarying, monotonous 16 *uniform*; cloying, satiating.

bored, twiddling one's thumbs, doodling, kicking one's heels 679 *inactive*; fed up to the back teeth, browned off, cheesed off, hacked off, had it up to here 829 *discontented*; jaded 684 *fatigued*; world-weary 834 *melancholic*; blasé 860 *indifferent*; satiated, cloyed 863 *sated*; sick of, sick and tired, fed up.

Vb. *be tedious*, pall, lose its novelty, cloy, jade, satiate 863 *sate*; bore, irk, try, weary 684 *fatigue*; bore to death, bore to tears, bore the pants off, bore stiff; weary to distraction, get one down, get on one's nerves, outstay one's welcome; make one yawn, send one to sleep; drag 278 *move slowly*; go on and on, never end; drone on, bang on, harp on; be prolix 570 *be diffuse*.

Adv. *boringly*, ad nauseam, to death.

839 Wit

N. *wit*, wittiness, pointedness, point; ready wit, badinage, repartee; Attic salt, elegance; sparkle, scintillation, brightness 498 *intelligence*; humour, sense of h.; wry humour, pawkiness, dryness; drollery, pleasantry, waggishness, facetiousness; jocularity 833 *merriment*; comicalness, absurdity 849 *ridiculousness*; flippancy 456 *inattention*; fun, joking, practical j., jesting, tomfoolery, buffoonery, clowning, funny business 497 *foolery*; comic turn, laugh a minute; broad humour, low h., vulgarity 847 *bad taste*; farce, broad f., knockabout comedy, slapstick, custard-pie humour, ham, high camp 594 *dramaturgy*; whimsicality, fancy 604 *whim*; cartoon, comic strip, caricature; biting wit, cruel humour, satire, sarcasm 851 *ridicule*; irony, spoof 850 *affectation*; black comedy, black humour, sick h.; wordplay, play upon words, punning.

witticism, witty remark; sally, mot, bon mot; epigram; pun, play upon words; punch line, throwaway l.; banter, chaff, badinage; repartee, quid pro quo, backchat 460 *answer*; sarcasm 851 *satire*; joke, standing j., private j., family j., in-joke; jest, good one, rib-tickler, side-splitter; quip, gag, one-liner; old joke, corny j., chestnut; practical joke, hoax, spoof, legpull; dirty joke, blue j., sick j.; story, funny s., shaggy-dog s.; limerick, clerihew.

humorist, wit, epigrammatist; life and soul of the party, wag, joker; jokesmith, funny man, gagster, punster; banterer, leg-puller, ragger, teaser; practical joker, hoaxer, spoof artist 545 *deceiver*; satirist, lampooner 926 *detractor*; comedian, comedienne, comic, standup c., slapstick c. 594 *entertainer*; comic writer, cartoonist, caricaturist; impersonator, parodist 20 *imitator*;

raconteur, raconteuse; jester, court j., clown, zany, buffoon, stooge 501 *fool*.

Adj. *witty*, nimble-witted, quick; elegant; pointed, pithy, epigrammatic; brilliant, sparkling, smart, clever, too clever by half 498 *intelligent*; salty, racy, piquant; fruity, risqué; snappy, biting, pungent, keen, sharp, sarcastic; ironic, dry, sly, pawky; facetious, flippant 456 *lightminded*; jocular, joking, jokey, waggish, roguish; comic, funny ha-ha, rib-tickling 849 *funny*; comical, humorous, droll; whimsical 604 *capricious*; playful, sportive, fooling 497 *absurd*.

Vb. *be witty*, scintillate, sparkle; jest, joke, crack a j., quip, wisecrack; tell a good story, raise a laugh, have the audience in stitches 837 *amuse*; pun, make a p., play upon words; pull one's leg, have one on, put one on, make fun of, poke fun at, get a rise out of 851 *ridicule*; caricature 851 *satirize*.

840 Dullness

N. *dullness*, heaviness 834 *dejection*; stuffiness, dreariness, dreichness, deadliness; monotony, boringness 838 *tedium*; colourlessness, drabness; lack of sparkle, lack of fire, lack of inspiration, want of originality; stodginess, turgidity; staleness, flatness 387 *insipidity*; banality; lack of humour, prosaicness.

Adj. *dull*, uninteresting, uninspiring; deadly dull, dull as ditchwater; stuffy, dreary, deadly; boring, tedious; colourless, drab; flat, bland, vapid, insipid 387 *tasteless*; unimaginative, uninventive, unoriginal, derivative; stupid 499 *unintelligent*; humourless, frumpish 834 *serious*; inelegant; heavy, heavy-footed, clod-hopping, ponderous, sluggish 278 *slow*; stodgy, turgid, prosaic, matter-of-fact, pedestrian; stale, banal, common-place, hackneyed, trite, platitudinous 610 *usual*.

841 Beauty

N. *beauty*, pulchritude; perfection; the sublime, splendour, gorgeousness; radiance; transfiguration 843 *beautification*; polish, gloss, ornament 844 *ornamentation*; scenic beauty, picturesqueness, scenery, view, landscape, seascape, snowscape, cloudscape 445 *spectacle*; regular features, classic f. 245 *symmetry*; physical beauty, loveliness, comeliness, fairness, handsomeness, bonniness, prettiness, chocolate-box p., picture-postcard p.; attraction, attractiveness, agreeableness, charm 826 *pleasurableness*; appeal, glamour, glitz, sex appeal, it, cuteness, attractions, physical a., charms; good looks, pretty face, beaux yeux; eyes of blue, ruby lips, schoolgirl complexion, peaches and cream c.; shapeliness, trim figure, curves, curvaceousness, vital statistics; gracefulness, grace 575 *elegance*;

chic, style, dress sense 848 *fashion*; delicacy, refinement 846 *good taste*; aesthetics.

a beauty, thing of beauty, work of art; garden, beauty spot; masterpiece 644 *exceller*; bijou, jewel, jewel in the crown, pearl, treasure 646 *paragon*; peacock, swan, flower, rosebud, rose, lily; belle, raving beauty, toast of the tour, idol 890 *favourite*; dream girl; jolie laide; beauty queen, Miss World, bathing belle, pin-up girl, cover girl, page 3 girl, centre-fold g., pin-up, cheesecake; beefcake, hunk, muscleman, Mr Universe, spunk, fine figure of a man *or* woman; blond(e), brunette, redhead; English rose; dream, a dream walking, vision, poem, picture, sight for sore eyes; angel, charmer, dazzler; knockout, eyeful, good-looker, looker; doll, dolly bird; glamour puss, glamour girl *or* boy; heartthrob, dreamboat; enchantress, femme fatale, vamp, seductress, siren, witch 983 *sorceress*; smasher, lovely, cutie, honey, beaut, peach, dish; bimbo; Venus, Aphrodite, Helen of Troy; Adonis, Narcissus.

Adj. *beautiful*, pulchritudinous, beauteous; lovely, fair, radiant; comely, bonny, pretty; pretty-pretty, pretty in a chocolate box way, picture-postcard, good enough to eat; pretty as a picture, photogenic; handsome, good-looking; well-built, husky, manly; tall, dark and handsome; statuesque, Junoesque; godlike, goddess-like, divine, pleasing to the eye, lovely to behold; picturesque, scenic, ornamental; aesthetic 846 *tasteful*; exquisite, perfect.

splendid, superb, fine 644 *excellent*; grand 868 *noble*; glorious, rich, gorgeous; resplendent, magnificent.

shapely, well-proportioned, of classic proportions 245 *symmetrical*; well-formed, well-turned; well-rounded, well-stacked, well-endowed, buxom, bosomy, curvaceous 248 *curved*; slinky; clean-limbed, straight, slender, slim, lissom, svelte, willowy 206 *lean*; graceful, elegant, chic, petite, dainty, delicate; perfect.

personable, prepossessing, agreeable; buxom, sonsy; attractive, dishy, phat, fetching, appealing 826 *pleasurable*; sexy, cute; charming, entrancing, alluring, enchanting, glamorous; winsome; fresh-faced, clean-cut, wholesome, blooming; rosy-cheeked, apple-c., cherry-lipped, fresh-complexioned, bright-eyed; sightly, becoming, easy on the eye; presentable, natty, trim; spruce, dapper, glossy, sleek; well-dressed, well turned out, smart, stylish, classy, chic, soigné(e) 848 *fashionable*; elegant, dainty, delicate, refined 846 *tasteful*.

Vb. *be beautiful*, – splendid etc. adj.; be entrancing 983 *bewitch*; take one's breath away, beggar all description; be photogenic, photo-

graph well; have good looks, bloom, dazzle 417 *shine*; be dressed to kill.

beautify, trim, improve; prettify, decorate; ornament; set off, grace, suit, become, go well, show one off, flatter; bring out the highlights, enhance one's looks, glamorize, transfigure; give a face-lift, smarten up; prink, titivate, do oneself up, do one's face, powder, rouge 843 *primp*.

842 Ugliness

N. *ugliness*, unsightliness, hideousness, repulsiveness; gracelessness, lumpishness, clumsiness 576 *inelegance*; asymmetry 246 *distortion*; unshapeliness 246 *deformity*; disfigurement 845 *blemish*; defacement; squalor, filth, grottiness, yuk 649 *uncleanness*; homeliness, plainness, ugly face; not much to look at, no beauty, no oil painting, wry face, forbidding countenance, haggardness; fading beauty, dim eyes, wrinkles, crow's-feet, hand of time, ravages of time 131 *age*.

eyesore, hideosity; blemish; offence to the eyes; blot on the landscape, architectural monstrosity, satanic mills; ugly person, fright, sight, frump; scarecrow, horror, death's-head, gargoyle; monster; harridan, witch; toad, gorilla, baboon, crow; plain Jane, ugly duckling; satyr, Caliban; Gorgon, Medusa; Beast.

Adj. *ugly*, ugly as sin, hideous, foul 649 *unclean*; frightful, shocking, monstrous; repulsive, repellent, odious, loathsome; beastly; not much to look at, short on looks, unprepossessing, homely, plain, plain-looking, without any looks; mousy, frumpish; ill-favoured, saturnine 893 *sullen*.

unsightly, ravaged, wrinkled 131 *ageing*; not fit to be seen, unseemly; marred; shapeless, formless 244 *amorphous*; grotesque, twisted, deformed, disfigured 246 *distorted*; defaced, vandalized, litter-strewn; ill-proportioned, misshapen; dumpy, squat 196 *dwarfish*; bloated 195 *fleshy*; ghastly; gruesome.

graceless, ungraceful 576 *inelegant*; unaesthetic; unattractive; badly dressed; tawdry; crude, uncouth 699 *artless*; clumsy, awkward, ungainly, cumbersome, hulky, hulking, slouching, clodhopping 195 *unwieldy*.

Vb. *be ugly*, be short on looks, lose one's l.; show one's age; look a wreck, look a mess, look a fright.

make ugly, uglify; sully 649 *make unclean*; deface, disfigure, mar, blemish; grimace; twist 246 *distort*; mutilate, vandalize 655 *impair*.

843 Beautification

N. *beautification*, beautifying 844 *ornamentation*; make-over, transfiguration 143 *transformation*;

landscape gardening 844 *ornamental art*; plastic surgery, cosmetic s., nose-job, skin-grafting, face-lift 658 *surgery*; beauty treatment, face-lifting, eyebrow-plucking, waxing, electrolysis; face mask, mud pack, facial, facial scrub; massage, body m.; manicure, buffing; pedicure, chiropody; tattooing 844 *ornamental art*; ear-piercing; sun-tanning; sun lamp, sun bed; toilet, grooming, make-up, cosmetology; cleansing, moisturizing, toning, creaming, rouging, painting, dyeing, powdering; soaping, shampooing; wash and brush up 648 *ablutions*.

hairdressing, trichology; shaving, clipping, trimming, thinning, singeing; depilation; cutting, haircut, bobbing, shingling; shave, hair cut, razor c., clip, trim, singe, short back and sides; hair style, coiffure, crop, Eton c., bob, shingle, pageboy, crewcut, urchin cut, bouffant c., coupe sauvage, spike; styling, hair-s., curling, frizzing, waving, setting, hair-straightening, defrizzing; hairdo, restyle, shampoo and set, set; blow-dry, finger-dry, scrunching; wave, blow w., marcel w., cold w.; permanent w., perm; curl 251 *coil*; bang, fringe, ponytail, bunches, pigtail, plaits, chignon, bun; pompadour, beehive, Afro 259 *hair*; hairpiece, toupee, switch, hair extension, hair weaving, hair implant; curling iron, tongs, curl papers, curlers, rollers, heated r.; bandeau, Alice band; comb, hairpin, hairgrip, bobby pin, Kirbigrip (tdmk), slide; hairnet, snood 228 *headgear*.

hairwash, shampoo, conditioner, rinse, highlights, bleach, tint, dye, henna, peroxide; hair mousse, hair gel, setting lotion, hair spray, lacquer, hair-cream, brilliantine; hair-restorer.

cosmetic, beauty aid, beauty spot; make-up, stick m.; greasepaint, warpaint, rouge, blusher, highlighter, cream, face c., cold c., cleansing c., vanishing c., moisturizing c., night c., lanolin 357 *unguent*; lipstick, lip gloss; nail polish, nail varnish, powder, face p., talcum p.; eye make-up, kohl, mascara, eye shadow, eyeliner, eyebrow pencil; hand lotion, skin toner, aftershave lotion, sun-tan l.; bath salts, bath oil, bath essence, bubble bath, foam b. 648 *cleanser*; antiperspirant, deodorant; scent, perfume, essence, cologne, eau de c., lavender water, toilet w.; false eyelashes; powder puff, compact; vanity case, manicure set, nail file, nail scissors, clippers; shaver, razor, electric r., depilatory, strip wax; toiletry, toiletries.

beautician, plastic surgeon; make-up artist; cosmetician; barber, hairdresser, hair stylist, coiffeur, coiffeuse; trichologist; manicurist, pedicurist, chiropodist.

Vb. *primp*, prettify, doll up, do up, dress up, ornament 844 *decorate*; prink, trick out; preen; titivate, make up, apply cosmetics, rouge, paint, powder; shave, pluck one's eyebrows, wax one's e., varnish one's nails, dye *or* tint one's hair; curl, wave, perm; have a hairdo, have a facial, have a manicure 841 *beautify*.

844 Ornamentation

N. *ornamentation*, decoration, adornment, garnish; ornateness 574 *ornament*; art deco, art nouveau, baroque, rococo; chinoiserie; richness, gilt, gaudiness 875 *ostentation*; enhancement, enrichment, embellishment; table decoration, centrepiece, silver, china, glass; floral decoration, flower arrangement, wreath, garland, bouquet, nosegay, posy, buttonhole; objet d'art, bric-a-brac, curio, bibelot.

ornamental art, landscape gardening, topiarism; architecture; interior decoration; statuary 554 *sculpture*; frieze, dado, triglyph; figurehead; boss, cornice, gargoyle; astragal, moulding, beading, fluting; fretting, tracery; varnishing 226 *facing*; veneering, panelling; ormolu, gilt, gold leaf; illumination, illustration, sign-painting, graphic art 551 *art*; stained glass; tie-dyeing, batik; heraldic art 547 *heraldry*; tattooing; etching 555 *engraving*; handiwork, handicraft, fancywork, woodwork, fretwork, open-work, filigree; whittling, carving, embossing, chasing, intaglio; inlay, inset, enamelling, mosaic, marquetry 437 *variegation*; metalwork; gem-cutting, setting; cut glass, engraved g.; wrought iron.

pattern, motif, print, design, composition 331 *structure*; detail; geometrical style, rose window, spandrel, cyma, ogee, fleuron, cusp, trefoil, fleur-de-lis; tracery, scrollwork, arabesque, flourish, curlicue 251 *coil*; weave 331 *texture*; argyle, Arran, paisley 222 *textile*; chevron; tartan, check 437 *chequer*; pin-stripe 437 *stripe*; spot, dot, polka d. 437 *maculation*; herringbone, zigzag, dogtooth, hound's tooth 220 *obliquity*; watermark, logo 547 *identification*.

needlework, cross-stitch; patchwork, appliqué; open work, drawn-thread w.; embroidery, smocking; crochet, lace, broderie anglaise; tatting, knitting 222 *network*; stitch, purl, plain, stocking stitch, garter s., moss s.; gros point, petit p., needle p.; chain stitch, cable s., hem s., stem s., blanket s., feather s., back s., satin s., herringbone s., French knot, lazy-daisy.

trimming, piping, valance, border, fringe, frieze, frill, flounce 234 *edging*; binding 589 *bookbinding*; trappings; braid, frog, lapel, epaulette, star, rosette, cockade 547 *badge*; bow 47 *fastening*; bobble, pompom; tassel, bead; ermine, fur 259 *hair*; feather, ostrich f., osprey, plume 259 *plumage*; streamer, ribbon.

finery, togs, gear, glad rags, Sunday best, best bib and tucker 228 *clothing*; frippery, frills and furbelows, ribbons, froufrou; trinket, knick-knack, gewgaw, fandangle; tinsel, spangle, sequin, diamante, costume jewellery, glass, paste, marcasite, rhinestone 639 *bauble*.

jewellery, bijouterie; crown jewels, diadem, tiara 743 *regalia*; costume jewellery; drop, pendant, locket 217 *hanging object*; crucifix; amulet, charm 983 *talisman*; rope, string, necklet, necklace, beads, pearls, choker, chain, watch c. 250 *loop*; armlet, anklet, bracelet, bangle; ring, earring, drop e., signet ring, wedding r., eternity r., engagement r., dress r. 250 *circle*; cameo, brooch, clasp, badge, crest; stud, pin, gold p., tie p., collar stud, cufflinks 47 *fastening*; medal, medallion.

gem, jewel, bijou; stone, precious s., semiprecious s.; uncut gem, cut g., cabochon; diamond, rock, ice; solitaire; ruby, pearl, cultured p., seed p.; opal, black o., fire o.; sapphire, turquoise, emerald, beryl, aquamarine; garnet, amethyst, topaz, chalcedony, cornelian, jasper, agate, onyx; heliotrope, bloodstone, moonstone, cat's-eye, zircon, jacinth, hyacinth, chrysolite; coral, ivory, mother of pearl, jet, amber, jade, lapis lazuli.

Adj. *ornamental*, decorative, decorated, patterned, fancy, arty-crafty; intricate, elaborate; picturesque, pretty-pretty, chocolate-box pretty; scenic; geometric; Doric, Ionic, Corinthian, Moresque, Romanesque, Decorated; baroque, rococo; gimmicky, with bells and whistles, all singing, all dancing.

Vb. *decorate*, adorn, embellish, enhance, enrich; set off 574 *ornament*; paint, bejewel; tart up, glamorize, prettify 841 *beautify*; garnish, trim; array, bedeck 228 *dress*; deck out, trick o., preen, titivate 843 *primp*; add the finishing touches; freshen, smarten, spruce up, furbish, burnish 648 *clean*; beribbon; stud, bespangle 437 *variegate*; whitewash, varnish, japan, lacquer 226 *coat*; enamel, gild, silver; emblazon, illuminate, illustrate 553 *paint*, 425 *colour*; trim 234 *hem*; work, pick out, embroider; inlay, engrave; encrust, emboss, bead, mould; fret, carve 262 *groove*, 260 *notch*; wreathe.

845 Blemish

N. *blemish*, scar, cicatrice, weal, welt, mark, pockmark; flaw, crack, defect 647 *imperfection*; disfigurement, deformity 246 *distortion*; stigma, blot, blot on the landscape 842 *eyesore*; graffiti; blotch, splotch, smudge 550 *obliteration*; smut, patch, smear, stain, tarnish, rust, patina 649 *dirt*; spot, speck, speckle, macula, spottiness 437 *maculation*; freckle, mole, birthmark, strawberry mark; excrescence, pimple, plook, zit, blackhead, whitehead, carbuncle, sebaceous cyst, wen, wart 253 *swelling*; acne, rosacea, eczema

651 *skin disease*; harelip, cleft palate; cast, squint; scratch, bruise, black eye, shiner, cauliflower ear, broken nose 655 *wound*.

Vb. *blemish*, flaw, crack, injure, damage 655 *impair*; blot, smudge, stain, smear, sully, soil 649 *make unclean*; stigmatize, brand 547 *mark*; scar, pit, pockmark; mar, spoil, spoil the look of 842 *make ugly*; deface, vandalize, disfigure, scratch 244 *deform*.

846 Good Taste

N. *good taste*, tastefulness, taste; simplicity 573 *plainness*; refinement, delicacy 950 *purity*; discernment, palate 463 *discrimination*; daintiness, finickiness, fikiness, kid gloves 862 *fastidiousness*; decency, seemliness 848 *etiquette*; tact, consideration, dignity, manners, table m., breeding, civility, social graces 884 *courtesy*; propriety, decorum; grace, polish, finish, sophistication, gracious living 575 *elegance*; cultivation, culture, connoisseurship; epicureanism, epicurism; aesthetics 480 *judgment*; artistry, virtuosity.

people of taste, connoisseur, cognoscente; epicurean, epicure, gourmet; aesthete, art critic 480 *estimator*; arbiter of taste; purist.

Adj. *tasteful*, in good taste, in the best of t.; exquisite 644 *excellent*; simple 573 *plain*; graceful, classical 575 *elegant*; refined, delicate 950 *pure*; aesthetic, artistic 819 *sensitive*; discerning, epicurean 463 *discriminating*; nice, dainty 862 *fastidious*; decent, seemly, becoming 24 *apt*; proper, correct, comme il faut 848 *fashionable*; mannerly 848 *well-bred*.

Vb. *have taste*, show good t., reveal fine feelings 463 *discriminate*; appreciate, value 480 *judge*; settle for nothing less than the best, be a perfectionist 862 *be fastidious*.

847 Bad Taste

N. *bad taste*, tastelessness, poor taste 645 *badness*; no taste; kitsch; commercialization; yellow press, gutter p.; unrefinement, coarseness, barbarism, vulgarism, philistinism 699 *artlessness*; vulgarity, gaudiness, garishness, loudness; tawdriness, shoddiness; paste, ersatz, imitation 639 *bauble*; insensitivity, crassness, grossness, coarseness; tactlessness, indelicacy, impropriety, unseemliness; bad joke, sick j., obscenity 951 *impurity*; dowdiness.

ill-breeding, vulgarity, commonness; loudness; provinciality, suburbanism, unfashionableness; bad form, lack of etiquette; bad manners, boorishness, impoliteness 885 *discourtesy*; ungentlemanliness; unladylikeness; misbehaviour, indecorum; rowdyism 61 *disorder*.

Adj. *vulgar*, unrefined 576 *inelegant*; tasteless, in bad taste, in the worst possible t.; gross, crass, coarse; philistine, yobbish, barbarian 699 *artless*; commercial, commercialized; tawdry, cheap, cheap and nasty, naff, kitschy, ersatz; flashy; blatant, loud, gaudy, garish; flaunting, shameless; excessive; schmaltzy; overdressed; common, common as muck, low, gutter, sordid 867 *disreputable*; improper, indelicate, indecorous; beyond the pale, scandalous, indecent, ribald 951 *impure*.

ill-bred, badly brought up; unpresentable, not to be taken anywhere; ungentlemanly, unladylike; hoydenish; ungenteel, non-U 869 *plebeian*; loud; tactless, insensitive, blunt; impolite, unmannerly, ill-mannered 885 *discourteous*; provincial, gone native; crude, rude, boorish, churlish, yobbish, loutish, clodhopping, uncouth, uncultured, unrefined 491 *ignorant*; unsophisticated, knowing no better 699 *artless*; uncivilized, barbaric; gauche 695 *clumsy*; rowdy 61 *disorderly*.

848 Fashion. Etiquette

N. *fashion*, style, mode, cut 243 *form*; method 624 *way*; vogue, cult 610 *habit*; prevailing taste, current fashion, trend 126 *modernism*; rage, fad, craze; new look, the latest, latest fashion, what's new, New Look 126 *newness* retro fashion; retro style; Gothic look; grunge; dernier cri, last word, ne plus ultra, height of fashion; dash 875 *ostentation* fashionableness; stylishness, flair, chic, anti-chic; dress sense; fashion show, mannequin parade 522 *exhibit*; haute couture, elegance; foppery 850 *affectation*.

etiquette, point of e. 875 *formality*; protocol, convention, custom, conventionality 610 *practice*; done thing, good form, what is expected; proprieties, appearances, Mrs Grundy; decorum, propriety, right note, correctness 846 *good taste*; courtesy; breeding, good b.; gentility, gentlemanliness, ladylike behaviour; manners, table m., good m.; best behaviour, savoir-faire, savvy 688 *conduct*.

beau monde, society, high s., civilization; Mayfair; St James's, court; top drawer, right people, smart set, upper ten 868 *nobility*; upper crust, cream of society 644 *elite*; beautiful people, glitterati, jet set; fashionable person; Sloane Ranger, Sloane; yuppy; man *or* woman about town, man *or* woman of fashion, slave to fashion, trend-setter; man *or* woman of the world, socialite, playboy 882 *sociable person*.

fop, buck; dandy, beau. Beau Brummel; popinjay, peacock, clothes-horse, fashion plate; coxcomb; swell, toff, dude, nob, His Nibs, Lady Muck; lounge lizard, gigolo, gallant; ladykiller.

Adj. *fashionable*, modish, stylish, voguish; in, in vogue, in fashion, à la mode, chichi; chic, elegant, colour-supplement, well-dressed, well-groomed 846 *tasteful*; clothes-conscious, foppish, dressy; dashing, snazzy, flashy 875 *showy*; smart, classy, ritzy, swanky, swish, posh; up-to-the-minute, bang up-to-date, ultrafashionable, new-fangled, all the rage 126 *modern*; cool, hip, hep, groovy, trendy, with it; dressed up to the nines, dressed to kill; from the top drawer, moving in the best circles, knowing the right people; in the swim 83 *conformable*.

well-bred, thoroughbred, blue-blooded 868 *noble*; civilized, urbane; well brought up, housetrained; U, gentlemanly, ladylike 868 *genteel*; civil, well-mannered, well-spoken 884 *courteous*; courtly 875 *formal*; poised; correct, conventional, decorous, proper; considerate 884 *amiable*; punctilious 929 *honourable*.

Vb. *be in fashion*, be done, catch on 610 *be wont*; be all the rage, be the latest, be the latest craze, be trendy 126 *modernize*; get with it, follow the fashion, jump on the band wagon, change with the times 83 *conform*; move in the best circles, be seen in the right places; keep up with the Jones's, keep up appearances; cut a dash, be a trend-setter, set the tone; have style.

849 Ridiculousness

N. *ridiculousness*, ludicrousness, risibility, laughability, height of nonsense, height of absurdity 497 *absurdity*; funniness, pricelessness, drollery 839 *wit*; quaintness, oddness, queerness, eccentricity 84 *nonconformity*; bathos, anticlimax 509 *disappointment*; extravagance, bombast 546 *exaggeration*; light relief, comic r.; light verse, comic v., nonsense v., doggerel, limerick 839 *witticism*; spoonerism, malapropism, bull; comic turn, comedy, farce, burlesque, slapstick, knockabout, clowning, buffoonery 594 *stage play*.

Adj. *ridiculous*, ludicrous, preposterous, monstrous, grotesque, fantastic, inappropriate 497 *absurd*; clownish 695 *clumsy*; silly 499 *foolish*; derisory 639 *unimportant*; laughable, risible; bizarre, rum, quaint, odd, queer 84 *unusual*; strange, outlandish 59 *extraneous*; stilted 850 *affected*; bombastic, extravagant, outré; crazy, crackpot.

funny, funny-peculiar 84 *abnormal*; funny-ha-ha, good for a laugh 837 *amusing*; comical, droll, humorous 839 *witty*; rich, priceless, side-splitting, wildly amusing, hilarious, a real hoot, a scream, too funny for words; light, comic; ironical, satirical; burlesque; doggerel; farcical, slapstick, clownish, custard-pie, knockabout.

Vb. *be ridiculous*, make one laugh, excite laughter, raise a laugh; tickle, make one fall about, give one the giggles; entertain 837 *amuse*; look silly, be a figure of fun, cut a ridiculous figure, be a laughingstock, fool, play the fool 497 *be absurd*; pass from the sublime to the ridiculous; make an exhibition of oneself 695 *act foolishly*.

850 Affectation

N. *affectation*, fad 848 *fashion*; affectedness, pretentiousness 875 *ostentation*; putting on airs, grand a. 873 *airs*; posing, posturing, attitudinizing; pose, public image, façade; artificiality, mannerism, literary affectation, grandiloquence; preciosity, euphuism 574 *ornament*; foppery, foppishness, dandyism 873 *vanity*; euphemism, mock modesty 874 *modesty*; theatricality, camp, histrionics.

pretension, pretensions, false p.; artifice, sham, humbug, quackery, charlatanism, fraud 542 *deception*; superficiality; stiltedness; pedantry 735 *severity*; prudery; sanctimony, sanctimoniousness 979 *pietism*.

Adj. *affected*, self-conscious; studied, mannered, euphuistic, precious, chichi 574 *ornate*; artificial, unnatural, stilted 875 *formal*; prim, priggish, prudish, goody-goody, mealy-mouthed, euphemistic, sanctimonious, self-righteous, holier than thou, smug, demure 979 *pietistic*; arch, sly, nudging, winking 833 *merry*; coquettish, coy, cute, twee, too-too, namby-pamby, mincing, simpering; hypocritical, tongue-in-cheek, ironical; bluffing; shallow, hollow, specious, pretentious, high-sounding; gushing, fulsome, stagy, theatrical, camp, over-dramatized 875 *ostentatious*; dandified, foppish, poncy, camp; conceited, la-di-da, giving oneself airs, putting on a., showing off, swanking, posturing, posing, striking poses, attitudinizing 873 *vain*; stuck up 871 *prideful*; name-dropping, keeping up appearances 847 *ill-bred*; bogus 541 *false*; for effect, assumed, put on, insincere, phoney; overdone.

Vb. *be affected*, affect, put on, assume; pretend, feign, go through the motions, make a show of, bluff 541 *dissemble*; make as if 20 *imitate*; act a part, play-act, role-play 594 *act*; overact, ham, barnstorm 546 *exaggerate*; do for effect, camp it up, play to the gallery; dramatize oneself, attitudinize, strike attitudes, posture, strike a p., prance, mince, ponce about 875 *be ostentatious*; put on airs, give oneself a., put on side, swank, show off, make an exhibition of oneself 873 *be vain*; air one's knowledge 490 *know*; euphuize.

851 Ridicule

N. *ridicule*, derision, derisiveness, poking fun; mockery, mimicry, scoffing; sniggering, grinning 835 *laughter*; teasing, making fun of, ribbing, banter, badinage, leg-pulling, chaff, leg-pull; buffoonery, horseplay, clowning, practical joke 497 *foolery*; snigger, scoff, mock;

irony, sarcasm, barbed shaft, backhanded compliment; catcall, hoot, hiss 924 *censure*; ribaldry 839 *witticism*.

satire, parody, burlesque, travesty, caricature, cartoon 552 *misrepresentation*; skit, spoof, send-up, take-off 20 *mimicry*; lampoon 926 *detraction*.

laughingstock, object of ridicule, figure of fun, butt; sport, game, fair g.; Aunt Sally; April fool, silly f., buffoon, clown, zany 501 *fool*; stooge, foil, feed, straight man; guy, caricature, travesty, mockery of, apology for; eccentric 504 *crank*; original, card, caution, queer fish, odd f.; fall guy, victim 728 *loser*.

Vb. *ridicule*, deride, pour scorn on, laugh at, smirk at; snigger, laugh in *or* up one's sleeve; banter, chaff, twit, rib, tease, rag, pull one's leg, poke fun, make fun of, make sport of, make game of, take the mickey out of, have one on, put one on, kid, fool, make a fool of, make a laughing-stock of, take the piss out of (vulg), make an April fool of; mock, scoff, jeer 926 *detract*; make a joke of 922 *hold cheap*; take down, deflate, debunk, take the wind out of one's sails, make one look silly, make one laugh on the other side of his face 872 *humiliate*.

satirize, lampoon 921 *not respect*; mock; mimic, send up, take off 20 *imitate*; parody, travesty, spoof, burlesque, caricature 552 *misrepresent*; pillory 928 *accuse*.

852 Hope

N. *hope*, hopes, expectations, presumption 507 *expectation*; high hopes, conviction 485 *belief*; reliance, trust, confidence, faith, assurance 473 *certainty*; reassurance 831 *relief*; security, anchor, mainstay, staff 218 *support*; last hope, ray of hope, glimmer of h. 469 *possibility*; good omen, favourable auspices, promise, bright prospect 511 *omen*; blue sky, silver lining, a break in the clouds; hopefulness; buoyancy, optimism 833 *cheerfulness*; wishful thinking, self-deception; rose-coloured spectacles, rosy picture.

aspiration, ambition, purpose 617 *intention*; pious hope, fond h.; vision, pipe dream, heart's desire; castles in the air, castles in Spain, El Dorado, fool's paradise 513 *fantasy*; the end of the rainbow, promised land, utopia, millennium, the day 617 *objective*.

hoper, aspirant, candidate, young hopeful, wannabe; optimist; utopian 513 *visionary*; Micawber.

Adj. *hoping*, aspiring, starry-eyed; ambitious, go-getting, would-be; dreaming, day-dreaming 513 *imaginative*; hopeful, in hopes 507 *expectant*; happy in the hope, in sight of, on the verge of; sanguine, confident 473 *certain*; buoyant, optimistic; hoping for the best, everhoping.

promising, full of promise, favourable, auspicious, propitious 730 *prosperous*; bright, fair, golden, rosy; hopeful, encouraging; likely 471 *probable*; utopian, millennial; visionary 513 *imaginary*.

Vb. *hope*, trust, have faith; rest assured, feel confident, put one's trust in, rely, bank on, count on, pin one's hopes on, hope and believe 485 *believe*; assume; look forward 507 *expect*; hope for, dream of, aspire, promise oneself, aim high 617 *intend*; have hopes, have high h., have expectations, live in hopes, keep one's fingers crossed; nurse hope; take hope, recover h., see light at the end of the tunnel; refuse to give up hope, see no cause for despair, hope against hope, keep hope alive, never say die; catch at straws, keep one's spirits up, look on the bright side, hope for the best 833 *be cheerful*; keep smiling 600 *persevere*; see life through rose-coloured spectacles; delude oneself 477 *reason badly*; anticipate, count one's chickens before they are hatched 135 *be early*; indulge in wishful thinking, dream 513 *imagine*.

Int. nil desperandum! never say die! while there's life there's hope! hope springs eternal!

853 Hopelessness

N. *hopelessness*, no hope, defeatism, despondency 834 *dejection*; pessimism, cynicism, despair, desperation, no way out, last hope gone; dashed hopes, hope extinguished 509 *disappointment*; resignation 508 *lack of expectation*; not a hope 470 *impossibility*; vain hope, forlorn h. 513 *fantasy*; poor lookout, no prospects; hopeless case, dead duck; hopeless situation, catch-22, bad business 700 *predicament*; Job's comforter.

Adj. *hopeless*, bereft of hope, devoid of h., despairing, in despair, desperate, suicidal; unhopeful, pessimistic, cynical, looking on the black side; defeatist, fearing the worst, sunk in despair, inconsolable, disconsolate 834 *dejected*; wringing one's hands 836 *lamenting*; disappointed; desolate, forlorn; ruined, undone, 731 *unfortunate*.

unpromising, hopeless 834 *cheerless*; desperate 661 *dangerous*; unpropitious, inauspicious 731 *adverse*; ill-omened, ominous 511 *presageful*; irremediable, incurable, inoperable, terminal; beyond hope, past recall, despaired of; incorrigible, irreparable, irrecoverable, irrevocable, irreversible, inevitable; out of the question 470 *impossible*.

Vb. *despair*, lose heart, lose hope; become despondent, give way to despair, wring one's hands 834 *be dejected*; have shot one's last bolt, have no cards up one's sleeves, give up hope;

abandon h., hope for nothing more from, write off 674 *stop using*; give up, turn one's face to the wall 721 *submit*.

854 Fear

N. *fear*, healthy f., dread, awe 920 *respect*; abject fear 856 *cowardice*; fright, stage f.; wind up, funk, blue funk; terror, mortal t.; state of terror, intimidation, trepidation, alarm, false a.; shock, flutter, flap, flat spin 318 *agitation*; fit, fit of terror, scare, stampede, panic, panic attack 318 *spasm*; flight, sauve qui peut; the creeps, horror, hair on end, cold sweat; dismay 853 *hopelessness*; defence mechanism, fight or flight.

nervousness, lack of confidence 856 *cowardice*; diffidence 874 *modesty*; timidity, timorousness, fearfulness, hesitation 620 *avoidance*; loss of nerve, cold feet, second thoughts, fears, suspicions, misgivings, qualms, mistrust, apprehension, apprehensiveness, uneasiness, disquiet, anxiety, angst, care 825 *worry*; perturbation, trepidation, fear and trembling, flutter, tremor, palpitation, trembling, quaking, shaking, shuddering, shivering, stuttering; nerves, willies, butterflies, collywobbles, creeps, shivers, jumps, jitters, heebie-jeebies 318 *agitation*; gooseflesh, hair on end, knees knocking, teeth chattering.

phobia, claustrophobia, agoraphobia, aerophobia, acrophobia, pyrophobia, frigophobia, pogonophobia, autophobia, phobophobia, acrophobia, zoophobia, algophobia, monophobia, aquaphobia, astrophobia, nyctophobia, triskaidekaphobia, homophobia, ailurophobia, canophobia; thanatophobia, fear of death; technophobia, cyberphobia, technofear; antisemitism, racial prejudice, xenophobia 888 *hatred*; McCarthyism, Reds under the beds, witch-hunting.

intimidation, deterrence, war of nerves, sabrerattling, arms build up, fee faw fum; threatening 900 *threat*; caution 664 *warning*; terror, terrorism, reign of terror 735 *severity*; alarmism, scaremongering; sword of Damocles, suspended sentence 963 *punishment*; deterrent 723 *weapon*; object of terror, goblin, hobgoblin 970 *demon*; spook, spectre 970 *ghost*; Gorgon, Medusa, scarecrow, tattie bogle, nightmare; bugbear, ogre 938 *monster*; skeleton, death's head, skull and crossbones.

alarmist, scaremonger, doom merchant, gloom and doom m., doom-watcher, doomster, ecodoomster, Cassandra, Calamity Jane; pessimist; terrorist; sabre-rattler.

Adj. *fearing*, afraid, frightened, funky, panicky; overawed 920 *respectful*; intimidated, terrorized; in mortal fear, in trepidation, in a cold sweat, in a flap, in a flat spin, in a panic, in a frenzy; panic-stricken; stampeding, scared, alarmed, startled; hysterical, having fits, in hysterics, in the grip of a panic attack; dismayed; frozen, petrified, stunned; aghast, horrorstruck, unmanned, scared out of one's wits, trembling with fear, paralysed by f., rooted to the spot with fear, frightened to death, white as a sheet, ashen-faced.

nervous, tense, uptight; waiting for the axe to fall; timid, timorous, shy, diffident, self-conscious 874 *modest*; wary, shrinking, treading warily 858 *cautious*; doubtful, distrustful, suspicious 474 *doubting*; windy, faint-hearted 601 *irresolute*; disturbed; apprehensive, uneasy, fearful, dreading, anxious, worried 825 *unhappy*; a prey to fears; highly-strung, afraid of one's own shadow, jittery, jumpy, nervy, on edge; shaking, trembling, quaking, cowering, cringing 856 *cowardly*; with one's heart in one's mouth, shaking like a leaf *or* a jelly; on pins and needles, palpitating, breathless.

frightening, shocking, startling, alarming etc. vb.; formidable, redoubtable; hazardous, hairy 661 *dangerous*; dreadful, awe-inspiring, fearsome, awesome 821 *impressive*; grim, grisly, hideous, ghastly, lurid, frightful, revolting; petrifying, horrifying, horrific, horrible, terrible, awful; mind-boggling, mind-blowing; hair-raising, flesh-creeping, blood-curdling; weird, eerie, creepy, scary, ghoulish, nightmarish, gruesome, macabre, sinister; portentous, ominous; intimidating, sabre-rattling, bullying, hectoring 735 *oppressive*; menacing; nerve-racking 827 *distressing*.

Vb. *fear*, funk, be afraid, – frightened etc. adj.; stand in fear *or* awe, go in fear and trembling, dread 920 *respect*; flap, be in a f., be in a bit of a state, have the wind up, have the willies; get the wind up, take fright, take alarm; panic, fall into p., have a panic attack, press the panic button, stampede, take to flight, fly 620 *run away*; start, jump 318 *be agitated*; faint, collapse.

quake, shake, tremble, quiver, shiver, shudder, stutter, quaver; quake in one's shoes, shake like a jelly, fear for one's life, be frightened to death, be scared out of one's wits; change colour, blench, pale, go white as a sheet, turn ashen; wince, flinch, shrink, shy, jib 620 *avoid*; quail, cower, crouch; stand aghast, be horrified, be petrified, be chilled with fear, freeze, freeze with horror, be rooted to the spot with terror, feel one's blood run cold, feel one's hair stand on end.

be nervous, – apprehensive etc. adj.; have misgivings; shrink, quail, funk it, put off the evil day; be anxious, dread, have qualms; hesitate, get cold feet, think twice, have second thoughts, think better of it, not dare 858 *be cau-*

tious; get the wind up, start at one's own shadow, be on edge, be all of a doodah 318 *be agitated*.

frighten, scare, panic, stampede; intimidate, menace 900 *threaten*; hang over 155 *impend*; alarm, cause a., raise the a., press the panic button, cry wolf; frighten to death, scare the living daylights out of, scare stiff, scare half to death; make one jump, give one a fright, give one a turn, startle, make one all of a doodah 318 *agitate*; disquiet, disturb, perturb, prey on the mind 827 *trouble*; put the wind up, make nervous, set on edge, rattle, shake, unnerve; play on one's nerves, throw into a nervous state; unman, make a coward of; put the fear of God into, overawe 821 *impress*; cow 727 *overmaster*; disconcert 63 *derange*; frighten off, daunt, deter; terrorize 735 *oppress*; browbeat, bully 827 *torment*; terrify; chill, freeze, paralyse, petrify, turn to stone, mesmerize 375 *render insensible*; make one's blood run cold; make one's hair stand on end *or* curl, make one's flesh creep, make one's knees knock, make one's teeth chatter, frighten out of one's wits, reduce one to a quivering jelly.

855 Courage

N. *courage*, bravery, valour, derring-do; courage of one's convictions 929 *probity*; courage in the face of the enemy, heroism, gallantry, chivalry; fearlessness, intrepidity, daring, nerve, bottle; boldness, audacity 857 *rashness*; spirit; mettle, dash, go, élan, panache 174 *vigorousness*; enterprise 672 *undertaking*; tenacity, survivability, bulldog courage 600 *perseverance*; stoutness of heart, resoluteness 599 *resolution*; gameness, pluck, smeddum, spunk, guts, heart, stout h., heart of oak, backbone, grit 600 *stamina*; Dutch courage; courage of despair; brave face, bold front 711 *defiance*; fresh courage, new heart, encouragement 612 *inducement*.

manliness, manhood, machismo 929 *probity*; chivalry; manly spirit; endurance, stiff upper lip 599 *resolution*.

prowess, derring-do, chivalry, heroism, act of courage, courage in the face of the enemy; feat, exploit, bold stroke, coup de grâce 676 *deed*; desperate venture 857 *rashness*; heroics.

brave person, hero, heroine, VC, GC, Croix de Guerre; knight; brave, warrior 722 *soldier*; man *or* woman of mettle, man *or* woman of spirit, plucky fellow, bulldog, braveheart, daredevil, stunt man *or* woman; fire-eater; Galahad, Lionheart; Joan of Arc, Boadicea, Amazon; knight-errant; the bravest of the brave; band of heroes, gallant company, SAS; forlorn hope 644 *elite*; lion, tiger, fighting cock, bulldog.

Adj. *courageous*, brave, valiant, gallant,

heroic; chivalrous, knightly; soldierly, martial, Amazonian 718 *warlike*; stout, manly, tough, macho, Ramboesque, red-blooded; aggressive, fire-eating; fierce; bold 711 *defiant*; audacious, daring, venturesome, bold as brass 857 *rash*; adventurous 672 *enterprising*; mettlesome, spirited, stouthearted, brave-h., braveheart, lionhearted, bold as a lion; full of courage, spunky; unbowed, firm, indomitable, never say die; determined 599 *resolute*; game, plucky, sporting; ready for the fray, ready for anything, unflinching 597 *willing*.

Vb. *be courageous*, – bold etc. adj.; have what it takes, have guts, come up to scratch, show spirit, show one's mettle 716 *fight*; venture, bell the cat, take the plunge, take the bull by the horns 672 *undertake*; dare 661 *face danger*; show fight, brave, face, outface, outdare, beard, defy; confront, look straight in the face, look in the eyes, be eyeball to eyeball with, eyeball; speak out, speak one's mind, speak up, stand up and be counted 532 *affirm*; face the music, stick one's neck out, show a bold front 599 *stand firm*; laugh at danger, mock at d. 857 *be rash*; grin and bear it, take one's medicine 825 *suffer*.

take courage, pluck up c., muster c., nerve or steel oneself, take one's courage in both hands; put a brave face on it, screw up one's courage 599 *be resolute*.

give courage, infuse c.; put heart into, hearten, make a man of; embolden 612 *incite*; buck up, rally 833 *cheer*; raise morale, bolster up, give confidence.

856 Cowardice

N. *cowardice*, abject fear, funk, blue f. 854 *fear*; cowardliness, no guts 601 *irresolution*; timidity; faintheartedness, chicken-heartedness; unmanliness, defeatism 853 *hopelessness*; leaving the sinking ship, desertion, quitting, shirking 918 *undutifulness*; white feather, yellow streak, faint heart, chicken liver; Dutch courage; cowering, skulking; overcaution 858 *caution*; moral cowardice.

coward, funk, poltroon, craven, lily-liver, chickenheart, wheyface; scaredycat, fraidycat, cowardly custard; coward at heart; sissy, milksop, mummy's boy, baby, big b., cry-b. 163 *weakling*; quitter, shirker, deserter; cur, chicken, rabbit, mouse, jellyfish, invertebrate, doormat; scaremonger.

Adj. *cowardly*, coward, craven, poltroonish; pusillanimous, timid, timorous, fearful, afraid of one's own shadow, unable to say boo to a goose, of a nervous disposition 854 *nervous*; soft, womanish, babyish, unmanly, sissy 163 *weak*; spiritless, spunkless, without grit, without guts, lacking smeddum, with no backbone,

faint-hearted, chicken-livered, yellow-l., lily-l., chicken; cowering, quailing; yellow, abject, base; unwarlike, cowed, defeatist 853 *hopeless*; unheroic, uncourageous 858 *cautious*; shy, coy 874 *modest*; infirm of purpose 601 *irresolute*.

Vb. *be cowardly*, lack courage, have no fight, have no pluck, have no grit, have no guts, lack smeddum, have no backbone, have no heart *or* stomach for, not dare 601 *be irresolute*; lose one's nerve, get the jitters, have cold feet 854 *be nervous*; shrink, funk, shy from, back out, chicken o. 620 *avoid*; hide, skulk, quail, cower, cringe 721 *knuckle under*; show a yellow streak, show the white feather, show fear, turn tail, cut and run, run for cover, panic, press the panic button, stampede, scuttle, show one's back, desert 620 *run away*; lead from behind, keep well to the rear 858 *be cautious*.

857 Rashness

N. *rashness*, lack of caution, incautiousness, unwariness, heedlessness 456 *inattention*; carelessness, neglect 458 *negligence*; imprudence, improvidence, indiscretion 499 *folly*; lack of consideration, irresponsibility; wildness, indiscipline 738 *disobedience*; daredevilry, recklessness, foolhardiness, temerity, audacity, presumption, over-confidence; hotheadedness, impatience 822 *excitability*; rushing into things, impetuosity, precipitance, hastiness, overhastiness 680 *haste*; quixotry; playing with fire, brinkmanship, game of chicken; desperation, courage of despair 855 *courage*; needless risk, leap in the dark 661 *danger*; too many eggs in one basket, underinsurance, counting one's chickens before they are hatched 661 *vulnerability*; reckless gamble, last throw 618 *gambling*; reckless expenditure 815 *prodigality*.

desperado, daredevil, madcap, hothead, adventurer, inveterate gambler 618 *gambler*; harumscarum, ne'er-do-well; one who sticks at nothing, gunman, terrorist, contra, guerrilla; bully 904 *ruffian*.

Adj. *rash*, ill-considered, ill-conceived, illadvised, harebrained, foolhardy, wildcat, injudicious, indiscreet, imprudent 499 *unwise*; careless, hit-and-miss, slapdash, free-and-easy 458 *negligent*; uncircumspect, lemming-like, incautious, unwary, heedless, thoughtless, inconsiderate, uncalculating 456 *inattentive*; frivolous, flippant, giddy, devil-may-care, harumscarum, slaphappy, trigger-happy 456 *light-minded*; irresponsible, reckless, regardless, couldn't-care-less, don't-care, damning the consquences, lunatic, wanton, wild, cavalier; bold, daring, audacious; overdaring, madcap, daredevil, do-or-die, breakneck, suicidal; overambitious, over the top, oversanguine, oversure, overconfident 852 *hoping*; overweening, presumptuous, arrogant 878 *insolent*; precipitate, headlong, hell-bent, desperate 680 *hasty*; unchecked, headstrong 602 *wilful*; 491 *ignorant*; impulsive, impatient, hot-blooded, hot-headed 822 *excitable*; venturesome 618 *speculative*; adventurous, thrill-seeking, risk-taking 672 *enterprising*; improvident 815 *prodigal*.

Vb. *be rash*, – reckless etc. adj.; lack caution, want judgment, lean on a broken reed; expose oneself, drop one's guard, stick one's neck out, take unnecessary risks, put one's head in the lion's cage, ride the tiger; go bull-headed at, charge at, rush at, rush into, rush one's fences 680 *hasten*; take a leap in the dark, leap before one looks, buy a pig in a poke, take something on trust; ignore the consequences, damn the c.; gamble, put all one's eggs into one basket, underinsure; not care 456 *be inattentive*; play fast and loose 634 *waste*; spend to the hilt 815 *be prodigal*; play the fool, play with fire, burn one's fingers; go out on a limb, risk one's neck, dice with death 661 *face danger*; play a desperate game, court disaster, ask for trouble, tempt providence, push one's luck, rush in where angels fear to tread; count one's chickens before they are hatched, aim too high 695 *act foolishly*.

Adv. *rashly*, incautiously; headlong, recklessly, like Gadarene swine, like lemmings.

858 Caution

N. *caution*, cautiousness, wariness, heedfulness, care, heed 457 *carefulness*; hesitation, doubt, second thoughts 854 *nervousness*; instinct of self-preservation 932 *selfishness*; looking before one leaps, looking twice, looking round, circumspection; guardedness, secretiveness, reticence 525 *secrecy*; calculation, counting the risk, safety first; nothing left to chance 669 *preparation*; deliberation, due d., mature consideration 480 *judgment*; sobriety, balance, level-headedness 834 *seriousness*; prudence, discretion, worldly wisdom 498 *wisdom*; insurance, precaution 662 *safeguard*; forethought 510 *foresight*; Fabian policy 823 *patience*; going slow, taking one's time, watching one's step, one step at a time, festina lente 278 *slowness*; wait-and-see policy, waiting game, cat-and-mouse 136 *delay*.

Adj. *cautious*, wary, watchful 455 *attentive*; heedful 457 *careful*; hesitating, doubtful, suspicious 854 *nervous*; taking no risks, insured, hedging; guarded, secret, secretive, incommunicative, cagey 525 *reticent*; experienced, taught by experience, once bitten, twice shy 669 *prepared*; on one's guard, circumspect, looking round, looking all ways, gingerly, stealthy, feel-

ing one's way, taking one's time, watching one's step, tentative 461 *experimental*; conservative 660 *safe*; responsible 929 *trustworthy*; prudent, discreet 498 *wise*; noncommittal 625 *neutral*; frugal, counting the cost 814 *economical*; canny; timid, slow-moving, overcautious, unenterprising, unadventurous; slow, deliberate, Fabian 823 *patient*; sober, cool-headed, level-h., cool; cold-blooded, calm, self-possessed 823 *inexcitable*.

Vb. *be cautious*, beware 457 *be careful*; take no risks, play it by the book, play safe, play a waiting game, play a cat-and-mouse g. 498 *be wise*; ca' canny, go slow, festina lente 278 *move slowly*; cover up, cover one's tracks 525 *conceal*; not talk 525 *keep* secret; keep under cover, keep on the safe side, keep in the rear, keep in the background, keep out of the limelight, hide 523 *lurk*; look out, see how the land lies 438 *scan*; see how the wind blows, feel one's way, play it by ear, put a toe in the water 461 *be tentative*; be on one's guard, tread warily, watch one's step, pussyfoot 525 *be stealthy*; think twice 455 *be mindful*; calculate, reckon 480 *judge*; consider the risk factor, count the cost, cut one's coat according to one's cloth 814 *economize*; know when to stop, take one's time; let well alone, let sleeping dogs lie, keep well out of 620 *avoid*; consider the consequences 511 *predict*; take precautions; look a gift horse in the mouth 480 *estimate*; make sure 473 *make certain*; cover oneself, insure, hedge; leave nothing to chance 669 *prepare*.

Adv. *cautiously*, gingerly; softly softly.

859 Desire

N. *desire*, wish, will and pleasure 595 *will*; summons, call, cry 737 *command*; demand; wanting, want, need, exigency 627 *requirement*; claim 915 *dueness*; nostalgia, nostalgie de la boue, homesickness 830 *regret*; wistfulness, longing, hankering, yearning, sheep's eyes; wishing, thinking, daydreaming, daydream, castles in the air 513 *fantasy*; ambition, aspiration 852 *hope*; yen, urge 279 *impulse*; itch; thrill-seeking, rubbernecking, curiousness, thirst for knowledge, intellectual curiosity 453 *curiosity*; avidity, eagerness, zeal 597 *willingness*; passion, ardour, warmth, impetuosity, impatience 822 *excitability*; rage, fury 503 *frenzy*; mania 503 *personality disorder*; craving, lust for, appetite, hunger, thirst; expansionism, a place in the sun; covetousness, cupidity, itching palm 816 *avarice*; graspingness, greediness, greed 786 *rapacity*; voracity, wolfishness, insatiability 947 *gluttony*; concupiscence, lust (**see** *libido*); incontinence 943 *intemperance*.

hunger, starvation, famine, famished condition, empty stomach 946 *fasting*; appetite, good a., keen a., voracious a., edge of a.; thirst, thirstiness 342 *dryness*; dipsomania 949 *alcoholism*.

liking, fancy, fondness, infatuation 887 *love*; stomach, appetite, zest, craving; relish, tooth, sweet t. 386 *taste*; leaning, penchant, propensity, trend 179 *tendency*; weakness, partiality; affinity; sympathy, involvement 775 *participation*; inclination, mind 617 *intention*; predilection, favour 605 *choice*; whim, whimsy 604 *caprice*; hobby, craze, fad, mania 481 *bias*; fascination, allurement, attraction, temptation, titillation, seduction 612 *inducement*.

libido, sexual urge; erotism, eroticism; erogenous zone, G-spot, Grafenberg spot; concupiscence, sexual desire, carnal d., passion, rut, heat, oestrus; mating season; libidinousness, prurience, lust, lecherousness, letch, the hots 951 *unchastity*; nymphomania, priapism, satyriasis 84 *abnormality*.

desired object, one's heart's desire, wish, desire 627 *requirement*; catch, prize, plum 729 *trophy*; cynosure 890 *favourite*; forbidden fruit, torment of Tantalus; envy, temptation; magnet, lure, draw 291 *attraction*; the unattainable; aim, goal, star, ambition, aspiration, dream 617 *objective*; ideal 646 *perfection*; height of one's ambition.

Adj. *greedy*, acquisitive 932 *selfish*; ambitious, status-seeking; voracious, omnivorous, openmouthed 947 *gluttonous*; unsated, unsatisfied, unslaked; insatiable, rapacious, grasping, retentive 816 *avaricious*.

hungry, hungering; unfilled, empty, supperless, dinnerless 946 *fasting*; half-starved, starving, famished 636 *underfed*; peckish, ready for, ravenous, hungry as a hunter, ready to eat a horse; thirsty, dry, drouthy, parched, dehydrated.

desired, wanted, liked; likable, desirable, worth having, enviable, coveted, to die for, in demand; acceptable, welcome; appetizing 826 *pleasurable*; fetching, catchy, attractive, appealing; wished, self-sought, invited 597 *voluntary*.

Vb. *desire*, want, miss, feel the lack of 627 *require*; ask for, cry out f., clamour f. 737 *demand*; call, summon, send for, ring for 737 *command*; invite 882 *be hospitable*; wish, make a w., pray; wish otherwise, unwish 830 *regret*; covet 912 *envy*; have a mind to, set one's heart on, set one's mind on, have designs on, set one's sights on, aim at, have at heart 617 *intend*; plan for, angle f., fish f. 623 *plan*; aspire, dream of, dream, daydream 852 *hope*; aim high; look for, expect 915 *claim*; wish in vain, whistle for, cry for the moon 695 *act foolishly*; pray for, intercede, invoke, wish on, call down on; wish ill 899 *curse*; wish one well; welcome, be glad

of, jump at, catch at, grasp at, clutch at 786 *take*; lean towards 179 *tend*; favour, prefer, select 605 *choose*; crave, itch for, hanker after, have a yen for, long for; long, yearn, pine, languish; pant for, gasp f., burn f., die f., be dying f. 636 *be unsatisfied*; thirst for, hunger f.; can't wait, must have; like, have a liking, have a taste for, care for 887 *love*; take to, warm to, take a fancy to, fall in love with, dote, dote on, be infatuated with, moon after, be in love, ogle, make eyes at, make passes, solicit, woo 889 *court*; set one's cap at, make a dead set at, run after, chase 619 *pursue*; lust, lust for, lust after, letch after, have the hots for 951 *be impure*; rut, be on heat.

be hungry, hunger, famish, starve, be ravenous, have an empty stomach, have an aching void, be ready to eat a horse 636 *be unsatisfied*; have a good appetite, lick one's chops, salivate, water at the mouth 301 *eat*; thirst, be dry, be dying for a drink, be parched, be dehydrated.

860 Indifference

N. *indifference*, unconcern, uninterestedness 454 *incuriosity*; lack of interest, halfheartedness, want of zeal, lukewarmness 598 *unwillingness*; coolness, coldness, faint praise; lovelessness, mutual indifference, nothing between them; anorexia, no appetite, loss of a.; no desire for; inertia, apathy 679 *inactivity*; nonchalance, insouciance 458 *negligence*; perfunctoriness, carelessness 456 *inattention*; don't-care attitude 734 *laxity*; recklessness, heedlessness 857 *rashness*; promiscuousness 464 *indiscrimination*; amorality; open mind, unbiased attitude, impartiality, equity 913 *justice*; neutrality 625 *middle way*; nothing to choose between, six of one and half a dozen of the other.

Adj. *indifferent*, unconcerned, uninterested 454 *incurious*; lukewarm, Laodicean, halfhearted 598 *unwilling*; impersonal, uninvolved, phlegmatic 820 *impassive*; unimpressed, blasé; calm, cool, cold 823 *inexcitable*; nonchalant, insouciant, careless, perfunctory 458 *negligent*; supine, lackadaisical, listless 679 *inactive*; unambitious, unaspiring; don't-care, easygoing 734 *lax*; unresponsive, unmoved, insensible to; fancy-free, uninvolved; disenchanted, disillusioned, out of love, cooling off; impartial; noncommittal 625 *neutral*.

unwanted, unwelcome, de trop, in the way; unwished for, unasked, uninvited; unvalued 458 *neglected*; on the shelf; unattractive, undesirable.

Vb. *be indifferent*, – unconcerned etc. adj.; be uninvolved, take no interest 456 *be inattentive*; not mind, care little for, not lose any sleep over, damn with faint praise; care nothing for, not give a fig *or* a thank-you for, not care a straw about, couldn't care less, take it or leave it; not think twice about, not care, not give a hoot, shrug off, dismiss, let go, make light of 922 *hold cheap*; not defend, hold no brief for, take neither side, sit on the fence 606 *be neutral*; grow indifferent, fall out of love, lose interest, cool off.

Int. never mind! what does it matter! who cares? so what?

861 Dislike

N. *dislike*, disinclination, no inclination for, no fancy for, no stomach for; reluctance, backwardness 598 *unwillingness*; displeasure 891 *resentment*; dissatisfaction 829 *discontent*; disagreement 489 *dissent*; shyness, aversion 620 *avoidance*; sudden *or* instant dislike, antipathy, allergy; rooted dislike, distaste, repugnance, repulsion, disgust, abomination, abhorrence, detestation, loathing; shuddering, horror, mortal h. 854 *fear*; xenophobia 854 *phobia*; prejudice 481 *bias*; animosity, bad blood, ill feeling, mutual hatred, common h. 888 *hatred*; nausea, queasiness, turn, heaving stomach, vomit 300 *voidance*; object of dislike, not one's type, bête noire, pet aversion, a red rag to a bull.

Vb. *dislike*, find not to one's taste; not care for, have no liking f., have no desire for; have no stomach for, have no heart for 598 *be unwilling*; not choose, prefer not to 607 *reject*; object 762 *deprecate*; mind 891 *resent*; take a dislike to, feel an aversion for, have a down on, have one's knife in, have it in for 481 *be biased*; react against 280 *recoil*; feel sick at 300 *vomit*; shun, turn away, shrink from, have no time for 620 *avoid*; look askance at 924 *disapprove*; turn up the nose at, sniff at, sneer at 922 *despise*; make a face, grimace; be unable to abide, not endure, can't stand, can't bear, detest, loathe, abominate, abhor 888 *hate*; not like the look of, shudder at 854 *fear*; unwish, wish undone 830 *regret*.

cause dislike, disincline, deter 854 *frighten*; go against the grain, rub the wrong way, antagonize, put one's back up 891 *enrage*; set against, set at odds, make bad blood; satiate, pall, jade 863 *sate*; disagree with, upset 25 *disagree*; put off, revolt 292 *repel*; offend, grate, jar 827 *displease*; get one's goat, get up one's nose, get on one's nerves 827 *torment*; disgust, stick in one's throat, nauseate, sicken, make one's gorge rise, turn one's stomach, make one sick; shock, scandalize, make a scandal 924 *incur blame*.

862 Fastidiousness

N. *fastidiousness*, niceness, nicety, daintiness, finicalness, finicality, fikiness, pernicketiness, delicacy; discernment, perspicacity, sublety 463 *discrimination*; refinement 846 *good taste*; connoisseurship, epicurism; meticulousness, preciseness 457 *carefulness*; idealism, overdeveloped conscience 917 *conscience*; perfectionism, fussiness, nit-picking, over-refinement, hypercriticalness, pedantry, hair-splitting; prudishness, Puritanism 950 *prudery*.

perfectionist, idealist, purist, rigorist, fusspot, pedant, nit-picker, stickler, hard taskmaster; picker and chooser, gourmet, epicure.

Adj. *fastidious*, nice, dainty, delicate, epicurean; perspicacious, discerning 463 *discriminating*; particular, demanding, choosy, finicky, finical, fiky; overnice, overparticular, scrupulous, meticulous, squeamish 455 *attentive*; punctilious, painstaking, conscientious, overconscientious, critical, hypercritical, overcritical, fussy, pernickety, hard to please, fault-finding, censorious 924 *disapproving*; pedantic, donnish, precise, rigorous, exacting, difficult 735 *severe*; prim, puritanical 950 *prudish*.

Vb. *be fastidious*, – choosy etc. adj.; settle for nothing less than the best; pick and choose 605 *choose*; over-refine, split hairs, mince matters 475 *argue*; draw distinctions 463 *discriminate*; find fault 924 *dispraise*; fuss, turn up one's nose, wrinkle one's n.; look a gift horse in the mouth, feel superior, disdain 922 *despise*; keep oneself to oneself.

863 Satiety

N. *satiety*, jadedness, fullness, repletion 54 *plenitude*; overfulness, plethora, overabundance, stuffing, engorgement, saturation, saturation point 637 *redundance*; glut, surfeit, too much of a good thing 838 *tedium*; overdose, excess 637 *superfluity*; spoiled child, spoilt brat.

Adj. *sated*, satiated, satisfied, replete, saturated, brimming 635 *filled*; overfull, surfeited, gorged, glutted, cloyed, sick of; jaded, blasé 838 *bored*.

Vb. *sate*, satiate; satisfy, quench, slake 635 *suffice*; fill up, overfill, saturate 54 *fill*; soak 341 *drench*; stuff, gorge, glut, surfeit, cloy, pall; overdose, overfeed; sicken 861 *cause dislike*; spoil, overindulge, kill with kindness; bore, weary 838 *be tedious*.

864 Wonder

N. *wonder*, state of wonder, wonderment, raptness; admiration, hero worship 887 *love*; awe, fascination; cry of wonder, gasp of admiration, whistle, wolf w., exclamation, exclamation mark; shocked silence 399 *silence*; open mouth, popping eyes, eyes on stalks; shock, surprise, surprisal 508 *lack of expectation*; astonishment, amazement; stupor, stupefaction; bewilderment, bafflement 474 *uncertainty*; consternation 854 *fear*.

miracle-working, wonder-working, spellbinding, magic 983 *sorcery*; stroke of genius, feat, exploit 676 *deed*; transformation scene, coup de théâtre 594 *dramaturgy*.

prodigy, portent, sign, eye-opener 511 *omen*; quite something, phenomenon, miracle, marvel, wonder; drama, sensation, cause célèbre, nine-days' wonder; object of wonder or admiration, wonderland, fairyland 513 *fantasy*; seven wonders of the world; sight 445 *spectacle*; infant prodigy, genius, man or woman of genius 696 *proficient person*; miracle-worker, thaumaturge, wizard, witch, fairy godmother 983 *sorcerer*; hero, heroine, wonder boy, superman, dream girl, superwoman, whiz kid 646 *paragon*; freak, sport, curiosity, oddity, guy, monster, monstrosity 84 *rara avis*; puzzle 530 *enigma*.

Adj. *wonderful*, to wonder at, wondrous, marvellous, miraculous, monstrous, prodigious, phenomenal; stupendous, fearful 854 *frightening*; admirable, exquisite 644 *excellent*; record-breaking 644 *best*; striking, overwhelming, awesome, awe-inspiring, breathtaking 821 *impressive*; dramatic, sensational; shocking, scandalizing; rare, exceptional, extraordinary, unprecedented 84 *unusual*; remarkable, noteworthy; strange, passing s., odd, very odd, outré, weird, weird and wonderful, unaccountable, mysterious, enigmatic 517 *puzzling*; exotic, outlandish, unheard of 59 *extraneous*; fantastic 513 *imaginary*; impossible, hardly possible, too good or bad to be true 472 *improbable*; unbelievable, incredible, inconceivable, unimaginable, indescribable; unutterable, unspeakable, ineffable 517 *inexpressible*; surprising 508 *unexpected*; mind-boggling, mind-blowing, astounding, amazing, shattering, bewildering etc. vb.; wonder-working; magic, like m. 983 *magical*.

Vb. *wonder*, marvel, admire, whistle; hold one's breath, gasp, gasp with admiration; stare, goggle at, gawk, open one's eyes wide, rub one's e., not believe one's e.; gape, gawp, open one's mouth, stand in amazement, look aghast 508 *not expect*; be awestruck, be overwhelmed 854 *fear*; have no words to express, not know what to say, be reduced to silence, be struck dumb 399 *be silent*.

be wonderful, – marvellous etc. adj.; do wonders, work miracles, achieve marvels; surpass belief, stagger b., boggle the mind 486 *cause doubt*; beggar all description, baffle d., beat everything; spellbind, enchant 983 *bewitch*; dazzle, strike with admiration, turn one's head; strike dumb, awe, electrify 821 *impress*; make one's eyes open, make one sit up

and take notice, take one's breath away; bowl over, stagger; blow one's mind, stun, daze, stupefy, petrify, dumbfound, confound, astound, astonish, amaze, flabbergast 508 *surprise*; baffle, bewilder 474 *puzzle*; startle 854 *frighten*; shock, scandalize 924 *incur blame*.

865 Lack of wonder

N. *lack of wonder*, irreverence, refusal to be impressed, blankness, stony indifference 860 *indifference*; composure, calmness, serenity, tranquillity 266 *quietude*; imperturbability, impassiveness, cold blood 820 *moral insensibility*; taking for granted 610 *habituation*; lack of imagination, unimaginativeness; disbelief 486 *unbelief*; matter of course, just what one thought, nothing to wonder at, nothing to write home about, nothing in it.

Vb. *not wonder*, see nothing remarkable 820 *be insensitive*; treat as a matter of course, not raise an eyebrow, take for granted, take as one's due; see it coming 507 *expect*.

866 Repute

N. *repute*, good r., high r.; reputation, good r.; report, good r.; title to fame, name, great n., good n., fair n., character, good c., high c., reputability, respectability 802 *credit*; regard, esteem 920 *respect*; opinion, good o., good odour, favour, high f., popular f., good books; popularity, vogue 848 *fashion*; acclaim, applause, approval, stamp of a., seal of a., cachet 923 *approbation*.

prestige, aura, mystique, magic; glamour, glitz, dazzle, éclat, lustre, splendour; brilliance, prowess; illustriousness, glory, honour, honour and glory, kudos, claim to fame, succès d'estime (**see** *famousness*); esteem, estimation, account, high a., worship 638 *importance*; face, izzat, caste; degree, rank, ranking, standing, footing, status, honorary s.; condition, position, position in society; top of the ladder or the tree, precedence 34 *superiority*; conspicuousness, prominence, eminence 443 *visibility*; distinction, greatness, high rank, exaltedness, majesty 868 *nobility*; impressiveness, dignity, stateliness, solemnity, grandeur, sublimity, awesomeness; name to conjure with 178 *influence*; paramountcy, ascendancy, hegemony, primacy 733 *authority*; leadership, acknowledged l. 689 *directorship*; prestigiousness, snob value; status symbol, trophy wife.

famousness, title to fame, celebrity, notability, remarkability; illustriousness, renown, stardom, fame, name, note; household name, synonym for; glory 727 *success*; notoriety 867 *disrepute*; talk of the town 528 *publicity*; claim to fame, place in history, posthumous fame 505 *memory*;

undying name, immortal n., immortality, deathlessness; remembrance, commemoration, niche in the hall of fame.

honours, honour, blaze of glory, crown of g.; crown, martyr's c.; halo, aureole, nimbus, glory; blushing honours, battle h.; laurels, bays, wreath, garland, favour; feather, feather in one's cap 729 *trophy;* order, star, garter, ribbon, medal 729 *decoration;* spurs, sword, shield, arms 547 *heraldry;* an honour, signal h., distinction, accolade, award 962 *reward;* compliment, bouquet, flattery, incense, laud, eulogy 923 *praise;* memorial, statue, bust, picture, portrait, niche, plaque, temple, monument 505 *reminder;* title of honour, dignity, handle 870 *title;* patent of nobility, knighthood, baronetcy, peerage 868 *nobility;* academic honour, baccalaureate, doctorate, degree, academic d., honours d., pass d., ordinary d., aegrotat d., honorary d., diploma, certificate 870 *academic title;* sports trophy, cup, cap, blue; source of honour, fount of h., College of Arms; honours list, birthday honours, roll of honour 87 *list.*

person of repute, honoured sir *or* madam, gentle reader; worthy, sound person, good citizen, loyal subject, pillar of society, pillar of the church, pillar of the state; man *or* woman of honour; knight, dame, peer 868 *person of rank;* somebody, great man, great woman, big shot, big noise, big gun, big name, big wheel, VIP 638 *bigwig;* someone of mark, notable, celebrity, notability, figure, public f.; champion 644 *exceller;* lion, star, rising star, luminary; man *or* woman of the hour, heroine of the hour, hero of the day, popular hero, icon; pop singer, idol 890 *favourite;* cynosure, model, mirror 646 *paragon;* cream, cream of society, crème de la crème 644 *elite;* choice spirit, master s., leading light 690 *leader;* grand old man, GOM 500 *sage;* noble army, great company, bevy, galaxy, constellation 74 *band.*

Adj. *reputable,* reputed, of repute, of good *or* sound reputation, of credit; creditworthy 929 *trustworthy;* gentlemanly 929 *honourable;* worthy, creditable, meritorious, prestigious 644 *excellent;* esteemed, respectable, regarded, well-r., well thought of; edifying, moral 933 *virtuous;* in good odour, in the good books, in favour, in high f. 923 *approved;* popular, modish 848 *fashionable;* sanctioned, allowed, admitted.

worshipful, reverend, honourable; admirable 864 *wonderful;* heroic 855 *courageous;* imposing, dignified, august, stately, grand, sublime 821 *impressive;* lofty, high; high and mighty, mighty 32 *great;* lordly, princely, kingly, queenly, majestic, royal, regal 868 *noble;* aristocratic, well-born, high-caste, heaven-born; glorious, in glory, full of g., full of honours, honoured,

titled, ennobled; time-honoured, ancient, age-old 127 *immemorial;* sacrosanct, sacred, holy 979 *sanctified;* honorific, dignifying.

noteworthy, notable, remarkable, extraordinary 84 *unusual;* wonderful; of mark, of distinction, distinguished, distingué(e) 638 *important;* conspicuous, prominent, public, in the public eye, in the limelight 443 *obvious;* eminent, preeminent, supereminent; peerless, nonpareil, foremost, in the forefront 34 *superior;* ranking, starring, leading, commanding; brilliant, bright, lustrous 417 *luminous;* illustrious, splendid, glorious 875 *ostentatious.*

renowned, celebrated, acclaimed; of renown, of glorious name, of fame; famous, fabled, legendary, famed, far-f.; historic, illustrious, great, noble, glorious 644 *excellent;* notorious 867 *disreputable;* known as, well-known, on the map 490 *known;* of note, noted (**see** *noteworthy);* talked of, resounding, on all lips, on every tongue, in the news; lasting, unfading, never-fading, evergreen, imperishable, deathless, immortal, eternal 115 *perpetual.*

Vb. *have a reputation,* enjoy a r., wear a halo; have a good name; rank, stand high, have status *or* standing, be looked up to, have a name for, be praised f. 920 *command respect;* stand well with, do oneself credit, win honour, win renown, gain prestige, gain recognition, build a reputation, earn a name; be somebody, make one's mark, set the heather on fire 730 *prosper;* win one's spurs, gain one's laurels, take one's degree, graduate 727 *succeed;* cut a figure, cut a dash, cover oneself with glory 875 *be ostentatious;* rise to fame, get to the top of the ladder *or* tree, flash to stardom; shine, excel 644 *be good;* outshine, eclipse, steal the show, throw into the shade, overshadow 34 *be superior;* have precedence, play first fiddle, take the lead, play the 1., star 64 *come before;* bask in glory, have fame, have a great name, hand down one's name to posterity; make history, live in h., be sure of immortality, carve a niche for oneself in the hall of fame 505 *be remembered.*

honour, revere, regard, look up to, hold in respect, hold in reverence, hold in honour 920 *respect;* stand in awe of 854 *fear;* bow down to, recognize as superior 981 *worship;* know how to value, appreciate, prize; value, tender, treasure 887 *love;* show honour, pay respect, pay due regard, pay one's respects to 920 *show respect;* be polite to 884 *be courteous;* compliment 925 *flatter;* grace with, honour w., dedicate to, inscribe to; praise, sing the praises, laud, glorify, acclaim 923 *applaud;* crown, grant the palm, deck with laurels, make much of, eulogize, lionize, chair, ask for one's autograph; credit, give c., honour for 907 *thank;* glorify, immortalize, eternize, commemorate, memorialize 505 *remember;* celebrate, renown, blazon 528 *proclaim;* reflect honour, redound to one's honour *or* one's credit, lend distinction *or* lustre to, do credit to, be a credit to.

dignify, glorify, exalt; canonize, beatify, deify, consecrate, dedicate 979 *sanctify;* install, enthrone, crown 751 *commission;* signalize, mark out, distinguish 547 *indicate;* aggrandize, advance, upgrade 285 *promote;* honour, delight to h., confer an h.; bemedal, beribbon 844 *decorate;* bestow a title, create, elevate, raise to the peerage, ennoble; confer a knighthood, dub, knight, give the accolade; give one his *or* her title, sir, bemadam 561 *name;* take a title, take a handle to one's name, accept a knighthood.

867 Disrepute

N. *disrepute,* disreputableness, bad reputation, bad name, bad character, shady reputation, past; disesteem 921 *disrespect;* notoriety, infamy, ill repute, ill fame, succès de scandale; no reputation, no standing, ingloriousness, obscurity; bad odour, ill favour, disfavour, bad books, discredit, black books, bad light; derogation, dishonour, disgrace, shame (**see** *slur*), smear campaign 926 *detraction;* ignominy, loss of honour, loss of reputation, faded r., withered laurels, tarnished honour; departed glory, Ichabod; loss of face, loss of rank, demotion, degradation, reduction to the ranks, dishonourable discharge; debasement, abasement, comedown 872 *humiliation;* abjectness, baseness, vileness, turpitude 934 *wickedness.*

slur, reproach 924 *censure;* imputation, brickbat, aspersion, reflection, slander, opprobrium, abuse 926 *calumny;* slight, insult, put-down 921 *indignity;* scandal, shocking s., disgrace, shame, burning s., crying s.; defilement, pollution 649 *uncleanness;* stain, smear, smudge 649 *dirt;* stigma, brand, mark, black m., spot, blot, tarnish, taint 845 *blemish;* dirty linen; bar sinister, blot on one's scutcheon, badge of infamy, scarlet letter, mark of Cain.

Adj. *disreputable,* not respectable, disrespectable, louche, shifty, shady; notorious, infamous, of ill fame, of ill repute, nefarious; arrant 645 *bad;* doubtful, dubious, questionable, objectionable 645 *not nice;* risqué, ribald, improper, indecent, obscene 951 *impure;* not thought much of, held in contempt, despised 922 *contemptible;* characterless, without references, of no repute *or* reputation; petty, pitiful 639 *unimportant;* outcast; down-and-out, degraded, base, abject, despicable, odious 888 *hateful;* mean, cheap, low 847 *vulgar;* shabby, squalid, dirty, scruffy 649 *unclean;* poor, down at heel, out at

elbows 655 *dilapidated;* in a bad light, under a cloud, in one's bad *or* black books, in the doghouse, in Coventry, unable to show one's face; discredited, disgraced, in disgrace (**see** *inglorious*); reproached; unpopular.

discreditable, no credit to, bringing discredit, reflecting upon one, damaging, compromising; ignoble, unworthy; improper, unbecoming 643 *inexpedient;* dishonourable 930 *dishonest;* despicable 922 *contemptible;* censurable 924 *blameworthy;* shameful, shame-making, disgraceful, infamous, scandalous, shocking, outrageous, unmentionable, disgusting; too bad 645 *not nice.*

degrading, lowering, demeaning, ignominious, opprobrious, mortifying, humiliating; derogatory, hurting one's dignity; beneath one, beneath one's dignity, infra dig.

inglorious, without repute, without prestige, without note; without a name, nameless 562 *anonymous;* unheroic 879 *servile;* unaspiring, unambitious 874 *modest;* unnoted, unremarked, unnoticed, unmentioned 458 *neglected;* unrenowned, unknown to fame, unheard of, obscure 491 *unknown;* unseen, unheard 444 *invisible;* unhymned, unsung, unglorified, unhonoured, undecorated; titleless 869 *plebeian;* deflated, put down, cut down to size, debunked, humiliated, mortified; sunk low, shorn of glory, faded, withered, tarnished; stripped of reputation, discredited, creditless, disgraced, dishonoured, out of favour, in the bad *or* black books, in eclipse; degraded, demoted, reduced to the ranks.

Vb. *have no repute,* have no reputation, have no character, have no name to lose, have a past; have no credit, rank low, stand low in estimation, have no standing, have little status, be a nobody, cut no ice; be out of favour, be in the bad *or* black books, be in bad odour, be unpopular, be discredited, be in disgrace, stink in the nostrils; play second fiddle, take a back seat, stay in the background 35 *be inferior;* blush unseen, hide one's light 444 *be unseen.*

lose repute, fall *or* go out of fashion, pass from the public eye, fall out of favour; come down in the world, fall, sink 309 *descend;* fade, wither; fall into disrepute, incur discredit, incur dishonour, incur disgrace, achieve notoriety, get a bad name for oneself 924 *incur blame;* spoil one's record, blot one's copybook, disgrace oneself, compromise one's name, risk one's reputation, lose one's r., outlive one's r.; tarnish one's glory, forfeit one's honour, lose one's halo, lose one's good name, earn no credit, earn no honour, win no glory 728 *fail;* come down in the eyes of, forfeit one's good opinion, sink in estimation, suffer in reputation, lose prestige, lose face, lose rank; admit defeat, slink away, crawl, crouch 721 *knuckle under*; look silly, look foolish, be a laughing-stock, cut a sorry figure, blush for shame, laugh on the wrong side of one's mouth 497 *be absurd*; be exposed, be brought to book 963 *be punished*.

demean oneself, lower o., degrade o.; condescend, stoop, marry beneath one; make oneself cheap, cheapen oneself, disgrace o., behave unworthily, have no sense of one's position; sacrifice one's pride, forfeit self-respect; have no pride, feel no shame, think no s.

shame, put to s., hold up to s.; pillory, expose, show up, post; scorn, mock 851 *ridicule*; snub, put down, take down a peg or two 872 *humiliate*; discompose, disconcert, discomfit, put out of countenance, put one's nose out of joint, deflate, cut down to size, debunk; strip of one's honours, strip of rank, deplume, degrade, downgrade, demote, disrate, reduce to the ranks, cashier, disbar, defrock, deprive, strip 963 *punish*; black-ball, ostracize 57 *exclude*; vilify, malign, disparage 926 *defame*; destroy one's reputation, take away one's good name, ruin one's credit; put in a bad light, reflect upon, taint; sully, mar, blacken, tarnish, stain, blot, besmear, smear, bespatter 649 *make unclean*; debase, defile, desecrate, profane 980 *be impious*; stigmatize, brand, cast a slur upon, tar 547 *mark*; dishonour, disgrace, discredit, give a bad name, bring into disrepute, bring shame upon, scandalize, be a public scandal 924 *incur blame*; heap shame upon, dump on, heap dirt u., drag through the mire *or* mud; trample, tread underfoot, ride roughshod over, outrage 735 *oppress*; contemn, disdain 922 *despise*; make one blush, outrage one's modesty 951 *debauch*; not spare one's blushes, eulogize, overpraise.

868 Nobility

N. *nobility*, nobleness, distinction, rank, high r., titled r., station, order 27 *degree*; royalty, kingliness, queenliness, princeliness, majesty, prerogative 733 *authority*; birth, high b., gentle b., gentility, noblesse; descent, high d., noble d., ancestry, long a., line, unbroken l., lineage, pedigree, ancient p. 169 *genealogy*; noble family, noble house, ancient h., royal h., dynasty, royal d. 11 *family*; blood, blue b., best b.; bloodstock, caste, high c.; badge of rank, patent of nobility, coat of arms, crest 547 *heraldry*.

aristocracy, patriciate, patrician order; nobility, hereditary n., lesser n., noblesse, ancien régime; lordship, lords, peerage, House of Lords, lords spiritual and temporal; dukedom, earldom, viscountcy, baronetcy; baronage, knightage; landed interest, squirearchy, squiredom; county family, county set, gentry, landed g., gentlefolk; the great, great folk, the high and the mighty, notables; life peerage.

upper class, upper classes, upper ten, upper crust, top layer, top drawer; first families, the quality, best people, better sort, chosen few 644 *elite*; high society, social register, high life, fashionable world 848 *beau monde*; ruling class, the twice-born, the Establishment 733 *authority*; high-ups, Olympians; the haves 800 *rich person*; salaried class, salariat.

aristocrat, patrician, nobleman *or* -woman; person of high caste, Brahman; bloodstock, thoroughbred; senator, magnifico, magnate, dignitary; don, grandee, caballero, hidalgo; gentleman, gentlewoman; squire, laird; boyar, Junker; emperor, king, queen, prince 741 *sovereign*; nob, swell, gent, toff 848 *fop*; panjandrum, superior person 638 *bigwig*.

person of rank, titled person, noble, nobleman *or* -woman, noble lord *or* lady, seigneur; princeling, lordling, aristo; lordship, milord; ladyship, milady; peer, hereditary p., life p.; peer of the realm, peeress; Prince of Wales, princess royal, duke, grand d., archduke, duchess; marquis, marquess, marquise, marchioness, margrave, margravine, count, countess, contessa; earl, belted e.; viscount, viscountess, baron, baroness, thane, baronet, knight, banneret, knight-bachelor, knight-banneret; rajah, bey, nawab, begum, emir, khan, sheikh 741 *potentate*, governor.

Adj. *noble*, chivalrous, knightly; gentlemanly, gentlemanlike, ladylike (**see** *genteel*); majestic, royal, regal, every inch a king *or* queen; kingly, queenly, princely, lordly; ducal, baronial, seigneurial; of royal blood, of high birth, of gentle b., of good family, pedigreed, well-born, high-b., born in the purple, born with a silver spoon in one's mouth; thoroughbred, blue-blooded; of rank, ennobled, titled, in Debrett, in Burke's Peerage; haughty, high, exalted, high-up, grand 32 *great*.

genteel, patrician, senatorial; aristocratic; superior, top-drawer, upper-crust, high-class, upper-c., cabin-c., classy, posh, U, highly respectable, comme il faut; of good breeding 848 *well-bred*.

869 Commonalty

N. *commonalty*, commons, third estate, bourgeoisie, middle classes, lower c.; plebs, plebeians; citizenry, democracy; townsfolk, country-folk; silent majority, grass roots; the public, general public; people at large, populace, the people, the common p.; vulgar herd, great unwashed; the many, the multitude, hoi polloi; the masses, mass of society, mass of the people, admass, proletariat; the general, rank and file, rag, tag and bobtail, Tom Dick and Harry 79 *everyman.*

rabble, mob, horde 74 *crowd*; clamjamphrie, rout, rabble r., varletry; riffraff, scum, off-scourings, dregs of society, the flotsam and jetsam, canaille, cattle, vermin.

lower classes, lower orders, one's inferiors 35 *inferior*; common sort, small fry, humble folk; working class, blue-collar workers, wage earners, servant class; steerage class, lower deck; second-class citizens, the have-nots, the underprivileged, the disadvantaged; proletariat, proles; down-and-outs, depressed class, outcasts, outcasts of society, poor whites, white trash; demi-monde, under-world, low company, low life.

middle classes, bourgeoisie 732 *averageness*; professional classes, salaried c., white-collar workers; Brown, Jones and Robinson; Middle England, Middle America.

commoner, bourgeois(e), plebeian, pleb; untitled person, plain Mr *or* Mrs; citizen, mere citizen, John Citizen, Joe Bloggs, joe soap; one of the people, man *or* woman of the p., democrat, republican; proletarian, prole; working man *or* woman 686 *worker*; town-dweller, country-d. 191 *native*; little man, man *or* woman in the street, everyman, everywoman, common type, average t. 30 *common man*; common person, groundling, pittite, galleryite 35 *inferior*; backbencher, private; underling 742 *servant*; ranker, upstart, parvenu, social climber, arriviste, nouveau riche, Philistine; a nobody, nobody one knows, nobody knows who 639 *nonentity*; low-caste person, outcaste; Untouchable; villein, serf 742 *slave.*

country-dweller, countryman *or* -woman, yeoman, rustic, swain, gaffer, peasant, son *or* daughter of the soil, tiller of the soil, ploughman, teuchter 370 *farmer*; boor, churl, bogtrotter; yokel, hind, clod, clodhopper, rube, redneck, hayseed, hick, backwoodsman; bumpkin, country b., Tony Lumpkin, country cousin, provincial, hillbilly; village idiot 501 *ninny.*

low fellow, fellow, varlet 938 *cad*; slum-dweller 801 *poor person*; guttersnipe, mudlark, street arab, gamin, ragamuffin, down-and-out, tramp, bag lady, bum, vagabond 268 *wanderer*; gaberlunzie, panhandler 763 *beggar*; low type, rough t., bully, ugly customer, plug ugly, ruffian, rowdy, rough, bit of rough, boot boy, bovver boy, roughneck 904 *raffian*; rascal 938 *knave*; gangster, hood, crook; criminal, delinquent, juvenile d. 904 *offender*; barbarian, savage, Goth, Vandal, Yahoo.

Adj. *plebeian*, common, simple, untitled, unennobled, without rank, titleless; ignoble,

below the salt; below-stairs, servant-class; lower-deck, rank and file 732 *middling*; mean, low, low-down, street-corner 867 *disreputable*; lowly, base-born, low-born, low-caste, of low birth, of low origin, of mean parentage, of mean extraction; slave-born, servile; humble, of low estate, of humble condition 35 *inferior*; unaristocratic, middle-class, lower m.-c., working-c., cloth-cap, non-U, proletarian; homely, homespun 573 *plain*; obscure 867 *inglorious*; coarse, brutish, uncouth, unpolished 847 *ill-bred*; unfashionable, cockney, bourgeois, Main Street, suburban, provincial, rustic; parvenu, risen from the ranks 847 *vulgar*; boorish, churlish, loutish, yobbish.

barbaric, barbarous, barbarian, wild, savage, brutish, yobbish; uncivilized, uncultured, without arts, philistine, primitive, neolithic 699 *artless.*

870 Title

N. *title*, title to fame, entitlement, claim 915 *dueness*; title of honour, courtesy title, handle, handle to one's name; honour, distinction, order, knighthood 866 *honours*; royal we, editorial we 875 *formality*; mode of address, style of a., Royal Highness, Serene H., Excellency, Grace, Lordship, Ladyship, noble, most n., my liege, my lord, my lady, dame; the Honourable, Right Honourable; Reverend, Very R., Right R., Most R., Monsignor, His Holiness; dom, padre; your reverence, your honour, your worship; sire, esquire, sir, dear s., madam, ma'am, master, mister, mistress, miss, Ms; monsieur, madame, mademoiselle; don, señor, señora, señorita; signore, signora, signorina; Herr, mynheer, Frau, Fraulein; babu, sahib, memsahib; bwana, effendi, mirza; citoyen, comrade, tovarich.

academic title, doctor, doctor honoris causa; doctor of philosophy, D Phil, PhD; doctor of literature, D Litt.; doctor of divinity, DD; doctor of laws, LLD; doctor of medicine, MD; doctor of music, Mus D; bachelor of arts, BA; bachelor of literature, B Litt; bachelor of science, BSc; bachelor of medicine and surgery, MBChB, MBBS; bachelor of education, B Ed; bachelor of law, BL; bachelor of music, Mus B; master of arts, MA; master of science, MSc; M Ed; M Litt, M Phil; Professor, Professor Emeritus; reader, lecturer; doctorate, baccalaureate.

871 Pride

N. *pride*, self-esteem, amour propre; self-respect, self-confidence; conceit, self-c., swelled *or* swollen head, swank, side 873 *vanity*; snobbery, inverted s. 850 *affectation*; false pride, touchiness 819 *moral sensibility*; dignity, reputation 866 *prestige*; stateliness, loftiness; condescension, hauteur, haughtiness, uppitiness, unapproachability, disdain 922 *contempt*; overweening pride, bumptiousness, arrogance, altitude, hubris 878 *insolence*; swelling pride, pomp, pomposity, grandiosity, show, display 875 *ostentation*; egoism, self-praise, vainglory 877 *boasting*; class-consciousness, race-prejudice, sexism 481 *prejudice*.

proud person, vain p., snob, parvenu; swelled head, swank; lady muck, lord of creation 638 *bigwig*; fine gentleman, grande dame 848 *fop*; peacock, turkey cock, cock of the walk, swaggerer, bragger; purse-proud plutocrat 800 *rich person*; class-conscious person 868 *aristocrat*.

Adj. *proud*, elevated, haughty, lofty, sublime 209 *high*; plumed, crested 875 *showy*; fine, grand 848 *fashionable*; grandiose, dignified, stately, statuesque 821 *impressive*; majestic, royal, kingly, queenly, lordly, aristocratic 868 *noble*; self-respecting, self-confident, proud-hearted, high-souled 855 *courageous*; high-stepping, high-spirited 819 *lively*; stiff-necked 602 *obstinate*; mighty, overmighty 32 *great*; imperious, commanding 733 *authoritative*; high-handed 735 *oppressive*; overweening, overbearing, hubristic, arrogant, with attitude 878 *insolent*; puffed-up, inflated, swelling, swollen, big-headed; overproud, high and mighty, stuck-up, toffee-nosed, snobbish, nose-in-the-air, snooty; upstage, uppish, uppity; on one's dignity, on one's high horse; haughty, disdainful, superior, holier than thou, supercilious, hoity-toity, high-hat, patronizing, condescending; standoffish, aloof; taking pride in, house-proud; proud of, bursting with pride, inches taller; strutting, swaggering, vainglorious; pleased with oneself, pleased as Punch, pleased as a dog with two tails, like the cat that got the cream; cocky, bumptious, conceited 873 *vain*; pretentious 850 *affected*; swanky, swanking, pompous 875 *showy*; proud as Lucifer, proud as a peacock.

Vb. *be proud*, have one's pride, have one's self-respect, be jealous of one's honour, guard one's reputation, hold one's head high, stand erect, refuse to stoop, bow to no one, stand on one's dignity, mount one's high horse; give oneself airs, toss one's head, hold one's nose in the air, think it beneath one, be too proud to, be too grand to; be stuck-up, be snooty, swank, show off, swagger, strut 875 *be ostentatious*; condescend, patronize; look down on, disdain 922 *despise*; display hauteur 878 *be insolent*; lord it, queen it, come it over, throw one's weight about, pull rank, overween 735 *oppress*.

872 Humility. Humiliation

N. *humility*, humbleness, humble spirit 874 *modesty*; abasement, lowness, lowliness; unpretentiousness, quietness; harmlessness, inoffensiveness 935 *innocence*; meekness, resignation, submissiveness, servility 721 *submission*; self-depreciation, self-effacement, self-abasement, mortification 931 *disinterestedness*; condescension, stooping 884 *courtesy*; mouse, violet, shrinking v.

humiliation, abasement, humbling, letdown, climbdown, comedown, slap in the face 921 *indignity*; crushing retort; rebuke 924 *reprimand*; shame, disgrace 867 *disrepute*; sense of shame, sense of disgrace, blush, suffusion, confusion; shamefaced look, hangdog expression, tail between the legs; chastening thought, mortification, hurt pride, injured p., offended dignity 891 *resentment*.

Adj. *humble*, humble-minded, self-deprecating, poor in spirit, lowly; meek, submissive, resigned, unprotesting, servile 721 *submitting*; self-effacing 931 *disinterested*; self-abasing, stooping, condescending 884 *courteous*; mouselike, harmless, inoffensive, unoffending 935 *innocent*; unassuming, unpretentious, without airs, without side 874 *modest*; mean, low 639 *unimportant*; of lowly birth 869 *plebeian*.

Vb. *be humble*, – lowly etc. adj.; have no sense of pride, have no self-conceit, humble oneself 867 *demean oneself*; play second fiddle, take a back seat 874 *be modest*; put others first, not think of oneself 931 *be disinterested*; condescend, unbend 884 *be courteous*; stoop, bow down, crawl, be a sycophant, sing small, eat humble pie, eat crow 721 *knuckle under*; turn the other cheek.

be humbled, – humiliated etc. adj.; receive a snub, be cold-shouldered, get a slap in the face, be put in one's place, be taken down a peg; be ashamed, be ashamed of oneself, feel shame; blush, colour up 431 *redden*; feel small, hide one's face, hang one's head, avert one's eyes, have nothing to say for oneself, wish to sink through the floor, wish the earth would swallow one up; stop swanking, come off it.

humiliate, humble, chasten, abash, disconcert, put to the blush; lower, take down a peg, put down, debunk, deflate; make one feel small, make one sing small, make one feel this high, teach one his place, make one crawl, rub one's nose in the dirt, rub one's nose in it; snub, cut, crush, squash, sit on, send away with a flea in their ear 885 *be rude*; slight 921 *not respect*; mortify, hurt one's pride, offend one's dignity, lower in all men's eyes, put to shame 867 *shame*; score off, put one's nose out of joint, make a fool of, make one look silly; put in the shade 306 *outdo*; outstare, outfrown, frown down, daunt 854 *frighten*; get the better of, gain the upper hand, triumph over, crow o. 727 *overmaster*.

873 Vanity

N. *vanity*, emptiness 4 *insubstantiality*; empty pride 871 *pride*; immodesty, conceit, conceitedness, self-importance, megalomania; swank, side, puffed-up chest, swelled head; cockiness, bumptiousness, assurance, self-a.; good opinion of oneself, self-conceit, self-esteem, amour propre; self-satisfaction, smugness; self-love, self-admiration, narcissism; self-complacency, self-approbation, self-praise, self-applause, self-flattery, self-congratulation, self-glorification, vainglory 877 *boasting*; self-sufficiency, self-centredness, egotism, me-ism 932 *selfishness*; exhibitionism, showing off, self-display 875 *ostentation*.

airs, fine a., airs and graces, mannerisms, pretensions, absurd p. 850 *affectation*; swank, side, pompousness 875 *ostentation*; coxcombry, priggishness, foppery.

vain person, self-admirer, Narcissus; self-centred person, me generation, egotist, coxcomb 848 *fop*; exhibitionist, peacock, turkey cock, show-off; know-all, bighead, God's gift to women; smarty-pants, smart alec, smart ass, cleverstick, clever dick, Mr Clever, Miss Clever 500 *wiseacre*; stuffed shirt, pompous twit 4 *insubstantial thing*.

Adj. *vain*, conceited, overweening, stuck-up, snooty, proud 871 *prideful*; egotistic, egocentric, self-centred, self-satisfied, self-complacent, full of oneself, self-important 932 *selfish*; smug, pleased with oneself; self-loving, narcissistic, stuck on oneself; wise in one's own conceit, dogmatic, opinionated, oversubtle, overclever, clever clever, too clever by half, too smart for one's own good 498 *intelligent*; swollen-headed, puffed-up, too big for one's boots, bigheaded, bumptious, cocky, perky, smart-ass 878 *insolent*; immodest, blatant; showing off, swaggering, vainglorious, self-glorious; pompous 875 *ostentatious*; pretentious, soi-disant, so-called, self-styled; coxcombical, fantastical, putting on airs 850 *affected*.

Vb. *be vain*, – conceited etc. adj.; have a swelled head, have one's head turned; have a high opinion of oneself, set a high value on o., think a lot of o., think too much of o., think oneself the cat's pyjamas, think o. God Almighty, regard oneself as God's gift; exaggerate one's own merits, blow one's own trumpet 877 *boast*; admire oneself, hug o., flatter o., give

oneself a pat on the back; plume oneself, preen o., pride o.; swank, strut, show off, put on airs, put on side, show one's paces, display one's talents, talk for effect, talk big, not hide one's light under a bushel, push oneself forward 875 *be ostentatious*; lap up flattery, fish for compliments; get above oneself, have pretentions, give oneself airs 850 *be affected*; play the fop, be overconcerned with one's appearance, dress up, doll oneself up, dandify 843 *primp*.

874 Modesty

N. *modesty*, lack of ostentation, shyness, retiring disposition; diffidence, timidness, timidity 854 *nervousness*; overmodesty, prudishness 950 *prudery*; bashfulness, blushing, blush; shamefacedness, shockability; chastity 950 *purity*; deprecation, self-depreciation, self-effacement, hiding one's light 872 *humility*; unobtrusiveness, unpretentiousness, unassuming nature; demureness, reserve; shrinking violet, mouse.

Adj. *modest*, without vanity, free from pride; self-effacing, unobtrusive, unseen, unheard 872 *humble*; self-deprecating, unboastful; unassertive, unpushing, unthrustful, unambitious; quiet, unassuming, unpretentious, unpretending; unimposing, unimpressive, moderate, mediocre 639 *unimportant*; shy, retiring, shrinking, timid, mouse-like, diffident, unselfconfident, unsure of oneself 854 *nervous*; overshy, awkward, constrained, embarrassed, inarticulate; deprecating, demurring; bashful, blushing, rosy; shamefaced, sheepish; reserved, demure, coy; shockable, overmodest, prudish 850 *affected*; chaste 950 *pure*.

Vb. *be modest*, show moderation; not blow one's trumpet, not push oneself forward, efface oneself, yield precedence 872 *be humble*; play second fiddle, keep in the background, merge into the background, take a back seat, be a back-room boy *or* girl, know one's place; blush unseen, shun the limelight, shrink from the public gaze, hide one's light under a bushel 456 *escape notice*; not look for praise, do good by stealth and blush to find it fame; retire, creep into one's shell, shrink, hang back, be coy 620 *avoid*; show bashfulness, blush, colour, go red, crimson 431 *redden*; preserve one's modesty 933 *be virtuous*.

875 Ostentation. Formality

N. *ostentation*, demonstration, display, parade, show 522 *manifestation*; unconcealment, blatancy, flagrancy, shamelessness, brazenness, exhibitionism 528 *publicity*; ostentatiousness, showiness, magnificence, delusions of grandeur, grandiosity; splendour, brilliance; selfconsequence, self-importance 873 *vanity*; pomposity, fuss, swagger, showing off, pretension, pretensions, airs and graces 873 *airs*; swank, side, thrown-out chest, strut; machismo, bravado, heroics 877 *boast*; theatricality, camp, histrionics, dramatization, dramatics, sensationalism 546 *exaggeration*; demonstrativeness, back-slapping, bonhomie 882 *sociability*; showmanship, effect, window-dressing; solemnity (**see** *formality*); grandeur, dignity, stateliness, impressiveness; declamation, rhetoric 574 *grandiloquence*; flourish, flourish of trumpets, fanfaronade, big drum 528 *publication*; pageantry, pomp, circumstance, pomp and c., bravery, pride, panache, waving plumes, fine feathers, flying colours, dash, splash, splurge 844 *finery*; frippery, gaudiness, glitter, tinsel 844 *ornamentation*; idle pomp, idle show, false glitter, unsubstantial pageant, mummery, mockery, idle m., hollow m., solemn m. 4 *insubstantiality*; tomfoolery 497 *foolery*; travesty 20 *mimicry*; exterior, gloss, veneer, polish, varnish 223 *exteriority*; pretence, profession 614 *pretext*; insincerity, lip service, tokenism 542 *deception*; formality, state, stateliness, dignity; ceremoniousness, stiffness, starchiness; royal we, editorial we 870 *title*; ceremony, ceremonial 988 *ritual*; drill, smartness, spit and polish, military bull; correctness, correctitude, protocol, form, good f., right f. 848 *etiquette*; punctilio, punctiliousness, preciseness 455 *attention*; routine, fixed r. 610 *practice*; solemnity, formal occasion, ceremonial o., state o., function, grand f., official f., red carpet 876 *celebration*; full dress, court d., robes, regalia, finery, black tie 228 *formal dress*; correct dress 228 *uniform*.

pageant, show 522 *exhibit*; fete, gala, gala performance, tournament, tattoo; field day, great doings 876 *celebration*; son et lumière 445 *spectacle*; set piece, tableau, scene, transformation s., stage effect 594 *stage set*; display, bravura, stunt; pyrotechnics; carnival, Lord Mayor's Show 837 *festivity*, *revel*; procession, promenade, march-past, fly-past; changing the guard, trooping the colour; turnout, review, grand r., parade, array 74 *assembly*.

Adj. *ostentatious*, showy, pompous; done for effect; window-dressing, for show, for the sake of appearance; for prestige, for the look of the thing; specious, seeming, hollow 542 *spurious*; consequential, self-important, pretentious, would-be 850 *affected*; showing off, swanking, swanky 873 *vain*; inflated, turgid, orotund, pontificating, windy, magniloquent, declamatory, high-sounding, high-flown; grand, highfalutin, splendiferous, splendid, brilliant, magnificent, grandiose, posh; superb, royal 813 *liberal*; sumptuous, diamond-studded, luxurious, de luxe,

plushy, ritzy, glitzy, costly, expensive, expense-account 811 *dear*; painted, glorified, tarted up.

showy, flashy, dressy, dressed to kill, all dolled up, foppish 848 *fashionable*; colourful, lurid, gaudy, gorgeous 425 *florid*; tinsel, glittering, garish, tawdry 847 *vulgar*; flaming, flaring, flaunting, flagrant, blatant, public; brave, dashing, gallant, gay, jaunty, rakish, sporty; spectacular, scenic, dramatic, histrionic, theatrical, camp, stagy; sensational, daring; exhibitionist, stunting.

formal, dignified, solemn, stately, majestic, grand, fine; ceremonious, standing on ceremony, punctilious, stickling, correct, precise, stiff, starchy; black-tie, white-tie, full-dress; of state, public, official; ceremonial, ritual 988 *ritualistic*; for a special occasion, for a gala o.

Vb. *be ostentatious*, - showy etc. adj.; observe the formalities, stand on ceremony; splurge, splash out, cut a dash, make a splash, make a figure; glitter, dazzle 417 *shine*; flaunt, sport 228 *wear*; dress up 843 *primp*; wave, flourish 317 *brandish*; blazon, trumpet, sound the t., beat the big drum 528 *proclaim*; stage a demonstration, wave banners 711 *defy*; demonstrate, exhibit 522 *show*; act the showman, make a display, put on a show; make the most of, put on a front, window-dress, stage-manage; see to the outside, paper the cracks, polish, veneer 226 *coat*; intend for effect, strive for e., sensationalize, camp up; talk for effect, shoot a line 877 *boast*; take the centre of the stage, grab or hog the limelight 455 *attract notice*; put oneself forward, advertise oneself, dramatize o.; play to the gallery, fish for compliments 850 *be affected*; show off, flaunt oneself, show one's paces, prance, promenade, swan around; parade, march, march past, fly past; peacock, strut, swank, put on side 873 *be vain*; make an exhibition of oneself, make a public spectacle of oneself, make people stare.

876 Celebration

N. *celebration*, performance, soleminization 676 *action*; commemoration 505 *remembrance*; observance, solemn o. 988 *ritual*; ceremony, ceremonial, function, occasion, do; formal occasion, coronation, enthronement, inauguration, installation, presentation 751 *commission*; debut, coming out 68 *beginning*; reception, welcome, hero's w., tickertape w., red-carpet treatment 875 *formality*; official reception 923 *applause*; festive occasion, fete, jubilee, diamond j. 837 *festivity*; jubilation, cheering, high-five, ovation, standing o., triumph, salute, salvo, tattoo, roll, roll of drums, fanfare, fanfaronade, flourish of trumpets, flying colours, flag waving, mafficking 835 *rejoic-*

ing; flags, banners, bunting, streamers, decorations, Chinese lanterns, illuminations; firework display; bonfire 379 *fire*; triumphal arch 729 *trophy*; harvest home, thanksgiving, Te Deum 907 *thanks*; paean, hosannah, hallelujah 886 *congratulation*; health, toast.

special day, day to remember, great day, red-letter d., gala d., flag d., field d.; Saint's day, feast d., fast d. 988 *holy day*; Armistice Day, D-Day, Remembrance Sunday; Fourth of July, Independence Day, Republic D., Bastille D.; birthday, name-day; wedding anniversary, silver wedding, golden w., diamond w., ruby w.; centenary, bicentenary, sesquicentenary 141 *anniversary*.

Vb. *celebrate*, solemnize; hallow, keep holy, keep sacred 979 *sanctify*; commemorate 505 *remember*; honour, observe; make it an occasion, mark the o.; make much of, welcome, kill the fatted calf, do one proud 882 *be hospitable*; do honour to, fete; chair, carry shoulder-high 310 *elevate*; mob, rush 61 *rampage*; garland, deck with flowers, wreathe, crown 962 *reward*; lionize, give a hero's welcome, fling wide the gates, roll out the red carpet, hang out the flags, put out the bunting, beat a tattoo, blow the trumpets, clash the cymbals, fire a salute, fire a salvo, fire a feu de joie 884 *pay one's respects*; cheer, jubilate, triumph, rejoice; make holiday 837 *revel*.

toast, pledge, clink glasses; drink to, raise one's glass to, drink a health 301 *drink*.

877 Boasting

N. *boasting*, bragging, boastfulness, fanfaronade; ostentation; self-glorification, swagger, swank 873 *vanity*; advertisement, hype 528 *publicity*; puffery 482 *overestimation*; grandiloquence, fine talk 515 *empty talk*; swaggering, swashbuckling, heroics, bravado; flag-wagging or -waving, chauvinism, jingoism 481 *bias*; defensiveness, blustering, bluster 854 *nervousness*; sabre-rattling, intimidation 900 *threat*.

boast, brag; hype 528 *advertisement*; flourish, fanfaronade, bravado, bombast, rant, tall talk 546 *exaggeration*; hot air, gas, bunkum 515 *empty talk*; bluff 542 *deception*; big talk, bluster, hectoring, idle threat 900 *threat*.

Vb. *boast*, brag, crow, vaunt, talk big, have a big mouth, shoot one's mouth, shoot a line, bluff, huff and puff, bluster, hector, shout; bid defiance 711 *defy*; vapour, prate, rant, gas 515 *mean nothing*; enlarge, magnify, lay it on thick, draw the longbow 546 *exaggerate*; trumpet, parade, flaunt, show off 528 *publish*; puff, crack up, cry one's wares 528 *advertise*; sell oneself, advertise o., be a self-publicist, blow one's own trumpet, blow hard, sing one's own praises,

bang the big drum 875 *be ostentatious*; flourish, wave 317 *brandish*; play the jingo, rattle the sabre 900 *threaten*; show off, strut, swagger, prance, swank, throw out one's chest 873 *be vain*; gloat, pat oneself on the back, hug oneself 824 *be pleased*; boast of, plume oneself on 871 *be proud*; glory in, crow over 727 *triumph*; exult 835 *rejoice*.

878 Insolence

N. *insolence*, arrogance, haughtiness attitude, loftiness 871 *pride*; domineering, tyranny 735 *severity*; bravado 711 *defiance*; bluster 900 *threat*; disdain 922 *contempt*; sneer, sneering 926 *detraction*; contumely 899 *scurrility*; assurance, self-a., self-assertion, bumptiousness, cockiness, brashness; presumption 916 *arrogation*; audacity, hardihood, boldness, effrontery, chutzpah, shamelessness, brazenness, brass neck, blatancy, flagrancy; face, front, hardened f., brazen face.

sauciness, disrespect, impertinence, impudence, pertness, freshness, sassiness; flippancy, nerve, gall, brass, cheek, cool c., neck; lip, mouth, sauce, crust, sass, snook, V-sign 547 *gesture*; taunt, personality, insult, affront 921 *indignity*; rudeness, incivility, throwaway manner 885 *discourtesy*; petulance, defiance, answer, provocation, answering back, backtalk, backchat 460 *rejoinder*; raillery, banter 851 *ridicule*.

insolent person, minx, hussy, baggage, madam; whippersnapper, pup, puppy; upstart, Jack-in-office, tin god 639 *non-entity*; blusterer, swaggerer, braggart; bantam-cock; bully, swashbuckler.

Adj. *insolent*, rebellious 711 *defiant*; sneering, insulting 921 *disrespectful*; injurious, scurrilous 899 *cursing*; lofty, supercilious, disdainful, contemptuous; undemocratic, snobbish, haughty, snooty, up-stage, high-hat, high and mighty 871 *proud*; arrogant, presumptuous, assuming; with attitude; brash, bumptious, bouncing 873 *vain*; flagrant, blatant; shameless, brazen, brazen-faced, brass-necked, bold as brass; bold, hardy, audacious 857 *rash*; overweening, overbearing, domineering, imperious, lordly, dictatorial, arbitrary, high-handed, harsh, tyrannical 735 *oppressive*.

impertinent, pert, forward, fresh; impudent, saucy, sassy, cheeky, smart-mouth, cool, cocky, cocksure, flippant, flip; cavalier, offhand, presumptuous, out of line, familiar, overfamiliar, free-and-easy 921 *disrespectful*; impolite, rude, uncivil, ill-mannered 885 *discourteous*; defiant, answering back, offensive.

Vb. *be insolent*, – arrogant etc. adj.; forget one's manners, get personal 885 *be rude*; have a nerve, cheek, sauce, sass, give lip, taunt, provoke 891 *enrage*; have the audacity to, have the brass neck to, have the cheek to; retort, answer back 460 *answer*; shout down 479 *confute*; get above oneself, get above one's station, teach one's grandmother to suck eggs; not know one's place, presume, be out-of-line, arrogate, assume, take on oneself, make bold to, make free with, get fresh; put on airs, hold one's nose in the air, look one up and down 871 *be proud*; look down on, sneer at 922 *despise*; banter, rally 851 *ridicule*; express contempt, sniff, snort; not give a fig 860 *be indifferent*; cock a snook, put one's tongue out, give the V-sign 711 *defy*; outstare, outface, brazen it out, brave it o.; take a high tone, lord it, queen it, lord it over; lay down the law, throw one's weight around; hector, bully, browbeat, grind down, trample on, ride roughshod over, treat with a high hand 735 *oppress*; swank, swagger, swell, look big 873 *be vain*; brag, talk big 877 *boast*; be a law unto oneself 738 *disobey*; tempt providence *or* fate.

879 Servility

N. *servility*, slavishness, no pride, lack of self-respect 856 *cowardice*; subservience 721 *submission*; submissiveness, obsequiousness, compliance, pliancy 739 *obedience*; time-serving 603 *change of mind*; abasement 872 *humility*; prostration, genuflexion, stooping, bent back, bow, scrape, bowing and scraping, duck, bob 311 *obeisance*; cringing, crawling, fawning, boot-licking, bumsucking, toadyism, sycophancy, ingratiation, soft soap 925 *flattery*; flunkeyism; servile condition, slavery 745 *servitude*.

toady, collaborator, Uncle Tom; yes-man, rubber stamp 488 *assenter*; lickspittle, bootlicker, backscratcher, bumsucker, apple-polisher, kowtower, groveller, crawler, creep; hypocrite, creeping Jesus, Uriah Heep; spaniel, fawner, courtier, fortune-hunter, lion-h. 925 *flatterer*; sycophant, parasite, leech, sponger, freeloader; jackal, hanger-on, gigolo 742 *dependant*; flunkey, lackey 742 *retainer*; born slave, slave; doormat, footstool, lapdog, poodle; tool, creature, puppet, dupe, cat's-paw 628 *instrument*.

Adj. *servile*, not free, dependent 745 *subject*; slavish 856 *cowardly*; mean-spirited, mean, abject, base, tame 745 *subjected*; subservient, submissive, deferential 721 *submitting*; pliant, putty-like, compliant, supple 739 *obedient*; time-serving; bowed, stooping, prostrate, boot-licking, backscratching, bumsucking, grovelling, kowtowing, bowing, scraping, cringing, cowering, crawling, sneaking, fawning; begging, whining; toadying, toadyish, sycophantic, parasitical; creepy, obsequious, unctuous, soapy, oily, slimy, overattentive, soft-soaping, ingratiating 925 *flattering*.

Vb. *be servile*, forfeit one's self-respect, stoop to anything 867 *demean oneself*; crawl, grovel, kiss the hands of, kiss the feet of, kiss the hem of one's garment, lick the boots of 721 *knuckle under*; bow and scrape, bend, kowtow, touch the forelock, make obeisance, kneel 311 *stoop*; swallow insults 872 *be humble*; make-up to cosy up to, toady to, suck up to, fawn, ingratiate oneself, soft-soap, pay court to, curry favour, worm oneself into f. 925 *flatter*; squire, attend, dance attendance on, fetch and carry for 742 *serve*; comply 739 *obey*; be the tool of, do one's dirty work, pander to, stooge for 628 *be instrumental*; let oneself be walked all over, be a doormat, act as a footstool; beg for favours, beg for crumbs 761 *beg*; play the parasite, batten on, sponge, sponge on; jump on the band wagon, run with the hare and hunt with the hounds 83 *conform*; serve the times 603 *tergiversate*.

SECTION THREE

Interpersonal emotion

880 Friendship

N. *friendship*, bonds of f., amity 710 *concord*; compatibility, mateyness, chumminess, palliness; friendly relations, social intercourse, hob-nobbing 882 *fellowship*; companionship, belonging, togetherness; alignment, fellowship, comradeship, sodality, freemasonry, brotherhood, sisterhood 706 *association*; solidarity, mutual support 706 *cooperation*; acquaintanceship, acquaintance, mutual a., familiarity, intimacy 490 *knowledge*; close friendship 887 *love*.

friendliness, amicability, kindliness, kindness, neighbourliness 884 *courtesy*; heartiness, cordiality, warmth 897 *benevolence*; fraternization, camaraderie, palliness, mateyness; hospitality 882 *sociability*; greeting, welcome, open arms, handclasp, handshake, hand-kissing, kissing, peck on the cheek, hug, rubbing noses 884 *courteous act*; regard, mutual r. 920 *respect*; goodwill, mutual g.; fellow feeling, sympathy, response 775 *participation*; understanding, same wavelength, entente, entente cordiale, hands across the sea.

friend, girlfriend, boyfriend 887 *loved one*; one's friends and acquaintances, one's circle of friends, acquaintance, intimate a.; friend of the family, lifelong friend, mutual f., friend of a friend, crony, old c. (**see** *chum*); neighbour, good n., fellow townsman *or* -woman, fellow countryman *or* -woman; cousin, clansman 11 *kinsman*; well-wisher, backer, angel 707 *patron*; second 660 *protector*; fellow, sister, brother, partner, associate 707 *colleague*; ally, brother-in-arms 707 *auxiliary*; collaborator, helper, friend in need 703 *aider*; guest, welcome g., frequent visitor, persona grata; young friend, protégé(e); host, kind h. 882 *sociable person*; former friend, fairweather f. 603 *tergiversator*.

close friend, best f.; soul mate, kindred spirit; best man, bridesmaid 894 *bridal party*; dear friend, good f., close f., f. in need; intimate, bosom friend, bosom pal, confidant(e), alter ego, other self, shadow; comrade, companion, boon c., drinking c.; good friends all, happy family; mutual friends, inseparables, band of brothers *or* sisters, Three Musketeers, David and Jonathan, Ruth and Naomi, Castor and Pollux; two minds with but a single thought, birds of a feather.

chum, crony; pal, mate, amigo, cobber, buddy, butty, marrow, sidekick, oppo; fellow, comrade, shipmate, messmate, roommate, stable companion 707 *colleague*; teammate, playmate, classmate, schoolmate, schoolfellow; pen friend, pen pal.

Adj. *friendly*, nonhostile, amicable, devoted 887 *loving*; loyal, faithful, staunch, fast, firm, tried and true 929 *trustworthy*; fraternal, brotherly, sisterly, cousinly; natural, unstrained, easy, harmonious; compatible, congenial, sympathetic, understanding; well-wishing, well-meaning, well-intentioned, philanthropic 897 *benevolent*; hearty, cordial, warm, welcoming, hospitable 882 *sociable*; effusive, demonstrative, back-slapping, hail-fellow-well-met; comradely, chummy, pally, matey, buddy-buddy, palsy-walsy; friendly with, good friends w., at home w.; acquainted 490 *knowing*; free and easy, on familiar terms, on visiting t., on intimate t., on the best of t., well in with, intimate, inseparable, thick, thick as thieves, hand in glove.

Vb. *be friendly*, be friends with, get on well w., be on friendly terms w.; have dealings w., rub along w., be palsy-walsy w., be buddy-buddy w.; fraternize, hobnob, keep company with, keep up w., keep in w., cosy up to, go about together, be inseparable 882 *be sociable*; have friends, make f., win f., have a wide circle of friends, have a large acquaintance; shake hands, clasp h., embrace 884 *greet*; welcome, entertain 882 *be hospitable*; sympathize 516 *understand*; like, warm to, become fond of 887 *love*; mean well, have the best intentions, have the friendliest feelings.

befriend, take up, take in tow, protect 703 *patronize*; gain one's friendship; extend the right hand of fellowship, make welcome; strike an acquaintance, scrape an a.; break the ice, make overtures 289 *approach*; seek one's friendship, cultivate one's f., pay one's addresses to

889 *court*; take to, warm to, click with, hit it off; fraternize with, frat, hobnob, get pally with, get matey w., get chummy w., chum up w., make friends w.

881 Enmity

N. *enmity*, inimicality, hostility, antagonism 704 *opposition*; no love lost, unfriendliness, incompatibility, antipathy 861 *dislike*; loathing 888 *hatred*; animosity, spite, grudge, ill feeling, ill will, bad blood, intolerance, persecution 898 *malevolence*; jealousy 912 *envy*; coolness, coldness 380 *ice*; estrangement, alienation, strain, tension, dissension; bitterness, hard feelings, rancour, soreness 891 *resentment*; unfaithfulness, disloyalty 930 *perfidy*; breach, open b., breach of friendship 709 *quarrel*; hostile act; conflict, hostilities, breaking off of diplomatic relations, state of war 718 *belligerency*; vendetta, feud, blood f.

enemy, no friend; ex-friend 603 *tergiversator*; traitor, viper in one's bosom 663 *troublemaker*; bad neighbour, ill-wisher; antagonist, opposite side, other s., them 705 *opponent*; competitor, rival 716 *contender*; open enemy, foe, foeman, hostile force 722 *combatant*; aggressor 712 *attacker*; enemy within the gates, fifth column, Trojan Horse; public enemy, sworn enemy, bitter e.; arch enemy; misanthropist, misogynist 902 *misanthrope*; xenophobe, Anglophobe, Francophobe, racialist, anti-Semite 481 *narrow mind*; persona non grata, pet aversion, bête-noire 888 *hateful object*.

Adj. *hostile*, inimical, unfriendly, ill-disposed, disaffected; disloyal, unfaithful 930 *perfidious*; aloof, distant, unwelcoming 883 *unsociable*; cool, chilly, frigid, icy 380 *cold*; antipathetic, incompatible, unsympathetic; loathing; hostile, antagonistic, warring, conflicting, actively opposed 704 *opposing*; antagonized, estranged, alienated, unreconciled, irreconcilable; bitter, embittered, rancorous 891 *resentful*; jealous, grudging 912 *envious*; spiteful 898 *malevolent*; bad friends with, on bad terms, not on speaking t.; at variance, at loggerheads, at daggers drawn 709 *quarrelling*; aggressive, militant, belligerent, at war with 718 *warring*; intolerant, persecuting 735 *oppressive*; dangerous, venomous, virulent, deadly, fell.

Vb. *be hostile*, – unfriendly etc. adj.; show hostility; harden one's heart, bear ill will, bear malice 898 *be malevolent*; grudge, nurse a g. 912 *envy*; hound, persecute 735 *oppress*; chase, hunt down 619 *hunt*; battle 716 *fight*; make war 718 *wage war*; take offence, take something the wrong way, take umbrage 891 *resent*; fall out, come to blows 709 *quarrel*; be incompatible, have nothing in common, be on different wavelengths, conflict, collide, clash 14 *be contrary*; withstand 704 *oppose*.

882 Sociality

N. *fellowship*, membership, membership of society, intercommunity, consociation 706 *association*; making one of, being one of, belonging; team spirit, esprit de corps; comradeship, companionship, society; camaraderie, fraternization, hobnobbing; social intercourse, familiarity, intimacy, palliness, mateyness, togetherness 880 *friendship*; social circle, home c., family c., one's friends and acquaintances 880 *friend*; social ambition, social climbing; society, the world.

sociability, group activity; compatibility 83 *conformity*; sociableness, gregariousness, sociable disposition 880 *friendliness*; social success, popularity, street credibility, street cred, social tact; social graces, savoir-vivre, good manners, easy m. 884 *courtesy*; urbanity 846 *good taste*; clubbability; affability 584 *interlocution*; acceptability, welcome, smiling reception, open door; greeting, glad hand, handshake, hand-clasp, embrace 884 *courteous act*; hospitality, entertaining, home from home, open house, Liberty Hall, pot luck 813 *liberality*; good company, good fellowship, geniality, cordiality, heartiness, back-slapping, bonhomie; conviviality, joviality, jollity, merrymaking 824 *enjoyment*; gaiety 837 *revel*; good cheer 301 *food*; festive board, the cup that cheers.

social gathering, forgathering, meeting 74 *assembly*; reunion, get-together, social; reception, at home, soirée, levee; entertainment 837 *amusement*; singsong, camp fire; party, do, shindig, thrash, hen party, stag p., tête-à-tête; housewarming, house party, weekend p., birthday p., coming-out p.; feast, banquet, orgy 301 *feasting*; communion, love feast 988 *ritual act*; coffee morning, tea party, bun fight, drinks, cocktail party, dinner p., supper p., garden p., picnic, barbecue, bottle party, byob (= bring your own bottle) p. 837 *festivity*; dance, ball, ceilidh, hop, disco 837 *dancing*.

social round, social activities, social whirl, season, social s., social entertainment; social calls, round of visits; seeing one's friends, visiting, calling, dropping in; weekending, stay, visit, formal v., call, courtesy c.; visiting terms, haunting 880 *friendship*; social demands, engagement, something on; dating, trysting, rendezvous, assignation, date, blind d.; meeting place, club, pub, local 76 *focus*.

sociable person, active member, keen m.; caller, visitor, dropper-in, frequenter, haunter, habitué; convivial person, bon vivant, bon viveur; good mixer, good company, life and soul

of the party; social success, catch, lion 890 *favourite*; boon companion, hobnobber, clubman, club woman; good neighbour 880 *friend*; hostess, host, mine h.; guest, welcome g., one of the family; parasite, freeloader, ligger, gatecrasher; gadabout, social butterfly; socialite, social climber 848 *beau monde*.

Adj. *sociable*, gregarious, social, sociably disposed, extrovert, outgoing, fond of company, party-minded; companionable, fraternizing, affable, conversable, chatty, gossipy; clubbable; couthie, cosy, folksy; neighbourly, matey, chummy, pally, palsy-walsy, buddy-buddy 880 *friendly*; hospitable, welcoming, smiling, cordial, warm, hearty, back-slapping, hail-fellow-well-met; convivial, jolly, jovial 833 *merry*; lively, witty 837 *amusing*; urbane 884 *courteous*; easy, free-and-easy.

Vb. *be sociable*, – gregarious etc. adj.; like company, have friends, make friends easily, hobnob, fraternize, socialize, mix with 880 *be friendly*; mix well, be a good mixer, get around, mix in society, go out, dine o.; freeload, lig, gate-crash; have fun, live it up, be the life and soul of the party 837 *amuse oneself*; join in, get together, make it a party, club together, go Dutch, share, go shares 775 *participate*; take pot luck 301 *eat*; join in a bottle, crack a b. 301 *drink*; toast; carouse 837 *revel*; make oneself at home, become one of the family; relax, unbend 683 *repose*; chat to 584 *converse*; make engagements, date, make a date; make friends, make friendly overtures 880 *befriend*; introduce oneself, exchange names, exchange telephone numbers; enlarge one's circle of acquaintances; keep up with, keep in touch w., write to 588 *correspond*.

visit, go visiting, pay a visit, be one's guest, sojourn, stay, weekend; see one's friends; go and see, look one up, call, call in, look in, drop in; leave a card; exchange visits, be on visiting terms.

be hospitable, keep open house 813 *be liberal*; invite, have round, ask in, be at home to, receive, open one's home to, keep open house; welcome, welcome with open arms; act the host, do the honours, preside; do proud, kill the fatted calf 876 *celebrate*; have company, entertain 301 *feed*; give a party, throw a p. 837 *revel*; cater for, provide entertainment 633 *provide*.

883 Unsociability. Seclusion

N. *unsociability*, unsociableness, unsocial habits, shyness 620 *avoidance*; introversion, autism; keeping one's own company, keeping oneself to oneself; staying at home; inhospitality 816 *parsimony*; standoffishness, unapproachability, distance, aloofness 871 *pride*;

unfriendliness, coolness, coldness, moroseness, 893 *sullenness*; silence, lack of conversation 582 *taciturnity*; ostracism, boycott 57 *exclusion*; blacklist 607 *rejection*.

seclusion, privacy, private world, world of one's own; island universe 321 *star*; peace and quiet 266 *quietude*; home life, domesticity; loneliness, solitariness, solitude; retreat, retirement, withdrawal; hiddenness 523 *latency*; confinement, solitary c., purdah 525 *concealment*; isolation, splendid i. 744 *independence*; division, estrangement 46 *separation*; renunciation 621 *relinquishment*; renunciation of the world, monasticism; self-exile, expatriation; sequestration, segregation, ghettoization, rustication, excommunication, house arrest, quarantine, deportation, banishment, exile 57 *exclusion*; reserve, reservation, ghetto, harem; gaol 748 *prison*; sequestered nook, godforsaken hole, back of beyond; island, desert, wilderness; hide-out, hideaway 527 *hiding-place*; den, study, sanctum, inner s., cloister, cell, hermitage 192 *retreat*; ivory tower, private quarters, shell; backwater.

solitary, unsocial person, iceberg; lonely heart; loner, lone wolf, rogue elephant; isolationist; introvert; stay-at-home, home-body; ruralist, recluse, anchorite, hermit; stylite; maroon, castaway 779 *derelict*; Robinson Crusoe.

outcast, pariah, leper, outsider; out-caste, untouchable; expatriate, alien 59 *foreigner*; exile, evictee, deportee, evacuee, refugee, political r., displaced person, homeless p., rough sleeper, skell; stateless p.; nonperson, unperson; proscribed person, outlaw, bandit; reject, flotsam and jetsam, the dregs 641 *rubbish*.

Adj. *unsociable*, unsocial, antisocial, introverted, morose; unassimilated, foreign 59 *extraneous*; unclubbable, stay-at-home, domestic; inhospitable, unwelcoming, forbidding, hostile, unneighbourly, unfriendly, uncongenial, unaffable, misanthropic; distant, aloof, unbending, stiff; stand-offish, haughty 871 *prideful*; unwelcoming, frosty, icy, cold 893 *sullen*; unforthcoming, in one's shell; unconversational, uncommunicative, close, silent 582 *taciturn*; cool, impersonal 860 *indifferent*; solitary, lonely, lone 88 *alone*; shy, reserved, retiring, withdrawn; wild, feral; celibate, unmarried; by the world forgot.

secluded, private, sequestered, cloistered, shut away, hidden, buried, tucked away 523 *latent*; veiled, in purdah; quiet, lonely, isolated, enisled, marooned; remote, out of the way; godforsaken, unfrequented, unexplored, unseen, unfamiliar, off the beaten track, far from the madding crowd 491 *unknown*; uninhabited, deserted 190 *empty*.

Vb. *seclude*, sequester, isolate, quarantine, segregate, ghettoize; keep in purdah; confine, shut up 747 *imprison*.

884 Courtesy

N. *courtesy*, chivalry, knightliness, gallantry; common courtesy, deference 920 *respect*; consideration, condescension 872 *humility*; graciousness, politeness, civility, urbanity, mannerliness, manners, good m., good behaviour; good breeding, gentlemanliness, ladylikeness, gentility 846 *good taste*; tactfulness, diplomacy; courtliness, correctness, correctitude, etiquette 875 *formality*; amiability, niceness, obligingness, kindness, kindliness 897 *benevolence*; gentleness, mildness 736 *leniency*; agreeableness, affability, social tact 882 *sociability*.

courteous act, act of courtesy, graceful gesture, courtesy, common c., civility, favour, kindness; compliment, bouquet 886 *congratulation*; kind words, fair w., sweet w. 889 *endearment*; introduction 880 *friendliness*; welcome, reception, invitation; acknowledgment, recognition, nod, salutation, salute, greeting, smile, kiss, kiss on the cheek, air-kiss, air-kissing, hug, squeeze, handclasp, hand-shake 920 *respects*; salaam, kowtow, bow, curtsy 311 *obeisance*; respects, regards, kind r., best r., remembrances, love, best wishes; love and kisses, farewell 296 *valediction*.

Adj. *courteous*, chivalrous, knightly, generous 868 *noble*; courtly, gallant, old-world, correct 875 *formal*; polite, civil, urbane, gentle, gentlemanly, ladylike, dignified, well-mannered, fine-m. 848 *well-bred*; gracious, mannerly 920 *respectful*; on one's best behaviour, minding one's P's and Q's 455 *attentive*; obliging, kind 897 *benevolent*; agreeable, suave; well-spoken.

amiable, nice, sweet, winning; affable, friendly, amicable 882 *sociable*; considerate, kind 897 *benevolent*; inoffensive, harmless 935 *innocent*; gentle, easy, mild, soft-spoken 736 *lenient*; good-tempered, sweet-t., good-natured, unruffled 823 *inexcitable*; well-behaved, good 739 *obedient*; peaceable 717 *peaceful*.

Vb. *be courteous*, be on one's best behaviour, mind one's P's and Q's; mind one's manners; show courtesy; make time for 455 *be attentive*; not forget one's manners, keep a civil tongue in one's head, make oneself agreeable, be all things to all men; take no offence, take in good part, 823 *be patient*; mend one's manners.

pay one's respects, give one's regards, send one's r., send one's compliments, do one the honour; pay compliments 925 *flatter*; drink to, toast; pay homage, show one's respect, kneel, kiss hands 920 *show respect*; honour 876 *celebrate*.

greet, send greetings (**see** *pay one's respects*); acknowledge, recognize, hold out one's hand 455 *notice*; shout *or* call out one's greeting, hail 408 *vociferate*; nod, wave, smile, kiss one's fingers, blow a kiss; say hallo, bid good morning 583 *speak to*; salute, raise one's hat; touch one's cap, tug one's forelock; bow, bob, curtsy, salaam, make obeisance, kiss hands, prostrate oneself, kowtow 311 *stoop*; shake hands, clasp h., shake the hand, press *or* squeeze *or* wring *or* pump the hand; escort 89 *accompany*; make a salute, fire a s., present arms, parade 876 *celebrate*; receive, do the honours, be mother; welcome 882 *be sociable*; welcome with open arms 824 *be pleased*; embrace, hug, kiss, kiss on both cheeks 889 *caress*; usher in, present, introduce 299 *admit*.

885 Discourtesy

N. *discourtesy*, impoliteness, bad manners, disgraceful table m.; no manners, want of courtesy, lack of politeness, lack of manners, incivility; churlishness, uncouthness, boorishness, yobbishness 847 *ill-breeding*; unpleasantness, nastiness, misbehaviour, misconduct, unbecoming conduct; tactlessness, want of consideration, stepping on one's toes.

rudeness, ungraciousness, gruffness, bluntness; sharpness, tartness, acerbity, acrimony, asperity; roughness, harshness 735 *severity*; offhandedness 456 *inattention*; shortness; sarcasm 851 *ridicule*; unparliamentary language, bad l., rude words, virulence 899 *scurrility*; rebuff, insult 921 *indignity*; impertinence, pertness, sauce, sassiness, lip, cheek, truculence 878 *insolence*; interruption, shouting 822 *excitability*; black look, sour l., scowl, frown, pulling faces, sticking out the tongue 893 *sullenness*; act of discourtesy, display of bad manners.

rude person, no gentleman, no lady; savage, barbarian, brute, lout, boor, yob, loudmouth; crab, bear; sourpuss, crosspatch, grouch, grouser, fault-finder, bellyacher, beefer, sulker 829 *malcontent*.

Adj. *discourteous*, unchivalrous; unceremonious, ungentlemanly, unladylike; impolite, uncivil, rude; mannerless, unmannerly, ill-mannered, bad-m.; boorish, loutish, yobbish, uncouth, brutish, beastly, savage, barbarian 847 *ill-bred*; insolent, impudent; cheeky, saucy, sassy, pert, forward 878 *impertinent*; unpleasant, disagreeable; unaccommodating 860 *indifferent*; offhanded, cavalier, tactless, inconsiderate 456 *inattentive*.

Vb. *be rude*, – mannerless etc. adj.; have no

manners, flout etiquette; know no better 699 *be artless*; forget one's manners, show discourtesy 878 *be insolent*; show no thought for others, step on everyone's toes, ride roughshod over everyone 921 *not respect*; have no time for 456 *be inattentive*; treat rudely, snub, turn one's back on, cold-shoulder, hand one the frozen mitt, cut, ignore, look right through, cut dead; show one the door, send away with a flea in their ear 300 *eject*; cause offence, miff, ruffle one's feelings 891 *huff*; insult, abuse; take liberties, make free with, make bold; stare, ogle 438 *gaze*; make one blush 867 *shame*; lose one's temper, shout, interrupt 891 *get angry*; curse, swear; snarl, growl, frown, scowl, lour, pout, sulk.

886 Congratulation

N. *congratulation*, congratulations, felicitations, compliments, bouquets, compliments of the season; good wishes, best w.; salute, toast; welcome, hero's w., official reception 876 *celebration*; thanks 907 *gratitude*.

Vb. *congratulate*, compliment, proffer bouquets; offer one's congratulations, wish one joy, wish many happy returns, wish a merry Christmas and a happy New Year, offer the season's greetings; send one's congratulations, send one's compliments 884 *pay one's respects*; give one a hero's welcome, give a standing ovation, give three cheers, clap 923 *applaud*; fete, lionize 876 *celebrate*; congratulate oneself, give oneself a pat on the back.

887 Love

N. *love*, affection, friendship, charity; brotherly love, sisterly l., Christian l.; true love, real thing; parental affection, paternal a., maternal a., mother-love; possessiveness 911 *jealousy*; conjugal love, uxoriousness; closeness, intimacy; sentiment 818 *feeling*; tenderness 897 *benevolence*; Platonic love 880 *friendship*; two hearts that beat as one, mutual love, mutual affection, mutual attraction, compatibility, sympathy, fellow feeling, understanding; fondness, liking, predilection, inclination 179 *tendency*; preference 605 *choice*; fancy 604 *caprice*; attachment, sentimental a.; devotion, patriotism 739 *loyalty*; courtly love, gallantry; sentimentality, susceptibility, amorousness 819 *moral sensibility*; power of love, fascination, enchantment, bewitchment 983 *sorcery*; lovesickness, yearning, longing 859 *desire*; eroticism, lust 859 *libido*; regard 920 *respect*; admiration, hero-worship, worship from afar 864 *wonder*; first love, calf l., puppy l., young l.; crush, pash, infatuation; worship 982 *idolatry*; romantic love, l. at first sight, coup de foudre, passion, tender p., flames of love, enthusiasm, rapture, ecstasy, transports of love

822 *excitable state*; narcissism, Oedipus complex; love-hate.

love affair, romantic a., affair of the heart, affaire de coeur; romance, love and the world well lost; flirtation, amour, entanglement; free love; liaison, intrigue, seduction, adultery 951 *illicit love*; falling in love, something between them; course of love, the old old story; betrothal, engagement, wedding bells 894 *marriage*; relationship, serial monogamy.

lovemaking, flirting, spooning, canoodling, necking, billing and cooing 889 *endearment*; courting, walking out, going with, going steady, pressing one's suit, laying siege 889 *wooing*; pursuit of love, flirting, coquetry, philandering; dalliance.

lover, love, true l., sweetheart; squeeze; young man, boyfriend, Romeo; young woman, girlfriend, bird; swain, beau, gallant, cavalier, squire, escort, date; steady, fiancé(e); wooer, courter, suitor, follower, admirer, hero-worshipper, adorer, votary, worshipper; aficionado, fan, devoted following, fan club; sugar daddy; gigolo, ladies' man, lady-killer, seducer, Lothario, Don Juan, Casanova; paramour, flirt, coquette, philanderer; gold-digger, vamp, cohabitee, common-law husband *or* wife, man, woman, live-in, bidie-in, POSSLQ (= person of opposite sex sharing living quarters).

loved one, beloved, love, true love, soul mate, heart's desire, light of one's life, one's own 890 *darling*; intimate 880 *close friend*; lucky man, intended, betrothed, affianced, fiancé(e), bride-to-be 894 *spouse*; conquest, inamorata, ladylove, girlfriend, girl, bird, bit, honey, baby, sweetie; angel, princess, goddess; sweetheart, valentine, flame, old f.; idol; hero; heartthrob, maiden's prayer, dream man, Alpha man, dream girl 859 *desired object*; favourite, mistress, concubine 952 *kept woman*; femme fatale.

Adj. *loving*, brotherly, sisterly; loyal, patriotic 931 *disinterested*; wooing; courting, cuddling, making love; affectionate, demonstrative; tender, motherly, wifely, conjugal; loverlike, gallant, romantic, sentimental, lovesick; mooning, moping, lovelorn, languishing 834 *dejected*; attached to, fond of, fond, mad about, uxorious, doting; possessive 911 *jealous*; admiring, adoring, devoted, enslaved (**see** *enamoured*); flirtatious, coquettish 604 *capricious*; amorous, ardent, passionate 818 *fervent*; yearning; lustful, libidinous 951 *lecherous*.

enamoured, in love, inclined to, sweet on, soft on, keen on, set on, stuck on, gone on, sold on; struck with, taken w., smitten, bitten, caught, hooked; charmed, enchanted, fascinated 983 *bewitched*; mad on, infatuated, besotted, crazy about, wild a., head over heels in love 503 *crazy*.

erotic, aphrodisiac, erogenous; sexy, page 3, pornographic 951 *impure*.

Vb. *love*, like, care, rather care for, quite like, take pleasure in, be partial to, take an interest in; sympathize with, feel w., be fond of, have a soft spot for; be susceptible, have a heart, have a warm h.; bear love towards, hold in affection, hold dear, care for, cherish, cling to, embrace; appreciate, value, prize, treasure, think the world of, regard, admire, revere 920 *respect*; adore, worship, idolize, only have eyes for; live for, live only f.; burn with love, be on fire with passion (**see** *be in love*); make love, bestow one's favours 45 *unite with*; make much of, spoil, indulge, pet, fondle, drool over, slobber o. 889 *caress*.

be in love, burn with love, dote 503 *be insane*; take a fancy to, take a shine to, cotton on to, take to, warm to, be taken with, be sweet on, dig, have a crush on, have a pash for; carry a torch for 859 *desire*; form an attachment, fall for, fall in love, get infatuated, get hooked on, have it bad; go crazy over, be nuts on 503 *go mad*; set one's heart on, lose one's heart, bestow one's affections; declare one's love, offer one's heart to, woo, sue, sigh, press one's suit, make one's addresses 889 *court*; set one's cap at, chase 619 *pursue*; enjoy one's favours; honeymoon 894 *wed*.

888 Hatred

N. *hatred*, hate, no love lost; love-hate; disillusion; aversion, antipathy, allergy, nausea 861 *dislike*; intense dislike, repugnance, detestation, loathing, abhorrence, abomination; disfavour, displeasure; disaffection, estrangement, alienation 709 *dissension*; hostility, antagonism 881 *enmity*; animosity, ill feeling, bad blood, bitterness, acrimony, rancour 891 *resentment*; malice, ill will, evil eye, spite, grudge, ancient g. 898 *malevolence*; jealousy 912 *envy*; wrath 891 *anger*; execration 899 *malediction*; scowl, black looks, snap, snarl, baring one's fangs 893 *sullenness*; phobia, xenophobia, Anglophobia, anti-Semitism, racialism, racism, colour prejudice 481 *prejudice*; misogyny 902 *misanthropy*; odium, disfavour, unpopularity 924 *disapprobation*; discredit, bad odour, bad books, black books 867 *disrepute*; odiousness, hatefulness, loathsomeness, beastliness, obnoxiousness; despicability, despisedness 922 *contemptibility*.

hateful object, anathema; unwelcome necessity, bitter pill; abomination; object of one's hate 881 *enemy*; not one's type, pet aversion, bête-noire, bugbear, Dr Fell, nobody's darling;

pest, menace, public nuisance, good riddance 659 *bane*; blackleg.

Adj. *hateful*, odious, unlovable, unloved; invidious, antagonizing, obnoxious, pestilential; beastly, nasty, horrid, from hell 645 *not nice*; abhorrent, loathsome, abominable; accursed, execrable; offensive, repulsive, repellent, nauseous, nauseating, revolting, disgusting; bitter, sharp 393 *sour*; unwelcome 860 *unwanted*.

Vb. *hate*, bear hatred, have no love for; hate one's guts; loathe, abominate, detest, abhor; turn away from, shrink f. 620 *avoid*; revolt from, recoil at 280 *recoil*; can't bear, can't stand, can't stomach 861 *dislike*; reject; spurn 922 *despise*; denounce 899 *curse*; bear malice, have a down on 898 *be malevolent*; bear a grudge, nurse resentment, have it in for 910 *be revengeful*, 891 *resent*; conceive a hatred for, fall out of love, become disenchanted with, turn to hate.

889 Endearment

N. *endearment*, blandishments, compliments, bouquets 925 *flattery*; loving words, pretty speeches, pet name; sweet nothings, lovers' vows; billing and cooing, holding hands, slap and tickle, footsie; fondling, cuddling, canoodling, lovemaking, petting, necking, smooching, snogging, kissing; caress, embrace, clasp, hug, bear h., cuddle, squeeze; salute, kiss, butterfly k., French k., smacker; nibble, bite, love b.; stroke, tickle, pat.

wooing, courting, spooning, flirting; love-play, lovemaking; flirtation, philandering, coquetry; courtship, suit, love s., addresses, advances 887 *lovemaking*; serenade, love song, love lyric, amorous ditty; love letter, billet-doux; love poem, sonnet; proposal, engagement, betrothal 894 *marriage*.

love token, true lover's knot, favour, ribbon, glove; ring, engagement r., wedding r., eternity r.; valentine, love letter, billet-doux; language of flowers, posy, red roses; arrow, heart; tattoo.

Vb. *pet*, pamper, spoil, indulge, over-indulge, spoonfeed, featherbed, mother, smother, kill with kindness; cosset, coddle; make much of, be all over one; nurse, rock, cradle, baby; sing to, croon over; coax, wheedle 925 *flatter*.

caress, fondle, dandle, take in one's lap; play with, stroke, smooth, pat, paw, pinch one's cheek, pat one on the head, chuck under the chin; kiss, brush one's cheek; embrace, enfold, fold in one's arms, press to one's bosom, hang on one's neck, fly into the arms of; open one's arms, clasp, hug, hold one tight, cling 778 *retain*; squeeze, cuddle; snuggle, nestle, nuzzle, nibble, give love bites; play, romp, wanton, toy,

trifle, dally, spark; make love, carry on, canoodle, spoon, bill and coo, hold hands, pet, neck, snog, smooch, play footsie.

court, make advances, give the glad eye; make eyes, make sheep's e., ogle, leer, eye 438 *gaze*; get off with, try to get off with, get fresh, make a pass, make passes, chat up, come on to, hit on, pat one's bottom, goose; philander, flirt, coquette; be sweet on 887 *be in love*; set one's cap at, run after, do all the running, chase 619 *pursue*; squire, escort 89 *accompany*; hang round, wait on 284 *follow*; date, make a date, take out; walk out with, go steady, go out with, go with; sue, woo, go a-wooing, go courting, pay court to, pay one's addresses to, pay suit to, press one's suit; lay siege to one's affections, whisper sweet nothings; serenade; sigh, pine, languish 887 *love*; offer one's heart, offer one's hand; ask for the hand of, propose, propose marriage, pop the question, plight one's troth, become engaged, announce one's engagement, publish the banns, make a match 894 *wed*.

890 Darling. Favourite

N. *darling*, dear, my dear; dear friend; dearest, dear one, only one; one's own, one's all; true-love, love, beloved 887 *loved one*; heart, dear h.; sweetheart, fancy, valentine; sweeting, sweetie, sugar, honeybaby, honeybunch; flower, precious, jewel, treasure; chéri(e), chou, mavourneen; angel, angel child, cherub; poppet, popsy, moppet, mopsy; pet, lamb, precious l., chick, chicken, duck, ducks, ducky, hen, dearie, lovey.

favourite, spoiled darling, spoiled child, mother's darling, teacher's pet; jewel, jewel in the crown, apple of one's eye, blue-eyed boy; persona grata, someone after one's own heart, one of the best, Mr *or* Miss Right; flavour of the month, the tops, salt of the earth; first choice, front runner, top seed, only possible choice 644 *exceller*; someone to be proud of, pride and joy; favourite son, man *or* woman of the hour 866 *person of repute*; idol, pop i., hero, heroine, golden girl *or* boy, icon; screen goddess, media personality, star, film s.; universal favourite, toast of the town; world's sweetheart, pinup girl 841 *a beauty*; centre of attraction, cynosure 291 *attraction*; catch, lion 859 *desired object*.

891 Resentment. Anger

n. *resentment*, dissatisfaction 829 *discontent*; huffiness, ill humour, the hump, sulks 893 *sullenness*; sternness 735 *severity*; rankling, rancour, soreness, painful feelings; growing impatience; indignation (**see** *anger*); umbrage, offence, taking o., huff, tiff, pique; bile, spleen, gall; acerbity, acrimony, bitterness, bitter resentment, smouldering r., hard feelings, daggers drawn; virulence, hate 888 *hatred*; animosity, grudge, ancient g., bone to pick 881 *enmity*; vindictiveness, revengefulness, spite 910 *revenge*; malice 898 *malevolence*; impatience, fierceness, hot blood 892 *irascibility*; cause of offence, red rag to a bull, sore point; pinprick, irritation 827 *annoyance*; provocation, aggravation, insult, affront, last straw 921 *indignity*; wrong, injury 914 *injustice*.

anger, wrathfulness, irritation, exasperation, vexation, indignation; dudgeon, high d., wrath, ire; rage, road r., air r., trolley r., fury, raging f., passion, towering p. 822 *excitable state*; crossness, temper, tantrum, tizzy, paddy, fume, fret, pet, fit of temper, burst of anger, outburst, explosion, storm, stew, ferment, taking, paroxysm, tears of rage 318 *agitation*; rampage, fire and fury, gnashing the teeth, stamping the foot; shout, roar 400 *loudness*; fierceness, angry look, glare, frown, scowl, black look; growl, snarl, bark, bite, snap, snappishness, asperity 892 *irascibility*; warmth, heat, words, high words, angry w. 709 *quarrel*; box on the ear, rap on the knuckles, slap in the face 921 *indignity*; blows, fisticuffs 716 *fight*.

Adj. *resentful*, piqued, stung, galled, huffed, miffed; hurt, sore, smarting 829 *discontented*; surprised, pained, hurt, offended; warm, indignant; unresigned, reproachful 924 *disapproving*; bitter, embittered, acrimonious, full of hate, rancorous, virulent; splenetic, spiteful 898 *malevolent*; full of revenge, vindictive; jealous, green with envy 912 *envious*; grudging 598 *unwilling*.

angry, displeased, not amused, stern, frowning 834 *serious*; impatient, cross, crabbit, waxy, ratty, wild, mad, livid; wroth, wrathy, wrathful, ireful, irate; peeved, nettled, rattled, annoyed, irritated, vexed, provoked, stung; worked up, wrought up, het up, hot, hot under the collar; angry with, mad at; indignant, angered, incensed, infuriated, beside oneself with rage, leaping up and down in anger; shirty, in a temper, in a paddy, in a wax, in a huff, in a rage, in a boiling r., in a fury, in a taking, in a passion; warm, fuming, boiling, burning; speechless, stuttering, gnashing, spitting with fury, crying with rage, stamping one's foot in rage; raging, foaming, savage, violent 176 *furious*; apoplectic, rabid, foaming at the mouth, mad as a hornet, hopping m., dancing, rampaging, rampageous 503 *frenzied*; seeing red, berserk; roaring, ramping, rearing; snarling, snapping, glaring, glowering 893 *sullen*; red with anger, flushed with rage, purple with r., red-eyed, bloodshot 431

red; blue in the face; pale with anger; dangerous, fierce 892 *irascible*.

Vb. *resent*, be piqued, – offended etc. adj.; find intolerable, not bear, be unable to stomach 825 *suffer*; mind, have a chip on one's shoulder, feel resentment, smart under 829 *be discontented*; take amiss, take ill, take the wrong way, not see the joke; feel insulted, take offence, take on the nose, take umbrage, take exception to 709 *quarrel*; jib, take in ill part, take in bad p., get sore, cut up rough; burn, smoulder, sizzle, simmer, boil with indignation; express resentment, vent one's spleen, indulge one's spite 898 *be malevolent*; take to heart, let it rankle, remember an injury, cherish a grudge, nurse resentment, bear malice 910 *be revengeful*; go green with envy 912 *envy*.

get angry, get cross, get wild, get mad; get peeved, get sore, get in a pet, go spare; kindle, grow warm, grow heated, colour, redden, go purple, flush with anger; take fire, flare up, start up, rear up, ramp; bridle, bristle, raise one's hackles, arch one's back; lose patience, lose one's temper, lose control of one's t., forget oneself; throw a tantrum, stamp, shout, throw things; get one's dander up, get one's monkey up, fall into a passion, fly into a temper, fly off the handle; let fly, burst out, let off steam, boil over, blow up, flip one's lid, blow one's top, explode; see red, go berserk, go mad, foam at the mouth 822 *be excitable*.

be angry, – impatient etc. adj.; show impatience, interrupt, chafe, fret, fume, fuss, flounce, dance, ramp, stamp, champ, champ the bit, paw the ground; carry on, create, perform, make a scene, make an exhibition of oneself, make a row, go on the warpath 61 *rampage*; turn nasty, cut up rough, raise Cain; rage, rant, roar, bellow, bluster, storm, thunder, fulminate 400 *be loud*; look like thunder, look black, look daggers, glare, glower, frown, scowl, growl, snarl; spit, snap, lash out; gnash one's teeth, grind one's t., weep with rage, boil with r., quiver with r., shake with passion, swell with fury, burst with indignation, stamp with rage, dance with fury, lash one's tail 821 *be excited*; breathe fire and fury, out-Lear Lear; let fly, express one's feelings, vent one's spleen.

huff, miff, pique, sting, nettle, rankle, smart; ruffle the dignity, ruffle one's feathers, wound, wound the feelings 827 *hurt*; antagonize, put one's back up, rub up the wrong way, get across, give umbrage, offend, cause offence, cause lasting o., put one's nose out of joint, embitter; stick in the throat, raise one's gorge 861 *cause dislike*; affront, insult, outrage 921 *not respect*.

enrage, upset, discompose, ruffle, disturb

one's equanimity, ruffle one's temper, irritate, wind up, rile, push one's buttons, peeve, miff; annoy, vex, pester, bug, bother 827 *trouble*; get on one's nerves, get under one's skin, get up one's nose, get one's goat, give one the pip; do it to annoy, tease, bait, pinprick, needle 827 *torment*; bite, fret, nag, gnaw; put in an ill humour, try one's patience, exasperate; push too far, make one lose one's temper, put into a temper, work into a passion; anger, incense, infuriate, madden, drive mad; goad, sting, taunt, trail one's coat, invite a quarrel, throw down the gauntlet; drive into a fury, lash into f., whip up one's anger, rouse one's ire, kindle one's wrath, excite indignation, stir the blood, stir one's bile, make one's gorge rise, raise one's hackles, get one's dander up; make one's blood boil, make one see red; cause resentment, embitter, poison; exasperate, add fuel to the fire *or* flame, fan the flame 832 *aggravate*; embroil, set at loggerheads, set by the ears 709 *make quarrels*.

892 Irascibility

N. *irascibility*, irritability, impatience 822 *excitability*; grumpiness, gruffness 883 *unsociability*; sharpness, tartness, asperity, gall 393 *sourness*; sensitivity 819 *moral sensibility*; huffness, touchiness, prickliness, readiness to take offence, pugnacity, bellicosity 709 *quarrelsomeness*; temperament, testiness, pepperiness, peevishness, petulance; captiousness, uncertain temper, doubtful t., sharp t., short t., quick t.; hot temper, fierce t., fiery t.; limited patience, snappishness, fierceness, dangerousness, hot blood, fieriness, inflammable nature; bad temper, dangerous t., foul t., nasty t., evil t.

Adj. *irascible*, impatient, choleric, irritable, peppery, testy, crusty, peevish, crotchety, cranky, cross-grained; short-tempered, hot-t., sharp-t.; prickly, touchy, tetchy, huffy, thin-skinned 819 *sensitive*; inflammable, like tinder; hot-blooded, fierce, fiery, passionate 822 *excitable*; quick, warm, hasty, overhasty, trigger-happy 857 *rash*; quick-tempered, easily roused 709 *quarrelling*; scolding, shrewish, vixenish, sharp-tongued 899 *cursing*; petulant, cantankerous, crabbed, crabbit, snarling, querulous; captious, bitter, vinegary 393 *sour*; splenetic, liverish; snappy, waspish; tart, sharp, short; uptight, edgy; fractious, fretful, moody, temperamental, changeable; gruff, grumpy, ratty, like a bear with a sore head 829 *discontented*; ill-humoured, cross, stroppy 893 *sullen*.

893 Sullenness

N. *sullenness*, sternness, grimness 834 *seriousness*; sulkiness, ill humour, pettishness; morosity, surliness, churlishness, crabbedness,

crustiness, unsociableness 883 *unsociability*; vinegar 393 *sourness*; grumpiness, grouchiness, pout, grimace 829 *discontent*; gruffness 885 *discourtesy*; crossness, peevishness, ill temper, bad t., savage t., shocking t. 892 *irascibility*; spleen, bile, liver; sulks, fit of the s., the hump, the pouts, mulligrubs, dumps, grouch, bouderie, moodiness, temperament; cafard, the blues, blue devils 834 *melancholy*; black look, hangdog l.; glare, glower, lour, frown, scowl; snort, growl, snarl, snap, bite.

Adj. *sullen*, forbidding, ugly; gloomy, saturnine, overcast, cloudy, sunless 418 *dark*; glowering, scowling; stern, frowning, unsmiling, grim 834 *serious*; sulky, sulking, cross, cross as two sticks, out of temper, out of humour, out of sorts, misanthropic 883 *unsociable*; surly, morose, dyspeptic, crabbed, crabbit, crusty, cross-grained, difficult; snarling, snapping, snappish, shrewish, vixenish, cantankerous, quarrelsome, stroppy 709 *quarrelling*; refractory, jibbing 738 *disobedient*; grouchy, grumbling, grousing, belly-aching, beefing, grumpy 829 *discontented*; acid, tart, vinegary 393 *sour*; gruff, rough, abrupt, brusque 885 *discourteous*; temperamental, moody, up and down 152 *changeful*; jaundiced, dyspeptic; blue, down, down in the dumps, depressed, melancholy 834 *melancholic*; petulant, pettish, peevish, shirty, ill-tempered, bad-t. 892 *irascible*; smouldering, sultry.

894 Marriage

N. *marriage*, matrimony, holy m., sacrament of m., one flesh; wedlock, wedded state, married s., state of matrimony, wedded bliss; match, union, alliance, partnership; conjugality, conjugal knot, nuptial bond, marriage tie, marriage bed, bed and board, cohabitation, living as man and wife, living together by habit and repute, living together, life together; banns, marriage certificate, marriage lines.

type of marriage, matrimonial arrangement, monogamy, serial m., monandry, bigamy, polygamy, Mormonism, polygyny, polyandry; digamy, deuterogamy, second marriage, remarriage, levirate; endogamy, exogamy; arranged match, marriage of convenience, mariage de convenance, mariage blanc; love-match; mixed marriage, intermarriage, miscegenation 43 *mixture*; mismarriage, mésalliance, misalliance, morganatic marriage, left-handed m.; companionate marriage, temporary m., trial m., open m., common-law m., marriage by habit and repute; free union, free love, concubinage; compulsory marriage, forcible wedlock, shotgun wedding; abduction, Sabine rape.

wedding, getting married, match, match-making, betrothal, engagement; nuptial vows, marriage v.; ring, wedding r.; bridal, nuptials; leading to the altar, tying the knot, getting spliced, getting hitched; marriage rites, marriage ceremony; wedding service, nuptial mass, nuptial benediction 988 *Christian rite*; church wedding, white w., civil marriage, registry-office m.; Gretna Green marriage, run-away match, elopement; solemn wedding, quiet w.; wedding day, wedding bells; marriage feast, wedding breakfast, reception; honeymoon; silver wedding, golden w., wedding anniversary 876 *special day*.

bridal party, groomsman, best man, maid *or* matron of honour, bridesmaid, best maid, page, train-bearer; attendant, usher.

spouse, one's promised, one's betrothed 887 *loved one*; man, wife; spouses, man and wife, Mr and Mrs, Darby and Joan; married couple, young marrieds, bridal pair, newlyweds, honeymooners; bride, blushing b.; bridegroom; consort, partner, mate, helpmate, helpmeet, better half, soul-mate; married man, husband, hubbie, man, old man, lord and master; much-married man, henpecked husband; injured husband; married woman, wife, wedded wife, lawful w., lady, matron, feme covert, partner of one's bed and board; wife of one's bosom, woman, old w., missus, wifey, better half, old dutch, rib, trouble and strife, squaw; common-law husband *or* wife, 887 *lover*.

Vb. *marry*, marry off, find a husband *or* wife for, match, mate; matchmake, make a match, arrange a m., arrange a marriage; betroth, affiance, publish the banns, announce the engagement; give in marriage, give away; join in marriage, declare man and wife; join, couple, splice, hitch, tie the knot.

wed, marry; take a wife, find a husband; ask for the hand of 889 *court*; give up one's freedom, renounce bachelorhood, take the plunge, get married, get hitched, get spliced, mate with, marry oneself to, unite oneself with, give oneself in marriage, bestow one's hand, accept a proposal, plight one's troth, become engaged, put up the banns; lead to the altar, walk down the aisle, say 'I do', take for better or worse, be made one 45 *unite with*; pair off, mate, couple; honeymoon, cohabit, live together, set up house together, share bed and board, live as man and wife; marry well, make a good match, make a marriage of convenience; mismarry, make a bad match, repent at leisure; make a love match 887 *be in love*; marry in haste, run away, elope; contract marriage, make an honest woman of, go through a form of marriage;

marry again, remarry; commit bigamy; intermarry, miscegenate.

895 Celibacy

N. *celibacy*, singleness, single state, unmarried s., single blessedness 744 *independence*; bachelorhood, bachelordom; misogamy, misogyny 883 *unsociability*; spinsterhood, spinsterdom, the shelf; monk-hood, the veil 985 *monasticism*; maidenhood, virginity 950 *purity*.

celibate, unmarried man, single m., bachelor; confirmed bachelor, born b., old b., gay b., not the marrying kind; misogamist, misogynist 902 *misanthrope*; monk; hermit 883 *solitary*.

spinster, unmarried woman, bachelor girl; maid, maiden, virgo intacta; maiden aunt, old maid; Vestal Virgin 986 *nun*.

896 Divorce. Widowhood

N. *divorce*, dissolution of marriage, putting away, repudiation; divorce decree, decree nisi, decree absolute; separation, legal s., judicial s.; annulment; nonconsummation; nullity, impediment, prohibited degree, consanguinity, affinity; desertion, living apart; alimony, aliment, palimony; marriage on the rocks, breakup, split-up, broken marriage, broken engagement, forbidding the banns; divorce court, divorce case; divorced person, divorcee, divorcé(e); corespondent; single parent.

Vb. *divorce*, separate, split up, break up, go one's separate ways, live separately, live apart, desert 621 *relinquish*; untie the knot 46 *disunite*; put away, sue for divorce, file a divorce suit; bring a charge of adultery; get a divorce, revert to bachelorhood, revert to the single state, regain one's freedom; put asunder, dissolve marriage, annul a m., grant a decree of nullity, grant a divorce, pronounce a decree absolute.

897 Benevolence

N. *benevolence*, good will, helpfulness 880 *friendliness*; ahimsa, harmlessness 935 *innocence*; benignity, kindly disposition, heart of gold; amiability, bonhomie 882 *sociability*; milk of human kindness, goodness of nature, warmth of heart, warm-heartedness, kind-heartedness, kindliness, kindness, loving-k., goodness and mercy, charity, Christian c. 887 *love*; godly love, brotherly l., brotherliness, fraternal feeling 880 *friendship*; tenderness, consideration 736 *leniency*; understanding, responsiveness, caring, concern, fellow feeling, empathy, sympathy, overflowing s. 818 *feeling*; condolence 905 *pity*; decent feeling, humanity, humaneness, humanitarianism 901 *philanthropy*; utilitarianism 901 *sociology*; charitableness, hospitality, unselfishness, generosity, magnanimity 813 *liberality*; gentleness, softness, mildness, tolerance, toleration 734 *laxity*; placability, mercy 909 *forgiveness*; God's love, grace of God; blessing, benediction.

Adj. *benevolent*, well meant, well-intentioned, with the best intentions, for the best 880 *friendly*; out of kindness, to oblige; out of charity, eleemosynary; kind of one, good of one, so good of; sympathetic, wishing well, well-wishing, favouring, praying for; kindly disposed, benign, benignant, kindly, kind-hearted, overflowing with kindness, full of the milk of human k., warm-hearted, large-h., golden-h.; kind, good, human, decent, Christian; affectionate 887 *loving*; fatherly, paternal; motherly, maternal; brotherly, fraternal; sisterly, cousinly; good-humoured, good-natured, easy, sweet, gentle 884 *amiable*; placable, merciful; tolerant, indulgent 734 *lax*; humane, considerate 736 *lenient*; soft-hearted, tender; pitiful, sympathizing, condolent 905 *pitying*; genial, hospitable 882 *sociable*; bounteous, bountiful 813 *liberal*; generous, magnanimous, unselfish, selfless, unenvious, unjealous, altruistic 931 *disinterested*; beneficent, charitable, humanitarian, doing good 901 *philanthropic*; obliging, accommodating, helpful 703 *aiding*; tactful, complaisant, gracious, gallant, chivalrous, chivalric 884 *courteous*.

do good, philanthropize, do good works, be a caring person, have a social conscience, serve the community, show public spirit, be a good Samaritan, do a good turn, do one a favour, render a service; care; get involved 678 *be active*; reform; relieve the poor, visit, nurse 703 *minister to*; mother 889 *pet*.

898 Malevolence

N. *malevolence*, ill will 881 *enmity*; truculence, cussedness, bitchiness, beastliness, evil intent, bad intention, worst intentions, cloven hoof; spite, gall, spitefulness, viciousness, despite, malignity, malignancy, malice, malice afore-thought; bad blood, hate 888 *hatred*; venom, virulence, deadliness, balefulness 659 *bane*; bitterness, acrimony, acerbity 393 *sourness*; mordacity 388 *pungency*; rancour, spleen 891 *resentment*; gloating, unholy joy 912 *envy*; evil eye 983 *spell*.

inhumanity, misanthropy, inconsiderateness, lack of concern; uncharitableness; intolerance, persecution 735 *severity*; harshness, mercilessness, implacability, hardness of heart, obduracy, heart of stone 906 *pitilessness*; cold feelings, unkindness; callousness 326 *hardness*; cruelty, barbarity, bloodthirstiness; barbarism,

savagery, ferocity, barbarousness, savageness, ferociousness; outrageousness; sadism, fiendishness, devilishness 934 *wickedness*; truculence, brutality, ruffianism; destructiveness, vandalism 165 *destruction*.

cruel act, brutality; ill-treatment, ill usage 675 *misuse*; abuse, child a., sexual a., disservice, ill turn; victimization, harassment, sexual h., bullying 735 *severity*; foul play, bloodshed 176 *violence*; act of inhumanity, atrocity, outrage; cruelty, torture, barbarities; cannibalism, murder 362 *homicide*; mass murder, genocide 362 *slaughter*.

Adj. *malevolent*, ill-wishing, ill-willed, evil-intentioned, ill-disposed, meaning harm 661 *dangerous*; ill-natured, churlish 893 *sullen*; nasty, bloody-minded, bitchy, cussed 602 *wilful*; malicious, catty, spiteful; mischievous, mischief-making; baleful, squint-eyed, malign, malignant 645 *harmful*; vicious, viperous, venomous 362 *deadly*; black-hearted, full of spite; jealous 912 *envious*; disloyal, treacherous 930 *perfidious*; bitter, rancorous 891 *resentful*; implacable, unforgiving, merciless 906 *pitiless*; vindictive, gloating; hostile, fell 881 *hostile*; intolerant, persecuting 735 *oppressive*.

unkind, ill-natured 893 *sullen*; unkindly; unchristian; cold, unfriendly, hostile, misanthropic 881 *hostile*; inhospitable 883 *unsociable*; unhelpful, disobliging; uncharitable; mean, nasty; unsympathetic, unmoved 820 *impassive*; stern 735 *severe*; inhuman.

cruel, grim, fell; hard-hearted, flint-h., stony-h.; callous, cold-blooded; heartless, ruthless, merciless 906 *pitiless*; tyrannical 735 *oppressive*; sadistic; blood-thirsty, cannibalistic 362 *murderous*; bloody 176 *violent*; atrocious, outrageous; feral, tigerish, wolfish; unnatural, subhuman, dehumanized, brutalized, brutish; brutal, rough, fierce, ferocious; savage, barbarous, wild, untamed; inhuman, ghoulish, fiendish, devilish, diabolical, demoniacal, satanic, hellish, infernal.

Vb. *be malevolent*, bear malice, cherish a grudge, nurse resentment, have it in for 888 *hate*; show ill will, spite, do one a bad turn; do one's worst, wreak one's spite, break a butterfly on a wheel, have no mercy 906 *be pitiless*; take one's revenge, exact r., victimize; take it out of one, bully, maltreat, abuse 645 *ill-treat*; molest, hurt, injure, annoy 645 *harm*; malign, run down, throw stones at 926 *detract*; tease, harass, harry, hound, persecute, tyrannize, torture 735 *oppress*; thirst for blood 362 *slaughter*; rankle, fester, poison, be a thorn in the flesh; create havoc, blight; blast, cast the evil eye 983 *bewitch*.

899 Maledicton

N. *malediction*, curse, imprecation, anathema; evil eye; ill wishes, execration, denunciation; fulmination, thunder; ban, proscription, excommunication; exorcism, bell, book and candle.

scurrility, ribaldry, vulgarity; profanity, swearing, profane s., cursing and swearing, blasting, effing and blinding, effing and ceeing; bad language, foul l., filthy l., blue l., shocking l., strong l., unparliamentary l., Limehouse, Billingsgate; naughty word, four-letter w., expletive, swearword, oath, swear, damn, curse, cuss, tinker's c.; invective, vituperation, abuse, volley of a.; mutual abuse, slanging match, stormy exchange; vain abuse, empty curse, more bark than bite 900 *threat*; no compliment, aspersion, reflection, vilification, slander 926 *calumny*; cheek, sauce 878 *sauciness*; personal remarks, epithet, insult 921 *indignity*; contumely, scorn 922 *contempt*; scolding, rough edge of one's tongue, lambasting, tongue-lashing 924 *reproach*.

Adj. *cursing*, evil-speaking, swearing, damning, blasting; profane, foul-mouthed, foul-tongued, foul-spoken, effing and ceeing, unparliamentary, scurrilous, scurrile, ribald 847 *vulgar*; blue; vituperative, abusive, vitriolic, injurious; scornful.

Vb. *curse*, cast the evil eye 983 *bewitch*; accurse, wish ill 898 *be malevolent*; wish on, call down on; wish one joy of; curse with bell, book and candle, curse up hill and down dale; anathematize, imprecate, invoke curses on, execrate, hold up to execration; fulminate, thunder against, rant and rail against, inveigh 924 *reprove*; denounce 928 *accuse*; excommunicate, damn 961 *condemn*; round upon, confound, send to the devil, send to blazes; abuse, vituperate, revile, rail, chide, heap abuse, pour vitriol 924 *reproach*.

cuss, curse, swear, damn, blast; blaspheme 980 *be impious*; swear like a trooper, use expletives, use Billingsgate, curse and swear, use four-letter words, eff and blind, eff and cee, turn the air blue; slang, abuse; rail at, scold, lash out at, give the rough edge of one's tongue, slag off.

Int. curse! a curse on! a plague on! woe to! woe betide! ill betide! confound it! devil take it! blast! damn! darn! drat! hang! the deuce! the dickens!

900 Threat

N. *threat*, menace; fulmination 899 *malediction*; minacity, ominousness; challenge, dare 711 *defiance*; blackmail 737 *demand*; battle cry, war whoop, sabre-rattling, war of nerves 854 *intimi-*dation; deterrent, big stick 723 *weapon*; black cloud, gathering clouds 511 *omen*; hidden fires, secret weapon 663 *pitfall*; impending danger, sword of Damocles 661 *danger*; danger signal, fair warning, writing on the wall 664 *warning*; bluster, idle threat, hollow t. 877 *boast*; bark, growl, snarl, bared teeth 893 *sullenness*; aggressive begging.

Vb. *threaten*, menace, use threats, hold out t., utter t.; demand with menaces, blackmail 737 *demand*; hijack, hold to ransom, take hostage; frighten, deter, intimidate, bully, wave the big stick 854 *frighten*; roar, bellow 408 *vociferate*; fulminate, thunder 899 *curse*; bark, talk big, bluster, hector 877 *boast*; shake, wave, flaunt 317 *brandish*; rattle the sabre, clench the fist, draw one's sword 711 *defy*; bare the fangs, snarl, growl, mutter; bristle, spit, look daggers, grow nasty 891 *get angry*; pull a gun on, hold at gunpoint; draw a bead on, cover, have one covered, keep one c. 281 *aim*; gather, mass, lour, hang over, hover 155 *impend*; bode ill, presage, disaster, mean no good, promise trouble, spell danger 511 *predict*; serve notice, caution, forewarn 664 *warn*; breathe revenge, threaten reprisals 910 *be revengeful*.

901 Philanthropy

N. *philanthropy*, humanitarianism, humanity, humaneness, the golden rule 897 *benevolence*; humanism, cosmopolitanism, internationalism; altruism 931 *disinterestedness*; idealism, ideals 933 *virtue*; the greatest happiness of the greatest number, utilitarianism, Benthamism; common good, socialism, communism; reformism; chivalry, knighterrantry; dedication, crusading spirit, missionary s., social conscience; good works, mission; Holy War, jihad, crusade, campaign, cause, good c.

sociology, social science, social planning; social care; poor relief, social security, benefit, dole; social services, Welfare State; social inclusion; dependency culture; community service, social service, social work, good works; care in the community, community care.

patriotism, civic ideals, good citizenship, public spirit, concern for the community, love of one's country; parochialism; nationalism, chauvinism, gung-hoism, my country right or wrong.

philanthropist, humanitarian, do-gooder, benefactor, social worker; community service worker, VSO, Peace Corps 597 *volunteer*; paladin, champion, crusader, knight, knight errant; Messiah 690 *leader*; missionary; idealist, altruist, flower people 513 *visionary*; reformist 654 *reformer;* utilitarian, Benthamite; Utopian, millenarian; humanist.

patriot, lover of one's country; nationalist, chauvinist.

Adj. *philanthropic,* humanitarian, humane, human 897 *benevolent;* charitable, aid-giving 703 *aiding;* enlightened, humanistic, liberal; idealistic, altruistic 931 *disinterested;* visionary, dedicated; socialistic, communistic; utilitarian.

patriotic, public-spirited, community-minded; nationalistic, chauvinistic; loyal, true, true-blue.

902 Misanthropy

N. *misanthropy,* cynicism 883 *unsociability;* misandry, misogyny; moroseness 893 *sullenness;* inhumanity.

misanthrope, misanthropist, man-hater, woman-h., misandrist, misogynist; cynic, Diogenes; world-hater.

903 Benefactor

N. *benefactor,* benefactress 901 *philanthropist;* Lady Bountiful, Father Christmas, Santa Claus 781 *giver;* fairy godmother, guardian angel, good genius 660 *protector;* founder, foundress, supporter, angel, backer 707 *patron;* protector of the people 901 *patriot;* saviour, redeemer, rescuer 668 *deliverance;* champion 713 *defender;* Good Samaritan; good neighbour 880 *friend;* helper, present help in time of trouble 703 *aider;* saint 937 *good person.*

904 Evildoer

N. *evildoer,* malefactor, wrongdoer, sinner 934 *wickedness;* villain, blackguard, bad lot, baddy; one up to no good, mischief-maker 663 *trouble-maker;* slanderer 926 *detractor;* snake in the grass, viper in the bosom, traitor 545 *deceiver;* saboteur, despoiler, wrecker, defacer, vandal, Hun, iconoclast 168 *destroyer;* terrorist, nihilist, anarchist 738 *revolter;* incendiary, arsonist 381 *incendiarism;* disturber of the peace 738 *rioter.*

ruffian, blackguard, rogue, football hooligan, scoundrel 938 *knave;* lout, lager lout, hooligan, hoodlum, boot boy, bovver boy, larrikin 869 *low fellow;* Hell's Angel, skinhead, yob, yobbo, punk; bully, terror, terror of the neighbourhood; rough, tough, rowdy, ugly customer, hard man, plug-ugly, bruiser, thug, bravo, desperado, assassin, hired a.; cutthroat, hatchet man, hit man, gunman, contract man, killer, butcher 362 *murderer;* genocide, mass murderer; plague, scourge, scourge of the human race, Attila 659 *bane;* petty tyrant; molester, brute, savage b., beast, savage, barbarian; homicidal maniac 504 *madman.*

offender, sinner, black sheep 938 *bad person;* suspect; culprit, guilty person, law-breaker; criminal, villain, crook, malefactor, wrongdoer, felon; delinquent, juvenile d., first offender; recidivist, backslider, old offender, hardened o., lag, old l., convict, ex-c., jailbird; lifer, gallowsbird, parolee, probationer, ticket-of-leave man; mafioso, mobster, gangster, racketeer; housebreaker 789 *thief, robber;* forger 789 *defrauder;* blackmailer, bloodsucker; poisoner 362 *murderer;* outlaw, public enemy 881 *enemy;* intruder, trespasser; criminal world, underworld, Mafia 934 *wickedness.*

905 Pity

N. *pity,* ruth; remorse, compunction 830 *regret;* charity, compassion, compassionateness, humanity 897 *benevolence;* soft heart, tender h., bleeding h.; gentleness, softness 736 *leniency;* commiseration, touched feelings, melting mood, tears of sympathy 825 *sorrow;* Weltschmerz 834 *dejection;* sympathy, empathy, understanding, fellow feeling; self-pity.

condolence, commiseration, sympathy, fellow feeling 775 *participation;* consolation, comfort 831 *relief;* keen, coronach, wake 836 *lament.*

mercy, tender mercies, quarter, grace; second chance; mercifulness, clemency, lenity, placability, forbearance, long-suffering 909 *forgiveness;* light sentence 963 *penalty;* let-off, pardon 960 *acquittal.*

Adj. *pitying,* compassionate, sympathetic, understanding, commiserating; sorry for, feeling for; merciful, clement, full of mercy 736 *lenient;* tender, tender-hearted, soft, soft-hearted 819 *impressible;* disposed to mercy; humane, charitable 897 *benevolent;* forbearing 823 *patient.*

Vb. *pity,* feel p; show compassion, show pity, take pity on; sympathize, sympathize with, empathize, feel for, feel with, share the grief of 775 *participate;* sorrow, grieve, bleed for, feel sorry for, weep f., lament f., commiserate, condole, express one's condolences, send one's c.; yearn over 836 *lament;* console, comfort, offer consolation, wipe away one's tears 833 *cheer;* have pity, have compassion.

show mercy, have m., spare, spare the life of, give quarter, commute (a sentence), pardon, grant a p.; forget one's anger 909 *forgive;* be slow to anger, forbear; give one a break, give one a second chance 736 *be lenient;* relent, not be too hard upon, go easy on, let one down gently; put out of their misery.

ask mercy, plead for m., appeal for m.; pray for m., beg for m., throw oneself upon another's mercy, fall at one's feet, cry mercy, ask for quarter, plead for one's life.

906 Pitilessness

N. *pitilessness*, lack of pity, heartlessness, ruthlessness, mercilessness; inclemency, intolerance, rigour, zero tolerance 735 *severity*; callousness, hardness of heart 898 *inhumanity*; inflexibility 326 *hardness*; inexorability, relentlessness, remorselessness, unforgivingness 910 *revengefulness*; letter of the law, pound of flesh; no pity, no heart, no feelings, short shrift, no quarter.

Adj. *pitiless*, unfeeling 820 *impassive*; unsympathetic; unmoved, dry-eyed; hard-hearted, stony-h.; callous 326 *hard*; harsh, rigorous, intolerant, persecuting 735 *severe*; brutal, sadistic 898 *cruel*; merciless, ruthless, heartless; inclement, unmerciful, unrelenting, relentless, remorseless, inflexible, inexorable, implacable.

Vb. *be pitiless*. – ruthless etc. adj.; have no heart, have no compassion, have no pity; not be moved, turn a deaf ear; show no pity, show no mercy, give no quarter; harden one's heart, be deaf to appeal; stand on the letter of the law, insist on one's pound of flesh 735 *be severe*; take one's revenge 910 *avenge*.

907 Gratitude

N. *gratitude*, gratefulness, thankfulness, grateful heart, sense of obligation; appreciativeness, appreciation.

thanks, hearty t., grateful t.; vote of t., thankyou; thanksgiving, eucharist, benediction, blessing; praises, Te Deum 876 *celebration*; grace; thankyou letter, bread-and-butter l.; credit, credit title, acknowledgment, due a., grateful a., recognition, grateful r.; tribute 923 *praise*; parting present, leaving p., recognition of one's services, golden handshake, token of one's gratitude, tip 962 *reward*.

Adj. *grateful*, thankful, appreciative; thanking; crediting, giving credit; obliged, under obligation, in one's debt, owing a favour, beholden, indebted.

Vb. *be grateful*, thank one's lucky stars; feel an obligation; accept gratefully, receive with open arms, not look a gift horse in the mouth.

thank, give thanks, express t.; acknowledge, credit, give due c., give full c. 158 *attribute*; show appreciation, tip 962 *reward*; return a favour.

Int. thanks! many t.! much obliged! thank you! ta! cheers! thank goodness! thank Heaven! Heaven be praised!

908 Ingratitude

N. *ingratitude*, lack of appreciation, ungratefulness, thanklessness; grudging thanks; taking everything as one's due, thankless task; ingrate.

Adj. *ungrateful*, unthankful 885 *discourteous*; unbeholden; unmindful of favours.

Vb. *be ungrateful*, take for granted, take as one's due; omit to thank; not give a thankyou for, look a gift horse in the mouth; forget a kindness, return evil for good.

Int. thank you for nothing! no thanks to.

909 Forgiveness

N. *forgiveness*, pardon, free p., full p., reprieve 506 *amnesty*; indemnity, grace, indulgence, plenary i. 905 *mercy*; cancellation, remission, absolution 960 *acquittal*; justification, exculpation, exoneration, excuse 927 *vindication*; conciliation, reconciliation 719 *pacification*; mercifulness, placability, lenity 905 *pity*; longsuffering, forbearance 823 *patience*.

Vb. *forgive*, pardon, reprieve, forgive and forget, think no more of, not give another thought 506 *forget*; remit, absolve, shrive; cancel, blot out, wipe the slate clean 550 *obliterate*; relent, unbend, accept an apology 736 *be lenient*; be merciful, not be too hard upon, let one down gently, let one off the hook 905 *show mercy*; bear with, put up w., forbear, tolerate, make allowances 823 *be patient*; take no offence, bear no malice, take in good part, pocket, stomach, not hold it against one; forget an injury, ignore a wrong, overlook, pass over, not punish, leave unavenged, turn the other cheek; return good for evil; connive, wink at, condone, make an issue of, turn a blind eye 458 *disregard*; excuse, find excuses for 927 *justify*; intercede 720 *mediate*; exculpate, exonerate 960 *acquit*; be ready to forgive, make the first move, bury the hatchet, let bygones be bygones, make it up, extend the hand of forgiveness, shake hands, kiss and be friends, kiss and make up, be reconciled 880 *be friendly*; restore to favour, kill the fatted calf 876 *celebrate*.

910 Revenge

N. *revengefulness*, thirst for revenge; vengefulness, vindictiveness, spitefulness, spite 898 *malevolence*; ruthlessness 906 *pitilessness*; remorselessness, relentlessness, implacability, irreconcilability, unappeasability; resentment.

revenge, sweet r.; crime passionel 911 *jealousy*; vengeance, day of reckoning 963 *punishment*; reprisal, reprisals, punitive expedition 714 *retaliation*; tit for tat, a Roland for an Oliver, measure for measure, eye for an eye, tooth for a tooth; vendetta, feud, blood f. 881 *enmity*.

Vb. *avenge*, avenge oneself, revenge o., take one's revenge, exact r., take vengeance, wreak v., take the law into one's own hands; exact retribution, get one's own back, repay, pay out, pay off *or* settle old scores, square an account, give someone what was coming to them, give someone his *or* her come-uppance; get back at, give tit for tat 714 *retaliate*; enjoy one's revenge, gloat.

be revengeful, get one's knife into 898 *be malevolent*; bear malice, promise vengeance 888 *hate*; nurse one's revenge, harbour a grudge, carry on a feud, conduct a blood feud, have a rod in pickle, have a bone to pick, have a score *or* accounts to settle 881 *be hostile*; let it rankle, remember an injury, refuse to forget 891 *resent*.

911 Jealousy

N. *jealousy*, pangs of j., jealousness; jaundiced eye, green-eyed monster; distrust, mistrust 486 *doubt*; resentment; enviousness 912 *envy*; hate 888 *hatred*; inferiority complex, emulation, competitiveness, competitive spirit, competition, rivalry, jealous r. 716 *contention*; possessiveness 887 *love*; sexual jealousy, eternal triangle, crime passionel 910 *revenge*; competitor, rival, hated r., the other man, the other woman; Othello.

Adj. *jealous*, green-eyed, yellow-e., jaundiced, envying 912 *envious*; devoured with jealousy, consumed with j., eaten up with j.; possessive 887 *loving*; suspicious, mistrusting, distrustful 474 *doubting*; emulative, competitive, rival, competing.

912 Envy

N. *envy*, envious eye, enviousness, covetousness 859 *desire*; rivalry 716 *contention*; jealousy; ill will, spite, spleen; mortification, unwilling admiration, grudging praise.

Adj. *envious*, envying, envious-eyed, green with envy 911 *jealous*; greedy, unsatisfied 829 *discontented*; covetous, longing, grudging.

Vb. *envy*, view with e., cast envious looks, cast covetous i., turn green with e., resent; covet, crave, lust after, must have for oneself, long to change places with 859 *desire*.

SECTION FOUR

Morality

913 Right

N. *right*, rightfulness, rightness, fitness, what is fitting, what ought to be, what should be; obligation 917 *duty*; fittingness, seemliness, propriety, decency 848 *etiquette*; normality 83 *conformity*; rules, rules and regulations 693 *precept*; ethicalness, morality, moral code, good morals 917 *morals*; righteousness 933 *virtue*; rectitude, uprightness, honour 929 *probity*; one's right, one's due, one's prerogative, deserts, merits, claim 915 *dueness*.

justice, freedom from wrong, justifiability; righting wrong, redress; reform 654 *reformism*; even-handed justice, impartial j.; scales of justice, justice under the law, process of 1. 953 *legality*; retribution, retributive justice, poetic j. 962 *reward*; give and take, retaliation; fair-mindedness, objectivity, lack of bias, disinterestedness, detachment, impartiality, equalness 28 *equality*; equity, equitableness, reasonableness, fairness; fair deal, square d., fair treatment, fair play; no discrimination, equal opportunity; fair society; good law, Queensberry rules.

Adj. *right*, rightful, proper, right and p., fitting, suitable, appropriate 24 *fit*; good 917 *ethical*; put right, redressed, reformed; normal, standard, classical 83 *conformable*.

just, upright, righteous, right-minded, high-principled, on the side of the angels 933 *virtuous*; fair-minded, disinterested, unprejudiced, unbiased, unswerving, undeflected 625 *neutral*; detached, impersonal, dispassionate, objective, open-minded; equal, egalitarian, impartial, even-handed; fair, square, fair and s., equitable, reasonable, fair enough; in the right, justifiable, justified, unchallengeable, unchallenged, unimpeachable; above-board, legitimate, according to law 953 *legal*; sporting, sportsmanlike 929 *honourable*; deserved, well-d., earned, merited, well-m., 915 *due*; overdue, demanded, claimed, rightly c., claimable 627 *required*.

914 Wrong

N. *wrong*, wrongness, something wrong, something amiss, oddness, queerness 84 *abnormality*; something rotten, curse, bane, scandal 645 *badness*; disgrace, shame, crying s., dishonour 867 *slur*; impropriety, indecorum 847 *bad taste*; wrongheadedness, unreasonableness 481 *misjudgment*; unjustifiability, what ought not to be, what must not be 916 *undueness*; inexcusability, culpability, guiltiness 936 *guilt*; immorality, vice, sin 934 *wickedness*; dishonesty, unrighteousness 930 *improbity*; irregularity, illegitimacy, criminality, crime, lawlessness 954 *illegality*; wrongfulness, misdoing, transgression, trespass, encroachment; misdeed, offence 936 *guilty act*; a wrong, injustice, mischief, outrage, foul; sense of wrong, complaint, charge 928 *accusation*; grievance, just g. 891 *resentment*; wrong-doer, unjust judge 938 *bad person*.

injustice, no justice; miscarriage of justice, wrong verdict 481 *misjudgment*; warped judgment, packed jury 481 *bias*; one-sidedness, inequity, unfairness; discrimination, race d., sex d., racism, sexism, heterosexism, ageism, classism, ableism; partiality, leaning, favouritism, favour, nepotism; preferential treatment, positive discrimination, affirmative action; partisanship, party spirit, old school tie 481 *prejudice*; unlawfulness, no law 954 *illegality*; justice denied, right withheld, privilege curtailed 916 *undueness*; unfair advantage, 'heads I win, tails you lose'; no equality, wolf and the lamb 29 *inequality*; not cricket; imposition, robbing Peter to pay Paul.

Adj. *wrong*, not right 645 *bad*; odd, queer, suspect 84 *abnormal*; unfitting, inappropriate, unseemly, improper 847 *vulgar*; wrongheaded, unreasonable; wrong from the start, out of court, inadmissible; irregular, against the rules, foul, unauthorized, unwarranted 757 *prohibited*; wrongful, illegitimate, illicit, felonious, criminal 954 *illegal*; condemnable, culpable, in the wrong, offside 936 *guilty*; unwarrantable, inexcusable, unpardonable, unforgivable, unjustifiable (**see** *unjust*); open to objection, objectionable, reprehensible, scandalous; injurious, mischievous 645 *harmful*; unrighteous 930 *dishonest*; iniquitous, sinful, vicious, immoral 934 *wicked*.

unjust, unjustifiable; uneven, weighted 29 *unequal*; inequitable, iniquitous, unfair; hard, hard on 735 *severe*; foul, not playing the game, not keeping to the rules, below the belt, unsportsmanlike; discriminatory, favouring, one-sided, leaning to one side, partial, partisan, prejudiced 481 *biased*; selling justice 930 *venal*; wresting the law 954 *illegal*.

do wrong, wrong, hurt, injure, do an injury 645 *harm*; be hard on, have a down on 735 *be severe*; not play the game, not play cricket, hit below the belt; break the rules, commit a foul; commit a crime, break the law, pervert the course of justice, be illegal; transgress, infringe, trespass 306 *encroach*; wink at, connive at, turn a blind eye; do less than justice, withhold justice, deny j., deny one's rights; weight, load the scales, pack the jury, rig the jury; lean, lean to one side, discriminate against, show partiality, show favouritism, discriminate 481 *be biased*; favour 703 *patronize*; go too far, overcompensate, lean over backwards; commit, perpetrate.

915 Dueness

N. *dueness*, what is due, what is owing; accountability, responsibility, obligation 917 *duty*; from each according to his ability and to each according to his need; the least one can do, bare minimum; what one looks for, expectations; dues 804 *payment*; something owed, indebtedness 803 *debt*; tribute, credit 158 *attribution*; recognition, acknowledgment 907 *thanks*; something to be said for, something in favour of, case for; qualification, merits, deserts, just d. 913 *right*;

justification 927 *vindication*; entitlement, claim, title 913 *right*; birthright, patriality, patrimony 777 *dower*; interest, vested i., prescriptive right, absolute r., inalienable r.; legal right, prescription, ancient lights; human rights, women's r., animal r. 744 *freedom*; constitutional right, civil rights, bill of r., Magna Carta; privilege, exemption, immunity 919 *nonliability*; prerogative, privilege; charter, warrant, licence 756 *permit*; liberty, franchise; bond, security 767 *title deed*; patent, copyright; recovery of rights, restoration, compensation 787 *restitution*; owner, title-holder 776 *possessor*; heir 776 *beneficiary*; claimant, plaintiff, pursuer, appellant; person with a grievance 763 *petitioner*.

Adj. *due*, owing, payable; ascribable, attributable, assignable; merited, well-m., deserved, well-d., richly-d., earned, well-e., coming to one; admitted, allowed, sanctioned, warranted, licit, lawful; constitutional, entrenched, untouchable, uninfringeable, unchallengeable, unimpeachable, inviolable; privileged, sacrosanct; confirmed, vested, prescriptive, inalienable, imprescriptible; secured by law, legalized, legitimate, rightful, of right, de jure, by habit and repute 953 *legal*; claimable, heritable, inheritable, earmarked, reserved, set aside; expected, fit, fitting, befitting 913 *right*; proper, en règle 642 *advisable*.

Vb. *claim*, claim as a right, lay claim to, stake a c., take possession 786 *appropriate*; claim unduly, arrogate; demand one's rights, assert one's r., stand up for one's r., vindicate one's r., insist on one's r., stand on one's r.; draw on, come down on for, take one's toll 786 *levy*; call in (debts), reclaim 656 *retrieve*; publish one's claims, declare one's right; sue, demand redress 761 *request*; enforce a claim, exercise a right; establish a right, patent, copyright.

deserve, merit, be worthy, be found w., have a claim on; have a right to, have right on one's side; earn, receive one's due, meet with one's deserts, get one's d.; have it coming to one, get one's come-uppance, have only oneself to thank; sow the wind and reap the whirlwind.

916 Undueness

N. *undueness*, not what one expects *or* would expect 508 *lack of expectation*; not the thing, not quite the t., impropriety, unseemliness, indecorum 847 *bad taste*; inappropriateness, unfittingness 643 *inexpedience*; unworthiness, demerit 934 *vice*; illicitness, illegitimacy, bastardy 954 *illegality*; no thanks to 908 *ingratitude*; absence of right, want of title, failure of t., nonentitlement; no claim, no right, no title, false t., courtesy t.; gratuitousness, gratuity, bonus, grace marks, unearned increment; inordinacy, excessiveness, too much, overpayment 637 *redundance*; imposition, exaction 735 *severity*; unfair share, lion's s.; violation, breach, infraction, infringement, encroachment 306 *overstepping*; profanation, desecration 980 *impiety*.

arrogation, assumption, unjustified a., presumption, unwarranted p.; pretendership, usurpation, tyranny; misappropriation 786 *expropriation*; encroachment, inroad, trespass 306 *overstepping*.

loss of right, disentitlement, disfranchisement, disqualification; denaturalization, detribalization 147 *conversion*; forfeiture 772 *loss*; deportation, dismissal, deprivation, dethronement 752 *deposal*; ouster, dispossession 786 *expropriation*; seizure, forcible s., robbery 788 *stealing*; cancellation 752 *abrogation*; waiver, abdication 621 *relinquishment*.

usurper, pretender 545 *impostor*; desecrator; violator, infringer, encroacher, trespasser, squatter, cuckoo in the nest.

Adj. *unwarranted*, unwarrantable; unauthorized, unsanctioned, unlicensed, unchartered, unconstitutional; unrightful, unlegalized, illicit, illegitimate, ultra vires 954 *illegal*; arrogated, usurped, stolen, borrowed; excessive, presumptuous, assuming 878 *insolent*; unjustified, unjustifiable 914 *wrong*; undeserved, unmerited, unearned; overpaid, underpaid; invalid, weak; forfeited, forfeit; false, bastard 542 *spurious*; fictitious, would-be, self-styled 850 *affected*.

Vb. *disentitle*, uncrown, dethrone 752 *depose*; disqualify, unfrock, disfranchise, alienize, denaturalize, detribalize, denationalize; invalidate 752 *abrogate*; disallow 757 *prohibit*; dispossess, expropriate 786 *deprive*; forfeit, declare f.; defeat a claim, mock the claims of; make illegitimate, illegalize, criminalize 954 *make illegal*; bastardize, debase 655 *impair*.

917 Duty

N. *duty*, what ought to be done, what is up to one, the right thing, the proper t., the decent t.; one's duty, bounden d., inescapable d.; obligation, liability, onus, responsibility, accountability 915 *dueness*; fealty, allegiance, loyalty 739 *obedience*; sense of duty, dutifulness, duteousness 597 *willingness*; discharge of duty, performance, acquittal, discharge 768 *observance*; call of duty, claims of conscience, case of c.; bond, tie, engagement, commitment, word, pledge 764 *promise*; task, office, charge 751 *commission*; walk of life, station, profession 622 *vocation*.

conscience, tender c., inner voice, 'still, small voice'.

code of duty, code of honour, unwritten code, professional c.; Ten Commandments, Hippocratic oath 693 *precept*.

morals, morality 933 *virtue*; honour 929 *probity*; moral principles, high p., ideals, high i., standards, high s., professional s.; moral high ground, moral majority; ethics, religious e., humanist e., professional e.; ethical investment, ethical shopping, ethology, deontology, casuistry, ethical philosophy, moral p., moral science, idealism, humanism, utilitarianism, behaviourism 449 *philosophy*.

Adj. *obliged*, duty-bound, on duty, bound by duty, called by d.; under duty, in duty bound, in the line of duty; obligated, beholden, under obligation; tied, bound, sworn, pledged, committed, engaged; unexempted, liable, chargeable, answerable, responsible, accountable; in honour bound, bound in conscience, answerable to God; plagued by conscience, conscience-stricken 939 *repentant*; conscientious, punctilious 768 *observant*; duteous, dutiful 739 *obedient*; vowed, under a vow.

obligatory, incumbent, imposed, behoving, up to one; binding, de rigueur, compulsory, mandatory, peremptory, operative 740 *compelling*; inescapable, unavoidable; strict, unconditional, categorical.

ethical, moral, principled 933 *virtuous*; honest, decent 929 *honourable*; moralistic, ethological, casuistical; moralizing; humanistic, idealistic; utilitarian.

Vb. *be one's duty*, be incumbent, behove, become, befit 915 *be due*; devolve on, belong to, be up to, pertain to, fall to, arise from one's functions, be part of the job; lie with, lie at one's door, rest with, rest on one's shoulders.

incur a duty, make it one's d., take on oneself, accept responsibility, shoulder one's r.; make oneself liable, commit oneself, pledge o., engage for 764 *promise*; assume one's functions, enter upon one's office, receive a posting; have the office, have the function, have the charge, have the duty; owe it to oneself, feel it up to one, feel it incumbent upon one; feel duty's call, accept the c., answer the c., submit to one's vocation.

do one's duty, fulfil one's d. 739 *obey*; discharge, acquit, perform, do the needful 676 *do*; do one's bit, play one's part; perform one's office, discharge one's functions 768 *observe*; be on duty, stay at one's post, go down with one's ship; come up to what is expected of one, come up to expectation, not be found wanting; keep faith with one's conscience, meet one's obligations, discharge an obligation, make good one's promise, redeem a pledge, be as good as one's word; honour, meet, pay up 804 *pay*.

impose a duty, require, oblige, look to, call

upon; devolve, call to office, swear one in, offer a post, post 751 *commission*; assign a duty, saddle with, detail, order, enjoin, decree 737 *command*; tax, overtax, task, overtask 684 *fatigue*; exact 735 *be severe*; demand obedience, expect it of one, expect too much of one 507 *expect*; bind, condition 766 *give terms*; bind over, take security 764 *take a pledge*.

Adv. *on duty*, at one's post; under an obligation; in the line of duty, as in duty bound; with a clear conscience; for conscience' sake.

918 Undutifulness

N. *undutifulness*, default, want of duty, dereliction of d.; neglect, wilful n.; culpable negligence 458 *negligence*; disrespect; malingering, evasion of duty, cop-out 620 *avoidance*; nonpractice, nonperformance 769 *non-observance*; idleness, laziness 679 *sluggishness*; forgetfulness 506 *oblivion*; noncooperation, want of alacrity 598 *unwillingness*; truancy, absenteeism 190 *absence*; absconding 667 *escape*; infraction, violation, breach of orders, indiscipline, mutiny, rebellion 738 *disobedience*; incompetence, mismanagement 695 *bungling*; obstruction, sabotage 702 *hindrance*; desertion, defection 603 *change of mind*; disloyalty, treachery, treason 930 *perfidy*; secession, breakaway 978 *schism*; irresponsibility, escapism; truant, absentee, malingerer, defaulter 620 *avoider*; slacker 679 *idler*; deserter, absconder 667 *escaper*; betrayer, traitor 603 *tergiversator*; saboteur; mutineer, rebel 738 *revolter*; seceder, splinter group 978 *schismatic*.

Adj. *undutiful*, wanting in duty, uncooperative 598 *unwilling*; unfilial, un-daughterly 921 *disrespectful*; mutinous, rebellious, seceding, breakaway 738 *disobedient*; disloyal, treacherous, treasonous 930 *perfidious*; irresponsible, unreliable; truant, absentee 190 *absent*; absconding.

Vb. *fail in duty*, neglect one's d., be wilfully negligent 458 *neglect*; ignore one's obligations 458 *disregard*; oversleep, sleep in 679 *sleep*; default, let one down, leave one in the lurch 509 *disappoint*; mismanage, bungle 495 *blunder*; not remember 506 *forget*; shirk, evade, wriggle out of, malinger, 620 *avoid*; wash one's hands of, pass the buck 919 *be exempt*; play truant, overstay leave 190 *be absent*; abscond 667 *escape*; quit, scuttle, scarper 296 *decamp*; abandon, abandon one's post, desert, desert the colours 621 *relinquish*; break orders, disobey o., violate o., exceed one's instructions 738 *disobey*; mutiny, rebel 738 *revolt*; be disloyal, prove treacherous, betray, commit treason 603 *tergiversate*; sabotage 702 *obstruct*; noncooperate, withdraw, walk out, break away, form a splinter group, secede.

919 Nonliability

N. *nonliability*, nonresponsibility, exemption, dispensation; conscience clause, escape c., letout c., force majeure 468 *qualification*; immunity, impunity, privilege, special treatment, special case, benefit of clergy; extraterritoriality, diplomatic immunity; franchise, charter 915 *dueness*; independence, liberty, the four freedoms 744 *freedom*; licence, leave 756 *permission*; compassionate leave, aegrotat, certificate of exemption 756 *permit*; excuse, exoneration, exculpation 960 *acquittal*; absolution, pardon, amnesty 909 *forgiveness*; discharge, release 746 *liberation*; renunciation 621 *relinquishment*; evasion of responsibility, escapism, self-exemption, washing one's hands, passing the buck 753 *resignation*.

Vb. *exempt*, set apart, set aside; eliminate, count out, rule o. 57 *exclude*; excuse, exonerate, exculpate 960 *acquit*; grant absolution, absolve, pardon 909 *forgive*; spare 905 *show mercy*; grant immunity, privilege, charter 756 *permit*; license, dispense, give dispensation, grant impunity; amnesty, declare an amnesty 506 *forget*; enfranchise, set free, set at liberty, release 746 *liberate*; pass over, stretch a point 736 *be lenient*.

be exempt, – exempted etc. adj.; owe no responsibility, be free from r., have no liability, not come within the scope of; enjoy immunity, enjoy diplomatic i., enjoy impunity, enjoy a privileged position, enjoy independence 744 *be free*; spare oneself the necessity, exempt oneself, excuse oneself, absent oneself, take leave, go on leave 190 *go away*; transfer the responsibility, pass the buck, shift the blame 272 *transfer*; evade *or* escape liability, get away with 667 *escape*; own *or* admit no responsibility, wash one's hands of 918 *fail in duty*.

920 Respect

N. *respect*, regard, consideration, esteem 923 *approbation*; high standing, honour, favour 866 *repute*; polite regard, attention, attentions, flattering a. 884 *courtesy*; due respect, respectfulness, deference, humbleness 872 *humility*; obsequiousness 879 *servility*; devotion 739 *loyalty*; admiration, awe 864 *wonder*; terror 854 *fear*, reverence, veneration, adoration 981 *worship*.

respects, regards, duty, kind regards, kindest r., greetings 884 *courteous act*; red carpet, guard of honour, address of welcome, illuminated address, salutation, salaam; nod, bob, duck, bow, scrape, curtsy, genuflexion, prostration, kowtow 311 *obeisance*; reverence, homage; salute, presenting arms; honours of war, flags flying.

Adj. *respectful*, deferential, knowing one's

place 872 *humble*; obsequious, boot-licking, kowtowing 879 *servile*; submissive 721 *submitting*; reverent, reverential; admiring, awestruck; polite 884 *courteous*; ceremonious, at the salute, saluting, cap in hand, bare-headed, forelock-tugging; kneeling, on one's knees, prostrate; bobbing, bowing, scraping, bowing and s., bending; showing respect, rising, standing, on one's feet, all standing.

Vb. *respect*, hold in r., hold in honour, hold in high regard, hold in high esteem, think well of, rank high, place h., look up to, esteem, regard, value; admire 864 *wonder*; reverence, venerate, exalt 866 *honour*; adore 981 *worship*; idolize; revere, stand in awe of, have a wholesome respect for 854 *fear*; know one's place, defer to, take a back seat to 721 *submit*; pay tribute to, take one's hat off to 923 *praise*; do homage to, make much of, lionize, chair, carry shoulder-high 876 *celebrate*.

show respect, render honour, pay homage, do the honours 884 *pay one's respects*; make way for, leave room for, keep one's distance, take a back seat to, know one's place; welcome, hail, salute, present arms, turn out the guard, roll out the red carpet, put out the bunting 884 *greet*; cheer, drink to 876 *toast*; bob, bow, bow and scrape, curtsy, kneel, kowtow, prostrate oneself 311 *stoop*; observe decorum, stand on ceremony, stand, rise, rise to one's feet, rise from one's seat, uncover, remove one's hat *or* cap, stand bareheaded; humble oneself, condescend 872 *be humble*.

command respect, inspire r., awe, strike with a., overawe, impose 821 *impress*; enjoy a reputation, rank high, stand h., stand well in the eyes of all 866 *have a reputation*; compel respect, demand r., command admiration 864 *be wonderful*; dazzle, bedazzle 875 *be ostentatious*; receive respect, gain honour, gain a reputation, receive bouquets 923 *be praised*.

921 Disrespect

N. *disrespect*, want of respect, scant r., disrespectfulness, irreverence, impoliteness, incivility, discourtesy 885 *rudeness*; dishonour, disfavour 924 *disapprobation*; neglect, undervaluation 483 *underestimation*; low esteem 867 *disrepute*; depreciation, disparagement 926 *detraction*; scorn 922 *contempt*; mockery 851 *ridicule*; desecration 980 *impiety*.

indignity, humiliation, mortification, affront, insult, slight, snub, slap in the face, outrage 878 *insolence*; snook, V-sign, Harvey Smith salute 878 *sauciness*; gibe, taunt, jeer 922 *contempt*; quip, sarcasm, mock, flout 851 *ridicule*; hiss, hoot, boo, catcall, brickbat, rotten eggs 924 *disapprobation*.

Adj. *disrespectful*, wanting in respect, slighting, neglectful 458 *negligent*; insubordinate 738 *disobedient*; irreverent, irreverential, aweless; sacrilegious 980 *profane*; outspoken, overcandid 573 *plain*; rude, impolite 885 *discourteous*; airy, breezy, offhand, offhanded, cavalier, familiar, cheeky, saucy 878 *impertinent*; insulting, outrageous 878 *insolent*; flouting, jeering, gibing, scoffing, mocking, satirical, cynical, sarcastic; injurious, contumelious, scurrilous 899 *cursing*; denigratory, depreciative, pejorative; snobbish, supercilious, disdainful, scornful; unflattering, uncomplimentary 924 *disapproving*.

Vb. *not respect*, be disrespectful; have no respect for, have no regard f., have no use f. 924 *disapprove*; misprize, undervalue, underrate 483 *underestimate*; look down on, have a low opinion of, marginalize, disdain, scorn 922 *despise*; run down, denigrate, disparage 926 *defame*; spit on, toss aside 607 *reject*; show disrespect, show no respect, lack courtesy, remain seated, remain covered, keep one's hat on, push aside, shove a., elbow a., crowd, jostle 885 *be rude*; ignore, turn one's back 458 *disregard*; snub, slight, insult, affront, outrage 872 *humiliate*; dishonour, disgrace, put to shame, drag in the mud 867 *shame*; trifle with, treat lightly 922 *hold cheap*; cheapen, lower, degrade; have no awe, not reverence, desecrate, profane 980 *be impious*; call names, abuse 899 *curse*; taunt, twit, cock a snook 878 *be insolent*; laugh at, guy, scoff, mock, flout, deride 851 *ridicule*; make mouths at, make faces at, jeer, hiss, hoot, heckle, boo, point at, spit at 924 *reproach*; mob, hound, chase 619 *pursue*; pelt, stone, heave a brick.

922 Contempt

N. *contempt*, utter c.; scorn, disdain, disdainfulness, superiority, loftiness 871 *pride*; contemptuousness, sniffiness; snootiness, superciliousness, snobbishness 850 *affectation*; superior airs, side, smile of contempt, curl of the lip, snort, sniff; slight, humiliation 921 *indignity*; sneer, dig at 926 *detraction*; derision, scoffing 851 *ridicule*; snub, rebuff 885 *discourtesy*.

contemptibility, unworthiness, despisedness, insignificance, puerility, pitiability, futility 639 *unimportance*; pettiness, meanness, littleness, paltriness 33 *smallness*; cause for shame, byword of reproach.

Adj. *contemptible*, despicable, beneath contempt; abject, worthless 645 *bad*; petty, paltry, little, mean 33 *small*; spurned, spat on; scorned, despised, contemned, low in one's estimation; trifling, pitiable, futile, of no account 639 *unimportant*.

Vb. *despise*, hold in contempt, feel utter contempt for, have no use for 921 *not respect*; look down on, consider beneath one, be too good for, be too grand for 871 *be proud*; disdain, spurn, sniff at, snort at 607 *reject*; come it over, turn up one's nose, wrinkle the n., curl one's lips, toss one's head, snort; snub, turn one's back on 885 *be rude*; scorn, whistle, hiss, boo, give a slow handclap, point at, point the finger of scorn 924 *reproach*; laugh at, have a dig at, laugh to scorn, scoff, scout, flout, gibe, jeer, mock, deride 851 *ridicule*; trample on, ride roughshod over 735 *oppress*; disgrace, roll in the mire 867 *shame*.

hold cheap, have a low opinion of 921 *not respect*; ignore, dismiss, discount, take no account of 458 *disregard*; belittle, disparage, fail to appreciate, underrate, undervalue 483 *underestimate*; decry 926 *detract*; marginalize, set no value on, set no store by, think nothing of, think small beer of, not care a rap for, not care a straw, not give a hoot *or* a damn, not give that for, laugh at, treat as a laughing matter, snap one's fingers at, shrug away, pooh-pooh; slight, trifle with, treat lightly, treat like dirt, denigrate, lower, degrade 872 *humiliate*.

Int. get lost!, get stuffed!, in your face!, get a life!

923 Approbation

N. *approbation*, approval, modified rapture; satisfaction 828 *content*; appreciation, recognition, acknowledgment 907 *gratitude*; good opinion, golden opinions, kudos, credit 866 *prestige*; regard, admiration, esteem 920 *respect*; good books, good graces, grace, favour, popularity, affection 887 *love*; adoption, acceptance, welcome, favourable reception 299 *reception*; sanction 756 *permission*; nod of approval, seal of a., blessing; nod, wink, thumbs up, consent 488 *assent*; countenance, patronage, championship, advocacy, backing 703 *aid*; friendly notice, favourable review, rave r. 480 *estimate*; good word, kind w., testimonial, written t., reference, commendation, recommendation 466 *credential*.

praise, loud p., praise and glory, laudation, benediction, blessing; compliment, eulogy, panegyric, glorification, adulation, idolatry 925 *flattery*; hero worship 864 *wonder*; overpraise 482 *overestimation*; faint praise, two cheers; shout of praise, hosanna, alleluia; praises, song of praise, hymn of p., paean of p., Te Deum; tribute, credit, due credit 907 *thanks*; complimentary reference, bouquet, accolade, citation, honourable mention, commendation, glowing terms; official biography, hagiography; self-praise, self-glorification 877 *boasting*; name in

lights, letters of gold; puff, blurb 528 *advertisement*.

applause, clamorous a., acclaim, universal a.; enthusiasm, excitement 821 *excitation*; warm reception, hero's welcome 876 *celebration*; acclamation, plaudits, clapping, stamping, whistling, cheering; clap, three cheers, paean, hosannah; thunderous applause, shout of a., chorus of a., round of a., salvo of a., storm of a., ovation, standing o., shouts of 'encore', shouts of 'more, more'; encore, curtain call; bouquet, pat on the back.

commender, praiser, eulogist, panegyrist; clapper, applauder, shouter; approver, friendly critic, admirer, devoted a., hero-worshipper, fan club, supporters' c.; advocate, recommender, supporter, speaker for the motion 707 *patron*; inscriber, dedicator; advertiser, blurb-writer, puffer, promotions manager, booster; agent, tout, touter, barker 528 *publicizer*; canvasser, electioneer, election agent.

Adj. *approving*, uncensorious, uncomplaining, satisfied 828 *content*; favouring, supporting, advocating 703 *aiding*; appreciative 907 *grateful*; approbatory, favourable, friendly, well-inclined; complimentary, commendatory, laudatory, eulogistic, panegyrical, lyrical; admiring, hero-worshipping, idolatrous; lavish, generous; fulsome, overpraising, uncritical, undiscriminating; acclamatory, clapping, applauding, thunderous 400 *loud*; ecstatic, rapturous, in raptures 821 *excited*.

approved, passed, tested, tried; uncensured, free from blame, stamped with approval, blessed; popular, in favour, in high f., in one's good books, in the good graces of, in good odour, in high esteem, thought well of 866 *reputable*; praised etc. vb.; commended, highly c.; favoured, backed, odds on 605 *chosen*.

Vb. *approve*, see nothing wrong with, sound pleased, have no fault to find, be unable to fault, have nothing but praise for, think highly of 920 *respect*; like well 887 *love*; think well of, admire, esteem, value, prize, treasure, cherish, set store by 866 *honour*; appreciate, give credit, give full c., give credit where credit is due, salute, take one's hat off to, hand it to, give full marks; think no worse of, think the better of; count it to one's credit, see the good points, see the good in one, think good, think perfect 8; think desirable 912 *envy*; think the best, award the palm; pronounce good, mark with approbation, give the seal *or* stamp of approval; accept, pass, tick, give marks for, give points for; nod, wink, nod one's approval, give one's assent 488 *assent*; sanction, bless, give one's blessing 756 *permit*; ratify 488 *endorse*; commend, recommend, advocate, support, back, favour, countenance, stand up for, speak up f., put in a good word for, give one a reference or a testimonial, act as referee for 703 *patronize*.

praise, compliment, pay compliments 925 *flatter*; speak well of, speak highly, swear by; bless 907 *thank*; salute, pay tribute to, hand it to, take one's hat off to; commend, give praise, hand out bouquets to, laud, eulogize, praise to the skies, sound the praises, sing the p., exalt, extol, glorify, magnify; wax lyrical, get carried away; not spare one's blushes 546 *exaggerate*; puff, inflate, overpraise, overestimate 482 *overrate*; lionize, hero-worship, idolize; trumpet, write up, cry up, puff up, hype up, crack up, boost 528 *advertise*; praise oneself, glorify o. 877 *boast*.

applaud, welcome, hail; acclaim, receive with acclamation, clap, clap one's hands, give a big hand, stamp, whistle, bring the house down, raise the roof; give a standing ovation; cheer, raise a c., give three cheers, give three times three; cheer to the echo, shout for, root for; clap on the back, pat on the back, hand out bouquets to; welcome, congratulate, garland, chair 876 *celebrate*; drink to 876 *toast*.

Int. bravo! well done! hear hear! encore! more, more! bis! three cheers! hurrah! hosannah! olé!

924 Disapprobation

N. *disapprobation*, disapproval, dissatisfaction 829 *discontent*; nonapproval, return 607 *rejection*; refusal; disfavour, displeasure, unpopularity 861 *dislike*; low opinion 921 *disrespect*; bad books, black b. 867 *disrepute*; disparagement, decrial, carping, niggling 926 *detraction*; censoriousness, fault-finding 862 *fastidiousness*; hostility 881 *enmity*; objection, exception, cavil 468 *qualification*; complaint, clamour, outcry, protest, tut-tut, sniffing 762 *deprecation*; indignation 891 *anger*; sibilation, hissing, hiss, boo, slow handclap, whistle, catcall; brickbats 851 *ridicule*; ostracism, boycott, bar, colour b., ban, nonadmission 57 *exclusion*; blackball, blacklist, Index.

censure, blame, impeachment, inculpation 928 *accusation*; home truth, no compliment, left-handed c., back-handed c.; criticism, stricture; lambasting, hypercriticism, fault-finding; onslaught 712 *attack*; brickbats, bad press, critical review, hostile r., slashing r., slating, panning; open letter, tirade, jeremiad, philippic, diatribe 704 *opposition*; conviction 961 *condemnation*; false accusation 928 *false charge*; slur, slander, aspersions, insinuation, innuendo 926 *calumny*; brand, stigma.

reproach, reproaches; recriminations 709 *quarrel*; home truths, invective, vituperation, calling

names, bawling out, shouting down 899 *scurrility*; execration 899 *malediction*; personal remarks, aspersion, reflection 921 *indignity*; taunt, sneer 878 *insolence*; sarcasm, irony, satire, biting wit, biting tongue, dig, cut, hit, brickbat 851 *ridicule*; rough side of one's tongue, tongue-lashing, lambasting, hard words, cutting w., bitter w. (**see** *reprimand*); silent reproach, disapproving look, dirty l., black l. 893 *sullenness*.

reprimand, remonstrance 762 *deprecation*; stricture, animadversion, reprehension, reprobation; censure, rebuke, flea in one's ear, reproof, snub; rocket, raspberry; piece of one's mind, expression of displeasure, mark of d., black mark; castigation, correction, rap over the knuckles, smack or slap on the wrist, box on the ears 963 *punishment*; inculpation, admonition, admonishment, tongue-lashing, chiding, talking-to, upbraiding, scolding, slating, strafing, trouncing, lambasting, dressing down, blowing up, roasting, wigging, carpeting; talking to, lecture, curtain 1.

Adj. *disapproving*, unapproving, not amused; shocked, scandalized; unimpressed; disillusioned 509 *disappointed*; sparing of praise, grudging; silent 582 *taciturn*; unfavourable, hostile 881 *hostile*; objecting, protesting, deprecatory; reproachful, chiding, scolding, upbraiding, vituperative, lambasting; critical, unflattering, uncomplimentary; withering, hard-hitting, pulling no punches, strongly worded; overcritical, hypercritical, captious, fault-finding, niggling, carping, cavilling; disparaging, defamatory, damaging; caustic, sharp, bitter, venomous, trenchant, mordant; sarcastic, sardonic, cynical; censorious, holier than thou; blaming, faulting, censuring, reprimanding, recriminative, denunciatory, accusatory, condemning, damning, damnatory.

blameworthy, blamable, open to criticism, censurable, condemnable 645 *bad*; reprehensible, dishonourable, unjustifiable 867 *discreditable*; unpraiseworthy, uncommendable, not to be thought of; reprobate, culpable, to blame.

Vb. *disapprove*, hold no brief for, have no regard for, not think much of, think little of, take a dim view of; think the worse of, think ill of 922 *despise*; not pass, fail, plough; return 607 *reject*; disallow 757 *prohibit*; cancel 752 *abrogate*; censor 550 *obliterate*; withhold approval, look grave, shake one's head, not hold with 489 *dissent*; disfavour, reprehend, lament, deplore 830 *regret*; abhor, reprobate 861 *dislike*; wash one's hands of, turn one's back on, disown, look askance, avoid, ignore; keep at a distance, draw the line, ostracize, ban, bar, blacklist 57 *exclude*; protest, tut-tut, sniff, remonstrate, object, take exception to, demur 762 *deprecate*; discountenance, show disapproval, exclaim, shout down, bawl d., hoot, boo, bay, heckle, hiss, whistle, give a slow handclap, give the bird, drive off the stage; hand out brickbats, throw mud, throw rotten eggs, throw bricks *or* stones; hound, chase, mob, lynch; make a face, grimace, make a moue, make mouths at, spit; look black; sullen; look daggers 891 *be angry*.

criticize, not recommend, give no marks *or* points to, damn with faint praise, damn 961 *condemn*; fault, find f., pick holes, niggle, cavil, carp, nitpick, deprecate, run down, belittle 926 *detract*; oppose, tilt at, shoot at, throw the book at 712 *attack*; weigh in, pitch into, hit out at, let fly, lay into, lam into, savage, maul, slash, slate, lambast, scourge, flay, put the boot in; inveigh, thunder, fulminate, storm against, rage a. 61 *rampage*; shout down, cry shame, slang, call names; gird, rail, revile, abuse, heap a., pour vitriol, objurgate, execrate 899 *curse*; vilify, blacken, denigrate 926 *defame*; stigmatize, brand, pillory; expose, denounce, recriminate 928 *accuse*; sneer, twit, taunt 921 *not respect*.

reprove, reprehend, reproach, rebuke, administer a r., snub, rebuff, send away with a flea in the eat; call to order, caution, wag one's finger, read the Riot Act 664 *warn*; book, give one a black mark; censure, reprimand, take to task, rap over the knuckles, smack *or* slap the wrist, box the ears; tick off, tell off, have one's head for, carpet, have on the carpet, haul over the coals, send before the beak; remonstrate, expostulate, admonish, castigate, chide, correct; lecture, read one a lecture, give one a talking to, give one a wigging, give one a dressing-down, lambast, trounce, roast, browbeat, blow up, tear strips off, come down hard on, come down on like a ton of bricks, chastise 963 *punish*.

blame, find fault, carp, cavil, nitpick, pick holes in; get at, henpeck; reprehend, hold to blame, pick on, put the blame on, hold responsible; throw the first stone, inculpate, incriminate, complain against, impute, impeach, charge, criminate 928 *accuse*; round on, return the charge, recriminate 714 *retaliate*; think the worst of 961 *condemn*.

reproach, heap reproaches on; upbraid, slate, rate, berate, rail, slag, strafe, shend, lambast, revile, abuse, denigrate, blackguard 899 *curse*; go for, inveigh against, bawl out, scold, tonguelash, lash, give the rough edge of one's tongue, rail in good set terms against, give one a piece of one's mind, give one what for, give it to one straight from the shoulder, give to one straight, not mince matters, not pull one's punches, let it rip.

incur blame, take the blame, take the rap, carry the can, catch it; be held responsible, have to answer for; be open to criticism, blot one's copy book, get a bad name 867 *lose repute*; be up on a charge, be carpeted, be up before the beak, be court-martialled, stand accused; stand corrected; be an example, be a scandal, scandalize, shock, revolt 861 *cause dislike*.

925 Flattery

N. *flattery*, cajolery, wheedling, getting round, blarney, blandishments, sweet talk; flannel, soft soap; adulation; voice of the charmer, honeyed words, sweet nothings 889 *endearment*; compliment, pretty speeches, bouquets; coquetry, winning ways; fawning, back-scratching; obsequiousness, flunkeyism, sycophancy, toadying 879 *servility*; unctuousness, smarminess, euphemism, insincerity, hypocrisy, tongue in cheek, lip-homage 542 *sham*.

flatterer, adulator, cajoler, wheedler; coquette, charmer; tout, puffer, hyper, promoter, booster, claqueur, claque 923 *commender*; courtier, yesman 488 *assenter*; creep, fawner, backscratcher, sycophant, parasite, minion, hanger-on 879 *toady*; fair-weather friend, hypocrite 545 *deceiver*.

Adj. *flattering*, overpraising, overdone; boosting, puffing, hyping, overpromoting; complimentary, overcomplimentary, full of compliments; fulsome, adulatory; sugary, saccharine; cajoling, wheedling, coaxing, blarneying, mealy-mouthed, glozing, canting; smooth-tongued, honey-t., bland; smooth, oily, unctuous, soapy, slimy, smarmy; obsequious, all over one, courtly, fawning, crawling, back-scratching, sycophantic 879 *servile*; specious, plausible, beguiling, ingratiating, insinuating; lulling, soothing; vote-catching, vote-snatching; false, insincere, tongue-in-cheek, unreliable 541 *hypocritical*.

Vb. *flatter*, deal in flattery, have kissed the Blarney Stone; compliment, hand out bouquets 923 *praise*; overpraise, overdo it, lard it on, lay it on thick, lay it on with a trowel, not spare one's blushes; puff, hype, promote, boost, cry up 482 *overrate*; adulate, burn incense to, assail with flattery, turn one's head; butter up, soften up, soft-soap; blarney, flannel; sweet-talk, sugar; wheedle, coax, cajole, coo; lull, soothe, beguile 542 *deceive*; humour, jolly along, pander to; gild the pill, sugar the p., make things pleasant, tell people what they want to hear; blandish, smooth, smarm; make much of, be all over one 889 *caress*; fawn, fawn on, cultivate, court, pay court to, play the courtier, massage one's ego; smirk 835 *smile*; scratch one's back, back-scratch, curry favour, make up to, suck up to;

toady to, pander to 879 *be servile*; insinuate one-self, worm oneself into favour, get on the right side of, creep into one's good graces; flatter one-self, have a swelled head 873 *be vain*.

926 Detraction

N. *detraction*, faint praise, two cheers, under-statement 483 *underestimation*; criticism, hostile c.; destructive c., flak, bad review, slating r., bad press 924 *disapprobation*; onslaught 712 *attack*; hatchet job; impeachment 928 *accusation*; exposure, bad light 867 *disrepute*; decrial, dispar-agement, depreciation, running down; lower-ing, derogation; slighting language, scorn 922 *contempt*; vilification, abuse, invective 899 *scur-rility*; defamation 543 *untruth*; backbiting, catti-ness, spite 898 *malevolence*; aspersion, reflection, snide remark (**see** *calumny*); whisper, innuendo, insinuation, imputation, whispering campaign; smear campaign, mud-slinging, smirching, denigration, character assassination; brand, stigma; muck-raking, scandal-mongering; disillusionment, cynicism 865 *lack of wonder*.

calumny, slander, libel, aspersion, false report, roorback 543 *untruth*; a defamation, defamatory remark, damaging report; smear, smear-word, dirty word 867 *slur*; offensive remark, personal r., insult, taunt, dig at; brickbat 921 *indignity*; scoff, sarcasm 851 *ridicule*; sneer, sniff; carica-ture 552 *misrepresentation*; skit, lampoon 851 *sat-ire*; scandal, scandalous talk, malicious gossip, bad mouth.

detractor, decrier, disparager, slighter; debunker, deflater, cynic; mocker, scoffer, satir-izer, satirist, lampooner; castigator, denouncer, reprover, censurer, censor; no respecter of persons, no flatterer, candid friend, candid critic; critic, hostile c., destructive c., attacker, arch-critic, chief accuser, impeacher 928 *accuser*; captious critic, knocker, fault-finder, carper, caviller, niggler, nit-picker, hair-splitter; heckler, barracker; Philistine; defamer, destroyer of reputations, hatchet man; smircher, smearer, slanderer, libeller; backbiter, gossiper, scandal-monger, muck-raker; gossip columnist, gutter press, chequebook journalist; denigrator, mud-slinger; brander, stigmatizer; vituperator, reviler; scold, poison pen.

Vb. *detract*, deprecate, disparage, run down, sell short; debunk, deflate, puncture, cut down to size 921 *not respect*; minimize 483 *under-estimate*; belittle, slight, diss 922 *hold cheap*; sneer at, sniff at 922 *despise*; decry, cry down, rubbish, damn with faint praise, fail to appreci-ate 924 *disapprove*; find nothing to praise, criticize, knock, bad mouth, slam, fault, find f., pick holes in, slate, pull to pieces, tear to rib-bons 924 *criticize*; caricature, guy 552 *misrep-resent*; lampoon, dip one's pen in gall 851 *satirize*; scoff, mock 851 *ridicule*; make catty remarks, get in a dig at; whisper, insinuate, cast aspersions.

defame, dishonour, damage, compromise, scandalize, degrade, lower, put to shame 867 *shame*; give a dog a bad name, lower *or* lessen one's reputation, destroy one's good name; denounce, expose, pillory, stigmatize, brand 928 *accuse*; libel, slander, traduce, malign; vil-ify, denigrate, blacken, tarnish, sully; reflect upon, put in a bad light; speak ill of, speak evil, gossip, badmouth, make scandal, talk about, backbite, talk behind one's back; discredit 486 *cause doubt*; smear, start a smear campaign, besmear, smirch, besmirch, spatter, bespatter, throw mud, fling dirt, drag in the gutter 649 *make unclean*; hound, witch-hunt 619 *hunt*; look for scandal, smell evil, muckrake, rake about in the gutter 619 *pursue*.

927 Vindication

N. *vindication*, restoration, rehabilitation 787 *res-titution*; triumph of justice, wrong righted; exon-eration, exculpation, clearance 960 *acquittal*; justification, good grounds, just cause, every excuse; apologetics, self-defence, apologia, defence, legal d., good d.; alibi, plea, excuse, whitewash, gloss 614 *pretext*; fair excuse, good e. 494 *truth*; extenuation, palliation, mitigation, mitigating circumstance, extenuating c., palli-ative 468 *qualification*; counterargument 479 *confutation*; reply, reply for the defence, rebuttal 460 *rejoinder*; recrimination, countercharge; accusation; bringing to book, poetic justice, just punishment 963 *punishment*.

Vb. *vindicate*, revenge 910 *avenge*; do justice to, give the devil his due; set right, restore, rehabilitate 787 *restitute*; maintain, speak up for, argue f., contend f., advocate 475 *argue*; undertake to prove, bear out, confirm, make good, prove the truth of, prove 478 *demonstrate*; champion, stand up for, stick up for 713 *defend*; support, offer moral support 703 *patronize*.

justify, warrant, justify by the event, give grounds for, provide justification, furnish an excuse, give one cause; put one in the right, put one in the clear, clear, clear one's name, free from blame, exonerate, exculpate, acquit; white-wash, varnish, gloss; salve one's conscience, jus-tify oneself, defend o. 614 *plead*; plead one's own cause, say in defence, rebut the charge, plead ignorance.

extenuate, excuse, make excuses for, make allowances; palliate, mitigate, soften, mince one's words, soft-pedal, slur, slur over, play down, downplay, gloss, gloss over, varnish, whitewash; take the will for the deed 736 *be lenient.*

928 Accusation

N. *accusation*, complaint, charge, home truth; censure, blame, stricture 924 *reproach*; challenge 711 *defiance*; countercharge, recrimination 460 *rejoinder*; twit, taunt 921 *indignity*; imputation, allegation, information, denunciation; plaint, suit, action 959 *litigation*; prosecution, impeachment, arraignment, indictment, citation, summons; bill of indictment, true bill; gravamen, substance of a charge; case, case to answer, case for the prosecution 475 *reasons*; evidence.

false charge, trumped-up c., put-up job, frame-up; false information, perjured testimony, false evidence; counterfeit evidence, plant; illegal prosecution; lie, libel, slander, scandal, stigma 926 *calumny*.

accuser, complainant, plaintiff, pursuer, petitioner, appellant, libellant, litigant; challenger, denouncer, charger; grass, supergrass, nark, copper's n. 524 *informer*; common informer, delator, relator, impeacher, indicter, prosecutor, public p., procurator fiscal; libeller, slanderer, calumniator, stigmatizer; hostile witness 881 *enemy*; the finger of suspicion.

accused person, the accused, prisoner, prisoner at the bar; defendant, respondent, corespondent; culprit; suspect, victim of suspicion, marked man; slandered person, libellee, victim.

Vb. *accuse*, challenge 711 *defy*; taunt; point a finger at, finger, cast the first stone, throw in one's teeth, reproach 924 *reprove*; stigmatize, brand, pillory, cast a slur on, cast aspersions, defame; impute, charge with, saddle w., tax w., hold against, lay to one's charge, lay at one's door, hold responsible, make r.; pick on, fix on, hold to blame, put the blame on, pin on, stick on, bring home to 924 *blame*; point at, expose, show up, name, name names 526 *divulge*; denounce, inform against, tell, tell on, clype, blab, squeal, sing, rat on, split on, turn Queen's evidence 524 *inform*; involve, implicate, incriminate; countercharge, rebut the charge, turn the tables upon 479 *confute*; make one a scapegoat, shift the blame; admit the charge, plead guilty 526 *confess*; implicate oneself, lay oneself open.

indict, impeach, arraign, inform against, lodge a complaint, lay information against; complain, charge, bring a charge, file charges, swear an indictment 959 *litigate*; book, cite, summon, serve with a writ, prosecute, sue; bring an action, bring a suit, bring a case; haul up, send before the beak, have up, put on trial,

put in the dock; throw the book at 712 *attack*; charge falsely, lie against 541 *be false*; frame, trump up a charge, cook the evidence, use false e., fake the e., plant the e. 541 *fake*.

Adv. *accusingly*, censoriously.

929 Probity

N. *probity*, rectitude, uprightness, goodness, sanctity 933 *virtue*; stainlessness 950 *purity*; good character, moral fibre, honesty, soundness, incorruptibility, integrity; high character, nobleness, nobility; honourableness, decent feelings, finer f., tender conscience; honour, personal h., sense of h., principles, high p.; conscientiousness 768 *observance*; scrupulousness, scrupulosity, punctiliousness, meticulousness 457 *carefulness*; ingenuousness, singleheartedness; trustworthiness, reliability, sense of responsibility; truthfulness 540 *veracity*; candour, plain-speaking 573 *plainness*; sincerity, good faith 494 *truth*; fidelity, faith, troth, faithfulness, trustiness, constancy 739 *loyalty*; clean hands, clear conscience 935 *innocence*; impartiality, fairness, sportsmanship 913 *justice*; respectability 866 *repute*; gentlemanliness, ladylikeness, chivalry; principle, point of honour, punctilio, code, code of honour, bushido 913 *right*; court of justice, court of honour, field of h.

Adj. *honourable*, upright, erect, of integrity, of honour 933 *virtuous*; correct, strict; lawabiding, honest, on the level; principled, high-p., above-board, on the up-and-up; scrupulous, conscientious, soul-searching; incorruptible, not to be bought off; incorrupt, immaculate 935 *innocent*; stainless, unstained, untarnished, unsullied 648 *clean*; noble, highminded, pure-m. 950 *pure*; ingenuous, unworldly 699 *artless*; good, straight, straight as a die, square, on the square, one hundred per cent; fair, fair-dealing, equitable, impartial 913 *just*; sporting, sportsmanlike, playing the game; gentlemanly, chivalrous, knightly, jealous of one's honour; careful of one's reputation, respectable 866 *reputable*; saintly 979 *pious*.

trustworthy, creditworthy, reliable, dependable, tried, tested, proven; trusty, true-hearted, true-blue, true to the core, sure, staunch, singlehearted, constant, unchanging, faithful, loyal 739 *obedient*; responsible, duteous, dutiful 768 *observant*; conscientious, religious, scrupulous, meticulous, punctilious 457 *careful*; candid, frank, open, open and above-board, openhearted, transparent, ingenuous, without guile, guileless 494 *true*; straightforward, truthful, truth-speaking, as good as one's word 540 *veracious*; unperjured, unperfidious, untreacherous.

930 Improbity

N. *improbity*, dishonesty; lack of principle; laxity; unconscientiousness 456 *inattention*; unscrupulousness, opportunism; insincerity, disingenuousness, unstraightforwardness, untrustworthiness, unreliability, undependability, untruthfulness 541 *falsehood*; unfairness, partiality, bias 914 *injustice*; shuffling, slipperiness, artfulness; suspiciousness, shadiness, deviousness, crookedness; corruption, sleaze, sleaze factor, corruptibility, venality, bribability, graft, palm-greasing, nepotism, simony, baseness, shabbiness, abjectness, debasement, shamefulness, disgrace, dishonour, shame 867 *disrepute*; worthlessness, good-for-nothingness, villainousness, villainy, knavery, roguery, rascality, spivvery, skulduggery, racketeering, black market, under-the-counter dealings; criminality, crime, complicity, aiding and abetting 954 *lawbreaking*; turpitude, moral t. 934 *wickedness*.

perfidy, perfidiousness, faithlessness, unfaithfulness, infidelity, unfaith 543 *untruth*; bad faith, divided allegiance, wavering loyalty, sitting on the fence, disloyalty 738 *disobedience*; running with the hare and hunting with the hounds, double-dealing, double-crossing, Judas kiss 541 *duplicity*; volte face, U-turn 603 *change of mind*; defection, desertion 918 *undutifulness*; betrayal, treachery, stab in the back, sell-out; treason, high t. 738 *sedition*; fifth column, Trojan horse; breach of faith, broken word, broken promise, breach of p., cry of treason, dirty trick, stab in the back; not playing the game, foul, hitting below the belt 914 *wrong*; professional foul 623 *contrivance*; trick, shuffle, chicanery 542 *trickery*; sharp practice, heads I win tails you lose; dirty work, job, deal, racket; under-the-counter dealing, fiddle, wangle, manipulation, gerrymandering, hanky-panky, monkey business; tax evasion 620 *avoidance*; malversation 788 *peculation*; crime, felony 954 *lawbreaking*.

Adj. *dishonest*, not on the level 914 *wrong*; unprincipled, unscrupulous; shameless, dead to honour, lost to shame; unethical, immoral 934 *wicked*; untrustworthy, unreliable, undependable, not to be trusted; disingenuous, economical with the truth, untruthful 543 *untrue*; two-faced, insincere 541 *hypocritical*; creeping, crawling; artful, dodging, opportunist, slippery, foxy 698 *cunning*; shifty, shuffling, prevaricating 518 *equivocal*; designing, scheming; sneaking, underhand 523 *latent*; up to something, on the fiddle, wangling; not straight, bent, crooked, devious, tortuous, winding; insidious, dark, sinister; shady, fishy, suspicious, doubtful, questionable; fraudulent 542 *spurious*; illicit 954

illegal; foul 645 *bad*; unclean 649 *dirty*; mean, shabby, dishonourable, infamous 867 *disreputable*; derogatory, unworthy, undignified; inglorious, ignominious 867 *degrading*; ignoble, unchivalrous, ungentlemanly; unsporting, unsportsmanlike, unfair.

venal, corruptible, bribable, mercenary; palm-greasing, corrupt, grafting, nepotistic.

perfidious, treacherous, unfaithful, inconstant, faithless 541 *false*; double-dealing, double-crossing; disloyal; false-hearted, traitorous, treasonous, untrue 738 *disobedient*; plotting, scheming, intriguing; Machiavellian; cheating; fraudulent 542 *spurious*.

Vb. *be dishonest*, have no morals, yield to temptation, be lost to shame; lack honesty, live by one's wits, lead a life of crime 954 *be illegal*; fiddle, finagle, wangle, gerrymander, racketeer; defraud; cheat, swindle 542 *deceive*; betray, play false, do the dirty on, stab in the back; run with the hare and hunt with the hounds, double-cross 541 *dissemble*; fawn 925 *flatter*; break faith, break one's word, go back on one's promises, tell lies 541 *be false*; shuffle, dodge, prevaricate 518 *be equivocal*; sell out, sell down the river 603 *apostatize*; sink into crime, sell one's honour 867 *lose repute*; smack of dishonesty, smell fishy.

931 Disinterestedness

N. *disinterestedness*, impartiality, lack of bias 913 *justice*; selflessness, self-effacement 872 *humility*; self-sacrifice, martyrdom; loftiness of purpose, idealism; magnanimity; quixotry; purity of motive, labour of love; altruism, thought for others; charity 887 *love*.

Adj. *disinterested*, impartial, without self-interest, without bias 913 *just*; incorruptible, uncorrupted; unselfish, selfless, self-sacrificing; altruistic, philanthropic; undesigning; sacrificial, unmercenary, for love, non-profitmaking; idealistic, quixotic, lofty, elevated; magnanimous.

Vb. *be disinterested*, – unselfish etc. adj.; sacrifice, sacrifice oneself; think of others, put oneself last, take a back seat 872 *be humble*; rise above petty considerations; have no axe to grind, have nothing to gain, have no ulterior motive, do for its own sake.

932 Selfishness

N. *selfishness*, self-love, self-admiration, narcissism, self-worship, self-praise 873 *vanity*; self-pity, self-indulgence, ego trip 943 *intemperance*; egocentricity; egoism, egotism; self-preservation, everyone for themselves; axe to grind, personal considerations, personal motives, private ends, personal advantage; self-seeking, self-aggrandizement, self-interest, looking after number one; no thought for others, 'I'm all right, Jack'; charity that begins at home, cupboard love; meanness 816 *parsimony*; greed, acquisitiveness 816 *avarice*; possessiveness 911 *jealousy*; 'heads I win tails you lose' 914 *injustice*; selfish ambition; power politics.

egotist, egoist, self-centred person, narcissist 873 *vain person*; self-seeker; go-getter, adventurer; monopolist, dog in the manger, hog, road h.; opportunist.

Adj. *selfish*, egocentric, self-centred, wrapped up in oneself; egoistic, egotistic, egotistical; personal, concerned with number one; self-interested, self-seeking; self-indulgent 943 *intemperate*; narcissistic 873 *vain*; not altruistic; uncharitable, mean, acquisitive, mercenary 816 *avaricious*; covetous 912 *envious*; hogging, monopolistic 859 *greedy*; possessive, dog-in-the-manger; designing, axe-grinding; go-getting, on the make, on the gravy train, opportunist; materialistic.

Vb. *be selfish*, – egoistic etc. adj.; put oneself first, think only of oneself, take care of number one; indulge oneself, spoil o.; have only oneself to please; feather one's nest, look out for oneself, have an eye to the main chance, know on which side one's bread is buttered; keep for oneself, hog, monopolize, be a dog in the manger 778 *retain*; have personal motives, have an axe to grind; pursue one's interests, advance one's own i., sacrifice the interests of others.

933 Virtue

N. *virtue*, virtuousness; goodness; saintliness, holiness, spirituality; odour of sanctity 979 *sanctity*; righteousness 913 *justice*; uprightness, rectitude, moral r., character, integrity, principles, high principle, honour 929 *probity*; guiltlessness 935 *innocence*; morality, ethics 917 *morals*; temperance, chastity 950 *purity*; straight and narrow path, virtuous conduct, christian c., good behaviour, well-spent life, duty done; clear conscience.

virtues, cardinal v., moral v.; theological virtues, faith, hope, charity; natural virtues, prudence, justice, temperance, fortitude; qualities, saving grace; merits; perfections 646 *perfection*; nobleness, magnanimity.

Adj. *virtuous*, moral 917 *ethical*; good, good as gold 644 *excellent*; stainless 950 *pure*; guiltless 935 *innocent*; irreproachable, above reproach, impeccable, above temptation 646 *perfect*; saintlike, seraphic, angelic, saintly, holy 979 *sanctified*; high-principled, right-minded, on the side of the angels 913 *right*; righteous 913 *just*; upright, honest 929 *honourable*; dutiful 739 *obedient*; generous, magnanimous, philan-

thropic 897 *benevolent*; sober 942 *temperate*; chaste, virginal; proper, exemplary; meritorious, worthy, praiseworthy, commendable 923 *approved*.

Vb. *be virtuous*, – good etc. adj.; have all the virtues, be a shining light 644 *be good*; behave, be on one's good *or* best behaviour; resist temptation 942 *be temperate*; have a soul above; keep to the straight and narrow path, follow one's conscience, fight the good fight; discharge one's obligations 917 *do one's duty*; go straight; hear no evil, see no evil, speak no evil; set a good example, be a shining e., shame the devil 644 *do good*.

934 Wickedness

N. *wickedness*, principle of evil 645 *badness*; Devil, cloven hoof 969 *Satan*; fallen nature, Old Adam; iniquity, sinfulness, sin 914 *wrong*; loss of innocence 936 *guilt*; ungodliness 980 *impiety*; amorality 860 *indifference*; hardness of heart 898 *malevolence*; naughtiness, bad behaviour 738 *disobedience*; immorality, turpitude, moral t.; loose morals, profligacy 951 *impurity*; degeneracy, degradation 655 *deterioration*; vice, corruption, depravity 645 *badness*; heinousness, flagrancy; bad character, viciousness, unworthiness, baseness, vileness; villainy; dishonesty 930 *improbity*; crime, criminality 954 *lawbreaking*; devilry, hellishness 898 *inhumanity*; devil worship 982 *idolatry*; scandal, abomination, enormity, infamy 867 *disrepute*; infamous conduct, misbehaviour, delinquency, wrongdoing, evil-doing, transgression, wicked ways, career of crime; primrose path, slippery slope; low life, criminal world, underworld, demi-monde; den of vice, sink of iniquity 649 *sink*.

vice, fault, demerit, unworthiness; human weakness, moral w., infirmity, frailty, human f., foible 163 *weakness*; imperfection, shortcoming, defect, deficiency, limitation, failing, flaw, fatal f., weak point, weakness of the flesh; transgression, trespass, injury, outrage, enormity 914 *wrong*; sin, besetting s., deadly s.; seven deadly sins, pride, covetousness, lust, anger, gluttony, envy, sloth; venial sin, small fault, slight transgression, peccadillo, scrape; impropriety, indecorum 847 *bad taste*; offence 936 *guilty act*; crime, felony, deadly crime, capital c., hanging matter 954 *illegality*.

Adj. *wicked*, unvirtuous, immoral; amoral, amoralistic 860 *indifferent*; unprincipled, unscrupulous 930 *dishonest*; callous; ungodly, irreligious, profane 980 *impious*; iniquitous 914 *unjust*; evil 645 *bad*; evil-minded, black-hearted 898 *malevolent*; evil-doing; misbehaving, bad, naughty 738 *disobedient*; erring, sinning, transgressing; sinful 936 *guilty*; unworthy; not in a state of grace, reprobate; unredeemed, irredeemable; accursed, godforsaken; hellish, infernal, devilish, fiendish, Mephistophelian, satanic 969 *diabolic*.

vicious, steeped in vice, sunk in iniquity; good-for-nothing, ne'er-do-well; past praying for; unworthy, graceless; villainous, miscreant; improper, indecent 847 *vulgar*; immoral; unvirtuous, intemperate 951 *unchaste*; profligate, dissolute, abandoned; corrupt, debauched, depraved, perverted, degenerate, sick, rotten, rotten to the core; brutalized, brutal 898 *cruel*.

frail, infirm, feeble 163 *weak*; having one's foibles, having a touch of human frailty, human, only h.; easily tempted 661 *vulnerable*; not above temptation, not perfect, fallen 647 *imperfect*; slipping, sliding, recidivous.

heinous, grave, serious, deadly; abysmal, hellish, infernal; sinful, immoral, wicked 914 *wrong*; criminal, nefarious, felonious 954 *lawbreaking*; monstrous, flagrant, scandalous, shocking, outrageous, obscene; gross, foul, rank; base, vile, abominable, accursed; despicable 645 *bad*; blameworthy, culpable; reprehensible, indefensible, unjustifiable 916 *unwarranted*; atrocious, brutal 898 *cruel*; unforgivable, unpardonable, inexcusable.

Vb. *be wicked*, – vicious, – sinful etc. adj.; not be in a state of grace; fall from grace, spoil one's record, blot one's copybook, lapse, relapse, backslide; fall into evil ways, go to the bad *or* to the dogs 655 *deteriorate*; do wrong, transgress, misbehave, carry on, be naughty, sow one's wild oats, kick over the traces; trespass, offend, sin, commit s.; leave *or* stray from the straight and narrow, deviate from the paths of virtue, err, stray, slip, trip, stumble, fall.

make wicked, corrupt, deform one's character, brutalize 655 *pervert*; mislead, lead astray, seduce 612 *tempt*; set a bad example, dehumanize.

935 Innocence

N. *innocence*, guiltlessness, clean hands; clear conscience, irreproachability; nothing to confess; blamelessness, freedom from blame, every excuse; declared innocence 960 *acquittal*; inexperience, unworldliness 699 *artlessness*; playfulness, harmlessness, inoffensiveness; freedom from sin, unfallen state, saintliness, purity of heart, state of grace 933 *virtue*; undefilement 950 *purity*; incorruptibility 929 *probity*; impeccability 646 *perfection*; days of innocence, golden age 824 *happiness*.

innocent, Holy Innocents, babe, newborn babe, babe unborn, babes and sucklings; child, ingénue; lamb, dove; angel, pure soul; milksop,

goody-goody; one in the right, innocent party, injured p.

Adj. *innocent*, pure, unspotted, stainless, unblemished, spotless, immaculate 648 *clean*; uncorrupted, undefiled; unfallen, free from sin, unerring, impeccable 646 *perfect*; green, inexperienced, callow, naive, unversed in crime 491 *ignorant*; unworldly, guileless 699 *artless*; innocuous, harmless, inoffensive, playful, gentle, lamb-like, dove-like, child-like, angelic, saintly; wide-eyed, looking as if butter would not melt in one's mouth; innocent as a lamb *or* a dove, innocent as a babe unborn, innocent as a child; Arcadian.

guiltless, free from guilt, not responsible, not guilty 960 *acquitted*; more sinned against than sinning; falsely accused, wrongly a., misunderstood; cleanhanded, bloodless; blameless, faultless, unblameworthy, not culpable; irreproachable, above reproach, above suspicion; unobjectionable, unexceptionable, unimpeachable; pardonable, forgivable, excusable, venial.

Vb. *be innocent*, know no wrong; live in a state of grace, not fall from g. 933 *be virtuous*; have every excuse, have no need to blush, have clean hands, have a clear conscience, have nothing to be ashamed of, have nothing to confess; know no better.

936 Guilt

N. *guilt*, guiltiness, red-handedness; culpability; criminality, delinquency 954 *illegality*; sinfulness, original sin 934 *wickedness*; involvement, complicity, aiding and abetting; liability, one's fault; burden of guilt 702 *encumbrance*; blame, censure 924 *reproach*; guilt complex 503 *eccentricity*; guilty feelings, guilty conscience, bad c.; guilty behaviour, suspicious conduct, blush, stammer, embarrassment; confession 526 *disclosure*; twinge of conscience, remorse, shame 939 *penitence*.

guilty act, sin, deadly s., venial s. 934 *vice*; misdeed, wicked deed, misdoing, sinning, transgression, trespass, offence, crime 954 *illegality*; misdemeanour, felony; misconduct, misbehaviour, malpractice; unprofessional conduct; indiscretion, impropriety, peccadillo; naughtiness, scrape; lapse, slip, faux pas, blunder 495 *mistake*; omission, sin of o. 458 *negligence*; fault, failure, dereliction of duty 918 *undutifulness*; injustice, injury 914 *wrong*; enormity, atrocity, outrage 898 *cruel act*.

Adj. *guilty*, found g., convicted 961 *condemned*; suspected, blamed, censured 924 *disapproved*; responsible 180 *liable*; in the wrong, at fault, to blame, culpable, chargeable; reprehensible, censurable 924 *blameworthy*; deadly

934 *heinous*; trespassing, transgressing, sinful 934 *wicked*; criminal 954 *illegal*; red-handed, caught in the act, flagrante delicto, caught with one's pants *or* trousers down; caught with one's hand in the till; hangdog, sheepish, shame-faced, blushing, ashamed.

Vb. *be guilty*, be at fault, be in the wrong, be to blame; have crimes to answer for, have blood on one's hands; be caught in the act, be caught red-handed, be caught with one's hand in the till; have nothing to say for oneself, plead guilty 526 *confess*; have no excuse, stand condemned; trespass, transgress, sin 934 *be wicked*.

937 Good person

N. *good person*, sterling character; pillar of society, model of virtue, salt of the earth, shining light 646 *paragon*; Christian, true C.; saint 979 *pietist*; angel 935 *innocent*; heart of gold; good neighbour, Good Samaritan 903 *bene-factor*; one of the best, one in a million, the tops 890 *favourite*; hero, heroine 855 *brave person*; goody, good guy, good sort, good old boy, stout fellow, brick, trump, sport.

938 Bad person

N. *bad person*, no saint, sinner, hardened s., limb of Satan, Antichrist 904 *evildoer*; fallen angel, lost sheep, lost soul; reprobate, scape-grace, good-for-nothing, ne'er-do-well, black sheep, the despair of; scallywag, scamp; rake, roué, profligate 952 *libertine*; wanton, hussy 952 *loose woman*; wastrel, waster, prodigal son 815 *prodigal*; scum; nasty type, ugly customer, undesirable, bad 'un, wrong 'un, thug, bully, boot boy, bovver boy, hitman, terrorist, roughneck 904 *ruffian*; bad lot, bad egg, bad hat, bad character, bad guy, baddy, villain; rotten apple; bad influence, bad example; bad child, naughty c., terror, holy t., enfant terrible, monkey, little devil 663 *troublemaker*; knave, wretch, rascal, 869 *low fellow*; rogue, criminal 904 *offender*; thief, pirate, freebooter 789 *robber*; villain, black-guard, scoundrel, miscreant; cheat, liar, crook; impostor, twister, conman 545 *trickster*; sneak, grass, supergrass, squealer, canary, rat 524 *informer*; renegade, recreant 603 *tergiversator*; betrayer, traitor, Quisling, Judas.

cad, utter cad, nasty bit of work, scoundrel, blackguard; rotter, out-and-out r., blighter, bas-tard, bounder, jerk, heel, slob, scab, son of a bitch; stinker, skunk, dirty dog, filthy beast; per-vert, degenerate; swine, rat, worm; louse, insect, vermin; pig, beast, cat, bitch.

monster, unspeakable villain; brute, savage, sadist; ogre 735 *tyrant*; fiend, demon, ghoul 969 *devil*; hellhound, fury; devil incarnate, ape-man, King Kong, Frankenstein's monster, bogy.

939 Penitence

N. *penitence*, repentance, contrition, attrition, compunction, remorse, self-reproach 830 *regret*; confession 988 *Christian rite*; weight on one's mind, voice of conscience, uneasy c., guilty c., bad c., twinge of c. 936 *guilt*; deathbed repent-ance, sackcloth and ashes, stool of repentance 941 *penance*; apology 941 *atonement*.

penitent, confessor; returned prodigal, a sad-der and a wiser man; reformed character.

Adj. *repentant*, contrite, remorseful, regretful, sorry, apologetic 830 *regretting*; ashamed; weeping 836 *lamenting*; conscience-stricken, plagued by c.; self-condemned; confessing; peni-tent, doing penance 941 *atoning*; chastened, sob-ered; reclaimed, reformed, converted, born again.

Vb. *be penitent*, repent, show compunction, feel remorse, feel shame, blush for s., feel sorry, say one is s., express regrets, apologize; reproach oneself, blame o.; go to confession 526 *confess*; do penance, repent in sackcloth and ashes 941 *atone*; bewail one's sins; beat one's breast, prostrate oneself; eat humble pie 721 *knuckle under*; rue, have regrets, wish undone 830 *regret*; have second thoughts, think better of; learn one's lesson, find out from bitter experience 536 *learn*; reform, be reformed, be a reformed character, be reclaimed, turn over a new leaf 654 *get better*; see the light, see the error of one's ways, be converted, return to the straight and narrow 147 *be turned to*.

940 Impenitence

N. *impenitence*, lack of contrition; refusal to recant, obduracy, stubbornness 602 *obstinacy*; hardness of heart 326 *hardness*; no apologies, no regrets, no remorse, no compunction 906 *pitilessness*; hardened sinner, despair of 938 *bad person*.

Adj. *impenitent*, unregretting; obdurate, invet-erate, stubborn 602 *obstinate*; unrepentant; without regrets; unrelenting, relentless; with-out compunction, without remorse, remorse-less, heartless 898 *cruel*; hard, hardened; conscienceless, unashamed, unblushing, brazen; incorrigible, irreclaimable, irredeem-able, hopeless, despaired of, lost 934 *wicked*; unshriven; unreformed, unreconciled; uncon-verted.

Vb. *be impenitent*, make no excuses, offer no apologies, have no regrets, not wish things otherwise, would do it again; not see the light, not see the error of one's ways, refuse to recant 602 *be obstinate*; make no confession; stay unrec-onciled, want no forgiveness; feel no compunc-tion, feel no remorse, harden one's heart, steel one's h. 906 *be pitiless*.

941 Atonement

N. *atonement*, making amends, amends, apology, satisfaction; reparation, compensation, indemnity, indemnification, blood money, conscience money 787 *restitution*; repayment, quits.

propitiation, expiation, satisfaction, reconciliation, conciliation 719 *pacification*; reclamation, redemption; sacrifice, offering, burnt o., peace o. 981 *oblation*; scapegoat, whipping boy 150 *substitute*.

penance, shrift, confession, acknowledgment 939 *penitence*; sacrament of penance, fasting, flagellation 945 *asceticism*; purgation; purgatory; penitent form, stool of repentance, cutty stool, corner 964 *pillory*; sackcloth and ashes, breast-beating 836 *lamentation*.

Adj. *atoning*, making amends 939 *repentant*; reparatory, compensatory, indemnificatory; conciliatory, apologetic; expiatory, purgatorial; sacrificial; penitential, penitentiary, doing penance 963 *punitive*.

Vb. *atone*, salve one's conscience, make amends, make reparation, indemnify, compensate, pay compensation, make it up to; apologize, make apologies, offer one's a.; propitiate, conciliate 719 *pacify*; give satisfaction, offer s. 787 *restitute*; make up for, make *or* put matters right; sacrifice to, offer sacrifice; expiate, pay the penalty, pay the forfeit, pay the cost; become the whipping boy, make oneself the scapegoat 931 *be disinterested*.

do penance, undergo p.; pray, fast, flagellate oneself, scourge o.; suffer purgatory; put on sackcloth and ashes, don a hair shirt, rend one's garments, stand in the corner, sit on the stool of repentance; take one's punishment, swallow one's medicine 963 *be punished*; salve one's conscience, go to confession 526 *confess*.

942 Temperance

N. *temperance*, temperateness, nothing in excess 177 *moderation*; self-denial 931 *disinterestedness*; self-restraint, self-control, self-discipline, keeping a stiff upper lip, stoicism 747 *restraint*; continence, chastity 950 *purity*; soberness 948 *sobriety*; forbearance 620 *avoidance*; renunciation 621 *relinquishment*; abstemiousness, abstinence, abstention, total abstinence, teetotalism; prohibition, prohibitionism 747 *restriction*; vegetarianism, veganism; dieting 946 *fasting*; frugality 814 *economy*; plain living, simple life, self-sufficiency, getting away from it all; frugal diet 945 *asceticism*.

abstainer, total a., teetotaller 948 *sober person*; prohibitionist; nonsmoker; vegetarian, vegan, demi-veg; dropout, dieter, faster; Spartan 945 *ascetic*.

Adj. *temperate*, not excessive, within bounds, within reasonable limits; tempered 177 *moderate*; plain, Spartan, sparing 814 *economical*; frugal 816 *parsimonious*; forbearing, abstemious, abstinent; dry, teetotal 948 *sober*; vegan, vegetarian, not self-indulgent, self-controlled, self-disciplined, continent 747 *restrained*; chaste 950 *pure*; self-denying 945 *ascetic*.

Vb. *be temperate*, – moderate etc. adj.; moderate, temper, keep within bounds, avoid excess, know when one has had enough, know when to stop; keep sober 948 *be sober*; forbear, refrain, abstain 620 *avoid*; control oneself, contain o. 747 *restrain*; deny oneself 945 *be ascetic*; take the pledge, go on the wagon; give up, swear off; ration oneself, restrict o., tighten one's belt, draw in one's b. 946 *starve*; diet, go on a d. 206 *make thin*.

943 Intemperance

N. *intemperance*, immoderation, abandon; excess, excessiveness, luxury 637 *redundance*; too much 637 *superfluity*; wastefulness, extravagance, profligacy, waste 815 *prodigality*; indiscipline, incontinence 734 *laxity*; indulgence, self-i., overindulgence; addiction, bad habit 610 *habit*; drug habit 949 *drug-taking*; high living, dissipation, licentiousness, debauchery 944 *sensualism*; overeating 947 *gluttony*; intoxication.

Adj. *intemperate*, immoderate, excessive 637 *redundant*; unlimited 635 *plentiful*; wasteful, extravagant, profligate, spendthrift 815 *prodigal*; luxurious 637 *superfluous*; hedonistic, indulgent, self-i., overindulgent, denying oneself nothing; unrestrained, uncontrolled, lacking self-control, undisciplined; incontinent 951 *unchaste*.

Vb. *be intemperate*, – immoderate etc. adj.; roll in, luxuriate, wallow; lack self-control, want discipline, lose control 734 *be lax*; deny oneself nothing, indulge oneself, give oneself up to; kick over the traces, have one's fling, sow one's wild oats 815 *be prodigal*; run to excess, run riot, exceed 306 *overstep*; observe no limits, go to any lengths, stick at nothing, not know when to stop, overindulge, burn the candle at both ends 634 *waste*; live it up, go on a spree, go on a binge, go on a bender 837 *revel*; drink like a fish, drink to excess, be a heavy drinker 949 *get drunk*; eat to excess, gorge, overeat, binge, make oneself sick 947 *gluttonize*; be incontinent, grow dissipated 951 *be impure*.

944 Sensualism

N. *sensualism*, earthiness, materialism 319 *materiality*; sensuality, carnality, sexuality, the flesh; grossness, beastliness, bestiality, wallowing; craze for excitement 822 *excitability*; love of pleasure, search for p., hedonism, epicurism, epicureanism 376 *pleasure*; voluptuousness, voluptuosity, softness, luxuriousness, dolce vita; luxury, lap of l. 637 *superfluity*; full life, life of pleasure, high living, fast l., wine, women and song 824 *enjoyment*; dissipation, abandon 943 *intemperance*; licentiousness, dissoluteness, debauchery 951 *impurity*; indulgence, self-i., overindulgence, greediness 947 *gluttony*; eating and drinking 301 *feasting*; bingeing, orgy, Bacchanalia 837 *revel*.

sensualist, pig, swine, hog, wallower; hedonist, playboy *or* -girl, pleasure-lover, thrill-seeker; luxury-lover, epicurean, bon vivant, bon viveur; epicure, gourmet, gourmand 947 *glutton*; hard drinker 949 *drunkard*; loose liver, profligate, rake 952 *libertine*; drug addict 949 *drugtaking*; degenerate, decadent.

Adj. *sensual*, earthy, gross, unspiritual 319 *material*; fleshly, carnal, bodily; sexual, venereal 887 *erotic*; bestial, beastly, brutish, swinish, hoggish, wallowing; pleasure-giving 826 *pleasurable*; voluptuous, pleasure-loving, thrill-seeking, living for kicks; hedonistic, epicurean, luxury-loving, luxurious; pampered, indulged, spoilt, self-i., overindulged, featherbedded; overfed 947 *gluttonous*; high-living, fast-l., incontinent 943 *intemperate*; licentious, dissipated, debauched 951 *impure*; riotous, orgiastic, bingeing, Bacchanalian 949 *drunken*.

Vb. *be sensual*, – voluptuous etc. adj.; live for pleasure, wallow in luxury, live off the fat of the land 730 *prosper*; indulge oneself, pamper o., spoil o., do oneself proud; run riot, live in the fast lane, burn the candle at both ends 943 *be intemperate*.

945 Asceticism
N. *asceticism*, austerity, mortification, flagellation 941 *penance*; ascetic practice, yoga; anchoritism 883 *seclusion*; holy poverty 801 *poverty*; plain living, simple fare, Spartan fare 946 *fasting*; fast day 946 *fast*; self-denial 942 *temperance*; frugality 814 *economy*; Puritanism, sackcloth, hair shirt.

ascetic, yogi, fakir, dervish, fire-walker; hermit, anchorite, recluse 883 *solitary*; flagellant 939 *penitent*; faster 942 *abstainer*; Puritan, Plymouth Brethren.

Adj. *ascetic*, yogic, self-mortifying, fasting, flagellating; hermit-like, anchoretic; puritanical; austere, rigorous 735 *severe*; Spartan.

Vb. *be ascetic*, live like a Spartan, live the simple life; fast 946 *starve*; live like a hermit, wear a hair shirt, put on sackcloth; lie on nails, walk through fire.

946 Fasting
N. *fasting*, abstinence from food; no appetite, anorexia, a. nervosa 651 *ill health*; cutting down

301 *dieting*; strict fast, hunger strike; lenten fare, bread and water, meagre diet, starvation d.; iron rations, short commons 636 *scarcity*; no food, starvation 859 *hunger*.

fast, fast day, Good Friday, Lent, Ramadan; day of abstinence; hunger strike 145 *strike*.

Adj. *fasting*, not eating, off one's food; abstinent 942 *temperate*; on hunger strike; without food, unfed, empty, with an empty stomach, supperless; poorly fed, half-starved 636 *underfed*; starved, starving, famished, famishing, ravenous, wasting away 206 *lean*; wanting food 859 *hungry*.

Vb. *starve*, famish 859 *be hungry*; waste with hunger, be a bag of bones; have no food, have nothing to eat, live on water, live on air 801 *be poor*; fast, go without food, abstain from f., eat no meat; keep Lent, keep Ramadan; give up eating, refuse one's food, go on hunger strike; eat less, diet, go on a d., go on a crash d., reduce, take off weight 37 *abate*; tighten one's belt, go on short commons, live on iron rations; eat sparingly, make a little go a long way, control one's appetite 942 *be temperate*; keep a poor table 816 *be parsimonious*.

947 Gluttony
N. *gluttony*, greediness, greed, insatiability, voracity, voraciousness, wolfishness, hoggishness, piggishness; insatiable appetite 859 *hunger*; good living, high l., indulgence, overeating, overfeeding 943 *intemperance*; guzzling, gorging, bingeing, gormandizing, gluttonizing, epicureanism, epicurism, foodism, pleasures of the table 301 *gastronomy*; bust, binge, blowout, masses of food, groaning table 301 *feasting*.

glutton, glutton for food, guzzler, gormandizer, bolter, gorger, crammer, stuffer, binger; locust, wolf, vulture, cormorant, pig, hog; trencherman *or* -woman, good eater, hearty e. 301 *eater*; greedy-guts, greedy pig; gourmand, gastronome, gourmet, epicure, bon vivant, bon viveur.

Adj. *gluttonous*, greedy; devouring, voracious, wolfish; omnivorous 464 *indiscriminating*; insatiable, never full 859 *hungry*; eating one's fill 301 *feeding*; guzzling, gorging, bingeing, stuffing, cramming, licking one's lips, licking one's chops, drooling, watering at the mouth; gastronomic, epicurean.

Vb. *gluttonize*, guzzle, bolt, wolf, gobble, gobble up, devour, gulp down; fill oneself, gorge, cram, stuff, binge; overeat 301 *eat*; eat one's head off, eat out of house and home; have a good appetite, be a good trencherman *or* -woman; eat like a trooper, eat like a horse, eat like a pig, have eyes bigger than one's stomach; make oneself sick; tickle one's palate; lick one's lips, lick one's chops, water at the mouth, drool at the sight of food; keep a good table; like one's food, live to eat, not eat to live, live only for eating.

948 Sobriety

N. *sobriety*, soberness 942 *temperance*; teetotalism; clear head, unfuddled brain, no hangover; dry area.

sober person, moderate drinker; teetotaller, total abstainer 942 *abstainer*; temperance society, Alcoholics Anonymous; prohibitionist.

Adj. *sober*, abstinent, abstemious; off drink, drying out, on the wagon; teetotal, strictly TT, prohibitionist, dry; clearheaded, with a clear head, sober as a judge, stone-cold sober, sobered up, without a hangover; dried out, off the bottle.

Vb. *be sober*, – abstemious, etc. adj.; not drink, never touch drink, drink moderately 942 *be temperate*; give up drinking, dry out, come off (drugs), go on the wagon, give up alcohol, become teetotal, sign the pledge; go dry; hold one's liquor, keep a clear head, be sober as a judge; sober up, clear one's head, sleep it off.

949 Drunkenness. Drug-taking

N. *drunkenness*, excessive drinking 943 *intemperance*; insobriety; weakness for liquor, fondness for the bottle; Dutch courage 855 *courage*; intoxication, inebriation; thick speech, slurred s. 580 *speech defect*; tipsiness, wooziness, staggering 317 *oscillation*; getting drunk, one for the road, one over the eight, drop too much, hard drinking; libations; hair of the dog that bit one; booze, liquor 301 *alcoholic drink, wine*; drinking bout, jag, lush, blind, binge, spree, bender, pub-crawl.

crapulence, crapulousness; morning after the night before, hangover, thick head, sick headache.

alcoholism, alcoholic addiction, alcohol abuse, dipsomania; delirium tremens, dt's, the horrors, heebiejeebies, jimjams, pink elephants.

drug-taking, drug abuse, drug addiction, drug dependence, drug habit, habit, substance abuse 943 *intemperance.*, smoking, snorting, freebasing, sniffing, glue-s., hitting up, shooting up, injecting, main-lining; pill-popping, chasing the dragon.

drug, hard drug, soft d., recreational d., drugs, substance, illegal s.; joint, reefer, spliff, roach; shot, fix; narcotic, dope, designer drug; nicotine 388 *tobacco*; cannabis, marijuana, ganja, hemp, hashish, hash, bhang, kef, pot, grass, Acapulco gold, sensemillia; cocaine, coke, basuer, basuker, snowy crack, rock, free-base, heroin, horme, junk, smack, scag, black bar, candy, nose candy,

dogfood, gumball, Mexican mud, trotsie role; methadone; downers; barbiturates, barbs, morphia, morphine, opium 658 *drug*; stimulant, pep pill, amphetamine, speed, purple hearts, dexies, uppers 821 *excitant*; performance-enhancing drug; intoxicant, hallucinogen, LSD, lysergic acid diethylamide, acid, Ecstasy, MDHA, phencyclidine, PCP, angel dust, mescalin, peyote, magic mushroom, drug addiction (**see** *drug-taking*); trip (**see** *drug experience*); drug-selling, drug-pushing (**see** *drug-peddler*); narcoterrorism; action against drugs, drug czar.

drug-taker, drug-user, user, drug addict, dope fiend, freak, head, acid-head, coke-head, base-head, junkie, mainliner, acid-scorer, drug-scorer. (**See** *drug-peddler*.)

drug-peddler, drug-dealer, drug-pusher, pusher, dope-peddler, drug-baron, drug-carrier, mule, stuffer; drug traffic; narco-terrorism.

drug experience, trip, acid t., bad t., freak-out; drying-out, withdrawal symptoms, cold turkey, bogue.

drunkard, drunk, sot, lush; slave to drink, wino, alcoholic, recovering alcoholic, dipsomaniac, dipso; drinker, social d., hard d., secret d.; tippler, toper, boozer, swiller, old soak; tosspot, barfly; pub-crawler.

Adj. *drunk*, inebriated, intoxicated, under the influence, having had a drop too much; in one's cups, in liquor, the worse for l.; half-seas over, three sheets to the wind, one over the eight; boozed up, ginned up, liquored up, lit up, flushed, merry, happy, high; full, fou, tanked up, bevvied up; roaring drunk, drunk and disorderly 61 *disorderly*.

tipsy, tiddly, squiffy, tight, half-cut, pissed, Brahms and Liszt; well-oiled, pickled, canned, bottled, stewed, well-lubricated; pixilated, fuddled; maudlin; tired and emotional, drunken, boozy, muzzy, woozy; pie-eyed; reeling, staggering; hiccupping.

dead drunk, smashed, sloshed, sozzled, soaked, soused, plastered; stinko, stoned; blind drunk, blind, blotto; legless, paralytic, stocious; in a drunken stupor; under the table; drunk as a lord; pissed as a newt, fou as a coot, fou as a wulk, etc.

crapulous, crapulent, with a hangover, with a thick head; dizzy, giddy, sick.

drugged, doped, high, zonked, spaced out, freaked o., in a trance; stoned 375 *insensible*; turned on, hooked on drugs, addicted.

drunken, never sober; gin-sodden; boozy, beery; fond of a drink, having a drink problem; tippling, boozing, toping, swilling, hard-drinking; pub-crawling; gouty, given to drink, a slave to d., addicted to d., on the bottle, alcoholic, dipsomaniac.

intoxicating, inebriating; exhilarating, going to the head, heady, winy, like wine 821 *exciting*; stimulant, intoxicant; opiate, narcotic; hallucinatory, psychedelic, psychotropic, mind-bending, mind-blowing; addictive, habit-forming; alcoholic, spirituous, vinous, beery; hard, potent, double-strength, overproof 162 *strong*; neat 44 *unmixed*.

Vb. *be drunk*, – tipsy etc. adj.; be under the influence of liquor, be under the influence, have had too much, have had one too many; have a weak head, not hold one's liquor, not walk straight, lurch, stagger, reel 317 *oscillate*.

get drunk, have too much, have one over the eight, drink like a fish; liquor up, tank up, crack a bottle, knock back a few, bend one's elbow, lush, bib, tipple, fuddle, booze, tope, swill, souse, hit the bottle 301 *drink*; go on the spree, go on a blind *or* a bender, go pub-crawling; drown one's sorrows; quaff, carouse, wassail.

drug oneself, smoke, sniff, snort, inject oneself, shoot, mainline; turn on, take a trip, blow one's mind; freak out.

950 Purity

N. *purity*, faultlessness 646 *perfection*; innocence; moral purity, morals, morality 933 *virtue*; decency, propriety, delicacy 846 *good taste*; shame, bashfulness 874 *modesty*; chastity 942 *temperance*; frigidity 820 *moral insensibility*; honour, one's h.; virginity, maidenhood, maidenhead 895 *celibacy*; prudery, prudishness; false modesty 874 *modesty*; demureness, gravity 834 *seriousness*; priggishness, primness, coyness 850 *affectation*; sanctimoniousness 979 *pietism*; Puritanism; euphemism, Grundyism, genteelism, mealy-mouthedness; censorship, expurgation, bowdlerization 550 *obliteration*.

virgin, maiden, vestal virgin, virgo intacta, maid, old maid, spinster 895 *celibate*; religious celibate 986 *monk*, *nun*; virtuous woman.

prude, prig, Victorian, euphemist; Puritan, wowser; guardian of morality, censor, Watch Committee, Mrs Grundy.

Adj. *pure*, faultless 646 *perfect*; undefiled, unfallen 935 *innocent*; maidenly, virgin, virginal, vestal, untouched; modest; coy, shy; chaste 942 *temperate*; impregnable, incorruptible 929 *honourable*; frigid 380 *cold*; immaculate, spotless, snowy 427 *white*; good, moral 933 *virtuous*; Platonic, purified; decent, decorous, delicate, refined 846 *tasteful*; censored, bowdlerized, expurgated.

prudish, squeamish, shockable, Victorian; prim 850 *affected*; straitlaced, narrow-minded, puritan, priggish; holy, sanctimonious 979 *pietistic*.

951 Impurity

N. *impurity*, impure thoughts, filthiness, defilement 649 *uncleanness*; indelicacy 847 *bad taste*; indecency, immodesty, shamelessness, exhibitionism; coarseness, grossness, nastiness; ribaldry, bawdiness, salaciousness; blue joke; double entendre; smut, dirt, filth, obscenity, obscene literature, adult l., erotic l., erotica; pornography, hard-core p., porn, soft porn, page 3, girlie magazine; blue film, skin flick, video nasty; prurience.

unchastity, promiscuity, wantonness; easy virtue, amorality; permissive society 734 *laxity*; vice, immorality; prurience, lust 859 *libido*; carnality, sexuality, eroticism, the flesh 944 *sensualism*; sexiness, lasciviousness, lewdness, salacity, lubricity; dissoluteness, dissipation, debauchery, licentiousness, licence, libertinism; seduction, defloration; lechery, fornication; womanizing, whoring, screwing around, sleeping a.; harlotry, whorishness.

illicit love, unlawful desires, forbidden fruit; extramarital relations; incest; perversion, pederasty, buggery, sodomy, bestiality; satyriasis, priapism, nymphomania; adultery, unfaithfulness, infidelity, marital i., cuckolding, cuckoldry; eternal triangle, liaison, intrigue, amour, seduction 887 *love affair*; free love, living together; wife-swapping.

rape, ravishment, violation, indecent assault, grope; date rape, acquaintance r., drug r., gang bang; sexual abuse, sex crime.

social evil, harlotry, whoredom; oldest profession, Mrs Warren's p.; streetwalking, prostitution, soliciting, hooking; indecent exposure, exposing oneself, flashing; pimping, pandering, brothel-keeping, living on immoral earnings, white slave traffic; vice squad.

brothel, bordello, whorehouse, bawdyhouse, cathouse, disorderly h., h. of ill fame, h. of ill repute; knocking-shop; red-light district, tolerance zone.

Adj. *impure*, defiled, unclean; unwholesome 653 *insalubrious*; vulgar, coarse, gross; ribald, loose; strong, racy, bawdy, Rabelaisian; uncensored, unexpurgated, unbowdlerized; suggestive, provocative, piquant, titillating, near the knuckle, near the bone; spicy; immoral, risqué, nudge-nudge wink-wink; naughty, wicked, blue; unmentionable, unquotable, unprintable; smutty, filthy, scatological, offensive; indecent, obscene, lewd, salacious; licentious, pornographic; prurient, erotic, priapic; sexual, sexy, hot.

unchaste, unvirtuous 934 *vicious*; fallen, seduced; of easy virtue, of loose morals, amoral, immoral; light, wanton, loose, fast, naughty; wild, rackety; immodest, daring, revealing;

unblushing, shameless, brazen, flaunting, scarlet, meretricious, whorish, tarty; promiscuous, sleeping around, screwing a.; street-walking, on the game.

lecherous, carnal; libidinous, lustful, goatish; prurient; on *or* in heat, rutting; turned-on, hot, randy; oversexed, sex-mad, sex-crazy, nymphomaniac; perverted, bestial; lewd, licentious, libertine; depraved, debauched, dissolute, dissipated, profligate 934 *vicious*.

Vb. *be impure*, – unchaste etc. adj.; have no morals; be unfaithful, commit adultery, cuckold; be dissipated 943 *be intemperate*; fornicate, womanize, whore, keep a mistress, have a lover; lech, lust, rut, be on heat, be hot, have the hots 859 *desire*; be promiscuous, sleep around, screw a.; become a prostitute, become a hooker, become a rent-boy, street-walk, be on the streets; pimp, pander, procure, keep a brothel.

debauch, defile, smirch 649 *make unclean*; proposition, seduce, lead astray; have one's way with; dishonour, deflower, disgrace 867 *shame*; prostitute, make a whore of; lay, screw, knock off, bed, go to bed with, lie with, sleep w. 45 *unite with*; rape, ravish, violate, molest, abuse, interfere with, assault, indecently a., sexually abuse.

952 Libertine

N. *libertine*, philanderer, flirt; free-lover, fast man *or* woman, gay dog, rip, rake, roué, debauchee 944 *sensualist*; lady-killer, gallant; fancy-man, gigolo, sugar daddy; seducer, deceiver, gay d., Lothario; corespondent, adulterer; cuckolder, bed-hopper, wife-swapper; Don Juan, Casanova; wolf, kerb-crawler; womanizer, fornicator, stud; whoremonger, whoremaster; voyeur, lecher, flasher, satyr, goat, dirty old man, DOM; sex maniac; rapist; male prostitute, rent-boy; pederast, sodomite, pervert 84 *nonconformist*.

loose woman, wanton, easy lay, anybody's; fast woman, sexpot, hot stuff; woman of easy virtue, one no better than she should be; flirt; bit, bint, wench, floozy, jade, hussy, minx, nymphet, sex kitten, Lolita, groupie; baggage, trash, trollop, slut; tart, chippy, scrubber, slapper, pickup; vamp, adventuress, temptress. seductress, femme fatale, scarlet woman, painted w.; Jezebel, Delilah; adultress, other woman; nymphomaniac, nympho.

kept woman, fancy w., mistress, paramour, concubine; bit of fluff, bit on the side, floozie, doxy, moll.

prostitute, pro; white slave, fallen woman; harlot, trollop, whore, strumpet; streetwalker, woman of the streets, broad, hustler, hooker, scrubber, slapper, pickup, callgirl; courtesan; male prostitute, rent-boy, gigolo.

bawd, go-between, pimp, ponce, pander, procurer, procuress, brothel-keeper, madam; white slaver.

953 Legality

N. *legality*, due process 959 *litigation*; letter of the law, four corners of the l.; respect for law, constitutionalism; judgment according to the law 480 *judgment*; keeping within the law, lawfulness, legitimateness, legitimacy, validity.

legislation, legislature, legislatorship, lawgiving, law-making, constitution-m.; legalization, legitimization, validation, ratification, confirmation 532 *affirmation*; passing into law, enacting, enactment, regulation; plebiscite 605 *vote*; law, statute, ordinance, order, bylaw 737 *decree*; canon, rule, edict 693 *precept*.

law, the law; body of law, constitution, written c., unwritten c.; charter, institution; statute book, legal code; Ten Commandments, penal code, civil c., Napoleonic c.; written law, common l., unwritten l., natural l.; canon law, ecclesiastical l.; international law, law of nations, law of the sea, law of the air; cyberlaw; law of commerce, commercial law, law of contract, criminal law, civil l., constitutional l., law of the land; arm of the law, legal process 955 *jurisdiction*; writ, summons, lawsuit 959 *legal trial*.

Adj. *legal*, lawful 913 *just*; law-abiding 739 *obedient*; legitimate, competent; licit, licensed, permissible, allowable; within the law, sanctioned by law, according to l., legally sound; statutory, constitutional; law-giving, legislative; legislated, enacted, passed, voted, made law, ordained, decreed, ordered, by order; legalized, legitimized, decriminalized, brought within the law; actionable; pertaining to law, jurisprudential.

Vb. *be legal*, – legitimate etc. adj.; stand up in law *or* court; come within the law, keep within the l., stay the right side of the l.

make legal, legalize, legitimize, decriminalize, validate, confirm, ratify, formalize 488 *endorse*; vest, establish 153 *stabilize*; legislate, make laws, give l.; pass, enact, ordain, enforce 737 *decree*.

954 Illegality

N. *illegality*, legal flaw, loophole, let-out, irregularity, error of law; wrong verdict, bad judgment 481 *misjudgment*; contradictory law; miscarriage of justice 914 *injustice*; wrong side of the law, unlawfulness; incompetence, illicitness, illegitimacy 757 *prohibition*.

lawbreaking, breach of law, violation of l., transgression, contravention, infringement, encroachment 306 *overstepping*; trespass, offence, offence against the law, civil wrong; malpractice; dishonesty 930 *improbity*; criminality 936 *guilt*; criminal activity, criminal offence, indictable o., crime, capital c., misdemeanour, felony; wrongdoing 914 *wrong*; criminology.

lawlessness, outlawry; breakdown of law and order, crime wave 734 *anarchy*; summary justice, vigilantism; kangaroo court, gang rule, mob law, lynch l.; riot, race r., rioting, hooliganism, ruffianism, rebellion 738 *revolt*; coup d'état, usurpation 916 *arrogation*; arbitrary rule, abolition of law; martial law; mailed fist, jackboot 735 *brute force*.

bastardy, bar *or* bend *or* baton sinister; bastardization, illegitimacy; bastard, illegitimate child, natural c., love c., by-blow.

Adj. *illegal*, illegitimate, illicit; contraband, black-market, hot; impermissible, verboten 757 *prohibited*; unauthorized, incompetent, without authority, unwarrantable, informal, unofficial; unlawful, wrongful 914 *wrong*; unlegislated, exceeding the l.; unchartered, unconstitutional, unstatutory; suspended, null and void, nullified, annulled; irregular; extrajudicial; on the wrong side of the law, against the l.; outside the law, outwith the l., outlawed, out of bounds; actionable, punishable.

lawbreaking, trespassing, transgressing, infringing, encroaching; sinning 934 *wicked*; offending 936 *guilty*; criminal, felonious; fraudulent, shady 930 *dishonest*.

lawless, chaotic; ungovernable, licentious; violent, summary; arbitrary, irresponsible, unanswerable, unaccountable; without legal backing, unofficial, cowboy; above the law; despotic, tyrannical 735 *oppressive*.

bastard, illegitimate, spurious; born out of wedlock, born on the wrong side of the blanket; without a father, without a name, without benefit of clergy; bastardized.

Vb. *be illegal*, be against the law, break the law; circumvent the l.; be lawless, defy the law, drive a coach and horses through the l. 914 *do wrong*; take the law into one's own hands, exceed one's authority, encroach; stand above the law; stand outside the law.

make illegal, – unlawful etc. adj.; outlaw; criminalize 757 *prohibit*; forbid by law, penalize 963 *punish*; bastardize; suspend, annul, cancel, make the law a dead letter 752 *abrogate*.

955 Jurisdiction

N. *jurisdiction*, portfolio 622 *function*; judicature, magistracy, commission of the peace; mayoralty; competence, legal c., legal authority, arm of the law 733 *authority*; administration of justice, legal administration, Home Office; local authority, corporation, municipality, county council, regional c., district c.,

parish c., community c., bailiwick 692 *council*; vigilance committee, watch c. 956 *tribunal*; office, bureau, secretariat 687 *workshop*; legal authority, competence, cognizance 751 *mandate*.

law officer, legal administrator, Lord Chancellor, Attorney General, Lord Advocate, Solicitor General, Queen's Proctor; Crown Counsel, public prosecutor; judge advocate, procurator fiscal, district attorney 957 *judge*; mayor, lord m., provost, lord p., sheriff 733 *position of authority*; court officer, clerk of the court, bailiff; summoner, Bow Street runner; beadle, macebearer 690 *official*.

police, forces of law and order, long arm of the law; police force, the force, the fuzz, Old Bill, the boys in blue; Scotland Yard; constabulary, gendarmerie, military police, transport p.; police officer, limb of the law, policeman *or* – woman, constable, community policeman, special c., copper, cop, traffic c., patrolman *or* – woman; bobby, flatfoot, rozzer, pig, smokey bear, flic; police sergeant, police inspector, police superintendent, commissioner of police, chief constable, provost marshal; watch, posse comitatus; special patrol group, SPG; plainclothes man, dick 459 *detective*.

956 Tribunal

N. *tribunal*, seat of justice, woolsack, throne; judgment seat, bar; confessional, Judgment Day; forum 692 *council*; public opinion, vox populi, electorate; judicatory, bench, board, bench of judges, panel of j., judge and jury; judicial assembly; Justices of the Peace.

lawcourt, court, open c.; court of law, court of justice, criminal court, civil c.; Federal Court, High Court, Court of Justiciary; Sheriff C., District Court, County Court; Supreme Court, appellate court, Court of Appeal; Court of Exchequer, Star Chamber; House of Lords 692 *parliament*; High Court of Justice, Queen's Bench, Queen's Bench Division, Court of Criminal Appeal; Admiralty Division; Probate Court, Divorce C.; Court of Chancery, court of equity, c. of arbitration; Court of Common Pleas; circuit court; assizes; Court of Session, sessions, quarter s., petty s.; Central Criminal Court, Old Bailey; magistrate's court, juvenile c., police c.; coroner's court; court of record, feudal c., manorial c., Stannary C., court baron, court leet; guild court, hustings; court-martial, summary court.

957 Judge

N. *judge*, justice, your Lordship, my lud, m'lud; justiciary, Lord Chancellor, Lord Chief Justice, Master of the Rolls, Lords of Appeal; military judge, Judge Advocate General; chief justice, puisné judge, county court j., recorder, Common Serjeant; sessions judge, assize j., circuit j.; district judge, subordinate j.; sheriff, sheriff substitute; magistrate, district m., city m., police m., stipendiary m.; coroner; honorary magistrate, justice of the peace, JP; bench, judiciary; hanging judge.

magistracy, the beak, his *or* her Worship, his *or* her Honour, his nibs, her nibs; arbiter, umpire, referee, assessor, arbitrator, Ombudsman 480 *estimator*; Recording Angel 549 *recorder*; Solomon, Daniel come to judgment.

jury, twelve good men and true; grand jury, special j., common j., petty j., trial j., coroner's j.; rigged j.; hung j.; juror's panel, jury list; juror, juryman *or* -woman, jurat; foreman *or* forewoman of the jury.

958 Lawyer

N. *lawyer*, legal practitioner, solicitor, member of the legal profession, man *or* woman of law; civil lawyer, criminal l.; one called to the bar, barrister, barrister-at-law, devil, advocate, counsel, learned c.; junior barrister, junior counsel; senior barrister, bencher, bencher of the Inns of Court; silk, leading counsel, King's C., K.C., Queen's C., Q.C.; serjeant, serjeant-at-law; circuit barrister; Philadelphia lawyer 696 *expert*; shyster, pettifogger, crooked lawyer.

law agent, attorney, public a., attorney at law, proctor, procurator; Writer to the Signet, solicitor before the Supreme Court; solicitor, legal adviser; legal representative, legal agent, pleader, advocate; conveyancer.

notary, notary public, commissioner for oaths; scrivener, petition-writer; clerk of the court 955 *law officer*; solicitor's clerk, barrister's c., barrister's devil.

jurist, legal adviser, legal expert; pundit, legalist; student of law.

bar, civil b., criminal b., English bar, Scottish b., junior b., senior b.; Inns of Chancery, Inns of Court, Gray's I., Lincoln's I., Inner Temple, Middle T.; barristership, advocacy.

Vb. *do law*, study l., go in for l., take up l.; be called to the bar; take silk; practise at the bar, accept a brief, take a case, advocate, plead; practise law; devil.

959 Litigation

N. *litigation*, going to law, litigiousness 709 *quarrelsomeness*; legal dispute 709 *quarrel*; issue, legal i.; lawsuit, suit at law, suit, case, cause, action; prosecution, arraignment, impeachment, charge 928 *accusation*; test case 461 *experiment*; claim, counter c. 915 *dueness*; plea, petition 761 *request*; affidavit, written state-

ment, averment, pleading, demurrer 532 *affirmation*.

legal process, proceedings, legal procedure, arm of the law 955 *jurisdiction*; citation, subpoena, summons, search warrant 737 *warrant*; arrest, apprehension, detention, committal 747 *restraint*; habeas corpus, bail, surety, security; injunction; writ.

legal trial, trial, justice seen to be done; trial by law, trial by jury, trial at the bar, trial in court, assize, sessions 956 *lawcourt*; inquest, inquisition, examination 459 *enquiry*; hearing, prosecution, defence; hearing of evidence, taking of e., recording of e. 466 *evidence*; examination, cross-e., objection sustained, objection overruled 466 *testimony*; pleadings, arguments 475 *reasoning*; counterargument, rebutter, rebuttal 460 *rejoinder*; proof 478 *demonstration*; disproof 479 *confutation*; summing-up, charge to the jury; ruling, finding, decision, verdict 480 *judgment*; majority verdict, hung jury; favourable verdict 960 *acquittal*; unfavourable verdict 961 *condemnation*; execution of judgment 963 *punishment*; appeal, motion of a.; successful appeal, reversal of judgment, retrial; precedent, case law; law reports; case record, dossier 548 *record*.

litigant, litigator, party, party to a suit, suitor 763 *petitioner*; claimant, plaintiff, pursuer, defendant, appellant, respondent, objector, intervener; accused, prisoner at the bar 928 *accused person*; prosecutor 928 *accuser*.

Vb. *litigate*, go to law, appeal to l., set the law in motion, institute legal proceedings, bring a suit, file a s., petition 761 *request*; prepare a brief, brief counsel; file a claim, contest at law 915 *claim*; have the law on one, take one to court, haul before the c., have one up, sue, arraign, impeach, accuse, charge, prefer charges, press c. 928 *indict*; cite, summon, serve notice on; prosecute, put on trial, bring to justice, bring to trial; call evidence 475 *argue*.

try a case, put down for hearing; call witnesses, examine, cross-examine, take statements; sit in judgment, rule, find, decide, adjudicate 480 *judge*; sum up, charge the jury; bring in a verdict, pronounce sentence; commit for trial.

stand trial, come up for trial, be put on t., stand in the dock; plead guilty, plead not guilty; submit to judgment, hear sentence; defend an action.

960 Acquittal

N. *acquittal*, favourable verdict, verdict of not guilty, verdict of not proven, benefit of the doubt; clearance, exculpation, exoneration 935 *innocence*; absolution, discharge; let-off, thumbs up 746 *liberation*; white-washing, justification, compurgation 927 *vindication*; successful defence; case dismissed; no case, withdrawal of the charge, quashing, quietus; reprieve, pardon 909 *forgiveness*; nonprosecution, exemption, impunity 919 *nonliability*.

Adj. *acquitted*, not guilty, not proven 935 *guiltless*; clear, cleared, in the clear, exonerated, exculpated, vindicated; immune, exempted, exempt; let off, let off the hook, discharged, without a stain on one's character; reprieved; recommended for mercy.

Vb. *acquit*, find *or* pronounce not guilty, prove innocent, find that the case is not proven, justify, whitewash, get one off 927 *vindicate*; clear, absolve, exonerate, exculpate; find there is no case to answer, not press charges, not prosecute 919 *exempt*; discharge, let go, let off 746 *liberate*; reprieve, respite, pardon, remit the penalty 909 *forgive*; quash, quash the conviction, set aside the sentence, allow an appeal 752 *abrogate*.

961 Condemnation

N. *condemnation*, unfavourable verdict; conviction; successful prosecution; damnation, perdition; blacklist. Index 924 *disapprobation*; excommunication 899 *malediction*; doom, judgment, sentence 963 *punishment*; writing on the wall 511 *omen*; outlawry, price on one's head, proscription, attainder; death warrant, condemned cell, execution chamber, electric chair, Death Row; black cap, thumbs down.

Adj. *condemned*, found guilty, made liable; convicted, sentenced; sentenced to death; proscribed, outlawed, with a price on one's head; having no case, without a leg to stand on; damned, in hell.

Vb. *condemn*, prove guilty, bring home the charge; find liable, find against; find guilty, pronounce g., convict, sentence; sentence to death, put on the black cap, sign one's death warrant, reject one's defence, reject one's appeal 607 *reject*; proscribe, outlaw, ban, put a price on one's head 954 *make illegal*; blacklist 924 *disapprove*; damn, excommunicate 899 *curse*; stand condemned out of one's own mouth 936 *be guilty*; plead guilty, sign a confession, be verballed 526 *confess*.

962 Reward

N. *reward*, remuneration, recompense; meed, deserts, just d. 913 *justice*; recognition, due r., acknowledgment, thanks 907 *gratitude*; tribute, bouquets, brownie points 923 *praise*; prize-giving, award, presentation, prize, Nobel P.; crown, cup, shield, certificate, medal 729 *trophy*; consolation prize, booby p.; honour 729

decoration; birthday honours 866 *honours*; letters after one's name, peerdom 870 *title*; prize money, cash p., jackpot; prize fellowship, scholarship, bursary, stipend, exhibition 703 *subvention*; reward for service, fee, retainer, refresher, honorarium, payment, payment in kind, remuneration, emolument, pension, salary, wage, wages, increment 804 *pay*; productivity bonus, overtime pay 612 *incentive*; perquisite, perks, expense account, fringe benefits; income, turnover 771 *earnings*; return, profit, margin of p., bottom line 771 *gain*; compensation, indemnification, satisfaction; consideration, quid pro quo; comeuppance 714 *retaliation*; reparation 787 *restitution*; bounty, gratuity, golden handshake, golden parachute, redundancy money; commission, rake-off; golden handcuffs; tip, douceur, sweetener, pourboire, trinkgeld, baksheesh 781 *gift*; tempting offer 759 *offer*; golden hello, bait, lure, bribe 612 *incentive*; slush fund, hush money, protection m., blackmail.

Vb. *reward*, recompense; award, give a prize, offer a reward; bestow a medal, honour with a title 866 *honour*; recognize, acknowledge, pay tribute, hand out bouquets, thank, show one's gratitude 907 *be grateful*; remunerate 804 *pay*; satisfy, requite 781 *give*; repay, requite 714 *retaliate*; compensate, indemnify, make reparation 787 *restitute*; offer a bribe, grease the palm, win over 612 *bribe*.

be rewarded, win a prize, get a medal, receive a title; be given an honorarium, get paid, draw a salary, earn an income, have a gainful occupation 771 *acquire*; accept payment 782 *receive*; take a bribe, have one's palm greased; have one's reward, get one's deserts, receive one's due 915 *deserve*; get one's comeuppance; reap a profit 771 *gain*.

963 Punishment

N. *punishment*, sentence 961 *condemnation*; execution of sentence; chastisement, heads rolling, zero tolerance; castigation, carpeting 924 *reprimana*, disciplinary action; dose, pill, bitter p., infliction, trial, visitation, carrying the can 731 *adversity*; just deserts, meet reward, comeuppance 915 *dueness*; doom, judgment, day of j., day of reckoning, divine justice 913 *justice*; poetic justice, retribution, Nemesis; reckoning, repayment 787 *restitution*; requital, reprisal 714 *retaliation*; penance 941 *atonement*; hara-kiri 362 *suicide*; penology.

corporal punishment, smacking, slapping, trouncing, hiding, beating, thrashing, kicking, punishment beating, caning, whipping, flogging, birching; scourging, flagellation; ducking, keel-hauling; slap, smack, rap over the knuckles, box on the ear; drubbing, blow, buffet, cuff, clout, stroke, stripe 279 *knock*; kick; third degree, torture, breaking on the wheel.

capital punishment, extreme penalty 361 *death*; death sentence, death warrant; execution 362 *killing*; decapitation, beheading, guillotining; hanging, drawing and quartering; strangulation, garrotte; hanging, long drop; electrocution, hot seat, electric chair; stoning; crucifixion, impalement, flaying alive; burning, burning at the stake; drowning; massacre, mass murder, mass execution, purge, genocide 362 *slaughter*; martyrdom, martyrization; lynching, lynch law, contract; judicial murder.

penalty, injury, damage 772 *loss*; imposition, task, lines, punishment exercise; sentence, tariff, three strikes and you are out, penalization; penal code, penology; community service, community penalties; devil to pay, liability, legal l. 915 *dueness*; damages, costs, compensation, restoration 787 *restitution*; fining, fine, compulsory payment 804 *payment*; ransom 809 *price*; forfeit, forfeiture, sequestration, confiscation, deprivation 786 *expropriation*; keeping in, gating, imprisonment 747 *detention*; suspension, rustication; binding over 747 *restraint*; penal servitude, hard labour; transportation; expulsion, deportation 300 *ejection*; ostracism, sending to Coventry, banishment, exile, proscription, ban, outlawing, blackballing 57 *exclusion*; reprisal 714 *retaliation*.

Adj. *punitive*, penal, punitory; castigatory, disciplinary, corrective; vindictive, retributive; in reprisal; penalizing, fining; confiscatory, expropriatory; scourging, flagellatory, torturing 377 *painful*.

Vb. *punish*, afflict 827 *hurt*; persecute, victimize, make an example of 735 *be severe*; inflict punishment, take disciplinary action; give *or* teach one a lesson, discipline, correct, chastise, castigate; reprimand, rebuke, tell off, rap across the knuckles, smack on the wrist; throw the book at, come down hard on, come down on like a ton of bricks, give one what for; penalize, impose a penalty, sentence 961 *condemn*; exact retribution, settle with, get even w., pay one out *or* back 714 *retaliate*; settle, fix, bring to book, give one what was coming to him, give one his/her come-uppance; fine, forfeit, deprive, sequestrate, confiscate 786 *take away*; unfrock, demote, degrade, downgrade, reduce to the ranks, suspend 867 *shame*; stand in a corner, send out of the room; tar and feather; pillory, set in the stocks; duck, keelhaul; lock up 747 *imprison*; transport.

spank, slap, smack; cuff, clout, box on the ears, rap over the knuckles, smack on the wrist; drub, trounce, beat, belt, strap, leather, lather, wallop, tan, cane, birch, whack, tan one's hide, give one a hiding, beat black and blue 279 *strike*.

flog, whip, horsewhip, thrash, hide, give a hiding, cudgel 279 *strike*; scourge, give one the cat; lash, birch, give one the birch, flay; flagellate.

torture, give the third degree; put on the rack, break on the wheel, kneecap, persecute, martyrize 827 *torment*.

execute, put to death 362 *kill*; lynch 362 *murder*; tear limb from limb; crucify; stone to death; shoot, fusillade; burn at the stake, send to the s.; necklace, give one a n.; garrotte, strangle; hang, hang by the neck, string up, bring to the gallows; hang, draw and quarter; send to the scaffold, behead, decapitate, guillotine; electrocute, send to the chair, send to the hot seat; gas, put in the gas chamber; commit genocide, hold mass executions, purge, massacre, decimate 362 *slaughter*.

be punished, suffer punishment, take the consequences, be for the high jump, have it coming to one, get one's comeuppance, catch it, catch *or* get it in the neck; take the rap, face the music; take one's medicine; get what one was asking for, get one's deserts; pay the ultimate price; lay one's head on the block; come to the gallows, swing; die the death.

964 Means of punishment

N. *scourge*, birch, cat, cat-o'-nine-tails, rope's end; whip, horsewhip, switch; lash, strap, tawse, thong, belt; cane, rattan; stick, big s., rod, ferule, cudgel, ruler, cosh 723 *club*; rubber hose, bicycle chain, sandbag.

pillory, stocks, whipping post, ducking stool; corner, dunce's cap; stool of repentance, cutty stool; chain, irons 748 *fetter*; prison house 748 *prison*.

instrument of torture, rack, thumbscrew, iron boot; Iron Maiden, wheel, treadmill; torture chamber.

means of execution, scaffold, block, gallows, gibbet; cross; stake; hemlock 659 *poison*; bullet; axe, guillotine, maiden, widow-maker; rope, noose; garrotte; necklace; electric chair, hot seat; death chamber, gas c.; condemned cell, Death Row 961 *condemnation*.

SECTION FIVE

Religion

965 Divineness

N. *divineness*, divinity, deity; godhead; divine principle, Brahma; mana; divine essence, the Good the True and the Beautiful; love,

Fatherhood; Brahmahood, nirvana; world soul;
divine nature, God's ways, Providence.

divine attribute, omnipresence 189 *presence*;
omniscience, wisdom 490 *knowledge*; omnipotence, almightiness 160 *power*; timelessness,
eternity 115 *perpetuity*; changelessness 153 *stability*; truth, sanctity, holiness, goodness, justice,
mercy; transcendence, sublimity, supremacy,
sovereignty, majesty, glory, light; glory of the
Lord.

the Deity, God, Supreme Being, Alpha and
Omega; the Almighty; the All-holy, the All-
merciful; Ruler of Heaven and Earth, Judge of
all men, Maker of all things, Creator, Preserver;
Allah; Elohim, Yahweh, Jehovah, Adonai, ineffable name, I AM; name of God, Tetragramma-
ton; God of Abraham, God of Moses, Lord of
Hosts, God of our fathers; our Father; All-
Father, Great Spirit; Krishna.

God the Son, Son of God, the Only Begotten;
Messiah, Son of David, the Lord's Anointed,
Christ; Immanuel; Lamb of God, Son of Man;
Son of Mary, Jesus, Jesu, Jesus Christ; Holy
Infant, Christ Child, Child of Bethlehem; Jesus
of Nazareth; the Good Shepherd, Saviour,
Redeemer, Friend; Lord, Master; Rock of Ages,
Bread of Life; the Way the Truth and the Life;
Light of the World, Sun of Righteousness; King
of Kings, Prince of Peace.

Adj. *divine*, holy, hallowed, sanctified,
sacred, sacrosanct, heavenly, celestial; transcendental, sublime, ineffable; mystical, religious,
spiritual, superhuman, supernatural, unearthly,
not of this world.

godlike, divine, superhuman; omnipresent
189 *ubiquitous*; immortal 115 *perpetual*; immutable, changeless 144 *permanent*; almighty, all-
powerful, omnipotent 160 *powerful*; creative
160 *dynamic*; all-wise, all-seeing, all-knowing,
omniscient 490 *knowing*; all-merciful, merciful;
compassionate 905 *pitying*; holy, all-h., wor-
shipped 979 *sanctified*; sovereign 34 *supreme*;
incarnate, in the image of God, deified; mes-
sianic, anointed; Christly, Christlike.

966 Deities in general

N. *deity*, god, goddess, deva, devi; the gods, the
immortals; Olympian 967 *Olympian deity*; false
god, idol, petty god, inferior g.; demigod, half-
god, divine hero, divine king; fetish, totem 982
idol; mumbo jumbo.

mythic deity, nature god *or* goddess, Pan,
Flora; earth goddess, Gaia; mother earth,
mother goddess, earth mother; fertility god,
Adonis, Marduk, Atys; god of the underworld,
Pluto, Dis 967 *Chthonian deity*; sky god, Zeus,
Jupiter; storm god, Indra, wind god, Aeolus; sun
god, Apollo, Hyperion, Helios, Ra, Mithras;

river god, sea g., Poseidon, Neptune; war god *or*
goddess, Mars, Bellona; god *or* goddess of love,
Cupid, Eros, Venus, Aphrodite; household
gods, Lares, Penates; the Fates 596 *fate*.

967 Pantheon: classical and nonclassical deities

N. *classical deities*, gods and goddesses of Greece
and Rome, Graeco-Roman pantheon; Homeric
deities, Hesiodic theogony; primeval deities,
Erebus, Nox; Ge, Gaia, Tellus, Uranus, Cronus,
Saturn, Rhea, Ops; Pontus, Oceanus, Tethys;
Helios, Sol, Hyperion, Phaethon; Titan, Atlas,
Prometheus; Giant, Enceladus; the Fates, Par-
cae, Clotho, Lachesis, Atropos.

Olympian deity, Olympian, Zeus, Jupiter, Jove,
president of the immortals; Pluto, Hades; Posei-
don, Neptune; Apollo, Phoebus; Hermes, Mer-
cury; Ares, Mars; Hephaestus, Vulcan;
Dionysus, Bacchus; Hera, Juno; Demeter, Ceres;
Persephone, Proserpina; Athena, Minerva;
Aphrodite, Venus; Artemis, Diana; Eros, Cupid;
Iris; Hebe.

Chthonian deity, Ge, Gaia, Dis Pater, Orcus,
Hades, Pluto, Persephone; Erectheus, Trophon-
ius, Pytho; Eumenides, Erinyes, Furies.

lesser deity, Pan, Silvanus, Flora, Faunus, Sil-
enus; Aurora, Eos; Luna, Selene; Aeolus, Boreas
352 *wind*; Triton, Nereus, Proteus, Glaucus; Ate,
Eris, Bellona, Nike; Astraea; Muses, tuneful
Nine, Erato, Euterpe, Terpsichore, Polyhymnia,
Clio, Calliope, Melpomene, Thalia, Urania;
Asclepius, Aesculapius; Hypnos, Somnus, Morpheus; Hymen; Hestia, Vesta; Lares, Penates;
local god, genius loci.

nymph, wood n., tree n., dryad, hamadryad;
mountain nymph, oread; water nymph, naiad;
sea nymph, nereid, Oceanid; Thetis, Calypso,
Callisto; Pleiades, Maia; Latona, Leto; siren 970
mythical being.

demigod, divine offspring, divine hero; Her-
acles, Hercules; Dioscuri, Castor and Pollux,
Castor and Polydeuces; Perseus, Achilles,
Aeneas, Memnon.

Hindu deities, Brahmanic d., Vedic d.; Dyaus
Pitar, Prithivi; Varuna (sky), Mitra (light), Indra
(thunder), Agni (fire), Surya (sun); Trimurti,
Brahma, Siva, Vishnu; Sakti, Uma *or* Parvat, Kali
or Durga; Ganesha (luck-bringer), Karttikeya
(fertility), Sarasvati (learning), Hanuman
(monkey-god), Sitala (smallpox), Manasa
(snakes), Lakshmi (wealth and fortune).

Egyptian deities, Nun, Atum; Shu (air), Tefnut
(moisture), Nut (sky), Geb (earth), Osiris, Isis,
Set, Nephthys; Ra *or* Re, Amon- *or* Amun-Ra,
Atum-ra, Aton; Horus, elder Horus, Ra-
Harakhte, Khepera; Amon, Min (all-father),
Hathor (all-mother), Neith, Anata; Ptah

(creator), Ma'at (truth), Imhotep (peace), Bes (dancing), Serapis (underworld); theriomorphic deity, theriocephalous d.; Apis (sacred bull), Thoth (ibis), Anubis (jackal), Sekhmet (lioness), Sebek (crocodile), Bast (cat), Setekh (hound), Uadjit (cobra), Taurt (hippopotamus).

Semitic deities, Nammu, Anu, Enlil, Enki *or* Ea; Shamash, Sin, Adad; Bel, Marduk; El, Baal, Aleyan-Baal; Moloch, Rimmon, Asshur; great mother, Ishtar, Ashtoreth, Astarte, Asherah, Inanna, Anat; fertility god, Tammuz, Atys; Mot, Allatu.

Nordic deities, Aesir, Vanir; Odin *or* Wotan, Frigg his wife; Thor (thunder god), his wife Sif, his son Ull; Tiu *or* Tyr (war), Heimdall, Balder the beautiful, Vidar the silent, Hoder the blind, Bragi (god of poetry), Hermoder (messenger), Vali (youngest son of Odin); Frey *or* Freyr (peace, fertility), Freya *or* Freyja (goddess of love), Njord *or* Nerthus (wealth and ships), Hoenir, Odmir; Skadi; Loki (evil and strife), Hel (goddess of the dead); Aegir (ocean), his wife Ran, Mimir (guardian of the spring of wisdom), Ymir (father of the Giants).

Celtic deities, Dagda, Math, Magog, Oengus *or* Dwyn; Ogma, Belinus, Esos, Teutates, Taranis; Mabon, Borvo *or* Bormo; Epona; Bilé *or* Beli, Govannon or Goibniu (smith), Diancecht (medecine); Lludd *or* Nudd *or* Nuada (sun); Gwydion, Amaethon; Lleu *or* Lug (light), Dylan (darkness); sea gods, Ler *or* Llyr, Bran *or* Branwen, Manannan *or* Manawydan; Dana *or* Don, Morrigan (war), Brigit, Blathnat, Arianrod, Blodeuwedd, Creirwy (love), Keridwen (poetry), Rhiannon (underworld).

Aztec deities, Nahuan d.; Cipactli (earth dragon); Coatlicue (ancient earth goddess); Red Tezcatlipoca, Black T., White T., Blue T., Xipe Topec (spring), Quetzalcoatl (culture), Huitzilopochti (warrior); god and goddess of creation, Tonacatecuhtli, Tonicacihuatl; deities of fertility, Cihuacoatl, Chicomecoatl, Centeotl, Tlazolteotl, Xochipilli; Tlaloc (rain), Chalcihuitlicue (water); Xiuhtecuhtli (fire), Tonatiuh (sun), Teccuciztecutl, Metztli (moon), Mixcoatl (sky), Mictlantecuhtli (death).

968 Angel. Saint. Madonna

N. *angel*, archangel, heavenly host; seraph, seraphim, cherub, cherubim; Michael, Gabriel, Raphael, Uriel, Zadkiel; Israfel, Azrael, angel of death; guardian angel.

saint, patron s., the blessed. . . .

Madonna. Our Lady, Blessed Virgin Mary, Mother of God; Mariolatry.

Adj. *angelic*, seraphic, cherubic; saintly.

969 Devil

N. *Satan*, Lucifer, fallen angel; Archfiend, Prince of Darkness; serpent, Tempter, Adversary, Antichrist, Common Enemy, Enemy of mankind; evil genie, Shaitan, Eblis; King of Hell, angel of the bottomless pit, Apollyon, Abaddon; the foul fiend, the Devil, the Evil One, Wicked O., Auld Nick, cloven hoof; Ahriman, Angra Mainyu.

Mephisto, Mephistopheles, His Satanic Majesty, the old one, the Old Gentleman, Old Nick, Auld N., Old Harry, Old Scratch, Auld Hornie, Clootie.

devil, fiend; familiar, imp of Satan 938 *bad person*; Tutivillus, Asmodeus, Azazel 970 *demon*; malevolent spirit; powers of darkness; fallen angel, lost soul, sinner, dweller in Pandemonium, denizen of Hell; Mammon, Belial, Beelzebub, Lord of the Flies; horns, cloven hoof.

diabolism, devilry, demonry, diablerie 898 *inhumanity*; Satanism, devilism; devil worship, demonism, demonolatry; demonomania, demoniac possession; witchcraft, black magic, Black Mass 983 *sorcery*; Satanology, demonology; demonization.

diabolist, Satanist, devil-worshipper, demonolater, demonist; demonologist, demonologer.

Adj. *diabolic*, diabolical, devil-like, satanic, Mephistophelean, fiendish, demonic, demoniacal, devilish 898 *malevolent*; infernal, hellish, hell-born; devil-worshipping; demoniac, possessed; demonological.

970 Fairy

N. *fairy*, elfland, fairyland, faerie; fairy folk, little people; fay, peri; good fairy, fairy godmother 903 *benefactor*; bad fairy, witch 983 *sorceress*; fairy queen, Mab, Queen M., Titania; fairy king, Oberon, Erl King; Puck, Robin Goodfellow; spirit of air, Ariel; sylph, sylphid; fairy ring; fairy tales; A Midsummer Night's Dream, The Faerie Queene.

elf, elves, elfin folk, pixie, brownie; gnome, dwarf, Nibelung; troll, trow; orc, goblin, flibbertigibbet; imp, sprite, hobgoblin; changeling; leprechaun; poltergeist, gremlin; Puck, Hob, Robin Goodfellow.

ghost, spirit, departed s.; shades, souls of the dead, Manes; zombie; revenant, haunter, poltergeist; spook, spectre, apparition, phantom, shade, wraith, presence, doppelganger 440 *visual fallacy*; White Lady, Grey L.

demon, flibbertigibbet; imp, familiar 969 *devil*; she-demon, banshee; kelpie, troll; ogre, ogress, giant, giantess; bugbear, bugaboo, bogle, bogy, bogyman 938 *monster*; ghoul, vampire, lycanthrope, werewolf; incubus, succubus, nightmare; fury, harpy; Gorgon.

mythical being 968 angel, 969 devil; demon, genie, jinn; houri; Valkyrie; centaur, satyr, faun; sea nymph, river n., water n., Oceanid, Naiad, kelpie, nix, nixie; merman, mermaid; Lorelei, Siren; water spirit, Undine 967 *nymph*; Lady of the Lake, Old Man of the Sea; Merlin 983 *sorcerer*; Wayland Smith, Green Man, Wodwose; Yeti, Abominable Snowman, Leviathan, Phoenix 84 *rara avis*.

Adj. *fairylike*, fairy, sylph-like 206 *lean*; dwarf-like 196 *dwarfish*; elf-like, elfin, elvish, impish, Puckish; magic 983 *magical*.

spooky, ghostly, ghoulish; haunted, hagridden; nightmarish, macabre 854 *frightening*; weird, uncanny, unearthly, eldritch 84 *abnormal*; eerie, supernatural; spectral, wraith-like; disembodied 320 *immaterial*; spiritualistic 984 *psychical*.

Vb. *haunt*, visit, walk.

971 Heaven

N. *heaven*, abode of G., kingdom of G., kingdom of heaven, heavenly kingdom, kingdom come; Paradise, abode of the saints, land of the leal, gates of St Peter; Abraham's bosom, eternal home, happy h.; eternal rest, blessed state; nirvana, seventh heaven; the Millennium, earthly Paradise, heaven on earth, Zion, Land of Beulah, New Jerusalem, Holy City, Celestial C.; afterlife, the hereafter, eternal life, eternity 124 *future state*; resurrection; assumption, glorification; deification, apotheosis.

mythic heaven, Olympus; Valhalla, Asgard; Elysium, Elysian fields, happy hunting grounds, the happy hunting grounds in the skies; Earthly Paradise, Eden, Garden of E., garden of the Hesperides, Islands of the Blest, the Happy Isles, Isle of Avalon 513 *fantasy*.

972 Hell

N. *hell*, place of the dead, nether regions, underworld; grave, limbo, Hades; purgatory; perdition, place of the damned, abode of evil spirits, inferno, Pandemonium; abyss, bottomless pit, Abaddon; place of torment, Gehenna, lake of fire and brimstone; hellfire.

mythic hell, Hel, Niflheim; realm of Pluto, Hades, Tartarus, Avernus, Erebus; river of hell, Acheron, Styx, Cocytus, Phlegethon, Lethe; Stygian Ferryman, Charon; infernal watchdog, Cerberus; infernal judge, Minos, Rhadamanthus; nether gods, Chthonians, Pluto, Osiris 967 *Chthonian deity*.

973 Religion

N. *religion*, religious belief, creed, dogma; deism; primitive religion; paganism 982 *idolatry*; dharma, revealed religion, incarnational r., sacramental r.; mysticism, Sufism; yoga, hathayoga, dharmayoga, jnanayoga, karmayoga, bhaktiyoga; Eightfold Path; theosophy 449 *philosophy*; theolatry 981 *worship*; religious cult, state religion 981 *cult*; atheism 974 *irreligion*.

deism, belief in a god, theism; animism, pantheism, polytheism, henotheism, monotheism, dualism; gnosticism.

religious faith, faith 485 *belief*; Christianity, the Cross; Judaism; Islam, Muhammedanism, the Crescent; Baha'ism, Zoroastrianism, Mazdaism; Vedic religion, Dharma; Hinduism, Brahmanism, Vedantism, Tantrism; Vaishnavism 978 *sectarianism*; Sikhism; Jainism; Buddhism, Theravada, Hinayana, Mahayana, Zen; Shintoism; Taoism, Confucianism; Theosophy; Scientology.

theology, natural theology, revealed t.; religious knowledge, religious learning, divinity; scholastic theology, scholasticism, Thomism; Rabbinism; demythologization; eschatology; hagiology, hagiography, iconology; dogmatics; symbolics, creedal theology; deposit of faith; religious doctrine, received d., defined d.; definition, canon; doxy, dogma; tenet; articles of faith, credo 485 *creed*; confession, Thirty-nine Articles; fundamentalism 976 *orthodoxism*; Bibliology; comparative religion.

theologian, divinity student, divine; rabbi, scribe, mufti, mullah; schoolman, scholastic, scholastic theologian, Thomist, Talmudist, canonist; theogonist, hagiologist, hagiographer, iconologist; psalmist, hymnographer, hymnwriter; textualist; scripturalist, fundamentalist, rabbinist.

religious teacher, prophet, rishi, inspired writer; guru, maharishi 500 *sage*; evangelist, apostle, missionary; reformer, religious r.; expected leader, Messiah, Mahdi, Invisible Imam, twelfth avatar of Vishnu; founder of Christianity, Christ, Jesus Christ; Prophet of God, Muhammad, Mohammed *or* Mahomet; Zoroaster *or* Zarathustra; Ramakrishna, Baha'ullah; Buddha, Gautama; Confucius, Laotzu; Joseph Smith, Mary Baker Eddy, Madame Blavatsky; expounder, hierophant, gospeller, catechist 520 *interpreter*.

religionist, deist, theist; monotheist, polytheist, pantheist, animist, fetishist; pagan, gentile 974 *heathen*; adherent, believer, orthodoxist; believer 979 *zealot*; Christian, Nazarene; Jew; Muslim, Moslem, Islamite, Mussulman,

Muhammedan; Sunnite, Shi'ite 978 *non-Christian sect*; Sufi, dervish; Baha'i; Parsee, Zoroastrian; Hindu, gymnosophist, Brahmanist; Sikh; Jain; Buddhist, Zen B.; Tantrist; Taoist; Confucianist; Shintoist; Theosophist; Mormon 978 *sect*; Rosicrucian 984 *occultist*; gnostic 977 *heretic*.

Adj. *religious*, divine, holy, sacred, spiritual, sacramental; deistic, theistic, pantheistic, monotheistic, dualistic; Christian, Islamic, Moslem, Jewish, Judaistic, Mosaic; Baha'i, Zoroastrian, Avestan; Confucian, Taoistic; Buddhistic, Hinduistic, Vedic, Brahminical, Upanashadic, Vedantic; yogic, mystic, Sufic; devotional, devout, practising.

974 Irreligion

N. *irreligion*, profaneness, ungodliness 980 *impiety*; heathenism 982 *idolatry*; atheism, disbelief 486 *unbelief*; humanism; agnosticism, scepticism; lack of faith; lapse from faith, recidivism, backsliding 603 *change of mind*; paganization; apathy 860 *indifference*.

heathen, non-Christian, pagan, paynim; misbeliever, infidel, giaour; gentile, the uncircumcised, the unbaptized, the unconverted; apostate, backslider, lapsed Christian 603 *tergiversator*.

Adj. *irreligious*, godless, profane 980 *impious*; atheistic, atheistical; humanistic; agnostic, doubting, sceptical, Pyrrhonic; free-thinking, rationalistic, non-practising; ungodly 934 *wicked*; amoral 860 *indifferent*; secular, worldly, materialistic, Mammonistic 944 *sensual*; lacking faith, backsliding, recidivous, lapsed, paganized; unchristian, non-Christian; anticlerical.

heathenish, unholy, unhallowed, unsanctified, unblest, unconsecrated 980 *profane*; unchristian, unbaptized, unconfirmed; gentile, uncircumcised; heathen, pagan, infidel; pre-Christian, unconverted, in darkness 491 *uninstructed*.

Vb. *be irreligious*, – atheistic etc. adj.; have no religion, lack faith; serve Mammon; lose one's faith, suffer a lapse of faith, give up the Church 603 *apostatize*; demythologize, rationalize; deny God, blaspheme 980 *be impious*.

975 Revelation

N. *revelation*, divine r., apocalypse 526 *disclosure*; illumination 417 *light*; inspiration, divine i.; prophecy; intuition, mysticism; Mosaic Law, Ten Commandments; God's word, gospel; God revealed, theophany, burning bush, epiphany, incarnation, Word made flesh; avatar, emanation, divine e.

scripture, word of God, sacred writings; Holy Scripture, Holy Writ, Bible, Holy B., the Book, the Good Book, the Word; Wyclif's Bible, Geneva or Breeches B., King James's Bible, Authorized Version, Revised V., Revised Standard Version, Jerusalem Bible, New English B., Good News B.; Vulgate, Douai Version, Greek version, Septuagint; canonical writings, canonical books, canon; Old Testament, Pentateuch, Hexateuch, Octateuch, Major Prophets, Minor P.; Torah, the Law and the Prophets, Hagiographa; New Testament, Gospels, Synoptic G., Epistles, Pastoral E., Pauline E., Johannine E., Petrine E.; Acts of the Apostles, Revelation, Apocalypse; noncanonical writings, Apocrypha, agrapha, logia, sayings, noncanonical gospel; patristic writings; psalter, psalmbook, breviary, missal; prayer book, Book of Common Prayer 981 *prayers*; hymn book, hymnal 981 *hymn*; post-Biblical writings (Hebrew), Targum, Talmud, Mishnah, Gemara; textual commentary, Masorah, Higher Criticism; fundamentalism, scripturalism.

non-Biblical scripture, Koran, the Glorious Koran, Qur'an; Hadith, Sunna; Hindu scripture, Veda, the Four Vedas, Rigveda, Yajurveda, Samaveda, Atharvaveda; Brahmana, Upanishad, Purana; Bhagavad Gita; sruti, smriti, shastra, sutra, tantra; Granth; Buddhist scripture, Pitaka, Tripitaka, Nikaya, Dhammapada; Iranian and Zoroastrian scripture, Avesta, Zend-Avesta; Book of the Dead (Egyptian); Book of Mormon.

Adj. *revelational*, inspirational, mystic; inspired, prophetic, revealed; visional; apocalyptic; prophetic, evangelical.

scriptural, sacred, holy; hierographic; revealed, inspired, prophetic; canonical 733 *authoritative*; biblical, Mosaic; gospel, evangelistic, apostolic; patristic, homiletic; Talmudic, Mishnaic; Koranic, uncreated; Vedic, Upanishadic, Puranic; textuary, textual, Masoretic.

976 Orthodoxy

N. *orthodoxy*, orthodoxness, correct opinion; sound theology, religious truth, gospel t., pure Gospel 494 *truth*; scripturality, canonicity; the Faith, the true faith; early Church, Apostolic age; ecumenicalism, catholicity, Catholicism; formulated faith, credo 485 *creed*; Apostles' Creed, Nicene C., Athanasian C.; Thirty-nine Articles, Tridentine decrees; textuary, catechism, Church Catechism.

orthodoxism, strictness, strict interpretation; scripturalism, textualism, fundamentalism, literalism, precisianism; Karaism (Jewish); traditionalism, institutionalism, ecclesiasticism; churchianity 985 *the church*; sound churchmanship 83 *conformity*; Christian practice 768 *observance*; intolerance, heresy-hunting, persecution; suppression of heresy, extermination of error, Counter-Reformation; religious censorship, Holy Office 956 *tribunal*; Inquisition 459 *interrogation*; Index, Index Expurgatorius, Index Librorum Prohibitorum 924 *disapprobation*; guaranteed orthodoxy, imprimatur 923 *approbation*.

Christendom, Christian world, the Church; undivided Church; Holy Church, Mother C.; Bride of Christ; Body of Christ, universal Church; Church Militant, Church on earth, visible Church; invisible Church, Church Triumphant; established Church, recognized C., denominational C.; Orthodox C., Eastern Orthodox C., Armenian C., Coptic C.; Church of Rome, Roman Catholic and Apostolic C.; Church of England, Episcopalian C.; Church of Scotland; United Free Church, Free Church; Church of South India; Reformed Church, Protestant C., Lutheran C., Calvinist C.; Ecumenical Council, World Council of Churches.

Catholicism, Orthodoxy, Eastern O.; Roman Catholicism, Romanism, popery, papistry, ultramontanism, Scarlet Woman; Counter-Reformation; Old Catholicism; Anglicanism, Episcopalianism, prelacy; Anglo-Catholicism, High Church; Tractarianism, Oxford Movement.

Protestantism, the Reformation, Anglicanism, Lutheranism, Zwinglianism, Calvinism; Presbyterianism, Congregationalism, United Reformed Church, Baptists; Quakerism, Society of Friends; Wesleyanism, Methodism, Primitive M. 978 *sect*.

Catholic, Orthodox, Eastern O.; Greek O., Russian O., Coptic; Roman Catholic, Romanist, papist, ultramontanist; Old Catholic, Anglo-C., Anglican, Episcopalian, High-Churchman, Tractarian.

Protestant, reformer, Anglican, Lutheran, Zwinglian, Calvinist, Huguenot, Anabaptist; Presbyterian, Wee Free, Congregationalist, United Reformist, Baptist, Wesleyan, Methodist, Wesleyan M., Primitive M.; Quaker, Friend; Plymouth Brother.

Adj. *orthodox*, right-minded; nonheretical, unschismatical 488 *assenting*; undivided 52 *whole*; unswerving, undeviating, loyal, devout 739 *obedient*; practising, conforming, conventional 83 *conformable*; churchy 979 *pietistic*; strict, pedantic; holier than thou, bible-thumping *or* bashing; intolerant, witch-hunting, inquisitional 459 *enquiring*; correct 494 *accurate*; doctrinal 485 *creedal*; authoritative, defined, canonical, biblical, scriptural, evangelical, gospel 494 *genuine*; textual, literal, fundamentalist, fundamentalistic; fundie; Trin-

itarian; Athanasian; catholic, ecumenical, universal; accepted, held, widely h., believed, generally b. 485 *credible*; traditional, customary 610 *usual*.

Roman Catholic, Catholic, Roman, Romish, Romanist, Romanizing, ultramontanist; popish, papistic.

Anglican, episcopalian; tractarian, Anglo-Catholic, High-Church, high; Low-Church; Broad-C., Latitudinarian.

Protestant, reformed; denominational 978 *sectarian*; Lutheran, Zwinglian, Calvinist, Calvinistic; Presbyterian, Congregational, United Reformed, Baptist, Methodist, Wesleyan, Quaker; bishopless, nonepiscopal.

977 Heterodoxy

N. *heterodoxy*, unorthodoxy; erroneous opinion, wrong belief, false creed, superstition 495 *error*; new teaching; perversion of the truth; heretical tendency, latitudinarianism, modernism, Higher Criticism; unscripturality, noncatholicity, partial truth; heresy, rank h.

heresy, heathen theology, Gnosticism; Monarchianism, Arianism; Socinianism; Unitarianism; Apollinarianism, Nestorianism; Monophysitism, Monothelitism; Pelagianism; Montanism, Donatism, Manichaeism, Albigensianism, Antinomianism; Lollardy; Erastianism, antipapalism.

heretic, arch-h., heresiarch; Gnostic, Manichee; Monarchian, Unitarian; Arius, Arian; Socinus, Socinian; Nestorius, Nestorian; Eutyches, Apollinaris, Apollinarian; Monophysite, Monothelite; Pelagius; Montanus, millenarian; Donatist; Manichaean, Cathar, Paulician, Albigensian; Antinomian; Wycliffite, Lollard, Hussite; Waldenses.

Adj. *heretical*, heretic; heathen, Gnostic, Manichean, Monarchian, Unitarian, Socinian; Arian, Eutychian, Apollinarian, Nestorian, Monophysitic, Monothelite; Pelagian; Montanist; Manichaean, Albigensian; Antinomian, Waldensian, Wycliffite, Lollard, Hussite.

978 Sectarianism

N. *sectarianism*, exclusiveness, clannishness, cliqueishness, sectionalism 481 *prejudice*; bigotry 481 *bias*; party spirit, factiousness 709 *quarrelsomeness*; separatism, schismatical tendency 738 *disobedience*; denominationalism, nonconformism, nonconformity 489 *dissent*; Lutheranism, Calvinism, Anabaptism, Pietism, Moravianism, Puritanism 976 *Protestantism*; Puseyism, Tractarianism 976 *Catholicism*.

schism, division, differences 709 *quarrel*; dissociation, breakaway, splintering, secession, withdrawal 46 *separation*; nonrecognition, mutual excommunication 883 *seclusion*; recusancy 769 *nonobservance*; religious schism, Great Schism.

sect, division, off-shoot, branch, group, faction, splinter group 708 *party*; order, religious o., brotherhood, sisterhood 708 *community*; nonconformist sect, chapel, conventicle 976 *Protestantism*; Society of Friends, Friends, Quakers; Unitarians; Moravians; Plymouth Brethren; Churches of Christ; Sabbatarians, Seventh-day Adventists; Church of Christ Scientist; Church of Jesus Christ of the Latter-Day Saints, Mormons; Jehovah's Witnesses; Salvation Army, Salvationists; Oxford Group, Moral Rearmament.

non-Christian sect, Jewish s.; Orthodox Jews, Reform J.; Pharisees, Sadducees; Hasidim, Rabbinists; Karaites; Nazarites, Essenes; paganochristian sect, Gnostics, Mandaeans, Euchites; Islamic sect, Sunnis, Shi'ites, Sufis, Wahhabis; Black Muslims; Rastafarians, Rastas; Hindu sect, Vedantists, Vaishnavas, Saivas, Shaktas; Brahmoists, Hare Krishna sect; Tantrists, Pure Land sect, Jodo s. 973 *religious faith*.

sectarian, particularist; follower, adherent, devotee; Sectary, Nonconformist, Independant; Puritan, Shaker; Quaker, Friend; Pentecostalist; Presbyterian, Wee Free, Covenanter 976 *Protestant*; Salvationist; Christian Scientist; Jehovah's Witness; Unitarian; Seventh-day Adventist, Mennonite; Mormon; Moonie; Christadelphian, Scientologist, Gnostic 977 *heretic*.

schismatic, separated brother; schismatics, separated brethren; separatist, separationist; seceder, secessionist; splinter group; factionary, factionist; rebel, mutineer 738 *revolter*; recusant, nonjuror; dissident, dissenter, nonconformist 489 *dissentient*; wrong believer 977 *heretic*; apostate 603 *tergiversator*.

Adj. *sectarian*, particularist; party-minded, partisan 481 *biased*; clannish, exclusive; Judaizer, Ebionite; Gallican; Erastian; High-Church, episcopalian 976 *Anglican*; Low-Church, evangelical 976 *Protestant*; Puritan, Independant, Presbyterian, Covenanting; revivalist, Pentecostalist; Vaishnavite, Saiva, Shakta, Tantrist; Ramakrishna; Rastafarian; Sunni, Shi'ite, Sufic; Essene, Pharisaic, Sadducean, Hasidic; Gnostic.

schismatical, schismatic, secessionist, seceding, breakaway; divided, separated 46 *separate*; excommunicated, excommunicable 977 *heretical*; dissentient, nonconformist 489 *dissenting*; recusant 769 *nonobservant*; rebellious, rebel, contumacious 738 *disobedient*; apostate.

979 Piety

N. *piety*, piousness, goodness 933 *virtue*; reverence, veneration, honour, decent respect 920 *respect*; dutifulness, attendance at worship, regular churchgoing 768 *observance*; churchmanship 976 *orthodoxy*; religiousness, religion, theism 973 *deism*; religious feeling; fear of God 854 *fear*; pious belief, faith, trust in God 485 *belief*; devotion, dedication 931 *disinterestedness*; devoutness, sincerity, earnestness, unction; enthusiasm, fervour, zeal; inspiration, exaltation, speaking in tongues, glossolalia 821 *excitation*; adoration, prostration 981 *worship*; meditation, retreat; contemplation, mysticism, communion with God, mystic communion 973 *religion*; faith healing 656 *restoration*; act of piety; good works; pilgrimage, hajj.

sanctity, sanctitude, holiness, hallowedness, sacredness, sacrosanctity; goodness, cardinal virtues 933 *virtue*; state of grace, odour of sanctity 950 *purity*; godliness, saintliness; spirituality, unworldliness, otherworldliness; spiritual life; sainthood, blessedness, blessed state; enlightenment; conversion, regeneration, rebirth, new birth 656 *revival*; sanctification; canonization, beatification, consecration, dedication.

pietism, show of piety, sanctimony; sanctimoniousness, unction, cant 542 *sham*; religionism, religiosity, religious mania; biblethumping *or* bashing; tender conscience; austerity 945 *asceticism*; formalism, Puritanism 481 *narrow mind*; literalness, fundamentalism, Bible-worship, bibliolatry 494 *accuracy*; sabbatarianism 978 *sectarianism*; churchiness, sacerdotalism, ritualism 985 *ecclesiasticism*; preachiness, unctuousness; bigotry, fanaticism 481 *prejudice*; persecution, witch-hunting, heresy-h. 735 *severity*.

pietist, pious person, real saint 937 *good person*; children of God, c. of light; the good, the righteous, the just; conformist 488 *assenter*; practising Christian, communicant 981 *worshipper*; confessor, martyr; saint, bodhissattva, marabout; man *or* woman of prayer, contemplative, mystic, sufi; holy man, sadhu, sannyasi, bhikshu, fakir, dervish 945 *ascetic*; hermit, anchorite 883 *solitary*; monk, nun, religious 986 *clergy*; devotee; convert, neophyte, catechumen, ordinand 538 *learner*; believer, the faithful; the chosen people, the elect; pilgrim, palmer, hajji; votary.

zealot, religionist, enthusiast, wowser, fanatic, bigot, image-breaker, iconoclast; formalist, precisian, Puritan; Pharisee; scribe, scribes and Pharisees; the unco guid, goody-goody; fundamentalist, fundie; in-errantist, Bible-worshipper, bibliolater, Sabbatarian 978 *sectarian*; bible-puncher *or* thumper *or* basher;

pulpiteer 537 *preacher*; evangelical, salvationist, hot-gospeller; missionary 901 *philanthropist*; revivalist, speaker in tongues, faith healer; champion of the faith, crusader; militant Christian; militant Islamite, ghazi; persecutor 735 *tyrant*.

Adj. *pious*, good, 933 *virtuous*; decent, reverent 920 *respectful*; faithful 739 *obedient*; conforming; believing 976 *orthodox*; sincere; pure, pure in heart, holy-minded; unworldly, otherworldly, spiritual; godly, God-fearing, religious, devout; praying, psalm-singing; happy-clappy; in retreat, meditative, contemplative, mystic; holy, saintly, saintlike; Christian.

pietistic, ardent, fervent, seraphic; enthusiastic, inspired; austere 945 *ascetic*; hermit-like, anchoretic 883 *unsociable*; earnest, pi, religiose, overreligious, overpious, self-righteous, holier than thou; overstrict, precise, Puritan; formalistic, Pharisaic, ritualistic 978 *sectarian*; priest-ridden, churchy; psalm-singing, hymn-s.; preachy, bible-thumping *or* bashing, sanctimonious, canting 850 *affected*; goody-goody, too good to be true 933 *virtuous*; crusading, evangelical, missionary-minded.

sanctified, consecrated, dedicated, enshrined; reverend, holy, sacred, solemn, sacrosanct 866 *worshipful*; haloed, sainted, canonized, beatified; chosen; saved, redeemed, ransomed; renewed, reborn, born again.

Vb. *be pious*, – religious etc. adj.; have one's mind on higher things; fear God 854 *fear*; have faith 485 *believe*; keep the faith, fight the good fight 162 *be strong*; walk humbly with one's God; go to church, be a regular churchgoer; pray, say one's prayers 981 *worship*; kneel, genuflect, bow 311 *stoop*; cross oneself, make the sign of the cross; make offering, sacrifice, devote 759 *offer*; give alms and oblations, lend to God 781 *give*; give to charity; glorify God 923 *praise*; give God the glory 907 *thank*; revere, show reverence 920 *show respect*; sermonize, preach at 534 *teach*; set a good example.

become pious, be converted, get religion; see the light, see the error of one's ways 603 *recant*; mend one's ways, reform, repent, repent of one's evil ways, receive Christ 939 *be penitent*; enter the church, become ordained, take holy orders, take vows, take the veil 986 *take orders*.

make pious, bring religion to, proselytize, convert 485 *convince*; Christianize, win for Christ, baptize, receive into the church 299 *admit*; Islamize, Judaize; spiritualize 648 *purify*; confirm in the faith 162 *strengthen*; inspire, fill with grace; redeem 656 *restore*.

sanctify, hallow, make holy, keep h. 866 *honour*; consecrate, dedicate, enshrine 866 *dig-*

nify; make a saint of, canonize, beatify, invest with a halo; bless, make the sign of the cross.

980 Impiety

N. *impiety*, impiousness; irreverence; godlessness 974 *irreligion*; scoffing, mockery, derision 851 *ridicule*; scorn, pride 922 *contempt*; sacrilegiousness, profanity; blasphemy, cursing, swearing 899 *malediction*; sacrilege, desecration, violation, profanation, perversion, abuse 675 *misuse*; immorality, sin, pervertedness 934 *wickedness*; lapse of faith, backsliding, apostasy; profaneness, unholiness, worldliness, materialism 319 *materiality*; paganism, heathenism.

false piety, sham p. 541 *falsehood*; sanctimoniousness, Pharisaism 979 *pietism*; hypocrisy, lip service 541 *duplicity*; cant 850 *affectation*.

impious person, blasphemer, curser, swearer 899 *malediction*; defamer 926 *detractor*; desecrator, violator, profaner 904 *offender*; gentile, pagan, infidel, unbeliever 974 *heathen*; atheist, sceptic; materialist, immoralist 944 *sensualist*; sinner, reprobate, children of darkness 938 *bad person*; recidivist, backslider, apostate; fallen angel 969 *Satan*.

Adj. *impious*, ungodly, anti-Christian; dissenting 977 *heretical*; unbelieving, nonbelieving, atheistical, godless 974 *irreligious*; nonpractising 769 *nonobservant*; scoffing, mocking, deriding; blasphemous, swearing 899 *cursing*; irreligious, irreverent; sacrilegious, profaning, desecrating, violating, iconoclastic 954 *lawless*; sinning, sinful, impure, perverted, reprobate 934 *wicked*; lapsing, backsliding, apostate.

profane, unholy, unhallowed, unsanctified, unblest; accursed; unconsecrated; infidel, pagan.

Vb. *be impious*, – sacrilegious etc. adj.; sin 934 *be wicked*; swear, blaspheme, take the name of the Lord in vain 899 *curse*; profane, desecrate, violate 675 *misuse*; commit sacrilege, defile, sully 649 *make unclean*; worship false gods; play false 541 *dissemble*; lapse, backslide 603 *apostatize*.

981 Worship

N. *worship*, honour, reverence, homage 920 *respect*; awe 854 *fear*; veneration, adoration; humbleness 872 *humility*; devotion, devotedness 979 *piety*; prayer, one's devotions, one's prayers; retreat, meditation, contemplation, communion with God.

cult, mystique; service of God, supreme worship, latria; inferior worship, dulia, hyperdulia; Christolatry, Mariolatry; iconolatry, image-worship; false worship 982 *idolatry*.

act of worship, rites; praises; glorification;

hymn-singing, psalm-s., psalmody, plainsong, chanting 412 *vocal music*; thanksgiving, blessing, benediction 907 *thanks*; offering, oblation, almsgiving, sacrifice, offering (**see** *oblation*); praying, saying one's prayers, reciting the rosary; self-examination 939 *penitence*; self-denial, self-discipline 945 *asceticism*; keeping fast 946 *fasting*; hajj, pilgrimage.

prayers, orisons, devotions; retreat, contemplation 449 *meditation*; prayer; petition, petitionary prayer 761 *request*; invocation, invocatory prayer 583 *allocution*; intercession, intercessory prayer, arrow p. 762 *deprecation*; suffrage, prayers for the dead, vigils; special prayer, intention; rogation, supplication, solemn s., litany, solemn l.; comminatory prayer, commination, denunciation 900 *threat*; imprecation, imprecatory prayer 899 *malediction*; excommunication, ban 883 *seclusion*; exorcism 300 *ejection*; benediction, benedicite, benison, grace 907 *thanks*; prayer for the day, collect; liturgical prayer, the Lord's Prayer, Paternoster, Our Father; Ave, Ave Maria, Hail Mary; Kyrie Eleison, Sursum Corda, Sanctus; Nunc Dimittis; dismissal, blessing; rosary, beads, bead-roll; prayer-wheel; prayer book, missal, breviary, book of hours; call to prayer, muezzin's cry 547 *call*.

hymn, song, psalm, metrical p.; religious song, spiritual; processional hymn, recessional; introit; plainsong, Gregorian chant, Ambrosian c., descant 412 *vocal music*; anthem, cantata, motet; antiphon, response; canticle, Te Deum, Benedicite; song of praise, paean, Magnificat; doxology, Gloria; greater doxology, Gloria in Excelsis; lesser doxology, Gloria Patri; paean, Hallelujah, Hosanna; Homeric hymn; Vedic hymn; hymn-singing, hymnody; psalm-singing, psalmody; hymnbook, hymnal, hymnary, psalter; Vedic hymns, Rigveda, Samaveda; hymnology, hymnography.

oblation, offertory, collection, alms and oblations 781 *offering*; pew rent, pewage; libation, incense; dedication, consecration; votive offering; scapegoat 150 *substitute*; burnt offering, holocaust; sacrifice, devotion; immolation, hecatomb 362 *slaughter*; human sacrifice 362 *homicide*; self-sacrifice 931 *disinterestedness*; self-immolation, suttee 362 *suicide*; expiation, propitiation 941 *atonement*; a humble and a contrite heart 939 *penitence*.

public worship, common prayer, intercommunion; agape, love-feast; service, divine service, divine office, mass, matins, evensong, benediction 988 *church service*; psalm-singing, psalmody, hymn-singing 412 *vocal music*; church, church-going, chapel-g. 979 *piety*; meeting for prayer, gathering for worship 74

assembly; prayer meeting, revival m.; open-air service, mission s., street evangelism, revivalism; temple worship, state religion 973 *religion*.

worshipper, fellow w., coreligionist; adorer, venerator; votary, devotee, oblate 979 *pietist*; glorifier, hymner, praiser, idolizer, admirer, ardent a., humble a. 923 *commender*; follower, server 742 *servant*; image-worshipper, iconolater; sacrificer, offerer 781 *giver*; invocator, invoker, caller 583 *allocution*; supplicator, suppliant, suppliant 763 *petitioner*, man *or* woman of prayer, beadsman, intercessor; contemplative, mystic, sufi, visionary; dervish, marabout, enthusiast, revivalist, prophet 973 *religious teacher*; celebrant, officiant 986 *clergy*; communicant, churchgoer, chapelgoer, temple worshipper; congregation, the faithful; psalm-singer, hymns., psalmodist, chanter, cantor; psalmist, hymn-writer, hymnologist; pilgrim, palmer, hajji 268 *traveller*.

Vb. *worship*, honour, revere, venerate, adore 920 *respect*; honour and obey 854 *fear*; pay homage to, acknowledge 917 *do one's duty*; make a god of one, deify; bow down before, kneel to, genuflect, prostrate oneself, lift up one's heart; extol, laud, magnify, glorify, give glory to 923 *praise*; celebrate 413 *sing*; light candles to, burn incense before, offer sacrifice to; pray, say a prayer, say one's prayers, recite the rosary; commune with God 979 *be pious*.

offer worship, celebrate, officiate, minister, administer the sacraments 988 *perform ritual*; lead the congregation, lead in prayer; sacrifice, make s., offer up 781 *give*; sacrifice to, propitiate, appease 719 *pacify*; vow, make vows 764 *promise*; dedicate, consecrate 979 *sanctify*, take vows, enter holy orders 986 *take orders*; go to church, go to chapel, go to meeting, meet for prayer 979 *be pious*; go to service, hear Mass, take the sacraments, receive the Eucharist, take Holy Communion; observe Lent 946 *starve*; deny oneself 945 *be ascetic*; go into retreat 449 *meditate*; chant psalms, sing hymns, sing praises.

982 Idolatry

N. *idolatry*, idolatrousness, false worship, superstition 981 *worship*; heathenism, paganism 973 *religion*; fetishism, anthropomorphism, zoomorphism; iconolatry, image worship; mumbo jumbo, hocus-pocus 983 *sorcery*; cult; sacrifice, human s. 981 *oblation*; heliolatry, sun worship; star worship, Sabaism; pyrolatry, fire worship; zoolatry, animal worship; ophiolatry, snake worship; necrolatry, worship of the dead, demonolatry, devil worship 969 *diabolism*; Mammonism, worship of wealth.

idol. image, graven i., fetish, totem pole; lingam, yoni; golden calf 966 *deity*; godling, joss; teraphim, lares et penates, totem; Mumbo-Jumbo; Juggernaut, Baal, Moloch.

983 Sorcery

N. *sorcery*, witchery, magic arts, enchantments; witchcraft; magic lore 490 *knowledge*; wizardry; wonder-working, thaumaturgy 864 *miracle-working*; magic, jugglery, illusionism 542 *sleight*; white magic; black magic, black art, necromancy; witch-doctoring, shamanism; obeah, obi, voodooism, voodoo, hoodoo; spirit-raising 511 *divination*, 984 *occultism*; spirit-laying, ghost-l., exorcism 988 *rite*; magic rite, incantation; coven, witches' sabbath, witches' coven; Walpurgisnacht, Hallowe'en; witching hour.

spell, charm, enchantment, cantrip, hoodoo, curse; evil eye, jinx, hex, influence; bewitchment, fascination 291 *attraction*; obsession, possession, demoniacal p.; incantation; magic sign; magic word, magic formula, abraxas, open sesame, abracadabra; hocus pocus, mumbo jumbo, fee faw fum 515 *lack of meaning*; philtre, love potion.

talisman, charm, countercharm; cross, phylactery; St Christopher medal 662 *safeguard*; juju, obeah, mojo, fetish 982 *idol*; periapt, amulet, mascot, lucky charm; rabbit's foot, four-leaf clover, horseshoe, black cat; pentacle, pentagram 547 *indication*; swastika, fylfot, gammadion; scarab; birthstone; emblem; relic, holy r.

magic instrument, bell, book and candle, broomstick; witches' brew, hellbroth, witches' cauldron; philtre, potion, moly; wand, magic w.; fairy w.; magic ring, wishing cap; Aladdin's lamp, flying carpet, magic c.; seven-league boots; Excalibur; wishing well, wishbone, merrythought.

sorcerer, wise man, seer, soothsayer; astrologer, alchemist 984 *occultist*; Druid, magus, the Magi; thaumaturgist, wonder-worker, miracle-w. 864 *miracle-working*; shaman, witch-doctor, medicine man, fetishist; obi-man, voodooist, hoodooist, spirit-raiser 984 *occultist*; conjuror, exorcist, ghost-buster; snake-charmer; juggler, illusionist; enchanter, wizard, warlock; magician, theurgist; necromancer 969 *diabolist*; familiar, imp, evil spirit 969 *devil*; sorcerer's apprentice; Merlin, Prospero, Gandalf; Faust, Pied Piper.

sorceress, wise woman, Sibyl 511 *diviner*; Druidess; enchantress, witch, weird sister; hag, hellcat; succubus, succuba; lamia; fairy godmother, wicked fairy, Morgan le Fay 970 *fairy*; Witch of Endor, Hecate, Circe, Medea; three witches in 'Macbeth'.

Adj. *magical*, otherworldly, supernatural,

uncanny, eldritch, weird 970 *fairy-like*; spell-like; voodooistic; talismanic, phylacteric; magic, charmed, enchanted 178 *influential*.

bewitched, enchanted, charmed, fey; hypnotized, fascinated, spellbound, under the evil eye; under a curse, cursed; blighted, blasted, withered; hag-ridden, haunted.

Vb. *bewitch*, charm, enchant, fascinate 291 *attract*; hypnotize; magic; spellbind, cast a spell on, weave a spell over, lay under a spell; put a voodoo on; cast the evil eye, blight, blast 898 *be malevolent*; put a curse on, lay under a curse 899 *curse*; taboo, make t. 757 *prohibit*; hag-ride.

984 Occultism

N. *occultism*, esotericism, hermeticism, mysticism, transcendentalism 973 *religion*; cabbalism, cabbala, gematria; theosophy, reincarnationism; yogism; sciosophy, hyperphysics, metaphysics; supernaturalism, psychicism, pseudopsychology; secret art, esoteric science, occult lore, alchemy, astrology, psychomancy, spiritualism, magic 983 *sorcery*; sortilege 511 *divination*; fortune-telling, crystal-gazing, palmistry, chiromancy, tea-leaf reading 511 *prediction*; clairvoyance, feyness, second sight 438 *vision*; sixth sense 476 *intuition*; animal magnetism, mesmerism, hypnotism; hypnosis, hypnotic trance 375 *insensibility*.

psychics, parapsychology, psychism 447 *psychology*; psychic science, psychical research; paranormal perception, extrasensory p., ESP; telaesthesia, clairvoyance, feyness, second sight 476 *intuition*; psychokinesis, fork-bending; telepathy, telergy; thought-reading, mind-r., thought transference; precognition, psi faculty; déjà vu.

spiritualism, spiritism; spirit communication, psychomancy 983 *sorcery*; sciomancy 511 *divination*; mediumism; séance; astral body, spirit b., ethereal b. 320 *immateriality*; spirit manifestation, materialization, ectoplasm 319 *materiality*; apport, telekinesis; poltergeists; spirit-rapping, table-tapping, table-turning; automatism, automatic writing, spirit w.; psychography 586 *writing*; spirit message, psychogram; spiritualistic apparatus, psychograph, planchette, ouija board; control 970 *ghost*; ghost-hunting; psychical research; exorcism.

occultist, mystic; cabbalist; theosophist, yogi; spiritualist; astrologer, fortune-teller, spaewife *or* man, crystalgazer, palmist 511 *diviner*.

psychic, clairvoyant; telepathist; mind reader, thought r.; mesmerist, hypnotist; medium, spirit-rapper, automatist, psychographer, spirit-writer; seer, prophet 511 *oracle*.

psychical, psychic, fey, second-sighted; prophetic 511 *predicting*; telepathic, clairvoyant;

thought-reading, mind-r.; spiritualistic, mediumistic; ectoplasmic, telekinetic, spirit-rapping; mesmeric, hypnotic.

paranormal, parapsychological, meta-psychological, supernatural, preternatural, supranormal, supranatural.

985 The Church

N. *the church*, theocracy 733 *authority*, church government, Canterbury, Vatican 733 *government*; ecclesiastical order; papalism, papacy, popedom; popishness, ultramontanism; prelatism, prelacy; episcopacy, episcopalianism; presbytery, presbyterianism, congregationalism, ecclesiology.

ecclesiasticism, clericalism, sacerdotalism; priestliness, priesthood, brahminhood; priest-dom, priestcraft; Brahminism; benefit of clergy 919 *nonliability*; Holy Office, Index Expurgatorius 757 *prohibition*.

monasticism, monastic life, monachism 895 *celibacy*; cenobitism 883 *seclusion*; monkhood, monkishness 945 *asceticism*.

holy orders, orders, minor o. 986 *cleric*; apostolic succession, ordination, consecration; induction, reading in; installation, enthronement; nomination, presentation, appointment 751 *commission*; preferment, translation, elevation 285 *progression*.

church office 689 *management*; ecclesiastical rank; priesthood; apostolate, apostleship; pontificate, papacy, Holy See, Vatican; cardinalate, cardinalship; patriarchate, exarchate, metropolitanate; primacy, primateship; archiepiscopate, archbishopric; see, bishopric, episcopate, episcopacy, prelacy, prelature; abbotship, abbacy, abbotric; priorate, priorship; archdeaconry, archdeaconate, archdeaconship; deanery, deanship; canonry, canonicate; prebendaryship; deaconate, deaconship; diaconate, subdiaconate; presbyterate, presbytership; eldership, moderatorship; ministership, pastorship, pastorate; rectorship, vicarship, vicariate; curacy, cure of souls; chaplainship, chaplaincy, chaplainry; incumbency, tenure, benefice 773 *possession*.

parish, deanery; presbytery; diocese, bishopric, see, archbishopric; metro-politanate, patriarchate, province 184 *district*.

benefice, incumbency, tenure; living, rectorship, parsonage; glebe, tithe; prebend, prebendal stall, canonry; temporalities, church lands, church endowments 777 *property*; patronage, advowson, right of presentation.

synod, provincial s., convocation, general council, ecumenical c. 692 *council*; college of cardinals, consistory, conclave; bench of bishops, episcopal bench; chapter, vestry; kirk

session, presbytery, synod, Sanhedrim 956 *tribunal*; consistorial court, Court of Arches.

Adj. *ecclesiastical*, ecclestiastic, churchly, ecclesiological, theocratic; infallible 733 *authoritative*; priest-ridden, ultramontane 976 *orthodox*; apostolic; hierarchical, pontifical, papal 976 *Roman Catholic*; patriarchal, metropolitan; episcopal, prelatic; episcopalian, presbyterian, Wee Free 978 *sectarian*; prioral, abbatial; conciliar, synodic, presbyteral, capitular; sanhedral, consistorial; provincial, diocesan, parochial.

986 Clergy

N. *clergy*, hierarchy; clerical order, parsondom, the cloth, the pulpit, the ministry; sacerdotal order, priesthood, secular clergy, regular clergy, religious.

cleric, clerk in holy orders, priest, deacon, sub-deacon, acolyte, exorcist, lector, ostiary; churchman *or* -woman, ecclesiastic, divine; Doctor of Divinity; clergyman, man *or* woman of the cloth, minister of the Gospel, servant of God; reverend, father, father in God; padre, sky pilot, Holy Joe; beneficed clergyman, beneficiary, pluralist, parson, minister, rector, incumbent, residentiary 776 *possessor*; hedgepriest, priestling 639 *nonentity*; ordinand, seminarist 538 *learner*.

pastor, shepherd, father in God, minister, woman m., parish priest, rector, vicar, perpetual curate, curate, abbé; chaplain; confessor, father c., penitentiary; spiritual director, spiritual adviser; pardoner; friar; preaching order, predicant; pulpiteer, lay preacher 537 *preacher*; field preacher, missioner, missionary 901 *philanthropist*; evangelist, revivalist, salvationist, hot-gospeller.

ecclesiarch, ecclesiastical potentate, hierarch, dignitary 741 *governor*; pope, Supreme Pontiff, Holy Father, Vicar of Christ, Bishop of Rome; cardinal, prince of the church; patriarch, exarch, metropolitan, primate, archbishop; prelate, diocesan, bishop; suffragan, assistant bishop, 'episcopal curate'; bench of bishops, episcopale, Lords Spiritual; episcopi vagantes; archpriest, archpresbyter; archdeacon, deacon, subdeacon; dean, subdean, rural dean; canon, canon regular, canon secular, residentiary; prebendary, capitular; archimandrite; Superior, Mother S.; abbot, abbess, prior, prioress, Grand Prior; elder, presbyter, moderator.

monk, monastic 895 *celibate*; hermit, cenobite, Desert Father 883 *solitary*; Orthodox monk, caloyer; Islamic monk, santon, marabout; sufi 979 *pietist*; dervish, fakir 945 *ascetic*; Buddhist monk, pongye, bonze; brother, regular, conventual; superior, archimandrite, abbot, prior; novice, lay brother; friar, begging f., mendicant f., discalced f., barefoot f.; monks, religious; fraternity, brotherhood, lay b., friary; order, religious o. 708 *community*; Black Monk, Benedictine, Cistercian, Bernardine, Trappist; Carthusian; Cluniac; Gilbertine; Premonstratensian, Mathurin, Trinitarian; Dominicans, Friars Majors, Black Friars; Franciscans, Poverelli, Grey Friars, Friars Minors, Capuchins; Augustines, Austin Friars; Carmelites, White Friars; Crutched Friars; Beghards; teaching order, missionary o., Society of Jesus, Jesuits; crusading order, Templars, Knights Templars; Hospitallers, Knights Hospitallers, Knights of the Hospital of St John of Jerusalem, Knights of Malta.

nun, clergywoman; anchoress, recluse; religious, bride of Christ; sister, mother; novice, postulant; lay sister; Superioress, Mother Superior, abbess, prioress, canoness, deaconess; sisterhood, lay s., beguinage, Beguine; Carmelites, Ursulines. Poor Clares, Little Sisters of the Poor, Sisters of Mercy.

church officer, elder, presbyter, deacon 741 *officer*; priest, chantry p., chaplain; curate in charge, minister; lay preacher, lay reader; acolyte, server, altar boy; crucifer, thurifer; chorister, choirboy, precentor, succentor, cantor 413 *choir*; sidesman *or* -woman; churchwarden; clerk, vestry c., parish c.; beadle, verger, pewopener; sacristan, sexton; grave digger, bellringer.

priest, chief p., high p., archpriest, hierophant; priestess, Vestal, Pythia, Pythoness, prophetess, prophet 511 *oracle*; Levite; rabbi; imam, mufti; Brahmin; bonze, lama, Dalai L., Panchen L.; pontifex, pontiff, flamen, archflamen; Druid, Druidess; shaman, witch doctor.

church title, Holy Father; Eminence; Monsignor, Monseigneur; Lordship, Lord Spiritual; Most Reverend, Right R., Very R.; the Reverend; parson, rector, vicar; father, brother, Dom; mother, sister.

monastery, monkery, bonzery, lamasery; friary; priory, abbey; cloister, convent, nunnery, beguinage; ashram, hermitage 192 *retreat*; community house 192 *abode*; theological college, seminary; cell 194 *chamber*.

parsonage, presbytery, rectory, vicarage; manse; deanery, archdeaconry 192 *abode*; palaee, bishop's p., patriarchate; Lambeth, Vatican; close, cathedral c., precincts 235 *enclosure*.

Adj. *monastic*, cloistered, enclosed; monkish, celibate; contemplative, in retreat; cowled, veiled; tonsured, shaven and shorn.

Vb. *take orders*, take holy orders, be ordained, enter the church, enter the ministry, become a minister *or* vicar, wear the cloth; take vows, take the tonsure, take the cowl; take the veil,

become a nun; enter a monastery *or* a nunnery, renounce the world.

987 Laity

N. *laity*, temporalty, lay people, people, civilians 869 *commonalty*; cure, charge, parish; flock, sheep, fold; diocesans, parishioners; brethren, congregation, society; lay brethren, lay sisterhood, lay community 708 *community*.

lay person, laic; lay rector, lay deacon; lay brother, lay sister; catechumen, ordinand, seminarist, novice, postulant 538 *learner*; lay preacher, lay reader; elder, deacon, deaconess 986 *church officer*; parishioner, diocesan, member of the flock; laicizer, secularizer.

988 Ritual

N. *ritual*, procedure, way of doing things, method, routine 624 *way*; prescribed procedure, due order 60 *order*; form, order, liturgy 610 *practice*; ceremonial, ceremony 875 *formality*.

rite, mode of worship 981 *cult*; observance, ritual practice 610 *practice*; form, order, ordinance, rubric, formula, formulary 693 *precept*; ceremony, solemnity, sacrament, mystery 876 *celebration*; rites, mysteries 551 *representation*; initiatory rite, rite of passage, circumcision, initiation, initiation rites, baptism 299 *reception*; christening; salat, puja.

ministration, functioning, officiating, performance 676 *action*; administration, celebration, solemnization; the pulpit, sermon, address, preaching 534 *teaching*; homily 534 *lecture*; homiletics 579 *oratory*; pastoral care, cure of souls; pastoral epistle, pastoral letter; confession, auricular c.; shrift, absolution, penance.

Christian rite, rites of the Church; sacrament, the seven sacraments; baptism, christening 299 *reception*; immersion, total i. 303 *immersion*; laying on of hands, confirmation, First Communion; Holy Communion, Eucharist, reservation of the sacraments; penitential rites 941 *penance*; absolution 960 *acquittal*; Holy Matrimony 894 *marriage*; Holy Orders 985 *the church*; Holy Unction, chrism; visitation of the sick, extreme unction, last rites, viaticum; burial of the dead; requiem mass; liturgy, order of service, order of baptism, marriage service, solemnization of matrimony, nuptial mass; churching of women; ordination, ordering of deacons, ordering of priests; consecration, consecration of bishops; exorcism 300 *ejection*; excommunication, ban, bell, book and candle; canonization, beatification; dedication, undedication.

Holy Communion, Eucharist, Blessed E.; mass, high m., missa solemnis; sung m., missa cantata; low mass; public mass, private m.; communion, the Lord's Supper; preparation, confession, asperges; service of the book, introit, the Kyries, the Gloria, the Lesson, the Gradual, the Collects, the Gospel, the creed; service of the Altar, the offertory, offertory sentence, offertory prayers, the biddings; the blessing, the thanksgiving, Sursum Corda, Preface, Sanctus, Great Amen; the breaking of the bread, the commixture; the Pax; consecration; elevation of the Host; Angus Dei; the Communion; kiss of peace; prayers of thanksgiving, the dismissal; the blessing.

the sacrament, the Holy Sacrament, the Blessed Eucharist; Corpus Christi, body and blood of Christ; real presence, transubstantiation, consubstantiation, impanation; the elements, bread and wine, altar bread; consecrated bread, host; reserved sacrament; viaticum.

church service, office, duty, service 981 *act of worship*; liturgy, celebration, concelebration; canonical hours, matins, lauds, prime, terce, sext, none, vespers, compline; the little hours; morning prayer, matins; evening prayer, evensong, benediction; Tenebrae; vigil, midnight mass, watchnight service; devotional service, three-hour s.; novena.

ritual act, symbolical act, sacramental, symbolism 551 *representation*; lustration, purification; thurification, incense-burning 338 *vaporization*; sprinkling, aspersion, asperges; circumambulation 314 *circuition*; procession 285 *progression*; stations of the cross 981 *act of worship*; obeisance, bowing, kneeling, genuflexion, prostration, homage, Toronto blessing 920 *respects*; crossing oneself, signation, sign of the cross 547 *gesture*; eucharistic rite, breaking the bread; intinction; elevating of the Host; kiss of peace; sacrifice.

ritual object, cross, rood, Holy Rood, crucifix; altar, Lord's table, communion t.; altar furniture, altar cloth, candle, candlestick; communion wine, communion bread; cup, chalice, grail, Holy Grail, Sangrail; cruet; paten, ciborium, pyx, pyx chest, tabernacle; monstrance, chrism, chrismatory; collection plate, salver; incense, incensory, censer, thurible; holy water; aspergillum; aspersorium; piscina; sacring bell, Sanctus bell; font, baptismal f., baptistery; baptismal garment, chrisom, christening gown; wedding garment, wedding dress, bridal veil, wedding ring; devotional object, relics, sacred relics; reliquary, shrine, casket 194 *box*; icon, Pietà, Holy Sepulchre, stations of the cross 551 *image*; osculatory, pax; Agnus Dei, rosary, beads, beadroll 981 *prayers*; votive candle; non-Christian objects, Ark of the Covenant, Mercy-seat; seven-branched candlestick; shewbread;

laver; hyssop; sackcloth and ashes; libation dish, patina; joss stick; prayer wheel; altar of incense; urim, thummim; temple veil.

hymnal, hymn book, hymnary; psalter, psalm-book, book of psalms 981 *hymn*.

holy day, feast, feast day, festival 837 *festivity*; fast day, meatless d. 946 *fast*; high day, day of observance, day of obligation 876 *celebration*; sabbath, sabbath day, day of rest 681 *leisure*; Lord's Day, Sunday; saint's day 141 *anniversary*; All Hallows, All Saints, All Souls, Lady Day, Feast of the Annunciation; Candlemas, Feast of the Purification; Feast of the Assumption; Lammas, Martinmas, Michaelmas; Advent; Christmas, Christmastide, Yuletide, Noel, Nativity, Epiphany, Twelfth Night; Lent, Shrove Tuesday, Ash Wednesday, Maundy Thursday, Good Friday; Holy Week, Passion Week; Easter, Eastertide, Easter Sunday, Ascension Day; Whitsuntide, Whitsun, Pentecost; Corpus Christi; Trinity Sunday; Passover; Feast of Weeks, Pentecost; Feast of Tabernacles, Feast of Ingathering; Feast of the Dedication, Hanukkah; Day of Atonement, Yom Kippur; Ramadan, Bairam; Muharram.

Adj. *ritual*, procedural; formal, solemn, ceremonial, liturgical; processional, recessional; symbolic, symbolical.

ritualistic, ceremonious, ceremonial, formulistic.

Vb. *perform ritual*, perform the rites, say office, celebrate, concelebrate, officiate; take the service, lead worship 981 *offer worship*; baptize, christen, confirm, ordain, lay on hands; minister, administer the sacraments, give communion; sacrifice, offer s., make s.; offer prayers, bless, give benediction; anathematize, ban, ban with bell, book and candle; excommunicate, unchurch, unfrock; dedicate, consecrate, deconsecrate; purify, lustrate, asperge; cense, burn incense; anoint, give extreme unction; confess, absolve, pronounce absolution, shrive; take communion, partake of Holy Communion, receive the sacraments; bow, kneel, genuflect, prostrate oneself; sign oneself, cross o., make the sign of the cross; take holy water; tell one's beads, say one's rosary; make one's stations; process, go in procession; circumambulate; fast, flagellate oneself, do penance.

989 Canonicals

N. *canonicals*, clericals, clerical dress, cloth, clerical black 228 *dress*; frock, soutane, cassock, scapular; cloak, gown, Geneva g. 228 *cloak*; robe, cowl, hood, capuche; lappet, bands, Geneva b.; clerical collar, dog c.; chimere, lawn sleeves; apron, gaiters, shovel hat; cardinal's hat; priests' cap, biretta, black b., purple b., red b.; skullcap, calotte, zucchetto; Salvation Army bonnet 228 *headgear*; tonsure, shaven crown 229 *bareness*; prayer-cap; tallith.

vestments, ephod, priestly vesture, canonical robes; pontificalia, pontificals; cassock, surplice, rochet; cope, tunicle, dalmatic, alb 228 *robe*; amice, chasuble; stole, deacon's s.; scarf, tippet, pallium; cingulum; maniple, fanon; mitre, tiara, triple crown 743 *regalia*; papal vestment, orale; crosier, crook, staff, pastoral s. 743 *badge of rank*; pectoral 222 *cross*; episcopal ring; orphrey or orfray, ecclesiastical embroidery 844 *ornamentation*.

990 Temple

N. *temple*, pantheon; shrine; joss house; house of God, tabernacle, the Temple, House of the Lord; place of worship 981 *worship*; masjid, mosque; house of prayer, oratory; pagoda, stupa, tope, dagoba, ziggurat 164 *edifice*; torii, toran, gopuram 263 *doorway*.

holy place, holy ground, sacred g.; sanctuary, adytum, cella, naos; Ark of the Covenant, Mercy-seat, Sanctum, Holy of Holies, oracle; martyry, sacred tomb, marabout, sepulchre, Holy Sepulchre; graveyard, God's Acre 364 *cemetery*; place of pilgrimage; Holy City, Zion, Jerusalem; Mecca, Benares.

church, God's house; parish church, daughter c., chapel of ease; cathedral, minster, pro-cathedral; basilica; abbey; kirk, chapel, tabernacle, temple, bethel, ebenezer; conventicle, meeting house, prayer h.; house of prayer, oratory, chantry, chantry chapel; synagogue, mosque.

altar, high a., sacrarium, sanctuary; altar stone, altar slab; altar table, Lord's t., communion t.; altar bread 988 *the sacrament*; altar pyx; prothesis, credence, credence table 988 *ritual object*; canopy, baldachin, altarpiece, diptych, triptych, altar screen, reredos; altar cloth, altar frontal, antependium; predella, altar rails.

church utensil, font, baptistry; ambry, stoup, piscina; chalice, paten 988 *ritual object*; pulpit, lectern; bible, chained b., hymnal, hymnary, prayer book 981 *prayers*; hassock, kneeler; salver, collection plate, offertory bag; organ, harmonium; bell, church b., carillon.

church interior, nave, aisle, apse, ambulatory, transept; chancel, chevet, choir, sanctuary; hagioscope, squint; chancel screen, rood screen, jube, rood loft, gallery, organ loft; stall, choir s., sedile, sedilia, misericorde; pew, box pew; pulpit, ambo; lectern; chapel, side c., Lady c., feretory; confessional; clerestory, triforium; spandrel; stained glass, stained-glass window, rose w., jesse w.; calvary, stations of the cross, Easter sepulchre; baptistry, font; aumbry, sacristy, vestry; undercroft, crypt, vault; rood, cross, crucifix.

church exterior, porch, narthex, galilee; tympanum 263 *doorway*; tower, steeple, spire 209 *high structure*; bell tower, bellcote, belfry, campanile; buttress, flying b. 218 *prop*; cloister, ambulatory; chapterhouse, presbytery 692 *council*; churchyard, kirkyard, lychgate; close 235 *enclosure*.

Adj. *churchlike*, basilican, cathedral-like, cathedralesque; cruciform 222 *crossed*; apsidal 248 *curved*; Romanesque, Norman, Gothic, Early English, Decorated, Perpendicular, baroque, Puginesque, Gothic revival.

Index

For a note on how to use the index, see p. xi

accidental death
decease 361 n.
acclaim
assent 488 vb.
honour 866 vb.
repute 866 n.
applaud 923 vb.
applause 923 n.
acclamation
conformity 83 n.
acclimatize
make conform
   83 vb.
break in 369 vb.
habituate 610 vb.
make ready
   669 vb.
acclivity
incline 220 n.
accolade
honours 866 n.
praise 923 n.
accommodate
adjust 24 vb.
equalize 28 vb.
comprise 78 vb.
make conform
   83 vb.
place 187 vb.
aid 703 vb.
lend 784 vb.
accommodation
adaptation 24 n.
inclusion 78 n.
conformity 83 n.
room 183 n.
quarters 192 n.
storage 632 n.
pacification 719 n.
accompaniment
accompaniment
   89 n.
concomitant 89 n.
musical piece
   412 n.
accompanist
concomitant 89 n.
instrumentalist
   413 n.
accompany
accompany 89 vb.
play music 413 vb.
accomplice
concomitant 89 n.
colleague 707 n.
accomplish
produce 164 vb.
do 676 vb.
carry out 725 vb.
succeed 727 vb.
accomplishment
production 164 n.
action 676 n.
skill 694 n.

completion 725 n.
success 727 n.
accord
accord 24 vb.
agreement 24 n.
attribute 158 vb.
permit 756 vb.
consent 758 n.
give 781 vb.
accordance
uniformity 16 n.
agreement 24 n.
according to
agreeing 24 adj.
accordion
organ 414 n.
accost
approach 289 vb.
speak to 583 vb.
request 761 vb.
account
statistics 86 n.
list 87 n.
report 524 n.
oration 579 n.
correspondence
   588 n.
description 590 n.
credit 802 n.
debt 803 n.
account 808 vb.
accounts 808 n.
prestige 866 n.
accountable
liable 180 adj.
obliged 917 adj.
accountancy
numeration 86 n.
accounts 808 n.
accountant
accountant 808 n.
account for
account for
   158 vb.
accounts
accounts 808 n.
accoutrements
adjunct 40 n.
dressing 228 n.
property 777 n.
accredited
credible 485 adj.
creedal 485 adj.
accretion
increment 36 n.
addition 38 n.
adjunct 40 n.
extraneousness
   59 n.
expansion 197 n.
accrue
augment 36 vb.
accrue 38 vb.
result 157 vb.

accumulate
grow 36 vb.
join 45 vb.
bring together
   74 vb.
store 632 n.
acquire 771 vb.
take 786 vb.
accurate
accurate 494 adj.
accursed
bad 645 adj.
damnable 645 adj.
harmful 645 adj.
unfortunate
   731 adj.
unhappy 825 adj.
unpleasant
   827 adj.
hateful 888 adj.
heinous 934 adj.
wicked 934 adj.
profane 980 adj.
accusation
vindication
   927 n.
accusation 928 n.
accuse
accuse 928 vb.
litigate 959 vb.
accused
prisoner 750 n.
accused person
   928 n.
litigant 959 n.
accustom
train 534 vb
habituate 610 vb.
accustomed
usual 610 adj.
accustomed to
habituated
   610 adj.
AC/DC
abnormal 84 adj.
double 91 adj.
ace
unit 88 n.
best 644 adj.
excellent 644 adj.
masterpiece 694 n.
skilful 694 adj.
proficient person
   696 n.
acerbity
pungency 388 n.
unsavouriness
   391 n.
sourness 393 n.
rudeness 885 n.
resentment 891 n.
malevolence 898 n.
acetic
sour 393 adj.

acetylene
fuel 385 n.
ache
feel pain 377 vb.
pang 377 n.
badness 645 n.
suffer 825 vb.
achieve
produce 164 vb.
do 676 vb.
carry out 725 vb.
succeed 727 vb.
achievement
production 164 n.
progression 285 n.
heraldry 547 n.
deed 676 n.
completion 725 n.
success 727 n.
Achilles' heel
weakness 163 n.
defect 647 n.
vulnerability
   661 n.
moral sensibility
   819 n.
Achilles' tendon
foot 214 n.
aching
pain 377 n.
painful 377 adj.
fatigued 684 adj.
suffering 825 adj.
paining 827 adj.
achromatic
colourless 426 adj.
acid
destroyer 168 n.
keen 174 adj.
unsavoury 391 adj.
sour 393 adj.
sourness 393 n.
sullen 893 adj.
drug-taking 949 n.
acid house
music 412 n.
acidity
pungency 388 n.
sourness 393 n.
acidosis
sourness 393 n.
digestive disorders
   651 n.
acid rain
poison 659 n.
acid test
experiment 461 n.
acidulous
sour 393 adj.
acknowledge
attribute 158 vb.
notice 455 vb.
answer 460 vb.
testify 466 vb.

assent 488 vb.
confess 526 vb.
correspond 588 vb.
observe 768 vb.
greet 884 vb.
thank 907 vb.
reward 962 vb.
worship 981 vb.
acknowledged
usual 610 adj.
acknowledgment
attribution 158 n.
answer 460 n.
assent 488 n.
disclosure 526 n.
correspondence
   588 n.
observance 768 n.
courteous act
   884 n.
thanks 907 n.
dueness 915 n.
approbation 923 n.
penance 941 n.
reward 962 n.
acme
summit 213 n.
**acme of
   perfection**
perfection 646 n.
acne
skin disease 651 n.
blemish 845 n.
acolyte
auxiliary 707 n.
church officer
   986 n.
cleric 986 n.
aconite
poisonous plant
   659 n.
acoustic
sounding 398 adj.
auditory 415 adj.
acquaint
inform 524 vb.
acquaintance
knowledge 490 n.
friend 880 n.
friendship 880 n.
**acquaintance
   rape**
rape 951 n.
acquiesce
concur 181 vb.
acquiesce 488 vb.
be willing 597 vb.
be content 828 vb.
acquiescence
conformity 83 n.
concurrence 181 n.
assent 488 n.
willingness 597 n.
submission 721 n.

nearly 200 adv.
all clear
  signal 547 n.
  safety 660 n.
  permit 756 n.
all comers
  opponent 705 n.
  contender 716 n.
allegation
  testimony 466 n.
  affirmation 532 n.
  pretext 614 n.
  accusation 928 n.
allege
  affirm 532 vb.
  plead 614 vb.
allegiance
  loyalty 739 n.
  subjection 745 n.
  duty 917 n.
allegory
  analogue 18 n.
  assimilation 18 n.
  comparison
    462 n.
  metaphor 519 n.
  latency 523 n.
  narrative 590 n.
allegro
  adagio 412 adv.
alleluia
  praise 923 n.
allergic
  sentient 374 adj.
  diseased 651 adj.
allergy
  excretion 302 n.
  sensibility 374 n.
  ill health 651 n.
  dislike 861 n.
  hatred 888 n.
alleviate
  abate 37 vb.
  assuage 177 vb.
  disencumber
    701 vb.
  relieve 831 vb.
alley
  road 624 n.
All Hallows
  holy day 988 n.
all hands
  everyman 79 n.
alliance
  relation 9 n.
  consanguinity
    11 n.
  union 45 n.
  combination 50 n.
  concurrence 181 n.
  association 706 n.
  society 708 n.
  compact 765 n.
  marriage 894 n.

alligator
  skin 226 n.
  reptile 365 n.
all in
  impotent 161 adj.
  fatigued 684 adj.
all-in
  complete 54 adj.
  inclusive 78 adj.
  educational
    534 adj.
all in all
  on the whole
    52 adv.
all-inclusive
  inclusive 78 adj.
all-in wrestling
  wrestling 716 n.
alliteration
  assimilation 18 n.
  recurrence 106 n.
  ornament 574 n.
  prosody 593 n.
all-knowing
  knowing 490 adj.
  godlike 965 adj.
all manner of
  different 15 adj.
allocate
  arrange 62 vb.
  mete out 465 vb.
  apportion 783 vb.
allocution
  allocution 583 n.
all one
  equivalent 28 adj.
allot
  arrange 62 vb.
  disperse 75 vb.
  dispose of 673 vb.
  use 673 vb.
  endow 777 vb.
  give 781 vb.
  apportion 783 vb.
allotment
  piece 53 n.
  arrangement 62 n.
  farm 370 n.
  garden 370 n.
  apportionment
    783 n.
  portion 783 n.
allotted span
  old age 131 n.
  life 360 n.
all out
  completely 54 adv.
  swiftly 277 adv.
  resolute 599 adj.
all over
  widely 183 adv.
all over, be
  be complete 54 vb.
  end 69 vb.

all over one, be
  pet 889 vb.
  flatter 925 vb.
all over with, be
  be destroyed
    165 vb.
allow
  subtract 39 vb.
  attribute 158 vb.
  make possible
    469 vb.
  acquiesce 488 vb.
  assent 488 vb.
  confess 526 vb.
  facilitate 701 vb.
  permit 756 vb.
  consent 758 vb.
  be patient 823 vb.
allowance
  extra 40 n.
  qualification
    468 n.
  subvention 703 n.
  permission 756 n.
  earnings 771 n.
  dower 777 n.
  gift 781 n.
  portion 783 n.
  money 797 n.
  receipt 807 n.
  due 915 adj.
allowing
  thus 8 adv.
allowing for
  provided 468 adv.
  qualifying
    468 adj.
alloy
  a mixture 43 n.
  mix 43 vb.
  compound 50 n.
  mineral 359 n.
all right
  not bad 644 adj.
all-rounder
  athlete 162 n.
  proficient person
    696 n.
  player 837 n.
All Saints
  holy day 988 n.
all-singing, all-dancing
  comprehensive
    52 adj.
  ornamental
    844 adj.
all set
  prepared 669 adj.
all sorts
  medley 43 n.
  everyman 79 n.
All Souls
  holy day 988 n.

all talk
  insubstantial thing
    4 n.
all the best
  good luck 730 int.
all the rage
  fashionable
    848 adj.
all there
  intelligent
    498 adj.
  sane 502 adj.
all the same
  nevertheless
    468 adv.
all the time
  while 108 adv.
all the time in the world
  slowness 278 n.
  leisure 681 n.
all the way
  throughout
    54 adv.
all together
  collectively
    52 adv.
  together 74 adv.
all told
  completely 54 adv.
all to the good
  well 615 adv.
allude
  imply 523 vb.
  hint 524 vb.
all up with, be
  be destroyed
    165 vb.
allure
  attract 291 vb.
  attraction 291 n.
  tempt 612 vb.
  delight 826 vb.
alluring
  exciting 821 adj.
  pleasurable
    826 adj.
  personable
    841 adj.
allusion
  referral 9 n.
  metaphor 519 n.
alluvium
  leavings 41 n.
  soil 344 n.
ally
  join 45 vb.
  combine 50 vb.
  assenter 488 n.
  aider 703 n.
  cooperate 706 vb.
  colleague 707 n.
  join a party
    708 vb.

  contract 765 vb.
  friend 880 n.
alma mater
  academy 539 n.
almanac
  directory 87 n.
  chronology 117 n.
almighty
  powerful 160 adj.
  godlike 965 adj.
Almighty, the
  the Deity 965 n.
almoner
  nurse 658 n.
almost
  almost 33 adv.
  on the whole
    52 adv.
  nearly 200 adv.
alms
  gift 781 n.
almshouse
  retreat 192 n.
aloes
  unsavouriness
    391 n.
alone
  alone 88 adj.
  singly 88 adv.
along
  longwise 203 adv.
alongside
  near 200 adv.
along with
  in addition 38 adv.
  with 89 adv.
aloof
  distant 199 adj.
  incurious 454 adj.
  impassive
    820 adj.
  proud 871 adj.
  hostile 881 adj.
  unsociable 883 adj.
aloud
  loudly 400 adv.
alp
  high land 209 n.
alpaca
  fibre 208 n.
  textile 222 n.
alpha
  beginning 68 n.
Alpha and Omega
  the Deity 965 n.
alphabet
  beginning 68 n.
  list 87 n.
  letter 558 n.
  lettering 586 n.
alphabetical order
  order 60 n.

**alpha-
fetoprotein
test**
obstetrics 167 n.
diagnostic 658 n.
alphanumeric
computerized
86 adj.
alpha plus
excellent 644 adj.
Alps
high land 209 n.
already
before 119 adv.
at present 121 adv.
Alsatian
dog 365 n.
also
in addition 38 adv.
also-ran
inferior 35 n.
loser 728 n.
altar
ritual object 988 n.
altar 990 n.
altar boy
church officer
986 n.
altarpiece
altar 990 n.
alter
change 143 vb.
modify 143 vb.
qualify 468 vb.
alteration
difference 15 n.
change 143 n.
transition 147 n.
altercation
quarrel 709 n.
contention 716 n.
alter ego
identity 13 n.
analogue 18 n.
colleague 707 n.
deputy 755 n.
close friend 880 n.
alternate
correlate 12 vb.
correlative 12 adj.
come after 65 vb.
sequential 65 adj.
be discontinuous
72 vb.
discontinuous
72 adj.
periodical 141 adj.
substitute 150 n.
vary 152 vb.
fluctuate 317 vb.
deputy 755 n.
alternately
correlatively
12 adv.

alternating
correlative 12 adj.
sequential 65 adj.
discontinuous
72 adj.
periodical 141 adj.
alternative
changeable
143 adj.
substitute 150 n.
choice 605 n.
contrivance 623 n.
alternative fuel
fuel 385 n.
choice 605 n.
**alternative
medicine**
dissent 489 n.
medical art 658 n.
**alternative
reading**
interpretation
520 n.
alternator
electronics 160 n.
although
although 182 adv.
provided 468 adv.
altimeter
angular measure
247 n.
meter 465 n.
altitude
quantity 26 n.
degree 27 n.
height 209 n.
alto
vocalist 413 n.
altogether
completely 54 adv.
altogether, the
bareness 229 n.
altruism
philanthropy
901 n.
disinterestedness
931 n.
altruistic
benevolent
897 adj.
philanthropic
901 adj.
disinterested
931 adj.
alumnus
student 538 n.
always
while 108 adv.
**Alzheimer's
disease**
old age 131 n.
helplessness 161 n.
mental disorder
503 n. ·

a.m.
o'clock 117 adv.
morning 128 n.
amah
domestic 742 n.
amalgam
a mixture 43 n.
compound 50 n.
amalgamation
mixture 43 n.
combination 50 n.
association 706 n.
amanuensis
recorder 549 n.
instrument 628 n.
auxiliary 707 n.
amass
join 45 vb.
bring together
74 vb.
store 632 vb.
take 786 vb.
amateur
ignorance 491 n.
beginner 538 n.
unskilled 695 adj.
bungler 697 n.
**amateur
dramatics**
drama 594 n.
amateurish
ignorant 491 adj.
bungled 695 adj.
unskilled 695 adj.
amaze
surprise 508 vb.
disappoint 509 vb.
impress 821 vb.
be wonderful
864 vb.
amazing
prodigious 32 adj.
unexpected
508 adj.
wonderful 864 adj.
Amazon
violent creature
176 n.
female 373 n.
soldier 722 n.
brave person
855 n.
ambassador
messenger 529 n.
envoy 754 n.
amber
resin 357 n.
brownness 430 n.
orange 432 n.
yellow 433 adj.
yellowness 433 n.
gem 844 n.
ambidextrous
dual 90 adj.

double 91 adj.
skilful 694 adj.
ambience
surroundings
230 n.
painting 553 n.
ambiguity
disagreement 25 n.
uncertainty 474 n.
connotation 514 n.
unintelligibility
517 n.
equivocalness
518 n.
imperspicuity
568 n.
ambition
motive 612 n.
intention 617 n.
aspiration 852 n.
desire 859 n.
desired object
859 n.
ambivalence
contrariety 14 n.
disagreement 25 n.
uncertainty 474 n.
equivocalness
518 n.
falsehood 541 n.
amble
gait 265 n.
pedestrianism
267 n.
ride 267 vb.
wander 267 vb.
move slowly
278 vb.
slowness 278 n.
ambulance
conveyance
267 n.
vehicle 274 n.
hospital 658 n.
ambush
surprise 508 vb.
ambush 527 n.
ambush 527 vb.
stratagem 698 n.
ameliorate
make better
654 vb.
amen
amen 488 int.
assent 488 n.
amenable
credulous 487 adj.
willing 597 adj.
obedient 739 adj.
amend
rectify 654 vb.
repaire 656 vb.
amendment
amendment 654 n.

amends
compensation
31 n.
restoration 656 n.
remedy 658 n.
restitution 787 n.
atonement 941 n.
amenity
pleasurableness
826 n.
amethyst
purpleness 436 n.
gem 844 n.
amiable
pleasurable
826 adj.
friendliness 880 n.
amiable 884 adj.
amicable
friendly 880 adj.
amiable 884 adj.
amid
among 43 adv.
between 231 adv.
amidst
among 43 adv.
between 231 adv.
amiss
amiss 616 adv.
badly 645 adv.
amity
friendship 880 n.
ammo
ammunition
723 n.
ammonia
stench 397 n.
ammunition
means 629 n.
ammunition
723 n.
amnesia
oblivion 506 n.
amnesty
amnesty 506 n.
forget 506 vb.
deliverance 668 n.
exempt 919 vb.
nonliability 919 n.
amniocentesis
obstetrics 167 n.
diagnostic 658 n.
among
among 43 adv.
between 231 adv.
amongst
among 43 adv.
between 231 adv.
amoral
wicked 934 adj.
unchaste 951 adj.
irreligious 974 adj.
amorous
loving 887 adj.

request 761 n.
request 761 vb.
approachable
accessible 289 adj.
possible 469 adj.
easy 701 adj.
approaching
relative 9 adj.
approaching
289 adj.
approbation
approbation 923 n.
appropriate
circumstantial
8 adj.
relevant 9 adj.
apt 24 adj.
special 80 adj.
appropriate
786 vb.
right 913 adj.
**appropriate
person**
parentage 169 n.
keeper 749 n.
approval
assent 488 n.
permission 756 n.
repute 866 n.
approbation 923 n.
approve
approve 923 vb.
approved
authoritative
733 adj.
approved 923 adj.
approximate
liken 18 vb.
similar 18 adj.
near 200 adj.
approach 289 vb.
approximately
almost 33 adv.
nearly 200 adv.
approximation
relativeness 9 n.
similarity 18 n.
nearness 200 n.
approach 289 n.
appurtenance(s)
addition 38 n.
adjunct 40 n.
component 58 n.
concomitant 89 n.
property 777 n.
APR
finance 797 n.
credit 802 n.
après
similar 18 adj.
April fool
dupe 544 n.
laughingstock
851 n.

April shower
brief span 114 n.
apron
stage set 594 n.
canonicals 989 n.
apron stage
stage set 594 n.
apron strings
subjection 745 n.
fetter 748 n.
apropos
concerning 9 adv.
apt 24 adj.
incidentally
137 vb.
apse
church interior
990 n.
apt
apt 24 adj.
intelligent 498 adj.
aptitude
aptitude 694 n.
aptness
fitness 24 n.
tendency 179 n.
accuracy 494 n.
aptitude 694 n.
aptness vitae
alcoholic drink
301 n.
apt to
liable 180 adj.
aquamarine
greenness 434 n.
blue 435 adj.
blueness 435 n.
gem 844 n.
aquarium
accumulation 74 n.
zoo 369 n.
collection 632 n.
aquatic
watery 339 adj.
aquavit
alcoholic drink
301 n.
aqua vitae
alcoholic drink
301 n.
aqueduct
conduit 351 n.
bridge 624 n.
aquiline
angular 247 adj.
curved 248 adj.
animal 365 adj.
arabesque
ballet 594 n.
pattern 844 n.
Arabic alphabet
letter 558 n.
Arabic numerals
number 85 n.

arable farm
farm 370 n.
arachnid
animal 365 n.
arbiter
adviser 691 n.
magistracy 957 n.
arbitrage
gamble 618 vb.
arbitrageur
gambler 618 n.
arbitrary
unrelated 10 adj.
illogical 477 adj.
volitional 595 adj.
capricious 604 adj.
authoritative
733 adj.
authoritarian
735 adj.
insolent 878 adj.
lawless 954 adj.
arbitrate
judge 480 vb.
mediate 720 vb.
arbitration
judgment 480 n.
concord 710 n.
mediation 720 n.
arbitrator
estimator 480 n.
adviser 691 n.
mediator 720 n.
magistracy 957 n.
arbor
pivot 218 n.
arboretum
wood 366 n.
garden 370 n.
arboriculture
agriculture 370 n.
arbour
arbour 194 n.
Arbroath smoky
fish food 301 n.
arc
part 53 n.
arc 250 n.
fire 379 n.
arcade
pavilion 192 n.
curve 248 n.
path 624 n.
emporium 796 n.
Arcadia
happiness 824 n.
arcane
unintelligible
517 adj.
latent 523 adj.
concealed 525 adj.
arch
consummate
32 adj.

supreme 34 adj.
bond 47 n.
foot 214 n.
support 218 n.
be curved 248 vb.
curve 248 n.
camber 253 n.
merry 833 adj.
affected 850 adj.
archaeologist
antiquarian
125 n.
detector 484 n.
chronicler 549 n.
archaeology
antiquity 125 n.
palaeology 125 n.
discovery 484 n.
archaic
antiquated
127 adj.
olden 127 adj.
archaism
archaism 127 n.
neology 560 n.
archangel
angel 968 n.
archbishop
governor 741 n.
ecclesiarch 986 n.
archdeacon
ecclesiarch 986 n.
archduke
potentate 741 n.
person of rank
868 n.
arched
arched 253 adj.
concave 255 adj.
arch enemy
enemy 881 n.
archery
propulsion 287 n.
arms 723 n.
sport 837 n.
archetypal
original 21 adj.
archetype
prototype 23 n.
**Archimedes'
screw**
irrigator 341 n.
archipelago
island 349 n.
architect
producer 164 n.
artist 556 n.
planner 623 n.
artisan 686 n.
architecture
composition 56 n.
form 243 n.
structure 331 n.
art 551 n.

ornamental art
844 n.
archives
record 548 n.
collection 632 n.
title deed 767 n.
archivist
recorder 549 n.
keeper 749 n.
archpriest
ecclesiarch 986 n.
priest 986 n.
archway
doorway 263 n.
arc light
lamp 420 n.
ardent
forceful 571 adj.
fervent 818 adj.
loving 887 adj.
pietistic 979 adj.
ardour
heat 379 n.
vigour 571 n.
resolution 599 n.
warm feeling
818 n.
desire 859 n.
arduous
laborious 682 adj.
difficult 700 adj.
area
quantity 26 n.
greatness 32 n.
measure 183 n.
space 183 n.
region 184 n.
place 185 n.
size 195 n.
arena
range 183 n.
arena 724 n.
areola
circle 250 n.
argent
heraldic 547 adj.
heraldry 547 n.
argil
soil 344 n.
argon
air 340 n.
argosy
merchant ship
275 n.
shipping 275 n.
navy 722 n.
argot
slang 560 adj.
arguable
possible 469 adj.
uncertain 474 adj.
argue
evidence 466 vb.
argue 475 vb.

asteroid
planet 321 n.

as . . . they say
proverbially
496 adv.

asthma
respiratory disease
651 n.

asthmatic
diseased 651 adj.
sick person 651 n.

astigmatic
dim-sighted
440 adj.

astigmatism
dim sight 440 n.

astir
busy 678 adj.
excited 821 adj.

as . . . to
concerning 9 adv.

astonish
surprise 508 vb.
be wonderful
864 vb.

astonishing
prodigious 32 adj.
unusual 84 adj.

astonishment
wonder 864 n.

astound
surprise 508 vb.
impress 821 vb.
be wonderful
864 vb.

astounding
prodigious 32 adj.
unexpected
508 adj.
wonderful 864 adj.

astrakhan
skin 226 n.

astral
immaterial
320 adj.
celestial 321 adj.

astral body
spiritualism 984 n.

astray
unrelated 10 adj.
lost 772 adj.

astringent
conjunctive 45 adj.
pungent 388 adj.
sour 393 adj.

astrodome
athletics 162 n.
meeting place
192 n.
view 438 n.

astrolabe
gauge 465 n.

astrologer
diviner 511 n.

sorcerer 983 n.
occultist 984 n.

astrological
astronomic
321 adj.

astrology
influence 178 n.
astronomy 321 n.
divination 511 n.
occultism 984 n.

astronaut
traveller 268 n.
aeronaut 271 n.

astronomer
spectator 441 n.

astronomic
astronomic
321 adj.

astronomical
exorbitant 32 adj.
astronomic
321 adj.

astronomy
astronomy 321 n.

astrophysics
astronomy 321 n.

astute
intelligent 498 adj.
cunning 698 adj.

asunder
apart 46 adv.
separate 46 adj.

as . . . well as
in addition 38 adv.

as . . . well not to
inexpedient
643 adj.

as . . . well to
advisable 642 adj.

asylum
retreat 192 n.
reception 299 n.
protection 660 n.
refuge 662 n.

asymmetric
distorted 246 adj.

asymmetrical
unrelated 10 adj.
nonuniform 17 adj.
unequal 29 adj.
abnormal 84 adj.

asymmetry
unrelatedness 10 n.
nonuniformity
17 n.
disagreement 25 n.
inequality 29 n.
distortion 246 n.
ugliness 842 n.

at a guess
about 33 adv.

at all times
perpetually
139 adv.

at a loose end
leisurely 681 adj.

at a loss, be
be uncertain
474 vb.
not know 491 vb.
be in difficulty
700 vb.

**at a loss for
words**
voiceless 578 adj.

at a pinch
with difficulty
700 adv.

at a standstill
quiescent 266 adj.
inactive 679 adj.

atavism
consanguinity
11 n.
recurrence
106 n.
reversion 148 n.
reproduction
166 n.
memory 505 n.

at bay
endangered
661 adj.
in difficulties
700 adj.

at close range
near 200 adv.

**at cross
purposes**
disagreeing 25 adj.

**at daggers
drawn**
opposing 704 adj.
quarrelling
709 adj.
hostile 881 adj.

at death's door
dying 361 adj.

at ease
tranquil 266 adj.
reposeful 683 adj.
free 744 adj.
content 828 adj.

atelier
chamber 194 n.

at fault
mistaken 495 adj.
guilty 936 adj.

at full pitch
loud 400 adj.

at full speed
swiftly 277 adv.

at gunpoint
by force 740 adv.

at half-cock
immature 670 adj.

at half-mast
lamenting 836 adj.

at hand
early 135 adj.
impending 155 adj.
near 200 adj.
useful 640 adj.

Atharvaveda
non-Biblical
scripture 975 n.

at heart
inside 224 adv.

atheism
philosophy 449 n.
unbelief 486 n.
religion 973 n.
irreligion 974 n.

atheroma
cardiovascular
disease 651 n.

athlete
athlete 162 n.

athlete's foot
skin disease 651 n.

athletics
athletics 162 n.
contention 716 n.
contest 716 n.

at home
apt 24 adj.
assembly 74 n.
inside 224 adv.

at home in
habituated
610 adj.

at intervals
periodically
141 adv.

at its height
great 32 adj.
beyond 34 adv.

at knifepoint
by force 740 adv.

Atlantis
fantasy 513 n.

at large
free 744 adj.

Atlas
athlete 162 n.
giant 195 n.
classical deities
967 n.

atlas
directory 87 n.
world 321 n.
map 551 n.

at last
finally 69 adv.
at last 113 adv.
late 136 adv.

at least
slightly 33 adv.

at length
late 136 adv.

at long last
finally 69 adv.

at last 113 adv.
late 136 adv.

ATM
treasury 799 n.

atmosphere
surroundings
230 n.
atmosphere 340 n.
painting 553 n.

atmospheric
airy 340 adj.

**atmospheric
pressure**
weather 340 n.

atmospherics
commotion 318 n.
discord 411 n.

at no time
never 109 adv.

at odds
disagreeing 25 adj.
quarrelling
709 adj.

atoll
island 349 n.

atom
small thing 33 n.
unit 88 n.
minuteness 196 n.
element 319 n.

atomic
dynamic 160 adj.

atomizer
pulverizer 332 n.
vaporizer 338 n.
air 340 n.

atonal
discordant 411 adj.

at one
agreeing 24 adj.

atone
atone 941 vb.

**at one's beck
and call**
obedient 739 adj.
serving 742 adj.

**at one's
convenience**
leisurely 681 adj.

at one's disposal
possessed 773 adj.

at one's ease
comfortable
376 adj.
in comfort
376 adv.

at one's feet
near 200 adv.

**at one's
fingertips**
near 200 adj.
near 200 adv.

at one's peak
strong 162 adj.

audiotypist
stenographer
586 n.
audiovisuals
sounding 398 adj.
auditory 415 adj.
educational
534 adj.
audit
number 86 vb.
enquire 459 vb.
enquiry 459 n.
account 808 vb.
accounts 808 n.
audition
hearing 415 n.
listening 415 n.
exam 459 n.
experiment 461 n.
dramaturgy 594 n.
auditorium
listener 415 n.
onlookers 441 n.
theatre 594 n.
auf
Wiedersehen
goodbye 296 int.
auger
sharp point 256 n.
perforator 263 n.
augment
augment 36 vb.
augmentation
increase 36 n.
increment 36 n.
expansion 197 n.
aggravation 832 n.
augur
predict 511 vb.
augury
divination 511 n.
august
great 32 adj.
notable 638 adj.
impressive 821 adj.
worshipful
866 adj.
Augustan Age
literature 557 n.
auk
animal 365 n.
auld lang syne
past time 125 n.
aumbry
church interior
990 n.
aunt
kinsman 11 n.
female 373 n.
Auntie
broadcasting
531 n.
auntie
kinsman 11 n.

female 373 n.
Aunt Sally
laughingstock
851 n.
au pair
resident 191 n.
domestic 742 n.
aura
surroundings
230 n.
prestige 866 n.
aural
auditory 415 adj.
aureole
light 417 n.
honours 866 n.
aureomycin
drug 658 n.
au revoir
goodbye 296 int.
auricular
auditory 415 adj.
auriscope
hearing aid 415 n.
detector 484 n.
diagnostic 658 n.
Aurora
morning 128 n.
aurora
glow 417 n.
aurora australis
heavens 321 n.
glow 417 n.
aurora borealis
heavens 321 n.
glow 417 n.
auspices
protection 660 n.
aid 703 n.
auspicious
opportune 137 adj.
predicting 511 adj.
palmy 730 adj.
promising 852 adj.
austere
plain 573 adj.
severe 735 adj.
ascetic 945 adj.
pietistic 979 adj.
austerity
unsavouriness
391 n.
plainness 573 n.
insufficiency
636 n.
severity 735 n.
asceticism 945 n.
pietism 979 n.
authentic
genuine 494 adj.
authenticate
testify 466 vb.
make certain
473 vb.

endorse 488 vb.
give security
767 vb.
title deed 767 n.
authenticity
authenticity 494 n.
author
cause 156 n.
author 589 n.
planner 623 n.
authoritarian
authoritarian
735 adj.
tyrant 735 n.
authoritative
evidential 466 adj.
certain 473 adj.
creedal 485 adj.
authoritative
733 adj.
commanding
737 adj.
orthodox 976 adj.
authorities, the
master 741 n.
authority
credential 466 n.
sage 500 n.
informant
524 n.
expert 696 n.
authority 733 n.
permit 756 n.
authorization
warrant 737 n.
permission 756 n.
security 767 n.
authorize
endorse 488 vb.
commission
751 vb.
permit 756 vb.
Authorized
Version
scripture 975 n.
authorship
composition 56 n.
causation 156 n.
production 164 n.
writing 586 n.
autism
intrinsicality 56 n.
learning disability
503 n.
unsociability
883 n.
autistic
intrinsic 5 adj.
*having a learning
disability* 503 adj.
auto
automobile 274 n.
autobahn
road 624 n.

autobiography
biography 590 n.
autobus
bus 274 n.
autochthones
native 191 n.
autocrat
autocrat 741 n.
autocratic
volitional 595 adj.
authoritative
733 adj.
authoritarian
735 adj.
autocrime
stealing 788 n.
autocue
broadcasting
531 n.
auto da fé
killing 362 n.
autograph
no imitation 21 n.
reminder 505 n.
identification
547 n.
label 547 n.
sign 547 vb.
script 586 n.
automated
dynamic 160 adj.
mechanical
630 adj.
automated
teller machine
treasury 799 n.
automatic
intrinsic 5 adj.
computerized
86 adj.
involuntary
596 adj.
spontaneous
609 adj.
instrumental
628 adj.
mechanical
630 adj.
pistol 723 n.
automatic pilot
aeronaut 271 n.
aircraft 276 n.
automatic reflex
spontaneity 609 n.
automation
uniformity 16 n.
electronics 160 n.
instrumentality
628 n.
automatism
spiritualism 984 n.
automaton
image 551 n.
machine 630 n.

automobile
automobile 274 n.
automotive
moving 265 adj.
autonomous
governmental
733 adj.
independent
744 adj.
autonomy
government 733 n.
independence
744 n.
autopilot
aeronaut 271 n.
aircraft 276 n.
autopsy
death 361 n.
inquest 364 n.
inspection 438 n.
enquiry 459 n.
autoroute
road 624 n.
autostrada
road 624 n.
autosuggestion
sense 374 n.
insensibility 375 n.
misjudgment
481 n.
fantasy 513 n.
autotheft
automobile 274 n.
stealing 788 n.
autumn
period 110 n.
autumn 129 n.
auxiliary
inferior 35 adj.
additional 38 adj.
aiding 703 adj.
auxiliary 707 n.
avail
benefit 615 vb.
utility 640 n.
available
accessible 289 adj.
possible 469 adj.
useful 640 adj.
used 673 adj.
avalanche
revolution 149 n.
descent 309 n.
snow 380 n.
redundance 637 n.
avant-garde
precursor 66 n.
modern 126 adj.
modernist 126 n.
front 237 n.
preceding 283 n.
dramatic 594 adj.
avarice
avarice 816 n.

barrier
barrier 235 n.
obstacle 702 n.
barrier
  contraceptive
contraception
  172 n.
barring
exclusive of
  57 adv.
barrister
combatant 722 n.
lawyer 958 n.
barrow
earthwork 253 n.
pushcart 274 n.
tomb 364 n.
monument
  548 n.
shop 796 n.
barrow boy
seller 793 n.
pedlar 794 n.
barry
heraldic 547 adj.
bar sinister
slur 867 n.
barter
correlate 12 vb.
interchange
  151 vb.
assign 780 vb.
barter 791 n.
trade 791 n.
pay 804 vb.
basalt
rock 344 n.
base
situation 186 n.
place 187 vb.
station 187 n.
abode 192 n.
base 214 n.
support 218 vb.
limit 236 n.
heraldry 547 n.
bad 645 adj.
cowardly 856 adj.
disreputable
  867 adj.
servile 879 adj.
heinous 934 adj.
baseball
ball game 837 n.
baseboard
base 214 n.
baseline
place 185 n.
basement
cellar 194 n.
lowness 210 n.
base 214 n.
base metal
mineral 359 n.

baseness
disrepute 867 n.
improbity 930 n.
wickedness 934 n.
bash
collide 279 vb.
strike 279 vb.
bashful
unwilling 598 adj.
modest 874 adj.
bashing
knock 279 n.
basic
simple 44 adj.
fundamental
  156 adj.
important 638 adj.
basics
reality 1 n.
learning 536 n.
basic training
learning 536 n.
basil
herb 301 n.
basilica
church 990 n.
basilisk
rara avis 84 n.
eye 438 n.
basin
stable 192 n.
bowl 194 n.
cavity 255 n.
conduit 351 n.
basis
reason why 156 n.
basis 218 n.
bask
be hot 379 vb.
basket
basket 194 n.
basketball
ball game 837 n.
basket chair
seat 218 n.
basketwork
network 222 n.
bask in
enjoy 376 vb.
be pleased
  824 vb.
basmatti rice
cereals 301 n.
bas-relief
sculpture 554 n.
bass
fish 365 n.
resonance 404 n.
vocalist 413 n.
basset
dog 365 n.
bassinet
basket 194 n.
bed 218 n.

bassoon
flute 414 n.
bastard
unwarranted
  916 adj.
cad 938 n.
bastard 954 adj.
bastardy 954 n.
bastardize
disentitle 916 vb.
make illegal
  954 vb.
baste
tie 45 vb.
cook 301 vb.
grease 357 vb.
Bastille Day
anniversary 141 n.
special day 876 n.
bastion
protection 660 n.
refuge 662 n.
fortification 713 n.
bacuco
drug 949 n.
bat
velocity 277 n.
strike 279 vb.
propel 287 vb.
mammal 365 n.
club 723 n.
batch
finite quantity
  26 n.
bunch 74 n.
group 74 n.
batch
  processing
computing 86 n.
bated breath
faintness 401 n.
voicelessness
  578 n.
bath
vessel 194 n.
water 339 n.
ablutions 648 n.
bath chair
pushcart 274 n.
bathe
swim 269 vb.
immerse 303 vb.
be wet 341 vb.
drench 341 vb.
clean 648 vb.
amuse oneself
  837 vb.
bathing beauty
sea nymph
  343 n.
bathing suit
beachwear 228 n.
bathos
absurdity 497 n.

ridiculousness
  849 n.
bathrobe
informal dress
  228 n.
bathroom
chamber 194 n.
ablutions 648 n.
bathroom scales
scales 322 n.
bath salts
cosmetic 843 n.
bathtub
ablutions 648 n.
bathymetric
deep 211 adj.
batik
textile 222 n.
printing 555 n.
ornamental art
  844 n.
batman
clothier 228 n.
domestic 742 n.
baton
support 218 n.
badge of rule
  743 n.
bat one's
  eyelashes
gesticulate 547 vb.
bats
crazy 503 adj.
bats in the
  belfry
eccentricity 503 n.
batsman
player 837 n.
battalion(s)
multitude 104 n.
formation 722 n.
batten
fastening 47 n.
strip 208 n.
battenburg cake
pastries and cakes
  301 n.
batten down the
  hatches
close 264 vb.
seek refuge 662 vb.
make ready
  669 vb.
batten on
eat 301 vb.
prosper 730 vb.
be servile 879 vb.
batter
demolish 165 vb.
deform 244 vb.
distort 246 vb.
collide 279 vb.
strike 279 vb.
pulpiness 356 n.

ill-treat 645 vb.
battering ram
ram 279 n.
club 723 n.
battery
accumulation 74 n.
electronics 160 n.
stable 192 n.
stock farm 369 n.
exam 459 n.
storage 632 n.
formation 722 n.
gun 723 n.
battery of tests
diagnostic 658 n.
battle
slaughter 362 n.
action 676 n.
contend 716 vb.
battle 718 n.
trophy 729 n.
be hostile 881 vb.
battleaxe
sharp edge 256 n.
axe 723 n.
battle cry
call 547 n.
danger signal
  665 n.
defiance 711 n.
war 718 n.
warfare 718 n.
threat 900 n.
battledress
uniform 228 n.
battlefield
battle 718 n.
battleground
  724 n.
battle front
battle 718 n.
battleground
battleground
  724 n.
battlement
notch 260 n.
fortification 713 n.
battle royal
fight 716 n.
battle 718 n.
battleship(s)
warship 722 n.
indoor game
  837 n.
battle station
battle 718 n.
batty
crazy 503 adj.
batwing sleeve
sleeve 228 n.
bauble
insubstantial thing
  4 n.
bauble 639 n.

Bauhaus
architectural
192 adj.
art 551 n.

bawbee
coinage 797 n.

bawdy
impure 951 adj.

bawl
cry 408 n.
vociferate 408 vb.
lamentation 836 n.
weep 836 vb.

bawl out
reproach 924 vb.

bay
compartment
194 n.
curve 248 n.
cavity 255 n.
horse 273 n.
gulf 345 n.
tree 366 n.
ululate 409 vb.
brown 430 adj.
disapprove 924 vb.

bayleaf
herb 301 n.

bayonet
pierce 263 vb.
kill 362 vb.
strike at 712 vb.
sidearms 723 n.

bayou
gulf 345 n.

bay window
window 263 n.

bazaar
request 761 n.
sale 793 n.
emporium 796 n.
shop 796 n.

bazooka
flute 414 n.
gun 723 n.
missile weapon
723 n.

BBC
broadcasting
531 n.

be
be 1 vb.
be situated 186 vb.
be present 189 vb.

beach
edge 234 n.
land 295 vb.
shore 344 n.
arena 724 n.

beachcomber
wanderer 268 n.

beacon
signal light 420 n.
signal 547 n.

warning 664 n.
danger signal
665 n.

bead
sphere 252 n.
decorate 844 vb.
trimming 844 n.

beading
ornamental art
844 n.

beadle
officer 741 n.
law officer 955 n.
church officer
986 n.

beads
jewellery 844 n.
prayers 981 n.
ritual object 988 n.

beagle
dog 365 n.

beak
protuberance
254 n.
teacher 537 n.

beak, the
magistracy 957 n.

beaker
cup 194 n.

**be-all and end-
all**
all 52 n.
important matter
638 n.

beam
beam 218 n.
laterality 239 n.
direction 281 n.
flash 417 n.
radiate 417 vb.
communicate
524 vb.
be cheerful 833 vb.
smile 835 vb.

beaming
luminous 417 adj.
happy 824 adj.
cheerful 833 adj.

bean
head 213 n.

bean curd
fruit and vegetables
301 n.

beanfeast
feasting 301 n.
meal 301 n.
enjoyment 824 n.
amusement 837 n.
festivity 837 n.

beanpole
thinness 206 n.
tall creature 209 n.

beans
food 301 n.

fruit and vegetables
301 n.

beansprouts
fruit and vegetables
301 n.

bear
reproduce itself
167 vb.
be fruitful 171 vb.
support 218 vb.
carry 273 vb.
mammal 365 n.
acquiesce 488 vb.
heraldry 547 n.
gambler 618 n.
seller 793 n.
feel 818 vb.
be patient 823 vb.
suffer 825 vb.
rude person 885 n.

bear a grudge
hate 888 vb.

beard
filament 208 n.
prickle 256 n.
hair 259 n.
print-type 587 n.
defy 711 vb.
be courageous
855 vb.

bearded
hairy 259 adj.

bear down on
approach 289 vb.

bearer bond
title deed 767 n.

bear fruit
reproduce itself
167 vb.
get better 654 vb.
be successful
727 vb.

beargarden
turmoil 61 n.
arena 724 n.

bear hug
retention 778 n.
endearment 889 n.

bear ill will
be hostile 881 vb.

bearing
relation 9 n.
pivot 218 n.
support 218 n.
direction 281 n.
look 445 n.
meaning 514 n.
heraldry 547 n.
conduct 688 n.

bear in mind
think 449 n.
be mindful 455 vb.

bearish
animal 365 adj.

salable 793 adj.
cheap 812 adj.

bearnaise sauce
sauce 389 n.

bear no malice
forgive 909 vb.

bear out
corroborate 466 vb.
demonstrate
478 vb.
vindicate 927 vb.

bear pit
zoo 369 n.

bearskin
headgear 228 n.
armour 713 n.

bear the brunt
stand firm 599 vb.
busy oneself
622 vb.
be in difficulty
700 vb.
withstand 704 vb.

**bear the mark
of**
be intrinsic 5 vb.

bear up
support 218 vb.
elevate 310 vb.

bear upon
be related 9 vb.
influence 178 vb.

bear with
forgive 909 vb.

**bear with a sore
head**
moper 834 n.

bear witness
testify 466 vb.
affirm 532 vb.

beast
violent creature
176 n.
animal 365 n.
eyesore 842 n.
ruffian 904 n.
cad 938 n.

beastly
animal 365 adj.
not nice 645 adj.
unpleasant
827 adj.
ugly 842 adj.
discourteous
885 adj.
hateful 888 adj.
sensual 944 adj.

beast of burden
beast of burden
273 n.
animal 365 n.
worker 686 n.

beat
be superior 34 vb.

periodicity 141 n.
territory 184 n.
place 185 n.
impulse 279 n.
strike 279 vb.
cook 301 vb.
pass 305 vb.
oscillate 317 vb.
oscillation 317 n.
agitate 318 vb.
be agitated 318 vb.
pulverize 332 vb.
roll 403 vb.
tempo 410 n.
play music
413 vb.
prosody 593 n.
chase 619 n.
hunt 619 vb.
clean 648 vb.
defeat 727 vb.
spank 963 vb.

**beat about the
bush**
sophisticate
477 vb.
be equivocal
518 vb.
dissemble 541 vb.
be diffuse 570 vb.

beat a retreat
regress 286 vb.
run away 620 vb.

beat a tattoo
roll 403 vb.
celebrate 876 vb.

beat down
demolish 165 vb.
bargain 791 vb.
cheapen 812 vb.

beaten
inferior 35 adj.
used 673 adj.
defeated 728 adj.

beaten track
habit 610 n.
bore 838 n.

beater
hunter 619 n.

beatific
pleasurable
826 adj.

beatify
dignify 866 vb.
sanctify 979 vb.

beating
periodical 141 adj.
impulse 279 n.
knock 279 n.
victory 727 n.
defeat 728 n.
*corporal
punishment*
963 n.

beat it
decamp 296 vb.
run away 620 vb.

beatnik
nonconformist
84 n.
unconformable
84 adj.

beat one's breast
lament 836 vb.
be penitent 939 vb.

**beat one's head
against a
brick wall**
waste effort
641 adj.

**beat swords into
ploughshares**
be at peace 717 vb.
make peace
719 vb.

**beat the big
drum**
proclaim 528 vb.
be ostentatious
875 vb.

beat the record
be superior 34 vb.

beat time
time 117 vb.
play music
413 vb.

beat up
force 176 vb.
strike 279 vb.
thicken 354 vb.
strike at 712 vb.

beau
male 372 n.
fop 848 n.
lover 887 n.

Beau Brummel
fop 848 n.

Beaujolais
wine 301 n.

beau monde
beau monde 848 n.

beaut
a beauty 848 n.

beautician
beautician 843 n.

beautiful
beautiful 841 adj.

beautify
ornament 574 vb.
beautify 841 vb.

beauty
beauty 841 n.

beauty, a
masterpiece 694 n.

beauty queen
a beauty 841 n.

beauty sleep
sleep 679 n.

beauty spot
a beauty 841 n.
cosmetic 843 n.

beaux yeux
beauty 841 n.

beaver
headgear 228 n.
hair 259 n.
mammal 365 n.
armour 713 n.

beaver away
be active 678 vb.
work 682 vb.

becalmed
quiescent 266 adj.
still 266 adj.
nonactive
677 adj.
hindered 702 adj.

because
hence 158 adv.

béchamel
sauce 389 n.

beck
stream 350 n.
gesture 547 n.
command 737 n.
command
737 vb.

beckon
gesticulate 547 vb.

become
become 1 vb.
be turned to
147 n.
happen 154 vb.
beautify 841 vb.
be one's duty
917 vb.

become one of
join a party
708 vb.

**become one of
the family**
be sociable 882 vb.

**become public
knowledge**
be disclosed
526 vb.

becoming
agreeing 24 adj.
converted 147 adj.
personable
841 adj.
tasteful 846 adj.

bed
unite with 45 vb.
place 187 vb.
layer 207 n.
base 214 n.
basis 218 n.
bed 218 n.
garden 370 n.
debauch 951 vb.

**bed and
breakfast**
inn 192 n.
provision 633 n.

bedaub
coat 226 vb.

bedazzle
shine 417 vb.
command respect
920 vb.

bed bug
insect 365 n.

bedclothes
coverlet 226 n.

bedding
bed 218 n.
coverlet 226 n.

bed down
place 187 vb.
sleep 679 vb.

bedevil
bedevil 63 vb.
trouble 827 vb.

bed jacket
nightwear 228 n.

bedlam, Bedlam
disorder 61 n.
turmoil 61 n.
loudness 400 n.
discord 411 n.
mental hospital
503 n.

bed linen
coverlet 226 n.

bed of nails
suffering 825 n.

bed of roses
palmy days 730 n.

bedouin
dweller 191 n.
wanderer 268 n.

bed out
implant 303 vb.
cultivate 370 vb.

bedpan
vessel 194 n.
latrine 649 n.

bedraggled
dirty 649 adj.

bedridden
sick 651 adj.
restrained 747 adj.

bedrock
reality 1 n.
permanence 144 n.
fixture 153 n.
source 156 n.
base 214 n.
basis 218 n.
chief thing 638 n.
important
638 adj.

bedroom
chamber 194 n.

bed settee
bed 218 n.

bedside manner
therapy 658 n.

bed-sitter
flat 192 n.

bedspread
coverlet 226 n.

bedstead
bed 218 n.

bedtime
clock time 117 n.
evening 129 n.

bedtime story
soporific 679 n.

bee
insect 365 n.

Beeb
broadcasting
531 n.

beech
tree 366 n.

beechmast
provender 301 n.

beef
meat 301 n.
deprecate 762 vb.
be discontented
829 vb.

beefcake
a beauty 841 n.

beefiness
vitality 162 n.
bulk 195 n.

beef up
strengthen 162 vb.

beefy
stalwart 162 adj.
fleshy 195 adj.
thick 205 adj.

beehive
nest 192 n.
dome 253 n.
stock farm 369 n.
hairdressing 843 n.

**bee in one's
bonnet**
prejudgment
481 n.
eccentricity 503 n.
whim 604 n.

bee-keeping
animal husbandry
369 n.

beeline
short distance
200 n.
straightness 249 n.
direction 281 n.

Beelzebub
devil 969 n.

beer
alcoholic drink
301 n.

beer and skittles
enjoyment 824 n.
festivity 837 n.

beery
drunken 949 adj.
intoxicating
949 adj.

bee's knees
exceller 644 n.

beestings
milk 301 n.

beeswax
fat 357 n.

beetle
be high 209 vb.
automobile 274 n.
hammer 279 n.
insect 365 n.

beetle-browed
projecting 254 adj.

beetle off
decamp 296 vb.

beetroot
fruit and vegetables
301 n.

beet sugar
sweet thing 392 n.

befall
happen 154 vb.

befitting
fit 24 adj.
due 915 adj.

before
before 64 adv.
before 119 adv.
in front 237 adv.

beforehand
before 119 adv.
beforehand
135 adv.

before long
betimes 135 adv.

**before-
mentioned**
preceding 64 adj.

before now
before 119 adv.

before one's eyes
in front 237 adv.
obvious 443 adj.
visible 443 adj.

before the Flood
antiquated
127 adj.
primal 127 adj.

before then
before 119 adv.

**before you could
say Jack
Robinson**
swiftly 277 adv.

beg
beg 761 vb.
acquire 771 vb.

biff
knock 279 n.
strike 279 vb.
bifid
bisected 92 adj.
bifocal
dual 90 adj.
bifurcate
bifurcate 92 vb.
cross 222 vb.
angular 247 adj.
diverge 294 vb.
big
great 32 adj.
large 195 adj.
bigamy
type of marriage
894 n.
Big Apple, the
city 184 n.
Big Bang
finance 797 n.
big bang theory
universe 321 n.
big battalions
bigwig 638 n.
army 722 n.
brute force 735 n.
Big Ben
timekeeper 117 n.
Big Brother
influence 178 n.
bigwig 638 n.
protection 660 n.
authority 733 n.
position of
authority 733 n.
tyrant 735 n.
autocrat 741 n.
master 741 n.
big business
business 622 n.
big drum
drum 414 n.
ostentation 875 n.
**big fish in a
small pool**
superior 34 n.
big game
animal 365 n.
big girl's blouse
fool 501 n.
bungler 697 n.
big gun
bigwig 638 n.
autocrat 741 n.
person of repute
866 n.
big-headed
proud 871 adj.
bight
curve 248 n.
cavity 255 n.
gulf 345 n.

big noise
influence 178 n.
bigwig 638 n.
person of repute
866 n.
bigot
dogmatist 473 n.
narrow mind
481 n.
zealot 979 n.
big shot
influence 178 n.
bigwig 638 n.
autocrat 741 n.
person of repute
866 n.
Big Smoke, the
city 184 n.
big stick
incentive 612 n.
compulsion 740 n.
threat 900 n.
scourge 964 n.
big toe
foot 214 n.
finger 378 n.
big top
canopy 226 n.
theatre 594 n.
big wheel
bigwig 638 n.
person of repute
866 n.
big white chief
bigwig 638 n.
bigwig
bigwig 638 n.
master 741 n.
bijou
little 196 adj.
a beauty 841 n.
gem 844 n.
bijou residence
small house 192 n.
bike
nest 192 n.
ride 267 vb.
bicycle 274 n.
bikini
beachwear 228 n.
bilateral
dual 90 adj.
lateral 239 adj.
contractual
765 adj.
bilberry
fruit and vegetables
301 n.
bile
resentment 891 n.
sullenness 893 n.
Bilé or Beli
Celtic deities
967 n.

bilge
leavings 41 n.
base 214 n.
silly talk 515 n.
rubbish 641 n.
bilharzia
infection 651 n.
See **tropical
disease**
tropical disease
651 n.
bilingual
linguistic 557 adj.
speaking 579 adj.
bilious
yellow 433 adj.
unhealthy
651 adj.
bilk
deceive 542 vb.
fleece 786 vb.
defraud 788 vb.
be in debt 803 vb.
not pay 805 vb.
bill
numerical result
85 n.
list 87 n.
protuberance
254 n.
exhibit 522 n.
advertise 528 vb.
advertisement
528 n.
label 547 n.
correspondence
588 n.
demand 737 vb.
title deed 767 n.
paper money
797 n.
credit 802 n.
account 808 vb.
accounts 808 n.
bill and coo
caress 889 vb.
billboard
advertisement
528 n.
billet
stopping place
145 n.
place 185 n.
place 187 n.
quarters 192 n.
apportion 783 vb.
billet-doux
correspondence
588 n.
love token 889 n.
wooing 889 n.
billfold
case 194 n.
treasury 799 n.

billhook
sharp edge 256 n.
billiard ball
sphere 252 n.
billiards
ball game 837 n.
Billingsgate
slang 560 adj.
scurrility 899 n.
billion
over one hundred
99 n.
billions
funds 797 n.
bill of exchange
title deed 767 n.
paper money
797 n.
bill of fare
list 87 n.
bill of lading
list 87 n.
bill of rights
dueness 915 n.
billow(s)
swelling 253 n.
ocean 343 n.
wave 350 n.
Billy Bunter
bulk 195 n.
billycan
pot 194 n.
billy goat
goat 365 n.
male animal
372 n.
bimbo
ignoramus 493 n.
dunce 501 n.
a beauty 841 n.
bin
vessel 194 n.
binary
computerized
86 adj.
dual 90 adj.
star 321 n.
binary system
number 85 n.
bind
tie 45 vb.
combine 50 vb.
bring together
74 vb.
stabilize 153 vb.
make smaller
198 vb.
cover 226 vb.
close 264 vb.
cultivate 370 vb.
repair 656 vb.
obstruct 702 vb.
compel 740 vb.
subjugate 745 vb.

fetter 747 vb.
restrain 747 vb.
bore 838 n.
impose a duty
917 n.
binder
bond 47 n.
farm tool 370 n.
binding
ligature 47 n.
wrapping 226 n.
edging 234 n.
bookbinding 589 n.
necessary 596 adj.
authoritative
733 adj.
compelling
740 adj.
trimming 844 n.
obligatory 917 adj.
bind oneself
promise 764 vb.
bind over
impose a duty
917 vb.
bindweed
plant 366 n.
bine
plant 366 n.
bin-ends
leavings 41 n.
piece 53 n.
binge
eat 301 vb.
festivity 837 n.
be intemperate
943 vb.
gluttonize 947 vb.
gluttony 947 n.
drunkenness 949 n.
bingo
gambling 618 n.
card game 837 n.
binnacle
sailing aid 269 n.
binocular
seeing 438 adj.
binoculars
telescope 442 n.
bint
female 373 n.
loose woman
952 n.
biochemistry
biology 358 n.
biodata
evidence 466 n.
biography 590 n.
biodiesel
fuel 385 n.
biodiversity
biology 358 n.
biogenetic
biological 358 adj.

disapproving
924 adj.
bittern
bird 365 n.
bitterness
sourness 393 n.
badness 645 n.
bane 659 n.
sorrow 825 n.
painfulness 827 n.
discontent 829 n.
enmity 881 n.
hatred 888 n.
resentment 891 n.
malevolence 898 n.
bitters
sourness 393 n.
bittersweet
contrary 14 adj.
painful 377 adj.
bitty
fragmentary
53 adj.
incomplete 55 adj.
bitumen
resin 357 n.
bivalve
marine life 365 n.
bivouac
place oneself
187 vb.
station 187 n.
abode 192 n.
dwell 192 vb.
biweekly
seasonal 141 adj.
bizarre
unusual 84 adj.
imaginative
513 adj.
ridiculous 849 adj.
blab
inform 524 vb.
divulge 526 vb.
accuse 928 vb.
black
set apart 46 vb.
exclude 57 vb.
formal dress 228 n.
horse 273 n.
darkness 418 n.
black 428 adj.
blacken 428 vb.
blackness 428 n.
evil 616 adj.
bad 645 adj.
dirty 649 adj.
prohibit 757 vb.
lamentation 836 n.
black and blue
blackish 428 adj.
blue 435 n.
black and white
polarity 14 n.

antiquated
127 adj.
achromatism
426 n.
blackness 428 n.
pied 437 adj.
painted 553 adj.
painting 553 n.
opposites 704 n.
**black-and-
white
television**
broadcasting
531 n.
black armband
badge 547 n.
black art
sorcery 983 n.
blackball
exclude 57 vb.
exclusion 57 n.
eject 300 vb.
reject 607 vb.
prohibit 757 vb.
shame 867 vb.
disapprobation
924 n.
black belt
proficient person
696 n.
blackberry
fruit and vegetables
301 n.
black thing 428 n.
blackbird
bird 365 n.
black thing 428 n.
blackboard
stationery 586 n.
black books
disrepute 867 n.
hatred 888 n.
disapprobation
924 n.
black bottom
dance 837 n.
black box
aircraft 276 n.
recording
instrument 549 n.
black cap
badge of rule
743 n.
condemnation
961 n.
black cat
omen 511 n.
talisman 983 n.
black cloud
threat 900 n.
black coffee
soft drink 301 n.
black comedy
stage play 594 n.

wit 839 n.
blackcurrant
fruit and vegetables
301 n.
Black Death
plague 651 n.
black diamond
coal 385 n.
black economy
escape 667 n.
swindling 788 n.
market 796 n.
nonpayment
805 n.
blacken
blacken 428 vb.
mark 547 vb.
shame 867 vb.
criticize 924 vb.
defame 926 vb.
black eye
black 428 adj.
black thing 428 n.
wound 655 n.
blemish 845 n.
blackfly
insect 365 n.
blackguard
evildoer 904 n.
ruffian 904 n.
reproach 924 vb.
bad person 938 n.
cad 938 n.
blackhead
skin disease 651 n.
blemish 845 n.
black hole
star 321 n.
black ice
wintriness 380 n.
**black
information**
information 524 n.
debt 803 n.
blacking
cleanser 648 n.
hindrance 702 n.
blackjack
vessel 194 n.
hammer 279 n.
strike 279 vb.
black lead
lubricant 334 n.
blacklead
blacken 428 vb.
black thing 428 n.
clean 648 vb.
cleanser 648 n.
blackleg
nonconformist
84 n.
apostatize 603 vb.
recanter 603 n.
revolter 738 n.

hateful object
888 n.
blacklist
set apart 46 vb.
list 87 n.
unsociability
883 n.
disapprobation
924 n.
disapprove
924 vb.
condemn 961 vb.
condemnation
961 n.
black look
rudeness 885 n.
anger 891 n.
sullenness 893 n.
reproach 924 n.
black magic
badness 645 n.
diabolism 969 n.
sorcery 983 n.
blackmail
demand 737 n.
demand 737 vb.
compel 740 vb.
compulsion 740 n.
request 761 n.
request 761 vb.
fleece 786 vb.
rapacity 786 n.
rob 788 vb.
swindling 788 n.
booty 790 n.
tax 809 n.
threat 900 n.
threaten 900 vb.
reward 962 n.
Black Maria
vehicle 274 n.
lockup 748 n.
black mark
slur 867 n.
reprimand 924 n.
black market
trade 791 n.
market 796 n.
improbity 930 n.
illegal 954 adj.
black metal
music 412 n.
Black Muslim
revolter 738 n.
non-Christian sect
978 n.
blackness
blackness 428 n.
blackout
insensibility 375 n.
darkening 418 n.
oblivion 506 n.
dramaturgy 594 n.
prohibition 757 n.

black pepper
condiment 389 n.
black pudding
meat 301 n.
Black Rod
badge 547 n.
badge of rule
743 n.
black sheep
offender 904 n.
bad person 938 n.
blacksmith
artisan 686 n.
black spot
danger 661 n.
blackthorn
tree 366 n.
black tie
formal dress 228 n.
ostentation 875 n.
**blackwater
fever**
tropical disease
651 n.
bladder
sphere 252 n.
blade
sharp edge 256 n.
bluntness 257 n.
propeller 269 n.
propellant 287 n.
foliage 366 n.
male 372 n.
sidearms 723 n.
blades
plaything 837 n.
blah-blah
empty talk 515 n.
blame
blame 924 vb.
censure 924 n.
accusation 928 n.
guilt 936 n.
blameless
guiltless 935 adj.
blanch
lose colour 426 vb.
whiten 427 vb.
blancmange
dessert 301 n.
blanco
whiten 427 vb.
bland
smooth 258 adj.
dull 840 adj.
flattering 925 adj.
blandishment(s)
inducement 612 n.
endearment 889 n.
flattery 925 n.
blank
nonexistence 2 n.
insubstantial 4 adj.
uniform 16 adj.

be wonderful
  864 vb.
bowls
  ball game 837 n.
bow out
  depart 296 vb.
bowsprit
  projection 254 n.
Bow-street
  runner
  law officer 955 n.
bow tie
  neckwear 228 n.
bow to
  be inferior 35 vb.
  submit 721 vb.
bow-wow
  dog 365 n.
box
  small house 192 n.
  box 194 n.
  compartment
    194 n.
  cover 226 vb.
  circumscribe
    232 vb.
  strike 279 vb.
  tree 366 n.
  theatre 594 n.
  fight 716 vb.
box, the
  broadcasting
    531 n.
box camera
  camera 442 n.
boxer
  dog 365 n.
  pugilist 722 n.
boxer shorts
  underwear 228 n.
box girder
  beam 218 n.
boxing
  defence 713 n.
  pugilism 716 n.
boxing match
  pugilism 716 n.
box-kite
  airship 276 n.
box office
  onlookers 441 n.
  theatre 594 n.
  treasury 799 n.
box-office hit
  dramaturgy
    594 n.
  success 727 n.
box of tricks
  stratagem 698 n.
box on the ear
  knock 279 n.
  anger 891 n.
  reprimand 924 n.
  corporal

  punishment
    963 n.
  spank 963 vb.
box pleat
  fold 261 n.
boxroom
  storage 632 n.
box the compass
  orientate 281 vb.
boy
  youngster 132 n.
  male 372 n.
boycott
  separation 46 n.
  set apart 46 vb.
  exclude 57 vb.
  exclusion 57 n.
  hindrance 702 n.
  unsociability
    883 n.
  disapprobation
    924 n.
boyfriend
  male 372 n.
  friend 880 n.
  lover 887 n.
boyhood
  youth 130 n.
boyish
  young 130 adj.
  immature 670 adj.
Boy Scouts
  band 74 n.
  society 708 n.
boys in blue, the
  police 955 n.
bra
  underwear 228 n.
brace
  fastening 47 n.
  group 74 n.
  duality 90 n.
  strengthen 162 vb.
  support 218 n.
  support 218 vb.
  notation 410 n.
  punctuation 547 n.
  refresh 685 vb.
brace and bit
  perforator 263 n.
bracelet
  circle 250 n.
  loop 250 n.
  jewellery 844 n.
brace oneself
  be resolute 599 vb.
  prepare oneself
    669 vb.
braces
  fastening 47 n.
  hanger 217 n.
  underwear 228 n.
bracing
  vigorous 174 adj.

  refreshing 685 adj.
bracken
  plant 366 n.
bracket
  equalize 28 vb.
  join 45 vb.
  bond 47 n.
  classification 77 n.
  pair 90 vb.
  shelf 218 n.
  support 218 n.
  See **shelf**
  angularity 247 n.
brackets
  punctuation 547 n.
bracket with
  liken 18 vb.
brackish
  salty 388 adj.
bradawl
  perforator 263 n.
Bradshaw
  directory 87 n.
  itinerary 267 n.
  guidebook 524 n.
brae
  high land 209 n.
brag
  defy 711 vb.
  boast 877 n.
  boast 877 vb.
  be insolent 878 vb.
braggart
  insolent person
    878 n.
Bragi
  Nordic deities
    967 n.
Brahma
  divineness 965 n.
  Hindu deities
    967 n.
Brahman
  aristocrat 868 n.
Brahmana
  non-Biblical
  scripture 975 n.
Brahmin
  priest 986 n.
Brahminism
  ecclesiasticism
    985 n.
braid
  tie 45 vb.
  ligature 47 n.
  strip 208 n.
  crossing 222 n.
  weave 222 vb.
  hair 259 n.
  fold 261 n.
  variegate 437 vb.
  trimming 844 n.
Braille
  blindness 439 n.

  writing 586 n.
brain
  head 213 n.
  kill 362 vb.
  render insensible
    375 vb.
  intellect 447 n.
  intelligence 498 n.
brain-child
  product 104 n.
  idea 451 n.
brain death
  decease 361 n.
brainless
  mindless 448 adj.
brains
  intellect 447 n.
  intelligence 498 n.
  planner 623 n.
brain scanner
  hospital 658 n.
brainstorm
  neurosis 503 n.
  contrivance 623 n.
brains trust
  interrogation
    459 n.
  consignee 754 n.
brain surgery
  head 213 n.
  surgery 658 n.
brain-teaser
  question 459 n.
  enigma 530 n.
brainwash
  convert 147 vb.
  influence 178 vb.
  teach 534 vb.
  habituate 610 vb.
  pervert 655 vb.
brainwave
  product 164 n.
  idea 451 n.
  intelligence 498 n.
  contrivance 623 n.
brainy
  intelligent
    498 adj.
braise
  cook 301 vb.
brake
  halt 145 vb.
  moderator 177 n.
  bring to rest
    266 vb.
  carriage 274 n.
  retard 278 vb.
  slowness 278 n.
  wood 366 n.
  safeguard 662 n.
  hinder 702 vb.
  restraint 747 vb.
  restraint 747 n.
  fetter 748 n.

brake light
  lamp 420 n.
bramble
  prickle 256 n.
  plant 366 n.
bran
  cereals 301 n.
  powder 332 n.
  grass 366 n.
  rubbish 641 n.
branch
  branch 53 n.
  be dispersed 75 vb.
  classification 77 n.
  descendant 170 n.
  extend 183 n.
  nest 192 n.
  filament 208 n.
  stream 350 n.
  foliage 366 n.
  tree 366 n.
  sect 978 n.
branch off
  bifurcate 92 vb.
  diverge 294 vb.
branch out
  be dispersed 75 vb.
  deviate 282 vb.
  diverge 294 vb.
brand
  sort 77 n.
  burn 381 n.
  burning 381 n.
  furnace 383 n.
  torch 420 n.
  identification
    547 n.
  label 547 n.
  mark 547 vb.
  blemish 845 vb.
  shame 867 vb.
  slur 867 n.
  censure 924 n.
  criticize 924 vb.
  defame 926 vb.
  detraction 926 n.
  accuse 928 vb.
branded
  proprietary
    777 adj.
brandish
  brandish 317 vb.
  use 673 vb.
brand-new
  new 126 adj.
brandy
  alcoholic drink
    301 n.
brandysnap
  pastries and cakes
    301 n.
brash
  piece 53 n.
  insolent 878 adj.

brushwood
wood 366 n.
fuel 385 n.
brushwork
painting 553 n.
brusque
concise 569 adj.
taciturn 582 adj.
sullen 893 adj.
brutal
violent 176 adj.
oppressive 735 adj.
cruel 898 adj.
pitiless 906 adj.
heinous 934 adj.
vicious 934 adj.
brutalize
pervert 655 vb.
make wicked
934 vb.
brute
violent creature
176 n.
animal 365 n.
tyrant 735 n.
rude person 885 n.
ruffian 904 n.
monster 938 n.
BSE
animal disease
651 n.
B-side
rear 238 n.
bubble
insubstantial thing
4 n.
brief span 114 n.
minuteness 196 n.
lightness 323 n.
flow 350 VB.
bubble 355 n.
bubble 355 vb.
deception 542 n.
bubble gum
sweets 301 n.
elasticity 328 n.
bubble pack
wrapping 226 n.
transparency
422 n.
bubbly
wine 301 n.
light 323 adj.
bubbly 355 adj.
fervent 818 adj.
lively 819 adj.
merry 833 adj.
buccaneer
mariner 270 n.
militarist 722 n.
robber 789 n.
buck
leap 312 vb.
mammal 365 n.

male animal
372 n.
coinage 797 n.
funds 797 n.
paper money
797 n.
bucket
vessel 194 n.
rain 350 vb.
bucket shop
stock exchange
618 n.
market 796 n.
buckle
join 45 vb.
break 46 vb.
fastening 47 n.
distort 246 vb.
distortion 246 n.
make concave
255 vb.
buckler
armour 713 n.
buckle to
be resolute 599 vb.
undertake 672 vb.
be active 678 vb.
buckshot
ammunition
723 n.
buck up
hurry up 680 int.
animate 821 vb.
relieve 831 vb.
be cheerful 833 vb.
cheer 833 vb.
give courage
855 vb.
bud
grow 36 vb.
origin 68 n.
source 156 n.
growth 157 n.
result 157 vb.
generate 167 vb.
expand 197 vb.
swelling 253 n.
implant 303 vb.
flower 366 n.
Buddhism
philosophy 449 n.
religious faith
973 n.
budding
beginning 68 adj.
young 130 adj.
buddy
male 372 n.
colleague 707 n.
chum 880 n.
budge
be in motion
265 vb.
move 265 vb.

budget
provide 633 vb.
account 808 vb.
accounts 808 n.
budget account
credit 802 n.
budgetary
monetary 797 adj.
accounting
808 adj.
buff
skin 226 n.
smooth 258 vb.
rub 333 vb.
brown 430 adj.
enthusiast 504 n.
clean 648 vb.
buff, the
bareness 229 n.
buffer
intermediary
231 n.
male 372 n.
protection 660 n.
obstacle 702 n.
defence 713 n.
buffet
café 192 n.
cabinet 194 n.
knock 279 n.
strike 279 vb.
evil 616 n.
ill-treat 645 vb.
corporal
punishment
963 n.
buffoon
fool 501 n.
bungler 697 n.
humorist 839 n.
laughingstock
851 n.
bug
insect 365 n.
hear 415 vb.
be curious 453 vb.
infection 651 n.
failure 728 n.
torment 827 vb.
enrage 891 vb.
bugbear
bane 659 n.
intimidation
854 n.
hateful object
888 n.
demon 970 n.
buggery
illicit love 951 n.
Buggin's turn
sequence 65 n.
buggy
automobile 274 n.
carriage 274 n.

pushcart 274 n.
bugle
play music 413 vb.
horn 414 n.
call 547 n.
build
compose 56 vb.
composition 56 n.
produce 164 vb.
form 243 n.
form 243 vb.
elevate 310 vb.
structure 331 n.
builder
producer 164 n.
artisan 686 n.
building
edifice 164 n.
place 185 n.
house 192 n.
building site
workshop 687 n.
building society
pawnshop 784 n.
treasury 799 n.
build up
augment 36 vb.
make complete
54 vb.
bring together
74 vb.
strengthen 162 vb.
enlarge 197 vb.
make higher
209 vb.
elevate 310 vb.
buildup
increase 36 n.
overestimation
482 n.
advertisement
528 n.
store 632 n.
built-in
intrinsic 5 adj.
component 58 adj.
interior 224 adj.
built-up area
district 184 n.
housing 192 n.
bulb
source 156 n.
sphere 252 n.
swelling 253 n.
plant 366 n.
lamp 420 n.
bulge
grow 36 vb.
increment 36 n.
convexity 253 n.
swelling 253 n.
bulging
full 54 adj.
convex 253 adj.

projecting 254 adj.
bulimia nervosa
eating 301 n.
disease 651 n.
bulk
quantity 26 n.
chief part 52 n.
bulk 195 n.
size 195 n.
enlarge 197 vb.
food content 301 n.
bulky
substantial 3 adj.
great 32 adj.
large 195 adj.
bull
cattle 365 n.
male animal
372 n.
mistake 495 n.
silly talk 515 n.
falsehood 541 n.
fool 542 vb.
fable 543 n.
exaggerate 546 vb.
gambler 618 n.
labour 682 n.
decree 737 n.
purchaser 792 n.
overcharge 811 vb.
ridiculousness
849 n.
bulldog
dog 365 n.
brave person
855 n.
bulldoze
demolish 165 vb.
collide 279 vb.
necessitate 596 vb.
compel 740 vb.
bulldozer
destroyer 168 n.
flattener 216 n.
smoother 258 n.
vehicle 274 n.
raw 279 n.
pulverizer 332 n.
bullet
sphere 252 n.
missile 287 n.
ammunition
723 n.
missile weapon
723 n.
means of execution
964 n.
bulletin
report 524 n.
news 529 n.
correspondence
588 n.
bulletproof
strong 162 adj.

*place of
amusement*
837 n.
cabbage
fruit and vegetables
301 n.
**Cabbage Patch
(tdmk) doll**
image 551 n.
plaything 837 n.
caber
missile 287 n.
cabin
small house 192 n.
chamber 194 n.
cabin boy
mariner 270 n.
naval man 722 n.
servant 742 n.
cabinet
cabinet 194 n.
chamber 194 n.
management
689 n.
director 690 n.
council 692 n.
cabinet-maker
artisan 686 n.
cable
cable 47 n.
information 524 n.
message 529 n.
telecommunication
531 n.
cablegram
information 524 n.
telecommunication
531 n.
cable railway
train 274 n.
cable stitch
needlework 844 n.
**cable television
or radio**
broadcasting
531 n.
caboodle
great quantity
32 n.
cache
concealment
525 n.
hiding-place 527 n.
store 632 n.
cachet
repute 866 n.
cack-handed
clumsy 695 adj.
**cack-
handedness**
sinistrality 242 n.
cackle
ululate 409 n.
chatter 581 n.

laugh 835 vb.
laughter 835 n.
cacophony
stridor 407 n.
discord 411 n.
cactus
prickle 256 n.
plant 366 n.
cad
cad 938 n.
cadaver
corpse 363 n.
caddy
small box 194 n.
carry 273 vb.
servant 742 n.
cadence
descent 309 n.
sound 398 n.
melody 410 n.
prosody 593 n.
cadet
posteriority 120 n.
subsequent
120 adj.
young 130 adj.
beginner 538 n.
subject 745 adj.
cadge
beg 761 vb.
take 786 vb.
cadre
party 708 n.
caecum
closure 264 n.
Caesar
sovereign 741 n.
Caesarian birth
extraction 304 n.
**Caesarian
(section)**
obstetrics 167 n.
caesura
discontinuity 72 n.
prosody 593 n.
café
café 192 n.
cafeteria
café 192 n.
cafetière
pot 194 n.
caffeine
tonic 658 n.
caftan
robe 228 n.
cage
stable 192 n.
compartment
194 n.
receptacle 194 n.
circumscribe
232 vb.
enclose 235 vb.
enclosure 235 n.

break in 369 vb.
imprison 747 vb.
lockup 748 n.
cagey
reticent 525 adj.
cunning 698 adj.
cautious 858 adj.
cairn
signpost 547 n.
monument 548 n.
caisson disease
depth 211 n.
diver 313 n.
cajole
fool 542 vb.
induce 612 vb.
request 761 vb.
flatter 925 vb.
cake
cohere 48 vb.
pastries and cakes
301 n.
be dense 324 vb.
solid body 324 n.
sweet thing 392 n.
make unclean
649 vb.
cakewalk
dance 837 n.
calamity
evil 616 n.
misfortune 731 n.
calcify
harden 326 vb.
calcium
food content 301 n.
calculate
number 86 vb.
measure 465 vb.
estimate 480 vb.
expect 507 vb.
intend 617 vb.
plan 623 vb.
be cautious 858 vb.
calculated
predetermined
608 adj.
calculated risk
intention 617 n.
calculation
numeration 86 n.
measurement
465 n.
estimate 480 vb.
intention 617 n.
caution 858 n.
calculator
*counting
instrument* 86 n.
calendar
directory 87 n.
list 87 n.
chronology 117 n.
time 117 vb.

reference book
589 n.
calendar month
period 110 n.
calender
smooth 258 vb.
calends
date 108 n.
calf
young creature
132 n.
skin 226 n.
leg 267 n.
cattle 365 n.
bookbinding 589 n.
calf love
love 887 n.
calibrate
graduate 27 vb.
gauge 465 vb.
calibre
sort 77 n.
size 195 n.
breadth 205 n.
intelligence 498 n.
firearm 723 n.
calico
textile 222 n.
caliph
sovereign 741 n.
call
enter 297 vb.
cry 408 vb.
ululate 409 vb.
ululation 409 n.
communicate
524 vb.
call 547 n.
name 561 vb.
motive 612 vb.
command 737 vb.
desire 859 n.
desire 859 vb.
social round 882 n.
visit 882 vb.
call centre
telecommunications
531 n.
**called to the
bar, be**
do law 958 vb.
caller
incomer 297 n.
sociable person
882 n.
worshipper 981 n.
callgirl
prostitute 952 n.
calligraphy
art 551 n.
lettering 586 n.
call in
bring together
74 vb.

admit 299 vb.
consult 691 vb.
visit 882 vb.
calling
motive 612 n.
vocation 622 n.
social round 882 n.
call in question
cause doubt
486 vb.
negate 533 vb.
calliper
support 218 n.
measure 465 vb.
callipers
gauge 465 n.
call it a day
terminate 69 vb.
cease 145 vb.
call of duty
duty 917 n.
call off
halt 145 vb.
abrogate 752 vb.
call one's bluff
defy 711 vb.
callosity
hardness 326 n.
callous
unfeeling 375 adj.
thick-skinned
820 adj.
cruel 898 adj.
pitiless 906 adj.
wicked 934 adj.
call out
halt 145 vb.
cry 408 vb.
defy 711 vb.
resist 715 vb.
callow
new 126 adj.
young 130 adj.
amorphous
244 adj.
unhabituated
611 adj.
immature 670 adj.
artless 699 adj.
innocent 935 adj.
call the shots
dominate 733 vb.
call the tune
motivate 612 vb.
dominate 733 vb.
call to arms
remember 505 vb.
call 547 n.
go to war 718 vb.
war 718 n.
war measures
718 n.
call to mind
remember 505 vb.

call up
bring together
74 vb.
go to war 718 vb.
call upon
command 737 vb.
impose a duty
917 vb.
callus
hardness 326 n.
calm
assuage 177 vb.
moderate 177 adj.
moderation 177 n.
flat 216 adj.
smooth 258 adj.
smoothness
258 n.
quietude 266 n.
tranquil 266 adj.
silent 399 adj.
inaction 677 n.
impassive 820 adj.
inexcitable
823 adj.
tranquillize
823 vb.
please 826 vb.
relieve 831 vb.
cautious 858 adj.
indifferent
860 adj.
calm as a
millpond
flat 216 adj.
smooth 258 adj.
calm before the
storm
reversion 148 n.
calorie(s)
energy 160 n.
dieting 301 n.
food content 301 n.
thermometry
379 n.
calumny
calumny 926 n.
Calvary
suffering 825 n.
Calvinistic
Protestant 976 adj.
calypso
vocal music 412 n.
calyx
receptacle 194 n.
flower 366 n.
camaraderie
friendliness 880 n.
fellowship 882 n.
camber
obliquity 220 n.
camber 253 n.
camcorder
camera 442 n.

camel
beast of burden
273 n.
mammal 365 n.
camel hair
fibre 208 n.
camellia
tree 366 n.
cameo
sculpture 554 n.
description 590 n.
acting 594 n.
jewellery 844 n.
camera
camera 442 n.
recording
instrument 549 n.
camisole
shirt 228 n.
underwear 228 n.
camouflage
assimilation 18 n.
imitate 20 vb.
mimicry 20 n.
transform 147 vb.
conceal 525 vb.
concealment
525 n.
disguise 527 n.
camp
place oneself
187 vb.
station 187 n.
abode 192 n.
dwell 192 vb.
art 551 n.
dramatic 594 adj.
shelter 662 n.
party 708 n.
amuse oneself
837 vb.
affectation 850 n.
affected 850 adj.
ostentation 875 n.
showy 875 adj.
campaign
undertaking 672 n.
action 676 n.
do 676 vb.
tactics 688 n.
fight 716 n.
fight 716 vb.
warfare 718 n.
philanthropy
901 n.
campanologist
instrumentalist
413 n.
camper
traveller 268 n.
automobile 274 n.
camp
follower(s)
retinue 67 n.

concomitant 89 n.
follower 284 n.
habitué 610 n.
dependant 742 n.
camphor
resin 357 n.
scent 396 n.
preserver 666 n.
camping
sport 837 n.
camp it up
act 594 vb.
be affected 850 vb.
campsite
station 187 n.
abode 192 n.
campus
focus 76 n.
meeting place
192 n.
academy 539 n.
arena 724 n.
campylobacter
infection 651 n.
can
be able 160 vb.
cup 194 n.
small box 194 n.
vessel 194 n.
preserve 666 vb.
prison 748 n.
canaille
rabble 869 n.
canal
cavity 255 n.
transport 272 n.
conduit 351 n.
access 624 n.
canapé
hors-d'oeuvres
301 n.
canary
bird 365 n.
bad person 938 n.
canasta
card game 837 n.
cancan
leap 312 n.
dance 837 n.
cancel
nullify 2 vb.
exclude 57 vb.
destroy 165 vb.
counteract 182 vb.
obliterate 550 vb.
relinquish 621 vb.
stop using 674 vb.
abrogate 752 vb.
not observe 769 vb.
not retain 779 vb.
forgive 909 vb.
disapprove 924 vb.
make illegal
954 vb.

cancellation
extinction 2 n.
counteraction
182 n.
negation 533 n.
obliteration 550 n.
relinquishment
621 n.
nonuse 674 n.
abrogation 752 n.
prohibition 757 n.
nonretention
779 n.
forgiveness 909 n.
loss of right 916 n.
cancer
badness 645 n.
cancer 651 n.
disease 651 n.
dilapidation 655 n.
blight 659 n.
candelabra
lamp 420 n.
candescent
fiery 379 adj.
candid
true 494 adj.
veracious 540 adj.
artless 699 adj.
trustworthy
929 adj.
candidate
respondent 460 n.
contender 716 n.
petitioner 763 n.
candle
lighter 385 n.
torch 420 n.
ritual object 988 n.
candlelight
evening 129 n.
light 417 n.
candlestick
lamp 420 n.
ritual object 988 n.
candlewick
textile 222 n.
candour
truth 494 n.
manifestation
522 n.
veracity 540 n.
artlessness 699 n.
probity 929 n.
candy
sweets 301 n.
sweeten 392 vb.
sweet thing 392 n.
candyfloss
sweets 301 n.
bubble 355 n.
sweet thing 392 n.
cane
support 218 n.

strike 279 vb.
spank 963 vb.
scourge 964 n.
canine
animal 365 adj.
dog 365 n.
caning
corporal
punishment
963 n.
canister
box 194 n.
small box 194 n.
canker
badness 645 n.
dilapidation 655 n.
blight 659 n.
cannabis
drug-taking 949 n.
cannelloni
dish 301 n.
cannibal
eater 301 n.
killer 362 n.
cannibalize
sunder 46 vb.
repair 656 vb.
canning
preservation 666 n.
cannon
collision 279 n.
recoil 280 n.
recoil 280 vb.
gun 723 n.
cannonball
sphere 252 n.
missile 287 n.
ammunition
723 n.
cannon fodder
soldiery 722 n.
cannula
tube 263 n.
canoe
row 269 vb.
rowing boat 275 n.
canon
rule 81 n.
musical piece
412 n.
vocal music 412 n.
creed 485 n.
maxim 496 n.
precept 693 n.
decree 737 n.
legislation 953 n.
theology 973 n.
scripture 975 n.
ecclesiarch 986 n.
canonize
dignify 866 vb.
sanctify 979 vb.
canoodle
caress 889 vb.

canopy
canopy 226 n.
screen 421 vb.
altar 990 n.

cant
be oblique 220 vb.
obliquity 220 n.
propel 287 vb.
duplicity 541 n.
falsehood 541 n.
dialectal 560 adj.
slang 560 adj.
pietism 979 n.
false piety 980 n.

cantankerous
quarrelling
   709 adj.
irascible 892 adj.
sullen 893 adj.

cantata
vocal music 412 n.
hymn 981 n.

canteen
café 192 n.
box 194 n.
chamber 194 n.

canter
gait 265 n.
ride 267 vb.

canticle
vocal music 412 n.
hymn 981 n.

cantilever
support 218 n.

canto
subdivision 53 n.

canton
district 184 n.
flag 547 n.
heraldry 547 n.

cantor
choir 413 n.
worshipper 981 n.
church officer
   986 n.

canvas
textile 222 n.
canopy 226 n.
sail 275 n.
picture 553 n.

canvass
enquire 459 vb.
enquiry 459 n.
divulge 526 vb.
publish 528 vb.
vote 605 vb.
do 676 vb.
request 761 vb.
sell 793 vb.

canyon
gap 201 n.
high land 209 n.
valley 255 n.
conduit 351 n.

caoutchouc
elasticity 328 n.

cap
be superior 34 vb.
culminate 34 vb.
crown 213 vb.
vertex 213 n.
cover 226 vb.
covering 226 n.
headgear 228 n.
close 264 vb.
stopper 264 n.
badge 547 n.
letter 558 n.
retaliate 714 vb.
explosive 723 n.
climax 725 vb.
decoration 729 n.
honours 866 n.

capable
fit 24 adj.
powerful 160 adj.
possible 469 adj.
intelligent
   498 adj.

capacious
great 32 adj.
spacious 183 adj.
large 195 adj.

capacitance
electricity 160 n.

capacity
greatness 32 n.
plenitude 54 n.
ability 160 n.
room 183 n.
size 195 n.
limit 236 n.
possibility 469 n.
intelligence
   498 n.
function 622 n.
means 629 n.
utility 640 n.
facility 701 n.

cape
cloak 228 n.

caper
ride 267 vb.
leap 312 n.
leap 312 vb.
amuse oneself
   837 vb.
dance 837 vb.

capercaillie
table bird 365 n.

capers
spice 301 n.
foolery 497 n.

capillary
narrow 206 adj.
narrowness 206 n.
filament 208 n.
tube 263 n.

cap in hand
supplicatory
   761 adj.
respectful 920 adj.

capital
supreme 34 adj.
summit 213 n.
topmost 213 adj.
deadly 362 adj.
means 629 n.
store 632 n.
important 638 adj.
super 644 adj.
estate 777 n.
funds 797 n.
wealth 800 n.

**capital gains
   tax**
tax 809 n.

capitalist
rich person 800 n.

capitalize
profit by 137 vb.

capitalize on
use 673 vb.

capital letter
letter 558 n.

**capital
   punishment**
capital punishment
   963 n.

capitals
print-type 587 n.

capitation
numeration 86 n.
statistics 86 n.

capitol
fort 713 n.

capitulate
submit 721 vb.

capon
poultry 365 n.
male animal
   372 n.

cappuccino
soft drink 301 n.

caprice
musical piece
   412 n.
caprice 604 n.
whim 604 n.

capricious
capricious 604 adj.

capsicum
fruit and vegetables
   301 n.

capsize
be unequal 29 vb.
derange 63 vb.
be inverted 221 vb.
invert 221 vb.
navigate 269 vb.
descent 309 n.
tumble 309 vb.

capsule
receptacle 194 n.
covering 226 n.
flower 366 n.
medicine 658 n.

captain
navigate 269 vb.
nautical personnel
   270 n.
direct 689 vb.
director 690 n.
leader 690 n.
army officer 741 n.
naval officer 741 n.

**captain of
   industry**
bigwig 638 n.
master 741 n.

caption
commentary 520 n.
indication 547 n.
label 547 n.
record 548 n.
name 561 n.
phrase 563 n.
script 586 n.
edition 589 n.
description 590 n.

captious
irascible 892 adj.
disapproving
   924 adj.

captivate
motivate 612 vb.
subjugate 745 vb.

captive
slave 742 n.
captive 750 adj.
prisoner 750 n.
take 786 vb.

captivity
servitude 745 n.
detention 747 n.

captor
master 741 n.
possessor 776 n.
taker 786 n.

capture
imagine 513 vb.
represent 551 vb.
describe 590 vb.
attack 712 vb.
overmaster 727 vb.
subjugate 745 vb.
arrest 747 vb.
acquire 771 vb.
take 786 vb.
taking 786 n.

car
conveyance 267 n.
automobile 274 n.
airship 276 n.

carafe
vessel 194 n.

caramel
sweets 301 n.
brownness 430 n.

carapace
covering 226 n.

carat
weighing 322 n.

caravan
small house 192 n.
cart 274 n.
follower 284 n.
traction 288 n.
amuse oneself
   837 vb.

caravan site
station 187 n.

caraway
spice 301 n.

carbine
firearm 723 n.

carbohydrates
food content 301 n.

carbolic
cleanser 648 n.
prophylactic 658 n.

carbonate
gasify 336 vb.
bubble 355 vb.

carbonated
gaseous 336 adj.

carbon copy
duplicate 22 n.
duplication 91 n.
record 548 n.

carbon dioxide
poison 659 n.

**carbon
   monoxide**
poison 659 n.

carbon paper
paper 631 n.

carbuncle
swelling 253 n.
blemish 845 n.

carcass
structure 331 n.
corpse 363 n.

carcinogenic
diseased 651 adj.
insalubrious
   653 adj.

carcinoma
growth 157 n.
swelling 253 n.
cancer 651 n.

car-clocking
swindling 788 n.

card
nonconformist
   84 n.
smoother 258 n.
sailing aid 269 n.
male 372 n.
label 547 n.

pied 437 adj.
enquire 459 vb.
enquiry 459 n.
experiment 461 n.
measurement
 465 n.
certainty 473 n.
make certain
 473 vb.
hinder 702 vb.
hindrance 702 n.
defeat 727 vb.
defeat 728 n.
adversity 731 n.
restrain 747 vb.
restraint 747 n.
loss 772 n.
pattern 844 n.
checkers
board game 837 n.
checking
measurement
 465 n.
restraining
 747 adj.
checklist
list 87 n.
comparison 462 n.
checkmate
halt 45 vb.
stop 145 n.
overmaster 727 vb.
victory 727 n.
defeat 728 n.
check on
enquire 459 vb.
checkout
recording
 instrument 549 n.
checkup
attention 455 n.
enquiry 459 n.
check with
compare 462 vb.
cheek
laterality 239 n.
be insolent 878 vb.
sauciness 878 n.
rudeness 885 n.
scurrility 899 n.
cheek by jowl
with 89 adv.
near 200 adv.
sideways 239 adv.
cheeky
impertinent
 878 adj.
discourteous
 885 adj.
disrespectful
 921 adj.
cheep
ululate 409 vb.
ululation 409 n.

cheer
cry 408 n.
cry 408 vb.
vociferate 408 vb.
gesture 547 n.
excite 821 vb.
be cheerful
 833 vb.
cheer 833 vb.
rejoice 835 vb.
celebrate 876 vb.
show respect
 920 vb.
applaud 923 vb.
cheerful
cheerful 833 adj.
cheerio
goodbye 296 int.
cheerleader
cry 408 n.
cheerless
cheerless 834 adj.
dejected 834 adj.
melancholic
 834 adj.
cheers
bon appétit
 301 int.
cheers 835 int.
rejoicing 835 n.
thanks 907 int.
cheer up
relieve 831 vb.
be cheerful
 833 vb.
cheery
cheerful 833 adj.
cheese
dairy product
 301 n.
cheesecake
pastries and cakes
 301 n.
a beauty 841 n.
cheesed off
discontented
 829 adj.
dejected 834 adj.
bored 838 adj.
cheese-paring
economical
 814 adj.
economy 814 n.
parsimonious
 816 adj.
parsimony 816 n.
cheetah
big cat 365 n.
chef
cookery 301 n.
caterer 633 n.
chef d'oeuvre
perfection 646 n.
masterpiece 694 n.

Chelsea
 pensioner
soldier 722 n.
chemise
dress 228 n.
underwear 228 n.
chemist
experimenter
 461 n.
druggist 658 n.
chemistry
conversion 147 n.
physics 319 n.
chemoprevention
prophylactic 658 n.
chemotherapy
therapy 658 n.
chenille
textile 222 n.
cheongsam
dress 228 n.
cheque
paper money
 797 n.
chequebook
record 548 n.
chequer
chequer 437 n.
variegate 437 vb.
chequered
changeable
 143 adj.
pied 437 adj.
Chequers
house 192 n.
chéri(e)
darling 890 n.
cherish
look after 457 vb.
safeguard 660 vb.
animate 821 vb.
love 887 vb.
approve 923 vb.
cherished
 number-plate
label 547 n.
cheroot
tobacco 388 n.
cherry
fruit and vegetables
 301 n.
redness 431 n.
cherub
child 132 n.
image 551 n.
darling 890 n.
angel 968 n.
cherubim
angel 968 n.
Cheshire cat
 grin
laughter 835 n.
chess
board game 837 n.

chessboard
chequer 437 n.
arena 724 n.
chess piece
plaything 837 n.
chest
box 194 n.
insides 224 n.
bosom 253 n.
treasury 799 n.
chesterfield
seat 218 n.
chestnut
repetition 106 n.
horse 273 n.
fruit and vegetables
 301 n.
brown 430 adj.
witticism 839 n.
chest of drawers
cabinet 194 n.
cheval glass
mirror 442 n.
chevet
church interior
 990 n.
chevron
obliquity 220 n.
angularity
 247 n.
heraldry 547 n.
badge of rank
 743 n.
pattern 844 n.
chew
chew 301 vb.
chewing
eating 301 n.
chewing gum
mouthful 301 n.
See **sweetmeat**
sweets 301 n.
elasticity 328 n.
chew the cud
graze 301 vb.
chewy
tough 329 adj.
chez
inside 224 adv.
chianti
wine 301 n.
chiaroscuro
darkening 418 n.
painted 553 adj.
painting 553 n.
chiasmus
inversion 221 n.
ornament 574 n.
chic
beauty 841 n.
personable
 841 adj.
shapely 841 adj.
fashion 848 n.

fashionable
 848 adj.
chicune
traffic control
 305 n.
chicanery
sophistry 477 n.
trickery 542 n.
perfidy 930 n.
chichi
fashionable
 848 adj.
affected 850 adj.
chick
young creature
 132 n.
youngster 132 n.
female 373 n.
darling 890 n.
chicken
young creature
 132 n.
weakling 163 n.
meat 301 n.
poultry 365 n.
coward 856 n.
cowardice 856 n.
cowardly 856 adj.
darling 890 n.
chickenfeed
small quantity
 33 n.
trifle 639 n.
easy thing 701 n.
money 797 n.
chicken-livered
cowardly 856 adj.
chicken out
be cowardly
 856 vb.
chickenpox
infection 651 n.
chicory
fruit and vegetables
 301 n.
chide
curse 899 vb.
reprove 924 vb.
chief
superior 34 n.
supreme 34 adj.
first 68 adj.
central 225 adj.
heraldry 547 n.
bigwig 638 n.
important 638 adj.
director 690 n.
potentate 741 n.
chief constable
police 955 n.
chieftain
potentate 741 n.
chiffon
textile 222 n.

transparency
422 n.
chiffonier
cabinet 194 n.
chignon
hair 259 n.
hairdressing 843 n.
chihuahua
dog 365 n.
chilblain(s)
coldness 380 n.
ulcer 651 n.
child
child 132 n.
innocent 935 n.
child abuse
painfulness
827 n.
cruel act 898 n.
child-bearing
female 373 adj.
child benefit
subvention 703 n.
childbirth
obstetrics 167 n.
childhood
youth 130 n.
childish
young 130 adj.
feeble 572 adj.
trivial 639 adj.
immature 670 adj.
childless
unproductive
172 adj.
childlike
young 130 adj.
artless 699 adj.
innocent 935 adj.
childminder
surveillance 457 n.
**child
psychology**
therapy 658 n.
children
kinsman 11 n.
child 132 n.
posterity 170 n.
children's home
shelter 662 n.
child's play
trifle 639 n.
easy thing 701 n.
chill
moderate 177 vb.
he cold 380 vb.
coldness 380 n.
refrigerate 382 vb.
adversity 731 n.
frighten 854 vb.
chilli
fruit and vegetables
301 n.
spice 301 n.

chilly
chilly 380 adj.
cold 380 adj.
hostile 881 adj.
chime
sound faint
401 vb.
roll 403 vb.
resonance 404 n.
resound 404 vb.
melody 410 n.
tune 412 n.
chime in
accord 24 vb.
chimera
insubstantial thing
4 n.
rara avis 84 n.
fantasy 513 n.
chimney
gap 201 n.
chimneypot
cylinder 252 n.
chimney stack
high structure
209 n.
chimneysweep
cleaner 648 n.
chimpanzee
mammal 365 n.
chin
protuberance
254 n.
china
weak thing
163 n.
pottery 381 n.
ornamentation
844 n.
china doll
image 551 n.
plaything 837 n.
chinaware
receptacle 194 n.
pottery 381 n.
chinchilla
skin 226 n.
chinese lantern
lamp 420 n.
celebration 876 n.
chink
gap 201 n.
narrowness 206 n.
furrow 262 n.
faintness 401 n.
sound faint
401 vb.
resonance 404 n.
resound 404 vb.
**chink in one's
armour**
defect 647 n.
vulnerability
661 n.

chinoiserie
ornamentation
844 n.
chinook
wind 352 n.
chintz
textile 222 n.
chinwag
speech 579 n.
chat 584 n.
converse 584 vb.
chip
small thing 33 n.
break 46 vb.
cut 46 vb.
piece 53 n.
label 547 n.
sculpt 554 vb.
chip away
make smaller
198 vb.
chip in
discontinue 72 vb.
interfere 231 vb.
aid 703 vb.
give 781 vb.
chipmunk
mammal 365 n.
**chip off the old
block**
analogue 18 n.
descendant 170 n.
chipolata
meat 301 n.
**chip on one's
shoulder**
discontent 829 n.
chipper
cheerful 833 adj.
chippy
loose woman
952 n.
chips
fruit and vegetables
301 n.
**chips are down,
the**
crisis 137 n.
chiromancy
occultism 984 n.
chiropodist
doctor 658 n.
beautician 843 n.
chiropractor
doctor 658 n.
chirp
ululate 409 vb.
sing 413 vb.
be cheerful 833 vb.
chirpy
cheerful 833 adj.
chirrup
ululate 409 vb.
sing 413 vb.

be cheerful 833 vb.
chisel
cut 46 vb.
produce 164 vb.
form 243 vb.
sharp edge 256 n.
sculpt 554 vb.
engraving 555 n.
tool 630 n.
chit
youngster 132 n.
dwarf 196 n.
credential 466 n.
reminder 505 n.
label 547 n.
correspondence
588 n.
permit 756 n.
chit-chat
chat 584 n.
chitter
be cold 380 vb.
chitterlings
meat 301 n.
chivalrous
male 372 adj.
courageous
855 adj.
noble 868 adj.
courteous 884 adj.
benevolent
897 adj.
honourable
929 adj.
chivalry
courage 855 n.
manliness 855 n.
prowess 855 n.
courtesy 884 n.
philanthropy
901 n.
probity 929 n.
chives
herb 301 n.
chlorinate
purify 648 vb.
make sanitary
652 adj.
safeguard 660 vb.
**chlorofluoro-
carbon**
propellant 287 n.
atmosphere 340 n.
poison 659 n.
chloroform
anaesthetic 375 n.
render insensible
375 vb.
chock-a-block
full 54 adj.
filled 635 adj.
chock-full
full 54 adj.
filled 635 adj.

chocolate
milk 301 n.
mouthful 301 n.
sweets 301 n.
brown 430 adj.
brownness 430 n.
choice
unusual 84 adj.
savoury 390 adj.
choice 605 n.
chosen 605 adj.
excellent 644 adj.
pleasurable
826 adj.
choir
choir 413 n.
church interior
990 n.
**choirboy or
-girl**
choir 413 n.
church officer
986 n.
choirmaster
choir 413 n.
trainer 537 n.
choirstall
compartment
194 n.
seat 218 n.
church interior
990 n.
choke
close 264 vb.
stopper 264 n.
kill 362 vb.
extinguish 382 vb.
rasp 407 vb.
superabound
637 vb.
hinder 702 vb.
choke back
restrain 747 vb.
choker
loop 250 n.
jewellery 844 n.
choky
lockup 748 n.
cholera
digestive disorders
651 n.
infection 651 n.
tropical disease
651 n.
choleric
irascible 892 adj.
cholesterol
food content 301 n.
chomp
chew 301 vb.
choose
choose 605 vb.
choosy
fastidious 862 adj.

chyle
fluid 335 n.
chypre
scent 396 n.
CIA
secret service
459 n.
ciabatta
cereals 301 n.
ciao
goodbye 296 int.
ciborium
ritual object 988 n.
cicada
insect 365 n.
cicatrice
blemish 845 n.
Cicero
speaker 579 n.
CID
police enquiry
459 n.
cider
alcoholic drink
301 n.
ci-devant
prior 119 adj.
cigar
tobacco 388 n.
cigar case
tobacco 388 n.
cigarette
tobacco 388 n.
cigarette card
picture 553 n.
cigarette case
case 194 n.
tobacco 388 n.
**cigarette
holder**
handle 218 n.
**cigarette
machine**
tobacco 388 n.
cilium
filament 208 n.
cinch
certainty 473 n.
dupe 544 n.
easy thing 701 n.
Cinderella
poor person 801 n.
**Cindy (tdmk)
doll**
image 551 n.
plaything 837 n.
cinema
cinema 445 n.
*place of
amusement*
837 n.
**Cinemascope
(tdmk)**
film 445 n.

cinematography
cinema 445 n.
photography
551 n.
**Cinerama
(tdmk)**
film 445 n.
cinerarium
cemetery 364 n.
cinerary
funereal 364 adj.
cingulum
vestments 989 n.
cinnabar
red pigment 431 n.
cinnamon
spice 301 n.
brownness 430 n.
cinquefoil
five 99 n.
heraldry 547 n.
Cinque Ports
five 99 n.
cipher
nonexistence 2 n.
insubstantial thing
4 n.
number 85 n.
zero 103 n.
secrecy 525 n.
enigma 530 n.
indication 547 n.
label 547 n.
writing 586 n.
nonentity 639 n.
circa
nearly 200 adv.
Circe
attraction 291 n.
motivator 612 n.
sorceress 983 n.
circle
continuity 71 n.
assembly 74 n.
group 74 n.
region 184 n.
circumscribe
232 vb.
circumscription
232 n.
circle 250 n.
fly 271 vb.
circle 314 vb.
onlookers 441 n.
informant 524 n.
theatre 594 n.
party 708 n.
circuit
continuity 71 n.
periodicity 141 n.
regular return
141 n.
revolution 149 n.
electricity 160 n.

region 184 n.
surroundings
230 n.
outline 233 n.
circle 250 n.
orbit 250 n.
land travel 267 n.
circle 314 vb.
circuition 314 n.
circuit 626 n.
circuit 626 vb.
circuit judge
judge 957 n.
circuitous
circuitous 314 adj.
roundabout
626 adj.
circular
continuous 71 adj.
round 250 adj.
information 524 n.
publication 528 n.
correspondence
588 n.
reading matter
589 n.
decree 737 n.
circularity
circularity 250 n.
circularize
publish 528 vb.
correspond 588 vb.
command 737 vb.
circular saw
notch 260 n.
rotator 315 n.
circulate
disperse 75 vb.
pass 305 vb.
circle 314 vb.
be published
528 vb.
publish 528 vb.
change hands
780 vb.
mint 797 vb.
circulation
dispersion 75 n.
orbit 250 n.
circuition 314 n.
rotation 315 n.
blood 335 n.
publication 528 n.
publicity 528 n.
circumcision
scission 46 n.
rite 988 n.
circumference
region 184 n.
size 195 n.
distance 199 n.
exteriority 223 n.
surroundings
230 n.

outline 233 n.
enclosure 235 n.
limit 236 n.
circle 250 n.
circuit 626 n.
circumflex
curved 248 adj.
**circumflex
accent**
punctuation 547 n.
circumlocution
obliquity 220 n.
trope 519 n.
phrase 563 n.
diffuseness 570 n.
circumnavigate
navigate 269 vb.
circle 314 vb.
circumscribe
circumscribe
232 vb.
circumspect
vigilant 457 adj.
cautious 858 adj.
circumstance
circumstance 8 n.
concomitant 89 n.
event 154 n.
ostentation 875 n.
circumstances
circumstance 8 n.
particulars 80 n.
estate 777 n.
**circumstances
beyond one's
control**
necessity 596 n.
circumstantial
circumstantial
8 adj.
**circumstantial
evidence**
evidence 466 n.
circumvent
avoid 620 vb.
circus
medley 43 n.
housing 192 n.
circle 250 n.
zoo 369 n.
stage show 594 n.
theatre 594 n.
arena 724 n.
pleasure ground
837 n.
cirrhosis
digestive disorders
651 n.
cirrocumulus
cloud 355 n.
cirrose
cloudy 355 adj.
cirrostratus
cloud 355 n.

cirrus
cloud 355 n.
cissy or sissy
weak 163 adj.
cist
interment 364 n.
tomb 364 n.
Cistercian
monk 986 n.
cistern
vat 194 n.
storage 632 n.
citadel
fort 713 n.
citation
referral 9 n.
evidence 466 n.
exhibit 522 n.
decoration 729 n.
warrant 737 n.
praise 923 n.
accusation 928 n.
legal process 959 n.
cite
specify 80 vb.
exemplify 83 vb.
repeat 106 vb.
manifest 522 vb.
command 737 vb.
indict 928 vb.
litigate 959 vb.
cithara
stringed instrument
414 n.
cithern
stringed instrument
414 n.
citizen
native 191 n.
subject 742 n.
free person 744 n.
commoner 869 n.
**Citizens' Band
radio**
broadcasting
531 n.
citrus fruit
fruit and vegetables
301 n.
City, city
city 184 n.
abode 192 n.
business 622 n.
*political
organization*
733 n.
city centre
focus 76 n.
city father
officer 741 n.
civet
scent 396 n.
civic
national 371 adj.

coal 385 n.
fuel 385 n.
black thing 428 n.
coalesce
be identical 13 vb.
combine 50 vb.
cooperate 706 vb.
coalface
store 632 n.
workshop 687 n.
coalfield
coal 385 n.
store 632 n.
coal gas
gas 336 n.
fuel 385 n.
coalition
union 45 n.
association 706 n.
political party
  708 n.
society 708 n.
coal mine
excavation 255 n.
store 632 n.
workshop 687 n.
coarse
rough 259 adj.
textural 331 adj.
indiscriminating
  464 adj.
inelegant 576 adj.
unclean 649 adj.
vulgar 847 adj.
plebeian 869 adj.
impure 951 adj.
coarse fishing
chase 619 n.
coarseness
roughness 259 n.
indiscrimination
  464 n.
plainness 573 n.
inelegance 576 n.
moral insensibility
  820 n.
bad taste 847 n.
impurity 951 n.
coast
edge 234 n.
flank 239 vb.
laterality 239 n.
be in motion
  265 vb.
ride 267 vb.
travel 267 vb.
voyage 269 vb.
pass 305 vb.
shore 344 n.
be neglectful
  458 vb.
not act 677 vb.
coastal
marginal 234 adj.

coaster
stand 218 n.
merchant ship
  275 n.
coastguard
nautical personnel
  270 n.
protector 660 n.
keeper 749 n.
coast home
do easily 701 vb.
coasting
water travel 269 n.
coastline
outline 233 n.
shore 344 n.
coat
layer 207 n.
coat 226 vb.
skin 226 n.
wrapping 226 n.
jacket 228 n.
overcoat 228 n.
See **jacket**
coatee
jacket 228 n.
coating
layer 207 n.
covering 226 n.
facing 226 n.
lining 227 n.
coat of arms
heraldry 547 n.
nobility 868 n.
coat-tail(s)
extremity 69 n.
hanging object
  217 n.
garment 228 n.
coax
tempt 612 vb.
request 761 vb.
pet 889 vb.
flatter 925 vb.
cob
pony 273 n.
cereals 301 n.
bird 365 n.
male animal
  372 n.
cobber
chum 880 n.
cobble
paving 226 n.
building material
  631 n
repair 656 vb.
cobbler
clothier 228 n.
mender 656 n.
cobblestone
paving 226 n.
cobble together
produce 164 vb.

cob nut
fruit and vegetables
  301 n.
cobra
reptile 365 n.
cobweb
weak thing 163 n.
filament 208 n.
network 222 n.
lightness 323 n.
dirt 649 n.
Coca Cola or
  Coke (tdmk)
soft drink 301 n.
cocaine
anaesthetic 375 n.
drug 658 n.
drug-taking 949 n.
coccyx
buttocks 238 n.
cochineal
pigment 425 n.
red pigment 431 n.
cochlea
ear 415 n.
cock
poultry 365 n.
male animal
  372 n.
make ready
  669 vb.
cockade
trimming 844 n.
cock-a-hoop
jubilant 833 adj.
cock and bull
  story
insubstantial thing
  4 n.
fable 543 n.
cock a snook
defy 711 vb.
disobey 738 vb.
not observe
  769 vb.
be insolent 878 vb.
not respect 921 vb.
cockatrice
rara avis 84 n.
eye 438 n.
heraldry 547 n.
cockerel
poultry 365 n.
male animal
  372 n.
cock-eyed
distorted 246 adj.
erroneous 495 adj.
absurd 497 adj.
cockfight
duel 716 n.
cockle
fish food 301 n.
marine life 365 n.

cockles of the
  heart
affections 817 n.
Cockney,
  cockney
native 191 n.
dialect 560 adj.
dialectal 560 adj.
plebeian 869 adj.
cockpit
chamber 194 n.
aircraft 276 n.
duel 716 n.
cockroach
insect 365 n.
cocktail
a mixture 43 n.
alcoholic drink
  301 n.
draught 301 n.
cocktail party
social gathering
  882 n.
cock-up
mistake 495 n.
cocky
proud 871 adj.
vain 873 adj.
impertinent
  878 adj.
cocoa
milk 301 n.
soft drink 301 n.
See **milk**
coconut
fruit and vegetables
  301 n.
cocoon
young creature
  132 n.
source 156 n.
receptacle 194 n.
wrapping 226 n.
safeguard 660 vb.
C.O.D.
pay 804 vb.
cod
fish food 301 n.
coda
adjunct 40 n.
sequel 67 n.
end 69 n.
rear 238 n.
melody 410 n.
musical piece
  412 n.
coddle
cook 301 vb.
please 826 vb.
pet 889 vb.
code
arrangement 62 n.
rule 81 n.
latency 523 n.

secrecy 525 n.
enigma 530 n.
writing 586 n.
precept 693 n.
probity 929 n.
codeine
drug 658 n.
codex
book 589 n.
codicil
adjunct 40 n.
sequel 67 n.
title deed 767 n.
codification
arrangement 62 n.
codpiece
garment 228 n.
coeducational
educational
  534 adj.
coefficient
numerical element
  85 n.
coerce
dominate 733 vb.
compel 740 vb.
coeval
contemporary
  123 n.
synchronous
  123 adj.
coexistence
accompaniment
  89 n.
synchronism
  123 n.
contiguity 202 n.
concord 710 n.
peace 717 n.
coffee
soft drink 301 n.
brownness 430 n.
coffee morning
social gathering
  882 n.
coffee table
stand 218 n.
coffee-table
  book
book 589 n.
coffer
box 194 n.
storage 632 n.
treasury 799 n.
coffin
place 185 n.
box 194 n.
funeral 364 n.
inter 364 vb.
interment 364 n.
cog
tooth 256 n.
notch 260 n.
notch 260 vb.

cogent
powerful 160 adj.
rational 475 adj.
forceful 571 adj.
compelling
  740 adj.
cogitate
think 449 vb.
See **meditate**
cognac
alcoholic drink
  301 n.
cognate
relative 9 adj.
verbal 559 adj.
cognition
intellect 447 n.
knowledge 490 n.
cognitive
knowing 490 adj.
cognizance
knowledge 490 n.
jurisdiction 955 n.
cognoscente
expert 696 n.
people of taste
  846 n.
cogwheel
notch 260 n.
cohabit
unite with 45 vb.
accompany 89 vb.
lover 887 n.
wed 894 vb.
cohere
cohere 48 vb.
coherent
sane 502 adj.
intelligible 516 adj.
cohesion
union 45 n.
coherence 48 n.
contiguity 202 n.
density 324 n.
toughness 329 n.
cohesive
cohesive 48 adj.
cohorts
army 722 n.
coiffure
hairdressing 843 n.
coil
complexity 61 n.
contraception
  172 n.
be curved 248 vb.
coil 251 n.
twine 251 vb.
coin
produce 164 vb.
form 243 vb.
circle 250 n.
imagine 513 vb.
coinage 797 n.

mint 797 vb.
coinage
neology 560 n.
coinage 797 n.
coincide
be 1 vb.
be identical 13 vb.
accord 24 vb.
synchronize
  123 vb.
be contiguous
  202 vb.
coincidence
identity 13 n.
conformance 24 n.
equality 28 n.
accompaniment
  89 n.
concomitant 89 n.
synchronism
  123 n.
event 154 n.
chance 159 n.
concurrence 181 n.
contiguity 202 n.
nondesign 618 n.
coincidental
casual 159 adj.
unintentional
  618 adj.
coincide with
be equal 28 vb.
Cointreau
  (tdmk)
alcoholic drink
  301 n.
coir
fibre 208 n.
coitus
coition 45 n.
coke
coal 385 n.
drug-taking 949 n.
colander
bowl 194 n.
porosity 263 n.
cold
excretion 302 n.
dead 361 adj.
unfeeling 375 adj.
cold 380 n.
coldness 380 n.
blue 435 adj.
mistaken 495 adj.
respiratory disease
  651 n.
uncooked 670 adj.
nonactive 677 adj.
adverse 731 adj.
adversity 731 n.
impassive 820 adj.
inexcitable
  823 adj.
indifferent 860 adj.

unsociable 883 adj.
unkind 898 n.
cold-blooded
animal 365 adj.
cautious 858 adj.
cruel 898 adj.
cold-calling
advertisement
  528 n.
cold cream
unguent 357 n.
cosmetic 843 n.
cold cuts
hors-d'oeuvres
  301 n.
cold feet
nervousness 854 n.
cold fish
unfeeling person
  820 n.
cold front
coldness 380 n.
wintriness 380 n.
coldness
coldness 380 n.
indifference 860 n.
enmity 881 n.
unsociability
  883 n.
cold-shoulder
exclude 57 vb.
repel 292 vb.
disregard 458 vb.
reject 607 vb.
avoid 620 vb.
be rude 885 vb.
cold storage
delay 136 n.
refrigeration
  382 n.
refrigerator 384 n.
preservation 666 n.
cold turkey
drug-taking 949 n.
cold water
moderator 177 n.
dissuasion 613 n.
coleslaw
hors-d'oeuvres
  301 n.
colic
pang 377 n.
digestive disorders
  651 n.
coliseum
arena 724 n.
colitis
digestive disorders
  651 n.
collaborate
assent 488 vb.
be willing 597 vb.
apostatize 603 vb.
cooperate 706 vb.

collaborator
collaborator 707 n.
toady 879 n.
friend 880 n.
collage
variegation 437 n.
art 551 n.
picture 553 n.
collapse
decrease 37 vb.
decomposition
  51 n.
cease 145 vb.
helplessness 161 n.
weakness 163 n.
ruin 165 n.
fall short 307 vb.
descend 309 vb.
descent 309 n.
be ill 651 vb.
illness 651 n.
deteriorate 655 vb.
dilapidation 655 n.
be fatigued 684 vb.
fatigue 684 n.
knuckle under
  721 vb.
defeat 728 n.
fail 728 vb.
failure 728 n.
fear 854 vb.
collar
garment 228 n.
See **neckwear**
neckwear 228 n.
loop 250 n.
arrest 747 vb.
fetter 748 n.
take 786 vb.
collarbone
support 218 n.
collate
compare 462 vb.
print 587 vb.
collateral
relative 9 adj.
lateral 239 adj.
security 767 n.
collateral
  damage
death roll 361 n.
collation
meal 301 n.
colleague
colleague 707 n.
collect
bring together
  74 vb.
congregate 74 vb.
understand 516 vb.
book 589 n.
abstract 592 vb.
acquire 771 vb.
receive 782 vb.

take 786 vb.
prayers 981 n.
collection
arrangement 62 n.
assemblage 74 n.
edition 589 n.
anthology 592 n.
collection 632 n.
acquisition 771 n.
offering 781 n.
receiving 782 n.
pay 804 n.
payment 804 n.
oblation 981 n.
collection plate
ritual object 988 n.
church utensil
  990 n.
collective
assemblage 74 n.
general 79 adj.
joint possession
  775 n.
collective
  bargaining
conditions 766 n.
collector
collector 492 n.
receiver 782 n.
collector's item
exhibit 522 n.
exceller 644 n.
masterpiece 694 n.
colleen
youngster 132 n.
female 373 n.
college
edifice 164 n.
academy 539 n.
collide
disagree 25 vb.
collide 279 vb.
be hostile 881 vb.
collide with
collide 279 vb.
meet 295 vb.
collie
dog 365 n.
collier
merchant ship
  275 n.
artisan 686 n.
colliery
excavation 255 n.
store 632 n.
workshop 687 n.
collimate
aim 281 vb.
collimation
parallelism 219 n.
direction 281 n.
collision
collision 279 n.
battle 718 n.

be disclosed
526 vb.
be published
528 vb.
relinquish 621 vb.
be inactive 679 vb.
resist 715 vb.
revolt 738 vb.
deprecate 762 vb.
come out with
manifest 522 vb.
confess 526 vb.
divulge 526 vb.
improvise 609 vb.
come over
be intelligible
516 vb.
come round
be restored 656 vb.
consent 758 vb.
comestibles
food 301 n.
comet
planet 321 n.
come through
be safe 660 vb.
come to
number 86 vb.
be turned to
147 vb.
live 360 vb.
be restored
656 vb.
be refreshed
685 vb.
cost 809 vb.
come to a head
culminate 34 vb.
be complete 54 vb.
come together
congregate 74 vb.
converge 293 vb.
come to life
live 360 vb.
come to nothing
pass away 2 vb.
fall short 307 vb.
miscarry 728 vb.
**come to one's
ears**
hear 415 vb.
be known 490 vb.
come to pass
happen 154 vb.
come under
be included 78 vb.
come upon
chance 159 vb.
meet 295 vb.
discover 484 vb.
comeuppance
retaliation 714 n.
reward 962 n.
punishment 963 n.

come what may
certainly 473 adv.
comfit
sweets 301 n.
comfort
assuage 177 vb.
repose 683 n.
facility 701 n.
aid 703 vb.
wealth 800 n.
please 826 vb.
content 828 n.
content 828 vb.
relief 831 n.
relieve 831 vb.
cheer 833 vb.
condolence 905 n.
pity 905 vb.
comfortable
tranquil 266 adj.
comfortable
376 adj.
prosperous 730 adj.
comforter
wrapping 226 n.
neckwear 228 n.
comfortless
unpleasant
827 adj.
cheerless 834 adj.
melancholic
834 adj.
comfy
comfortable
376 adj.
comic
fool 501 n.
the press 528 n.
dramatic 594 adj.
entertainer 594 n.
laughing 835 adj.
humorist 839 n.
witty 839 adj.
funny 849 adj.
comical
absurd 497 adj.
laughing 835 adj.
witty 839 adj.
funny 849 adj.
coming
future 124 adj.
approach 289 n.
arrival 295 n.
**coming and
going**
reversion 148 n.
fluctuation 317 n.
shadowy 419 adj.
busy 678 adj.
coming out
debut 68 n.
celebration 876 n.
coming to one
due 915 adj.

comma
punctuation 547 n.
command
advantage 34 n.
be superior 34 vb.
be high 209 vb.
style 566 n.
governance 733 n.
command 737 n.
command 737 vb.
commandant
army officer 741 n.
commandeer
compel 740 vb.
appropriate
786 vb.
commander
superior 34 n.
nautical personnel
270 n.
army officer 741 n.
naval officer 741 n.
**commander-in-
chief**
army officer 741 n.
commanding
superior 34 adj.
influential 178 adj.
authoritative
733 adj.
commanding
737 adj.
noteworthy
866 adj.
proud 871 adj.
commandment
precept 693 n.
command 737 n.
Commandoes
armed force 722 n.
tasteful 846 adj.
genteel 868 adj.
commemorate
remind 505 vb.
honour 866 vb.
celebrate 876 vb.
**commemorative
stamp**
*postal
communication*
531 n.
commence
begin 68 vb.
commend
advise 691 vb.
approve 923 vb.
praise 923 vb.
commendation
approbation 923 n.
praise 923 n.
commensal
resident 191 n.
commensurable
numerical 85 adj.

comment
estimate 480 n.
maxim 496 n.
commentary 520 n.
affirm 532 vb.
affirmation 532 n.
speech 579 n.
article 591 n.
commentary
commentary 520 n.
oration 579 n.
dissertation 591 n.
commentator
estimator 480 n.
interpreter 520 n.
informant 524 n.
broadcaster 531 n.
dissertator 591 n.
comment on
interpret 520 vb.
comment upon
notice 455 vb.
dissertate 591 vb.
commerce
interlocution
584 n.
business 622 n.
vocation 622 n.
trade 791 n.
commercial
advertisement
528 n.
broadcast 531 n.
bad taste 847 n.
vulgar 847 adj.
commercialize
trade 791 vb.
commercialized
vulgar 847 adj.
commination
prayers 981 n.
commiserate
lament 836 vb.
pity 905 vb.
commissar
officer 741 n.
commissariat
provisions 301 n.
provision 633 n.
commission
increment 36 n.
band 74 n.
job 622 n.
action 676 n.
precept 693 n.
command 737 n.
commission 751 n.
commission
751 adj.
mandate 751 n.
permit 756 n.
earnings 771 n.
portion 783 n.
pay 804 n.

price 809 n.
discount 810 n.
reward 962 n.
commissionaire
doorkeeper 264 n.
courier 529 n.
servant 742 n.
**commissioned
officer**
army officer 741 n.
commissioner
official 690 n.
officer 741 n.
commit
transfer 272 vb.
do 676 vb.
commission
751 vb.
give 781 vb.
do wrong 914 adj.
commitment
resolution 599 n.
perseverance 600 n.
promise 764 n.
debt 803 n.
duty 917 n.
committal
transference 272 n.
commission 751 n.
legal process 959 n.
committee
band 74 n.
party 708 n.
authority 733 n.
consignee 754 n.
commode
cabinet 194 n.
latrine 649 n.
commodious
spacious 183 adj.
commodity
object 319 n.
utility 640 n.
merchandise
795 n.
commodore
nautical personnel
270 n.
naval officer 741 n.
common
general 79 adj.
typical 83 adj.
frequent 139 adj.
plain 348 n.
aphoristic 496 adj.
linguistic 557 adj.
usual 610 adj.
unpossessed
774 adj.
joint possession
775 n.
lands 777 n.
vulgar 847 adj.
plebeian 869 adj.

condolence
benevolent
897 adj.
condolence 905 n.
condom
contraception
172 n.
condominium
joint possession
775 n.
condone
be patient 823 vb.
forgive 909 vb.
conducive
instrumental
628 adj.
useful 640 adj.
conduct
come before 64 vb.
accompany 89 vb.
transfer 272 vb.
carry 273 vb.
precede 283 vb.
play music 413 vb.
conduct 688 n.
deal with 688 vb.
direct 689 vb.
manage 689 vb.
conduction
electricity 160 n.
motion 265 n.
transference 272 n.
conductivity
motion 265 n.
conduct oneself
do 676 vb.
behave 688 vb.
conductor
living model 23 n.
electricity 160 n.
musician 413 n.
See **orchestra**
orchestra 413 n.
leader 690 n.
conduit
conduit 351 n.
cone
cone 252 n.
flower 366 n.
confectionery
pastries and cakes
301 n.
sweets 301 n.
sweet thing 392 n.
confederacy
association 706 n.
society 708 n.
confederate
colleague 707 n.
confer
confer 584 vb.
give 781 vb.
conference
conference 584 n.

confess
confess 526 vb.
perform ritual
988 vb.
confession
testimony 466 n.
assent 488 n.
disclosure 526 n.
affirmation 532 n.
guilt 936 n.
penitence 939 n.
penance 941 n.
theology 973 n.
Holy Communion
988 n.
ministration
988 n.
confessional
creedal 485 adj.
disclosure 526 n.
tribunal 956 n.
church interior
990 n.
confessor
penitent 939 n.
pietist 979 n.
pastor 986 n.
confetti
small thing 33 n.
confidant(e)
adviser 691 n.
retainer 742 n.
servant 742 n.
close friend 880 n.
confide
inform 524 vb.
divulge 526 vb.
confide in
consult 691 vb.
confidence
positiveness 473 n.
expectation 507 n.
information 524 n.
safety 660 n.
hope 852 n.
confidence trick
trickery 542 n.
swindling 788 n.
confident
positive 473 adj.
expectant 507 adj.
assertive 532 adj.
hoping 852 adj.
confidential
private 80 adj.
concealed 525 adj.
configuration
outline 233 n.
form 243 n.
confine
hem 234 vb.
enclose 235 vb.
limit 236 vb.
conceal 525 vb.

imprison 747 vb.
seclude 883 vb.
confinement
obstetrics 167 n.
circumscription
232 n.
concealment
525 n.
detention 747 n.
seclusion 883 n.
confines
region 184 n.
place 185 n.
edge 234 n.
confirm
stabilize 153 vb.
strengthen 162 vb.
corroborate 466 vb.
make certain
473 vb.
judge 480 vb.
affirm 532 vb.
consent 758 vb.
contract 765 vb.
vindicate 927 vb.
make legal 953 vb.
perform ritual
988 vb.
confirmation
evidence 466 n.
certainty 473 n.
assent 488 n.
affirmation 532 n.
consent 758 n.
legislation 953 n.
Christian rite
988 n.
confirmed
habituated
610 adj.
due 915 adj.
confiscate
deprive 786 vb.
punish 963 vb.
conflagration
fire 379 n.
burning 381 n.
conflate
abstract 592 vb.
conflict
contrariety 14 n.
differ 15 vb.
disagreement 25 n.
counteraction
182 n.
opposition 704 n.
quarrel 709 n.
quarrel 709 vb.
contention 716 n.
fight 716 n.
be hostile 881 vb.
enmity 881 n.
confluence
union 45 n.

approach 289 n.
convergence 293 n.
current 350 n.
conform
adjust 24 vb.
conform 83 vb.
make conform
83 vb.
modify 143 vb.
conformist
conformist 83 n.
pietist 979 n.
confound
bedevil 63 vb.
confute 479 vb.
be wonderful
864 vb.
curse 899 vb.
confounded
damnable 645 adj.
confront
disagree 25 vb.
be present 189 vb.
be in front 237 vb.
be opposite 240 vb.
collide 279 vb.
compare 462 vb.
show 522 vb.
withstand 704 vb.
resist 715 vb.
go to war 718 vb.
be courageous
855 vb.
confrontation
contrariety 14 n.
disagreement
25 n.
contiguity 202 n.
collision 279 n.
convergence 293 n.
quarrel 709 n.
confuse
derange 63 vb.
blur 440 vb.
puzzle 474 vb.
confused
mixed 43 adj.
shadowy 419 adj.
indistinct 444 adj.
indiscriminate
464 adj.
poorly reasoned
477 adj.
unclear 568 adj.
confusion
psychosis 503 n.
humiliation 872 n.
confute
confute 479 vb.
conga
dance 837 n.
congé
valediction 296 n.
deposal 752 n.

congeal
be dense 324 vb.
thicken 354 vb.
congenial
pleasant 376 adj.
friendly 880 adj.
congenital
genetic 5 adj.
congestion
crowd 74 n.
redundance 637 n.
conglomerate
cohere 48 vb.
bring together
74 vb.
congregate 74 vb.
be dense 324 vb.
solid body 324 n.
corporation 708 n.
conglomeration
medley 43 n.
coherence 48 n.
accumulation 74 n.
congratulate
congratulate
886 vb.
applaud 923 vb.
congratulate
oneself
be pleased 824 vb.
be content 828 vb.
rejoice 835 vb.
congratulate
886 vb.
congratula-
tions
rejoicing 835 n.
congratulation
886 n.
congregate
congregate 74 vb.
congregation
assembly 74 n.
council 692 n.
community 708 n.
worshipper 981 n.
laity 987 n.
congress
union 45 n.
convergence 293 n.
council 692 n.
parliament 692 n.
congruent
identical 13 adj.
agreeing 24 adj.
equal 28 adj.
symmetrical
245 adj.
congruity
similarity 18 n.
conformance 24 n.
symmetry 245 n.
conical
convergent 293 adj.

constant
identical 13 adj.
identity 13 n.
uniform 16 adj.
continuous 71 adj.
regular 81 adj.
number 85 n.
lasting 113 adj.
perpetual 115 adj.
frequent 139 adj.
periodical 141 adj.
fixture 153 n.
unchangeable
 153 adj.
accurate 494 adj.
resolute 599 adj.
obedient 739 adj.
trustworthy
 929 adj.
constellation
group 74 n.
star 321 n.
person of repute
 866 n.
consternation
wonder 864 n.
constipation
closure 264 n.
defecation 302 n.
condensation
 324 n.
digestive disorders
 651 n.
constituency
district 184 n.
electorate 605 n.
constituency list
list 87 n.
constituency MP
official 690 n.
councillor 692 n.
constituent
part 53 n.
component 58 adj.
component 58 n.
included 78 adj.
electorate 605 n.
constitute
constitute 56 vb.
be included 78 vb.
produce 164 vb.
constitution
character 5 n.
composition 56 n.
beginning 68 n.
inclusion 78 n.
structure 331 n.
precept 693 n.
law 953n.
legislation 953 n.
constitutional
intrinsic 5 adj.
land travel 267 n.

pedestrianism
 267 n.
habit 610 n.
exercise 682 n.
governmental
 733 adj.
due 915 adj.
legal 953 adj.
constraint
limit 236 n.
compulsion 740 n.
subjection 745 n.
restraint 747 n.
constrict
tighten 45 vb.
make smaller
 198 vb.
constriction
compression 198 n.
restriction 747 n.
construct
make complete
 54 vb.
compose 56 vb.
produce 164 vb.
form 243 vb.
construction
composition 56 n.
arrangement 62 n.
production 164 n.
structure 331 n.
connotation 514 n.
interpretation
 520 n.
constructive
semantic 514 adj.
interpretative
 520 adj.
aiding 703 adj.
construe
interpret 520 vb.
consul
official 690 n.
officer 741 n.
envoy 754 n.
consulate
house 192 n.
position of
 authority 733 n.
envoy 754 n.
consult
consult 691 vb.
consultant
sage 500 n.
oracle 511 n.
teacher 537 n.
doctor 658 n.
adviser 691 n.
expert 696 n.
consultation
enquiry 459 n.
conference 584 n.
preparation 669 n.
advice 691 n.

consume
decompose 51 vb.
disable 161 vb.
consume 165 vb.
destroy 165 vb.
dispose of 673 vb.
use 673 vb.
expend 806 vb.
consumer
eater 301 n.
purchaser 792 n.
consumer durables
merchandise
 795 n.
consummate
consummate
 32 adj.
terminate 69 vb.
crown 213 vb.
perfect 646 adj.
perfect 646 vb.
consumption
contraction 198 n.
thinness 206 n.
reception 299 n.
eating 301 n.
requirement 627 n.
infection 651 n.
respiratory disease
 651 n.
use 673 n.
loss 772 n.
consumptive
lean 206 adj.
diseased 651 adj.
sick person 651 n.
contact
connect 45 vb.
union 45 n.
be contiguous
 202 vb.
contiguity 202 n.
transference 272 n.
touch 378 n.
communicate
 524 vb.
informant 524 n.
messenger 529 n.
contact lens
eyeglass 442 n.
contagious
diseased 651 adj.
infectious 653 adj.
contain
contain 56 vb.
surround 230 vb.
possess 773 vb.
retain 778 vb.
container
receptacle 194 n.
transport 272 n.
carrier 273 n.
storage 632 n.

containerize
load 193 vb.
transpose 272 vb.
contain oneself
be temperate
 942 vb.
contaminate
transfer 272 vb.
make unclean
 649 vb.
impair 655 vb.
contaminated
diseased 651 adj.
contemplate
scan 438 vb.
meditate 449 vb.
intend 617 vb.
contemplation
look 438 n.
meditation 449 n.
attention 455 n.
expectation 507 n.
piety 979 n.
prayers 981 n.
worship 981 n.
contemplative
thoughtful 449 adj.
pietist 979 n.
pious 979 adj.
worshipper 981 n.
monastic 986 adj.
contemporaneous
present 121 adj.
synchronous
 123 adj.
contemporary
present 121 adj.
contemporary
 123 n.
synchronous
 123 adj.
modern 126 adj.
contempt
contempt 922 n.
contemptible
bad 645 adj.
contemptible
 922 adj.
contemptuous
insolent 878 adj.
contend
affirm 532 vb.
contend 716 vb.
contender
contender 716 n.
contend with
resist 715 vb.
content
structure 331 n.
content 828 adj.
content 828 n.
content 828 vb.
contention
contention 716 n.

contentions
quarrelling
 709 adj.
contentment
euphoria 376 n.
content 828 n.
contents
contents 193 n.
topic 452 n.
meaning 514 n.
edition 589 n.
compendium
 592 n.
contest
contend 716 vb.
contest 716 n.
contestant
opponent 705 n.
contender 716 n.
context
circumstance 8 n.
relation 9 n.
concomitant 89 n.
connotation 514 n.
meaning 514 n.
contiguous, be
be contiguous
 202 vb.
continence
temperance 942 n.
continent
region 184 n.
land 344 n.
temperate 942 adj.
continental
extraneous 59 adj.
continental quilt
coverlet 226 n.
contingency
extrinsicality 6 n.
juncture 8 n.
event 154 n.
possibility 469 n.
uncertainty 474 n.
expectation 507 n.
contingent
extrinsic 6 adj.
circumstantial
 8 adj.
part 53 n.
caused 157 adj.
liable 180 adj.
qualifying 468 adj.
possible 469 adj.
uncertain 474 adj.
conditional
 766 adj.
contingent, be
be possible 469 vb.
continual
continuous 71 adj.
perpetual 115 adj.
frequent 139 adj.

badness 645 n.
uncleanness 649 n.
deterioration
655 n.
dilapidation 655 n.
improbity 930 n.
wickedness 934 n.
corset
make smaller
198 vb.
support 218 n.
underwear 228 n.
hardness 326 n.
cortège
retinue 67 n.
follower 284 n.
obsequies 364 n.
retainer 742 n.
cortex
exteriority 223 n.
skin 226 n.
cortical
exterior 223 adj.
cortisone
drug 658 n.
coryza
excretion 302 n.
coldness 380 n.
respiratory disease
651 n.
cosh
hammer 279 n.
strike 279 vb.
club 723 n.
scourge 964 n.
cosmetic
spurious 542 adj.
cosmetic 843 n.
cosmetic
  surgery
surgery 658 n.
beautification
843 n.
cosmic
extensive 32 adj.
comprehensive
52 adj.
cosmic 321 adj.
cosmonaut
aeronaut 271 n.
cosmopolitan
universal 79 adj.
national 371 adj.
cosmos
whole 52 n.
arrangement 62 n.
universe 321 n.
cosset
pet 889 vb.
cost
appraise 465 vb.
account 808 vb.
cost 809 n.
cost 809 vb.

price 809 vb.
dearness 811 n.
costermonger
seller 793 n.
pedlar 794 n.
costive
dense 324 adj.
costly
destructive 165 adj.
valuable 644 adj.
dear 811 adj.
ostentatious
875 adj.
cost of living
statistics 86 n.
expenditure 806 n.
cost 809 n.
costs
expenditure 806 n.
cost 809 n.
penalty 963 n.
costume
suit 228 n.
stage set 594 n.
costume
  jewellery
finery 844 n.
jewellery 844 n.
cosy
little 196 adj.
comfortable
376 adj.
pleasurable
826 adj.
content 828 adj.
sociable 882 adj.
cosy up to
be servile 879 vb.
be friendly with
880 vb.
cot
small house 192 n.
bed 218 n.
cotangent
ratio 85 n.
coterie
band 74 n.
group 74 n.
classification 77 n.
association 706 n.
community 708 n.
party 708 n.
cotillion
dance 837 n.
cottage
small house 192 n.
cottage industry
business 622 n.
cotton
fibre 208 n.
textile 222 n.
cotton on to
understand 516 vb.
be in love 887 vb.

cotton wool
fibre 208 n.
cotyledon
foliage 366 n.
couch
be horizontal
216 vb.
bed 218 n.
seat 218 n.
couchant
supine 216 adj.
heraldic 547 adj.
couch potato
idler 679 n.
cougar
big cat 365 n.
cough
eruct 300 vb.
excrete 302 vb.
excretion 302 n.
breathe 352 vb.
rasp 407 vb.
respiratory disease
651 n.
cough up
eject 300 vb.
confess 526 vb.
pay 804 vb.
couldn't care
  less
be incurious
454 vb.
negligence 458 n.
negligent 458 adj.
apathetic 820 adj.
be indifferent
860 vb.
council
conference 584 n.
council 692 n.
council house
house 192 n.
councillor
councillor 692 n.
officer 741 n.
council tax
tax 809 n.
counsel
advice 691 n.
advise 691 vb.
adviser 691 n.
consignee 754 n.
lawyer 958 n.
counselling
advice 691 n.
counsellor
estimator 480 n.
adviser 691 n.
aider 703 n.
consignee 754 n.
count
comprise 78 vb.
number 86 vb.
numeration 86 n.

measure 465 vb.
motivate 612 vb.
person of rank
868 n.
count as
substitute 150 vb.
count down
number 86 vb.
countdown
start 68 vb.
numeration 86 n.
countenance
face 237 n.
look 445 n.
approbation 923 n.
approve 923 vb.
counter
counteract 182 vb.
shelf 218 n.
stand 218 n.
answer 460 vb.
label 547 n.
be obstructive
702 vb.
oppose 704 vb.
retaliate 714 vb.
plaything 837 n.
counteract
counteract 182 vb.
counterattack
attack 712 n.
retaliation 714 n.
counter-
  attraction
influence 178 n.
counterbalance
be equal 28 vb.
influence 178 vb.
counteract 182 vb.
counteraction
182 n.
countercharge
rejoinder 460 n.
vindication 927 n.
accusation 928 n.
accuse 928 vb.
counterclaim
rejoinder 460 n.
counterevidence
467 n.
request 761 n.
deprecation 762 n.
counterevidence
counterevidence
467 n.
counterfeit
copy 20 vb.
imitation 20 n.
imitative 20 adj.
substituted
150 adj.
dissemble 541 vb.
duplicity 541 n.
fake 541 vb.

false 541 adj.
deceive 542 vb.
sham 542 n.
spurious 542 adj.
be untrue 543 vb.
mint 797 vb.
counterfoil
credential 466 n.
label 547 n.
title deed 767 n.
receipt 807 n.
counterirritant
counteraction
182 n.
antidote 658 n.
countermand
command 737 vb.
abrogate 752 vb.
prohibit 757 vb.
counterpane
coverlet 226 n.
counterpart
analogue 18 n.
compeer 28 n.
counterpoint
contrariety 14 n.
combination 50 n.
melody 410 n.
music 412 n.
counter-
  revolution
reversion 148 n.
revolution 149 n.
countersign
testify 466 vb.
endorse 488 vb.
give security
767 vb.
countess
person of rank
868 n.
count for
substitute 150 vb.
count heads
number 86 vb.
vote 605 vb.
counting
inclusive 78 adj.
numeration 86 n.
countless
multitudinous
104 adj.
infinite 107 adj.
count on
believe 485 vb.
hope 852 vb.
count one's
  blessings
be content 828 vb.
count one's
  chickens
  before they
  are hatched
expect 507 vb.

jewellery 844 n.
nobility 868 n.
crestfallen
disappointed
509 adj.
dejected 834 adj.
crest of the
wave
superiority 34 n.
summit 213 n.
cretin
fool 501 n.
person with a
learning disability
504 n.
cretonne
textile 222 n.
Creutzfeldt-
Jakob disease
mental disorder
503 n.
crevasse
gap 201 n.
pitfall 663 n.
crevice
gap 201 n.
crew
component 58 n.
band 74 n.
operate 173 vb.
resident 191 n.
navigate 269 vb.
mariner 270 n.
personnel 686 n.
party 708 n.
crew cut
shortness 204 n.
hairdressing 843 n.
crew neck
jersey 228 n.
neckline 228 n.
crib
copy 20 vb.
copy 22 vb.
basket 194 n.
bed 218 n.
translation 520 n.
borrow 785 vb.
steal 788 vb.
cribbage
card game 837 n.
crick
pang 377 n.
cricket
insect 365 n.
ball game 837 n.
cricketer
player 837 n.
cricket pitch
arena 724 n.
cri de coeur
request 761 n.
crier
publicizer 528 n.

crime
deed 676 n.
disobedience
738 n.
wrong 914 n.
improbity 930 n.
perfidy 930 n.
vice 934 n.
wickedness 934 n.
guilty act 936 n.
lawbreaking 954 n.
crime passionel
homicide 362 n.
revenge 910 n.
jealousy 911 n.
crime wave
lawlessness 954 n.
criminal
nonconformist
84 n.
unconformable
84 adj.
low fellow 869 n.
offender 904 n.
wrong 914 adj.
heinous 934 adj.
guilty 936 adj.
bad person 938 n.
lawbreaking
954 adj.
criminal
investigation
police enquiry
459 n.
criminal
offence
lawbreaking 954 n.
criminology
lawbreaking 954 n.
crimp
crinkle 251 vb.
notch 260 vb.
crimson
red 431 adj.
redden 431 vb.
redness 431 n.
be modest 874 vb.
cringe
stoop 311 vb.
knuckle under
721 vb.
be cowardly
856 vb.
crinkle
crinkle 251 vb.
crinoline
skirt 228 n.
cripple
disable 161 vb.
make useless
641 adj.
sick person 651 n.
impair 655 vb.
hinder 702 vb.

crisis
degree 27 n.
present time 121 n.
crisis 137 n.
crisis of
conscience
unbelief 486 n.
crisp
harden 326 vb.
rigid 326 adj.
brittle 330 adj.
concise 569 adj.
crispbread
cereals 301 n.
crisps
mouthful 301 n.
crisscross
crossed 222 adj.
crossing 222 n.
crit
estimate 480 n.
criterion
prototype 23 n.
testing agent
461 n.
comparison 462 n.
gauge 465 n.
critic
estimator 480 n.
dissentient 489 n.
interpreter 520 n.
bookperson 589 n.
dissertator 591 n.
malcontent 829 n.
detractor 926 n.
critical
circumstantial
8 adj.
crucial 137 adj.
discriminating
463 adj.
literary 557 adj.
important 638 adj.
sick 651 adj.
dangerous 661 adj.
unsafe 661 adj.
difficult 700 adj.
discontented
829 adj.
fastidious 862 adj.
disapproving
924 adj.
critical moment
juncture 8 n.
criticism
estimate 480 n.
interpretation
520 n.
affirmation 532 n.
literature 557 n.
article 591 n.
advice 691 n.
censure 924 n.
detraction 926 n.

criticize
dissertate 591 vb.
be discontented
829 vb.
criticize 924 vb.
detract 926 vb.
critique
discrimination
463 n.
estimate 480 n.
interpretation
520 n.
article 591 n.
croak
die 361 vb.
rasp 407 vb.
ululate 409 vb.
ululation 409 n.
crochet
tie 45 vb.
network 222 n.
weave 222 vb.
needlework 844 n.
crock
vessel 194 n.
sick person 651 n.
crockery
receptacle 194 n.
pottery 381 n.
crocodile
line 203 n.
skin 226 n.
reptile 365 n.
crocodile tears
duplicity 541 n.
lament 836 n.
Croesus
rich person 800 n.
croft
house 192 n.
farm 370 n.
croissant
cereals 301 n.
crone
old woman 133 n.
crony
colleague 707 n.
chum 880 n.
friend 880 n.
crook
support 218 n.
angularity 247 n.
be curved 248 vb.
deflect 282 vb.
punctuation 547 n.
thief 789 n.
low fellow 869 n.
offender 904 n.
bad person 938 n.
vestments 989 n.
crooked
distorted 246 adj.
angular 247 adj.
cunning 698 adj.

dishonest 930 adj.
croon
sound faint
401 vb.
sing 413 vb.
crooner
vocalist 413 n.
entertainer 594 n.
crop
great quantity
32 n.
growth 157 n.
product 164 n.
stomach 194 n.
shorten 204 vb.
hair 259 n.
graze 301 vb.
agriculture 370 n.
cultivate 370 vb.
benefit 615 n.
store 632 n.
acquire 771 vb.
earnings 771 n.
take 786 vb.
hairdressing 843 n.
crop circle
circle 250 n.
farming 370 n.
cropped
incomplete 55 adj.
cropper
descent 309 n.
crop up
happen 154 vb.
chance 159 vb.
be visible 443 vb.
croquet
ball game 837 n.
croquettes
dish 301 n.
crosier
badge of rule
743 n.
vestments 989 n.
cross
hybrid 43 n.
mix 43 vb.
counteract 182 vb.
cross 222 n.
cross 222 n.
crossed 222 adj.
traverse 267 vb.
pass 305 vb.
obsequies 364 n.
assent 488 n.
badge 547 n.
heraldry 547 n.
indication 547 n.
label 547 n.
mark 547 vb.
bane 659 n.
encumbrance
702 n.
opposing 704 adj.

cut short
cut 46 vb.
halt 145 vb.
suppress 165 vb.
shorten 204 vb.
be concise 569 vb.
concise 569 adj.
cut straws
gamble 618 vb.
cut the Gordian knot
disencumber 701 vb.
cut the ground from under one's feet
hinder 702 vb.
defeat 727 vb.
cutter
sharp edge 256 n.
boat 275 n.
sailing ship 275 n.
cut-throat
destructive 165 adj.
cutthroat
murderer 362 n.
ruffian 904 n.
cut-throat competition
contention 716 n.
cut through
cut 46 vb.
pierce 263 vb.
be resolute 599 vb.
cutting
scission 46 n.
excavation 255 n.
sharp 256 adj.
plant 366 n.
cinema 445 n.
railway 624 n.
hairdressing 843 n.
cutting edge
sharp edge 256 n.
cuttings
record 548 n.
anthology 592 n.
cuttlefish
marine life 365 n.
cut to pieces
slaughter 362 vb.
cut to the quick
excite 821 vb.
hurt 827 vb.
cut up
cut 46 vb.
unhappy 825 adj.
melancholic 834 adj.
cut up about
suffering 825 adj.
cut up rough
be angry 891 vb.
resent 891 vb.

cv
biography 590 n.
cyanide
poison 659 n.
cyanosis
blueness 435 n.
cybercafe
restaurant 192 n.
cyberlaw
computing 86 n.
law 953 n.
cybernetics
computing 86 n.
cyberpet
animal 365 n.
cybersex
computing 86 n.
sexual intercourse 45 n.
cybershopping
purchase 792 n.
cyberspace
computing 86 n.
cycle
continuity 71 n.
recurrence 106 n.
era 110 n.
periodicity 141 n.
regular return 141 n.
orbit 250 n.
motion 265 n.
ride 267 vb.
bicycle 274 n.
poem 593 n.
stage play 594 n.
cycle track
road 624 n.
cyclic
periodical 141 adj.
round 250 adj.
cyclical
continuous 71 adj.
cycling
land travel 267 n.
exercise 682 n.
sport 837 n.
cyclist
rider 268 n.
cyclometer
meter 465 n.
cyclone
storm 176 n.
vortex 315 n.
weather 340 n.
gale 352 n.
Cyclops
giant 195 n.
cyclostyle
copy 20 vb.
cyclotron
nucleonics 160 n.
cygnet
young creature 132 n.

bird 365 n.
cylinder
cylinder 252 n.
cyma
pattern 844 n.
cymbals
gong 414 n.
cyme
flower 366 n.
cynic
underestimation 483 n.
unbeliever 486 n.
misanthrope 902 n.
detractor 926 n.
cynical
impassive 820 adj.
hopeless 853 adj.
disrespectful 921 adj.
disapproving 924 adj.
cynicism
philosophy 449 n.
moral insensibility 820 n.
dejection 834 n.
hopelessness 853 n.
misanthropy 902 n.
detraction 926 n.
cynosure
focus 76 n.
attraction 291 n.
desired object 859 n.
person of repute 866 n.
favourite 890 n.
cyst
swelling 253 n.
skin disease 651 n.
ulcer 651 n.
cystitis
digestive disorders 651 n.
cytology
biology 358 n.
czardas
dance 837 n.

D

dab
small thing 33 n.
knock 279 n.
touch 378 vb.
dabble
be inactive 679 vb.
dabble in
not know 491 vb.

amuse oneself 837 vb.
dabchick
bird 365 n.
dab hand
proficient person 696 n.
dabs
trace 548 n.
dactyl
prosody 593 n.
dad
paternity 169 n.
Dada
school of painting 553 n.
Dadaist
artist 556 n.
daddy
paternity 169 n.
daddy longlegs
insect 365 n.
dado
base 214 n.
lining 227 n.
ornamental art 844 n.
daffodil
plant 366 n.
yellowness 433 n.
heraldry 547 n.
daft
foolish 499 adj.
crazy 503 adj.
dagger
sharp point 256 n.
punctuation 547 n.
sidearms 723 n.
daggers drawn
resentment 891 n.
dahlia
plant 366 n.
daily
often 139 adv.
periodically 141 adv.
seasonal 141 adj.
journal 528 n.
the press 528 n.
usual 610 adj.
cleaner 648 n.
servant 742 n.
daily dozen
exercise 682 n.
daily help
cleaner 648 n.
servant 742 n.
dainty
small 33 adj.
flimsy 163 adj.
little 196 adj.
savouriness 390 n.
pleasurableness 826 n.

personable 841 adj.
shapely 841 adj.
tasteful 846 adj.
fastidious 862 adj.
dairy
chamber 194 n.
workshop 687 n.
dairy farm
stock farm 369 n.
farm 370 n.
dairymaid
herdsman 369 n.
dais
stand 218 n.
daisy
plant 366 n.
daisy wheel
stationery 586 n.
Dalai Lama
sovereign 741 n.
priest 986 n.
dale
plain 348 n.
Dalek
image 551 n.
dalliance
lovemaking 887 n.
dally
be inactive 679 vb.
caress 889 vb.
Dalmatian
dog 365 n.
mottle 437 n.
dam
exclusion 57 n.
maternity 169 n.
close 264 vb.
irrigator 341 n.
lake 346 n.
staunch 350 vb.
obstacle 702 n.
obstruct 702 vb.
damage
break 46 vb.
derange 63 vb.
tell against 467 vb.
evil 616 n.
waste 634 n.
waste 634 vb.
badness 645 n.
harm 645 vb.
impair 655 vb.
impairment 655 n.
cost 809 n.
blemish 845 vb.
defame 926 vb.
penalty 963 n.
damages
compensation 31 n.
restitution 787 n.
pay 804 n.
cost 809 n.
penalty 963 n.

damaging
wasteful 634 adj.
harmful 645 adj.
discreditable
867 adj.
disapproving
924 adj.

damask
textile 222 n.
red 431 adj.

dame
female 373 n.
master 741 n.
person of repute
866 n.
title 870 n.

dammed
born 360 adj.

damn
trifle 639 n.
curse 899 int.
curse 899 vb.
cuss 899 vb.
scurrility 899 n.
criticize 924 vb.
condemn 961 vb.

damnable
damnable 645 adj.

damnably
extremely 32 vb.

damnation
future state 124 n.
suffering 825 n.
condemnation
961 n.

damned
damnable 645 adj.
condemned
961 adj.

damning
evidential 466 adj.
cursing 899 adj.
disapproving
924 adj.

**damn with faint
praise**
be indifferent
860 vb.
criticize 924 vb.
detract 926 vb.

damp
moderate 177 vb.
gas 336 n.
water 339 n.
humid 341 adj.
moisture 341 n.
extinguish 382 vb.
depress 834 vb.

damp course
base 214 n.

damp down
abate 37 vb.
extinguish 382 vb.
hinder 702 vb.

restrain 747 vb.
dampen
moderate 177 vb.
moisten 341 vb.
mute 401 vb.
dissuade 613 vb.
depress 834 vb.

damper
moderator 177 n.
stopper 264 n.
heater 383 n.
nonresonance
405 n.
piano 414 n.
dissuasion 613 n.
moper 834 n.

dampness
moisture 341 n.

damp-proof
strong 162 adj.
coat 226 vb.

damp squib
disappointment
509 n.
failure 728 n.

damsel
youngster 132 n.
female 373 n.

damson
fruit and vegetables
301 n.
purpleness 436 n.

**damson-
coloured**
purple 436 adj.

dam up
staunch 350 vb.
obstruct 702 vb.

dan
proficient person
696 n.

dance
vary 152 vb.
be in motion
265 vb.
walk 267 vb.
leap 312 vb.
oscillate 317 vb.
be agitated 318 vb.
shine 417 vb.
ballet 594 n.
be excited 821 vb.
be cheerful 833 vb.
rejoice 835 vb.
dance 837 n.
dance 837 vb.
dancing 837 vb.
social gathering
882 n.
be angry 891 vb.

**dance
attendance on**
follow 284 vb.
be servile 879 vb.

dance band
band 74 n.

dance floor
smoothness 258 n.

dance hall
place of amusement
837 n.

dance music
music 412 n.

**dance of the
seven veils**
uncovering 229 n.
dance 837 n.

dancer
entertainer 594 n.

dance step
leap 312 n.

dancing
motion 265 n.
merry 833 adj.
dancing 837 n.
angry 891 adj.

dancing girl
entertainer 594 n.

dandelion
plant 366 n.
yellowness 433 n.

dandle
caress 889 vb.

dandruff
powder 332 n.
dirt 649 n.

dandy
super 644 adj.
fop 848 n.

danegeld
tax 809 n.

danger
destiny 155 n.
danger 661 n.

danger of
vulnerability 661 n.

dangerous
dangerous 661 adj.
hostile 881 adj.
angry 891 adj.

danger signal
danger signal
665 n.
threat 900 n.

dangle
come unstuck
49 vb.
hang 217 vb.
pendency 217 n.
oscillate 317 vb.

**Daniel come to
judgment**
sage 500 n.
magistracy 957 n.

dank
humid 341 adj.

dapper
orderly 60 adj.

personable
841 adj.

dappled
mixed 43 adj.
pied 437 adj.

Darby and Joan
duality 90 n.
old couple 133 n.
spouse 894 n.

dare
be resolute 599 vb.
oppose 704 vb.
defiance 711 n.
defy 711 vb.
be free 744 vb.
be courageous
855 vb.
threat 900 n.

daredevil
brave person
855 n.
desperado 857 n.
rash 857 adj.

dare say
assume 471 vb.
suppose 512 vb.

daring
resolution 599 n.
danger 661 n.
enterprising
672 adj.
defiance 711 n.
courage 855 n.
courageous
855 adj.
rash 857 adj.
showy 875 adj.
unchaste 951 adj.

dark
evening 129 n.
dark 418 adj.
darkness 418 n.
black 428 adj.
blackish 428 adj.
brown 430 adj.
blind 439 adj.
unknown 491 adj.
latency 523 n.
cheerless 834 adj.
dishonest 930 adj.

Dark Ages
era 110 n.
antiquity 125 n.
ignorance 491 n.

darken
darken 418 vb.
screen 421 vb.
be unseen 444 vb.

darkening
darkening 418 n.
blackness 428 n.

**darken the
doors**
enter 297 vb.

dark glasses
shade 226 n.
screen 421 n.
semitransparency
424 n.
eyeglass 442 n.
misinterpretation
521 n.

dark-headed
black 428 adj.

dark horse
unknown thing
491 n.
latency 523 n.
secret 530 n.

darkish
dim 419 adj.

darkness
darkness 418 n.
ignorance 491 n.

darkroom
darkness 418 n.

dark-skinned
blackish 428 adj.

darling
darling 890 n.

darn
join 45 vb.
modify 143 vb.
weave 222 vb.
repair 656 vb.
curse 899 int.

darned
damnable 645 adj.

darning
network 222 n.
repair 656 vb.

dart
vary 152 vb.
be in motion
265 vb.
move fast 277 vb.
missile 287 n.
propel 287 vb.
missile weapon
723 n.

darting
speedy 277 adj.

darts
indoor game 837 n.

Darwinism
evolution 316 n.
biology 358 n.

dash
small quantity
33 n.
tincture 43 n.
bond 47 n.
vigorousness
174 n.
move fast 277 vb.
spurt 277 n.
strike 279 vb.
be agitated 318 vb.

impossibility
470 n.
inaction 677 n.
difficulty 700 n.
obstacle 702 n.
noncompletion
726 n.
defeat 728 n.
dead loss
lost labour 641 n.
loss 772 n.
deadly
deadly 362 adj.
dull 840 adj.
hostile 881 adj.
heinous 934 adj.
guilty 936 adj.
deadly
 nightshade
plant 366 n.
poisonous plant
659 n.
dead men
 (empty
 bottles)
emptiness 190 n.
dead of night
midnight 129 n.
darkness 418 n.
dead-on
accurate 494 adj.
dead pan
seriousness 834 n.
deadpan
still 266 adj.
impassive
820 adj.
inexcitable
823 adj.
serious 834 adj.
dead ringer
identity 13 n.
analogue 18 n.
Dead Sea
ocean 343 n.
dead to
thick-skinned
820 adj.
dead to the
 world
sleepy 679 adj.
dead weight
rubbish 641 n.
encumbrance
702 n.
deaf
deaf 416 adj.
deaf-aid
hearing aid 415 n.
deaf and dumb
deaf 416 adj.
voiceless 578 adj.
deaf as a post
deaf 416 adj.

deaf ears
inattention 456 n.
deafen
be loud 400 vb.
deafen 416 vb.
deafening
loud 400 adj.
deaf-mute
deaf 416 adj.
deafness 416 n.
deaf to
deaf 416 adj.
thick-skinned
820 adj.
deal
great quantity
32 n.
arrange 62 vb.
disperse 75 vb.
deed 676 n.
compact 765 n.
apportionment
783 n.
portion 783 n.
trade 791 n.
perfidy 930 n.
deal, a
greatly 32 vb.
deal a
 deathblow
kill 362 vb.
dealer
agent 686 n.
seller 793 n.
merchant 794 n.
dealing
barter 791 n.
dealings
deed 676 n.
conduct 688 n.
deal out
disperse 75 vb.
give 781 vb.
apportion 783 vb.
deal with
be related to 9 vb.
dissertate 591 vb.
do business
622 vb.
deal with 688 vb.
make terms
766 vb.
trade 791 vb.
dean
teacher 537 n.
director 690 n.
ecclesiarch
986 n.
dear
known 490 adj.
dear 811 adj.
pleasurable
826 adj.
darling 890 adj.

dear departed
the dead 361 n.
dearest
darling 890 n.
dear heart
darling 890 n.
dearly
greatly 32 vb.
dearly-bought
dear 811 adj.
dearness
dearness 811 n.
dear sir
title 870 n.
dearth
unproductiveness
172 n.
scarcity 636 n.
death
death 361 n.
deathbed
late 136 adj.
decease 361 n.
deathbed
 repentance
decease 361 n.
penitence 939 n.
deathblow
end 69 n.
death 361 n.
killing 362 n.
evil 616 n.
defeat 728 n.
death
 certificate
death roll 361 n.
label 547 n.
record 548 n.
death chamber
means of execution
964 n.
death duty
tax 809 n.
death knell
death 361 n.
warning 664 n.
deathless
perpetual 115 adj.
renowned 866 adj.
deathly
dying 361 adj.
deadly 362 adj.
colourless 426 adj.
evil 616 adj.
deathly pale
colourless 426 adj.
death mask
copy 22 n.
sculpture 554 n.
death rate
statistics 86 n.
death roll 361 n.
death rattle
decease 361 n.

death roll
death roll 361 n.
Death Row
lockup 748 n.
condemnation
961 n.
means of execution
964 n.
death's door
suffering 825 n.
Death sentence
capital punishment
963 n.
death's-head
corpse 363 n.
moper 834 n.
eyesore 842 n.
intimidation
854 n.
deathtrap
trap 542 n.
danger 661 n.
pitfall 663 n.
death warrant
condemnation
961 n.
capital punishment
963 n.
deathwatch
surveillance
457 n.
deathwatch
 beetle
insect 365 n.
death wish
dejection 834 n.
debacle
revolution 149 n.
ruin 165 n.
defeat 728 n.
debag
uncover 229 vb.
debar
exclude 57 vb.
obstruct 702 vb.
prohibit 757 vb.
refuse 760 vb.
debar from
restrain 747 vb.
debarkation
arrival 295 n.
debase
abase 311 vb.
impair 655 vb.
pervert 655 vb.
disentitle 916 vb.
debasement
lowness 210 n.
lowering 311 n.
deterioration
655 n.
disrepute 867 n.
improbity 930 n.

debatable
uncertain 474 adj.
debate
argue 475 vb.
argument 475 n.
confer 584 vb.
conference 584 n.
be irresolute
601 vb.
contention 716 n.
debauched
vicious 934 adj.
sensual 944 adj.
lecherous 951 adj.
debenture
title deed 767 n.
debilitated
weakened 163 adj.
debility
old age 131 n.
weakness 163 n.
ill health 651 n.
sluggishness 679 n.
debit
debt 803 n.
account 808 vb.
debouchment
egress 298 n.
Debrett
directory 87 n.
debris
remainder 41 n.
piece 53 n.
accumulation 74 n.
powder 332 n.
rubbish 641 n.
debt
debt 803 n.
debt-collector
receiver 782 n.
debt counselling
advice 691 n.
debt 803 n.
debug
computerize 86 vb.
rectify 654 vb.
debunk
abase 311 vb.
disclose 526 vb.
ridicule 851 vb.
shame 867 vb.
humiliate 872 vb.
detract 926 vb.
debut
debut 68 n.
celebration 876 n.
debutant
beginner 538 n.
decade
over five 99 n.
period 110 n.
decadent
literary 557 adj.
sensualist 944 n.

depravity
badness 645 n.
deterioration 655 n.
wickedness 934 n.
deprecate
deprecate 762 vb.
criticize 924 vb.
detract 926 vb.
deprecatory
disapproving
924 adj.
depreciate
abate 37 vb.
underestimate
483 vb.
discount 810 vb.
be cheap 812 vb.
depreciated
monetary 797 adj.
depreciation
decrease 37 n.
underestimation
483 n.
loss 772 n.
finance 797 n.
cheapness 812 n.
disrespect 921 n.
detraction 926 n.
depress
abate 37 vb.
make concave
255 vb.
lower 311 vb.
depress 834 vb.
depressed
concave 255 adj.
dejected 834 adj.
sullen 893 adj.
depressing
unpleasant
827 adj.
cheerless 834 adj.
tedious 838 adj.
depression
inferiority 35 n.
lowness 210 n.
depth 211 n.
cavity 255 n.
concavity 255 n.
valley 255 n.
lowering 311 n.
weather 340 n.
neurosis 503 n.
deterioration 655 n.
adversity 731 n.
poverty 801 n.
dejection 834 n.
melancholy 834 n.
depressive
psychotic 503 adj.
neurotic 504 n.
deprivation
absence 190 n.
ejection 300 n.

scarcity 636 n.
deposal 752 n.
loss 772 n.
nonownership
774 n.
expropriation
786 n.
loss of right 916 n.
penalty 963 n.
deprive
weaken 163 vb.
deprive 786 vb.
shame 867 vb.
punish 963 vb.
deprived
poor 801 adj.
depth
depth 211 n.
blackness 428 n.
metrology 465 n.
depths
lowness 210 n.
deputation
commission 751 n.
deputize
deputize 755 vb.
deputy
councillor 692 n.
deputy 755 n.
derailment
displacement
188 n.
deranged
mentally disordered
503 adj.
derationing
liberation 746 n.
derby
headgear 228 n.
Derby, the
racing 716 n.
deregulate
liberate 746 vb.
not retain 779 vb.
deregulation
liberation 746 n.
derelict
disused 674 adj.
derelict 779 n.
not retained
779 adj.
dereliction of
duty
undutifulness
918 n.
guilty act 936 n.
derestriction
laxity 734 n.
deride
reject 607 vb.
laugh 835 vb.
ridicule 851 vb.
not respect 921 vb.
despise 922 vb.

impious 980 adj.
de rigueur
usual 610 adj.
obligatory 917 adj.
derision
unbelief 486 n.
laughter 835 n.
ridicule 851 n.
contempt 922 n.
impiety 980 n.
derisory
laughing 835 adj.
ridiculous 849 adj.
derisory
amount, a
fewness 105 n.
derivation
origin 68 n.
reversion 148 n.
source 156 n.
effect 157 n.
attribution 158 n.
connotation 514 n.
word 559 n.
derivative
imitative 20 adj.
numerical element
85 n.
caused 157 adj.
effect 157 n.
verbal 559 adj.
word 559 n.
dull 840 adj.
derive
acquire 771 vb.
derive from
result 157 vb.
attribute 158 vb.
dermatitis
skin disease 651 n.
dermatology
medical art 658 n.
derogatory
degrading 867 adj.
dishonest 930 adj.
derring-do
courage 855 n.
prowess 855 n.
derris
poison 659 n.
derv
fuel 385 n.
dervish
ascetic 945 n.
religionist 973 n.
pietist 979 n.
worshipper 981 n.
monk 986 n.
desalinate
purify 648 vb.
descant
tune 412 n.
vocal music 412 n.
sing 413 vb.

be diffuse 570 vb.
hymn 981 n.
descend
descend 309 vb.
descendant
successor 67 n.
posteriority 120 n.
descendant 170 n.
descender
print-type 587 n.
descend from
result 157 vb.
descending
order
decrease 37 n.
series 71 n.
descent
consanguinity
11 n.
sequence 65 n.
continuity 71 n.
posteriority 120 n.
source 156 n.
genealogy 169 n.
presence 189 n.
descent 309 n.
nobility 868 n.
describe
describe 590 vb.
describe a circle
circumscribe
232 vb.
outline 233 vb.
circle 314 vb.
represent 551 vb.
description
literature 557 n.
name 561 n.
nomenclature
561 n.
description 590 n.
descriptive
descriptive 590 adj.
descry
see 438 vb.
understand 516 vb.
desecrate
make unclean
649 vb.
impair 655 vb.
misuse 675 vb.
shame 867 vb.
not respect 921 vb.
be impious 980 vb.
deselect
vote 605 vb.
reject 607 vb.
desert
desert 172 n.
unproductive
172 adj.
empty 190 adj.
dry 342 adj.
disregard 458 vb.

apostatize 603 vb.
change one's mind
603 vb.
run away 620 vb.
relinquish 621 vb.
goodness 644 n.
not observe 769 vb.
be cowardly
856 vb.
seclusion 883 n.
divorce 896 vb.
fail in duty 918 vb.
deserted
alone 88 adj.
empty 190 adj.
neglected 458 adj.
secluded 883 adj.
deserter
recanter 603 n.
avoider 620 n.
coward 856 n.
undutifulness
918 n.
desertification
unproductiveness
172 n.
dryness 342 n.
desertion
change of mind
603 n.
relinquishment
621 n.
disobedience
738 n.
cowardice 856 n.
divorce 896 n.
undutifulness
918 n.
perfidy 930 n.
desert island
desert 172 n.
desertization
unproductiveness
172 n.
dryness 342 n.
deserts
conduct 688 n.
retaliation 714 n.
right 913 n.
dueness 915 n.
reward 962 n.
deserve
deserve 915 vb.
deserved
just 913 adj.
due 915 adj.
déshabillé
informal dress
228 n.
uncovering 229 n.
desiccated
dry 342 adj.
desiccator
dryer 342 n.

dialysis
cleansing 648 n.
surgery 658 n.
diamante
finery 844 n.
diameter
dividing line 92 n.
breadth 205 n.
diamond
angular figure
247 n.
hardness 326 n.
exceller 644 n.
gem 844 n.
diamond jubilee
anniversary 141 n.
celebration 876 n.
diamond
wedding
anniversary 141 n.
special day 876 n.
Diana
moon 321 n.
hunter 619 n.
Olympian deity
967 n.
diaphanous
transparent
422 adj.
diaphragm
middle 70 n.
contraception
172 n.
musical instrument
414 n.
diarist
chronologist
117 n.
chronicler 549 n.
author 589 n.
diarrhoea
defecation 302 n.
digestive disorders
651 n.
diary
list 87 n.
chronology 117 n.
reminder 505 n.
record 548 n.
reference book
589 n.
biography 590 n.
diatonic scale
key 410 n.
diatribe
oration 579 n.
censure 924 n.
diazepam
drug 658 n.
dice
cut 46 vb.
cook 301 vb.
oracle 511 n.
gambling 618 n.

amuse oneself
837 vb.
dice game
gambling game
837 n.
dice with death
face danger
661 vb.
be rash 857 vb.
dicey
casual 159 adj.
speculative
618 adj.
dangerous 661 adj.
dichotomy
disunion 46 n.
scission 46 n.
bisection 92 n.
dick
detective 459 n.
police 955 n.
dickens, the
curse 899 int.
See **perish**
dickey
garment 228 n.
dicky
seat 218 n.
unsafe 661 adj.
Dictaphone
(tdmk)
hearing aid 415 n.
recording
instrument 549 n.
dictate
teach 534 vb.
speak 579 vb.
necessitate 596 vb.
direct 689 vb.
dominate 733 vb.
rule 733 vb.
command 737 n.
command 737 vb.
decree 737 n.
compel 740 vb.
dictation
teaching 534 n.
oration 579 n.
command 737 n.
dictator
tyrant 735 n.
autocrat 741 n.
dictatorial
narrow-minded
481 adj.
volitional 595 adj.
authoritative
733 adj.
authoritarian
735 adj.
commanding
737 adj.
insolent 878 adj.
dictatorship
directorship 689 n.

despotism 733 n.
brute force 735 n.
diction
phrase 563 n.
style 566 n.
dictionary
dictionary 559 n.
dictum
maxim 496 n.
affirmation 532 n.
speech 579 n.
command 737 n.
didactic
educational
534 adj.
diddled, be
be duped 544 vb.
didicoi
wanderer 268 n.
die
mould 23 n.
be past 125 vb.
die 361 vb.
See **perish**
be unseen 444 vb.
fate 596 n.
gambling 618 n.
die down
decrease 37 vb.
be quiescent
266 vb.
blow 352 vb.
extinguish 382 vb.
die for
desire 859 vb.
diehard
permanent
144 adj.
die out
pass away 2 vb.
end 69 vb.
perish 361 vb.
diesel engine
locomotive 274 n.
diet
make smaller
198 vb.
make thin 206 vb.
dieting 301 n.
eating 301 n.
be temperate
942 vb.
starve 946 vb.
dietetics
dieting 301 n.
die the death
be punished
963 vb.
dietician
doctor 658 n.
differ
differ 15 vb.
disagree 25 vb.
dissent 489 vb.

difference
difference 15 n.
numerical result
85 n.
dissent 489 n.
difference of
opinion
dissent 489 n.
differences
dissension 709 n.
schism 978 n.
different
different 15 adj.
different ball
game, a
variant 15 n.
differentia
difference 15 n.
differential
difference 15 n.
degree 27 n.
numerical 85 adj.
numerical element
85 n.
earnings 771 n.
differentiate
differentiate 15 vb.
different kettle
of fish
variant 15 n.
differing
different 15 adj.
dissenting
489 adj.
difficult
difficult 700 adj.
disobedient
738 adj.
discontented
829 adj.
fastidious 862 adj.
sullen 893 adj.
difficulties
poverty 801 n.
difficulty
unintelligibility
517 n.
difficulty 700 n.
diffidence
nervousness 854 n.
modesty 874 n.
diffident
doubting 474 adj.
nervous 854 adj.
modest 874 adj.
diffraction
dispersion 75 n.
reflection 417 n.
diffuse
disperse 75 vb.
generalize 79 vb.
disappear 446 vb.
publish 528 vb.
diffuse 570 adj.

diffusion
disunion 46 n.
dispersion 75 n.
presence 189 n.
transference 272 n.
ingress 297 n.
dig
antiquity 125 n.
excavation 255 n.
make concave
255 vb.
knock 279 n.
agitate 318 vb.
agitation 318 n.
cultivate 370 vb.
search 459 n.
search 459 vb.
understand 516 vb.
work 682 vb.
be in love 887 vb.
reproach 924 n.
digamy
type of marriage
894 n.
dig at
contempt 922 n.
calumny 926 n.
dig down
descend 309 vb.
digest
arrangement 62 n.
modify 143 vb.
absorb 299 vb.
eat 301 vb.
compendium
592 n.
be patient 823 vb.
digestible
edible 301 adj.
digestion
combination 50 n.
reception 299 n.
eating 301 n.
digestive
purgative 658 n.
remedial 658 adj.
dig for
search 459 vb.
pursue 619 vb.
dig in
place oneself
187 vb.
defend 713 vb.
dig in one's
heels
persevere 600 vb.
be obstinate
602 vb.
refuse 760 vb.
dig into
enquire 459 vb.
digit
number 85 n.
feeler 378 n.

digital
numerical 85 adj.
computerized
86 adj.
statistical 86 adj.
digital clock
timekeeper 117 n.
digital
computer
counting
instrument 86 n.
digital
television
broadcast 531 n.
digital watch
timekeeper 117 n.
digitize
computerize 86 vb.
dignified
elegant 575 adj.
authoritative
733 adj.
impressive 821 adj.
worshipful
866 adj.
proud 871 adj.
formal 875 adj.
courteous 884 adj.
dignitary
officer 741 n.
aristocrat 868 n.
ecclesiarch 986 n.
dignity
conduct 688 n.
good taste 846 n.
honours 866 n.
prestige 866 n
pride 871 n.
ostentation 875 n.
digress
deviate 282 vb.
be inattentive
456 vb.
be diffuse 570 vb.
digression
obliquity 220 n.
deviation 282 n.
overstepping
306 n.
diffuseness 570 n.
oration 579 n.
digs
quarters 192 n.
dig up
extract 304 vb.
exhume 364 vb.
be curious 453 vb.
dike
gap 201 n.
fence 235 n.
furrow 262 n.
conduit 351 n.
obstacle 702 n.
defences 713 n.

diktat
decree 737 n.
dilapidated
dilapidated
655 adj.
dilatation
dilation 197 n.
rarity 325 n.
dilatation and
curettage
surgery 658 n.
dilate
grow 36 vb.
expand 197 vb.
rarefy 325 vb.
blow up 352 vb.
dilatoriness
delay 136 n.
dilatory
late 136 adj.
slow 278 adj.
dilemma
circumstance 8 n.
dubiety 474 n.
choice 605 n.
predicament 700 n.
dilettante
dabbling 491 adj.
collector 492 n.
dabbler 493 n.
diligent
attentive 455 adj.
careful 457 adj.
studious 536 adj.
observant 768 adj.
dilly-dally
be irresolute
601 vb.
be inactive 679 vb.
dilute
abate 37 vb.
weaken 163 vb.
rarefy 325 vb.
moisten 341 vb.
dim
darken 418 vb.
dim 419 adj.
dim 419 vb.
be dim-sighted
440 vb.
blur 440 vb.
unintelligent
499 adj.
dime
small thing 33 n.
coinage 797 n.
dimension
quantity 26 n.
measure 183 n.
appearance 445 n.
dimensions
quantity 26 n.
greatness 32 n.
size 195 n.

metrology 465 n.
diminish
abate 37 vb.
subtract 39 vb.
render few 105 vb.
moderate 177 vb.
shorten 204 vb.
diminuendo
contraction 198 n.
adagio 412 adv.
diminution
smallness 33 n.
diminution 37 n.
subtraction 39 n.
diminutive
small 33 adj.
little 196 adj.
word 559 n.
name 561 n.
part of speech
564 n.
diminutiveness
smallness 33 n.
littleness 196 n.
dimple
cavity 255 n.
concavity 255 n.
notch 260 n.
lowering 311 n.
dimwit
dunce 501 n.
fool 501 n.
dim-witted
weak 163 adj.
unintelligent
499 adj.
din
greatness 32 n.
commotion 318 n.
be loud 400 vb.
loudness 400 n.
roll 403 n.
discord 411 n.
dinar
coinage 797 n.
dine
eat 301 vb.
feed 301 vb.
dine out
eat 301 vb.
be sociable
882 vb.
diner
café 192 n.
eater 301 n.
ding
resound 404 vb.
dingbat
fool 501 n.
dingdong
roll 403 n.
dinghy
boat 275 n.
rowing boat 275 n.

dingle
valley 255 n.
dingo
dog 365 n.
dingy
dim 419 adj.
colourless 426 adj.
dirty 649 adj.
dilapidated
655 adj.
din in
emphasize 532 vb.
educate 534 vb.
dining
eating 301 n.
dining room
chamber 194 n.
dinky
little 196 adj.
dinner
meal 301 n.
festivity 837 n.
dinner jacket
formal dress 228 n.
jacket 228 n.
dinner party
social gathering
882 n.
dinosaur
fossil 125 n.
archaism 127 n.
giant 195 n.
animal 365 n.
dint
concavity 255 n.
make concave
255 vb.
notch 260 n.
collide 279 vb.
knock 279 n.
diocese
district 184 n.
parish 985 n.
Diogenes
misanthrope
902 n.
dioxin
poison 659 n.
dip
be oblique 220 vb.
incline 220 n.
cavity 255 n.
valley 255 n.
swim 269 vb.
impel 279 vb.
immerse 303 vb.
descend 309 vb.
descent 309 n.
lower 311 vb.
lowering 311 n.
plunge 313 n.
plunge 313 vb.
be wet 341 vb.
drench 341 vb.

dim 419 vb.
torch 420 n.
colour 425 vb.
ablutions 648 n.
clean 648 vb.
diphtheria
infection 651 n.
respiratory disease
651 n.
diphthong
speech sound
398 n.
voice 577 n.
dip into
be curious 453 vb.
study 536 vb.
diploma
credential 466 n.
record 548 n.
mandate 751 n.
honours 866 n.
diplomacy
tactics 688 n.
cunning 698 n.
mediation 720 n.
conditions 766 n.
courtesy 884 n.
diplomat
expert 696 n.
mediator 720 n.
envoy 754 n.
diplomatic
hypocritical
541 adj.
skilful 694 adj.
diplomatic
excuse
untruth 543 n.
diplomatic
immunity
freedom 744 n.
nonliability 919 n.
diplomatic
incident
predicament 700 n.
diplomatic
service
vocation 622 n.
diplomatist
expert 696 n.
mediator 720 n.
envoy 754 n.
dipper
ladle 194 n.
bird 365 n.
dippy
crazy 503 adj.
dipso
drunkard 949 n.
dipsomaniac
the maladjusted
504 n.
drunkard 949 n.
drunken 949 adj.

fastidiousness
862 n.
discharge
displace 188 vb.
propulsion 287 n.
shoot 287 vb.
outflow 298 n.
dismiss 300 vb.
ejection 300 n.
empty 300 vb.
excretion 302 n.
escape 667 n.
deliverance 668 n.
stop using 674 vb.
do 676 vb.
carry out 725 vb.
liberate 746 vb.
liberation 746 n.
deposal 752 n.
observance 768 n.
observe 768 vb.
not retain 779 vb.
pay 804 vb.
do one's duty
917 vb.
duty 917 n.
nonliability 919 n.
acquit 960 vb.
acquittal 960 n.
**discharge an
obligation**
do one's duty
917 vb.
dischuffed
disappointed
509 adj.
discontented
829 adj.
disciple
listener 415 n.
learner 538 n.
auxiliary 707 n.
disciplinarian
tyrant 735 n.
disciplinary
punitive 963 adj.
**disciplinary
action**
punishment 963 n.
discipline
order 60 n.
teaching 534 n.
severity 735 n.
obedience 739 n.
compel 740 vb.
restrain 747 vb.
restraint 747 n.
punish 963 vb.
disc jockey
broadcaster 531 n.
disclaim
negate 533 vb.
recant 603 vb.
reject 607 vb.

abrogate 752 vb.
refuse 760 vb.
not retain 779 vb.
disclaimer
negation 533 n.
recantation 603 n.
resignation 753 n.
refusal 760 vb.
disclose
disclose 526 vb.
disco
dancing 831 n.
*place of
amusement*
837 n.
social gathering
882 n.
discoid
round 250 adj.
discoloration
hue 425 n.
achromatism
426 n.
impairment 655 n.
wound 655 n.
discolour
modify 143 vb.
colour 425 vb.
variegate 437 vb.
discomfit
defeat 727 vb.
trouble 827 vb.
shame 867 vb.
discomfiture
defeat 728 n.
discomfort
pain 377 n.
evil 616 n.
suffering 825 n.
discompose
derange 63 vb.
agitate 318 vb.
trouble 827 vb.
shame 867 vb.
enrage 891 vb.
discomposure
disorder 61 n.
derangement
63 n.
disconcert
derange 63 vb.
distract 456 vb.
defeat 727 vb.
trouble 827 vb.
frighten 854 vb.
shame 867 vb.
humiliate 872 vb.
disconcerted
unexpecting
508 adj.
suffering 825 adj.
disconnect
disunite 46 vb.
discontinue 72 vb.

disconsolate
unhappy 825 adj.
discontented
829 adj.
melancholic
834 adj.
hopeless 853 adj.
discontent
suffering 825 n.
discontent 829 n.
discontented
discontented
829 adj.
discontinue
terminate 69 vb.
discontinue 72 vb.
be inactive 679 vb.
abrogate 752 vb.
discord
contrariety 14 n.
difference 15 n.
discord 411 n.
discord 411 vb.
discordant
unrelated 10 adj.
contrary 14 adj.
different 15 adj.
discordant 411 adj.
florid 425 adj.
discordant note
dissension 709 n.
discothèque
*place of
amusement*
837 n.
discount
disregard 458 vb.
underestimate
483 vb.
discount 810 n.
discount 810 vb.
hold cheap 922 vb.
discountenance
disapprove
924 vb.
discounting
qualifying 468 vb.
discourage
dissuade 613 vb.
prohibit 757 vb.
cause discontent
829 vb.
depress 834 vb.
discouragement
dissuasion 613 n.
hindrance 702 n.
discourse
lecture 534 n.
teach 534 vb.
oration 579 n.
speech 579 n.
dissertation 591 n.
discourse upon
dissertate 591 vb.

discourteous
discourteous
885 adj.
discourtesy
nonobservance
769 n.
discourtesy 885 n.
disrespect 921 n.
discover
see 438 vb.
discover 484 vb.
discoverer
precursor 66 n.
producer 164 n.
detector 484 n.
discovery
discovery 484 n.
manifestation
522 n.
disclosure 526 n.
discredit
cause doubt
486 vb.
disbelieve 486 vb.
unbelief 486 n.
disrepute 867 n.
shame 867 vb.
hatred 888 n.
defame 926 vb.
discredited
erroneous 495 adj.
disused 674 adj.
disreputable
867 adj.
inglorious
867 adj.
discreet
soft-hued 425 adj.
discriminating
463 adj.
reticent 525 adj.
taciturn 582 adj.
cautious 858 adj.
discrepancy
difference 15 n.
disagreement 25 n.
discrete
separate 46 adj.
discontinuous
72 adj.
discretion
discrimination
463 n.
judgment 480 n.
sagacity 498 n.
will 595 n.
choice 605 n.
caution 858 n.
discriminate
make unlike
19 vb.
discriminate
463 vb.
do wrong 914 adj.

**discriminate
against**
be biased 481 vb.
do wrong 914 adj.
discriminating
discriminating
463 adj.
discrimination
inequality 29 n.
separation 46 n.
exclusion 57 n.
discrimination
463 n.
prejudice 418 n.
injustice 914 n.
discriminatory
biased 481 adj.
unjust 914 adj.
discursive
rational 475 adj.
prolix 570 adj.
discus
circle 250 n.
missile 287 n.
argue 475 vb.
publish 528 vb.
confer 584 vb.
dissertate 591 vb.
discussion
enquiry 459 n.
answer 460 n.
argument 475 n.
conference 584 n.
dissertation 591 n.
disdain
reject 607 vb.
be fastidious
862 vb.
shame 867 vb.
be proud 871 vb.
pride 871 n.
insolence 878 n.
not respect 921 vb.
contempt 922 n.
despise 922 vb.
disdainful
proud 871 adj.
insolent 878 adj.
disrespectful
921 adj.
disease
disease 651 n.
disembark
navigate 269 vb.
voyage 269 vb.
land 295 vb.
disembodied
immaterial
320 adj.
spooky 970 adj.
disembowel
empty 300 vb.
disemployed
powerless 161 adj.

cruel act 898 n.
dissidence
disagreement 25 n.
nonconformity
84 n.
dissent 489 n.
dissident
misfit 25 n.
nonconformist
84 n.
unconformable
84 adj.
dissentient 489 n.
dissenting 489 adj.
opponent 705 n.
revolter 738 n.
discontented
829 adj.
malcontent 829 n.
schismatic 978 n.
dissimilar
dissimilar 19 adj.
dissimulate
dissemble 541 vb.
dissipate
disperse 75 vb.
destroy 165 vb.
disappear 446 vb.
waste 634 vb.
be prodigal 815 vb.
dissipated
weakened 163 adj.
prodigal 815 adj.
sensual 944 adj.
lecherous 951 adj.
dissipation
dispersion 75 n.
pleasure 376 n.
disappearance
446 n.
waste 634 n.
loss 772 n.
prodigality 815 n.
intemperance
943 n.
sensualism 944 n.
unchastity 951 n.
dissociate
disunite 46 vb.
**dissociate
oneself**
negate 533 vb.
oppose 704 vb.
dissolute
vicious 934 adj.
lecherous 951 adj.
dissolution
disunion 46 n.
separation 46 n.
decomposition
51 n.
finality 69 n.
destruction 165 n.
liquefaction 337 n.

disappearance
446 n.
abrogation 752 n.
**dissolution of
marriage**
nonretention
779 n.
divorce 896 n.
dissolve
pass away 2 vb.
be dispersed 75 vb.
destroy 165 vb.
liquefy 337 vb.
disappear 446 vb.
abrogate 752 vb.
dissolve in tears
weep 836 vb.
**dissolve
marriage**
not retain 779 vb.
divorce 896 n.
dissonant
discordant 411 adj.
dissuade
dissuade 613 vb.
distaff
weaving 222 n.
distaff side, the
womankind 373 n.
distance
distance 199 n.
progress 285 vb.
invisibility 444 n.
unsociability
883 n.
distant
distant 199 adj.
muted 401 adj.
incurious 454 adj.
impassive 820 adj.
hostile 881 adj.
unsociable
883 adj.
distant future
futurity 124 n.
distasteful
unpleasant
827 adj.
distemper
coat 226 vb.
facing 226 n.
colour 425 vb.
pigment 425 n.
animal disease
651 n.
distend
augment 36 vb.
enlarge 197 vb.
expand 197 vb.
distil
exude 298 vb.
extract 304 vb.
vaporize 338 vb.
purify 648 vb.

distillation
essential part 5 n.
extraction 304 n.
vaporization
338 n.
distillery
vaporizer 338 n.
workshop 687 n.
distinct
different 15 adj.
separate 46 adj.
definite 80 adj.
sounding 398 adj.
obvious 443 adj.
intelligible 516 adj.
distinction
differentiation
15 n.
speciality 80 n.
discrimination
463 n.
reasoning 475 n.
importance 638 n.
honours 866 n.
prestige 866 n.
nobility 868 n.
title 870 n.
distinctive
distinctive 15 adj.
special 80 adj.
distinctness
difference 15 n.
visibility 443 n.
distinguish
differentiate 15 vb.
make unlike 19 vb.
set apart 46 vb.
see 438 vb.
discriminate
463 vb.
understand 516 vb.
dignify 866 vb.
distinguishable
separate 46 adj.
intelligible 516 adj.
distinguished
different 15 adj.
remarkable
32 adj.
superior 34 adj.
notable 638 adj.
noteworthy
866 adj.
distinguishing
distinctive 15 adj.
discriminating
463 adj.
distort
distort 246 vb.
distorted
distorted 246 adj.
imperfect 647 adj.
distract
distract 456 vb.

distracted
distracted 456 adj.
excited 821 adj.
distraction
abstractedness
456 n.
inattention 456 n.
frenzy 503 n.
distrait(e)
abstracted 456 adj.
excited 821 adj.
distraught
frenzied 503 adj.
excited 821 adj.
distress
give pain 377 vb.
pain 377 n.
evil 616 n.
ill-treat 645 vb.
adversity 731 n.
impress 821 vb.
suffering 825 n.
worry 825 n.
hurt 827 vb.
distressing
distressing 827 adj.
distribute
arrange 62 vb.
publish 528 vb.
provide 633 vb.
apportion 783 vb.
distribution
arrangement 62 n.
dispersion 75 n.
transference 272 n.
provision 633 n.
apportionment
783 n.
sale 793 n.
distributor
electronics 160 n.
district
district 184 n.
land 344 n.
district nurse
nurse 658 n.
aider 703 n.
distrust
doubt 486 n.
doubt 486 vb.
jealousy 911 n.
distrustful
doubting 474 adj.
nervous 854 adj.
jealous 911 adj.
disturb
decompose 51 vb.
derange 63 vb.
mistime 138 vb.
displace 188 vb.
agitate 318 vb.
distract 456 vb.
trouble 827 vb.
frighten 854 vb.

disturbance
turmoil 61 n.
derangement 63 n.
untimeliness
138 n.
commotion 318 n.
quarrel 709 n.
disturbed
violent 176 adj.
nervous 854 adj.
disunity
disagreement
25 n.
dissension 709 n.
disuse
desuetude 611 n.
relinquishment
621 n.
nonuse 674 n.
abrogation 752 n.
nonretention
779 n.
ditch
gap 201 n.
partition 231 n.
fence 235 n.
cavity 255 n.
furrow 262 n.
fly 271 vb.
conduit 351 n.
drain 351 n.
cultivate 370 vb.
change one's mind
603 vb.
reject 607 vb.
relinquish 621 vb.
stop using 674 vb.
stratagem 698 n.
obstacle 702 n.
defences 713 n.
not retrain 779 vb.
dither
be agitated 318 vb.
be uncertain
474 vb.
be irresolute
601 vb.
ditto
be identical 13 vb.
identically 13 adv.
identity 13 n.
do likewise 20 vb.
accord 24 vb.
again 106 vb.
repeat 106 vb.
repetition 106 n.
ditty
vocal music 412 n.
doggerel 593 n.
diuretic
purgative 658 n.
diurnal
seasonal 141 adj.

diva
vocalist 413 n.
actor 594 n.
divan
bed 218 n.
seat 218 n.
dive
tavern 192 n.
navigate 269 vb.
swim 269 vb.
fly 271 vb.
move fast 277 vb.
spurt 277 n.
descend 309 vb.
descent 309 n.
tumble 309 vb.
plunge 313 n.
plunge 313 vb.
amuse oneself
837 vb.
diver
diver 313 n.
bird 365 n.
diverge
disagree 25 vb.
be oblique 220 vb.
diverge 294 vb.
diverge from
differ 15 vb.
divergence
difference 15 n.
nonuniformity
17 n.
dissimilarity 19 n.
disagreement 25 n.
divergence 294 n.
divergent
nonuniform 17 adj.
divergent 294 adj.
divers
multiform 82 adj.
many 104 adj.
diverse
different 15 adj.
nonuniform
17 adj.
dissimilar 19 adj.
multiform 82 adj.
diversification
variegation 437 n.
diversify
modify 143 vb.
variegate 437 vb.
diversion
irrelevance 10 n.
change 143 n.
deviation 282 n.
traffic control
305 n.
pleasure 376 n.
inattention 456 n.
trickery 542 n.
circuit 626 n.
amusement 837 n.

diversity
unrelatedness 10 n.
difference 15 n.
nonuniformity
17 n.
multiformity 82 n.
variegation 437 n.
divert
deflect 282 vb.
distract 456 vb.
obstruct 702 vb.
not pay 805 vb.
amuse 837 vb.
diverting
amusing 837 adj.
divertissement
pleasure 376 n.
musical piece
412 n.
amusement 837 n.
**divert one's
attention**
distract 456 vb.
divest
subtract 39 vb.
uncover 229 vb.
relinquish 621 vb.
depose 752 vb.
deprive 786 vb.
divide
sunder 46 vb.
part 53 vb.
class 62 vb.
bisect 92 vb.
partition 231 vb.
limit 236 n.
mete out 465 vb.
divided
fragmentary
53 adj.
quarrelling
709 adj.
schismatical
978 adj.
**divided
allegiance**
perfidy 930 n.
divided skirt
skirt 228 n.
dividend
part 53 n.
numerical element
85 n.
gain 771 n.
portion 783 n.
dividers
gauge 465 n.
divide up
sunder 46 vb.
apportion 783 vb.
dividing
separate 46 adj.
interjacent
231 adj.

divination
intuition 476 n.
divination 511 n.
divine
foresee 510 vb.
divine 511 vb.
beautiful 841 adj.
divine 965 adj.
godlike 965 adj.
religious 973 adj.
theologian 973 n.
cleric 986 n.
diviner
diviner 511 n.
divine right
authority 733 n.
divining rod
detector 484 n.
divinity
divineness 965 n.
theology 973 n.
divisible
numerical 85 adj.
division
scission 46 n.
decomposition
51 n.
subdivision 53 n.
arrangement 62 n.
discontinuity 72 n.
classification 77 n.
district 184 n.
partition 231 n.
vote 605 n.
formation 722 n.
apportionment
783 n.
seclusion 883 n.
schism 978 n.
sect 978 n.
divisor
numerical element
85 n.
divorce
disunite 46 vb.
separate 46 vb.
divorce 896 n.
divorce 896 vb.
divorcé(e)
divorce 896 n.
divorced
separate 46 adj.
not retained
779 adj.
divot
piece 53 n.
divulge
manifest 522 vb.
divulge 526 vb.
Dixieland
music 412 n.
DIY
repair 656 n.
repair 656 vb.

dizzy
unequal 29 adj.
changeful 152 adj.
high 209 adj.
crazy 503 adj.
crapulous 949 adj.
dizzy height
height 209 n.
DJ
broadcaster 531 n.
DMs (tdmk)
footwear 228 n.
DNA
heredity 5 n.
organism 358 n.
**DNA
fingerprinting**
evidence 466 n.
identification
547 n.
diagnostic 658 n.
D notice
restraint 747 n.
do
accord 24 vb.
unite with 45 vb.
feasting 301 n.
study 536 vb.
deceive 542 vb.
suffice 635 vb.
be expedient
642 vb.
do 676 vb.
overcharge 811 vb.
amusement 837 n.
celebration 876 n.
social gathering
882 n.
do a bunk
run away 620 vb.
do a favour
do good 644 vb.
do again
repeat 106 vb.
do away with
destroy 165 vb.
kill 362 vb.
dobbin
horse 273 n.
**Dobermann
pinscher**
dog 365 n.
doch-an-dorris
valediction 296 n.
draught 301 n.
docile
willing 597 adj.
obedient 739 adj.
dock
subtract 39 vb.
cut 46 vb.
sunder 46 vb.
place 187 vb.
dwell 192 vb.

stable 192 n.
shorten 204 vb.
edge 234 n.
navigate 269 vb.
arrive 295 vb.
storage 632 n.
shelter 662 n.
workshop 687 n.
lockup 748 n.
docker
displacement
188 n.
boatman 270 n.
worker 686 n.
docket
list 87 n.
list 87 vb.
credential 466 n.
label 547 n.
mark 547 vb.
record 548 n.
abstract 592 vb.
dockyard
workshop 687 n.
**Doc Martens
(tdmk)**
footwear 228 n.
doctor
mix 43 vb.
modify 143 vb.
sage 500 n.
be false 541 vb.
doctor 658 n.
doctor 658 vb.
account 808 vb.
academic title
870 n.
**doctor-assisted
suicide**
suicide 361 n.
doctorate
honours 866 n.
academic title
870 n.
**doctor of
divinity,
literature,
medicine,
philosophy
etc.**
academic title
870 n.
doctrinaire
positive 473 adj.
doctrinal
creedal 485 adj.
educational
534 adj.
orthodox 976 adj.
doctrine
creed 485 n.
document
corroborate 466 vb.
evidence 466 n.

demonstrate
478 vb.
record 548 n.
record 548 vb.
book 589 n.
documentary
film 445 n.
information 524 n.
informative
524 adj.
broadcast 531 n.
lecture 534 n.
descriptive 590 adj.
documentation
evidence 466 n.
demonstration
478 n.
record 548 n.
documented
evidential 466 adj.
dod
bulk 195 n.
solid body 324 n.
doddering
ageing 131 adj.
doddle
easy thing 701 n.
dodecahedron
over five 99 n.
angular figure
247 n.
dodge
vary 152 vb.
be oblique 220 vb.
be in motion 265 vb.
disregard 458 vb.
sophisticate 477 vb.
be stealthy 525 vb.
dissemble 541 vb.
trickery 542 vb.
avoid 620 vb.
avoidance 620 n.
contrivance 623 n.
elude 667 vb.
means of escape
667 n.
skill 694 n.
be cunning 698 vb.
stratagem 698 n.
not observe
769 vb.
be dishonest
930 vb.
dodgem car
vehicle 274 n.
dodgy
dangerous 661 adj.
dodo
archaism 127 n.
animal 365 n.
doe
mammal 365 n.
female animal
373 n.

doer
doer 676 n.
doeskin
textile 222 n.
skin 226 n.
do for
destroy 165 vb.
kill 362 vb.
murder 362 vb.
provide 633 vb.
harm 645 vb.
minister to 703 vb.
defeat 727 vb.
serve 742 vb.
do for oneself
provide 633 vb.
dog
accompany 89 vb.
be behind 238 vb.
follow 284 vb.
dog 365 n.
male animal 372 n.
pursue 619 vb.
dogcart
carriage 274 n.
dog collar
neckwear 228 n.
canonicals 989 n.
doge
officer 741 n.
dog-eared
dilapidated
655 adj.
used 673 adj.
dog-eat-dog
anarchy 734 n.
dog-end
tobacco 388 n.
dogfight
fight 716 n.
battle 718 n.
dogfish
fish food 301 n.
fish 365 n.
dogged
obstinate 602 adj.
doggedness
perseverance 600 n.
obstinacy 602 n.
doggerel
absurdity 497 n.
doggerel 593 n.
poetic 593 adj.
funny 849 adj.
ridiculousness
849 n.
doggy
animal 365 adj.
doghouse
stable 192 n.
dog in the
manger
possessor 776 n.
egotist 932 n.

selfish 932 adj.
dogma
creed 485 n.
religion 973 n.
theology 973 n.
dogmatic
certain 473 adj.
positive 473 adj.
narrow-minded
481 adj.
creedal 485 adj.
assertive 532 adj.
obstinate 602 adj.
vain 873 adj.
do-gooder
volunteer 597 n.
philanthropist
901 n.
dogs, the
racing 716 n.
dogsbody
worker 686 n.
auxiliary 707 n.
servant 742 n.
dog's breakfast
bungling 695 n.
dog's home
shelter 662 n.
dogsleigh
sled 274 n.
Dog star
star 321 n.
dog-tired
fatigued 684 adj.
dogtooth
notch 260 n.
pattern 844 n.
dog track
meeting place
192 n.
arena 724 n.
dog-watches
evening 129 n.
do in
destroy 165 vb.
kill 362 vb.
murder 362 vb.
doing
agency 173 n.
action 676 n.
doings
affairs 154 n.
deed 676 n.
do-it-yourself
artless 699 adj.
do justice to
eat 301 vb.
vindicate 927 vb.
do one's duty
do one's duty
917 vb.
do one's utmost
exert oneself
682 vb.

doldrums
weather 340 n.
inaction 677 n.
inactivity 679 n.
dejection 834 n.
dole
small quantity
33 n.
insufficiency
636 n.
gift 781 n.
sociology 901 n.
doleful
melancholic
834 adj.
lamenting 836 adj.
dole out
disperse 75 vb.
mete out 465 vb.
give 781 vb.
apportion 783 vb.
pay 804 vb.
doll
dwarf 196 n.
female 373 n.
image 551 n.
plaything 837 n.
a beauty 841 n.
dollar
coinage 797 n.
dollar bill
paper money
797 n.
dollop
portion 783 n.
doll's house
plaything 837 n.
doll up
primp 843 vb.
dolly
little 196 adj.
dolly bird
a beauty 841 n.
dolman sleeve
sleeve 228 n.
dolmen
tomb 364 n.
monument 548 n.
dolour
suffering 825 n.
dolphin
mammal 365 n.
dolt
dunce 501 n.
dom
male 372 n.
title 870 n.
domain
classification
77 n.
territory 184 n.
lands 777 n.
domaine
function 622 n.

dome
edifice 164 n.
house 192 n.
high structure
209 n.
head 213 n.
dome 253 n.
Domesday Book
list 87 n.
domestic
native 191 adj.
provincial 192 adj.
interior 224 adj.
animal 365 n.
domestic 742 n.
unsociable 883 adj.
domestic
violence
violence 176 n.
domesticate
break in 369 vb.
habituate 610 vb.
domicile
abode 192 n.
domiciliary
native 191 adj.
dominant
supreme 34 adj.
influential 178 adj.
musical note
410 n.
authoritative
733 adj.
dominate
influence 178 vb.
be high 209 vb.
dominate 733 vb.
subjugate 745 vb.
domination
superiority 34 n.
influence 178 n.
governance 733 n.
domineer
oppress 735 vb.
domineering
authoritative
733 adj.
authoritarian
735 adj.
oppressive 735 adj.
insolence 878 n.
insolent 878 adj.
dominie
teacher 537 n.
dominion
territory 184 n.
governance 733 n.
political
organization
733 n.
lands 777 n.
domino
disguise 527 n.
plaything 837 n.

eclipse
be superior 34 vb.
darken 418 vb.
darkening 418 n.
be unseen 444 vb.
disappearance
446 n.
conceal 525 vb.
have a reputation
866 vb.

E coli
infection 651 n.

ecology
situation 186 n.
biology 358 n.

e-commerce
business 622 n.
trade 791 n.

economical
cheap 812 adj.
economical
814 adj.

economics
management
689 n.

economize
economize 814 vb.

economy
management
689 n.
cheap 812 adj.
economy 814 n.

**economy of
truth**
falsehood 541 n.
untruth 543 n.

economy size
large 195 adj.
cheap 812 adj.

ecosphere
situation 186 n.
world 321 n.

ecosystem
situation 186 n.
organism 358 n.

ecotage
preservation 666 n.

ecotype
organism 358 n.

ecowarrior
dissentient 489 n.
preserver 666 n.

ecru
whitish 427 adj.
brown 430 adj.

ecstasy
pleasure 376 n.
frenzy 503 n.
imagination 513 n.
warm feeling 818 n.
excitable state
822 n.
joy 824 n.
love 887 n.

Ecstasy
drug 949 n.

ecstatic
impressed 818 adj.
rejoicing 835 adj.
approving 923 adj.

ECT
therapy 658 n.

ectopic
unconformable
84 adj.

ectoplasm
spiritualism 984 n.

ecumenical
universal 79 adj.
orthodox 976 adj.

eczema
skin disease 651 n.
blemish 845 n.

eddy
changeable thing
152 n.
rotate 315 vb.
eddy 350 n.

Eden
mythic heaven
971 n.

edge
advantage 34 n.
be oblique 220 vb.
circumscribe
232 vb.
edge 234 n.
hem 234 vb.
limit 236 vb.
flank 239 vb.
sharpen 256 vb.
pungency 388 n.
victory 727 n.

edge in
introduce 231 vb.
enter 297 vb.

edge out
depose 752 vb.
not retain 779 vb.

edging
edging 234 n.
lateral 239 adj.

edgy
excitable 822 adj.
irascible 892 adj.

edible
edible 301 adj.

edict
publication 528 n.
decree 737 n.
legislation 953 n.

edification
teaching 534 n.
benefit 615 n.

edifice
edifice 164 n.

edify
educate 534 vb.

See **teach**
benefit 615 vb.
do good 644 vb.

edit
modify 143 vb.
interpret 520 vb.
publish 528 vb.
rectify 654 vb.

edition
the press 528 n.
edition 589 n.

editor
interpreter 520 n.
author 589 n.
bookperson 589 n.
dissertator 591 n.
reformer 654 n.

editorial
interpretative
520 adj.
publicity 528 n.
article 591 n.

EDP
computing 86 n.

educate
produce 164 vb.
educate 534 vb.

education
culture 490 n.
knowledge 490 n.
education 534 n.
teaching 534 n.
vocation 622 n.

educational
educational
534 adj.

educationalist
teacher 537 n.

EEC
society 708 n.
trade 791 n.
market 796 n.

EEG
diagnostic 658 n.

eel
serpent 251 n.
fish food 301 n.
fish 365 n.

eerie
frightening 854 adj.
spooky 970 adj.

efface
destroy 165 vb.
obliterate 550 vb.

efface oneself
be modest 874 vb.

effect
cause 156 vb.
caused 157 adj.
effect 157 n.
produce 164 vb.
sense 374 n.
appearance 445 n.
spectacle 445 n.

carry out 725 vb.
succeed 727 vb.
ostentation 875 n.

effective
powerful 160 adj.
influential 178 adj.
appearing 445 adj.
forceful 571 adj.
instrumental
628 adj.
useful 640 adj.
successful 727 adj.

effects
property 777 n.

effectual
powerful 160 adj.
operative 173 adj.
useful 640 adj.

effeminate
weak 163 adj.
female 373 adj.

effervescent
vigorous 174 adj.
gaseous 336 adj.
bubbly 355 adj.
lively 819 adj.
excited 821 adj.
excitable 822 adj.
merry 833 adj.

effete
impotent 161 adj.
weakened 163 adj.

efficacious
powerful 160 adj.
operative 173 adj.
useful 640 adj.
successful 727 adj.

efficacy
ability 160 n.
instrumentality
628 n.
utility 640 n.

efficiency
ability 160 n.
agency 173 n.
utility 640 n.

efficient
operative 173 adj.
useful 640 adj.
industrious
678 adj.

effigy
copy 22 n.
image 551 n.

efflorescence
powder 332 n.
ripening 669 n.

effluence
outflow 298 n.
current 350 n.

effluvial
gaseous 336 adj.

effluvium
gas 336 n.

efflux
egress 298 n.
outflow 298 n.

effort
power 160 n.
vigorousness
174 n.
attempt 671 n.
action 676 n.
exertion 682 n.

effortless
easy 701 adj.

effrontery
insolence 878 n.

effulgence
light 417 n.

effusion
outflow 298 n.
ejection 300 n.
diffuseness 570 n.

effusive
diffuse 570 adj.
feeling 818 adj.
friendly 880 adj.

E-fit
representation
551 n.

eft
amphibian 365 n.

EFTPOS
payment 804 n.

egalitarian
uniformist 16 n.
just 913 adj.

egest
emit 300 vb.

egg
origin 68 n.
source 156 n.
product 164 n.
genitalia 167 n.

eggcup
cup 194 n.

egg donation
propagation 167 n.

egghead
intellectual 492 n.
sage 500 n.

egg on
invigorate 174 vb.
incite 612 vb.
animate 821 vb.

eggshell
weak thing 163 n.
brittle 330 adj.
brittleness 330 n.

eggspoon
ladle 194 n.

egg timer
timekeeper 117 n.

ego
intrinsicality 5 n.
self 80 n.
subjectivity 320 n.

elements, the
weather 340 n.
elephant
giant 195 n.
tall creature 209 n.
beast of burden
273 n.
mammal 365 n.
elephantine
large 195 adj.
unwieldy 195 adj.
animal 365 adj.
elevate
elevate 310 vb.
purify 648 vb.
make better
654 vb.
delight 826 vb.
dignify 866 vb.
elevated
proud 871 adj.
disinterested
931 adj.
elevation
height 209 n.
verticality 215 n.
elevation 310 n.
feature 445 n.
map 551 n.
cheerfulness 833 n.
holy orders 985 n.
elevator
conveyance 267 n.
ascent 308 n.
eleven
band 74 n.
over five 99 n.
party 708 n.
elevenses
meal 301 n.
eleventh hour
late 136 adj.
lateness 136 n.
crisis 137 n.
elf
elf 970 n.
elfin
little, 196 adj.
fairylike 970 adj.
elicit
cause 156 vb.
extract 304 vb.
discover 484 vb.
manifest 522 vb.
excite 821 vb.
eligible
included 78 adj.
eliminate
render few 105 vb.
eject 300 vb.
empty 300 vb.
extract 304 vb.
obliterate 550 vb.
exempt 919 vb.

elision
contraction 198 n.
prosody 593 n.
elite
elite 644 n.
elitism
government 733 n.
elixir
medicine 658 n.
remedy 658 n.
elk
mammal 365 n.
ellipse
arc 250 n.
ellipsis
punctuation 547 n.
grammar 564 n.
imperspicuity
568 n.
conciseness 569 n.
elliptic
round 250 adj.
concise 569 adj.
elm
tree 366 n.
elocution
pronunciation
577 n.
eloquence 579 n.
oratory 579 n.
speech 579 n.
elongate
lengthen 203 vb.
elope
decamp 296 vb.
run away 620 vb.
escape 667 vb.
wed 894 vb.
eloquence
eloquence 579 n.
eloquent
intelligible
516 adj.
stylistic 566 adj.
eloquent 579 adj.
else
in addition 38 adv.
elucidate
be intelligible
516 vb.
interpret 520 vb.
elude
elude 667 vb.
not observe 769 vb.
elusive
impracticable
470 adj.
puzzling 517 adj.
elves
elf 970 n.
Elysium
happiness 824 n.
mythic heaven
971 n.

em
print-type 587 n.
emaciated
lean 206 adj.
underfed 636 adj.
unhealthy 651 adj.
e-mail
telecommunication
531 n.
emanate
happen 154 vb.
result 157 vb.
emerge 298 vb.
be plain 522 vb.
emanation
egress 298 n.
excretion 302 n.
appearance 445 n.
revelation 975 n.
emancipated
free 744 adj.
emancipation
freedom 744 n.
independence
744 n.
liberation 746 n.
emasculated
impotent 161 adj.
feeble 572 adj.
embalm
inter 364 vb.
preserve 666 vb.
embankment
support 218 n.
earthwork 253 n.
railway 624 n.
safeguard 662 n.
obstacle 702 n.
defences 713 n.
embargo
exclusion 57 n.
quiescence 266 n.
hindrance 702 n.
command 737 n.
restrain 747 vb.
restraint 747 n.
prohibition 757 n.
nonpayment
805 n.
embark
voyage 269 vb.
start out 296 vb.
embarkation
start 68 n.
departure 296 n.
embark on
begin 68 vb.
undertake 672 vb.
embarras de
richesses
greatness 32 n.
productiveness
171 n.
plenty 635 n.

redundance 637 n.
superfluity 637 n.
embarrass
trouble 827 vb.
embarrassment
predicament 700 n.
annoyance 827 n.
guilt 936 n.
embassy
house 192 n.
commission 751 n.
envoy 754 n.
embed
place 187 vb.
implant 303 vb.
embellish
add 38 vb.
make better
654 vb.
decorate 844 vb.
embers
coal 385 n.
embezzle
defraud 788 vb.
embittered
discontented
829 adj.
hostile 881 adj.
resentful 891 adj.
emblazon
colour 425 vb.
mark 547 vb.
decorate 844 vb.
emblem
badge 547 n.
indication 547 n.
talisman 983 n.
emblematic
insubstantial 4 adj.
heraldic 547 adj.
embody
combine 50 vb.
contain 56 vb.
comprise 78 vb.
materialize 319 vb.
represent 551 vb.
embolism
interjection 231 n.
closure 264 n.
cardiovascular
disease 651 n.
embonpoint
bulk 195 n.
emboss
mark 547 vb.
sculpt 554 vb.
decorate 844 vb.
embrace
join 45 vb.
unite with 45 vb.
cohere 48 vb.
contain 56 vb.
comprise 78 vb.
surround 230 vb.

circumscribe
232 vb.
enclose 235 vb.
choose 605 vb.
be wont 610 vb.
retain 778 vb.
retention 778 n.
be friendly 880 vb.
sociability 882 n.
greet 884 vb.
love 887 vb.
caress 889 vb.
endearment 889 n.
embrasure
window 263 n.
embrocation
unguent 357 n.
balm 658 n.
embroider
variegate 437 vb.
fake 541 vb.
exaggerate 546 vb.
decorate 844 vb.
embroidery
adjunct 40 n.
exaggeration
546 n.
art 551 n.
ornament 574 n.
needlework 844 n.
embroil
bedevil 63 vb.
enrage 891 vb.
embryo
young creature
132 n.
source 156 n.
undevelopment
670 n.
embryonic
beginning 68 adj.
converted 147 adj.
impending 155 adj.
amorphous
244 adj.
immature 670 adj.
emend
rectify 654 vb.
repair 656 vb.
emendation
amendment 654 n.
repair 656 n.
emerald
green 434 adj.
greenness 434 n.
gem 844 n.
emerge
begin 68 vb.
emerge 298 vb.
emergence
beginning 68 n.
egress 298 n.
emergency
crisis 137 n.

enunciate
affirm 532 vb.
voice 577 vb.
envelop
comprise 78 vb.
consume 165 vb.
dress 228 vb.
circumscribe
232 vb.
envelope
receptacle 194 n.
cover 226 vb.
covering 226 n.
enclosure 235 n.
correspondence
588 n.
envelopment
circumscription
232 n.
enviable
desired 859 adj.
envious
discontented
829 adj.
envious 912 adj.
environment
circumstance 8 n.
relation 9 n.
locality 187 n.
surroundings
230 n.
environmental
extrinsic 6 adj.
circumstantial
8 adj.
**environment-
alist**
preserver 666 n.
environs
locality 187 n.
surroundings
230 n.
envisage
imagine 513 vb.
envoi
adjunct 40 n.
sequel 67 n.
end 69 n.
verse form 593 n.
envoy
envoy 754 n.
envy
desired object
859 n.
envy 912 n.
envy 912 vb.
vice 934 n.
enzyme
leaven 323 n.
organism 358 n.
eolithic
primal 127 adj.
epaulette
badge 547 n.

badge of rank
743 n.
trimming 844 n.
ephemeral
ephemeral 114 adj.
dying 361 adj.
epic
film 445 n.
prolix 570 adj.
narrative 590 n.
poem 593 n.
epicene
abnormal 84 adj.
epicentre
centre 225 n.
epicure
eater 301 n.
people of taste
846 n.
perfectionist 862 n.
sensualist 944 n.
glutton 947 n.
epicurean
culinary 301 adj.
sensuous 376 adj.
savoury 390 adj.
people of taste
846 n.
tasteful 846 adj.
fastidious 862 adj.
sensual 944 adj.
sensualist 944 n.
gluttonous 947 adj.
epidemic
extensive 32 adj.
comprehensive
52 adj.
generality 79 n.
universal 79 adj.
plague 651 n.
infectious 653 adj.
epidermis
skin 226 n.
epidural
obstetrics 167 n.
anaesthetic 375 n.
epigram
maxim 496 n.
trope 519 n.
phrase 563 n.
conciseness 569 n.
witticism 839 n.
epilepsy
spasm 318 n.
frenzy 503 n.
disease 651 n.
nervous disorders
651 n.
epileptic
diseased 651 adj.
epileptic fit
frenzy 503 n.
epilogue
sequel 67 n.

extremity 69 n.
dramaturgy 594 n.
epiphany
revelation 975 n.
holy day 988 n.
episcopacy
church office
985 n.
the church 985 n.
episcopal
ecclesiastical
985 adj.
Episcopalian
Catholic 976 n.
episcopalian
Anglican 976 adj.
sectarian 978 adj.
ecclesiastical
985 adj.
episcopalianism
the church 985 n.
episcopate
church office
985 n.
ecclesiarch 986 n.
episode
event 154 n.
interjection 231 n.
narrative 590 n.
episodic
unrelated 10 adj.
discontinuous
72 adj.
interjacent 231 adj.
prolix 570 adj.
epistemology
knowledge 490 n
epistle
script 586 n.
correspondence
588 n.
epitaph
valediction 296 n.
obsequies 364 n.
indication 547 n.
phrase 563 n.
description 590 n.
epithet
name 561 n.
scurrility 899 n.
epitome
miniature 196 n.
contraction 198 n.
conciseness 569 n.
compendium
592 n.
epitomize
shorten 204 vb.
abstract 592 vb.
epoch
era 110 n.
chronology 117 n.
eponym
name 561 n.

nomenclature
561 n.
equable
uniform 16 adj.
equal 28 adj.
inexcitable
823 adj.
equal
be equal 28 vb.
compeer 28 n.
equal 28 adj.
just 913 adj.
equality
equality 28 n.
equalize
equalize 28 vb.
**equal
opportunity**
equality 28 n.
justice 913 n.
equals sign
punctuation 547 n.
equanimity
inexcitability
823 n.
equate
identify 13 vb.
equalize 28 vb.
equation
equalization
28 n.
equivalence 28 n.
number 85 n.
numerical result
85 n.
equator
middle 70 n.
dividing line 92 n.
limit 236 n.
circle 250 n.
equatorial
middle 70 adj.
astronomy 321 n.
warm 379 adj.
equerry
retainer 742 n.
equestrian
rider 268 n.
equidistant
equal 28 adj.
middle 70 adj.
equilateral
equal 28 adj.
symmetrical
245 adj.
**equilateral
triangle**
angular figure
247 n.
equilibrium
equilibrium 28 n.
quiescence 266 n.
inexcitability
823 n.

equine
equine 273 adj.
animal 365 adj.
equinoctial
celestial 321 adj.
equip
dress 228 vb.
provide 633 vb.
make ready
669 vb.
equipage
carriage 274 n.
equipment
contents 193 n.
means 629 n.
equipment 630 n.
provision 633 n.
equipoise
equilibrium 28 n.
weighing 322 n.
equitable
equal 28 adj.
just 913 adj.
honourable
929 adj.
equitation
equitation 267 n.
equity
indifference 860 n.
justice 913 n.
equivalent
identical 13 adj.
analogue 18 n.
compeer 28 n.
equivalence 28 n.
equivalent 28 adj.
semantic 514 adj.
equivocal
equivocal
518 adj.
equivocate
sophisticate
477 vb.
be equivocal
518 vb.
misinterpret
521 vb.
era
era 110 n.
eradicate
subtract 39 vb.
exclude 57 vb.
revolutionize
149 vb.
destroy 165 vb.
displace 188 vb.
eject 300 vb.
extract 304 vb.
erase
destroy 165 vb.
rub 333 vb.
disappear 446 vb.
obliterate 550 vb.
clean 648 vb.

tax 809 n.
excise officer
receiver 782 n.
excision
subtraction 39 n.
extraction 304 n.
excitable
excitable 822 adj.
excitation
increase 36 n.
activity 678 n.
excitation 821 n.
excite
cause feeling
374 vb.
excite 821 vb.
excited
excited 821 adj.
excitement
stimulation 174 n.
excitation 821 n.
applause 923 n.
exciting
exciting 821 adj.
exclaim
cry 408 vb.
voice 577 vb.
disapprove 924 vb.
exclamation
cry 408 n.
voice 577 n.
wonder 864 n.
**exclamation
mark**
punctuation
547 n.
wonder 864 n.
exclude
exclude 57 vb.
make impossible
470 vb.
excluded, be
be excluded 57 vb.
excluding
unmixed 44 adj.
excluding 57 adj.
exclusion
exclusion 57 n.
exclusive
excluding 57 adj.
private 80 adj.
news 529 n.
excellent 644 adj.
possessed 773 adj.
dear 811 adj.
sectarian 978 adj.
exclusivity
restriction 747 n.
excommunicate
exclude 57 vb.
eject 300 vb.
prohibit 757 vb.
curse 899 vb.
condemn 961 vb.

perform ritual
988 vb.
excommunicated
schismatical
978 adj.
excoriate
uncover 129 vb.
rub 333 vb.
excrement
excrement 302 n.
excrescence
swelling 253 n.
blemish 845 n.
excreta
excrement 302 n.
excrete
excrete 302 vb.
excretion
excretion 302 n.
excruciating
painful 377 adj.
paining 827 adj.
exculpate
forgive 909 vb.
exempt 919 vb.
justify 927 vb.
acquit 960 vb.
excursion
land travel 267 n.
enjoyment 824 n.
amusement 837 n.
excuse
exclude 57 vb.
reason why 156 n.
disregard 458 vb.
qualify 468 vb.
pretext 614 n.
deliver 668 vb.
stratagem 698 n.
forgive 909 vb.
forgiveness 909 n.
exempt 919 vb.
nonliability 919 n.
extenuate 927 vb.
vindication 927 n.
excuse oneself
plead 614 vb.
refuse 760 vb.
be exempt 919 vb.
ex-directory
concealed 525 adj.
execrable
bad 645 adj.
damnable 645 adj.
unpleasant
827 adj.
hateful 888 adj.
execration
hatred 888 n.
malediction 899 n.
reproach 924 n.
executant
interpreter 520 n.
doer 676 n.

agent 686 n.
execute
produce 164 vb.
operate 173 vb.
play music 413 vb.
undertake 672 vb.
do 676 vb.
deal with 688 vb.
carry out 725 vb.
contract 765 vb.
give security
767 vb.
observe 768 vb.
execute 963 vb.
execution
production 164 n.
agency 173 n.
death 361 n.
killing 362 n.
action 676 n.
skill 694 n.
completion 725 n.
capital punishment
963 n.
executioner
destroyer 168 n.
violent creature
176 n.
killer 362 n.
executive
producer 164 n.
doer 676 n.
agent 686 n.
worker 686 n.
manager 690 n.
executor
doer 676 n.
agent 686 n.
manager 690 n.
consignee 754 n.
executor, be
deputize 755 vb.
executrix
agent 686 n.
exemplar
prototype 23 n.
example 83 n.
exemplary
typical 83 adj.
interpretative
520 adj.
excellent 644 adj.
virtuous 933 adj.
exemplify
exemplify 83 vb.
manifest 522 vb.
exempt
separate 46 adj.
set apart 46 vb.
exclude 57 vb.
qualifying 468 adj.
reject 607 vb.
free 744 adj.
exempt 919 vb.

acquitted 960 adj.
exempt from
absent 190 adj.
relieve 831 vb.
exemption
separation 46 n.
exclusion 57 n.
nonconformity
84 n.
qualification
468 n.
rejection 607 n.
escape 667 n.
deliverance 668 n.
freedom 744 n.
permission 756 n.
relief 831 n.
dueness 915 n.
nonliability 919 n.
acquittal 960 n.
exercise
agency 173 n.
motion 265 n.
curriculum 534 n.
train 534 vb.
learn 536 vb.
job 622 n.
make ready
669 vb.
prepare oneself
669 vb.
undertaking 672 n.
use 673 n.
use 673 vb.
deed 676 n.
do 676 vb.
exercise 682 n.
labour 682 n.
exert
use 673 vb.
exertion
vigorousness
174 n.
exertion 682 n.
exert oneself
exert oneself
682 vb.
exfoliation
uncovering 229 n.
**ex gratia
payment**
gift 781 n.
pay 804 n.
exhale
exude 298 vb.
emit 300 vb.
vaporize 338 vb.
breathe 352 vb.
smell 394 vb.
exhaust
abate 37 vb.
disable 161 vb.
rarefy 325 vb.
blowing 352 n.

blow up 352 vb.
impair 655 vb.
fatigue 684 vb.
exhaustion
decrease 37 n.
helplessness 161 n.
weakness 163 n.
waste 634 n.
deterioration
655 n.
use 673 n.
fatigue 684 n.
dejection 834 n.
exhaustive
complete 54 adj.
exhaust pipe
outlet 298 n.
blowing 352 n.
air pipe 353 n.
exhibit
appear 445 vb.
evidence 466 n.
exhibit 522 n.
show 522 vb.
indicate 547 vb.
be ostentatious
875 vb.
exhibition
appearance 445 n.
spectacle 445 n.
exhibit 522 n.
manifestation
522 n.
collection 632 n.
market 796 n.
reward 962 n.
**exhibition
centre**
exhibit 522 n.
exhibitionism
vanity 873 n.
ostentation 875 n.
impurity 951 n.
exhibitor
exhibitor 522 n.
exhilarate
excite 821 vb.
delight 826 vb.
cheer 833 vb.
exhort
incite 612 vb.
advise 691 vb.
exhortation
oration 579 n.
inducement 612 n.
exhume
exhume 364 vb.
exigency
needfulness 627 n.
desire 859 n.
exiguous
small 33 adj.
exile
exclude 57 vb.

facetious
witty 839 adj.
face to face
near 200 adv.
in front 237 adv.
against 240 adv.
opposite 240 adj.
opposing 704 adj.
face up to
be in front 237 vb.
face value
appearance 445 n.
price 809 n.
facial
exterior 223 adj.
friction 333 n.
beautification
843 n.
facile
easy 701 adj.
facilitate
facilitate 701 vb.
aid 703 vb.
facilities
means 629 n.
good policy 642 n.
facility 701 n.
facility
willingness 597 n.
facility 701 n.
facing
near 200 adj.
facing 226 n.
lining 227 n.
frontal 237 adj.
against 240 adv.
opposite 240 adj.
fold 261 n.
directed 281 adj.
towards 281 adv.
facsimile
copy 22 n.
sham 542 n.
representation
551 n.
fact
reality 1 n.
event 154 n.
evidence 466 n.
certainty 473 n.
truth 494 n.
faction
disagreement 25 n.
part 53 n.
dissent 489 n.
dissentient 489 n.
broadcast 531 n.
literature 557 n.
description 590 n.
narrative 590 n.
opposition 704 n.
party 708 n.
revolt 738 n.
sect 978 n.

factions
opposites 704 n.
factious
quarrelling
709 adj.
fact of life
reality 1 n.
factor
part 53 n.
component 58 n.
numerical element
85 n.
cause 156 n.
influence 178 n.
element 319 n.
farmer 370 n.
manager 690 n.
consignee 754 n.
deputy 755 n.
factor VIII
blood 335 n.
factorize
simplify 44 vb.
sunder 46 vb.
decompose 51 vb.
factors
circumstance 8 n.
factory
workshop 687 n.
factory farming
production 164 n.
agriculture 370 n.
factory ship
fishing boat 275 n.
factotum
busy person 678 n.
worker 686 n.
servant 742 n.
facts
evidence 466 n.
accuracy 494 n.
truth 494 n.
information 524 n.
facts and figures
accounts 808 n.
facts of life
propagation 167 n.
factual
real 1 adj.
evidential 466 adj.
certain 473 adj.
true 494 adj.
veracious 540 adj.
faculty
classification 77 n.
ability 160 n.
teacher 537 n.
aptitude 694 n.
skill 694 n.
fad
eccentricity 503 n.
whim 604 n.
fashion 848 n.
affectation 850 n.

liking 859 n.
faddy
misjudging
481 adj.
capricious 604 adj.
fade
decrease 37 vb.
be transient
114 vb.
be old 127 vb.
be weak 163 vb.
be dim 419 vb.
lose colour 426 vb.
whiten 427 vb.
be unseen 444 vb.
photography
551 n.
deteriorate 655 vb.
lose repute 867 vb.
fade away
cease 145 vb.
sound faint
401 vb.
disappear 446 vb.
faded
dim 419 adj.
soft-hued 425 adj.
colourless 426 adj.
inglorious
867 adj.
fade out
cease 145 vb.
dim 419 vb.
fading
decrease 37 n.
decreasing 37 adj.
transient 114 adj.
achromatism
426 n.
colourless 426 adj.
deterioration
655 n.
faeces
excrement 302 n.
dirt 649 n.
faerie
fairy 970 n.
fag
tobacco 388 n.
labour 682 n.
fatigue 684 vb.
worker 686 n.
servant 742 n.
fag end
remainder 41 n.
extremity 69 n.
tobacco 388 n.
fag for
serve 742 vb.
fagged out
fatigued 684 adj.
faggot
bunch 74 n.
fuel 385 n.

faience
pottery 381 n.
fail
decrease 37 vb.
be weak 163 vb.
close 264 vb.
fall short 307 vb.
be dim-sighted
440 vb.
not suffice 636 vb.
be ill 651 vb.
deteriorate 655 vb.
be inactive 679 vb.
be fatigued 684 vb.
fail 728 vb.
not observe 769 vb.
not pay 805 vb.
disapprove 924 vb.
failed
unskilful 695 adj.
unsuccessful
728 adj.
failing
inferior 35 adj.
ageing 131 adj.
deficient 307 adj.
vice 934 n.
failure
inferiority 35 n.
insufficiency
636 n.
imperfection
647 n.
bungler 697 n.
failure 728 n.
loser 728 n.
guilty act 936 n.
faint
small 33 adj.
helplessness 161 n.
be weak 163 vb.
weak 163 adj.
weakly 163 adj.
insensibility 375 n.
silent 399 adj.
muted 401 adj.
dim 419 adj.
colourless 426 adj.
indistinct 444 adj.
be inactive 679 vb.
inactive 679 adj.
be fatigued 684 vb.
fear 854 vb.
faint-hearted
irresolute 601 adj.
nervous 854 adj.
cowardly 856 adj.
fainting
illness 651 n.
faintly
slightly 33 adv.
faintness
faintness 401 n.
dimness 419 n.

faint praise
indifference 860 n.
praise 923 n.
detraction 926 n.
fair
dry 342 adj.
warm 379 adj.
undimmed
417 adj.
colourless 426 adj.
whitish 427 adj.
rational 475 adj.
exhibit 522 n.
not bad 644 adj.
palmy 730 adj.
middling 732 adj.
market 796 n.
festivity 837 n.
pleasure ground
837 n.
beautiful 841 adj.
promising 852 adj.
just 913 adj.
honourable
929 adj.
fair and square
just 913 adj.
fair enough
just 913 adj.
fair exchange
equivalence 28 n.
barter 791 n.
fair game
dupe 544 n.
laughingstock
851 n.
fairground
arena 724 n.
place of
amusement
837 n.
fairly
greatly 32 vb.
slightly 33 adv.
fair name
repute 866 n.
fairness
beauty 841 n.
justice 913 n.
probity 929 n.
fair offer
offer 759 n.
fair play
justice 913 n.
fair sex
womankind
373 n.
fair-sized
great 32 adj.
large 195 adj.
fair-skinned
colourless 426 adj.
fair to middling
middling 732 adj.

guiltless 935 adj.
pure 950 adj.
faultlessness
perfection 646 n.
purity 950 n.
faulty
inexact 495 adj.
bad 645 adj.
imperfect 647 adj.
faun
mythical being 970 n.
fauna
animality 365 n.
Faust
sorcerer 983 n.
faute de mieux
instead 150 adv.
Fauvism
school of painting 553 n.
faux pas
mistake 495 n.
failure 728 n.
guilty act 936 n.
favour
resemble 18 vb.
advantage 34 n.
influence 178 n.
promote 285 vb.
be biased 481 vb.
badge 547 n.
choice 605 n.
choose 605 vb.
benefit 615 n.
aid 703 n.
gift 781 n.
desire 859 vb.
liking 859 n.
honours 866 n.
repute 866 n.
courteous act 884 n.
love token 889 n.
do wrong 914 adj.
injustice 914 n.
respect 920 n.
approbation 923 n.
approve 923 vb.
favourable
opportune 137 adj.
predicting 511 adj.
beneficial 644 adj.
palmy 730 adj.
promising 852 adj.
approving 923 adj.
favourable verdict
legal trial 959 n.
acquittal 960 n.
favourably
well 615 adv.
favourite
chosen 605 adj.

contender 716 n.
loved one 887 n.
favourite 890 n.
favouritism
prejudice 481 n.
injustice 914 n.
fawn
young creature 132 n.
mammal 365 n.
brown 430 adj.
be servile 879 vb.
flatter 925 vb.
be dishonest 930 vb.
fawn on
flatter 925 vb.
fax
message 529 n.
telecommunication 531 n.
fay
fairy 970 n.
FBI
police enquiry 459 n.
fealty
loyalty 739 n.
duty 917 n.
fear
fear 854 n.
fear 854 vb.
fear for one's life
quake 854 vb.
fearful
nervous 854 adj.
cowardly 856 adj.
wonderful 864 adj.
fearing
fearing 854 adj.
fear of death
phobia 854 n.
fear of God
piety 979 n.
fears
nervousness 854 n.
fearsome
frightening 854 adj.
feasibility
possibility 469 n.
facility 701 n.
feasible
possible 469 adj.
easy 701 adj.
feast
eat 301 vb.
feasting 301 n.
feed 301 vb.
pleasure 376 n.
plenty 635 n.
enjoyment 824 n.
revel 837 vb.

social gathering 882 n.
holy day 988 n.
feast day
festivity 837 n.
special day 876 n.
holy day 988 n.
feat
contrivance 623 n.
deed 676 n.
masterpiece 694 n.
success 727 n.
prowess 855 n.
miracle-working 864 n.
feather
sort 77 n.
filament 208 n.
row 269 vb.
lightness 323 n.
trifle 639 n.
trimming 844 n.
honours 866 n.
feather bed
softness 327 n.
featherbed
soften 327 vb.
aid 703 n.
be lax 734 vb.
be lenient 736 vb.
pet 889 vb.
featherbrain
fool 501 n.
featherbrained
light-minded 456 adj.
foolish 499 adj.
feather in one's cap
success 727 n.
trophy 729 n.
honours 866 n.
feather one's nest
prosper 730 vb.
get rich 800 vb.
be selfish 932 vb.
feathers
skin 226 n.
plumage 259 n.
wing 271 n.
softness 327 n.
featherweight
light 323 adj.
pugilist 722 n.
feathery
light 323 adj.
feature
component 58 n.
speciality 80 n.
feature 445 n.
show 522 vb.
advertise 528 vb.
broadcast 531 n.

dramatize 594 vb.
feature film
film 445 n.
features
character 5 n.
outline 233 n.
face 237 n.
febrifuge
antidote 658 n.
febrile
hot 379 adj.
diseased 651 adj.
feckless
capricious 604 adj.
useless 641 adj.
unskilful 695 adj.
FE college
academy 539 n.
school 539 n.
fecund
prolific 171 adj.
fecundity
propagation 167 n.
productiveness 171 n.
federal
cooperative 706 adj.
federalism
government 733 n.
federation
association 706 n.
society 708 n.
political organization 733 n.
fed up
have enough 635 vb.
bored 838 adj.
fee
estate 777 n.
gift 781 n.
pay 804 n.
price 809 n.
reward 962 n.
feeble
small 33 adj.
inferior 35 n.
impotent 161 adj.
powerless 161 adj.
weak 163 adj.
muted 401 adj.
poorly reasoned 477 adj.
feeble 572 adj.
lax 734 adj.
frail 934 adj.
feeble-minded
weak 163 adj.
unintelligent 499 adj.
having a learning disability 503 adj.

feebleness
weakness 163 n.
feebleness 572 n.
feed
eat 301 vb.
feed 301 vb.
graze 301 vb.
meal 301 n.
provender 301 n.
provide 633 vb.
provision 633 n.
laughingstock 851 n.
feedback
computing 86 n.
reversion 148 n.
answer 460 n.
feeding frenzy
exaggeration 546 n.
feed on
eat 301 vb.
fee faw fum
intimidation 854 n.
spell 983 n.
feel
texture 331 n.
touch 378 vb.
be tentative 461 n.
feel 818 vb.
feeler
feeler 378 n.
question 459 n.
empiricism 461 n.
offer 759 n.
feel for
search 459 vb.
pity 905 vb.
feel-good factor
happiness 824 n.
content 828 n.
feeling
touch 378 n.
feeling 818 adj.
feeling 818 n.
feelings
affections 817 n.
feel like
be willing 597 vb.
feel sorry
be penitent 939 vb.
feel sorry for
pity 905 vb.
feel the pinch
be in difficulty 700 vb.
have trouble 731 vb.
be poor 801 vb.
feet
foot 214 n.
conveyance 267 n.

dance 837 vb.

foxy
animal 365 adj.
dishonest 930 adj.

foyer
quarters 192 n.
lobby 194 n.
theatre 594 n.

fracas
turmoil 61 n.
quarrel 709 n.
fight 716 n.

fractal
line 203 n.
distortion 246 n.

fraction
quantity 26 n.
small quantity
  33 n.
part 53 n.
numerical element
  85 n.
fraction 102 n.

fractional
fragmentary
  53 adj.
numerical 85 adj.
fractional 102 adj.

fractionate
sunder 46 vb.

fractious
irascible 892 adj.

fracture
break 46 vb.
separation 46 n.
discontinuity 72 n.
disable 161 vb.
force 176 vb.
gap 201 n.
pain 377 n.
wound 655 n.

fragile
insubstantial 4 adj.
small 33 adj.
ephemeral 114 adj.
flimsy 163 adj.
brittle 330 adj.

fragment
small quantity
  33 n.
small thing 33 n.
break 46 vb.
sunder 46 vb.
part 53 n.
See **piece**
part 53 vb.
piece 53 n.
fraction 102 n.
pulverize 332 vb.

fragmentary
fragmentary
  53 adj.
uncompleted
  726 adj.

fragmentation
  bomb
bomb 723 n.

fragrant
fragrant 396 adj.

frail
small 33 adj.
ephemeral 114 adj.
flimsy 163 adj.
weak 163 adj.
brittle 330 adj.
unsafe 661 adj.
frail 934 adj.

frailty
transience 114 n.
weakness 163 n.
brittleness 330 n.
vice 934 n.

frame
mould 23 n.
affix 45 vb.
sort 77 n.
produce 164 vb.
receptacle 194 n.
frame 218 n.
support 218 vb.
weaving 222 n.
circumscribe
  232 vb.
outline 233 n.
outline 233 vb.
edging 234 n.
enclose 235 vb.
enclosure 235 n.
form 243 n.
form 243 vb.
matter 319 n.
garden 370 n.
fake 541 vb.
photography
  551 n.
predetermine
  608 vb.
plan 623 vb.
plot 623 vb.
indict 928 vb.

frame of mind
temperament 5 n.
state 7 n.
affections 817 n.

frame of
  reference
referral 9 n.
prototype 23 n.
conditions 766 n.

frame tent
canopy 226 n.

frame-up
duplicity 541 n.
trap 542 n.
untruth 543 n.
predetermination
  608 n.
plot 623 n.

false charge 928 n.

framework
frame 218 n.
outline 233 n.
structure 331 n.

franc
coinage 797 n.

franchise
vote 605 n.
dueness 915 n.
nonliability 919 n.

Franciscans
monk 986 n.

frangible
brittle 330 adj.

frangipani
scent 396 n.

Franglais
dialect 560 adj.

frank
veracious 540 adj.
artless 699 adj.
trustworthy
  929 adj.

Frankenstein
  food
food 301 n.

Frankenstein's
  monster
monster 938 n.

frankfurter
meat 301 n.

frankincense
resin 357 n.
scent 396 n.

frankly
openly 263 adv.

frankness
truth 494 n.
plainness 573 n.
artlessness 699 n.

frantic
disorderly 61 adj.
furious 176 adj.
absurd 497 adj.
frenzied 503 adj.
active 678 adj.
excited 821 adj.

fraternal
akin 11 adj.
friendly 880 adj.
benevolent
  897 adj.

fraternity
family 11 n.
association 706 n.
cooperation 706 n.
community 708 n.
monk 986 n.

fraternize
accord 24 vb.
combine 50 vb.
concord 710 vb.
be friendly 880 vb.

be sociable 882 vb.

fraternize with
befriend 880 vb.

fratricide
homicide 362 n.

Frau
female 373 n.
title 870 n.

fraud
duplicity 541 n.
trickery 542 n.
impostor 545 n.
slyboots 698 n.
swindling 788 n.
pretension 850 n.

fraudulent
false 541 adj.
thieving 788 adj.
dishonest 930 adj.
perfidious 930 adj.
lawbreaking
  954 adj.

fraught, be
carry 273 vb.

fraught with
  danger
dangerous 661 adj.

Fraulein
female 373 n.
title 870 n.

fray
rend 46 vb.
rub 333 vb.
fight 716 n.

fray, the
activity 678 n.

freak
variant 15 n.
nonuniformity
  17 n.
misfit 25 n.
nonconformist
  84 n.
enthusiast 504 n.
the maladjusted
  504 n.
whim 604 n.
prodigy 864 n.
drug-taking 949 n.

freakish
abnormal 84 adj.
unconformable
  84 adj.
unexpected
  508 adj.
capricious 604 adj.

freak out
be unconformable
  84 vb.
drug oneself
  949 vb.

freckle
mottle 437 n.
variegate 437 vb.

skin disease 651 n.
blemish 845 n.

free
disunite 46 vb.
extract 304 vb.
interpretative
  520 adj.
deliver 668 vb.
disencumber
  701 vb.
free 744 adj.
liberate 746 vb.
unpossessed
  774 adj.
not retain 779 vb.
given 781 adj.
uncharged 812 adj.

free agent
free person 744 n.

free-and-easy
lax 734 adj.
free 744 adj.
rash 857 adj.
impertinent
  878 adj.
friendly 880 adj.
sociable 882 adj.

free-base
drug-taking 949 n.

freebie
extra 40 n.
incentive 612 n.
free 744 adj.
acquisition 771 n.
gift 781 n.
given 781 adj.
no charge 812 n.

freebooter
militarist 722 n.
robber 789 n.
bad person 938 n.

freeborn
free 744 adj.

Free Church
Christendom
  976 n.

freedom
noncoherence 49 n.
freedom 744 n.

freedom fighter
soldier 722 n.

freedom of
  action
freedom 744 n.
independence
  744 n.

freedom of
  choice
opportunity 137 n.
choice 605 n.
independence
  744 n.

free fall
aeronautics 271 n.

free for all
turmoil 61 n.
contest 716 n.
fight 716 n.
anarchy 734 n.
free 744 adj.
scope 744 n.
free gift
extra 40 n.
acquisition 771 n.
gift 781 n.
free, gratis and for nothing
uncharged 812 adj.
free hand
facility 701 n.
scope 744 n.
permit 756 n.
liberality 813 n.
free hand, a
scope 744 n.
freehold
independence 744 n.
estate 777 n.
lands 777 n.
proprietary 777 adj.
free house
tavern 192 n.
freelance
author 589 n.
do business 622 vb.
worker 686 n.
independent 744 adj.
free person 744 n.
freeloader
idler 679 n.
beggar 763 n.
toady 879 n.
sociable person 882 n.
free love
freedom 744 n.
love affair 887 n.
type of marriage 894 n.
illicit love 951 n.
Freemasonry
society 708 n.
free of charge
uncharged 812 adj.
free pardon
amnesty 506 n.
forgiveness 909 n.
free port
way in 297 n.
scope 744 n.
emporium 796 n.
no charge 812 n.
freesheet
the press 528 n.

free speech
freedom 744 n.
free spirit
free person 744 n.
free-thinking
free 744 adj.
irreligious 974 adj.
free time
leisure 681 n.
free trade
ingress 297 n.
scope 744 n.
trade 791 n.
no charge 812 n.
free verse
verse form 593 n.
freewheel
ride 267 vb.
travel 267 vb.
not act 677 vb.
do easily 701 vb.
free will
will 595 n.
freedom 744 n.
freewill
volitional 595 adj.
freeze
halt 145 vb.
come to rest 266 vb.
quiescence 266 n.
stop 266 int.
be dense 324 vb.
harden 326 vb.
render insensible 375 vb.
be cold 380 vb.
wintriness 380 n.
refrigerate 382 vb.
preserve 666 vb.
restriction 747 n.
nonpayment 805 n.
not pay 805 vb.
frighten 854 vb.
quake 854 vb.
freeze-dry
dry 342 vb.
refrigerate 382 vb.
preserve 666 vb.
freezer
cabinet 194 n.
refrigerator 384 n.
storage 632 n.
preserver 666 n.
freezing
contraction 198 n.
cold 380 adj.
refrigeration 382 n.
freezing point
coldness 380 n.
freight
fill 54 vb.
contents 193 n.

load 193 vb.
transport 272 n.
gravity 322 n.
merchandise 795 n.
freight train
train 274 n.
French beans
fruit and vegetables 301 n.
French cricket
ball game 837 n.
French dressing
hors-d'oeuvres 301 n.
sauce 389 n.
French fries
fruit and vegetables 301 n.
French horn
horn 414 n.
French kiss
endearment 889 n.
French knickers
underwear 228 n.
French leave
absence 190 n.
escape 667 n.
French letter
contraception 172 n.
French polish
smoother 258 n.
French poodle
dog 365 n.
French window
window 263 n.
frenetic
furious 176 adj.
frenzied 503 adj.
frenzied
frenzied 503 adj.
fervent 818 adj.
frenzy
turmoil 61 n.
violence 176 n.
frenzy 503 n.
activity 678 n.
excitable state 822 n.
frequency
degree 27 n.
frequency 139 n.
periodicity 141 n.
electricity 160 n.
oscillation 317 n.
frequency band
oscillation 317 n.
frequency wave
radiation 417 n.
frequent
frequent 139 adj.
recur 139 vb.
go on 146 vb.

be present 189 vb.
dwell 192 vb.
be wont 610 vb.
frequently
often 139 adv.
fresco
picture 553 n.
fresh
original 21 adj.
lasting 113 adj.
new 126 adj.
airy 340 adj.
humid 341 adj.
windy 352 adj.
cold 380 adj.
remembered 505 adj.
unhabituated 611 adj.
clean 648 adj.
salubrious 652 adj.
impertinent 878 adj.
fresh air
air 340 n.
salubrity 652 n.
freshen
invigorate 174 vb.
aerate 340 vb.
purify 648 vb.
revive 656 vb.
refresh 685 vb.
decorate 844 vb.
freshen up
make better 654 vb.
repair 656 vb.
refresh 685 vb.
fresher
student 538 n.
fresh-faced
personable 841 adj.
freshness
originality 21 n.
newness 126 n.
youth 130 n.
coldness 380 n.
cleanness 648 n.
sauciness 878 n.
fresh-water lake
lake 346 n.
fret
rend 46 vb.
rub 333 vb.
give pain 377 vb.
cry 408 vb.
stringed instrument 414 n.
restlessness 678 n.
hasten 680 vb.
disobey 738 vb.
be excitable 822 vb.

excitable state 822 n.
suffer 825 vb.
torment 827 vb.
decorate 844 vb.
anger 891 n.
be angry 891 vb.
enrage 891 vb.
fretful
capricious 604 adj.
active 678 adj.
discontented 829 adj.
irascible 892 adj.
fretwork
network 222 n.
ornamental art 844 n.
friable
brittle 330 adj.
powdery 332 adj.
friar
monk 986 n.
pastor 986 n.
friary
monastery 986 n.
monk 986 n.
fricassee
dish 301 n.
fricative
speech sound 398 n.
friction
counteraction 182 n.
friction 333 n.
opposition 704 n.
dissension 709 n.
painfulness 827 n.
fridge
refrigerator 384 n.
storage 632 n.
fridge-freezer
cabinet 194 n.
refrigerator 384 n.
storage 632 n.
friend
friend 880 n.
friend at court
influence 178 n.
latency 523 n.
patron 707 n.
friendly
pleasant 376 adj.
friendly 880 adj.
amiable 884 adj.
approving 923 adj.
friendly fire
mistake 495 n.
bungling 695 n.
friendship
friendship 880 n.
love 887 n.

Friesian
cattle 365 n.

frieze
textile 222 n.
ornamental art
844 n.
trimming 844 n.

frigate
sailing ship 275 n.
warship 722 n.

fright
eyesore 842 n.
fear 854 n.

frighten
frighten 854 vb.
threaten 900 vb.

frightened
fearing 854 adj.

frightening
frightening
854 adj.

frightful
prodigious 32 adj.
ugly 842 adj.
frightening
854 adj.

frigid
cold 380 adj.
impassive 820 adj.
inexcitable
823 adj.
hostile 881 adj.
pure 950 adj.

frigidity
coldness 380 n.
moral insensibility
820 n.
inexcitability
823 n.
purity 950 n.

frill
edging 234 n.
plumage 259 n.
fold 261 n.
fold 261 vb.
trimming 844 n.

fringe
adjunct 40 n.
extremity 69 n.
contiguity 202 n.
filament 208 n.
edge 234 n.
edging 234 n.
hem 234 vb.
hair 259 n.
unimportant
639 adj.
hairdressing 843 n.
trimming 844 n.

fringe benefits
earnings 771 n.
reward 962 n.

fringe medicine
medical art 658 n.

frippery
clothing 228 n.
bauble 639 n.
finery 844 n.
ostentation 875 n.

frisk
be in motion
265 vb.
move fast 277 vb.
leap 312 vb.
search 459 vb.
be cheerful 833 vb.
rejoice 835 vb.

frisky
active 678 adj.
merry 833 adj.

frisson
agitation 318 n.

fritter away
waste 634 vb.
misuse 675 vb.
lose 772 vb.
be prodigal 815 vb.

fritters
dish 301 n.

frivolous
changeful 152 adj.
light-minded
456 adj.
capricious 604 adj.
trivial 639 adj.
merry 833 adj.
rash 857 adj.

frizzy
undulatory
251 adj.
hairy 259 adj.

frock
dress 228 n.
canonicals 989 n.

frock coat
overcoat 228 n.

Froebel system
education 534 n.

frog
fastening 47 n.
amphibian 365 n.
trimming 844 n.

frogman
diver 313 n.

frogmarch
impel 279 vb.

frolic
leap 312 n.
be cheerful 833 vb.
rejoice 835 vb.
amuse oneself
837 vb.
revel 837 n.

frolicsome
merry 833 adj.

fromage frais
dairy products
301 n.

from A to Z
including 78 adv.

from hell
not nice 645 adj.
hateful 888 adj.

**from pillar to
post**
round about
626 adv.

from scratch
initially 68 adv.

**from time to
time**
sometimes
139 adv.

frond
foliage 366 n.

front
put in front 64 vb.
beginning 68 n.
first 68 adj.
impend 155 vb.
coat 226 vb.
be in front 237 vb.
front 237 n.
frontal 237 adj.
appearance 445 n.
duplicity 541 n.
path 624 n.
battle 718 n.
battleground
724 n.
insolence 878 n.

frontage
situation 186 n.
face 237 n.

frontal
frontal 237 adj.

frontier
extremity 69 n.
contiguity 202 n.
edge 234 n.
limit 236 n.

fronting
near 200 adj.

frontispiece
prelude 66 n.
front 237 n.

**frontman or
-woman**
broadcaster 531 n.

front of house
theatre 594 n.

front room
chamber 194 n.

front runner
contender 716 n.
favourite 890 n.

front tooth
tooth 256 n.

frost
cover 226 vb.
wintriness 380 n.
opacity 423 n.

whiten 427 vb.
blight 659 n.

frost-bite
coldness 380 n.
refrigerate 382 vb.

frosted
rough 259 adj.
cooled 382 adj.
opaque 423 adj.
semitransparent
424 adj.
white 427 adj.
grey 429 adj.

frosted glass
screen 421 n.
semitransparency
424 n.

frosting
covering 226 n.
powderiness 332 n.

frosty
cold 380 adj.
white 427 adj.
unsociable 883 adj.

froth
effervesce 318 vb.
moisture 341 n.
bubble 355 n.
bubble 355 vb.
dirt 649 n.
be excitable
822 vb.

frothy
light 323 adj.
bubbly 355 adj.
ornate 574 adj.

frottage
picture 553 n.

frou-frou
faintness 401 n.
sibilation 406 n.
finery 844 n.

frown
distort 246 vb.
fold 261 n.
gesticulate 547 vb.
gesture 547 n.
discontent 829 n.
be rude 885 vb.
rudeness 885 n.
be angry 891 vb.
sullenness 893 n.

frown upon
depress 834 vb.

frozen
cohesive 48 adj.
fixed 153 adj.
still 266 adj.
dense 324 adj.
hard 326 adj.
insensible 375 adj.
chilly 380 adj.
cooled 382 adj.

preserved 666 adj.
impassive 820 adj.
fearing 854 adj.

frozen assets
estate 777 n.
debt 803 n.

frozen food
provisions 301 n.

frozen mitt
rejection 607 n.

frozen shoulder
rheumatism 651 n.

fructification
productiveness
171 n.

fructose
food content
301 n.
sweet thing 392 n.

frugal
economical
814 adj.
cautious 858 adj.
temperate 942 adj.

frugivorous
feeding 301 adj.

fruit
nonconformist
84 n.
growth 157 n.
product 164 n.
reproduce itself
167 vb.
flower 366 n.
plant 366 n.

fruitful
increasing 36 adj.
prolific 171 adj.
successful 727 adj.
gainful 771 adj.

fruit growing
agriculture 370 n.

fruition
propagation 167 n.
ripening 669 n.
completion 725 n.

fruit juice
soft drink 301 n.

fruitless
unproductive
172 adj.
profitless 641 adj.
unsuccessful
728 adj.

fruit machine
gambling 618 n.

fruity
tasty 386 adj.
fragrant 396 adj.
witty 839 adj.

frump
eyesore 842 n.

frustrate
disappoint 509 vb.

gainsay
negate 533 vb.

gait
gait 265 n.
way 624 n.

gaiters
legwear 228 n.
badge of rule
743 n.
canonicals 989 n.

gala
festivity 837 n.
pageant 875 n.

galactic
cosmic 321 adj.

galactose
sweet thing 392 n.

gala day
amusement 837 n.
special day 876 n.

Galahad
brave person
855 n.

**gala
performance**
pageant 875 n.

galaxy
group 74 n.
star 321 n.
luminary 420 n.
person of repute
866 n.

gale
velocity 277 n.
gale 352 n.
windy 352 adj.

**gales of
laughter**
laughter 835 n.

gall
swelling 253 n.
give pain 377 vb.
sourness 393 n.
hurt 827 vb.
torment 827 vb.
sauciness 878 n.
resentment 891 n.
irascibility 892 n.
malevolence 898 n.

gallant
fop 848 n.
courageous
855 adj.
showy 875 adj.
courteous 884 adj.
lover 887 n.
loving 887 adj.
benevolent
897 adj.
libertine 952 n.

gallantry
courage 855 n.
courtesy 884 n.
love 887 n.

galleon
merchant ship
275 n.
warship 722 n.

gallery
lobby 194 n.
tunnel 263 n.
listener 415 n.
onlookers 441 n.
exhibit 522 n.
playgoer 594 n.
theatre 594 n.
collection 632 n.
church interior
990 n.

galley
chamber 194 n.
rowing boat
275 n.
cookery 301 n.
heater 383 n.

galley proof
print 587 n.

galley slave
boatman 270 n.
busy person
678 n.
slave 742 n.
prisoner 750 n.

galliard
dance 837 n.

gallimaufry
medley 43 n.

galling
annoying 827 adj.

gallivant
wander 267 vb.

gallon
metrology 465 n.

gallons
great quantity
32 n.

gallop
be transient
114 vb.
gait 265 n.
ride 267 vb.
move fast 277 vb.
spurt 277 n.

gallows
hanger 217 n.
means of execution
964 n.

gallstones
digestive disorders
651 n.

**Gallup poll
(tdmk)**
statistics 86 n.
enquiry 459 n.
vote 605 n.

galoot
ninny 501 n.
bungler 697 n.

galore
great quantity
32 n.
many 104 adj.
plenty 635 n.

galumph
be clumsy 695 vb.

galvanize
invigorate 174 vb.
move 265 vb.
incite 612 vb.
excite 821 vb.

gambit
debut 68 n.
attempt 671 n.
tactics 688 n.

gamble
empiricism 461 n.
uncertainty
474 n.
conjecture 512 n.
gamble 618 vb.
gambling 618 n.
be rash 857 vb.

gambler
gambler 618 n.
player 837 n.

gambling
gambling 618 n.

gambling den
gaming-house
618 n.

gambol
leap 312 n.
leap 312 vb.
be cheerful 833 vb.
amuse oneself
837 vb.

game
crippled 163 adj.
meat 301 n.
animal 365 n.
trickery 542 n.
resolute 599 adj.
objective 617 n.
chase 619 n.
plot 623 n.
stratagem 698 n.
contest 716 n.
amuse oneself
837 vb.
revel 837 n.
laughingstock
851 n.
courageous
855 adj.

game bird
table bird 365 n.

gamekeeper
keeper 749 n.

gameness
willingness 597 n.
stamina 600 n.
courage 855 n.

**game not worth
the candle**
lost labour 641 n.

game preserve
wood 366 n.
stock farm 369 n.

games
exercise 682 n.
contest 716 n.
sport 837 n.

**game, set and
match**
victory 727 n.

gamesmanship
tactics 688 n.
cunning 698 n.
contention 716 n.
sport 837 n.

**gaming
machine**
gambling 618 n.

gamma ray
radiation 417 n.

gammer
old woman 133 n.

gammon
meat 301 n.

gammy
crippled 163 adj.

gamp
shade 226 n.

gamut
series 71 n.
key 410 n.
musical note
410 n.

gamy
pungent 388 adj.
savoury 390 adj.

gander
bird 365 n.
male animal
372 n.

gang
band 74 n.
be in motion
265 vb.
personnel 686 n.
party 708 n.

gang agley
miscarry 728 vb.

gang bang
rape 951 n.

ganger
worker 686 n.
manager 690 n.

gangling
unwieldy 195 adj.
narrow 206 adj.
clumsy 695 adj.

ganglion
centre 225 n.

gangplank
bridge 624 n.

gangrene
decay 51 n.
decompose 51 vb.
infection 651 n.
ulcer 651 n.

gangster
murderer 362 n.
robber 789 n.
low fellow 869 n.
offender 904 n.

gang up
congregate 74 vb.
cooperate 706 vb.

gangway
doorway 263 n.
access 624 n.
bridge 624 n.

gannet
eater 301 n.
bird 365 n.

gantry
stand 218 n.

gaol
prison 748 n.
seclusion 883 n.

gap
incompleteness
55 n.
gap 201 n.
concavity 255 n.
requirement 627 n.

gape
space 201 vb.
open 263 vb.
gaze 438 vb.
watch 441 vb.
be curious 453 vb.
wonder 864 vb.

gaping
open 263 adj.
opening 263 n.

gap year
lull 145 n.
interval 201.
leisure 681 n.

garage
stable 192 n.
chamber 194 n.
music 412 n.
storage 632 n.
store 632 vb.
safeguard 660 vb.

garage sale
sale 793 n.

garb
dress 228 vb.
dressing 228 n.

garbage
dirt 649 n.

garble
mislead 495 vb.
misinterpret
521 vb.
be false 541 vb.

gawky
clumsy 695 adj.

gawp
gaze 438 vb.
scan 438 vb.
not expect 508 vb.
wonder 864 vb.

gay
abnormal 84 adj.
nonconformist
84 n.
luminous 417 adj.
florid 425 adj.
merry 833 adj.
showy 875 adj.

gay abandon
merriment 833 n.
rejoicing 835 n.

gay lib
freedom 744 n.

gaze
gaze 438 vb.
look 438 n.

gazebo
arbour 194 n.

gazelle
mammal 365 n.

gazette
journal 528 n.
record 548 n.

gazetteer
directory 87 n.
guidebook 524 n.
reference book
589 n.

gazpacho
hors-d'oeuvres
301 n.

GCE
exam 459 n.

GCSE
exam 459 n.

gear
accumulation 74 n.
sort 77 n.
box 194 n.
clothing 228 n.
dressing 228 n.
form 243 n.
equipment 630 n.
property 777 n.
finery 844 n.

gearing
machine 630 n.
debt 803 n.

gear oneself up
prepare oneself
669 vb.

gears
machine 630 n.

gecko
reptile 365 n.

geegaw
bauble 639 n.

gee-gee
horse 273 n.

geek
fool 501 n.
enthusiast 504 n.
bore 838 n.

gefilte fish
fish food 301 n.

Geiger counter
radiation 417 n.
meter 465 n.
detector 484 n.

gel
thicken 354 vb.
viscidity 354 n.

gelatine
thickening 354 n.

geld
subtract 39 vb.
unman 161 vb.

gelding
horse 273 n.
male animal
372 n.

gelignite
explosive 723 n.

gell or jell
be dense 324 vb.
harden 326 vb.

gem
gem 844 n.

gen
information 524 n.

gendarmerie
police 955 n.

gender
classification 77 n.
grammar 564 n.

**gender
  discrimination**
prejudice 481 n.

gender equality
equality 28 n.

gene
heredity 5 n.
organism 358 n.

genealogy
genealogy 169 n.

general
general 79 adj.
national 371 adj.
army officer 741 n.

**general
  anaesthetic**
anaesthetic 375 n.
synod 985 n.

general election
vote 605 n.

generality
generality 79 n.

generalization
whole 52 n.
generality 79 n.
reasoning 475 n.

inexactness 495 n.

**general
  knowledge**
erudition 490 n.

generally
generally 79 adv.
often 139 adv.

**general
  practitioner**
doctor 658 n.

general public
social group 371 n.
commonalty
869 n.

generalship
tactics 688 n.

generate
generate 167 vb.

generation
coition 45 n.
era 110 n.

generations
long duration
113 n.

generator
electronics 160 n.

generic
general 79 adj.

generic drug
medicine 658 n.

generosity
liberality 813 n.
benevolence 897 n.

generous
great 32 adj.
many 104 adj.
liberal 813 adj.
courteous 884 adj.
benevolent
897 adj.
approving 923 adj.
virtuous 933 adj.

genesis
origin 68 n.
source 156 n.

gene therapy
therapy 658 n.

genetic
genetic 5 adj.

genetic map
heredity 5 n.

**genetically-
  modified food**
food 301 n.

**genetic
  counselling**
heredity 5 n.

**genetic
  engineering**
heredity 5 n.
biology 358 n.

**genetic
  fingerprint**
label 547 n.

**genetic
  fingerprinting**
evidence 466 n.
identification
547 n.
diagnostic 658 n.

genetics
heredity 5 n.
biology 358 n.

geneva
alcoholic drink
301 n.

**Geneva
  Convention**
treaty 765 n.

genial
pleasant 376 adj.
warm 379 adj.
pleasurable
826 adj.
cheerful 833 adj.
benevolent 897 adj.

genie
mythical being
970 n.

genitalia
genitalia 167 n.

genitals
genitalia 167 n.

genius
identity 13 n.
analogue 18 n.
tendency 179 n.
intellect 447 n.
spirit 447 n.
intellectual 492 n.
intelligence 498 n.
sage 500 n.
exceller 644 n.
aptitude 694 n.
proficient person
696 n.
prodigy 864 n.

genius loci
lesser deity 967 n.

genned-up
informed 524 adj.

genocide
destruction 165 n.
homicide 362 n.
See **slaughter**
slaughter 362 n.
cruel act 898 n.
ruffian 904 n.
capital punishment
963 n.

genome
heredity 5 n.

genotype
breed 77 n.

genre
sort 77 n.

gent
male 372 n.

aristocrat 868 n.

genteel
genteel 868 adj.

gentian violet
purpleness 436 n.

gentile
religionist 973 n.
heathen 974 n.
heathenish
974 adj.
impious person
980 n.

gentility
etiquette 848 n.
nobility 868 n.
courtesy 884 n.

gentle
muted 401 adj.
lenient 736 adj.
amiable 884 adj.
courteous 884 adj.
benevolent
897 adj.
innocent 935 adj.

gentlefolk
aristocracy 868 n.

gentleman
adult 134 n.
male 372 n.
aristocrat 868 n.

gentlemanly
male 372 n.
well-bred 848 adj.
reputable 866 adj.
noble 868 adj.
courteous 884 adj.
honourable
929 adj.

**gentleman's
  agreement**
unreliability 474 n.
promise 764 n.
compact 765 n.

gentleness
moderation 177 n.
leniency 736 n.
courtesy 884 n.
benevolence 897 n.
pity 905 n.

gentle sex
womankind 373 n.

gentlewoman
female 373 n.
aristocrat 868 n.

gentrification
restoration 656 n.

gentry
aristocracy 868 n.

Gents
latrine 649 n.

genuflexion
obeisance 311 n.
submission 721 n.
servility 879 n.

respects 920 n.
ritual act 988 n.
genuine
genuine 494 adj.
genuine article, the
no imitation 21 n.
authenticity 494 n.
genuineness
identity 13 n.
no imitation 21 n.
authenticity 494 n.
genus
group 74 n.
breed 77 n.
geocentric
central 225 adj.
celestial 321 adj.
geodesy
earth sciences 321 n.
measurement 465 n.
geographic
geographic 321 adj.
geography
situation 186 n.
earth sciences 321 n.
geology
earth sciences 321 n.
mineralogy 359 n.
geomancy
production 104 n.
plan 623 n.
geometric
ornamental 844 adj.
geometrical
statistical 86 adj.
geometrical progression
ratio 85 n.
geometry
mathematics 86 n.
geometry 465 n.
geomorphology
earth sciences 321 n.
George Cross
badge 547 n.
decoration 729 n.
georgette
textile 222 n.
Georgian
architectural 192 adj.
geranium
redness 431 n.
gerbil
animal 365 n.
geriatric
ageing 131 adj.

geriatrics
gerontology 131 n.
medical art 658 n.
germ
origin 68 n.
source 156 n.
infection 651 n.
poison 659 n.
germane
apt 24 adj.
German measles
infection 651 n.
germicide
prophylactic 658 n.
poison 659 n.
germinate
begin 68 vb.
result 157 vb.
reproduce itself 167 vb.
be fruitful 171 vb.
vegetate 366 vb.
germ warfare
warfare 718 n.
weapon 723 n.
gerontology
gerontology 131 n.
medical art 658 n.
gerrymandering
cunning 698 n.
perfidy 930 n.
Gestalt psychology
psychology 447 n.
Gestalt therapy
therapy 658 n.
Gestapo
police enquiry 459 n.
gestation
propagation 167 n.
See **obstetrics**
ripening 669 n.
gesticulate
gesticulate 547 vb.
gesture
move 265 vb.
look 445 n.
gesticulate 547 vb.
gesture 547 n.
deed 676 n.
behave 688 vb.
gesture politics
publicity 528 n.
get
be turned to 147 vb.
generate 167 vb.
know 490 vb.
understand 516 vb.
acquire 771 vb.
possess 773 vb.
receive 782 vb.

get above oneself
be vain 873 vb.
be insolent 878 vb.
get across
mean 514 vb.
be intelligible 516 vb.
communicate 524 vb.
huff 891 vb.
get ahead
come before 64 vb.
progress 285 vb.
get a life
contempt 922 int.
get a move on
accelerate 277 vb.
move fast 277 vb.
progress 285 vb.
hurry up 680 int.
get around
travel 267 vb.
be sociable 882 vb.
get at
blame 924 vb.
get away
recede 290 vb.
disappear 446 vb.
escape 667 vb.
achieve liberty 746 vb.
getaway
departure 296 n.
escape 667 n.
get back
recoup 31 vb.
retrieve 656 vb.
acquire 771 vb.
get back at
be restored 656 vb.
avenge 910 vb.
get better
get better 654 vb.
get cracking
begin 68 vb.
move fast 277 vb.
get down to it
be related 9 vb.
work 682 vb.
get in the way
be clumsy 695 vb.
hinder 702 vb.
get in touch
be contiguous 202 vb.
communicate 524 vb.
get nowhere
waste effort 641 adj.
get off
land 295 vb.
descend 309 vb.

escape 667 vb.
get off with
court 889 vb.
get on
progress 285 vb.
prosper 730 vb.
get one down
cause discontent 829 vb.
depress 834 vb.
be tedious 838 vb.
get one's come-uppance
deserve 915 vb.
be punished 963 vb.
get on one's nerves
displease 827 vb.
be tedious 838 vb.
cause dislike 861 vb.
enrage 891 vb.
get on with
accord 24 vb.
do 676 vb.
get out
come along 267 int.
land 295 vb.
extract 304 vb.
publish 528 vb.
escape 667 vb.
get over
be restored 656 vb.
get rid of
destroy 165 vb.
eject 300 vb.
kill 362 vb.
relinquish 621 vb.
deliver 668 vb.
not retain 779 vb.
get round
fool 542 vb.
induce 612 vb.
avoid 620 vb.
get shot of
eject 300 vb.
carry through 725 vb.
get the better of
be superior 34 vb.
confute 479 vb.
defeat 727 vb.
humiliate 872 vb.
get the picture
know 490 vb.
understand 516 vb.
get there
arrive 295 vb.
getting warm, be
approaching 289 adj.

detect 484 vb.
getting well
healthy 650 adj.
get-together
assembly 74 n.
amusement 837 n.
social gathering 882 n.
get to one's feet
be vertical 215 vb.
lift oneself 310 vb.
get up
produce 164 vb.
ascend 308 vb.
lift oneself 310 vb.
blow 352 vb.
study 536 vb.
fake 541 vb.
get-up
form 243 n.
get-up-and-go
vigour 571 n.
restlessness 678 n.
get wind of
smell 394 vb.
discover 484 vb.
be informed 524 vb.
get with it
modernize 126 vb.
be in fashion 848 vb.
get worse
be inferior 35 vb.
deteriorate 655 vb.
gewgaw
finery 844 n.
geyser
outflow 298 n.
water 339 n.
stream 350 n.
heat 379 n.
heater 383 n.
gharry
cab 274 n.
ghastly
not nice 645 adj.
distressing 827 adj.
unpleasant 827 adj.
unsightly 842 adj.
frightening 854 adj.
ghat
gap 201 n.
ghazal
verse form 593 n.
ghazi
zealot 979 n.
ghee
food 301 n.
fat 357 n.
gherkins
sauce 389 n.

gloat
be pleased 824 vb.
rejoice 835 vb.
boast 877 vb.
avenge 910 vb.

global
extensive 32 adj.
comprehensive
52 adj.
inclusive 78 adj.
universal 79 adj.
spacious 183 adj.
broad 205 adj.
rotund 252 adj.
indiscriminate
464 adj.

globe
whole 52 n.
sphere 252 n.
universe 321 n.
world 321 n.
map 551 n.

globe-trotter
traveller 268 n.
spectator 441 n.

globular
rotund 252 adj.

globule
sphere 252 n.

glockenspiel
gong 414 n.

gloom
darkness 418 n.
dimness 419 n.
adversity 731 n.
sorrow 825 n.
dejection
834 n.

**gloom and
doom**
dejection 834 n.

gloomy
dark 418 adj.
black 428 adj.
cheerless 834 adj.
dejected 834 adj.
melancholic
834 adj.
sullen 893 adj.

glorified
ostentatious
875 adj.

glorify
augment 36 vb.
dignify 866 vb.
honour 866 vb.
praise 923 vb.
worship 981 vb.

glorious
great 32 adj.
excellent 644 adj.
super 644 adj.
palmy 730 adj.
splendid 841 adj.

noteworthy
866 adj.
renowned 866 adj.
worshipful
866 adj.

glory
success 727 n.
famousness 866 n.
honours 866 n.
prestige 866 n.
divine attribute
965 n.

glory hole
chamber 194 n.

gloss
smoothness 258 n.
light 417 n.
reflection 417 n.
maxim 496 n.
commentary 520 n.
interpret 520 vb.
sham 542 n.
untruth 543 n.
facilitate 701 vb.
beauty 841 n.
ostentation 875 n.
extenuate 927 vb.
justify 927 vb.
vindication 927 n.

glossary
word list 87 n.
commentary 520 n.
dictionary 559 n.

glossolalia
piety 979 n.

gloss over
neglect 458 vb.
sophisticate
477 vb.
mislead 495 vb.
conceal 525 vb.
fake 541 vb.
plead 614 vb.
extenuate 927 vb.

gloss paint
pigment 425 n.

glossy
luminous 417 adj.
personable
841 adj.

glossy magazine
journal 528 n.

glottal stop
speech sound
398 n.
pronunciation
577 n.

glove
glove 228 n.
love token 889 n.

glove puppet
image 551 n.

glow
be hot 379 vb.

heat 379 n.
glow 417 n.
shine 417 vb.
hue 425 n.
redden 431 vb.
vigour 571 n.
warm feeling
818 n.

glower
gaze 438 vb.
be angry 891 vb.
sullenness 893 n.

glowering
angry 891 adj.
sullen 893 adj.

glowing terms
praise 923 n.

glow-worm
insect 365 n.

glucose
food content 301 n.
sweet thing 392 n.

glue
join 45 vb.
adhesive 47 n.
viscidity 354 n.

glue-sniffing
drug-taking 949 n.

glum
melancholic
834 adj.

glut
productiveness
171 n.
redundance 637 n.
superabound
637 vb.
superfluity 637 n.
cheapness 812 n.
sate 863 vb.
satiety 863 n.

gluten
viscidity 354 n.

glutton
glutton 947 n.

gluttony
vice 934 n.
gluttony 947 n.

glycerine
lubricant 334 n.
fat 357 n.

G.M.T.
clock time 117 n.

gnarled
distorted 246 adj.
rough 259 adj.
dense 324 adj.

gnash
rub 333 vb.

**gnash one's
teeth**
gesticulate 547 vb.
regret 830 vb.
be angry 891 vb.

gnat
small thing 33 n.
insect 365 n.

gnaw
abate 37 vb.
rend 46 vb.
chew 301 vb.
give pain 377 vb.
hurt 827 vb.
enrage 891 vb.

gnome
elf 970 n.

gnostic
religionist 973 n.
heretic 977 n.
heretical 977 adj.
sectarian 978 adj.
sectarian 978 n.

gnu
mammal 365 n.

go
pass away 2 vb.
period 110 n.
periodicity 141 n.
operate 173 vb.
vigorousness
174 n.
be in motion
265 vb.
travel 267 vb.
walk 267 vb.
recede 290 vb.
excrete 302 vb.
disappear 446 vb.
vigour 571 n.
function 622 vb.
restlessness 678 n.
board game 837 n.
courage 855 n.

go about
undertake 672 vb.

goad
stimulant 174 n.
sharp point 256 n.
impel 279 vb.
incentive 612 n.
incite 612 vb.
hasten 680 vb.
animate 821 vb.
excitant 821 n.
excite 821 vb.
engage 891 vb.

go against
counteract
182 vb.
oppose 704 vb.

**go against the
grain**
be difficult 700 vb.
displease 827 vb.
cause dislike
861 vb.

go-ahead
vigorous 174 adj.

progressive
285 adj.
assent 488 n.
enterprising
672 adj.
permit 756 n.

goal
limit 236 n.
goal 295 n.
attempt 671 n.
success 727 n.
desired object
859 n.

goalkeeper
player 837 n.

go along with
concur 181 vb.
assent 488 vb.
consent 758 vb.

goat
goat 365 n.
libertine 952 n.

go back
revert 148 vb.
turn round 282 vb.
turn back 286 vb.
recede 290 vb.

go back on
recant 603 vb.
not observe
769 vb.

gobbet
small thing 33 n.

gobbledygook
lack of meaning
515 n.
neology 560 n.
slang 560 adj.

gobble (up)
consume 165 vb.
absorb 299 vb.
ululate 409 vb.
gluttonize 947 vb.

go-between
intermediary
231 n.
informant 524 n.
messenger 529 n.
instrument 628 n.
mediator 720 n.

goblet
cup 194 n.

goblin
intimidation
854 n.
elf 970 n.

gobs
great quantity
32 n.

gobsmacked
unexpecting
508 adj.

go by
elapse 111 vb.

go-cart
automobile 274 n.
pushcart 274 n.
God
cause 156 n.
the Deity 965 n.
god, goddess
deity 966 n.
godchild
family 11 n.
godfather
bigwig 638 n.
godforsaken
empty 190 adj.
distant 199 adj.
secluded 883 adj.
wicked 934 adj.
godhead
divineness 965 n.
godless
irreligious 974 adj.
impious 980 adj.
godlike
beautiful 841 adj.
godlike 965 adj.
godly
pious 979 adj.
go down
be destroyed
165 vb.
descend 309 vb.
founder 313 vb.
godparent
parentage
169 n.
godsend
benefit 615 n.
gods (the)
onlookers 441 n.
playgoer 594 n.
theatre 594 n.
go Dutch
compromise
770 vb.
participate
775 vb.
defray 804 vb.
be sociable 882 vb.
go easy (on)
be lenient 736 vb.
show mercy
905 vb.
goffer
groove 262 vb.
go for
attack 712 vb.
cost 809 vb.
reproach 924 vb.
go-getter
doer 676 n.
egotist 932 n.
goggle
gaze 438 vb.
not expect 508 vb.

wonder 864 vb.
goggles
eyeglass 442 n.
shelter 662 n.
go-go
speedy 277 adj.
progression 285 n.
progressive
285 adj.
enterprising
672 adj.
gogo dancer
entertainer 594 n.
go in for
be resolute 599 vb.
be wont 610 vb.
busy oneself
622 vb.
undertake 672 vb.
going begging
superfluous
637 adj.
free 744 adj.
unpossessed
774 adj.
going beyond
overstepping
306 n.
going cheap
cheap 812 adj.
going down
decreasing 37 adj.
**going for a
song**
cheap 812 adj.
going rate
price 809 n.
go into
dissertate 591 vb.
go it alone
be free 744 vb.
goitre
swelling 253 n.
skin disease
651 n.
gold
orange 432 n.
yellow 433 adj.
yellowness 433 n.
incentive 612 n.
money 797 n.
gold-digger
enquirer 459 n.
lover 887 n.
golden
yellow 433 adj.
palmy 730 adj.
promising 852 adj.
Golden Age
era 110 n.
literature 557 n.
palmy days 730 n.
happiness 824 n.
innocence 935 n.

**golden girl or
boy**
favourite 890 n.
**golden
handcuffs**
reward 962 n.
**golden
handshake**
extra 40 n.
ejection 300 n.
resignation 753 n.
earnings 771 n.
pay 804 n.
thanks 907 n.
reward 962 n.
golden hello
extra 40 n.
arrival 295 n.
reward 962 n.
golden mean
average 30 n.
moderation 177 n.
middle way 625 n.
averageness 732 n.
golden oldie
archaism 127 n.
golden rule
maxim 496 n.
precept 693 n.
philanthropy
901 n.
golden wedding
period 110 n.
anniversary 141 n.
special day 876 n.
wedding 894 n.
goldfish
animal 365 n.
gold-medallist
proficient person
696 n.
gold-mine
store 632 n.
wealth 800 n.
gold standard
finance 797 n.
golf
ball game 837 n.
golf course
pleasure ground
837 n.
Goliath
athlete 162 n.
giant 195 n.
gondola
rowing boat 275 n.
airship 276 n.
gone
past 125 adj.
absent 190 adj.
dead 361 adj.
lost 772 adj.
gong
timekeeper 117 n.

resound 404 vb.
gong 414 n.
gonorrhoea
venereal disease
651 n.
goo
viscidity 354 n.
good
good 615 adj.
good 615 n.
excellent 644 adj.
skilful 694 adj.
obedient 739 adj.
pleasurable
826 adj.
amiable 884 adj.
benevolent
897 adj.
right 913 adj.
honourable
929 adj.
virtuous 933 adj.
pure 950 adj.
pious 979 adj.
good, be
be good 644 vb.
good behaviour
conduct 688 n.
courtesy 884 n.
virtue 933 n.
good books
repute 866 n.
approbation 923 n.
good breeding
etiquette 848 n.
courtesy 884 n.
goodbye
goodbye 296 int.
good cause
philanthropy
901 n.
good chance
fair chance 159 n.
possibility 469 n.
probability 471 n.
good cheer
enjoyment 824 n.
merriment 833 n.
sociability 882 n.
good company
sociability 882 n.
sociable person
882 n.
good faith
loyalty 739 n.
probity 929 n.
good form
practice 610 n.
etiquette 848 n.
ostentation 875 n.
**good-for-
nothing**
powerless 161 adj.
idler 679 n.

vicious 934 adj.
bad person 938 n.
good fortune
chance 159 n.
good 615 n.
success 727 n.
prosperity 730 n.
happiness 824 n.
good graces
approbation 923 n.
good-humoured
benevolent
897 adj.
good in parts
imperfect 647 adj.
good intentions
intention 617 n.
good living
gastronomy 301 n.
gluttony 947 n.
good looks
beauty 841 n.
good luck
chance 159 n.
good 615 n.
nondesign 618 n.
good luck 730 int.
prosperity 730 n.
goodly
good 615 adj.
**good
management**
economy 814 n.
good manners
conduct 688 n.
etiquette 848 n.
sociability 882 n.
courtesy 884 n.
good name
repute 866 n.
good-natured
amiable 884 adj.
benevolent
897 adj.
good neighbour
aider 703 n.
friend 880 n.
sociable person
882 n.
benefactor 903 n.
good person 937 n.
goodness
goodness 644 n.
probity 929 n.
virtue 933 n.
divine attribute
965 n.
piety 979 n.
sanctity 979 n.
good offices
protection 660 n.
aid 703 n.
pacification 719 n.
mediation 720 n.

grim
resolute 599 adj.
obstinate 602 adj.
not nice 645 adj.
distressing 827 adj.
serious 834 adj.
frightening
854 adj.
sullen 893 adj.
cruel 898 adj.
grimace
distort 246 vb.
distortion 246 n.
agitation 318 n.
look 438 n.
gesticulate 547 vb.
gesture 547 n.
discontent 829 n.
make ugly 842 vb.
dislike 861 vb.
sullenness 893 n.
disapprove 924 vb.
grime
dirt 649 n.
grin
laughter 835 n.
smile 835 vb.
grin and bear it
stand firm 599 vb.
knuckle under
721 vb.
be patient 823 vb.
suffer 825 vb.
be cheerful
833 vb.
be courageous
855 vb.
grind
break 46 vb.
rend 46 vb.
demolish 165 vb.
make smaller
198 vb.
deform 244 vb.
sharpen 256 vb.
chew 301 vb.
pulverize 332 vb.
rub 333 vb.
rasp 407 vb.
study 536 n.
wound 655 vb.
labour 682 n.
work 682 n.
oppress 735 vb.
grind down
abase 311 vb.
be insolent 878 vb.
**grind one's
   teeth**
be angry 891 vb.
grindstone
pulverizer 332 n.
labour 682 n.
bore 838 n.

grip
join 45 vb.
unite with 45 vb.
fastening 47 n.
vitality 162 n.
vigorousness
174 n.
influence 178 n.
bag 194 n.
gesture 547 n.
tool 630 n.
governance 733 n.
restrain 747 vb.
possess 773 vb.
possession 773 n.
retain 778 vb.
retention 778 n.
take 786 vb.
impress 821 vb.
gripe
give pain 377 vb.
be discontented
829 vb.
grisly
frightening
854 adj.
grist
powder 332 n.
gristle
solid body 324 n.
hardness 326 n.
toughness 329 n.
grist to the mill
provision 633 n.
grit
strength 162 n.
vigorousness
174 n.
hardness 326 n.
texture 331 n.
powder 332 n.
resolution 599 n.
stamina 600 n.
courage 855 n.
grit one's teeth
gesticulate 547 vb.
be resolute 599 vb.
See **stand firm**
persevere 600 vb.
gritty
hard 326 adj.
textural 331 adj.
powdery 332 adj.
grizzled
whitish 427 adj.
grey 429 adj.
pied 437 adj.
grizzly
grey 429 adj.
groan
feel pain 377 vb.
cry 408 vb.
deprecate 762 vb.
discontent 829 n.

be dejected 834 vb.
lamentation 836 n.
weep 836 vb.
grocer
tradespeople
794 n.
groceries
provisions 301 n.
groggy
weakly 163 adj.
sick 651 adj.
sleepy 679 adj.
groin
angularity 247 n.
groom
animal husbandry
369 n.
groom 369 vb.
clean 648 vb.
make ready
669 vb.
domestic 742 n.
servant 742 n.
groom for
fit 24 adj.
groomsman
bridal party
894 n.
groove
regularity 81 n.
place 185 n.
receptacle 194 n.
gap 201 n.
cavity 255 n.
furrow 262 n.
groove 262 vb.
habit 610 n.
grope
move slowly
278 vb.
touch 378 vb.
be tentative
461 vb.
be uncertain
474 vb.
not know 491 vb.
be clumsy 695 vb.
rape 951 vb.
grope for
search 459 vb.
gross
consummate
32 adj.
whole 52 adj.
manifest 522 adj.
bad 645 adj.
not nice 645 adj.
acquire 771 vb.
receive 782 vb.
take 786 vb.
vulgar 847 adj.
heinous 934 adj.
sensual 944 adj.
impure 951 adj.

gross, a
over one hundred
99 n.
grotesque
unusual 84 adj.
absurd 497 adj.
imaginative
513 adj.
unsightly 842 adj.
ridiculous
849 adj.
grotto
pavilion 192 n.
arbour 194 n.
cavity 255 n.
grotty
trivial 639 adj.
bad 645 adj.
unclean 649 adj.
sick 651 adj.
grouch
be discontented
829 vb.
malcontent 829 n.
rude person 885 n.
sullenness 893 n.
ground
fragmentary
53 adj.
reason why 156 n.
region 184 n.
territory 184 n.
situation 186 n.
base 214 n.
flatten 216 vb.
basis 218 n.
support 218 vb.
navigate 269 vb.
powdery 332 adj.
land 344 n.
educate 534 vb.
arena 724 n.
grounded
fixed 153 adj.
ground floor
base 214 n.
groundless
unreal 2 adj.
insubstantial 4 adj.
illogical 477 adj.
erroneous 495 adj.
grounds
leavings 41 n.
territory 184 n.
park 192 n.
grassland 348 n.
evidence 466 n.
reasons 475 n.
motive 612 n.
dirt 649 n.
lands 777 n.
ground swell
commotion 318 n.
wave 350 n.

ground troops
armed force 722 n.
groundwork
source 156 n.
base 214 n.
basis 218 n.
preparation 669 n.
group
combine 50 vb.
part 53 n.
subdivision 53 n.
arrange 62 vb.
arrangement 62 n.
class 62 vb.
bring together
74 vb.
group 74 n.
network 222 n.
party 708 n.
air force 722 n.
sect 978 n.
groupie
concomitant 89 n.
follower 284 n.
habitué 610 n.
grouse
meat 301 n.
table bird 365 n.
be discontented
829 vb.
grout
adhesive 47 n.
coat 226 vb.
grove
wood 366 n.
grovel
knuckle under
721 vb.
be servile 879 vb.
grow
become 1 vb.
augment 36 vb.
grow 36 vb.
produce 164 vb.
breed stock 369 vb.
cultivate 370 vb.
mature 669 vb.
growing
increasing 36 adj.
young 130 adj.
grow into
evolve 316 vb.
growl
ululate 409 vb.
ululation 409 n.
See **ululate**
be rude 885 vb.
anger 891 n.
be angry 891 vb.
sullenness 893 n.
threat 900 n.
threaten 900 vb.
grown-up
adult 134 n.

gusto
vigorousness
174 n.
pleasure 376 n.
taste 386 n.
vigour 571 n.
enjoyment 824 n.
gut
demolish 165 vb.
destroy 165 vb.
tube 263 n.
empty 300 vb.
cook 301 vb.
extract 304 vb.
involuntary
596 adj.
gut reaction
absence of thought
450 n.
intuition 476 n.
guts
vitality 162 n.
vigorousness
174 n.
insides 224 n.
vigour 571 n.
resolution 599 n.
stamina 600 n.
courage 855 n.
gutter
furrow 262 n.
conduit 351 n.
drain 351 n.
guttersnipe
low fellow 869 n.
guttural
speech sound
398 n.
hoarse 407 adj.
stridor 407 n.
guy
cable 47 n.
support 218 n.
male 372 n.
be absurd 497 vb.
image 551 n.
laughingstock
851 n.
prodigy 864 n.
not respect 921 vb.
detract 926 vb.
Guy Fawkes
deceiver 545 n.
image 551 n.
guzzle
eat 301 vb.
gluttonize 947 vb.
gybe
navigate 269 vb.
gym
arena 724 n.
gymkhana
equitation 267 n.
contest 716 n.

amusement 837 n.
gymnasium
athletics 162 n.
meeting place
192 n.
academy 539 n.
arena 724 n.
gymnast
athlete 162 n.
proficient person
696 n.
gymnastics
athletics 162 n.
motion 265 n.
exercise 682 n.
contest 716 n.
sport 837 n.
gynaecologist
obstetrics 167 n.
doctor 658 n.
gynaecology
female 373 n.
medical art 658 n.
gypsy
extraneous 59 adj.
nonconformist
84 n.
wanderer 268 n.
gyrate
rotate 315 vb.
gyrocompass
sailing aid 269 n.
gyroscope
rotator 315 n.

H

haar
moisture 341 n.
cloud 355 n.
dimness 419 n.
opacity 423 n.
invisibility 444 n.
habeas corpus
transference 272 n.
warrant 737 n.
legal process 959 n.
haberdasher
clothier 228 n.
tradespeople 794 n.
habit
state 7 n.
habit 610 n.
vocation 622 n.
drug taking 949 n.
habitat
place 185 n.
situation 186 n.
locality 187 n.
abode 192 n.
habitation
edifice 164 n.
abode 192 n.

habit-forming
habitual 610 adj.
intoxicating
949 adj.
habitual
typical 83 adj.
repeated 106 adj.
habitual 610 adj.
habitué
habitué 610 n.
sociable person
882 n.
hacienda
house 192 n.
stock farm 369 n.
farm 370 n.
lands 777 n.
hack
cut 46 vb.
computerize 86 vb.
roughen 259 vb.
roughness 259 n.
ride 267 vb.
saddle horse 273 n.
coldness 380 n.
author 589 n.
wound 655 vb.
worker 686 n.
bungler 697 n.
servant 742 n.
hacker
computer 86 n.
hackle
plumage 259 n.
hackneyed
imitative 20 adj.
known 490 adj.
aphoristic 496 adj.
feeble 572 adj.
usual 610 adj.
used 673 adj.
dull 840 adj.
hacksaw
notch 260 n.
had, be
be duped 544 vb.
pay too much
811 vb.
haddock
fish food 301 n.
had enough
be defeated
728 vb.
Hades
destiny 155 n.
death 361 n.
the dead 361 n.
hell 972 n.
mythic hell 972 n.
had it
dying 361 adj.
defeated 728 adj.
haematologist
doctor 658 n.

haematology
blood 335 n.
haemoglobin
blood 335 n.
haemophilia
haemorrhage
302 n.
blood 335 n.
fluidity 335 n.
blood disease
651 n.
haemorrhage
haemorrhage
302 n.
blood disease
651 n.
haemorrhoids
swelling 253 n.
digestive disorders
651 n.
hag
old woman 133 n.
sorceress 983 n.
haggard
lean 206 adj.
fatigued 684 adj.
suffering 825 adj.
haggis
meat 301 n.
haggle
make terms
766 vb.
bargain 791 vb.
trade 791 vb.
cheapen 812 vb.
be parsimonious
816 vb.
hagiography
biography 590 n.
praise 923 n.
theology 973 n.
ha-ha
gap 201 n.
fence 235 n.
laugh 835 vb.
haiku
verse form 593 n.
hail
crowd 74 n.
rain 350 n.
rain 350 n.
wintriness 380 n.
cry 408 n.
cry 408 vb.
call 547 n.
speak to 583 vb.
great 884 vb.
show respect
920 vb.
applaud 923 vb.
hail-fellow-well-met
friendly 880 adj.
sociable 882 adj.

hailstone
wintriness 380 n.
hair
small thing 33 n.
fibre 208 n.
hair 259 n.
hairdo
hairdressing 843 n.
hairdresser
beautician 843 n.
hairless
hairless 229 adj.
**hair of the dog
that bit one**
drunkenness 949 n.
hairpin bend
curve 248 n.
hair-raising
exciting 821 adj.
frightening
854 adj.
hair's breadth
short distance
200 n.
narrowness 206 n.
hair shirt
asceticism 945 n.
hair-splitting
discrimination
463 n.
argument 475 n.
sophistry 477 n.
fastidiousness
862 n.
hairy
hairy 259 adj.
frightening
854 adj.
hajj
piety 979 n.
act of worship
981 n.
halberd
axe 723 n.
spear 723 n.
halcyon
tranquil 266 adj.
peaceful 717 adj.
palmy 730 adj.
halcyon days
weather 340 n.
palmy days 730 n.
joy 824 n.
hale and hearty
healthy 650 adj.
half
part 53 n.
bisection 92 n.
half a chance
fair chance 159 n.
half-a-dozen
over five 99 n.
half a loaf
compromise 770 n.

writing 586 n.
handy
little 196 adj.
near 200 adj.
light 323 adj.
useful 640 adj.
skilful 694 adj.
handyman
mender 656 n.
proficient person
696 n.
servant 742 n.
hang
hang 217 vb.
pendency 217 n.
kill 362 vb.
curse 899 int.
execute 963 vb.
hang (a picture)
show 522 vb.
hang about
wait 136 vb.
be in motion
265 vb.
be inactive 679 vb.
hangar
stable 192 n.
air travel 271 n.
hang around
expect 507 vb.
See **await**
hang back
be late 136 vb.
avoid 620 vb.
refuse 760 vb.
be modest 874 vb.
hang by a
thread
be uncertain
474 vb.
be in danger
661 vb.
hangdog
guilty 936 adj.
hang down
hang 217 vb.
descend 309 vb.
hang, draw and
quarter
execute 963 vb.
hanger
hanger 217 n.
hanger-on
successor 67 n.
concomitant 89 n.
follower 284 n.
dependant 742 n.
toady 879 n.
flatterer 925 n.
hang fire
wait 136 vb.
pause 145 vb.
move slowly
278 vb.

be unwilling
598 vb.
not act 677 vb.
be inactive 679 vb.
refuse 760 vb.
hang-gliding
aeronautics 271 n.
sport 837 n.
hanging
hanging 217 adj.
pendency 217 n.
killing 362 n.
capital punishment
963 n.
hangings
hanging object
217 n.
covering 226 n.
hangman
destroyer 168 n.
killer 362 n.
indoor game 837 n.
hang on
affix 45 vb.
wait 136 vb.
go on 146 vb.
persevere 600 vb.
hang oneself
kill oneself 362 vb.
hang on to
hang 217 vb.
store 632 vb.
retain 778 vb.
hang out
jut 254 vb.
dry 342 vb.
amuse oneself
637 vb.
be inactive 679 vb.
hangout
abode 192 n.
hang over
impend 155 vb.
be high 209 vb.
hang 217 vb.
fly 271 vb.
frighten 854 vb.
threaten 900 vb.
hangover
sequel 67 n.
crapulence 949 n.
hang together
accord 24 vb.
unite with 45 vb.
cohere 48 vb.
concur 181 vb.
be reasonable
475 vb.
hang up
terminate 69 vb.
cease 145 vb.
hang 217 vb.
hang-up
idea 451 n.

attention 455 n.
prejudgment 481 n.
eccentricity 503 n.
hang upon
depend 157 vb.
hank
bunch 74 n.
hanker after
regret 830 vb.
desire 859 vb.
hanky-panky
deception 542 n.
perfidy 930 n.
hansom
cab 274 n.
haphazard
nonuniform 17 adj.
casual 159 adj.
indiscriminate
464 adj.
hapless
unfortunate
731 adj.
happen
happen 154 vb.
be true 494 vb.
happening
event 154 n.
happiness
pleasure 376 n.
happiness 824 n.
cheerfulness 833 n.
happy
apt 24 adj.
opportune 137 adj.
comfortable
376 adj.
elegant 575 adj.
willing 597 adj.
good 615 adj.
happy 824 adj.
pleased 824 adj.
drunk 949 adj.
happy-clappy
fervent 818 adj.
pious 979 adj.
happy ending
good 615 n.
success 727 n.
happy event
propagation 167 n.
happy-go-lucky
cheerful 833 adj.
happy medium
average 30 n.
middle way 625 n.
hara-kiri
suicide 362 n.
punishment 963 n.
harangue
teach 534 vb.
be diffuse 570 vb.
diffuseness 570 n.
orate 579 vb.

oration 579 n.
harass
oppress 735 vb.
torment 827 vb.
be malevolent
898 vb.
harbinger
precursor 66 n.
omen 511 n.
informant 524 n.
messenger 529 n.
harbour
stopping place
145 n.
goal 295 n.
shelter 662 n.
harbourage
shelter 662 n.
hard
hard 326 adj.
puzzling 517 adj.
unclear 568 adj.
laborious 682 adj.
difficult 700 adj.
adverse 731 adj.
thick-skinned
820 adj.
paining 827 adj.
unjust 914 adj.
impenitent
940 adj.
intoxicating
949 adj.
hard-bitten
thick-skinned
820 adj.
hard-boiled
severe 735 adj.
thick-skinned
820 adj.
hard by
near 200 adj.
near 200 adv.
hard cash
money 797 n.
hard-core
obstinate 602 adj.
hard drug
drug 949 n.
harden
harden 326 vb.
mature 669 vb.
be dear 811 vb.
harden one's
heart
be severe 735 vb.
refuse 760 vb.
be hostile 881 vb.
be pitiless 906 vb.
be impenitent
940 vb.
hard feelings
feeling 818 n.
enmity 881 n.

resentment 891 n.
hard frost
wintriness 380 n.
hard going
difficulty 700 n.
hard-headed
severe 735 adj.
hard-hearted
cruel 898 adj.
pitiless 906 adj.
hard-hitting
disapproving
924 adj.
hard labour
labour 682 n.
penalty 963 n.
hard lines
misfortune 731 n.
hard luck
nondesign 618 n.
misfortune 731 n.
hardly
slightly 33 adv.
seldom 140 adv.
hardly any
few 105 adj.
hardly ever
seldom 140 adv.
hardness
hardness 326 n.
difficulty 700 n.
hardness of
hearing
deafness 416 n.
hard-nosed
obstinate
602 adj.
hard of hearing
deaf 416 adj.
hard on
nearly 200 adv.
oppressive 735 adj.
unjust 914 adj.
hard-pressed
hasty 680 adj.
in difficulties
700 adj.
hard put to it
in difficulties
700 adj.
poor 801 adj.
hard sell
advertisement
528 n.
inducement 612 n.
sale 793 n.
hardship
adversity 731 n.
annoyance 827 n.
hard shoulder
road 624 n.
hard stuff
alcoholic drink
301 n.

heap
great quantity
32 n.
chief part 52 n.
accumulation 74 n.
bring together
74 vb.
bunch 74 n.
bulk 195 n.
store 632 n.
store 632 vb.
acquire 771 vb.
acquisition 771 n.
wealth 800 n.
heaps
finite quantity
26 n.
great quantity
32 n.
multitude 104 n.
funds 797 n.
hear
have feeling
374 vb.
hear 415 vb.
enquire 459 vb.
judge 480 vb.
heard
known 490 adj.
hearer
listener 415 n.
hear, hear
amen 488 int.
bravo 923 int.
hearing
sense 374 n.
auditory 415 adj.
hearing 415 n.
listening 415 n.
legal trial 959 n.
hearing aid
hearing aid 415 n.
hearing dog
dog 365 n.
hearken
hear 415 vb.
hearsay
evidence 466 n.
information 524 n.
rumour 529 n.
hearse
vehicle 274 n.
funeral 364 n.
heart
essence 1 n.
essential part 5 n.
middle 70 n.
focus 76 n.
insides 224 n.
interiority 224 n.
centre 225 n.
life 360 n.
spirit 447 n.
chief thing 638 n.

affections 817 n.
courage 855 n.
love token 889 n.
darling 890 n.
heartache
pain 377 n.
suffering 825 n.
dejection 834 n.
heart attack
cardiovascular
disease 651 n.
heartbreaking
distressing 827 adj.
heart-broken
unhappy 825 adj.
heartburn
digestive disorders
651 n.
heart condition
cardiovascular
disease 651 n.
hearten
invigorate 174 vb.
aid 703 vb.
animate 821 vb.
relieve 831 vb.
cheer 833 vb.
give courage
855 vb.
heart failure
cardiovascular
disease 651 n.
hearth
home 192 n.
furnace 383 n.
refuge 662 n.
heartily
greatly 32 vb.
heartland
district 184 n.
interiority 224 n.
land 344 n.
heartless
impassive 820 adj.
cruel 898 adj.
pitiless 906 adj.
impenitent
940 adj.
heart-melting
pleasurable
826 adj.
heart-rending
distressing
827 adj.
hearts
card game 837 n.
heart's blood
essential part 5 n.
interiority 224 n.
life 360 n.
heart's desire
objective 617 n.
aspiration 852 n.
loved one 887 n.

heart-shaped
curved 248 adj.
heartstrings
affections 817 n.
heartthrob
a beauty 841 n.
loved one 887 n.
heart-to-heart
chat 584 n.
heart trouble
cardiovascular
disease 651 n.
heart-warming
pleasant 376 adj.
pleasurable
826 adj.
hearty
vigorous 174 adj.
healthy 650 adj.
feeling 818 adj.
cheerful 833 adj.
friendly 880 adj.
sociable 882 adj.
heat
part 53 n.
heat 379 n.
heat 381 vb.
contest 716 n.
libido 859 n.
anger 891 n.
heated
hot 379 adj.
heated 381 adj.
heater
heater 383 n.
heath
desert 172 n.
plain 348 n.
wood 366 n.
heathen
unbeliever 486 n.
heathen 974 n.
heathenish
974 adj.
heresy 977 n.
heretical 977 adj.
heather
plant 366 n.
purpleness 436 n.
Heath Robinson
imaginative
513 adj.
heating
heating 381 adj.
heating 381 n.
heave
carry 273 vb.
impel 279 vb.
impulse 279 n.
propel 287 vb.
draw 288 vb.
vomit 300 vb.
oscillate 317 vb.
breathe 352 vb.

exertion 682 n.
work 682 vb.
show feeling
818 vb.
heaven
summit 213 n.
heaven 971 n.
heavenly
celestial 321 adj.
super 644 adj.
pleasurable
826 adj.
divine 965 adj.
heaven-sent
opportune 137 adj.
good 615 adj.
heave to
bring to rest
266 vb.
navigate 269 vb.
heavy
substantial 3 adj.
great 32 adj.
strong 162 adj.
inert 175 adj.
alcoholic drink
301 n.
weighty 322 adj.
dense 324 adj.
the press 528 n.
forceful 571 adj.
bad 645 adj.
inactive 679 adj.
laborious 682 adj.
severe 735 adj.
tedious 838 adj.
dull 840 adj.
heavy-going
serious 834 adj.
heavy-handed
violent 176 adj.
weighty 322 adj.
oppressive 735 adj.
heavy-hearted
unhappy 825 adj.
melancholic
834 adj.
heavyweight
athlete 162 n.
weighty 322 adj.
bigwig 638 n.
pugilist 722 n.
heavy with
impending 155 adj.
fertilized 167 adj.
prolific 171 adj.
hecatomb
oblation 981 n.
heckle
interrogate 459 vb.
be obstructive
702 vb.
torment 827 vb.
not respect 921 vb.

disapprove 924 vb.
hector
boast 877 vb.
be insolent 878 vb.
threaten 900 vb.
hedge
partition 231 n.
edge 234 n.
fence 235 n.
wood 366 n.
screen 421 n.
avoid 620 vb.
shelter 662 n.
obstacle 702 n.
defend 713 vb.
be cautious 858 vb.
hedgehog
mammal 365 n.
hedgerow
fence 235 n.
wood 366 n.
hedonism
pleasure 376 n.
philosophy 449 n.
enjoyment 824 n.
sensualism 944 n.
heed
attention 455 n.
be attentive
455 vb.
be careful 457 vb.
carefulness 457 n.
obey 739 vb.
observe 768 vb.
caution 858 n.
heedless
inattentive
456 adj.
negligent 458 adj.
forgetful 506 adj.
rash 857 adj.
heel
foot 214 n.
be oblique 220 vb.
rear 238 n.
repair 656 vb.
cad 938 n.
hefty
stalwart 162 adj.
Hegira
departure 296 n.
heifer
young creature
132 n.
cattle 365 n.
female animal
373 n.
height
height 209 n.
high land 209 n.
metrology 465 n.
heighten
augment 36 vb.
enlarge 197 vb.

egotist 932 n.
sensualist 944 n.
glutton 947 n.

hoi polloi
crowd 74 n.
everyman 79 n.
averageness 732 n.
commonalty
869 n.

hoist
elevate 310 vb.
elevation 310 n.
flag 547 n.

**hoist with one's
own petard**
defeated 728 adj.

hoity-toity
proud 871 adj.

hold
fastening 47 n.
contain 56 vb.
comprise 78 vb.
stay 144 vb.
cease 145 vb.
go on 146 vb.
influence 178 n.
prevail 178 vb.
be present 189 vb.
cellar 194 n.
receptacle 194 n.
base 214 n.
support 218 vb.
believe 485 vb.
be of the opinion
that 485 vb.
be true 494 vb.
affirm 532 vb.
storage 632 n.
store 632 vb.
preserve 666 vb.
wrestling 716 n.
governance 733 n.
arrest 747 vb.
imprison 747 vb.
restrain 747 vb.
possess 773 vb.
possession 773 n.
retain 778 vb.
retention 778 n.
impress 821 vb.

holdall
bag 194 n.
storage 632 n.

hold back
pause 145 vb.
doubt 486 vb.
be unwilling
598 vb.
avoid 620 vb.
hinder 702 vb.
compel 740 vb.
restrain 747 vb.
retain 778 vb.

holder
receptacle 194 n.
handle 218 n.
storage 632 n.
possessor 776 n.

hold fast
cohere 48 vb.
persevere 600 vb.
retain 778 vb.

hold forth
teach 534 vb.
orate 579 vb.

hold good
be 1 vb.
stay 144 vb.
be proved 478 vb.
be true 494 vb.
be wont 610 vb.

holding
inclusive 78 adj.
territory 184 n.
enclosure 235 n.
farm 370 n.
store 632 n.
possession 773 n.
estate 777 n.
lands 777 n.

hold it
stay 144 vb.
stop 266 int.

held off
be distant 199 vb.
avoid 620 vb.
not use 674 vb.
resist 715 vb.

hold on
wait 136 vb.
stay 144 vb.
stop 266 int.
progress 285 vb.
retain 778 vb.

hold one's own
be equal 28 vb.
withstand 704 vb.
be successful
727 vb.

hold out
affirm 532 vb.
stand firm 599 vb.
persevere 600 vb.
resist 715 vb.
offer 759 vb.
promise 764 vb.

hold over
put off 136 vb.

**hold the whip
hand**
prevail 178 vb.

hold tight
retain 778 vb.

hold up
put off 136 vb.
halt 145 vb.
support 218 vb.

elevate 310 vb.
hinder 702 vb.
retain 778 vb.
rob 788 vb.

holdup
delay 136 n.
hitch 702 n.
stealing 788 n.

hold water
be reasonable
475 vb.
be proved 478 vb.
be true 494 vb.

hole
circumstance 8 n.
disunion 46 n.
place 185 n.
dwelling 192 n.
small house 192 n.
receptacle 194 n.
gap 201 n.
cavity 255 n.
opening 263 n.
orifice 263 n.
pierce 263 vb.
insert 303 vb.
refuge 662 n.
shelter 662 n.
predicament 700 n.

hole-and-corner
stealthy 525 adj.

holiday
lull 145 n.
absence 190 n.
leisure 681 n.
repose 683 n.
reposeful 683 adj.
permit 756 n.
amusement 837 n.

holier than thou
aphoristic 496 adj.
affected 850 adj.
proud 871 adj.
disapproving
924 adj.
orthodox 976 adj.
pietistic 979 adj.

holiness
virtue 933 n.
divine attribute
965 n.
sanctity 979 n.

**holistic
medicine**
medical art 658 n.

holler
vociferate 408 vb.

hollow
empty 190 adj.
lowness 210 n.
be deep 211 vb.
depth 211 n.
cavity 255 n.
concave 255 adj.

make concave
255 vb.
furrow 262 n.
opening 263 n.
lower 311 vb.
lowering 311 n.
rare 325 adj.
resonant 404 adj.
hoarse 407 adj.
affected 850 adj.
ostentatious
875 adj.

hollow-eyed
fatigued 684 adj.

Hollywood
cinema 445 n.
drama 594 n.

holocaust
slaughter 362 n.
fire 379 n.
burning 381 n.
oblation 981 n.

hologram
image 551 n.
photography
551 n.

holster
case 194 n.
arsenal 723 n.

holy
worshipful
866 adj.
virtuous 933 adj.
prudish 950 adj.
divine 965 adj.
godlike 965 adj.
religious 973 adj.
scriptural 975 adj.
pious 979 adj.
sanctified 979 adj.

Holy Bible
scripture 975 n.

**Holy
Communion**
Christian rite
988 n.
Holy Communion
988 n.

holy day
holy day 988 n.

Holy Grail
objective 617 n.
ritual object 988 n.

holy ground
holy place 990 n.

Holy of Holies
ritual object 988 n.
holy place 990 n.

holy terror
violent creature
176 n.
bad person 938 n.

Holy Week
holy day 988 n.

homage
submission 721 n.
respects 920 n.
worship 981 n.
ritual act 988 n.

home
native 191 adj.
abode 192 n.
home 192 n.
house 192 n.
retreat 192 n.
near 200 adj.
interior 224 adj.
limit 236 n.
social gathering
882 n.

home alone
neglected 458 adj.

homecoming
return 286 n.
arrival 295 n.

home economics
cookery 301 n.

home help
cleaner 648 n.

homeland
territory 184 n.
home 192 n.

homeless
unrelated 10 adj.
alone 88 adj.
poor 801 adj.

homely
comfortable
376 adj.
plain 573 adj.
pleasurable
826 adj.
ugly 842 adj.
plebeian
869 adj.

homemade
artless 699 adj.

homesickness
suffering 825 n.
regret 830 n.
melancholy 834 n.
desire 859 n.

homespun
textile 222 n.
roughness 259 n.
textural 331 adj.
plain 573 adj.
plainness 573 n.
artless 699 adj.
plebeian 869 adj.

homestead
home 192 n.
lands 777 n.

home truth
truth 494 n.
veracity 540 n.
censure 924 n.
accusation 928 n.

hors de combat
useless 641 adj.
hors d'oeuvre
prelude 66 n.
savouriness 390 n.
hors-d'oeuvres
hors-d'oeuvres
301 n.
horse
horse 273 n.
mammal 365 n.
male animal
372 n.
drug-taking 949 n.
horse about
be absurd 497 vb.
horse-breeding
animal husbandry
369 n.
horse chestnut
tree 366 n.
horsemanship
skill 694 n.
horseplay
fight 716 n.
ridicule 851 n.
horsepower
energy 160 n.
strength 162 n.
vehicle 274 n.
metrology 465 n.
horse racing
equitation 267 n.
gambling 618 n.
racing 716 n.
horse sense
intelligence 498 n.
horseshoe
curve 248 n.
omen 511 n.
talisman 983 n.
horse-trading
conditions 766 n.
barter 791 n.
horsewhip
flog 963 vb.
scourge 964 n.
horticulture
flower 366 n.
agriculture 370 n.
hosanna
cheers 835 int.
rejoicing 835 n.
celebration 876 n.
applause 923 n.
bravo 923 int.
praise 923 n.
hymn 981 n.
hose
legwear 228 n.
tube 263 n.
water 339 n.
irrigate 341 vb.
irrigator 341 n.

conduit 351 n.
extinguisher 382 n.
hosier
clothier 228 n.
hospice
retreat 192 n.
hospital 658 n.
shelter 662 n.
hospitable
liberal 813 adj.
friendly 880 adj.
sociable 882 adj.
benevolent
897 adj.
hospital
hospital 658 n.
hospitality
liberality 813 n.
friendliness 880 n.
sociability 882 n.
benevolence 897 n.
hospital trust
hospital 658 n.
host
band 74 n.
multitude 104 n.
infection 651 n.
army 722 n.
friend 880 n.
sociable person
882 n.
the sacrament
988 n.
hostage
prisoner 750 n.
security 767 n.
taking 786 n.
hostel
station 187 n.
quarters 192 n.
retreat 192 n.
hostelry
inn 192 n.
hostess
sociable person
882 n.
hostile
contrary 14 adj.
disagreeing 25 adj.
separate 46 adj.
opposing 704 adj.
adverse 731 adj.
hostile 881 adj.
unsociable 883 adj.
malevolent
898 adj.
unkind 898 adj.
disapproving
924 adj.
hostile, be
be hostile 881 vb.
hostilities
fight 716 n.
belligerency 718 n.

enmity 881 n.
hostility
contrariety 14 n.
disagreement 25 n.
hindrance 702 n.
opposition 704 n.
dissension 709 n.
enmity 881 n.
hatred 888 n.
disapprobation
924 n.
hot
violent 176 adj.
hot 379 adj.
pungent 388 adj.
red 431 adj.
angry 891 adj.
impure 951 adj.
lecherous 951 adj.
illegal 954 adj.
hot air
insubstantial thing
4 n.
polarity 14 n.
lightness 323 n.
be hot 379 vb.
heater 383 n.
overestimation
482 n.
empty talk 515 n.
chatter 581 n.
excited 821 adj.
boast 877 n.
hotbed
abundance 171 n.
heater 383 n.
badness 645 n.
pitfall 663 n.
hot-button
important 638 adj.
hotching with
full 54 adj.
multitudinous
104 adj.
hotchpotch
nonuniformity
17 n.
medley 43 n.
disorder 61 n.
hot dog
meal 301 n.
hotel
inn 192 n.
hotelier
caterer 633 n.
hotfoot
hasty 680 adj.
hot-headed
hasty 680 adj.
fervent 818 adj.
excitable 822 adj.
rash 857 adj.
hothouse
arbour 194 n.

garden 370 n.
heater 383 n.
hot line
telecommunication
531 n.
hotpot
dish 301 n.
hot potato
difficulty 700 n.
hot-rod
automobile 274 n.
hot seat
predicament 700 n.
hotting
automobile 274 n.
hot toddy
alcoholic drink
301 n.
**hot under the
collar**
excited 821 adj.
angry 891 adj.
hot up
heat 381 vb.
hot water
heat 379 n.
predicament 700 n.
hour
juncture 8 n.
period 110 n.
hourglass
timekeeper 117 n.
contraction 198 n.
curved 248 adj.
house
race 11 n.
genealogy 169 n.
place 187 vb.
abode 192 n.
house 192 n.
music 412 n.
onlookers 441 n.
class 538 n.
playgoer 594 n.
safeguard 660 vb.
sovereign 741 n.
house arrest
detention 747 n.
seclusion 883 n.
houseboat
small house 192 n.
boat 275 n.

house-breaking
stealing 788 n.
household
family 11 n.
group 74 n.
home 192 n.
known 490 adj.
usual 610 adj.
household name
famousness 866 n.
housekeeper
resident 191 n.
caterer 633 n.
manager 690 n.
domestic 742 n.
retainer 742 n.
servant 742 n.
keeper 749 n.
housekeeping
management
689 n.
housemaid
domestic 742 n.
houseman
doctor 658 n.
house of cards
weak thing 163 n.
**House of
Commons**
parliament 692 n.
House of Lords
parliament 692 n.
housetop
vertex 213 n.
roof 226 n.
housewarming
start 68 n.
festivity 837 n.
social gathering
882 n.
housewife
resident 191 n.
case 194 n.
female 373 n.
caterer 633 n.
manager 690 n.
housework
labour 682 n.
housing
housing 192 n.
frame 218 n.
dressing 228 n.
hovel
small house
192 n.
hover
vary 152 vb.
impend 155 vb.
be high 209 vb.
hang 217 vb.
be in motion
265 vb.
wander 267 vb.
fly 271 vb.

ill repute
disrepute 867 n.
ill-spent
profitless 641 adj.
ill-treat
ill-treat 645 vb.
be severe 735 vb.
illuminate
make bright
417 vb.
colour 425 vb.
interpret 520 vb.
paint 553 vb.
decorate 844 vb.
illumination
light 417 n.
lighting 420 n.
discovery 484 n.
knowledge 490 n.
interpretation
520 n.
art 551 n.
painting 553 n.
ornamental art
844 n.
revelation 975 n.
illusion
appearance 445 n.
error 495 n.
deception 542 n.
sleight 542 n.
illusory
erroneous 495 adj.
imaginary 513 adj.
illustrate
exemplify 83 vb.
interpret 520 vb.
represent 551 vb.
decorate 844 vb.
illustration
example 83 n.
interpretation
520 n.
representation
551 n.
picture 553 n.
edition 589 n.
ornamental art
844 n.
illustrator
artist 556 n.
illustrious
noteworthy
866 adj.
renowned 866 adj.
ill will
badness 645 n.
adversity 731 n.
enmity 881 n.
hatred 888 n.
malevolence 898 n.
envy 912 n.
image
copy 22 n.

appearance 445 n.
ideality 513 n.
show 522 vb.
indication 547 n.
image 551 n.
idol 982 n.
imagery
imagination 513 n.
metaphor 519 n.
imaginary
imaginary 513 adj.
imagination
imagination 513 n.
imaginative
imaginative
513 adj.
imagine
perceive 447 adj.
imagine 513 vb.
image-maker
publicizer 528 n.
imbalance
inequality 29 n.
changeableness
152 n.
distortion 246 n.
imbecile
weak 163 adj.
foolish 499 adj.
unintelligent
499 adj.
fool 501 n.
*having a learning
disability* 503 adj.
imbibe
absorb 299 vb.
drink 301 vb.
imbroglio
medley 43 n.
complexity 61 n.
disorder 61 n.
predicament
700 n.
imbue
mix 43 vb.
combine 50 vb.
pervade 189 vb.
drench 341 vb.
colour 425 vb.
educate 534 vb.
habituate 610 vb.
imitate
imitate 20 vb.
imitation
imitation 20 n.
imitative 20 adj.
substituted
150 adj.
false 541 adj.
sham 542 n.
spurious 542 adj.
bad taste 847 n.
imitative
imitative 20 adj.

imitator
imitator 20 n.
immaculate
perfect 646 adj.
clean 648 adj.
honourable
929 adj.
innocent 935 adj.
pure 950 adj.
immanent
intrinsic 5 adj.
immaterial
irrelevant 10 adj.
immaterial
320 adj.
unimportant
639 adj.
immature
immature 670 adj.
immeasurable
infinite 107 adj.
immediacy
instantaneity
116 n.
punctuality 135 n.
haste 680 n.
immediate
instantaneous
116 adj.
early 135 adj.
impending 155 adj.
speedy 277 adj.
hasty 680 adj.
immemorial
great 32 adj.
immense
enormous 32 adj.
infinite 107 adj.
huge 195 adj.
immerse
immerse
303 vb.
plunge 313 vb.
immersion
ingress 297 n.
plunge 313 n.
Christian rite
988 n.
immigrant
extraneous 59 adj.
foreigner 59 n.
settler 191 n.
incomer 297 n.
immigrate
travel 267 vb.
enter 297 vb.
immigration
ingress 297 n.
imminent
future 124 adj.
early 135 adj.
impending 155 adj.
approaching
289 adj.

immobile
permanent
144 adj.
fixed 153 adj.
still 266 adj.
nonactive 677 adj.
immobilize
bring to rest
266 vb.
make inactive
679 vb.
immoderate
violent 176 adj.
redundant 637 adj.
intemperate
943 adj.
immodest
vain 873 adj.
unchaste 951 adj.
immolate
kill 362 vb.
immoral
wrong 914 adj.
dishonest 930 adj.
heinous 934 adj.
vicious 934 adj.
wicked 934 adj.
impure 951 adj.
unchaste 951 adj.
immorality
wrong 914 n.
wickedness 934 n.
unchastity 951 n.
impiety 980 n.
immortal
existing 1 adj.
perpetual 115 adj.
renowned 866 adj.
godlike 965 adj.
immortalize
perpetuate
115 vb.
honour 866 vb.
immovable
firm 45 adj.
fixed 153 adj.
still 266 adj.
resolute 599 adj.
obstinate 602 adj.
immune
invulnerable
660 adj.
free 744 adj.
acquitted
960 adj.
immunity
safety 660 n.
escape 667 n.
freedom 744 n.
dueness 915 n.
nonliability 919 n.
immunize
doctor 658 vb.
safeguard 660 vb.

immure
circumscribe
232 vb.
enclose 235 vb.
imprison 747 vb.
immutable
perpetual 115 adj.
permanent
144 adj.
unchangeable
153 adj.
godlike 965 adj.
imp
demon 970 n.
elf 970 n.
sorcerer 983 n.
impact
affix 45 vb.
influence 178 n.
collision 279 n.
impulse 279 n.
excitation 821 n.
impacted
firm 45 adj.
impaired
incomplete 55 adj.
crippled 163 adj.
impairment
incompleteness
55 n.
impairment 655 n.
impale
pierce 263 vb.
impalpability
insubstantiality
4 n.
immateriality
320 n.
impart
inform 524 vb.
give 781 vb.
impartial
equal 28 adj.
neutral 625 adj.
indifferent 860 adj.
just 913 adj.
honourable
929 adj.
disinterested
931 adj.
impassable
closed 264 adj.
difficult 700 adj.
impasse
stop 145 n.
closure 264 n.
impossibility
470 n.
difficulty 700 n.
obstacle 702 n.
impassioned
forceful 571 adj.
fervent 818 adj.
excited 821 adj.

impassive
impassive 820 adj.
inexcitable
823 adj.
impatient
unwise 499 adj.
willing 597 adj.
hasty 680 adj.
fervent 818 adj.
excitable 822 adj.
rash 857 adj.
angry 891 adj.
irascible 892 adj.
impeachment
censure 924 n.
detraction 926 n.
accusation 928 n.
litigation 959 n.
impeccable
perfect 646 adj.
virtuous 933 adj.
innocent 935 adj.
impecunious
poor 801 adj.
impede
hinder 702 vb.
impediment
difficulty 700 n.
hindrance 702 n.
obstacle 702 n.
divorce 896 n.
impel
impel 279 vb.
impending
impending 155 adj.
impenetrable
closed 264 adj.
dense 324 adj.
impracticable
470 adj.
unintelligible
517 adj.
latent 523 adj.
difficult 700 adj.
thick-skinned
820 adj.
impenitent
impenitent
940 adj.
imperative
necessary 596 adj.
important 638 adj.
commanding
737 adj.
compelling
740 adj.
imperceptible
inconsiderable
33 adj.
slow 278 adj.
dim 419 adj.
invisible 444 adj.
imperceptive
insensible 375 adj.

indiscriminating
464 adj.
imperfect
imperfect 647 adj.
imperfection
insufficiency
636 n.
imperfection 647 n.
nonpreparation
670 n.
vice 934 n.
imperial
great 32 adj.
hair 259 n.
metrical 465 adj.
paper 631 n.
ruling 733 adj.
imperialism
nation 371 n.
governance 733 n.
imperil
endanger 661 vb.
imperious
authoritative
733 adj.
proud 871 adj.
insolent 878 adj.
impermanence
transience 114 n.
changeableness
152 n.
impermeable
strong 162 adj.
closed 264 adj.
dense 324 adj.
thick-skinned
820 adj.
impersonal
general 79 adj.
material 319 adj.
impassive 820 adj.
indifferent 860 adj.
unsociable 883 adj.
just 913 adj.
impersonate
represent 551 vb.
act 594 vb.
imperspicuity
imperspicuity
568 n.
impertinent
irrelevant 10 adj.
impertinent
878 adj.
imperturbable
impassive 820 adj.
inexcitable
823 adj.
impervious
closed 264 adj.
dense 324 adj.
obstinate 602 adj.
thick-skinned
820 adj.

impetigo
skin disease 651 n.
impetuous
furious 176 adj.
hasty 680 adj.
fervent 818 adj.
excitable 822 adj.
impetus
energy 160 n.
vigorousness
174 n.
spurt 277 n.
impulse 279 n.
motive 612 n.
impiety
impiety 980 n.
impinge
collide 279 vb.
encroach 306 vb.
touch 378 vb.
impious
impious 980 adj.
impish
fairylike 970 adj.
implacable
resolute 599 adj.
obstinate 602 adj.
severe 735 adj.
malevolent
898 adj.
pitiless 906 adj.
implant
affix 45 vb.
place 187 vb.
implant 303 vb.
educate 534 vb.
implausible
improbable
472 adj.
erroneous 495 adj.
implement
produce 164 vb.
instrument
628 n.
tool 630 n.
do 676 vb.
carry out 725 vb.
implementation
action 676 n.
completion 725 n.
implicate
accuse 928 vb.
implication
relation 9 n.
complexity 61 n.
meaning 514 n.
latency 523 n.
implicit
intrinsic 5 adj.
tacit 523 adj.
implore
entreat 761 vb.
imploring
entreaty 761 n.

supplicatory
761 adj.
imply
comprise 78 vb.
imply 523 vb.
hint 524 vb.
indicate 547 vb.
impolite
ill-bred 847 adj.
impertinent
878 adj.
discourteous
885 adj.
disrespectful
921 adj.
impolitic
foolish 499 adj.
inexpedient
643 adj.
import
relation 9 n.
transference 272 n.
ingress 297 n.
admit 299 vb.
reception 299 n.
meaning 514 n.
importance 638 n.
importance
importance 638 n.
important
necessary 596 adj.
important 638 adj.
importation
transference 272 n.
ingress 297 n.
reception 299 n.
importer
carrier 273 n.
merchant 794 n.
importunate
annoying 827 adj.
importune
request 761 vb.
torment 827 vb.
impose
place 187 vb.
print 587 vb.
necessitate 596 vb.
command 737 vb.
compel 740 vb.
command respect
920 vb.
imposing
notable 638 adj.
impressive 821 adj.
worshipful
866 adj.
imposition
addition 38 n.
bane 659 n.
command 737 n.
demand 737 n.
tax 809 n.
injustice 914 n.

undueness 916 n.
penalty 963 n.
impossible
impossible 470 adj.
annoying 827 adj.
intolerable 827 adj.
wonderful 864 adj.
impostor
impostor 545 n.
bad person 938 n.
imposture
duplicity 541 n.
deception 542 n.
cunning 698 n.
impotent
impotent 161 adj.
powerless 161 adj.
unproductive
172 adj.
impound
imprison 747 vb.
impoverished
weakened 163 adj.
poor 801 adj.
impracticable
unapt 25 adj.
impracticable
470 adj.
useless 641 adj.
difficult 700 adj.
impractical
misjudging
481 adj.
imaginative
513 adj.
imprecation
entreaty 761 n.
malediction 899 n.
prayers 981 n.
imprecise
inexact 495 adj.
unclear 568 adj.
impregnable
strong 162 adj.
invulnerable
660 adj.
pure 950 adj.
impregnation
mixture 43 n.
propagation 167 n.
impresario
exhibitor 522 n.
stage manager
594 n.
impress
effect 157 n.
make concave
255 vb.
mark 547 vb.
engrave 555 vb.
compel 740 vb.
impress 821 vb.
impressible
soft 327 adj.

impressible
819 adj.
impression
copy 22 n.
concavity 255 n.
sense 374 n.
spectacle 445 n.
idea 451 n.
opinion 485 n.
indication 547 n.
label 547 n.
representation
551 n.
printing 555 n.
print 587 n.
edition 589 n.
feeling 818 n.
impressionable
sentient 374 adj.
impressible
819 adj.
excitable 822 adj.
Impressionism
school of painting
553 n.
impressive
appearing 445 adj.
impressive 821 adj.
impress on
emphasize 532 vb.
imprimatur
assent 488 n.
permit 756 n.
orthodoxism
976 n.
imprint
copy 22 n.
concavity 255 n.
identification
547 n.
See **label**
label 547 n.
mark 547 vb.
imprison
imprison 747 vb.
improbable
improbable
472 adj.
impromptu
musical piece
412 n.
extempore
609 adv.
spontaneity 609 n.
spontaneous
609 adj.
unprepared
670 adj.
improper
unapt 25 adj.
unwise 499 adj.
inexpedient
643 adj.
not nice 645 adj.

vulgar 847 adj.
discreditable
867 adj.
disreputable
867 adj.
wrong 914 adj.
vicious 934 adj.
improper
fraction
numerical element
85 n.
impropriety
inaptitude 25 n.
inelegance 576 n.
inexpedience
643 n.
bad taste 847 n.
wrong 914 n.
undueness 916 n.
vice 934 n.
guilty act 936 n.
improve
grow 36 vb.
flourish 615 vb.
do good 644 vb.
get better 654 vb.
make better
654 vb.
beautify 841 vb.
improvement
improvement
654 n.
improve on
be superior 34 vb.
make better
654 vb.
improvident
negligent 458 adj.
prodigal 815 adj.
rash 857 adj.
improvise
compose music
413 vb.
play music 413 vb.
improvise 609 vb.
imprudent
inexpedient
643 adj.
rash 857 adj.
impudent
impertinent
878 adj.
discourteous
885 adj.
impugn
negate 533 vb.
impulse
impulse 279 n.
intuition 476 n.
necessity 596 n.
whim 604 n.
spontaneity 609 n.
motive 612 n.
feeling 818 n.

impulsive
intuitive 476 adj.
involuntary
596 adj.
spontaneous
609 adj.
hasty 680 adj.
excitable 822 adj.
rash 857 adj.
impunity
nonliability 919 n.
acquittal 960 n.
impure
impure 951 adj.
impious 980 adj.
impurity
impurity 951 n.
impute
attribute 158 vb.
blame 924 vb.
accuse 928 vb.
in
inside 224 adv.
usual 610 adj.
fashionable
848 adj.
inability
impotence 161 n.
uselessness 641 n.
unskilfulness
695 n.
inaccessible
impracticable
470 adj.
inaccurate
negligent 458 adj.
indiscriminating
464 adj.
inexact 495 adj.
inactive
inactive 679 adj.
inactivity
weakness 163 n.
inactivity 679 n.
inadequate
unequal 29 adj.
incomplete 55 adj.
powerless 161 adj.
deficient 307 adj.
insufficient
636 adj.
imperfect 647 adj.
unskilful 695 adj.
inadmissible
unapt 25 adj.
extraneous 59 adj.
inexpedient
643 adj.
wrong 914 adj.
inadvertent
inattentive
456 adj.
unintentional
618 adj.

inadvisable
inexpedient
643 adj.
inalienable
due 915 adj.
inane
insubstantial 4 adj.
empty 190 adj.
foolish 499 adj.
meaningless
515 adj.
feeble 572 adj.
inanimate
mindless 448 adj.
inactive 679 adj.
in a nutshell
proverbially
496 adv.
concisely 569 adv.
inapplicable
irrelevant 10 adj.
unapt 25 adj.
useless 641 adj.
inapposite
irrelevant 10 adj.
inappreciable
unimportant
639 adj.
inappropriate
unrelated 10 adj.
unapt 25 adj.
inexpedient
643 adj.
ridiculous 849 adj.
wrong 914 adj.
inaptitude
inaptitude 25 n.
in arrears
nonpaying 805 adj.
inarticulate
voiceless 578 adj.
taciturn 582 adj.
modest 874 adj.
inartistic
bungled 695 adj.
inasmuch
concerning 9 adv.
inattentive
inattentive
456 adj.
inaudible
silent 399 adj.
muted 401 adj.
deaf 416 adj.
unintelligible
517 adj.
voiceless 578 adj.
inaugural
precursory 66 adj.
beginning 68 adj.
inauguration
debut 68 n.
mandate 751 n.
celebration 876 n.

inauspicious
inopportune
138 adj.
predicting 511 adj.
evil 616 adj.
adverse 731 adj.
unpromising
853 adj.
in black and
white
written 586 adj.
inborn
genetic 5 adj.
with affections
817 adj.
inbred
genetic 5 adj.
extrinsic 6 adj.
ethnic 11 adj.
combined 50 adj.
with affections
817 adj.
incalculable
multitudinous
104 adj.
infinite 107 adj.
casual 159 adj.
incandescent
fiery 379 adj.
luminous 417 adj.
incantation
sorcery 983 n.
spell 983 n.
incapable
powerless 161 adj.
unskilful 695 adj.
incapacitated
impotent 161 adj.
crippled 163 adj.
incarcerate
imprison 747 vb.
incarnate
material 319 adj.
materialize
319 adj.
alive 360 adj.
manifest 522 vb.
godlike 965 adj.
incarnation
essential part 5 n.
materiality 319 n.
manifestation
522 n.
representation
551 n.
revelation 975 n.
incendiary
destructive 165 adj.
violent 176 adj.
violent creature
176 n.
arson 381 n.
heating 381 adj.
evildoer 904 n.

inflect
voice 577 vb.
inflexible
unchangeable
153 adj.
straight 249 adj.
rigid 326 adj.
resolute 599 adj.
obstinate 602 adj.
severe 735 adj.
pitiless 906 adj.
inflexion
adjunct 40 n.
sequel 67 n.
extremity 69 n.
change 143 n.
curvature 248 n.
word 559 n.
grammar 564 n.
part of speech
564 n.
pronunciation
577 n.
inflict
be severe 735 vb.
compel 740 vb.
inflorescence
flower 366 n.
influence
influence 178 n.
influence 178 vb.
importance 638 n.
manage 689 vb.
spell 983 n.
influential
influential 178 adj.
influenza
infection 651 n.
influx
ingress 297 n.
info
information 524 n.
inform
inform 524 vb.
inform against
inform 524 vb.
accuse 928 vb.
indict 928 vb.
informal
lax 734 adj.
nonobservant
769 adj.
illegal 954 adj.
informal dress
informal dress
228 n.
informality
laxity 734 n.
scope 744 n.
nonobservance
769 n.
informant
witness 466 n.
informant 524 n.

informatics
information 524 n.
information
erudition 490 n.
information 524 n.
accusation 928 n.
**information
superhighway**
computing 86 n.
information 524 n.
informative
expressive 516 adj.
informative
524 adj.
informer
secret service
459 n.
informer 524 n.
infraction
nonconformity
84 n.
disobedience
738 n.
undueness 916 n.
undutifulness
918 n.
infra dig
degrading 867 adj.
infrangible
tough 329 adj.
**infrared
radiation**
radiation 417 n.
infrastructure
base 214 n.
frame 218 n.
structure 331 n.
infrequent
infrequent 140 adj.
infringement
nonconformity
84 n.
overstepping 306 n.
opposition 704 n.
attack 712 n.
disobedience
738 n.
nonobservance
769 n.
borrowing 785 n.
undueness 916 n.
lawbreaking 954 n.
infuriate
make mad 503 vb.
enrage 891 vb.
infuse
educate 534 vb.
infusion
a mixture 43 n.
mixture 43 n.
tincture 43 n.
reception 299 n.
draught 301 n.
insertion 303 n.

solution 337 n.
medicine 658 n.
tonic 658 n.
ingenious
imaginative
513 adj.
skilful 694 adj.
cunning 698 adj.
ingenue
acting 594 n.
innocent 935 n.
ingenuous
veracious 540 adj.
artless 699 adj.
honourable
929 adj.
trustworthy
929 adj.
ingest
absorb 299 vb.
eat 301 vb.
inglenook
home 192 n.
inglorious
inglorious
867 adj.
dishonest 930 adj.
ingrained
intrinsic 5 adj.
combined 50 adj.
fixed 153 adj.
habitual 610 adj.
with affections
817 adj.
ingrate
ingratitude 908 n.
**ingratiate
oneself**
be servile 879 vb.
ingratitude
ingratitude 908 n.
ingredient
adjunct 40 n.
tincture 43 n.
part 53 n.
component 58 adj.
component 58 n.
element 319 n.
ingredients
contents 193 n.
ingress
ingress 297 n.
ingrown
firm 45 adj.
interior 224 adj.
inhabit
be present 189 vb.
dwell 192 vb.
possess 773 vb.
inhabitant
dweller 191 n.
inhalation
reception 299 n.
respiration 352 n.

inhale
absorb 299 vb.
breathe 352 vb.
smoke 388 vb.
smell 394 vb.
inharmonious
discordant 411 adj.
inherent
intrinsic 5 adj.
component 58 adj.
included 78 adj.
inherit
be intrinsic 5 vb.
come after 65 vb.
reproduce 166 vb.
inherit 771 vb.
receive 782 vb.
inheritance
sequel 67 n.
posterity 170 n.
acquisition 771 n.
possession 773 n.
dower 777 n.
transfer 780 n.
receiving 782 n.
receipt 807 n.
inhibit
counteract 182 vb.
obstruct 702 vb.
restrain 747 vb.
inhibition
hindrance 702 n.
prohibition 757 n.
inhospitable
unsociable 883 adj.
unkind 898 adj.
inhuman
harmful 645 adj.
impassive 820 adj.
cruel 898 adj.
unkind 898 adj.
inhumanity
inhumanity
898 n.
misanthropy
902 n.
inhume
inter 364 vb.
inimical
hostile 881 adj.
inimitable
inimitable 21 adj.
iniquitous
evil 616 adj.
unjust 914 adj.
wrong 914 adj.
wicked 934 adj.
initial
beginning 68 n.
first 68 adj.
sign 547 vb.
spell 558 vb.
initials
label 547 n.

initiate
auspicate 68 vb.
initiate 68 vb.
admit 299 vb.
train 534 vb.
learner 538 n.
initiative
beginning 68 n.
vigorousness
174 n.
willingness 597 n.
restlessness 678 n.
inject
pierce 263 vb.
irrigate 341 vb.
doctor 658 vb.
injection
insertion 303 n.
medicine 658 n.
injudicious
unwise 499 adj.
inexpedient
643 adj.
rash 857 adj.
injunction
requirement
627 n.
precept 693 n.
command 737 n.
prohibition 757 n.
legal process 959 n.
injure
weaken 163 vb.
harm 645 vb.
impair 655 vb.
hurt 827 vb.
blemish 845 vb.
be malevolent
898 vb.
do wrong 914 adj.
injury
evil 616 n.
badness 645 n.
impairment 655 n.
wound 655 n.
resentment 891 n.
vice 934 n.
guilty act 936 n.
penalty 963 n.
injustice
injustice 914 n.
wrong 914 n.
guilty act 936 n.
ink
blacken 428 vb.
black thing 428 n.
inkling
knowledge 490 n.
hint 524 n.
inky
dark 418 adj.
black 428 adj.
inlaid work
chequer 437 n.

indifferent 860 adj.
inspect
scan 438 vb.
inspection
inspection 438 n.
surveillance 457 n.
inspector
spectator 441 n.
enquirer 459 n.
estimator 480 n.
manager 690 n.
inspiration
causation 156 n.
influence 178 n.
respiration 352 n.
intuition 476 n.
intelligence 498 n.
imagination 513 n.
diffuseness 570 n.
spontaneity 609 n.
contrivance 623 n.
warm feeling
818 n.
excitation 821 n.
revelation 975 n.
piety 979 n.
inspire
cause 156 vb.
influence 178 vb.
incite 612 vb.
animate 821 vb.
make pious 979 vb.
instability
changeableness
152 n.
weakness 163 n.
excitability 822 n.
install
place 187 vb.
commission
751 vb.
dignify 866 vb.
installation
location 187 n.
celebration 876 n.
holy orders 985 n.
instance
example 83 n.
exemplify 83 vb.
instant
instant 116 n.
instantaneous
116 adj.
present 121 adj.
impending 155 adj.
ready-made
669 adj.
instantaneous
instantaneous
116 adj.
instead
instead 150 adv.
instep
foot 214 n.

curve 248 n.
instigate
incite 612 vb.
induce 612 vb.
instil
mix 43 vb.
combine 50 vb.
educate 534 vb.
instinct
intellect 447 n.
absence of thought
450 n.
empiricism 461 n.
intuition 476 n.
necessity 596 n.
spontaneity 609 n.
habit 610 n.
nondesign 618 n.
feeling 818 n.
instinctive
intrinsic 5 adj.
intuitive 476 adj.
involuntary
596 adj.
spontaneous
609 adj.
institute
cause 156 vb.
produce 164 vb.
academy 539 n.
corporation
708 n.
institution
beginning 68 n.
practice 610 n.
law 953 n.
institutionalize
make uniform
16 vb.
instruct
inform 524 vb.
educate 534 vb.
command 737 vb.
instruction
culture 490 n.
information 524 n.
teaching 534 n.
advice 691 n.
precept 693 n.
instructions
command 737 n.
instructive
influential 178 adj.
informative
524 adj.
educational
534 adj.
instrument
instrument 628 n.
title deed 767 n.
instrumental
musical 412 adj.
instrumental
628 adj.

instrumentalist
instrumentalist
413 n.
instrumentation
composition 56 n.
melody 410 n.
music 412 n.
musical piece
412 n.
instrumentality
628 n.
insubordinate
disobedient
738 adj.
disrespectful
921 adj.
insubstantial
insubstantial 4 adj.
insufferable
intolerable 827 adj.
insufficient
insufficient
636 adj.
insular
unrelated 10 adj.
separate 46 adj.
alone 88 adj.
narrow-minded
481 adj.
insulate
set apart 46 vb.
cover 226 vb.
line 227 vb.
be hot 379 vb.
heat 381 vb.
safeguard 660 vb.
insulated
heated 381 adj.
insulation
lining 227 n.
insulin
drug 658 n.
insult
annoyance 827 n.
hurt 827 vb.
slur 867 n.
sauciness 878 n.
be rude 885 vb.
rudeness 885 n.
huff 891 vb.
resentment 891 n.
scurrility 899 n.
indignity 921 n.
not respect 921 vb.
calumny 926 n.
insuperable
impracticable
470 adj.
difficult 700 adj.
insupportable
intolerable 827 adj.
insurance
protection 660 n.
promise 764 n.

security 767 n.
caution 858 n.
insurance policy
title deed 767 n.
insure
prepare 669 vb.
promise 764 vb.
contract 765 vb.
give security
767 vb.
be cautious 858 vb.
insurgent
revolter 738 n.
insurmountable
impracticable
470 adj.
insurrection
resistance 715 n.
revolt 738 n.
intact
intact 52 adj.
undamaged
646 adj.
safe 660 adj.
intaglio
mould 23 n.
concavity 255 n.
sculpture 554 n.
ornamental art
844 n.
intake
size 195 n.
ingress 297 n.
reception 299 n.
requirement 627 n.
intangible
unreal 2 adj.
immaterial
320 adj.
integer
whole 52 n.
number 85 n.
unit 88 n.
integral
intrinsic 5 adj.
whole 52 adj.
complete 54 adj.
numerical 85 adj.
numerical element
85 n.
integrate
combine 50 vb.
make complete
54 vb.
**integrated
circuit**
electronics 160 n.
integration
mixture 43 n.
combination 50 n.
whole 52 n.
completeness 54 n.
inclusion 78 n.
unity 88 n.

integrity
whole 52 n.
probity 929 n.
virtue 933 n.
integument
layer 207 n.
exteriority 223 n.
skin 226 n.
intellect
intellect 447 n.
intellectual
mental 447 adj.
intellectual 492 n.
wise 498 adj.
proficient person
696 n.
intelligence
secret service
459 n.
intelligence 498 n.
information 524 n.
news 529 n.
**intelligence
quotient**
intellect 447 n.
intelligence 498 n.
intelligent
intelligent
498 adj.
intelligentsia
intellectual 492 n.
intelligible
intelligible 516 adj.
intemperate
violent 176 adj.
vicious 934 adj.
intemperate
943 adj.
intend
intend 617 vb.
intended
impending 155 adj.
expected 507 adj.
volitional 595 adj.
loved one 887 n.
intense
great 32 adj.
vigorous 174 adj.
florid 425 adj.
feeling 818 adj.
fervent 818 adj.
intensify
augment 36 vb.
invigorate 174 vb.
enlarge 197 vb.
animate 821 vb.
aggravate 832 vb.
intensity
degree 27 n.
greatness 32 n.
vigorousness
174 n.
light 417 n.
hue 425 n.

alive 360 adj.
in the red
poor 801 adj.
in the red, be
lose 772 vb.
be in debt 803 vb.
**in the running
for, be**
offer oneself
759 vb.
in the same boat
with 89 adv.
in the teeth of
with difficulty
700 adv.
in opposition
704 adv.
in the thick of
between 231 adv.
In the way
near 200 adv.
unwanted 860 adv.
intifada
revolt 738 n.
intimacy
relation 9 n.
coition 45 n.
knowledge 490 n.
friendship 880 n.
fellowship 882 n.
love 887 n.
intimate
conjunctive 45 adj.
private 80 adj.
near 200 adj.
interior 224 adj.
knowing 490 adj.
known 490 adj.
hint 524 vb.
inform 524 vb.
close friend 880 n.
friendly 880 adj.
loved one 887 n.
intimation
knowledge 490 n.
hint 524 n.
information 524 n.
news 529 n.
intimidate
oppress 735 vb.
frighten 854 vb.
threaten 900 vb.
intimidation
fear 854 n.
intimidation
854 n.
boasting 877 n.
into
obsessed 455 adj.
intolerable
intolerable 827 adj.
intolerant
biased 481 adj.
harmful 645 adj.

severe 735 adj.
hostile 881 adj.
malevolent
898 adj.
pitiless 906 adj.
orthodox 976 adj.
intonation
sound 398 n.
voice 577 n.
intoxicate
invigorate 174 vb.
excite 821 vb.
delight 826 vb.
intoxication
excitation 821 n.
excitable state
822 n.
intemperance
943 n.
drunkenness 949 n.
intractable
rigid 326 adj.
wilful 602 adj.
difficult 700 adj.
disobedient
738 adj.
intransigent
strong 162 adj.
rigid 326 adj.
resolute 599 adj.
obstinate 602 adj.
intrapreneur
doer 676 n.
intravenous
interior 224 adj.
intricacy
complexity 61 n.
crossing 222 n.
convolution 251 n.
enigma 530 n.
difficulty 700 n.
intricate
tied 45 adj.
complex 61 adj.
intricate 251 adj.
ornamental
844 adj.
intrigue
latency 523 n.
motivate 612 vb.
plot 623 n.
plot 623 vb.
be cunning 698 vb.
sedition 738 n.
impress 821 vb.
love affair 887 n.
illicit love 951 n.
intriguing
cunning 698 adj.
perfidious 930 adj.
intrinsic
intrinsic 5 adj.
introduce
add 38 vb.

come before 64 vb.
initiate 68 vb.
introduce 231 vb.
precede 283 vb.
admit 299 vb.
insert 303 vb.
offer 759 vb.
greet 884 vb.
introduction
prelude 66 n.
beginning 68 n.
reception 299 n.
insertion 303 n.
teaching 534 n.
courteous act
884 n.
introit
vocal music 412 n.
hymn 981 n.
Holy Communion
988 n.
introspective
intrinsic 5 adj.
thoughtful 449 adj.
introverted
intrinsic 5 adj.
unsociable 883 adj.
intrude
intrude 297 vb.
insert 303 vb.
intruder
unrelatedness 10 n.
intruder 59 n.
interjector 231 n.
offender 904 n.
intrusion
interjection 231 n.
ingress 297 n.
overstepping 306 n.
intrusive
unrelated 10 adj.
extraneous 59 adj.
interjacent 231 adj.
intuition
intuition 476 n.
feeling 818 n.
revelation 975 n.
intumescence
dilation 197 n.
inundate
drench 341 vb.
flow 350 vb.
superabound
637 vb.
inure
train 534 vb.
habituate 610 vb.
make ready
669 vb.
invade
congregate 74 vb.
interfere 131 vb.
encroach 306 vb.
attack 712 vb.

go to war 718 vb.
invader
intruder 59 n.
incomer 297 n.
attacker 712 n.
invalid
helplessness 161 n.
powerless 161 adj.
weaking 163 n.
illogical 477 adj.
useless 641 adj.
sick person 651 n.
unwarranted
916 adj.
invalidate
disable 161 vb.
weaken 163 vb.
destroy 165 vb.
confute 479 vb.
negate 533 vb.
abrogate 752 vb.
disentitle 916 vb.
invalided
sick 651 adj.
invalidity
impotence 161 n.
lack of meaning
515 n.
invaluable
profitable 640 adj.
valuable 644 adj.
of value 811 adj.
invariable
identical 13 adj.
uniform 16 adj.
unchangeable
153 adj.
usual 610 adj.
invasion
crowd 74 n.
ingress 297 n.
attack 712 n.
warfare 718 n.
invective
oration 579 n.
oratory 579 n.
scurrility 899 n.
reproach 924 n.
detraction 926 n.
inveigh
curse 899 vb.
criticize 924 vb.
inveigle
ensnare 542 vb.
tempt 612 vb.
invent
initiate 68 vb.
cause 156 vb.
produce 164 vb.
perceive 447 adj.
think 449 vb.
discover 484 vb.
imagine 513 vb.
manifest 522 vb.

be false 541 vb.
fake 541 vb.
plan 623 vb.
invention
beginning 68 n.
causation 156 n.
production 164 n.
idea 451 n.
discovery 484 n.
falsehood 541 n.
fable 543 n.
untruth 543 n.
contrivance 623 n.
inventive
original 21 adj.
new 126 adj.
imaginative
513 adj.
inventor
precursor 66 n.
cause 156 n.
producer 164 n.
detector 484 n.
planner 623 n.
inventory
all 52 n.
arrangement 62 n.
number 86 vb.
list 87 n.
list 87 vb.
contents 193 n.
inverse
contrariety 14 n.
contrary 14 adj.
contraposition
240 n.
opposite 240 adj.
invert
invert 221 vb.
invertebrate
animal 365 adj.
animal 365 n.
coward 856 n.
invest
place 187 vb.
dress 228 vb.
circumscribe
232 vb.
store 632 vb.
commission
751 vb.
lend 784 vb.
speculate 791 vb.
expend 806 vb.
investigate
enquire 459 vb.
investigation
enquiry 459 n.
police enquiry
459 n.
search 459 n.
study 536 n.
investiture
dressing 228 n.

worry 825 n.
painfulness 827 n.
discontent 829 n.
aggravation
832 n.
anger 891 n.
resentment 891 n.
irruption
ingress 297 n.
Islam
religious faith
973 n.
island
region 184 n.
traffic control
305 n.
island 349 n.
seclusion 883 n.
islander
dweller 191 n.
isle
land 344 n.
island 349 n.
isobar
weather 340 n.
isolate
set apart 46 vb.
seclude 883 vb.
isolation
unrelatedness 10 n.
disunion 46 n.
unity 88 n.
seclusion 883 n.
isometrics
exercise 682 n.
**isosceles
triangle**
angular figure
247 n.
isotope
element 319 n.
I-spy
indoor game
837 n.
issue
kinsman 11 n.
subdivision 53 n.
event 154 n.
happen 154 vb.
effect 157 n.
result 157 vb.
posterity 170 n.
egress 298 n.
emerge 298 vb.
outflow 298 n.
flow 350 vb.
topic 452 n.
publish 528 vb.
the press 528 n.
edition 589 n.
reading matter
589 n.
completion 725 n.
coinage 797 n.

mint 797 vb.
litigation 959 n.
isthmus
bond 47 n.
contraction 198 n.
narrowness 206 n.
land 344 n.
bridge 624 n.
it
identity 13 n.
attraction 291 n.
authenticity 494 n.
inducement 612 n.
pleasurableness
826 n.
beauty 841 n.
IT
information
524 n.
italic
letter 558 n.
lettering 586 n.
written 586 adj.
print-type 587 n.
italicize
emphasize 532 vb.
itch
agitation 318 n.
tingling 378 n.
skin disease 651 n.
desire 859 n.
item
in addition
38 adv.
part 53 n.
component 58 n.
unit 88 n.
duality 90
object 319 n.
itemize
specify 80 vb.
list 87 vb.
iteration
duplication 91 n.
repetition 106 n.
itinerant
traveller 268 n.
itinerary
itinerary 267 n.
guidebook 524 n.
IVF
propagation
167 n.
ivory
hardness 326 n.
white thing
427 n.
whitish 427 adj.
gem 844 n.
ivory tower
refuge 662 n.
seclusion 883 n.
ivy
tree 366 n.

J

jab
knock 279 n.
insertion 303 n.
touch 378 vb.
wound 655 n.
medicine 658 n.
jabber
empty talk 515 n.
mean nothing
515 vb.
speak 579 vb.
be loquacious
581 vb.
chatter 581 n.
Jabberwocky
rara avis 84 n.
fantasy 513 n.
jabot
neckwear 228 n.
jack
support 218 n.
missile 287 n.
rotator 315 n.
male animal
372 n.
flag 547 n.
tool 630 n.
jackal
mammal 365 n.
dependant 742 n.
toady 879 n.
jackass
fool 501 n.
jackboot
conduct 688 n.
brute force 735 n.
tyrant 735 n.
lawlessness 954 n.
jackdaw
bird 365 n.
jacket
skin 226 n.
jacket 228 n.
bookbinding 589 n.
**Jack-in-the-
box**
plaything 837 n.
**jack-of-all-
trades**
busy person 678 n.
proficient person
696 n.
jackpot
acquisition 771 n.
reward 962 n.
Jacuzzi (tdmk)
vortex 315 n.
water 339 n.
eddy 350 n.
heater 383 n.
ablutions 648 n.

jade
saddle horse 273 n.
female 373 n.
greenness 434 n.
be tedious 838 vb.
gem 844 n.
cause dislike
861 vb.
sate 863 vb.
loose woman
952 n.
jaded
bored 838 adj.
sated 863 adj.
jag
notch 260 vb.
drunkenness 949 n.
jagged
angular 247 adj.
sharp 256 adj.
rough 259 adj.
jaguar
big cat 365 n.
jail
prison 748 n.
jailer
doorkeeper 264 n.
gaoler 749 n.
jalopy
automobile 274 n.
jam
circumstance 8 n.
affix 45 vb.
join 45 vb.
crowd 74 n.
halt 145 vb.
make smaller
198 vb.
be quiescent
266 vb.
viscidity 354 n.
pulpiness 356 n.
sweet thing 392 n.
play music 413 vb.
predicament 700 n.
obstruct 702 vb.
jamb
pillar 218 n.
jamboree
amusement 837 n.
jam in
fill 54 vb.
jam session
dancing 837 n.
jam tomorrow
neverness 109 n.
future state 124 n.
incentive 612 n.
jangle
resound 404 vb.
rasp 407 vb.
discord 411 n.
discord 411 vb.
dissension 709 n.

jar
disagree 25 vb.
misfit 25 n.
vessel 194 n.
agitation 318 n.
give pain 377 vb.
rasp 407 vb.
discord 411 vb.
dissension 709 n.
cause dislike
861 vb.
jargon
speciality 80 n.
absurdity 497 n.
lack of meaning
515 n.
unintelligibility
517 n.
language 557 n.
neology 560 n.
slang 560 adj.
jar on
displease 827 vb.
jasmine
yellow 433 adj.
jasper
gem 844 n.
jaundice
yellowness 433 n.
bias 481 n.
digestive disorders
651 n.
jaunt
land travel 267 n.
amusement
837 n.
jaunty
cheerful 833 adj.
showy 875 adj.
javelin
missile 287 n.
missile weapon
723 n.
spear 723 n.
jaw
protuberance
254 n.
empty talk 515 n.
be loquacious
581 vb.
jaws
stomach 194 n.
orifice 263 n.
jay
bird 365 n.
jazz
music 412 n.
JCB (tdmk)
vehicle 274 n.
jealous
discontented
829 adj.
hostile 881 adj.
resentful 891 adj.

journal
chronology 117 n.
journal 528 n.
the press 528 n.
record 548 n.
journalism
publicity 528 n.
writing 586 n.
journalist
enquirer 459 n.
publicizer 528 n.
news reporter
529 n.
chronicler 549 n.
author 589 n.
journey
land travel
267 n.
travel 267 vb.
passage 305 n.
journeyman
artisan 686 n.
jousting
duel 716 n.
jovial
merry 833 adj.
sociable 882 adj.
jowl
laterality 239 n.
joy
joy 824 n.
joyful
happy 824 adj.
merry 833 adj.
joyous
happy 824 adj.
joy-ride
automobile 274 n.
stealing 788 n.
jubilant
jubilant 833 adj.
jubilation
merriment 833 n.
rejoicing 835 n.
celebration 876 n.
jubilee
twenty and over
99 n.
period 110 n.
anniversary
141 n.
merriment 833 n.
celebration 876 n.
Judaism
religious faith
973 n.
judder
agitation 318 n.
be agitated 318 vb.
judge
estimator 480 n.
judge 480 vb.
officer 741 n.
judge 957 n.

judgment
intellect 447 n.
judgment 480 n.
sagacity 498 n.
condemnation
961 n.
punishment
963 n.
Judgment Day
tribunal 956 n.
judgment seat
tribunal 956 n.
judicial
judicial 480 adj.
judicious
discriminating
463 adj.
judicial 480 adj.
wise 498 adj.
advisable 642 adj.
judo
defence 713 n.
wrestling 716 n.
jug
vessel 194 n.
water 339 n.
prison 748 n.
juggernaut
destroyer 168 n.
flattener 216 n.
carrier 273 n.
lorry 274 n.
idol 982 n.
juggle
deceive 542 vb.
be cunning 698 vb.
juggler
entertainer 594 n.
slyboots 698 n.
sorcerer 983 n.
jugular vein
essential part 5 n.
juice
fluid 335 n.
moisture 341 n.
semiliquidity
354 n.
fuel 385 n.
juice bar
café 192 n.
juice box
soft drink 301 n.
juicy
new 126 adj.
soft 327 adj.
humid 341 adj.
super 644 adj.
pleasurable
826 adj.
jujitsu
defence 713 n.
wrestling 716 n.
jujube
sweet thing 392 n.

jukebox
gramophone
414 n.
jumble
medley 43 n.
disorder 61 n.
jumble 63 vb.
deform 244 vb.
jumbo
giant 195 n.
large 195 adj.
jumbo jet
aircraft 276 n.
jump
interval 201 n.
gait 265 n.
fly 271 vb.
move fast 277 vb.
spurt 277 n.
progression 285 n.
ascent 308 n.
leap 312 n.
leap 312 vb.
agitation 318 n.
be agitated 318 vb.
be excited 821 vb.
be excitable
822 vb.
amuse oneself
837 vb.
fear 854 vb.
jump at
be willing 597 vb.
consent 758 vb.
desire 859 vb.
jumped-up
unimportant
639 adj.
jumper
dress 228 n.
jersey 228 n.
horse 273 n.
**jump on the
bandwagon**
do likewise 20 vb.
conform 83 vb.
acquiesce 488 vb.
be in fashion
848 vb.
be servile 879 vb.
jump the gun
do before 119 vb.
be early 135 vb.
jump the queue
be disordered
61 vb.
come before 64 vb.
do before 119 vb.
precede 283 vb.
**jump to
conclusions**
prejudge 481 vb.
jump to it
be active 678 vb.

jumpy
active 678 adj.
nervous 854 adj.
junction
joint 45 n.
union 45 n.
bond 47 n.
focus 76 n.
passage 305 n.
access 624 n.
railway 624 n.
road 624 n.
juncture
juncture 8 n.
joint 45 n.
present time 121 n.
occasion 137 n.
jungle
wood 366 n.
music 412 n.
junior
inferior 35 adj.
inferior 35 n.
subsequent
120 adj.
young 130 adj.
subject 745 adj.
junk
sailing ship 275 n.
reject 607 vb.
rubbish 641 n.
drug-taking 949 n.
junket
dairy product
301 n.
meal 301 n.
milk 301 n.
amusement 837 n.
revel 837 n.
revel 837 vb.
junketing
revel 837 n.
junk food
provisions 301 n.
junkie
the maladjusted
504 n.
drug-taking 949 n.
jurisdiction
jurisdiction 955 n.
jury
jury 957 n.
just
veracious 540 adj.
just 913 adj.
justice
justice 913 n.
virtues 933 n.
judge 957 n.
divine attribute
965 n.
justification
counterevidence
467 n.

justify
demonstrate
478 vb.
print 587 vb.
justify 927 vb.
acquit 960 vb.
just so
accurate 494 adj.
jut
jut 254 vb.
jute
fibre 208 n.
textile 222 n.
juvenile
young 130 adj.
youngster 132 n.
feeble 572 adj.
immature 670 adj.
**juvenile
delinquent**
low fellow 869 n.
offender 904 n.
juvenilia
reading matter
589 n.
juxtaposition
contiguity 202 n.
comparison 462 n.

K

kagoule
jacket 228 n.
kaizen
production 164 n.
improvement
654 n.
kaleidoscope
medley 43 n.
multiformity
82 n.
changeable thing
152 n.
variegation 437 n.
spectacle 445 n.
kangaroo
mammal 365 n.
kangaroo court
lawlessness 954 n.
kaolin
soil 344 n.
kapok
fibre 208 n.
lining 227 n.
kaput
powerless 161 adj.
dead 361 adj.
useless 641 adj.

pretext 614 n.
forgiveness 909 n.
dueness 915 n.
vindication 927 n.
acquittal 960 n.

arrest 747 vb.
take away 786 vb.
steal 788 vb.
kidney
sort 77 n.
meal 301 n.
kidney donor
giver 781 n.
good giver 813 n.
kidney machine
hospital 658 n.
kidology
deception 542 n.
kids' stuff
easy thing 701 n.
kill
kill 362 vb.
prohibit 757 vb.
killer
destroyer 168 n.
killer 362 n.
murderer 362 n.
ruffian 904 n.
killing fields
slaughter 362 n.
killjoy
moderator 177 n.
dissuasion 613 n.
moper 834 n.
kill oneself
kill oneself 362 vb.
kill time
pass time 108 vb.
be inactive 679 vb.
amuse oneself
837 vb.
kiln
furnace 383 n.
kilo
weighing 322 n.
kilometre
long measure
203 n.
kilt
shorten 204 vb.
skirt 228 n.
kimono
robe 228 n.
kin
kinsman 11 n.
breed 77 n.
genealogy 169 n.
kind
degree 27 n.
sort 77 n.
form 243 n.
aiding 703 adj.
amiable 884 adj.
courteous 884 adj.
benevolent
897 adj.
kindergarten
nonage 130 n.
school 539 n.

kind-hearted
benevolent
897 adj.
kindle
cause 156 vb.
invigorate 174 vb.
be hot 379 vb.
kindle 381 vb.
incite 612 vb.
feel 818 vb.
excite 821 vb.
be excitable
822 vb.
get angry 891 vb.
kindliness
friendliness 880 n.
courtesy 884 n.
benevolence 897 n.
kindly
benevolent
897 adj.
kindness
leniency 736 n.
friendliness 880 n.
courteous act
884 n.
courtesy 884 n.
benevolence 897 n.
kindred
relative 9 adj.
akin 11 adj.
consanguinity
11 n.
kinsman 11 n.
kinetics
motion 265 n.
king
sovereign 741 n.
plaything 837 n.
aristocrat 868 n.
kingdom
breed 77 n.
territory 184 n.
political
organization
733 n.
kingpin
bigwig 638 n.
chief thing 638 n.
manager 690 n.
king size
large 195 adj.
size 195 n.
kink
complexity 61 n.
nonconformity
84 n.
be curved 248 vb.
loop 250 n.
coil 251 n.
convolution 251 n.
roughen 259 vb.
roughness 259 n.
eccentricity 503 n.

whim 604 n.
defect 647 n.
kinky
abnormal 84 adj.
undulatory
251 adj.
kiosk
pavilion 192 n.
small house 192 n.
shop 796 n.
kipper
dry 342 vb.
season 388 vb.
preserve 666 vb.
kippers
fish food 301 n.
kirk
church 990 n.
kismet
fate 596 n.
kiss
be contiguous
202 vb.
touch 378 vb.
courteous act
884 n.
greet 884 vb.
caress 889 vb.
endearment 889 n.
kit
accumulation 74 n.
sort 77 n.
unit 88 n.
clothing 228 n.
viol 414 n.
equipment 630 n.
kitbag
bag 194 n.
kitchen
chamber 194 n.
cookery 301 n.
heater 383 n.
workshop
687 n.
kitchen sink
sink 649 n.
kitchen-sink
drama
stage play 594 n.
kite
airship 276 n.
bird 365 n.
kite-flying
empiricism 461 n.
publication 528 n.
indication 547 n.
kith and kin
kinsman 11 n.
kit out
provide 633 vb.
kitsch
inferiority 35 n.
art 551 n.
bad taste 847 n.

kitten
young creature
132 n.
weakling 163 n.
reproduce itself
167 vb.
cat 365 n.
kittenish
merry 833 adj.
kitty
store 632 n.
association 706 n.
joint possession
775 n.
kleptomaniac
neurotic 503 adj.
neurotic 504 n.
thieving 788 adj.
thief 789 n.
knack
habit 610 n.
aptitude 694 n.
knackered
fatigued 684 adj.
knave
bad person 938 n.
knead
mix 43 vb.
form 243 n.
soften 327 vb.
knee
joint 45 n.
angularity 247 n.
leg 267 n.
kneecap
leg 267 n.
torture 963 vb.
knee-deep
deep 211 adj.
knee-high to a
grasshopper
dwarfish 196 adj.
short 204 adj.
kneel
stoop 311 vb.
knuckle under
721 vb.
be servile 879 vb.
pay one's respects
884 vb.
show respect
920 vb.
be pious 979 vb.
perform ritual
988 vb.
kneeler
cushion 218 n.
church utensil
990 n.
knees-up
revel 837 n.
knell
ruin 165 n.
obsequies 364 n.

play music
413 vb.
signal 547 n.
raise the alarm
665 vb.
lament 836 n.
knickerbockers
trousers 228 n.
knickers
underwear 228 n.
knick-knack
bauble 639 n.
finery 844 n.
knife
cut 46 vb.
sharp edge 256 n.
kill 362 vb.
tool 630 n.
sidearms 723 n.
knife-edge
narrowness 206 n.
edge 234 n.
knight
rider 268 n.
cavalry 722 n.
combatant 722 n.
plaything 837 n.
brave person
855 n.
dignify 866 vb.
person of repute
866 n.
person of rank
868 n.
philanthropist
901 n.
knight errant
rider 268 n.
defender 713 n.
brave person
855 n.
philanthropist
901 n.
knighthood
honours 866 n.
title 870 n.
knit
join 45 vb.
tie 45 vb.
compose 56 vb.
produce 164 vb.
weave 222 vb.
jersey 228 n.
close 264 vb.
knitting
network 222 n.
formation 243 n.
needlework
844 n.
knob
hanger 217 n.
handle 218 n.
sphere 252 n.
swelling 253 n.

knock
knock 279 n.
strike 279 vb.
be loud 400 vb.
loudness 400 vb.
bang 402 n.
detract 926 vb.
knock about
travel 267 vb.
misuse 675 vb.
knockabout
dramatic 594 adj.
funny 849 adj.
ridiculousness
849 n.
knock down
demolish 165 vb.
flatten 216 vb.
strike 279 vb.
fell 311 vb.
knock-down
price
discount 810 n.
cheapness 812 n.
knocker
signal 547 n.
detractor 926 n.
knocking
loudness 400 n.
roll 403 n.
knock it back
drink 301 vb.
knock-kneed
crippled 163 adj.
deformed 246 adj.
angular 247 adj.
convergent 293 adj.
knock off
subtract 39 vb.
unite with 45 vb.
cease 145 vb.
take 786 vb.
steal 788 vb.
debauch 951 vb.
knock out
disable 161 vb.
destroy 165 vb.
strike 279 vb.
render insensible
375 vb.
defeat 727 vb.
knockout
end 69 n.
exceller 644 n.
victory 727 n.
a beauty 841 n.
knot
tie 45 vb.
ligature 47 n.
complexity 61 n.
band 74 n.
crowd 74 n.
long measure
203 n.

cross 222 vb.
distort 246 vb.
swelling 253 n.
solid body 324 n.
difficulty 700 n.
knots
velocity 277 n.
knotty
dense 324 adj.
difficult 700 adj.
know
unite with 45 vb.
know 490 vb.
know-all
dogmatist 473 n.
intellectual 492 n.
wiseacre 500 n.
vain person 873 n.
know-how
knowledge 490 n.
intelligence 498 n.
way 624 n.
means 629 n.
skill 694 n.
cunning 698 n.
knowing
knowing 490 adj.
knowledge 490 n.
intelligent 498 adj.
cunning 698 n.
knowingly
purposely 617 adv.
knowledge
knowledge 490 n.
knowledgeable
wise 498 adj.
know one's
place
be modest 874 vb.
respect 920 vb.
show respect
920 vb.
know one's stuff
discriminate
463 vb.
know 490 vb.
knuckle
joint 45 n.
angularity 247 n.
swelling 253 n.
meat 301 n.
knuckle under
be inferior 35 vb.
knuckle under
721 vb.
Koran
non-Biblical
scripture 975 n.
kosher
edible 301 adj.
clean 648 adj.
kowtow
obeisance 311 n.
stoop 311 vb.

knuckle under
721 vb.
be servile 879 vb.
courteous act
884 n.
greet 884 vb.
respects 920 n.
show respect
920 vb.
kraal
dwelling 192 n.
Kremlin
master 741 n.
kudos
prestige 866 n.
approbation 923 n.
Ku Klux Klan
society 708 n.
kungfu
wrestling 716 n.

L

laager
station 187 n.
fort 713 n.
labarum
flag 547 n.
label
class 62 vb.
heraldry 547 n.
label 547 n.
mark 547 vb.
labial
marginal 234 adj.
speech sound
398 n.
laboratory
testing agent
461 n.
workshop 687 n.
laborious
laborious 682 adj.
labouring 682 adj.
Labour
political party
708 n.
labour
be unrelated
10 vb.
obstetrics 167 n.
move slowly
278 vb.
emphasize
532 vb.
exaggerate 546 vb.
action 676 n.
do 676 vb.
labour 682 n.
work 682 vb.
personnel 686 n.
labour camp
prison camp 748 n.

laboured
irrelevant 10 adj.
inelegant 576 adj.
matured 669 adj.
laborious 682 adj.
labourer
producer 164 n.
worker 686 n.
servant 742 n.
labour in vain
fall short 307 vb.
attempt the
impossible
470 vb.
waste 634 vb.
lost labour 641 n.
waste effort
641 adj.
act foolishly
695 vb.
fail 728 vb.
labour of love
voluntary work
597 n.
vocation 622 n.
undertaking 672 n.
gift 781 n.
no charge 812 n.
amusement 837 n.
disinterestedness
931 n.
labour of
Sisyphus
lost labour 641 n.
labour-saving
mechanical
630 adj.
leisurely 681 adj.
economical
814 adj.
economy 814 n.
labour the
obvious
waste effort
641 adj.
laburnum
tree 366 n.
labyrinth
complexity 61 n.
meandering 251 n.
ear 415 n.
enigma 530 n.
labyrinthine
difficult 700 adj.
lace
mix 43 vb.
join 45 vb.
tie 45 vb.
ligature 47 n.
network 222 n.
textile 222 n.
transparency
422 n.
needlework 844 n.

lace into
strike 279 vb.
attack 712 vb.
laceration
scission 46 n.
wound 655 n.
lachrymose
lamenting 836 adj.
lack
be inferior 35 vb.
be incomplete
55 vb.
deficit 55 n.
absence 190 n.
fall short 307 vb.
shortfall 307 n.
necessity 596 n.
require 627 vb.
not suffice 636 vb.
scarcity 636 n.
noncompletion
726 n.
be poor 801 vb.
be discontented
829 vb.
lackadaisical
inactive 679 adj.
apathetic 820 adj.
inexcitable
823 adj.
dejected 834 adj.
indifferent 860 adj.
lackey
instrument 628 n.
dependant 742 n.
domestic 742 n.
toady 879 n.
lacking
incomplete 55 adj.
absent 190 adj.
deficient 307 adj.
necessitous
627 adj.
insufficient
636 adj.
imperfect 647 adj.
lost 772 adj.
lacklustre
weakly 163 adj.
dim 419 adj.
dimness 419 n.
colourless
426 adj.
dejected 834 adj.
laconic
concise 569 adj.
taciturn 582 adj.
lacquer
coat 226 vb.
facing 226 n.
resin 357 n.
colour 425 vb.
hairwash 843 n.
decorate 844 vb.

lie detector
detector 484 n.
lie doggo
lurk 523 vb.
be stealthy 525 vb.
lie down
be horizontal
216 vb.
repose 683 vb.
lie flat
be horizontal
216 vb.
liege
master 741 n.
subject 742 n.
subject 745 adj.
lie in wait
ambush 527 vb.
ensnare 542 vb.
lie low
be unseen 444 vb.
disappear 446 vb.
lurk 523 vb.
elude 667 vb.
lie of the land
circumstance 8 n.
direction 281 n.
lieutenant
nautical personnel
270 n.
aider 703 n.
auxiliary 707 n.
soldiery 722 n.
army officer 741 n.
naval officer 741 n.
deputy 755 n
life
essential part 5 n.
time 108 n.
affairs 154 n.
vigorousness
174 n.
life 360 n.
biography 590 n.
vocation 622 n.
activity 678 n.
life-and-death
necessary 596 adj.
life belt
wrapping 226 n.
safeguard 662 n.
lightness 323 n.
lifeblood
essential part 5 n.
blood 335 n.
life 360 n.
lifeboat
boat 275 n.
safeguard 662 n.
life coach
teacher 537 n.
lifeguard
protector 660 n.
defender 713 n.

Life Guards
armed force 722 n.
life jacket
wrapping 226 n.
aircraft 276 n.
lightness 323 n.
safeguard 662 n.
lifeless
inert 175 adj.
dead 361 adj.
inactive 679 adj.
lifelike
lifelike 18 adj.
lifeline
bond 47 n.
safeguard 662 n.
lifelong
lasting 113 adj.
life peer
person of rank
868 n.
life-saving
deliverance 668 n.
life sciences, the
science 490 n.
life-size
large 195 adj.
size 195 n.
**life story or
history**
biography 590 n.
lifestyle
state 7 n.
habit 610 n.
vocation 622 n.
way 624 n.
conduct 688 n.
**life-support
machine**
support 218 n.
lifetime
time 108 n.
long duration
113 n.
life 360 n.
life to come
future state 124 n.
life 360 n.
lift
copy 20 vb.
displace 188 vb.
conveyance 267 n.
land travel 267 n.
carry 273 vb.
progression 285 n.
promote 285 vb.
draw 288 vb.
ascent 308 n.
elevate 310 vb.
elevation 310 n.
make bright
417 vb.
improvement
654 n.

exertion 682 n.
aid 703 n.
liberate 746 vb.
steal 788 vb.
relieve 831 vb.
lift-off
space travel 271 n.
ascent 308 n.
ligament
ligature 47 n.
ligature
ligature 47 n.
light
shallow 212 adj.
window 263 n.
descend 309 vb.
light 323 adj.
kindle 381 vb.
lighter 385 n.
light 417 n.
luminous 417 adj.
make bright
417 vb.
soft-hued 425 adj.
white 427 adj.
guide 520 n.
easy 701 adj.
funny 849 adj.
unchaste 951 adj.
divine attribute
965 n.
lighten
assuage 177 vb.
lighten 323 vb.
make bright
417 vb.
disencumber
701 vb.
relieve 831 vb.
lighter
boat 275 n.
lighter 385 n.
light-fingered
thieving 788 adj.
light-headed
light-minded
456 adj.
light-hearted
cheerful 833 adj.
lighthouse
sailing aid 269 n.
signal light 420 n.
signpost 547 n.
safeguard 662 n.
lighting
lighting 420 n.
lightly
slightly 33 adv.
light music
music 412 n.
lightness
lightness 323 n.
achromatism
426 n.

lightning
electricity 160 n.
velocity 277 n.
flash 417 n.
luminary 420 n.
light on
land 295 n.
light relief
contrariety 14 n.
ridiculousness
849 n.
lights
insides 224 n.
light upon
chance 159 vb.
meet 295 vb.
acquire 771 vb.
lightweight
inconsiderable
33 adj.
weak 163 adj.
weakling 163 n.
light 323 adj.
nonentity 639 n.
trivial 639 adj.
light year
period 110 n.
distance 199 n.
long measure
203 n.
ligneous
wooden 366 adj.
lignite
fuel 385 n.
likable
desired 859 adj.
like
relative 9 adj.
similar 18 adj.
similarly 18 adv.
equal 28 adj.
enjoy 376 vb.
be pleased 824 vb.
desire 859 vb.
be friendly
880 vb.
love 887 vb.
like lemmings
rashly 857 adv.
likelihood
liability 180 n.
possibility 469 n.
probability 471 n.
likely
probable 471 adj.
credible 485 adj.
promising 852 adj.
like magic
wonderful 864 adj.
like-minded
agreeing 24 adj.
assenting 488 adj.
liken
liken 18 vb.

likeness
analogue 18 n.
similarity 18 n.
equivalence 28 n.
appearance 445 n.
comparison 462 n.
metaphor 519 n.
representation
551 n.
likes of, the
analogue 18 n.
likewise
similarly 18 adv.
in addition 38 adv.
liking
tendency 179 n.
liking 859 n.
love 887 n.
lilac
tree 366 n.
purple 436 adj.
purpleness 436 n.
Lilliputian
dwarf 196 n.
dwarfish 196 adj.
little 196 adj.
lilting
melodious 410 adj.
lily
plant 366 n.
white thing 427 n.
a beauty 841 n.
lily-livered
weak 163 adj.
cowardly 856 adj.
limb
branch 53 n.
limb 53 n.
piece 53 n.
leg 267 n.
foliage 366 n.
tree 366 n.
limber
war chariot
274 n.
flexible 327 adj.
limber up
begin 68 vb.
prepare oneself
669 vb.
limbless
crippled 163 adj.
limbo
hell 972 n.
lime
adhesive 47 n.
fertilizer 171 n.
fruit and vegetables
301 n.
tree 366 n.
sourness 393 n.
bleacher 426 n.
greenness 434 n.
take 786 vb.

list
be unequal 29 vb.
list 87 n.
list 87 vb.
be oblique 220 vb.
obliquity 220 n.
navigate 269 vb.
hear 415 vb.

listed building
archaism 127 n.
preservation 666 n.

listen
hear 415 vb.
be curious 453 vb.
be attentive
455 vb.
obey 739 vb.

listener
listener 415 n.

listen in
hear 415 vb.
be curious 453 vb.

listless
weakly 163 adj.
inactive 679 adj.
dejected 834 adj.
indifferent 860 adj.

lists
duel 716 n.

lit
fiery 379 adj.
luminous 417 adj.

litany
prayers 981 n.

literacy
culture 490 n.

literal
narrow-minded
481 adj.
accurate 494 adj.
true 494 adj.
mistake 495 n.
semantic
514 adj.
interpretative
520 adj.
verbal 559 adj.
orthodox 976 adj.

literally
truly 494 adv.

literal-minded
narrow-minded
481 adj.
accurate 494 adj.

literary
linguistic 557 adj.
literary 557 adj.
stylistic 566 adj.

literature
erudition 490 n.
information 524 n.
literature 557 n.
reading matter
589 n.

lithe
flexible 327 adj.

lithography
printing 555 n.
print 587 n.

litigant
accuser 928 n.
litigant 959 n.

litigation
litigation 959 n.

litigious
quarrelling
709 adj.

litmus paper
testing agent
461 n.

litotes
underestimation
483 n.
trope 519 n.

litre
metrology 465 n.

litter
leavings 41 n.
disorder 61 n.
group 74 n.
be dispersed
75 vb.
young creature
132 n.
reproduce itself
167 vb.
posterity 170 n.
bed 218 n.
vehicle 274 n.
waste 634 n.
rubbish 641 n.
dirt 649 n.

litter lout
slut 61 n.
dirty person
649 n.

litter-strewn
unsightly 842 adj.

little
slightly 33 adv.
few 105 adj.
seldom 140 adv.
little 196 adj.
contemptible
922 adj.

little bird
informant 524 n.

little by little
by degrees 27 adv.
slightly 33 adv.
slowly 278 adv.

littleness
inferiority 35 n.
littleness 196 n.
contemptibility
922 n.

little pitcher
listener 415 n.

liturgy
Christian rite
988 n.
church service
988 n.
ritual 988 n.

live
be 1 vb.
at present 121 adv.
stay 144 vb.
be situated 186 vb.
dwell 192 vb.
alive 360 adj.
live 360 vb.
dramatic 594 adj.
active 678 adj.
feel 818 vb.

live and let live
give scope 744 vb.
compromise
770 vb.
be patient 823 vb.

lived in
occupied 191 adj.

live in
dwell 192 vb.
live 360 vb.

live-in
lover 887 n.

**live in a state of
grace**
be innocent
935 vb.

live in the past
remember 505 vb.

live it up
revel 837 vb.
be sociable 882 vb.
be intemperate
943 vb.

livelihood
vocation 622 n.

livelong
lasting 113 adj.

lively
speedy 277 adj.
imaginative
513 adj.
busy 678 adj.
feeling 818 adj.
lively 819 adj.
sociable 882 adj.

live music
music 412 n.

liven up
liven 360 vb.
be cheerful 833 vb.

live on
eat 301 vb.
be remembered
505 vb.

liver
insides 224 n.
meat 301 n.

sullenness 893 n.

liverish
irascible 892 adj.

livery
hue 425 n.

livestock
animal 365 n.
cattle 365 n.

live theatre
drama 594 n.

live together
wed 894 vb.

live with
unite with 45 vb.
accompany
89 vb.

livid
colourless 426 adj.
blackish 428 adj.
grey 429 adj.
blue 435 adj.
excited 821 adj.
angry 891 adj.

living
existing 1 adj.
alive 360 adj.
life 360 n.
linguistic
557 adj.
vocation 622 n.
aware 777 n.
benefice 985 n.

living image
analogue 18 n.
duplication 91 n.

living room
chamber 194 n.

living soul
person 371 n.

living will
title deed 767 n.

lizard
reptile 365 n.

llanos
plain 348 n.

load
finite quantity
26 n.
addition 38 n.
fill 54 vb.
bunch 74 n.
contents 193 n.
load 193 vb.
transport 272 n.
gravity 322 n.
weigh 322 vb.
store 632 n.
make ready
669 vb.
adversity 731 n.
worry 825 n.

loaded
weighty 322 adj.
moneyed 800 adj.

loads
great quantity
32 n.
multitude 104 n.

loadstone
traction 288 n.

load the dice
deceive 542 vb.

load with
hinder 702 vb.

loaf
head 213 n.
cereals 301 n.
intelligence 498 n.
be inactive 679 vb.

loam
soil 344 n.

loan
subvention 703 n.
lend 784 vb.
lending 784 n.
borrowing 785 n.
credit 802 n.

loan word
word 559 n.
neology 560 n.

loath
dissenting 489 adj.
unwilling 598 adj.

loathe
dislike 861 vb.
hate 888 vb.

loathsome
unsavoury 391 adj.
not nice 645 adj.
unpleasant
827 adj.
ugly 842 adj.
hateful 888 adj.

lob
strike 279 vb.
propel 287 vb.
elevate 310 vb.

lob (cricket)
propulsion 287 n.

lobby
influence 178 n.
influence 178 vb.
lobby 194 n.
incite 612 vb.
motivator 612 n.
petitioner 763 n.

lobbyist
motivator 612 n.
petitioner 763 n.

lobe
hanging object
217 n.
ear 415 n.

lobotomy
surgery 658 n.

lobster
fish food 301 n.
marine life 365 n.

gambling game
837 n.
lotus-eater
idler 679 n.
load
loud 400 adj.
florid 425 adj.
manifest 522 adj.
ill-bred 847 adj.
vulgar 847 adj.
loud hailer
megaphone 400 n.
hearing aid 415 n.
publicity 528 n.
loudly
loudly 400 adv.
loudmouth
rude person 885 n.
loudness
loudness 400 n.
hue 425 n.
bad taste 847 n.
ill-breeding 847 n.
loudspeaker
sound 398 n.
megaphone 400 n.
hearing aid 415 n.
publicity 528 n.
lounge
chamber 194 n.
be inactive 679 vb.
repose 683 vb.
lounge bar
tavern 192 n.
lour
impend 155 vb.
hang 217 vb.
be dark 418 vb.
be dim 419 vb.
predict 511 vb.
warn 664 vb.
be rude 885 vb.
sullenness 893 n.
threaten 900 vb.
Lourdes
focus 76 n.
louse
insect 365 n.
cad 938 n.
louse-up
mistake 495 n.
lousy
not nice 645 adj.
unclean 649 adj.
lousy with
full 54 adj.
multitudinous
104 adj.
lout
rude person 885 n.
ruffian 904 n.
love
zero 103 n.
enjoy 376 vb.

courteous act
884 n.
love 887 n.
love 887 vb.
loved one 887 n.
lover 887 n.
darling 890 n.
divineness 965 n.
love affair
love affair 887 n.
love child
descendant 170 n.
bastardy 954 n.
loved one
loved one 887 n.
love letter
correspondence
588 n.
love token 889 n.
wooing 889 n.
lovelorn
loving 887 adj.
lovely
pleasant 376 adj.
excellent 644 adj.
super 644 adj.
pleasurable
826 adj.
a beauty 841 n.
beautiful 841 adj.
lovemaking
lovemaking 887 n.
endearment
889 n.
wooing 889 n.
love-play
wooing 889 n.
lover
concomitant 89 n.
lover 887 n.
lovesick
loving 887 adj.
loving cup
cup 194 n.
draught 301 n.
loving words
endearment 889 n.
low
small 33 adj.
inferior 35 adj.
inferiority 35 n.
weak 163 adj.
low 210 adj.
muted 401 adj.
ululate 409 vb.
not nice 645 adj.
dejected 834 adj.
vulgar 847 adj.
disreputable
867 adj.
plebeian 869 adj.
humble 872 adj.
low-born
plebeian 869 adj.

lowbrow
uninstructed
491 adj.
ignoramus 493 n.
unintelligent
499 adj.
low-budget
cheap 812 adj.
lowdown
truth 494 n.
information 524 n.
low ebb
lowness 210 n.
lower
inferior 35 adj.
low 210 adj.
be deep 211 vb.
lower 311 vb.
pervert 655 vb.
humiliate 872 vb.
not respect 921 vb.
hold cheap 922 vb.
defame 926 vb.
Lower House
parliament 692 n.
lower level
lowness 210 n.
lower oneself
descend 309 vb.
sit down 311 vb.
demean oneself
867 vb.
**lower one's
sights**
abase 311 vb.
lower the light
darken 418 vb.
lowest point
inferiority 35 n.
lowness 210 n.
depth 211 n.
base 214 n.
low-fat food
food 301 n.
low fellow
low fellow 869 n.
low gear
slowness 278 n.
low-key
moderate 177 adj.
lowlands
lowness 210 n.
land 344 n.
plain 348 n.
low-level
low 210 adj.
unimportant
639 adj.
lowly
inferior 35 adj.
plebeian 869 adj.
humble 872 adj.
lowness
lowness 210 n.

humility 872 n.
low on
insufficient
636 adj.
lowpaid
poor 801 adj.
lox
fish food 301 n.
loyal
conformable
83 adj.
obedient 739 adj.
observant 768 adj.
friendly 880 adj.
loving 887 adj.
patriotic 901 adj.
trustworthy
929 adj.
orthodox 976 adj.
loyalist
conformist 83 n.
auxiliary 707 n.
defender 713 n.
loyalty
willingness 597 n.
loyalty 739 n.
duty 917 n.
loyalty card
purchase 729 n.
lozenge
sweet thing 392 n.
heraldry 547 n.
medicine 658 n.
LP
gramophone
414 n.
LSD
drug-taking 949 n.
Lsd
money 797 n.
lubricant
lubricant 334 n.
lubricate
lubricate 334 vb.
lubricating oil
oil 357 n.
lubrication
lubrication 334 n.
lubricator
smoother 258 n.
lubricant 334 n.
lubricious
smooth 258 adj.
lubricity
changeableness
152 n.
smoothness 258 n.
lubrication 334 n.
lucent
transparent
422 adj.

lucerne
provender 301 n.
lucid
orderly 60 adj.
luminous 417 adj.
undimmed
417 adj.
transparent
422 adj.
sane 502 adj.
intelligible 516 adj.
lucidity
transparency
422 n.
sanity 502 n.
intelligibility
516 n.
perspicuity 567 n.
lucid moment
sanity 502 n.
lucid prose
perspicuity 567 n.
Lucifer
planet 321 n.
luminary 420 n.
Satan 969 n.
lucifer
lighter 385 n.
luck
changeable thing
152 n.
chance 159 n.
good 615 n.
nondesign 618 n.
prosperity 730 n.
luckless
unfortunate
731 adj.
luck of the draw
chance 159 n.
nondesign 618 n.
See **gambling**
prosperity 730 n.
lucky
opportune 137 adj.
prosperous 730 adj.
happy 824 adj.
lucky break
prosperity 730 n.
lucky charm
talisman 983 n.
lucky dip
nonuniformity
17 n.
medley 43 n.
equal chance
159 n.
lucrative
gainful 771 adj.
Luddite
destroyer 168 n.
rioter 738 n.
ludicrous
absurd 497 adj.

foolish 499 adj.
ridiculous 849 adj.
ludo
board game 837 n.
lug
handle 218 n.
carry 273 vb.
sail 275 n.
draw 288 vb.
ear 415 n.
luggage
box 194 n.
transport 272 n.
lugubrious
cheerless 834 adj.
lamenting 836 adj.
lugworm
creepy-crawly
365 n.
lukewarm
median 30 adj.
warm 379 adj.
unwilling 598 adj.
irresolute 601 adj.
neutral 625 adj.
apathetic 820 adj.
indifferent 860 adj.
lull
lull 145 n.
assuage 177 vb.
bring to rest
266 vb.
silence 399 n.
silence 399 vb.
inactivity 679 n.
make inactive
679 vb.
tranquillize
823 vb.
please 826 vb.
content 828 vb.
relieve 831 vb.
flatter 925 vb.
lullaby
moderator 177 n.
musical piece
412 n.
vocal music 412 n.
soporific 679 n.
lumbago
pang 377 n.
rheumatism 651 n.
lumbar
back 238 adj.
lumber
leavings 41 n.
disorder 61 n.
walk 267 vb.
move slowly
278 vb.
wood 366 n.
rubbish 641 n.
work 682 vb.
be clumsy 695 vb.

lumbered with
hindered 702 adj.
lumbering
unwieldy 195 adj.
clumsy 695 adj.
luminary
luminary 420 n.
sage 500 n.
person of repute
866 n.
luminescent
luminous 417 adj.
luminous
luminous 417 adj.
lump
great quantity
32 n.
piece 53 n.
bulk 195 n.
convexity 253 n.
swelling 253 n.
gravity 322 n.
solid body 324 n.
hardness 326 n.
lumpectomy
bosom 253 n.
surgery 658 n.
**lump in one's
throat**
feeling 818 n.
lumpish
inert 175 adj.
unwieldy 195 adj.
inactive 679 adj.
lump sum
funds 797 n.
lump together
join 45 vb.
combine 50 vb.
bring together
74 vb.
lumpy
unwieldy 195 adj.
thick 205 adj.
convex 253 adj.
rough 259 adj.
dense 324 adj.
lunacy
folly 499 n.
mental disorder
503 n.
lunar
curved 248 adj.
celestial 321 adj.
lunar month
period 110 n.
lunatic
mentally disordered
503 adj.
madman 504 n.
rash 857 adj.
lunch
eat 301 vb.
meal 301 n.

lunch box
genitalia 167 n.
small box 194 n.
luncheon
meal 301 n.
lung cancer
respiratory disease
651 n.
lunge
move fast 277 vb.
impulse 279 n.
strike at 712 vb.
lunge at
strike 279 vb.
lungs
insides 224 n.
respiration 352 n.
voice 577 n.
lupin
plant 366 n.
lupine
animal 365 adj.
lurch
obliquity 220 n.
walk 267 vb.
move slowly
278 vb.
descent 309 n.
fluctuation 317 n.
oscillate 317 vb.
be agitated 318 vb.
show feeling
818 vb.
be drunk 949 vb.
lurching
fitfulness 142 n.
lure
attract 291 vb.
attraction 291 n.
ensnare 542 vb.
trap 542 n.
incentive 612 n.
tempt 612 vb.
desired object
859 n.
reward 962 n.
lurid
luminous 417 adj.
florid 425 adj.
frightening
854 adj.
showy 875 adj.
lurk
lurk 523 vb.
lurking
invisible 444 adj.
latent 523 adj.
stealthy 525 adj.
luscious
sweet 392 adj.
pleasurable
826 adj.
lush
prolific 171 adj.

vigorous 174 adj.
plentiful 635 adj.
rich 800 adj.
drunkard 949 n.
drunkenness
949 n.
get drunk 949 vb.
lust
desire 859 n.
See **libido**
desire 859 vb.
libido 859 n.
love 887 n.
vice 934 n.
be impure
951 vb.
unchastity 951 n.
lust after
desire 859 vb.
envy 912 vb.
lustful
loving 887 adj.
lecherous 951 adj.
lustration
ritual act 988 n.
lustre
light 417 n.
See **reflection**
reflection 417 n.
prestige 866 n.
lustrous
luminous
417 adj.
noteworthy
866 adj.
lusty
strong 162 adj.
vigorous 174 adj.
fleshy 195 adj.
healthy 650 adj.
lute
stringed instrument
414 n.
luvvy
actor 594 n.
luxuriant
prolific 171 adj.
dense 324 adj.
ornate 574 adj.
plentiful 635 adj.
luxuriate
abound 635 vb.
superabound
637 vb.
be intemperate
943 vb.
luxurious
comfortable
376 adj.
superfluous
637 adj.
rich 800 adj.
pleasurable
826 adj.

ostentatious
875 adj.
intemperate
943 adj.
sensual 944 adj.
luxury
plenty 635 n.
superfluity 637 n.
prosperity 730 n.
wealth 800 n.
intemperance
943 n.
sensualism
944 n.
lycanthrope
demon 970 n.
lychgate
doorway 263 n.
funeral 364 n.
See **obsequies**
church exterior
990 n.
lyddite
explosive 723 n.
lye
solution 337 n.
lying
erroneous 495 adj.
false 541 adj.
falsehood 541 n.
untrue 543 adj.
lymph
blood 335 n.
fluid 335 n.
lymphatic
haematic
335 adj.
watery 339 adj.
lymphogram
diagnostic 658 n.
lynch
kill 362 vb.
disapprove 924 vb.
execute 963 vb.
lynx
big cat 365 n.
eye 438 n.
lyre
stringed instrument
414 n.
lyric
musical 412 adj.
vocal music 412 n.
poetic 593 adj.
lyrical
melodious 410 adj.
poetic 593 adj.
impressed 818 adj.
rejoicing 835 adj.
approving 923 adj.
lyrics
vocal music 412 n.
reading matter
589 n.

new 126 adj.
youngster 132 n.
female 373 n.
spinster 895 n.
virgin 950 n.
means of execution
964 n.
maiden aunt
spinster 895 n.
maidenhead
purity 950 n.
maidenhood
celibacy 895 n.
purity 950 n.
maiden name
name 561 n.
maiden speech
debut 68 n.
maiden's prayer
loved one 887 n.
maiden voyage
debut 68 n.
**maid or matron
of honour**
bridal party 894 n.
mail
covering 226 n.
send 272 vb.
*postal
communications*
531 n.
correspondence
588 n.
safeguard 662 n.
armour 713 n.
mailed fist
brute force 735 n.
lawlessness 954 n.
mailing list
information 524 n.
correspondence
588 n.
mail order
send 272 vb.
purchase 792 n.
maim
disable 161 vb.
impair 655 vb.
main
great 32 adj.
supreme 34 adj.
ocean 343 n.
important
638 adj.
main chance
chief thing 638 n.
mainframe
*counting
instrument* 86 n.
mainland
land 344 n.
mainline
drug oneself
949 vb.

mainly
greatly 32 vb.
on the whole
52 adv.
generally 79 adv.
main road
road 624 n.
mainsail
sail 275 n.
mainstay
support 218 n.
chief thing 638 n.
refuge 662 n.
aider 703 n.
hope 852 n.
maintain
stay 144 vb.
sustain 146 vb.
support 218 vb.
vitalize 360 vb.
believe 485 vb.
affirm 532 vb.
persevere 600 vb.
provide 633 vb.
preserve 666 vb.
vindicate 927 vb.
maintenance
continuance 146 n.
provisions 301 n.
perseverance 600 n.
provision 633 n.
subvention 703 n.
dower 777 n.
receipt 807 n.
maisonette
flat 192 n.
maître d'hôtel
caterer 633 n.
maize
cereals 301 n.
food 301 n.
majestic
elegant 575 adj.
authoritative
733 adj.
ruling 733 adj.
impressive 821 adj.
worshipful
866 adj.
noble 868 adj.
proud 871 adj.
formal 875 adj.
majesty
greatness 32 n.
superiority 34 n.
authority 733 n.
prestige 866 n.
nobility 868 n.
divine attribute
965 n.
major
great 32 adj.
first 68 adj.
older 131 adj.

important 638 adj.
army officer 741 n.
majordomo
retainer 742 n.
majority
finite quantity
26 n.
degree 27 n.
chief part 52 n.
plurality 101 n.
adultness 134 n.
majuscule
letter 558 n.
make
unite with 45 vb.
compose 56 vb.
constitute 56 vb.
sort 77 n.
convert 147 vb.
cause 156 vb.
produce 164 vb.
form 243 vb.
arrive 295 vb.
structure 331 n.
estimate 480 vb.
make better
654 vb.
acquire 771 vb.
gain 771 vb.
**make a balls-up
of**
impair 655 vb.
**make a beeline
for**
steer for 281 vb.
**make a break
for it**
decamp 296 vb.
**make a clean
breast of it**
confess 526 vb.
be truthful 540 vb.
**make a clean
sweep (of)**
revolutionize
149 vb.
empty 300 vb.
clean 648 vb.
**make a
comeback**
recoup 31 vb.
be restored 656 vb.
**make a dead set
at**
desire 859 vb.
make advances
court 889 vb.
make a face
dislike 861 vb.
disapprove 924 vb.
make a fool of
be absurd 497 vb.
fool 542 vb.
ridicule 851 vb.

humiliate 872 vb.
make a go of
succeed 727 vb.
**make a guinea
pig of**
experiment 461 vb.
make a killing
gain 771 vb.
get rich 800 vb.
**make
alterations**
differ 15 vb.
make a man of
do good 644 vb.
give courage
855 vb.
make amends
compensate 31 vb.
restore 656 vb.
restitute 787 vb.
atone 941 vb.
make a mint
get rich 800 vb.
make an aside
voice 577 vb.
soliloquize 585 vb.
make a packet
get rich 800 vb.
make a pass
court 889 vb.
make a point of
compel 740 vb.
make a scene
be angry 891 vb.
make a show of
show 522 vb.
dissemble 541 vb.
be affected 850 vb.
make a stand
resist 715 vb.
**make a storm in
a teacup**
exaggerate 546 vb.
make away with
destroy 165 vb.
kill 362 vb.
murder 362 vb.
make-believe
fantasy 513 n.
imaginary 513 adj.
imagine 513 vb.
hypocritical
541 adj.
sham 542 n.
spurious 542 adj.
be untrue 543 vb.
untrue 543 adj.
**make capital
out of**
plead 614 vb.
find useful 640 adj.
use 673 vb.
make do with
substitute 150 vb.

make ends meet
vitalize 360 vb.
make fast
tighten 45 vb.
stabilize 153 vb.
make for
congregate 74 vb.
navigate 269 vb.
promote 285 vb.
make free with
be free 744 vb.
appropriate
786 vb.
be insolent 878 vb.
be rude 885 vb.
make fun of
fool 542 vb.
be witty 839 vb.
ridicule 851 vb.
make good
compensate 31 vb.
succeed 727 vb.
vindicate 927 vb.
**make hay while
the sun shines**
profit by 137 vb.
make headway
progress 285 vb.
get better 654 vb.
**make inroads
on**
encroach 306 vb.
make into
convert 147 vb.
make it
triumph 727 vb.
prosper 730 vb.
make it up
make peace
719 vb.
forgive 909 vb.
make light of
underestimate
483 vb.
do easily 701 vb.
be indifferent
860 vb.
make love
unite with 45 vb.
love 887 vb.
caress 889 vb.
make merry
rejoice 835 vb.
revel 837 vb.
make money
flourish 615 vb.
prosper 730 vb.
acquire 771 vb.
gain 771 vb.
get rich 800 vb.
make off with
steal 788 vb.
make one
compel 740 vb.

future state 124 n.
futurity 124 n.
delay 136 n.
inactivity 679 n.
man-at-arms
cavalry 722 n.
combatant 722 n.
soldier 722 n.
soldiery 722 n.
Mandarin
language 557 n.
mandarin
fruit and vegetables
301 n.
bigwig 638 n.
officer 741 n.
mandate
government 733 n.
*political
organization*
733 n.
mandate 751 n.
mandatory
necessary 596 adj.
authoritative
733 adj.
commanding
737 adj.
compelling
740 adj.
obligatory 917 adj.
mandolin
stringed instrument
414 n.
mane
hair 259 n.
man-eater
eater 301 n.
killer 362 n.
animal 365 n.
hunter 619 n.
man-eating
eating 301 n.
murderous 362 adj.
manège
equitation 267 n.
animal husbandry
369 n.
man Friday
worker 686 n.
aider 703 n.
manful
manly 162 adj.
mange
animal disease
651 n.
skin disease 651 n.
manger
bowl 194 n.
mangetout
fruit and vegetables
301 n.
mangle
flattener 216 n.

distort 246 vb.
smoother 258 n.
dry 342 vb.
dryer 342 n.
wound 655 vb.
mangrove
tree 366 n.
mangy
bad 645 adj.
unclean 649 adj.
manhandle
touch 378 vb.
misuse 675 vb.
man-hater
misanthrope
902 n.
manhole
orifice 263 n.
manhood
adultness 134 n.
male 372 n.
manliness 855 n.
man-hours
labour 682 n.
manhunt
chase 619 n.
mania
psychosis 503 n.
warm feeling
818 n.
desire 859 n.
liking 859 n.
maniac
madman 504 n.
maniacal
psychotic 503 adj.
manic
psychotic 503 adj.
**manic
depression**
psychosis 503 n.
Manichaeism
heresy 977 n.
manicure
beautification
843 n.
manicurist
beautician 843 n.
manifest
list 87 n.
manifest 522 adj.
manifest 522 vb.
manifestation
manifestation
522 n.
manifest itself
be visible 443 vb.
manifesto
publication 528 n.
electorate 605 n.
command 737 n.
decree 737 n.
manifold
multiform 82 adj.

many 104 adj.
manikin
small thing 33 n.
dwarf 196 n.
image 551 n.
manila
fibre 208 n.
**man or woman
in the street**
common man
30 n.
everyman 79 n.
social group 371 n.
commoner 869 n.
maniple
vestments 989 n.
manipulate
touch 378 vb.
fake 541 vb.
fool 542 vb.
motivate 612 vb.
plot 623 vb.
doctor 658 vb.
use 673 vb.
misuse 675 vb.
do 676 vb.
deal with 688 vb.
**manipulative
therapy**
alternative therapy
658 n.
mankind
humankind
371 n.
manliness
male 372 n.
manliness 855 n.
manly
grown-up 134 adj.
manly 162 adj.
animal 365 adj.
male 372 adj.
beautiful 841 adj.
courageous
855 adj.
man-made
imitative 20 adj.
spurious 542 adj.
manna
food 301 n.
**manna from
heaven**
gift 781 n.
manned
occupied 191 adj.
mannequin
living model 23 n.
exhibitor 522 n.
manner
modality 7 n.
sort 77 n.
style 566 n.
way 624 n.
conduct 688 n.

mannered
stylistic 566 adj.
affected 850 adj.
mannerism
speciality 80 n.
nonconformity
84 n.
identification
547 n.
phrase 563 n.
style 566 n.
habit 610 n.
affectation 850 n.
mannerly
tasteful 846 adj.
courteous 884 adj.
manners
practice 610 n.
conduct 688 n.
good taste 846 n.
etiquette 848 n.
courtesy 884 n.
mannish
male 372 adj.
manoeuvre
be in motion
265 vb.
motion 265 n.
deed 676 n.
do 676 vb.
tactics 688 n.
be cunning 698 vb.
stratagem 698 n.
**man or woman
of means**
rich person 800 n.
**man or woman
of the world**
expect 696 n.
beau monde 848 n.
manor
house 192 n.
lands 777 n.
man-o'-war
warship 722 n.
man of straw
insubstantial thing
4 n.
changeable thing
152 n.
sham 542 n.
nonentity 639 n.
manpower
band 74 n.
power 160 n.
means 629 n.
personnel 686 n.
manqué
unsuccessful
728 adj.
manse
parsonage 986 n.
mansion
edifice 164 n.

place 185 n.
house 192 n.
man-size
large 195 adj.
manslaughter
homicide 362 n.
mantelpiece
shelf 218 n.
mantilla
headgear 228 n.
mantissa
numerical element
85 n.
mantle
sequence 65 n.
cover 226 vb.
wrapping 226 n.
dress 228 vb.
screen 421 n.
badge of rule
743 n.
mantra
maxim 496 n.
mantrap
trap 542 n.
manual
handed 378 adj.
musical note
410 n.
organ 414 n.
piano 414 n.
guidebook 524 n.
instrumental
628 adj.
manual worker
worker 686 n.
manufacture
produce 164 vb.
product 164 n.
production 164 n.
business 622 n.
manufacturer
producer 164 n.
manure
fertilizer 171 n.
excrement 302 n.
cultivate 370 vb.
manuscript
no imitation 21 n.
prototype 23 n.
script 586 n.
written 586 adj.
book 589 n.
many
great 32 adj.
many 104 adj.
many-sided
multiform 82 adj.
plural 101 adj.
lateral 239 adj.
Maoism
government 733 n.
map
outline 233 vb.

material
substantiality 3 n.
textile 222 n.
material 319 adj.
matter 319 n.
information 524 n.
materials 631 n.
materialism
existence 1 n.
materiality 319 n.
philosophy 449 n.
sensualism 944 n.
impiety 980 n.
materialistic
material 319 adj.
selfish 932 adj.
irreligious 974 adj.
materialize
happen 154 vb.
materialize 319 vb.
be visible 443 vb.
appear 445 vb.
maternal
akin 11 adj.
parental 169 adj.
benevolent
897 adj.
maternity
propagation 167 n.
maternity 169 n.
parentage 169 n.
maternity leave
absence 190 n.
mate with
wed 894 vb.
matey
pleasant 376 adj.
friendly 880 adj.
sociable 882 adj.
mathematical
statistical 86 adj.
mathematics
mathematics 86 n.
matinée
evening 129 n.
dramaturgy 594 n.
matinee jacket
jacket 228 n.
mating
coition 45 n.
matins
morning 128 n.
public worship
981 n.
church service
988 n.
matriarchal
governmental
733 adj.
matriarchy
family 11 n.
female 373 n.
matriculation
exam 459 n.

matrimony
marriage 894 n.
matrix
mould 23 n.
number 85 n.
surroundings 230 n.
print-type 587 n.
matron
adult 134 n.
maternity 169 n.
female 373 n.
nurse 658 n.
manager 690 n.
spouse 894 n.
matronly
ageing 131 adj.
grown-up 134 adj.
parental 169 adj.
female 373 adj.
matt
dim 419 adj.
matted
crossed 222 adj.
hairy 259 adj.
dense 324 adj.
dirty 649 adj.
matter
excrement 302 n.
matter 319 n.
universe 321 n.
fluid 335 n.
semiliquidity
354 n.
topic 452 n.
meaning 514 n.
dirt 649 n.
matter of course
practice 610 n.
lack of wonder
865 n.
matter of fact
reality 1 n.
event 154 n.
certainty 473 n.
narrow-minded
481 adj.
truth 494 n.
mattock
sharp edge 256 n.
mattress
cushion 218 n.
treasury 799 n.
maturation
ripening 669 n.
completion 725 n.
mature
ageing 131 adj.
grown-up 134 adj.
mature 669 vb.
matured 669 adj.
maturity
oldness 127 n.
middle age 131 n.
adultness 134 n.

completion 725 n.
maudlin
foolish 499 adj.
feeling 818 adj.
impressible
819 adj.
tipsy 949 adj.
maul
hammer 279 n.
strike 279 vb.
ill-treat 645 vb.
wound 655 vb.
attack 712 vb.
criticize 924 vb.
maundering
folly 499 n.
foolish 499 adj.
mausoleum
edifice 164 n.
high structure
209 n.
tomb 364 n.
monument 548 n.
mauve
purple 436 adj.
purpleness 436 n.
maverick
nonconformist
84 n.
revolter 738 n.
independent
744 adj.
maw
stomach 194 n.
mawkish
feeling 818 adj.
impressible
819 adj.
maxim
prototype 23 n.
rule 81 n.
maxim 496 n.
maximize
augment 36 vb.
overestimate
482 vb.
exaggerate 546 vb.
use 673 vb.
maximum
great 32 adj.
greatness 32 n.
superiority 34 n.
plenitude 54 n.
size 195 n.
may
tree 366 n.
be possible 469 vb.
mayday
call 547 n.
mayfly
brief span 114 n.
insect 365 n.
mayhem
disorder 61 n.

mayonnaise
hors-d'oeuvres
301 n.
sauce 389 n.
mayor
official 690 n.
councillor 692 n.
officer 741 n.
law officer 955 n.
mayoress
officer 741 n.
maypole
high structure
209 n.
maze
complexity 61 n.
meandering 251 n.
enigma 530 n.
difficulty 700 n.
mazurka
musical piece
412 n.
dance 837 n.
MC
leader 690 n.
m-commerce
business 622 n.
trade 791 n.
MCP
male 372 n.
me
subjectivity 320 n.
ME
disease 651 n.
mead
alcoholic drink
301 n.
grassland 348 n.
sweet thing 392 n.
meadow
grassland 348 n.
meagre
small 33 adj.
lean 206 adj.
feeble 572 adj.
economical
814 adj.
meal
cereals 301 n.
meal 301 n.
powder 332 n.
mealy-mouthed
hypocritical
541 adj.
affected 850 adj.
flattering 925 adj.
mean
average 30 n.
median 30 adj.
middle 70 adj.
middle 70 n.
comprise 78 vb.
statistics 86 n.
interjacent 231 adj.

mean 514 vb.
bad 645 adj.
parsimonious
816 adj.
disreputable
867 adj.
plebeian 869 adj.
humble 872 adj.
servile 879 adj.
unkind 898 adj.
contemptible
922 adj.
dishonest 930 adj.
selfish 932 adj.
mean business
be resolute 599 vb.
meandering
meandering 251 n.
moving 265 adj.
roundabout
626 adj.
meaning
meaning 514 n.
indication 547 n.
intention 617 n.
meaningful
substantial 3 adj.
meaningful
514 adj.
expressive 516 adj.
meaningless
meaningless
515 adj.
mean it
be truthful 540 vb.
meanness
smallness 33 n.
insufficiency
636 n.
parsimony 816 n.
contemptibility
922 n.
selfishness 932 n.
means
means 629 n.
means test
enquiry 459 n.
meantime
while 108 adv.
mean to
intend 617 vb.
mean well
be friendly 880 vb.
meanwhile
while 108 adv.
measles
infection 651 n.
measly
unimportant
639 adj.
bad 645 adj.
measure
finite quantity
26 n.

mermaid
rara avis 84 n.
sea nymph 343 n.
mythical being
970 n.
merman
rara avis 84 n.
sea god 343 n.
mythical being
970 n.
merriment
enjoyment 824 n.
merriment 833 n.
amusement 837 n.
merry
merry 833 adj.
drunk 949 adj.
merry-go-round
rotator 315 n.
merry-making
enjoyment 824 n.
merriment 833 n.
merry 833 adj.
rejoicing 835 n.
festivity 837 n.
sociability 882 n.
mésalliance
misfit 25 n.
type of marriage
894 n.
mescalin
drug-taking 949 n.
mesh
unite with 45 vb.
gap 201 n.
space 201 vb.
cross 222 vb.
network 222 n.
meshuga
crazy 503 adj.
mesmerism
influence 178 n.
occultism 984 n.
mesmerize
influence 178 vb.
render insensible
375 vb.
convince 485 vb.
frighten 854 vb.
mesolithic
primal 127 adj.
mess
disorder 61 n.
jumble 63 vb.
chamber 194 n.
eat 301 vb.
predicament 700 n.
message
topic 452 n.
message 529 n.
messenger
traveller 268 n.
messenger 529 n.
servant 742 n.

Messiah
philanthropist
901 n.
God the Son 965 n.
religious teacher
973 n.
messiah
leader 690 n.
mess up
jumble 63 vb.
blunder 495 vb.
impair 655 vb.
messy
dirty 649 adj.
metabolism
transformation
143 n.
metabolize
modify 143 vb.
metal
hardness 326 n.
mineral 359 n.
heraldry 547 n.
materials 631 n.
metalanguage
language 557 n.
metallic
strident 407 adj.
metallurgy
mineralogy 359 n.
metal rule
gauge 465 n.
metamorphosis
transformation
143 n.
revolution 149 n.
metaphor
analogue 18 n.
assimilation 18 n.
substitute 150 n.
metaphor 519 n.
phrase 563 n.
ornament 574 n.
metaphorical
compared 462 adj.
semantic 514 adj.
figurative 519 adj.
metaphysics
existence 1 n.
philosophy 449 n.
metasomatism
transformation
143 n.
metastasis
transference 272 n.
metathesis
interchange 151 n.
inversion 221 n.
transference 272 n.
trope 519 n.
metazoon
animal 365 n.
mete
mete out 465 vb.

meteor
brief span 114 n.
meteor 321 n.
meteoric
brief 114 adj.
speedy 277 adj.
celestial 321 adj.
meteorite
meteor 321 n.
meteorological
airy 340 adj.
meteorology
weather 340 n.
meter
gauge 465 vb.
meter 465 n.
meter maid
traffic control
305 n.
methadone
drug-taking 949 n.
methane
gas 336 n.
fuel 385 n.
method
uniformity 16 n.
order 60 n.
arrangement 62 n.
regularity 81 n.
way 624 n.
means 629 n.
conduct 688 n.
fashion 848 n.
ritual 988 n.
methodical
orderly 60 adj.
arranged 62 adj.
regular 81 adj.
Methodism
Protestantism
976 n.
methodology
order 60 n.
methylated
spirit
fuel 385 n.
meticulous
attentive 455 adj.
careful 457 adj.
accurate 494 adj.
observant 768 adj.
fastidious
862 adj.
trustworthy
929 adj.
métier
vocation 622 n.
skill 694 n.
metonymy
trope 519 n.
metre
long measure
203 n.
prosody 593 n.

metric
metrical 465 adj.
metrical
metrical 465 adj.
poetic 593 adj.
metric system
metrology 465 n.
metro
tunnel 263 n.
railway 624 n.
metronome
prototype 23 n.
timekeeper 117 n.
oscillation 317 n.
tempo 410 n.
meter 465 n.
metropolis
city 184 n.
metropolitan
dweller 191 n.
central 225 adj.
ecclesiastical
985 adj.
ecclesiarch 986 n.
mettle
vigorousness
174 n.
resolution 599 n.
affections 817 n.
courage 855 n.
mettlesome
vigorous 174 adj.
active 678 adj.
courageous
855 adj.
mew
ululate 409 vb.
ululation 409 n.
mewl
cry 408 vb.
ululate 409 vb.
weep 836 vb.
mews
flat 192 n.
stable 192 n.
Mexican wave
gesture 547 n.
mezzanine floor
layer 207 n.
mezze
hors-d'oeuvres
301 n.
mezzo
middle 70 adj.
mezzo floor
middle 70 n.
mezzo-soprano
vocalist 413 n.
miaow
ululate 409 vb.
ululation 409 n.
miasma
gas 336 n.
stench 397 n.

poison 659 n.
miasmic
gaseous 336 adj.
deadly 362 adj.
fetid 397 adj.
Michaelmas
autumn 129 n.
holy day 988 n.
microbiology
biology 358 n.
medical art 658 n.
microcomputer
counting
instrument 86 n.
microcosm
small thing 33 n.
whole 52 n.
miniature 196 n.
universe 321 n.
microfiche
copy 22 n.
miniature 196 n.
record 548 n.
photography
551 n.
microfilm
copy 22 n.
miniature 196 n.
record 548 n.
photography
551 n.
microlight
aircraft 276 n.
micrometer
gauge 465 n.
meter 465 n.
micrometry
long measure
203 n.
accuracy 494 n.
micron
small quantity
33 n.
long measure
203 n.
microphone
megaphone 400 n.
hearing aid 415 n.
telecommunication
531 n.
microprocessor
counting
instrument 86 n.
electronics 160 n.
microscope
microscope 442 n.
microscopie
small 33 adj.
indistinct 444 adj.
microvirus
computing 86 n.
microwave
cook 301 vb.
cookery 301 n.

furnace 383 n.
radiation 417 n.
micturate
excrete 302 vb.
mid
middle 70 adj.
between 231 adv.
Midas touch
prosperity 730 n.
wealth 800 n.
midday
noon 128 n.
midden
accumulation 74 n.
rubbish 641 n.
sink 649 n.
middle
middle 70 adj.
middle 70 n.
middling 732 adj.
middle age
middle age 131 n.
Middle Ages
era 110 n.
antiquity 125 n.
middle classes
social group 371 n.
commonalty
869 n.
middle classes
869 n.
middle course
middle point 30 n.
middle way 625 n.
Middle England
middle classes
869 n.
middle ground
middle point 30 n.
middleman
intermediary
231 n.
agent 686 n.
mediator 720 n.
consignee 754 n.
merchant 794 n.
tradespeople 794 n.
**middle-of-the-
road**
median 30 adj.
middle point 30 n.
moderate 177 adj.
middle way 625 n.
neutral 625 adj.
not bad 644 adj.
middling 732 adj.
middle youth
youth 130 n.
middle age 131 n.
middling
not bad 644 adj.
middling 732 adj.
midge
insect 365 n.

midget
small thing 33 n.
dwarf 196 n.
midline
middle 70 n.
midnight
midnight 129 n.
midpoint
middle point 30 n.
middle 70 n.
centre 225 n.
midriff
middle 70 n.
centrality 225 n.
midshipman
nautical personnel
270 n.
midst
middle 70 n.
between 231 adv.
midstream
middle 70 n.
middle way 625 n.
midsummer
summer 128 n.
midway
middle point 30 n.
midwife
obstetrics 167 n.
instrument 628 n.
doctor 658 n.
midwinter
middle 70 n.
winter 129 n.
mien
look 445 n.
miffed
unhappy 825 adj.
discontented
829 adj.
resentful 891 adj.
might
greatness 32 n.
power 160 n.
strength 162 n.
be possible 469 vb.
might and main
power 160 n.
exertion 682 n.
mighty
great 32 adj.
greatly 32 adv.
powerful 160 adj.
strong 162 adj.
influential 178 adj.
huge 195 adj.
worshipful
866 adj.
proud 871 adj.
migraine
pang 377 n.
illness 651 n.
migrant
foreigner 59 n.

dweller 191 n.
wanderer 268 n.
incomer 297 n.
bird 365 n.
migrate
travel 267 vb.
wander 267 vb.
migration
departure 296 n.
mike
megaphone 400 n.
hearing aid 415 n.
mild
alcoholic drink
301 n.
warm 379 adj.
lenient 736 adj.
amiable 884 adj.
mildew
destroyer 168 n.
dim 419 vb.
be unclean 649 vb.
dirt 649 n.
deteriorate 655 vb.
dilapidation 655 n.
impair 655 vb.
blight 659 n.
mildness
moderation 177 n.
leniency 736 n.
courtesy 884 n.
benevolence 897 n.
mile
long measure
203 n.
mileage
distance 199 n.
length 203 n.
utility 640 n.
milestone
degree 27 n.
serial place 73 n.
event 154 n.
situation 186 n.
limit 236 n.
itinerary 267 n.
gauge 465 n.
signpost 547 n.
important matter
638 n.
milieu
circumstance 8 n.
relation 9 n.
locality 187 n.
surroundings
230 n.
militant
violent creature
176 n.
active 678 adj.
busy person 678 n.
opposing 704 adj.
political party
708 n.

quarrelling
709 adj.
defiant 711 adj.
warlike 718 adj.
warring 718 adj.
militarist 722 n.
hostile 881 adj.
**Militant
Tendency**
political party
708 n.
militaristic
warlike 718 adj.
military
warlike 718 adj.
militate
influence 178 vb.
counteract 182 vb.
do 676 vb.
oppose 704 vb.
militia
defender 713 n.
army 722 n.
milk
moderator 177 n.
empty 300 vb.
milk 301 n.
soft drink 301 n.
extract 304 vb.
fluid 335 n.
white thing 427 n.
use 673 vb.
acquire 771 vb.
take 786 vb.
milk and honey
prosperity 730 n.
milk and water
weak 163 adj.
weak thing 163 n.
milkmaid
herdsman 369 n.
servant 742 n.
**milk of human
kindness**
benevolence 897 n.
milksop
weakling 163 n.
ninny 501 n.
coward 856 n.
innocent 935 n.
milky
fatty 357 adj.
opaque 423 adj.
semitransparent
424 adj.
whitish 427 adj.
Milky Way
star 321 n.
luminary 420 n.
mill
produce 164 vb.
pulverize 332 vb.
pulverizer 332 n.
workshop 687 n.

mill around
congregate 74 vb.
rotate 315 vb.
be agitated 318 vb.
millennium
over one hundred
99 n.
period 110 n.
future state 124 n.
fantasy 513 n.
aspiration 852 n.
heaven 971 n.
millennium bug
computing 86 n.
miller
pulverizer 332 n.
millet
cereals 301 n.
grass 366 n.
milliard
over one hundred
99 n.
milligram
weighing 322 n.
millimetre
small quantity
33 n.
short distance
200 n.
long measure
203 n.
millinery
dressing 228 n.
headgear 228 n.
million
over one hundred
99 n.
multitude 104 n.
**millionaire,
millionairess**
rich person 800 n.
millions
great quantity
32 n.
multitude 104 n.
funds 797 n.
millpond
smoothness 258 n.
quietude 266 n.
lake 346 n.
millstone
pulverizer 332 n.
encumbrance
702 n.
mime
imitate 20 vb.
imitator 20 n.
mimicry 20 n.
gesticulate 547 vb.
gesture 547 n.
represent 551 vb.
representation
551 n.
act 594 vb.

mistaken
mistaken 495 adj.
mistime
mistime 138 vb.
mistletoe
plant 366 n.
mistral
wind 352 n.
mistreatment
misuse 675 n.
mistress
female 373 n.
master 741 n.
owner 776 n.
title 870 n.
loved one 887 n.
kept woman 952 n.
mistrust
doubt 486 n.
doubt 486 vb.
nervousness 854 n.
jealousy 911 n.
misty
insubstantial 4 adj.
humid 341 adj.
cloudy 355 adj.
dim 419 adj.
opaque 423 adj.
indistinct 444 adj.
uncertain 474 adj.
misunderstand
not know 491 vb.
err 495 vb.
misinterpret
521 vb.
**misunder-
standing**
error 495 n.
misinterpretation
521 n.
misuse
use 673 n.
misuse 675 n.
misuse 675 vb.
mite
small quantity
33 n.
small thing 33 n.
child 132 n.
dwarf 196 n.
insect 365 n.
insufficiency
636 n.
mitigate
abate 37 vb.
moderate 177 vb.
qualify 468 vb.
relieve 831 vb.
extenuate 927 vb.
mitre
join 45 vb.
joint 45 n.
badge of rule
743 n.

vestments 989 n.
mitt
glove 228 n.
mitten
glove 228 n.
mix
mix 43 vb.
mixed-ability
educational
534 adj.
mixed bag
nonuniformity
17 n.
medley 43 n.
accumulation 74 n.
mixed blessing
inexpedience
643 n.
mixed farming
agriculture 370 n.
mixed grill
dish 301 n.
mixer
soft drink 301 n.
mixing bowl
bowl 194 n.
mix it
fight 716 vb.
cause discontent
829 vb.
mixture
mixture 43 n.
medicine 658 n.
mix-up
disorder 61 n.
mnemonic
remembering
505 adj.
reminder 505 n.
moan
blow 352 vb.
faintness 401 n.
sound faint
401 vb.
cry 408 vb.
be discontented
829 vb.
lamentation 836 n.
weep 836 vb.
moat
fence 235 n.
cavity 255 n.
furrow 262 n.
conduit 351 n.
protection 660 n.
obstacle 702 n.
defences 713 n.
mob
rampage 61 vb.
crowd 74 n.
multitude 104 n.
redundance 637 n.
rabble 869 n.
celebrate 876 vb.

not respect 921 vb.
disapprove 924 vb.
mobile
changeable thing
152 n.
hanging object
217 n.
moving 265 adj.
telecommunications
531 n.
mobile home
small house 192 n.
cart 274.
mobile phone
telecommunications
531 n.
mobility
changeableness
152 n.
motion 265 n.
mobilize
bring together
74 vb.
move 265 vb.
make ready
669 vb.
go to war 718 vb.
mob law
anarchy 734 n.
lawlessness 954 n.
moccasins
footwear 228 n.
mocha
brown 430 adj.
mock
simulating 18 adj.
imitative 20 adj.
substituted
150 adj.
disbelieve 486 vb.
fool 542 vb.
spurious 542 adj.
laugh 835 vb.
ridicule 851 vb.
ridicule 851 vb.
satirize 851 vb.
shame 867 vb.
indignity 921 n.
not respect 921 vb.
despise 922 vb.
detract 926 vb.
mockery
insubstantial thing
4 n.
mimicry 20 n.
unbelief 486 n.
deception 542 n.
sham 542 n.
ridicule 851 n.
ostentation 875 n.
disrespect 921 n.
impiety 980 n.
mockingbird
imitator 20 n.

mock-up
prototype 23 n.
exhibit 522 n.
mod
assembly 74 n.
youngster 132 n.
music 412 n.
modality
modality 7 n.
mode
modality 7 n.
statistics 86 n.
key 410 n.
style 566 n.
practice 610 n.
way 624 n.
fashion 848 n.
model
copy 22 n.
be an example
23 vb.
living model
23 n.
prototype 23 n.
composition 56 n.
rule 81 n.
example 83 n.
little 196 adj.
miniature 196 n.
form 243 n.
comparison 462 n.
exhibit 522 n.
exhibitor 522 n.
image 551 n.
represent 551 vb.
sculpt 554 vb.
sculpture 554 n.
plan 623 n.
paragon 646 n.
perfect 646 adj.
plaything 837 n.
person of repute
866 n.
modelling
sculpture 554 n.
mode of address
title 870 n.
moderate
median 30 adj.
small 33 adj.
decrease 37 vb.
moderate 177 adj.
moderate 625 n.
political party
708 n.
lenient 736 adj.
inexcitable
823 adj.
tranquillize
823 vb.
relieve 831 vb.
modest 874 adj.
be temperate
942 vb.

moderation
smallness 33 n.
moderation 177 n.
leniency 736 n.
modern
modern 126 adj.
modernism
modernism 126 n.
art subject 553 n.
heterodoxy 977 n.
modernize
modernize 126 vb.
modest
inconsiderable
33 adj.
small 33 adj.
modest 874 adj.
pure 950 adj.
modesty
modesty 874 n.
modicum
small quantity
33 n.
portion 783 n.
modification
difference 15 n.
chang 143 n.
qualification
468 n.
modify
differ 15 vb.
make unlike 19 vb.
modify 143 vb.
modish
fashionable
848 adj.
reputable 866 adj.
modulate
adjust 24 vb.
modify 143 vb.
harmonize 410 vb.
voice 577 vb.
module
prototype 23 n.
curriculum 534 n.
modus operandi
way 624 n.
modus vivendi
substitute 150 n.
mogul
bigwig 638 n.
mohair
fibre 208 n.
textile 222 n.
hair 259 n.
**Mohammed or
Mahomet**
religious teacher
973 n.
moiety
bisection 92 n.
moire
textile 222 n.
variegation 437 n.

moist
  watery 339 adj.
  humid 341 adj.
moisten
  moisten 341 vb.
moisture
  moisture 341 n.
moisturizing
  beautification
  843 n.
moke
  beast of burden
  273 n.
molar
  tooth 256 n.
  pulverizer 332 n.
molasses
  sweet thing 392 n.
mole
  mammal 365 n.
  spectator 441 n.
  secret service
  459 n.
  latency 523 n.
  informer 524 n.
  identification
  547 n.
  skin disease 651 n.
  collaborator 707 n.
  blemish 845 n.
molecule
  minuteness 196 n.
  element 319 n.
molehill
  minuteness 196 n.
  dome 253 n.
molest
  harm 645 vb.
  torment 827 vb.
  be malevolent
  898 vb.
  debauch 951 vb.
moll
  female 373 n.
  kept woman 952 n.
mollify
  assuage 177 vb.
  pacify 719 vb.
mollusc
  animal 365 n.
  marine life 365 n.
moment
  juncture 8 n.
  small quantity
  33 n.
  date 108 n.
  brief span 114 n.
  instant 116 n.
  cause 156 n.
  importance 638 n.
momentary
  brief 114 adj.
momentous
  crucial 137 adj.

influential 178 adj.
  important 638 adj.
momentum
  energy 160 n.
  impulse 279 n.
monad
  existence 1 n.
  unit 88 n.
monarch
  sovereign 741 n.
  owner 776 n.
  heretical 977 adj.
Monarchianism
  heresy 977 n.
monarchist
  revolter 738 n.
monarchy
  government 733 n.
monastery
  monastery 986 n.
monastic
  monastic 986 adj.
  monk 986 n.
monaural
  sounding 398 adj.
monetary
  monetary
  797 adj.
money
  money 797 n.
moneybags
  rich person 800 n.
moneybox
  box 194 n.
  storage 632 n.
  treasury 799 n.
moneyed
  moneyed 800 adj.
money for jam
  or old rope
  easy thing 701 n.
moneylender
  lender 784 n.
money-making
  gainful 771 adj.
mongoloid
  mentally
  handicapped
  503 adj.
mongoose
  mammal 365 n.
mongrel
  hybrid 43 n.
  mixed 43 adj.
  abnormal 84 adj.
  nonconformist
  84 n.
  dog 365 n.
monies
  funds 797 n.
moniker
  name 561 n.
monism
  unity 88 n.

monitor
  reptile 365 n.
  listener 415 n.
  look after 457 vb.
  enquire 459 vb.
monk
  celibate 895 n.
  pietist 979 n.
  monk 986 n.
monkey
  ram 279 n.
  mammal 365 n.
  be cunning 698 vb.
  funds 797 n.
  bad person 938 n.
monkey
  business
  deception 542 n.
  cunning 698 n.
  perfidy 930 n.
monkey tricks
  foolery 497 n.
  disobedience
  738 n.
  revel 837 n.
monkey with
  impair 655 vb.
monkey wrench
  tool 630 n.
mono
  one 88 adj.
  sound 398 n.
  sounding 398 adj.
monochrome
  uniform 16 adj.
  achromatism
  426 n.
  painting 553 n.
monocle
  eyeglass 442 n.
monogamy
  type of marriage
  894 n.
monogram
  indication 547 n.
  label 547 n.
monograph
  dissertation 591 n.
monolingual
  dictionary
  dictionary 559 n.
monolith
  uniformity 16 n.
  coherence 48 n.
  unit 88 n.
  monument 548 n.
monolithic
  identical 13 adj.
  uniform 16 adj.
  simple 44 adj.
  cohesive 48 adj.
  indivisible 52 adj.
  one 88 adj.
  dense 324 adj.

monologue
  uniformity 16 n.
  unit 88 n.
  oration 579 n.
  soliloquy 585 n.
  stage play 594 n.
monomania
  prejudgment
  481 n.
monophonic
  sounding 398 adj.
monoplane
  aircraft 276 n.
monopolize
  prevail 178 vb.
  absorb 449 vb.
  possess 773 vb.
  appropriate
  786 vb.
  be selfish 932 vb.
monopoly
  exclusion 57 n.
  corporation 708 n.
  restriction 747 n.
  possession 773 n.
  sale 793 n.
monorail
  railway 624 n.
monosyllable
  word 559 n.
monotheism
  unity 88 n.
  deism 973 n.
monotheist
  religionist 973 n.
monotone
  uniform 16 adj.
  uniformity 16 n.
  musical note
  410 n.
  painting 553 n.
monotonous
  identical 13 adj.
  uniform 16 adj.
  continuous 71 adj.
  repeated 106 adj.
  feeble 572 adj.
  tedious 838 adj.
monotony
  uniformity 16 n.
  continuity 71 n.
  tedium 838 n.
  dullness 840 n.
monounsaturated
  fat
  fat 357 n.
Monseigneur
  church title 986 n.
monsieur
  male 372 n.
  title 870 n.
monsoon
  rain 350 n.
  wind 352 n.

monster
  abnormality 84 n.
  nonconformist
  84 n.
  giant 195 n.
  eyesore 842 n.
  prodigy 864 n.
  monster 938 n.
monstrosity
  abnormality 84 n.
  deformity 246 n.
  prodigy 864 n.
monstrous
  exorbitant 32 adj.
  unusual 84 adj.
  huge 195 adj.
  harmful 645 adj.
  not nice 645 adj.
  ugly 842 adj.
  ridiculous 849 adj.
  wonderful 864 adj.
  heinous 934 adj.
montage
  cinema 445 n.
  picture 553 n.
month
  period 110 n.
monthly
  periodically
  141 adv.
  seasonal 141 adj.
  journal 528 n.
  usual 610 adj.
month of
  Sundays
  neverness 109 n.
  long duration
  113 n.
monument
  monument 548 n.
  honours 866 n.
monumental
  enormous 32 adj.
  large 195 adj.
moo
  ululate 409 vb.
  ululation 409 n.
mooch
  beg 761 vb.
  take 786 vb.
mood
  temperament 5 n.
  state 7 n.
  tendency 179 n.
  grammar 564 n.
  whim 604 n.
  conduct 688 n.
  affections 817 n.
  moral sensibility
  819 n.
moody
  fitful 142 adj.
  changeful 152 adj.
  capricious 604 adj.

excitable 822 adj.
melancholic
834 adj.
irascible 892 adj.
sullen 893 adj.
moon
changeable thing
152 n.
follower 284 n.
moon 321 n.
satellite 321 n.
luminary 420 n.
be inattentive
456 vb.
moon after
desire 859 vb.
moonlight
moon 321 n.
light 417 n.
work 682 vb.
not pay 805 vb.
moonlighting
escape 667 n.
swindling 788 n.
moonlit
undimmed
417 adj.
moonshine
insubstantial thing
4 n.
alcoholic drink
301 n.
moon 321 n.
light 417 n.
empty talk 515 n.
fable 543 n.
moonstone
gem 844 n.
moor
affix 45 vb.
tie 45 vb.
desert 172 n.
place 187 vb.
high land 209 n.
navigate 269 vb.
arrive 295 vb.
plain 348 n.
mooring
station 187 n.
arrival 295 n.
moose
mammal 365 n.
moot
interrogate
459 vb.
propound 512 vb.
moot point
topic 452 n.
question 459 n.
mop
hair 259 n.
dry 342 vb.
dryer 342 n.
clean 648 vb.

cleaning utensil
648 n.
mope
be dejected 834 vb.
moped
conveyance 267 n.
bicycle 274 n.
moped rider
rider 268 n.
mop up
destroy 165 vb.
absorb 299 vb.
empty 300 vb.
dry 342 vb.
clean 648 vb.
carry through
725 vb.
moraine
leavings 41 n.
piece 53 n.
soil 344 n.
moral
judgment 480 n.
maxim 496 n.
phrase 563 n.
good 615 adj.
precept 693 n.
reputable 866 adj.
ethical 917 adj.
virtuous 933 adj.
pure 950 adj.
moral certainty
positiveness
473 n.
morale
state 7 n.
morale-boosting
aiding 703 adj.
**moral high
ground**
morals 917 n.
moralistic
ethical 917 adj.
morality
right 913 n.
morals 917 n.
virtue 933 n.
purity 950 n.
moralize
teach 534 vb.
**moral
philosophy**
morals 917 n.
morals
conduct 688 n.
morals 917 n.
purity 950 n.
morass
marsh 347 n.
moratorium
delay 136 n.
lull 145 n.
nonpayment
805 n.

morbid
diseased 651 adj.
morbidity
badness 645 n.
mordant
keen 174 adj.
pigment 425 n.
concise 569 adj.
disapproving
924 adj.
more
finite quantity
26 n.
beyond 34 adv.
additional 38 adj.
in addition 38 adv.
bravo 923 int.
moreish
edible 301 adj.
savoury 390 adj.
more or less
about 33 adv.
nearly 200 adv.
moreover
in addition 38 adv.
mores
habit 610 n.
practice 610 n.
conduct 688 n.
morgue
death 361 n.
interment 364 n.
inactivity 679 n.
moribund
ageing 131 adj.
dying 361 adj.
**Mori poll
(tdmk)**
vote 605 n.
Mormon
religionist 973 n.
sectarian 978 n.
morn
morning 128 n.
morning
period 110 n.
morning 128 n.
perpetually
139 adv.
**morning after
the night
before**
crapulence 949 n.
morning dress
formal dress 228 n.
morning star
planet 321 n.
luminary 420 n.
morocco
skin 226 n.
bookbinding 589 n.
moron
fool 501 n.
person with a

learning disability
504 n.
moronic
mindless 448 adj.
absurd 497 adj.
unintelligent
499 adj.
having a learning
disability 503 adj.
morose
melancholic
834 adj.
unsociable 883 adj.
sullen 893 adj.
morpheme
word 559 n.
part of speech
564 n.
morphia
drug 658 n.
drug-taking 949 n.
morphine
anaesthetic 375 n.
drug 658 n.
soporific 679 n.
drug-taking 949 n.
morphology
form 243 n.
biology 358 n.
zoology 367 n.
morris dance
dance 837 n.
morse
fastening 47 n.
telecommunication
531 n.
signal 547 n.
morsel
small quantity
33 n.
piece 53 n.
mouthful 301 n.
mortal
ephemeral 114 adj.
destructive 165 adj.
dying 361 adj.
deadly 362 adj.
person 371 n.
evil 616 n.
mortality
transience 114 n.
death 361 n.
death roll 361 n.
humankind 371 n.
mortar
adhesive 47 n.
gun 723 n.
mortgage
encumbrance
702 n.
give security
767 vb.
security 767 n.
lending 784 n.

borrow 785 vb.
borrowing 785 n.
credit 802 n.
debt 803 n.
mortification
decay 51 n.
death 361 n.
sorrow 825 n.
annoyance 827 n.
discontent 829 n.
regret 830 n.
humiliation 872 n.
humility 872 n.
envy 912 n.
indignity 921 n.
asceticism 945 n.
mortified
unhappy 825 adj.
discontented
829 adj.
inglorious 867 adj.
mortify
decompose 51 vb.
hurt 827 vb.
cause discontent
829 vb.
humiliate 872 vb.
mortise
join 45 vb.
receptacle 194 n.
introduce 231 vb.
furrow 262 n.
mortuary
death 361 n.
funereal 364 adj.
interment 364 n.
Mosaic
religious 973 adj.
scriptural 975 adj.
mosaic
nonuniformity
17 n.
medley 43 n.
multiform 82 adj.
chequer 437 n.
variegated 437 adj.
picture 553 n.
ornamental art
844 n.
mosey along
wander 267 vb.
mosey around
be curious 453 vb.
Moslem
religionist 973 n.
religious 973 adj.
mosque
church 990 n.
temple 990 n.
mosquito
insect 365 n.
bane 659 n.
moss
plant 366 n.

mum's the word
hush 399 int.
munch
chew 301 vb.
municipality
district 184 n.
jurisdiction 955 n.
munificent
liberal 813 adj.
munitions
arms 723 n.
mural
picture 553 n.
murder
homicide 362 n.
killing 362 n.
murder 362 vb.
indoor game 837 n.
cruel act 898 n.
murderer
murderer 362 n.
murderous
murderous 362 adj.
murk
darkness 418 n.
dimness 419 n.
murky
dense 324 adj.
dark 418 adj.
opaque 423 adj.
murmur
flow 350 VB.
faintness 401 n.
sound faint
401 vb.
roll 403 n.
imply 523 vb.
deprecate 762 vb.
deprecation 762 n.
Murphy's law
rule 81 n.
axiom 496 n.
muscle
ligature 47 n.
power 160 n.
vitality 162 n.
exertion 682 n.
muscle in
intrude 297 vb.
muscleman
athlete 162 n.
bulk 195 n.
a beauty 841 n.
muscular
stalwart 162 adj.
**muscular
dystrophy**
nervous disorders
651 n.
muse
meditate 449 vb.
be inattentive
456 vb.
poetry 593 n.

excitation 821 n.
Muses
poetry 593 n.
lesser deity 967 n.
museum
accumulation 74 n.
antiquity 125 n.
exhibit 522 n.
collection 632 n.
museum piece
archaism 127 n.
exhibit 522 n.
exceller 644 n.
mush
face 237 n.
orifice 263 n.
pulpiness 356 n.
mushroom
grow 36 vb.
new 126 adj.
be fruitful 171 vb.
expand 197 vb.
dome 253 n.
fruit and vegetables
301 n.
plant 366 n.
whitish 427 adj.
brown 430 adj.
mushy
soft 327 adj.
music
music 412 n.
broadcast 531 n.
musical
melodious 410 adj.
musical 412 adj.
vocal music 412 n.
film 445 n.
stage play 594 n.
pleasurable
826 adj.
musical chairs
indoor game 837 n.
musical comedy
vocal music 412 n.
stage play 594 n.
**musical
instrument**
musical instrument
414 n.
music centre
gramophone
414 n.
musician
musician 413 n.
music-making
music 412 n.
musicologist
musician 413 n.
**music to one's
ears, be**
delight 826 vb.
musk
scent 396 n.

musket
firearm 723 n.
musketeer
soldiery 722 n.
musky
fragrant 396 adj.
Muslim
religionist 973 n.
muslin
textile 222 n.
semitransparency
424 n.
mussel
fish food 301 n.
marine life 365 n.
must, a
necessity 596 n.
requirement 627 n.
mustang
saddle horse 273 n.
mustard
condiment 389 n.
yellowness 433 n.
mustard gas
poison 659 n.
weapon 723 n.
muster
bring together
74 vb.
number 86 vb.
statistics 86 n.
musty
fetid 397 adj.
dirty 649 adj.
mutable
changeable
143 adj.
changeful 152 adj.
mutant
nonconformist
84 n.
mutation
variant 15 n.
nonuniformity
17 n.
misfit 25 n.
abnormality 84 n.
change 143 n.
conversion 147 n.
deformity 246 n.
mute
silent 399 adj.
mute 401 vb.
nonresonance
405 n.
voiceless 578 adj.
taciturn 582 adj.
muted
muted 401 adj.
soft-hued 425 adj.
serious 834 adj.
mutilate
subtract 39 vb.
destroy 165 vb.

deform 244 vb.
impair 655 vb.
make ugly 842 vb.
mutineer
revolter 738 n.
undutifulness
918 n.
schismatic 978 n.
mutinous
quarrelling
709 adj.
defiant 711 adj.
resisting 715 adj.
disobedient
738 adj.
undutiful 918 adj.
mutiny
strike 145 n.
resist 715 vb.
revolt 738 n.
revolt 738 vb.
fail in duty 918 vb.
undutifulness
918 n.
mutt
dog 365 n.
mutter
blow 352 vb.
sound faint
401 vb.
roll 403 n.
cry 408 vb.
voice 577 n.
stammer 580 vb.
threaten 900 vb.
mutton
meat 301 n.
mutton-chops
hair 259 n.
mutual
relative 9 adj.
correlative 12 adj.
muzak
music 412 n.
muzzle
disable 161 vb.
protuberance
254 n.
orifice 263 n.
stopper 264 n.
silence 399 vb.
make mute
578 vb.
hinder 702 vb.
firearm 723 n.
restrain 747 vb.
fetter 748 n.
muzzy
tipsy 949 adj.
mycology
botany 368 n.
myna bird
imitator 20 n.
bird 365 n.

myopia
dim sight 440 n.
myriad
over one hundred
99 n.
many 104 adj.
myrrh
resin 357 n.
interment 364 n.
scent 396 n.
myself
self 80 n.
subjectivity 320 n.
mysterious
unusual 84 adj.
invisible 444 adj.
uncertain 474 adj.
unknown 491 adj.
puzzling 517 adj.
occult 523 adj.
concealed 525 adj.
unclear 568 adj.
wonderful 864 adj.
mystery
invisibility 444 n.
unknown thing
491 n.
latency 523 n.
secrecy 525 n.
enigma 530 n.
secret 530 n.
rite 988 n.
mystery play
stage play 594 n.
mystic
occult 523 adj.
religious 973 adj.
revelational
975 adj.
pietist 979 n.
pious 979 adj.
worshipper 981 n.
occultist 984 n.
mystical
divine 965 adj.
mysticism
meditation 449 n.
latency 523 n.
religion 973 n.
revelation 975 n.
piety 979 n.
occultism 984 n.
mystify
puzzle 474 vb.
sophisticate
477 vb.
deceive 542 vb.
mystique
prestige 866 n.
cult 981 n.
myth
fantasy 513 n.
fable 543 n.
narrative 590 n.

mythical
erroneous 495 adj.
mythology
tradition 127 n.
myxomatosis
animal disease
651 n.

N

n
many 104 adj.
Naafi
café 192 n.
nab
alcoholic drink
301 n.
ensnare 542 vb.
arrest 747 vb.
take 786 vb.
nabob
officer 741 n.
nadir
inferiority 35 n.
extremity 69 n.
zero 103 n.
lowness 210 n.
depth 211 n.
base 214 n.
naff
useless 641 adj.
bad 645 adj.
vulgar 847 adj.
naff off
go away 190 vb.
nag
horse 273 n.
saddle horse 273 n.
incite 612 vb.
animate 821 vb.
torment 827 vb.
enrage 891 vb.
naiad
nymph 967 n.
mythical being
970 n.
nail
affix 45 vb.
fastening 47 n.
hanger 217 n.
sharp point 256 n.
perforator 263 n.
tool 630 n.
nail bomb
bomb 723 n.
nail file
smoother 258 n.
cosmetic 843 n.
naive
credulous 487 adj.
ignorant 491 adj.
artless 699 adj.
innocent 935 adj.

naked
simple 44 adj.
uncovered 229 adj.
visible 443 adj.
vulnerable 661 adj.
namby-pamby
weak 163 adj.
weakling 163 n.
affected 850 adj.
name
inform 524 vb.
indicate 547 vb.
label 547 n.
name 561 n.
name 561 vb.
famousness 866 n.
repute 866 n.
accuse 928 vb.
name-dropping
affected 850 adj.
nameless
anonymous
562 adj.
inglorious 867 adj.
namely
namely 80 adv.
in plain words
520 adv.
namesake
name 561 n.
nan
maternity 169 n.
cereals 301 n.
nancy
nonconformist
84 n.
nanny
protector 660 n.
domestic 742 n.
retainer 742 n.
servant 742 n.
keeper 749 n.
nanny goat
goat 365 n.
female animal
373 n.
nap
weaving 222 n.
texture 331 n.
sleep 679 n.
sleep 679 vb.
card game 837 n.
nape
rear 238 n.
narcissism
vanity 873 n.
love 887 n.
selfishness 932 n.
narcolepsy
insensibility
375 n.
narcoterrorism
drug 949 n.
drug peddler 949 n.

narcotic
anaesthetic 375 n.
drug 658 n.
remedial 658 adj.
drug-taking 949 n.
intoxicating
949 adj.
nark
informer 524 n.
accuser 928 n.
narrate
communicate
524 vb.
describe 590 vb.
narrative
narrative 590 n.
narrator
speaker 579 n.
narrow
become small
198 vb.
make smaller
198 vb.
narrow 206 adj.
narrow-minded
481 adj.
narrowboat
boat 275 n.
narrowcasting
publication 528 n.
narrow escape
danger 661 n.
escape 667 n.
narrow-minded
narrow-minded
481 adj.
prudish 950 adj.
narrows
narrowness 206 n.
nasal
speech sound
398 n.
nascent
beginning 68 adj.
nasty
not nice 645 adj.
unclean 649 adj.
dangerous 661 adj.
unpleasant
827 adj.
hateful 888 adj.
malevolent
898 adj.
unkind 898 adj.
natal
first 68 adj.
nation
race 11 n.
nation 371 n.
community 708 n.
national
universal 79 adj.
native 191 adj.
native 191 n.

national 371 adj.
subject 742 n.
National
Curriculum
education 534 n.
national
emblem
heraldry 547 n.
nationalism
nation 371 n.
patriotism 901 n.
nationalist
patriot 901 n.
nationalistic
biased 481 adj.
patriotic 901 adj.
nationality
consanguinity
11 n.
nation 371 n.
nationalization
association 706 n.
joint possession
775 n.
transfer 780 n.
trade 791 n.
National
Lottery
equal chance
159 n.
gambling 618 n.
gambling game
301 n.
national
monument
monument 548 n.
national service
war measures
718 n.
nationwide
universal 79 adj.
native
genetic 5 adj.
intrinsic 5 adj.
component 58 adj.
native 191 adj.
native 191 n.
artless 699 adj.
native heath
home 192 n.
native wit
ability 160 n.
Nativity
holy day 988 n.
nativity
origin 68 n.
propagation 167 n.
life 360 n.
natter
chat 584 n.
converse 584 vb.
natty
personable
841 adj.

natural
real 1 adj.
substantial 3 adj.
intrinsic 5 adj.
typical 83 adj.
material 319 adj.
musical note
410 n.
genuine 494 adj.
person with a
learning disability
504 n.
plain 573 adj.
usual 610 adj.
artless 699 adj.
friendly 880 adj.
natural gas
gas 336 n.
fuel 385 n.
naturalistic
literary 557 adj.
naturalized
converted 147 adj.
native 191 adj.
habituated
610 adj.
naturalness
plainness 573 n.
artlessness 699 n.
natural
philosophy
physics 319 n.
philosophy 449 n.
science 490 n.
nature
essence 1 n.
character 5 n.
composition 56 n.
sort 77 n.
tendency 179 n.
affections 817 n.
nature study
biology 358 n.
naturism
uncovering 229 n.
naturist
stripper 229 n.
naturopathy
medical art 658 n.
naught
insubstantiality
4 n.
zero 103 n.
naughty
difficult 700 adj.
disobedient
738 adj.
wicked 934 adj.
impure 951 adj.
unchaste 951 adj.
nausea
voidance 300 n.
digestive disorders
651 n.

nephew
kinsman 11 n.
male 372 n.
nephritis
digestive disorders
651 n.
ne plus ultra
superiority 34 n.
completeness 54 n.
extremity 69 n.
summit 213 n.
limit 236 n.
exceller 644 n.
perfection 646 n.
completion 725 n.
fashion 848 n.
nepotism
consanguinity
11 n.
injustice 914 n.
Neptune
planet 321 n.
sea god 343 n.
mythic deity 966 n.
Olympian deity
967 n.
nereid
nymph 967 n.
nerve
stability 153 n.
vitality 162 n.
courage 855 n.
sauciness 878 n.
nerve gas
poison 659 n.
weapon 723 n.
nerve-racking
frightening
854 adj.
nerves
neurosis 503 n.
ill health 651 n.
excitability 822 n.
nervousness
854 n.
nervous
excitable 822 adj.
nervous 854 adj.
nervous
breakdown
neurosis 503 n.
nervous disorders
651 n.
nervous system
sense 374 n.
nervy
active 678 adj.
excitable 822 adj.
nervous 854 adj.
nest
origin 68 n.
group 74 n.
dwell 192 vb.
nest 192 n.

nest egg
store 632 n.
preparation 669 n.
wealth 800 n.
nestle
dwell 192 vb.
caress 889 vb.
nestling
young creature
132 n.
net
remaining 41 adj.
bring together
74 vb.
receptacle 194 n.
cross 222 vb.
network 222 n.
textile 222 n.
enclosure 235 n.
semitransparency
424 n.
ensnare 542 vb.
trap 542 n.
hunt 619 vb.
acquire 771 vb.
receive 782 vb.
take 786 vb.
Net, the
computing 86 n.
information 524 n.
netball
ball game 837 n.
nether
low 210 adj.
net profit
gain 771 n.
netting
network 222 n.
nettle
prickle 256 n.
bane 659 n.
hurt 827 vb.
huff 891 vb.
nettlerash
tingling 378 n.
skin disease
651 n.
network
connect 45 vb.
union 45 n.
bond 47 n.
network 222 n.
broadcasting
531 n.
cooperate 706 vb.
networking
latency 523 n.
cooperation 706 n.
neuralgia
pang 377 n.
neuritis
pang 377 n.
neurology
medical art 658 n.

neuropath
neurotic 504 n.
neurosis
neurosis 503 n.
neurosurgery
head 213 n.
neurotic
neurotic 503 adj.
neurotic 504 n.
neuter
unman 161 vb.
material 319 adj.
grammatical
564 adj.
neutral
inert 175 adj.
colourless 426 adj.
grey 429 adj.
greyness 429 n.
moderate 625 n.
neutral 625 adj.
pacifist 717 n.
peaceful 717 adj.
free person 744 n.
neutrality
middle point 30 n.
disunion 46 n.
moderation 177 n.
no choice 606 n.
middle way 625 n.
peace 717 n.
indifference 860 n.
neutralize
nullify 2 vb.
disable 161 vb.
weaken 163 vb.
assuage 177 vb.
counteract 182 vb.
neutron
minuteness 196 n.
element 319 n.
neutron bomb
bomb 723 n.
never
never 109 adv.
never-ending
perpetual 115 adj.
prolix 570 adj.
never-never, the
borrowing 785 n.
purchase 792 n.
nevertheless
nevertheless
468 adv.
new
new 126 adj.
unknown 491 adj.
unhabituated
611 adj.
New Age
traveller
nonconformist
84 n.
wanderer 268 n.

new boy
intruder 59 n.
incomer 297 n.
beginner 538 n.
new broom
newness 126 n.
busy person 678 n.
newcomer
intruder 59 n.
successor 67 n.
incomer 297 n.
new departure
originality 21 n.
newfangled
unusual 84 adj.
modern 126 adj.
changeable
143 adj.
unknown 491 adj.
fashionable
848 adj.
new leaf
newness 126 n.
improvement
654 n.
new look
modernism 126 n.
change 143 n.
repair 656 n.
revival 656 n.
fashion 848 n.
newlyweds
spouse 894 n.
New Man
male 372 n.
new moon
moon 321 n.
news
new 529 n.
broadcast 531 n.
newsagent
tradespeople
794 n.
newscaster
news reporter
529 n.
broadcaster 531 n.
news flash
news 529 n.
broadcast 531 n.
newsletter
publicity 528 n.
the press 528 n.
newspaper
the press 528 n.
reading matter
589 n.
newspeak
equivocalness
518 n.
neology 560 n.
newsprint
script 586 n.
paper 631 n.

newsreader
new reporter 529 n.
broadcaster 531 n.
newsreel
film 445 n.
publicity 528 n.
new 529 n.
newssheet
the press 528 n.
newsworthy
notable 638 adj.
newsy
informative
524 adj.
loquacious
581 adj.
newt
amphibian 365 n.
new technology
production 164 n.
means 629 n.
next
after 65 adv.
sequential 65 adj.
subsequent
120 adj.
subsequently
120 adv.
next-door to
near 200 adj.
next-of-kin
akin 11 adj.
kinsman 11 n.
beneficiary 776 n.
nib
vertex 213 n.
sharp point 256 n.
stationery 586 n.
nibble
eat 301 vb.
graze 301 vb.
mouthful 301 n.
taste 386 n.
be duped 544 vb.
caress 889 vb.
endearment 889 n.
nice
pleasant 376 adj.
careful 457 adj.
discriminating
463 adj.
accurate 494 adj.
pleasurable
826 adj.
tasteful 846 adj.
fastidious
862 adj.
amiable 884 adj.
niceness
pleasurableness
826 n.
fastidiousness
862 n.
courtesy 884 n.

nicety
differentiation
15 n.
discrimination
463 n.
fastidiousness
862 n.
niche
place 185 n.
compartment
194 n.
shelf 218 n.
angularity 247 n.
cavity 255 n.
hiding-place 527 n.
honours 866 n.
nick
small thing 33 n.
cut 46 vb.
notch 260 n.
notch 260 vb.
ensnare 542 vb.
indication 547 n.
mark 547 vb.
wound 655 n.
wound 655 vb.
arrest 747 n.
lockup 748 n.
steal 788 vb.
nickel
coinage 797 n.
nicker
coinage 797 n.
nickname
name 561 n.
name 561 vb.
misname 562 vb.
misnomer 562 n.
nick of time
occasion 137 n.
nicotine
tobacco 388 n.
tonic 658 n.
drug-taking 949 n.
nictitate
be dim-sighted
440 vb.
nidus
nest 192 n.
niece
kinsman 11 n.
female 373 n.
niff
odour 394 n.
stench 397 n.
stink 397 vb.
nifty
speedy 277 adj.
niggardly
insufficient
636 adj.
niggle
cause discontent
829 vb.

criticize 924 vb.
nigh
future 124 adj.
near 200 adv.
night
darkness 418 n.
night and day
continuously
71 adv.
perpetually
139 adv.
fluctuation 317 n.
nightbird
bird 365 n.
nightcap
moderator 177 n.
nightwear 228 n.
valediction 296 n.
draught 301 n.
soporific 679 n.
nightclothes
nightwear 228 n.
night club
meeting place
192 n.
theatre 594 n.
place of
amusement
837 n.
night cream
cosmetic 843 n.
nightdress
nightwear 228 n.
nightfall
evening 129 n.
darkness 418 n.
nightingale
bird 365 n.
nightly
seasonal 141 adj.
nightmare
fantasy 513 n.
suffering 825 n.
intimidation
854 n.
demon 970 n.
night-owl
evening 129 n.
nightshirt
nightwear 228 n.
night
   watchman
doorkeeper 264 n.
spectator 441 n.
protector 660 n.
keeper 749 n.
nihilism
extinction 2 n.
nonexistence 2 n.
disorder 61 n.
philosophy 449 n.
sedition 738 n.
nihilistic
disorderly 61 adj.

violent 176 adj.
nil
nonexistence 2 n.
zero 103 n.
nimble
speedy 277 adj.
active 678 adj.
skilful 694 adj.
nimbus
light 417 n.
honours 866 n.
nincompoop
fool 501 n.
ninny 501 n.
nine
over five 99 n.
nine days'
   wonder
insubstantial thing
4 n.
over five 99 n.
brief span 114 n.
prodigy 864 n.
ninepins
ball game 837 n.
nineteen to the
   dozen
swiftly 277 adv.
ninety
twenty and over
99 n.
ninety-nine per
   cent
chief part 52 n.
ninjutsu
wrestling 716 n.
ninny
fool 501 n.
ninny 501 n.
ninth
musical note
410 n.
nip
make smaller
198 vb.
make thin 206 vb.
move fast 277 vb.
draught 301 n.
give pain 377 vb.
pang 377 n.
touch 378 vb.
refrigerate 382 vb.
nip and tuck
equal 28 adj.
synchronism
123 n.
near 200 adj.
nip in the bud
be early 135 vb.
destroy 165 vb.
suppress 165 vb.
shorten 204 vb.
kill 362 vb.
hinder 702 vb.

nipper
youngster 132 n.
nippers
pincers 778 n.
nipple
bosom 253 n.
nippy
vigorous 174 adj.
cold 380 adj.
active 678 adj.
nirvana
extinction 2 n.
happiness 824 n.
divineness 965 n.
heaven 971 n.
Nissen hut
small house 192 n.
nit
insect 365 n.
nit-picking
trivial 639 adj.
discontent 829 n.
fastidiousness
862 n.
nitrates
fertilizer 171 n.
nitrogen
air 340 n.
nitroglycerine
explosive 723 n.
nitty-gritty
reality 1 n.
substance 3 n.
essential part 5 n.
chief part 52 n.
particulars 80 n.
source 156 n.
base 214 n.
interiority 224 n.
element 319 n.
meaning 514 n.
chief thing 638 n.
nitwit
dunce 501 n.
nix
zero 103 n.
mythical being
970 n.
No
stage play 594 n.
no
_no_ 489 adv.
negation 533 n.
refusal 760 n.
Noah's Ark
ship 275 n.
zoo 369 n.
nob
head 213 n.
fop 848 n.
aristocrat 868 n.
nobble
disable 161 vb.
take 786 vb.

steal 788 vb.
nobbly
projecting 254 adj.
Nobel prize
reward 962 n.
nobility
aristocracy 868 n.
nobility 868 n.
probity 929 n.
noble
important 638 adj.
coinage 797 n.
renowned 866 adj.
noble 868 adj.
person of rank
868 n.
title 870 n.
honourable
929 adj.
nobleman or -
   woman
aristocrat 868 n.
person of rank
868 n.
noblesse
aristocracy 868 n.
nobility 868 n.
nobody
zero 103 n.
nobody 190 n.
nonentity 639 n.
nobody's
unpossessed
774 adj.
nobody's fool
sage 500 n.
nocturnal
dark 418 adj.
nocturne
musical piece
412 n.
art subject 553 n.
nod
hang 217 vb.
obeisance 311 n.
stoop 311 vb.
fluctuation 317 n.
oscillate 317 vb.
be inattentive
456 vb.
be neglectful
458 vb.
assent 488 n.
assent 488 vb.
hint 524 n.
gesticulate 547 vb.
gesture 547 n.
sleep 679 vb.
be fatigued
684 vb.
command 737 n.
command 737 vb.
permit 756 vb.
consent 758 vb.

**not trouble
oneself**
be incurious
454 vb.
not turn a hair
be insensitive
820 vb.
keep calm 823 vb.
not up to it
insufficient
636 adj.
not with it
antiquated
127 adj.
abstracted 456 adj.
notwithstanding
although 182 adv.
**not worth the
effort**
profitless 641 adj.
nougat
sweets 301 n.
nought
zero 103 n.
**noughts and
crosses**
indoor game 837 n.
noun
name 561 n.
part of speech
564 n.
nourish
feed 301 vb.
nourishment
food 301 n.
nous
intelligence 498 n.
nouveau riche
new 126 adj.
prosperous person
730 n.
rich person 800 n.
commoner 869 n.
nouvelle cuisine
cookery 301 n.
dieting 301 n.
nouvelle vague
film 445 n.
nova
star 321 n.
novel
dissimilar 19 adj.
original 21 adj.
new 126 adj.
unknown 491 adj.
novel 590 n.
novelette
novel 590 n.
novelist
author 589 n.
novelty
dissimilarity 19 n.
originality 21 n.
newness 126 n.

bauble 639 n.
pleasurableness
826 n.
novena
over five 99 n.
church service
988 n.
novice
ignoramus 493 n.
beginner 538 n.
bungler 697 n.
monk 986 n.
nun 986 n.
lay person 987 n.
now
at present 121 adv.
nowadays
at present 121 adv.
present time
121 n.
now and then
sometimes
139 adv.
no way
impossibility
470 n.
impossibly
470 adv.
not likely 472 int.
no 489 adv.
now or never
at present 121 adv.
noxious
fetid 397 adj.
harmful 645 adj.
insalubrious
653 adj.
nozzle
projection 254 n.
orifice 263 n.
outlet 298 n.
air pipe 353 n.
nuance
differentiation
15 n.
degree 27 n.
small quantity
33 n.
hue 425 n.
discrimination
463 n.
nub
substance 3 n.
essential part 5 n.
focus 76 n.
centre 225 n.
chief thing 638 n.
nubile
grown-up 134 adj.
nuclear
dynamic 160 adj.
central 225 adj.
nuclear bomb
bomb 723 n.

nuclear fallout
radiation 417 n.
poison 659 n.
nuclear family
family 11 n.
nuclear missile
nucleonics 160 n.
rocket 276 n.
nuclear reactor
nucleonics 160 n.
nuclear weapon
weapon 723 n.
nuclear winter
winter 129 n.
nucleonics 160 n.
blight 659 n.
nucleate
make smaller
198 vb.
centralize 225 vb.
be dense 324 vb.
nucleolus
centre 225 n.
organism 358 n.
nucleonics
nucleonics 160 n.
nucleus
essential part 5 n.
middle 70 n.
source 156 n.
minuteness 196 n.
centre 225 n.
element 319 n.
solid body 324 n.
organism 358 n.
chief thing 638 n.
nude
uncovered 229 adj.
art subject 553 n.
nudge
knock 279 n.
agitate 318 vb.
agitation 318 n.
hint 524 n.
hint 524 vb.
gesticulate 547 vb.
gesture 547 n.
indication 547 n.
warning 664 n.
nudge-nudge
impure 951 adj.
nudism
uncovering 229 n.
nudist
stripper 229 n.
nudity
bareness 229 n.
nugget
solid body 324 n.
nuisance
evil 616 n.
hindrance 702 n.
obstacle 702 n.
annoyance 827 n.

nuke
destroy 165 vb.
null
insubstantial 4 adj.
not one 103 adj.
null and void
nonexistent 2 adj.
powerless 161 adj.
unproductive
172 adj.
illegal 954 adj.
nullify
nullify 2 vb.
not be 4 vb.
negate 533 vb.
abrogate 752 vb.
numb
inert 175 adj.
insensible 375 adj.
number
subdivision 53 n.
number 85 n.
number 86 vb.
abode 192 n.
mark 547 vb.
grammar 564 n.
reading matter
589 n.
numbered
statistical 86 adj.
number one
self 80 n.
numberplate
label 547 n.
numbness
helplessness 161 n.
insensibility 375 n.
moral insensibility
820 n.
numeracy
culture 490 n.
numeral
number 85 n.
numerical 85 adj.
numeration
numeration 86 n.
numerator
numerical element
85 n.
numerical
numerical 85 adj.
numerous
many 104 adj.
numismatics
coinage 797 n.
numismatist
collector 492 n.
numskull
ignoramus 493 n.
dunce 501 n.
nun
female 373 n.
virgin 950 n.

pietist 979 n.
nun 986 n.
nunnery
monastery 986 n.
nuptials
wedding 894 n.
nurse
feed 301 vb.
look after 457 vb.
cure 656 vb.
doctor 658 vb.
nurse 658 n.
safeguard 660 vb.
minister to 703 vb.
domestic 742 n.
retainer 742 n.
servant 742 n.
keeper 749 n.
please 826 vb.
pet 889 vb.
do good 897 adj.
nurse a grudge
be discontented
829 vb.
be hostile 881 vb.
nursemaid
teacher 537 n.
protector 660 n.
domestic 742 n.
retainer 742 n.
servant 742 n.
keeper 749 n.
nursery
nonage 130 n.
abundance 171 n.
chamber 194 n.
farm 370 n.
workshop 687 n.
**nurseryman or
woman**
gardener 370 n.
nursery rhyme
doggerel 593 n.
nursery slope
lowness 210 n.
incline 220 n.
nursing
therapy 658 n.
nurture
feed 301 vb.
food 301 n.
breed stock 369 vb.
educate 534 vb.
mature 669 vb.
ripening 669 n.
nut
fastening 47 n.
head 213 n.
fruit and vegetables
301 n.
flower 366 n.
madman 504 n.
the maladjusted
504 n.

hypocritical
541 adj.
dirty 649 adj.
servile 879 adj.
flattering 925 adj.
ointment
lubricant 334 n.
unguent 357 n.
balm 658 n.
OK
assent 488 n.
not bad 644 n.
okra
fruit and vegetables
301 n.
old
antiquated
127 adj.
olden 127 adj.
ageing 131 adj.
weak 163 adj.
old age
old age 131 n.
helplessness
161 n.
Old Bailey
lawcourt 956 n.
old boy
old man 133 n.
learner 538 n.
old-boy network
latency 523 n.
old crony
friend 880 n.
See **chum**
old dog
expert 696 n.
olden
olden 127 adj.
olden days
past time 125 n.
older
older 131 adj.
olde worlde
antiquated
127 adj.
old-fashioned
anachronistic
118 adj.
antiquated
127 adj.
old flame
loved one 887 n.
old fogy
archaism 127 n.
old man 133 n.
old girl
old woman 133 n.
learner 538 n.
old gold
orange 432 n.
old hand
old man 133 n.
expert 696 n.

old hat
antiquated
127 adj.
unwonted 611 adj.
old lag
prisoner 750 n.
offender 904 n.
old maid
female 373 n.
card game 837 n.
spinster 895 n.
virgin 950 n.
old master
picture 553 n.
artist 556 n.
Old Nick
Mephisto 969 n.
old offender
offender 904 n.
**old people's
home**
gerontology 131 n.
retreat 192 n.
shelter 662 n.
old salt
mariner 270 n.
old-school
antiquated
127 adj.
opinionatedness
602 n.
old-school tie
injustice 914 n.
old stager
old man 133 n.
expert 696 n.
Old Testament
scripture 975 n.
old wives' tales
error 495 n.
fable 543 n.
old-world
antiquated
127 adj.
courteous 884 n.
oleograph
picture 553 n.
'O' level
exam 459 n.
olfaction
odour 394 n.
oligarchy
government 733 n.
olive
green 434 adj.
olive branch
peace offering
719 n.
olive oil
oil 357 n.
Olympics
contest 716 n.
ombudsman
estimator 480 n.

mediator 720 n.
magistracy 957 n.
omega
extremity 69 n.
omelette
dish 301 n.
omen
omen 511 n.
ominous
predicting 511 adj.
harmful 645 adj.
dangerous 661 adj.
adverse 731 adj.
unpromising
853 adj.
frightening
854 adj.
omission
deficit 55 n.
incompleteness
55 n.
exclusion 57 n.
negligence 458 n.
failure 728 n.
nonobservance
769 n.
guilty act 936 n.
omission mark
punctuation 547 n.
omit
be incomplete
55 vb.
exclude 57 vb.
neglect 458 vb.
be taciturn 582 vb.
not observe 769 vb.
omnibus
comprehensive
52 adj.
bus 274 n.
omnibus edition
edition 589 n.
omnipotent
powerful 160 adj.
strong 162 adj.
godlike 965 adj.
omnipresent
ubiquitous 189 adj.
godlike 965 adj.
omniscient
knowing 490 adj.
godlike 965 adj.
omnivorous
feeding 301 adj.
greedy 859 adj.
gluttonous 947 adj.
omophagous
feeding 301 n.
OMOV
vote 605 n.
on
concerning 9 adv.
forward 285 adv.
shown 522 adj.

on account of
hence 158 adv.
**on a hiding to
nothing, be**
waste effort
641 adj.
face danger
661 vb.
be defeated 728 vb.
on all cylinders
actively 678 adv.
on and on
for ever 115 adv.
diffusely 570 adv.
on a par
equal 28 adj.
**on appro,
approval**
chosen 605 adj.
purchase 792 n.
on call
expectant 507 adj.
prepared 669 adj.
once
singly 88 adv.
**once (and) for
all**
singly 88 adv.
**once bitten,
twice shy**
cautious 858 adj.
**once in a blue
moon**
seldom 140 adv.
once-over
inspection 438 n.
**once upon a
time**
when 108 adv.
formerly 125 adv.
oncology
medical art 658 n.
oncoming
frontal 237 adj.
approaching
289 adj.
on demand
enough 635 adv.
on display
shown 522 adj.
on duty
obliged 917 adj.
on duty 917 adv.
one
one 88 adj.
unit 88 n.
person 371 n.
one and only
identical 13 adj.
dissimilar 19 adj.
inimitable 21 adj.
one 88 adj.
one another
correlation 12 n.

correlatively
12 adv.
**one-armed
bandit**
gambling 618 n.
one by one
severally 80 adv.
singly 88 adv.
**one degree
under**
weakly 163 adj.
sick 651 adj.
on edge
expectantly
507 adv.
excitable 822 adj.
nervous 854 adj.
one for the road
valediction 296 n.
draught 301 n.
drunkenness 949 n.
one-horse
lesser 35 adj.
little 196 adj.
trivial 639 adj.
**one in the eye
for**
disappointment
509 n.
on end
vertical 215 adj.
oneness
simpleness 44 n.
whole 52 n.
unity 88 n.
one-off
one 88 adj.
**one over the
eight**
over five 99 n.
redundant 637 adj.
drunk 949 adj.
drunkenness 949 n.
one-piece
uniform 16 adj.
onerous
difficult 700 adj.
annoying 827 adj.
one's betters
superior 34 n.
**oneself again,
be**
be restored 656 vb.
one-sided
biased 481 adj.
unjust 914 adj.
one's own
possessed 773 adj.
loved one 887 n.
darling 890 n.
one's own way
scope 744 n.
one's stars
destiny 155 n.

sociability 882 n.
opener
opener 263 n.
open fire
initiate 68 vb.
shoot 287 vb.
open-handed
not retain 779 vb.
liberal 813 adj.
liberality 813 n.
**open-heart
surgery**
surgery 658 n.
open hostilities
go to war 718 vb.
open house
liberality 813 n.
sociability 882 n.
opening
disunion 46 n.
scission 46 n.
prelude 66 n.
debut 68 n.
entrance 68 n.
opportunity 137 n.
room 183 n.
gap 201 n.
uncovering 229 n.
open 263 adj.
opening 263 n.
open space 263 n.
way in 297 n.
job 622 n.
open letter
publicity 528 n.
correspondence
588 n.
deprecation 762 n.
censure 924 n.
openly
openly 263 adv.
open-minded
doubting 474 adj.
just 913 adj.
open-mouthed
open 263 adj.
greedy 859 adj.
openness
uncovering 229 n.
opening 263 n.
open out
open 263 vb.
open question
uncertainty 474 n.
open secret
knowledge 490 n.
known 490 adj.
publicity 528 n.
open sesame
opener 263 n.
answer 460 n.
discovery 484 n.
identification
547 n.

instrument 628 n.
spell 983 n.
open the eyes
disclose 526 vb.
educate 534 vb.
open to
liable 180 adj.
open up
cause 156 vb.
accelerate 277 vb.
manifest 522 vb.
disclose 526 vb.
make better
654 vb.
open verdict
dubiety 474 n.
opera
vocal music 412 n.
operable
possible 469 adj.
medical 658 adj.
operate
produce 164 vb.
operate 173 vb.
doctor 658 vb.
operatic
musical 412 adj.
dramatic 594 adj.
operation
agency 173 n.
way 624 n.
instrumentality
628 n.
surgery 658 n.
undertaking 672 n.
action 676 n.
deed 676 n.
labour 682 n.
operational
operative 173 adj.
prepared 669 adj.
operations
warfare 718 n.
operative
powerful 160 adj.
operative 173 adj.
secret service
459 n.
machinist 630 n.
useful 640 adj.
doer 676 n.
worker 686 n.
obligatory
917 adj.
operator
number 85 n.
machinist 630 n.
doer 676 n.
agent 686 n.
merchant 794 n.
operetta
vocal music 412 n.
ophthalmic
seeing 438 adj.

ophthalmologist
vision 438 n.
doctor 658 n.
opiate
moderator 177 n.
soporific 679 n.
intoxicating
949 adj.
opinion
opinion 485 n.
repute 866 n.
opinionated
positive 473 adj.
narrow-minded
481 adj.
obstinate 602 adj.
vain 873 adj.
opinion poll
vote 605 n.
opium
moderator 177 n.
anaesthetic 375 n.
drug 658 n.
soporific 679 n.
drug-taking 949 n.
opponent
opponent 705 n.
opportune
apt 24 adj.
opportune 137 adj.
advisable 642 adj.
opportunist
recanter 603 n.
enterprising
672 adj.
dishonest 930 adj.
egotist 932 n.
selfish 932 adj.
opportunity
juncture 8 n.
present time 121 n.
opportunity 137 n.
good policy 642 n.
oppose
be opposite 240 vb.
tell against 467 vb.
oppose 704 vb.
contend 716 vb.
refuse 760 vb.
criticize 924 vb.
opposing
opposing 704 adj.
resisting 715 adj.
adverse 731 adj.
opposite
correlative 12 adj.
difference 15 n.
opposite 240 adj.
**opposite
number**
correlation 12 n.
compeer 28 n.
opposites
opposites 704 n.

opposition
contraposition
240 n.
opposition 704 n.
**opposition
party**
opponent 705 n.
oppress
weigh 322 vb.
oppress 735 vb.
oppression
badness 645 n.
severity 735 n.
subjection 745 n.
dejection 834 n.
oppressive
weighty 322 adj.
warm 379 adj.
oppressive 735 adj.
annoying 827 adj.
oppressor
bane 659 n.
tyrant 735 n.
opprobrium
slur 867 n.
opt for
choose 605 vb.
optical
luminous 417 adj.
seeing 438 adj.
optical illusion
insubstantial thing
4 n.
visual fallacy
440 n.
optician
vision 438 n.
doctor 658 n.
optics
electronics 160 n.
eye 438 n.
optimism
cheerfulness
833 n.
hope 852 n.
optimistic
optimistic 482 adj.
cheerful 833 adj.
hoping 852 adj.
optimum
best 644 adj.
option
will 595 n.
willingness 597 n.
choice 605 n.
optional
volitional 595 adj.
voluntary 597 adj.
opt out
reject 607 vb.
refuse 760 vb.
opulent
plentiful 635 adj.
rich 800 adj.

opus
product 164 n.
musical piece
412 n.
or
heraldic 547 adj.
heraldry 547 n.
Oracle (tdmk)
computing 86 n.
broadcasting
531 n.
oracle
answer 460 n.
dogmatist 473 n.
oracle 511 n.
adviser 691 n.
holy place 990 n.
oral
informative
524 adj.
speaking 579 adj.
orange
fruit and vegetables
301 n.
orange 432 adj.
orange 432 n.
orangeade
soft drink 301 n.
orange peel
rubbish 641 n.
**oranges and
lemons**
indoor game 837 n.
orang-outang
mammal 365 n.
oration
oration 579 n.
orator
speaker 579 n.
motivator 612 n.
oratorio
vocal music
412 n.
oratory
oratory 579 n.
church 990 n.
temple 990 n.
orb
region 184 n.
circle 250 n.
badge 547 n.
regalia 743 n.
orbit
influence 178 n.
orbit 250 n.
fly 271 vb.
space travel 271 n.
passage 305 n.
circle 314 vb.
circuition 314 n.
rotate 315 vb.
function 622 n.
route 624 n.
circuit 626 n.

overview
whole 52 n.
inspection 438 n.
overweening
rash 857 adj.
proud 871 adj.
vain 873 adj.
insolent 878 adj.
overweight
be unequal 29 vb.
unequal 29 adj.
fleshy 195 adj.
huge 195 adj.
unwieldy 195 adj.
make heavy
322 vb.
redundance 637 n.
overwhelm
fill 54 vb.
be many 104 vb.
destroy 165 vb.
confute 479 vb.
superabound
637 vb.
attack 712 vb.
impress 821 vb.
overwhelming
prodigious 32 adj.
strong 162 adj.
destructive 165 adj.
violent 176 adj.
liberal 813 adj.
fervent 818 adj.
impressive 821 adj.
wonderful 864 adj.
overwork
waste 634 vb.
use 673 vb.
exertion 682 n.
be fatigued
684 vb.
fatigue 684 vb.
overwrought
excited 821 adj.
ovoid
round 250 adj.
rotund 252 adj.
ovule
flower 366 n.
ovum
genitalia 167 n.
owe
be in debt 803 vb.
owing
impending 155 adj.
due 915 adj.
owing to
caused 157 adj.
hence 158 adv.
owl
bird 365 n.
omen 511 n.
owlish
animal 365 adj.

own
assent 488 vb.
confess 526 vb.
possess 773 vb.
owner
owner 776 n.
dueness 915 n.
ownership
possession
773 n.
own goal
mistake 495 n.
bungling 695 n.
own up
confess 526 vb.
ox
beast of burden
273 n.
cattle 365 n.
male animal
372 n.
Oxbridge
educational
534 adj.
academy 539 n.
oxen
beast of burden
273 n.
cattle 365 n.
oxtail
meat 301 n.
oxygen
air 340 n.
oxygen tent
respiration 352 n.
hospital 658 n.
oyster
fish food 301 n.
marine life 365 n.
greyness 429 n.
ozone
air 340 n.
ozone layer
atmosphere 340 n.

P

pabulum
food 301 n.
pace
synchronize
123 vb.
long measure
203 n.
gait 265 n.
motion 265 n.
walk 267 vb.
velocity 277 n.
measure 465 vb.
pacemaker
living model 23 n.
substitute 150 n.
leader 690 n.

pacesetter
leader 690 n.
pace up and
down
walk 267 vb.
pachyderm
mammal 365 n.
pacific
moderate 177 adj.
peaceful 717 adj.
pacifier
moderator 177 n.
mediator 720 n.
pacifist
pacifist 717 n.
peaceful 717 adj.
pacify
pacify 719 vb.
pack
fill 54 vb.
bring together
74 vb.
bunch 74 n.
group 74 n.
load 193 vb.
cover 226 vb.
line 227 vb.
animal 365 n.
hunter 619 n.
store 632 n.
pack (a jury)
fake 541 vb.
predetermine
608 vb.
do wrong 914 adj.
package
bring together
74 vb.
bunch 74 n.
inclusion 78 n.
unit 88 n.
load 193 vb.
package deal
inclusion 78 n.
packaging
receptacle 194 n.
wrapping 226 n.
lining 227 n.
enclosure 235 n.
pack a punch
be strong 162 vb.
packed
firm 45 adj.
full 54 adj.
false 541 adj.
predetermined
608 adj.
packer
worker 686 n.
packet
bunch 74 n.
small box 194 n.
ship 275 n.
store 632 n.

funds 797 n.
wealth 800 n.
packhorse
beast of burden
273 n.
packing
lining 227 n.
pack-mule
ibeast of burden
273 n.
pack up
decamp 296 vb.
be fatigued
684 vb.
fail 728 vb.
pact
agreement 24 n.
compact 765 n.
pad
abode 192 n.
enlarge 197 vb.
foot 214 n.
seat 218 n.
line 227 vb.
walk 267 vb.
saddle horse 273 n.
softness 327 n.
faintness 401 n.
stationery 586 n.
defend 713 vb.
padded cell
mental hospital
503 n.
padding
increment 36 n.
adjunct 40 n.
lining 227 n.
stopper 264 n.
softness 327 n.
diffuseness 570 n.
superfluity 637 n.
paddle
be in motion
265 vb.
walk 267 vb.
propeller 269 n.
row 269 vb.
swim 269 vb.
propellant 287 n.
be wet 341 vb.
paddle one's
own canoe
behave 688 vb.
be free 744 vb.
paddle steamer
ship 275 n.
paddlewheel
propellant 287 n.
paddock
place 185 n.
enclosure 235 n.
amphibian 365 n.
paddyfield
farm 370 n.

padlock
fastening 47 n.
barrier 235 n.
pad out
augment 36 vb.
be diffuse 570 vb.
padre
title 870 n.
cleric 986 n.
paean
rejoicing 835 n.
celebration 876 n.
applause 923 n.
hymn 981 n.
paean of praise
praise 923 n.
paediatrics
medical art 658 n.
paella
dish 301 n.
pagan
ignorant 491 adj.
religionist 973 n.
heathen 974 n.
heathenish
974 adj.
impious person
980 n.
profane 980 adj.
page
part 53 n.
courier 529 n.
mark 547 vb.
edition 589 n.
domestic 742 n.
retainer 742 n.
a beauty 841 n.
erotic 887 adj.
bridal party 894 n.
impurity 951 n.
pageant
spectacle 445 n.
pageant 875 n.
pageantry
spectacle 445 n.
ostentation 875 n.
pageboy
servant 742 n.
hairdressing
843 n.
pager
telecommunication
531 n.
signal 547 n.
paginate
number 86 vb.
mark 547 vb.
print 587 vb.
pagoda
high structure
209 n.
temple 990 n.
pail
vessel 194 n.

be subject 745 vb.
give 781 vb.
respect 920 vb.
praise 923 vb.
reward 962 vb.
pay up
keep faith 768 vb.
pay 804 vb.
do one's duty
917 vb.
pc
message 529 n.
correspondence
588 n.
PC
computing 86 n.
conformity 83 n.
conformable
83 adj.
p.d.q.
swiftly 277 adv.
pea
sphere 252 n.
peace
agreement 24 n.
hush 399 int.
silence 399 n.
peace 717 n.
pleasurableness
826 n.
peaceable
moderate 177 adj.
peaceful 717 adj.
amiable 884 adj.
peace camp
pacifist 717 n.
pacification 719 n.
peaceful
tranquil 266 adj.
silent 399 adj.
reposeful 683 adj.
peaceful 717 adj.
inexcitable
823 adj.
pleasurable
826 adj.
**peace-keeping
force**
mediator 720 n.
peacemaker
moderator 177 n.
pacifist 717 n.
mediator 720 n.
peace offering
peace offering
719 n.
offering 781 n.
propitiation 941 n.
peace process
peace 717 n.
pacification 719 n.
mediation 720 n.
peacetime
peace 717 n.

peaceful 717 adj.
peach
fruit and vegetables
301 n.
a beauty 841 n.
peacock
table bird 365 n.
a beauty 841 n.
fop 848 n.
proud person
871 n.
vain person 873 n.
be ostentatious
875 vb.
peak
superiority 34 n.
completeness 54 n.
extremity 69 n.
be high 209 vb.
high land 209 n.
summit 213 n.
sharp point 256 n.
perfection 646 n.
climax 725 vb.
palmy days 730 n.
**peak of
perfection**
summit 213 n.
peaky
lean 206 adj.
colourless 426 adj.
unhealthy 651 adj.
peal
be loud 400 vb.
loudness 400 n.
bang 402 n.
roll 403 n.
roll 403 vb.
resonance 404 n.
tune 412 n.
gong 414 n.
call 547 n.
peanut
fruit and vegetables
301 n.
peanuts
small quantity
33 n.
trifle 639 n.
easy thing 701 n.
money 797 n.
pear
fruit and vegetables
301 n.
pearl
sphere 252 n.
semitransparency
424 n.
white thing 427 n.
exceller 644 n.
a beauty 841 n.
gem 844 n.
pearls
jewellery 844 n.

pearly
semitransparent
424 adj.
soft-hued 425 adj.
whitish 427 adj.
grey 429 adj.
pear-shaped
curved 248 adj.
round 250 adj.
peas
fruit and vegetables
301 n.
peasant
dweller 191 n.
farmer 370 n.
country-dweller
869 n.
pea-souper
cloud 355 n.
opacity 423 n.
peat
heater 383 n.
fuel 385 n.
pebble
hardness 326 n.
soil 344 n.
pebbledash
coat 226 vb.
facing 226 n.
pebbly
hard 326 adj.
pecan
fruit and vegetables
301 n.
peccadillo
trifle 639 n.
vice 934 n.
guilty act 936 n.
peck
great quantity
32 n.
eat 301 vb.
metrology 465 n.
peck at
eat 301 vb.
peckish
hungry 859 adj.
pectin
thickening
354 n.
pectoral
cross 222 n.
vestments 989 n.
peculiar
special 80 adj.
unusual 84 adj.
crazy 503 adj.
peculiarity
temperament 5 n.
speciality 80 n.
nonconformity
84 n.
pecuniary
monetary 797 adj.

pedagogic
educational
534 adj.
severe 735 adj.
pedagogy
teaching 534 n.
pedal
propel 287 vb.
propellant 287 n.
play music 413 vb.
tool 630 n.
pedantic
careful 457 adj.
narrow-minded
481 adj.
ornate 574 adj.
obstinate 602 adj.
severe 735 adj.
fastidious 862 adj.
orthodox 976 adj.
peddle
trade 791 vb.
sell 793 vb.
pederast
libertine 952 n.
pedestal
base 214 n.
stand 218 n.
pedestrian
pedestrian 268 n.
feeble 572 adj.
prosaic 593 adj.
dull 840 adj.
**pedestrian
crossing**
traffic control
305 n.
access 624 n.
road 624 n.
refuge 662 n.
pedigree
list 87 n.
genealogy 169 n.
nobility 868 n.
pediment
summit 213 n.
pedlar
pedlar 794 n.
pedometer
meter 465 n.
peek
gaze 438 vb.
look 438 n.
scan 438 vb.
be curious 453 vb.
enquire 459 vb.
peel
abate 37 vb.
subtract 39 vb.
leavings 41 n.
disunite 46 vb.
layer 207 n.
skin 226 n.
uncover 229 vb.

rubbish 641 n.
peel off
come unstuck
49 vb.
peep
ululate 409 vb.
gaze 438 vb.
look 438 n.
scan 438 vb.
be curious 453 vb.
enquire 459 vb.
peeping
inspection 438 n.
inquisitive 453 adj.
peeping Tom
inspection 438 n.
spectator 441 n.
peep show
spectacle 445 n.
peer
compeer 28 n.
gaze 438 vb.
scan 438 vb.
be dim-sighted
440 vb.
enquire 459 vb.
councillor 692 n.
colleague 707 n.
person of repute
866 n.
person of rank
868 n.
peerage
honours 866 n.
aristocracy 868 n.
peer group
group 74 n.
contemporary
123 n.
peerless
dissimilar 19 adj.
supreme 34 adj.
best 644 adj.
noteworthy
866 adj.
peer out
emerge 298 vb.
peeved
unhappy 825 adj.
angry 891 adj.
peevish
discontented
829 adj.
irascible 892 adj.
sullen 893 adj.
peg
degree 27 n.
fastening 47 n.
hanger 217 n.
stopper 264 n.
draught 301 n.
tool 630 n.
peg out
dry 342 vb.

pickpocket
thief 789 n.
pick up
elevate 310 vb.
get better 654 vb.
be restored 656 vb.
arrest 747 vb.
acquire 771 vb.
take 786 vb.
pick-up
loose woman
952 n.
prostitute 952 n.
pick up the tab
defray 804 vb.
pickup truck
lorry 274 n.
picnic
meal 301 n.
easy thing 701 n.
victory 727 n.
amusement 837 n.
amuse oneself
837 vb.
social gathering
882 n.
pictorial
painted 553 adj.
picture
composition 56 n.
photography
551 n.
represent 551 vb.
picture 553 n.
describe 590 vb.
description 590 n.
a beauty 841 n.
honours 866 n.
picture house
cinema 445 n.
theatre 594 n.
picture postcard
picture 553 n.
pictures
film 445 n.
picturesque
painted 553 adj.
impressive 821 adj.
pleasurable
826 adj.
beautiful 841 adj.
ornamental
844 adj.
picture window
window 263 n.
piddling
trivial 639 adj.
pidgin English
language 557 n.
dialect 560 adj.
pie
dish 301 n.
pastries and cakes
301 n.

bird 365 n.
print-type 587 n.
piebald
horse 273 n.
pied 437 adj.
piece
piece 53 n.
component 58 n.
unit 88 n.
product 164 n.
textile 222 n.
dish 301 n.
meal 301 n.
musical piece
412 n.
reading matter
589 n.
coinage 797 n.
pièce de
résistance
dish 301 n.
elite 644 n.
exceller 644 n.
masterpiece 694 n.
piece of cake
easy thing 701 n.
piece of one's
mind
reprimand 924 n.
piece rate
price 809 n.
piece together
join 45 vb.
make complete
54 vb.
decipher 520 vb.
repair 656 vb.
piecework
labour 682 n.
pie chart
statistics 86 n.
pied-à-terre
abode 192 n.
pie-eyed
tipsy 949 adj.
pie in the sky
fantasy 513 n.
pier
stable 192 n.
pillar 218 n.
stand 218 n.
support 218 n.
See **pillar**
projection 254 n.
goal 295 n.
arena 724 n.
pierce
be sharp 256 vb.
pierce 263 vb.
refrigerate 382 vb.
impress 821 vb.
piercing
cold 380 adj.
loud 400 adj.

strident 407 adj.
pierrot
entertainer 594 n.
piety
feeling 818 n.
piety 979 n.
piffling
meaningless
515 adj.
trivial 639 adj.
pig
pig 365 n.
dirty person 649 n.
cad 938 n.
sensualist 944 n.
glutton 947 n.
police 955 n.
pigeon
bird 365 n.
function 622 n.
pigeon-chested
deformed 246 adj.
pigeon-fancier
breeder 369 n.
pigeonhole
class 62 vb.
sorting 62 n.
classification 77 n.
put off 136 vb.
place 185 n.
compartment
194 n.
receptacle 194 n.
orifice 263 n.
be neglectful
458 vb.
pigeon post
postal
communications
531 n.
pigeon-toed
deformed 246 adj.
pig-farming
animal husbandry
369 n.
piggery
stock farm 369 n.
piggybank
treasury 799 n.
pig-headed
obstinate 602 adj.
wilful 602 adj.
pig in a poke
uncertainty 474 n.
gambling 618 n.
piglet
young creature
132 n.
pig 365 n.
pigment
colour 425 vb.
pigment 425 n.
pigmentation
hue 425 n.

blackness 428 n.
pigmy
dwarf 196 n.
dwarfish 196 adj.
little 196 adj.
pigpen
stable 192 n.
pig's ear
bungling 695 n.
pigskin
skin 226 n.
bookbinding 589 n.
pigsty
cattle pen 369 n.
sink 649 n.
pigswill
provender 301 n.
pigtail
hanging object
217 n.
crossing 222 n.
hair 259 n.
hairdressing 843 n.
pike
high land 209 n.
sharp point 256 n.
fish 365 n.
spear 723 n.
pikestaff
high structure
209 n.
pilaff
dish 301 n.
pilaster
pillar 218 n.
pilau
dish 301 n.
pilchard
fish food 301 n.
pile
fastening 47 n.
accumulation
74 n.
bring together
74 vb.
edifice 164 n.
high structure
209 n.
pillar 218 n.
weaving 222 n.
texture 331 n.
heraldry 547 n.
store 632 vb.
acquisition 771 n.
funds 797 n.
wealth 800 n.
piledriver
ram 279 n.
pile in
fill 54 vb.
start out 296 vb.
enter 297 vb.
pile it on
exaggerate 546 vb.

superabound
637 vb.
piles
swelling 253 n.
digestive disorders
651 n.
pile up
bring together
74 vb.
exaggerate 546 vb.
store 632 vb.
acquire 771 vb.
pileup
accumulation 74 n.
collision 279 n.
pilfer
steal 788 vb.
pilgrim
traveller 268 n.
pietist 979 n.
worshipper 981 n.
pilgrimage
land travel 267 n.
undertaking 672 n.
piety 979 n.
act of worship
981 n.
pill
contraception
172 n.
sphere 252 n.
medicine 658 n.
punishment
963 n.
pillage
plundering 788 n.
rob 788 vb
booty 790 n.
pillar
fixture 153 n.
high structure
209 n.
pillar 218 n.
monument 548 n.
pillar of society
person of repute
866 n.
good person 937 n.
Pillbox
headgear 228 n.
cylinder 252 n.
fort 713 n.
pillion
seat 218 n.
pillory
fetter 747 vb.
lockup 748 n.
satirize 851 vb.
shame 867 vb.
criticize 924 vb.
defame 926 vb.
accuse 928 vb.
punish 963 vb.
pillory 964 n.

pillow
cushion 218 n.
support 218 vb.
softness 327 n.

pilot
precursor 66 n.
driver 268 n.
navigate 269 vb.
navigator 270 n.
aeronaut 271 n.
director 690 n.

pilotage
navigation 269 n.

pilot light
lighter 385 n.

pilot scheme
experiment 461 n.
plan 623 n.
preparation 669 n.

pimp
provide 633 vb.
be impure 951 vb.
bawd 952 n.

pimple
lowness 210 n.
swelling 253 n.
skin disease 651 n.
blemish 845 n.

pimply
convex 253 adj.

PIN
label 547 n.
treasury 799 n.

pin
join 45 vb.
fastening 47 n.
sharp point 256 n.
perforator 263 n.
trifle 639 n.
restrain 747 vb.
retain 778 vb.
jewellery 844 n.

pinball
ball game 837 n.

pince-nez
eyeglass 442 n.

pincers
tool 630 n.
pincers 778 n.

pinch
small quantity
33 n.
make smaller
198 vb.
make thin 206 vb.
notch 260 vb.
give pain 377 vb.
pang 377 n.
touch 378 vb.
refrigerate 382 vb.
adversity 731 n.
arrest 747 vb.
steal 788 vb.
poverty 801 n.

economize 814 vb.
be parsimonious
816 vb.

pinched
lean 206 adj.
narrow 206 adj.

pincushion
receptacle 194 n.
porosity 263 n.

pin down
place 187 vb.
compel 740 vb.
retain 778 vb.

pine
tree 366 n.
desire 859 vb.
court 889 vb.

pineapple
fruit and vegetables
301 n.

ping
roll 403 n.
roll 403 vb.
resonance 404 n.
resound 404 vb.

pingpong
ball game 837 n.

pinion
tie 45 vb.
wing 271 n.
fetter 747 vb.
fetter 748 n.
take 786 vb.

pink
moderate 177 adj.
notch 260 vb.
pierce 263 vb.
plant 366 n.
red 431 adj.

pink elephants
alcoholism 949 n.

**pink of
condition**
health 650 n.

pin money
dower 777 n.
money 797 n.
receipt 807 n.

pinnacle
superiority 34 n.
crown 213 vb.
summit 213 n.
perfection 646 n.

pin on
affix 45 vb.
accuse 928 vb.

**pin one's hopes
on**
believe 485 vb.
hope 852 vb.

pinpoint
small thing 33 n.
specify 80 vb.
place 185 n.

place 187 vb.
minuteness 196 n.
orientate 281 vb.

pinprick
small thing 33 n.
shallowness 212 n.
trifle 639 n.
annoyance 827 n.
painfulness 827 n.
enrage 891 vb.
resentment 891 n.

**pins-and-
needles**
pang 377 n.
tingling 378 n.

pin-stripe
pattern 844 n.

pint
metrology 465 n.

pint-size
little 196 adj.

pin-up
picture 553 n.
a beauty 841 n.

pioneer
come before 64 vb.
precursor 66 n.
initiate 68 vb.
settler 191 n.
front 237 n.
traveller 268 n.
preceding 283 n.
prepare 669 vb.

pious
pious 979 adj.

pip
timekeeper 117 n.
flower 366 n.
signal 547 n.

pip at the post
be cunning
698 vb.

pipe
vat 194 n.
cylinder 252 n.
tube 263 n.
conduit 351 n.
blow 352 vb.
air pipe 353 n.
ululate 409 vb.
play music 413 vb.
sing 413 vb.
flute 414 n.
metrology 465 n.

pipe band
orchestra 413 n.

pipe cleaner
tobacco 388 n.
cleaning utensil
648 n.

piped music
music 412 n.

pipe down
cease 145 vb.

be quiescent
266 vb.
be silent 399 vb.
hush 399 int.
be taciturn 582 vb.

pipe dream
insubstantial thing
4 n.
fantasy 513 n.
pleasurableness
826 n.
aspiration 852 n.

pipeline
tube 263 n.
transport 272 n.
conduit 351 n.
store 632 n.
provision 633 n.

pipe of peace
tobacco 388 n.
peace 717 n.
peace offering
719 n.

piper
instrumentalist
413 n.

pipette
vessel 194 n.
tube 263 n.

pipe up
cry 408 vb.
speak 579 vb.

piping
edging 234 n.
hem 234 vb.
tube 263 n.
stridor 407 n.
trimming 844 n.

piping hot
hot 379 adj.

pips
broadcast 531 n.
badge 547 n.
badge of rank
743 n.

pipsqueak
dwarf 196 n.

piquant
pungent 388 adj.
savoury 390 adj.
exciting 821 adj.
witty 839 adj.
impure 951 adj.

pique
excite 821 vb.
hurt 827 vb.
discontent 829 n.
huff 891 vb.
resentment 891 n.

piracy
imitation 20 n.
copy 22 n.
borrowing 785 n.
taking 786 n.

plundering 788 n.

piranha
fish 365 n.

pirate
copy 20 vb.
imitator 20 n.
mariner 270 n.
militarist 722 n.
borrow 785 vb.
appropriate
786 vb.
steal 788 vb.
robber 789 n.
thief 789 n.
bad person 938 n.

pirate radio
broadcasting
531 n.

pirate ship
warship 722 n.

pirouette
rotate 315 vb.
rotation 315 n.
ballet 594 n.

pistil
flower 366 n.

pistol
pistol 723 n.

piston
stopper 264 n.

pit
depth 211 n.
interiority 224 n.
cavity 255 n.
excavation 255 n.
tunnel 263 n.
listener 415 n.
onlookers 441 n.
trap 542 n.
playgoer 594 n.
theatre 594 n.
pitfall 663 n.
workshop 687 n.
stratagem 698 n.
blemish 845 vb.

pit-a-pat
agitation 318 n.
faintness 401 n.
roll 403 n.

pitch
adjust 24 vb.
degree 27 n.
serial place 73 n.
territory 184 n.
place 85 n.
height 209 n.
summit 213 n.
be oblique 220 vb.
obliquity 220 n.
coat 226 n.
voyage 269 vb.
propel 287 vb.
fluctuation 317 n.
oscillate 317 vb.

plate
plate 194 n.
coat 226 vb.
covering 226 n.
circle 250 n.
tooth 256 n.
photography
551 n.
picture 553 n.
print-type 587 n.
edition 589 n.
plateau
high land 209 n.
vertex 213 n.
horizontality
216 n.
plain 348 n.
plate glass
transparency
422 n.
platelet
blood 335 n.
platform
layer 207 n.
horizontality
216 n.
stand 218 n.
publication 528 n.
publicity 528 n.
policy 623 n.
railway 624 n.
arena 724 n.
platinum
white thing
427 n.
**platinum
blond(e)**
achromatism
426 n.
whitish 427 adj.
yellowness 433 n.
platitude
truth 494 n.
maxim 496 n.
lack of meaning
515 n.
Platonic
pure 950 adj.
Platonic love
love 887 n.
platoon
band 74 n.
formation 722 n.
platter
plate 194 n.
horizontality
216 n.
gramophone 414 n.
plaudits
rejoicing 835 n.
applause 923 n.
plausible
plausible 471 adj.
credible 485 adj.

hypocritical
541 adj.
flattering 925 adj.
play
composition 56 n.
operate 173 vb.
influence 178 n.
range 183 n.
ascend 308 vb.
oscillate 317 vb.
flow 350 vb.
play music 413 vb.
act 594 vb.
stage play 594 n.
action 676 n.
contend 716 vb.
amusement 837 n.
amuse oneself
837 vb.
revel 837 vb.
caress 889 vb.
play-acting
duplicity 541 n.
hypocritical
541 adj.
acting 594 n.
play at
be inattentive
456 vb.
amuse oneself
837 vb.
playback
repetition 106 n.
gramophone 414 n.
play ball
cooperate 706 vb.
**playboy,
playgirl**
beau monde
848 n.
sensualist 944 n.
play down
moderate 177 vb.
underestimate
483 vb.
extenuate 927 vb.
player
musician 413 n.
interpreter 520 n.
actor 594 n.
gambler 618 n.
doer 676 n.
agent 686 n.
player 837 n.
play footsie
caress 889 vb.
play for time
be cunning 698 vb.
be obstructive
702 vb.
playful
merry 833 adj.
witty 839 adj.
innocent 935 adj.

play games
amuse oneself
837 vb.
playground
arena 724 n.
pleasure ground
837 n.
playgroup
school 539 n.
play havoc with
harm 645 n.
impair 655 vb.
playing
music 412 n.
playing field
arena 724 n.
pleasure ground
837 n.
**play into one's
hands**
blunder 495 vb.
play it by ear
intuit 476 vb.
be cautious 858 vb.
**play it by the
book**
be cautious 858 vb.
play on
use 673 vb.
playmate
colleague 707 n.
chum 880 n.
playroom
chamber 194 n.
play safe
be cautious 858 vb.
**play the
concertina**
play music 413 vb.
play the fool
rampage 61 vb.
be absurd 497 vb.
be foolish 499 vb.
amuse oneself
837 vb.
be ridiculous
849 vb.
be rash 857 vb.
play the game
behave 688 vb.
plaything
plaything 837 n.
**plaything of the
gods**
unlucky person
731 n.
**play to the
gallery**
act 594 vb.
be affected 850 vb.
be ostentatious
875 vb.
play tricks on
fool 542 vb.

play truant
be absent 190 vb.
disappear 446 vb.
run away 620 vb.
relinquish 621 vb.
fail in duty 918 vb.
play up
overestimate
482 vb.
be obstructive
702 vb.
disobey 738 vb.
play upon
motivate 612 vb.
play with fire
be in danger
661 vb.
be rash 857 vb.
playwright
author 589 n.
dramatist 594 n.
plea
testimony 466 n.
argument 475 n.
pretext 614 n.
request 761 n.
vindication 927 n.
litigation 959 n.
plead
testify 466 vb.
argue 475 vb.
plead 614 vb.
do law 958 vb.
plead guilty
assent 488 vb.
confess 526 vb.
accuse 928 vb.
be guilty 936 vb.
stand trial 959 vb.
condemn 961 vb.
pleasant
pleasant 376 adj.
pleasurable
826 adj.
amusing 837 adj.
pleasantry
wit 839 n.
please
please 826 vb.
amuse 837 vb.
pleased
willing 597 adj.
pleased 824 adj.
content 828 adj.
**pleased as a dog
with two tails**
proud 871 adj.
**pleased as
Punch**
pleased 824 adj.
proud 871 adj.
pleasurable
pleasurable
826 adj.

pleasure
pleasure 376 n.
amusement 837 n.
pleat
garment 228 n.
fold 261 n.
plebeian
commoner 869 n.
plebeian 869 adj.
plebiscite
judgment 480 n.
vote 605 n.
decree 737 n.
legislation 953 n.
plectrum
stringed instrument
414 n.
pledge
drink 301 vb.
affirm 532 vb.
oath 532 n.
promise 764 n.
promise 764 vb.
give security
767 vb.
security 767 n.
toast 876 vb.
duty 917 n.
plenary
complete 54 adj.
plenitude
greatness 32 n.
plenitude 54 n.
plenteous
plentiful 635 adj.
liberal 813 adj.
plentiful
great 32 adj.
plentiful 635 adj.
plenty
plenty 635 n.
plethora
redundance 637 n.
satiety 863 n.
pleurisy
respiratory disease
651 n.
pliable
flexible 327 adj.
pliant
conformable
83 adj.
flexible 327 adj.
irresolute 601 adj.
tractable 701 adj.
submitting
721 adj.
servile 879 adj.
pliers
tool 630 n.
pincers 778 n.
plight
state 7 n.
circumstance 8 n.

polka
musical piece
412 n.
dance 837 n.
polka dot
mottle 437 n.
pattern 844 n.
poll
number 86 vb.
numeration 86 n.
statistics 86 n.
head 213 n.
enquiry 459 n.
judgment 480 n.
vote 605 n.
vote 605 vb.
pollard
make smaller
198 vb.
tree 366 n.
pollen
genitalia 167 n.
powder 332 n.
flower 366 n.
pollinate
generate 167 vb.
polling
vote 605 n.
polling booth
electorate 605 n.
polls
vote 605 n.
pollster
enquirer 459 n.
poll tax
tax 809 n.
pollute
harm 645 vb.
make unclean
649 vb.
impair 655 vb.
misuse 675 vb.
pollution
uncleanness 649 n.
infection 651 n.
insalubrity 653 n.
impairment 655 n.
poison 659 n.
misuse 675 n.
slur 867 n.
polo
ball game 837 n.
polo neck
jersey 228 n.
neckline 228 n.
shirt 228 n.
poltergeist
elf 970 n.
ghost 970 n.
spiritualism 984 n.
poltroon
coward 856 n.
poly
academy 539 n.

poly bag
bag 194 n.
carrier 273 n.
polyester
textile 222 n.
polyethylene
materials 631 n.
polygamy
type of marriage
894 n.
polyglot
speaking 579 adj.
polygon
plurality 101 n.
angular figure
247 n.
polymorphous
multiform 82 adj.
polyp
swelling 253 n.
polystyrene
wrapping 226 n.
lining 227 n.
materials 631 n.
polysyllabic
long 203 adj.
diffuse 570 adj.
polytechnic
academy 539 n.
polythene
wrapping 226 n.
materials 631 n.
polythene bag
bag 194 n.
polyunsaturates
food content 301 n.
polyurethane
resin 357 n.
pomade
unguent 357 n.
pomander
scent 396 n.
pomegranate
fruit and vegetables
301 n.
pomelo
fruit and vegetables
301 n.
pommel
handle 218 n.
sphere 252 n.
pomp
pride 871 n.
ostentation 875 n.
**pomp and
circumstance**
ostentation 875 n.
pompom
trimming 844 n.
pompous
proud 871 adj.
vain 873 adj.
ostentatious
875 adj.

ponce
bawd 952 n.
ponce about
be affected 850 vb.
pond
shallowness 212 n.
lake 346 n.
ponder
meditate 449 vb.
think 449 vb.
estimate 480 vb.
ponderous
weighty 322 adj.
dull 840 adj.
pong
odour 394 n.
smell 394 vb.
stench 397 n.
stink 397 vb.
deteriorate 655 vb.
pontiff
sovereign 741 n.
priest 986 n.
pontificate
dogmatize 473 vb.
affirm 532 vb.
teach 534 vb.
church office
985 n.
pontoon
boat 275 n.
card game 837 n.
pontoon bridge
bridge 624 n.
pony
twenty and over
99 n.
cup 194 n.
pony 273 n.
funds 797 n.
ponytail
hair 259 n.
hairdressing 843 n.
pony-trekking
sport 837 n.
pooch
dog 365 n.
poodle
dog 365 n.
toady 879 n.
poof
nonconformist
84 n.
poofter
nonconformist
84 n.
pooh-pooh
disregard 458 vb.
underestimate
483 vb.
hold cheap 922 vb.
pool
combine 50 vb.
lake 346 n.

store 632 n.
store 632 vb.
association 706 n.
acquisition 771 n.
joint possession
775 n.
ball game 837 n.
pool resources
cooperate 706 vb.
pools
gambling 618 n.
pool table
arena 724 n.
pooped
fatigued 684 adj.
poor
incomplete 55 adj.
weak 163 adj.
unproductive
172 adj.
feeble 572 adj.
insufficient
636 adj.
bad 645 adj.
unfortunate
731 adj.
poor 801 adj.
unhappy 825 adj.
disreputable
867 adj.
poorhouse
retreat 192 n.
poverty 801 n.
poor lookout
adversity 731 n.
hopelessness
853 n.
poorly
slightly 33 adv.
weakly 163 adj.
sick 651 adj.
poor show
bungling 695 n.
poor turnout
fewness 105 n.
poor visibility
dimness 419 n.
invisibility 444 n.
pop
paternity 169 n.
jut 254 vb.
soft drink 301 n.
bang 402 n.
bang 402 vb.
music 412 n.
give security
767 vb.
borrow 785 vb.
pop art
art 551 n.
popcorn
mouthful 301 n.
pope
sovereign 741 n.

ecclesiarch 986 n.
pop-eyed
projecting 254 adj.
pop-fastener
fastening 47 n.
pop group
band 74 n.
orchestra 413 n.
popgun
plaything 837 n.
pop in
enter 297 vb.
popinjay
fop 848 n.
poplar
tree 366 n.
poplin
textile 222 n.
pop music
music 412 n.
amusement 837 n.
pop off
die 361 vb.
pop out
jut 254 vb.
emerge 298 vb.
popper
fastening 47 n.
poppet
darling 890 n.
poppy
plant 366 n.
redness 431 n.
poppycock
empty talk 515 n.
pop singer
vocalist 413 n.
entertainer 594 n.
person of repute
866 n.
**pop the
question**
interrogate 459 vb.
request 761 vb.
court 889 vb.
populace
social group
371 n.
commonalty
869 n.
popular
general 79 adj.
native 191 adj.
governmental
733 adj.
reputable 866 adj.
approved 923 adj.
popularity
repute 866 n.
sociability 882 n.
approbation 923 n.
**popular
misconception**
error 495 n.

predestined
impending 155 adj.
fated 596 adj.
predetermined
608 adj.
predetermine
necessitate 596 vb.
predetermine
608 vb.
predicament
predicament 700 n.
predicate
part of speech
564 n.
predict
predict 511 vb.
predictable
unchangeable
153 adj.
prediction
prediction 511 n.
predilection
tendency 179 n.
prejudice 481 n.
choice 605 n.
affections 817 n.
liking 859 n.
love 887 n.
predispose
bias 481 vb.
motivate 612 vb.
predisposition
tendency 179 n.
willingness 597 n.
affections 817 n.
predominant
powerful 160 adj.
influential 178 adj.
authoritative
733 adj.
predominate
predominate 34 vb.
pre-embryo
origin 68 n.
young creature
132 n.
source 156 n.
preeminent
supreme 34 adj.
authoritative
733 adj.
noteworthy
866 adj.
preempt
exclude 57 vb.
do before 119 vb.
be early 135 vb.
precede 283 vb.
acquire 771 vb.
preemptive
excluding 57 vb.
preen
primp 843 vb.
decorate 844 vb.

preexistence
existence 1 n.
priority 119 n.
preexisting
prior 119 adj.
prefab
house 192 n.
prefabricated
ready-made
669 adj.
preface
add 38 vb.
come before 64 vb.
put in front 64 vb.
prelude 66 n.
front 237 n.
edition 589 n.
prefatory
preceding 64 adj.
precursory 66 adj.
beginning 68 adj.
prior 119 adj.
prefect
official 690 n.
officer 741 n.
prefer
choose 605 vb.
desire 859 vb.
preferable
excellent 644 adj.
prefer charges
litigate 959 vb.
preference
precedence 64 vb.
will 595 n.
choice 605 n.
love 887 n.
preferential
treatment
injustice 914 n.
preferment
progression 285 n.
holy orders 985 n.
prefigure
predict 511 vb.
indicate 547 vb.
prefix
add 38 vb.
adjunct 40 n.
affix 45 vb.
put in front 64 vb.
precursor 66 n.
front 237 n.
part of speech
564 n.
pregnancy
fertilized 167 adj.
propagation 167 n.
prolific 171 adj.
meaningful
514 adj.
important 638 adj.
pregnant with
impending 155 adj.

prehensile
tactual 378 adj.
retentive 778 adj.
prehistoric
prior 119 adj.
past 125 adj.
olden 127 adj.
prejudge
do before 119 vb.
prejudge 481 vb.
prejudgment
prejudgment 481 n.
prejudice
influence 178 vb.
tendency 179 n.
bias 481 vb.
prejudice 481 n.
error 495 n.
motivate 612 vb.
affections 817 n.
dislike 861 n.
prejudiced
biased 481 adj.
erroneous 495 adj.
unjust 914 adj.
prejudice the
issue
prejudge 481 vb.
prejudicial
evil 616 adj.
harmful 645 adj.
prelate
ecclesiarch 986 n.
preliminaries
beginning 68 n.
preparation 669 n.
preliminary
preceding 64 adj.
precursory 66 adj.
prelude 66 n.
prior 119 adj.
preparatory
669 adj.
prelims
exam 459 n.
edition 589 n.
prelude
prelude 66 n.
preceding 283 n.
musical piece
412 n.
play music 413 vb.
premature
early 135 adj.
ill-timed 138 adj.
immature 670 adj.
prematurely
beforehand
135 adv.
premedication
preparation 669 n.
premeditated
predetermined
608 adj.

premeditated
murder
homicide 362 n.
premeditation
foresight 510 n.
predetermination
608 n.
preparation 669 n.
premier
superior 34 n.
director 690 n.
officer 741 n.
premier cru
wine 301 n.
premiere
debut 68 n.
dramaturgy 594 n.
premise
premise 475 n.
premises
place 185 n.
evidence 466 n.
premium
interest 803 n.
receipt 807 n.
price 809 n.
premium bond
equal chance
159 n.
gambling 618 n.
paper money
797 n.
premonition
precursor 66 n.
foresight 510 n.
warning 664 n.
prenatal
prior 119 adj.
preoccupation
attention 455 n.
preoccupied
obsessed 455 adj.
distracted 456 adj.
preordained
fated 596 adj.
predetermined
608 adj.
prep
curriculum 534 n.
study 536 n.
preparation 669 n.
preparation
teaching 534 n.
study 536 n.
medicine 658 n.
preparation 669 n.
preparatory
preceding 64 adj.
preparatory
669 adj.
prepare
prepare 669 vb.

prepared
prepared 669 adj.
prepared, be
foresee 510 vb.
prepare for
prepare 669 vb.
preponderance
inequality 29 n.
preposition
precursor 66 n.
part of speech
564 n.
prepossessing
personable
841 adj.
preposterous
exorbitant 32 adj.
absurd 497 adj.
imaginative
513 adj.
ridiculous 849 adj.
prep school
school 539 n.
prequel
precursor 66 n.
priority 119 n.
front 237 n.
preceding 283 n.
reading matter
589 n.
prerequisite
qualification
468 n.
required 627 adj.
requirement 627 n.
prerogative
authority 733 n.
freedom 744 n.
nobility 868 n.
dueness 915 n.
presage
predict 511 vb.
indicate 547 vb.
threaten 900 vb.
presbyopic
dim-sighted
440 adj.
presbyter
church officer
986 n.
ecclesiarch 986 n.
Presbyterianism
Protestantism
976 n.
presbytery
seniority 131 n.
parish 985 n.
synod 985 n.
the church 985 n.
parsonage 986 n.
church exterior
990 n.
prescribe
doctor 658 vb.

general 79 adj.
universal 79 adj.
powerful 160 adj.
influential 178 adj.
known 490 adj.
prevaricate
be equivocal
518 vb.
dissemble 541 vb.
be dishonest
930 vb.
prevent
counteract 182 vb.
obstruct 702 vb.
prohibit 757 vb.
preventative
counteraction
182 n.
prevention
counteraction
182 n.
avoidance 620 n.
hindrance 702 n.
restraint 747 n.
preventive
excluding 57 adj.
counteraction
182 n.
prophylactic 658 n.
preventive
measure
protection 660 n.
preventive
medicine
medical art 658 n.
preservation 666 n.
preview
precursor 66 n.
do before 119 vb.
priority 119 n.
inspection 438 n.
film 445 n.
manifestation
522 n.
dramaturgy
594 n.
previous
preceding 64 adj.
anachronistic
118 adj.
prior 119 adj.
previous
engagement
pretext 614 n.
prewar
prior 119 adj.
antiquated
127 adj.
peaceful 717 adj.
prey
animal 365 n.
objective 617 n.
chase 619 n.
sufferer 825 n.

prey on
eat 301 vb.
prey on one's
mind
absorb 449 vb.
trouble 827 vb.
frighten 854 vb.
priapism
libido 859 n.
illicit love 951 n.
price
price 809 n.
price 809 vb.
priceless
profitable 640 adj.
valuable 644 adj.
of value 811 adj.
funny 849 adj.
price war
contention 716 n.
prick
small thing 33 n.
cut 46 vb.
stimulant 174 n.
be sharp 256 vb.
sharp point 256 n.
pierce 263 vb.
give pain 377 vb.
incite 612 vb.
wound 655 n.
wound 655 vb.
excitant 821 n.
prickle
prickle 256 n.
foliage 366 n.
prickly
sharp 256 adj.
irascible 892 adj.
prickly heat
tingling 378 n.
skin disease 651 n.
prick out
implant 303 vb.
cultivate 370 vb.
prick up (one's
ears)
elevate 310 vb.
hear 415 vb.
be curious 453 vb.
be attentive
455 vb.
pricy
dear 811 adj.
pride
pride 871 n.
ostentation 875 n.
vice 934 n.
impiety 980 n.
pride (lions)
group 74 n.
pride and joy
favourite 890 n.
pride of place
precedence 64 n.

preceding 283 n.
authority 733 n.
priest
church officer
986 n.
cleric 986 n.
priest 986 n.
priestess
priest 986 n.
priesthole
retreat 192 n.
hiding place 527 n.
priesthood
church office
985 n.
ecclesiasticism
985 n.
clergy 986 n.
prig
prude 950 n.
priggish
affected 850 adj.
prudish 950 adj.
prim
serious 834 adj.
affected 850 adj.
fastidious 862 adj.
prudish 950 adj.
primacy
prestige 866 n.
church office
985 n.
prima donna
superior 34 n.
vocalist 413 n.
actor 594 n.
bigwig 638 n.
proficient person
696 n.
prima facie
evidence
evidence 466 n.
primal
primal 127 adj.
primarily
initially 68 adv.
primary
original 21 adj.
simple 44 adj.
first 68 adj.
fundamental
156 adj.
educational
534 adj.
vote 605 n.
important 638 adj.
primary care
medical art 658 n.
primary colour
colour 425 n.
primate
superior 34 n.
mammal 365 n.
ecclesiarch 986 n.

prime
numerical 85 adj.
primal 127 adj.
educate 534 vb.
important 638 adj.
elite 644 n.
excellent 644 adj.
make ready
669 vb.
palmy days 730 n.
church service
988 n.
primed
informed 524 adj.
prepared 669 adj.
prime minister
superior 34 n.
director 690 n.
officer 741 n.
prime mover
cause 156 n.
producer 164 n.
prime number
number 85 n.
prime of life
salad days 130 n.
middle age 131 n.
adultness 134 n.
primeval
beginning 68 adj.
primal 127 adj.
priming
preparation
669 n.
explosive 723 n.
primitive
past 125 adj.
primal 127 adj.
fundamental
156 adj.
artist 556 n.
artless 699 adj.
barbaric 869 adj.
primogeniture
priority 119 n.
seniority 131 n.
primordial
original 21 adj.
beginning 68 adj.
primal 127 adj.
fundamental
156 adj.
primp
primp 843 vb.
primrose
plant 366 n.
yellowness 433 n.
primrose path
way 624 n.
deterioration
655 n.
wickedness 934 n.
primula
plant 366 n.

primus stove
furnace 383 n.
prince
potentate 741 n.
sovereign 741 n.
aristocrat 868 n.
princely
ruling 733 adj.
liberal 813 adj.
worshipful
866 adj.
noble 868 adj.
Prince of Wales
check
chequer 437 n.
Prince of
Wales's
feathers
regalia 743 n.
princess
sovereign 741 n.
loved one 887 n.
principal
supreme 34 adj.
first 68 adj.
teacher 537 n.
director 690 n.
master 741 n.
principal boy or
girl
acting 594 n.
principality
political
organization
733 n.
principally
eminently 34 adv.
principle
essential part 5 n.
rule 81 n.
source 156 n.
element 319 n.
idea 451 n.
premise 475 n.
opinion 485 n.
axiom 496 n.
motive 612 n.
precept 693 n.
probity 929 n.
principles
creed 485 n.
conduct 688 n.
probity 929 n.
virtue 933 n.
prink
dress 228 vb.
beautify 841 vb.
primp 843 vb.
print
copy 22 n.
effect 157 n.
indication 547 n.
photograph
551 vb.

induce 612 vb.
provide 633 vb.
acquire 771 vb.
be impure 951 vb.
procurement
agency 173 n.
acquisition 771 n.
procurer
bawd 952 n.
procuress
bawd 952 n.
prod
stimulant 174 n.
impel 279 vb.
gesticulate 547 vb.
incentive 612 n.
incite 612 vb.
prodigal
prodigal 815 adj.
prodigal 815 n.
prodigal son
prodigal 815 n.
bad person 938 n.
prodigious
prodigious 32 adj.
wonderful 864 adj.
prodigy
intellectual 492 n.
exceller 644 n.
prodigy 864 n.
prodromal
preceding 64 adj.
produce
growth 157 n.
produce 164 vb.
product 164 n.
lengthen 203 vb.
agriculture 370 n.
manifest 522 vb.
dramatize 594 vb.
provision 633 n.
producer
producer 164 n.
stage manager 594 n.
product
numerical result 85 n.
event 154 n.
product 164 n.
production
product 164 n.
production 164 n.
dramaturgy 594 n.
production line
production 164 n.
workshop 687 n.
productive
prolific 171 adj.
productivity
production 164 n.
productiveness 171 n.
diffuseness 570 n.

plenty 635 n.
utility 640 n.
profane
make unclean 649 vb.
impair 655 vb.
shame 867 vb.
cursing 899 adj.
not respect 921 vb.
wicked 934 adj.
irreligious 974 adj.
be impious 980 vb.
profane 980 adj.
profanity
scurrility 899 n.
impiety 980 n.
profess
affirm 532 vb.
plead 614 vb.
profession
assent 488 n.
affirmation 532 n.
pretext 614 n.
vocation 622 n.
promise 764 n.
ostentation 875 n.
duty 917 n.
professional
expert 694 adj.
expert 696 n.
professionalism
skill 694 n.
professor
scholar 492 n.
teacher 537 n.
expert 696 n.
academic title 870 n.
professor emeritus
teacher 537 n.
academic title 870 n.
proffer
offer 759 n.
offer 759 vb.
promise 764 vb.
proficiency
culture 490 n.
skill 694 n.
proficient
knowing 490 adj.
expert 694 adj.
profile
outline 233 n.
outline 233 vb.
laterality 239 n.
form 243 n.
feature 445 n.
estimate 480 n.
picture 553 n.
description 590 n.
profiling
psychology 447 n.

profit
growth 157 n.
incentive 612 n.
benefit 615 n.
benefit 615 vb.
utility 640 n.
be expedient 642 vb.
good policy 642 n.
be profitable 771 vb.
gain 771 n.
reward 962 n.
profitable
profitable 640 adj.
beneficial 644 adj.
profit by
profit by 137 vb.
use 673 vb.
profiteer
prosper 730 vb.
prosperous person 730 n.
speculate 791 vb.
overcharge 811 vb.
profligate
prodigal 815 adj.
prodigal 815 n.
vicious 934 adj.
bad person 938 n.
intemperate 943 adj.
sensualist 944 n.
lecherous 951 adj.
profound
great 32 adj.
deep 211 adj.
wise 498 adj.
unclear 568 adj.
profoundly deaf
deaf 416 adj.
profundity
depth 211 n.
thought 449 n.
imperspicuity 568 n.
profuse
many 104 adj.
diffuse 570 adj.
plentiful 635 adj.
liberal 813 adj.
prodigal 815 adj.
profusion
great quantity 32 n.
abundance 171 n.
plenty 635 n.
prodigality 815 n.
progenitor
source 156 n.
paternity 169 n.
progenitrix
maternity 169 n.

progeny
posterity 170 n.
prognosis
foresight 510 n.
prediction 511 n.
medical art 658 n.
prognostication
foresight 510 n.
prediction 511 n.
program
class 62 vb.
computerize 86 vb.
computing 86 n.
programme
list 87 n.
foresight 510 n.
prediction 511 n.
publication 528 n.
broadcast 531 n.
plan 623 n.
policy 623 n.
undertaking 672 n.
tactics 688 n.
progress
increase 36 n.
continuance 146 n.
motion 265 n.
progress 285 n.
progression 285 n.
way 624 n.
improvement 654 n.
success 727 n.
progression
order 60 n.
series 71 n.
ratio 85 n.
progression 285 n.
progressive
increasing 36 adj.
continuous 71 adj.
moving 265 adj.
progressive 285 adj.
improving 654 adj.
reformer 654 n.
enterprising 672 adj.
progressiveness
increase 36 n.
continuity 71 n.
progression 285 n.
prohibit
prohibit 757 vb.
prohibition
prohibition 757 n.
temperance 942 n.
prohibitive
excluding 57 adj.
dear 811 adj.
project
make extrinsic 6 vb.
jut 254 vb.

propel 287 vb.
emerge 298 vb.
be visible 443 vb.
curriculum 534 n.
intend 617 vb.
plan 623 n.
plan 623 vb.
undertaking 672 n.
projectile
missile 287 n.
ammunition 723 n.
projecting
projecting 254 adj.
projection
extrinsicality 6 n.
distortion 246 n.
convexity 253 n.
projection 254 n.
propulsion 287 n.
cinema 445 n.
ideality 513 n.
map 551 n.
projector
lamp 420 n.
cinema 445 n.
prolapse
descend 309 vb.
prolepsis
anachronism 118 n.
proletarian
commoner 869 n.
plebeian 869 adj.
proletariat
commonalty 869 n.
lower classes 869 n.
proliferate
grow 36 vb.
be fruitful 171 vb.
abound 635 vb.
prolific
prolific 171 adj.
prolix
prolix 570 adj.
prolixity
diffuseness 570 n.
speech 579 n.
loquacity 581 n.
tedium 838 n.
prologue
prelude 66 n.
oration 579 n.
dramaturgy 594 n.
prolong
augment 36 vb.
continue 71 adj.
sustain 146 vb.
lengthen 203 vb.
preserve 666 vb.
prolongation
sequence 65 n.

select 605 vb.
intend 617 vb.
advise 691 vb.
patronize 703 vb.
offer 759 vb.
court 889 vb.
propose
  marriage
  court 889 vb.
proposition
  topic 452 n.
  supposition 512 n.
  plan 623 n.
  advice 691 n.
  offer 759 n.
  request 761 n.
  debauch 951 vb.
propound
  propound 512 vb.
proprietary
  proprietary
  777 adj.
proprietary
  drug
  medicine 658 n.
proprieties
  etiquette 848 n.
proprietor
  owner 776 n.
proprietress
  owner 776 n.
proprietrix
  owner 776 n.
propriety
  relevance 9 n.
  fitness 24 n.
  elegance 575 n.
  good policy
  642 n.
  good taste 846 n.
  etiquette 848 n.
  right 913 n.
  purity 950 n.
props
  stage set 594 n.
propulsion
  propulsion 287 n.
prop up
  preserve 666 vb.
  aid 703 vb.
pro rata
  pro rata 783 adv.
prosaic
  typical 83 adj.
  feeble 572 adj.
  plain 573 adj.
  prosaic 593 adj.
  tedious 838 adj.
  dull 840 adj.
pros and cons
  reasons 475 n.
proscenium
  stage set 594 n.
  theatre 594 n.

proscribe
  command 737 vb.
  prohibit 757 vb.
  condemn 961 vb.
proscription
  prohibition 757 n.
  malediction 899 n.
  condemnation
  961 n.
prose
  prose 593 n.
prosecute
  do 676 vb.
  indict 928 vb.
  litigate 959 vb.
prosecution
  accusation 928 n.
  legal trial 959 n.
  litigation 959 n.
prosecutor
  accuser 928 n.
  litigant 959 n.
proselyte
  learner 538 n.
prosody
  prosody 593 n.
prospect
  futurity 124 n.
  destiny 155 n.
  range 183 n.
  view 438 n.
  search 459 vb.
  be tentative
  461 vb.
  expectation 507 n.
  prediction 511 n.
  art subject 553 n.
  intention 617 n.
prospective
  future 124 adj.
  expected 507 adj.
  foreseeing
  510 adj.
prospector
  enquirer 459 n.
  experimenter
  461 n.
  detector 484 n.
prospectus
  list 87 n.
  foresight 510 n.
  prediction 511 n.
  compendium
  592 n.
  policy 623 n.
prosper
  grow 36 vb.
  get better 654 vb.
  prosper 730 vb.
prosperity
  prosperity 730 n.
prosperous
  prosperous 730 adj.

prostate
  genitalia 167 n.
prosthesis
  precedence 64 n.
  substitute 150 n.
  leg 267 n.
  surgery 658 n.
prostitute
  pervert 655 vb.
  misuse 675 vb.
  debauch 951 vb.
  prostitute 952 n.
prostitution
  deterioration
  655 n.
  misuse 675 n.
  social evil 951 n.
prostrate
  disable 161 vb.
  low 210 adj.
  flatten 216 vb.
  supine 216 adj.
  fell 311 vb.
  sick 651 adj.
  fatigue 684 vb.
  fatigued 684 adj.
  submitting
  721 adj.
  suffering 825 adj.
  sadden 834 vb.
  servile 879 adj.
  respectful 920 adj.
prostrated
  impotent 161 adj.
prostrate
  oneself
  stoop 311 vb.
  greet 884 vb.
  show respect
  920 vb.
  be penitent 939 vb.
  worship 981 vb.
  perform ritual
  988 vb.
prostration
  helplessness 161 n.
  weakness 163 n.
  lowness 210 n.
  lowering 311 n.
  illness 651 n.
  fatigue 684 n.
  submission 721 n.
  sorrow 825 n.
  dejection 834 n.
  servility 879 n.
  respects 920 n.
  piety 979 n.
  ritual act 988 n.
prosy
  prolix 570 adj.
protagonist
  actor 594 n.
protean
  multiform 82 adj.

changeful 152 adj.
protect
  accompany 89 vb.
  screen 421 vb.
  safeguard 660 vb.
  preserve 666 vb.
  defend 713 vb.
  befriend 880 vb.
protected
  safe 660 adj.
  preserved 666 adj.
  restrained 747 adj.
protected
  species
  preservation 666 n.
protection
  protection 660 n.
  safeguard 662 n.
  trade 791 n.
protectionism
  restriction 747 n.
protection
  factor
  protection 660 n.
protection
  racket
  swindling 788 n.
protective
  clothing
  shelter 662 n.
  armour 713 n.
protective
  custody
  detention 747 n.
protector
  protector 660 n.
  master 741 n.
protectorate
  territory 184 n.
  protection 660 n.
  political
  organization
  733 n.
protectress
  protector 660 n.
protégé(e)
  dependant 742 n.
  friend 880 n.
protein
  food content 301 n.
  organism 358 n.
protest
  dissent 489 n.
  dissent 489 vb.
  affirm 532 vb.
  negate 533 vb.
  negation 533 n.
  be unwilling
  598 vb.
  unwillingness
  598 n.
  be active 678 vb.
  oppose 704 vb.
  resist 715 vb.

resistance 715 n.
revolt 738 vb.
refusal 760 n.
refuse 760 vb.
deprecation 762 n.
nonobservance
  769 n.
be discontented
  829 vb.
disapprobation
  924 n.
disapprove 924 vb.
Protestantism
  Protestantism
  976 n.
protester
  dissentient 489 n.
  agitator 738 n.
protest march
  deprecation 762 n.
prothesis
  altar 990 n.
protocol
  practice 610 n.
  etiquette 848 n.
  ostentation 875 n.
proton
  minuteness 196 n.
  element 319 n.
protoplasm
  prototype 23 n.
  origin 68 n.
  matter 319 n.
  organism 358 n.
  life 360 n.
prototype
  prototype 23 n.
  preparation 669 n.
protract
  put off 136 vb.
  sustain 146 vb.
  lengthen 203 vb.
  be diffuse 570 vb.
  be obstructive
  702 vb.
protractor
  angular measure
  247 n.
  gauge 465 n.
protrude
  jut 254 vb.
protrusion
  convexity 253 n.
protuberance
  convexity 253 n.
  protuberance
  254 n.
protuberant
  projecting 254 adj.
proud
  proud 871 adj.
  vain 873 adj.
proud flesh
  swelling 253 n.

ptarmigan
table bird 365 n.
pterodactyl
animal 365 n.
pub
focus 76 n.
tavern 192 n.
social round 882 n.
pub-crawl
drunkenness 949 n.
puberty
propagation 167 n.
pubescence
youth 130 n.
pubic hair
hair 259 n.
public
social group 371 n.
known 490 adj.
manifest 522 adj.
shown 522 adj.
noteworthy
866 adj.
formal 875 adj.
showy 875 adj.
public, the
commonalty
869 n.
**public address
system**
megaphone 400 n.
hearing aid 415 n.
publicity 528 n.
publican
caterer 633 n.
receiver 782 n.
publication
publication 528 n.
book 589 n.
public baths
ablutions 648 n.
**public
convenience**
latrine 649 n.
public domain
joint possession
775 n.
public enemy
enemy 881 n.
offender 904 n.
public enquiry
enquiry 459 n.
adviser 691 n.
public eye
publicity 528 n.
public figure
person of repute
866 n.
public house
tavern 192 n.
publicist
exhibitor 522 n.
publicizer 528 n.
dissertator 591 n.

publicity
publicity 528 n.
publicize
attract notice
455 vb.
manifest 522 vb.
communicate
524 vb.
divulge 526 vb.
advertise 528 vb.
**public
knowledge**
knowledge 490 n.
public library
library 589 n.
public life
vocation 622 n.
**public limited
company**
corporation 708 n.
publicly
remarkably 32 vb.
public nuisance
hateful object
888 n.
public opinion
belief 485 n.
consensus 488 n.
tribunal 956 n.
**public opinion
poll**
enquiry 459 n.
**public
prosecutor**
accuser 928 n.
law officer 955 n.
public purse
treasury 799 n.
public relations
publicity 528 n.
public school
school 539 n.
public speaking
oratory 579 n.
public-spirited
patriotic 901 adj.
public transport
vehicle 274 n.
publish
publish 528 vb.
publisher
publicizer 528 n.
bookperson 589 n.
publishing
publication 528 n.
**publish the
banns**
court 889 vb.
marry 894 vb.
puce
brown 430 adj.
purple 436 adj.
Puck
elf 970 n.

fairy 970 n.
puck
missile 287 n.
pucker
become small
198 vb.
fold 261 n.
fold 261 vb.
pudding
sequel 67 n.
dessert 301 n.
dish 301 n.
puddle
shallowness 212 n.
lake 346 n.
pudenda
genitalia 167 n.
pudgy
fleshy 195 adj.
puerile
foolish 499 adj.
trivial 639 adj.
immature 670 adj.
puff
vary 152 vb.
dilation 197 n.
enlarge 197 vb.
emit 300 vb.
pastries and cakes
301 n.
blow 352 vb.
breathe 352 vb.
breeze 352 n.
smoke 388 vb.
overestimate
482 vb.
advertise 528 vb.
advertisement
528 n.
exaggerate 546 vb.
be fatigued
684 vb.
boast 877 vb.
praise 923 n.
praise 923 vb.
flatter 925 vb.
puff adder
reptile 365 n.
puffball
plant 366 n.
puffery
boasting 877 n.
puffin
bird 365 n.
puff out
enlarge 197 vb.
puff up
enlarge 197 vb.
elevate 310 vb.
praise 923 vb.
puffy
fleshy 195 adj.
pug
dog 365 n.

pugilism
pugilism 716 n.
sport 837 n.
pugilistic
warlike 718 adj.
pugnacious
quarrelling
709 adj.
warlike 718 adj.
pugnacity
quarrelsomeness
709 n.
attack 712 n.
bellicosity 718 n.
irascibility 892 n.
pug-nosed
short 204 adj.
puke
voidance 300 n.
vomit 300 vb.
pulchritude
beauty 841 n.
pule
cry 408 vb.
ululate 409 vb.
weep 836 vb.
pull
advantage 34 n.
force 176 vb.
influence 178 n.
move 265 vb.
row 269 vb.
transpose 272 vb.
deflect 282 vb.
propel 287 vb.
propulsion 287 n.
draw 288 vb.
traction 288 n.
attract 291 vb.
attraction 291 n.
extract 304 vb.
extraction 304 n.
smoke 388 vb.
reading matter
589 n.
motivate 612 vb.
doctor 658 vb.
exertion 682 n.
work 682 vb.
pull a fast one
deceive 542 vb.
be cunning 698 vb.
pull a long face
be dejected 834 vb.
pull back
draw 288 vb.
pull down
demolish 165 vb.
pullet
young creature
132 n.
poultry 365 n.
pulley
wheel 250 n.

tool 630 n.
pull in
arrive 295 vb.
pull it off
succeed 727 vb.
pull no punches
be concise 569 vb.
be severe 735 vb.
pull off
print 587 vb.
pull oneself up
lift oneself 310 vb.
**pull oneself up
by one's
bootstraps**
succeed 727 vb.
pull one's leg
fool 542 vb.
be witty 839 vb.
ridicule 851 vb.
**pull one's
weight**
participate 775 vb.
pull out
subtract 39 vb.
displace 188 vb.
enlarge 197 vb.
lengthen 203 vb.
fly 271 vb.
draw 288 vb.
decamp 296 vb.
start out 296 vb.
eject 300 vb.
extract 304 vb.
**pull out all the
stops**
be vigorous
174 vb.
exert oneself
682 vb.
**pull out of the
hat**
surprise 508 vb.
pullover
jersey 228 n.
pull rank
be proud 871 vb.
pull strings
influence 178 vb.
plot 623 vb.
be instrumental
628 vb.
pull the plug on
terminate 69 vb.
**pull the rug
from under
one's feet**
hinder 702 vb.
fire at 712 vb.
**pull the wool
over one's eyes**
deceive 542 vb.
pull through
be restored 656 vb.

puree
hors-d'oeuvres
301 n.
pulpiness 356 n.
purgative
opener 263 n.
purgative 658 n.
purgatory
suffering 825 n.
penance 941 n.
hell 972 n.
purge
slaughter 362 n.
slaughter 362 vb.
purify 648 vb.
purgative 658 n.
capital punishment
963 n.
execute 963 vb.
purification
inodorousness
395 n.
cleansing 648 n.
ritual act 988 n.
purify
purify 648 vb.
perform ritual
988 vb.
purist
people of taste
846 n.
perfectionist 862 n.
Puritan
sectarian 978 adj.
sectarian 978 n.
pietistic 979 adj.
zealot 979 n.
puritanical
severe 735 adj.
fastidious 862 adj.
ascetic 945 adj.
purity
simpleness 44 n.
purity 950 n.
purl
needlework 844 n.
purler
overturning
221 n.
descent 309 n.
purlieus
district 184 n.
locality 187 n.
purloin
defraud 788 vb.
steal 788 vb.
purple
purple 436 adj.
purpleness 436 n.
purple hearts
drug-taking 949 n.
purple prose
imperspicuity
568 n.

purport
mean 514 vb.
meaning 514 n.
purpose
will 595 n.
be resolute 599 vb.
intention 617 n.
aspiration 852 n.
purposeful
resolute 599 adj.
purposeless
useless 641 adj.
purposely
purposely 617 adv.
purpure
heraldic 547 adj.
heraldry 547 n.
purr
faintness 401 n.
sound faint
401 n.
ululate 409 vb.
sing 413 vb.
rejoice 835 vb.
purse
become small
198 vb.
treasury 799 n.
purse one's lips
gesticulate 547 vb.
purser
consignee 754 n.
treasurer 798 n.
purse strings
finance 797 n.
pursuance
sequence 65 n.
following 284 n.
pursuit 619 n.
pursue
pursue 619 vb.
do 676 vb.
pursuer
hunter 619 n.
dueness 915 n.
accuser 928 n.
litigant 959 n.
pursuit
following 284 n.
pursuit 619 n.
business 622 n.
pursuivant
heraldry 547 n.
purulent
diseased 651 adj.
toxic 653 adj.
purveyor
caterer 633 n.
pus
excrement 302 n.
fluid 335 n.
semiliquidity
354 n.
dirt 649 n.

push
vigorousness
174 n.
move 265 vb.
transpose 272 vb.
impel 279 vb.
impulse 279 n.
propel 287 vb.
propulsion 287 n.
ejection 300 n.
gesture 547 n.
motivate 612 vb.
be active 678 vb.
restlessness 678 n.
haste 680 n.
attack 712 n.
strike at 712 vb.
sell 793 vb.
push around
impel 279 vb.
push-button
instrumental
628 adj.
pushchair
pushcart 274 n.
pusher
raw 279 n.
propellant 287 n.
busy person 678 n.
drug-taking 949 n.
push on
progress 285 vb.
**push oneself
forward**
be vain 873 vb.
push one's luck
gamble 618 vb.
be rash 857 vb.
push out
eject 300 vb.
pushover
weakling 163 n.
dupe 544 n.
easy thing 701 n.
victory 727 n.
push too far
enrage 891 vb.
**push up the
daisies**
die 361 vb.
pusillanimous
cowardly 856 adj.
puss
cat 365 n.
pussy
cat 365 n.
pussyfoot
be stealthy 525 vb.
avoid 620 vb.
be cautious 858 vb.
pussy willow
tree 366 n.
pustule
skin disease 651 n.

put
firm 45 adj.
place 187 vb.
put about
navigate 269 vb.
circle 314 vb.
publish 528 vb.
**put a brave face
on it**
be patient 823 vb.
take courage
855 vb.
put across
convince 485 vb.
**put a damper
on**
moderate 177 vb.
depress 834 vb.
**put a false
construction
on**
be false 541 vb.
put an end to
terminate 69 vb.
destroy 165 vb.
defeat 727 vb.
put aside
set apart 46 vb.
exclude 57 vb.
be neglectful
458 vb.
neglected 458 adj.
store 632 vb.
**put a spoke in
one's wheel**
disable 161 vb.
make useless
641 adj.
be obstructive
702 vb.
put a stop to
terminate 69 vb.
halt 145 vb.
be severe 735 vb.
restrain 747 vb.
putative
supposed 512 adj.
put away
destroy 165 vb.
mentally disordered
503 adj.
divorce 896 vb.
put by
store 632 vb.
put down
destroy 165 vb.
suppress 165 vb.
place 187 vb.
let fall 311 vb.
kill 362 vb.
overmaster 727 vb.
inglorious 867 adj.
shame 867 vb.
humiliate 872 vb.

put-down
slur 867 n.
put down to
attribute 158 vb.
put forth
expand 197 vb.
propound 512 vb.
put forward
affirm 532 vb.
offer 759 vb.
**put in a good
word for**
approve 923 vb.
**put in an
appearance**
be present 189 vb.
put in for
offer oneself
759 vb.
request 761 vb.
**put in one's
place, be**
be humbled
872 vb.
put in order
compose 56 vb.
arrange 62 vb.
**put in
perspective**
relate 9 vb.
put in the shade
abate 37 vb.
humiliate
872 vb.
put into force
compel 740 vb.
**put into
operation**
move 265 vb.
use 673 vb.
**put into
practice**
use 673 vb.
do 676 vb.
deal with 688 vb.
put in touch
connect 45 vb.
put in writing
write 586 vb.
**put it another
way**
mean 514 vb.
put it bluntly
affirm 532 vb.
put off
put off 136 vb.
influence 178 vb.
repel 292 vb.
distracted 456 adj.
dissuade 613 vb.
be obstructive
702 vb.
cause dislike
861 vb.

quin
five 99 n.
quincentennial
seasonal 141 adj.
quinine
antidote 658 n.
prophylactic 658 n.
quinquennial
periodic 110 adj.
seasonal 141 adj.
quinquennium
period 110 n.
quinquereme
five 99 n.
quintal
weighing 322 n.
quintessence
essential part 5 n.
goodness 644 n.
perfection 646 n.
quintet
five 99 n.
orchestra 413 n.
quintuplet
five 99 n.
quip
be witty 839 vb.
witticism 839 n.
indignity 921 n.
quire
paper 631 n.
quirk
speciality 80 n.
nonconformity
84 n.
eccentricity 503 n.
whim 604 n.
quisling
recanter 603 n.
collaborator 707 n.
revolter 738 n.
bad person 938 n.
quit
separate 46 vb.
depart 296 vb.
relinquish 621 vb.
resign 753 vb.
fail in duty 918 vb.
quite
greatly 32 vb.
slightly 33 adv.
completely 54 adv.
quite something
prodigy 864 n.
**quite the
reverse**
contrariety 14 n.
inversely 221 adv.
quit one's post
relinquish 621 vb.
quits
equal 28 adj.
equivalence 28 n.
atonement 941 n.

quiver
accumulation 74 n.
case 194 n.
oscillate 317 vb.
agitation 318 n.
be agitated 318 vb.
feel pain 377 vb.
be cold 380 vb.
storage 632 n.
arsenal 723 n.
feeling 818 n.
show feeling
818 vb.
be excited 821 vb.
quake 854 vb.
quiverful
contents 193 n.
quixotic
disinterested
931 adj.
quiz
gaze 438 vb.
watch 441 vb.
be curious 453 vb.
interrogate 459 vb.
interrogation
459 n.
broadcast 531 n.
indoor game 837 n.
quizzical
enquiring 459 adj.
quod
prison 748 n.
quoits
ball game 837 n.
Quorn (tdmk)
fruit and vegetables
301 n.
quorum
finite quantity
26 n.
plenitude 54 n.
electorate 605 n.
sufficiency 635 n.
parliament 692 n.
quota
finite quantity
26 n.
part 53 n.
portion 783 n.
quotable
relevant 9 adj.
quotation
referral 9 n.
part 53 n.
repetition 106 n.
evidence 466 n.
exhibit 522 n.
price 809 n.
**quotation
marks**
punctuation 547 n.
quote
part 53 n.

exemplify 83 vb.
repeat 106 vb.
manifest 522 vb.
quotidian
seasonal 141 adj.
quotient
quantity 26 n.
numerical element
85 n.

R

rabbet
join 45 vb.
furrow 262 n.
rabbi
theologian 973 n.
priest 986 n.
rabbit
mammal 365 n.
beginner 538 n.
coward 856 n.
rabbit on
be diffuse 570 vb.
be loquacious
581 vb.
rabbit punch
knock 279 n.
rabbit warren
abundance 171 n.
rabble
rabble 869 n.
rabble-rouser
motivator 612 n.
agitator 738 n.
excitant 821 n.
Rabelaisian
impure 951 adj.
rabid
furious 176 adj.
frenzied 503 adj.
excitable
822 adj.
angry 891 adj.
rabies
animal disease
651 n.
infection 651 n.
raccoon
mammal 365 n.
race
race 11 n.
travel 267 vb.
hasten 680 vb.
conduct 688 n.
community 708 n.
contend 716 vb.
racing 716 n.
amuse oneself
837 vb.
**race against
time**
haste 680 n.

racecourse
meeting place
192 n.
gaming-house
618 n.
racing 716 n.
arena 724 n.
racehorse
horse 273 n.
racetrack
path 624 n.
arena 724 n.
racewalking
pedestrianism
267 n.
racing 716 n.
sport 837 n.
racial
ethnic 11 adj.
parental 169 adj.
racialism
prejudice 481 n.
hatred 888 n.
racialist
biased 481 adj.
narrow mind
481 n.
enemy 881 n.
racing
speedy 277 adj.
flowing 350 adj.
hasty 680 adj.
racing 716 n.
sport 837 n.
racism
prejudice 481 n.
hatred 888 n.
injustice 914 n.
racist
biased 481 adj.
narrow mind
481 n.
rack
compartment
194 n.
hanger 217 n.
shelf 218 n.
distort 246 vb.
pain 377 n.
suffering 825 n.
torment 827 vb.
instrument of
torture 964 n.
rack and ruin
ruin 165 n.
racket
turmoil 61 n.
commotion 318 n.
loudness 400 n.
roll 403 n.
discord 411 n.
trickery 542 n.
plot 623 n.
quarrel 709 n.

perfidy 930 n.
racketeer
robber 789 n.
offender 904 n.
be dishonest
930 vb.
rackets
ball game 837 n.
**rack one's
brains**
think 449 vb.
remember 505 vb.
raconteur
humorist 839 n.
racy
vigorous 174 adj.
stylistic 566 adj.
forceful 571 adj.
lively 819 adj.
witty 839 adj.
impure 951 adj.
radar
location 187 n.
sailing aid 269 n.
detector 484 n.
telecommunication
531 n.
indicator 547 n.
raddle
redden 431 vb.
radially
longwise 203 adv.
radian
angular measure
247 n.
radiance
glow 417 n.
light 417 n.
beauty 841 n.
radiant
divergent 294 adj.
luminous 417 adj.
happy 824 adj.
cheerful 833 adj.
beautiful 841 adj.
radiate
separate 46 vb.
be dispersed 75 vb.
diverge 294 vb.
radiate 417 vb.
radiation
dispersion 75 n.
divergence 294 n.
radiation 417 n.
radiator
heater 383 n.
radical
numerical 85 adj.
revolutionary
149 adj.
revolutionist
149 n.
fundamental
156 adj.

relive the past
describe 590 vb.
regret 830 vb.
relocate
change 143 vb.
place 187 vb.
be in motion
265 vb.
transpose 272 vb.
relocation
change 143 n.
transition 147 n.
location 187 n.
transference 272 n.
reluctance
slowness 278 n.
dissent 489 n.
unwillingness
598 n.
dislike 861 n.
reluctant
dissenting 489 adj.
unwilling 598 adj.
resisting 715 adj.
rely
hope 852 vb.
rely on
be certain 473 vb.
believe 485 vb.
take a pledge
764 vb.
rem
radiation 417 n.
remain
be left 41 vb.
continue 108 vb.
last 113 vb.
outlast 113 vb.
stay 144 vb.
go on 146 vb.
dwell 192 vb.
be quiescent
266 vb.
remainder
remainder 41 n.
book 589 n.
sell 793 vb.
remains
remainder 41 n.
trace 548 n.
remake
repeat 106 vb.
repetition 106 n.
reproduce 166 vb.
film 445 n.
restore 656 vb.
remand
command 737 vb.
detention 747 n.
imprison 747 vb.
remark
maxim 496 n.
affirm 532 vb.
speech 579 n.

remarkable
remarkable 32 adj.
unusual 84 adj.
visible 443 adj.
wonderful
864 adj.
noteworthy
866 adj.
remark on
notice 455 vb.
remarks
estimate 480 n.
remarry
wed 894 vb.
remedial
improving 654 adj.
remedial 658 adj.
remedy
repair 656 vb.
remedy 658 n.
remedy 658 vb.
remember
remember 505 vb.
give 781 vb.
remembrance
remembrance
505 n.
famousness 866 n.
remembrances
courteous act
884 n.
remind
remind 505 vb.
reminder
reminder 505 n.
remind oneself
remember 505 vb.
reminisce
remember 505 vb.
describe 590 vb.
reminiscence
remembrance
505 n.
narrative 590 n.
reminiscent
remembering
505 adj.
remiss
negligent 458 adj.
unwilling 598 adj.
lax 734 adj.
remission
fitfulness 142 n.
lull 145 n.
moderation 177 n.
forgiveness 909 n.
remit
send 272 vb.
forgive 909 vb.
remittance
transference
272 n.
funds 797 n.
payment 804 n.

remittance man
recipient 782 n.
remnant
remainder 41 n.
remnants
leavings 41 n.
remodel
transform 147 vb.
revolutionize
149 vb.
rectify 654 vb.
repair 656 vb.
remonstrance
dissuasion 613 n.
deprecation 762 n.
reprimand 924 n.
remonstrate
dissuade 613 vb.
deprecate 762 vb.
disapprove 924 vb.
reprove 924 vb.
remorse
sorrow 825 n.
regret 830 n.
pity 905 n.
guilt 936 n.
penitence 939 n.
remorseful
unhappy 825 adj.
regretting 830 adj.
repentant 939 adj.
remorseless
pitiless 906 adj.
impenitent
940 adj.
remote
irrelevant 10 adj.
inconsiderable
33 adj.
distant 199 adj.
invisible 444 adj.
secluded 883 adj.
remould
modify 143 vb.
reproduce 166 vb.
rectify 654 vb.
removal
subtraction 39 n.
exclusion 57 n.
displacement
188 n.
transference 272 n.
departure 296 n.
extraction 304 n.
deposal 752 n.
taking 786 n.
remove
degree 27 n.
subtract 39 vb.
disunite 46 vb.
exclude 57 vb.
serial place 73 n.
destroy 165 vb.
displace 188 vb.

transpose 272 vb.
depart 296 vb.
extract 304 vb.
class 538 n.
depose 752 vb.
take 786 vb.
take away 786 vb.
remuneration
earnings 771 n.
pay 804 n.
receipt 807 n.
reward 962 n.
remunerative
profitable 640 adj.
gainful 771 adj.
Renaissance
era 110 n.
architectural
192 adj.
renaissance
recurrence 106 n.
life 360 n.
revival 656 n.
rend
rend 46 vb.
demolish 165 vb.
force 176 vb.
hurt 827 vb.
render
convert 147 vb.
transform 147 vb.
coat 226 vb.
liquefy 337 vb.
play music
413 vb.
translate 520 vb.
give 781 vb.
rendering
facing 226 vb.
translation 520 n.
building material
631 n.
**render null and
void**
nullify 2 vb.
abrogate 752 vb.
rendezvous
union 45 n.
congregate 74 vb.
focus 76 n.
place 185 n.
goal 295 n.
meet 295 vb.
social round
882 n.
**rend the
heartstrings**
hurt 827 vb.
renegade
recanter 603 n.
bad person 938 n.
renege on
not observe
769 vb.

renew
double 91 vb.
repeat 106 vb.
reproduce 166 vb.
make better
654 vb.
repair 656 vb.
restore 656 vb.
renewal
duplication 91 n.
repetition 106 n.
newness 126 n.
reproduction
166 n.
repair 656 n.
revival 656 n.
**renew one's
efforts**
persevere 600 vb.
renounce
negate 533 vb.
recant 603 vb.
relinquish 621 vb.
resign 753 vb.
not retain 779 vb.
renovate
modernize 126 vb.
reproduce 166 vb.
make better
654 vb.
repair 656 vb.
restore 656 vb.
renovation
newness 126 n.
reproduction
166 n.
amendment 654 n.
repair 656 n.
renown
greatness 32 n.
famousness 866 n.
honour 866 vb.
renowned
renowned 866 adj.
rent
disunion 46 n.
gap 201 n.
assign 780 vb.
purchase 792 vb.
price 809 n.
rental
transfer 780 n.
price 809 n.
rent-boy
libertine 952 n.
prostitute 952 n.
rent out
lease 784 vb.
renunciation
negation 533 n.
recantation 603 n.
relinquishment
621 n.
laxity 734 n.

resounding
sounding 398 adj.
resonant 404 adj.
renowned 866 adj.
resource
contrivance 623 n.
resourceful
progressive
285 adj.
imaginative
513 adj.
skilful 694 adj.
cunning 698 adj.
resources
means 629 n.
materials 631 n.
estate 777 n.
wealth 800 n.
respect
relation 9 n.
observe 768 vb.
respect 920 n.
respect 920 vb.
respectability
repute 866 n.
probity 929 n.
respectable
great 32 adj.
not bad 644 adj.
reputable 866 adj.
honourable
929 adj.
respectful
respectful
920 adj.
respective
relative 9 adj.
respectively
severally 80 adv.
pro rata 783 adv.
respects
courteous act
884 n.
respects 920 n.
respiration
respiration 352 n.
respirator
respiration 352 n.
hospital 658 n.
safeguard 662 n.
preserver 666 n.
**respiratory
disease**
disease 651 n.
respiratory disease
651 n.
respire
breathe 352 vb.
respite
delay 136 n.
lull 145 n.
deliverance 668 n.
repose 683 n.
acquit 960 vb.

resplendent
luminous
417 adj.
splendid 841 adj.
respond
accord 24 vb.
answer 460 vb.
cooperate 706 vb.
concord 710 vb.
feel 818 vb.
respondent
respondent 460 n.
accused person
928 n.
litigant 959 n.
response
effect 157 n.
sense 374 n.
answer 460 n.
feeling 818 n.
friendliness 880 n.
hymn 981 n.
responsible
liable 180 adj.
observant 768 adj.
cautious 858 adj.
obliged 917 adj.
trustworthy
929 adj.
guilty 936 adj.
responsive
sentient 374 adj.
feeling 818 adj.
impressible
819 adj.
rest
be left 41 vb.
remainder 41 n.
be discontinuous
72 vb.
stay 144 vb.
cease 145 vb.
lull 145 n.
pause 145 vb.
go on 146 vb.
stability 153 n.
inertness 175 n.
support 218 n.
be quiescent
266 vb.
come to rest
266 vb.
quiescence 266 n.
quietude 266 n.
silence 399 n.
notation 410 n.
inaction 677 n.
be inactive 679 vb.
leisure 681 n.
repose 683 n.
repose 683 vb.
relief 831 n.
rest assured
believe 485 vb.

hope 852 vb.
restate
repeat 106 vb.
restaurant
café 192 n.
cookery 301 n.
restauranteur
caterer 633 n.
restful
tranquil 266 adj.
comfortable
376 adj.
reposeful 683 adj.
restitution
restitution 787 n.
restive
excited 821 adj.
excitable 822 adj.
discontented
829 adj.
restless
transient 114 adj.
fitful 142 adj.
moving 265 adj.
irresolute 601 adj.
active 678 adj.
excited 821 adj.
excitable 822 adj.
restock
replenish 633 vb.
**rest on one's
laurels**
be quiescent
266 vb.
not act 677 vb.
restoration
newness 126 n.
repair 656 n.
restoration 656 n.
dueness 915n.
vindication 927 n.
penalty 963 n.
restorative
stimulant 174 n.
remedial 658 adj.
tonic 658 n.
restore
compensate
31 vb.
make better
654 vb.
restore 656 vb.
relieve 831 vb.
vindicate 927 vb.
**restore one's
faith**
convince 485 vb.
restrain
restrain 747 vb.
tranquillize
823 vb.
restrained
plain 573 adj.
restrained 747 adj.

restrain oneself
restrain 747 vb.
restraint
moderation 177 n.
restraint 747 n.
restrict
make smaller
198 vb.
limit 236 vb.
qualify 468 vb.
hinder 702 vb.
restrain 747 vb.
prohibit 757 vb.
restricted
small 33 adj.
moderate 177 adj.
concealed 525 adj.
restrained 747 adj.
restricted area
restriction 747 n.
restriction
diminution 37 n.
hindrance 702 n.
restriction 747 n.
prohibition 757 n.
restrictive
excluding 57 adj.
restraining
747 adj.
**restrictive
practice**
restriction 747 n.
restrict oneself
be temperate
942 vb.
rest room
latrine 649 n.
restructuring
arrangement 62 n.
revolution 149 n.
rest with
be one's duty
917 vb.
restyle
hairdressing 843 n.
result
be left 41 vb.
remainder 41 n.
sequel 67 n.
end 69 n.
event 154 n.
effect 157 vb.
product 164 n.
judgment 480 n.
instrumentality
628 n.
completion 725 n.
resultant
remaining 41 adj.
caused 157 adj.
resultant action
effect 157 n.
result in
result 157 vb.

results
answer 460 n.
resume
repeat 106 vb.
acquire 771 vb.
résumé
abstract 592 vb.
compendium
592 n.
resumption
repetition 106 n.
restoration 656 n.
resurface
repair 656 vb.
resurgence
reproduction
166 n.
revival 656 n.
resurrect
reproduce 166 vb.
revive 656 vb.
resurrection
newness 126 n.
reproduction
166 n.
revival 656 n.
heaven 971 n.
resurrectionist
thief 789 n.
resuscitate
reproduce 166 vb.
revive 656 vb.
animate 821 vb.
retail
communicate
524 vb.
sell 793 vb.
retailer
intermediary
231 n.
seller 793 n.
merchant 794 n.
tradespeople 794 n.
retail price
price 809 n.
retail therapy
purchase 792 n.
retain
stabilize 153 vb.
understand 516 vb.
retain 778 vb.
retainer
inferior 35 n.
retainer 742 n.
reward 962 n.
retake
retrieve 656 vb.
retaliate
retaliate 714 vb.
retaliation
retaliation 714 n.
justice 913 n.
retard
put off 136 vb.

rough and tumble
turmoil 61 n.
fight 716 n.
roughcast
coat 226 vb.
facing 226 n.
rough 259 adj.
roughen 259 vb.
rough diamond
amorphism 244 n.
undevelopment 670 n.
roughen
roughen 259 vb.
rough going
roughness 259 n.
rough guess
conjecture 512 n.
roughhewn
incomplete 55 adj.
immature 670 adj.
roughhouse
turmoil 61 n.
violence 176 n.
fight 716 n.
roughly
nearly 200 adv.
roughneck
low fellow 869 n.
bad person 938 n.
roughness
violence 176 n.
roughness 259 n.
pungency 388 n.
stridor 407 n.
inelegance 576 n.
painfulness 827 n.
rudeness 885 n.
rough out
outline 233 vb.
represent 551 vb.
rough side of one's tongue
reproach 924 n.
rough sleeper
displaced person 188 n.
wanderer 268 n.
outcast 883 n.
roulette
gambling 618 n.
gambling game 837 n.
roulette wheel
rotator 315 n.
round
equal 28 adj.
part 53 n.
continuity 71 n.
serial place 73 n.
numerical 85 adj.
recurrence 106 n.
period 110 n.

periodicity 141 n.
fleshy 195 adj.
be curved 248 vb.
circle 250 n.
round 250 adj.
cylinder 252 n.
land travel 267 n.
navigate 269 vb.
circle 314 vb.
bang 402 n.
vocal music 412 n.
circuit 626 n.
pugilism 716 n.
round about
around 230 adv.
round about 626 adv.
roundabout
crossing 222 n.
circle 250 n.
traffic control 305 n.
prolix 570 adj.
road 624 n.
roundabout 626 adj.
roundabout way
circuition 314 n.
circuit 626 n.
roundelay
vocal music 412 n.
rounders
ball game 837 n.
round number
number 85 n.
round of applause
applause 923 n.
round off
equalize 28 vb.
make complete 54 vb.
round on
attack 712 vb.
retaliate 714 vb.
blame 924 vb.
round robin
continuity 71 n.
report 524 n.
correspondence 588 n.
request 761 n.
deprecation 762 n.
roundsman
traveller 268 n.
seller 793 n.
round sum
funds 797 n.
round table
council 692 n.
round the bend or the twist
crazy 503 adj.

round the clock
all along 113 adv.
round trip
reversion 148 n.
land travel 267 n.
circuition 314 n.
round up
bring together 74 vb.
break in 369 vb.
roundup
assemblage 74 n.
round upon
curse 899 vb.
roup
sale 793 n.
rouse
invigorate 174 vb.
incite 612 vb.
excite 821 vb.
rouse curiosity
impress 821 vb.
rousing
vigorous 174 adj.
eloquent 579 adj.
excitation 821 n.
exciting 821 adj.
rousing cheer
stimulant 174 n.
rejoicing 835 n.
rout
disperse 75 vb.
confute 479 vb.
defeat 727 vb.
defeat 728 n.
rabble 869 n.
route
itinerary 267 n.
passage 305 n.
route 624 n.
way 624 n.
route march
marching 267 n.
routine
uniformity 16 n.
order 60 n.
continuity 71 n.
regularity 81 n.
recurrence 106 n.
regular return 141 n.
permanence 144 n.
habit 610 n.
habitual 610 adj.
habituation 610 n.
practice 610 n.
way 624 n.
action 676 n.
conduct 688 n.
ostentation 875 n.
ritual 988 n.
roux
sauce 389 n.

rove
wander 267 vb.
roving commission
uncertainty 474 n.
row
turmoil 61 n.
series 71 n.
violence 176 n.
housing 192 n.
layer 207 n.
row 269 vb.
loudness 400 n.
discord 411 n.
quarrel 709 n.
fight 716 vb.
rowan
tree 366 n.
rowdy
violent 176 adj.
violent creature 176 n.
loud 400 adj.
combatant 722 n.
rioter 738 n.
ill-bred 847 adj.
low fellow 869 n.
ruffian 904 n.
rowing
aquatics 269 n.
water travel 269 n.
See **aquatics**
traction 288 n.
sport 837 n.
rowing boat
rowing boat 275 n.
rowlock
pivot 218 n.
royal
sail 275 n.
ruling 733 adj.
liberal 813 adj.
impressive 821 adj.
worshipful 866 adj.
noble 868 adj.
proud 871 adj.
ostentatious 875 adj.
Royal Commission
council 692 n.
royal jelly
tonic 658 n.
Royal Marines
naval man 722 n.
Royal Navy
naval man 722 n.
royalty
authority 733 n.
position of authority 733 n.
sovereign 741 n.

receipt 807 n.
nobility 868 n.
RSVP
answer 460 vb.
rub
be contiguous 202 vb.
friction 333 n.
rub 333 vb.
difficulty 700 n.
rub along with
be friendly 880 vb.
rub away
abate 37 vb.
rubber
elasticity 328 n.
friction 333 n.
obliteration 550 n.
contest 716 n.
rubber band
elasticity 328 n.
rubbernecking
inspection 438 n.
curiosity 453 n.
desire 859 n.
rubber of bridge
card game 837 n.
rubber of whist
card game 837 n.
rubberstamp
assent 488 vb.
endorse 488 vb.
rubbery
elastic 328 adj.
tough 329 adj.
rubbing
duplicate 22 n.
rubbish
absurdity 497 n.
silly talk 515 n.
falsehood 541 n.
rubbish 641 n.
detract 926 vb.
rubbish bin
vessel 194 n.
rubble
piece 53 n.
rub down
smooth 258 vb.
rub 333 vb.
groom 369 vb.
rubella
infection 651 n.
Rubicon
limit 236 n.
Rubik's cube (tdmk)
enigma 530 n.
Rubik's magic (tdmk)
enigma 530 n.
rub in
rub 333 vb.
emphasize 532 vb.

wanderer 268 n.
speedy 277 adj.
recanter 603 n.
avoider 620 n.
escaper 667 n.
runaway
  victory
victory 727 n.
run away
  with
take away 786 vb.
run before the
  wind
navigate 269 vb.
run down
decrease 37 vb.
cease 145 vb.
weakly 163 adj.
collide 279 vb.
underestimate
  483 vb.
sick 651 adj.
dilapidated
  655 adj.
be malevolent
  898 vb.
not respect 921 vb.
criticize 924 vb.
detract 926 vb.
rundown
compendium
  592 n.
rune
indication
  547 n.
letter 558 n.
run for
offer oneself
  759 vb.
run for cover
be cowardly
  856 vb.
run for it
run away 620 vb.
rung
degree 27 n.
serial place 73 n.
stand 218 n.
cylinder 252 n.
ascent 308 n.
run in
begin 68 vb.
initiate 68 vb.
enter 297 vb.
arrest 747 vb.
imprison 747 vb.
take 786 vb.
run in one's
  mind
be remembered
  505 vb.
run in the
  family
be intrinsic 5 vb.

run into
collide 279 vb.
meet 295 vb.
run its course
elapse 111 vb.
run neck and
  neck
synchronize
  123 vb.
runner
young plant 132 n.
hanger 217 n.
pedestrian 268 n.
courier 529 n.
contender 716 n.
servant 742 n.
runner beans
fruit and vegetables
  301 n.
running
continuous 71 adj.
continuously
  71 adv.
motion 265 n.
speedy 277 adj.
blood 335 adj.
flowing 350 adj.
dramatic 594 adj.
hasty 680 adj.
management
  689 n.
sport 837 n.
running battle
contention 716 n.
running jump
leap 312 n.
running repairs
repair 656 n.
running sore
outflow 298 n.
evil 616 n.
wound 655 n.
bane 659 n.
painfulness 827 n.
running track
path 624 n.
arena 724 n.
running water
fluid 335 n.
water 339 n.
stream 350 n.
runny
blood 335 adj.
flowing 350 adj.
run off
empty 300 vb.
flow 350 vb.
print 587 vb.
run of the mill
generality 79 n.
run-of-the-mill
imitative 20 adj.
median 30 adj.
general 79 adj.

run on
continue 71 vb.
go on 146 vb.
progress 285 vb.
be loquacious
  581 vb.
requirement 627 n.
run-on
continuous 71 adj.
run one's eye
  over
scan 438 vb.
run out
end 69 vb.
past 125 adj.
cease 145 vb.
impel 279 vb.
dismiss 300 vb.
not suffice 636 vb.
run out on
relinquish 621 vb.
run over
collide 279 vb.
study 536 vb.
abstract 592 vb.
run riot
exaggerate 546 vb.
superabound
  637 vb.
be active 678 vb.
be excitable
  822 vb.
be intemperate
  943 vb.
be sensual 944 vb.
run round in
  circles
be active 678 vb.
run short
fall short 307 vb.
runt
dwarf 196 n.
run the
  gauntlet
face danger
  661 vb.
defy 711 vb.
run the risk of
be liable 180 vb.
be in danger
  661 vb.
run through
make uniform
  16 vb.
pervade 189 vb.
pierce 263 vb.
insert 303 vb.
kill 362 vb.
strike at 712 vb.
run to
request 761 vb.
run to seed
waste 634 vb.
deteriorate 655 vb.

run up
produce 164 vb.
elevate 310 vb.
runway
air travel 271 n.
path 624 n.
run with the
  hare and hunt
  with the
  hounds
be false 541 vb.
be servile 879 vb.
be dishonest
  930 vb.
rupee
coinage 797 n.
rupture
disagreement 25 n.
break 46 vb.
separation 46 n.
gap 201 n.
wound 655 n.
dissension 709 n.
rural
provincial 192 adj.
ruse
trickery 542 n.
stratagem 698 n.
rush
rampage 61 vb.
crowd 74 n.
move fast 277 vb.
spurt 277 n.
be agitated 318 vb.
commotion 318 n.
flow 350 vb.
grass 366 n.
film 445 n.
be active 678 vb.
haste 680 n.
hasten 680 vb.
hasty 680 adj.
attack 712 n.
celebrate 876 vb.
rushed
hasty 680 adj.
rushed off one's
  feet
busy 678 adj.
rush hour
crowd 74 n.
period 110 n.
traffic control
  305 n.
rushing
excited 821 adj.
rush in where
  angels fear to
  tread
be rash 857 vb.
rush one's
  fences
hasten 680 vb.
be rash 857 vb.

rusk
cereals 301 n.
russet
fruit and vegetables
  301 n.
brown 430 adj.
red 431 adj.
Russian roulette
gambling 618 n.
rust
abate 37 vb.
decay 51 n.
decompose 51 vb.
oldness 127 n.
destroyer 168 n.
blunt 257 vb.
dim 419 vb.
desuetude 611 n.
be unclean 649 vb.
dirt 649 n.
deteriorate 655 vb.
dilapidation 655 n.
impair 655 vb.
blight 659 n.
not act 677 vb.
be inactive 679 vb.
blemish 845 n.
rustic
native 191 n.
provincial 192 adj.
country-dweller
  869 n.
plebeian 869 adj.
rustication
seclusion 883 n.
penalty 963 n.
rustle
faintness 401 n.
sound faint
  401 vb.
hiss 406 vb.
sibilation 406 n.
steal 788 vb.
rustler
thief 789 n.
rusty
strident 407 adj.
dim 419 adj.
red 431 adj.
unhabituated
  611 adj.
dilapidated
  655 adj.
inactive 679 adj.
rut
continuity 71 n.
regularity 81 n.
permanence 144 n.
roughness 259 n.
furrow 262 n.
groove 262 vb.
habit 610 n.
bore 838 n.
desire 859 vb.

violent creature
176 n.
ignorant 491 adj.
ill-treat 645 vb.
wound 655 vb.
attack 712 vb.
severe 735 adj.
barbaric 869 adj.
low fellow 869 n.
discourteous
885 adj.
rude person 885 n.
angry 891 adj.
cruel 898 adj.
ruffian 904 n.
criticize 924 vb.
monster 938 n.
savagery
violence 176 n.
ignorance 491 n.
inhumanity 898 n.
savages
humankind 371 n.
savanna
plain 348 n.
savant(e)
scholar 492 n.
save
exclusive of
57 adv.
store 632 vb.
preserve 666 vb.
deliver 668 vb.
liberate 746 vb.
acquire 771 vb.
retain 778 vb.
economize 814 vb.
relieve 831 vb.
save by the bell
deliver 668 vb.
saved
sanctified 979 adj.
save one's bacon
be safe 660 vb.
escape 667 vb.
save one's skin
deliver 668 vb.
save up
store 632 vb.
acquire 771 vb.
saving
qualifying 468 adj.
preservation 666 n.
economical
814 adj.
economy 814 n.
saving grace
virtues 933 n.
savings
store 632 vb.
gain 771 n.
economy 814 n.
savings account
store 632 n.

funds 797 n.
accounts 808 n.
Saviour
God the Son 965 n.
saviour
preserver 666 n.
benefactor 903 n.
savoir-faire
knowledge 490 n.
conduct 688 n.
skill 694 n.
etiquette 848 n.
savory
herb 301 n.
savour
taste 386 n.
taste 386 vb.
be pleased 824 vb.
savour of
resemble 18 vb.
taste 386 vb.
mean 514 vb.
savoury
dish 301 n.
mouthful 301 n.
savouriness 390 n.
savoury 390 adj.
savoy
fruit and vegetables
301 n.
savvy
know 490 vb.
knowledge 490 n.
intelligence 498 n.
understand 516 vb.
etiquette 848 n.
saw
cut 46 vb.
tooth 256 n.
notch 260 n.
rasp 407 vb.
discord 411 vb.
play music 413 vb.
maxim 496 n.
sawdust
leavings 41 n.
powder 332 n.
sawmill
workshop 687 n.
sawn-off
short 204 adj.
**sawn-off
shotgun**
firearm 723 n.
sax
flute 414 n.
saxophone
flute 414 n.
say
about 33 adv.
affirm 532 vb.
speak 579 vb.
say after
repeat 106 vb.

say a prayer
worship 981 vb.
saying
maxim 496 n.
affirmation 532 n.
phrase 563 n.
say in unison
synchronize
123 vb.
say of
attribute 158 vb.
say one is sorry
be penitent 939 vb.
say so
decree 737 vb.
say-so
affirmation 532 n.
command 737 n.
**say what is in
one's mind**
be artless 699 vb.
scab
nonconformist
84 n.
layer 207 n.
covering 226 n.
recanter 603 n.
wound 655 n.
revolter 738 n.
cad 938 n.
scabbard
case 194 n.
arsenal 723 n.
scabby
rough 259 adj.
unclean 649 adj.
scads
great quantity
32 n.
funds 797 n.
wealth 800 n.
scaffold
structure 331 n.
means of execution
964 n.
scaffolding
frame 218 n.
scag
drug-taking 949 n.
scald
burn 381 vb.
ulcer 651 n.
wound 655 n.
scalding
hot 379 adj.
paining 827 adj.
scale
degree 27 n.
graduate 27 vb.
be great–large
32 vb.
piece 53 n.
series 71 n.
plate 194 n.

layer 207 n.
skin 226 n.
climb 308 vb.
scales 322 n.
key 410 n.
musical note
410 n.
See **key**
opacity 423 n.
gauge 465 n.
scale down
abate 37 vb.
render few 105 vb.
scale drawing
plan 623 n.
scalene
unequal 29 adj.
distorted 246 adj.
scalene triangle
angular figure
247 n.
scales
scales 322 n.
scales of justice
justice 913 n.
scallion
fruit and vegetables
301 n.
scallop
edging 234 n.
convolution
251 n.
notch 260 n.
notch 260 vb.
fish food 301 n.
scallywag
bad person 938 n
scalp
head 213 n.
skin 226 n.
uncover 229 vb.
trophy 729 n.
scalpel
sharp edge 256 n.
scaly
rough 259 adj.
scamp
neglect 458 vb.
not complete
726 vb.
bad person 938 n.
scamped
hasty 680 adj.
uncompleted
726 adj.
scamped work
negligence 458 n.
scamper
move fast 277 vb.
spurt 277 n.
scampi
fish food 301 n.
scan
scan 438 vb.

photograph
551 vb.
photography
551 n.
poetize 593 vb.
scandal
rumour 529 n.
badness 645 n.
slur 867 n.
wrong 914 n.
calumny 926 n.
false charge 928 n.
wickedness 934 n.
scandalize
displease 827 vb.
cause dislike
861 vb.
be wonderful
864 vb.
shame 867 vb.
incur blame
924 vb.
defame 926 vb.
**scandal-
mongering**
detraction 926 n.
scandalous
bad 645 adj.
vulgar 847 adj.
discreditable
867 adj.
wrong 914 adj.
heinous 934 adj.
scanner
enquirer 459 n.
hospital 658 n.
scanning
photography
551 n.
poetic 593 adj.
diagnostic 658 n.
scansion
prosody 593 n.
scant
small 33 adj.
incomplete 55 adj.
few 105 adj.
insufficient
636 adj.
scant respect
disrespect 921 n.
scanty
small 33 adj.
few 105 adj.
short 204 adj.
insufficient
636 adj.
scapegoat
substitute 150 n.
unlucky person
731 n.
deputy 755 n.
sufferer 825 n.
propitiation 941 n.

scion
branch 53 n.
young plant 132 n.
descendant 170 n.
tree 366 n.

scission
scission 46 n.

scissors
sharp edge 256 n.

sclerosis
hardness 326 n.

scoff
food 301 n.
ridicule 851 n.
ridicule 851 vb.
not respect 921 n.
despise 922 vb.
calumny 926 n.
detract 926 vb.

scoff at
disbelieve 486 vb.

scold
violent creature
176 n.
cuss 899 vb.
reproach 924 vb.
detractor 926 n.

scolding
irascible 892 adj.
scurrility 899 n.
disapproving
924 adj.
reprimand 924 n.

scolloped
undulatory
251 adj.

sconce
head 213 n.

scone
cereals 301 n.

scoop
ladle 194 n.
information 524 n.
news 529 n.
acquisition 771 n.

scoop out
make concave
255 vb.

scoot
move fast 277 vb.
run away 620 vb.

scooter
conveyance 267 n.
bicycle 274 n.

scope
degree 27 n.
function 622 n.
scope 744 n.

scorch
move fast 277 vb.
dry 342 vb.
be hot 379 vb.
burn 381 vb.
impair 655 vb.

go to war 718 vb.

scorched
dry 342 adj.
hot 379 adj.

**scorched earth
policy**
unproductiveness
172 n.
warfare 718 n.

score
degree 27 n.
cut 46 vb.
compose 56 vb.
composition 56 n.
arrange 62 vb.
arrangement 62 n.
numerical result
85 n.
number 86 vb.
numeration 86 n.
list 87 n.
notch 260 n.
furrow 262 n.
groove 262 vb.
harmonize 410 vb.
notation 410 n.
music 412 n.
compose music
413 vb.
indication 547 n.
mark 547 vb.
register 548 vb.
wound 655 vb.
triumph 727 vb.
credit 802 n.
accounts 808 n.

score, a
twenty and over
99 n.

score a point
succeed 727 vb.

scoreboard
record 548 n.

score off
confute 479 vb.
triumph 727 vb.
humiliate
872 vb.

scores
multitude 104 n.

scorn
unbelief 486 n.
shame 867 vb.
scurrility 899 n.
disrespect 921 n.
not respect 921 vb.
contempt 922 n.
despise 922 vb.
detraction 926 n.
impiety 980 n.

scornful
cursing 899 adj.
disrespectful
921 adj.

scorpion
creepy-crawly
365 n.

**Scotchtape
(tdmk)**
adhesive 47 n.
fastening 47 n.
ligature 47 n.

Scotch whisky
alcoholic drink
301 n.

scot-free
free 744 adj.
uncharged 812 adj.

Scotland Yard
police 955 n.

Scottie
dog 365 n.

scoundrel
ruffian 904 n.
bad person 938 n.
cad 938 n.

scour
traverse 267 vb.
pass 305 vb.
rub 333 vb.
search 459 vb.
clean 648 vb.

scourge
evil 616 n.
plague 651 n.
bane 659 n.
adversity 731 n.
oppress 735 vb.
ruffian 904 n.
criticize 924 vb.
flog 963 vb.
scourge 964 n.

scourings
leavings 41 n.
rubbish 641 n.
dirt 649 n.

scout
precursor 66 n.
front 237 n.
traverse 267 vb.
male 372 n.
scan 438 vb.
spectator 441 n.
watch 441 vb.
enquirer 459 n.
warner 664 n.
domestic 742 n.
despise 922 vb.

scout out
watch 441 vb.

scout's honour
veracity 540 n.

scowl
look 438 n.
gesticulate 547 vb.
gesture 547 n.
discontent 829 n.
be rude 885 vb.

rudeness 885 n.
hatred 888 n.
anger 891 n.
be angry 891 vb.
sullenness 893 n.

Scrabble (tdmk)
board game 837 n.

scrabble
search 459 vb.

scraggy
lean 206 adj.

scram
come along
267 int.
decamp 296 vb.
run away 620 vb.

scramble
mix 43 vb.
disorder 61 n.
cook 301 vb.
climb 308 vb.
activity 678 n.
haste 680 n.
fight 716 vb.

scrambled eggs
dish 301 n.

scramble for
take 786 vb.

scrap
small quantity
33 n.
piece 53 n.
picture 553 n.
reject 607 vb.
rubbish 641 n.
stop using 674 vb.
fight 716 n.
fight 716 vb.
battle 718 n.

scrapbook
reminder 505 n.
record 548 n.
picture 553 n.
anthology 592 n.

scrape
abate 37 vb.
make smaller
198 vb.
be contiguous
202 vb.
collision 279 n.
stoop 311 vb.
friction 333 n.
rub 333 vb.
touch 378 vb.
rasp 407 vb.
stridor 407 n.
discord 411 vb.
play music 413 vb.
foolery 497 n.
engrave 555 vb.
clean 648 vb.
predicament 700 n.
economize 814 vb.

be parsimonious
816 vb.
servility 879 n.
respects 920 n.
vice 934 n.
guilty act 936 n.

**scrape an
acquaintance**
befriend 880 vb.

scrape home
win 727 vb.

scraper
sharp edge 256 n.

scrape together
bring together
74 vb.
acquire 771 vb.

scraping
friction 333 n.
hoarse 407 adj.
discordant 411 adj.
parsimonious
816 adj.
parsimony 816 n.
servile 879 adj.
respectful 920 adj.

scrappy
fragmentary
53 adj.
incomplete 55 adj.

scraps
leavings 41 n.
rubbish 641 n.

scratch
cut 46 vb.
rend 46 vb.
shallowness
212 n.
be rough 259 vb.
notch 260 n.
furrow 262 n.
groove 262 vb.
friction 333 n.
rub 333 vb.
touch 378 vb.
faintness 401 n.
rasp 407 vb.
stridor 407 n.
indication 547 n.
mark 547 vb.
trace 548 n.
change one's mind
603 vb.
relinquish 621 vb.
trifle 639 n.
ill-treat 645 vb.
wound 655 n.
wound 655 vb.
unprepared
670 adj.
fight 716 vb.
resign 753 vb.
blemish 845 n.
blemish 845 vb.

scratch a living
be poor 801 vb.
scratch card
equal chance
159 n.
gambling 618 n.
gambling game
837 n.
**scratch one's
back**
minister to 703 vb.
flatter 925 vb.
scratch out
eject 300 vb.
obliterate 550 vb.
scratchy
strident 407 adj.
scrawl
lack of meaning
515 n.
be unintelligible
517 vb.
unintelligibility
517 n.
lettering 586 n.
script 586 n.
write 586 vb.
scrawny
lean 206 adj.
scream
blow 352 vb.
be loud 400 vb.
loudness 400 n.
shrill 407 vb.
cry 408 n.
cry 408 vb.
weep 836 vb.
scream, a
funny 849 adj.
scree
piece 53 n.
incline 220 n.
screech
blow 352 vb.
rasp 407 vb.
shrill 407 vb.
stridor 407 n.
cry 408 n.
cry 408 vb.
ululate 409 vb.
ululation 409 n.
screech owl
bird 365 n.
screechy
strident 407 adj.
screed
facing 226 n.
oration 579 n.
script 586 n.
screeds
great quantity
32 n.
screen
exclusion 57 n.

porosity 263 n.
screen 421 n.
screen 421 vb.
enquire 459 vb.
show 522 vb.
stage set 594 n.
protection 660 n.
defence 713 n.
screening
diagnostic 658 n.
screen off
set apart 46 vb.
exclude 57 vb.
screenplay
cinema 445 n.
reading matter
589 n.
stage play 594 n.
screw
affix 45 vb.
fastening 47 n.
distort 246 n.
distortion 246 n.
coil 251 n.
propeller 269 n.
saddle horse 273 n.
propellant 287 n.
rotator 315 n.
tool 630 n.
gaoler 749 n.
earnings 771 n.
rob 788 vb.
debauch 951 vb.
screwdriver
tool 630 n.
screwed up
bungled 695 adj.
screw loose
deficit 55 n.
defect 647 n.
hitch 702 n.
screw loose, a
eccentricity
503 n.
screw on
affix 45 vb.
screw up
tighten 45 vb.
blunder 495 vb.
**screw up one's
courage**
strengthen 162 vb.
screwy
crazy 503 adj.
scribacious
prolific 171 adj.
diffuse 570 adj.
scribble
lack of meaning
515 n.
mean nothing
515 vb.
be unintelligible
517 vb.

unintelligibility
517 n.
mark 547 vb.
lettering 586 n.
script 586 n.
write 586 vb.
scribe
mark 547 vb.
recorder 549 n.
instrument 628 n.
theologian 973 n.
zealot 979 n.
scrimmage
quarrel 709 n.
fight 716 n.
fight 716 n.
scrimp
shorten 204 vb.
be parsimonious
816 vb.
scrip
title deed 767 n.
paper money
797 n.
script
cinema 445 n.
lettering 586 n.
script 586 n.
writing 586 n.
book 589 n.
reading matter
589 n.
stage play 594 n.
scriptural
scriptural
975 adj.
orthodox 976 adj.
scripture
credential 466 n.
scripture 975 n.
scrivener
notary 958 n.
scroll
computerize 86 vb.
list 87 n.
coil 251 n.
lettering 586 n.
book 589 n.
Scrooge
niggard 816 vb.
scrotum
genitalia 167 n.
scrounge
beg 761 vb.
take 786 vb.
steal 788 vb.
scrounger
idler 679 n.
beggar 763 n.
scrub
rub 333 vb.
wood 366 n.
clean 648 vb.
abrogate 752 vb.

scrubber
loose woman
952 n.
prostitute 952 n.
**scruff of the
neck**
rear 238 n.
scruffy
bad 645 adj.
unclean 649 adj.
disreputable
867 adj.
scrum
crowd 74 n.
fight 716 n.
scrumptious
savoury 390 adj.
super 644 adj.
scrumpy
alcoholic drink
301 n.
scrunch
rend 46 vb.
chew 301 vb.
pulverize 332 vb.
rasp 407 vb.
scrunching
hairdressing 843 n.
scruple
small quantity
33 n.
weighing 322 n.
doubt 486 n.
doubt 486 vb.
be unwilling
598 vb.
unwillingness
598 n.
scruples
carefulness 457 n.
scrupulous
careful 457 adj.
accurate 494 adj.
fastidious 862 adj.
honourable
929 adj.
trustworthy
929 adj.
scrutineer
enquirer 459 n.
scrutinize
scan 438 vb.
be attentive
455 vb.
enquire 459 vb.
scrutiny
attention 455 n.
enquiry 459 n.
scuba diver
diver 313 n.
scud
navigate 269 vb.
move fast 277 vb.
cloud 355 n.

scuff
rub 333 vb.
scuffle
fight 716 n.
fight 716 vb.
scull
propeller 269 n.
row 269 vb.
scullery
chamber 194 n.
sculling
aquatics 269 n.
scullion
domestic 742 n.
sculpt
compose 56 vb.
sculpt 554 vb.
sculpture
composition 56 n.
produce 164 vb.
sculpt 554 vb.
sculpture 554 n.
scum
leavings 41 n.
layer 207 n.
bubble 355 n.
rubbish 641 n.
purify 648 vb.
dirt 649 n.
rabble 869 n.
bad person 938 n.
scupper
suppress 165 vb.
slaughter 362 vb.
scurf
leavings 41 n.
powder 332 n.
dirt 649 n.
scurrilous
insolent 878 adj.
cursing 899 adj.
disrespectful
921 adj.
scurry
move fast 277 vb.
be active 678 vb.
haste 680 n.
hasten 680 vb.
scurvy
disease 651 n.
scut
rear 238 n.
scuttle
suppress 165 vb.
vessel 194 n.
move fast 277 vb.
decamp 296 vb.
lower 311 vb.
plunge 313 vb.
run away 620 vb.
be cowardly
856 vb.
fail in duty
918 vb.

army officer 741 n.
serial
continuous 71 adj.
recurrence 106 n.
periodical 141 adj.
journal 528 n.
reading matter
589 n.
narrative 590 n.
serialize
continue 71 adj.
publish 528 vb.
seriate
continuous 71 adj.
sericulture
animal husbandry
369 n.
series
order 60 n.
sequence 65 n.
series 71 n.
number 85 n.
recurrence 106 n.
key 410 n.
broadcast 531 n.
edition 589 n.
serif
print-type 587 n.
serious
great 32 adj.
attentive 455 adj.
resolute 599 adj.
important 638 adj.
sick 651 adj.
dangerous 661 adj.
serious 834 adj.
heinous 934 adj.
serjeant-at-law
lawyer 958 n.
sermon
lecture 534 n.
diffuseness 570 n.
oration 579 n.
allocution 583 n.
dissertation 591 n.
ministration
988 n.
sermonize
teach 534 vb.
be pious 979 vb.
serous
blood 335 adj.
haematic 335 adj.
serpent
serpent 251 n.
reptile 365 n.
horn 414 n.
deceiver 545 n.
bane 659 n.
slyboots 698 n.
Satan 969 n.
serpentine
snaky 251 adj.
animal 365 adj.

serpigo
skin disease 651 n.
serrated
angular 247 adj.
sharp 256 adj.
toothed 256 adj.
serried
cohesive 48 adj.
dense 324 adj.
serried ranks
coherence 48 n.
serum
blood 335 n.
fluid 335 n.
servant
servant 742 n.
serve
unite with 45 vb.
operate 173 vb.
concur 181 vb.
propel 287 vb.
be instrumental
628 vb.
provide 633 vb.
suffice 635 vb.
be expedient
642 vb.
work 682 vb.
serve 742 vb.
be subject 745 vb.
apportion 783 vb.
serve as
function 622 vb.
serve notice
communicate
524 vb.
threaten 900 vb.
serve notice on
litigate 959 vb.
serve up
provide 633 vb.
**serve with a
writ**
indict 928 vb.
service
agency 173 n.
job 622 n.
provide 633 vb.
provision 633 n.
utility 640 n.
repair 656 n.
restore 656 vb.
preserve 666 vb.
use 673 n.
aid 703 n.
gift 781 n.
public worship
981 n.
church service
988 n.
serviceable
instrumental
628 adj.
useful 640 adj.

service charge
price 809 n.
service flat
flat 192 n.
service provider
computing 86 n.
services
instrumentality
628 n.
services, the
army 722 n.
servile
conformable
83 adj.
plebeian 869 adj.
humble 872 adj.
servile 879 adj.
servility
humility 872 n.
servility 879 n.
serving
serving 742 adj.
servitude
servitude 745 n.
servomechanism
machine 630 n.
servomotor
machine 630 n.
sesquicentenary
special day 876 n.
sesquicentennial
seasonal 141 adj.
sesquipedalian
long 203 adj.
session
council 692 n.
sessions
lawcourt 956 n.
legal trial 959 n.
sestet
verse form 593 n.
set
uniformity 16 n.
affix 45 vb.
firm 45 adj.
join 45 vb.
coherence 48 n.
component 58 n.
arrange 62 vb.
series 71 n.
accumulation 74 n.
band 74 n.
group 74 n.
classification 77 n.
sort 77 n.
inclusion 78 n.
number 85 n.
unit 88 n.
young plant 132 n.
stabilize 153 vb.
tendency 179 n.
place 187 vb.
hang 217 vb.
pendency 217 n.

support 218 vb.
form 243 n.
direction 281 n.
descend 309 vb.
be dense 324 vb.
dense 324 adj.
harden 326 vb.
rigid 326 adj.
cultivate 370 vb.
spectacle 445 n.
be true 494 vb.
educational
534 adj.
class 538 n.
printed 587 adj.
edition 589 n.
stage set 594 n.
usual 610 adj.
collection 632 n.
doctor 658 vb.
make ready
669 vb.
association 706 n.
party 708 n.
contest 716 n.
hairdressing 843 n.
set a course
navigate 269 vb.
set against
set apart 46 vb.
dissuade 613 vb.
make quarrels
709 vb.
cause dislike
861 vb.
set alight
burn 381 vb.
set an example
be an example
23 vb.
motivate 612 vb.
behave 688 vb.
set apart
separate 46 adj.
set apart 46 vb.
exempt 919 vb.
set aside
set apart 46 vb.
displace 188 vb.
reject 607 vb.
store 632 vb.
abrogate 752 vb.
not observe
769 vb.
due 915 adj.
exempt 919 vb.
set at liberty
liberate 746 vb.
exempt 919 vb.
set at naught
defy 711 vb.
set a trap for
ambush 527 vb.
ensnare 542 vb.

set back
put off 136 vb.
setback
descent 309 n.
disappointment
509 n.
dissuasion 613 n.
evil 616 n.
deterioration
655 n.
hitch 702 n.
adversity 731 n.
loss 772 n.
suffering 825 n.
set by the ears
make quarrels
709 vb.
enrage 891 vb.
set down
place 187 vb.
let fall 311 vb.
affirm 532 vb.
set down to
attribute 158 vb.
set fair
warm 379 adj.
be auspicious
730 vb.
palmy 730 adj.
set fire to
burn 381 vb.
kindle 381 vb.
set foot in
enter 297 vb.
set forth
start out 296 vb.
set free
disunite 46 vb.
deliver 668 vb.
disencumber
701 vb.
give scope 744 vb.
liberate 746 vb.
exempt 919 vb.
set in
stay 144 vb.
set in motion
initiate 68 vb.
dispose of 673 vb.
**set in one's
ways, be**
be wont 610 vb.
set in order
compose 56 vb.
make ready
669 vb.
set no store by
underestimate
483 vb.
doubt 486 vb.
hold cheap 922 vb.
set off
correlate 12 vb.
initiate 68 vb.

shoot 287 vb.
show 522 vb.
beautify 841 vb.
decorate 844 vb.
set off on a wild-
goose chase
deflect 282 vb.
set of rules
precept 693 n.
set of teeth
tooth 256 n.
set on
attack 712 vb.
enamoured
887 adj.
set on an even
keel
equalize 28 vb.
set one back
hinder 702 vb.
cost 809 vb.
set on edge
roughen 259 vb.
give pain 377 vb.
frighten 854 vb.
set one's cap at
pursue 619 vb.
desire 859 vb.
be in love 887 vb.
court 889 vb.
set one's face
against
oppose 704 vb.
refuse 760 vb.
set one's hand to
the plough
undertake 672 vb.
set one's heart
on
be resolute 599 vb.
desire 859 vb.
be in love 887 vb.
set one's mind
at rest
tranquillize
823 vb.
set one's mind
on
desire 859 vb.
set one's
shoulder to
the wheel
undertake 672 vb.
set one's sights
aim 281 vb.
set one's sights
on
desire 859 vb.
set one's teeth
on edge
be sour 393 vb.
set on fire
burn 381 vb.
excite 821 vb.

set out
arrange 62 vb.
travel 267 vb.
start out 296 vb.
show 522 vb.
dissertate 591 vb.
set piece
pageant 875 n.
set right
disclose 526 vb.
rectify 654 vb.
vindicate 927 vb.
set sail
navigate 269 vb.
start out 296 vb.
set speech
oration 579 n.
set square
angular measure
247 n.
gauge 465 n.
set store by
approve 923 vb.
sett
dwelling 192 n.
paving 226 n.
settee
seat 218 n.
setter
dog 365 n.
set the ball
rolling
initiate 68 vb.
set the cat
among the
pigeons
surprise 508 vb.
set the heather
on fire
have a reputation
866 vb.
set theory
mathematics 86 n.
set the pace
motivate 612 vb.
set the seal on
carry through
725 vb.
set the stage
make ready
669 vb.
set the teeth on
edge
rasp 407 vb.
displease 827 vb.
set the Thames
on fire
attempt the
impossible
470 vb.
setting
situation 186 n.
surroundings
230 n.

musical piece
412 n.
view 438 n.
stage set 594 n.
hairdressing 843 n.
ornamental art
844 n.
settle
arrange 62 vb.
terminate 69 vb.
prevail 178 vb.
place oneself
187 vb.
dwell 192 vb.
seat 218 n.
travel 267 vb.
descend 309 vb.
weigh 322 vb.
murder 362 vb.
answer 460 vb.
make certain
473 vb.
judge 480 vb.
defeat 727 vb.
contract 765 vb.
appropriate
786 vb.
punish 963 vb.
settle an
account
pay 804 vb.
set a score
pay 804 vb.
settled
native 191 adj.
quiescent 266 adj.
settled decision
certainty 473 n.
judgment 480 n.
settle down
be quiescent
266 vb.
sleep 679 vb.
settle for
bargain 791 vb.
settle in
enter 297 vb.
settlement
territory 184 n.
location 187 n.
station 187 n.
compact 765 n.
transfer 780 n.
giving 781 n.
payment 804 n.
settle on
choose 605 vb.
settle one's hash
defeat 727 vb.
settler
settler 191 n.
incomer 297 n.
settle upon
possess 773 vb.

settle with
punish 963 vb.
set to
begin 68 vb.
eat 301 vb.
be resolute 599 vb.
undertake 672 vb.
work 682 vb.
fight 716 vb.
set-to
quarrel 709 n.
fight 716 n.
set to music
harmonize 410 vb.
musical 412 adj.
compose music
413 vb.
set to rights
repair 656 vb.
set to work
begin 68 vb.
prepare 669 vb.
set up
compose 56 vb.
arrange 62 vb.
stabilize 153 vb.
cause 156 vb.
strengthen 162 vb.
produce 164 vb.
place 187 vb.
elevate 310 vb.
set-up
circumstance 8 n.
composition 56 n.
structure 331 n.
set upon
resolute 599 adj.
set up shop
undertake 672 vb.
seven
over five 99 n.
seven deadly
sins
vice 934 n.
seven-league
boots
magic instrument
983 n.
seven lean years
scarcity 636 n.
seven
sacraments,
the
Christian rite
988 n.
seven seas, the
ocean 343 n.
Seventh-day
Adventist
sect 978 n.
seventh heaven
summit 213 n.
happiness 824 n.
heaven 971 n.

seventy
twenty and over
99 n.
seven wonders
of the world
prodigy 864 n.
sever
subtract 39 vb.
disunite 46 vb.
several
many 104 adj.
severally
severally 80 adv.
severance
subtraction 39 n.
separation 46 n.
severe
exorbitant 32 adj.
violent 176 adj.
accurate 494 adj.
plain 573 adj.
severe 735 adj.
severity
plainness 573 n.
severity 735 n.
Sèvres china
pottery 381 n.
sew
join 45 vb.
tie 45 vb.
produce 164 vb.
sewage
leavings 41 n.
sewer
tunnel 263 n.
drain 351 n.
stench 397 n.
badness 645 n.
sink 649 n.
insalubrity 653 n.
sewerage
cleansing 648 n.
dirt 649 n.
sewing-bee
assembly 74 n.
sewn
tied 45 adj.
sewn up
completed 725 adj.
sex
coition 45 n.
classification 77 n.
propagation 167 n.
life 360 n.
sexagenarian
twenty and over
99 n.
sexagenary
multifid 100 adj.
sexagesimal
multifid 100 adj.
sex appeal
attraction 291 n.
inducement 612 n.

shame into
motivate 612 vb.
shameless
thick-skinned
820 adj.
vulgar 847 adj.
insolent 878 adj.
dishonest 930 adj.
unchaste 951 adj.
shamming
imitative 20 adj.
shammy
cleaning cloth
648 n.
shampoo
rub 333 vb.
ablutions 648 n.
clean 648 vb.
cleanser 648 n.
hairwash 843 n.
shamrock
three 93 n.
plant 366 n.
heraldry 547 n.
shandy
alcoholic drink
301 n.
shanghai
ensnare 542 vb.
take away 786 vb.
steal 788 vb.
Shangri-la
fantasy 513 n.
shank
leg 267 n.
print-type 587 n.
Shanks's pony
conveyance 267 n.
pedestrianism
267 n.
shantung
textile 222 n.
shanty
small house
192 n.
vocal music 412 n.
poem 593 n.
shanty town
housing 192 n.
shape
modality 7 n.
sort 77 n.
convert 147 vb.
produce 164 vb.
outline 233 n.
form 243 n.
form 243 vb.
appearance 445 n.
feature 445 n.
educate 534 vb.
identification
547 n.
represent 551 vb.
plan 623 vb.

shape a course
travel 267 vb.
plan 623 vb.
shapeless
abnormal 84 adj.
amorphous
244 adj.
unsightly 842 adj.
shapely
shapely 841 adj.
**shape of things
to come**
prediction 511 n.
shard
piece 53 n.
share
part 53 n.
bisect 92 vb.
mete out 465 vb.
title deed 767 n.
participate 775 vb.
portion 783 n.
feel 818 vb.
be sociable 882 vb.
**share and share
alike**
participate 775 vb.
shareholder
participator 775 n.
owner 776 n.
share in
participate 775 vb.
share out
part 53 vb.
mete out 465 vb.
apportion 783 vb.
share-out
gain 771 vb.
participation
775 n.
portion 783 n.
shares
apportionment
783 n.
share shop
stock exchange
618 n.
market 796 n.
sharing
equal 28 adj.
shark
fish 365 n.
trickster 545 n.
taker 786 n.
defrauder 789 n.
sharkskin
textile 222 n.
Sharon fruit
fruit and vegetables
301 n.
sharp
keen 174 adj.
sharp 256 adj.
sentient 374 adj.

sour 393 adj.
musical note
410 n.
discordant 411 adj.
intelligent 498 adj.
descriptive 590 adj.
cunning 698 adj.
paining 827 adj.
unpleasant
827 adj.
witty 839 adj.
hateful 888 adj.
irascible 892 adj.
disapproving
924 adj.
sharp ear
hearing 415 n.
sharpen
sharpen 256 vb.
sharpen the wits
educate 534 vb.
sharper
trickster 545 n.
slyboots 698 n.
defrauder 789 n.
sharp-eyed
seeing 438 adj.
attentive 455 adj.
vigilant 457 adj.
sharply
greatly 32 vb.
sharp note
stridor 407 n.
sharp practice
duplicity 541 n.
trickery 542 n.
cunning 698 n.
perfidy 930 n.
sharp-tempered
irascible 892 adj.
sharp-tongued
irascible 892 adj.
sharp-witted
intelligent 498 adj.
shatter
break 46 vb.
demolish 165 vb.
pulverize 332 vb.
shattering
wonderful 864 adj.
shatterproof
strong 162 adj.
hard 326 adj.
tough 329 adj.
invulnerable
660 adj.
shave
cut 46 vb.
make smaller
198 vb.
shorten 204 vb.
smooth 258 vb.
touch 378 vb.
hairdressing 843 n.

primp 843 vb.
shaver
cosmetic 843 n.
shavings
leavings 41 n.
rubbish 641 n.
she
female 373 adj.
female 373 n.
sheaf
bunch 74 n.
cultivate 370 vb.
shear
subtract 39 vb.
power 160 n.
make smaller
198 vb.
shorten 204 vb.
distortion 246 n.
fleece 786 vb.
shears
sharp edge 256 n.
farm tool 370 n.
sheath
contraception
172 n.
case 194 n.
receptacle 194 n.
covering 226 n.
arsenal 723 n.
sheathe
layer 207 n.
cover 226 vb.
dress 228 vb.
sheath knife
sharp edge 256 n.
shebeen
tavern 192 n.
shed
decrease 37 vb.
small house 192 n.
emit 300 vb.
let fall 311 vb.
disaccustom
611 vb.
relinquish 621 vb.
shed blood
kill 362 vb.
go to war 718 vb.
oppress 735 vb.
shed tears
weep 836 vb.
sheen
light 417 n.
reflection 417 n.
sheep
imitator 20 n.
sheep 365 n.
laity 987 n.
sheepdog
dog 365 n.
sheep farming
animal husbandry
369 n.

sheepfold
stable 192 n.
enclosure 235 n.
cattle pen 369 n.
shelter 662 n.
sheepish
animal 365 adj.
modest 874 adj.
guilty 936 adj.
sheep-like
obedient 739 adj.
sheep's eyes
look 438 n.
desire 859 n.
sheepshank
ligature 47 n.
sheepskin
skin 226 n.
sheer
absolute 32 adj.
simple 44 adj.
vertical 215 adj.
sloping 220 adj.
transparent
422 adj.
sheer off
deviate 282 vb.
recede 290 vb.
sheet
part 53 n.
coverlet 226 n.
dress 228 vb.
edition 589 n.
paper 631 n.
abound 635 vb.
sheet lightning
luminary 420 n.
sheets
great quantity
32 n.
sheikh
potentate 741 n.
person of rank
868 n.
shekel
coinage 797 n.
shekels
shekels 797 n.
shelf
shelf 218 n.
projection 254 n.
storage 632 n.
shelf, the
celibacy 895 n.
shell
remainder 41 n.
emptiness 190 n.
exteriority 223 n.
covering 226 n.
skin 226 n.
uncover 229 vb.
rowing boat 275 n.
missile 287 n.
hardness 326 n.

shred
small thing 33 n.
cut 46 vb.
piece 53 n.
fraction 102 n.
strip 208 n.
cook 301 vb.
shrew
mammal 365 n.
female 373 n.
shrewd
judicial 480 adj.
knowing 490 adj.
intelligent 498 adj.
skilful 694 adj.
cunning 698 adj.
shrewd idea
conjecture 512 n.
shriek
loudness 400 n.
stridor 407 n.
cry 408 n.
weep 836 vb.
**shrieks of
laughter**
laughter 835 n.
shrift
penance 941 n.
ministration
988 n.
shrike
bird 365 n.
shrill
loud 400 adj.
shrill 407 vb.
strident 407 adj.
shrimp
small thing 33 n.
dwarf 196 n.
fish food 301 n.
marine life 365 n.
hunt 619 vb.
shrine
tomb 364 n.
ritual object 988 n.
temple 990 n.
shrink
be small 33 vb.
abate 37 vb.
decrease 37 vb.
become small
198 vb.
make smaller
198 vb.
recoil 280 vb.
recede 290 vb.
psychologist 447 n.
mental disorder
503 n.
avoid 620 vb.
deteriorate 655 vb.
doctor 658 n.
be nervous 854 vb.
quake 854 vb.

be cowardly
856 vb.
be modest 874 vb.
shrinkage
decrease 37 n.
contraction 198 n.
shortness 204 n.
shrink from
dislike 861 vb.
hate 888 vb.
shrinking
decrease 37 n.
recession 290 n.
avoidance 620 n.
nervous 854 adj.
modest 874 adj.
shrinking violet
humility 872 n.
modesty 874 n.
shrinkproof
unchangeable
153 adj.
shrink-wrapped
invulnerable
660 adj.
shrive
forgive 909 vb.
perform ritual
988 vb.
shrivel
become small
198 vb.
dry 342 vb.
heat 381 vb.
deteriorate 655 vb.
shroud
cover 226 vb.
wrapping 226 n.
dress 228 vb.
grave clothes
364 n.
screen 421 vb.
conceal 525 vb.
Shrove Tuesday
holy day 988 n.
shrub
tree 366 n.
shrubbery
wood 366 n.
garden 370 n.
shrug
jersey 228 n.
gesticulate 547 vb.
gesture 547 n.
shrug off
underestimate
483 vb.
be indifferent
860 vb.
**shrug one's
shoulders**
dissent 489 vb.
not know 491 vb.
gesticulate 547 vb.

submit 721 vb.
shrunk
dwarfish 196 adj.
shudder
agitation 318 n.
be agitated 318 vb.
be cold 380 vb.
show feeling
818 vb.
quake 854 vb.
shudder at
dislike 861 vb.
shuffle
mix 43 vb.
jumble 63 vb.
substitution 150 n.
interchange 151 n.
interchange
151 vb.
vary 152 vb.
be in motion
265 vb.
gait 265 n.
walk 267 vb.
transpose 272 vb.
move slowly
278 vb.
sophisticate
477 vb.
gesticulate 547 vb.
be excitable
822 vb.
dance 837 vb.
be dishonest
930 vb.
perfidy 930 n.
**shuffle off this
mortal coil**
die 361 vb.
shuffle the cards
make ready
669 vb.
shufti
inspection 438 n.
shun
avoid 620 vb.
dislike 861 vb.
shunt
transpose 272 vb.
deflect 282 vb.
shut
close 264 vb.
shut down
cease 145 vb.
close 264 vb.
lower 311 vb.
shutdown
stop 145 n.
inactivity 679 n.
shut-eye
sleep 679 n.
shut in
interior 224 adj.
surround 230 vb.

close 264 vb.
imprison 747 vb.
**shut one's eyes
to**
permit 756 vb.
shut one up
make mute 578 vb.
shut out
exclude 57 vb.
shutter
covering 226 n.
stopper 264 n.
darken 418 vb.
curtain 421 n.
camera 442 n.
shutters
shade 226 n.
shut the door on
exclude 57 vb.
prohibit 757 vb.
shut the eyes to
be blind 439 vb.
**shut the stable
door after the
horse has
bolted**
lose a chance
138 vb.
shuttle
interchange
151 vb.
vary 152 vb.
weaving 222 n.
travel 267 vb.
fluctuate 317 vb.
fluctuation 317 n.
**shuttle
diplomacy**
periodicity 141 n.
shuttlewise
correlatively
12 adv.
to and fro 317 adv.
shuttling
reversion 148 n.
transference 272 n.
fluctuation 317 n.
shut up
decrease 37 vb.
cease 145 vb.
hush 399 int.
confute 479 vb.
be mute 578 vb.
hush 582 int.
imprison 747 vb.
seclude 883 vb.
shut up shop
terminate 69 vb.
cease 145 vb.
shy
recoil 280 vb.
propel 287 vb.
propulsion 287 n.
reticent 525 adj.

unwilling 598 adj.
be irresolute
601 vb.
avoid 620 vb.
artless 699 adj.
restrained 747 adj.
nervous 854 adj.
quake 854 vb.
cowardly 856 adj.
modest 874 adj.
unsociable 883 adj.
pure 950 adj.
shy from
be cowardly
856 vb.
Shylock
lender 784 n.
shyness
restraint 747 n.
dislike 861 n.
modesty 874 n.
unsociability
883 n.
shy of
incomplete 55 adj.
shyster
trickster 545 n.
lawyer 958 n.
Siamese Cat
cat 365 n.
Siamese twins
duality 90 n.
Siberia
coldness 380 n.
sibilant
speech sound
398 n.
sibilation 406 n.
sibling
akin 11 adj.
kinsman 11 n.
Sibyl
oracle 511 n.
sorceress 983 n.
sic
truly 494 adv.
siccative
dryer 342 n.
sick
vomiting 300 n.
sick 651 adj.
vicious 934 adj.
crapulous
949 adj.
sick and tired
bored 838 adj.
sick as a dog
vomiting 300 n.
sick as a parrot
dejected 834 adj.
sick building
edifice 164 n.
sicken
be weak 163 vb.

be unpalatable
391 vb.
be ill 651 vb.
deteriorate 655 vb.
displease 827 vb.
cause dislike
861 vb.
sate 863 vb.
sickening
not nice 645 adj.
sick joke
witticism 839 n.
bad taste 847 n.
sickle
angularity 247 n.
curve 248 n.
sharp edge 256 n.
farm tool 370 n.
sick list
list 87 n.
sickly
weakly 163 adj.
colourless 426 adj.
unhealthy 651 adj.
sickness
badness 645 n.
digestive disorders
651 n.
illness 651 n.
sick of
bored 838 adj.
sated 863 adj.
sickroom
hospital 658 n.
sick to one's
stomach
vomiting 300 n.
sick with worry
suffering 825 adj.
side
part 53 n.
situation 186 n.
edge 234 n.
flank 239 vb.
lateral 239 adj.
laterality 239 n.
appearance 445 n.
party 708 n.
pride 871 n.
airs 873 n.
vanity 873 n.
ostentation 875 n.
contempt 922 n.
side against
oppose 704 vb.
sidearms
sidearms 723 n.
sideboard
cabinet 194 n.
stand 218 n.
sideburns
hair 259 n.
side by side
cohesive 48 adj.

with 89 adv.
near 200 adv.
sideways 239 adv.
sidecar
bicycle 274 n.
side dish
dish 301 n.
side-effect
effect 157 n.
sidekick
inferior 35 n.
chum 880 n.
sideline
edge 234 n.
laterality 239 n.
sidelong
lateral 239 adj.
sideways 239 adv.
sidereal
celestial 321 adj.
sidereal year
period 110 n.
siderite
meteor 321 n.
side-slip
aeronautics 271 n.
fly 271 vb.
side-splitting
funny 849 adj.
sidestep
be oblique 220 vb.
flank 239 vb.
laterality 239 n.
deviate 282 vb.
deviation 282 n.
avoid 620 vb.
side street
road 624 n.
side to side
to and fro 317 adv.
sidetrack
deflect 282 vb.
sidewalk
paving 226 n.
path 624 n.
road 624 n.
sideways
sideways 239 adv.
directed 281 adj.
sideways look
look 438 n.
side with
assent 488 vb.
join a party
708 vb.
siding
laterality 239 n.
railway 624 n.
sidle
be oblique 220 vb.
flank 239 vb.
deviate 282 vb.
sidle in
enter 297 vb.

siege
circumscription
232 n.
hindrance 702 n.
attack 712 n.
Siegfried Line
defences 713 n.
sierra
high land 209 n.
roughness 259 n.
siesta
sleep 679 n.
sieve
exclude 57 vb.
class 62 vb.
sorting 62 n.
porosity 263 n.
discriminate
463 vb.
cleaning utensil
648 n.
purify 648 vb.
sift
exclude 57 vb.
class 62 vb.
cultivate 370 vb.
enquire 459 vb.
discriminate
463 vb.
select 605 vb.
purify 648 vb.
sift through
search 459 vb.
sigh
blow 352 vb.
breathe 352 vb.
respiration 352 n.
faintness 401 n.
sound faint
401 vb.
cry 408 n.
cry 408 vb.
suffer 825 vb.
be dejected 834 vb.
melancholy 834 n.
lament 836 vb.
lamentation
836 n.
weep 836 vb.
be in love 887 vb.
court 889 vb.
sigh for
lament 836 vb.
sigh of relief
relief 831 n.
sight
sense 374 n.
see 438 vb.
vision 438 n.
telescope 442 n.
visibility 443 n.
spectacle 445 n.
firearm 723 n.
eyesore 842 n.

prodigy 864 n.
sight, a
greatly 32 vb.
sight for sore
eyes
spectacle 445 n.
pleasurableness
826 n.
a beauty 841 n.
sightless
blind 439 adj.
invisible 444 adj.
sightly
personable
841 adj.
sight of, a
multitude 104 n.
sights
direction 281 n.
sight-seeing
inspection 438 n.
curiosity 453 n.
sigmatism
speech defect
580 n.
sign
number 85 n.
evidence 466 n.
testify 466 vb.
make certain
473 vb.
omen 511 n.
exhibit 522 n.
manifestation
522 n.
badge 547 n.
gesticulate
547 vb.
gesture 547 n.
indication 547 n.
label 547 n.
sign 547 vb.
signal 547 n.
letter 558 n.
warning 664 n.
command 737 n.
command 737 vb.
contract 765 vb.
give security
767 vb.
prodigy 864 n.
signal
remarkable 32 adj.
manifest 522 adj.
hint 524 n.
gesture 547 n.
signal 547 n.
signal 547 vb.
railway 624 n.
notable 638 adj.
command 737 n.
command 737 vb.
signalize
dignify 866 vb.

signalling
telecommunication
531 n.
signally
remarkably 32 vb.
signatory
signatory 765 n.
signature
key 410 n.
notation 410 n.
credential 466 n.
assent 488 n.
identification
547 n.
label 547 n.
name 561 n.
script 586 n.
edition 589 n.
compact 765 n.
title deed 767 n.
signature tune
tune 412 n.
signet
label 547 n.
badge of rule
743 n.
signet ring
jewellery 844 n.
significant
evidential 466 adj.
meaningful
514 adj.
important 638 adj.
signification
connotation 514 n.
indication 547 n.
signify
predict 511 vb.
mean 514 vb.
inform 524 vb.
indicate 547 vb.
sign language
mimicry 20 n.
deafness 416 n.
gesture 547 n.
language 557 n.
voicelessness
578 n.
speech 579 n.
sign off
resign 753 vb.
sign of the cross
ritual act 988 n.
sign of the times
indication 547 n.
sign on
join a party
708 vb.
sign one's death
warrant
condemn 961 vb.
sign on the
dotted line
acquiesce 488 vb.

obey 739 vb.
promise 764 vb.
contract 765 vb.
give security
767 vb.
bargain 791 vb.
signor
male 372 n.
signora
female 373 n.
title 870 n.
signore
title 870 n.
signorina
female 373 n.
title 870 n.
signpost
orientate 281 vb.
point to 281 vb.
indicate 547 vb.
signpost 547 n.
**signs of the
times**
omen 511 n.
**signs of the
zodiac**
zodiac 321 n.
sign the pledge
be sober 948 vb.
sign-writing
writing 586 n.
Sikh
religionist 973 n.
silage
provender 301 n.
silence
hush 399 int.
silence 399 n.
silence 399 vb.
confute 479 vb.
defeat 727 vb.
restrain 747 vb.
unsociability
883 n.
silent
silent 399 adj.
reticent 525 adj.
stealthy 525 adj.
voiceless 578 adj.
unsociable 883 adj.
disapproving
924 adj.
silent film
film 445 n.
silent majority
commonalty
869 n.
silhouette
outline 233 n.
outline 233 vb.
form 243 n.
form 243 vb.
darken 418 vb.
darkness 418 n.

feature 445 n.
image 551 n.
picture 553 n.
silica
hardness 326 n.
silicone implant
bosom 253 n.
insertion 303 n.
silicosis
respiratory disease
651 n.
silk
fibre 208 n.
textile 222 n.
smoothness 258 n.
lawyer 958 n.
silky
smooth 258 adj.
soft 327 adj.
textural 331 adj.
sill
base 214 n.
shelf 218 n.
threshold 234 n.
projection 254 n.
rock 344 n.
silly
absurd 497 adj.
foolish 499 adj.
fool 501 n.
ridiculous 849 adj.
silly season
absurdity 497 n.
silo
space travel
271 n.
storage 632 n.
gun 723 n.
silt
leavings 41 n.
solid body 324 n.
soil 344 n.
semiliquidity
354 n.
silver
coat 226 vb.
white 427 adj.
whiten 427 vb.
white thing 427 n.
greyness 429 n.
money 797 n.
decorate 844 vb.
ornamentation
844 n.
silver jubilee
anniversary 141 n.
silver lining
relief 831 n.
hope 852 n.
silverplate
coat 226 vb.
silver screen
cinema 445 n.
drama 594 n.

silverside
meat 301 n.
silversmith
artisan 686 n.
silver-tongued
eloquent 579 adj.
silver wedding
anniversary 141 n.
special day 876 n.
wedding 894 n.
silvery
white 427 adj.
grey 429 adj.
simian
animal 365 adj.
similar
similar 18 adj.
similarity
similarity 18 n.
simile
analogue 18 n.
comparison 462 n.
metaphor 519 n.
ornament 574 n.
similitude
similarity 18 n.
comparison 462 n.
simmer
cook 301 vb.
effervesce 318 vb.
bubble 355 vb.
be excited 821 vb.
resent 891 vb.
simony
improbity 930 n.
simoom
gale 352 n.
heat 379 n.
simper
laughter 835 n.
simple
simple 44 adj.
soft-hued 425 adj.
credulous 487 adj.
ignorant 491 adj.
intelligible
516 adj.
plain 573 adj.
tasteful 846 adj.
plebeian 869 adj.
simple interest
gain 771 n.
interest 803 n.
simple-minded
artless 699 adj.
simpleton
ignoramus 493 n.
ninny 501 n.
simplicity
simpleness 44 n.
indiscrimination
464 n.
credulity 487 n.
ignorance 491 n.

intelligibility
516 n.
plainness 573 n.
artlessness 699 n.
facility 701 n.
good taste 846 n.
simplify
simplify 44 vb.
be intelligible
516 vb.
facilitate 701 vb.
simply
singly 88 adv.
simulacrum
sham 542 n.
simulate
imitate 20 vb.
dissemble 541 vb.
simulated
simulating 18 adj.
erroneous 495 adj.
false 541 adj.
hypocritical
541 adj.
spurious 542 adj.
untrue 543 adj.
simultaneous
synchronous
123 adj.
sin
badness 645 n.
disobedience
738 n.
wrong 914 n.
be wicked 934 vb.
vice 934 n.
wickedness 934 n.
be guilty 936 vb.
guilty act 936 n.
be impious
980 vb.
impiety 980 n.
since
subsequently
120 adv.
hence 158 adv.
sincere
simple 44 adj.
veracious 540 adj.
artless 699 adj.
pious 979 adj.
sincerity
no imitation 21 n.
veracity 540 n.
artlessness 699 n.
feeling 818 n.
probity 929 n.
piety 979 n.
sine
ratio 85 n.
sinecure
inaction 677 n.
leisure 681 n.
easy thing 701 n.

sine die
never 109 adv.
sine qua non
essential part 5 n.
speciality 80 n.
concomitant 89 n.
qualification
468 n.
supposition 512 n.
necessity 596 n.
requirement 627 n.
chief thing 638 n.
conditions 766 n.
sinews
vitality 162 n.
sinewy
stalwart 162 adj.
tough 329 adj.
sinful
bad 645 adj.
wrong 914 adj.
heinous 934 adj.
wicked 934 adj.
guilty 936 adj.
impious 980 adj.
sing
roll 403 vb.
resound 404 vb.
ululate 409 vb.
sing 413 vb.
confess 526 vb.
be cheerful
833 vb.
accuse 928 vb.
singe
burn 381 vb.
brown 430 vb.
hairdressing 843 n.
singer
vocalist 413 n.
singing
roll 403 n.
resonance 404 n.
vocal music 412 n.
merry 833 adj.
single
simple 44 adj.
one 88 adj.
unit 88 n.
gramophone 414 n.
independent
144 adj.
single currency
money 197 n.
single file
line 203 n.
single-handed
alone 88 adj.
single-minded
obsessed 455 adj.
resolute 599 adj.
singleness
unity 88 n.
celibacy 895 n.

sit up
be vertical 215 vb.
**sit up and take
notice**
be attentive
455 vb.
six
over five 99 n.
sixer
over five 99 n.
six feet under
dead 361 adj.
six-footer
tall creature 209 n.
**six of one and
half a dozen of
the other**
equivalence 28 n.
sixpence
coinage 797 n.
six-shooter
pistol 723 n.
sixth
musical note
410 n.
sixth sense
sense 374 n.
intellect 447 n.
intuition 476 n.
occultism 984 n.
sixty
twenty and over
99 n.
**sixty-four-
thousand-
dollar
question, the**
question 459 n.
difficulty 700 n.
sizable
great 32 adj.
large 195 adj.
size
make uniform
16 vb.
degree 27 n.
adhesive 47 n.
arrange 62 vb.
size 195 n.
coat 226 vb.
viscidity 354 n.
importance 638 n.
sizeism
prejudice 481 n.
size up
appraise 465 vb.
measure 465 vb.
estimate 480 vb.
sizzle
effervesce 318 vb.
be hot 379 vb.
crackle 402 vb.
hiss 406 vb.
be excited 821 vb.

resent 891 vb.
skate
be in motion
265 vb.
travel 267 vb.
sled 274 n.
fish food 301 n.
amuse oneself
837 vb.
skateboard
sled 274 n.
plaything 837 n.
skate on thin ice
be in danger
661 vb.
skate over
neglect 458 vb.
skating
motion 265 n.
sport 837 n.
skating rink
arena 724 n.
pleasure ground
837 n.
skean-dhu
sidearms 723 n.
skedaddle
come along
267 int.
move fast 277 vb.
decamp 296 vb.
run away 620 vb.
skein
bunch 74 n.
group 74 n.
crossing 222 n.
skeletal
remainder
163 adj.
lean 206 adj.
skeleton
remainder 41 n.
chief part 52 n.
incompleteness
55 n.
thinness 206 n.
frame 218 n.
outline 233 n.
structure 331 n.
corpse 363 n.
compendium
592 n.
plan 623 n.
intimidation
854 n.
**skeleton at the
feast**
moper 834 n.
**skeleton in the
cupboard**
secret 530 n.
skeleton key
opener 263 n.
instrument 628 n.

skelter
move fast 277 vb.
skerry
rock 344 n.
island 349 n.
sketch
copy 22 n.
prototype 23 n.
incompleteness
55 n.
outline 233 n.
outline 233 vb.
form 243 vb.
record 548 n.
represent 551 vb.
representation
551 n.
paint 553 vb.
picture 553 n.
describe 590 vb.
description 590 n.
compendium
592 n.
stage play 594 n.
plan 623 n.
prepare 669 vb.
**sketch in the
background**
relate 9 vb.
sketch out
outline 233 n.
represent 551 vb.
abstract 592 vb.
plan 623 vb.
sketchy
incomplete
55 adj.
uncompleted
726 adj.
skew
statistics 86 n.
distort 246 vb.
deflect 282 vb.
skewer
fastening 47 n.
sharp point 256 n.
perforator 263 n.
pierce 263 vb.
ski
be in motion
265 vb.
travel 267 vb.
amuse oneself
837 vb.
skid
gait 265 n.
deviate 282 vb.
skier
pedestrian 268 n.
skiff
boat 275 n.
rowing boat 275 n.
skiffle
music 412 n.

skiing
sport 837 n.
skilful
skilful 694 adj.
skill
skill 694 n.
skillet
pot 194 n.
skim
be contiguous
202 vb.
travel 267 vb.
move fast 277 vb.
purify 648 vb.
skim off
select 605 vb.
skimp
shorten 204 vb.
neglect 458 vb.
be parsimonious
816 vb.
skimpy
small 33 adj.
short 204 adj.
insufficient
636 adj.
skim through
scan 438 vb.
skin
subtract 39 vb.
leavings 41 n.
disunite 46 vb.
skin 226 n.
uncover 229 vb.
rub 333 vb.
fleece 786 vb.
overcharge 811 vb.
skin-and-bone
lean 206 adj.
underfed 636 adj.
skin-deep
shallow 212 adj.
exterior 223 adj.
skin diving
sport 837 n.
skinflick
film 445 n.
impurity 951 n.
skinflint
niggard 816 n.
skinhead
youngster 132 n.
ruffian 904 n.
skinny
weakly 163 adj.
lean 206 adj.
narrow 206 adj.
skin-search
search 459 n.
search 459 vb.
skintight
cohesive 48 adj.
skip
be absent 190 vb.

vessel 194 n.
gait 265 n.
walk 267 vb.
decamp 296 vb.
leap 312 n.
leap 312 vb.
neglect 458 vb.
study 536 vb.
escape 667 vb.
not complete
726 vb.
rejoice 835 vb.
skipper
mariner 270 n.
direct 689 vb.
director 690 n.
skirl
be loud 400 vb.
shrill 407 vb.
stridor 407 n.
skirmish
fight 716 n.
fight 716 vb.
battle 718 n.
skirt
be contiguous
202 vb.
base 214 n.
hanging object
217 n.
skirt 228 n.
edge 234 n.
flank 239 n.
meat 301 n.
pass 305 vb.
circle 314 vb.
female 373 n.
circuit 626 vb.
skirt round
avoid 620 vb.
skis
sled 274 n.
skit
stage play 594 n.
satire 851 n.
calumny 926 n.
skitter
be in motion
265 vb.
skittish
capricious 604 adj.
exitable 822 adj.
skittle alley
arena 724 n.
skittles
ball game 837 n.
skive
be absent 190 vb.
be inactive 679 vb.
not complete
726 vb.
skivvy
domestic 742 n.
servant 742 n.

skol
bon appétit
301 int.
skua
bird 365 n.
skulduggery
trickery 542 n.
improbity 930 n.
skulk
wander 267 vb.
be stealthy 525 vb.
be cowardly
856 vb.
skull
head 213 n.
dome 253 n.
corpse 363 n.
skull and
crossbones
cross 222 n.
flag 547 n.
heraldry 547 n.
intimidation
854 n.
skullcap
headgear 228 n.
canonicals 989 n.
skunk
mammal 365 n.
stench 397 n.
cad 938 n.
sky
space 183 n.
height 209 n.
summit 213 n.
propel 287 vb.
heavens 321 n.
skydiving
aeronautics
271 n.
sky-high
enormous 32 adj.
high 209 adj.
dear 811 adj.
skyjack
steal 788 vb.
stealing 788 n.
skylab
satellite 321 n.
skylarking
foolery 497 n.
revel 837 n.
skylight
window 263 n.
skyline
distance 199 n.
horizontality
216 n.
outline 233 n.
edge 234 n.
limit 236 n.
visibility 443 n.
skyscraper
edifice 164 n.

high structure
209 n.
slab
piece 53 n.
horizontality
216 n.
shelf 218 n.
slabber
moisture 341 n.
slack
weak 163 adj.
inert 175 adj.
slow 278 adj.
soft 327 adj.
coal 385 n.
negligent 458 adj.
be inactive 679 vb.
lazy 679 adj.
lax 734 adj.
slacken
decrease 37 vb.
disunite 46 vb.
moderate 177 vb.
decelerate 278 vb.
be inactive 679 vb.
slacken off
cease 145 vb.
decelerate 278 vb.
slacks
informal dress
228 n.
trousers 228 n.
slag
leavings 41 n.
slut 61 n.
rubbish 641 n.
reproach 924 vb.
slag heap
rubbish 641 n.
slag off
cuss 899 vb.
slake
assuage 177 vb.
sate 863 vb.
slake one's
thirst
drink 301 vb.
slalom
racing 716 n.
slam
close 264 vb.
impel 279 vb.
impulse 279 n.
strike 279 vb.
propel 287 vb.
be loud 400 vb.
loudness 400 n.
bang 402 n.
bang 402 vb.
victory 727 n.
detract 926 vb.
slammer
lockup 748 n.
prison 748 n.

slander
slur 867 n.
scurrility 899 n.
censure 924 n.
calumny 926 n.
defame 926 vb.
false charge 928 n.
slang
speciality 80 n.
unintelligibility
517 n.
language 557 n.
slang 560 n.
cuss 899 vb.
criticize 924 vb.
slanging match
interlocution
584 n.
quarrel 709 n.
scurrility 899 n.
slant
be oblique 220 vb.
obliquity 220 n.
idea 451 n.
bias 481 n.
slap
knock 279 n.
strike 279 vb.
bang 402 n.
crackle 402 vb.
corporal
punishment
963 n.
spank 963 vb.
slapdash
negligent 458 adj.
hasty 680 adj.
bungled 695 adj.
clumsy 695 adj.
rash 857 adj.
slaphead
uncovered person
229 n.
slap in the face
refusal 760 n.
humiliation 872 n.
anger 891 n.
indignity 921 n.
slapper
loose woman
952 n.
slapstick
dramatic 594 adj.
stage play 594 n.
wit 839 n.
funny 849 adj.
ridiculousness
849 n.
slap-up
liberal 813 adj.
slash
cut 46 vb.
rend 46 vb.
shorten 204 vb.

notch 260 vb.
furrow 262 n.
wound 655 vb.
discount 810 vb.
cheapen 812 vb.
criticize 924 vb.
slat
strip 208 n.
slate
brittleness 330 n.
greyness 429 n.
stationery 586 n.
policy 623 n.
building material
631 n.
criticize 924 vb.
reproach 924 vb.
detract 926 vb.
slating
roof 226 n.
censure 924 n.
reprimand 924 n.
slats
shade 226 n.
slattern
slut 61 n.
dirty person 649 n.
bungler 697 n.
slaughter
slaughter 362 n.
slaughter 362 vb.
slave
instrument 628 n.
be active 678 vb.
minister to
703 vb.
servant 742 n.
slave 742 n.
toady 879 n.
slave away
work 682 vb.
slave-driver
tyrant 735 n.
slavery
labour 682 n.
compulsion 740 n.
servitude 745 n.
detention 747 n.
servility 879 n.
slave to, a
subject 745 adj.
slavish
imitative 20 adj.
conformable
83 adj.
subjected 745 adj.
servile 879 adj.
slay
kill 362 vb.
amuse 837 vb.
sleaze
improbity 930 n.
sled
sled 274 n.

sledge
be in motion
265 vb.
sled 274 n.
sledgehammer
hammer 279 n.
pulverizer 332 n.
sleek
smooth 258 adj.
personable
841 adj.
sleep
sleep 679 n.
sleep 679 vb.
sleep around
be impure 951 vb.
sleeper
basis 218 n.
train 274 n.
secret service
459 n.
book 589 n.
sleep in
fail in duty 918 vb.
sleeping bag
bag 194 n.
sleeping dog
latency 523 n.
pitfall 663 n.
sleeping pill
moderator 177 n.
drug 658 n.
soporific 679 n.
sleeping
policeman
traffic control
305 n.
sleepless
active 678 adj.
sleep on it
wait 136 vb.
meditate 449 vb.
sleepwalking
pedestrianism
267 n.
sleep 679 n.
sleep with
unite with 45 vb.
debauch 951 vb.
sleepy
sleepy 679 adj.
sleet
rain 350 n.
rain 350 vb.
wintriness 380 n.
sleeve
sleeve 228 n.
sleigh
sled 274 n.
sleight
sleight 542 n.
sleight of hand
sleight 542 n.
skill 694 n.

cunning 698 n.
slender
small 33 adj.
narrow 206 adj.
insufficient
636 adj.
shapely 841 adj.
sleuth
detective 459 n.
informer 524 n.
hunter 619 n.
pursue 619 vb.
'S' level
exam 459 n.
slew
deviate 282 vb.
deviation 282 n.
rotate 315 vb.
slice
cut 46 vb.
piece 53 n.
ladle 194 n.
notch 260 vb.
deflect 282 vb.
propel 287 vb.
be clumsy 695 vb.
bungling 695 n.
portion 783 n.
slice (golf)
propulsion 287 n.
slice of the cake
portion 783 n.
slick
smooth 258 adj.
skilful 694 adj.
cunning 698 adj.
slick down
smooth 258 vb.
slide
fastening 47 n.
elapse 111 vb.
obliquity 220 n.
smoothness 258 n.
be in motion
265 vb.
gait 265 n.
travel 267 vb.
descent 309 n.
photography
551 n.
deteriorate 655 vb.
not act 677 vb.
fail 728 vb.
hairdressing 843 n.
slide rule
counting
instrument 86 n.
gauge 465 n.
sliding
motion 265 n.
frail 934 adj.
slight
inconsiderable
33 adj.

small 33 adj.
weak 163 adj.
narrow 206 adj.
shallow 212 adj.
rare 325 n.
disregard 458 vb.
underestimate
483 vb.
trivial 639 adj.
slur 867 n.
humiliate 872 vb.
indignity 921 n.
not respect 921 vb.
contempt 922 n.
hold cheap 922 vb.
detract 926 vb.
slightly
slightly 33 adv.
slightly-built
weak 163 adj.
narrow 206 adj.
slightness
weakness 163 n.
slim
small 33 adj.
make smaller
198 vb.
make thin 206 vb.
narrow 206 adj.
shapely 841 adj.
slim down
render few 105 vb.
slime
moisture 341 n.
semiliquidity
354 n.
dirt 649 n.
slimming
dieting 301 n.
slimy
humid 341 adj.
viscid 354 adj.
dirty 649 adj.
unpleasant
827 adj.
servile 879 adj.
flattering 925 adj.
sling
bag 194 n.
propel 287 vb.
propellant 287 n.
propulsion 287 n.
surgical dressing
658 n.
missile weapon
723 n.
sling out
reject 607 vb.
**slings and
arrows**
evil 616 n.
slink
lurk 523 vb.
be stealthy 525 vb.

slink off
run away 620 vb.
slinky
narrow 206 adj.
shapely 841 adj.
slip
small thing 33 n.
come unstuck
49 vb.
branch 53 n.
elapse 111 vb.
young plant 132 n.
youngster 132 n.
dwarf 196 n.
thinness 206 n.
underwear 228 n.
gait 265 n.
descend 309 vb.
blunder 495 vb.
mistake 495 n.
deteriorate 655 vb.
failure 728 n.
be wicked 934 vb.
guilty act 936 n.
slip away
go away 190 vb.
decamp 296 vb.
slip back
revert 148 vb.
regress 286 vb.
fall short 307 vb.
relapse 657 vb.
slip by
elapse 111 vb.
slip knot
ligature 47 n.
**slip of the
pen**
mistake 495 n.
solecism 565 n.
**slip of the
tongue**
mistake 495 n.
solecism 565 n.
**slip one's
memory**
be forgotten
506 vb.
slippage
deficit 55 n.
incompleteness
55 n.
shortness 204 n.
shortfall 307 n.
descent 309 n.
requirement 627 n.
insufficiency
636 n.
scarcity 636 n.
slipper
footwear 228 n.
slippers
informal dress
228 n.

slippery
smooth 258 adj.
unsafe 661 adj.
cunning 698 adj.
dishonest 930 adj.
slippery slope
ruin 165 n.
danger 661 n.
predicament 700 n.
wickedness 934 n.
sliproad
road 624 n.
slips
workshop 687 n.
slipshod
negligent 458 adj.
lax 734 adj.
**slip through
one's fingers**
escape 667 vb.
**slip 'twixt the
cup and the
lip**
disappointment
509 n.
slip up
blunder 495 vb.
slip-up
mistake 495 n.
slipway
smoothness 258 n.
slit
cut 46 vb.
disunion 46 n.
rend 46 vb.
See **cut**
sunder 46 vb.
gap 201 n.
furrow 262 n.
wound 655 vb.
slither
be in motion
265 vb.
sliver
small thing 33 n.
piece 53 n.
slivovitz
alcoholic drink
301 n.
Sloane Ranger
idler 679 n.
beau monde 848 n.
Sloane Rangers
elite 644 n.
slob
bungler 697 n.
cad 938 n.
slobber
exude 298 vb.
emit 300 vb.
excrement 302 n.
excrete 302 vb.
be wet 341 vb.
moisture 341 n.

sloe
tree 366 n.
sourness 393 n.
black thing 428 n.
slog
strike 279 vb.
propel 287 vb.
be active 678 vb.
work 682 vb.
slogan
maxim 496 n.
advertisement
528 n.
phrase 563 n.
instrument 628 n.
slog away
persevere 600 vb.
sloop
sailing ship 275 n.
slop
let fall 311 vb.
moisten 341 vb.
semiliquidity
354 n.
be clumsy 695 vb.
slope
high land 209 n.
be oblique
220 vb.
obliquity 220 n.
ascent 308 n.
descent 309 n.
slope off
travel 267 vb.
decamp 296 vb.
run away 620 vb.
sloping
sloping 220 adj.
written 586 adj.
sloppy
humid 341 adj.
negligent 458 adj.
feeble 572 adj.
slosh
strike 279 vb.
drench 341 vb.
flow 350 vb.
sloshed
dead drunk
949 adj.
slot
sorting 62 n.
serial place 73 n.
classification 77 n.
place 185 n.
receptacle 194 n.
gap 201 n.
furrow 262 n.
groove 262 vb.
orifice 263 n.
sloth
inertness 175 n.
sluggishness 679 n.
vice 934 n.

slothful
lazy 679 adj.
slot in
place 187 vb.
slot machine
shop 796 n.
treasury 799 n.
slouch
move slowly
278 vb.
slowcoach 278 n.
stoop 311 vb.
be inactive 679 vb.
slough
leavings 41 n.
gulf 345 n.
marsh 347 n.
relinquish 621 vb.
dirt 649 n.
stop using 674 vb.
difficulty 700 n.
**Slough of
Despond**
marsh 347 n.
adversity 731 n.
dejection 834 n.
slough off
disaccustom
611 vb.
slovenly
negligent 458 adj.
dirty 649 adj.
clumsy 695 adj.
slow
slow 278 adj.
inexact 495 adj.
unintelligent
499 adj.
impassive 820 adj.
tedious 838 adj.
cautious 858 adj.
slowcoach
slowcoach 278 n.
slow down
decelerate 278 vb.
repose 683 vb.
hinder 702 vb.
slow handclap
disapprobation
924 n.
slowly
slowly 278 adv.
**slowly but
surely**
by degrees 27 adv.
slow motion
motion 265 n.
slowness 278 n.
slow-motion
slow 278 adj.
slowness
slowness 278 n.
unintelligence
499 n.

unskilfulness
695 n.
moral insensibility
820 n.
**slow on the
uptake**
unintelligent
499 adj.
slow up
decelerate 278 vb.
slowworm
reptile 365 n.
slubbed
rough 259 adj.
sludge
leavings 41 n.
semiliquidity
354 n.
dirt 649 n.
slug
knock 279 n.
strike 279 vb.
draught 301 n.
creepy-crawly
365 n.
print-type 587 n.
ammunition
723 n.
sluggard
slowcoach 278 n.
idler 679 n.
sluggish
late 136 adj.
inert 175 adj.
slow 278 adj.
nonactive 677 adj.
inactive 679 adj.
lazy 679 adj.
apathetic 820 adj.
dejected 834 adj.
dull 840 adj.
sluice
outlet 298 n.
drench 341 vb.
irrigator 341 n.
conduit 351 n.
clean 648 vb.
slum
housing 192 n.
sink 649 n.
insalubrity 653 n.
dilapidation 655 n.
poverty 801 n.
slumber
quietude 266 n.
sleep 679 n.
sleep 679 vb.
slump
decrease 37 n.
decrease 37 vb.
unproductiveness
172 n.
contraction 198 n.
regress 286 vb.

regression 286 n.
fall short 307 vb.
descend 309 vb.
descent 309 n.
tumble 309 vb.
deteriorate 655 vb.
deterioration
655 n.
be inactive 679 vb.
inactivity 679 n.
adversity 731 n.
poverty 801 n.
cheapness 812 n.
slur
speech defect
580 n.
stammer 580 vb.
slur 867 n.
censure 924 n.
extenuate 927 vb.
slush
semiliquidity
354 n.
pulpiness 356 n.
slush fund
incentive 612 n.
gift 781 n.
reward 962 n.
slushy
humid 341 adj.
marshy 347 adj.
slut
slut 61 n.
dirty person 649 n.
loose woman 952 n.
sly
hypocritical
541 adj.
cunning 698 adj.
merry 833 adj.
witty 839 adj.
affected 850 adj.
smack
tincture 43 n.
sailing ship 275 n.
knock 279 n.
strike 279 vb.
taste 386 n.
bang 402 n.
crackle 402 vb.
drug 949 n.
*corporal
punishment*
963 n.
spank 963 vb.
smacker
funds 797 n.
endearment 889 n.
smack of
resemble 18 vb.
taste 386 vb.
indicate 547 vb.
smack one's lips
enjoy 376 vb.

be pleased 824 vb.
rejoice 835 vb.
**smack on the
wrist**
reprimand 924 n.
punish 963 vb.
spank 963 vb.
small
small 33 adj.
lesser 35 adj.
unimportant
639 adj.
small ad
information 524 n.
advertisement
528 n.
small arms
firearm 723 n.
small beer
alcoholic drink
301 n.
nonentity 639 n.
trifle 639 n.
small-beer
lesser 35 adj.
small-built
small 33 adj.
small change
trifle 639 n.
coinage 797 n.
money 797 n.
smaller
small 33 adj.
lesser 35 adj.
smallest room
chamber 194 n.
small fry
inferior 35 n.
child 132 n.
weakling 163 n.
nonentity 639 n.
lower classes
869 n.
smallholding
farm 370 n.
small hours
morning 128 n.
midnight 129 n.
lateness 136 n.
small letter
letter 558 n.
**small-
mindedness**
narrow mind
481 n.
smallness
smallness 33 n.
invisibility 444 n.
smallpox
infection 651 n.
small print
conditions 766 n.
smalls
underwear 228 n.

small screen
broadcasting
531 n.
small-sized
small 33 adj.
small talk
chatter 581 n.
chat 584 n.
smarmy
flattering 925 adj.
smart
speedy 277 adj.
feel pain 377 vb.
pang 377 n.
intelligent 498 adj.
active 678 adj.
skilful 694 adj.
cunning 698 adj.
suffer 825 vb.
suffering 825 n.
witty 839 adj.
personable
841 adj.
fashionable
848 adj.
huff 891 vb.
smart alec
wiseacre 500 n.
vain person 873 n.
smart ass
wiseacre 500 n.
vain person
873 n.
smart-ass
vain 873 adj.
smart card
payment 804 n.
smarten
decorate 844 vb.
smarten up
beautify 841 vb.
smart under
feel 818 vb.
resent 891 vb.
smash
break 46 vb.
demolish 165 vb.
ruin 165 n.
force 176 vb.
collision 279 n.
strike 279 vb.
propel 287 vb.
pulverize 332 vb.
wound 655 vb.
smash (tennis)
propulsion 287 n.
**smash and grab
raid**
stealing 788 n.
smashed
dead drunk
949 adj.
smash hit
dramaturgy 594 n.

exceller 644 n.
masterpiece 694 n.
success 727 n.
smashing
super 644 adj.
smash up
demolish 165 vb.
smashup
collision 279 n.
smattering
erudition 490 n.
knowledge 490 n.
sciolism 491 n.
smear
coat 226 vb.
dim 419 vb.
make unclean
649 vb.
blemish 845 n.
blemish 845 vb.
shame 867 vb.
slur 867 n.
calumny 926 n.
defame 926 vb.
smear campaign
discontent 829 n.
disrepute 867 n.
detraction 926 n.
smear test
diagnostic 658 n.
smell
small quantity
33 n.
have feeling
374 vb.
sense 374 n.
odour 394 n.
smell 394 vb.
stink 397 vb.
trace 548 n.
be unclean 649 vb.
deteriorate 655 vb.
smell a rat
detect 484 vb.
doubt 486 vb.
smelling salts
pungency 388 n.
tonic 658 n.
**smell of the
lamp**
ornament 574 vb.
smell out
smell 394 vb.
discover 484 vb.
smelly
odorous 394 adj.
fetid 397 adj.
smelt
liquefy 337 vb.
smelter
workshop 687 n.
smidgen
small quantity
33 n.

fewness 105 n.
smile
gesticulate 547 vb.
gesture 547 n.
be pleased 824 vb.
be cheerful 833 vb.
laughter 835 n.
smile 835 vb.
courteous act
884 n.
greet 884 vb.
smile on
be auspicious
730 vb.
smirch
defame 926 vb.
debauch 951 vb.
smirk
laughter 835 n.
smile 835 vb.
flatter 925 vb.
smirk at
ridicule 851 vb.
smite
strike 279 vb.
smith
artisan 686 n.
smithereens
small thing 33 n.
smitten
enamoured
887 adj.
smock
shirt 228 n.
fold 261 vb.
smocking
needlework
844 n.
smog
powder 332 n.
cloud 355 n.
opacity 423 n.
insalubrity 653 n.
poison 659 n.
smoke
emit 300 vb.
powder 332 n.
gas 336 n.
vaporize 338 vb.
dry 342 vb.
be hot 379 vb.
season 388 vb.
smoke 388 vb.
tobacco 388 n.
odour 394 n.
make unclean
649 vb.
preserve 666 vb.
mature 669 vb.
drug oneself
949 vb.
smokeless
coal 385 n.

smokeless zone
air 340 n.
smoke out
eject 300 vb.
extract 304 vb.
smoker
train 274 n.
tobacco 388 n.
smoke-screen
screen 421 n.
opacity 423 n.
invisibility 444 n.
concealment
525 n.
disguise 527 n.
trickery 542 n.
pretext 614 n.
defences 713 n.
smoking
fiery 379 adj.
hot 379 adj.
tobacco 388 n.
drug-taking 949 n.
smoking jacket
informal dress
228 n.
smoky
dense 324 adj.
powdery 332 adj.
vaporific 338 adj.
heated 381 adj.
pungent 388 adj.
fetid 397 adj.
dim 419 adj.
opaque 423 adj.
black 428 adj.
grey 429 adj.
dirty 649 adj.
smooch
caress 889 vb.
smooth
continuous
71 adj.
flat 216 adj.
symmetrical
245 adj.
smooth 258 adj.
smooth 258 vb.
hypocritical
541 adj.
caress 889 vb.
flatter 925 vb.
flattering 925 adj.
smooth down
flatten 216 vb.
smoothen
smooth 258 vb.
smooth the way
make possible
469 vb.
smoothing-iron
smoother 258 n.
smoothly
easily 701 adv.

**smooth one's
ruffled
feathers**
pacify 719 vb.
smooth over
assuage 177 vb.
smooth 258 vb.
smooth sailing
easy thing 701 n.
smooth-tongued
hypocritical
541 adj.
eloquent 579 adj.
flattering 925 adj.
smorgasbord
hors-d'oeuvres
301 n.
smother
disable 161 vb.
suppress 165 vb.
moderate 177 vb.
cover 226 vb.
close 264 vb.
kill 362 vb.
murder 362 vb.
extinguish 382 vb.
conceal 525 vb.
pet 889 vb.
smoulder
be hot 379 vb.
lurk 523 vb.
be inactive 679 vb.
resent 891 vb.
smudge
blur 440 vb.
defect 647 n.
dirt 649 n.
make unclean
649 vb.
blemish 845 n.
blemish 845 vb.
slur 867 n.
smug
affected 850 adj.
vain 873 adj.
smuggle
steal 788 vb.
smuggling
trade 791 n.
smut
powder 332 n.
black thing 428 n.
dirt 649 n.
blemish 845 n.
impurity 951 n.
smutty
black 428 adj.
unclean 649 adj.
impure 951 adj.
snack
small quantity
33 n.
eat 301 vb.
meal 301 n.

mouthful 301 n.
snaffle
take 786 vb.
steal 788 vb.
snag
defect 647 n.
danger 661 n.
pitfall 663 n.
difficulty 700 n.
hitch 702 n.
obstacle 702 n.
snail
slowcoach 278 n.
creepy-crawly
365 n.
snail mail
*postal
communication*
531 n.
snail's pace
slowness 278 n.
snake
meander 251 vb.
serpent 251 n.
reptile 365 n.
bane 659 n.
slyboots 698 n.
finance 797 n.
**snake in the
grass**
latency 523 n.
deceiver 545 n.
badness 645 n.
bane 659 n.
troublemaker
663 n.
evildoer 904 n.
**snakes and
ladders**
board game 837 n.
snaky
snaky 251 adj.
animal 365 adj.
snap
break 46 vb.
instantaneous
116 adj.
vigorousness
174 n.
bang 402 n.
crackle 402 vb.
ululate 409 vb.
ululation 409 n.
gesticulate 547 vb.
photograph 551 vb.
photography 551 n.
picture 553 n.
spontaneous
609 adj.
unprepared
670 adj.
card game 837 n.
hatred 888 n.
anger 891 n.

soak up
absorb 299 vb.
drink 301 vb.
dry 342 vb.

so and so
person 371 n.
no name 562 n.

soap
softness 327 n.
lubricant 334 n.
lubricate 334 vb.
fat 357 n.
clean 648 vb.
cleanser 648 n.

soapbox
publicity 528 n.
oratory 579 n.

soap opera
broadcast 531 n.
narrative 590 n.

soap powder
cleanser 648 n.

soapsuds
bubble 355 n.

soapy
smooth 258 adj.
bubbly 355 adj.
fatty 357 adj.
white 427 adj.
servile 879 adj.
flattering 925 adj.

soar
be great–large
32 vb.
be high 209 vb.
fly 271 vb.
ascend 308 vb.
be light 323 vb.
be dear 811 vb.

soar above
outdo 306 vb.

sob
respiration 352 n.
rasp 407 vb.
cry 408 n.
cry 408 vb.
voicelessness
578 n.
lamentation
836 n.
weep 836 vb.

sober
moderate 177 vb.
plain 573 adj.
depress 834 vb.
serious 834 adj.
cautious 858 adj.
virtuous 933 adj.
sober 948 adj.

sober as a judge
serious 834 adj.
sober 948 adj.

sobersides
moper 834 n.

sober up
be sober 948 vb.

sobriety
inexcitability
823 n.
seriousness 834 n.
caution 858 n.
sobriety 948 n.

sobriquet
name 561 n.

sob-stuff
excitation 821 n.

so-called
supposed 512 adj.
spurious 542 adj.
untrue 543 adj.
named 561 adj.
vain 873 adj.

soccer
ball game 837 n.

sociable
sociable 882 adj.

social
national 371 adj.
sociable 882 adj.
social gathering
882 n.

**social
anthropology**
anthropology
371 n.

social butterfly
sociable person
882 n.

social circle
fellowship 882 n.

social class
degree 27 n.
serial place 73 n.
classification 77 n.
community 708 n.

social climber
commoner 869 n.
sociable person
882 n.

social disease
venereal disease
651 n.

social exclusion
poverty 801 n.

social graces
good taste 846 n.
sociability 882 n.

socialism
government 733 n.
joint possession
775 n.
philanthropy
901 n.

Socialists
political party
708 n.

socialite
beau monde 848 n.

sociable person
882 n.

socialize
make better
654 vb.
be sociable 882 vb.

social science
anthropology
371 n.
sociology 901 n.

social security
safety 660 n.
subvention 703 n.
sociology 901 n.

social services
sociology 901 n.

social whirl
festivity 837 n.
social round 882 n.

social work
sociology 901 n.

societal
national 371 adj.

society
accompaniment
89 n.
social group 371 n.
society 708 n.
beau monde 848 n.
fellowship 882 n.
laity 987 n.

sociology
sociology 901 n.

sociopath
the maladjusted
504 n.

sock
strike 279 vb.
drama 594 n.

socket
place 185 n.
receptacle
194 n.
cavity 255 n.

sock it to
strike 279 vb.

socks
legwear 228 n.

sod
piece 53 n.
soil 344 n.
grass 366 n.

soda
soft drink 301 n.

soda water
soft drink 301 n.
water 339 n.

sodomy
illicit love 951 n.

sod's law
rule 81 n.
axiom 496 n.

sofa
seat 218 n.

soft
small 33 adj.
smooth 258 adj.
soft 327 adj.
hush 399 int.
silent 399 adj.
muted 401 adj.
luminous 417 adj.
soft-hued 425 adj.
foolish 499 adj.
lax 734 adj.
lenient 736 adj.
cowardly 856 adj.
pitying 905 adj.

soft drink
soft drink 301 n.

soft drug
drug-taking 949 n.

soften
soften 327 vb.
mute 401 vb.
relieve 831 vb.
extenuate 927 vb.

softening
weakness 163 n.
soft 327 adj.

**softening of the
brain**
mental disorder
503 n.

soften up
weaken 163 vb.
induce 612 vb.
prepare 669 vb.
flatter 925 vb.

soft fruit
fruit and vegetables
301 n.

soft-hearted
impressible
819 adj.
benevolent
897 adj.
pitying 905 adj.

softly
slightly 33 adv.

softly softly
cautiously
858 adv.

soft mark
dupe 544 n.

soft on
enamoured
887 adj.

soft option
easy thing 701 n.

soft-pedal
moderate 177 vb.
move slowly
278 vb.
silence 399 vb.
mute 401 vb.
underestimate
483 vb.

extenuate 927 vb.

soft porn
impurity 951 n.

soft sell
advertisement
528 n.
inducement 612 n.
sale 793 n.

soft-soap
be servile 879 vb.
flatter 925 vb.

soft-spoken
speaking 579 adj.
amiable 884 adj.

soft spot
defect 647 n.
moral sensibility
819 n.

soft touch
dupe 544 n.
easy thing 701 n.

software
computing 86 n.

soggy
soft 327 adj.
unsavoury 391 adj.

soi-disant
named 561 adj.
vain 873 adj.

soigné(e)
elegant 575 adj.
personable
841 adj.

soil
region 184 n.
soil 344 n.
make unclean
649 vb.
blemish 845 vb.

soirée
evening 129 n.
social gathering
882 n.

sojourn
be present 189 vb.
dwell 192 vb.
visit 882 vb.

solace
relief 831 n.
relieve 831 vb.
amusement 837 n.

solar
celestial 321 adj.

solar heating
heating 381 n.

solarium
arbour 194 n.
heater 383 n.

solar plexus
insides 224 n.

solar system
sun 321 n.

solder
join 45 vb.

spittle
excrement 302 n.
lubricant 334 n.
moisture 341 n.
spittoon
sink 649 n.
splash
small quantity
33 n.
disperse 75 vb.
water 339 n.
moisten 341 vb.
flow 350 vb.
hiss 406 vb.
sibilation 406 vb.
mottle 437 n.
make unclean
649 vb.
ostentation 875 n.
splashdown
space travel 271 n.
descent 309 n.
splash out
expend 806 vb.
be ostentatious
875 vb.
splatter
moisten 341 vb.
splay
disperse 75 vb.
expand 197 vb.
obliquity 220 n.
diverge 294 vb.
splay-footed
deformed 246 adj.
spleen
insides 224 n.
discontent 829 n.
melancholy 834 n.
resentment 891 n.
sullenness 893 n.
malevolence 898 n.
envy 912 n.
splendid
luminous 417 adj.
excellent 644 adj.
pleasurable
826 adj.
splendid 841 adj.
noteworthy
866 adj.
ostentatious
875 adj.
splendiferous
excellent 644 adj.
ostentatious
875 adj.
splendour
light 417 n.
beauty 841 n.
prestige 866 n.
ostentation 875 n.
splenetic
resentful 891 adj.

irascible 892 adj.
splice
affix 45 vb.
joint 45 n.
tie 45 vb.
cross 222 vb.
introduce 231 vb.
repair 656 vb.
marry 894 vb.
splint
support 218 n.
hardness 326 n.
surgical dressing
658 n.
splinter
small thing 33 n.
break 46 vb.
piece 53 n.
thinness 206 n.
strip 208 n.
splinter group
dissentient 489 n.
party 708 n.
revolter 738 n.
undutifulness
918 n.
schismatic 978 n.
sect 978 n.
split
break 46 vb.
disunion 46 n.
separate 46 vb.
sunder 46 vb.
decompose 51 vb.
discontinuity 72 n.
bisect 92 vb.
bisected 92 adj.
be weak 163 vb.
be destroyed
165 vb.
gap 201 n.
space 201 vb.
furrow 262 n.
open 263 vb.
opening 263 n.
crackle 402 vb.
inform 524 vb.
divulge 526 vb.
dissension 709 n.
quarrel 709 n.
apportion 783 vb.
portion 783 n.
split hairs
argue 475 vb.
sophisticate
477 vb.
be fastidious
862 vb.
split on
accuse 928 vb.
split one's sides
laugh 835 vb.
split personality
multiformity 82 n.

duality 90 n.
spirit 447 n.
personality disorder
503 n.
split second
instant 116 n.
**split the
difference**
average out 30 vb.
compromise
770 vb.
splitting
separation 46 n.
opening 263 n.
brittle 330 adj.
split up
disunite 46 vb.
separate 46 vb.
divorce 896 vb.
splodge
mottle 437 n.
splurge
be prodigal 815 vb.
prodigality 815 n.
be ostentatious
875 vb.
ostentation 875 n.
splutter
emit 300 vb.
hiss 406 vb.
sibilation 406 vb.
stammer 580 vb.
Spode china
pottery 381 n.
spoil
derange 63 vb.
modify 143 vb.
tell against 467 vb.
deteriorate 655 vb.
impair 655 vb.
be clumsy 695 vb.
be lax 734 vb.
be lenient 736 vb.
blemish 845 vb.
sate 863 vb.
love 887 vb.
pet 889 vb.
spoilage
impairment 655 n.
spoiled child
satiety 863 n.
favourite 890 n.
spoiler
equilibrium 28 n.
stabilizer 153 n.
spoiling
impairment 655 n.
**spoiling for a
fight, be**
make quarrels
709 vb.
attack 712 vb.
spoil oneself
be selfish 932 vb.

be sensual 944 vb.
spoils
booty 790 n.
spoils of war
trophy 729 n.
booty 790 n.
spoilsport
dissuasion 613 n.
moper 834 n.
spoilt
inferior 35 adj.
sensual 944 adj.
**spoil the ship
for a ha'porth
of tar**
act foolishly
695 vb.
be parsimonious
816 vb.
spoke
line 203 n.
spoken
informative
524 adj.
linguistic 557 adj.
speaking 579 adj.
**spokesman or
-woman or
-person**
interpret 520 vb.
interpreter 520 n.
informant 524 n.
messenger 529 n.
speaker 579 n.
agent 686 n.
deputy 755 n.
sponge
fossil 125 n.
cavity 255 n.
porosity 263 n.
absorb 299 vb.
dry 342 vb.
dryer 342 n.
pulpiness 356 n.
clean 648 vb.
cleaning utensil
648 n.
beg 761 vb.
fleece 786 vb.
be servile
879 vb.
sponge bag
bag 194 n.
sponge on
be servile 879 vb.
sponger
idler 679 n.
beggar 763 n.
toady 879 n.
spongy
concave 255 adj.
porous 263 adj.
rare 325 adj.
soft 327 adj.

marshy 347 adj.
sponsor
witness 466 n.
stage manager
594 n.
aider 703 n.
patronize 703 vb.
patron 707 n.
sponsorship
protection 660 n.
aid 703 n.
security 767 n.
spontaneous
volitional 595 adj.
spontaneous
609 adj.
spontaneousness
will 595 n.
willingness 597 n.
spoof
imitate 20 vb.
mimicry 20 n.
copy 22 n.
deceive 542 vb.
fool 542 vb.
trickery 542 n.
wit 839 n.
witticism 839 n.
satire 851 n.
satirize 851 vb.
spook
spectator 441 n.
secret service
459 n.
informer 524 n.
intimidation
854 n.
ghost 970 n.
spooky
spooky 970 adj.
spool
rotate 315 vb.
rotator 315 n.
photography
551 n.
spoon
ladle 194 n.
caress 889 vb.
spoonerism
inversion 221 n.
mistake 495 n.
neology 560 n.
ridiculousness
849 n.
spoonfeed
aid 703 vb.
be lax 734 vb.
be lenient 736 vb.
pet 889 vb.
spoonful
finite quantity
26 n.
small quantity
33 n.

stigma
flower 366 n.
indication 547 n.
blemish 845 n.
slur 867 n.
censure 924 n.
detraction 926 n.
false charge 928 n.
stigmata
indication 547 n.
stigmatize
blemish 845 vb.
shame 867 vb.
criticize 924 vb.
defame 926 vb.
accuse 928 vb.
stile
ascent 308 n.
access 624 n.
obstacle 702 n.
stiletto
sharp point 256 n.
perforator 263 n.
sidearms 723 n.
stiletto heels
footwear 228 n.
still
assuage 177 vb.
moderate 177 adj.
quiescent 266 adj.
still 266 adj.
vaporizer 338 n.
heater 383 n.
silence 399 n.
silent 399 adj.
nevertheless
468 adv.
photography
551 n.
make mute 578 vb.
inactive 679 adj.
stillborn
dead 361 adj.
unsuccessful
728 adj.
still life
art subject 553 n.
stillroom
chamber 194 n.
storage 632 n.
still water
water 339 n.
stilted
ornate 574 adj.
inelegant 576 adj.
ridiculous 849 adj.
affected 850 adj.
stilts
leg 267 n.
plaything 837 n.
stimulant
stimulant 174 n.
drug 658 n.
refreshment 685 n.

drug-taking 949 n.
intoxicating
949 adj.
stimulate
augment 36 vb.
cause 156 vb.
invigorate 174 vb.
incite 612 vb.
refresh 685 vb.
animate 821 vb.
stimulator
excitant 821 n.
stimulus
cause 156 n.
stimulant 174 n.
incentive 612 n.
sting
be sharp 256 vb.
sharpness 256 n.
sharp point 256 n.
give pain 377 vb.
pang 377 n.
pungency 388 n.
duplicity 541 n.
badness 645 n.
wound 655 vb.
bane 659 n.
fleece 786 vb.
overcharge 811 vb.
excitant 821 n.
excite 821 vb.
suffering 825 n.
torment 827 vb.
enrage 891 vb.
huff 891 vb.
stingray
fish 365 n.
stingy
insufficient
636 adj.
parsimonious
816 adj.
stink
odour 394 n.
stench 397 n.
stink 397 vb.
uncleanness 649 n.
stink bomb
stench 397 n.
stinker
cad 938 n.
stinking
unsavory 391 adj.
fetid 397 adj.
not nice 645 adj.
unclean 649 adj.
unpleasant
827 adj.
stint
degree 27 n.
time 108 n.
period 110 n.
labour 682 n.
restrain 747 vb.

portion 783 n.
be parsimonious
816 vb.
stipend
subvention 703 n.
reward 962 n.
stipple
variegate 437 vb.
paint 553 vb.
engrave 555 vb.
stipulate
postulate 475 vb.
give terms 766 vb.
stir
mix 43 vb.
stimulation 174 n.
be in motion
265 vb.
motion 265 n.
cook 301 vb.
agitate 318 vb.
be agitated 318 vb.
commotion 318 n.
activity 678 n.
prison 748 n.
excite 821 vb.
stir-fry
cook 301 vb.
dish 301 n.
stir it
make quarrels
709 vb.
**stir one's
stumps**
travel 267 vb.
move fast 277 vb.
be active 678 vb.
stirring
mixture 43 n.
active 678 adj.
busy 678 adj.
exciting 821 adj.
stirrup
support 218 n.
stirrup cup
valediction 296 n.
draught 301 n.
stir up
move 265 vb.
agitate 318 vb.
**stir up a
hornet's nest**
be in difficulty
700 vb.
stitch
join 45 vb.
tie 45 vb.
fastening 47 n.
component 58 n.
pang 377 n.
needlework 844 n.
stitching
joint 45 n.
bookbinding 589 n.

stitch in time, a
anticipation 135 n.
stoat
mammal 365 n.
stock
race 11 n.
great quantity
32 n.
ligature 47 n.
accumulation 74 n.
source 156 n.
genealogy 169 n.
hors-d'oeuvres
301 n.
animal 365 n.
tree 366 n.
sauce 389 n.
aphoristic 496 adj.
usual 610 adj.
store 632 n.
provide 633 vb.
property 777 n.
merchandise
795 n.
stockade
barrier 235 n.
enclosure 235 n.
protection 660 n.
shelter 662 n.
defences 713 n.
stock and barrel
all 52 n.
stock-breeding
animal husbandry
369 n.
stockbroker
consignee 754 n.
merchant 794 n.
**stockbroker
belt**
district 184 n.
stock car
automobile 274 n.
stock exchange
stock exchange
618 n.
market 796 n.
finance 797 n.
stockholder
participator 775 n.
owner 776 n.
stocking
treasury 799 n.
stockings
legwear 228 n.
stock-in-trade
means 629 n.
equipment 630 n.
store 632 n.
stockpile
store 632 n.
store 632 vb.
stockroom
storage 632 n.

stocks
lockup 748 n.
pillory 964 n.
**stocks and
shares**
means 629 n.
estate 777 n.
**stocks and
stones**
absence of intellect
448 n.
stock-still
still 266 adj.
stock up
store 632 n.
provide 633 vb.
stocky
stalwart 162 adj.
fleshy 195 adj.
short 204 adj.
stodgy
tedious 838 adj.
dull 840 adj.
stoic
unfeeling person
820 n.
patient 823 adj.
stoical
impassive 820 adj.
patient 823 adj.
Stoicism
philosophy 449 n.
stoicism
feeling 818 n.
moral insensibility
820 n.
inexcitability
823 n.
patience 823 n.
temperance 942 n.
stoke
augment 36 vb.
stoke up
heat 381 vb.
stole
neckwear 228 n.
vestments 989 n.
stolen goods
booty 790 n.
stolid
inactive 679 adj.
impassive 820 adj.
serious 834 adj.
stomach
stomach 194 n.
insides 224 n.
knuckle under
721 vb.
be patient 823 vb.
liking 859 n.
forgive 909 vb.
stomp
dance 837 n.
dance 837 vb.

trustworthy
929 adj.
**straight
forwards**
towards 281 adv.
**straight from
the shoulder**
genuine 494 adj.
assertive 532 adj.
veracious 540 adj.
straight line
line 203 n.
straightness 249 n.
strain
temperament 5 n.
be unrelated 10 vb.
race 11 n.
quantity 26 n.
small quantity
33 n.
tincture 43 n.
derange 63 vb.
breed 77 n.
power 160 n.
weaken 163 vb.
genealogy 169 n.
agency 173 n.
force 176 vb.
make smaller
198 vb.
distort 246 vb.
distortion 246 n.
exude 298 vb.
overstep 306 vb.
pain 377 n.
sound 398 n.
tune 412 n.
exaggerate 546 vb.
style 566 n.
be resolute 599 vb.
purify 648 vb.
impairment 655 n.
bane 659 n.
attempt 671 vb.
exertion 682 n.
exert oneself
682 vb.
labour 682 n.
fatigue 684 n.
fatigue 684 vb.
affections 817 n.
worry 825 n.
enmity 881 n.
**strain at a gnat
and swallow a
camel**
reason badly
477 vb.
act foolishly
695 vb.
strainer
sorting 62 n.
bowl 194 n.
porosity 263 n.

**strain every
nerve**
exert oneself
682 vb.
strain one's eyes
scan 438 vb.
strait
narrow 206 adj.
narrowness 206 n.
gulf 345 n.
access 624 n.
**straitened
circumstances**
poverty 801 n.
straitjacket
restraint 747 n.
fetter 748 n.
straitlaced
severe 735 adj.
prudish 950 adj.
straits
predicament 700 n.
strand
fibre 208 n.
filament 208 n.
edge 234 n.
hair 259 n.
shore 344 n.
stranded
fixed 153 adj.
hindered 702 adj.
strange
unrelated 10 adj.
extraneous 59 adj.
unusual 84 adj.
unknown 491 adj.
puzzling 517 adj.
ridiculous 849 adj.
wonderful 864 adj.
stranger
foreigner 59 n.
**stranger in our
midst**
intruder 59 n.
stranger to, a
ignorant 491 adj.
strangle
disable 161 vb.
suppress 165 vb.
make smaller
198 vb.
close 264 vb.
kill 362 vb.
murder 362 vb.
retain 778 vb.
execute 963 vb.
stranglehold
retention 778 n.
strangulation
compression 198 n.
closure 264 n.
killing 362 n.
capital punishment
963 n.

strap
tie 45 vb.
strip 208 n.
strike 279 vb.
spank 963 vb.
scourge 964 n.
strapping
stalwart 162 adj.
fleshy 195 adj.
support 218 n.
healthy 650 adj.
stratagem
tactics 688 n.
stratagem
698 n.
strategic
planned 623 adj.
**Strategic
Defence
Initiative**
rocket 276 n.
arms 723 n.
strategist
motivator 612 n.
planner 623 n.
expert 696 n.
slyboots 698 n.
strategy
sagacity 498 n.
policy 623 n.
tactics 688 n.
warfare 718 n.
strathspey
musical piece
412 n.
dance 837 n.
stratification
covering 226 n.
stratosphere
height 209 n.
atmosphere
340 n.
stratum
layer 207 n.
horizontality
216 n.
stratus
cloud 355 n.
straw
lightness 323 n.
grass 366 n.
flute 414 n.
trifle 639 n.
strawberry
fruit and vegetables
301 n.
**strawberry
blond(e)**
yellowness 433 n.
**strawberry
mark**
identification
547 n.
blemish 845 n.

**straw in the
wind**
indication 547 n.
straw poll
enquiry 459 n.
vote 605 n.
stray
casual 159 adj.
be in motion
265 vb.
wanderer 268 n.
stray 282 vb.
derelict 779 n.
be wicked
934 vb.
streak
small quantity
33 n.
tincture 43 n.
line 203 n.
narrowness
206 n.
strip 208 n.
furrow 262 n.
groove 262 vb.
move fast 277 vb.
flash 417 n.
stripe 437 n.
variegate 437 vb.
make unclean
649 vb.
streaker
stripper 229 n.
streaking
bareness 229 n.
**streak of
lightning**
velocity 277 n.
stream
congregate 74 vb.
crowd 74 n.
group 74 n.
classification 77 n.
tendency 179 n.
be in motion
265 vb.
be wet 341 vb.
flow 350 vb.
rain 350 vb.
stream 350 n.
flash 417 n.
class 538 n.
store 632 n.
abound 635 vb.
streamer
advertisement
528 n.
flag 547 n.
trimming 844 n.
streamers
celebration 876 n.
streamlined
smooth 258 adj.
speedy 277 adj.

**stream of
consciousness**
intellect 447 n.
idea 451 n.
soliloquy 585 n.
narrative 590 n.
streams
great quantity
32 n.
plenty 635 n.
street
locality 187 n.
abode 192 n.
housing 192 n.
road 624 n.
street furniture
traffic control
305 n.
streets ahead
superior 34 adj.
streetwalker
prostitute 952 n.
streetwise
intelligent 498 adj.
strength
greatness 32 n.
strength 162 n.
pungency 388 n.
vigour 571 n.
strengthen
strengthen 162 vb.
strenuous
vigorous 174 adj.
forceful 571 adj.
labouring 682 adj.
stress
quantity 26 n.
power 160 n.
strengthen 162 vb.
distortion 246 n.
pain 377 n.
attract notice
455 vb.
trope 519 n.
affirmation 532 n.
emphasize 532 vb.
vigour 571 n.
pronunciation
577 n.
voice 577 vb.
prosody 593 n.
importance 638 n.
bane 659 n.
exertion 682 n.
fatigue 684 vb.
difficulty 700 n.
worry 825 n.
stretch
be great–large
32 vb.
augment 36 vb.
period 110 n.
range 183 n.
space 183 n.

personable
841 adj.
fashionable
848 adj.
stylistic
stylistic 566 adj.
stylite
solitary 883 n.
stylo
stationery 586 n.
stylus
sharp point 256 n.
gramophone 414 n.
stymie
be obstructive
702 vb.
obstruct 702 vb.
Styx
the dead 361 n.
mythic hell 972 n.
suave
smooth 258 adj.
courteous 884 adj.
sub
inferior 35 n.
substitute 150 n.
publish 528 vb.
subaltern
inferior 35 adj.
inferior 35 n.
army officer 741 n.
servant 742 n.
subaqua
sport 837 n.
subconscious
intuition 476 n.
intuitive 476 adj.
latency 523 n.
latent 523 adj.
subconscious, the
spirit 447 n.
subcutaneous
interior 224 adj.
subdivision
scission 46 n.
subdivision 53 n.
subdue
moderate 177 vb.
prevail 178 vb.
overmaster
727 vb.
subjugate 745 vb.
restrain 747 vb.
subedit
publish 528 vb.
rectify 654 vb.
subfusc
formal dress 228 n.
subgroup
subdivision 53 n.
subhuman
animal 365 adj.
cruel 898 adj.

subject
living model 23 n.
inferior 35 adj.
inferior 35 n.
topic 452 n.
part of speech
564 n.
overmaster 727 vb.
subject 742 n.
subject 745 adj.
subject, be
be subject 745 vb.
subjective
intrinsic 5 adj.
intuitive 476 adj.
misjudging
481 adj.
subjectivity
intrinsicality 5 n.
subjectivity 320 n.
subject matter
topic 452 n.
meaning 514 n.
subject to
liable 180 adj.
provided 468 adv.
subject 745 adj.
on terms 766 adv.
subject to terms
conditional
766 adj.
subjoin
insert 303 vb.
sub judice
sub judice 480 adv.
subjugate
prevail 178 vb.
subjugate 745 vb.
sublet
lease 784 vb.
lending 784 n.
sub-lieutenant
nautical personnel
270 n.
naval officer 741 n.
sublimate
vaporize 338 vb.
make better
654 vb.
sublime
high 209 adj.
worshipful
866 adj.
proud 871 adj.
divine 965 adj.
subliminal
latent 523 adj.
involuntary
596 adj.
sublimity
height 209 n.
prestige 866 n.
divine attribute
965 n.

submachine gun
gun 723 n.
submarine
low 210 adj.
deep 211 adj.
depth 211 n.
ship 275 n.
warship 722 n.
submerge
suppress 165 vb.
immerse 303 vb.
descend 309 vb.
plunge 313 vb.
drench 341 vb.
irrigate 341 vb.
be unseen 444 vb.
obliterate 550 vb.
submerse
plunge 313 vb.
submission
argument 475 n.
supposition 512 n.
affirmation 532 n.
submission 721 n.
entreaty 761 n.
submissive
willing 597 adj.
inactive 679 adj.
tractable 701 adj.
peaceful 717 adj.
submitting
721 adj.
obedient 739 adj.
subjected 745 adj.
humble 872 adj.
servile 879 adj.
respectful 920 adj.
submit
propound 512 vb.
affirm 532 vb.
advise 691 vb.
submit 721 vb.
submit a report
communicate
524 vb.
submultiple
numerical element
85 n.
subnormal
inferior 35 adj.
abnormal 84 adj.
unintelligent
499 adj.
*having a learning
disability* 503 adj.
subordinate
extrinsic 6 adj.
inferior 35 adj.
inferior 35 n.
servant 742 n.
subject 745 adj.
**subordinate
clause**
subdivision 53 n.

subordination
inferiority 35 n.
order 60 n.
arrangement 62 n.
sequence 65 n.
subjection 745 n.
suborn
bribe 612 vb.
subplot
narrative 590 n.
dramaturgy 594 n.
subpoena
command 737 vb.
warrant 737 n.
legal process 959 n.
subrogation
substitution 150 n.
subscribe
testify 466 vb.
sign 547 vb.
join a party
708 vb.
contract 765 vb.
give security
767 vb.
give 781 vb.
subscriber
assenter 488 n.
signatory 765 n.
giver 781 n.
subscribe to
endorse 488 vb.
patronize 703 vb.
subscription
giving 781 n.
offering 781 n.
pay 804 n.
payment 804 n.
subsection
classification 77 n.
subsequence
posteriority 120 n.
following 284 n.
subsequent
subsequent
120 adj.
subservient
subjected 745 adj.
servile 879 adj.
subset
classification 77 n.
subside
decrease 37 vb.
be quiescent
266 vb.
recede 290 vb.
descend 309 vb.
blow 352 vb.
subsidence
decrease 37 vb.
quiescence 266 n.
descent 309 n.
subsidiary
extrinsic 6 adj.

inferior 35 adj.
inferior 35 n.
additional 38 adj.
unimportant
639 adj.
aiding 703 adj.
subsidize
aid 703 vb.
give 781 vb.
subsidy
subvention 703 n.
gift 781 n.
pay 804 n.
subsist
be 1 vb.
pass time 108 vb.
stay 144 vb.
subsistence
existence 1 n.
subsistence level
insufficiency
636 n.
poverty 801 n.
subsoil
base 214 n.
soil 344 n.
subsonic flight
aeronautics 271 n.
subspecies
subdivision 53 n.
breed 77 n.
substance
substance 3 n.
quantity 26 n.
matter 319 n.
structure 331 n.
meaning 514 n.
chief thing 638 n.
importance 638 n.
estate 777 n.
wealth 800 n.
drug 949 n.
substance abuse
misuse 675 n.
substandard
inferior 35 adj.
abnormal 84 adj.
deficient 307 adj.
cheap 812 adj.
substantial
substantial 3 adj.
great 32 adj.
strong 162 adj.
material 319 adj.
dense 324 adj.
meaningful
514 adj.
substantiate
specify 80 vb.
materialize 319 vb.
corroborate 466 vb.
demonstrate
478 vb.
be true 494 vb.

ageing 131 adj.
disused 674 adj.
superannuation
earnings 771 n.
superb
excellent 644 adj.
splendid 841 adj.
ostentatious
875 adj.
superbug
disease 651 n.
supercharged
dynamic 160 adj.
supercilious
proud 871 adj.
insolent 878 adj.
disrespectful
921 adj.
superficial
insubstantial 4 adj.
inconsiderable
33 adj.
shallow 212 adj.
exterior 223 adj.
appearing 445 adj.
inattentive
456 adj.
negligent 458 adj.
dabbling 491 adj.
irresolute 601 adj.
trivial 639 adj.
uncompleted
726 adj.
superfluity
greatness 32 n.
great quantity
32 n.
diffuseness 570 n.
superfluity 637 n.
superfluous
remaining 41 adj.
superfluous
637 adj.
supergiant
star 321 n.
supergrass
witness 466 n.
informer 524 n.
accuser 928 n.
bad person 938 n.
superhuman
divine 965 adj.
godlike 965 adj.
superimpose
add 38 vb.
modify 143 vb.
cover 226 vb.
superintend
manage 689 vb.
superintendent
manager 690 n.
superior
superior 34 adj.
superior 34 n.

notable 638 adj.
genteel 868 adj.
proud 871 adj.
superiority
superiority 34 n.
contempt 922 n.
superlative
distinctive 15 adj.
supreme 34 adj.
grammatical
564 adj.
excellent 644 adj.
superman,
woman
superior 34 n.
exceller 644 n.
paragon 646 n.
prodigy 864 n.
supermarket
shop 796 n.
supernatural
extraneous 59 adj.
abnormal 84 adj.
unusual 84 adj.
divine 965 adj.
spooky 970 adj.
magical 983 adj.
paranormal 984 n.
supernova
star 321 n.
supernumerary
additional 38 adj.
extra 40 n.
superfluous
637 adj.
superpower
influence 178 n.
bigwig 638 n.
political
organization
733 n.
supersede
substitute 150 vb.
displace 188 vb.
stop using 674 vb.
not retain 779 vb.
supersonic
sounding 398 adj.
supersonic
flight
aeronautics 271 n.
velocity 277 n.
superstition
credulity 487 n.
ignorance 491 n.
error 495 n.
heterodoxy 977 n.
idolatry 982 n.
superstitious
misjudging
481 adj.
erroneous 495 adj.
supertax
tax 809 n.

supervene
accrue 38 vb.
ensue 120 vb.
happen 154 vb.
supervention
addition 38 n.
supervise
manage 689 vb.
supervision
inspection 438 n.
supervisor
manager 690 n.
supine
supine 216 adj.
inactive 679 adj.
submitting
721 adj.
apathetic 820 adj.
indifferent 860 adj.
supper
meal 301 n.
supplant
come after 65 vb.
substitute 150 vb.
supple
flexible 327 adj.
servile 879 adj.
supplement
augment 36 vb.
increment 36 n.
add 38 vb.
addition 38 n.
adjunct 40 n.
make complete
54 vb.
sequel 67 n.
enlarge 197 vb.
the press 528 n.
edition 589 n.
price 809 n.
supplementary
increasing 36 adj.
additional 38 adj.
supplicant
petitioner 763 n.
worshipper 981 n.
supplicate
entreat 761 vb.
supplies
means 629 n.
provision 633 n.
supply
substitute 150 vb.
store 632 n.
provide 633 vb.
provision 633 n.
support
agency 173 n.
support 218 n.
support 218 vb.
corroborate 466 vb.
assent 488 n.
endorse 488 vb.
act 594 vb.

choose 605 vb.
inducement 612 n.
safeguard 660 vb.
preservation 666 n.
aid 703 n.
aider 703 n.
subvention 703 n.
be patient 823 vb.
approve 923 vb.
vindicate 927 vb.
supporter
follower 284 n.
assenter 488 n.
enthusiast 504 n.
patron 707 n.
benefactor 903 n.
commender 923 n.
supporting
assenting 488 adj.
aiding 703 adj.
approving 923 adj.
supporting role
inferiority 35 n.
supportive
aiding 703 adj.
suppose
suppose 512 vb.
suppose so
suppose 512 vb.
supposing
thus 8 adv.
provided 468 adv.
supposition
supposition 512 n.
suppository
surgical dressing
658 n.
suppress
suppress 165 vb.
keep secret 525 vb.
overmaster 727 vb.
suppression
exclusion 57 n.
destruction 165 n.
counteraction
182 n.
lowering 311 n.
concealment
525 n.
restraint 747 n.
abrogation 752 n.
prohibition 757 n.
suppurate
deteriorate 655 vb.
suppuration
excretion 302 n.
infection 651 n.
supra
before 64 adv.
supremacy
superiority 34 n.
importance 638 n.
authority 733 n.
governance 733 n.

divine attribute
965 n.
supreme
supreme 34 adj.
ending 69 adj.
strong 162 adj.
supremely
greatly 32 vb.
eminently
34 adv.
surcharge
price 809 n.
surd
number 85 n.
numerical 85 adj.
speech sound
398 n.
voiceless 578 adj.
voicelessness
578 n.
sure
certain 473 adj.
positive 473 adj.
expectant 507 adj.
safe 660 adj.
trustworthy
929 adj.
surefooted
skilful 694 adj.
sure thing
fair chance 159 n.
probability 471 n.
certainty 473 n.
necessary 596 adj.
necessity 596 n.
easy thing 701 n.
surety
protection 660 n.
security 767 n.
legal process 959 n.
surf
wave 350 n.
bubble 355 n.
amuse oneself
837 vb.
surface
space 183 n.
shallow 212 adj.
exterior 223 adj.
exteriority 223 n.
navigate 269 vb.
emerge 298 vb.
ascend 308 vb.
be light 323 vb.
texture 331 n.
be visible 443 vb.
road 624 n.
surface-to-air
missile
missile weapon
723 n.
surfboard
sled 274 n.
plaything 837 n.

surfeit
superfluity 637 n.
sate 863 vb.
satiety 863 n.
surfing
computing 86 n.
aquatics 269 n.
surge
grow 36 vb.
increase 36 n.
congregate 74 vb.
flow 350 vb.
be active 678 vb.
surgeon
doctor 658 n.
surgery
hospital 658 n.
surgery 658 n.
surly
sullen 893 adj.
surmise
*be of the opinion
that* 485 vb.
opinion 485 n.
foresee 510 vb.
conjecture 512 n.
suppose 512 vb.
surmount
be superior 34 vb.
be high 209 vb.
crown 213 vb.
climb 308 vb.
surmountable
possible 469 adj.
surname
name 561 n.
surpass
be superior 34 vb.
outdo 306 vb.
surplice
vestments
989 n.
surplus
extra 40 n.
remainder 41 n.
remaining 41 adj.
part 53 n.
superfluity 637 n.
superfluous
637 adj.
surprise
sequel 67 n.
lack of expectation
508 n.
surprise 508 vb.
attack 712 n.
wonder 864 n.
Surrealism
art 551 n.
school of painting
553 n.
literature 557 n.
surrealistic
literary 557 adj.

surrender
relinquish 621 vb.
nonuse 674 n.
submission 721 n.
submit 721 vb.
resign 753 vb.
resignation 753 n.
surreptitious
stealthy 525 adj.
surrogate
substitute 150 n.
consignee 754 n.
deputy 755 n.
**surrogate
mother**
family 11 n.
maternity 169 n.
surround
surround 230 vb.
outline 233 n.
enclose 235 vb.
enclosure 235 n.
close 264 vb.
besiege 712 vb.
surroundings
locality 187 n.
surroundings
230 n.
**surround-sound
system**
sound 398 n.
surtax
tax 809 n.
surveillance
inspection 438 n.
surveillance 457 n.
survey
inspection 438 n.
scan 438 vb.
enquire 459 vb.
enquiry 459 n.
measure 465 vb.
estimate 480 n.
represent 551 vb.
dissertate 591 vb.
dissertation 591 n.
compendium
592 n.
surveyor
enquirer 459 n.
estimator 480 n.
survivability
strength 162 n.
toughness 329 n.
life 360 n.
courage 855 n.
survival
remainder 41 n.
durability 113 n.
life 360 n.
**survival of the
fittest**
biology 358 n.
contention 716 n.

survive
be left 41 vb.
continue 108 vb.
outlast 113 vb.
go on 146 vb.
support 218 vb.
live 360 vb.
persevere 600 vb.
be restored 656 vb.
escape 667 vb.
survivor
escaper 667 n.
susceptible
liable 180 adj.
sentient 374 adj.
impressible
819 adj.
sushi
fish food 301 n.
sus out
enquire 459 vb.
suspect
be uncertain
474 vb.
*be of the opinion
that* 485 vb.
doubt 486 vb.
not know 491 vb.
offender 904 n.
wrong 914 adj.
accused person
928 n.
suspend
nullify 2 vb.
discontinue 72 vb.
pause 145 vb.
hang 217 vb.
stop using 674 vb.
abrogate 752 vb.
depose 752 vb.
prohibit 757 vb.
make illegal
954 vb.
punish 963 vb.
suspended
powerless 161 adj.
inert 175 adj.
hanging 217 adj.
nonactive 677 adj.
inactive 679 adj.
illegal 954 adj.
**suspended
animation**
insensibility 375 n.
suspender
fastening 47 n.
hanger 217 n.
legwear 228 n.
suspense
dubiety 474 n.
expectation 507 n.
suspension
exclusion 57 n.
delay 136 n.

lull 145 n.
pendency 217 n.
softness 327 n.
elasticity 328 n.
solution 337 n.
tempo 410 n.
nonuse 674 n.
inaction 677 n.
inactivity 679 n.
abrogation 752 n.
prohibition 757 n.
penalty 963 n.
suspicion
small quantity
33 n.
tincture 43 n.
doubt 486 n.
knowledge 490 n.
conjecture 512 n.
hint 524 n.
suspicious
uncertain 474 adj.
nervous 854 adj.
cautious 858 adj.
jealous 911 adj.
dishonest 930 adj.
sustain
continue 108 vb.
stay 144 vb.
sustain 146 vb.
strengthen 162 vb.
support 218 vb.
feed 301 vb.
corroborate 466 vb.
preserve 666 vb.
aid 703 vb.
sustenance
food 301 n.
provisions 301 n.
suttee
suicide 362 n.
burning 381 n.
oblation 981 n.
suture
joint 45 n.
tie 45 vb.
svelte
narrow 206 adj.
shapely 841 adj.
swab
dry 342 vb.
dryer 342 n.
clean 648 vb.
cleaning utensil
648 n.
surgical dressing
658 n.
**swaddling
clothes**
clothing 228 n.
swag
hang 217 vb.
descend 309 vb.
booty 790 n.

swagger
gait 265 n.
be proud 871 vb.
ostentation 875 n.
boast 877 vb.
boasting 877 n.
be insolent 878 vb.
swain
male 372 n.
country-dweller
869 n.
lover 887 n.
swallow
absorb 299 vb.
draught 301 n.
eat 301 vb.
mouthful 301 n.
bird 365 n.
believe 485 vb.
be credulous
487 vb.
be patient 823 vb.
**swallow one's
words**
stammer 580 vb.
swamp
fill 54 vb.
be many 104 vb.
destroy 165 vb.
drench 341 vb.
marsh 347 n.
swampy
marshy 347 adj.
swan
bird 365 n.
white thing 427 n.
a beauty 841 n.
swank
be affected 850 vb.
be proud 871 vb.
pride 871 n.
proud person
871 n.
airs 873 n.
be vain 873 vb.
vanity 873 n.
be ostentatious
875 vb.
ostentation 875 n.
boast 877 vb.
boasting 877 n.
be insolent 878 vb.
swanky
fashionable
848 adj.
proud 871 adj.
ostentatious
875 adj.
swansong
end 69 n.
decease 361 n.
attempt 671 n.
completion 725 n.
lament 836 n.

take things easy
keep calm 823 vb.
take time off or out
repose 683 vb.
take to
habituate 610 vb.
desire 859 vb.
befriend 880 vb.
be in love 887 vb.
take to flight
run away 620 vb.
be defeated 728 vb.
fear 854 vb.
take to heart
feel 818 vb.
be discontented 829 vb.
be dejected 834 vb.
resent 891 vb.
take to one's heels
run away 620 vb.
take to pieces
sunder 46 vb.
decompose 51 vb.
make useless 641 adj.
take to task
reprove 924 vb.
take to the cleaners
fleece 786 vb.
take umbrage
be hostile 881 vb.
resent 891 vb.
take up
shorten 204 vb.
elevate 310 vb.
study 536 vb.
be resolute 599 vb.
be wont 610 vb.
busy oneself 622 vb.
undertake 672 vb.
avail oneself of 673 vb.
receive 782 vb.
take 786 vb.
befriend 880 vb.
take up one's cross
suffer 825 vb.
take upon oneself
undertake 672 vb.
take up the challenge
contend 716 vb.
take up the cudgels for
patronize 703 vb.
defend 713 vb.

taking
taking 786 n.
anger 891 n.
takings
earnings 771 n.
receiving 782 n.
taking 786 n.
receipt 807 n.
talc
powder 332 n.
talcum powder
powder 332 n.
cosmetic 843 n.
tale
fable 543 n.
narrative 590 n.
talebearer
informer 524 n.
talent
tendency 179 n.
intelligence 498 n.
aptitude 694 n.
coinage 797 n.
talented
intelligent 498 adj.
gifted 694 adj.
talisman
talisman 983 n.
talk
cry 408 n.
empty talk 515 n.
inform 524 vb.
confess 526 vb.
divulge 526 vb.
rumour 529 n.
broadcast 531 n.
lecture 534 n.
language 557 n.
oration 579 n.
speak 579 vb.
speech 579 n.
be loquacious 581 vb.
allocution 583 n.
chat 584 n.
interlocution 584 n.
talkative
speaking 579 adj.
loquacious 581 adj.
talk behind one's back
defame 926 vb.
talk down
be loquacious 581 vb.
talkdown
aeronautics 271 n.
talkie
film 445 n.
talking head
broadcaster 531 n.

broadcasting 531 n.
talking-to
reprimand 924 n.
talk into
induce 612 vb.
talk it over
confer 584 vb.
talk out of
dissuade 613 vb.
talk round
induce 612 vb.
talks
conference 584 n.
talk shop
be loquacious 581 vb.
talk through one's hat
be absurd 497 vb.
be foolish 499 vb.
talk to oneself
orate 579 vb.
talk turkey
be concise 569 vb.
speak plainly 573 vb.
tall
great 32 adj.
tall 209 adj.
tallboy
cabinet 194 n.
tall order
undertaking 672 n.
hard task 700 n.
tallow
fat 357 n.
tall story
news 529 n.
fable 543 n.
exaggeration 546 n.
tally
accord 24 vb.
numerical result 85 n.
numeration 86 n.
list 87 n.
record 548 n.
credit 802 n.
debt 803 n.
accounts 808 n.
tally-ho
cry 408 n.
chase 619 n.
Talmud
scripture 975 n.
talon
foot 214 n.
sharp point 256 n.
finger 378 n.
pincers 778 n.
tambourine
drum 414 n.

tame
moderate 177 vb.
break in 369 vb.
train 534 vb.
habituate 610 vb.
habituated 610 adj.
oppress 735 vb.
obedient 739 adj.
subjugate 745 vb.
servile 879 adj.
tameness
obedience 739 n.
tammy
headgear 228 n.
tamp
impel 279 vb.
tamp down
close 264 vb.
tamper
derange 63 vb.
ram 279 n.
impair 655 vb.
meddle 678 vb.
tamper with
mix 43 vb.
modify 143 vb.
be false 541 vb.
tampon
stopper 264 n.
surgical dressing 658 n.
tan
be hot 379 vb.
burning 381 n.
colour 425 vb.
brown 430 adj.
brown 430 vb.
spank 963 vb.
tandem
bicycle 274 n.
cooperation 706 n.
tandoori
dish 301 n.
tang
taste 386 n.
pungency 388 n.
odour 394 n.
tangent
ratio 85 n.
contiguity 202 n.
straightness 249 n.
convergence 293 n.
tangential
convergent 293 adj.
tangerine
fruit and vegetables 301 n.
orange 432 n.
tangible
real 1 adj.
substantial 3 adj.
material 319 adj.
tactual 378 adj.

visible 443 adj.
true 494 adj.
tangle
complexity 61 n.
bedevil 63 vb.
roughen 259 vb.
tango
dance 837 n.
dance 837 vb.
tangy
tasty 386 adj.
pungent 388 adj.
tank
vat 194 n.
war chariot 274 n.
storage 632 n.
cavalry 722 n.
tankard
cup 194 n.
tanker
lorry 274 n.
merchant ship 275 n.
tanned
blackish 428 adj.
brown 430 adj.
tanner
coinage 797 n.
tannoy
hearing aid 415 n.
tantalize
tempt 612 vb.
tantamount
equivalent 28 adj.
semantic 514 adj.
tantra
non-Biblical scripture 975 n.
tantrum
anger 891 n.
tap
stopper 264 n.
impulse 279 n.
knock 279 n.
strike 279 n.
outlet 298 n.
empty 300 vb.
extract 304 vb.
water 339 n.
conduit 351 n.
touch 378 n.
touch 378 vb.
bang 402 n.
crackle 402 vb.
roll 403 vb.
play music 413 vb.
hear 415 vb.
store 632 n.
acquire 771 vb.
take 786 vb.
tap dancing
dancing 837 n.
tape
cable 47 n.

team
band 74 n.
group 74 n.
personnel 686 n.
party 708 n.

team spirit
cooperation 706 n.
concord 710 n.
fellowship 882 n.

team up
cooperate 706 vb.

team up with
combine 50 vb.
join a party
708 vb.

tea party
social gathering
882 n.

tea planter
farmer 370 n.

teapot
pot 194 n.

tear
disunion 46 n.
rend 46 vb.
See **sunder**
force 176 vb.
gap 201 n.
groove 262 vb.
move fast 277 vb.
give pain 377 vb.
ill-treat 645 vb.
wound 655 vb.
hurt 827 vb.
lamentation 836 n.

tear down
demolish 165 vb.

teardrop
moisture 341 n.
lamentation 836 n.

tearful
unhappy
825 adj.
melancholic
834 adj.
lamenting 836 adj.

tear gas
poison 659 n.

tearing hurry
haste 680 n.

tear into
attack 712 vb.

tear-jerking
distressing 827 adj.
lamenting 836 adj.

tear off
uncover 229 vb.
move fast 277 vb.
hasten 680 vb.

**tear oneself
away**
depart 296 vb.
be unwilling
598 vb.

tear one's hair
gesticulate 547 vb.
lament 836 vb.

tearoom
café 192 n.

tear out
extract 304 vb.

tears
water 339 n.
moisture 341 n.
lamentation 836 n.

tear strips off
reprove 924 vb.

tear to bits
demolish 165 vb.

tear up
demolish 165 vb.
destroy 165 vb.
abrogate 752 vb.

tease
tempt 612 vb.
excite 821 vb.
torment 827 vb.
ridicule 851 vb.
enrage 891 vb.
be malevolent
898 vb.

teaser
example 83 n.
priority 119 n.
advertisement
528 n.
difficulty 700 n.
worry 825 n.
humorist 839 n.

tea service
cup 194 n.

tea set
cup 194 n.

teashop
café 192 n.

teasing
exciting 821 adj.
ridicule 851 n.

teaspoon
ladle 194 n.

teat
bosom 253 n.

tea towel
cleaning cloth
648 n.

technicality
means of escape
667 n.

technician
machinist 630 n.
expert 696 n.

**Technicolor
(tdmk)**
colour 425 n.
film 445 n.

technique
painting 553 n.
way 624 n.

means 629 n.
skill 694 n.

techno
music 412 n.

technology
physics 319 n.
science 490 n.
business 622 n.
means 629 n.

technospeak
neology 560 n.
slang 560 adj.

Ted
youngster 132 n.

teddy
underwear 228 n.

teddy bear
image 551 n.
plaything 837 n.

tedious
tedious 838 adj.
dull 840 adj.

tedium
tedium 838 n.

tee-hee
laugh 835 vb.
laughter 835 n.

teem
reproduce itself
167 vb.
be fruitful
171 vb.
abound 635 vb.

teem with
be many 104 vb.
superabound
637 vb.

teenage
young 130 adj.

teenager
youngster 132 n.

teens
over five 99 n.

teeny
small 33 adj.
dwarf 196 n.
little 196 adj.

tee shirt
shirt 228 n.

teeter
vary 152 vb.
be weak 163 vb.
move slowly
278 vb.
oscillate 317 vb.
be agitated 318 vb.
be uncertain
474 vb.
be irresolute
601 vb.

**teeter on the
edge**
be in danger
661 vb.

teeth
vigorousness 174 n.
white thing 427 n.
weapon 723 n.
pincers 778 n.

**teething
troubles**
beginning 68 n.
learning 536 n.
difficulty 700 n.
hitch 702 n.

teetotal
temperate 942 adj.
sober 948 adj.

tee up
make ready
669 vb.

tegument
skin 226 n.

**Teletubbies
(tdmk)**
plaything 837 n.

telecast
communicate
524 vb.
publication 528 n.
publish 528 vb.
broadcast 531 n.

**telecommuni-
cation**
telecommuni-
cation 531 n.

telegram
information 524 n.
message 529 n.
telecommunication
531 n.

telegraph
velocity 277 n.
communicate
524 vb.
signal 547 n.

telegraphese
neology 560 n.
conciseness 569 n.

telegraphic
concise 569 adj.

telegraphy
telecommunication
531 n.

telekinesis
spiritualism 984 n.

telemedicine
medicular 658 n.

telemessage
information 524 n.
message 529 n.
telecommunication
531 n.

tele-ordering
purchase 792 n.

telepathic
intuitive 476 adj.
psychical 984 n.

telepathy
sense 374 n.
thought 449 n.
intuition 476 n.
psychics 984 n.

telephone
sound 398 n.
hearing aid 415 n.
communicate
524 vb.
telecommunication
531 n.

**telephone
directory**
directory 87 n.
guidebook 524 n.

telephonist
telecommunication
531 n.

telephony
telecommunication
531 n.

telephotography
photography
551 n.

telephoto lens
camera 442 n.

teleprinter
telecommunication
531 n.
recording
instrument 549 n.

telescope
shorten 204 vb.
astronomy 321 n.
telescope 442 n.
be concise 569 vb.

telescopic
distant 199 adj.
astronomic
321 adj.
visible 443 adj.

teleshopping
purchase 792 vb.

teletext
computing 86 n.
broadcasting
531 n.

televise
show 522 vb.
communicate
524 vb.
publish 528 vb.

television
electronics 160 n.
spectacle 445 n.
publicity 528 n.
broadcasting
531 n.
amusement 837 n.

**television
channel**
broadcasting
531 n.

teleworker
worker 686 n.
telex
communicate
524 vb.
information 524 n.
telecommunication
531 n.
tell
number 86 vb.
inform 524 vb.
divulge 526 vb.
describe 590 vb.
command 737 vb.
accuse 928 vb.
tell against
tell against 467 vb.
teller
informant 524 n.
treasurer 798 n.
**tell its own
story**
evidence 466 vb.
be intelligible
516 vb.
be plain 522 vb.
tell lies
be false 541 vb.
be dishonest
930 vb.
tell off
reprove 924 vb.
punish 963 vb.
tell on
inform 524 vb.
divulge 526 vb.
accuse 928 vb.
telltale
witness 466 n.
informer 524 n.
tell tales
inform 524 vb.
tell-tale sign
disclosure 526 n.
indication 547 n.
**tell that to the
marines**
God forbid 489 int.
tell upon
influence 178 vb.
tellurian
native 191 adj.
native 191 n.
telly
broadcasting
531 n.
temerity
rashness 857 n.
temp
deputy 755 n.
temper
temperament 5 n.
state 7 n.
mix 43 vb.

strengthen 162 vb.
moderate 177 vb.
harden 326 vb.
qualify 468 vb.
mature 669 vb.
affections 817 n.
excitation 821 n.
excitable state
822 n.
relieve 831 vb.
anger 891 n.
be temperate
942 vb.
tempera
art style 553 n.
temperament
temperament 5 n.
moral sensibility
819 n.
irascibility 892 n.
sullenness 893 n.
temperamental
nonuniform 17 adj.
capricious 604 adj.
excitable 822 adj.
irascible 892 adj.
sullen 893 adj.
temperance
virtue 933 n.
virtues 933 n.
temperance 942 n.
temperate
warm 379 adj.
temperate
942 adj.
temperature
illness 651 n.
tempest
storm 176 n.
velocity 277 n.
commotion 318 n.
excitable state
822 n.
tempestuous
disorderly 61 adj.
violent 176 adj.
speedy 277 adj.
windy 352 adj.
excitable 822 adj.
temple
head 213 n.
refuge 662 n.
honours 866 n.
church 990 n.
temple 990 n.
tempo
tendency 179 n.
motion 265 n.
velocity 277 n.
tempo 410 n.
temporal
continuing
108 adj.
transient 114 adj.

temporary
circumstantial
8 adj.
inferior 35 adj.
ephemeral 114 adj.
substituted
150 adj.
**temporary
measure**
substitute 150 n.
temporize
put off 136 vb.
tempt
cause 156 vb.
tempt 612 vb.
temptation
attraction 291 n.
inducement 612 n.
difficulty 700 n.
request 761 n.
desired object
859 n.
liking 859 n.
tempting
tasty 386 adj.
savoury 390 adj.
tempting offer
incentive 612 n.
reward 962 n.
**tempt
providence or
fate**
face danger
661 vb.
be rash 857 vb.
be insolent 878 vb.
ten
over five 99 n.
tenable
rational 475 adj.
credible 485 adj.
invulnerable
660 adj.
tenacious
cohesive 48 adj.
tough 329 adj.
resolute 599 adj.
obstinate 602 adj.
retentive 778 adj.
tenacity
coherence 48 n.
toughness 329 n.
resolution 599 n.
perseverance 600 n.
obstinacy 602 n.
retention 778 n.
courage 855 n.
tenancy
time 108 n.
possession 773 n.
nonownership
774 n.
tenant
resident 191 n.

dwell 192 vb.
possessor 776 n.
**Ten Command-
ments**
over five 99 n.
fixture 153 n.
precept 693 n.
code of duty 917 n.
law 953 n.
revelation 975 n.
tend
tend 179 vb.
look after 457 vb.
doctor 658 vb.
serve 742 vb.
tendency
tendency 179 n.
tender
locomotive 274 n.
boat 275 n.
ship 275 n.
follower 284 n.
soft 327 adj.
sentient 374 adj.
painful 377 adj.
soft-hued
425 adj.
lenient 736 adj.
offer 759 n.
offer 759 vb.
sensitive 819 adj.
paining 827 adj.
honour 866 vb.
loving 887 adj.
benevolent
897 adj.
pitying 905 adj.
tender age
nonage 130 n.
youth 130 n.
tenderfoot
intruder 59 n.
beginner 538 n.
tender-hearted
feeling 818 adj.
impressible
819 adj.
pitying 905 adj.
tenderize
soften 327 vb.
tender mercies
severity 735 n.
mercy 905 n.
tenderness
weakness 163 n.
softness 327 n.
sensibility 374 n.
pain 377 n.
leniency 736 n.
moral sensibility
819 n.
painfulness 827 n.
love 887 n.
benevolence 897 n.

**tender one's
resignation**
resign 753 vb.
tending
possible 469 adj.
tendon
ligature 47 n.
tendril
ligature 47 n.
branch 53 n.
filament 208 n.
coil 251 n.
foliage 366 n.
pincers 778 n.
tenements
flat 192 n.
housing 192 n.
tenet
precept 693 n.
theology 973 n.
tenets
creed 485 n.
tenner
over five 99 n.
funds 797 n.
tennis
ball game 837 n.
tennis ball
missile 287 n.
tennis court
arena 724 n.
pleasure ground
837 n.
tennis elbow
rheumatism 651 n.
tennis-player
player 837 n.
tenon
projection 254 n.
tenor
degree 27 n.
tendency 179 n.
direction 281 n.
stridor 407 n.
vocalist 413 n.
meaning 514 n.
tenor sax
flute 414 n.
tense
tied 45 adj.
time 108 n.
rigid 326 adj.
grammar 564 n.
feeling 818 adj.
fervent 818 adj.
excited 821 adj.
excitable 822 adj.
nervous 854 adj.
tensile
elastic 328 adj.
tension
quantity 26 n.
energy 160 n.
dissension 709 n.

excitation 821 n.
worry 825 n.
enmity 881 n.
tent
dwell 192 vb.
dwelling 192 n.
pavilion 192 n.
small house 192 n.
canopy 226 n.
tentacle
feeler 378 n.
pincers 778 n.
tentative
slow 278 adj.
enquiring 459 adj.
experimental
461 adj.
clumsy 695 adj.
cautious 858 adj.
tenth
multifid 100 adj.
ten to one
probably 471 adv.
tenuous
flimsy 163 adj.
rare 325 adj.
tenure
time 108 n.
possession 773 n.
estate 777 n.
lands 777 n.
benefice 985 n.
church office
985 n.
tepee
dwelling 192 n.
canopy 226 n.
tepid
warm 379 adj.
tequila
alcoholic drink
301 n.
teratogen
poison 659 n.
teratoid
abnormal 84 adj.
unusual 84 adj.
teratology
deformity 246 n.
terce
church service
988 n.
tercentenary
triplication 94 n.
tercentennial
seasonal 141 adj.
tercet
verse form 593 n.
tergiversate
change one's mind
603 vb.
term
end 69 n.
serial place 73 n.

date 108 n.
time 108 n.
period 110 n.
limit 236 n.
word 559 n.
name 561 n.
name 561 vb.
termagant
violent creature
176 n.
terminal
ending 69 adj.
extremity 69 n.
stopping place
145 n.
distant 199 adj.
limit 236 n.
air travel 271 n.
goal 295 n.
deadly 362 adj.
unpromising
853 adj.
**terminal illness
or disease**
decease 361 n.
terminate
terminate 69 vb.
termination
end 69 n.
effect 157 n.
completion 725 n.
**terminological
inexactitude**
falsehood 541 n.
deception 542 n.
untruth 543 n.
terminology
nomenclature
561 n.
phrase 563 n.
terminus
extremity 69 n.
stopping place
145 n.
limit 236 n.
goal 295 n.
completion 725 n.
termite
insect 365 n.
terms
conditions 766 n.
**terms of
reference**
function 622 n.
mandate 751 n.
conditions 766 n.
tern
bird 365 n.
terotechnology
economy 814 n.
Terpsichorean
dramatic 594 adj.
terrace
housing 192 n.

horizontality
216 n.
terracotta
pottery 381 n.
terra firma
basis 218 n.
land 344 n.
terrain
space 183 n.
region 184 n.
land 344 n.
arena 724 n.
terra incognita
unknown thing
491 n.
secret 530 n.
terrapin
reptile 365 n.
terrarium
zoo 369 n.
terrestrial
native 191 adj.
native 191 n.
terrible
not nice 645 adj.
frightening
854 adj.
terribly
extremely 32 vb.
terrier
dog 365 n.
terrific
prodigious 32 adj.
excellent 644 adj.
terrify
frighten 854 vb.
terrine
bowl 194 n.
hors-d'oeuvres
301 n.
territorial
soldier 722 n.
territorial army
army 722 n.
**territorial
waters**
territory 184 n.
territory
territory 184 n.
land 344 n.
terror
violent creature
176 n.
fear 854 n.
intimidation
854 n.
ruffian 904 n.
respect 920 n.
bad person 938 n.
terrorist
violent creature
176 n.
murderer 362 n.
attacker 712 n.

revolter 738 n.
robber 789 n.
alarmist 854 n.
desperado 857 n.
evildoer 904 n.
bad person 938 n.
terrorize
oppress 735 vb.
frighten 854 vb.
terry towelling
textile 222 n.
terse
short 204 adj.
concise 569 adj.
tertiary
treble 94 adj.
**tertiary
education**
education 534 n.
tessellated
variegated 437 adj.
test
enquire 459 vb.
enquiry 459 n.
exam 459 n.
experiment 461 n.
experiment 461 vb.
diagnostic 658 n.
hard task 700 n.
testament
testimony 466 n.
testator
owner 776 n.
testatrix
owner 776 n.
test case
experiment 461 n.
litigation 959 n.
testicles
genitalia 167 n.
testify
testify 466 vb.
testimonial
credential 466 n.
reminder 505 n.
approbation 923 n.
testimony
testimony 466 n.
test match
contest 716 n.
test tube
vessel 194 n.
testing agent
461 n.
test-tube baby
propagation
167 n.
testy
discontented
829 adj.
irascible 892 adj.
tetanus
spasm 318 n.
infection 651 n.

tetchy
irascible 892 adj.
tête-à-tête
dual 90 adj.
near 200 adv.
chat 584 n.
interlocution
584 n.
advice 691 n.
social gathering
882 n.
tether
affix 45 vb.
tie 45 vb.
place 187 vb.
obstacle 702 n.
fetter 747 vb.
fetter 748 n.
Tethys
ocean 343 n.
classical deities
967 n.
tetrad
quaternity 96 n.
tetragon
quaternity 96 n.
angular figure
247 n.
tetrahedron
quaternity 96 n.
tetrameter
quaternity 96 n.
prosody 593 n.
tetrapod
quaternity 96 n.
tetrarchy
quaternity 96 n.
text
prototype 23 n.
part 53 n.
topic 452 n.
maxim 496 n.
meaning 514 n.
reading matter
589 n.
stage play 594 n.
textile
crossed 222 adj.
textile 222 n.
textural 331 adj.
textual
scriptural
975 adj.
orthodox 976 adj.
texture
weaving 222 n.
texture 331 n.
**textured
vegetable
protein**
meat 301 n.
thalassaemia
blood disease
651 n.

thank
thank 907 vb.
reward 962 vb.
thank goodness
thanks 907 int.
thank Heaven
thanks 907 int.
thankless
profitless 641 adj.
unpleasant
827 adj.
thankless task
hard task 700 n.
ingratitude 908 n.
**thank one's
lucky stars**
rejoice 835 vb.
be grateful
907 vb.
thanks
congratulation
886 n.
thanks 907 int.
thanks 907 n.
reward 962 n.
thanksgiving
rejoicing 835 n.
celebration 876 n.
thanks 907 n.
act of worship
981 n.
thanks to
hence 158 adv.
through 628 adv.
thank you
thanks 907 int.
thankyou
thanks 907 n.
thatch
coat 226 vb.
roof 226 n.
hair 259 n.
building material
631 n.
repair 656 vb.
that is
in plain words
520 adv.
that is to say
namely 80 adv.
thaumaturgy
sorcery 983 n.
thaw
come unstuck
49 vb.
soften 327 vb.
liquefaction 337 n.
liquefy 337 vb.
semiliquidity
354 n.
be hot 379 vb.
heat 381 vb.
thaw out
heat 381 vb.

theatre
region 184 n.
meeting place
192 n.
theatre 594 n.
arena 724 n.
*place of
amusement*
837 n.
theatre, the
drama 594 n.
theatregoer
spectator 441 n.
playgoer 594 n.
theatre of war
battle 718 n.
battleground
724 n.
theatrical
dramatic 594 adj.
affected 850 adj.
showy 875 adj.
theft
acquisition 771 n.
stealing 788 n.
theism
deism 973 n.
piety 979 n.
them
master 741 n.
enemy 881 n.
thematic
topical 452 adj.
theme
melody 410 n.
musical piece
412 n.
topic 452 n.
dissertation 591 n.
theme pub
tavern 192 n.
theme song
tune 412 n.
themselves
self 80 n.
thence
hence 158 adv.
theocracy
government 733 n.
the church 985 n.
theodolite
angular measure
247 n.
gauge 465 n.
theolatry
religion 973 n.
theologian
theologian 973 n.
theology
theology 973 n.
theophany
revelation 975 n.
theorem
topic 452 n.

axiom 496 n.
theoretical
mental 447 adj.
theorize
account for
158 vb.
meditate 449 vb.
suppose 512 vb.
theory
attribution 158 n.
idea 451 n.
opinion 485 n.
supposition 512 n.
theosophy
philosophy 449 n.
religion 973 n.
religious faith
973 n.
occultism 984 n.
therapeutic
remedial 658 adj.
therapeutics
medical art 658 n.
therapy 658 n.
therapy
therapy 658 n.
thereabouts
about 33 adv.
nearly 200 adv.
thereafter
subsequently
120 adv.
therefore
hence 158 adv.
thereupon
subsequently
120 adv.
therm
thermometry
379 n.
thermal
ascent 308 n.
thermal springs
heat 379 n.
**thermal
underwear**
underwear 228 n.
**thermo-
dynamics**
physics 319 n.
thermometry
379 n.
thermography
thermometry
379 n.
**thermo-
luminescence**
glow 417 n.
thermometer
thermometry
379 n.
meter 465 n.
thermonuclear
dynamic 160 adj.

**thermonuclear
flask (tdmk)**
pot 194 n.
preserver 666 n.
**thermonuclear
reaction**
nucleonics 160 n.
thermostat
thermometry
379 n.
thesaurus
word list 87 n.
dictionary 559 n.
reference book
589 n.
collection 632 n.
the sign of, be
indicate 547 vb.
thesis
topic 452 n.
argument 475 n.
supposition 512 n.
affirmation 532 n.
dissertation 591 n.
Thespian
actor 594 n.
dramatic
594 adj.
Thetis
sea nymph 343 n.
nymph 967 n.
they
group 74 n.
authority 733 n.
thick
great 32 adj.
middle 70 n.
multitudinous
104 adj.
thick 205 adj.
dense 324 adj.
dim 419 adj.
opaque 423 adj.
unintelligent
499 adj.
friendly 880 adj.
thick and fast
often 139 adv.
thick as thieves
friendly 880 adj.
**thick as two
short planks**
unintelligent
499 adj.
thicken
augment 36 vb.
grow 36 vb.
enlarge 197 vb.
be dense 324 vb.
thicken 354 vb.
thicket
bunch 74 n.
multitude 104 n.
wood 366 n.

thickness
quantity 26 n.
layer 207 n.
density 324 n.
semiliquidity
354 n.
opacity 423 n.
metrology 465 n.
**thick of the
action**
activity 678 n.
thick of things
middle 70 n.
activity 678 n.
**thick on the
ground**
multitudinous
104 adj.
frequent 139 adj.
thickset
stalwart 162 adj.
short 204 adj.
thick 205 adj.
thick-skinned
thick 205 adj.
unfeeling 375 adj.
thick-skinned
820 adj.
thief
thief 789 n.
bad person 938 n.
thieve
steal 788 vb.
thigh
leg 267 n.
thimbleful
finite quantity
26 n.
small quantity
33 n.
thin
insubstantial
4 adj.
small 33 adj.
incomplete 55 adj.
render few 105 vb.
weak 163 adj.
weaker 163 vb.
make smaller
198 vb.
lean 206 adj.
narrow 206 adj.
shallow 212 adj.
rare 325 adj.
rarefy 325 vb.
transparent
422 adj.
feeble 572 adj.
insufficient
636 adj.
thin air
insubstantial thing
4 n.
air 340 n.

toreador
killer 362 n.
combatant 722 n.
Tories
political party
708 n.
torment
give pain 377 vb.
pain 377 n.
bane 659 n.
suffering 825 n.
torment 827 vb.
tornado
turmoil 61 n.
storm 176 n.
vortex 315 n.
gale 352 n.
torpedo
suppress 165 vb.
fire at 712 vb.
bomb 723 n.
torpid
inert 175 adj.
inactive 679 adj.
inexcitable
823 adj.
torpor
inertness 175 n.
inactivity 679 n.
sluggishness
679 n.
torque
quantity 26 n.
loop 250 n.
torrent
great quantity
32 n.
outbreak 176 n.
velocity 277 n.
stream 350 n.
torrential
violent 176 adj.
torrid
hot 379 adj.
warm 379 adj.
torso
remainder 41 n.
chief part 52 n.
piece 53 n.
incompleteness
55 n.
image 551 n.
sculpture 554 n.
tortilla
cereals 301 n.
mouthful 301 n.
tortoise
slowcoach 278 n.
animal 365 n.
reptile 365 n.
tortoiseshell
covering 226 n.
variegated 437 adj.
variegation 437 n.

tortuous
convoluted
251 adj.
unclear 568 adj.
dishonest 930 adj.
torture
force 176 vb.
violence 176 n.
pain 377 n.
suffering 825 n.
be malevolent
898 vb.
cruel act 898 n.
corporal
punishment
963 n.
torture 963 vb.
to scale
relative 9 adj.
relatively 9 adv.
tosh
silly talk 515 n.
toss
small quantity
33 n.
derange 63 vb.
jumble 63 vb.
voyage 269 vb.
propel 287 vb.
propulsion 287 n.
oscillate 317 vb.
agitation 318 n.
be agitated 318 vb.
trifle 639 n.
toss and turn
be excited 821 vb.
toss aside
not respect 921 vb.
toss one's head
be proud 871 vb.
despise 922 vb.
toss up
elevate 310 vb.
gamble 618 vb.
toss-up
equal chance
159 n.
uncertainty 474 n.
tot
dwarf 196 n.
draught 301 n.
total
quantity 26 n.
consummate
32 adj.
add 38 vb.
addition 38 n.
all 52 n.
whole 52 adj.
complete 54 adj.
inclusive 78 adj.
numerical result
85 n.
number 86 vb.

totalitarianism
uniformity 16 n.
despotism 733 n.
brute force 735 n.
totality
whole 52 n.
completeness 54 n.
totalizator
counting
instrument 86 n.
totally
completely 54 adv.
tote
counting
instrument 86 n.
carry 273 vb.
gaming-house
618 n.
totem
badge 547 n.
See **indication**
deity 966 n.
idol 982 n.
totem pole
idol 982 n.
**to the four
winds**
widely 183 adv.
to the letter
truly 494 adv.
to flemax
extremely 32 adv.
to the point
relevant 9 adj.
apt 24 adj.
brief 114 adj.
rational 475 adj.
concise 569 adj.
to the purpose
apt 24 adj.
to the utmost
completely
54 adv.
totter
come unstuck
49 vb.
vary 152 vb.
be weak 163 vb.
walk 267 vb.
move slowly
278 vb.
oscillate 317 vb.
be agitated 318 vb.
deteriorate 655 vb.
tot up to
number 86 vb.
touch
be related 9 vb.
small quantity
33 n.
tincture 43 n.
derange 63 vb.
be situated 186 vb.
limit 236 n.

have feeling
374 vb.
sense 374 n.
touch 378 n.
touch 378 vb.
gesture 547 n.
request 761 vb.
excite 821 vb.
children's games
837 n.
touch and go
unreliability
474 n.
unreliable 474 adj.
unsafe 661 adj.
touch down
fly 271 vb.
land 295 n.
descend 309 vb.
touchdown
aeronautics 271 n.
air travel 271 n.
arrival 295 n.
touched
crazy 503 adj.
impressed 818 adj.
impressible
819 adj.
touch for
borrow 785 vb.
touching
concerning 9 adv.
contiguity 202 n.
tactual 378 adj.
borrowing 785 n.
distressing
827 adj.
touchline
limit 236 n.
touch off
cause 156 vb.
kindle 381 vb.
excite 821 vb.
touch on
relate 9 vb.
notice 455 vb.
inform 524 vb.
touchpaper
burning 381 n.
lighter 385 n.
touchstone
prototype 23 n.
testing agent
461 n.
touch up
colour 425 vb.
exaggerate 546 vb.
paint 553 vb.
make better
654 vb.
repair 656 vb.
touchy
sensitive 819 adj.
irascible 892 adj.

touchy-feely
feeling 818 adj.
tough
violent creature
176 n.
tough 329 adj.
difficult 700 adj.
resisting 715 adj.
thick-skinned
820 adj.
courageous
855 adj.
ruffian 904 n.
toughen
strengthen 162 vb.
harden 326 vb.
toupee
hair 259 n.
hairdressing 843 n.
tour
time 108 n.
period 110 n.
land travel 267 n.
travel 267 n.
circuition 314 n.
tour de force
contrivance 623 n.
deed 676 n.
masterpiece 694 n.
success 727 n.
tourism
land travel 267 n.
tourist
traveller 268 n.
bicycle 274 n.
spectator 441 n.
tournament
contest 716 n.
duel 716 n.
pageant 875 n.
tourniquet
ligature 47 n.
stopper 264 n.
surgical dressing
658 n.
tousle
jumble 63 vb.
roughen 259 vb.
tout
publicizer 528 n.
gambler 618 n.
request 761 vb.
petitioner 763 n.
sell 793 vb.
seller 793 n.
commender 923 n.
flatterer 925 n.
tout à fait
truly 494 adv.
tow
fibre 208 n.
navigate 269 vb.
draw 288 vb.
traction 288 n.

tremble in the balance
be uncertain 474 vb.
be in danger 661 vb.

trembling
agitation 318 n.
See **spasm**
feeling 818 n.
nervous 854 adj.
nervousness 854 n.

tremendous
prodigious 32 adj.

tremolo
roll 403 n.
musical note 410 n.
adagio 412 adv.

tremor
outbreak 176 n.
oscillation 317 n.
agitation 318 n.
feeling 818 n.
nervousness 854 n.

tremulousness
agitation 318 n.

trenail
fastening 47 n.

trench
gap 201 n.
fence 235 n.
excavation 255 n.
furrow 262 n.
conduit 351 n.
cultivate 370 vb.
refuge 662 n.
defences 713 n.

trenchant
keen 174 adj.
assertive 532 adj.
concise 569 adj.
disapproving 924 adj.

trench coat
overcoat 228 n.

trencherman, woman
eater 301 n.
glutton 947 n.

trenches
battleground 724 n.

trend
modality 7 n.
similarity 18 n.
continuity 71 n.
tendency 179 n.
form 243 n.
direction 281 n.
fashion 848 n.
liking 859 n.

trend-setter
living model 23 n.

precursor 66 n.
beau monde 848 n.

trendy
modern 126 adj.
modernist 126 n.
fashionable 848 adj.

trepanning
surgery 658 n.

trepidation
agitation 318 n.
excitable state 822 n.
fear 854 n.
nervousness 854 n.

trespass
interfere 231 vb.
ingress 297 n.
intrude 297 vb.
encroach 306 vb.
disobey 738 vb.
appropriate 786 vb.
do wrong 914 adj.
wrong 914 n.
arrogation 916 n.
be wicked 934 vb.
vice 934 n.
be guilty 936 vb.
guilty act 936 n.
lawbreaking 954 n.

trespasser
intruder 59 n.
offender 904 n.
usurper 916 n.

tresses
hair 259 n.

trestle
frame 218 n.

trews
trousers 228 n.

triad
three 93 n.
musical note 410 n.

triage
medical art 658 n.

trial
enquiry 459 n.
empiricism 461 n.
experiment 461 n.
experimental 461 adj.
preparation 669 n.
attempt 671 n.
difficulty 700 n.
contest 716 n.
suffering 825 n.
legal trial 959 n.
punishment 963 n.

trial and error
empiricism 461 n.

trial of strength
hard task 700 n.
contest 716 n.

trial run
enquiry 459 n.
experiment 461 n.
preparation 669 n.

trials
experiment 461 n.
preparation 669 n.
adversity 731 n.

trials and tribulations
painfulness 827 n.

triangle
three 93 n.
angular figure 247 n.
gong 414 n.

triangular
three 93 adj.

tribal
ethnic 11 adj.
national 371 adj.

tribe
family 11 n.
race 11 n.
group 74 n.
breed 77 n.
multitude 104 n.
genealogy 169 n.
native 191 n.
community 708 n.

tribesman
kinsman 11 n.

tribulation
difficulty 700 n.
suffering 825 n.
painfulness 827 n.

tribunal
tribunal 956 n.

tributary
inferior 35 adj.
stream 350 n.
subject 745 adj.

tribute
gift 781 n.
receiving 782 n.
pay 804 n.
payment 804 n.
tax 809 n.
thanks 907 n.
dueness 915 n.
praise 923 n.
reward 962 n.

trice
instant 116 n.

trichology
hairdressing 843 n.

trick
deceive 542 vb.
fool 542 vb.
trickery 542 n.

habit 610 n.
contrivance 623 n.
skill 694 n.
be cunning 698 vb.
stratagem 698 n.
revel 837 n.
perfidy 930 n.

trick cyclist
psychologist 447 n.

trickery
trickery 542 n.

trickle
small quantity 33 n.
fewness 105 n.
move slowly 278 vb.
be wet 341 vb.
flow 350 vb.

trick out
primp 843 vb.
decorate 844 vb.

tricks of the trade
trickery 542 n.
stratagem 698 n.

trickster
trickster 545 n.

tricky
difficult 700 adj.

tricolour
three 93 adj.
flag 547 n.

tricorn
three 93 adj.

tricycle
three 93 n.
bicycle 274 n.
plaything 837 n.

trident
three 93 n.

tried
certain 473 adj.
matured 669 adj.
expert 694 adj.
approved 923 adj.
trustworthy 929 adj.

tried and true
friendly 880 adj.

triennial
seasonal 141 adj.

triennium
three 93 n.

trifle
dessert 301 n.
be inattentive 456 vb.
trifle 639 n.
be inactive 679 vb.
caress 889 vb.

trifle with
not respect 921 vb.

hold cheap 922 vb.

trifling
inconsiderable 33 adj.
light-minded 456 adj.
negligence 458 n.
trivial 639 adj.
unimportant 639 adj.
contemptible 922 adj.

trifoliate
three 93 adj.

triform
three 93 adj.

trifurcate
trisect 95 vb.

trigger
handle 218 n.
tool 630 n.
firearm 723 n.

trigger-happy
murderous 362 adj.
defiant 711 adj.
excitable 822 adj.
rash 857 adj.
irascible 892 adj.

trigger off
initiate 68 vb.
cause 156 vb.

triglyceride
fat 357 n.

triglyph
ornamental art 844 n.

trigonometry
mathematics 86 n.
angular measure 247 n.
measurement 465 n.

trihedral
treble 94 adj.

trike
bicycle 274 n.

trilateral
three 93 adj.
treble 94 adj.
lateral 239 adj.

trilby
headgear 228 n.

trill
flow 350 vb.
roll 403 n.
roll 403 vb.
musical note 410 n.
sing 413 vb.
pronunciation 577 n.
voice 577 vb.

escaper 667 n.
undutiful 918 adj.
undutifulness
918 n.
truce
lull 145 n.
interval 201 n.
quiescence 266 n.
deliverance 668 n.
peace 717 n.
pacification 719 n.
truck
carrier 273 n.
carry 273 vb.
lorry 274 n.
pushcart 274 n.
train 274 n.
trudge
walk 267 vb.
move slowly
278 vb.
true
inimitable 21 adj.
straight 249 adj.
accurate 494 adj.
true 494 adj.
artless 699 adj.
patriotic 901 adj.
true blue
conformable
83 adj.
permanent
144 adj.
political party
708 n.
patriotic 901 adj.
trustworthy
929 adj.
true to life
lifelike 18 adj.
true 494 adj.
descriptive 590 adj.
truffle
fruit and vegetables
301 n.
trug
basket 194 n.
truism
truth 494 n.
axiom 496 n.
maxim 496 n.
lack of meaning
515 n.
truly
truly 494 adv.
trump
be superior 34 vb.
masterpiece 694 n.
overmaster 727 vb.
success 727 n.
good person 937 n.
trump card
advantage 34 n.
contrivance 623 n.

chief thing 638 n.
success 727 n.
trumped-up
spurious 542 adj.
untrue 543 adj.
trumpery
bauble 639 n.
trumpet
resound 404 vb.
shrill 407 vb.
ululate 409 vb.
play music 413 vb.
horn 414 n.
proclaim 528 vb.
publicizer 528 n.
call 547 n.
be ostentatious
875 vb.
boast 877 vb.
praise 923 vb.
trump up
fake 541 vb.
truncated
short 204 adj.
concise 569 adj.
truncheon
club 723 n.
badge of rule
743 n.
trundle
move 265 vb.
propel 287 vb.
rotate 315 vb.
trunk
remainder 41 n.
chief part 52 n.
piece 53 n.
incompleteness
55 n.
box 194 n.
support 218 n.
cylinder 252 n.
protuberance
254 n.
tree 366 n.
trunks
beachwear 228 n.
legwear 228 n.
truss
tie 45 vb.
bring together
74 vb.
bunch 74 n.
beam 218 n.
support 218 n.
support 218 vb.
trust
transference 272 n.
transport 272 n.
belief 485 n.
believe 485 vb.
expectation 507 n.
association 706 n.
corporation 708 n.

mandate 751 n.
hope 852 n.
hope 852 vb.
trustee
consignee 754 n.
recipient 782 n.
treasurer 798 n.
trustful
credulous 487 adj.
trust in
be certain 473 vb.
trustworthy
credible 485 adj.
trustworthy
929 adj.
trusty
credible 485 adj.
trustworthy
929 adj.
truth
truth 494 n.
maxim 496 n.
veracity 540 n.
artlessness 699 n.
divine attribute
965 n.
truthful
true 494 adj.
veracious 540 adj.
trustworthy
929 adj.
try
enquire 459 vb.
judge 480 vb.
be willing
597 vb.
persevere 600 vb.
attempt 671 n.
attempt 671 vb.
avail oneself of
673 vb.
do 676 vb.
exert oneself
682 vb.
torment 827 vb.
be tedious 838 vb.
trying
annoying 827 adj.
try it on
be tentative
461 vb.
deceive 542 vb.
behave 688 vb.
**try one's hand
at**
attempt 671 vb.
try out
experiment 461 vb.
trysting
social round 882 n.
tsarism
despotism 733 n.
tsetse fly
insect 365 n.

tub
vat 194 n.
vessel 194 n.
bulk 195 n.
ship 275 n.
water 339 n.
ablutions 648 n.
tuba
horn 414 n.
tubby
fleshy 195 adj.
thick 205 adj.
tube
electronics 160 n.
excavation 255 n.
tube 263 n.
tunnel 263 n.
railway 624 n.
tuber
plant 366 n.
tubercular
diseased 651 adj.
tuberculosis
infection 651 n.
respiratory disease
651 n.
tub-thumping
eloquent 579 adj.
oration 579 n.
oratory 579 n.
tuck
fold 261 n.
food 301 n.
tuck in
place 187 vb.
load 193 vb.
eat 301 vb.
tuck into
insert 303 vb.
tuck up
place 187 vb.
shorten 204 vb.
Tudor
architectural
192 adj.
tuft
bunch 74 n.
fewness 105 n.
hair 259 n.
tug
move 265 vb.
boat 275 n.
ship 275 n.
draw 288 vb.
traction 288 n.
attract 291 vb.
attraction 291 n.
extraction 304 n.
exertion 682 n.
work 682 vb.
tugboat
boat 275 n.
tug of love
opposition 704 n.

contest 716 n.
tug of war
traction 288 n.
opposition
704 n.
contest 716 n.
**tug one's
forelock**
greet 884 vb.
tuition
teaching 534 n.
tulle
textile 222 n.
tumble
unite with 45 vb.
jumble 63 vb.
descent 309 n.
tumble 309 vb.
tumbledown
flimsy 163 adj.
dilapidated
655 adj.
tumble-dry
dry 342 vb.
tumbler
athlete 162 n.
cup 194 n.
tumble to
discover 484 vb.
understand 516 vb.
tumbril
vehicle 274 n.
tumefaction
dilation 197 n.
tumescence
dilation 197 n.
convexity 253 n.
tumid
convex 253 adj.
tummy
stomach 194 n.
insides 224 n.
tumour
dilation 197 n.
swelling 253 n.
cancer 651 n.
tumult
turmoil 61 n.
commotion 318 n.
loudness 400 n.
discord 411 n.
activity 678 n.
revolt 738 n.
tumultuous
disorderly 61 adj.
violent 176 adj.
tumulus
earthwork 253 n.
tun
vat 194 n.
tuna
fish food 301 n.
tundra
plain 348 n.

turnpike
road 624 n.
**turn Queen's
evidence**
inform 524 vb.
confess 526 vb.
accuse 928 vb.
turn round
be inverted 221 vb.
turn round 282 vb.
circle 314 vb.
turnstile
barrier 235 n.
recording
instrument 549 n.
access 624 n.
obstacle 702 n.
treasury 799 n.
turntable
rotator 315 n.
gramophone 414 n.
turn tail
regress 286 vb.
run away 620 vb.
be cowardly
856 vb.
turn the air blue
cuss 899 vb.
**turn the clock
back**
revert 148 vb.
turn the corner
change 143 vb.
get better 654 vb.
be restored 656 vb.
**turn the other
cheek**
be patient 823 vb.
be humble 872 vb.
forgive 909 vb.
turn the scale
predominate 34 vb.
modify 143 vb.
cause 156 vb.
influence 178 vb.
prevail 178 vb.
dominate 733 vb.
**turn the
stomach**
be unpalatable
391 vb.
**turn the tables
on**
retaliate 714 vb.
accuse 928 vb.
turn to
be turned to
147 vb.
speak to 583 vb.
avail oneself of
673 vb.
turn topsy-turvy
bedevil 63 vb.
be inverted 221 vb.

invert 221 vb.
turn up
happen 154 vb.
chance 159 vb.
be present 189 vb.
shorten 204 vb.
fold 261 vb.
arrive 295 vb.
be visible 443 vb.
turnup
fold 261 n.
**turn up one's
nose**
be unwilling
598 vb.
reject 607 vb.
be fastidious
862 vb.
despise 922 vb.
**turn up one's
toes**
die 361 vb.
**turn upside
down**
bedevil 63 vb.
modify 143 vb.
turn up trumps
be successful
727 vb.
get rich 800 vb.
turpitude
disrepute 867 n.
improbity 930 n.
wickedness 934 n.
turquoise
blue 435 adj.
blueness 435 n.
gem 844 n.
turret
high structure
209 n.
fort 713 n.
turtle
reptile 365 n.
tusk
tooth 256 n.
tussle
contend 716 vb.
contention 716 n.
contest 716 n.
fight 716 n.
tussock
bunch 74 n.
tussore
fibre 208 n.
tutelage
teaching 534 n.
learning 536 n.
protection 660 n.
subjection 745 n.
tutor
educate 534 vb.
teach 534 vb.
teacher 537 n.

domestic 742 n.
keeper 749 n.
tutorial
educational
534 adj.
teaching 534 n.
tutoring
teaching 534 n.
tut-tut
deprecate 762 vb.
deprecation 762 n.
disapprobation
924 n.
disapprove 924 vb.
tutu
skirt 228 n.
tuxedo
formal dress 228 n.
jacket 228 n.
TV
broadcasting
531 n.
twaddle
absurdity 497 n.
silly talk 515 n.
twain
duality 90 n.
twang
sound 398 n.
resound 404 vb.
rasp 407 vb.
stridor 407 n.
play music 413 vb.
pronunciation
577 n.
speech defect
580 n.
tweak
draw 288 vb.
give pain 377 vb.
twee
affected 850 adj.
tweed
textile 222 n.
roughness 259 n.
**Tweedledum
and
Tweedledee**
duality 90 n.
tweeds
suit 228 n.
tweet
ululate 409 vb.
tweezers
tool 630 n.
pincers 778 n.
twelfth
multifid 100 adj.
Twelfth Night
holy day 988 n.
twelve
over five 99 n.
twelve noon
noon 128 n.

twelve o'clock
noon 128 n.
twelve tribes
over five 99 n.
twenty
twenty and over
99 n.
twenty-five
twenty and over
99 n.
**twenty
questions**
indoor game 837 n.
twerp
fool 501 n.
twice
double 91 adj.
twice removed
akin 11 adj.
twiddle
rotate 315 vb.
touch 378 vb.
**twiddle one's
thumbs**
not act 677 vb.
be inactive 679 vb.
twig
branch 53 n.
young plant 132 n.
foliage 366 n.
tree 366 n.
know 490 vb.
understand 516 vb.
twilight
evening 129 n.
light 417 n.
darkness 418 n.
dim 419 adj.
half-light 419 n.
deterioration
655 n.
twill
crossed 222 adj.
weave 222 vb.
twin
kinsman 11 n.
identity 13 n.
analogue 18 n.
liken 18 vb.
similar 18 adj.
be equal 28 vb.
compeer 28 n.
concomitant 89 n.
dual 90 adj.
double 91 adj.
double 91 vb.
contemporary
123 n.
synchronous
123 adj.
twine
tie 45 vb.
cable 47 n.
fibre 208 n.

twine 251 vb.
twine round
cohere 48 vb.
twinge
give pain 377 vb.
pang 377 n.
suffering 825 n.
twinkle
instant 116 n.
vary 152 vb.
agitation 318 n.
be agitated 318 vb.
flash 417 n.
shine 417 vb.
gesticulate 547 vb.
gesture 547 n.
laughter 835 n.
smile 835 vb.
twinkling
instant 116 n.
flash 417 n.
**twinkling of an
eye, the**
instant 116 n.
twins
duality 90 n.
twin set
jersey 228 n.
twirl
coil 251 n.
twine 251 vb.
rotate 315 vb.
rotation 315 n.
twist
tie 45 vb.
complexity 61 n.
derange 63 vb.
make conform
83 vb.
disable 161 vb.
force 176 vb.
bag 194 n.
fibre 208 n.
obliquity 220 n.
deform 244 vb.
distort 246 vb.
distortion 246 n.
coil 251 n.
convolution 251 n.
twine 251 vb.
be in motion
265 vb.
deviate 282 vb.
draw 288 vb.
circle 314 vb.
tobacco 388 n.
bias 481 vb.
eccentricity 503 n.
misinterpret
521 vb.
pervert 655 vb.
dance 837 n.
dance 837 vb.
make ugly 842 vb.

independent
744 adj.
uncommon
remarkable 32 adj.
infrequent 140 adj.
uncommonly
remarkably 32 vb.
uncommunicative
reticent 525 adj.
unsociable 883 adj.
uncompetitive
peaceful 717 adj.
uncomplaining
patient 823 adj.
content 828 adj.
approving 923 adj.
uncompleted
uncompleted
726 adj.
uncomplicated
simple 44 adj.
artless 699 adj.
easy 701 adj.
**uncompli-
mentary**
disrespectful
921 adj.
disapproving
924 adj.
**uncomprehend-
ing**
ignorant 491 adj.
uncompromising
resolute 599 adj.
obstinate 602 adj.
severe 735 adj.
unconcealed
manifest 522 adj.
shown 522 adj.
unconcerned
incurious 454 adj.
indifferent 860 adj.
unconditional
obligatory 917 adj.
unconfirmed
weak 163 adj.
heathenish
974 adj.
unconformity
nonconformity
84 n.
uncongenial
cheerless 834 adj.
unsociable 883 adj.
unconnected
unrelated 10 adj.
unconquerable
strong 162 adj.
unconquered
independent
744 adj.
**unconscientious-
ness**
improbity 930 n.

unconscionable
exorbitant 32 adj.
lasting 113 adj.
unconscious
impotent 161 adj.
insensible 375 adj.
ignorant 491 adj.
involuntary
596 adj.
inactive 679 adj.
sleepy 679 adj.
impassive 820 adj.
unconsciousness
helplessness 161 n.
insensibility 375 n.
ignorance 491 n.
sleep 679 n.
unconsecrated
heathenish
974 adj.
profane 980 adj.
unconsenting
unwilling 598 adj.
unconstitutional
unwarranted
916 adj.
illegal 954 adj.
uncontaminated
perfect 646 adj.
uncontested
undisputed
473 adj.
uncontrived
artless 699 adj.
uncontrollable
violent 176 adj.
frenzied 503 adj.
wilful 602 adj.
fervent 818 adj.
excited 821 adj.
uncontrolled
independent
744 adj.
intemperate
943 adj.
uncontroversial
undisputed
473 adj.
unconventional
nonuniform 17 adj.
unconformable
84 adj.
unwonted 611 adj.
independent
744 adj.
unconverted
impenitent
940 adj.
heathenish
974 adj.
unconvincing
improbable
472 adj.
feeble 572 adj.

uncooked
uncooked 670 adj.
uncooperative
unwilling 598 adj.
undutiful 918 adj.
uncork
uncover 229 vb.
open 263 vb.
liberate 746 vb.
uncorrected
inexact 495 adj.
uncorroborated
erroneous 495 adj.
uncorrupted
disinterested
931 adj.
innocent 935 adj.
uncounted
many 104 adj.
uncouple
disunite 46 vb.
uncouth
amorphous
244 adj.
clumsy 695 adj.
graceless 842 adj.
ill-bred 847 adj.
plebeian 869 adj.
discourteous
885 adj.
uncover
uncover 229 vb.
open 263 vb.
discover 484 vb.
show respect
920 vb.
uncritical
indiscriminating
464 adj.
approving 923 adj.
uncross (legs)
straighten 249 vb.
unction
lubrication 334 n.
unctuousness
357 n.
unguent 357 n.
warm feeling
818 n.
pietism 979 n.
piety 979 n.
unctuous
feeling 818 adj.
servile 879 adj.
flattering 925 adj.
uncultivated
unproductive
172 adj.
uninstructed
491 adj.
uncultured
uninstructed
491 adj.
ill-bred 847 adj.

barbaric 869 adj.
uncurl
straighten 249 vb.
evolve 316 vb.
uncustomary
unusual 84 adj.
uncut
intact 52 adj.
long 203 adj.
immature 670 adj.
uncut gem
gem 844 n.
undamaged
undamaged
646 adj.
undaughterly
undutiful 918 adj.
undaunted
resolute 599 adj.
undebatable
undisputed
473 adj.
undeceive
disclose 526 vb.
undecided
doubting 474 adj.
uncertain 474 adj.
irresolute 601 adj.
undecipherable
unintelligible
517 adj.
undeclared
tacit 523 adj.
undefended
vulnerable
661 adj.
undefiled
unmixed 44 adj.
innocent 935 adj.
pure 950 adj.
undefinable
uncertain 474 adj.
undefined
amorphous
244 adj.
shadowy 419 adj.
indiscriminate
464 adj.
uncertain 474 adj.
undemanding
easy 701 adj.
lax 734 adj.
lenient 736 adj.
undemocratic
authoritarian
735 adj.
insolent 878 adj.
**undemon-
strative**
impassive 820 adj.
undeniable
undisputed
473 adj.
creedal 485 adj.

undependable
unreliable 474 adj.
dishonest 930 adj.
under
low 210 adj.
under 210 adv.
underachieve
fall short 307 vb.
under-age
young 130 adj.
under arrest
imprisoned
747 adj.
captive 750 adj.
underbelly
insides 224 n.
undercapitalized
unprovided
636 adj.
undercarriage
frame 218 n.
support 218 n.
carrier 273 n.
aircraft 276 n.
undercharge
cheapen 812 vb.
underclothes
underwear 228 n.
undercoat
layer 207 n.
pigment 425 n.
under control
obedient 739 adj.
restrained 747 adj.
undercover
latent 523 adj.
concealed 525 adj.
**undercover
agent**
secret service
459 n.
informer 524 n.
undercurrent
current 350 n.
latency 523 n.
undercurrents
cause 156 n.
undercut
sell 793 vb.
cheapen 812 vb.
underdeveloped
incomplete 55 adj.
immature 670 adj.
underdog
inferior 35 n.
loser 728 n.
unlucky person
731 n.
underdone
culinary 301 adj.
unsavoury 391 adj.
uncooked 670 adj.
under duress
by force 740 adv.

unforgettable
remembered
505 adj.
notable 638 adj.
unforgivable
wrong 914 adj.
heinous 934 adj.
unforgiving
severe 735 adj.
malevolent
898 adj.
unformed
amorphous
244 adj.
immature 670 adj.
unforthcoming
impassive 820 adj.
unsociable 883 adj.
unfortified
unmixed 44 adj.
weak 163 adj.
unfortunate
inopportune
138 adj.
unfortunate
731 adj.
annoying 827 adj.
unfounded
unreal 2 adj.
insubstantial 4 adj.
illogical 477 adj.
erroneous 495 adj.
untrue 543 adj.
unfrequented
secluded 883 adj.
unfriendly
opposing 704 adj.
hostile 881 adj.
unsociable 883 adj.
unkind 898 adj.
unfrock
depose 752 vb.
deprive 786 vb.
disentitle 916 vb.
punish 963 vb.
perform ritual
988 vb.
unfruitful
unproductive
172 adj.
unfulfilled
  expectation
expectation 507 n.
unfunny
serious 834 adj.
unfurl
lengthen 203 vb.
straighten 249 vb.
evolve 316 vb.
manifest 522 vb.
disclose 526 vb.
unfurnished
unprovided
636 adj.

unequipped
670 adj.
unfussy
plain 573 adj.
ungainly
clumsy 695 adj.
graceless 842 adj.
ungarbled
veracious 540 adj.
ungarnished
uncooked 670 adj.
ungenerous
parsimonious
816 adj.
ungenial
cheerless 834 adj.
ungentlemanly
ill-bred 847 adj.
discourteous
885 adj.
dishonest 930 adj.
ungodly
wicked 934 adj.
irreligious 974 adj.
impious 980 adj.
ungovernable
violent 176 adj.
disobedient
738 adj.
lawless 954 adj.
ungraceful
inelegant 576 adj.
graceless 842 adj.
ungraciousness
conduct 688 n.
rudeness 885 n.
ungrateful
ungrateful 908 adj.
ungrounded
illogical 477 adj.
erroneous 495 adj.
untrue 543 adj.
ungrudging
willing 597 adj.
unguarded
neglected 458 adj.
negligent 458 adj.
vulnerable 661 adj.
unprepared
670 adj.
unguent
unguent 357 n.
ungulate
mammal 365 n.
unhand
not retain 779 vb.
unhappy
inopportune
138 adj.
inexpedient
643 adj.
unfortunate
731 adj.
unhappy 825 adj.

dejected 834 adj.
unharmed
safe 660 adj.
unharness
liberate 746 vb.
unhatched
immature 670 adj.
unhealthy
inexpedient
643 adj.
harmful 645 adj.
unhealthy 651 adj.
insalubrious
653 adj.
dangerous 661 adj.
unheard
unknown 491 adj.
inglorious 867 adj.
modest 874 adj.
unheated
cold 380 adj.
unheeded
neglected 458 adj.
unheeding
inattentive
456 adj.
unhelpful
inexpedient
643 adj.
unkind 643 adj.
unheralded
unexpected
508 adj.
unheroic
cowardly 856 adj.
inglorious
867 adj.
unhinge
derange 63 vb.
make mad 503 vb.
unhitch
disunite 46 vb.
unholy
heathenish
974 adj.
profane 980 adj.
unhook
disunite 46 vb.
unhopeful
dejected 834 adj.
hopeless 853 adj.
unhouse
displace 188 vb.
unhurried
tranquil 266 adj.
slow 278 adj.
leisurely 681 adj.
inexcitable
823 adj.
unhurt
undamaged
646 adj.
unhygienic
unclean 649 adj.

insalubrious
653 adj.
unicameral
one 88 adj.
unicellular
one 88 adj.
unicorn
rara avis 84 n.
animal 365 n.
heraldry 547 n.
unicycle
bicycle 274 n.
unidentified
unrelated 10 adj.
unknown 491 adj.
unification
union 45 n.
combination 50 n.
unity 88 n.
association 706 n.
unified
simple 44 adj.
combined 50 adj.
uniform
uniform 16 adj.
clothing 228 n.
uniform 228 n.
badge of rank
743 n.
uniformity
uniformity 16 n.
unify
identify 13 vb.
join 45 vb.
combine 50 vb.
unilateral
unrelated 10 adj.
one 88 adj.
lateral 239 adj.
independent
744 adj.
unimaginable
unusual 84 adj.
impossible 470 adj.
wonderful 864 adj.
unimaginative
imitative 20 adj.
indiscriminating
464 adj.
narrow-minded
481 adj.
impassive 820 adj.
thick-skinned
820 adj.
dull 840 adj.
unimagined
unborn 2 adj.
unimpaired
intact 52 adj.
unimpeachable
undisputed
473 adj.
just 913 adj.
due 915 adj.

guiltless 935 adj.
unimportant
unimportant
639 adj.
unimposing
modest 874 adj.
unimpressed
indifferent 860 adj.
disapproving
924 adj.
unimpressive
modest 874 adj.
uninfluenced
free 744 adj.
independent
744 adj.
uninformative
reticent 525 adj.
uninformed
uninstructed
491 adj.
unexpecting
508 adj.
uninhabitable
empty 190 adj.
uninhabited
empty 190 adj.
secluded 883 adj.
uninitiated
ignorant 491 adj.
unskilled 695 adj.
uninspired
feeble 572 adj.
plain 573 adj.
prosaic 593 adj.
apathetic 820 adj.
impassive 820 adj.
thick-skinned
820 adj.
tedious 838 adj.
uninspiring
feeble 572 adj.
dull 840 adj.
unintelligent
mindless 448 adj.
unintelligent
499 adj.
unintelligible
unintelligible
517 adj.
unintended
involuntary
596 adj.
unintentional
618 adj.
unintentional
unintentional
618 adj.
uninterested
incurious 454 adj.
inattentive
456 adj.
inactive 679 adj.
apathetic 820 adj.

user friendly
computerized
86 adj.

use up
disable 161 vb.
dispose of 673 vb.
use 673 vb.
expend 806 vb.

usher
accompany 89 vb.
retainer 742 n.
bridal party 894 n.

usher in
come before 64 vb.
initiate 68 vb.
precede 283 vb.
admit 299 vb.
predict 511 vb.
greet 884 vb.

usual
general 79 adj.
usual 610 adj.

usual suspects
practice 610 n.

usurer
lender 784 n.

usurp
encroach
306 vb.
take authority
733 vb.
appropriate
786 vb.
deprive 786 vb.

usurper
impostor 545 n.
taker 786 n.
usurper 916 n.

usury
gain 771 n.
lending 784 n.
interest 803 n.

utensil
tool 630 n.

uterus
genitalia 167 n.
insides 224 n.

utilitarian
useful 640 adj.
philanthropic
901 adj.
philanthropist
901 n.
ethical 917 adj.

utility
utility 640 n.

utilize
find useful 640 adj.
use 673 vb.

utmost
limit 236 n.

Utopia
fantasy 513 n.
aspiration 852 n.

utter
consummate
32 adj.
simple 44 adj.
divulge 526 vb.
publish 528 vb.
voice 577 vb.
speak 579 vb.

utterance
voice 577 n.
speech 579 n.

utterly
greatly 32 vb.
completely 54 adv.

uttermost
limit 236 n.

U-turn
change 143 n.
reversion 148 n.
curve 248 n.
return 286 n.
circuition 314 n.
change of mind
603 n.

uxorious
loving 887 adj.

V

vacancy
insubstantiality
4 n.
emptiness 190 n.
job 622 n.
nonownership
774 n

vacant
insubstantial 4 adj.
empty 190 adj.
unintelligent
499 adj.
free 744 adj.
unpossessed
774 adj.

vacate
go away 190 vb.
relinquish 621 vb.

vacation
absence 190 n.
leisure 681 n.
repose 683 n.
permit 756 n.

vaccinate
implant 303 vb.
doctor 658 vb.
safeguard 660 vb

vaccine
prophylactic 658 n.

vacillate
change 143 vb.
vary 152 vb.
be uncertain
474 vb.

be irresolute
601 vb.
be capricious
604 vb.

vacuous
insubstantial 4 adj.
empty 190 adj.
mindless 448 adj.

vacuum
nonexistence 2 n.
emptiness 190 n.
rarity 325 n.
clean 648 vb.

vacuum cleaner
cleaning utensil
648 n.

vacuum flask
pot 194 n.

vacuum sealed
invulnerable
660 adj.

vade mecum
guidebook 524 n.

vagabond
wanderer 268 n.
low fellow 869 n.

vagary
foolery 497 n.
ideality 513 n.
whim 604 n.

vagina
genitalia 167 n.
orifice 263 n.

vagrant
changeful 152 adj.
wanderer 268 n.
derelict 779 n.
poor person 801 n.

vague
insubstantial 4 adj.
general 79 adj.
amorphous
244 adj.
shadowy 419 adj.
indistinct 444 adj.
uncertain 474 adj.
reticent 525 adj.
unclear 568 adj.

vain
profitless 641 adj.
useless 641 adj.
unsuccessful
728 adj.
vain 873 adj.

vainglorious
proud 871 adj.
vain 873 adj.

valance
edging 234 n.
trimming 844 n.

vale
valley 255 n.

valediction
valediction 296 n.

valentine
correspondence
588 n.
loved one 887 n.
love token 889 n.
darling 890 n.

valet
clothier 228 n.
clean 648 vb.
minister to 703 vb.
domestic 742 n.
serve 742 vb.

valetudinarian
sick person 651 n.

Valhalla
mythic heaven
971 n.

valiant
courageous
855 adj.

valid
powerful 160 adj.
strong 162 adj.
genuine 494 adj.
useful 640 adj.

validate
stabilize 153 vb.
corroborate 466 vb.
testify 466 vb.
make legal 953 vb.

validity
authenticity 494 n.
legality 953 n.

valise
box 194 n.

Valium (tdmk)
moderator 177 n.
drug 658 n.

valkyrie
soldier 722 n.
mythical being
970 n.

valley
valley 255 n.

valour
courage 855 n.

valuable
valuable 644 adj.

valuables
estate 777 n.

valuation
degree 27 n.
measurement
465 n.
estimate 480 n.

value
degree 27 n.
equivalence 28 n.
appraise 465 vb.
estimate 480 vb.
importance 638 n.
utility 640 n.
goodness 644 n.
account 808 vb.

price 809 n.
price 809 vb.
tax 809 vb.
dearness 811 n.
have taste 846 vb.
honour 866 vb.
love 887 vb.
respect 920 vb.
approve 923 vb.

value-added tax
tax 809 n.

valueless
trivial 639 adj.
profitless 641 adj.

valuer
estimator 480 n.

valve
electronics 160 n.
stopper 264 n.
conduit 351 n.

vamoose
decamp 296 vb.
escape 667 vb.

vamp
play music 413 vb.
improvise 609 vb.
motivator 612 n.
a beauty 841 n.
lover 887 n.
loose woman
952 n.

vampire
taker 786 n.
demon 970 n.

van
beginning 68 n.
lorry 274 n.
preceding 283 n.

vandal
destroyer 168 n.
violent creature
176 n.
troublemaker
663 n.

vandalism
destruction 165 n.
violence 176 n.
waste 634 n.
inhumanity
898 n.

vandalize
waste 634 vb.
impair 655 vb.
make ugly 842 vb.
blemish 845 vb.

vane
weather 340 n.

vanguard
precursor 66 n.
front 237 n.
preceding 283 n.
armed force 722 n.

vanish
pass away 2 vb.

be ostentatious
875 vb.
ostentation 875 n.
venerable
great 32 adj.
olden 127 adj.
ageing 131 adj.
venerate
respect 920 vb.
worship 981 vb.
venereal
conjunctive 45 adj.
diseased 651 adj.
sensual 944 adj.
venereal disease
venereal disease
651 n.
venetian blind
shade 226 n.
curtain 421 n.
vengeance
revenge 910 n.
venial
guiltless 935 adj.
venial sin
vice 934 n.
guilty act 936 n.
venison
meat 301 n.
venogram
diagnostic 658 n.
venom
poison 659 n.
malevolence 898 n.
venomous
toxic 653 adj.
hostile 881 adj.
malevolent
898 adj.
disapproving
924 adj.
vent
orifice 263 n.
outlet 298 n.
air pipe 353 n.
divulge 526 vb.
means of escape
667 n.
ventilate
aerate 340 vb.
blow 352 vb.
divulge 526 vb.
publish 528 vb.
dissertate 591 vb.
purify 648 vb.
make sanitary
652 adj.
refresh 685 vb.
ventilation
ventilation 352 n.
publicity 528 n.
cleansing 648 n.
ventilator
air 340 n.

ventilation 352 n.
vent one's
  spleen
be angry 891 vb.
resent 891 vb.
ventricle
compartment
194 n.
ventriloquist
imitator 20 n.
entertainer 594 n.
venture
be tentative
461 vb.
gamble 618 vb.
gambling 618 n.
business 622 n.
danger 661 n.
attempt 671 n.
attempt 671 vb.
undertaking 672 n.
speculate 791 vb.
be courageous
855 vb.
venturesome
dangerous 661 adj.
enterprising
672 adj.
courageous
855 adj.
rash 857 adj.
venue
focus 76 n.
locality 187 n.
Venus
planet 321 n.
luminary 420 n.
a beauty 841 n.
mythic deity
966 n.
Olympian deity
967 n.
veracity
veracity 540 n.
verandah
lobby 194 n.
verb
part of speech
564 n.
verbal
testimony 466 n.
semantic 514 adj.
informative
524 adj.
verbal 559 adj.
grammatical
564 adj.
speaking 579 adj.
verbalize
form 243 vb.
phrase 563 vb.
voice 577 vb.
verballed, be
condemn 961 vb.

verbatim
accurate 494 adj.
true 494 adj.
truly 494 adv.
verbally 559 adv.
verbiage
empty talk 515 n.
word 559 n.
imperspicuity
568 n.
diffuseness 570 n.
verbose
verbal 559 adj.
diffuse 570 adj.
loquacious
581 adj.
verboten
prohibited 757 adj.
illegal 954 adj.
verdant
prolific 171 adj.
green 434 adj.
verdict
judgment 480 n.
legal trial 959 n.
verdigris
greenness 434 n.
verdure
foliage 366 n.
grass 366 n.
greenness 434 n.
verge
extremity 69 n.
tend 179 vb.
nearness 200 n.
edge 234 n.
limit 236 n.
road 624 n.
badge of rule
743 n.
verger
officer 741 n.
servant 742 n.
church officer
986 n.
verification
experiment 461 n.
evidence 466 n.
certainty 473 n.
demonstration
478 n.
assent 488 n.
title deed 767 n.
verify
corroborate 466 vb.
make certain
473 vb.
demonstrate
478 vb.
give security
767 vb.
verisimilitude
probability 471 n.
accuracy 494 n.

truth 494 n.
veracity 540 n.
verity
truth 494 n.
vermicelli
dish 301 n.
vermicular
animal 365 adj.
vermiform
snaky 251 adj.
vermifuge
antidote 658 n.
vermilion
red 431 adj.
red pigment 431 n.
vermin
insect 365 n.
dirt 649 n.
rabble 869 n.
cad 938 n.
vernacular
native 191 adj.
provincial 192 adj.
language 557 n.
linguistic 557 adj.
dialect 560 adj.
dialectal 560 adj.
plainness 573 n.
vernier
gauge 465 n.
verruca
swelling 253 n.
skin disease 651 n.
versatile
multiform 82 adj.
changeful 152 adj.
useful 640 adj.
skilful 694 adj.
verse
subdivision 53 n.
poetry 593 n.
verse form 593 n.
versed in
knowing 490 adj.
expert 694 adj.
versification
poem 593 n.
poetry 593 n.
See **prosody**
prosody 593 n.
version
sort 77 n.
speciality 80 n.
transformation
143 n.
translation 520 n.
description 590 n.
See **narrative**
verso
rear 238 n.
sinistrality 242 n.
edition 589 n.
versus
towards 281 adv.

in opposition
704 adv.
vertebrae
pillar 218 n.
centre 225 n.
vertebral
central 225 adj.
back 238 adj.
vertebral
  column
pillar 218 n.
vertebrate
animal 365 adj.
animal 365 n.
vertex
extremity 69 n.
vertex 213 n.
vertical
vertical 215 adj.
vertical takeoff
aeronautics 271 n.
vertigo
weakness 163 n.
illness 651 n.
verve
vigorousness
174 n.
vigour 571 n.
moral sensibility
819 n.
very
greatly 32 vb.
very moment,
  the
instant 116 n.
very one, the
identity 13 n.
very thing, the
fitness 24 n.
vesicle
sphere 252 n.
swelling 253 n.
vespers
evening 129 n.
church service
988 n.
vessel
vessel 194 n.
ship 275 n.
vest
jacket 228 n.
underwear 228 n.
make legal
953 vb.
vestal
pure 950 adj.
vested
due 915 adj.
vested in, be
belong 773 vb.
vested interest
influence 178 n.
master 741 n.
dueness 915 n.

vestibule
lobby 194 n.
access 624 n.
vestige
small quantity
33 n.
remainder 41 n.
trace 548 n.
vestigial
remaining 41 adj.
vestments
clothing 228 n.
uniform 228 n.
vestments 989 n.
vestry
council 692 n.
synod 985 n.
church interior
990 n.
vet
animal husbandry
369 n.
doctor 658 n.
veteran
olden 127 adj.
old man 133 n.
matured 669 adj.
expert 694 adj.
expert 696 n.
soldier 722 n.
veterinary
surgeon
animal husbandry
369 n.
doctor 658 n.
veto
restrain 747 vb.
restraint 747 n.
prohibit 757 vb.
prohibition 757 n.
vetting
protection 660 n.
vex
torment 827 vb.
enrage 891 vb.
vexation
difficulty 700 n.
sorrow 825 n.
annoyance
827 n.
anger 891 n.
vexed
unhappy 825 adj.
discontented
829 adj.
angry 891 adj.
vexed question
question 459 n.
enigma 530 n.
VHF
radiation 417 n.
via
towards 281 adv.
via 624 adv.

viable
alive 360 adj.
possible 469 adj.
viaduct
crossing 222 n.
bridge 624 n.
Viagra (tdmk)
drug 658 n.
stimulant 174 n.
vial
vessel 194 n.
viands
food 301 n.
vibes
gong 414 n.
feeling 818 n.
vibrant
vigorous 174 adj.
resonant 404 adj.
feeling 818 adj.
vibrate
vary 152 vb.
oscillate 317 vb.
be agitated 318 vb.
roll 403 vb.
resound 404 vb.
show feeling
818 vb.
vibrations
sound 398 n.
feeling 818 n.
vibrato
roll 403 n.
musical note
410 n.
adagio 412 adv.
vibrator
oscillation 317 n.
vicar
deputy 755 n.
church title 986 n.
pastor 986 n.
vicarage
house 192 n.
parsonage 986 n.
vicarious
substituted
150 adj.
vice
badness 645 n.
pincers 778 n.
wrong 914 n.
vice 934 n.
wickedness 934 n.
unchastity 951 n.
vice-captain
deputy 755 n.
vice-like
retentive 778 adj.
vice-president
deputy 755 n.
viceroy
governor 741 n.
deputy 755 n.

vice versa
correlatively 12 adv.
contrarily 14 adv.
inversely 221 adv.
against 240 adv.
vicinity
locality 187 n.
nearness 200 n.
surroundings
230 n.
vicious
furious 176 adj.
bad 645 adj.
malevolent
898 adj.
wrong 914 adj.
vicious 934 adj.
vicious circle
obstacle 702 n.
vicissitude
changeable thing
152 n.
adversity 731 n.
victim
corpse 363 n.
dupe 544 n.
chase 619 n.
unlucky person
731 n.
sufferer 825 n.
laughingstock
851 n.
accused person
928 n.
victimize
fool 542 vb.
ill-treat 645 vb.
oppress 735 vb.
be malevolent
898 vb.
punish 963 vb.
victor
victor 727 n.
Victorian
antiquated
127 adj.
architectural
192 adj.
prude 950 n.
prudish 950 adj.
victorious
superior 34 adj.
strong 162 adj.
successful 727 adj.
victory
victory 727 n.
victuals
food 301 n.
vicuna
fibre 208 n.
textile 222 n.
video
spectacle 445 n.
broadcasting 531 n.

record 548 vb.
amusement 837 n.
videocassette
broadcasting
531 n.
videocassette
recorder
broadcasting
531 n.
recording
instrument 549 n.
videorecorder
broadcasting
531 n.
video game
computing 86 n.
indoor game
837 n.
videotape
broadcasting
531 n.
record 548 vb.
videotape
recorder
recording
instrument 549 n.
view
inspection 438 n.
scan 438 vb.
see 438 vb.
view 438 n.
watch 441 vb.
appearance 445 n.
estimate 480 n.
opinion 485 n.
intention 617 n.
beauty 841 n.
viewdata
computing 86 n.
information
524 n.
viewer
spectator 441 n.
broadcasting
531 n.
viewfinder
telescope 442 n.
vie with
oppose 704 vb.
contend 716 vb.
viewpoint
view 438 n.
opinion 485 n.
vigil
precursor 66 n.
surveillance 457 n.
church service
988 n.
vigilance
attention 455 n.
carefulness 457 n.
surveillance 457 n.
sagacity 498 n.
restlessness 678 n.

vigilant
seeing 438 adj.
vigilant 457 adj.
vigilante
doorkeeper 264 n.
protector 660 n.
defender 713 n.
keeper 749 n.
vigils
prayers 981 n.
vignette
picture 553 n.
description 590 n.
acting 594 n.
vigorous
strong 162 adj.
vigorous 174 adj.
healthy 650 adj.
vigour
energy 160 n.
vitality 162 n.
vigorousness
174 n.
vigour 571 n.
resolution 599 n.
warm feeling 818n.
vile
bad 645 adj.
heinous 934 adj.
vilify
shame 867 vb.
criticize 924 vb.
defame 926 vb.
villa
house 192 n.
village
district 184 n.
housing 192 n.
village green
focus 76 n.
meeting place
192 n.
pleasure ground
837 n.
village idiot
country-dweller
869 n.
villager
dweller 191 n.
native 191 n.
villain
evildoer 904 n.
offender 904 n.
bad person 938 n.
villainous
bad 645 adj.
vicious 934 adj.
villainy
improbity 930 n.
wickedness 934 n.
villein
farmer 370 n.
slave 742 n.
commoner 869 n.

vim
vitality 162 n.
vigorousness
174 n.
vigour 571 n.
vinaigrette
sauce 389 n.
vinculum
bond 47 n.
vindicate
vindicate 927 vb.
vindictive
resentful 891 adj.
malevolent
898 adj.
punitive 963 adj.
vine
plant 366 n.
vinegar
sourness 393 n.
painfulness 827 n.
sullenness 893 n.
vinegary
sour 393 adj.
irascible 892 adj.
sullen 893 adj.
vineyard
farm 370 n.
vingt-et-un
card game 837 n.
viniculture
agriculture 370 n.
vino
wine 301 n.
vinous
intoxicating
949 adj.
vintage
date 108 n.
olden 127 adj.
product 164 n.
agriculture 370 n.
tasty 386 adj.
store 632 n.
excellent 644 adj.
goodness 644 n.
vintage car
automobile 274 n.
vinyl
floor-cover 226 n.
viol
viol 414 n.
violate
unite with 45 vb.
force 176 vb.
ill-treat 645 vb.
misuse 675 vb.
disobey 738 vb.
not observe
769 vb.
debauch 951 vb.
be impious 980 vb.
violation
misuse 675 n.

nonobservance
769 n.
undueness 916 n.
undutifulness
918 n.
rape 951 n.
impiety 980 n.
violent
great 32 adj.
violent 176 adj.
excited 821 adj.
angry 891 adj.
lawless 954 adj.
violet
purple 436 adj.
purpleness 436 n.
humility 872 n.
violin
viol 414 n.
VIP
person 371 n.
bigwig 638 n.
autocrat 741 n.
person of repute
866 n.
viper
reptile 365 n.
bane 659 n.
virago
female 373 n.
virgin
intact 52 adj.
new 126 adj.
youngster 132 n.
female 373 n.
unknown
491 adj.
unprepared
670 adj.
pure 950 adj.
virgin 950 n.
virginal
new 126 adj.
young 130 adj.
virtuous 933 adj.
pure 950 adj.
virginity
unproductiveness
172 n.
celibacy 895 n.
purity 950 n.
virile
grown-up 134 adj.
manly 162 adj.
vigorous 174 adj.
male 372 adj.
virility
adultness 134 n.
vitality 162 n.
vigorousness
174 n.
male 372 n.
virtually
almost 33 adv.

on the whole
52 adv.
virtual reality
computing 86 n.
virtue
essential part 5 n.
ability 160 n.
utility 640 n.
goodness 644 n.
virtue 933 n.
virtuosity
goodness 644 n.
skill 694 n.
good taste 846 n.
virtuoso
superior 34 n.
musician 413 n.
proficient person
696 n.
virtuous
virtuous 933 adj.
virulent
keen 174 adj.
hostile 881 adj.
resentful 891 adj.
virus
disease 651 n.
illness 651 n.
infection 651 n.
poison 659 n.
visa
credential 466 n.
assent 488 n.
permit 756 n.
visage
face 237 n.
feature 445 n.
vis-à-vis
concerning 9 adv.
against 240 adv.
opposite 240 adj.
viscera
insides 224 n.
viscid
tough 329 adj.
viscid 354 adj.
viscosity
fluidity 335 n.
viscidity 354 n.
viscount
person of rank
868 n.
viscountess
person of rank
868 n.
viscous
cohesive 48 adj.
blood 335 adj.
viscid 354 adj.
visible
visible 443 adj.
vision
insubstantial thing
4 n.

vision 438 n.
visual fallacy
440 n.
appearance 445 n.
spectacle 445 n.
foresight 510 n.
fantasy 513 n.
manifestation
522 n.
objective 617 n.
a beauty 841 n.
aspiration 852 n.
visionary
unreal 2 adj.
insubstantial 4 adj.
misjudging
481 adj.
imaginary 513 adj.
imaginative
513 adj.
visionary 513 n.
promising 852 adj.
philanthropic
901 adj.
worshipper 981 n.
visit
presence 189 n.
land travel 267 n.
travel 267 vb.
social round
882 n.
visit 882 vb.
do good 897 adj.
haunt 970 vb.
visitation
blight 659 n.
adversity 731 n.
severity 735 n.
suffering 825 n.
punishment 963 n.
visitor
resident 191 n.
traveller 268 n.
arrival 295 n.
incomer 297 n.
sociable person
882 n.
visor
shade 226 n.
screen 421 n.
disguise 527 n.
armour 713 n.
vista
open space 263 n.
view 438 n.
visual
seeing 438 adj.
appearing 445 adj.
visual aid
visibility 443 n.
image 551 n.
**visual display
unit**
computing 86 n.

visualize
see 438 vb.
imagine 513 vb.
**visually
challenged**
blind 439 adj.
vital
alive 360 adj.
necessary 596 adj.
required 627 adj.
important 638 adj.
lively 819 adj.
cheerful 833 adj.
vitality
vitality 162 n.
life 360 n.
vigour 571 n.
restlessness 678 n.
cheerfulness 833 n.
vitalize
vitalize 360 vb.
vitals
insides 224 n.
vital statistics
statistics 86 n.
beauty 841 n.
vitamins
dieting 301 n.
See **food
content**
food content 301 n.
viticulture
agriculture 370 n.
vitreous
hard 326 adj.
vitrify
harden 326 vb.
vitriol
burning 381 n.
poison 659 n.
vitriolic
paining 827 adj.
cursing 899 adj.
vituperate
curse 899 vb.
viva
exam 459 n.
vivacious
forceful 571 adj.
active 678 adj.
feeling 818 adj.
lively 819 adj.
cheerful 833 adj.
vivaciousness
moral sensibility
819 n.
vivacity
vigour 571 n.
restlessness 678 n.
moral sensibility
819 n.
cheerfulness 833 n.
vivarium
zoo 369 n.

wade
walk 267 vb.
swim 269 vb.
waders
footwear 228 n.
wadi
stream 350 n.
conduit 351 n.
wads
great quantity
32 n.
funds 797 n.
wealth 800 n.
wafer
adhesive 47 n.
strip 208 n.
cereals 301 n.
wafer-thin
narrow 206 adj.
waffle
cereals 301 n.
mean nothing
515 vb.
be equivocal
518 vb.
be diffuse 570 vb.
diffuseness
570 n.
be loquacious
581 vb.
chatter 581 vb.
waft
carry 273 vb.
be light 323 vb.
blow 352 vb.
breeze 352 n.
wag
brandish 317 vb.
fluctuation 317 n.
oscillate 317 vb.
agitate 318 vb.
be agitated 318 vb.
humorist 839 n.
wage
do 676 vb.
earnings 771 n.
reward 962 n.
wager
uncertainty 474 n.
gamble 618 vb.
gambling 681 n.
contend 716 vb.
contest 716 n.
wages
pay 804 n.
receipt 807 n.
reward 962 n.
waggish
witty 839 adj.
waggle
brandish 317 vb.
oscillate 317 vb.
agitate 318 vb.
be agitated 318 vb.

waggon
cart 274 n.
train 274 n.
wagtail
bird 365 n.
waif
wanderer 268 n.
derelict 779 n.
wail
cry 408 n.
cry 408 vb.
ululate 409 vb.
be discontented
829 vb.
lament 836 vb.
lamentation 836 n.
weep 836 vb.
wain
cart 274 n.
wainscotting
lining 227 n.
waistband
belt 228 n.
waistcoat
jacket 228 n.
waistline
centrality 225 n.
garment 228 n.
See **belt**
wait
continue 108 vb.
wait 136 vb.
go on 146 vb.
wait and see
wait 136 vb.
be tentative
461 vb.
be uncertain
474 vb.
not act 677 vb.
waiter
servant 742 n.
waiting
future 124 adj.
traffic control
305 n.
dubiety 474 n.
expectant 507 adj.
expectation
507 n.
waiting game
caution 858 n.
waiting list
list 87 n.
record 548 n.
waiting room
lobby 194 n.
wait on
result 157 vb.
follow 284 vb.
minister to 703 vb.
court 889 vb.
waitress
servant 742 n.

waits
choir 413 n.
waive
relinquish 621 vb.
not retain 779 vb.
waiver
resignation 753 n.
loss of right 916 n.
wake
adjunct 40 n.
retinue 67 n.
continuity 71 n.
effect 157 n.
rear 238 n.
water travel 269 vb.
follower 284 n.
eddy 350 n.
obsequies 364 n.
trace 548 n.
excite 821 vb.
lament 836 n.
condolence 905 n.
wakeful
attentive 455 adj.
active 678 adj.
wake up
have feeling
374 vb.
walk
park 192 n.
gait 265 n.
pedestrianism
267 n.
walk 267 vb.
path 624 n.
conduct 688 n.
haunt 970 vb.
walkabout
pedestrianism
267 n.
walker
pedestrian 268 n.
traveller 268 n.
walkie-talkie
hearing aid 415 n.
telecommunication
531 n.
walking
motion 265 n.
land travel 267 n.
pedestrianism
267 n.
walk it
win 727 vb.
Walkman
(tdmk)
gramophone 414 n.
walk off with
win 727 vb.
steal 788 vb.
walk of life
state 7 n.
vocation 622 n.
conduct 688 n.

duty 917 n.
walk out
cease 145 vb.
decamp 296 vb.
relinquish 621 vb.
resist 715 vb.
deprecate 762 vb.
fail in duty 918 vb.
walkout
stop 145 n.
strike 145 n.
departure 296 n.
egress 298 n.
dissent 489 n.
relinquishment
621 n.
walk out on
change one's mind
603 vb.
walk out with
accompany 89 vb.
court 889 vb.
walkover
easy thing 701 n.
victory 727 n.
wall
exclusion 57 n.
support 218 n.
partition 231 n.
barrier 235 n.
enclose 235 vb.
fence 235 n.
screen 421 n.
obstacle 702 n.
defences 713 n.
fortification 713 n.
wallaby
mammal 365 n.
wallet
case 194 n.
treasury 799 n.
wall-eyed
dim-sighted
440 adj.
wallflower
rejection 607 n.
wall in
cover 226 vb.
wallop
strike 279 vb.
spank 963 vb.
wallow
be agitated 318 vb.
be pleased 824 vb.
be intemperate
943 vb.
wallow in
enjoy 376 vb.
wallpaper
covering 226 n.
line 227 n.
lining 227 n.
wall-to-wall
floor-cover 226 n.

wall up
cover 226 vb.
enclose 235 vb.
kill 362 vb.
obstruct 702 vb.
imprison 747 vb.
wally
fool 501 n.
walnut
fruit and vegetables
301 n.
tree 366 n.
brownness 430 n.
walrus
mammal 365 n.
waltz
rotate 315 vb.
rotation 315 n.
musical piece
412 n.
dance 837 n.
dance 837 vb.
waltz away
with
win 727 vb.
waltztime
music 412 n.
wan
weakly 163 adj.
dim 419 adj.
colourless
426 adj.
feeble 572 adj.
wand
badge of rule
743 n.
magic instrument
983 n.
wander
be unrelated 10 vb.
wander 267 vb.
be foolish 499 vb.
be insane 503 vb.
be diffuse 570 vb.
wandering
irrelevant 10 adj.
unrelated 10 adj.
extraneous 59 adj.
unconformable
84 adj.
changeful 152 adj.
mistaken 495 adj.
folly 499 n.
foolish 499 adj.
crazy 503 adj.
frenzied 503 adj.
prolix 570 adj.
wane
decrease 37 n.
decrease 37 vb.
become small
198 vb.
be dim 419 vb.
deteriorate 655 vb.

wasp
insect 365 n.
bane 659 n.
waspish
irascible 892 adj.
wasp-waisted
narrow 206 adj.
wassail
festivity 837 n.
get drunk 949 vb.
wastage
waste 634 n.
rubbish 641 n.
loss 772 n.
waste
decrease 37 vb.
leavings 41 n.
desert 172 n.
unproductive
172 adj.
space 183 n.
emptiness 190 n.
plain 348 n.
waste 634 n.
waste 634 vb.
rubbish 641 n.
impair 655 vb.
impairment 655 n.
intemperance
943 n.
waste away
decompose 51 vb.
become small
198 vb.
wasteful
wasteful 634 adj.
profitless 641 adj.
prodigal 815 adj.
intemperate
943 adj.
wastelands
desert 172 n.
waste one's time
waste effort
641 adj.
wastepaper
rubbish 641 n.
wastepipe
drain 351 n.
waster
bad person 938 n.
wastrel
prodigal 815 n.
bad person 938 n.
watch
period 110 n.
timekeeper 117 n.
mariner 270 n.
look 438 n.
scan 438 vb.
watch 441 vb.
attention 455 n.
be attentive
455 vb.

invigilate 457 vb.
surveillance 457 n.
protection 660 n.
protector 660 n.
warner 664 n.
defend 713 vb.
defender 713 n.
keeper 749 n.
police 955 n.
watchdog
dog 365 n.
protector 660 n.
warner 664 n.
keeper 749 n.
watchful
attentive 455 adj.
vigilant 457 adj.
intelligent 498 adj.
active 678 adj.
observant 768 adj.
cautious 858 adj.
watchful eye
surveillance 457 n.
restlessness 678 n.
watchmaker
artisan 686 n.
watchman
spectator 441 n.
protector 660 n.
warner 664 n.
keeper 749 n.
watch one's step
be careful 457 vb.
be cautious 858 vb.
watch out for
scan 438 vb.
invigilate 457 vb.
expect 507 vb.
watch over
safeguard 660 vb.
watchword
maxim 496 n.
identification
547 n.
instrument 628 n.
water
cause 156 vb.
weak thing 163 n.
soft drink 301 n.
excrement 302 n.
element 319 n.
fluid 335 n.
water 339 n.
irrigate 341 vb.
cultivate 370 vb.
extinguisher 382 n.
transparency
422 n.
provide 633 vb.
cleanser 648 n.
**water at the
mouth**
exude 298 vb.
eat 301 vb.

be hungry 859 vb.
gluttonize 947 vb.
water closet
cleansing 648 n.
latrine 649 n.
watercolours
pigment 425 n.
watercourse
stream 350 n.
conduit 351 n.
watercress
fruit and vegetables
301 n.
water divining
discovery 484 n.
water down
mix 43 vb.
waterfall
waterfall 350 n.
water feature
lake 346 n.
stream 350 n.
garden 370 n.
waterfront
edge 234 n.
watergate
conduit 351 n.
waterhole
lake 346 n.
water lily
plant 366 n.
waterlogged
marshy 347 adj.
hindered 702 adj.
Waterloo
ruin 165 n.
defeat 728 n.
watermark
label 547 n.
pattern 844 n.
waterproof
strong 162 adj.
coat 226 vb.
overcoat 228 n.
dry 342 adj.
invulnerable
660 adj.
preserve 666 vb.
resisting 715 adj.
water rat
mammal 365 n.
watershed
serial place 73 n.
reversion 148 n.
event 154 n.
summit 213 n.
partition 231 n.
limit 236 n.
divergence 294 n.
water skiing
aquatics 269 n.
sport 837 n.
watersports
aquatics 269 n.

sport 837 n.
water table
layer 207 n.
horizontality
216 n.
watertight
dry 342 adj.
waterworks
excretion 302 n.
water 339 n.
watery
weak 163 adj.
watery 339. adj.
tasteless 387 adj.
feeble 572 adj.
insufficient
636 adj.
watt
electronics 160 n.
metrology 465 n.
wattle
network 222 n.
wattle and daub
building material
631 n.
wave
vary 152 vb.
be curved 248 vb.
crinkle 251 vb.
be in motion
265 vb.
elevate 310 vb.
brandish 317 vb.
oscillate 317 vb.
agitate 318 vb.
wave 350 n.
blow 352 vb.
gesticulate 547 vb.
gesture 547 n.
hairdressing 843 n.
primp 843 vb.
be ostentatious
875 vb.
boast 877 vb.
greet 884 vb.
threaten 900 vb.
waveband
radiation 417 n.
wavelength
long measure
203 n.
oscillation 317 n.
radiation 417 n.
wave lengths
broadcasting
531 n.
wave on
signal 547 vb.
waver
vary 152 vb.
decelerate 278 vb.
be uncertain
474 vb.
doubt 486 vb.

be irresolute
601 vb.
wave to
gesticulate 547 vb.
waving
gesture 547 n.
hairdressing 843 n.
wavy
curved 248 adj.
undulatory
251 adj.
wax
grow 36 vb.
be turned to
147 vb.
changeable thing
152 n.
expand 197 vb.
stripper 229 n.
smooth 258 vb.
smoothness 258 n.
hardness 326 n.
softness 327 n.
rub 333 vb.
lubricant 334 n.
lubricate 334 vb.
viscidity 354 n.
fat 357 n.
sculpture 554 n.
cleanser 648 n.
wax and wane
change 143 vb.
vary 152 vb.
waxen
fatty 357 adj.
whitish 427 adj.
waxing moon
moon 321 n.
wax lyrical
praise 923 vb.
waxwork
image 551 n.
sculpture 554 n.
waxy
soft 327 adj.
fatty 357 adj.
angry 891 adj.
way
modality 7 n.
degree 27 n.
room 183 n.
water travel 269 n.
direction 281 n.
progression 285 n.
way in 297 n.
habit 610 n.
way 624 n.
wayfarer
traveller 268 n.
way in
approach 289 n.
way in 297 n.
waylay
ambush 527 vb.

whipping
  knock 279 n.
  corporal
    punishment
    963 n.
whipping boy
  substitute 150 n.
  propitiation 941 n.
whip-round
  gift 781 n.
  payment 804 n.
whip up
  thicken 354 vb.
  excite 821 vb.
whirl
  rotate 315 vb.
  rotation 315 n.
  vortex 315 n.
  be agitated 318 vb.
  activity 678 n.
  haste 680 n.
  excitable state
    822 n.
  dance 837 n.
whirligig
  changeable thing
    152 n.
  rotator 315 n.
whirlpool
  coil 251 n.
  vortex 315 n.
  commotion 318 n.
  eddy 350 n.
  pitfall 663 n.
whirlpool bath
  vortex 315 n.
  eddy 350 n.
whirlwind
  turmoil 61 n.
  vortex 315 n.
  commotion 318 n.
  gale 352 n.
whirlybird
  aircraft 276 n.
whirr
  be agitated 318 vb.
  faintness 401 n.
  roll 403 n.
  roll 403 vb.
  resound 404 vb.
  ululate 409 vb.
whisk
  move fast 277 vb.
  cook 301 vb.
  rotate 315 vb.
  rotator 315 n.
  agitate 318 vb.
whisker
  filament 208 n.
  feeler 378 n.
whisky
  carriage 274 n.
  alcoholic drink
    301 n.

whisper
  small quantity
    33 n.
  faintness 401 n.
  sound faint
    401 vb.
  imply 523 vb.
  hint 524 n.
  hint 524 vb.
  rumour 529 n.
  voice 577 n.
  voice 577 vb.
  voicelessness
    578 n.
  speak 579 vb.
  detract 926 vb.
  detraction 926 n.
whist
  hush 399 int.
  card game 837 n.
whist drive
  amusement 837 n.
whistle
  blow 352 vb.
  be loud 400 vb.
  megaphone 400 n.
  hiss 406 vb.
  shrill 407 vb.
  cry 408 vb.
  ululate 409 vb.
  play music 413 vb.
  sing 413 vb.
  flute 414 n.
  signal 547 n.
  be cheerful 833 vb.
  wonder 864 vb.
  wonder 864 vb.
  despise 922 vb.
  applaud 923 vb.
  disapprobation
    924 n.
  disapprove 924 vb.
whistle-blowing
  warning 664 n.
whistle for
  desire 859 vb.
whistle-stop
  stopping place
    145 n.
whistle-stop
  tour
  vote 605 n.
whit
  small quantity
    33 n.
  trifle 639 n.
white
  white 427 adj.
  whiten 427 vb.
  whiteness 427 n.
  eye 438 n.
white-collar
  worker
  worker 686 n.

whited
  sepulchre
  sham 542 n.
  deceiver 545 n.
white elephant
  bane 659 n.
white feather
  cowardice 856 n.
white flag
  flag 547 n.
  peace offering
    719 n.
  submission 721 n.
white goods
  merchandise
    795 n.
white-haired
  ageing 131 adj.
white hope
  proficient person
    696 n.
white horses
  wave 350 n.
white-hot
  hot 379 adj.
  white 427 adj.
  fervent 818 adj.
white
  information
  information
    524 n.
  credit 802 n.
white lie
  equivocalness
    518 n.
  concealment
    525 n.
  untruth 543 n.
  stratagem 698 n.
white lines
  traffic control
    305 n.
white meat
  meat 301 n.
whiten
  whiten 427 vb.
whiteness
  whiteness 427 n.
  cleanness 648 n.
white-out
  dimness 419 n.
White Paper
  report 524 n.
  record 548 n.
white pepper
  condiment 389 n.
white sauce
  sauce 389 n.
white-skinned
  white 427 adj.
white slave
  prostitute 952 n.
white-tie
  formal 875 adj.

whitewash
  coat 226 vb.
  facing 226 n.
  colour 425 vb.
  pigment 425 n.
  whiten 427 vb.
  sophisticate
    477 vb.
  overestimate
    482 vb.
  mislead 495 vb.
  conceal 525 vb.
  sham 542 n.
  clean 648 vb.
  cleanser 648 n.
  decorate 844 vb.
  extenuate 927 vb.
  justify 927 vb.
  vindication 927 n.
  acquit 960 vb.
whiting
  fish food 301 n.
whitish
  whitish 427 adj.
whittle
  abate 37 vb.
  subtract 39 vb.
  cut 46 vb.
  form 243 vb.
  sculpt 554 vb.
whittle away
  make smaller
    198 vb.
whiz kid
  busy person 678 n.
  victor 727 n.
  prosperous person
    730 n.
  prodigy 864 n.
whizz
  move fast 277 vb.
  spurt 277 n.
  hiss 406 vb.
whoa
  stop 266 int.
whodunit
  novel 590 n.
whole
  whole 52 adj.
  whole 52 n.
  numerical 85 adj.
  universe 321 n.
whole bang
  shoot, the
  all 52 n.
whole caboodle,
  the
  all 52 n.
wholefood
  food 301 n.
whole-hearted
  resolute 599 adj.
whole hog
  actively 678 adv.

whole lot
  great quantity
    32 n.
  all 52 n.
wholemeal
  cereals 301 n.
whole number
  whole 52 n.
  number 85 n.
wholesale
  extensive 32 adj.
  greatly 32 vb.
  comprehensive
    52 adj.
  complete 54 adj.
  inclusive 78 adj.
  indiscriminate
    464 adj.
  sell 793 vb.
wholesome
  nourishing
    301 adj.
  beneficial 644 adj.
  healthy 650 adj.
  salubrious 652 adj.
  personable
    841 adj.
whole truth
  disclosure 526 n.
wholly
  completely
    54 adv.
whoop
  loudness 400 n.
  cry 408 n.
  cry 408 vb.
  be cheerful 833 vb.
  rejoice 835 vb.
whoopee
  revel 837 n.
whooping
  loud 400 adj.
whooping-
  cough
  infection 651 n.
  respiratory disease
    651 n.
whopper
  untruth 543 n.
whore
  be impure 951 vb.
  prostitute 952 n.
whorl
  weaving 222 n.
  coil 251 n.
whosoever
  everyman 79 n.
Who's Who
  directory 87 n.
whydunit
  novel 590 n.
wick
  filament 208 n.
  torch 420 n.

give 781 vb.
yin and yang
polarity 14 n.
duality 90 n.
yob
youngster 132 n.
rude person 885 n.
ruffian 904 n.
yobbo
ruffian 904 n.
yodel
cry 408 n.
sing 413 vb.
yoga
philosophy 449 n.
exercise 682 n.
asceticism 945 n.
religion 973 n.
yoghourt
dairy product 301 n.
dessert 301 n.
yogi
sage 500 n.
ascetic 945 n.
occultist 984 n.
yoke
affix 45 vb.
join 45 vb.
bond 47 n.
duality 90 n.
pair 90 vb.
support 218 n.
break in 369 vb.
servitude 745 n.
subjection 745 n.
fetter 748 n.
yokel
native 191 n.
country-dweller 869 n.
yon
distant 199 adj.
yonder
distant 199 adj.
yoni
idol 982 n.
yonks
long duration 113 n.
yoof
youth 132 n.
young
young 130 adj.
product 164 n.
posterity 170 n.
young creature
young creature 132 n.
younger
inferior 35 n.

subsequent 120 adj.
young 130 adj.
younger generation
modernist 126 n.
youth 130 n.
young hopeful
youngster 132 n.
young person
youngster 132 n.
youngster
youngster 132 n.
your honour
title 870 n.
yourself
self 80 n.
youth
youth 130 n.
youngster 132 n.
youthful
young 130 adj.
strong 162 adj.
youth hostel
inn 192 n.
yowl
cry 408 vb.
vociferate 408 vb.
ululate 409 vb.
yoyo
oscillation 317 n.
plaything 837 n.
yukky
unclean 649 adj.
Yule log
fuel 385 n.
Yuletide
holy day 988 n.
yummy
savoury 390 adj.
yuppy
modernist 126 n.
beau monde 848 n.

Z

zaitech
finance 797 n.
zany
fool 501 n.
humorist 839 n.
laughingstock 851 n.
zap
move fast 277 vb.
spurt 277 n.
Z-bend
obliquity 220 n.
curve 248 n.

zeal
curiosity 453 n.
resolution 599 n.
warm feeling 818 n.
desire 859 n.
piety 979 n.
zealot
dogmatist 473 n.
narrow mind 481 n.
enthusiast 504 n.
zealot 979 n.
zealotry
opinionatedness 602 n.
zealous
active 678 adj.
fervent 818 adj.
zebra
mammal 365 n.
See **cattle**
stripe 437 n.
zebra crossing
traffic control 305 n.
access 624 n.
road 624 n.
refuge 662 n.
Zen
philosophy 449 n.
religious faith 973 n.
zenith
superiority 34 n.
completeness 54 n.
extremity 69 n.
height 209 n.
summit 213 n.
perfection 646 n.
palmy days 730 n.
zephyr
breeze 352 n.
zero
not one 103 adj.
zero 103 n.
zero-based budgeting
accounts 808 n.
zero-emission vehicle
automobile 274 n.
zero hour
start 68 n.
date 108 n.
departure 296 n.
zero in on
bring together 74 vb.
congregate 74 vb.
focus 76 vb.

centralize 225 vb.
converge 293 vb.
aim at 617 vb.
zero option
necessity 596 n.
choice 605 n.
no choice 606 n.
zero-rated
uncharged 812 adj.
zero-rated goods
tax 809 n.
zero tolerance
severity 735 n.
pitilessness 906 n.
punishment 963 n.
zest
vigorousness 174 n.
pleasure 376 n.
taste 386 n.
enjoyment 824 n.
pleasurableness 826 n.
liking 859 n.
zesty
pungent 388 adj.
zeugma
ornament 574 n.
ziggurat
high structure 209 n.
temple 990 n.
zigzag
be oblique 220 vb.
obliquity 220 n.
angular 247 adj.
angularity 247 n.
meander 251 vb.
meandering 251 n.
deviate 282 vb.
deviation 282 n.
to and fro 317 adv.
pattern 844 n.
zilch
nonexistence 2 n.
insubstantiality 4 n.
zero 103 n.
zillion
over one hundred 99 n.
zing
vigorousness 174 n.
move fast 277 vb.
spurt 277 n.
Zion
focus 76 n.
heaven 971 n.

holy place 990 n.
zip
fastening 47 n.
energy 160 n.
vigorousness 174 n.
move fast 277 vb.
spurt 277 n.
zip up
join 45 vb.
close 264 vb.
zircon
gem 844 n.
zit
blemish 845 n.
zither
stringed instrument 414 n.
zloty
coinage 797 n.
zodiac
circle 250 n.
zodiac 321 n.
zombie
fool 501 n.
ghost 970 n.
zone
set apart 46 vb.
region 184 n.
territory 184 n.
layer 207 n.
land 344 n.
apportion 783 vb.
zonked
drugged 949 adj.
zoo
zoo 369 n.
zoological
biological 358 adj.
animal 365 adj.
zoology
zoology 367 n.
zoom
move fast 277 vb.
spurt 277 n.
ascend 308 vb.
ascent 308 n.
photography 551 n.
zoom lens
camera 442 n.
zoomorphism
animality 365 n.
idolatry 982 n.
zucchini
fruit and vegetables 301 n.
zymotic
light 323 adj.

READ MORE IN PENGUIN

In every corner of the world, on every subject under the sun, Penguin represents quality and variety – the very best in publishing today.

For complete information about books available from Penguin – including Puffins, Penguin Classics and Arkana – and how to order them, write to us at the appropriate address below. Please note that for copyright reasons the selection of books varies from country to country.

In the United Kingdom: Please write to *Dept. EP, Penguin Books Ltd, Bath Road, Harmondsworth, West Drayton, Middlesex UB7 0DA*

In the United States: Please write to *Consumer Services, Penguin Putnam Inc., 405 Murray Hill Parkway, East Rutherford, New Jersey 07073-2136*. VISA and MasterCard holders call 1-800-631-8571 to order Penguin titles

In Canada: Please write to *Penguin Books Canada Ltd, 10 Alcorn Avenue, Suite 300, Toronto, Ontario M4V 3B2*

In Australia: Please write to *Penguin Books Australia Ltd, 487 Maroondah Highway, Ringwood, Victoria 3134*

In New Zealand: Please write to *Penguin Books (NZ) Ltd, Private Bag 102902, North Shore Mail Centre, Auckland 10*

In India: Please write to *Penguin Books India Pvt Ltd, 11 Community Centre, Panchsheel Park, New Delhi 110017*

In the Netherlands: Please write to *Penguin Books Netherlands bv, Postbus 3507, NL-1001 AH Amsterdam*

In Germany: Please write to *Penguin Books Deutschland GmbH, Metzlerstrasse 26, 60594 Frankfurt am Main*

In Spain: Please write to *Penguin Books S. A., Bravo Murillo 19, 1°B, 28015 Madrid*

In Italy: Please write to *Penguin Italia s.r.l., Via Vittorio Emanuele 45/a, 20094 Corsico, Milano*

In France: Please write to *Penguin France, 12, Rue Prosper Ferradou, 31700 Blagnac*

In Japan: Please write to *Penguin Books Japan Ltd, Iidabashi KM-Bldg, 2-23-9 Koraku, Bunkyo-Ku, Tokyo 112-0004*

In South Africa: Please write to *Penguin Books South Africa (Pty) Ltd, P.O. Box 751093, Gardenview, 2047 Johannesburg*

READ MORE IN PENGUIN

LITERARY CRITICISM

The Practice of Writing David Lodge

This lively collection examines the work of authors ranging from the two Amises to Nabokov and Pinter; the links between private lives and published works; and the different techniques required in novels, stage plays and screenplays. 'These essays, so easy in manner, so well-built and informative, offer a fine blend of creative writing and criticism' *Sunday Times*

A Lover's Discourse Roland Barthes

'May be the most detailed, painstaking anatomy of desire we are ever likely to see or need again ... The book is an ecstatic celebration of love and language ... readers interested in either or both ... will enjoy savouring its rich and dark delights' *Washington Post*

The New Pelican Guide to English Literature Edited by Boris Ford

The indispensable critical guide to English and American literature in nine volumes, erudite yet accessible. From the ages of Chaucer and Shakespeare, via Georgian satirists and Victorian social critics, to the leading writers of the twentieth century, all literary life is here.

The Structure of Complex Words William Empson

'Twentieth-century England's greatest critic after T. S. Eliot, but whereas Eliot was the high priest, Empson was the *enfant terrible* ... *The Structure of Complex Words* is one of the linguistic masterpieces of the epoch, finding in the feel and tone of our speech whole sedimented social histories' *Guardian*

Vamps and Tramps Camille Paglia

'Paglia is a genuinely unconventional thinker ... Taken as a whole, the book gives an exceptionally interesting perspective on the last thirty years of intellectual life in America, and is, in its wacky way, a celebration of passion and the pursuit of truth' *Sunday Telegraph*

READ MORE IN PENGUIN

LANGUAGE/LINGUISTICS

Language Play David Crystal

We all use language to communicate information, but it is language play which is truly central to our lives. Full of puns, groan-worthy gags and witty repartee, this book restores the fun to the study of language. It also demonstrates why all these things are essential elements of what makes us human.

Swearing Geoffrey Hughes

'A deliciously filthy trawl among taboo words across the ages and the globe' *Observer*. 'Erudite and entertaining' Penelope Lively, *Daily Telegraph*

The Language Instinct Stephen Pinker

'Dazzling ... Pinker's big idea is that language is an instinct, as innate to us as flying is to geese ... Words can hardly do justice to the superlative range and liveliness of Pinker's investigations' *Independent*. 'He does for language what David Attenborough does for animals, explaining difficult scientific concepts so easily that they are indeed absorbed as a transparent stream of words' John Gribbin

Mother Tongue Bill Bryson

'A delightful, amusing and provoking survey, a joyful celebration of our wonderful language, which is packed with curiosities and enlightenment on every page' *Sunday Express*. 'A gold mine of language-anecdote. A surprise on every page ... enthralling' *Observer*

Longman Guide to English Usage
Sidney Greenbaum and Janet Whitcut

Containing 5000 entries compiled by leading authorities on modern English, this invaluable reference work clarifies every kind of usage problem, giving expert advice on points of grammar, meaning, style, spelling, pronunciation and punctuation.

READ MORE IN PENGUIN

DICTIONARIES

Abbreviations
Ancient History
Archaeology
Architecture
Art and Artists
Astronomy
Biographical Dictionary of
  Women
Biology
Botany
Building
Business
Challenging Words
Chemistry
Civil Engineering
Classical Mythology
Computers
Contemporary American History
Curious and Interesting Geometry
Curious and Interesting Numbers
Curious and Interesting Words
Design and Designers
Economics
Eighteenth-Century History
Electronics
English and European History
English Idioms
Foreign Terms and Phrases
French
Geography
Geology
German
Historical Slang
Human Geography
Information Technology

International Finance
International Relations
Literary Terms and Literary
  Theory
Mathematics
Modern History 1789–1945
Modern Quotations
Music
Musical Performers
Nineteenth-Century World
  History
Philosophy
Physical Geography
Physics
Politics
Proverbs
Psychology
Quotations
Quotations from Shakespeare
Religions
Rhyming Dictionary
Russian
Saints
Science
Sociology
Spanish
Surnames
Symbols
Synonyms and Antonyms
Telecommunications
Theatre
The Third Reich
Third World Terms
Troublesome Words
Twentieth-Century History
Twentieth-Century Quotations